American Government
and Politics Today
▽
Second Edition

American Government and Politics Today

Second Edition

Steffen W. Schmidt
Iowa State University

Mack C. Shelley, II
Iowa State University

Barbara A. Bardes
Loyola University of Chicago

West Publishing Company
St. Paul   New York   Los Angeles   San Francisco

Copy Editor: Elaine Linden
Composition: Parkwood Composition Service
Illustrations: John Foster and Rolin Graphics

Photo Credits Follow Index

Copyright © 1985 By West Publishing Company
Copyright © 1987 By West Publishing Company
           50 West Kellogg Boulevard
           P.O. Box 64526
           St. Paul, MN 55164-1003
All rights reserved

Printed in the United States of America

Library of Congress Cataloging-in-Publication Data

Schmidt, Steffen W.
  American government and politics today.

  Includes bibliographies and index.
  1. United States—Politics and government.
I. Shelley, Mack C., 1950–   . II. Bardes, Barbara A. III. Title.
JK274.S428 1987   320.973   86-29018
ISBN 0-314-30389-8

Contents in Brief

Part One

The American System   1

Chapter 1
American Democracy and Political Culture   3
WHAT IF . . . The United States Had Been a Colony of Spain?   4
GETTING INVOLVED: Your Political Profile 26

Chapter 2
The Constitution   29
WHAT IF . . . The Constitution Had Not Been Ratified?   30
GETTING INVOLVED: How Can You Affect the U.S. Constitution?   57

Chapter 3
Federalism   61
WHAT IF . . . The United States Had a National School System?   62
GETTING INVOLVED: Contemporary Issues Concerning Federalism   91

Part Two

Civil Rights and Liberties   95

Chapter 4
Civil Liberties   97
WHAT IF . . . There Were No Habeas Corpus?   98
GETTING INVOLVED: Your Civil Liberties: Search and Seizure   127

Chapter 5
Minority Rights 131
WHAT IF . . . The North Had Lost the Civil War?   132
GETTING INVOLVED: Citizenship and Immigration Rights   161

Chapter 6
New Groups, New Demands   165
WHAT IF . . . Women's Suffrage Had Failed?   166

Part Three

▽

People and Politics   191

Chapter 7
Public Opinion   193
WHAT IF . . . Public Opinion Polls Made Law?   194
GETTING INVOLVED: How to Read a Public Opinion Poll   222

Chapter 8
Political Parties   225
WHAT IF . . . We Had a Multiparty Political System in the United
    States?   226
GETTING INVOLVED: Electing Convention Delegates   254

Chapter 9
The Media   257
WHAT IF . . . There Were Only One National Network?   258
GETTING INVOLVED: Being a Critical Consumer of the News   287

Chapter 10
Campaigns, Candidates, and Elections   289
WHAT IF . . . Voting Were Compulsory?   290
GETTING INVOLVED: Voting   336

Chapter 11
Interest Groups   339
WHAT IF . . . Interest Groups' Campaign Spending Were Limited to $1.00
    Per Member?   340
GETTING INVOLVED: The Gun Control Issue   364

Part Four

▽

Political Institutions   367

Chapter 12
The Presidency   369
WHAT IF . . . The United States Had a Plural Executive?   370
GETTING INVOLVED: Influencing the Presidency   405

Chapter 13
The Congress   13
WHAT IF . . . Bills Could Not Be Amended?   408
GETTING INVOLVED: Contacting Your Congressperson   446

Chapter 14
The Bureaucracy 449
WHAT IF . . . There Were No Civil Service? 450
GETTING INVOLVED: What Does the Government Know About You? 477

Chapter 15
The Judiciary 15
WHAT IF . . . The United States Had a Napoleonic Law Code? 480
GETTING INVOLVED: Changing the Legal System 513

Part Five

▽

Public Policy   517

Chapter 16
Political Economy 519
WHAT IF . . . The Federal Budget Had to Be Balanced? 520
GETTING INVOLVED: The Importance of Government in Your Life 542

Chapter 17
Domestic Policy 545
WHAT IF . . . Nuclear Power Were Banned in the U.S.? 546
GETTING INVOLVED: Working for a Clean Environment 574

Chapter 18
Foreign and Defense Policy 577
WHAT IF . . . The United States Withdrew from the United Nations? 578
GETTING INVOLVED: Reducing the Nuclear Threat 617

Part Six

▽

State and Local Politics   621

Chapter 19
State and Local Government 623
WHAT IF . . . Every State Had the Same Constitution? 624
GETTING INVOLVED: Organizing in Your Community 651

Appendix A   The U.S. Constitution   654
Appendix B   The Declaration of Independence   657
Appendix C   The Presidents of the U.S.   674
Appendix D   Federalist Papers 10 and 51   676

Glossary   681
Index   698

Contents

▽

Chapter 1
American Democracy and Political Culture   3

WHAT IF . . . *The United States Had Been a Colony of Spain?*   *4*
The Political System in 1986   5
The 1986 Elections   6
The Candidate-Centered Campaign   7
The Message of the Election   7
Politics   9
Government   11
Authority   11
Legitimacy   11
Power   12
Who Governs   12
The Athenian Model of Direct Democracy   12
The Founders' Fear of Direct Democracy   13
Representative Democracy   14
PROFILE: *Thomas Jefferson*   *15*
   Principles of Democratic Government   *16*
   Constitutional Democracy   *16*
Democracy: Ideal and Real   16
Elitism   17
Pluralism   18
American Political Culture   18
HIGHLIGHT: *Religion and American Political Culture*   *19*
A Political Consensus   21
   Liberty   *21*
   Equality   *22*
   Property   *22*
   Political Socialization   *22*
Subcultures and Political Conflict   23
An Overview of This Book   24
GETTING INVOLVED: *Your Political Profile*   *26*
Chapter Summary   27
Questions for Review and Discussion   27
Selected References   27

Part One
▽
**The American
System
1**

Chapter 2
The Constitution 29

WHAT IF . . . *The Constitution Had Not Been Ratified?* 30

The Starving Time 31
Pilgrims, the *Mayflower*, and the Compact 32
More Colonies, More Government 33
British Restrictions and Colonial Grievances 33
The Colonial Response: The Continental Congress 34
Declaring Independence 35
The Resolution of Independence 35
July 4, 1776 35
The Rise of Republicanism 36
The Articles of Confederation: Promise and Reality 37
Accomplishments under the Articles 38
Weaknesses of the Articles 38
Shays's Rebellion and the Need for Revision of the Articles 39
The Philadelphia Convention: Drafting the Constitution 39
The Proceedings 40
Not a Commoner Among Them 40
The Working Environment 41
Factions Among the Delegates 41
Politicking and Compromises 42
    The Virginia Plan 42
    The New Jersey Plan 43
    The "Great Compromise" 43
    Other Issues, Other Compromises 43
Working Toward the Final Document 44
The Difficult Road to Ratification 45

CRITICAL PERSPECTIVE: *The Madisonian Argument for Separation of Powers* 46

The Federalists Push for Ratification 46

PROFILE: *Benjamin Franklin* 47

    The Federalist Papers 48
    The Anti-Federalist Response 48
    The March to the Finish 49
Was the Constitution Truly Favored by the Majority 49
The Bill of Rights 49
Madison's Task 49
The Importance of Mandatory Imperatives 50

HIGHLIGHT: *The Bill of Rights: A Second Thought* 51

Altering the Constitution 51
The Formal Amendment Process 51
    Many Amendments Proposed, Few Accepted 52

CRITICAL PERSPECTIVE: *Alternative Constitutions* 53

    The National Convention Provision 54
Informal Methods of Constitutional Change 55
Judicial Review 55
Interpretation, Custom and Usage 55
The Result: It Has Lasted 56

GETTING INVOLVED: *How Can You Affect the U.S. Constitution?* 57

Chapter Summary 58
Questions for Review and Discussion 58
Selected References 59

Chapter 3
Federalism   61

WHAT IF . . . *The United States Had a National School System?*   62

Three Systems of Government   63
A Unitary System of Government   63
A Confederal System   63
A Federal System   64
Why a Federal System?   64
The Historical Reasons for Federalism   64
 Common Problems   64
 Size and Regional Isolation   65
 Sectionalism and Political Subcultures   65
Other Arguments for Federalism   66

PROFILE: *Alexander Hamilton   67*
The Constitutional Basis for American Federalism   67
Powers Delegated to the National Government   68
 Expressed Powers   68
 Implied Powers   69
 Resulting Powers   69
 Inherent Powers   69
Reserved Powers of the State Governments   69
Concurrent Powers   70
Horizontal Federalism   70
The Full Faith and Credit Clause   71
Privileges and Immunities   71
Interstate Extradition   72
The Peaceful Settlement of Differences between States   72
The Supremacy of the National Constitution   72

HIGHLIGHT: *Extradition is Not Always so Simple: The Case of Dennis Banks*   73

Milestones in National Government Supremacy   74
McCulloch v. Maryland (1819)   74
 The Constitutional Question   74
 Marshall's Decision   75
Gibbons v. Ogden (1824)   75
 The Issue Before the Court   75

HIGHLIGHT: *The Seedier Side of Gibbons v. Ogden*   76

 Marshall's Decision   76
The Civil War   77
 Nullification and Secession   77

HIGHLIGHT: *The Webster-Calhoun Debate in 1833*   78

 War and the Growth of the National Government   79
The Continuing Dispute over the Division of Power   79
Duel Federalism   80
Cooperative Federalism   80
The Growth of National-Level Powers   81
The New Federalism   82
 The Decentralization of Federal Programs   83
 Opposition to the New Federalism   83
The Fiscal Side of Federalism   84
Categorical Grants-in-Aid   84
Block Grants   85

CRITICAL PERSPECTIVE: *Are There Nine Nations in North America?*   86
General Grants-in-Aid, or Revenue Sharing   86

Federalism Versus Regionalism: The Shift of Power from the Snowbelt to the
    Sunbelt   88
    GETTING INVOLVED: *Contemporary Issues Concerning Federalism*   91
Chapter Summary   92
Questions for Review and Discussion   93
Selected References   93

Part Two

▽

Civil Rights and Liberties
95

Chapter 4
Civil Liberties   97

WHAT IF . . . *There Were No Habeas Corpus?*   98
Civil Rights and the Fear of Government   99
The Bill of Rights   99
The Nationalization of the Bill of Rights   99
The Incorporation Issue   100
Freedom of Religion   101
The Separation of Church and State   101
    The Issue of School Prayer   102

HIGHLIGHT: *Public Opinion about School Prayer*   103

    Forbidding the Teaching of Evolution   103
    Aid to Church-Related Schools   104
The Free Exercise of Religious Beliefs   104
Freedom of Expression   105
Early Restrictions on Expression   105
    The Alien and Sedition Acts   105

HIGHLIGHT: *Is Espionage on the Rise?*   106

    The Espionage Act   106
    Clear and Present Danger   107
    The Bad-Tendency Rule   108
    No Prior Restraint   108
The Protection of Symbolic Speech   108

HIGHLIGHT: *No Prior Restraint: The Case of the Pentagon Papers*   109

The Protection of Commercial Speech   110
Unprotected Speech: Obscenity   110

HIGHLIGHT: *An Invitation to Testify*   111

Unprotected Speech: Slander   112
Fighting Words and Hecklers' Veto   112
Freedom of the Press   113
Defamation in Writing   113
A Free Press Versus a Fair Trial: Gag Orders   113
Confidentiality and Reporters' Work Papers   114
Other Informed Channels: Motion Pictures, Radio, and TV   115
    Motion Pictures: Some Prior Restraint   115
    Radio and TV: Limited Protection   115
The Right to Assemble and to Petition the Government   115
More Liberties Under Scrutiny   117
The Right to Privacy   117
The Right to Abortion   118

PROFILE: *Justice Harry Blackmun*   119

▽

The Rights of Severely Disabled Infants—The "Baby Doe" Rule   119

The Great Balancing Act: The Rights of the Accused Versus the Rights of Society   120

Rights of the Accused   120

Extending the Rights of the Accused: *Miranda v. Arizona*   121

Recent Rulings and Their Impact on *Miranda*   122

The Exclusionary Rule   122

HIGHLIGHT: *The Case of Clarence Earl Gideon*   *123*

Capital Punishment: Cruel and Unusual?   124

GETTING INVOLVED: *Your Civil Liberties: Search and Seizure*   *127*

Chapter Summary   128

Questions for Review and Discussion   128

Selected References   129

Chapter 5
Minority Rights   131

WHAT IF . . . *The North Had Lost the Civil War?*   *132*

The Diversity of American Society   133

The Traditional Minorities: An Overview   134

Blacks: The Consequences of Slavery in the United States   134

The Civil Rights Acts of 1865–1877

The Nullification of the Civil Rights Acts   136

   The Civil Rights Cases   *136*

HIGHLIGHT: *And Now the Bad News*   *137*

   Plessy v. Ferguson: Separate but Equal   *137*

The End of Separate but Equal Doctrine   138

   Brown v. Board of Education   *138*

   "With All Deliberate Speed"   *138*

Reactions to School Integration   138

The Controversy Continues: Busing   139

The Civil Rights Movement   141

HIGHLIGHT: *"I Have a Dream"*   *142*

1960s Civil Rights Legislation and Its Implementation   143

The Civil Rights Act of 1964   144

The Civil Rights Act of 1968   144

Employment and Affirmative Action   145

Reverse Discrimination: Backlash   145

HIGHLIGHT: *Affirmative Action and Public Opinion*   *146*

   The Bakke Case   *146*

   The Weber Case   *147*

The Court's Most Recent Record on Reverse Bias   147

The Voting Rights Act of 1965   148

Historical Barriers to Black Political Participation   148

Provisions of the Act   150

PROFILE: *Coretta Scott King*   *151*

Hispanics in American Society   151

Mexican Americans   151

   Political Participation   *153*

   Political Organizations   *153*

Puerto Ricans   154
Cuban Americans   155
Bilingual Education   155
Native Americans: An American Tragedy   155
Economic and Social Status   156
The Appropriation of Indian Lands   156
Native American Political Response   157

HIGHLIGHT: *Skeletons in the Smithsonian's Closet*   *158*

Asian Americans   159
Melting Pot of Ethnic Stew   159

GETTING INVOLVED: *Citizenship and Immigration Rights*   *161*

Chapter Summary   162
Questions and Review and Discussion   162
Selected References   163

Chapter 6
New Groups, New Demands   165

WHAT IF . . . *Women's Suffrage Had Failed?*   *166*

Women's Position in Society: Historical Background   167
The Early Feminist Movement in the United States   168
The Suffrage Issue and the Fifteenth Amendment   168
The Continued Struggle for Equal Status   169
The National Organization for Women (NOW)   170

PROFILE: *Eleanor Smeal*   *171*

NOW and the Equal Rights Amendment   171
Opposition to ERA: The Conservative Reaction   172

HIGHLIGHT: *Two Women Run for Governor*   *173*

Federal Responses to Sex Discrimination in Jobs   173
Sex Discrimination and Title VII   173
The Equal Pay Act of 1963   175
Comparable Worth, or Pay Equity   176
The Status of the Elderly   177
The Burden of Medical Costs   177
The Inability to Find Work   178
Age Discrimination in Employment   178
   Court Actions   *179*
   Congressional Actions   *179*

PROFILE: *Claude Pepper*   *180*

The Elderly and Politics   180
   The Elderly as Voters   *180*
   The Elderly as Legislators   *181*
The Elderly as Activists   182
The Rights of the Handicapped   183
The Rights and Status of Juveniles   183
Voting, Marriage, and the Young   183
The Rights of Children in Civil and Criminal Proceedings   184
   Private Contract Rights   *184*
   Criminal Rights   *185*
   Procedural Rights in Criminal Trials   *185*
   The Other Side of the Coin   *186*

The Rights and Status of Gays   186
The Law and Public Attitudes   186

HIGHLIGHT: *The Impact of Aids on Gay Politics*   *187*

Gays and Politics   188

GETTING INVOLVED: *What To Do with Discrimination*   *189*

Chapter Summary   189
Questions for Review and Discussion   190
Selected References   190

Chapter 7
Public Opinion   193

WHAT IF . . . *Public Opinion Polls Made Law?*   *194*
Defining and Measuring Public Opinion   196
The Qualities of Public Opinion   197
Intensity   197
Fluidity   198
Stability   198
Quiescence   198
Relevance   198
Political Knowledge   199
Consensus and Division   200
Measuring Public Opinion: Polling Techniques   200
The History of Opinion Polls   200
Sampling Techniques   201

HIGHLIGHT: *Straw Polls and Front-Runners*   *202*

The Polls and the 1984 Election   204
Problems with Opinion Polls   206
How Public Opinion Is Formed   206

HIGHLIGHT: *When Polls Are Wrong*   *207*

The Importance of the Family   208
Educational Influence on Political Opinion   209
Peers and Peer Group Influence   209
Religious Influence   209

HIGHLIGHT: *The Reverend Jerry Falwell and the Moral Majority*   *210*

The Influence of Economic Status and Occupation   211
Opinion Leaders' Influence   212
Media Influence   212
The Influence of Demographic Traits   212

PROFILE: *Patrick Caddell*   *213*

The Gender Gap   215
The Political Culture of Americans   215

CRITICAL PERSPECTIVE: *On Political Thinking*   *216*

Public Opinion about Government   218
Political Ideology   219
Public Opinion and the Political Process   221

GETTING INVOLVED: *How to Read a Public Opinion Poll*   *222*

Chapter Summary   223
Questions for Review and Discussion   223
Selected References   224

Part Three
▽
People and Politics
191

Chapter 8
Political Parties   225

WHAT IF . . . *We Had a Multiparty Political System in the United States?*   226

What is a Political Party?   227
Why Do People Join Political Parties?   227
Political Parties in Other Countries   228
Functions of Political Parties in the United States   229
A Short History of Political Parties in the United States   229
The Formative Years: Federalists and Anti-Federalists   231
The Era of Personal Politics   231
National Two-Party Rule: Democrats and Whigs   231
The Post-Civil War Period   232
The Progressive Movement   232
The Modern Era: From the New Deal to the Present   233
The Structure of Political Parties   234
The National Party Organization   235
    Choosing the National Committee   235

CRITICAL PERSPECTIVE: *The Rise and Fall of the Major Party*   236

    Picking a National Chairperson   237
The State Organization   237
Local Party Machinery: The Grass Roots   238
The Two-Party System in American Politics   239

HIGHLIGHT: *Tammany Hall: The Quintessential Local Political Machine*   240

The Historical Foundation of the Two-Party System   242
Self-Perpetuation of the Two-Party System   242
The Political Culture of the United States   243
The Winner-Take-All Electoral System   244
State and Federal Laws Favoring the Two Parties   244

HIGHLIGHT: *The Rise of Republicanism in the 1980s*   245

How Do the Democratic and Republican Parties Differ?   246
The Role of Minor Parties in U.S. Political History   248
Historically Important Minor Parties   248

PROFILE: *Lyndon H. LaRouche, Jr.*   249

Spin-off Minor Parties   250
Other Minor Parties   251
The Impact of Minor Parties   251
Is The Party Over?   252

GETTING INVOLVED: *Electing Convention Delegates*   254

Chapter Summary   255
Questions for Review and Discussion   255
Selected References   256

Chapter 9
The Media   257

WHAT IF . . . *There Were Only One National Network?*   258

The Media's Functions   260
Entertainment   260
Reporting the News   261
Identifying Public Problems   261

HIGHLIGHT: *The Bill Cosby Phenomenon* 262

Socializing New Generations 262
Providing a Political Forum 263
Making Profits 263
History of the Media in the United States 263
The Rise of the Political Press 264
The Development of Mass-Readership Newspapers 264
The Popular Press and Yellow Journalism 265
The Age of the Electromagnetic Signal 266
The Revolution in Electronic Media 267
The Primacy of Television 267
The Political Power of the Media 268

PROFILE: *Ted Koppel* 269

Paid-for Political Announcements 269
Management of News Coverage 270

HIGHLIGHT: *Selling Candidates* 271

The Campaign Technique of Presidential Debates 271
The 1960 Debates 272
The 1976 Debates 272
The 1980 Debates 273
The 1984 Debates 274

CRITICAL PERSPECTIVE: *What's in the News?* 275

Investigating the Government 277
The Media and Public Attitudes 277
The Media and the Presidency 277
Setting the Public Agenda 278
Government Regulation of the Media 281
The First Amendment and the Press: A Review 281
The Electronic Media and Government Control 281

HIGHLIGHT: *Satellite Freedom* 282

The FCC's Fairness Doctrine 283
Does National Security Justify Suppression of the News? 284
The Public's Rights to Media Access 285
Bias in the Media 285

GETTING INVOLVED: *Being a Critical Consumer of the News* 287

Chapter Summary 287
Questions for Review and Discussion 288
Selected References 288

Chapter 10
Campaigns, Candidates, and Elections 289

WHAT IF . . . *Voting Were Compulsory?* 290
The People Who Run for Political Office 291
Why They Run 292
Who Runs? 293
The Modern Campaign Machine 295
The Changing Campaign 296
The Professional Campaign 297
Financing the Campaign 297

HIGHLIGHT: *Some Big Spenders in the History of Campaign Spending* 298

Media Coverage   298
    Scheduling Campaign Events   298
    Recruiting Assistants for Fieldwork   298
    Conducting Research   299
Campaign Workers   299
Campaign Strategy   **300**

PROFILE: *Jesse Jackson*   *301*

The Value of Campaign Polls   303
Campaign Financing and Reform   **304**
The Federal Election Campaign Acts of 1972 and 1974   306
    The Impact of the 1974 Act   307
    The Loan Strategy   307
    The Growth in Political Action Committees (PACs)   307
The Primaries and the Presidential Election   **307**
Primary Reform   308
Types of Primaries   310
A National Presidential Primary?   311
On to the National Convention   312
The Mechanics of Elections   312
    Office-Block and Party-Column Ballots   313
    Long Versus Short Ballots   313
Counting the Votes and Avoiding Fraud   315
The Electoral College   **316**
The Choice of Electors   316
The Elector's Commitment   318
Criticisms of the Electoral College   318
Proposed Reforms   319
Voting in National, State, and Local Elections   **319**

HIGHLIGHT: *How the Cities Vote*   *322*

The Effect of Low Voter Turnout   322
Factors Influencing Who Votes   323
Why Citizens Do Not Vote: The Rational Ignorance Effect   324

CRITICAL PERSPECTIVE; *On Voting Choices*   *325*

Legal Restrictions on Voting   **325**
Historical Restrictions   326
Current Eligibility and Registration Requirements   327
Determinants of Voter Choice   **328**
Socioeconomic and Demographic Factors   328
    Education   328
    Income and Socioeconomic Class   328
    Religion   329
    Ethnic Background   329
    Sex   329
    Age   330
    Geographic Region   330
Psychological Factors   331
    Party Identification   332
    Perception of the Candidates   332
    Issue Preferences   333
Elections and Campaigns: A State of Constant Change   **335**

GETTING INVOLVED: *Voting*   *336*

Chapter Summary   337
Questions for Review and Discussion   338
Selected References   338

Chapter 11
Interest Groups   339

WHAT IF . . . *Interest Groups' Campaign Spending Were Limited to $1.00 Per Member?*   340
The Role of Interest Groups   341
What Is an Interest Group?   341
How Widespread Are Interest Groups?   342
Major Interest Groups   342
Business Interest Groups   342
    The National Association of Manufacturers (NAM)   342
    The U.S. Chamber of Commerce   344
    Business Roundtable   344
    Other Business-Oriented Pressure Groups   345
Agricultural Pressure Groups   345

HIGHLIGHT: *Honey and Money*   346

Labor Interest Groups   346

PROFILE: *Lane Kirkland*   348

Public Employee Pressure Groups   349

CRITICAL PERSPECTIVE: *The Logic of Collective Action*   350

Professional Pressure Groups   351
Public Interest Pressure Groups   351
Single-Interest Groups   352
Foreign Governments   352
Interest Group Strategies   353
Direct Techniques   354
    Lobbying Techniques   354
    The Ratings Game   354

HIGHLIGHT: *High-Tech Lobbying*   355

    Campaign Assistance   356
    PACs and Political Campaigns   356
Indirect Techniques   358
    Generating Public Pressure   359
    Using Constituents as Lobbyists   359
    Building Alliances   360
Regulating Lobbyists   360

HIGHLIGHT: *Lobbying by Former Government Officials*   361

Why Interest Groups Have So Much Power   362

GETTING INVOLVED: *The Gun Control Issue*   364

Chapter Summary   365
Questions for Review and Discussion   365
Selected References   365

Chapter 12
The Presidency   369

WHAT IF . . . *The United States Had a Plural Executive?*   370
Historical Development of the Presidency   371
PROFILE: *George Washington*   372

Part Four
▽
Political
Institutions
367

▽
xix

Who Can Become President?   372
The Process of Becoming President   373
HIGHLIGHT: *Presidential Elections*   *374*
The Many Powers of the President   375
Chief of State   376
Chief Executive   377
   The Powers of Appointment and Removal   *377*
   The Power to Grant Reprieves and Pardons   *379*
Commander in Chief   379
Chief Diplomat   381
   Recognition Power   *381*
   Proposal and Ratification of Treaties   *383*
   Executive Agreements   *383*
Chief Legislator   384
   Getting Legislation Passed   *385*
   Saying No to Legislation   *385*
   Measuring the Success of a President's Legislative Program   *386*
Other Presidential Powers   386
The President as Party Chief and Super Politician   388

CRITICAL PERSPECTIVE: *The President's Personality*   *389*

The Special Uses of Presidential Power   392
Emergency Powers   392
Executive Orders   392
Executive Immunity   393
Impoundment of Funds   394
Abuses of Executive Power: Impeachment   394

HIGHLIGHT: *Watergate: A Crime of Power?*   *395*
The Executive Organization   396
The Cabinet   396
The Executive Office of the President   399
   Council of Economic Advisers (CEA)   *399*
   Office of Management and Budget (OMB)   *399*
   National Security Council (NSC)   *400*
The Vice Presidency   400
The Vice President's Job   400
Presidential Succession   401
The Twenty-fifth Amendment   402
When the Vice Presidency Becomes Vacant   402

HIGHLIGHT: *The Presidential Sickbed*   *403*

Is the Power of the Presidency Increasing or Decreasing?   403

GETTING INVOLVED: *Influencing the Presidency*   *405*

Chapter Summary   405
Questions for Review and Discussion   406
Selected References   406

Chapter 13
The Congress   13

WHAT IF . . . *Bills Could Not Be Amended?*   *408*
Why Was Congress Created?   409
Enumerated Powers   411
The Necessary and Proper Clause   412
The Functions of Congress   412

The Lawmaking Function   413
Service to Constituents   414
The Representative Function   415
    The Trustee View of Representation   415
    The Instructed-Delegate View of Representation   415
The Oversight Function   415
The Public Education Function   416
The Conflict Resolution Function   416
House-Senate Differences   416
Size and Rules   417
Debate and Filibustering   418
Prestige   418
Other Differences   418
Congresspersons and the Citizenry—A Comparison   419

PROFILE: *Edward Moore Kennedy*   420

Congressional Elections   421
Candidates for Congressional Elections   421
    Reasons for Making the Race   422
    The Nomination Process   422

HIGHLIGHT: *Congress on the Air*   423

    Who Wins, and Why?   424
The Power of Incumbency   424
The 1986 Congressional Elections   425

CRITICAL PERSPECTIVE: *At Home with House Members*   426

Congressional Reapportionment   427
Pay, Perks, and Privileges   428

HIGHLIGHT: *Globe-Trotting Legislators*   430

Permanent Professional Staffs   430
Privileges and Immunities Under the Law   431
The Committee Structure   431
Types of Congressional Committees   432
    Standing Committees   432
    Select Committees   434
    Joint Committees   434
    Conference Committees   434
    The House Rules Committee   434
The Selection of Committee Members   435
The Formal Leadership   435
Leadership in the House   436
    The Speaker   436
    The Majority Leader   436
    The Minority Leader   437
    Whips   437
    What Determines the House Leadership's Success?   437
Leadership in the Senate   438
How Members of Congress Decide   440
How a Bill Becomes Law   441
The Question of Congressional Ethics   442
New Directions from Old   444

GETTING INVOLVED: *Contacting Your Congressperson*   446

Chapter Summary   446
Questions for Review and Discussion   447
Selected References   447

Chapter 14
The Bureaucracy   449

WHAT IF . . . *There Were No Civil Service?*   *450*

Controlling the Federal Bureaucracy   451
The Nature of Bureaucracy   452
The Size of the Bureaucracy   454

PROFILE: *Elizabeth Hanford Dole*   *455*

The Organization of the Federal Bureaucracy   456
Cabinet Departments   456
Independent Executive Agencies   457
    General Services Administration (GSA)   *458*
    National Aeronautics and Space Administration (NASA)   *459*
    Veterans Administration (VA)   *459*
Independent Regulatory Agencies   459

HIGHLIGHT: *NASA and the Space Shuttle Disaster*   *460*

Government Corporations   463
    Tennessee Valley Authority (TVA)   *464*
    U.S. Postal Service   *464*
    AMTRAK   *465*
Staffing the Bureaucracy   465
A Short History of the Federal Civil Service   466
    To The Victor Belongs the Spoils   *466*
    The Civil Service Reform Act of 1883   *466*
    The Hatch Act of 1939   *467*
The Carter Reforms   468
    The Office of Personnel Management   *468*
    The Merit Systems Protection Board   *468*
    The Senior Executive Service   *469*
The Reagan Reforms   469
Current Attempts at Bureaucratic Reform   470
Grade Banding   470
Sunshine Laws   471
Sunset Laws   471
Helping Out the Whistle-Blowers   472
Bureaucrats as Politicians and Policy Makers   472

HIGHLIGHT: *How to Save $400 Billion*   *473*

The Iron Triangle   474
Congressional Control of the Bureaucracy   475
The American Bureaucracy   476

GETTING INVOLVED: *What Does the Government Know About You?*   *477*

Chapter Summary   477
Questions for Review and Discussion   478
Selected References   478

Chapter 15
The Judiciary   15

WHAT IF . . . *The United States Had a Napoleonic Law Code?*   *480*

What is the Law   481
The Foundation of American Law: The Courts and *Stare Decisis*   482

More Recent Sources of Law   483
Constitutions   483
Judicial Review   483

HIGHLIGHT: *Judicial Review—Marbury v. Madison* (1803)   484

Court Jurisdiction   485
General Jurisdiction and Special, or Limited, Jurisdiction   486
Original and Appellate Jurisdiction   486
The Court Systems in the United States   487
The Federal Court System   487
 District Courts   487
 U.S. Court of Appeals   488
 The Supreme Court of the United States   488
Jurisdiction of Federal Courts   489
How the Supreme Court Functions   490
Which Cases Reach the Supreme Court?   490
 Appeal   490
 Writ of Certiorari   491
Decisions and Options   491
The Supreme Court at Work   492
 Deciding a Case: Private Research   493
 Deciding a Case: The Friday Conference   493
How Federal Judges are Selected   495
Nominating Judicial Candidates   495
District Court Judgeship Nominations   495
Courts of Appeals Appointments   495
The President and Supreme Court Appointments   496
Who Are the Federal Judges?   496
The Background of Supreme Court Justices   496

PROFILE: *Sandra Day O'Connor*   498

The Background of Lower Court Judges   499

HIGHLIGHT: *The Impeachment of a Federal Judge*   500

Qualifications of Federal Judges   500
The Effect of Party Affiliation   501
Judicial Activism and Judicial Restraint   502
A Contrast in Courts: The Warren Court and the Burger Court   503
The Warren Court   503
 Protecting Personal Rights   503
 Widening The Meaning of Personal Rights   504
 Extending the Civil Rights of Minorities   505
The Burger Court   505
 Judicial Activism Continued   506
 Liberal or Conservative?   507
The Rehnquist/Reagan Court   509

PROFILE: *Chief Justice Rehnquist*   510

What Checks Our Courts?   511
Legislative Checks   511
Executive Checks   511
The Rest of the Judiciary   511
The Public Has A Say   511

GETTING INVOLVED: *Changing the Legal System*   513

Chapter Summary   514
Questions for Review and Discussion   514
Selected References   515

Part Five

▽

Public Policy

517

Chapter 16
Political Economy   519

WHAT IF . . . *The Federal Budget Had to Be Balanced?*   **520**

Monetary and Fiscal Policy   **521**

Monetary Policy   521

    Full Employment Without Inflation: Incomes Policy   522

    The Politics of Monetary Policy   522

Fiscal Policy   522

HIGHLIGHT: *The "Misery Index"*   **523**

    Current Fiscal Policies   524

    Fiscal Policy and the Federal Budgeting Process   524

The Political Business Cycle and Monetary and Fiscal Policy   524

HIGHLIGHT: *The Great Depression, 1929–1941*   **525**

    The Theory of a Political Business Cycle   526

    The Evidence   526

The Budget Process   **526**

Presidential Budgeting   526

    OMB's Spring and Fall Preview   527

    What the President Does   527

Congressional Budgeting   528

HIGHLIGHT: *The Day You Could Not Go to Trial*   **529**

The Five Decision Categories in Congressional Budget Making   529

Supplemental Appropriations   529

Nonpolitical Budgeting: The Uncontrollables   530

Our Federal Tax System   **530**

The Types of Taxes   530

HIGHLIGHT: *Backdoor Funding*   **531**

What Is a Fair Type of Tax System?   532

    Three Types of Taxation   532

    Horizontal Versus Vertical Equity   532

    Ability-to-Pay Principle   533

    Benefits-Received Principle   533

Tax Reform   533

    The Politics of Tax Reform   533

    The Players in the Tax Reform Debate   534

The Basic Question of Fairness   535

When Spending Exceeds Revenues: The Public Debt   **536**

Is the Public Debt a Burden?   536

HIGHLIGHT: *Republicans: Fiscal Conservatives?*   **537**

CRITICAL PERSPECTIVE: *Is The Budget Deficit a Red Herring?*   **538**

The Problem of "Crowding Out"   539

PROFILE: *William Philip Gramm*   **540**

Testing the Constitutionality of Gramm-Rudman   540

Congress Reacts   541

GETTING INVOLVED: *The Importance of Government in Your Life*   **542**

Chapter Summary   542

Questions for Review and Discussion   543

Selected References   543

Chapter 17
Domestic Policy 545

WHAT IF . . . Nuclear Power Were Banned in the U.S.? 546
Providing Income Security for Retirement: Social Security 547
How It Works 548
The Economic and Political Crisis Facing Social Security 548
    How Did the Short-Term Crisis Occur? 549
    Now for the Long Run 549
Providing for Medical Care: Medicare and Medicaid 549
Poverty on the Rise? 551
Defining Poverty 552
Who Are the Poor? 553
Other Basic Programs for the Poor 554
Supplemental Security Income (SSI) and Aid to Families with Dependent Children
    (AFDC) 554

CRITICAL PERSPECTIVE: *Is There a Poverty-Welfare Curve?* 555

    Food Stamps 556
    Additional Programs 556
Why Are People Poor? 556
Providing Income Security for Farmers 557
A Short History of the Farmers' Dilemma 557
Problems with Current Farm Programs 558
    Deficiency Payments and Target Prices 558
    The Dairy Program 558
    Price Supports and Suppluses 559
Who Benefits from Price Supports? 559

HIGHLIGHT: *Can We Save the Small Farm?* 560

Labor-Management Regulation 560
Labor's Political Agenda 561
Labor Legislation 562
    Norris-LaGuardia Act of 1932 562
    National Labor Relations Act of 1935 562
    The Forty-Hour Work Week and the Prohibition Against Child Labor 562

PROFILE: *Florence Kelley* 563

    The Taft-Hartley Act of 1947 563
    The Landrum-Griffin Act of 1959 564
Regulating Worker Safety and Health 565
OSHA 565
Protection for Workers on the Decline 565
Energy and the Environment 566

HIGHLIGHT: *Why What Happened at Chernobyl Didn't Happen
  at Three Mile Island* 567

Nuclear Power 567

HIGHLIGHT: *Is Biotechnology a Threat?* 569

The Environment 569
The Government's Response to Pollution Problems 570
    The National Environmental Policy Act 572
    Acid Rain: A Current Environmental Policy Question 572

GETTING INVOLVED: *Working for a Clean Environment* 574

Chapter Summary 575
Questions for Review and Discussion 575
Selected References 575

Chapter 18
Foreign and Defense Policy   577

WHAT IF . . . The United States Withdrew from the United Nations?   578

The United States Is Just a Part of the World   580
Economic Interdependence   581
Military Interdependence   581
Cultural Interdependence   581
What Is Foreign Policy?   582
National Security Policy   582
Diplomacy   583
A Short History of U.S. Foreign Policy   583
The Formative Years   583
Nineteenth-Century Isolationism   584
The Beginning of Interventionism and World War I   584
Post-World War I Isolationism   585
World War II—The Era of Internationalism   585
The End of World War II and the Beginning of the Cold War   586
　The Marshall Plan   587
　Mutual Security Pacts   588
　Confrontation with the Soviet Union   588

CRITICAL PERSPECTIVE: *Who Started the Cold War?*   590

　Containment: A New Foreign Policy   590

PROFILE: *George F. Kennan*   592

　Confrontation in a Nuclear War   593
A Period of Détente   594
A Change in Direction?   594
Terrorism   596

HIGHLIGHT: *Are United States Defenses Spread Too Thin?*   597

The Iranian Connection   599
Who Makes Foreign Policy?   600
Constitutional Powers of the President   600
Informal Techniques of Presidential Leadership   602
Sources of Foreign Policy Making Within the Executive Branch   602
　The Department of State   603
　The National Security Council   605
　The Intelligence Community   605
　The Department of Defense   607
The Military-Industrial Complex   607
Eisenhower's Farewell to the Nation   609
A Symbiotic Relationship   609
Limiting the President's Power   610
Foreign Economic Policy   611
Multinational Corporations: A New Force in Foreign Policy   611

HIGHLIGHT: *The Roller-Coaster Dollar*   612

The Nuclear Freeze Movement   614
Would Nuclear War Be World Suicide?   615
Impetus for a Nuclear Freeze   615

GETTING INVOLVED: *Reducing the Nuclear Threat*   617

Chapter Summary   618
Questions for Review and Discussion   619
Selected References   619

Chapter 19
State and Local Government   623

WHAT IF . . . *Every State Had the Same Constitution?*   *624*
State and Local Government Spending   626
Paying for State and Local Government   627
Raising Revenue   627
The Era of Tax Revolt   628
  Enter Proposition 13   *628*
PROFILE: *Tom Bradley*   *629*
  Effects of Tax Limitation Measures   *629*
The U.S. Constitution and the States   630
State Constitutions   631
Why Are State Constitutions So Long?   631
The Constitutional Convention and the Constitutional Initiative   634
The State Executive Branch   634
A Weak Executive   634
Reforming the System   635
The Governor's Veto Power   636
Off-Year Election of Governors   636
The State Legislature   636
Legislative Apportionment   638
Direct Democracy: The Initiative, Referendum, and Recall   639
  The Initiative   *639*
  The Referendum   *639*
  The Recall   *640*
The State Judiciary   640
How Local Government Operates   641
The Legal Existence of Local Government   641
PROFILE: *Henry Cisneros*   *642*
Local Governmental Units   643
  Municipalities   *643*
  Counties   *644*
  Towns and Townships   *644*
  Special Districts   *645*
Consolidation of Governments   646
How Municipalities Are Governed   647
  The Commission Plan   *647*
  The Council-Manager Plan   *648*
  The Mayor-Administrator Plan   *648*
  Mayor-Council Plan   *648*
Machine Versus Reform in City Politics   648
HIGHLIGHT: *Three Tables and Some Chairs—$180,000*   *649*
GETTING INVOLVED: *Organizing in Your Community*   *651*
Chapter Summary   652
Questions for Review and Discussion   652
Selected References   653

Appendix A   The U.S. Constitution   654
Appendix B   The Declaration of Independence   657
Appendix C   The Presidents of the U.S.   674
Appendix D   Federalist Papers 10 and 51   676

Glossary   681
Index   698

Part Six
▽
State and Local Politics
621

Preface

▽

As the United States prepared to celebrate the bicentennial of the Constitution, the national political scene gave evidence of both stability and change. While the 1986 election reaffirmed the relative ineffectiveness of presidential campaigning for Congress, it also revealed the continued growth of the Republican party, particularly at the state level. Most analysts characterized the mood of the nation as "centrist" and predicted few major political upheavals in the next few years.

The goal of this textbook is to enable students to perceive and understand both the dynamics of political change and those structures and patterns which reinforce the stability of the system. We believe that it is important for students to gain a comprehensive understanding of the system and its historical roots while at the same time catching the excitement of current political events. The inclusion of the most up-to-date material available increases the student's enthusiasm for the political process, and, therefore, enhances their desire to learn.

A Total Learning/Teaching Package

▽

This text, along with its numerous supplements, constitutes what we believe to be a total learning/teaching package. Specifically, the text itself contains numerous pedagogical aids and high-interest additions, such as:

1. A Preview of Contents to Each Chapter. To give the student an understanding of what is to come, each chapter starts out with a topical outline of its contents.
2. What if . . .? In order to stimulate student interest in the chapter topics, each chapter begins with a hypothetical situation that we call "What If . . .?" For example, in Chapter 2 we asked the hypothetical question, "What if . . . the Constitution had not been ratified?"
3. Marginal Definitions. Since terminology is often a stumbling block to understanding, each important term is printed in boldface. More importantly, in the margins adjacent to the boldfaced terms termed is a glossary definition of those terms.
4. Did You Know? Throughout the text, within the margins, are various facts and figures that we call "Did You Know?" They add relevance, humor, and a certain amount of fun to the student's task of learning about American government and politics.
5. Profiles and Highlights. Every chapter is enlivened with profiles of key individuals, who have made unique contributions to the American political system. Also included in every chapter are Highlight boxes, which take a closer look at some of the interest aspects of topics discussed in the chapter.
6. Getting Involved. Because we believe that the best way for students to get a firmer understanding of the American political system is by getting involved, we offer suggestions on ways for them to get involved in the system. At the end of each chapter there are suggestions of where to write, whom to call, and what to do.

7. **Point-by-Point Chapter Summary.** At the end of each chapter the essential points in the chapter are presented in a point-by-point format for ease of review and understanding.

8. **Questions for Review and Discussion.** In order to elicit student interest and discussion in and out of class, there are two to five questions for review and discussion at the end of each chapter.

9. **Selected References.** Important and understandable references are given at the end of each chapter. Each reference is annotated to indicate its usefulness and the area that it covers.

10. **Tables, Charts, and Photos.** As you can readily see, the text uses tables and charts, as well as photos, to summarize and illustrate important institutional, historical, or economic facts.

New to the Second Edition—Critical Perspectives

▽

We have added what we believe to be a major, high-interest, effective teaching device to the majority of chapters in this Second Edition. They are entitled Critical Perspectives. In these short essays, we examine a number of newer theories about either what has happened in American political history, what is happening currently, or what might happen in the future. The student is asked to examine a particular theory in a more critical fashion than he or she might normally do within the text itself. The Critical Perspectives that we have chosen for this edition are:

Chapter 2: The Madisonian Argument for Separation of Powers
             Alternative Constitutions
Chapter 3: Are There Nine Nations in North America?
Chapter 7: On Political Thinking
Chapter 8: The Rise and Fall of the Major Party
Chapter 9: What's in the News?
Chapter 10: On Voting Choices
Chapter 11: The Logic of Collective Action
Chapter 12: The President's Personality
Chapter 13: A Home with House Members
Chapter 16: Is the Budget Deficit a Red Herring?
Chapter 17: Is There a Poverty-Welfare Curve?
Chapter 18: Who Started the Cold War?

Updating in Other Parts of the Learning/Teaching Package

Whenever appropriate, we have updated or changed the What If sections, the Did You Knows, the Profiles, the Highlights, and the Getting Involved sections. The Selected References have also been thoroughly updated, with the most appropriate references clearly annotated for the student at the end of each chapter.

Appendices

▽

So that this book can serve as a reference, we have included important documents for the student of American government to have at close hand. The documents included are:

▽ The U.S. Constitution
▽ The Declaration of Independence
▽ A list of presidents of the United States
▽ New to the Second Edition. We have added the Federalist Papers 10 and 51 to the Appendix, at the request of a number of adopters. We hope this addition will prove useful to everyone using the text.

And Some Reorganization

Although we have followed the basic format and organization of the First Edition, we have changed Part Three on People and Politics. There is now a separate chapter (7) on public opinion and a separate chapter (11) on special-interest groups. Another new chapter combining elements of several previous ones is Chapter 10 on campaigns, voting behavior, and elections.

Several of the public policy chapters have been completely rewritten to better mirror the policy concerns of today. Chapter 16 concerns itself exclusively with political economy, including the important questions surrounding rising federal budget deficits and the Gramm-Rudman-Hollings Act. Tax reform is also examined, not only in the context of the changes in our federal tax code, but also in the context of how our tax code mirrors the values that we hold. Chapter 17 now deals exclusively with domestic policy with increased coverage of poverty and its elimination, management-labor relations, Medicare and Medicaid, and the agricultural sector.

The Latest Election Results Tallied and Analyzed

Because we believe that currency is important in maintaining student interest in the subject matter, we have made sure that all of the latest congressional election results from November 1986 are included in the edition. We analyze them in Chapter 1 on the American Democracy and Political Culture and Chapter 8 on Political Parties, Chapter 9 on the Media, Chapter 10 on Campaigns, Voting Behavior, and Elections, Chapter 13 on the Congress, and Chapter 19 on State and Local Government.

The Student Study Guide
▽

The Student Study Guide was written by James McElyea of Tulsa Junior College, Oklahoma. Each chapter provides learning objectives, a topical outline, a list of terms and concepts, and a variety of self-study questions.

Instructor's Manual with Test Bank
▽

The Instructor's Manual was written by Michael Dinneen of Tulsa Junior College and includes learning objectives and an annotated outline with teaching suggestions, examples, ideas for presentation, and supplemental lecture ideas. The extensive test bank is organized by chapter subtitle.

Computerized Testing

▽

The test bank is available on WesTest II magnetic tape for use on mainframe computers. Also, MicroTest II diskettes are available to adopters who want to generate tests using Apple, IBM PC, or TRS 80 micrcomputers.

Software

▽

A computerized Study Guide for Apple microcomputers is available to adopters. The program was designed to incorporate the authors' teaching objectives. Twenty questions are available for each chapter presented in three basic formats—a review, a race, and a quiz. Upon completion of a session, the summary sequence provides students with a listing of the questions missed by chapter, page, and topic.

A Videotape on the History of Political Advertising

▽

"And If I'm Elected," a videotape available in VHS and Beta formats, is a retrospective of political television commercials hosted by the Smothers Brothers. It chronicles the sometimes humorous and sometimes surprising nature of American political campaigning, and we strongly recommend it as a wonderful teaching tool to all adopters of this text.

Enrichment Lectures

▽

We have added a new teaching device to this edition. Each chapter has an enrichment lecture that includes full references plus one transparency. These provide additional lecture topics in outline form.

Transparency Masters

▽

A number of transparencies and transparency masters are available to adopters of this text. These transparencies are of critical graphs and tables from the text itself.

Acknowledgments:

▽

Since we started this project a number of years ago, a sizable cadre of individuals has helped us in various phases of the undertaking. The following academic reviewers offered numerous constructive criticisms, comments, and suggestions during the preparation of the first edition of this text:

Kevin Bailey
North Harris Community College, Texas

Ralph Bunch
Portland State University

Robert E. Craig
University of New Hampshire

Doris Daniels
Nassau Community College, New York

George C. Edwards, III
Texas A&M University

Stefan D. Haag
Austin Community College, Texas

Robert M. Herman
Moorpark College, California

J. C. Horton
San Antonio College, Texas

Loch K. Johnson
University of Georgia

John D. Kay
Santa Barbara City College, California

Charles W. Kegley
University of South Carolina

Dale Krane
Mississippi State University

Samuel Krislov
University of Minnesota

Carl Lieberman
University of Akron, Ohio

Orma Linford
Kansas State University

James D. McElyea
Tulsa Junior College, Oklahoma

William P. McLauchlan
Purdue University

William S. Maddox
University of Florida

J. David Martin
Midwestern State University, Texas

Bruce B. Mason
Arizona State University

Charles Prysby
University of North Carolina

Donald R. Ranish
Antelope Valley College, California

Curt Reichel
University of Wisconsin

Eleanor A. Schwab
South Dakota State University

Len Shipman
Mount San Antonio College, California

Scott Shrewsbury
Mankato State University, Minnesota

John R. Todd
North Texas State University

B. Oliver Walter
University of Wyoming

Further, we would like to thank the following individuals for their incitful reviews of the manuscript for the second edition:

Clyde W. Barrow
University of California at Los Angeles

Carol Cassell
University of Alabama

Willoughby Jarrell
Kennesaw College, Georgia

James McElyea
Tulsa Junior College, Oklahoma

John P. Pelissero
Loyola University of Chicago

Gerald S. Strom
University of Illinois at Chicago

Allan Wiese
Mankato State University, Minnesota

In addition, we wish to thank Roger L. Miller who revised the chapters on economics and on the legal system. He also offered suggestions concerning changes in the format of this edition. In addition, we are indebted to the following persons for their editorial and research assistance in this undertaking: Bill Stryker, Julie Sobeleski, Steve Davis, and Cara Bardes. Finally, we wish to thank Sharon Marsh for her management of the project details and Clyde Perlee, of West Publishing Company, who continues to be our faithful editor and arbitrator, attempting to coordinate three authors. Any remaining errors are definitely our own. We welcome any and all comments from both instructors and students. We feel that the comments we received on the First Edition helped us improve it, but we know that we will need to continue to make changes as the needs of instructors and students change.

Steffen Schmidt
Mack Shelley
Barbara Bardes

1
THE AMERICAN SYSTEM

Chapter 1

▽

American Democracy and Political Culture

Contents

▽

The Political System in 1986

Politics

Who Governs

Democracy: Real and Ideal

American Political Culture

Overview

What If . . .

The United States Had Been a Colony of Spain?

The formation of new nation states, such as the United States, seems in retrospect a natural and inevitable process. We can't imagine it to have been any other way. However, it could have been very different. In fact, one event alone might have altered the history of North America fundamentally—the Battle of the Spanish Armada in 1588.

Under the Spanish King Philip the Prudent, Spain's power and influence were stunning. Between 1559 and 1609, Spain was the dominant power in European affairs. Not content with his domain, Philip tried to roll back the Protestant Reformation in Europe and continue to expand the Spanish Empire, which flourished following the discovery of America by Christopher Columbus in 1492.

One of Philip's ambitions had been to reclaim England for Roman Catholicism and in the process to expand Spanish influence and control to the British Isles. His move came in 1588 after the execution of Mary Queen of Scots and following complicated and exciting plots and counterplots in England.

In July of that year, Philip ordered the Spanish naval fleet (the Armada) to enter the English channel, attack

and defeat the British fleet, and then seize England and bring it into his realm. While formidable, the Spanish fleet was defeated, in large measure because the British and their allies the Dutch were better able to maneuver in shallow coastal waters with their flat-bottomed boats and to harass and finally drive away the Spanish contingents.

If Spain had been victorious, North American history would have taken a very different course. In the first place, the northeastern parts of the New World would likely not have been intensively explored and settled. Spain already had a strong foothold and colonial settlements in the southern parts of the Americas. These gradually expanded north and westward, and this pattern would have continued. The Mayflower would not have sailed, and early settlements such as Jamestown (1607) would probably not have existed.

Second, Roman Catholicism, one of the driving forces behind Philip's expansion in Europe, would clearly have become the only permissible religion in the Americas. North American Indians, like their brethren in the south, would have been converted.

Third, a Spanish viceroy would have been appointed as administrator and representative of the Spanish crown. His seat would likely have been in Florida and would have extended as far north as Spanish exploration allowed.

With Spanish rule would have come several fundamental institutions, such as Roman law, which is based on elaborate legal statutes and codes and allows the judge no interpretive discretion, as does English common law. A highly centralized form of government accountable directly to Spain through an elaborate bureaucracy would also have prevailed. Moreover, Span-

ish would have been the official language.

Such a gigantic Spanish colonial empire would have generated even more elaborate resources for Spain, allowing that country to become a political and economic giant. The Latin American wars of independence against Spain (1810–1820) might never have erupted, as it was partly the example of the American Revolution and U.S. independence that inspired the Latin American leaders to break with Spain. If, however, independence movements had occurred, the result could have been a large Spanish-speaking state in North America, possibly more homogeneous in population and resembling more closely some of the other Latin American superstates such as Brazil or Argentina.

▽

Having a Spanish tradition would have greatly influenced all of the early attempts at self-government by the Founding Fathers. The idea of the people writing their own charter for government would have been foreign to the Spanish culture in the 17th century. Instead, as descendents of English culture, colonial elites assumed a certain right of self government and carried their English background and ideas to the writing of our Constitution.

As the last representatives to the Constitutional Convention in 1787 were putting their signatures to the document, Benjamin Franklin looked at the back of the president's chair on which a rising sun was painted and observed, "I have often and often in the course of the session, and the vicissitudes of my hopes and fears as to its issue, looked at that sun behind the president without being able to tell whether it was rising or setting. But now at length I have the happiness to know that it is a rising and not a setting sun."[1]

Even with his optimism, Franklin could not have imagined how prosperous and successful the new nation would become. The United States has developed a unique **political system.** We live under the oldest written constitution in the world, its essential features unchanged since its **ratification** in 1789. Virtually nowhere do more people vote in free, competitive elections. Nowhere are so many public officials, or holders of local, state, or national positions, accountable to the **electorate** at such regular intervals. The constitutional structure of the United States and the free exercise of the vote have sustained stable, adaptable, and effective political processes.

The American political system is neither flawless nor without its critics. The **institutions** of government can act very slowly, and the political process of lawmaking is hard pressed to respond to rapid economic and social changes in the nation. The rights of minority groups within the population have been denied at various times in our history, and the promise of equality for all citizens has not been fulfilled. Although citizens exercise extraordinary freedom in speech, press, and religion, these rights have not always been safeguarded. One fact is certain: Political life in the United States is ever changing in response to societal and technological changes, to the pressures of the international environment, and to the increasing demands of individuals and groups for governmental action. The political situation of the United States in the late 1980s reflects this unceasing activity and suggests some of the political conflicts that lie ahead.

The Political System in 1986
▽

Although the political contests of 1986 lacked the dramatic flair of presidential years, the election campaign underscored the stability of the political system while at the same time hinting at its future. Generally, the mid-1980s saw a resurgence of patriotic feeling in the United States. Perhaps those feelings were best symbolized by Liberty Weekend, 1986, which celebrated the restoration of the Statue of Liberty and its centennial. As millions of Americans watched on television, thousands of immigrants were sworn in as new citizens, a parade of tall ships saluted the statue, and lavish entertainment spectacles took place in New York City. In the same year, the United States issued a series of gold coins, the first in many decades, which sold out to collectors and investors. Americans also seemed to be aware, to a limited extent, of problems in the nation. Thousands joined in the "Hands Across America" project to raise money for the hungry although turnout and pledges fell short of the sponsors' goals.

The national sense of well-being was paralleled by the unprecedented popularity of Ronald Reagan. In his sixth year of office, the president remained personally popular with the majority of Americans although they disapproved of many of his

[1]Max Farrand, ed., *The Records of the Federal Convention of 1787*, vol. 2, rev. ed. (New Haven: Yale University Press, 1937), p. 648.

Chapter 1
American Democracy and Political Culture
▽

Political System

A set of institutions, practices, and policies through which political questions are resolved.

Ratification

Formal approval and consent by an authorized political body.

Electorate

All citizens entitled to vote.

Institutions

Long-standing, identifiable structures or associations that perform functions for society.

For more analysis of the impact of the 1986 election see discussions of:

- Nebraska governor's race, page 173
- State politics, page 238
- The LaRouche effort, page 249
- Exit polls, page 304
- The new Congress, page 419
- Congressional elections, page 425
- State referenda, page 640

▽

President Reagan campaigning in South Dakota for Republicans in 1986.

policies. Given the president's approval levels in the polls, the low rate of inflation, and overall state of economic health in the nation, analysts anticipated low turnout and issueless debates in the 1986 elections.

The 1986 Elections
▽

The longterm stakes were high in the 1986 elections although public interest was low until the last days of the campaign. The Democrats saw an opportunity to regain control of the United States Senate which they had lost in 1980. Their chances were improved by the ratio of Senators seeking reelection. Twenty-two Republican seats were up for grabs as compared to twelve for the Democrats and many of the Republican Senators had originally won their seats by riding on Reagan's coattails.

Many political analysts also saw the elections as a test of the possible realignment of the political parties. Would the trend toward increasing Republican party identification continue to increase, particularly among the younger voters and Southern whites? If the Republicans kept their Southern Senatorial seats and increased their control at the state level, the two parties would be more competitive than they had been since 1932.

The outcome of the election could also be seen as predicting the issues and trends for the last two years of the Reagan presidency. A strong Republican showing would give the president a claim to popular support for some of his programs and enable him to control the political agenda. Losses might seriously impair his legendary ability to persuade Congress.

The Candidate-Centered Campaign

Few national issues sparked public debate in 1986. In a rare display of bipartisanship, the Congress had passed a tax reform bill before the November elections. The president was immensely popular, so few candidates saw much advantage to attacking him or his programs. Polls taken after the failed Rykjavik summit indicated public support for the president's Strategic Defense Initiative and for his stance toward the Soviet Union.

Given the issueless national political arena, campaigns focused on local issues and on the candidates themselves. Many candidates had raised enough money to produce extensive media campaigns in which they attacked their opponents' positions and credibility. Local issues became increasingly important: In the farm states, the plight of the agricultural sector became the central issue and trade reform became the hot topic in the textile producing states. The president himself contributed to the focus on candidates by entering the campaign during the last two weeks. He made personal appearances on behalf of many Republican candidates, asking the voters to return Republicans to Washington to support his programs.

The Message of the Election

The outcome of the 1986 elections held no great surprises for the parties or for political analysts, yet it suggested a number of possibilities for the future. The president, like others before him, was very ineffective in getting voters to support his choices for office. In fact, the Democrats showed surprising strength, regaining control of the Senate with a net gain of eight seats in that body. Republicans,

Joe Kennedy, son of Robert Kennedy, campaigning for Tip O'Neill's House seat in Massachusetts.

Chapter 1
American Democracy and
Political Culture
▽
7

however, showed resilience and the power of incumbency, in holding onto most
of their House seats. For the sixth year of a presidency, their net loss was extremely
low. Republicans also gained a number of governorships but made no gains in
state legislative bodies.

The results confirmed the trends of the campaigns: the 1986 elections were
heavily candidate-centered. Voters picked and chose carefully among the parties.
In many states, both Democratic and Republican office-holders were returned by
large margins. New York's Democratic Governor Cuomo, a possible presidential
candidate, won by more than 65% of the vote while Republican Senator D'Amato
captured more than 58%. Local issues and personalities decided the races in most
states so that no overall pattern of support for either party emerged.

Democrats claimed that there had been no increase in Republican strength
among the voters and, pointing to the Southern Senatorial races, announced that
"Democrats had come home." Republicans noted that a large proportion of Southern whites had voted for Republicans and that they now held governorships in
South Carolina, Alabama, and Texas. Neither party could really claim that it had
captured new groups in the voting public.

What did the election results portend for the future? With Democrats firmly in
control of both houses of Congress, the President lost the ability to set the legislative
agenda. Issues which would probably reach Congress would be trade reform to ease
unemployment in Democratic areas and agricultural programs for the farmers. The
President can expect much more difficulty in obtaining aid for the *contras* in
Nicaragua and support for the Star Wars defense system. His judicial appointments
will encounter intense scrutiny in the Senate and possible opposition.

During the week of the election, a new issue arose which looked as if it would
change the national agenda for the last years of the Reagan presidency. The president's deal to send arms to Iran as a possible ploy to gain the freedom of hostages
held in Beirut immediately raised questions of judgment and legality. When it
became known that profits from the Iranian arms deal were intended for contra
forces in Nicaragua, the credibility of the White House and many of the President's
closest advisors declined rapidly. The secret policy immediately raised the level of

*Barbara Mikulski celebrates her election
to the U.S. Senate with Sen. Paul Sar-
banes.*

Dante Fascell (left), Chairman of the House Foreign Relations Committee, on the first day of hearings on the sale of arms to Iran. Lt. Col. Oliver North (above) appears on television after being dismissed from his position on the National Security Council.

political conflict in the system. To begin our investigation of the processes of American politics and the ways in which the system responds to political conflict, let us begin by looking at some of the fundamental concepts of American politics, the study of which is political science.

Politics
▽

You may be surprised to learn that there is not a single definition of **politics** that is acceptable to all political scientists. Indeed, the discipline recognizes various definitions, each differing from the others in subtle ways. This should not concern us, however, because definitions are not ends in themselves; they are tools we use to understand a complicated subject.

Still, currently used definitions of politics share certain meanings and lead us to look at certain kinds of activities. Most major definitions of politics are based on the idea of **social conflict.**

All national societies require cohesion and a high level of cooperation among their members to survive and prosper. At the same time, each nation must deal with conflict among its citizens. To maintain a vital degree of unity and cooperation, ways must be found to channel and to resolve conflict in order to keep it from threatening the very existence of the society.

Conflicts arise in societies because their members are distinct individuals with their own unique needs, values, and perspectives. Individuals and groups compete with one another in at least three respects. First, because of their differing beliefs, rooted in religious or personal values, individuals may disagree over basic issues of right and wrong. The intensely bitter debate that has raged in recent years over abortion is an example of this kind of conflict. Second, because of their differing needs and values, individuals may disagree about society's priorities. In the 1980s, Americans debated about whether the government's main concern should be social justice and welfare or national defense. This is the latest version of the "guns or butter" dilemma that has faced nations for centuries. Third, individuals compete

Politics
According to David Easton, the "authoritative allocation of values" for a society; according to Harold Lasswell, "who gets what, when, and how" in a society.

Social Conflict
Disagreements arising in society because of differing beliefs, values, and attitudes; conflicts over society's priorities and competition for scarce resources.

Conflict resolution in a congressional committee.

for scarce resources. Income is a good example. There is never enough of it to go around to satisfy everyone's demands. Thus many political debates can be analyzed in terms of the distribution of income. Underlying most debates about taxes, for example, is the question of which group will part with some of its income to pay for the nation's priorities.

Harold Lasswell, one of this century's most influential political scientists, fashioned a definition of politics that captures these various kinds of social conflicts: Politics is a process that determines "who gets what, when, and how" for a society. This definition implies that people (who) are in conflict over values (what). Another implication is that a society needs to have a set of procedures to resolve the question of who gets what. Thus politics not only involves the reality of social conflict but the need for ways to solve these conflicts. It is important to note that conflict is seen as natural and inevitable in any social system. Differences of opinion or values are not inherently bad in a society. The process of resolving conflict can be an opportunity for clarifying values and making change possible.

Another leading political scientist, David Easton, has formulated one of the most widely used definitions of politics, one which is similar to Lasswell's. Easton defined politics as the "authoritative allocation of values" for a society. This means that politics encompasses all of the activities involved in the conflict over who receives benefits from the society. These benefits or values may include status, welfare payments, or a law dealing with prayer in the public schools. Easton further specifies an authoritative conflict resolution. Authoritative decisions are those that can be backed up by legitimate power. This concept of **authority** is very important for helping us understand politics and the role of government in society.

Authority

An agency that is generally recognized and accepted as having the deciding voice. For most societies, government is the ultimate authority in the allocation of values.

Government

If politics refers to conflict and conflict resolution, **government** refers to the structured arrangement through which the decisions resolving conflict are made, or, in Easton's terms, "allocating values." Some societies, such as families or tribes, may be small enough that they do not need permanent structures to make these decisions. The group may collectively and in very informal ways allocate values for the whole society. This would be a community that has politics but no government. But once a society reaches a certain level of complexity, there is likely to emerge a particular person or group of people who make decisions allocating values for the society. With the establishment of these decision makers, we have arrived at the concept of government.

Authority

Authority is central to the question of compliance with the decision as to who gets what. For example, the United States government makes laws and rules designed to ensure that all residents who receive a certain level of income will pay income taxes. In 1986, more than one hundred million tax returns were filed with the Internal Revenue Service from which the government derived more than $360 billion in revenue. Every year, millions of Americans struggle to fill out their tax forms or pay someone else to do it for them. By April 15 (sometimes at midnight), they have mailed these forms to the government, many with a check attached. Although the IRS employs a staff of more than eighty-four thousand people to collect the taxes, the system is for the most part voluntary. Comedians make jokes about the tax system, yet most Americans obey the law even though it takes part of their personal income and may require considerable personal effort to learn how to comply.

Why, in spite of these disadvantages to themselves, do vast numbers of Americans comply with the law by reporting their incomes and paying the appropriate taxes? It is a matter of authority. To say that a government is authoritative implies a reasonable expectation that there will be **compliance** with its decisions. What prompts this reasonable expectation that there will be general compliance with Internal Revenue Service rules?

Legitimacy

Some people comply with taxes because they are afraid of the possible sanctions the government might impose on them if they do not. But considerations of power do not explain every instance of compliance. Many people obey the tax laws because they think it is right to do so. In other words, they see the laws as having **legitimacy.** The laws are an appropriate use of power by the legally constituted government following correct decision-making procedures. Legitimacy implies rightfulness, as do the terms used in the preceding sentence: *appropriate, legally constituted,* and *correct.* To say that authority is legitimate is to strongly suggest an obligation to comply with its decisions—even a moral obligation.

It is also possible that a good many people obey because they have developed the **habit of compliance.** Habits of compliance are rooted in perceptions of the legitimacy and power of the government. They are also closely related to the beliefs

---

Government
Individuals, institutions, and processes that make society's rules about conflict resolution and the allocation of resources and that possess the power to enforce them.

Compliance
Accepting and carrying out authoritative decisions.

Legitimacy
A status conferred by the people on the government's officials, acts, and institutions through their belief that the government's actions are an appropriate use of power by a legally constituted governmental authority following correct decision-making policies; regarded as rightful and entitled to compliance and obedience on the part of citizens.

Habits of Compliance
Learned obedience without thinking much about power or legitimacy, although these reinforce such habits.

▽

Launch of a Pershing II missile.

Political Culture

The pattern of political beliefs and values characteristic of a community or population.

Power

The ability to cause others to modify their behavior and to conform to what the power holder wants.

Democracy

A system of government in which ultimate political authority is vested in the people. Derived from the Greek words *demos* ("the people") and *kratos* ("authority").

Direct Democracy

A system of government in which political decisions are made by the people directly, rather than by their elected representatives; probably possible only in small political communities.

Legislature

A government body primarily responsible for the making of laws.

and attitudes that people have toward their country. Although few individuals feel patriotic when filling out their tax returns, they act in part on an underlying belief in what the country stands for. Such beliefs and ideals form a significant part of what political scientists sometimes refer to as the **political culture.**

Power

Another and perhaps more fundamental answer to why we comply with onerous tax forms is because we understand that the government has the **power** to enforce these laws. Although we may pay out of compliance and acknowledge the legitimacy of the income tax, we support the right of the government to use force to make other citizens pay their share.

Power is a particular kind of relationship between two actors. If Smith is able to make Brown do something that Brown would otherwise not do, we say that Smith has power over Brown. That power may be exercised through persuasion, command, or physical coercion, as well as myriad other ways. In the same way, we perceive an interest group such as the National Rifle Association as powerful if it is successful in having gun control regulations weakened. Often, we talk of the power of the president when he is able to convince the Congress to pass legislation that he has requested. In many respects, power is at the heart of "who gets what."

Who Governs

▽

The ultimate location of the power to decide which groups and individuals benefit from the government and to make the laws that all must obey is central to our understanding of politics. The United States is a **democracy;** in its derivation from the Greek, this means government by the people. Although the definition seems clear, it is worth considering how much democracy we have in this nation. Although the political culture instills the abstract principles of democratic government in most citizens, the practice of democracy may take several alternate forms.

The Athenian Model of Direct Democracy

The government of the ancient Greek city-state of Athens is often considered to be the historic model for a **direct democracy.** In fact, the system was not a pure system of direct democracy because the average Athenian was not a participant in every political decision. Nonetheless, all major issues, even if decided by the committees of the ruling Council, were put before the assembly of all citizens for a vote. Moreover, about one in six citizens held some political office in any given year. Since positions were usually held only for one year they were rotated from one citizen to another quite often, most citizens did, in fact, participate in governing. The most important feature of Athenian democracy was that the **legislature** was composed of all of the citizens. Women, foreigners, and slaves, not being citizens, were excluded.

Athenian direct democracy is considered an ideal form of democracy because it demanded a high level of participation from every citizen. All important decisions were put to a vote of the entire citizenry so that public debate over political issues

was a constant feature of social life. Furthermore, the idea of rotation in office allowing many individuals the chance to serve in government meant that no one politician could gain too much power.

Direct democracy also has been practiced in some Swiss cantons, in New England town meetings, and in some midwestern township meetings in the United States. New England town meetings, which include all of the voters who live in the town, continue to make important decisions for the community—such as levying taxes, hiring city officials, and deciding local ordinances—by majority vote. Some states provide a modern adaptation of direct democracy for their citizens: In thirty-nine states, representative democracy is supplemented by the **initiative** or the **referendum**—a process by which the people may vote directly on laws or constitutional amendments. The **recall** process, which is available in thirteen states, allows the people to vote to remove a politician from state office.

The Founders' Fear of Direct Democracy

Although they were aware of the Athenian model, the framers of the U.S. Constitution—for the most part—were opposed to such a system. For many centuries preceding this country's establishment, any form of democracy was considered to be dangerous and to lead to instability. But in the eighteenth and nineteenth centuries, the idea of government based on the **consent of the people** gained increasing popularity. Such a government was the main aspiration of the American and French revolutions, as well as of many subsequent ones. Few of the revolutions' advocates, however, were ready to embrace direct democracy on the Athenian model. Generally, the masses were considered to be too uneducated to govern themselves, too prone to the influence of demagogues, and too likely to abrogate minority rights.

In the *Federalist Papers*, James Madison defended the new scheme of republican government in the Constitution, while warning of the problems inherent in a "pure democracy":

Initiative
A procedure whereby voters can propose a law or a constitutional amendment.

Referendum
An act of referring legislative (statutory) or constitutional measures to the voters for approval or disapproval.

Recall
A procedure allowing the people to vote to dismiss an elected official from state office before his or her term has expired.

Consent of the People
The idea that governments and laws derive their legitimacy from the consent of the people living under them.

[A] pure democracy . . . can admit of no cure for the mischiefs of faction. A common passion or interest will, in almost every case, be felt by a majority of the whole . . . and there is nothing to check the inducements to sacrifice the weaker party or an obnoxious individual. Hence it is that such democracies have ever been spectacles of turbulence and contention, and have ever been found incompatible with personal security or the rights of property; and have in general been as short in their lives as they have been violent in their deaths.[2]

Like many other politicians of his time, Madison feared that pure, or direct, democracy would deteriorate into mob rule. What would keep the majority of the people, if given direct decision-making power, from abusing the rights of individuals?

Representative Democracy

Representative Democracy

A form of government in which representatives elected by the people make laws and policies.

The framers of the U.S. Constitution settled on a republican form of government, which is also known as a **representative democracy.** The people hold the ultimate power over the government through the election process, but policy decisions are all made by national officials. Even this distance between the people and the government was not sufficient; other provisions in the Constitution made sure that the Senate and the president would be selected by political elites rather than by the people. This moderate form of democratic government came to be widely

[2]James Madison, in Alexander Hamilton, James Madison, and John Jay, *The Federalist Papers*, No. 10 (New York: Mentor Books, 1961), p. 81.

The right to vote.

Profile

▽

Thomas Jefferson

There is perhaps no better representative of the spirit of the early American political climate and no clearer proponent of the modern American political culture than Thomas Jefferson. It was Jefferson's eloquence, for example, that crafted the strong statements in the Declaration of Independence that established the foundation for our views about the relationship between the people and their government:

"We hold these truths to be self-evident, that all men are created equal, that they are endowed by their Creator with certain unalienable Rights, that among these are Life, Liberty, and the pursuit of Happiness.—That to secure these rights, Governments are instituted among Men, deriving their just powers from the consent of the governed,—That whenever any Form of Government becomes destructive of these ends, it is the Right of the People to alter or to abolish it, and to institute new Government, laying its foundation on such principles and organizing its powers in such form, as to them shall seem most likely to effect their Safety and Happiness."

Not all of Jefferson's views were written into the Declaration of Independence, however; for example, Jefferson's attacks on King George III of England for failing to abolish the slave trade (even though Jefferson was a slave owner) were stricken from the final version of the document.

Thomas Jefferson was born at Shadwell, Virginia, on April 13, 1743. He attended the College of William and Mary and subsequently studied law, science, and philosophy. After drafting

"I have sworn upon the altar of God eternal hostility against every form of tyranny over the mind of man."

the Declaration of Independence while a member of the Continental Congress, he was elected to the Virginia House of Delegates in 1776. Three years later, he became governor of Virginia. British occupation and political complexities led him to retire to his home at Monticello, Virginia. He became a member of the Continental Congress again in 1783, where he drafted provisions for the subsequent Northwest Ordinance that forbade slavery north of the Ohio river and helped establish the decimal system.

Jefferson was appointed minister to France in 1785 and secretary of state in 1789. He resigned that cabinet post in 1793 because of continued differences with Secretary of the Treasury Alexander Hamilton over plans for a strong, centralized, executive-centered government bordering on monarchy. He ran as the Democratic-Republican nominee for president in 1796, lost to John Adams, and became Adams's vice president. Jefferson and Aaron Burr received equal numbers of electoral votes in the 1800 presidential contest, but Jefferson became president by a vote of the House of Representatives when Hamilton threw his Federalist support in the House to Jefferson. His first term was highlighted by the Louisiana Purchase, which brought huge western territories into the union. Following reelection against Federalist Charles C. Pinckney in 1804, Jefferson pursued an unpopular embargo policy to try to keep the United States out of the Napoleonic Wars that ravaged Europe.

He retired to Monticello in 1809, later founded the University of Virginia, and developed his interests in education, science, architecture, and music. He died at Monticello on July 4, 1826, the same day that John Adams passed away.

It has been said that the greatest assemblage of intellectual talent that ever gathered in the White House occurred when Thomas Jefferson dined alone.

Universal Suffrage

The right of all people to vote for their representatives.

Canton

A political division in Switzerland comparable to one of the states in the United States.

Majority

More than 50 percent.

Majority Rule

A basic principle of democracy asserting that the greatest number of citizens in any political unit should select officials and determine policies.

Limited Government

A form of government based on the principle that the powers of government should be clearly limited either through a written document or through wide public understanding; characterized by institutional checks to ensure that governments serve the public rather than private interests.

Principles of Democratic Government

As practiced in the United States and many European countries, democratic government emphasizes certain values and procedures. All representative democracies rest on the rule of the people as expressed through the election of government officials. In the twentieth century, **universal suffrage** is the rule. In the 1790s, only free white males were able to vote and, in some states, they had to be property owners as well. Women did not receive the right to vote in the United States until 1920, whereas in Switzerland women of all **cantons** were only granted the franchise in 1981.

Granting every person the right to participate in the election of officials recognizes the equal voting power of each citizen. This emphasis on the equality of every individual before the law is central to the American system. Since everyone's vote counts equally, the only way to make fair decisions is by some form of **majority** will. However, to ensure that **majority rule** does not become oppressive, modern democracies also provide certain guarantees of minority rights. If certain democratic principles did not protect minorities, the majority might violate the fundamental rights of members of certain groups, especially groups that are unpopular or dissimilar to the majority population. In the past, the majority has imposed such limitations on blacks, Native Americans, women, and Japanese Americans, to name only a few.

One way to guarantee the continued existence of a representative democracy is to hold free, competitive elections. Thus the minority always has the opportunity to win elective office. For such elections to be totally open, freedom of the press and speech must be preserved so that opposition candidates may present their criticisms of the government. Americans are not always prepared to tolerate the political opinions of parties or individuals that run counter to our political culture, and in times of crisis, our tolerance tends to be even lower.

Constitutional Democracy

Another key feature of Western representative democracy is that it is based on the principle of **limited government.** Not only is the government dependent on popular sovereignty but also the powers of the government are clearly limited, either through a written document or through widely shared beliefs. The Constitution sets down the fundamental structure of the government and the limits to its activities. Such limits are intended to prevent political decisions based on the whims or ambitions of individuals in government rather than on constitutional principles.

Democracy: Ideal and Real

▽

The sheer size and complexity of American society make it unsuitable for direct democracy on a national scale. Some scholars suggest that representative democracy is also difficult to achieve in any modern state. They point to the low level of turnout for presidential elections and the even lower turnout for local ones. Research based on polling the public during election campaigns has shown that many Americans are neither particularly interested in politics nor well informed. Few are able to name the persons running for Congress in their district and even fewer can discuss the positions that candidates have espoused. Members of Congress claim to represent their constituents, but few constituents follow the issues, much less communicate their views to the representatives. For the average citizen, the national government is too remote, too powerful, and too bureaucratic to be influenced by one vote.

Elitism

If the ordinary citizens are not really making policy decisions with their votes, who is? One answer to this question is proposed by a group of theorists who suggest that **elites** really govern the United States. Proponents of **elite theory** see society much like Alexander Hamilton, who said,

> All communities divide themselves into the few and the many. The first are the rich and the wellborn, the other the mass of the people . . . The people are turbulent and changing; they seldom judge or determine right. Give therefore to the first class a distinct, permanent share in the government. They will check the unsteadiness of the second, and as they cannot receive any advantage by a change, they therefore will ever maintain good government.

The elitist perspective on the American political scene sees the mass population as uninterested in politics and willing to let the leaders make the decisions. Some versions of elite theory describe a relatively limited number of individuals within a cohesive elite class, whereas others, holding a more democratic view, suggest that voters choose among competing elites. New members of the elite are recruited through the educational system so that the brightest children of the masses allegedly have the opportunity to join the elite strata.

In such a political system, the primary goal of the government is stability, because elites do not want any change in their status. Major social and economic change only takes place if elites see their resources threatened. This selfish interest of the

Elites
The upper socioeconomic classes who control political and economic affairs.

Elite Theory
A perspective that holds that society is ruled by the elite.

The Kennedy compound at Hyannisport, Massachusetts.

Today there are national governments whose official names include the following terms:

—democratic republic
—people's socialist republic
—democratic and popular republic
—principality
—people's republic
—republic
—commonwealth
—state
—kingdom
—federative republic
—socialist republic
—united republic
—federal Islamic republic
—Arab republic
—socialist
—dominion
—federal republic
—people's revolutionary republic
—cooperative republic
—Islamic republic
—democratic people's republic
—people's democratic republic
—socialist people's Arab Jamahiriya
—grand duchy
—united states
—sultanate
—most serene republic
—confederation
—united republic
—union of soviet socialist republics
—united Arab emirates
—united kingdom
—state of Vatican city
—oriental republic
—socialist federal republic

Pluralism

A theory that views politics as conflict among interest groups. Political decision making is characterized by bargaining and compromise.

Culture

Habitual modes of thought and behavior characteristic of a particular society; everything that a people consciously creates.

▽

18

elites does not mean, however, that they are necessarily undemocratic. In fact, American elites are perceived as more devoted to democratic principles and rights than are most members of the mass public.[3]

Elite theory can neither be proved nor disproved, since it is not possible to identify with certainty the members of the ruling elite. Some governmental policies, such as tax loopholes for the wealthy, may be perceived as elitist in nature, whereas others benefit many members of the public. Elite theory does increase our awareness of the power of the elected leaders, even in a democracy.

Pluralism

A different school of thought looks at the characteristics of the American electorate and finds that our form of democracy is based on group activities. Even if the average citizen cannot keep up with political issues or cast a deciding vote in any election, the individual's interests will be protected by groups that represent him or her.

Theorists who subscribe to **pluralism** as a way of understanding American politics see all persons as naturally social and inclined to form associations. These groups of like-minded individuals will present their demands to government. In the pluralists' view, politics is the struggle among groups to gain benefits for their members. Given the structures of the American political system, group conflicts tend to be settled by compromise and accommodation so that each interest is satisfied to some extent.[4]

Pluralists see public policy as resulting from group interactions carried out within Congress and the executive branch. Because there are a multitude of interests, no one group can dominate the political process. Furthermore, since most individuals have more than one interest, conflict among groups does not divide the nation into hostile camps.

There are a number of flaws in some of the basic assumptions of this approach. Among these are the relatively low number of people who formally join interest groups, the real disadvantages of pluralism for the poorer citizens, and pluralism's belief that group decision making always reflects the best interests of the nation.

Both pluralism and elite theory attempt to explain the real workings of American democracy. Neither approach is complete, nor can either be proven. The elitist perspective reminds us that the Founders were not great defenders of the mass public and suggests that people need constant motivation to stay involved in the political system. In contrast, the pluralist view underscores both the advantages and the disadvantages of Americans' inclination to join, to organize, and to pursue benefits for themselves. It points out all of the places within the American system where interest groups find it comfortable to work. With this knowledge, the system can be adjusted to keep interest groups within the limits of the public good.

American Political Culture

▽

Every nation has a particular **culture,** which consists of its language and history, art, work habits, and virtually the entire body of beliefs and customs held by its

[3]Thomas Dye and Harmon Ziegler, *The Irony of Democracy,* 5th ed. (Duxbury, Mass.: Wadsworth, 1981); C. Wright Mills, *The Power Elite* (New York: Oxford University Press, 1956).

[4]David Truman, *The Governmental Process* (New York: Knopf, 1951); Robert Dahl, *Who Governs* (New Haven, Conn.: Yale University Press, 1961).

Highlight

Religion and American Political Culture

Given the strongly religious origins of the founders of the United States in the seventeenth and eighteenth centuries, it may not seem surprising that American culture is replete with religious symbols and practices. These practices spill over into the political arena on many occasions. Our coins and paper currency bear the motto, "In God We Trust," daily sessions of Congress begin with a prayer, and presidents are sworn into office with one hand on the Bible.

This cultural norm of religious expression in politics is traceable to patterns of belief shown in recent public opinion polls. A Gallup poll study published in May 1985 showed the following attitudes toward religion: 61 percent of respondents agreed that "religion can answer all or most of today's problems," whereas just 22 percent felt that "religion is largely old-fashioned and out of date"; two-thirds reported that they were a member of a church or synagogue; almost 90 percent said they have prayed to God, and about one-third reported praying twice a day or more. Seventy-two percent believe the Bible to be the word of God, whereas only 23 percent hold that it is not; 95 percent believe in "God or a universal spirit," only 66 percent believe in a personal God who watches over and judges people like the God of biblical revelation; 71 percent expressed

a belief in life after death, with an identical 71 percent believing in a heaven and 53 percent in a hell. Twenty-two percent, or 35 million adult Americans, fit the definition of "evangelicals," meaning they describe themselves as "born-again Christians," have encouraged other people to believe in Jesus Christ, and believe in a literal interpretation of the Bible.

In some respects, these results suggest a very different social climate for the growth of a political system than exists in other countries in the world. Of sixteen countries in a 1981 study, Americans ranked behind only South Africans in the extent to which they believe that God is extremely important in their lives.

Belief in life after death also sets Americans apart from much of the rest of the world. For the same sixteen countries, only the Republic of Ireland and Northern Ireland have higher proportions of believers in an afterlife—76 percent and 71 percent, respectively. At the other end of the spectrum of belief is Denmark, where only 26 percent believe in life after death.

Some changes have taken place in the religious underpinnings of American society, as measured by public opinion surveys. Gallup reports, for example, a decline from 81 percent to 61 percent between 1957 and 1985 in the percentage of Americans who believe

that religion can answer all or most of today's problems; also, the percentage saying that religion is very important in their lives declined from 75 percent in 1952 to 56 percent in 1984, whereas the proportion of adults who can be classified as "evangelicals" increased from 17 percent in 1981 to 22 percent in 1984.

Given results like these, it is possible to understand why Jimmy Carter was successful with his open "born-again" posture as a presidential candidate in 1976, why Ronald Reagan and the Republican party have so ardently pursued the votes of evangelicals, why moral issues like abortion or prayer in public schools can spark so much political activity, and why ministers such as Jesse Jackson, Martin Luther King, Jr., Pat Robertson, or Jerry Falwell can have such an impact on American politics as candidates or as supporters of major pressure groups. This information also helps us understand the way in which political debates have been shaped throughout this nation's history on issues such as slavery, civil rights, apartheid in South Africa, hunger, or poverty, where Americans' approaches to resolving these problems have often been influenced by matters of faith.

SOURCE: *The Gallup Report*, May 1985, pp. 18, 22, 38, 40, 45, 47, 50, 53. Note that these results are *not* all taken from Gallup polls and that they cover different surveys and different time periods.

---

residents. Culture includes everything that we consciously create. A formal definition of culture is the habitual modes of thought and behavior characteristic of a particular society.

The term *political culture*, then, refers to a subset of the national culture as a whole. Our political culture concerns itself with ideas, beliefs, attitudes, and symbols related to the authoritative allocation of values. It includes, for most Americans,

Political Socialization

The process through which individuals learn a set of political attitudes and form opinions about social issues. The family and the public school system are two of the most important forces in the political socialization process.

Hands across America.

the idea of being a Democrat or a Republican, the symbolism of the flag and the Statue of Liberty, and such beliefs as a person is innocent until proven guilty.

For a political culture to exist, a nation's citizens must have a *patterned* way of thinking about government—a more or less automatic response to or attitude about a political object or symbol. These attitudes are learned primarily through the process of **political socialization.** The family and the school are two of the most important means of teaching the political culture to children, although the process takes place gradually and unconsciously so that most of us do not remember being "taught" about being American.

Efforts by recording artists to raise aid for famine victims in Africa.

A Political Consensus

Usually, the more homogeneous a population, the easier it is to have a political culture that can be characterized by a political consensus. One of the reasons that Great Britain maintains a limited government without a written charter is that there exists considerable consensus within the population on the political decision-making process of government. Even when a nation is heterogeneous in geography and ethnic background, such as the United States, it is possible for shared cultural ideas to develop. We have already discussed one of the most fundamental ideas in American political culture, democracy. There are other concepts related to the notion of democracy that are also so fundamental to American political culture that they are beyond debate, although individual Americans may interpret their meaning quite differently. Among these are liberty, equality, and property.

Liberty

Liberty can be defined as the greatest freedom of individuals that is consistent with the freedom of other individuals in the society. In the United States, liberty includes religious freedom, both the right to practice whatever religion one chooses and freedom from any state-imposed religion. The basic guarantees of liberty are found not in the body of the U.S. Constitution but in the Bill of Rights, the first ten amendments to the Constitution. The process of ensuring liberty for all Americans did not end with the adoption of the Bill of Rights but has continued through the political struggles of groups like blacks, women, and those who hold unpopular opinions.

The concept of liberty has both personal and political dimensions. Most Americans feel that each individual has the right to free expression and to choose whatever path he or she might want to take, economically, socially, and politically. The idea of liberty also has a specific meaning in the political process. Freedom of speech, freedom of the press, and the freedom to organize groups for political action are essential to maintaining competition for office and for the free and open

Liberty
The greatest freedom of individuals that is consistent with the freedom of other individuals in the society.

Anti-nuclear weapons protest demonstrates freedom of speech and assembly.

▽

21

discussion of political issues. One of the key conflicts in American politics has centered on whether freedom of expression should be granted to those who do not believe in the American political culture.

Equality

The Declaration of Independence states, "All men are created equal." Today, that statement has been amended by the political culture to include groups other than white males—women, blacks, native Americans, Asians, and others. The definition of **equality,** however, still is unclear to most Americans. Does equality mean simply political equality—the right to register, to vote, and to run for political office? Does equality mean equal opportunity for individuals to develop their talents and skills? If the latter is the meaning of equality, what should the United States do to ensure equal opportunities for those who are born poor, handicapped, or female? Most Americans believe strongly that all persons should have the opportunity to fulfill their potential, but many disagree about whether it is the government's responsibility to eliminate all economic and social differences.

Property

Many Americans probably remember that the **inalienable rights** asserted in the Declaration of Independence are the rights to "life, liberty, and the pursuit of happiness." The inspiration for that phrase, however, came from the writings of an English philosopher, John Locke, who clearly stated that man's rights were to life, liberty, and **property.** In American political culture, the pursuit of happiness and property are considered to be closely related. Americans place tremendous value on owning land, on acquiring material possessions, and on the monetary value of jobs rather than on social status. Property can be seen as giving its owner political power and the liberty to do whatever he or she wants. At the same time, the ownership of property immediately creates inequality in society. However, the desire to own property is so widespread among all classes of Americans that socialist movements, which advocate the redistribution of wealth and property, have had a difficult time securing a wide following here.

Democracy, liberty, equality, and property—these concepts lie at the core of American political culture. Other issues such as majority rule, **popular sovereignty,** and **fraternity** are closely related to them. For most Americans these fundamental principles are so deeply ingrained that they rarely think about what they might mean today.

Political Socialization

The degree to which Americans subscribe to a single set of values is surprising if you consider that most U.S. citizens are descended from immigrants. The process by which such beliefs and values are transmitted to individuals is known as political socialization. Historically, the political parties played an important role in teaching new residents how to participate in the system in return for their votes. Frequently, the parties also provided the first economic opportunity in the form of jobs to immigrants and their families.

Another major force for the socialization of Americans—past and present—has been the school system. The educational process continues to socialize children of immigrants and native-born Americans by explicitly teaching such basic political

---

Equality

A concept that all people are of equal worth.

Inalienable Rights

Rights held to be inherent in natural law and not dependent on government; as asserted in the Declaration of Independence, the rights to "life, liberty, and the pursuit of happiness."

Property

As conceived by the political philosopher John Locke, a natural right superior to human law (laws made by government).

Popular Sovereignty

The natural rights concept that ultimate political authority rests with the people.

Fraternity

From the Latin *fraternus* ("brother"), the term *fraternity* came to mean, in the political philosophy of the eighteenth century, the condition in which each individual considers the needs of all others; a brotherhood. In the French Revolution of 1789, the popular cry was "liberty, equality, and fraternity."

values as equality and liberty. Perhaps the school system is even more successful in teaching loyalty to the system. From the introduction of a benevolent police image to first-graders to the playing of the national anthem at high school graduation, American schools emphasize patriotism and citizenship.

Subcultures and Political Conflict

Not all Americans share equally in this dominant political culture. There are a number of subcultures for which these beliefs have little relevance or value. Studies show that children from poor, black families or from communities in Appalachia do not internalize the same patriotic support for the system as do middle-class children. Native Americans and Hispanic citizens have tried to preserve their respective cultures and languages in the face of pressure to conform to the national standard. Still other groups in the nation have rejected the majority emphasis on individual economic achievement and material possessions and advocate instead communities based on the sharing of resources and true direct democracy.

In addition to alternative or minority subcultures, which reject part or all of the dominant culture, there exist multiple perspectives on how fundamental values relate to today's policy dilemmas. Indeed, political conflict over the application of these ideas, over choices among policies, and even over which problems are most in need of solving, is inevitable and unending. What the political culture does is

A Native American delegate at the 1984 Democratic Convention.

Affirmative Action

Job-hiring policies that give special consideration or compensatory treatment to traditionally disadvantaged groups in an effort to overcome present effects of past discrimination.

Reverse Discrimination

The charge that affirmative action programs requiring preferential treatment or "quotas" discriminate against those who have no minority status.

Public Policies

Policies reflecting various courses of action chosen by government officials.

to provide a common ground for the debate and a common set of rules within which debate, however intense, can be carried on.

We can see how conflicts arise if we consider the personal implications of issues such as **affirmative action** and **reverse discrimination,** which involve individual liberty, equality, and the right to property. Telling any individual that he or she should give up the right to a promotion (and therefore higher salary or property) to ensure that some other individual should have an "equal opportunity" to fulfill his or her dreams is distressing to many Americans. Why should one person's liberty or property be taken away for another's equality? If everyone is not, however, considered equal, then some people are being denied the freedom to achieve and to live the American dream. Finally, can the democratic process be used to resolve these conflicts when not everyone has equal political power?

An Overview of This Book

▽

Now that we have a brief acquaintance with the major concepts of politics in general and of the American political system in particular, we can begin to explore American government and politics today. In the following chapters, we examine the process of who gets what or the authoritative allocation of values as it takes place within a society, the United States, that holds certain beliefs as essential in the political process. This political culture interacts with the formal institutions of government and other less structured political organizations to create a unique political system.

In Part I, we examine the formal structures of government—the Constitution, federalism, and the Bill of Rights—and how each of these has evolved and changed over time. Many of the ideas and beliefs of American political culture are closely linked to the formal structures of government; they provide public support and, in the case of the Constitution, reverence for the government, making drastic structural change very unlikely. Part II discusses the expansion of civil liberties within the framework of the Bill of Rights (Chapter 4); the extension of civil rights to minorities (Chapter 5); and the response to the demands of newly emerging political groups (Chapter 6).

In Part III, we look at the broad panorama of American politics beyond the formal institutions. The activities of the media, interest groups, political parties, campaigns, and elections present demands that government must fill and conflicts that it must resolve. Through such political activities, society can exert democratic control over the institutions of government and the officials who make decisions.

The formal governmental institutions—the presidency, Congress, the Supreme Court, the bureaucracy—are the subjects of Part IV. How are policy decisions made and by whom? How does the government respond to the demands of the people and how are political conflicts resolved?

In Part V, we focus attention on the results of government and politics—**public policies.** To what extent do the policies decided on and implemented by government resolve political conflicts or postpone them? In this part, we discuss some of the most important problems that government has dealt with in recent years—economic policy, policies concerning energy and the environment, and foreign and national security policy. These public policies are in fact the value allocations of the political process, although they can and will change in response to future events.

In Part VI, we briefly survey the state and local governments in the United States. Each of these institutions makes important decisions affecting the daily lives of its citizens. The study of state and local governments is particularly interesting because local political systems, although closely related to national models, bear the imprint of local culture and political practice. Thus state and local governments are not clones of the national system but are instead unique adaptations of it. By examining politics at the state or local level, we can learn how the national political system might have developed differently.

A person's political affiliation and political beliefs are determined by a complex combination of factors that make up her or his "political profile." The following exercise sets up a self-evaluation matrix. Check the box to the left of each item that best describes you.

Look at the page opposite. Here you will find the results of the 1985 Gallup poll asking the same questions and indicating the percentages of respondents in each category who are Republican, Democrat, or Independent. Where do you fit in, in terms of party affiliation?

SEX
☐ Male
☐ Female

AGE
☐ 18–24 years
☐ 25–29 years
☐ 30–49 years
☐ 50–64 years
☐ 65 & older

REGION
☐ East
☐ Midwest
☐ South
☐ West

RACE
☐ White
☐ Non-white
☐ Black
☐ Hispanic

EDUCATION
☐ College graduate
☐ College incomplete
☐ High school graduate
☐ Not high school graduate

OCCUPATION OF CHIEF WAGE EARNER (YOUR FAMILY)
☐ Professional & business
☐ Clerical & sales
☐ Manual worker
☐ Skilled worker
☐ Unskilled worker

HOUSEHOLD INCOME (YOUR FAMILY)
☐ $50,000 & over
☐ $35,000–$49,999
☐ $25,000–$34,999
☐ $15,000–$24,999
☐ $10,000–$14,999
☐ Under $10,000

RELIGION
☐ Protestant
☐ Catholic

LABOR UNION
☐ Labor union family
☐ Non-union family

Political Affiliation—4th Quarter 1985

QUESTION: *In politics, as of today, do you consider yourself a Republican, a Democrat, or an Independent?*

	Percent Republican	Percent Democrat	Percent Independent
SEX			
Men	34	36	29
Women	31	44	25
AGE			
18–24 years	36	30	33
25–29 years	33	36	31
30–49 years	30	40	30
50–64 years	32	45	23
65 & older	35	48	17
REGION			
East	31	43	26
Midwest	34	46	30
South	32	43	25
West	35	38	27
RACE			
Whites	35	36	29
Non-whites	10	77	13
Blacks	6	81	13
Hispanics	23	57	20
EDUCATION			
College graduates	40	31	29
College incomplete	39	34	27
High school graduates	31	41	28
Not high school grads.	23	52	25
OCCUPATION OF CHIEF WAGE EARNER			
Professional & business	40	32	28
Clerical & sales	35	37	28
Manual workers	26	44	30
Skilled workers	32	36	32
Unskilled workers	27	46	27
HOUSEHOLD INCOME			
$50,000 & over	44	27	29
$35,000–$49,999	37	32	31
$25,000–$34,999	34	35	31
$15,000–$24,999	34	43	23
$10,000–$14,999	30	45	25
Under $10,000	22	52	26
RELIGION			
Protestants	36	39	25
Catholics	30	44	26
LABOR UNION			
Labor union families	25	49	26
Non-union families	35	38	27

Gallup Report, Jan.–Feb. 1986.

Chapter Summary

1. Most definitions of politics are based on the idea of social conflict, which invariably arises because of differing beliefs and values, and competition for scarce resources.

2. Harold Lasswell defined politics as a process that determines "who gets what" in a society. David Easton defined politics as the "authoritative allocation of values" within a society.

3. For most complex societies, government is the ultimate authority that allocates values and makes decisions about conflict resolution.

4. To say that a government is authoritative implies a reasonable expectation that there will be compliance with its value-allocating decisions. This authority is based on the power to enforce rules, legitimacy, and habits of compliance.

5. The framers of the Constitution warned against the inherent problems of a pure direct democracy: the inability of uneducated masses to govern themselves, the potentially disruptive influence of demagogues, and the threat to minority rights.

6. The U.S. political system is a representative, rather than a direct, democracy. The people hold ultimate power over the government through the election process, but they empower representatives to make decisions on their behalf.

7. Since everyone has an equal vote in a democracy, decisions are made by majority rule. To prevent oppression by the majority, certain rights are protected for the minority.

8. Elite theory sees the power in society resting with a small group of leaders who come from the upper social and economic classes. The masses are viewed as apathetic and uninterested in politics.

9. Pluralism assumes that groups are the basis of all political activity. Public policy results from group conflict and from bargaining among groups within Congress and the other institutions of government.

10. Concepts that are fundamental to American political culture are learned through a process of political socialization. Among these core concepts are liberty, equality, and property. These principles, subscribed to by men like Thomas Paine, Thomas Jefferson, and James Madison, sometimes conflict when applied to current problems.

Questions for Review and Discussion

▽

1. What decisions does the national government make that affect your life and work? What direct power does the national government have over you?

2. How might a direct democracy work in the United States? What percentage of Americans would participate in elections on national laws? How might modern technology be used to make direct democracy possible?

3. Think about how political decisions are made in your city or community. Are there certain individuals or social groups which seem to predominate in decision-making? How are such elite groups controlled by the voters?

4. Think about your own family and schooling. How did you learn about the concepts of liberty, equality, and opportunity? How did you find out the difference between Republicans and Democrats? Has your political socialization continued in your adult years? Through what agencies, or sources of information?

Selected References

▽

Robert A. Dahl, *Modern Political Analysis*, 4th ed. (Englewood Cliffs, N.J.: Prentice-Hall, 1984). Definitions and explanations of politics and political analysis, influence, systems, and socialization.

Robert A. Dahl, *A Preface to Economic Democracy* (Berkeley: University of California Press, 1985). Dahl argues that social and political equality in the United States can be achieved within a framework of liberty if "workplace democracy" would be realized. Liberty, justice, and efficiency, he proposes, could all be achieved with such a radical transformation of the American social vision.

Harold Lasswell, *Politics: Who Gets What, When and How* (New York: McGraw-Hill, 1936). A classic work defining the nature of politics.

Linda J. Medcalf and Kenneth M. Dolbeare, *Neopolitics: American Political Ideas in the 1980s* (New York: Random House, 1985). An incisive examination of labels such as liberalism, neoliberalism, democratic neopopulism, democratic socialism, neoconservatism, conservatism, and New Right populist conservatism in modern American political thought.

Jack C. Plano and Milton Greenberg. *The American Political Dictionary*, 6th ed. (New York: Holt, Rinehart and Winston, 1982). Nearly 1,200 terms, organizations, court cases, and important statutes are defined in this useful reference work.

Alexis de Tocqueville, *Democracy in America*, edited by Phillips Bradley (New York: Vintage Books, 1945). An account of life in the United States by a French writer who traveled through the nation in the 1820s.

Chapter 2
▽
The Constitution

Contents
▽

The Starving Time
British Restrictions and Colonial Grievances
The Colonial Response: The Continental Congresses
Declaring Independence
The Rise of Republicanism
The Articles of Confederation: Promise and Reality
The Philadelphia Convention: Drafting the Constitution
The Difficult Road to Ratification
The Bill of Rights
Altering the Constitution
The Result: It Has Lasted

WHAT IF . . .
▽
The Constitution
Had Not Been Ratified?

In the 1780s, the United States were far from united. Indeed, the several states that had been loosely joined together under the Articles of Confederation (1781–1787) had many features of independent nations. What would have happened if the Articles had not been superseded by the Constitution and by the establishment of a more centralized governing authority?

It seems likely that each of the thirteen states would have gradually become more independent from the others. Under the Articles of Confederation, a two-thirds vote in Congress was necessary before the central government could create a common currency, levy taxes, regulate interstate commerce, and make treaties with foreign governments. Considering the widely different economic and social interests of the states—particularly between the northern and southern states—it is hard to imagine that a two-thirds vote on any major issue could have been readily attained. Certainly, the history of the United States under the Articles makes this conclusion clear.

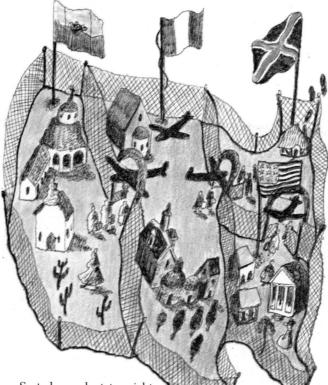

So today each state might well be a separate nation. Congregationalism might still be the established state religion in New York. New York City could have emerged as an independent city-state like Singapore or Hong Kong. On the whole, Puritans probably would be running New England. Certain states in the South could have evolved into countries resembling today's South Africa. All in all, the internal political system would have looked much different than it does today.

In addition, the inability to carry out a united foreign policy would have made any defense system against the European powers extraordinarily difficult, if not impossible. Further intervention by the British in American domestic affairs would not have been too unlikely, especially if one or more of the states were weakened by economic or social crises rendering them more vulnerable to outside influence and control. Finally, it

would have been difficult for the government under the Articles to make the treaty arrangements and territorial purchases that brought French and Spanish territories into the Union. The map of the United States would probably be quite different today: Florida might still be a Spanish territory, Texas an independent (and probably Spanish-speaking) country, and California and the Southwest a part of Mexico. It is possible that the Louisiana Purchase—which gave the land between the Mississippi and the Rockies to the United States—might never have been made.

▽

We cannot predict with certainty what would have evolved from the confederation. It seems clear, however, that the ratification of the Constitution paved the way for the growth of the United States by providing the mechanisms to deal with political conflicts within the new nation. The Constitution also created a central government sufficiently strong to establish the nation's independence in the world.

We the People of the United States, in Order to form a more perfect Union, establish Justice, insure domestic Tranquility, provide for the common defense, promote the general Welfare, and secure the Blessings of Liberty to ourselves and our Posterity, do ordain and establish this Constitution for the United States of America.

Every school child in America has at one time or another been exposed to these famous words from the Preamble to the United States Constitution. The document itself is remarkable: As constitutions go, it is short; and since its ratification on June 21, 1788, relatively few amendments have been added to it. What is even more remarkable is the fact that it has remained largely intact for almost two hundred years, making it the oldest written constitution in the world today.

How and why this Constitution was created is a story that has been told and retold. It is worth repeating because the historical and political context in which this country's governmental machinery was formed is essential to understanding American government and politics today. The Constitution was not the result of completely creative thinking, nor were its provisions ungrounded in political thought. The delegates to the Constitutional Convention in 1789 brought with them two important sets of influences: their political culture and their political experience. In the years between the first settlements in the New World and the end of the Confederation, Americans had developed a political philosophy about how people should be governed and had tried out numerous forms of government. These experiences provided the tools with which the Constitution was constructed.

The Starving Time
▽

The first British outpost in North America was set up by Sir Walter Raleigh in the 1580s for the purpose of harassing the Spanish treasure fleets. Located in Roanoke Island Colony, it stands as one of history's great mysteries: After a short absence for supplies, Raleigh's captain, John White, returned in 1590 to find no trace—living or dead—of the small colony's inhabitants. Roanoke has ever after been

The starving time.

Representative Assembly

A legislature composed of individuals who represent the population.

referred to as the "lost colony." To try to reconstruct in our imaginations the experiences of the vanished colonists helps us understand the great hardships faced by newcomers to America.

In 1607, the Plymouth Company landed a group of settlers near the mouth of the Sagadahoc River in Maine. Those who survived the winter ordeals packed up and returned to England. In the same year, a group of farmers were sent over to establish a trading post, Jamestown, in what is now Virginia. Indeed, the Virginia Company of London was the first to successfully establish a permanent British colony in the Americas. The king of England gave the backers of this colony a charter granting them "full power and authority" to make laws "for the good and welfare" of the settlement. The Jamestown colonists instituted a **representative assembly,** setting a precedent in government that was to be observed in later colonial adventures.

Unfortunately, Jamestown was not a commercial success. Of the 105 men who landed, 67 died within the first year. But 800 new arrivals in 1609 added to their numbers. By the spring of the next year, frontier hazards had cut their numbers to 60! These disheartened few were actually heading downriver to leave for England when new supplies and more settlers on three ships arrived to change their plans. In this way Jamestown eventually won the honor of being the first permanent British settlement in North America. Of the 6,000 people who left England for Virginia between 1607 and 1623, 4,000 of them perished. The distinguished historian Charles Andrews has called this the "starving time for Virginia."[1]

Pilgrims, the *Mayflower,* and the Compact

The first New England colony was established by the Plymouth Company in 1620. A group of English Puritans, calling themselves pilgrims, came over on the ship

[1]Charles M. Andrews, *The Colonial Period of American History*, vol. 1 (New Haven: Yale University Press, 1934), p. 110.

The signing of the Compact aboard the Mayflower.

Mayflower to the New World, landing at Plymouth (Massachusetts). Before going on shore, the adult males (women were not considered to have any political status) drew up the Mayflower Compact, which was signed by forty-one of the forty-four men aboard the ship on November 21, 1620. The reason for the compact was obvious: Being outside the jurisdiction of the London Company, and fearful of the consequences of having no political institutions, the pilgrim leadership wanted to form a government.

Rather than being a constitution, the compact was a political agreement reflecting the seventeenth-century ideas of a **social contract**. Its historical and political significance is that it served as a prototype for similar compacts (in American history) and that it depended on the consent of the individuals involved. The compact bound the signers to majority-rule government, pending receipt of a royal charter. According to Samuel Eliot Morison, the compact proved the determination of the English immigrants to live under the rule of law, based on the *consent of the people.*[2]

More Colonies, More Government

A second outpost in New England was set up by the Massachusetts Bay Colony in 1630. Then followed Rhode Island, Connecticut, New Hampshire, and others. By 1732, the last of the thirteen colonies, Georgia, was established. During the colonial period, Americans developed a concept of limited government, which followed from the establishment of the first colonies under Crown charters. The colonists were able to make their own laws, as in the Fundamental Orders of Connecticut in 1639. The Massachusetts Body of Liberties in 1641 supported the protection of individual rights and was made a part of colonial law. In 1682, Pennsylvania Frame of Government was passed. It, along with the 1701 Pennsylvania Charter of Privileges, established the rationale for our modern Constitution and Bill of Rights. All of this legislation enabled the colonists to acquire crucial political experience. After independence in 1776, the states quickly set up their own constitutions.

British Restrictions and Colonial Grievances

▽

The Navigation Acts of 1651–1750 were the earliest general restrictions on colonial activity. These acts imposed the condition that only English ships (including ships of its colonies) could be used for trade within the British Empire. Starting in 1763, British restrictions were intensified. The Proclamation of 1763 declared that no colonial settlement could be established west of the Appalachians. In 1764, the Sugar Act was passed to pay for wars that the British had waged (to a significant degree, on behalf of the colonies). As with the previous Molasses Act of 1733, many colonists were unwilling to pay the required tax.

Further oppressive legislation was to come. In 1765, the British Parliament passed the Stamp Act, providing for internal taxation, or, as the colonists' Stamp Act Congress assembled in 1765 called it, "taxation without representation." The col-

[2]See Morison's "The Mayflower Compact," in *An American Primer*, ed. Daniel J. Boorstin (Chicago: University of Chicago Press, 1966), p. 18.

Social Contract

An agreement between individuals to establish a government and to abide by its rules. Early theorists saw the social contract as an agreement between the ruler and the people.

Milestones in U.S. Political History	
1585	British outpost set up in Roanoke
1607	Jamestown established, Plymouth Company lands settlers
1620	Mayflower Compact signed
1630	Massachusetts Bay Colony set up
1639	Fundamental Orders of Connecticut adopted
1641	Massachusetts Body of Liberties adopted
1682	Pennsylvania Frame of Government passed
1701	Pennsylvania Charter of Privileges written
1732	Last of thirteen colonies established
1756	French and Indian War declared
1765	Stamp Act, Stamp Act Congress meets
1770	Boston Massacre
1774	First Continental Congress
1775	Second Continental Congress, Revolutionary War begins
1776	Declaration of Independence signed
1777	Articles of Confederation drafted
1781	Last state signs Articles of Confederation
1783–1789	"Critical period" in U.S history, weak national government
1786	Shays's Rebellion
1787	Constitutional Convention

▽

King George III

onists boycotted the Stamp Act, and the success of the boycott (the Stamp Act was repealed a year later) generated a feeling of unity within the colonies. However, the British continued to try to raise revenue in the colonies. When duties on glass, lead, paint, and other items were passed in 1767, the colonists boycotted the purchase of English commodities in return. Continuous negotiations between the colonists and the British took place until 1773. Finally, the Coercive Acts ("Intolerable Acts") were passed in 1774, closing Boston Harbor and placing the government of Boston under direct British control. The colonists were outraged—and they responded.

The Colonial Response: The Continental Congresses

▽

New York, Pennsylvania, and Rhode Island proposed the convening of a colonial congress. The Massachusetts House of Representatives requested that all colonies hold conventions to select delegates to be sent to Philadelphia for such a congress. The First Continental Congress was held at Carpenter's Hall on September 5, 1774. It was a gathering of delegates from twelve of the thirteen colonies (Georgia did not attend until 1775). At that meeting, there was little talk of independence. The Congress passed a resolution requesting that the colonies send a petition to King George III expressing their grievances. Resolutions were also passed requiring that the colonies raise their own troops and boycott British trade. The British government condemned the Congress's actions, treating them as open acts of rebellion.

What is important politically is that the First Continental Congress represented the nation's first formal act of cooperation among the colonies. The congressional delegates declared that in every county and city a committee was to be formed whose mission was to spy on the conduct of friends and neighbors and to report to the press any violators of the trade ban. In spite of the antilibertarian nature of these committees, their formation was another act of cooperation among the colonies, which represented a step toward the formation of a national government.

By the time the Second Continental Congress met in May 1775 (this time all the colonies were represented), fighting had already broken out between the British and the colonists. One of the main actions of the Second Congress was to establish an army. It did this by declaring the militia that had gathered around Boston an army and naming George Washington as commander in chief. The participants in that Congress still attempted to reach a peaceful settlement with the British Parliament. One declaration of the Congress stated explicitly that "we have not raised armies with ambitious designs of separating from Great Britain, and establishing independent states." But by the beginning of 1776 military encounters had become increasingly frequent.

Public debate was acrimonious. Then Thomas Paine's pamphlet *Common Sense* appeared in Philadelphia bookstores. It was a colonial best-seller.[3] Everyone agreed that Paine did make common sense when he argued:

> A government of our own is our natural right: and when a man seriously reflects on the precariousness of human affairs, he will become convinced, that it is infinitely wiser

[3]To do as well today, a book would have to sell between eight and ten million copies in its first year of publication.

and safer, to form a constitution of our own in a cool and deliberate manner, while we have it in our power, than to trust such an interesting event to time and chance.[4]

Paine attacked virtually every claim that had ever been made for loyalty to kings. He wanted the new nation to become a model in a world where all other nations were overrun with oppression. Students of Paine's pamphlet point out that his arguments were not new—they were common in tavern debates throughout the land. Rather, it was the near poetry of his words—which were at the same time as plain as the alphabet—that struck his readers.

Declaring Independence
▽

The Resolution of Independence

South Carolina created its own constitution in March 1776 and set up an independent government with John Rutledge as president. On April 6, 1776, the Second Continental Congress voted for free trade at all American ports for all countries except Great Britain. This act could be interpreted as an implicit declaration of independence. The next month, the Congress suggested that each of the remaining twelve colonies establish state governments unconnected to Britain. Finally, on July 2, the Resolution of Independence was adopted by the Second Continental Congress:

> RESOLVED, That these United Colonies are, and of right ought to be free and independent States, that they are absolved from allegiance to the British Crown, and that all political connection between them and the state of Great Britain is, and ought to be, totally dissolved.

The Resolution also recommended that foreign alliances be established as quickly as possible and that a plan of confederation be prepared and transmitted to the colonies for their consideration and approval. The actual Resolution of Independence was not legally significant. On the one hand, it was not judicially enforceable, for it established no legal rights or duties. On the other hand, the colonies were already, in their own judgment, self-governing and independent of Britain. Rather, the Resolution of Independence and the subsequent Declaration of Independence were necessary to establish the **legitimacy** of the new nation in the eyes of foreign governments, as well as in the eyes of the colonists themselves. What the new nation needed most was supplies for its armies and a commitment of foreign military aid. Unless it projected an image as being separate and independent from Britain, no foreign government would enter into a contract with its leaders.

Copyright 1985 Sidney Harris.

Legitimacy
Legal authority.

July 4, 1776

By June 1776, Thomas Jefferson was already writing drafts of the Declaration of Independence in the second-floor parlor of a bricklayer's house in Philadelphia. Upon adoption of the Resolution of Independence, Jefferson had argued that a declaration putting forth clearly the causes that compelled the colonies to separate

[4]*The Political Writings of Thomas Paine*, vol. 1 (Boston: J. P. Mendum Investigator Office, 1870), p. 46.

The signing of the Declaration of Independence.

Natural Rights

Rights held to be inherent in natural law, not dependent on governments. John Locke stated that natural law, being superior to human law, specifies certain rights of "life, liberty, and property." These rights, slightly altered to become "life, liberty, and the pursuit of happiness," are asserted in the Declaration of Independence.

Consent of the Governed

The government is based on the consent or will of the people and can be abolished by them.

from England was necessary. He did that in the task assigned to him, enumerating the major grievances. Some of his work was amended to gain unanimous acceptance (his condemnation of slavery was eliminated to satisfy Georgia and North Carolina), but the bulk of it was passed intact on July 4, 1776. On July 19, the modified draft became "the unanimous declaration of the thirteen United States of America." On August 2, it was signed by the members of the Continental Congress. The first printed version carried only the signatures of the congress's president, John Hancock, and secretary, Charles Thompson.

Perhaps the most revolutionary concept in the Declaration was the assumption that people have **natural rights** ("inalienable Rights") including "life, liberty, and the pursuit of happiness." Governments are established to secure these rights, and governments derive their power "from the **consent of the governed**." The Declaration went even farther and claimed that whenever any form of government "becomes destructive to these ends, it is the Right of the People to alter or to abolish it, and to institute a new government."

The Declaration has had

"a decisive impact on the development of our system of government because it set forth the ideals and standards which have been called the American Creed. This Creed, with its stress on the rights of people, equality under the law, limited government, and government by consent of the governed, infuses the structures and practices of the Constitution. The Declaration remains the American Conscience: A constant challenge to those who would subvert our democratic process or deny persons their unalienable rights."[5]

The Rise of Republicanism

▽

Not everyone had agreed with the notion of independence. There were recalcitrant colonists in the middle and lower southern colonies who demanded as a condition

[5]Edward S. Corwin and J. W. Peltason, *Corwin and Peltason's Understanding the Constitution*, 8th ed. (New York: Holt, Rinehart and Winston, 1979).

of independence that it be preceded by the formation of a strong central government. But the anti-Royalists in New England and Virginia, who called themselves Republicans, were against a strong central government, opposing monarchy, executive authority, and virtually any form of restraint upon the power of local groups. These so-called Republicans were a major political force from 1776 to 1780. Indeed, they almost prevented victory over the British by their unwillingness to cooperate with central authority.

During this time, all the states adopted written constitutions. Eleven of the constitutions were completely new, whereas two of them—those of Connecticut and Rhode Island—were old royal charters with minor modifications. Republican sentiment led to increased power for the legislatures. In Pennsylvania and Georgia, **unicameral** (one-body) **legislatures** were unchecked by executive or judicial authority. Basically, the Republicans attempted to maintain the politics of 1776: In almost all states, the executive branch was emasculated; the legislative branch was expanded.

The Articles of Confederation: Promise and Reality

▽

The fear of a powerful central government led to the passage of the Articles of Confederation. The term **confederation** is important; it means a voluntary association of *independent* states, in which the member states agree to only limited restraints on their freedom of action. As a result, confederations seldom have an effective executive authority.

Even though Richard Henry Lee first proposed the establishment of the confederation on June 6, 1776, it wasn't until November 15, 1777, that the Second Continental Congress agreed to a draft for the Articles and March 1, 1781, that the last state, Maryland, agreed to sign.

Under the Articles, the thirteen original colonies, now states, established a government of the states on March 1, 1781—the Congress of the Confederation. The Congress was a unicameral assembly of so-called ambassadors from each state, with each state possessing a single vote. The Congress was authorized to appoint an executive committee of the states "to execute in the recess of Congress, such of the powers of Congress as the United States, in Congress assembled, by the consent of nine [of the thirteen] states, shall from time to time think expedient to vest with them. . . ." The Congress was also allowed to appoint other committees and civil officers necessary for managing the general affairs of the United States. The Articles did not establish a separate judicial institution, although Congress had certain judicial functions. In addition, the Congress could regulate foreign affairs and establish coinage and weights and measures, but it lacked an independent source of revenue and any executive machinery to enforce its desires on individual citizens throughout the land. Figure 2–1 illustrates the structure of the confederal government under the Articles of Confederation; Table 2–1 summarizes the powers—and the lack of powers—of Congress under that system.

The Articles guaranteed each state its sovereignty:

Each state retains its sovereignty, freedom and independence, and every power, jurisdiction, and right, which is not by this Confederation expressly delegated to the United States in congress assembled.

Figure 2–1

▽

The Structure of the Confederal Government under the Articles of Confederation

Congress

Congress had one house. Each state had two to seven members, but only one vote. The exercise of most powers required approval of at least nine states. Amendments to the Articles required the consent of all the states.

Committee of the States

A committee of representatives from all the states was empowered to act in the name of Congress between sessions.

Officers

Congress appointed officers to do some of the executive work.

The States

Table 2–1
▽
Powers of the Congress of the Confederation

Congress Had Power To	Congress Lacked Power To
• Declare war and make peace	• Provide for effective treaty-making power and control foreign relations; it could not compel states to respect treaties
• Enter into treaties and alliances	
• Establish and control armed forces	• Compel states to meet military quotas; it could not draft soldiers
• Requisition men and money from states	
• Regulate coinage	• Regulate interstate and foreign commerce; it left each state free to set up its own tariff system
• Borrow money and issue bills of credit	
• Fix uniform standards of weight and measurement	• Collect taxes directly from the people; it had to rely on states to collect and forward taxes
• Create admiralty courts	
• Create a postal system	• Compel states to pay their share of government costs
• Regulate Indian affairs	
• Guarantee citizens of each state the rights and privileges of citizens in the several states when in another state	• Provide and maintain a sound monetary system or issue paper money; this was left up to the states, and monies in circulation differed tremendously in value
• Adjudicate disputes between states upon state petition	

Accomplishments under the Articles

Although the Articles of Confederation had many defects, there were also some accomplishments during the eight years of their existence. Certain states' claims to western lands were settled. Maryland had objected to the claims of Massachusetts, New York, Connecticut, Virginia, the Carolinas, and Georgia. It was only after these states consented to give up their land claims to the United States as a whole that Maryland signed the Articles of Confederation. Another accomplishment under the Articles was the Northwest Ordinance, which established a basic pattern of government for new territories north of the Ohio River.

Finally, the Articles created a sort of "first draft" for the Constitution of the United States that was to follow. In a sense, it was an unplanned applied experiment to try out some of the principles of government set forth in the Declaration of Independence. Moreover, the Articles allowed the states to judge in practice the strengths and weaknesses of these ideas. Without the experience of the Confederation, it probably would have been difficult, if not impossible, to arrive at the compromises that were later incorporated into the Constitution.

Weaknesses of the Articles

Although Congress had the legal right to declare war and to conduct foreign policy, it did not have the right to demand revenues from the states. It could only ask for them. Also, the actions of Congress required the consent of nine states, and any amendments to the Articles required the unanimous consent of the Congress. Further, the Articles did not create a national system of courts.

Basically, the functioning of the government under the Articles depended on the good will of the states. Article III of the Articles simply establishes a "league of friendship" among the states—no national government was intended.

Perhaps the most telling weakness of the Articles was their inability to give the Continental Congress the power to tax. When states refused to send money to support the government, Congress resorted to selling off western lands to speculators or issuing bonds that sold for less than their face value. Faced with a lack of resources, the Continental Congress was forced to disband the army, even in the face of serious Spanish and British military threats. Although it was permitted to do so, Congress really did not have the power to raise and maintain an army.

Shays's Rebellion and the Need for Revision of the Articles

By 1786, in the city of Concord, Massachusetts, the scene of one of the first battles of the Revolution, there were three times as many people in prison for debts as there were for all other crimes combined. In Worcester County, the ratio was even higher—20 to 1. Most of the prisoners were small farmers who couldn't pay their debts owing to the disorganized state of the economy. In August 1786, mobs of musket-bearing farmers led by former revolutionary captain Daniel Shays seized county courthouses and disrupted the trials of the debtors. Shays's men then launched an attack on the federal arsenal at Springfield, but they were repulsed. The rebellion continued to grow into the winter. George Washington wrote to a friend:

Shays's Rebellion.

> For God's sake, tell me what is the cause of these commotions? Do they proceed from licentiousness, British influence disseminated by the Tories, or real grievances which admit to redress? If the latter, why were they delayed until the public mind had become so agitated? If the former, why are not the powers of government tried at once?

Shays's Rebellion demonstrated the economic decline of the nation. Interstate trade conflicts, inflation, disruption of overseas trade, and the collapse of the U.S. bond market frightened individual citizens and businesses. The Articles of Confederation could not provide the type of central government that would ensure the growth of the country.

The Philadelphia Convention: Drafting the Constitution
▽

Shays's Rebellion was but one indication that America was in crisis by the winter of 1786–87. Finally, when the Continental Congress was unable to pass an amendment giving itself an independent source of revenue from import duties, its members became desperate. But as it was clearly impossible for the Congress to achieve unanimity on any important issue, there seemed little reason to call a constitutional convention.

As an alternative, the Virginia legislature called for a meeting of all the states, presumably to discuss commercial problems only. It was evident to those in attendance (including Alexander Hamilton and James Madison) that the national government had serious weaknesses, which had to be addressed if it were to survive. Among the most important problems to be solved were the relationship between the states and the central government, the powers of the national legislature, the need for executive leadership, and the establishment of policies for economic

Did You Know?

▽

That a royal British proclamation in 1763, at the end of the Seven Years War (also called the French and Indian Wars), prohibited whites from settling west of the Appalachian mountains and reserved that territory for the Indians?

stability. At this Annapolis meeting, a call was issued to all the states for a general convention to meet in Philadelphia in May of 1787 "to consider the exigencies of the union." When the members of the Second Continental Congress realized that the Philadelphia meeting would in fact take place, they approved the convention in February 1787, but they made it explicit that the convention was "for the sole and express purpose of revising the Articles of Confederation." Those in favor of a stronger national government—the Federalists, as they were to be called—had different ideas.

The Proceedings

The designated date for the opening of the convention was May 14, 1787. Since few of the delegates had actually arrived in Philadelphia by that time, however, it was not formally opened in the East Room of the Pennsylvania State House[6] until May 25. By this time, fifty-five of the seventy-four delegates chosen for the convention had arrived. Rhode Island was the only state that refused to send delegates; Republicans, who opposed a strong central government, were fully in charge in Rhode Island and wanted no part in creating a national government that might interfere in that state's internal affairs.

Not a Commoner Among Them

Who were the fifty-five delegates? They certainly did not represent a cross section of eighteenth-century American society. Consider the following facts:

1. Thirty-three were members of the legal profession.
2. Three were physicians.

[6]The State House was later named Independence Hall. This was the same room in which the Declaration of Independence had been signed eleven years earlier.

George Washington presiding at the Constitutional Convention in 1787.

3. Almost 50 percent were college graduates.
4. Seven were former chief executives of their respective states.
5. Six were large plantation owners.
6. Eight were important businessmen.[7]

They were also relatively young by today's standards: James Madison was thirty-six, Alexander Hamilton was only thirty-two, and Jonathan Dayton of New Jersey was twenty-six. The venerable Benjamin Franklin, however, was eighty-one and had to be carried in on a portable chair borne by four prisoners from a local jail. Not counting Franklin, the average age was just over forty-two.

Although some historians have suggested that the delegates were representatives of the economic elite and drafted the Constitution to protect their own interests, others note their lack of common concerns. Certainly, the interests of southern planters were not those of the merchants of New York. The delegates may also be characterized as astute politicians who were attempting to develop a pragmatic plan to save the new nation.[8] With the exception of age, they were quite similar to the members of Congress today. In the One Hundredth Congress (1987–89), for example, 184 representatives and 62 senators were lawyers, whereas blacks and women were underrepresented.

The Working Environment

The conditions under which the Founding Fathers worked for 115 days were far from ideal and were made even worse by the necessity of maintaining total secrecy. The framers of the Constitution felt that if public debate were started on particular positions, delegates would have a more difficult time compromising or backing down to reach agreement. Consequently, the windows were usually shut in the East Room of the State House. Since the summer was quickly upon the delegates, the air became heavy, humid, and hot by noon of each day. Also, when the windows were open, flies swarmed into the room. The delegates did, however, have a nearby tavern and inn to which they retired each evening. The Indian Queen became the informal headquarters of the delegates when the sun went down.

Factions Among the Delegates

Fortunately, we know much about the proceedings at the convention because James Madison kept a daily, detailed personal journal. A majority of the delegates were strong nationalists—they wanted a central government with real power, unlike that of the central government under the Articles of Confederation. Washington and Franklin preferred a limited national authority based on a separation of powers, but they were apparently willing to accept any type of national government, as long as the other delegates approved it. A few pronationalists, led by Gouverneur Morris of Pennsylvania and John Rutledge of South Carolina, distrusted the ability of the common people to engage in self-government.

Among the nationalists were several monarchists, including Alexander Hamilton, who was responsible for the Annapolis Convention's call for the Constitutional

[7]Charles Warren, *The Making of the Constitution* (New York: Barnes & Noble, 1967), pp. 55–60.

[8]John Roche, "The Founding Fathers: A Reform Caucus in Action," *American Political Science Review*, 61 (December 1961), pp. 799–816.

"*You know, the idea of taxation with representation doesn't appeal to me very much either.*"

Drawing by Handelsman; © 1970 The New Yorker Magazine, Inc.

Elbridge Gerry

Convention. In a long speech on June 18, he presented his views: "I have no scruple in declaring . . . that the British government is the best in the world and that I doubt much whether anything short of it will do in America." Hamilton wanted the American president to hold office for life and to have absolute veto power over the legislature. Further, he wanted a central government to appoint state governors who would also have absolute veto power over their own legislatures. In other words, the states would have no power because the central government would have unlimited sovereignty.

Another important group of nationalists were of a more democratic stripe. Led by James Madison of Virginia and James Wilson of Pennsylvania, these democratic nationalists wanted a central government founded on popular support.

Still another faction consisted of nationalists who would only support a central government if it were founded on very narrowly defined republican principles. This group was a relatively small number of individuals, including Edmund Randolph and George Mason of Virginia, Elbridge Gerry of Massachusetts, and Luther Martin and John Francis Mercer of Maryland.

Most of the other delegates of Maryland, New Hampshire, Connecticut, New Jersey, and Delaware were concerned about only one thing—claims to western lands. As long as those lands became the common property of all states, they were willing to support a central government.

Finally, there was a group of delegates who were totally against a national authority. Two of the three delegates from New York quit the convention when they saw the nationalist direction of its proceedings, leaving Alexander Hamilton alone.

Politicking and Compromises

The debates at the convention started on the first day. James Madison had spent months reviewing European political theory. When his Virginia delegation arrived ahead of most of the others, it got to work immediately. By the time Washington opened the convention, Governor Edmund Randolph of Virginia was immediately able to present fifteen resolutions. In retrospect this was a masterful stroke on the part of the Virginia delegation: It immediately set the agenda for the remainder of the convention. There was no talk about whether the convention should go beyond its initial mandate, even though the delegates had, in principle, been sent to Philadelphia for the sole purpose of amending the Articles of Confederation, not to write a new Constitution.

The Virginia Plan

Bicameral Legislature

A legislature made up of two chambers or parts. The United States Congress, composed of the House of Representatives and the Senate, is a bicameral legislature.

Randolph's fifteen resolutions proposed an entirely new national government under a constitution. It was, however, a plan that not surprisingly favored the large states, including Virginia. Basically, it called for the following:

1. A **bicameral** (two-house) **legislature,** the lower house chosen by the people and the upper chosen by the elected members of the lower house. The number of representatives would be proportional to population, thus favoring the large states. The legislature could void any unconstitutional state laws.
2. The creation of an unspecified national executive, elected by the legislature.
3. The creation of a national judiciary appointed by the legislature.

It did not take long for the smaller states to realize they would fare poorly under the Virginia plan. The debate on the plan lasted about two weeks. It was time for the small states to come up with their own plan.

The New Jersey Plan

On June 15, lawyer William Paterson of New Jersey offered an alternative plan. After all, argued Paterson, under the Articles of Confederation all states had equality; therefore, the convention had no power to change this arrangement. He proposed the following:

1. The fundamental principle of the Articles of Confederation—one state, one vote—would be retained.
2. Congress would be able to regulate trade and impose taxes.
3. All acts of Congress would be the supreme law of the land.
4. Several people would be elected by Congress to form an executive office.
5. The executive office would appoint a supreme court.

Basically, the New Jersey plan was simply an amendment of the Articles of Confederation. Its only notable feature was its reference to the **supremacy doctrine**, which was later included in the Constitution.

The "Great Compromise"

The delegates were at an impasse. Most wanted a strong national government and were unwilling even to consider the New Jersey plan. But when the Virginia plan was brought up again, the small states threatened to leave. It wasn't until July 16 that the **Great Compromise** was achieved. Roger Sherman of Connecticut proposed the following:

1. A bicameral legislature in which the House of Representatives would be apportioned according to the number of free inhabitants in each state, plus three-fifths of the slaves.
2. An upper house, the Senate, which would have two members from each state elected by the state legislatures.

This plan, often called the Connecticut Compromise, broke the deadlock. The large-state versus small-state controversy had been resolved. So too had another major issue—how to deal with slaves in the representational scheme. Slavery was legal everywhere except in Massachusetts, but it was concentrated in the South. The South wanted slaves to be counted equally in determining representation in Congress (but equal representation meant equal taxation). The South wanted to avoid equal taxation. Sherman's three-fifths compromise solved the issue, satisfying those northerners who felt that slaves should not be counted at all and those southerners who wanted them to be counted as free whites. Actually, Sherman's Connecticut plan spoke of three-fifths of "all other persons" (and that is the language in the Constitution itself). It is not hard to figure out, though, who those other persons were.

Other Issues, Other Compromises

The slavery issue was not completely eliminated by the three-fifths compromise. Many delegates were opposed to slavery and wanted it banned entirely in the United

Supremacy Doctrine
A doctrine that asserts the superiority of national law over state or regional laws. This principle is rooted in Article VI of the Constitution, which provides that the Constitution, the laws passed by the national government under its constitutional powers, and all treaties comprise the supreme law of the land.

Great Compromise
The compromise between the New Jersey and the Virginia plans that created one chamber of the Congress based on population and one chamber that represented each state equally.

Independence Hall, Philadelphia, Pennsylvania.

States. Finally, the delegates agreed that Congress could limit the importation of slaves after 1808. The compromise meant that the issue of slavery itself was never addressed.

The agrarian South and the mercantile North were in conflict. The South was worried that the northern majority in Congress would pass legislation unfavorable to its economic interests. Since the South depended on exports of its agricultural products, it feared the imposition of export taxes. The South won—export taxes, even today, are prohibited; the United States is one of the few countries that does not tax its exports. Further, in return for acceding to the northern demand that Congress be given the power to regulate commerce among the states and with other nations, the South was permitted to engage in the slave trade for another twenty years.

These compromises as well as others resulted from the recognition that if one group of states refused to ratify, the Constitution was doomed.

Working Toward the Final Document

The Connecticut Compromise was reached by mid-July. The makeup of the executive branch and the judiciary, however, was left unsettled. The remaining work of the convention was turned over to a five-man Committee of Detail, which presented a rough draft of the Constitution on August 6. It made the executive and judicial branches subordinate to the legislative branch.

The major issue of **separation of powers** had not yet been resolved. The delegates were concerned with structuring the government to prevent the imposition of tyranny—either by the majority or by a minority. It was Madison who devised a governmental scheme—sometimes called the Madisonian model—to achieve this: The executive, legislative, and judicial powers of government were to be separated so that no one branch had enough power to dominate the others. The separation of powers was by function, as well as by personnel, with Congress passing laws, the president enforcing and administering laws, and the courts interpreting laws in individual circumstances.

Each of the three branches of government would be independent of the others, but they would have to cooperate to govern. Figure 2–2 outlines these **checks and balances.** The president has veto power over congressional acts. Congress controls the budget and must approve presidential appointments. The Supreme Court consists of judges appointed by the president but with the advice and consent of the Senate.[9] Madison also wanted to prevent branches from abdicating their power to other branches. Note that our Constitution forces cooperation between at least two branches. But with checks and balances, we see simultaneous protection of the independence of each branch, yet forced dependence: Congress can pass a law; the executive branch must enforce and administer it.

Some delegates favored a plural executive made up of representatives from the various regions. This was abandoned in favor of a single chief executive. Others argued that Congress should choose the executive. However, to make the presidency completely independent of the proposed Congress, an **electoral college** was adopted, probably at Franklin's suggestion. To be sure, the electoral college (discussed in

Separation of Powers

The principle of dividing governmental powers among the executive, the legislative, and the judicial branches of government.

Checks and Balances

A major principle of the American governmental system whereby each branch of the government exercises a check upon the actions of the others. Separation of powers, divided power, and checks and balances limit government's power by pitting power against power. The president checks Congress by holding veto power, Congress has the purse strings, and Congress approves presidential appointments.

Electoral College

A group of persons called electors selected by the voters in each state; this group officially elects the president and vice president of the United States. The number of electors in each state is equal to the number of each state's representatives in both houses of Congress.

---

[9]After *Marbury v. Madison* in 1803 (1 Cranch 137), the Supreme Court became part of this checks and balances system through judicial review and the limited right to declare the policies of the other two branches of government unconstitutional.

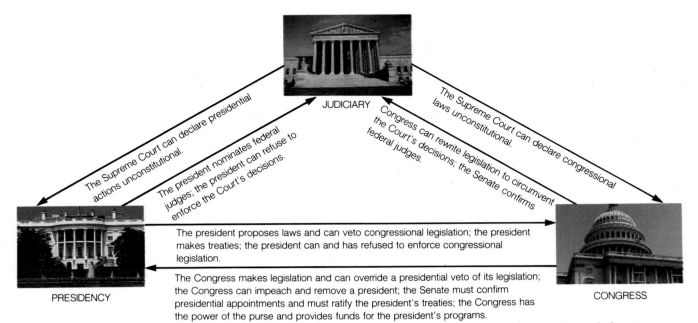

The president nominates federal judges; the president can refuse to enforce the Court's decisions.

The Supreme Court can declare presidential actions unconstitutional.

Congress can rewrite legislation to circumvent the Court's decisions; the Senate confirms federal judges.

The Supreme Court can declare congressional laws unconstitutional.

JUDICIARY

The president proposes laws and can veto congressional legislation; the president makes treaties; the president can and has refused to enforce congressional legislation.

The Congress makes legislation and can override a presidential veto of its legislation; the Congress can impeach and remove a president; the Senate must confirm presidential appointments and must ratify the president's treaties; the Congress has the power of the purse and provides funds for the president's programs.

PRESIDENCY

CONGRESS

Figure 2–2
▽
Checks and balances.

The major checks and balances among the three branches are illustrated here. Some of these checks are not mentioned in the Constitution, such as judicial review— the ability to declare congressional laws unconstitutional—or the president's ability to refuse to enforce judicial decisions or congressional legislation. Checks and balances can be thought of as a confrontation of powers or responsibilities. Each branch delays or checks the action of another; two branches in conflict have powers that can result in balances or stalemates, requiring one branch to give in or both to reach a compromise.

Chapter 12) made for a cumbersome presidential election process, but it further buttressed the notion of separation of powers (and mainly insulated the president from direct popular control). The seven-year single term that some of the delegates had proposed was replaced by a four-year term and the possibility of reelection.

On September 17, 1787, the Constitution was approved by thirty-nine delegates. Of the fifty-five who had originally attended, only forty-two remained. Only three delegates refused to sign the Constitution. Others disapproved of at least parts of it but signed anyway to begin the ratification debate.

The Constitution that was to be ratified gave us the following fundamental principles:

1. Popular sovereignty
2. A republican, or representative, government
3. Limited government
4. Separation of powers with checks and balances among branches
5. A federal system that allowed for states' rights

The Difficult Road to Ratification
▽

The Founding Fathers knew that **ratification** of the Constitution was far from certain. Indeed, since it was almost guaranteed that state legislatures would not ratify it, the delegates agreed that each state should hold a special convention at which elected delegates would discuss and vote on the Constitution. Further defying the Articles of Confederation, the delegates agreed that as soon as nine states (rather than all thirteen) approved the Constitution, it would take effect and the Congress could begin to organize the new government.

Delaware was the first to ratify on December 7, 1787, less than three months after the signing of the final document. The vote was unanimous. Pennsylvania and New Jersey ratified soon thereafter, on December 12 and 18, respectively. The Pennsylvania vote was 43 to 23, while the New Jersey convention was unanimous.

Ratification
Formal approval.

Chapter 2
The Constitution
▽
45

The Madisonian Argument for Separation of Powers

In a classic work entitled *A Preface to Democratic Theory,** political scientist Robert A. Dahl summarized the Madisonian argument for separation of powers as follows:

▽ *Hypothesis 1:* If unrestrained by external checks, any given individual or group of individuals will tyrannize over others.

▽ *Hypothesis 2:* The accumulation of all powers, legislative, executive, and judicial, in the same hands implies the elimination of external checks.

▽ *Hypothesis 3:* If unrestrained by external checks, a minority of individuals will tyrannize over a majority of individuals.

▽ *Hypothesis 4:* If unrestrained by external checks, a majority of individuals will tyrannize over a minority of individuals.

▽ *Hypothesis 5:* At least two conditions are necessary for the existence of a nontyrannical republic:

First Condition: The accumulation of all powers, legislative, executive, and judicial, in the same hands, whether of one, a few,

*Chicago: University of Chicago Press, 1956, chap. 1.

or many, and whether hereditary, self-appointed, or elective, must be avoided.

Second Condition: Factions must be so controlled that they do not succeed in acting adversely to the rights of other citizens or to the permanent and aggregate interests of the community.

▽ *Hypothesis 6:* Frequent popular elections will not provide an external check sufficient to prevent tyranny.

▽ *Hypothesis 7:* If factions are to be controlled and tyranny is to be avoided, this must be attained by controlling the effects of faction.

▽ *Hypothesis 8:* If a faction consists of less than a majority, it can be controlled by the operation of "the republican principle."

▽ *Hypothesis 9:* The development of majority factions can be limited if the electorate is numerous, extended, and diverse in interests.

▽ *Hypothesis 10:* To the extent that the electorate is numerous, extended, and diverse in interests, a majority faction is less likely to exist, and, if it does exist, it is less likely to act as a unity.

The Federalists Push for Ratification

Federalists

The name given to those who were in favor of the adoption of the United States Constitution and the creation of a federal union. They favored a strong central government.

Anti-Federalists

Those individuals who opposed the ratification of the new Constitution in 1787.

The two opposing forces in the battle of ratification were the Federalists and anti-Federalists. The **Federalists**—those in favor of a strong central government and the new Constitution—had an advantage over the **anti-Federalists,** who wanted to prevent the Constitution (in its then-current form) from being ratified. In the first place, the Federalists had assumed a positive name, leaving their opposition the negative label of *anti*-Federalist. More importantly, the Federalists had attended the Constitutional Convention and knew of all the deliberations that had taken place, whereas their opponents had no such knowledge since those deliberations were not open to the public. Thus the anti-Federalists were at a disadvantage in terms of information about the document. The Federalists also had time, power, and money on their side. Communications were slow, and those who had access to the best communications were Federalists—mostly wealthy bankers, lawyers, plantation owners, and merchants living in urban areas where communication was better. The Federalist campaign was organized relatively quickly and effectively to elect Federalists as delegates to the state ratifying conventions. The anti-Federalists, however, had at least one strong point in their favor: They stood for the status quo. In general, the greater burden is placed on those advocating affirmative change.

A national debate of unprecedented proportions arose over ratification. One powerful force aiding the Federalists throughout the debate was the publication of *The Federalist Papers,* numbers 10 and 51 of which can be found in the appendices at the back of this book.

Profile

▽

Benjamin Franklin

"Remember that *time* is money. He that can earn ten shillings a day by his labour, and goes abroad, or sits idle, one half of that day, though he spends but sixpence during his diversion of idleness, ought not to reckon *that* his only expense; he has really spent, or rather thrown away, five shillings besides." Such were the words of Benjamin Franklin in his *Advice to a Young Tradesman*, published in 1748. A better example of the cost of time would be hard to find.

Franklin's aphorisms were undoubtedly colored by his strict Calvinist upbringing. The true Calvinist was a driven man, described by British economist R. H. Tawney as "tempered by self-examination, self-discipline, self-control . . . the practical ascetic, whose victories are won not in the cloister, but on the battlefield, in the counting house, and in the market." Calvin himself referred to God as the "great task maker" and looked around for tasks man should undertake. Ben Franklin claimed that he was a free-thinker, but his father's continual exhortations—like "Seest thou a man diligent in his business. He shall stand before kings"—must have had some effect.

Young Ben was born in 1706 and raised in Boston. Family funds were insufficient for him to aim for Harvard, so he turned his hand to printing and went to Philadelphia in 1723. Deciding he needed to perfect his printing knowledge in London, he spent two years there working and living the Bohemian life. Within a few years he began to prosper as a master printer. His simple writing style and great clarity of

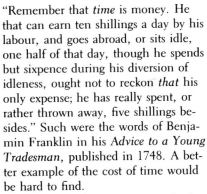

"*We must indeed all hang together, or, most assuredly, we shall all hang separately.*"

expression also started to bring in rewards. *Poor Richard's Almanac*, published annually between 1732 and 1757, was one of Franklin's most profitable enterprises, selling ten thousand copies a year. When he was twenty-three years old, Franklin wrote his first treatise on economics: *A Modest Inquiry into the Nature and Necessity of a Paper Currency* (1729). Coincidentally, Franklin was the first to start printing Pennsylvania paper currency, and he stayed in this business for quite some time.

Franklin was a crusader for learning and also a good businessman. He introduced printing and news publications to many communities throughout the colonies. He also helped start the present University of Pennsylvania in 1751. In 1753, he was named deputy postmaster general of the colonies.

Ben Franklin was also one of the first persons in America to use the techniques of advertising to increase business. When he started his *General Magazine,* he advertised his own "Pennsylvania Fire Place." The copy he wrote was persuasive: Franklin criticized ordinary fireplaces because they caused drafts that made "women . . . get cold in the head, rheums, and defluxions, which fall into their jaws and gums . . . [destroying] . . . early, many a fine set of teeth."

During the Revolution, Franklin helped draft the Declaration of Independence, which he also signed. Dispatched as envoy of the new government to France in 1776, proclaiming "our cause is the cause of all mankind," he began the successful diplomatic mission that enlisted foreign support for the Revolution. He signed the first U.S. treaty of alliance with France in 1778 and the treaty of peace with Great Britain in 1783. He died in 1790.

To practical men, especially the officers of savings banks ("a penny saved is a penny earned"), Ben Franklin seemed to be the epitome of good sense and morality. To others he appeared to be a materialistic opportunist. But, as John Adams once said, Franklin's "reputation was more universal than that of Leibniz, Newton, or Voltaire, and he was the first civilized American."

John Jay

The Federalist Papers

In New York opponents of the Constitution were quick to attack it. Alexander Hamilton answered their attacks in newspaper columns over the signature "Caesar." When the Caesar letters had little effect, Hamilton switched to the classical pseudonym Publius and brought on board two collaborators—John Jay and James Madison. In a very short period of time, those three political figures wrote a series of eighty-five essays in defense of the Constitution and of a republican form of government. These widely read essays appeared in New York newspapers from October 1787 to May 1788 and were reprinted in the newspapers of other states. Although we do not know for certain who wrote every one, it is apparent that Hamilton was responsible for about two-thirds of the essays, including the most important ones interpreting the Constitution, explaining the various powers of the three branches, and presenting a theory of judicial review. Madison's *Federalist Paper* No. 10, however, is considered a classic in political theory, dealing with the nature of groups—or factions, as he called them. In spite of the rapidity with which *The Federalist Papers* were written, they are considered the best example of political theorizing ever produced in the United States.[10]

The Anti-Federalist Response

The anti-Federalists used such pseudonyms as Montezuma and Philadelphiensis in their replies. Many of their attacks against the Constitution were also brilliant. They claimed that it was a document written by aristocrats and would lead to aristocratic tyranny. More importantly, the anti-Federalists believed the Constitution would create an overbearing and overburdening central government inimical to personal liberty. (It is true that the Constitution said nothing about liberty of the press, freedom of religion, or any other individual liberties.) Finally, the anti-Federalists decried the weakening of the power of the states.

The anti-Federalists cannot be dismissed as a bunch of unpatriotic extremists. Rather, they were arguing what had been the most prevalent view of the time, derived from the French political philosopher Montesquieu, who believed that liberty was only safe in relatively small societies governed by direct democracy or by a large legislature with small districts. The Madisonian view favoring a large republic, particularly expressed in *The Federalist Papers* Nos. 10 and 51, was actually the more *un*popular view of the time. Madison was probably convincing because citizens were already persuaded that a strong national government was necessary to combat foreign enemies and to prevent domestic insurrections. Still, some researchers believe it was mainly the bitter experiences with the Articles of Confederation that created the setting for the ratification of the Constitution, rather than Madison's arguments.[11]

---

[10]Some scholars believe that *The Federalist Papers* played only a minor role in securing ratification of the Constitution. Even if this is true, they still have lasting value as an authoritative explanation of the Constitution.

[11]Of particular interest is a current view of the anti-Federalist position contained in Herbert J. Storing, *What the Anti-Federalists Were For* (Chicago: University of Chicago Press, 1981). Storing also edited seven volumes of the anti-Federalist writings, *The Complete Anti-Federalist* (Chicago: University of Chicago Press, 1981). See also Jackson Turner Main, *The Anti-Federalist* (Chapel Hill: University of North Carolina Press, 1961).

The March to the Finish

The struggle for ratification continued. After Delaware, Pennsylvania, and New Jersey, Georgia ratified unanimously on January 2, 1788, and, on January 9, Connecticut voted for ratification by a margin of 3 to 1. There was a bitter struggle in Massachusetts, but clever politicking by the Federalists brought a close but successful ratification vote on February 6, 1788, even though some historians believe the anti-Federalists were a majority in the state at that time. In the spring of 1788, Maryland and South Carolina ratified by sizable majorities. On June 21, 1788, by a 57 to 46 margin, New Hampshire became the ninth state to ratify. The Constitution was now formally in effect, but that meant little without the large states of New York and Virginia. In New York, Hamilton used forceful arguments to fend off strong anti-Federalist opposition. During that summer, New York and Virginia agreed to the new Constitution by slender majorities. It took another sixteen months for North Carolina to ratify. Rhode Island did not ratify until May 29, 1790, and then by a margin of only two votes. Vermont waited until January 10, 1791.

Was the Constitution Truly Favored by the Majority?

Political scientists and historians still debate whether the Constitution was actually favored by the popular majority. The delegates at the various state ratifying conventions had been selected by only 150,000 of the approximately four million citizens of that time. That does not seem very democratic—at least not by today's standards. Even Federalist John Marshall believed that in some of the adopting states a majority of the people opposed the Constitution.[12] We have to realize, however, that the adoption of the Constitution was probably as open a process as was reasonable at that time. Transportation and communication were rudimentary and slow. It would have been difficult to discover the true popular opinion, even if the leaders of the new nation had been concerned to do so.

In any event, as soon as the Constitution was ratified, the movement to place limits on the power of the national government began.

The Bill of Rights
▽

Madison's Task

Bills of rights had been included in state constitutions at least as early as 1776 when George Mason of Virginia wrote the Virginia Declaration of Rights. That document was modeled on the traditional rights established in England and present in the British Bill of Rights of 1688.

Ratification in several important states could not have proceeded if the Federalists had not assured the states that amendments to the Constitution would be passed to protect individual liberties against incursions by the national government. Many

---

[12]Charles A. Beard, *An Economic Interpretation of the Constitution* (New York: Macmillan, 1913), p. 299.

of the recommendations of the state ratifying conventions included specific rights that were later considered by James Madison as he labored to draft what became the Bill of Rights.

Ironically, Madison had a year earlier told Jefferson, "I have never thought the omission [of the bill of rights] a material defect" of the Constitution. But Jefferson's enthusiasm for a bill of rights apparently influenced Madison, as did his desire to gain popular support for his election to Congress. He promised in his campaign letter to voters that once elected he would force Congress to "prepare and recommend to the states for ratification, the most satisfactory provisions for all essential rights."

Madison had to cull through more than two hundred state recommendations. It was no small task, and in retrospect he chose remarkably well. (One of the rights appropriate for constitutional protection that he left out was equal protection under the laws—but that was not commonly regarded as a basic right at that time.)

The final number of amendments that Madison came up with was sixteen. Congress tightened the language somewhat and eliminated four of the amendments. Of the remaining twelve, two—dealing with the apportionment of representatives and the compensation of the members of Congress—were not ratified by the states.

The Importance of Mandatory Imperatives

The state ratifying conventions had couched their proposals, with which Madison had worked, in terms of "ought" and "ought not." Those words sound weak to Americans who are used to seeing "Congress shall make no law . . . ," "no soldier shall . . . ," and "the accused shall . . . ." The oughts and ought nots were typical of the language contained in the English Bill of Rights and in the Virginia Declaration of Rights.

Consider one constitutional amendment proposed by Virginia's state ratifying convention: "That excessive bail ought not to be required, nor excessive fines imposed, nor cruel and unusual punishments inflicted." Madison changed that wording to read, "Excessive bail shall not be required, nor excessive fines imposed, nor cruel and unusual punishments inflicted." This was to become the Eighth Amendment, proposed by Madison on June 8, 1789. The difference between ought and ought not, and shall and shall not, is the difference between effective and ineffective legal language. A *mandatory imperative* was written into the amendments by Madison, and this has probably done more to safeguard the rights of individuals than any other change in the language of the proposed amendments on which he worked. Wishful thinking is not good enough or bold enough. Madison required the language of command.

On December 15, 1791, the national Bill of Rights was adopted when Virginia agreed to ratify the ten amendments. The basic structure of American government had already been established, and now the fundamental rights of individuals were protected, at least in theory, at the national level. Unfortunately, the proposed amendment that Madison characterized as "the most valuable amendment in the whole lot"—which would have prohibited the *states* from infringing on the freedoms of conscience, press, and jury trial—had been eliminated by the Senate. Thus the Bill of Rights as adopted did not limit state power, and the individual had to rely on the guarantees contained in the particular state constitution or state bill of rights. The country had to wait until the violence of the Civil War before significant limitations on state power became part of the national Constitution.

James Madison

Since many state ratifying conventions had been assured of action to include a bill of rights at the first session of the new Congress, it may seem surprising that James Madison could not get his proposed amendments considered the many times he rose in the House of Representatives to present them. The House was involved in a debate on import and tonnage duties. Madison kept asserting that the Bill of Rights was more important business, but to no avail. House members believed the discussion would take up more time than the House could then spare. Indeed, even in 1886, legal scholar Sir Henry Maine referred to the American Bill of Rights as a "certain number of amendments on comparatively unimportant points." How could this be?

At the time that Madison attempted to get the House to consider his amendments, the new Congress was in the midst of creating a new structure for government and solving more urgent problems, at least to the thinking of most of the Federalist members. As Representative Vining pointed out, "It strikes me that the great amendment which the Government wants is expedition in the despatch of business. The wheels of the national government cannot turn, until the impost and collection bill are perfected: these are the desiderata which the public mind is anxiously expecting."

Madison countered these objections by reminding the Congress that two of the states had not yet ratified the new Constitution and that the amendments had been promised to the people. He made a truly political argument to his colleagues, suggesting that if the Congress took action on the amendments, it might cause those who were opposed to the Constitution in the first place, or who hesitated to support the Federalist party, to change their minds. The House listened to Madison's plea and then postponed any consideration of the amendments for a month. After frequent reminders by Madison, work by a select committee, and several postponements, the amendments were finally approved by the House on August 24, 1789.*

*Bernard Schwartz, *The Bill of Rights: A Documentary History*, (New York: McGraw Hill Co. and Chelsea House Publishers, 1971).

Altering the Constitution
▽
The Formal Amendment Process

The U.S. Constitution is short (see Appendix B). One of the major reasons it has remained so is because the formal amending procedure does not allow for changes to be made easily. Article V of the Constitution outlines the way in which amendments may be proposed and ratified (see Figure 2–3).

Two formal methods of proposing an amendment to the Constitution are available: (1) a two-thirds vote in each house of Congress or (2) a national convention called by Congress at the request of two-thirds of the state legislatures. There has yet to be a successful amendment proposal using the second method, although the proposed balanced budget amendment—first proposed in 1975—has come close.

Ratification can occur by one of two methods: (1) by a positive vote in three-fourths of the legislatures of the various states or (2) by special conventions called in the states for the specific purpose of ratifying the proposed amendment, and a positive vote in three-fourths of them. The second method has been used only once, to repeal Prohibition. That situation was exceptional because it involved an amendment—the Twenty-first—to repeal an amendment—the Eighteenth, which had created Prohibition. Conventions were necessary for repeal because the "pro-dry" legislatures in the more conservative states would never have passed the repeal.

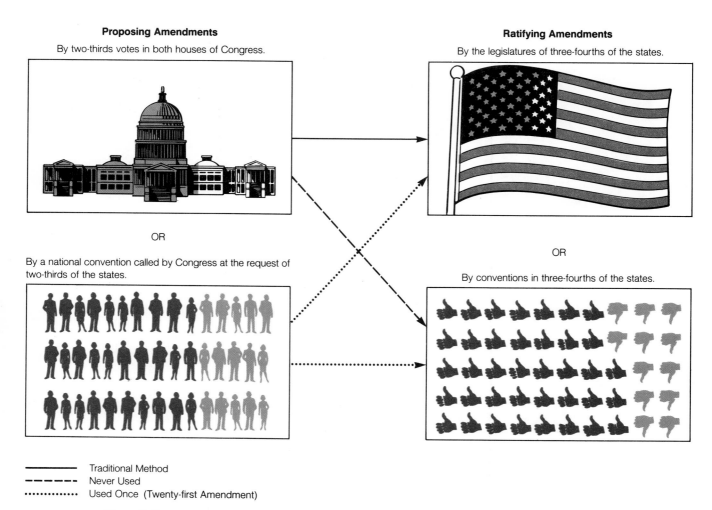

Proposing Amendments

By two-thirds votes in both houses of Congress.

OR

By a national convention called by Congress at the request of two-thirds of the states.

Ratifying Amendments

By the legislatures of three-fourths of the states.

OR

By conventions in three-fourths of the states.

——————— Traditional Method

– – – – – Never Used

·············· Used Once (Twenty-first Amendment)

Figure 2–3

▽

The Formal Constitutional Amending Procedure

There are two ways of proposing amendments to the U.S. Constitution and there are two ways of ratifying proposed amendments. Among the four possibilities, the usual route has been proposal by Congress and ratification by state legislatures. Only in the case of ratification of the Twenty-First Amendment in 1933 repealing the Eighteenth Amendment (Prohibition) was ratification by ratifying state conventions used. The Constitution has never been amended by two-thirds of the states requesting a national convention to be called by Congress and then having the proposed amendment ratified by the legislatures of three-fourths of the states.

▽

52

(It should be noted that Congress determines the method of constitutional amendment ratification to be used by all states.)

Many Amendments Proposed, Few Accepted

Congress has considered more than seven thousand amendments to the Constitution. Only thirty-three that were submitted by the states have been passed by Congress, and only twenty-six have been ratified. It should be clear that the process is much more difficult than a chart like Figure 2–3 can indicate. Because of competing social and economic interests, the requirement that two-thirds of both the House and Senate approve the amendments is difficult to achieve. Thirty-four senators, representing only seventeen sparsely populated states, could block any amendment. After approval by Congress, the process becomes even more arduous. Three-fourths of the state legislatures must approve the amendment, and it therefore must have wide popular support across parties and in all regions of the country.

The proposed Twenty-seventh Amendment—the Equal Rights Amendment (ERA)—failed to obtain ratification by the legislatures of three-fourths of the states

Alternative Constitutions

Since the ratification of our Constitution, major alternatives have been suggested, although obviously none have been accepted. These alternatives, however, are serious proposals that deserve consideration.

For the United States of the World

In 1872, Victoria Woodhull, purportedly the first female stockbroker in the United States and a noted feminist and political activist, proposed a new "Constitution for the United States of the World." She advocated a national railroad, the abolition of taxes on imports, and a modification of our capitalist economic system to one approaching socialism. Her idea

Victoria Woodhull, lecturer, reformer, and candidate for president in the 1880s.

for a constitution centered around absolute equality of all persons. At that time, the U.S. Senate, which was not popularly elected until 1913, was an inherently undemocratic body. Woodhull proposed that the Senate be abolished on the vote of three-fourths of the national electorate. House members were to serve a maximum of five terms. All bills would originate in the House. Any presidential veto could be overridden by a simple majority. Then, all bills would become law only after a majority of voters approved them in a national election. Woodhull also recommended that all state constitutions be prescribed by Congress and be identical. She was, in effect, proposing to eliminate federalism.

Frederick Adams's Ideas

In an 1897 novel published under the name President John Smith, Chicago writer Frederick Upham Adams proposed a constitution that would engender a new system of government dominated by majority rule, but oriented toward economic guarantees of jobs and work for every person. He wanted a direct vote for the president and a popularly elected cabinet. The legislature would be a single body of two hundred members, annually elected. All legislation would be subject to the approval of the voters. Presidential Supreme Court nominees would be ratified by popular vote. Unpopular justices could be removed by majority vote. Justices would serve as advisers to the Congress. The Supreme Court would have no power of judicial review. The constitution itself could be amended by majority vote and adopted by a three-fourths majority of the voters. Adams, like Woodhull, was moved by a profound and mystical sense of faith in "the people" as the last repository of wisdom, common sense, and ultimate prosperity.

Constitution for the Newstates of America

Prominent Roosevelt New Dealer Rexford G. Tugwell published a model constitution in 1970, then expanded it into the "Constitution for the Newstates of America." A product of an activist government during the Great Depression, he proposed that the government have two new branches—the planning branch and the regulatory branch. National planning and severe economic regulation were at the forefront of his model constitution. He also proposed that the president be elected for a single nine-year term and that he or she have two vice presidents to help.

James Sundquist's Ideas

A number of recent suggestions have been made for amending the U.S. Constitution, including a nine-point proposal made by political observer James Sundquist in *Constitutional Reform and Effective Government*.* Wanting to avoid a divided government, Sundquist sees the Constitution allowing for a "team ticket" for each political party, including candidates for vice president, Senate, and House. He recommends a four-year House and an eight-year Senate term. He also wants to see a national referendum to break deadlocks, a limited item veto for the president, and a war power provision limiting the president's use of the military.

Whatever the merit of these proposals, Americans are cautious about tampering with their Constitution and have a deep sentimental attachment for the time-tested document that reached its two-hundredth birthday in 1987.

*Washington, D.C.: Brookings Institution, 1986, pp. 240–241.

within the time limits set by Congress, although it was reintroduced into Congress in 1985. The proposed Twenty-eighth Amendment, which would have guaranteed congressional representation to the District of Columbia, fell far short of the thirty-eight needed before the August 22, 1985 deadline.

A reading of Article V of the Constitution reveals that the framers of the Constitution specified no time limit on the ratification process. The courts nonetheless have held that amendments must be ratified within a "reasonable" time. Congress is to decide what is reasonable. Since the early 1900s, most proposed amendments have included a requirement that ratification be obtained within seven years. This was the case in the proposed ERA. When three-fourths of the states had not ratified in time, Congress extended the limit for an additional three years and three months. That extension expired on June 30, 1982, without the amendment being ratified.

The National Convention Provision

The Constitution provides for a national convention requested by legislatures of two-thirds of the states to propose a constitutional amendment. This procedure has never been used, but there is a possibility that two-thirds of the legislatures will in fact jump on the bandwagon of the proposed amendment to require a balanced

federal budget. By 1986, thirty-two of the required thirty-four states had called for a constitutional convention to draft a balanced budget amendment. What if the required thirty-four states passed resolutions to have such a convention? The Constitution is silent about the procedures to be followed. There is no precedent. Can the convention be limited to one specific issue? Does Congress have the legal authority to set the ground rules? There is also another problem: The resolutions passed by the various states and sent to Congress are not identical; they seek at least ten different forms of a constitutional amendment to balance the budget. What would be the format for drafting a single amendment? Congress has proposed a "Constitutional Convention Procedures Act" to exert control over a constitutional convention if in fact it were to occur. The federal government lawmakers are clearly worried about a convention free-for-all adding numerous amendments to the Constitution.

Informal Methods of Constitutional Change

Formal amendments are one way of changing our Constitution, and, as is obvious by their small number, they have not been resorted to very frequently. If we discount the first ten amendments (the Bill of Rights), which passed soon after the ratification of the Constitution, there have been only sixteen formal alterations of the Constitution in the two hundred years of its existence.

But looking at the sparse number of formal constitutional changes gives us an incomplete view. The brevity and ambiguity of the original document has permitted great changes in the Constitution by way of changing interpretations over the course of time. As the United States grew, both in population and territory, new social and political realities emerged, and Congress, presidents, and the courts found it necessary to interpret the Constitution's provisions in light of these new realities. The Constitution has proved to be a remarkably flexible document, adapting itself time and again to new events and concerns.

Judicial Review

Another way of changing the Constitution—or of making it more flexible—is through the power of **judicial review**. In the case of *Marbury v. Madison*[13] in 1803, the Supreme Court ruled a provision of an act of Congress to be unconstitutional. Chief Justice Marshall declared that it is "the province and duty of the Judiciary department to say what the law is." Although the case was primarily concerned with the power of the Supreme Court in relation to the other two branches of the federal government, the principle of judicial review itself opened the way for Congress and the executive branch to test the elasticity of the Constitution—that is, it allowed them to see how far and in what ways it could be "stretched" without breaking.

Judicial Review
The power of the Supreme Court or any court to declare federal or state laws and other acts of government unconstitutional.

Interpretation, Custom and Usage

The Constitution has also been changed through its interpretation by both Congress and the president. Originally, the president had a staff consisting of personal sec-

[13]1803 (1 Cranch 137).

Former Chief Justice Warren Burger, chair of the bicentennial celebration of the Constitution.

retaries and a few others. Today, because Congress delegates specific tasks to the president and the chief executive assumes political leadership, the executive office staff alone has increased to several thousand persons. The executive provides legislative leadership far beyond the intentions of the Constitution.

Changes in the ways of doing political business have also changed the Constitution. The Constitution does not mention political parties, yet these informal, "nonconstitutional" organizations make the nominations for offices, run the campaigns, organize the members of Congress, and in fact change the election system from time to time. Perhaps most strikingly, the Constitution has been adapted from serving the needs of a small, rural republic with no international prestige to providing a framework of government for an industrial giant with vast geographic, natural, and human resources.

The Result: It Has Lasted

▽

There are those who say the Constitution has lasted because it furnished only an outline for government. Much was left unsaid so that political circumstances could be accounted for. Others might give credit for the flexibility of the document to the sharing of power among the three branches and the compromises this sharing encourages. Still others suggest that the doctrine of federalism solved the problems of governing many diverse territories within one nation. Most importantly, the Constitution articulates certain principles of democratic government—such as representation, majority rule, and protection for minorities—that have become the core of American political culture and that are the accepted "rules of the game" from the smallest town council to the halls of Congress.

The Constitution is an enduring document that has survived two hundred years of turbulent history. However, it is also a changing document. Twenty-six amendments have been added to the original Constitution. How can you, as an individual, actively help to rewrite the Constitution?

One of the best ways is to work for (or against) a constitutional amendment. At the time of this writing, three major issues are the subject of efforts to enact constitutional amendments—equal rights for women, antiabortion laws, and limitation of the size of the federal government. These three proposed amendments are supported and opposed by national coalitions of interest groups. If you want an opportunity to change the Constitution—or to assure that it isn't changed—you could work for or with one of the alliances of groups interested in the fate of these amendments.

The following contacts should help you get started on efforts to directly affect the U.S. Constitution:

Equal Rights for Women
▽

One group exclusively dedicated to the passage of the ERA has been Catholic Women for the ERA, 2706 Glenview Ave., Cincinnati, OH 45206. Its main activity is to contact and lobby state legislators to encourage them to vote for a national equal rights amendment.

Perhaps the most active organization working against the ERA has been Eagle Forum, Box 618, Alton, IL 62002 (618-462-5415). Its founder and president, Phyllis Schlafly, has been a major opponent of the amendment.

Abortion
▽

One of the organizations whose primary goal is to secure the passage of the Human Life Amendment is the American Life Lobby, Route 6, Box 162-F, Stafford, VA 22554 (703-659-4193). The Human Life Amendment

would recognize in law the "personhood" of the unborn, secure human rights' protections for the fetus from the time of fertilization, and prohibit abortion under any circumstances.

The National Abortion Rights Action League, 1424 K St., NW, Washington, D.C. 20005 (202-347-7774) is a political action and information organization working on behalf of "pro-choice" issues—that is, the right of women to have control over reproduction. The organization has roughly 150,000 members.

Government Reform
▽

An organization whose goal is to "reduce the size and cost of federal government to those functions specified in the U.S. Constitution" is the Liberty Amendment Committee of the U.S.A., P.O. Box 20888, El Cajon, CA 92021. The ultimate goal of LACUSA is to see the so-called Liberty Amendment (now pending in Congress) ratified and then to abolish the income tax.

An even more general goal—namely, to encourage Congress to call a constitutional convention (the most open-ended way to change the Constitution)—is pursued by Conservatives for a Constitutional Convention, P.O. Box 582, Desert Hot Springs, CA 92240.

The Movement for Economic Justice, 1638 R St., NW, Washington, D.C. is an activist organization seeking grass-roots involvement. Its goals are to encourage greater government responsiveness in such areas as revenue-sharing, inflation, and "fundamental economic reform." It conducts programs and training conferences and issues newsletters.

Chapter Summary

1. In 1607, the Virginia Company of London established the first permanent British settlement in North America. Of the 6,000 persons who left England between 1607 and 1623, 4,000 perished.

2. The first New England colony was established by the Plymouth Company in 1620. Its settlers drew up the May-flower Compact, which was based on the consent of the signers.

3. During the colonial period, Americans developed a concept of limited government.

4. Starting in 1763, British restrictions on colonial activity intensified. The colonies responded through the First Continental Congress, their first formal act of cooperation, in which resolutions were passed expressing their grievances.

5. By the time the Second Continental Congress met in 1775, fighting had begun. Thomas Paine's *Common Sense*—recommending separation from Great Britain—was well received.

6. The Resolution of Independence was adopted on July 2, 1776, by the Second Continental Congress. It was necessary to establish the legitimacy of the new nation in the eyes of foreign governments and in the eyes of Americans.

7. The Declaration of Independence was signed on August 2, 1776. It was based on the consent of the governed and assumed people had natural and "inalienable" rights.

8. Some colonists demanded the formation of a strong central government. The first "Republicans" opposed a strong central government.

9. On March 1, 1781, the newly established states passed the Articles of Confederation. Although some accomplishments took place during the eight-year existence of the Articles, they did not provide the type of central government that would ensure the growth of the country.

10. It became evident that the national government had serious weaknesses under the Articles of Confederation. A call was issued to all states for a general convention to meet in Philadelphia in May of 1787 "to consider the exigencies of the union."

11. The fifty-five delegates, mostly educated, upper-class individuals, met in secrecy to frame a new constitution. Trying to balance a number of competing interests—small states versus large states, North versus South, slave states versus nonslave states—they finally agreed on the "Great Compromise."

12. The framers divided the central government into the executive, legislative, and judicial branches (separation of powers) operating within a system whereby no one branch could dominate the other two (checks and balances).

13. Once the Constitution was signed by the delegates in September of 1787, it had to be ratified by nine of the thirteen states. The Federalists, favoring a strong central government, fought for its ratification. The anti-Federalists sought to prevent ratification. By July 1788, supporters had persuaded the necessary nine states to ratify.

14. The framers did not initially consider the Bill of Rights necessary to protect the rights of citizens. They were persuaded by Madison and Jefferson, however, and in 1791 the national Bill of Rights was adopted in the form of the first ten amendments to the Constitution.

15. Amendments to the Constitution can be proposed by (a) a two-thirds vote in each house of Congress or (b) a national convention called by Congress at the request of two-thirds of the state legislatures. Ratification can occur by (a) a positive vote of three-fourths of the legislatures of the various states or (b) special conventions called in the states for the specific purpose of ratifying the proposed amendment and a positive vote in three-fourths of them. Only twenty-six amendments to the Constitution have been ratified.

16. The Constitution has been adapted to meet the needs of a changing nation through the informal means of judicial review and by congressional and presidential interpretations.

Questions for Review and Discussion

1. The writing of the Constitution can be seen as the first real working of group interest or pluralism in the United States. What kinds of bargains or compromises were struck in the writing of this document? How were the various interests in the thirteen colonies protected by the provisions of the Constitution?

2. Although the Constitution calls for separation of powers, a more accurate description of the system might be one of "separate branches sharing powers." What provisions of the Constitution require that the branches cooperate or "share" power in order for the government to function?

3. List all the ways that the rights of the individual states are protected in the Constitution. Which provisions make it clear that the federal government has the ultimate power?

4. Why have so few amendments been added to the Constitution? How do the amendments which have passed reflect broad societal changes which have taken place since 1789?

Selected References

Charles A. Beard, *An Economic Interpretation of the Constitution* (New York: Macmillan, 1913). A classic interpretation of the motives of the founders of the republic, which emphasizes their own economic interests in the success of the nation.

Edward S. Corwin, *The Constitution and What It Means Today*, 14th ed. rev. by Harold W. Chase and Craig R. Ducat (Princeton: Princeton University Press, 1978). A detailed analysis of the meaning and interpretation of the Constitution through court cases.

Alexander Hamilton, James Madison, and John Jay, *The Federalist Papers* (Cambridge: Harvard University Press, 1961). The complete set of columns from the *New York Packet* defending the new Constitution.

Cecelia M. Kenyon, ed., *The Anti-Federalist* (Indianapolis: Bobbs-Merrill, 1966). This is a collection of "anti-Federalist papers" derived from speeches delivered at a state ratifying convention, newspaper articles, and popular pamphlets.

Leonard W. Levy, Kenneth L. Karst, and Dennis J. Mahoney, eds., *Encyclopedia of the American Constitution* (Riverside, N.J.: Macmillan, 1986). This truly remarkable resource book contains roughly 2,000 articles by 262 leading constitutional scholars, covering every major aspect of the Constitution and including a discussion of all the current, hotly debated issues.

Clinton Rossiter, *1787: The Grand Convention* (New York: Macmillan, 1966). A readable and interesting account of the Constitutional Convention in Philadelphia.

Edward Conrad Smith, ed., *The Constitution of the United States: With Case Summaries*, 11th ed. (New York: Barnes & Noble, 1979). A discussion of the Constitution's origins, content, and interpretation, including many documents.

Page Smith, *The Constitution: A Documentary and Narrative History* (New York: William Morrow, 1978). An analysis of the debates of the Constitutional Convention and subsequent interpretations and abuses of the resulting document.

James L. Sundquist, *Constitutional Reform and Effective Government* (Washington, D.C.: Brookings Institution, 1986). The author reviews the heated debate over constitutional reform, first analyzing the basic assumptions of the 1787 debates and then exploring the workable and desirable modifications that could strengthen and modernize American government.

Gordon S. Wood, *The Creation of the American Republic, 1776–1789* (New York: W. W. Norton, 1969). The distinctiveness of the American system of politics and the new political culture that emerged after the Revolution.

Chapter 3
▽
Federalism

Contents
▽

Three Systems of Government
Why a Federal System?
The Constitutional Basis for American Federalism
Horizontal Federalism
The Supremacy of the National Constitution
Milestones in National Government Supremacy
The Continuing Dispute over the Division of Power
The Fiscal Side of Federalism
Federalism Versus Regionalism

What If . . .

▽

The United States Had a National School System?

With our federal system, relatively few educational policies for public school systems are set by national authorities. Most decisions remain firmly in the hands of members of local boards of education who often decide what textbooks may be used, who will be certified to teach, which courses students must take, and which grades they must receive to graduate.

Such is certainly not the case in most other countries. It was often said that the French minister of education in Paris could look at the clock on the wall and know exactly what was being taught at that time in every classroom in the entire country. In England, students take examinations at age eleven that determine if they can go on to an academically-oriented secondary school. A similar structure of exams is given at an early age in Japan. In England and Japan, access to universities is rigidly controlled by rigorous national entrance exams. The Soviet Union is even more regimented—its students wear uniforms as well as learn from a standard national curriculum whose topics are mandated by the central government with some regional variations.

What would education be like in the United States if we also had a national school system? In Washington, D.C., a centralized ministry of education with regional offices in major cities would implement educational policy legislated by Congress. There would certainly be standardized exams for continuation through the various grades or levels of the school system and for entrance into college. The same textbook would be taught by each teacher, who had already passed the uniform certification program run by the ministry. A national ministry of education might even have a role in college-level instruction, such as the course in American government or political science you are now taking. Some young people in college today might not have been able to enter under a national education system because they might not have passed the rigorous test for university-bound students given at a very young age, such as in Japan and England. Also, sports would probably be downgraded under a centralized education system.

Some private education might be offered, mainly through religious institutions such as in France or high-cost programs such as in England. There would probably still be some degree of regional variation such as exists in the Soviet Union; however, the basic education available would be the same virtually everywhere throughout the country. All written learning materials, as well as curricula, would be consistent throughout the country. The only differences, for the most part, that students would experience would depend on differences in teachers.

▽

Think about these possibilities. Would you be in favor of having a national education system in this country? What is the best argument against such a system, and what is the single best argument for it?

How many separate governments do you think exist in the United States? One national government and fifty state governments, plus local governments, create a grand total of more than 80,000 governments in all! The breakdown can be seen in Table 3–1. Those 80,000 governments contain about 500,000 elected office-holders. Visitors from France or the Soviet Union are often awestruck by the complexity of our system of government. Consider that a criminal action can be defined by state law, by national law, or by both. Thus the alleged criminal can be prosecuted in the state court system or in the national court system (or both). Often economic regulation over exactly the same matter exists at the local level, the state level, and the national level—generating multiple forms to be completed, procedures to be followed, and laws to be obeyed. Numerous programs are funded by the national government but administered by state and local governments.

There are various ways of ordering relations between central governments and local units. Federalism is one of these ways. Understanding federalism and how it differs from other forms of government is important in understanding the current American political system.

Three Systems of Government
▽

There are basically three ways of ordering relations between central governments and local units: (1) a unitary system, (2) a confederal system, and (3) a federal system. The most popular, both historically and today, is the unitary system.

A Unitary System of Government

A **unitary system** of government is the easiest to define: Unitary systems allow ultimate governmental authority to rest in the hands of the national, or central, government. Consider a typical unitary system—France. There are departments in France and municipalities. Within the departments and the municipalities are separate government entities with elected and appointed officials. So far, the French system appears to be very similar to the United States system; but the similarity is only superficial. Under the unitary French system, the decisions of the governments of the departments and the municipalities can be overruled by the national government. Also, the national government can cut off the funding of many departmental and municipal government activities. Moreover, in a unitary system such as in France, all questions related to education, police, the use of land, and welfare are handled by the national government.[1]

Unitary System
A centralized governmental system in which local or subdivisional governments exercise only those powers given to them by the central government.

A Confederal System

We were introduced to the elements of a **confederal system** of government in Chapter 2, when we examined the Articles of Confederation. A confederation is the opposite of a unitary regime. It is a league of independent states, wherein a central government or administration handles only those matters of common con-

Confederal System
A league of independent states, each having essentially sovereign powers, wherein the central government created by such a league has only limited powers over the states.

---

[1]New legislation is altering somewhat the unitary character of the French political system, however. In March of 1982, a major decentralization law was adopted by the socialist government of François Mitterand.

Table 3–1
▽

The Number of Governments in the United States Today

With more than 80,000 separate governmental units in the United States today, it is no wonder that intergovernmental relations in the United States are so complicated. Actually, the number of school districts has decreased over time, but the number of special districts created for single purposes, such as flood control, has increased from only about eight thousand during World War II to the current almost thirty thousand.

Federal government		1
State governments		50
Local governments		82,290
Counties	3,041	
Municipalities	19,076	
(mainly cities or towns)		
Townships	16,734	
(less extensive powers)		
Special districts	28,588	
(water, sewer, etc.)		
School districts	14,851	
	82,290	
TOTAL		82,341

SOURCE: U.S. Department of Commerce, *Statistical Abstract of the United States*, 1986, Washington D.C.: U.S. Government Printing Office, 1986), p. 272.

Federal System

A system of government in which power is divided by a written constitution between a central government and regional, or subdivisional, governments. Each level must have some domain in which its policies are dominant and some genuine political or constitutional guarantee of its authority.

Extraordinary Majority

A majority which is greater than 50% plus one. For example, ratification of amendments requires the approval of two-thirds of the House and the Senate and three-fourths of the states.

cern expressly delegated to it by the member states. The central governmental unit has no ability to make laws directly applicable to individuals unless the member states explicitly support such laws.

A Federal System

Between the unitary and confederal forms of government lies the **federal system.** In this system, authority is divided, usually by a written constitution, between a central government and regional, or subdivisional, governments (often called constituent governments). The central government and the constituent governments both act directly on the people through laws and through actions of elected and appointed governmental officials. Within each government's sphere of authority, each is supreme in theory. Contrast a federal system to a unitary one in which the central government is supreme and the constituent governments derive their authority from it. A key feature of all federal systems is that changes in their written constitution must be approved by **extraordinary majorities** of the legislature of both the national government and some of the subnational units (the states, in the United States). See Figure 3–1 for a comparison among the three systems.

Why a Federal System?
▽

There are currently 180 countries in the world. Virtually none of them has a confederal system of government. Almost all have a unitary system. The United States is one of the few nations that has a truly federal system of government power. There are historical, as well as practical, reasons why the United States developed in that direction.

The Historical Reasons for Federalism

Common Problems

As we have seen in Chapter 2, the historical basis of our federal system was laid down in Philadelphia at the Constitutional Convention where strong national government advocates opposed equally strong states' rights advocates. This dichotomy continued through to the ratifying conventions in the several states. The resulting federal system was a compromise. Few, if any, delegates to the Philadelphia Convention wanted to continue with a confederal system, which had proved too weak to allow the government to face common problems, such as defense, that were national in scope. However, the independent states could never have accepted the idea of a union if the resulting political system had permitted extreme concentration of power in one central government. The appeal of federalism was that it retained state traditions and local power, while establishing a strong national government capable of handling common problems. Dealing with common problems was not the only reason that a federal system seemed to suit the United States well. A variety of characteristics—social and geographical—created the need for some type of federal system.

UNITARY	CONFEDERATE	FEDERAL

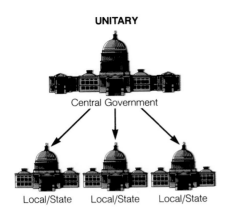

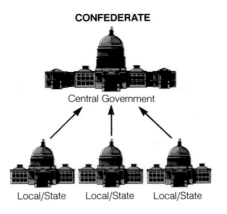

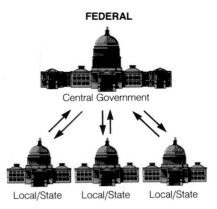

Central Government   Central Government   Central Government

Local/State   Local/State   Local/State   Local/State   Local/State   Local/State   Local/State   Local/State   Local/State

Figure 3–1

▽

The Flow of Power in Three Systems

Size and Regional Isolation

At the time of the Philadelphia Convention, the thirteen colonies taken together were geographically larger than England or France. Slow travel and communication combined with geographical spread contributed to the isolation of many regions within the colonies. It could, for example, take up to several weeks for all of the colonies to be informed about one particular political decision. Even if the colonial leaders had agreed on the desirability of a unitary system, the problems of size and regional isolation would have made such a system operationally difficult.

In a unitary system, the flow of power is from the central government uniquely to the local and state governments. In a confederal system, the flow of power is in the opposite direction—from the state and local governments to the central government. Finally, in a federal system the flow of power is, in principle, both ways.

Sectionalism and Political Subcultures

The American way of life has always been characterized by a number of political subcultures, dividing along the lines of race, wealth, education, religion, sexual

California lifestyle.

Did You Know?

▽

That local governments, which can be created as well as abolished by their state, have no independent existence according to the Constitution, unlike the state and national governments?

preferences, and age. These subcultures naturally developed because different groups of individuals became concentrated in different regions. For example, the Puritans who founded New England had, according to Daniel Elazar, a moralist subculture, viewing politics as the road to a good society.[2] The agricultural society of the South generated a traditionalist subculture, stressing not only tradition but also family and community. Finally, the Middle Atlantic states seemed to engender an individualist subculture, where politics was viewed as simply another business.

The existence of diverse political subcultures would appear to be at odds with a political authority concentrated solely in a central government. Had the United States developed into a unitary system, the various political subcultures certainly would have been less able to influence government behavior (relative to their own regions) than they have done and continue to do in our federal system.

Other Arguments for Federalism

The arguments for federalism in the United States and elsewhere involve a complex set of factors, some of which we have already noted. First, for big countries, such as the United States, India, and Nigeria, federalism allows many functions to be "farmed out" by the central government to the states or provinces; the lower level of government, accepting these responsibilities, can thereby become the focus of political dissatisfaction rather than the national authorities. Second, even with modern transportation and communication systems, the sheer geographic or population size of some nations makes it impractical to locate all political authority in one place. Third, strong regional differences within a nation can be partly diffused by a federal arrangement of political power. Federalism is in part a means by which conflicting language groups (as in Canada), ethnic national groups (as in Yugoslavia), religious groups (as in India), tribal groups (as in Nigeria), or regional nationalist groups can find local outlets for their social and political interests and can therefore be better accommodated as a whole. Finally, federalism brings government closer to the people, allowing more direct access to and influence on government agencies and policies, rather than leaving the population restive and dissatisfied with a remote, faceless, all-powerful central authority.

In the United States, in particular, federalism has historically had special benefits as well as drawbacks. State government has long been a training ground for future national leaders. Recent presidents like Jimmy Carter and Ronald Reagan first made their political mark as state governors, and many federal judges and members of Congress were initiated into politics and government on state courts or in state legislatures.

Many people argue that the states have also been testing grounds for the introduction of bold new government initiatives. This was true, for example, with unemployment compensation, which began in Wisconsin; the enfranchisement of eighteen-year-old voters, where Georgia pioneered the way; state lotteries, which were spearheaded in their modern form in New Hampshire; and air pollution control, which was first initiated in California. Of course, not everyone agrees that all of these developments were entirely beneficial, and other actions pioneered at the state level—such as Prohibition or Jim Crow laws—were either disastrous or morally bankrupt.

[2]Daniel J. Elazar, *American Federalism: A View from the States* (New York: Crowell, 1966).

Alexander Hamilton

The modern form of American federalism, consisting of a strong national government and subsidiary states, was endorsed both in theory and in practice by Alexander Hamilton. A New York lawyer educated at King's College (now Columbia University), Hamilton was a colleague of George Washington and a delegate to the Philadelphia Constitutional Convention. He later led the forces in favor of ratification of the Constitution in the New York State convention. Hamilton's successful politicking for ratification in that state was highlighted by a series of eighty-five public letters, which were printed in New York City newspapers from October 27, 1787 to August 16, 1788. The letters represented the joint work of Hamilton, James Madison, and John Jay and have come to be known as *The Federalist Papers.* About two-thirds of them are attributable to Hamilton.

Hamilton's admiration for a strong and energetic national government is evident in *The Federalist Papers.* He wrote that "the vigor of government is essential to the security of liberty" and that the fledgling nation confronted the alternatives of "adoption of the new Constitution or a dismemberment of the Union." History and common sense showed that "if these States should either be wholly disunited, or

"The more close the union of the states, and the more complete the authority of the whole, the less opportunity will be allowed the stronger states to injure the weaker."

Alexander Hamilton

only united in partial confederacies, the subdivisions into which they might be thrown would have frequent and violent contests with each other." A divided nation of sovereign states would also be easy prey for the divide-and-

conquer tactics of other nations. "A firm Union will be of the utmost moment to the peace and liberty of the States as a barrier against domestic faction and insurrection," whereas weak confederations would lead to "incurable disorder and imbecility in the government." The Constitution was not designed to abolish state governments, but to make them "constituent parts of the national sovereignty" by Senate representation and by their reserved powers.

A vigorous national government working for a common interest would also provide economic benefits from "an active commerce, an extensive navigation, [and] a flourishing marine," and the nation would be able to compete against European commercial power. "An unrestricted intercourse between the States themselves will advance the trade of each by an interchange of their respective productions, not only for the supply of reciprocal wants at home, but for exportation to foreign markets."

Hamilton, who became the nation's first secretary of the treasury in the cabinet of George Washington from 1789 to 1795, worked vigorously to implement these ideas. His views about strong national government have become dominant in U.S. history.

The Constitutional Basis for American Federalism

▽

No mention of the designation "federal system" can be found in the United States Constitution. Nor is it possible to find a systematic division of governmental authority between the national and state governments in that document. Rather, the Constitution sets out different types of powers (Figure 3–2). These powers can be classified as (1) the delegated powers of the national government, both expressed and implied, as well as resulting powers and the special category of inherent powers;

Figure 3–2
▽

The American Federal System—Division of Powers between the National Government and the State Governments.

We can separate the division of powers between national and state governments by looking at the powers granted by the Constitution to both the national governments and the state governments together. Then we look at the powers denied by the Constitution to each level of government.

(2) the reserved powers of the states; (3) concurrent powers; and (4) prohibited powers.

Powers Delegated to the National Government

Expressed Powers

Most of the powers expressly delegated to the national government are found in Article I, Section 8, of the Constitution. Some expressly delegated powers include setting standards for weights and measures, making uniform naturalization laws, admitting new states, establishing post offices, and declaring war.

POWERS GRANTED BY THE CONSTITUTION

NATIONAL
GOVERNMENT

Implied
"To make all laws which shall be necessary and proper for carrying into execution the foregoing powers, and all other powers vested by this Constitution in the Government of the United States, or in any Department or Officer thereof." (Article 1, Section 8:18)

Expressed
- To coin money
- To conduct foreign relations
- To regulate interstate commerce
- To levy and collect taxes
- To declare war
- To raise and support military forces
- To establish post offices
- To establish courts inferior to the Supreme Court
- To admit new states

NATIONAL
AND STATE
GOVERNMENTS

Concurrent
- To levy and collect taxes
- To borrow money
- To make and enforce laws
- To establish courts
- To provide for the general welfare
- To charter banks and corporations

STATE
GOVERNMENTS

Reserved to the States
- To regulate intrastate commerce
- To conduct elections
- To provide for public health, safety, and morals
- To establish local governments
- To ratify amendments to the federal constitution

POWERS DENIED BY THE CONSTITUTION

National
- To tax articles exported from any state
- To violate the Bill of Rights
- To change state boundaries

National and State
- To grant titles of nobility
- To permit slavery
- To deny citizens the right to vote

State
- To tax imports or exports
- To coin money
- To enter into treaties
- To impair obligations of contracts
- To abridge the privileges or immunities of citizens or deny due process and equal protection of the laws

Implied Powers

Article I, Section 8:18, states that the Congress shall have the power

> to make all laws which shall be necessary and proper for carrying into execution the foregoing powers, and all other powers vested by this Constitution in the Government of the United States, or in any Department or Officer thereof.

This clause is sometimes called the **elastic clause**, or the **necessary and proper clause**, because it gives elasticity to our constitutional system. It was first used in the Supreme Court decision of *McCulloch v. Maryland*[3] (discussed later in this chapter) to develop the concept of implied powers, through which the national government has succeeded in strengthening the scope of its authority to meet the numerous problems that the framers of the Constitution did not, and could not, anticipate.

Resulting Powers

Resulting powers are national powers that result when several expressed powers are added together. For example, the central government's authority to make paper money legal tender for the payment of debts is the result of adding together the expressed powers to coin money, to borrow money, and to regulate interstate commerce.

Inherent Powers

A special category of national powers that are not implied by the necessary and proper clause consists of what have been labeled the inherent powers of the national government. These powers derive from the fact that the United States is a sovereign power among nations, and, as such, its national government must be the only government that deals with other nations. Under international law, it is assumed that all nation-states, regardless of their size or power, have *inherent* in their existence as nations the right to ensure their own survival. To do this, each nation must have the ability to act in its own interest among and with the community of nations—by, for instance, making treaties, waging war, and seeking trade.[4] Some constitutional scholars categorize inherent powers as a third type of power, completely distinct from the delegated powers (both expressed and implied) of the national government.

Reserved Powers of the State Governments

The Tenth Amendment states that the powers not delegated to the United States by the Constitution, nor prohibited by it to the states, are reserved to the states respectively, or to the people. These are the reserved powers that the national government cannot usurp from, or deny to, the states. Such powers include each state's right to regulate commerce within its borders and to provide for a state militia. States also have the reserved power to make laws on all matters not pro-

Elastic Clause or Necessary and Proper Clause
The clause in Article I, Section 8, which grants Congress the power to do whatever is necessary to execute its specific powers.

---

[3]4 Wheaton 316 (1819).

[4]See especially *United States v. Curtiss-Wright Export Co.*, 299 U.S. 304 (1936), which upheld the validity of a joint resolution of Congress delegating the power to the president to prohibit armed shipments to foreign belligerents.

hibited to the states by the national or state constitutions and not expressly, or by implication, delegated to the national government. On occasion, states have used their power to pass discriminatory legislation, such as antimiscegenation laws prohibiting interracial marriages. These laws were passed on the assumption that since the Constitution did not grant such regulatory power to the national government, that power was reserved to the states acting through their legislatures. But when such laws were declared to be unconstitutional,[5] they immediately became unenforceable by the states.

Concurrent Powers

In certain areas, the Constitution gives national and state governments an equal right to pass legislation and to regulate certain activities. These are called concurrent powers. An example of a concurrent power is the power to tax. However, the types of taxation are divided between the levels of government. States may not levy a tariff (a set of taxes on imported goods); the federal government may not tax real estate; and neither may tax the facilities of the other. If the state governments did not have the power to tax, they would not be able to function other than on a ceremonial basis.

Other concurrent powers that are not specifically stated in the Constitution but only implied include the power to borrow money, to establish courts, and to charter banks and corporations. These powers are normally limited to the geographical area of the state and to those functions not preempted by the Constitution or by the national government—such as the coinage of money and the negotiation of treaties.

The foregoing discussion of the constitutional basis for state power might give the impression that the power of the states today is derived solely from the Constitution. This would be a mistake, for the independence of the states rests, in large part, on the commitment of American citizens to the idea of local self-government. In addition, and perhaps more importantly, members of the national government— senators and representatives—are elected by their local constituencies. Except for the president, politicians in the national government have obtained their power by satisfying those local constituencies, rather than by satisfying some ill-defined, broad national constituency. Furthermore, many of the programs paid for and undertaken by the national government are carried out by the state and local governmental units—for example, the interstate highway system, most of the welfare system, job creation programs, and environmental cleanup programs.

Horizontal Federalism

▽

So far we have examined only the relationship between central and constituent governmental units. But, of course, the constituent units have numerous commercial, social, and other dealings among themselves. These interstate activities, problems, and policies make up what can be called horizontal federalism. The national Constitution imposes certain "rules of the road" on horizontal federalism, which have had the effect of preventing any one state from setting itself apart from

[5]*Loving v. Virginia*, 388 U.S. 1 (1967).

the other states. The three most important clauses in the Constitution relating to horizontal federalism, all taken from the Articles of Confederation, require that

1. Each state give full faith and credit to every other state's public acts, records, and judicial proceedings
2. Each state extend to every other state's citizens the privileges and immunities of its own citizens
3. Each state agree to render persons who are fleeing from justice in another state back to their home state when requested to do so

The Full Faith and Credit Clause

Article IV, Section 1, of the Constitution provides that "full faith and credit shall be given in each state to the public acts, records, and judicial proceedings of every other state." This clause applies only to civil matters. It ensures that rights established under deeds, wills, contracts, and the like in one state will be honored by other states and any judicial decision with respect to such property rights will be honored as well as enforced in all states. The **full faith and credit clause** was originally put in the Articles of Confederation to promote mutual friendship among the people of the different states. In fact, it has contributed to the unity of American citizens because it protects their legal rights as they move about from state to state. This is extremely important in a country with a very mobile citizenry.

Privileges and Immunities

Privileges and immunities are defined as special rights and exemptions provided by law. Article IV, Section 2, indicates that "the citizens of each state shall be entitled to all privileges and immunities of citizens in the several states." This clause indicates the obligations of the states in their relations with each other's citizens.

Full Faith and Credit Clause
A section of the Constitution that requires states to recognize one another's laws and court decisions. It ensures that rights established under deeds, wills, contracts, and other civil matters in one state will be honored by other states.

Privileges and Immunities
A section of the Constitution requiring states not to discriminate against one another's citizens. A resident of one state cannot be treated as an alien when in another state; he or she may not be denied such privileges and immunities as legal protection, access to courts, travel rights, or property rights.

The Constitution requires freedom of travel between states.

Extradite

To surrender an accused criminal to the authorities of the state from which he or she has fled; to return a fugitive criminal to the jurisdiction of the accusing state.

Interstate Compacts

Agreements between two or more states. Agreements on minor matters are made without congressional consent, but any compact that tends to increase the power of the contracting states relative to other states or relative to the national government generally requires the consent of Congress. Such compacts serve as a means by which states can solve regional problems.

Supremacy Clause

The constitutional provision that makes the Constitution and federal laws superior to all state and local legislation.

It means, quite simply, that a resident of Alabama cannot be treated as an alien when that person is in California or New York. He or she must have access to the courts of each state, to travel rights, and to property rights.[6]

Interstate Extradition

Article IV, Section 2, states that "a person charged in any state with treason, felony, or another crime who shall flee from justice and be found in another state, shall on demand of the executive authority of the state from which he fled, be delivered up, to be removed to the state having jurisdiction of the crime." The language here appears clear, yet governors of one state have not been legally required to **extradite** (render to another state) a fugitive from justice. The federal courts will not order such an action. It is rather the moral duty of a governor to do so, and, in fact, extradition is routinely followed in most cases. Governors who refuse to extradite are inviting retaliation from other states. In many cases, the question is moot because Congress has made it a federal crime to flee across state lines to avoid prosecution for certain felonies. Therefore, apprehension by federal agents puts the fugitive in national government hands, and that person is usually turned over to the state from which he or she fled.

The Peaceful Settlement of Differences between States

States are supposed to settle their differences peacefully. In so doing, they may enter into agreements called **interstate compacts**—if consented to by Congress. In reality, congressional consent is necessary only if such a compact increases the power of the contracting states relative to other states (or to the national government). Typical examples of interstate compacts are the establishment of the Port of New York Authority by the states of New York and New Jersey and the regulation of the production of crude oil and natural gas by the Interstate Oil and Gas Compact of 1935. The U.S. Supreme Court plays a major role in dealing with legal disputes between the states. Also, the Supreme Court plays a major role in dealing with disputes between the national government and the state governments. We consider the judicial system in more detail in Chapter 15.

The Supremacy of the National Constitution

The supremacy of the national constitution over subnational laws and actions can be found in the **supremacy clause** of the Constitution. The supremacy clause (Article VI, Paragraph 2) states:

This Constitution, and the laws of the United States which shall be made in pursuance thereof; and all Treaties made . . . under the Authority of the United States, shall be the supreme law of the Land; and the Judges in every State shall be bound thereby; any Thing in the Constitution or Laws of any State to the Contrary notwithstanding.

In other words, states cannot use their reserved or concurrent powers to thwart national policies. All national and state officers, as well as judges, must be bound

[6]Out-of-state residents have been denied lower tuition rates at state universities, voting rights, and immediate claim to welfare benefits. Actually, the courts have never established a precise meaning of the term *privileges and immunities*.

Extradition is Not Always so Simple: The Case of Dennis Banks

Extradition is ordinarily so routine that most people, once arrested, waive the right to contest it. Few who fight extradition win more than a brief delay before being handed over to the authorities of the state from which they fled. Not so in the case of Dennis Banks, a Native American activist who managed to evade capture for nearly ten years.

In 1975, Banks was convicted of rioting and assault with a deadly weapon in connection with a riot which followed a protest against the stabbing of an Indian youth by police in Custer, South Dakota. Before sentencing, he jumped bail and fled to California to seek sanctuary. In 1976, the FBI—at South Dakota's behest—picked him up in San Francisco. Jane Fonda and Marlon Brando took up his cause, and a petition supporting Banks amassed 1.4 million signatures. Saying that he feared Banks's life might be in danger if Banks were returned to South Dakota, Governor Edmund G. Brown, Jr., spurned the extradition request.

Meanwhile, Banks's nemesis, former Attorney General William Janklow, was elected governor of South Dakota.

Dennis Banks.

Determined that Banks would face justice, Janklow asked that the California Supreme Court overrule Governor Brown's decision. The court ruled that the matter was entirely in Brown's

hands and that it had no authority under the federal constitution or its own state law to compel the governor to extradite Banks. A public battle between the two governors ensued. At one point, it was rumored that Janklow had vowed to send "every crook in the state" to California.

The story changed when George Deukmejian was sworn in as California's new governor in 1982. Throughout his campaign, he had vowed that, if elected, he would not continue to shelter Banks. But, when a sergeant appeared at Banks's front door with a South Dakota fugitive warrant shortly after Deukmejian was sworn in, it was too late. Dennis Banks was already on the Onondaga Indian Reservation in upstate New York where he sought and received sanctuary. In September 1984, Banks surrendered to law enforcement officials in South Dakota. According to his attorney, the Indian leader was tired of being restricted to the New York reservation and wanted to "get on with his life."

New York Times, Sept. 13, 1984.

by oath to support the Constitution. Hence any legitimate exercise of national governmental power supersedes any conflicting state action.[7] Of course, deciding whether a conflict actually exists is a judicial matter, as we will see in the case of *McCulloch v. Maryland*, although such decisions may be politically charged.

Some political scientists believe that national supremacy is critical for the longevity and smooth functioning of a federal system. Nonetheless, the application of this principle has been a continuous source of conflict. Indeed, the most extreme result of this conflict was the Civil War, which we explore in more detail later.

[7]An excellent example of this is President Eisenhower's disciplining of Arkansas Governor Orville Faubus by calling up the National Guard to enforce the court-ordered desegregation of Little Rock High School. See R. Neustadt, *Presidential Power: The Politics of Leadership from FDR to Carter* (New York: Wiley, 1980).

Milestones in National Government Supremacy

▽

Numerous court decisions and political events and even more numerous instances of bureaucratic decision making have given our national government a preponderance of significant political power. Such was not the case during the early days of the American republic, however. Historically, there are at least three milestones on the route to today's relatively more powerful national government. They are as follows:

1. The Supreme Court case of *McCulloch v. Maryland* (1819),[8] in which the doctrine of implied powers of the national government was clarified.
2. The Supreme Court case of *Gibbons v. Ogden* (1824),[9] in which the national government's power over commerce was defined for the first time in an expansive way.
3. The Civil War (1861–1865)

McCulloch v. Maryland (1819)

The U.S. Constitution says nothing about establishing a national bank. Article I, Section 8, gives Congress the power "to coin money, regulate the value thereof, and of foreign coin, and fix the standards of weights and measures. . . ." Nonetheless, at different times Congress chartered two banks—the First and Second Banks of the United States—and provided part of their initial capital; they were thus national banks.

Maryland was one of many states that opposed the existence of the Second Bank of the United States, claiming that it represented unfair competition against state banks and an extension of centralized political power. Yielding to pressure from its state banks, the government of Maryland imposed a tax on the Second Bank's Baltimore branch. The branch's cashier, James William McCulloch, refused to pay the Maryland tax. Maryland took McCulloch to its state court. In that suit, the state of Maryland won. Since similar taxes were being levied in other states, the national government appealed the case to the Supreme Court, then headed by Chief Justice John Marshall.

The Constitutional Question

The question before the Supreme Court was of monumental proportions. The very heart of national power under the Constitution, as well as the relationship between the national government and the states, was at issue. Congress has the authority to make all laws that are "necessary and proper" for the execution of Congress's enumerated powers. Strict constructionists looked at the word *necessary* and contended that the national government had only those powers *indispensable* to the exercise of its designated powers. To them, chartering and contributing capital to a bank was not necessary, for example, to coin money and regulate its value. Nothing was specifically stated in the Constitution about the creation by the national government of a national bank.

Loose constructionists disagreed. They believed that the word *necessary* could not be looked at in its strictest sense. If one were to interpret the necessary and

[8] 4 Wheaton 316 (1819).
[9] 9 Wheaton 1 (1824).

proper clause literally, it would have no practical effect. As Hamilton once said, "It is essential to the being of the national Government, that so erroneous a conception of the meaning of the word *necessary* should be exploded."

Marshall's Decision

John Marshall probably made his decision in this case even before he heard the opposing arguments. He adopted the Hamiltonian, or Federalist, approach. It is true, Marshall said, that Congress's power to establish a national bank was not expressed in the Constitution. However, he went on, if establishing such a national bank aided the national government in the exercise of its designated powers, then the authority to set up such a bank could be implied. To Marshall, the "necessary and proper" clause embraced "all means which are appropriate" to carry out "the legitimate ends" of the Constitution. Only when such actions are forbidden by the letter and spirit of the Constitution are they thereby unconstitutional. There was nothing in the Constitution, according to Marshall, "which excludes incidental or implied powers; and which requires that everything granted shall be expressly and minutely described."

John Marshall

Marshall felt that the Constitution was a living instrument that had to be interpreted to meet the "practical" needs of government. Marshall's decision became the basis for strengthening the national government's power from that day on. By refusing to bind the national government by the literal limits of its expressed powers, the Marshall Court enabled the national government to grow and to meet problems that the Founding Fathers were unable to foresee. Today, practically every expressed power of the national government has been expanded in one way or another by use of the necessary and proper clause.

Gibbons v. Ogden (1824)

One of the more important parts of the Constitution included in Article I, Section 8, is the so-called **commerce clause,** in which Congress is given the power "to regulate commerce with foreign nations, and among the several states, and with the Indian tribes. . . ." What exactly does "to regulate commerce mean"? What does "commerce" entail? The issue here is essentially the same as that raised by *McCulloch v. Maryland*—how strict an interpretation should be given to a constitutional phrase? As can be expected, since Marshall interpreted the necessary and proper clause liberally in *McCulloch v. Maryland*, he also, five years later, used the same approach in interpreting the commerce clause.

Commerce Clause
The section of the Constitution in which Congress is given the power to regulate trade among the states and with foreign countries.

The Issue Before the Court

Robert Fulton, inventor of the steamboat, and Robert Livingston, American minister to France, secured a monopoly of steam navigation on the waters in New York State from the New York legislature in 1803. They licensed Aaron Ogden to operate steam-powered ferryboats between New York and New Jersey. Thomas Gibbons decided to compete with Ogden, but he did so without New York's permission. Ogden sued Gibbons. The New York state courts granted Ogden an **injunction,** prohibiting Gibbons from operating in New York waters. Gibbons appealed to the Supreme Court.

Injunction
An order issued by a court in an equity proceeding to compel or restrain the performance of an act by an individual or government official.

What at first glance seems like a straightforward legal issue was actually a sensational battle between two men, a battle that physically and financially almost wrecked them. Gibbons was a belligerent southern planter. His sordid past included being campaign manager in an election where there were more votes than voters. The loser in that election, James Jackson, attacked Gibbons in Congress, telling everyone who would listen about "this person . . . whose soul is faction and whose life has been a scene of political corruption. . . ." Gibbons obviously did not appreciate Jackson's remarks. He proposed a duel; shots were exchanged, though neither man was hit.

Gibbon's legal battle against Ogden (who was a former governor of New Jersey and a U.S. senator) became a personal vendetta. No expenditure was too large to make sure that Ogden lost. Daniel Webster was one of the prestigious attorneys that Gibbons hired. Gibbons even put a $40,000 contingency provision in his will to carry on the legal battle if he died before it was resolved.

During the lengthy litigation, Gibbons decided to visit Ogden's home.

He challenged Ogden to a duel. Ogden instead sued and won $5,000 against Gibbons for trespassing.

By the time the case ended, both Gibbons and Ogden had spent the greater part of their fortunes on legal fees.

Thomas Gibbons

Aaron Ogden

Marshall's Decision

Marshall defined commerce as all commercial intercourse—that is, all business dealings. The Court ruled against Ogden's monopoly, reversing the injunction against Gibbons. Marshall used this opportunity not only to expand the definition of commerce but also to validate and increase the power of the national legislature to regulate commerce. Said Marshall, "What is this power? It is the power . . . to prescribe the rule by which commerce is to be governed. This power, like all others vested in Congress, is complete in itself." In other words, the power of the national government to regulate commerce has no limitations, other than those specifically found in the Constitution.

As a result of Marshall's decision, the commerce clause allowed the national government to exercise increasing authority over all areas of economic affairs throughout the land. Some scholars believe that Marshall's decision in *Gibbons v. Ogden* welded the people of the United States into a unit by the force of their commercial interests. In any event, today few areas of economic activity remain outside the regulatory power of the national legislature.

The Civil War

We usually think of the Civil War simply as the fight to free the slaves and of Abraham Lincoln as the Great Emancipator. The facts are quite different. Freedom was an important aspect of the Civil War, but not the only one and certainly not the most important one, say many scholars. After all, Lincoln claimed on taking office that he would not attack slavery as an institution. He even wanted a constitutional amendment that would make the right to own slaves irrevocable.[10]

At the heart of the controversy that led to the Civil War was the issue of national government supremacy versus the rights of the separate states. The Civil War brought to an ultimate and violent climax the ideological debate that had been outlined by the Federalist and anti-Federalist parties in the early years of the nation. This debate was sparked anew by the passage of the Tariff Acts of 1828 and 1830 by the national government, which the southern states believed were against their interests. The state of South Carolina attempted to nullify the tariffs, claiming that in cases of conflict between a state and the national government, the state should have the ultimate authority over its citizens.

Nullification and Secession

Defending the concept of **nullification** was a well-educated and articulate senator from South Carolina, John C. Calhoun. Not a newcomer to politics, Calhoun had served the government in several capacities—as vice president under John Quincy Adams and Andrew Jackson, as secretary of state, and as secretary of war. Calhoun viewed the federal system as simply a compact (as in the Articles of Confederation) among sovereign states. The national government was not the final judge of its own power—the ultimate sovereign authority rested with the several states. It followed that the national government could not force a state and its citizens to accept a law against their will. In such cases, Calhoun argued, the state had the right to declare a national law to be *null and void* and therefore not binding on its citizens. Within this theory of nullification is the concept of **interposition,** in which a state places itself between its citizens and the national government as a protector, shielding its citizens from any national legislation that may be harmful to them.[11]

Calhoun also espoused the political doctrine of the **concurrent majority,** in which he maintained that democratic decisions could be made only with the concurrence of all major segments of society, and without that agreement a decision should not be binding on those whose interests it violates.

Calhoun's concurrent majority thesis was used by others later as a justification for the **secession** of the southern states from the Union. The ultimate defeat of the South, however, permanently lay to waste any idea that a state within our Union can successfully claim the right to secede. We live in "the indestructible union of indestructible states," as the Supreme Court has said. It is not without irony that the Civil War, brought about in large part because of the South's desire for increased

Nullification

The act of nullifying or rendering void. Basing his argument on the assumption that ultimate sovereign authority rested with the several states, John C. Calhoun asserted that a state had the right to declare a national law to be null and void and therefore not binding on its citizens.

Interposition

The act in which a state places itself between its citizens and the national government as a protector, shielding its citizens from any national legislation that may be harmful to them. The doctrine of interposition has been rejected by the federal courts as contrary to the national supremacy clause of Article VI in the Constitution.

Concurrent Majority

A principle advanced by John C. Calhoun whereby democratic decisions could be made only with the concurrence of all major segments of society. Without the concurrence, a decision should not be binding on those whose interests it violates.

Secession

The act of formally withdrawing from membership in an alliance; withdrawal of a state from the federal union.

[10]See Richard Hofstadter, *The American Political Tradition and the Men Who Made It* (New York: Vintage Books, 1948), p. 126.

[11]Thomas Jefferson and James Madison also used the theory of interposition in the Kentucky and Virginia Resolutions of 1799, written to protest the Alien and Sedition Acts of 1798.

Highlight

The Webster-Calhoun Debate in 1833

Proud, sensitive, high-strung John C. Calhoun rose to take the floor of the Senate to debate the Force Bill introduced by the Jackson administration to compel the states, and especially Calhoun's native South Carolina, to enforce the tariff laws of 1828 and 1832—by military means if necessary. Calhoun argued passionately in favor of state sovereignty and the right to resist national government actions if a state opposes them.

The purpose of the Force Bill, he said, was to "make war against one of the free and sovereign members of this confederation . . . thus exhibiting the impious spectacle of this Government, the creature of the States, making war against the power to which it owes its existence." The bill was, he continued, ill advised because it assumed that the "entire sovereignty of this country belongs to the American people, as forming one great community; and regards the States as mere fractions or counties, and not as an integral part of the Union, having no more right to resist the encroachments of the Government than a county has to resist the author-

Daniel Webster

ity of a state. . . ." He reproached the government for treating resistance to the Force Bill as "the lawless acts of so many individuals, without possessing sovereign or political rights."

Calhoun went on to discuss his compact theory of federalism: "The terms union, federal, united, all imply a combination of sovereignties, a confederation of States . . . the sovereignty is in the several States, and . . . our system is a union of . . . sovereign powers, under a constitutional compact. . . ." He then propounded his theory of concurrent majorities by which "the Government should be organized upon the principle of the absolute majority, or rather of two absolute majorities combined," which were a majority of states in the Senate and a majority of the people of the states in the House of Representatives.

The crowded Senate floor and gallery awaited the reply from the great orator from Massachusetts, Daniel Webster, who began to speak as soon as Calhoun had finished. In attacking Calhoun's confederal view of the Union, Webster stated: "By the Constitution, we mean, not a 'constitutional compact,' but, simply and directly, the Constitution, the fundamental law; and if there be one word in the language which the people of the United States understand, this is that word."

Webster argued that to allow nullification and secession was the equivalent of dismembering the entire government. In fact, he said, the very reason that the Articles of Confederation had been replaced by the Constitution was to protect against disunion and to keep each state from imposing its individual will against the other states. In direct reply to Calhoun, Webster maintained

that the Constitution of the United States was not a league, confederacy, or a compact between the several states in their sovereign capacities but a government "founded on the adoption of the people, and creating direct relations between itself and individuals." Only revolution could "dissolve these relations," and "there can be no such thing as secession without revolution." Any attempt by a state to "abrogate, annul, or nullify an act of Congress, or to arrest its operation within her limits, on the ground that . . . such law is unconstitutional, is a direct usurpation on the just powers of the general government" and "a plain violation of the Constitution."

Concluding his defense of the Union, Webster pledged to "exert every faculty I possess in aiding to prevent the Constitution from being nullified, destroyed, or impaired; and even should I see it fall, I will still, with a voice feeble, perhaps, but earnest as ever issued from human lips, and with fidelity and zeal which nothing shall extinguish, call on the *people* to come to its rescue."

John C. Calhoun

states' rights, in fact resulted in the opposite—an increase in the political power of the national government.

War and the Growth of the National Government

Thousands of new employees were hired to run the Union war effort and to deal with the social and economic problems that had to be handled in the aftermath of war. A billion-dollar ($1.3 billion, which is about $8.9 billion in today's dollars) national government budget was passed for the first time in 1865 to cover the increased government expenditures. The first (temporary) income tax was imposed on citizens to help pay for the war. Civil liberties were curtailed in both the Union and in the Confederacy in the name of the wartime emergency. The distribution of pensions and widows' benefits also boosted the national government's social role.

The nation was set on the path to a modern, industrial economy and society by the victory of the North. Slavery, on which the agrarian economy of the old South had crucially depended, was ended, and the emancipated slaves were promised equality by the **Reconstruction** of southern government and by the passage of the Thirteenth, Fourteenth, and Fifteenth Amendments to the Constitution. That promise was briefly realized as the ex-slaves gained control of several state governments in the South, but violent reestablishment of white dominance through the physical repression by the **Ku Klux Klan** and the passage of discriminatory **Jim Crow laws** submerged the struggle for equality for a hundred years. Among the white population of the nation, however, the principles of "due process" and "equal protection," enshrined in the Fourteenth Amendment, were to increase greatly the social and economic role of the national government.

The Continuing Dispute over the Division of Power
▽

As we have noted, *McCulloch v. Maryland* expanded the implied powers of the federal government. The dispute, and its ultimate outcome, can be viewed as part of a continuing debate about the boundaries between federal and state authority with the Supreme Court as the boundary setter, or referee. As we might expect, the character of the referee will have an impact on the ultimate outcome of any boundary dispute. While John Marshall was head of the Supreme Court, he did much to increase the power of the national government and reduce that of the states. During the Jacksonian era (1829–1837), a shift back to states' rights began. In particular, the business community preferred state regulation (or, better yet, no regulation) of commerce. The question of the regulation of commerce became one of the major issues in federal-state relations.

The issue was often resolved in favor of the states under U.S. Supreme Court Justice Roger Taney, who headed the Court from 1836 until 1864. Taney's goal was to shift the constitutional emphasis from the national level and return power to the states, particularly with respect to the regulation of business and other activities within state borders like public health, safety, and morals. Under Taney, the **police power** of the states became the basic instrument through which property was controlled in the "public interest."

The continuing dispute over the division of power between the national government and the states can be looked at in terms of the historical phases of federalism in the United States: dual federalism, cooperative federalism, and the new federalism.

Reconstruction

The period following the Civil War when the Reconstruction Acts were passed to reconstruct the southern government and to grant full citizenship to blacks.

Ku Klux Klan

A white supremacist organization founded in 1865 by a small group of ex-Confederate soldiers to resist Reconstructionist policies and to restore state sovereignty.

Jim Crow Laws

State laws enforcing racial segregation in public accommodations and conveyances.

Police Power

The authority to legislate for the protection of the health, morals, safety, and welfare of the people. In the United States police power is a reserved power of the states. The federal government is able to legislate for the welfare of its citizens only through specific congressional powers such as control over interstate commerce.

Dual Federalism

Dual Federalism

A system of government in which each of the states and the national government remain supreme within their own spheres. The doctrine looks on nation and state as coequal sovereign powers and holds that acts of states within their reserved powers could be limitations on the powers of the national government.

Economic Regulation

The regulation of business practices by government agencies.

The legal doctrine of **dual federalism** emphasized a distinction between federal and state spheres of authority, particularly in the area of **economic regulation.** The distinction between intrastate commerce (which was not under the control of the national government) and interstate commerce (which was under the control of the national government) became of overriding importance. For example, in 1918, the U.S. Supreme Court ruled that a 1916 federal law banning child labor was unconstitutional. Why? Because it was a local problem and the power to deal with it was reserved to the states.[12] Even as recently as 1976, the Court held that a federal law regulating wages and overtime pay could not be applied to state government employees, as that would mean a violation of state sovereignty.[13] Political historians date the end of the legal doctrine of dual federalism to around 1937, when the United States was in the depths of the greatest depression it had ever experienced.

Cooperative Federalism

Franklin D. Roosevelt was inaugurated on March 4, 1933, as the thirty-second president of the United States. In the previous year, 1932, nearly 1,500 banks had failed (and 4,000 more would fail in 1933). Thirty-two thousand businesses closed down and one-fourth of the labor force was unemployed. The national government had been expected to do something about the disastrous state of the economy. But for the first three years of the Great Depression, the national government did very little. The new Democratic administration was marked by energetic intervention in the economy. FDR's "New Deal" included numerous government spending and

[12]*Hammer v. Dagenhart*, 247 U.S. 251 (1918). This decision was overruled in *U.S. v. Darby*, 312 U.S. 100 (1940).
[13]*National League of Cities v. Usery*, 426 U.S. 833 (1976); recently altered by *EEOC v. Wyoming*, 460 U.S. (1982).

WPA project during the Depression.

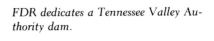
FDR dedicates a Tennessee Valley Authority dam.

welfare programs, in addition to voluminous regulations on economic activity. The U.S. Supreme Court, still abiding by the legal doctrine of dual federalism, rejected as unconstitutional virtually all of Roosevelt's national regulation of business. It was not until 1937 that the Court, responding to Roosevelt's Court-packing threat and two new Roosevelt-appointed justices, ruled that manufacturing could be regulated as interstate commerce by the national government.[14]

Some political scientists have labeled the era since 1937 as one of **cooperative federalism,** in which the states and the national government cooperate in solving complex common problems. Others see the 1937 decision as the beginning of an era of national supremacy, in which the power of the states has been consistently diminished. In particular, Congress can pass virtually any law that regulates almost any kind of economic activity, no matter where that activity is located. For all intents and purposes, the doctrine of dual federalism has been dead for quite some time, although, as we shall see, there have been attempts at reviving it during the Reagan administration.

Cooperative Federalism
The theory that the states and the national government should cooperate in solving problems.

The Growth of National-Level Powers

Even if the Great Depression had not occurred, we probably still would have witnessed a growth of national-level powers as the country became increasingly populated, industrial, and a world power. This meant that problems and situations that were once treated locally would begin to have a profound impact on Americans hundreds or even thousands of miles away.

For example, if one state is unable to maintain an adequate highway system, the economy of the entire region may suffer. If another state maintains a substandard

[14]*NLRB v. Jones & Laughlin Steel Corporation,* 301 U.S. 1 (1937). For a different view of the historical significance of this decision, see Morton Grodzins, "Centralization and Decentralization in the American Federal System," in Robert A. Goldwin, ed., A *Nation of States: Essays on the American Federal System* (Chicago: Rand McNally, 1963).

New Federalism

A plan to limit the national government's power to regulate and to restore power to state governments. Essentially, the new federalism was designed to give the states an increased ability to decide for themselves how government revenues should be spent.

Revenue-Sharing Program

A program in which the federal government allocates funds to states and cities with virtually no strings attached. Recipient governments can use the funds in any way they see fit.

Figure 3–3
▽
The Shift Toward Central Government Spending

Before the Great Depression, local governments accounted for 60 percent of all government spending, with the federal government only accounting for 17 percent. During Franklin D. Roosevelt's New Deal, in 1939, the federal government increased its spending to 47 percent of total government spending, with local government spending dropping to only 30 percent. By 1960, federal government spending was up to 64 percent, local governments accounted for only 19 percent, and the remainder was spent by state governments. The estimate for 1987 is that the federal government accounts for 65 percent and local governments for 16 percent.

SOURCE: *Government Finances*, U.S. Department of Commerce, Bureau of the Census, 1986.

educational system, the quality of the work force, the welfare rolls, and the criminal justice agencies in other states may be affected. So the death of dual federalism and the ascendancy of national supremacy had a very logical and very real set of causes. Our more mobile, industrial, and increasingly interdependent nation demanded more uniform and consistent sets of rules, regulations, and governmental programs. The shift toward the increasing role of the central government in the United States can nowhere better be seen than in the shift toward increased central government spending as a percentage of total government spending. Figure 3–3 shows that back in 1929, on the eve of the Great Depression, local governments accounted for 60 percent of all government outlays, whereas the federal government accounted for only 17 percent. After Roosevelt's New Deal was in place for several years during the Great Depression, local government gave up half of its share of the government spending pie, dropping to 30 percent, and the federal government increased its share to 47 percent. By 1987, the federal government accounted for about 65 percent of all government spending.

The degree to which the national government regulates the economic activity of citizens is also determined by the political process. Some citizens want regulation, and to the extent that Congress responds to those desires and passes appropriate legislation, regulation will exist. Other citizens oppose it. These forces continually struggle to win the support of the voters and politicians.

The Advisory Commission on Intergovernmental Relations has conducted an annual poll for the past fourteen years asking the public to rate the levels of government—federal, state, and local—on effectiveness. This survey is a way of indirectly judging public confidence and conducting a performance appraisal of government. Figure 3–4 shows the responses in selected categories for 1982 and 1985.

The New Federalism

The third phase of federalism was labeled by President Richard Nixon as the **new federalism.** Its goal is to reduce the restrictions attached to federal grants—that is, to allow local officials to make the decisions about how the money is to be spent. The centerpiece of Nixon's new federalism was a **revenue-sharing program** that gave local and state officials considerable freedom in spending decisions.

President Ronald Reagan continued Nixon's emphasis on the new federalism. "It is my intention . . . [to restore] the powers granted to the federal government

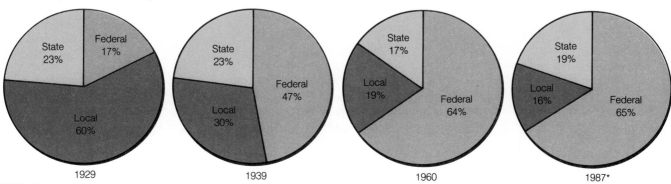

*Estimated

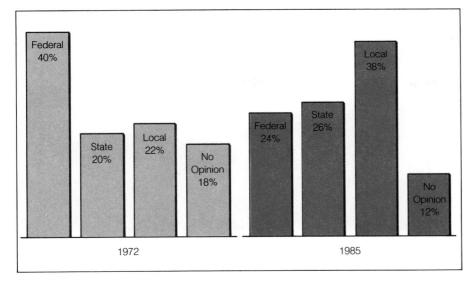

Figure 3–4
▽

**Opinions on Government Effectiveness
by Level**

*In response to the question, Which level
of government—federal, state, or local—
is most effective? 40 percent of respondents answered federal in 1972, but only
24 percent answered federal in 1985. The
percentage of those polled who believed
the state and local governments were most
effective had increased.*

SOURCE: Advisory Commission on Intergovernmental Relations, 1986.

and those reserved to the states and to the people," said President Reagan in his
first State of the Union address in 1982. Although President Reagan was referring
to the boundaries between the powers of the national government and of the states,
his new federalism, like Nixon's, was essentially a plan to give the states an increased
ability to decide for themselves how government revenues should be spent.

The Decentralization of Federal Programs

At first, President Reagan proposed a swap of about $47 billion in revenue in
government programs between the states and the national government, beginning
with the 1984 **fiscal year.** Congress was to decentralize and dismantle forty of the
domestic social, transportation, and community development programs that it had
created over the previous fifty years; it would then give back to the states the revenues
to help pay for those programs. In a July 1982 proposal, the Reagan administration
sought also to eliminate completely federal grants for environmental programs and
to shift such responsibility entirely to the states. As for welfare, the federal government was to pay for all the costs of the Medicaid health program, and the states,
in turn, would assume responsibility for food stamps and Aid to Families with
Dependent Children (AFDC).

Opposition to the New Federalism

The Reagan administration's plan for a new federalism came under increasing
criticism. From the beginning, almost every state governor rejected the program,
seeing it simply as a ploy to cut federal government expenditures on needed programs. What early support did exist for the new federalism soon began to decline
when about two-thirds of the Reagan budget cuts fell on state and local governments.
In spite of federal expectations to the contrary, the states were largely unable to
compensate for the loss of revenue from Washington out of their own resources.
Welfare benefits were reduced in some states and did no better than hold steady
in most other states. These problems were made worse by the deep recession in
the early 1980s. The poorer states, with fewer financial resources, were particularly

Fiscal Year

A period of twelve months, which can
begin at any time during the calendar
year, used by businesses for accounting
purposes; since 1976, the federal government's accounting period, or fiscal year,
runs from October 1 to September 30 of
the following year.

Students protest raising the legal drinking age to 21. If states did not pass such a law, federal highway funds could be cut.

affected by the loss of federal aid; yet the Reagan administration resisted the idea that the federal government should try to equalize any wealth differences across the states.

In the face of mounting criticism, the Reagan administration modified its proposals somewhat. The most important new provisions were that the federal government would retain the food stamp program and that local governments would be guaranteed the same share of state aid they formerly received from federal payments.

By 1984, the specific provisions of Reagan's plan quietly disappeared from the legislative agenda. Opposition from governors, Republican and Democratic, coupled with the fears of legislators that their own states would suffer unduly from the new arrangements, made the program politically weak. The administration then dropped the proposals from its list of policy priorities.

The Fiscal Side of Federalism

▽

Today, the national government collects over 60 percent of all tax dollars. As part of our system of cooperative federalism, the national government gives back to the states (and local governments) a significant amount—almost $95 billion dollars in fiscal year 1985, although this amount represents a decline over earlier years. (The first decline in three decades occurred in fiscal year 1981–82.) There are basically three separate methods by which the national government returns nationally collected tax dollars to state and local governments: categorical grants-in-aid, block grants, and general grants-in-aid (general revenue sharing).

Categorical Grants-in-Aid

The modern concept of a federal government grant-in-aid was derived from a 1902 law providing that revenues from the sale of public lands were to be shared with certain states and territories for irrigation and land reclamation. Not until the administration of Franklin Roosevelt did restrictions and regulations accompany the **categorical grants.** These involved the establishment of agricultural extension programs, highway construction, vocational education, and maternal and child health. During Roosevelt's first two terms in office, categorical grants-in-aid increased from $200 million annually to $3 billion.

The number and scope of the categorical grants expanded further as part of the Great Society programs of President Lyndon Johnson. Grants now became available in the fields of education, pollution control, conservation, recreation, and highway construction and maintenance. By 1984, more than $80 billion a year was channeled to the states by these grants. For some of the categorical grant programs, the state and local governments must put up a share of the money, usually called **matching funds.** For other types of programs, the funds are awarded according to a formula that takes into account the relative wealth of the state, a process known as **equalization.**

Although all state and local officials, as well as their congressional representatives, enjoy taking credit for the results of projects paid for by categorical grants, many would prefer to get the money with fewer restrictions. Local officials argue that wage rates determined in Washington are not appropriate to their locality or that the materials specified as suitable for a highway project in the South are not the best ones for roads in the North. It can also be argued that these specifications are necessary to achieve a national goal or to raise local standards and practices to a uniform level. In general, categorical grants have remained under fairly tight control by Congress. In a move to bypass the states, Congress established the **project grant** approach, which allows state and local agencies to apply directly for assistance to local offices that administer the federal funds. This way the funds can be directly placed where—in the eyes of Congress—they are most needed.

Categorical Grants

Federal grants-in-aid to states or local governments which are for very specific programs or projects.

Matching Funds

For many categorical grant programs, the state must "match" the federal funds. Some programs only require the state to raise 10% of the funds, whereas others approach an even share.

Equalization

A method for adjusting the amount of money that a state must put up to receive federal funds that takes into account the wealth of the state or its ability to tax its citizens.

Project Grant

An assistance grant that can be applied for directly by state and local agencies; established under a national program grant. Project grants allow Congress (and the administration) to bypass state governments and thereby to place the money directly where it is supposedly the most needed.

Block Grants

Although not originating with him, **block grants** were an important part of President Reagan's new federalism, which he outlined in his first State of the Union message in 1982. Introduced in 1966, these programs transfer funds to state and local governments in broadly defined areas such as health and criminal justice. Reagan supported block grants as an alternative to general grants-in-aid, partly because it is politically easier to reduce block grants than it is to reduce categorical grants-in-aid. A categorical grant-in-aid affects one particular group. That group is often willing to spend considerable effort and resources to prevent a budget cut affecting its funds. A block grant, however, affects many specific programs in some general area. It is therefore politically more difficult to muster the necessary opposition to prevent a budget cut for a block grant.

The Reagan administration's philosophy on block grants was well summarized by Reagan's assistant for intergovernmental affairs, Richard S. Williamson:

Block Grants

Federal programs that provide funding to the state and local governments for general functional areas such as criminal justice or mental health programs.

> Just as we believe economic decisions should be made in the freedom of an unburdened economic marketplace, so too should political and governmental decisions be made in the free and open political process. There will be winners and losers. But at least decisions can be made at a local level where decision-makers can be held accountable for their actions. None of us in this administration has any misconception that block grants are a magic panacea. But we are convinced that they will help make government work again. The pressing needs of individuals and institutions in this nation will continue to be met.

Are There Nine Nations in North America?*

We are used to thinking of American politics in terms of a standard division of the country into regions of Northeast, South, Midwest, East, and so on or some variation of these, like Sunbelt and Snowbelt. Joel Garreau presents another way of thinking about the regional basis of political differences, however, in which he divides North America, including Canada and Mexico, as well as the United States, into nine regions (see map):

1. The Foundry—the declining industrial area of the Northeast
2. Dixie—the traditional Southeast
3. Ecotopia—the northern Pacific Rim area with its new high-tech industries
4. MexAmerica—the far southwestern United States, plus Mexico
5. New England—the poorest of the regions economically but the most steeped in the traditions of civilization
6. Quebec—the culturally distinctive Francophone nation of North America

*Joel Garreau, *The Nine Nations of North America* (New York: Avon, 1981.)

7. The Islands—southern Florida and the islands of the Caribbean, distinguished by leisure-time industries and drug-related crime
8. The Empty Quarter—encompasses most of the reserve mineral wealth of the continent, mainly in northwestern Canada
9. The Breadbasket—the predominantly agricultural food-producing region in the Midwest and north into Canada

Garreau's typology is challenging to the imagination because it cuts across national, state, and traditional regional lines to emphasize similarities in culture, economics, and politics that are otherwise missed or not explained as neatly. As with most other attempts to assess the regional basis of federalism in the United States, Garreau emphasizes the conflicts over national policy decisions that are at the heart of his particular regional divisions. By calling his regions "nations," he focuses on the political dimensions of these conflicts and the extent to which the nine regions act almost as though they were sovereign countries only loosely affiliated on the continent.

The only real losers from block grants will be the bureaucratic middlemen—the grantsmen—who siphon off funds from those greatest in need.[15]

Opponents of the block grant approach to federalism argue that overall federal aid is reduced as a consequence, that state and local officials are not as capable of administering the programs as are federal officials, and that state and local officials do not have sufficient information about, or interest in, the people who are supposed to benefit from the programs. In addition, critics say, a block grant approach to federalism contributes to increasing inequality among the states and is potentially harmful to the poor, because state legislatures are less likely to spend funds on social welfare programs than is the national government.

President Reagan apparently was not too worried about the continuing inequality among the states in terms of government expenditures per capita. He gradually formulated a concept of **"shifting" federalism** in which he proposed to turn many of the grants over to the states on a continuing basis.

"Shifting" Federalism
President Reagan's concept of turning over federal grants to the states.

General Grants-in-Aid, or Revenue Sharing

In an effort to move away from national government involvement with categorical grants, the Nixon administration in 1972 asked Congress to remit to the states and

[15]Richard S. Williamson, "Block Grants—A Federalist Tool," *State Government* 54, no. 4, pp. 114–117.

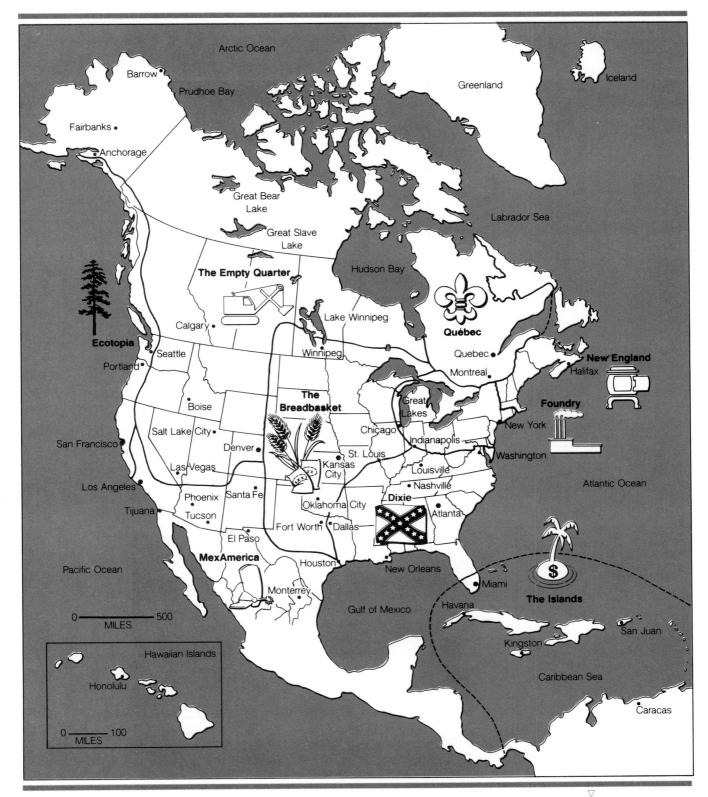

Arctic Ocean

Barrow •
Prudhoe Bay •

Greenland

Iceland

Fairbanks •

Anchorage •

Great Bear
Lake

Labrador Sea

The Empty Quarter

Great Slave
Lake

Hudson Bay

Calgary •

Lake Winnipeg

Québec

Ecotopia

Winnipeg

Quebec •

New England

Seattle •

Montreal •

Halifax •

Portland •

**The
Breadbasket**

Great
Lakes

Boise •

Chicago •

Foundry

Salt Lake City •

New York •

San Francisco •

Denver •

St. Louis •

Indianapolis •

Washington

Las Vegas •

Kansas
City

Louisville •

Los Angeles •

Phoenix •

Santa Fe •

Nashville •

Atlantic Ocean

Tijuana •

Tucson •

Oklahoma City •

Dixie

Atlanta •

El Paso •

Fort Worth • Dallas

MexAmerica

Houston •

New Orleans •

Pacific Ocean

Monterrey •

Miami •

Havana

The Islands

Gulf of Mexico

0 — 500
MILES

San Juan

Kingston •

Hawaiian Islands

Caribbean Sea

Honolulu •

Caracas •

0 — 100
MILES

local governments a certain percentage of tax income each year, on a more or less automatic basis, with few strings attached. Congress complied. One-third of the funds went to the states and two-thirds were sent directly to local governments. It is clear that the major impetus behind revenue sharing was President Nixon's desire to reduce the role of the national government while increasing that of the state and local governments. Figure 3–5 shows general revenue sharing in relation to other kinds of aid to states and to local governments from 1973 through 1987. One reason for the decline of revenue sharing relative to other types of assistance was the exclusion of state governments from the program in 1980. Although some argue that revenue-sharing funds are wasted on less important problems, many mayors and county officials see the funds as a way to pay for needed facilities and to reduce the local tax burden. The budget crisis confronting the federal government in the mid-1980s led Congress to abolish revenue sharing to local governments at the end of 1986.

Federalism Versus Regionalism:
The Shift of Power from the Snowbelt to the Sunbelt

▽

Figure 3–6 shows what happened to the United States population in the thirty-year period from 1950 to 1980. The Snowbelt states of the North increased 33.5 percent in population overall, whereas the Sunbelt states of the South and West increased 81.2 percent. This shifting population has meant an increasing amount of national government benefits obtained by the citizens of the Sunbelt states relative to those of the Snowbelt states. This has intensified regional conflict as the Snowbelt

Figure 3–5

▽

General Revenue Sharing in Relation to Other Kinds of Aid to States, 1972– 1987 (in millions)

General revenue sharing reached its peak in 1980 and has fallen since then. Block, broad-based, and categorical grants have been on the rise, however.

SOURCE: U.S. Office of Management and Budgets, Special Analysis, *Budget for Fiscal Year 1987.*

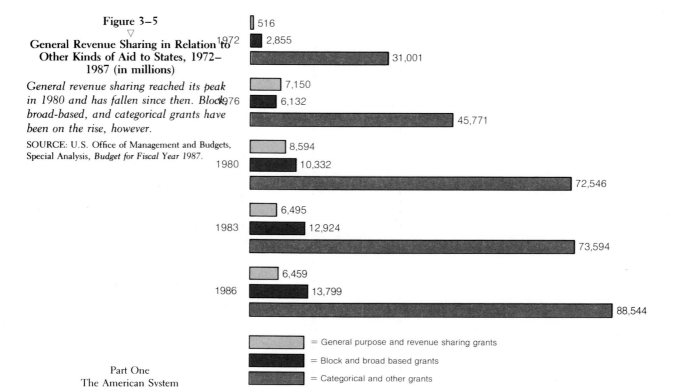

1972

516
2,855
31,001

1976

7,150
6,132
45,771

1980

8,594
10,332
72,546

1983

6,495
12,924
73,594

1986

6,459
13,799
88,544

= General purpose and revenue sharing grants

= Block and broad based grants

= Categorical and other grants

states have attempted to counter the changing power structure across the states. In part, this is a problem in horizontal federalism.

In the 1980s, shifting population has combined with a reduction of the role of the federal government in domestic social programs to make regionalism a more significant force in national politics. We can expect to see increasing battles over how national government funds are to be allocated regionally. The 1982 reapportionment of the House of Representatives decreased the representation of the Snowbelt states by seventeen seats, which were given to the Sunbelt states. This will undoubtedly intensify the Snowbelt coalition's efforts to obtain more funds, but its success is problematic because the South and the West now have a congressional majority for the first time.

Regionalism has been powered to a great extent by the reduction in inflation-adjusted federal aid to state and local governments, but another cause can be found in the rise of regional organizations. As early as 1976, the Democratic governors of seven northeastern states formed a Coalition of Northeast Governors to present a united front in Congress on specific economic issues, whereas bipartisan Northeast-Midwest Congressional Coalitions organized in both the House and the Senate. In reaction, Sunbelt representatives formed a Sunbelt Council in June 1981. Other Sunbelt caucuses on Capitol Hill include the Senate Western Coalition, which

Figure 3–6

▽

The Population Shift from the Snowbelt to the Sunbelt States, 1950–1980

From 1950 to 1980, the total U.S. population increased almost 50 percent. Some states experienced a much greater increase and others experienced a much smaller increase. On average, those states defined as the Snowbelt increased only 33 percent and those designated Sunbelt increased more than 80 percent.

SOURCE: *Information Please Almanac, 1982.*

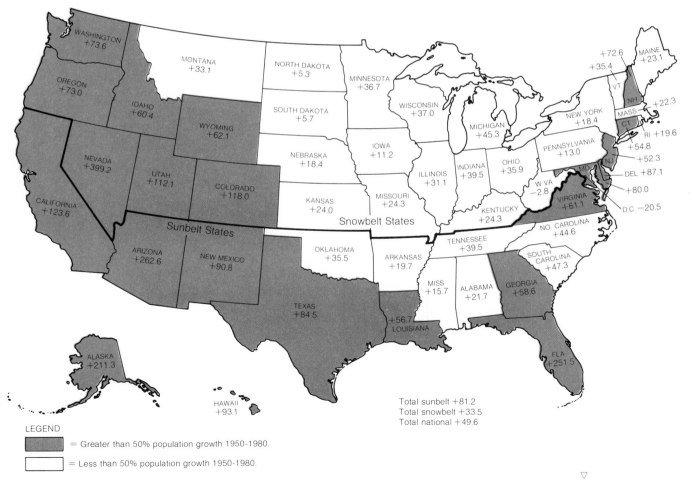

LEGEND

■ = Greater than 50% population growth 1950-1980.

□ = Less than 50% population growth 1950-1980.

Street repair in a snowbelt city.

focuses on land-use problems, energy, and water resources, and a Gulf Coast Working Group concerned about military facilities and immigration reform. A related development is the establishment of the Southern Governors' Association's office in Washington, D.C., paralleling the move of the northeastern governors.

Other forces tending to regionalize American politics include stronger and more coordinated state governments, greater grass-roots local activism on national issues, emphasis on the fundamentally local issue of education, a self-help philosophy by the state and local governments in the face of uncertain economic stimuli from Washington, and profound economic changes such as the industrial decline of the Great Lakes states and the growing diversity of southern economies. In the mid-1970s, these trends combined to spark the Snowbelt-Sunbelt clash as the northern states tried to arrest what they saw as a disproportionate flow of federal funds into the Sunbelt and the flow of jobs to the South and West.

Recent political efforts by Snowbelt states may be showing results. Studies suggest that federal dollars are being distributed more evenly among the states—not withstanding the fact that Uncle Sam continues to spend more money in the South and West relative to the taxes those states pay and sends less money back to the Northeast and Midwest than those states contribute to the federal treasury. Changes in the relative federal expenditure levels between the Snowbelt and the Sunbelt can be traced predominantly to redistribution of defense spending; military contracts more often go to companies based in southern states.[16] Snowbelt forces have also been generally successful in channeling federal emergency aid to help people in colder climates who must pay for more winter heating, but the fact that the Sunbelt is energy rich and the Snowbelt is energy dependent guarantees that federal government assistance in this area will remain a point of continued controversy along regional lines.[17]

[16]Joel Havemann and Rochelle L. Stanfield, " 'Neutral' Federal Policies Are Reducing Frostbelt-Sunbelt Spending Imbalances," *National Journal*, February 7, 1981, pp. 233–236.

[17]Richard Corrigan and Rochelle L. Stanfield, "Rising Energy Prices—What's Good for Some States is Bad for Others," *National Journal*, March 22, 1980, pp. 468–474.

The debate surrounding federalism—how power should be distributed among the local, state, and federal governments—is an old one. The argument comes up frequently, partly because the imagery on both sides is so compelling. Advocates of decentralization, a shift of power from federal to state or local governments, argue that we must recognize the right of states to design their own destiny and master their own fate. Concentrated power may be dangerous and offer little protection for individual rights in a highly diversified United States. Local and state governments have a better idea of how to cope with unique local problems than does a single remote bureaucracy. The right to govern lies with the people of the state.

Advocates of centralization pose an equally convincing argument. They see such a shift in power as undermining the national purpose, common interests, and responsibilities that bind us together in pursuit of national goals. It is, they state, a callous attempt to balance the budget on the backs of the poor, the handicapped, and the dependent, since state and local governments have demonstrated neither the resources nor the inclination to fund social service agencies. The national government has the responsibility to see that law and justice are distributed equally among its citizens, regardless of which section of the country in which they are born. The United States is an association of people under one constitution, united in power and resources.

A colorful revival of this controversy is the so-called Sagebrush Revolution, which has swept the western states. It began when the Nevada legislature passed a law declaring that forty-nine million acres of federal land properly belonged to the state. This idea struck a responsive chord in other western states since the federal government owns most of Alaska and Nevada, the bulk of Utah, Idaho, and Oregon, and nearly half of Wyoming and California. The movement united an otherwise maverick group of states and rugged individualists with a sense of common cause.

Certain groups in the western states claim that a powerful and absentee landlord, the federal government, is regulating them to death. They see Washington as Big Brother and the East as unsympathetic to their region's unique vital concerns. As Nevada Attorney General Rich Bryan asserted, "We're tired of being pistol-whipped by the bureaucrats and dry-gulched by federal regulations."* Said Nevada Senator Norm Glaser: "We're not just a bunch of wild-eyed cowboys out to lynch some federal officials. We're serious people asking for a serious look at the unfair treatment the West is receiving."**

The other side claims that despite their complaints, westerners often come out quite well under Big Government on issues such as meat import quotas and vital water reclamation projects. They argue that the West is living in a fantasy if they think they can survive without the federal government. "If you pulled the Federal presence out of Colorado, the state would collapse," says Senator Gary Hart.*** Eastern and Western environmentalists argue that if the federal government doesn't step in, the West will sell out and exploit its rare environment. The Idaho Environmental Council said that federal management for the most part "has been far superior to that of the various land boards of the western states managing state-owned public lands."†

Information about the general scope of this debate is available through the western regional office of the Bureau of Land Management and the Forest Service. The bureau has substantial materials available, and the Freedom of Information Act permits access to most of them.

If you are sympathetic to the priorities of environmentalists and conservation, you can get directly involved with one of the following organizations, either through the national office or in local chapters:

The Sierra Club
330 Pennsylvania Avenue, S.E.
Washington, D.C. 20003

Friends of the Earth
530 7th Street, S.E.
Washington, D.C. 20003

Time Magazine, September 17, 1979, p. 10.
**Ibid.*, p. 38.
***Ibid.*, p. 17.
†*New York Times*, September 2, 1979, p. E5.

▽

National Public Lands Taskforce
P.O. Box 1245
Carson City, Nevada 89701

Public Lands Institute
1740 High Street
Denver, Colorado 80218

The Wilderness Society
1901 Pennsylvania Avenue, N.W.
Washington, D.C. 20006

Working for the expansion of state control over these lands and less federal management are a number of organizations.

You can contact the following:

National Cattleman's Association
425 13th Street, N.W., Suite 1020
Washington, D.C. 20004

Sagebrush Rebellion, Inc.
P.O. Box 545
Boise, Idaho 83701

Western Coalition for Public Lands Clearinghouse
Legislative Council Bureau
Legislative Building, Room 215
Carson City, Nevada 89710

Chapter Summary

▽

1. There are three basic models of ordering relations between central governments and local units: (a) a unitary system, (b) a confederal system, and (c) a federal system.

2. A unitary system, such as France has, is one in which the national government has ultimate authority. This system is most common.

3. A confederal system is a league of independent states, each having essentially sovereign powers. The central government handles only matters of common concern that have been expressly delegated to it by member states.

4. Somewhere between the unitary and the confederal forms of government lies the federal system. Here authority is divided between the central government and the regional, or subdivisional, governments.

5. The American federal system resulted from a compromise between the strong national government advocates and the strong states' rights advocates.

6. Federalism is probably the best arrangement in large countries because of their size and consequent regional isolation and political subcultures. Division of power between local and national governments brings government closer to the people and allows government to meet the local needs of its citizens. State governments in the United States have also served as testing grounds for future national leaders and bold new initiatives.

7. The Constitution expressly delegated certain powers to the national government in Article I, Section 8.

8. The framers of the Constitution knew these powers would not be sufficient so they included the "elastic clause," giving Congress the right to pass laws "necessary and proper" to carrying out its enumerated powers.

9. Resulting powers are those held by the national government when several expressed powers are added together. Inherent powers are those held by the national government by virtue of its being a sovereign state with the right to preserve itself.

10. The Tenth Amendment to the Constitution states that powers that are not delegated to the United States by the Constitution, nor prohibited by it to the states, are reserved to the states respectively, or to the people.

11. In certain areas, the Constitution provides for concurrent powers, held by both national and state governments. The classic example of a concurrent power is the power to tax.

12. The supremacy clause of the Constitution states that the Constitution, congressional laws, and national treaties are the supreme law of the land. States cannot use their reserved or concurrent powers to override national policies.

13. The three most important clauses in the Constitution relating to horizontal federalism require that (a) each state give full faith and credit to every other state's public acts, records, and judicial proceedings; (b) each state extend to every other state's citizens the privileges and immunities of its own citizens; and (c) each state agree to render persons who are fleeing from justice to another state back to their home state when requested to do so.

14. *McCulloch v. Maryland* (1819) enhanced the implied

power of the federal government through Chief Justice John Marshall's broad interpretation of the "necessary and proper" clause of Article I of the Constitution. The effects of the decision are part of a continuing debate about the boundaries between federal and state authority.

15. *Gibbons v. Ogden* (1824) enhanced and consolidated national power over commerce. Chief Justice Marshall interpreted the commerce clause of the Constitution broadly and held that commerce power was complete in itself, with no limitations other than those found specifically in the Constitution. The regulation of commerce became one of the major issues in federal-state relations.

16. At the heart of the controversy that led to the Civil War was the issue of national government supremacy versus the right of the separate states. The notion of nullification eventually led to the secession of the Confederate states from the Union. The South's desire for increased states' rights led rather to an increase in the political power of the national government.

17. In dual federalism, each of the states and the federal government remain supreme within its own sphere.

18. The era since the Depression has sometimes been labeled as one of cooperative federalism, in which states and the national government cooperate in solving complex common problems. Others view it as the beginning of an era of national supremacy.

19. Because of the growth in population and industrialization and its status as a world power, the United States has witnessed a growth in national powers.

20. The third phase of federalism was labeled a new federalism by President Nixon and has been revived by President Reagan. The goal of the new federalism is to decentralize federal programs, giving more responsibility to the states.

21. There are basically three separate methods by which the national government returns nationally collected tax dollars to state and local governments: (a) categorical grants-in-aid, (b) block grants, and (c) general grants-in-aid (revenue sharing). The grants differ in the restrictions and regulations attached to them by the federal government.

22. Population shifts in the United States have created a change in the amount of benefits obtained by the citizens of the Sunbelt states relative to those of the Snowbelt states in the form of national revenues and programs. We can expect to see increasing battles over how national government funds are to be allocated regionally.

Questions for Review and Discussion
▽

1. The Constitution and federal law are supreme over state and local legislation. Can you think of several areas of law where local governments should have complete authority? Should the national government take full responsibility for protecting the environment?

2. Are the states unlikely to fund social welfare programs on their own if the federal government no longer sends grants for them? Why does the Congress prefer to keep control of such programs at the national level?

3. Should the federal government be responsible for distributing benefits and federal contracts equally among all of the states? If population and industries shift from one region of the nation to another—i.e., from the Snowbelt to the Sunbelt—is the federal government obligated to provide assistance for the states whose economies suffer?

4. By choosing a federal form for our government, the Founding Fathers assured the continued existence of regional differences. Choose four states from different sections of the country and list the ways in which their political interests differ from each other. On what kinds of national legislation will these differences surface? How do these differences affect the outcome of presidential elections?

Selected References
▽

Daniel J. Elazar, *American Federalism: A View from the States*, 3rd ed. (New York: Harper and Row, 1985). This is a classic book on the subject, with a focus on the politics of federalism—bargaining, negotiation, and cooperation. It also emphasizes the political subcultures of America and their impact on the states.

Marilyn Gittel, ed., *State Politics and the New Federalism* (White Plains, N.Y.: Longman, 1986). This book brings together readings and analysis that help shed light on the impact of the Reagan administration on state government and contemporary federalism.

Morton Grodzins, *The American System* (Chicago: Rand, McNally, 1974). A classic understanding of the modern federal system.

Robert B. Hawkins, Jr., ed., *American Federalism: A New Partnership for the Republic* (San Francisco, CA: Institute for Contemporary Studies, 1982). Scholars and policymakers analyze the implications of the 'new federalism.' The book treats the problem of returning power and responsibility to the states and the difficulty of generating revenues for local services.

Kirkpatrick Sale, *Power Shift: The Rise of the Southern Rim and Its Challenge to the Eastern Establishment* (New York: Vintage Books, 1975). The Sunbelt-Frostbelt conflict in terms of Cowboys and Yankees.

James C. Smith, *Emerging Conflicts in the Doctrine of Federalism: The Intergovernmental Predicament* (Lanham, Md.: University Press of America, 1984). Intergovernmental problems that interfere with the smooth operation and performance of government institutions, in particular the role of different levels and jurisdictions, are concisely explored in this study.

Deil S. Wright, *Understanding Intergovernmental Relations*, 2nd edition (Monterey, CA: Brooks/Cole Publishing Co., 1982). National political authorities' relations with state and local officials, emphasizing the practice and problems of federalism.

2
CIVIL RIGHTS AND LIBERTIES

Chapter 4

Civil Liberties

Contents
Civil Rights and the Fear of Government

The Bill of Rights

Freedom of Religion

Freedom of Expression

Freedom of the Press

The Right to Assemble and to Petition the Government

More Liberties Under Scrutiny

The Great Balancing Act: The Rights of the Accused Versus
the Rights of Society

What If . . .
There Were No Habeas Corpus?

Article 1, Section 9, of the Constitution allows for the suspension of the privilege of the **writ of habeas corpus** in cases of rebellion or invasion when public safety may require it. Suppose that just such a situation occurred and that Congress suspended the habeas corpus guarantee.

An unmarked car with three men pulls up at the curb. It is three o'clock in the morning. They knock on the door. You awaken confused at the unexpected interruption and open the door. The men inform you that you are under arrest, tell you to dress, and minutes later whisk you away to a detention center. Here, together with other detainees, you are held for weeks. Your relatives don't know what has happened to you. You are not informed about the charges against you. There is no way of communicating with the outside world. You have not been

allowed to make any telephone calls. You do not have access to legal counsel, and the authorities are not required to justify your detention.

Your family and friends search for you and hear that many people are being held at the prison where you have been languishing. They hire an attorney who makes inquiries and is told that you are being held for "acts against the state." The lawyer contacts one of the courts and requests a hearing. The judge agrees, and several days later your family and the attorney ask the judge to intervene on your behalf. In particular, the lawyer requests that the judge issue a writ of habeas corpus to the authorities holding you. This court order would require the au-

thorities to justify your detention to the court.

When you finally get an attorney who goes in front of a judge, all the judge would have to do is cite the public law just passed by Congress that suspended your ability to have your detention justified. In many countries in the world today, habeas corpus does not exist. But in only two cases in the U.S. has such a cherished civil liberty been suspended—President Lincoln suspended the writ in 1863 and President Roosevelt suspended it in Hawaii following the bombing of Pearl Harbor in 1941. Judging by what has happened in other countries, without the provision of habeas corpus writs as part of our system of protecting individual rights, the use of coercion and intimidation could greatly increase.

▽

The writ of habeas corpus is just one of the Constitutional guarantees that protect all individuals in the United States.

Most Americans believe they have more individual freedom than virtually any other people on earth. For the most part, this opinion is accurate. The freedoms that we take for granted—religion, speech, press, and assembly—are relatively unknown in many parts of the world. In many nations today, citizens have little chance of living without government harassment if they choose to criticize openly, through speech or print, the government or its actions. Indeed, if the United States suddenly had the same rules, laws, and procedures about verbal and printed expression that exist in many other countries, our jails would be filled overnight with transgressors.

Civil Rights and the Fear of Government
▽

Without government, people live in a state of anarchy. With unbridled government, men and women may end up living in a state of tyranny. The Founding Fathers wanted neither extreme. As we pointed out in Chapter 2, the Declaration of Independence was based on the idea of natural rights. These are rights discoverable in nature and history, according to such philosophers as John Locke and John Dickinson, who wrote that natural rights "are born with us; exist with us; and cannot be taken away from us by any human power."[1] Linked directly to the strong prerevolutionary sentiment for natural rights was the notion that a right was first and foremost a *limitation* on any government's ruling power. To obtain ratification of the Constitution by the necessary nine states, the Federalists had to deal with the colonists' fears of a too-powerful national government. The Bill of Rights was the result. When we speak of civil liberties in the United States, we are mostly referring to the specific limitations on government outlined in the first ten amendments to the U.S. Constitution, which were passed by Congress on September 25, 1789, and ratified by three-fourths of the states by December 15, 1791.

Writ of Habeas Corpus
Literally, "you should have the body." An order to bring a party before a court or judge.

The Bill of Rights
▽

The First Amendment to the Constitution is for many the most significant part of the **Bill of Rights,** as well as the mainstay of the Declaration of Independence statement that all people should be able to enjoy life, liberty, and the pursuit of happiness. For it is in this First Amendment that our basic freedoms of religion, speech, the press, assembly, and the right of petition are set forth. The first part of this chapter examines each of these freedoms in detail.

The second part of the chapter looks at our criminal justice system and at the rights of the accused. The basis for the rights of the accused and the limits on governmental search and seizure are outlined in Amendments IV, V, VI, VII, and VIII. These amendments express the concern of the framers of the Constitution about an overzealous police state.

Bill of Rights
The first ten amendments to the United States Constitution. They contain a listing of the rights a person enjoys and which cannot be infringed upon by the government, such as the freedoms of speech, press, and religion.

The Nationalization of the Bill of Rights

Most citizens do not realize that, as originally presented, the Bill of Rights limited only the power of the national government, not that of the states. In other words, a citizen in the State of Virginia in 1795 could not successfully sue in federal court

[1]Quoted in Bernard Bailyn, *The Ideological Origins of the American Revolution* (Cambridge, Mass.: Harvard University Press, 1967), p. 77.

against a law passed in Virginia that violated one of the amendments in the Bill of Rights. Each state had (and still has) its own constitution with its own Bill of Rights. Whereas the states' bills of rights were similar to the national one, there were some differences, and, perhaps more importantly, each state's judicial system interpreted the rights differently. A citizen in one state effectively had a different set of civil liberties than a citizen in another state. It was not until the Fourteenth Amendment was ratified in 1868 that our Constitution explicitly guaranteed to everyone due process of the law. Section 1 of that amendment provides that

> no state shall make or enforce any law which shall abridge the privileges or immunities of citizens of the United States; nor shall any State deprive any person of life, liberty, or property, without due process of law; nor deny to any person within its jurisdiction the equal protection of the laws.

Section 5 of the amendment explicitly gives Congress the power to enforce by appropriate legislation the provisions of the amendment. Note the use of the terms *citizens* and *person*. *Citizens* have political rights, such as voting and running for office, but no *person*, citizen or alien, can be denied civil rights (speech, press, and religion) nor have his or her property taken without equal recourse to the legal system.[2]

Positive Law

Laws made in and by legislatures to fit a particular circumstance.

The Fourteenth Amendment itself was, as Kenneth Karst wrote, an act of "**positive law**,"[3] that is, a law made to fit a particular circumstance. At the time of its passage, the sponsors of the Fourteenth Amendment had wished to extend to the South "a system of liberties and equality under the law that already existed elsewhere in the nation."[4]

The Incorporation Issue

The Fourteenth Amendment was passed as a standard that would guarantee both due process and equal protection under the laws for all persons. The courts did not agree. Many jurists still believed, as John Marshall did, that the states were "distinct governments framed by different persons and for different purposes."[5] Marshall's statement in the *Barron* decision was plain: The Bill of Rights limits only the national government and not the state governments. The *Barron* decision is still the general rule of law. We shall see, though, that it has been greatly modified in practice through interpretations of the Fourteenth Amendment.

Dual Citizenship

The condition of being a citizen of two sovereign political units; being a citizen of both a state and the nation.

In 1873 in the Slaughterhouse Cases,[6] the U.S. Supreme Court upheld the principle of **dual citizenship,** arguing that to deprive states of their authority and their identity would "fetter and degrade state governments."

Incorporation Theory

The view that the protections of the Bill of Rights are incorporated into the Fourteenth Amendment's protection against state governments.

Only gradually, and never completely, did the Supreme Court accept the **incorporation theory**—that no state could act in violation of the U.S. Bill of Rights. The practical implementation of the Fourteenth Amendment has taken place relatively slowly.

---

[2]Note also that there is a distinction between the technical definitions of a civil *right* and a civil *liberty:* The former is government granted, the latter is inherent.

[3]Kenneth L. Karst, "Not One Law at Rome and Another at Athens: The Fourteenth Amendment in Nationwide Application," *Washington University Law Quarterly,* no. 3 (Summer 1972), p. 383.

[4]Ibid.

[5]*Barron v. Baltimore,* 7 Peters 243 (1833).

[6]16 Wall. 36 (1873).

The last hundred years of Supreme Court decisions have bound the fifty states to accept most of the guarantees for their respective citizens that are contained in the U.S. Bill of Rights. The exceptions have usually involved the right to bear arms and to refuse to quarter soldiers and the right to a grand jury hearing. Thus, for all intents and purposes, the Bill of Rights provisions of the national Constitution must be uniformly applied by individual state governments to their laws and practices.

Just as judicial interpretation of the Fourteenth Amendment required more than a hundred years to "nationalize" the Bill of Rights, judicial interpretation has shaped the true nature of those rights as they apply to individuals in the United States. As we shall see in the following pages, there have been numerous conflicts over the meaning of such simple phrases as freedom of press and freedom of religion. To understand what freedoms we actually have, we have to examine some of those conflicts.

Freedom of Religion
▽

In the United States freedom of religion consists of two principal precepts as they are presented in the First Amendment. The first has to do with separation of church and state and the second guarantees free exercise of religion.

The Separation of Church and State

Congress shall make no law respecting an establishment of religion . . . .

In the words of President Jefferson, the establishment clause was designed to create a "wall of separation of Church and State."[7] Perhaps Jefferson was thinking about the religious intolerance that characterized the first colonies. Although many of the American colonies were founded by groups in pursuit of religious freedom,

[7]See Frank J. Sorauf, *Wall of Separation* (Princeton, N.J.: Princeton University Press, 1976).

Fundamentalists Vicki Frost and her husband who challenged textbooks as being too secular and violating their freedom of religion.

Establishment Clause

The part of the First Amendment prohibiting the establishment of a church officially supported by the national government. It is applied to questions of state and local government aid to religious organizations and schools, of the legality of allowing or requiring school prayers, and of the teaching of evolution versus fundamentalist theories of creation.

Children praying in school.

they were nonetheless quite intolerant of religious dissent within their communities. He undoubtedly was also aware that state religions were the rule; among the original thirteen American colonies, nine of them had official religions.

The **establishment clause** in the First Amendment means at least the following:

> Neither a state nor the federal government can set up a church. Neither can pass laws which aid one religion, aid all religions, or prefer one religion over another. Neither can force nor influence a person to go to or to remain away from church against his will or force him to profess a belief or disbelief in any religion. No person can be punished for entertaining or professing religious beliefs or disbeliefs, for church attendance or non-attendance. No tax in any amount, large or small, can be levied to support any religious activities or institutions, whatever they may be called, or whatever form they may adopt to teach or practice religion. Neither a state nor the federal government can, openly or secretly, participate in the affairs of any religious organizations or groups and vice versa.[8]

The establishment clause covers all conflicts about such matters as state and local government aid to religious organizations and schools, the legality of allowing or requiring school prayers, and the teaching of evolution versus fundamentalist theories of creation.

The Issue of School Prayer

Do the states have the right to promote religion in general, without making any attempt to establish a particular religion? That is the main question in the issue of school prayer and was the precise question presented in 1962 in *Engel v. Vitale*,[9] the so-called Regents' Prayer Case in New York. The State Board of Regents of New York had suggested that a prayer be spoken aloud in the public schools at the beginning of each day. The recommended prayer was:

> Almighty God, we acknowledge our dependence upon Thee,
> And we beg Thy blessings upon us, our parents, our teachers, and our Country.

Such a prayer was implemented in many New York public schools.

A number of students' parents challenged the action of the regents, maintaining that it violated the establishment clause of the First Amendment. At trial the parents lost. The court said that the state action did not constitute the "establishment of religion." When the case finally reached the U.S. Supreme Court, however, a different interpretation was made. The Supreme Court ruled that the regents' action was unconstitutional because "the constitutional prohibition against laws respecting an establishment of a religion must at least mean that in this country it is no part of the business of government to compose official prayers for any group of the American people to recite as part of a religious program carried on by any government."[10] The Court's conclusion was based to a great extent upon the "historical fact that governmentally established religions and religious persecutions go hand in hand."[11] Finally, the Court inferred that if the regents' actions were sanctioned, it might be the "foot in the door" that could lead to a broader state intervention in the future.

---

[8]*Everson v. Board of Education of Ewing Township*, 330 U.S. 1 (1947).
[9]370 U.S. 421 (1962).
[10]Ibid.
[11]Ibid.

In 1963 in two related decisions the Supreme Court outlawed daily readings of the Bible and recitation of the Lord's Prayer in public schools.[12]

Although the Supreme Court has over and over again ruled against officially sponsored prayer and Bible-reading sessions in public schools, other means for bringing some form of religious expression into public education have been attempted. In 1983, the Tennessee legislature passed a bill requiring public school classes to begin each day with a minute of silence. This followed several years of efforts by the Tennessee legislature to bring "meditation, prayer, or silent reflection into school." Alabama also had a similar law. In 1985, the Supreme Court struck down as unconstitutional the Alabama law authorizing one minute of silence in all public schools for prayer or meditation. The majority of the court indicated that since the law specifically endorsed prayer, it appeared to support religion.[13]

Many school districts, particularly in the South, continue to operate in violation of the Court's prayer ban. A coalition of conservatives and southerners has proposed a constitutional amendment that would overturn the 1963 rulings. President Reagan gave them moral support in a speech he made on March 8, 1983, to a convention of Protestant evangelicals in Orlando, Florida, when he said, "Let our children pray." He has indicated that he considers it "nonsense" that "we are told our children have no right to pray in school. . . . Sometimes I can't help but feel the First Amendment is being turned on its head."[14] But on March 20, 1984, the Senate rejected the proposed constitutional amendment to permit organized, recited prayers in the nation's public schools. In a 56–44 vote, the measure fell eleven votes short of the two-thirds majority needed to pass it.

Forbidding the Teaching of Evolution

A rather short-lived effort by certain religious groups took place to forbid the teaching of evolution in public schools. One such law was passed in Arkansas only to be

[12]*Abington School District v. Schempp*, 374 U.S. 203 (1963); *Murray v. Curlett*, 374 U.S. 203 (1963).

[13]*Wallace v. Jafree*, 105 S.Ct. 2479 (1985).

[14]Quoted in Steven Wermiel, "Church and State: High Court's Ruling Against School Is Often Violated," *Wall Street Journal*, March 5, 1984, p. 1.

struck down by the Supreme Court in the 1968 *Epperson v. Arkansas* case.[15] The Court held that the Alabama legislation violated the separation of church and state, for it imposed religious beliefs on students. The Arkansas legislature then passed a law requiring the teaching of the biblical story of creation alongside with evolution. In the 1982 Supreme Court case *McLean v. Arkansas*, this law was declared unconstitutional.

Aid to Church-Related Schools

Throughout the United States, all property owners except religious, educational, fraternal, literary, scientific, and similar nonprofit institutions must pay property taxes. A large part of the proceeds of such taxes go to support public schools. But not all school-age children attend public schools. Fully 12 percent attend private schools, of which 85 percent have religious affiliations. Numerous cases have reached the Supreme Court in which that Court has tried to draw a fine line between permissible public aid to students in church-related schools and impermissible public aid to religion.

It is at the elementary and secondary level where these issues have arisen most often. In a series of cases, the Supreme Court has allowed states to use tax funds for lunches, textbooks, speech-and-hearing-problem diagnostic services, standardized tests, and transportation in church-operated elementary and secondary schools.[16] However, in a number of cases, the Supreme Court has held unconstitutional state programs helping church-related schools. In *Lemon v. Kurtzman*,[17] the Court judged that direct state aid might not be used to subsidize religious instruction. The Court in the *Lemon* case gave its most general statement on the constitutionality of governmental aid to religious schools, stating that the aid had to be secular in aim and that the government must avoid "an excessive entanglement with religion."

The Free Exercise of Religious Beliefs

Free Exercise Clause

That part of the First Amendment constraining Congress from prohibiting the free exercise of religion.

The First Amendment constrains Congress from prohibiting the free exercise of religion. Does this **free exercise clause** mean that no type of religious practice can be prohibited or restricted by government? Certainly, a person can hold any religious belief that she or he wants; or a person can have no religious belief. When, however, religious *practices* work against public policy and the public welfare, the government can act. For example, regardless of a child's or parent's religious beliefs, the government can require certain types of vaccinations. The sale and use of marijuana for religious purposes has been held illegal because a religion cannot make legal what would otherwise be illegal. Conducting religious rites that result in beheaded and gutted animals left in public streets normally is not allowed.

The courts and lawmakers are constantly faced with a dilemma. On the one hand, no law may be made that requires someone to do something contrary to his or her religious beliefs or teachings because this would interfere with the free exercise of religion. On the other hand, if certain individuals, because of their religious beliefs, are exempted from specific laws, then such exemptions might tend to favor

[15]393 U.S. 97 (1968).

[16]See, *Everson v. Board of Education of Ewing Township*, 330 U.S. 1 (1947), *Meek v. Pittenger*, 421 U.S. 349 (1975), and *Wolman v. Walter*, 433 U.S. 229 (1977).

[17]403 U.S. 602 (1971).

religion and be contrary to the establishment clause. So what we have is a maze of exceptions and counterexceptions to legal precedents. For instance, children of Jehovah's Witnesses are not required to say the Pledge of Allegiance at school,[18] but their parents cannot prevent them from accepting medical treatment (such as blood transfusions) if in fact their life is in danger.

The military draft and conscientious objection often revolve around religious issues and the conflict between religious belief and public policy. Draft laws have exempted conscientious objectors from military duty with the concurrence of the Supreme Court. The Court even went further in *Welsh v. United States*[19] by stating that individuals cannot be drafted even if they do not believe in a supreme being or do not belong to any religious tradition. All that is required is that "their consciences, spurred by deeply held moral, ethical, or religious beliefs, would give them no rest or peace if they allowed themselves to become part of an instrument of war."[20]

Freedom of Expression
▽

Perhaps the most frequently invoked freedom that Americans have is the right to free speech and a free press without government interference. For the most part, Americans can criticize public officials and their actions without fear of reprisal or imprisonment by any branch of the government. Nonetheless, at various times, restrictions on expression have been legislated.

Early Restrictions on Expression

The Alien and Sedition Acts

In 1798, less than a decade after the ratification of the Bill of Rights, Congress passed the **Alien and Sedition Acts,** which were designed to curb criticism of the government. At that time, war with France seemed a real possibility. In an attempt to quiet critics of government policy and to protect government against subversion, the Federalist government under President John Adams passed four laws. The Naturalization Act required fourteen years' residency for citizenship instead of the previous five-year requirement. The Alien Act authorized the president to deport foreigners who were "considered" to be dangerous. The Alien Enemies Act enabled the deportation or confinement of aliens during a war. The most notorious of the Alien and Sedition Acts was the Sedition Act itself. The debate that ensued over the act was an effort to define the acceptable limits of public criticism of government. The act made it a crime punishable by fine and imprisonment to speak, write, or publish false and scandalous statements about the president, Congress, or the government "with intent to defame" or with intent to "excite against the government the hatred of the people."

Several dozen individuals were prosecuted under the act. Ten were actually convicted. The act expired on March 3, 1801, the day that Jefferson assumed the presidency. He pardoned all those convicted under the Sedition Act.

Alien and Sedition Acts
Four acts passed in 1798 by the Federalist party designed to curb criticism of the government.

[18]*West Virginia State Board of Education v. Barnette*, 319 U.S. 624 (1943).
[19]398 U.S. 333 (1970).
[20]Ibid.

An apparent rash of espionage incidents occurred in the mid-1980s. In June 1986, a federal jury in Baltimore, Maryland, convicted Ronald Pelton for espionage against the United States. He had sold top secret information to the Soviet Union. In the same week, a jury in Washington, D.C., found Jonathan Pollard guilty of selling secrets to Israel.

Pelton had been very straightforward about his espionage. He was desperate for money and simply called the Soviet Embassy in Washington, D.C. offering his services. The FBI had taped the conversation. A former coworker of Pelton's at the National Security Agency recognized his voice on the FBI tapes. Pelton was interviewed by the FBI and arrested. He then admitted that he earned $35,000 plus $5,000 in expenses for selling the Russians details about the National Security Agency's electronic spying and code-breaking operations. Pollard apparently received $45,000 for the information he gave to the Israelis. This was a strange case because the United States and Israel are in principle friends and allies.

Other espionage cases that made the press included selling stealth bomber secrets to the Russians, revealing CIA agents' names, and selling secrets to the Chinese government by one CIA analyst between 1952 and 1980.

In one of the most heavily publicized espionage cases, the "Walker family" ring—Retired Navy Commander Arthur J. Walker, his brother,

Michael Lance Walker being arrested.

John, and John's son, Michael—were all involved in passing highly classified military information to the Russians. This case has been called the most damaging espionage event in U.S. history.

In an effort to stem espionage, federal law has been changed to make it easier for the courts to prosecute espionage cases. In the past, defendants had used "graymailing," the threat of revealing top secret information in the course of their trial, unless the government would plea bargain with them for a reduced penalty. Congress passed the Classified Information Procedures Act in 1980 allowing defense lawyers to obtain security clearance, to discuss in private with the judge the evidence they plan to use at trial, and to permit the trial judge to exclude classified data without jeopardizing the defendant's chances of a fair trial.

One of the most interesting aspects of this recent rash of spying in the United States is that the prime motivation appears to be money rather than ideology or sympathy with the cause of the client. In the past spying was often done, at least on the surface, because the spies felt that they were helping a "cause."

The Espionage Act

The United States did not enter World War I until 1917, but the government's fear of espionage and sabotage by Germans and Austrians was evident even before its entry. Conspiracy to commit illegal acts and to overthrow our government was considered to be a serious problem. During World War I, the Socialist Party led an antiwar, antidraft movement. Since many of the Socialist party leaders were foreign born and frequently German, there was popular sentiment to "do something" to stop their propagandizing activities. So, in June 1917, Congress passed the **Espionage Act,** which prohibited all activities that obstructed the war effort. It had very little to do with espionage and much to do with suppressing the Socialist Party. Two provisions limited free speech. One made it a crime to send through the mails any material violating the act by "advocating or urging treason, insurrection, or forcible resistance to any law of the United States." The second made it a crime to utter false statements with the intent to interfere with American military forces or "to cause insubordination, disloyalty, mutiny, or refusal of duty" among American military personnel.

One famous case brought under the Espionage Act was *Adams v. United States,*[21] which went to the Supreme Court in 1919. On August 23, 1918, passersby at the corner of Houston and Crosby streets in New York City were showered by leaflets thrown from a loft window. The leaflets contained an explicit attack against the U.S. government policy of sending American troops to Siberia. The authors of the leaflet, supporters of the Russian Revolution, urged a workers' general strike. Six of the Russian factory workers who had printed and distributed the leaflets were arrested by the police. The Supreme Court upheld their convictions, holding that even though their primary intent had been to help the Russian Revolution, they would have obstructed the American war effort against Germany if they had been successful in causing a general strike. In a famous dissenting opinion, Justice Oliver Wendell Holmes claimed that the First Amendment guaranteed the "free trade in ideas." Holmes believed that the "silly" leaflets published by unknown individuals posed no danger of resistance to the war effort.

Three other laws—the Trading with the Enemy Act (1917), the Sabotage Act (1918), and the Sedition Act (1918)—were also enacted during this period. The most famous case resulting from this legislation was the conviction of Eugene V. Debs, a trade union leader, pacifist, and socialist, who was sentenced to ten years' imprisonment for speaking out against the war. He ran for president from his jail cell in the Atlanta Penitentiary, receiving almost one million votes. President Warren G. Harding commuted his sentence in 1921.

These laws pertained to espionage, but their principal effect was to restrict freedom of speech. Like the Espionage Act, they were a by-product of the anti-German hysteria during World War I.

Clear and Present Danger

When a person's remarks present a clear and present danger to the peace or public order, they can be constitutionally curtailed. Justice Holmes used this reasoning in 1919 when examining the case of a socialist who had been convicted for violating the Espionage Act. Holmes stated:

> The question in every case is whether the words are used in such circumstances and are of such a nature as to create a *clear and present danger* that they will bring about the substantive evils that Congress has a right to prevent. It is a question of proximity and degree.[22] (Emphasis added)

Thus according to the **clear and present danger test,** expression may be restricted if evidence exists that such expression would cause a condition, actual or imminent, that Congress has the power to prevent. Commenting on this test, Justice Brandeis in 1920 said, "Correctly applied, it will reserve the right of free speech . . . from

Espionage Act

An act passed in 1917 prohibiting espionage, sabotage, and obstruction of the war effort.

Clear and Present Danger Test

The test proposed by Justice Holmes for determining when government may restrict free speech. Restrictions are permissible, he argued, only when speech provokes a "clear and present danger" to the public order.

[21]*Abrams v. United States,* 250 U.S. 616 (1919).
[22]*Schenck v. United States,* 249 U.S. 47 (1919).

Preferred-Position Test

A court test used in determining the limits of free expression guaranteed by the First Amendment, requiring that limitations only be applied on speech to avoid imminent, serious, and important evils.

Sliding-Scale Test

Used as a criterion in cases where a careful examination of the facts of each individual case must be undertaken.

Bad-Tendency Rule

Speech or other First Amendment freedoms may permissibly be curtailed if there is a possibility that such expression might lead to some "evil."

Prior Restraint

Restraining an action before the activity has actually occurred. It involves censorship as opposed to subsequent punishment.

Symbolic Speech

Nonverbal expression of beliefs, which is given substantial protection by the courts.

suppression by tyrannists, well-meaning majorities, and from abuse by irresponsible, fanatical minorities."[23]

A related test includes the **preferred-position test.** This test comes almost as close to the position that freedom of expression may never be curtailed as is possible. Only if the government is able to show that limitations on speech are absolutely necessary to avoid imminent, serious, and important evils are such limitations allowed. Another test is called the **sliding-scale test.** Careful examination of the facts of each individual case must be undertaken.

The Bad-Tendency Rule

According to the **bad-tendency rule,** speech or other First Amendment freedoms may permissibly be curtailed if there is a possibility that such expression might lead to some "evil." In *Gitlow v. New York,*[24] a member of a left-wing group was convicted of violating New York state's criminal anarchy statute when he published and distributed a pamphlet urging the violent overthrow of the United States government. In its majority opinion, the Court held that although the First Amendment afforded protection against state incursions on freedom of expression, Gitlow could be legally punished in this particular instance because his expression would tend to bring about evils that the state had a right to prevent.

Two dissenting justices, Oliver Wendell Holmes and Louis Brandeis, believed that Gitlow's action did not represent a "clear and present danger," so his actions were constitutionally protected.

No Prior Restraint

Prior restraint is defined as restraining an activity before that activity has actually occurred. It involves censorship as opposed to subsequent punishment. Prior restraint of expression would require, for example, a permit before a speech could be made, a newspaper published, or a movie or TV show exhibited. Most, if not all, Supreme Court justices have been especially critical of any governmental action that imposes prior restraint on expression:

> A prior restraint on expression comes to this Court with a "heavy presumption" against its constitutionality. . . . The government thus carries a heavy burden of showing justification for the enforcement of such a restraint.[25]

The Protection of Symbolic Speech

Not all expression is in words or in writing. Gestures, movements, articles of clothing, and so on may under certain circumstances be considered **symbolic,** or nonverbal, **speech,** and such speech is given substantial protection today by our courts. During the Vietnam war when students around the country began wearing black armbands in protest, a Des Moines, Iowa, school administrator issued a regulation prohibiting students in the Des Moines School District from wearing them. The U.S. Supreme Court ruled that such a ban violated the free speech

---

[23]*Schaefer v. United States,* 251 U.S. 466 (1920).

[24]268 U.S. 652 (1925).

[25]*Nebraska Press Association v. Stuart,* 427 U.S. 539 (1976). See also *Near v. Minnesota,* 283 U.S. 697 (1931).

Highlight

▽

No Prior Restraint:
The Case of the Pentagon Papers

On June 13, 1971, the *New York Times* carried the first article on a forty-seven volume, classified U.S. government history of American policy in Vietnam from 1945 to 1967. The second article appeared the following day. A few days later, on June 18, the *Washington Post* also began a series on the secret study, based on documents it had secured. U.S. Attorney General John Mitchell obtained an injunction ordering the suspension of the publication of this material by both the *Times* and the *Post*. By June 24 both cases, *New York Times Co. v. United States* and *United States v. The Washington Post*, were before the Supreme Court.*

*403 U.S. 713 (1971); 403 U.S. 713 (1971), respectively.

The Justices were deeply divided on the constitutional issues raised by these cases.**

The key issue in the so-called Pentagon Papers cases was whether Americans had the right to know (and the press the right to inform them) of information that the government claimed might endanger national security. The First Amendment to the Constitution did not grant absolute rights to the press in publishing such material, and thus under certain circumstances prior restraint (government censorship) might be justified. Was this such a case? Would further publication immediately

**According to Bob Woodward and Scott Armstrong, *The Brethren* (New York: Simon and Schuster, 1979).

endanger national security or the lives and rights, for example, of hundreds of U.S. soldiers? Would publication jeopardize U.S. national security in the long run?

In an unusually speedy decision, reached after only four days in conference, the Court ruled 6 to 3 in favor of the newspapers' right to publish the information. The case affirmed the no prior restraint doctrine but left intact the government's right to prosecute after publication if the act of the publishers was claimed to be illegal.

Mary Beth Tinker and her brother John displaying the armbands that the Court ruled were "symbolic speech."

clause of the First Amendment. It reasoned that the school district was unable to show that the wearing of the black armbands had disrupted normal school activities. Furthermore, the school's ruling was discriminatory as it selected certain forms of symbolic speech for banning; lapel crosses and fraternity rings, for instance, symbolically speak of a person's affiliations, but these were not banned.[26]

The free speech clause also normally protects the symbolic speech of peaceful picketing. The courts do allow, however, reasonable regulation of the number of pickets and the location of picketing.[27]

The Protection of Commercial Speech

Commercial Speech
Advertising statements which have increasingly been given First Amendment protection.

Commercial speech is usually defined as advertising statements. Can advertisers use their First Amendment rights to prevent restrictions on the content of commercial advertising? Until the 1970s, the Supreme Court held that such speech was not protected by the First Amendment. By the mid-1970s, however, more and more commercial speech was brought under First Amendment protection. According to Justice Harry A. Blackmun, "Advertising, however tasteless and excessive it sometimes may seem, is nonetheless dissemination of information as to who is producing and selling what product for what reason and at what price."[28] If consumers are to make more intelligent marketplace decisions, they need to have the "free flow of commercial information," according to Blackmun and the Court.

Nonadvertising "speech" by businesses has also achieved First Amendment protection. In *First National Bank v. Belotti*,[29] the Supreme Court examined a Massachusetts statute prohibiting corporations from spending money to influence "the vote on any question submitted to the voters, other than one materially affecting any of the property, business, or assets of the corporation." That statute was struck down as unconstitutional because it unnecessarily prohibited "free speech." Some critics of the Court see in such decisions a strong bias toward property rights (the rights of corporations to use their property without regulation) and against the interests of consumers and the general citizenry—often called the "economic interpretation of politics."

Unprotected Speech: Obscenity

Numerous state and federal statutes make it a crime to disseminate obscene materials. All such state and federal statutes prohibiting obscenity have been deemed constitutional if the definition of obscenity conforms with that of the then current U.S. Supreme Court. Basically, the courts have not been willing to extend constitutional protections of free speech to what they consider obscene materials. For example, in *Roth v. United States*,[30] the Supreme Court states, "Obscenity is not within the area of constitutionally protected speech or press."

[26]*Tinker v. Des Moines School District*, 393 U.S. (1969).

[27]*Cox v. Louisiana*, 379 U.S. 559 (1965), and *International Brotherhood of Teamsters, Local 695, v. Vogt*, 354 U.S. 284 (1957).

[28]*Virginia State Board of Pharmacies v. The Virginia Citizens Consumer Council, Inc.*, 425 U.S. 748 (1976).

[29]435 U.S. 765 (1978).

[30]354 U.S. 476 (1957).

Highlight
▽
An Invitation to Testify

In February 1986, the Federal Commission on Pornography sent a letter to twenty-three retail chains inviting representatives of the stores to testify on the issue of whether those stores were selling pornographic materials. Publishers of erotic material and civil libertarians both claimed that the letter was an effort to intimidate the stores into refusing to carry such publications as *Playboy* and *Penthouse*. Indeed, six chains, including 7-Eleven, with more than eight thousand stores, pulled such magazines from their shelves. In its controversial final report, the commission concluded, among other things, that certain types of pornography led to sexual abuse and violence.

But what is obscenity? As Justice Potter Stewart once said, even though he could not define it, "I know it when I see it."[31] The problem, of course, is that even if it were agreed on, the definition of obscenity changes with the times. Victorians deeply disapproved of the "loose" morals of the Elizabethan Age. The works of Mark Twain and Edgar Rice Burroughs have at times been considered obscene (after all, Tarzan and Jane were not legally wed). Major literary works were often impossible to obtain legally in the United States because their importation or domestic publication was prohibited by the courts. James Joyce's *Ulysses* (1922) was not allowed into the country until 1934, for example, nor was D. H. Lawrence's *Lady Chatterley's Lover* (1928) until 1944.

The Supreme Court has grappled from time to time with the problem of specifying an operationally effective definition of obscenity. In the *Roth* case in 1957, the Court coined the phrase "redeeming social importance or value." Since then Supreme Court justices have viewed numerous films to determine if they met this criterion. By the 1970s, the justices had recognized the failure of the *Roth* definition. In the *Miller* case, Chief Justice Burger ultimately created a formal list of requirements, known as the Roth-Miller test of obscenity, that currently must be met for material to be legally obscene: (1) The average person finds that it violates contemporary community standards. (2) The work taken as a whole must appeal to prurient interest in sex. (3) The work shows patently offensive sexual conduct. (4) The work lacks serious redeeming literary, artistic, political, or scientific merit.[32]

[31]*Jacobellis v. Ohio*, 378 U.S. 184 (1964).
[32]*Miller v. California*, 413 U.S. 5 (1973).

Demonstration against pornography.

The problem, of course, is that one person's prurient interest is another person's artistic pleasure. The Court went on to state that the definition of prurient interest would be determined by the community's standards. The Court avoided presenting a definition of obscenity, leaving this determination to local and state authorities. Consequently, the *Miller* case has had widely inconsistent applications. Obscenity is still a constitutionally unsettled area, whether it deals with speech or printed or filmed materials. From what appears to be an increased amount of violence in pornography and from the trend toward child pornography has come a push by feminists, often in alliance with religious fundamentalists, to enact new antipornography laws.

Unprotected Speech: Slander

Can you say anything you want about someone else? Not really. Individuals are protected from **defamation of character,** which is defined as wrongfully hurting a person's good reputation. The law has imposed a general duty on all persons to refrain from making false, defamatory statements about others. Breaching this duty orally involves the wrongdoing called **slander.**[33]

Legally, slander is the public uttering of a statement that holds a person up for contempt, ridicule, or hatred. Slanderous public uttering means that the defamatory statements are made to, or within the hearing of, persons other than the defamed party. If one person calls another dishonest, unattractive, and incompetent when no one else is around, that does not constitute slander. The message is not communicated to a third party. If, however, a third party accidentally overhears defamatory statements, the courts have generally held that this constitutes public uttering and therefore slander, which is prohibited. Furthermore, any individual who repeats defamatory statements is liable, even if that person reveals the source of such statements. Hence most radio stations have instituted seven-second delays for live broadcasts, such as talk shows, allowing them to "bleep" out possibly defamatory statements.

Defamation of Character

Wrongfully hurting a person's good reputation. The law has imposed a general duty on all persons to refrain from making false, defamatory statements about others.

Slander

The public uttering of a statement that holds a person up for contempt, ridicule, or hatred, where the defamatory statement is made to, or within the hearing of, persons other than the defamed party.

Fighting Words

Those words that when uttered by a public speaker are so inflammatory that they could provoke the average listener to violence, usually of a racial, religious, or ethnic type.

Hecklers' Veto

Boisterous and generally prohibiting behavior by listeners of public speakers that, in effect, vetoes the public speaker's right to speak.

Fighting Words and Hecklers' Veto

The Supreme Court has created a limited class of speech "which by their very utterance inflict injury or intend to incite an immediate breach of peace that governments may constitutionally punish. . . ."[34] The reference here is to a prohibition on public speakers from using **fighting words.** These may include racial, religious, or ethnic slurs that are so inflammatory that they will provoke the "average" listener to fight. Under the Supreme Court leadership of Chief Justice Burger, fighting words have been more and more narrowly construed. For example, a four-letter word used about the draft and emblazoned on a sweater is not considered a fighting word, unless it is directed at a specific person.

Members of a crowd listening to a speech are similarly prohibited from exercising a **hecklers' veto.** When hecklers do so, they are threatening disruption or violence and they are vetoing the essential rights of the speaker.[35]

[33]Breaching it in writing involves the wrongdoing called *libel,* which is discussed in the next section.
[34]*Cohen v. California,* 403 U.S. 15 (1971).
[35]*Edwards v. South Carolina,* 372 U.S. 299 (1963).

Freedom of the Press

Freedom of the press can be regarded as a special instance of freedom of speech. Of course, at the time of the framing of the Constitution, the press meant only newspapers, magazines, and perhaps pamphlets. As technology has modified the ways we disseminate information, so too have the laws touching on freedom of the press been modified. But what can and cannot be printed still occupies an important place in constitutional law.

Defamation in Writing

As slander is oral defamation, **libel** is defamation in writing. As with slander, the wrongdoing of libel is **actionable** only if the defamatory statements are observed by a third party. If one person writes another a private letter accusing him or her of embezzling funds, that does not constitute libel. It is interesting that the courts have generally held that dictating a letter to a secretary constitutes publication, and therefore if defamation has occurred, the wrongdoing of libel is actionable.

Libel
Defamation of character in writing.

Actionable
Furnishing grounds for a lawsuit.

Newspapers are often involved in libel suits. *New York Times Co. v. Sullivan* explored an important question about public officials and liability.[36] Sullivan, a commissioner of the city of Montgomery, Alabama, sued the *New York Times* for libel because it had printed an advertisement critical of the actions of Montgomery officials during the Civil Rights movement. Under Alabama law, the jury found that the statements were in fact libelous on their face, so that damages could be awarded to Mr. Sullivan without proof of the extent of any injury to him. The jury awarded him a half-million dollars and the Alabama Supreme Court upheld the judgment.

The U.S. Supreme Court, however, unanimously reversed the judgment. It found that Alabama's rule of liability as applied to public officials in performance of their duty deprived critics of their rights of free speech under the First and Fourteenth Amendments.[37] Speaking for the Court, Justice William J. Brennan, Jr., stated that libel laws such as those in Alabama would inhibit the unfettered discussion of public issues. The Court indicated that only when a statement was made with **actual malice** against a public official could damages be obtained. The burden of proof shifted to the plaintiff who had to prove that statements were made with actual malice. In an even broader interpretation of the First Amendment, Justices Black, Goldberg, and Douglas stated in the same case that all statements about public officials, even those made with actual malice, are protected.

Actual Malice
Actual desire and intent to see another suffer by one's actions.

A Free Press Versus a Fair Trial: Gag Orders

Another major freedom of the press issue concerns newspaper reports of criminal trials. Amendment VI of the Bill of Rights guarantees a fair trial. In other words, the accused have rights. But the Bill of Rights also guarantees freedom of the press. What if the two appear to be in conflict? Which one prevails?

Jurors certainly may be influenced by reading news stories about the trial in which they are participating. In the 1970s, judges increasingly issued **"gag" orders**

"Gag" Orders
Orders issued by judges restricting publication of news about a trial in progress or a pretrial hearing to protect the accused's right to a fair trial.

[36]376 U.S. 254 (1964).

[37]Remember that the Fourteenth Amendment "nationalizes" most of the liberties listed in the Bill of Rights. (See page 100).

A widely publicized libel suit—Carol Burnett v. The National Enquirer

which restricted the publication of news about a trial in progress or even a pretrial hearing. A landmark case was decided by the Supreme Court in 1976,[38] involving the trial of E. C. Simants, who was charged with the murder of a neighboring family. Since the murder occurred in the course of a sexual assault, details of the crime were quite lurid. A local judge issued an order prohibiting the press from reporting information gleaned in a pretrial hearing; since there were only 860 people in the town, the judge believed that such publicity would prejudice potential jurors.

The Supreme Court unanimously ruled that the Nebraska judge's gag order had violated the First Amendment's freedom of the press clause. Chief Justice Burger indicated that even pervasive adverse pretrial publicity did not necessarily lead to an unfair trial, and that prior restraints on publication were not justified. Some justices even went so far as to indicate that gag orders are never justified.

In spite of the Nebraska Press Association ruling, the Court upheld certain types of gag orders. In *Gannett Company, Inc., v. De Pasquale,*[39] the highest court held that if a judge found a reasonable probability that news publicity would harm a defendant's right to a fair trial, the court could impose a gag rule: "Members of the public have no constitutional right under the Sixth and Fourteenth Amendments to *attend* criminal trials." The *Nebraska* and *Gannett* cases, however, involved pretrial hearings. Could a judge impose a gag order on an entire trial, including pretrial hearings? In *Richmond Newspapers, Inc., v. Virginia,*[40] the Court ruled that actual trials must be open to the public except under unusual circumstances.

Confidentiality and Reporters' Work Papers

By the 1980s, the courts had begun to influence cases that involved the press's responsibility to law-enforcement agencies. In one, Myron Farber, a *New York Times* reporter who had possession of extensive notes related to a murder case, was jailed in 1978 in New Jersey for not turning this material over to law-enforcement officials. The Supreme Court refused to review the case.[41]

Moreover, in several cases the police were permitted to search newspaper offices for documents related to cases under investigation. In general, the trend of the courts has moved in the direction of requiring the press to cooperate in criminal investigations to a much greater degree than it had before. These cases obviously raise a serious question about the confidentiality of working papers and background information that reporters obtain in the course of doing stories or investigative reporting. The question is not only who has the legitimate ownership and the right to privacy of those notes, but also whether these decisions compromise the freedom of the press guaranteed by the Constitution.

One important case involved the *Stanford Daily.*[42] The campus newspaper of Stanford University had its offices searched by police officers with a search warrant who were looking for photographs that would identify demonstrators who may have been responsible for injuries to the police. In this particular case, the Court ruled

[38]*Nebraska Press Association v. Stuart,* 427 U.S. 539 (1976).

[39]443 U.S. 368 (1979).

[40]448 U.S. 555 (1980).

[41]*New York Times Co. v. Jascalevich,* 439 U.S. 1317 (1978). *New York Times Co. v. New Jersey,* 439 U.S. 886 (1978).

[42]*Zurcher v. Stanford Daily,* 436 U.S. 547 (1978).

that the protection of confidentiality, and therefore the protection of the First Amendment's guarantees of a free press, was less important under the specific circumstances than the needs of law-enforcement agencies to secure information necessary for prosecution.

Other Informed Channels: Motion Pictures, Radio, and TV

The Founding Fathers could not have imagined the ways in which information is disseminated today. Nonetheless, they fashioned the Constitution into a flexible instrument that could respond to social and technological changes. First Amendment freedoms have been applied differently to newer forms of information dissemination.

Motion Pictures: Some Prior Restraint

The most onerous of all forms of government interference with expression is prior restraint. As we noted, the Supreme Court has not declared all forms of censorship unconstitutional but does require an exceptional justification for such restraint. Only in a few cases has the Supreme Court upheld prior restraint of published materials.

The Court's reluctance to accept prior restraint is less evident in the case of motion pictures. Throughout the last several decades, films have been routinely submitted to censorship boards.

Radio and TV: Limited Protection

Of all forms of communication, television is perhaps the most important and radio runs a close second. Radio and television broadcasting has the most limited First Amendment protection. In 1934, the national government established the Federal Communications Commission (FCC) to regulate electromagnetic wave frequencies. No one has a right to use the airwaves without a license granted by the FCC. The FCC grants licenses for limited periods and imposes numerous regulations on broadcasting. Although Congress has denied the FCC the authority to censor what is transmitted, the FCC can impose sanctions on those radio or TV stations broadcasting "filthy words," even if the words are not legally obscene.[43] Also, the FCC has occasionally refused to renew licenses of broadcasters who have presumably not "served the public interest." Perhaps one of the more controversial of the FCC's rulings has been its **fairness doctrine,** imposing on owners of broadcast licenses an obligation to present "both" sides of significant public issues (see Chapter 9 for a more detailed discussion).

Fairness Doctrine
An FCC regulation affecting broadcasting media, which requires that "equal time" be made available to legitimate opposing political groups or individuals.

The Right to Assemble and to Petition the Government
▽

The First Amendment prohibits Congress from making any law that abridges "the right of the people peaceably to assemble and to petition the Government for a redress of grievances." Inherent in such a right is the ability of private citizens to communicate their ideas on public issues to government officials as well as to other

[43]*Federal Communications Commission v. Pacifica Foundation*, 438 U.S. 726 (1978).

individuals. The Supreme Court has often put this freedom on a par with the freedom of speech and press. Nonetheless, it has allowed municipalities to require permits for parades, sound trucks, and demonstrations,[44] so that public officials may control traffic or prevent demonstrations from turning into riots. This became a major issue in 1977 when the American Nazi party wanted to march through the largely Jewish suburb of Skokie, Illinois. The American Civil Liberties Union (ACLU) defended the Nazis' right to march (in spite of its opposition to the Nazi philosophy). The Supreme Court let stand a lower court's ruling that the city of Skokie had violated the Nazis' First Amendment guarantees[45] by denying them a permit to do so.

The right to assemble has been broadly defined. For example, municipal and state governments do not have the right to require any organization to publish its membership list. This was decided in *NAACP v. Alabama*[46] when the state of Alabama required the National Association for the Advancement of Colored People to publish a list of its members. The Supreme Court held that the requirement was unconstitutional because it violated the NAACP's right of assembly, which the Court addressed in terms of freedom of association.

The courts have generally interpreted the right to parade and protest more narrowly than pure forms of speech or assembly. The Supreme Court has generally upheld the right of individuals to parade and protest in public places, but it has ruled against parades and protests when matters of public safety were at issue. In *Cox v. New Hampshire*[47] in 1941, the Court ruled that sixty-eight Jehovah's Witnesses had violated a statute prohibiting parading without a permit and upheld the right of a municipality to control its public streets.

[44]*Davis v. Massachusetts*, 167 U.S. 43 (1897).

[45]*Collin v. Smith*, 439 U.S. 916 (1978).

[46]357 U.S. 499 (1958).

[47]312 U.S. 569 (1941).

Nazi party members demonstrating for their views.

More Liberties Under Scrutiny

▽

During the past several years, a number of civil liberties have become important social issues. Among the most important are the right to privacy and the right to have an abortion.

The Right to Privacy

No explicit reference is made anywhere in the Constitution to a person's right to privacy. There is a serious constitutional issue about whether all of us, as private individuals, have the right to be left alone. The courts did not take a very positive approach toward the right to privacy until relatively recently. For example, during Prohibition suspected bootleggers' telephones were routinely tapped and the information obtained was used as a legal basis for prosecution. In *Olmstead v. U.S.*,[48] the Supreme Court upheld such invasion of privacy. However, Justice Louis Brandeis, a champion of personal freedoms, strongly dissented when he argued that the framers of the Constitution gave every citizen the right to be left alone. He called such a right "the most comprehensive of rights and the right most valued by civilized men."

In the 1960s, the highest court began to modify its view. In *Griswold v. Connecticut*[49] in 1965, the Supreme Court overthrew a Connecticut law that prohibited the sale or distribution of contraceptives on the basis of the right to privacy. Justice William O. Douglas formulated a unique way of reading this right into the Bill of Rights. He claimed that the First, Third, Fourth, Fifth, and Ninth Amendments created "penumbras, formed by emanations from those guarantees that help give them life and substance," and went on to talk about zones for privacy that are guaranteed by these rights. When we read the Ninth Amendment, we can see the foundation for his reasoning: "The enumeration in the Constitution of certain rights, shall not be construed to deny or disparage others retained by the people." In other words, just because the Constitution, including its amendments, does not specifically talk about the right to privacy does not mean this right is denied to the people.

An important right to privacy issue, created in part by the new technology, is the amassing of information on individuals by government. The average American citizen has personal information filed away in dozens of agencies—such as the Social Security Administration and the Internal Revenue Service. Because of the threat of indiscriminate use of private information by nonauthorized individuals, Congress passed the Privacy Act in 1974. This was the first law regulating the use of federal government information about private individuals. Under the Privacy Act, every citizen has the right to obtain copies of personal records collected by federal agencies and to correct inaccuracies in such records. In addition, the act established a Privacy Protection Study Commission, which has found a wide range of abuses in this area. The IRS has occasionally been called a lending library because it has been so quick to turn over tax returns to virtually any government agency requesting them. Indeed, the IRS has at times been asked to harass "enemies" of the executive office. President Nixon used the powers of the federal government to monitor the activities of people placed on what was called the Nixon enemies

---

[48]277 U.S. 438 (1928). This decision was reversed later in *Katz v. United States,* 389 U.S. 347 (1967).
[49]381 U.S. 479 (1965).

list. In an astonishingly frank memorandum, Richard Nixon's counsel, John Dean, wrote on August 16, 1971:

> This memorandum addresses the matter of how we can maximize the fact of our incumbency in dealing with persons known to be active in their opposition to our administration. Stated a bit more bluntly, how can we use the available federal machinery to screw our political enemies?[50]

The Right to Abortion

Does a woman have the right to an abortion? The arguments for and against this extremely sensitive issue revolve around when and who, if anyone, has the right to control reproduction. Before 1973 performance of an abortion was a criminal offense in most states. In 1973, however, the Supreme Court altered the law. In *Roe v. Wade*[51] the Court accepted the argument that the laws against abortion violated Jane Roe's right to privacy under the Constitution. The Court refused to answer the question of when life begins. It simply said that "the right to privacy is broad enough to encompass a woman's decision whether or not to terminate her pregnancy." Note, though, that the Court did not say such a right was absolute. Rather, it asserted that any state could impose certain regulations that would safeguard the health of the mother and protect potential life.

Thus the Court was balancing different issues when it decided that during the first trimester of pregnancy the state could not limit abortions except to require that they be performed by licensed physicians. During the second trimester, the state is allowed to specify the conditions under which an abortion can be performed. During the final trimester, the state may regulate or even outlaw abortions to protect a "viable" fetus.

In the summer of 1986, the Supreme Court again reaffirmed its 1973 decision by striking down a Pennsylvania law that greatly restricted abortions. In so doing,

[50]William Safire, *Safire's Political Dictionary* (New York: Random House, 1978), p. 203.
[51]410 U.S. 113 (1973).

Profile
▽
Justice Harry Blackmun

Justice Harry Blackmun had been on the Court for not much more than a year when he was given the assignment of writing the majority opinion in abortion cases that the Supreme Court had heard during its 1971 term. Although he was new on the Court, Justice Blackmun was not at all new to medical issues as they related to the law. Blackmun had been general counsel at the Mayo Clinic in Rochester, Minnesota, and had advised the staff there on the legality of abortions performed by the hospital.

In looking through available common law on the subject and examining the history of abortion in the United States and Great Britain, one of the things Blackmun discovered was that abortion had been a fairly accepted practice for many centuries, and it was only in the nineteenth century that it became a crime in the United States. Antiabortion laws were enacted largely to protect pregnant women since abortion was a very risky operation. But the medical reality had changed. Abortion is now a relatively safe procedure with the use of modern drugs and surgical techniques, particularly in early pregnancy.

During the summer of 1972, Blackmun went back to Rochester and researched the question of abortion at the Mayo Clinic Medical Library. The basic issue that found its way into Blackmun's opinion on abortion was

"When those trained in the respective disciplines of medicine, philosophy, and theology are unable to arrive at any consensus, the judiciary, at this point in the development of man's knowledge, is not in a position to speculate as to the answer."

whether a woman had an absolute right to privacy or if and at what point a state government or the federal government had the right to step in to prevent the pregnant woman from doing with her body what she wished.

There was little guidance in the law about the point at which the state's interests should override the interests of the pregnant woman. Blackmun used the results of medical research and accepted medical practice as his guide: Pregnancy was divided into three trimesters of roughly equal stages of three months each. The basic conclusion in the medical world was that abortions were generally safe in the first trimester and with proper medical controls could be performed safely in the second trimester as well—that is, up until the time a woman is about six months pregnant. After the second trimester, though, the fetus becomes capable of surviving outside the womb.

Blackmun's conclusion then was that at the end of the second trimester, some strong prohibitions would probably have to be included against a woman having an absolute right to an abortion. The sense of Blackmun's opinion was relatively liberal concerning abortion during the first two trimesters of pregnancy but rather conservative after the second trimester had ended and the third begun. On January 22, 1973, the U.S. Supreme Court handed down its ruling in *Roe v. Wade* and *Doe v. Bolton*, incorporating Harry Blackmun's opinion based on his medical background and legal expertise.

SOURCE: Bob Woodward and Scott Armstrong, *The Brethren* (New York: Simon and Schuster, 1979).

the high Court's majority spurned a suggestion by the Reagan administration that it overrule its landmark *Roe v. Wade* decision.

The Rights of Severely Disabled Infants—The "Baby Doe" Rule

What are the rights of severely disabled infants? The Reagan administration relied on a 1973 law prohibiting institutions that received federal funds from discrimi-

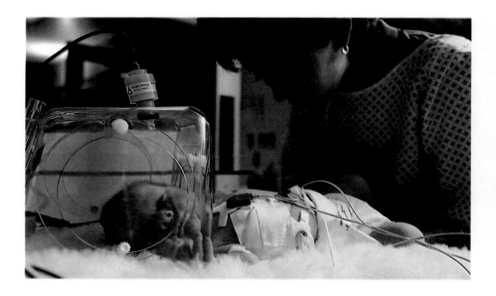

nating against the handicapped. Federal officials argued that refusing to treat severely handicapped infants was a type of discrimination based on handicap. A final version of the "Baby Doe" rule was passed in 1984. In effect, the federal government was policing the care hospitals gave to infants born with severe defects. In 1986, the Supreme Court invalidated the Reagan administration's "Baby Doe" rule. The Court pointed out that there was no known case in which care had been refused by a federally assisted hospital because of discrimination against a handicapped baby. Rather, it was always the parents who refused to give permission. The Court in essence ruled that the difficult decision about treating handicapped newborns rests primarily with the child's parents.

The Great Balancing Act: The Rights of the Accused Versus the Rights of Society

▽

The United States has one of the highest violent crime rates in the world. The statistics are quite shocking. Given so much crime in the United States, it is not surprising that many citizens have extremely strong opinions about the rights of those accused of criminal offenses. When an accused person, especially one who has confessed to some criminal act, is set free because of an apparent legal "technicality," many people may feel that the rights of the accused are being given more weight than the rights of society and of potential or actual victims.

So the courts and the police must constantly engage in a balancing act of competing rights. At the basis of all discussions about the appropriate balance is, of course, the U.S. Bill of Rights. The Fourth, Fifth, Sixth, and Eighth Amendments specifically deal with the rights of criminal defendants.

Rights of the Accused

The basic rights of criminal defendants can be outlined as follows. Where appropriate, the specific amendment on which a right is based is given also.

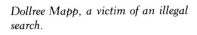
Dollree Mapp, a victim of an illegal search.

Limits on Conduct of Police and Prosecutors
▽ No unreasonable or unwarranted searches and seizures (Amend. IV)
▽ No arrest except on probable cause (Amend. IV)
▽ No coerced confessions or illegal interrogation (Amend. V)
▽ No entrapment
▽ Upon questioning, suspect must be informed of rights

Defendant's Pretrial Rights
▽ Writ of habeas corpus (Article I, Section 9)
▽ Prompt arraignment (Amend. VI)
▽ Legal counsel (Amend. VI)
▽ Reasonable bail (Amend. VIII)
▽ Defendant must be informed of charges (Amend. VI)
▽ Right to remain silent (Amend. V)

Trial Rights
▽ Speedy and public trial before a jury (Amend. VI)
▽ Impartial jury selected from cross section of community (Amend. VI and VII)
▽ Trial atmosphere free of prejudice, fear, and outside interference
▽ Confront all witnesses (cross-examination) (Amend. VI)
▽ No compulsory self-incrimination (Amend. V)
▽ Adequate counsel (Amend. VI)
▽ No cruel or unusual punishment (Amend. VIII)
▽ Appeal convictions
▽ No double jeopardy (Amend. V)

Extending the Rights of the Accused: *Miranda v. Arizona*

In 1963, near Phoenix, Arizona, a young woman was kidnapped and raped. A twenty-three-year old, mentally disturbed individual, Ernesto Miranda, was arrested soon after the crime took place. After two hours of questioning, he confessed and was later convicted.

Miranda's counsel appealed his conviction. They argued that the police had never informed Miranda that he had the right to remain silent and the right to be represented by counsel. In 1966, a 5-to-4 majority of the U.S. Supreme Court ruled in Miranda's favor:

> Prior to any questioning, the person must be warned that he has a right to remain silent, that any statement he does make may be used against him, and that he has a right to the presence of an attorney, either retained or appointed.[52]

The majority voted to reverse the conviction on the basis of the Fifth and Sixth Amendments, but the minority complained that the majority was distorting the Constitution by placing the rights of criminal suspects above the rights of society as a whole—the balancing act was again in question. Police officials sided with the minority view, but many agreed with the majority that criminal law enforcement would be more reliable if it were based on independently secured evidence rather than on confessions obtained under adverse interrogation conditions in the absence of counsel.

Recent Rulings and Their Impact on *Miranda*

Exclusionary Rule

A policy forbidding the admission of illegally seized evidence at trial.

The Supreme Court under Chief Justice Warren Burger did not expand the *Miranda* ruling but rather reduced its scope and effectiveness. Also, Congress in 1968 passed the Omnibus Crime Control and Safe Streets Act, which provided—among other things—that in federal cases a voluntary confession could be used in evidence, even if the accused was not warned of his or her rights.

Today, juries can accept confessions as valid even when they may not be convinced were voluntary.[53] Even in cases that are not tried in federal court, confessions made by criminal suspects who have not been completely informed of their legal rights may be taken into consideration.[54] In 1984, the Court added another exception to the *Miranda* rule by allowing the introduction of evidence into the courtroom that was voluntarily given by the suspect before he had been informed of his rights. The Court held that when "public safety" required (in this case to find the loaded gun), police could interrogate the suspect before advising him of his right to remain silent.[55]

The Exclusionary Rule

At least since 1914, a judicial policy has existed forbidding the admission of illegally seized evidence at trial. This is the so-called **exclusionary rule.** Improperly obtained evidence, no matter how telling, until recently could not be used by prosecutors. The reasoning behind the exclusionary rule is that it forces police officers to gather evidence properly, in which case their due diligence will be rewarded by a conviction. There have always been critics of the exclusionary rule who argued that it permits guilty persons to be freed because of innocent errors.

In a recent case in Massachusetts, the court seemed to be loosening the severity of the exclusionary rule. A Boston police officer suspected a man of murder and

[52]*Miranda v. Arizona,* 384 U.S. 436 (1966).

[53]See especially *Lego v. Twomey,* 404 U.S. 477 (1972).

[54]*Michigan v. Tucker,* 417 U.S. 433 (1974).

[55]*New York v. Quarles,* 461 U.S. 942 (1982).

Highlight

▽

The Case of Clarence Earl Gideon

In 1962, Clarence Earl Gideon sent a petition to the Supreme Court to review his most recent conviction, for breaking into a pool hall and stealing some money in Panama City, Florida. That petition would not only change Gideon's life but would become a landmark case in Constitutional law as well.

Clarence Gideon was not someone you would call a lucky man; in fact, he had been in trouble with the law during much of his life and in jail at least four times before for various crimes. He just couldn't seem to keep a steady job, gambled a lot, and at times resorted to theft to supplement his income. Those who knew him, including his jailers, found him rather likeable and relatively harmless.

Gideon's petition to the Supreme Court took the form of an *in forma pauperis* application: Gideon claimed he was unable to afford to pay a lawyer to file the petition for him. In the petition, Gideon claimed that his conviction and sentencing to a five-year term in prison violated the due process clause of the Fourteenth Amendment to the Constitution, which states that "no state shall . . . deprive any person of life, liberty, or property, without due process of the law." Gideon reported that at the time of his trial, when he asked for the assistance of a lawyer, the court refused this aid. The heart of Gideon's petition lay in his notion that "to try a poor man for a felony without giving him a lawyer was to deprive him of due process of law."

The problem with Gideon's argument was that the Supreme Court had established a precedent twenty years earlier in *Betts v. Brady*,* when it held that criminal defendants were not automatically guaranteed the right to have a lawyer present when they were tried in court except in capital cases. The *Betts v. Brady* decision had taken many by surprise and remained a source of dispute. Gideon, however, did not even refer to the earlier decision in his five-page summary, which showed a fairly sophisticated knowledge of the law. Gideon kept pressing the Court to hear his case on the grounds that he had been denied due process.

Gideon was successful, with the help of the American Civil Liberties Union (ACLU) and its appointed lawyer, Abe Fortas, who later was appointed to the Supreme Court by President Johnson. In the case of *Gideon v. Wainwright*** the Court decided in Gideon's favor, saying that persons who can demonstrate that they are unable to afford to have a lawyer present and are accused of felonies must be given a lawyer at the expense of the government. Gideon was retried, represented by an attorney appointed by the court, and found innocent of the charges.

*316 U.S. 455 (1942).
**372 U.S. 335 (1963).

SOURCE: Anthony Lewis, *Gideon's Trumpet* (New York: Vintage Books, 1964).

wished to search his residence. He used a technically incorrect search warrant form. The Massachusetts Appeals Court threw out the conviction because of this technical defect. But the Supreme Court held that the officer acted in good faith and thereby created the "good faith exception."[56] A similar good faith exception principle was applied to a federal case, *United States v. Leon*.[57]

Capital Punishment: Cruel and Unusual?

Amendment VIII prohibits cruel and unusual punishment. Until a Supreme Court decision in 1972,[58] the death penalty was not considered cruel and unusual punishment. Indeed, a number of states had imposed the death penalty for a variety of crimes and allowed juries to decide when the condemned could be sentenced to death.

But many believed, and in 1972 the Court agreed, that the imposition of the death penalty was random and arbitrary. For example, 53 percent of all persons executed from 1930 to 1965 were black, even though blacks only constituted less than 10 percent of the population during that period. Changing attitudes toward the death penalty could be seen in the fact that the number of individuals who actually were executed dropped dramatically since the 1930s. In the decade 1930–1939, 1,666 persons were executed; from 1960 to 1969, less than 200 persons were executed.

The Supreme Court's 1972 decision stated that the death penalty as currently applied violated the Eighth and Fourteenth Amendments. In its opinion, the Court invited the states to make more precise laws so that the death penalty would be applied more consistently. A plurality of states have done so in the last fifteen years. In the 1980s, an increasing number of states are actually executing death row inmates. Table 4–1 shows the number of death row inmates in various states and the type of execution authorized in each state where the death penalty exists.

[56]*Massachusetts v. Sheppard*, 468 U.S. 981 (1984).

[57]468 U.S. 897 (1984).

[58]*Furman v. Georgia*; *Jackson v. Georgia*; *Branch v. Texas*, 408 U.S. 238 (1972).

Lethal injection gurney.

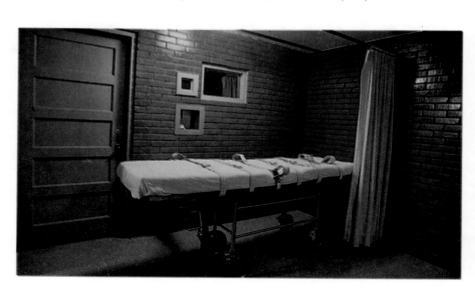

Table 4–1

▽

Death Row Inmates and Types of Execution Authorized by State

As of May 1, 1986, thirty-seven states had authorized the death penalty. They are listed below, along with the number of inmates currently on death row. The authorized form of execution is listed in the last column.

State	Number	Type of Execution Authorized
Alabama	82	Electrocution
Arizona	64	Gas Chamber
Arkansas	29	Lethal injection
California	177	Gas chamber
Colorado	1	Gas chamber
Connecticut	0	
Delaware	5	Lethal injection
Florida	231	Electrocution
Georgia	107	Electrocution
Idaho	13	Lethal injection
Illinois	89	Lethal injection
Indiana	35	Electrocution
Kentucky	26	Electrocution
Louisiana	47	Electrocution
Maryland	20	Gas chamber
Mississippi	46	Gas chamber
Missouri	41	Gas chamber
Montana	5	Lethal injection/hanging
Nebraska	13	Electrocution
Nevada	32	Lethal injection
New Hampshire	0	Lethal injection
New Jersey	20	Lethal injection
New Mexico	5	Lethal injection
North Carolina	58	Gas chamber/lethal injection
Ohio	66	Electrocution
Oklahoma	57	Lethal injection
Oregon	1	Lethal injection
Pennsylvania	83	Electrocution
South Carolina	42	Electrocution
South Dakota	0	
Tennessee	57	Electrocution
Texas	221	Lethal injection
Utah	7	Firing squad
Vermont	0	Lethal injection
Virginia	30	Electrocution
Washington	7	Lethal injection/hanging
Wyoming	3	Gas chamber

SOURCE: NAACP Legal Defense and Education Fund, *Death Row U.S.A. Report*, May 1, 1986.

This trend may be short-lived, however. On June 26, 1986, the Supreme Court stated that the U.S. Constitution bars states from executing convicted killers who have become insane while waiting on death row.[59] The case involved Alvin Bernard Ford, sentenced to death in 1974 for shooting a police officer twice and then standing over him and shooting him once more in the head. Ford's lawyers contended that he became insane while on death row. The Supreme Court further stated that the inmate's lawyer must be given an opportunity to present evidence to the official making the decision on the prisoner's sanity. This ruling created concern among psychiatrists, who see themselves in a dilemma. Effective psychiatric care of a convicted murderer, thereby rendering him sane, would in essence shorten his life.

Capital punishment remains one of the most debated aspects of our criminal justice system. Those in favor of it maintain that it serves as a deterrent to serious crime and satisfies society's need for justice and fair play. Those opposed to the death penalty do not believe it has any deterrent value and hold that it constitutes a barbaric act in an otherwise civilized society. Recent public opinion polls have demonstrated that an increasing percentage of Americans is in favor of using the death penalty more frequently.

[59]*Ford v. Wainwright*, 106 S.Ct. 2595 (1986).

Your Civil Liberties: Search and Seizure

What happens if you are stopped by members of the police force? Your civil liberties are such that your name and address are the only pieces of information you must provide. Indeed, you are not really required to produce evidence of identification, although it is a good idea to show this to the officers. Normally, even if you have not been placed under arrest, the officers have the right to frisk you for weapons and you must let them proceed. The officers cannot, however, check your person or your clothing further if, in their judgment, no weaponlike object is produced. Only if the officers have a search warrant or probable cause that they will likely find incriminating evidence if the search is conducted may they search you. Normally, it is unwise to physically resist the officers' attempt to search you if they do not have probable cause or a warrant; it is usually best simply to orally refuse to give permission for the search, preferably in the presence of a witness. Also, it is usually advisable to tell the officer as little as possible about yourself and the situation that is under investigation. Being polite and courteous, though firm, is better than acting out of anger or frustration, and making the officers irritable. If you are told not to leave, that means you are under arrest. At that point, it is best to keep quiet until you can speak with a lawyer.

If you are in your car and stopped by the police, the same fundamental rules apply. Always be ready to show your driver's license and car registration quickly. You may be asked to get out of the car. The officers may use a flashlight to peer into it if it is too dark to see otherwise. None of this constitutes a search. A true search requires either a warrant or probable cause. No officer has the legal right to search your car simply to find out if you may have committed a crime. Passengers in your car that has been stopped by the police are legally required only to give a name and address. Passengers are not even obligated to produce a piece of identification.

If you are in your residence and a police officer with a search warrant appears, you should examine the warrant before granting entry. A correctly made out warrant will state the exact place or persons to be searched, a description of the object sought, the date of the warrant (which should be no more than ten days old), and a signature of a judge or magistrate. If the search warrant is in order, you should not make any statement. If you believe it to be invalid, you should make it clear orally that you have not consented to the search, preferably in the presence of a witness. If the warrant is later proven to be invalid, normally any evidence obtained would be considered illegal. Officers who attempt to enter your home without a search warrant can do so only if they are pursuing a suspected felon into the house. Rarely is it advisable to give permission for a warrantless search. You must be the one to give permission for any evidence obtained to be legal. The landlord, manager, or head of a college dormitory cannot give legal permission. A roommate, however, can give permission for a search of his or her room, which may allow the police to search those areas in which you have personal belongings. If you find yourself a guest in a location for which there is a legal search, you may be legally searched also. But unless you have been placed under arrest, you cannot be compelled to go to the police station or into a squad car.

If you would like to find out more about your rights and obligations under the laws of search and seizure, you might wish to contact:

The American Civil Liberties Union
22 East 40th Street
New York, NY 10016
(212) 725-1222

Legal Defense Fund
67 Winthrop Street
Cambridge, MA 02138
(617) 864-8680

Chapter Summary

▽

1. When we speak of civil liberties in the United States, for the most part we are referring to the specific limitations on government outlined in the first ten amendments to the U.S. Constitution. These include our basic freedoms of religion, speech, press, and assembly, and the right to petition.

2. As originally presented, the Bill of Rights limited only the power of the national government, not that of the states. It was not until the Fourteenth Amendment was ratified in 1868 that our Constitution explicitly guaranteed to everyone due process of the law.

3. For the most part, the last hundred years of Supreme Court interpretations of the Fourteenth Amendment have bound the fifty states to accept most of the guarantees for their respective citizens that are contained in the Bill of Rights.

4. The First Amendment freedom of religion implies both free exercise of religion and the separation of church and state.

5. The Supreme Court has ruled against officially sponsored prayer and Bible-reading sessions in public schools. A constitutional amendment to permit organized, recited prayers in public schools was rejected in the Senate on March 20, 1984. In cases regarding government financial aid to church-related schools, the Supreme Court has attempted to distinguish between permissible public aid to students as opposed to impermissible public aid to religion. As for the exercise of religion, when religious practices work against public policy and public welfare, the government can intervene.

6. At various times, restrictions on the freedom of expression have been imposed in the name of national security. The Alien and Sedition Acts of 1798 were designed to curb criticism of government. The Espionage Act of 1917 prohibited activities obstructing the war effort.

7. The clear and present danger test is used in determining the limits of free expression. Other tests include the preferred-position test (more rigorous standards of review required because of importance), the sliding-scale test (careful examination of facts of each individual case must be undertaken), and the bad-tendency test (speech having a tendency to bring "evil").

8. Prior restraint on expression and laws that are too vague or broad may be deemed unconstitutional.

9. The free speech clause normally protects symbolic speech. Commercial speech and advertising statements have gradually been brought under the protection of the First Amendment.

10. Basically, the courts have not been willing to extend constitutional protections of free speech to what are considered obscene materials and to slander.

11. Abuses of free speech have included defamation of character in writing, or libel, and news reports of criminal trials when they interfere with a fair trial. The courts have moved in the direction of requiring the press to cooperate in criminal investigations if they have pertinent information.

12. The Supreme Court has not declared all forms of prior restraint or censorship to be unconstitutional but does require exceptional justification for such restraint.

13. Radio and television broadcasting has the most limited First Amendment protection.

14. The First Amendment protects the right to peaceably assemble and petition the government. The courts have generally upheld the right of the individual to parade and to protest in public places, but have ruled against such activities when public safety was threatened.

15. During the past several years, a number of civil liberties have become important social issues, including the right to privacy, the right to have an abortion, and the rights of severely disabled infants.

16. The police and the courts are constantly engaged in a balancing act between the rights of the accused versus the rights of society. The Fourth, Fifth, Sixth, and Eighth Amendments specifically deal with the rights of criminal defendants.

17. In *Miranda v. Arizona* (1966), the Supreme Court ruled that criminal suspects must be immediately informed of their right to remain silent, that any statement they make can be used against them, and that they have the right to the presence of an attorney.

18. Amendment VIII prohibits cruel and unusual punishment. Capital punishment has been debated under this amendment.

Questions for Review and Discussion

▽

1. Although the Communist party was strictly outlawed in the United States for many years, today its candidates compete openly in presidential and other elections. What activities—speeches, printed publications, demonstrations—of the Communist party do you think could be considered illegal under the current laws?

2. Most conflicts concerning civil liberties involve the rights of the individual versus the rights of society as a whole. What religious practices might be considered a threat to society? On the other hand, what activities of certain missionary groups may be violating your rights to be left alone?

3. The punishment of convicted criminals serves not only as retribution for the crime but also to satisfy the community's sense of justice. How should the courts balance the rights of

the criminal against the rights of society—and the rights of the victim—to ensure fair treatment?

4. The criminal justice system in the United States is extremely overburdened. Many accused persons are either released owing to a failure in the system or agree to plea bargaining and forfeit a trial. What reforms might you suggest to make the judicial process both more efficient and more effective for the accused and for the courts?

5. The electronic era has created many legal situations that are not covered by the Constitution. To what extent should radio and television be covered by freedom of the press? Should videotape rentals be regulated to prevent the spread of pornography, especially to minors? Should computer communications be protected by the right to privacy?

Selected References

Henry Abraham and Grace Doherty, *Freedom and the Court: Civil Rights and Liberties in the United States*, 3rd edition (Oxford University Press, 1977). This detailed analysis of the Bill of Rights examines the role of the Court in extending rights and freedoms.

John Brigham, *Civil Liberties and American Democracy* (Washington, D.C.: Congressional Quarterly Press, 1984). This book discusses fundamental civil liberties in the U.S. and the Supreme Court's role in guaranteeing those rights. Freedom of expression, press, speech, due process, and property rights are specifically treated.

William A. Donohue, *The Politics of the American Civil Liberties Union* (New Brunswick, N.J.: Transaction Books, 1985). An interesting study of one of the most visible and active civil liberties groups in the United States, with specific emphasis given to the role of ideology and the liberal-left orientation of the ACLU.

Robert Booth Fowler, *Religion and Politics in America* (Metuchen, N.J.: Scarecrow Press, 1985). This book is an excellent analysis of the impact and role of religion in American politics with special emphasis on Roman Catholics, Jews, liberal Protestants, and evangelicals and fundamentalists.

Nat Hentoff, *The First Freedom: The Tumultuous History of Free Speech in America* (New York: Delacorte, 1980). This is a lively account of the evolution of freedom of speech.

Anthony Lewis, *Gideon's Trumpet* (New York: Vintage, 1964). Absolutely essential reading for understanding how criminal rights cases reach the Supreme Court.

D. F. B. Tucker, *Law, Liberalism and Free Speech* (Totowa, N.J.: Rowman and Littlefield, 1986). Using the ideas of major contemporary philosophers, this book explores fundamental principles of freedom of speech and also provides specific applications to privacy, the public interest, the media, and authority.

Chapter 5

▽

Minority Rights

Contents

▽

The Diversity of American Society

The Traditional Minorities: An Overview

Blacks: The Consequences of Slavery in the United States

The Civil Rights Movement

1960s Civil Rights Legislation and Its Implementation

The Voting Rights Act of 1965

Hispanics in American Society

Native Americans: An American Tragedy

Asian Americans

Melting Pot or Ethnic Stew?

What If . . .
The North Had Lost the Civil War?

The scene is the Appomattox courthouse in the mid-1860s. The Civil War is about to end. But it is the northern general, Ulysses Simpson Grant, who has left his defeated troops to surrender to the victorious southern commander, Robert E. Lee. In a series of daring maneuvers, General Lee had encircled the Union forces near Washington, D.C., and dealt them a decisive setback as the nation's capital reeled under unrelenting Confederate artillery barrages and a Confederate naval blockade.

What if this had come to pass? There would probably be two separate nations between Mexico and Canada and two independent governments with their own national constitutions and political institutions. In defeat, the North would likely have never implemented the provisions of freedom from slavery, rights of citizenship, and universal male suffrage contained in the Thirteenth, Fourteenth, and Fifteenth Amendments. Most recent civil rights legislation, providing for equal employment and voting opportunities, would probably not exist.

In victory, the South would probably have retained slave institutions for a while and tried to expand them to the western territories, some of which would likely have become slave states. The abolition of slavery and perhaps equal rights would only gradually have been adopted. Unless the northern pattern of industrialization, rapidly expanding access to education, better employment opportunities, and the rise of a liberal middle class could have been repeated in the South, that nation would likely have remained a largely agricultural, socially static, and culturally insulated collection of loosely organized separate states.

The Civil War ended the institution of slavery in the United States. The war could not, however, abolish the discriminatory treatment of blacks and other minorities. It has taken more than a century of struggle—carried out in the Congress, in the courts, and, in some instances, in the streets—to begin to achieve equality for all Americans.

> We hold these truths to be self-evident,
> that all Men are created equal . . .

These are beautiful words, to be sure. But when they were written in 1776, the term *men* had a somewhat different meaning than it has today. It did not include slaves or women or Native Americans. So individuals in these groups were not considered equal. It has taken this nation two hundred years to approach even a semblance of equality among all Americans.

The struggle for equality has not been easy. In this chapter, we show that it is still continuing. It is a struggle perhaps best described as an effort to strengthen and to expand constitutional guarantees to *all* persons in our society. In this chapter and in the one that follows, we examine the rights of various minorities: blacks, Mexican Americans and other Hispanics, Native Americans, Asian Americans, women, gays, the elderly, and juveniles.

Minority rights have often been called civil rights and the quest for the expansion of minority rights has been called the civil rights movement. Since the civil rights movement started with the struggle for black equality, that story is told first. We begin by taking a look at the makeup of American society.

The Diversity of American Society
▽

A foreign visitor whose first stop in the United States is, say, a small town in the Midwest or a Los Angeles suburb might receive the impression that the population is entirely WASP (White Anglo-Saxon Protestants). But the facts are quite different. The United States is much more heterogeneous than it would seem at first glance and certainly more heterogeneous than any Western European country. The projection of population by race for 1990 shows that although whites will still constitute a large majority of Americans, blacks will make up 12.6 percent, Mexican Amer-

Table 5–1
▽
The Six Largest Ethnic Groups in the United States in 1980

Ancestry	Number (in millions)	Percentage of Population
English	49.6	26.3
German	49.2	26.1
Irish	40.2	21.3
African	20.9	11.1
French	12.9	6.8
Italian	12.2	6.5

SOURCE: *Statistical Abstract of the United States, 1984*, p. 84.

Figure 5–1
▽
Religious Groups in the United States, 1985

SOURCE: Adapted from *Information Please Almanac*.

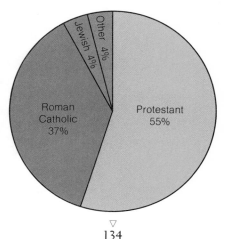

icans and other Hispanics 7.2 percent, and Asians 5.5 percent of the population of the United States.

In terms of national origin, Table 5–1 shows that Anglo-Saxons are the largest group, but nearly as numerous are those claiming German or Irish descent. Also the religious makeup of the American population certainly isn't homogeneous (Figure 5–1). Of those who express a religious affiliation in the United States, 55 percent are Protestant, 37 percent are Roman Catholic, 4 percent are Jewish, and 4 percent are of other religious persuasions. WASPs may constitute a large portion of our population, but this country is nonetheless made up of many diverse groups.

The Traditional Minorities: An Overview
▽

There are many ways to describe the relative condition of a minority. One way is simply to compare the economic situation of a specific minority group with the situation of the dominant groups in our society. Table 5–2 shows the median income of whites, blacks, and people of Spanish origin. Information on the number of years of schooling completed is also given.

Some observers, looking at the information in Table 5–2, simply conclude that the economic position of the traditional minorities is bad, but that it was worse in the past. Recent data do not, however, support such a view. Table 5–3 shows the median income of whites, blacks, and Hispanic families at three different times since 1972. It is apparent that the relative position among the three groups, in terms of median income, has not changed very dramatically.

Blacks: The Consequences of Slavery in the United States
▽

Article I, Section 2, of the Constitution stated that congressional representatives and direct taxes were to be apportioned among the states according to their respective numbers, obtained by adding to the total number of free persons "three-fifths of all other Persons." The "other persons" were, of course, slaves. A slave was thus equal to three-fifths of a white person.[1] As Lincoln stated sarcastically, "All men are created equal, except Negroes." Before 1861, the Constitution thus protected slavery and made equality impossible in the sense we use the word today. Black leader Frederick Douglass pointed out that "Liberty and Slavery—opposite as Heaven and Hell—are both in the Constitution."

The constitutionality of slavery was confirmed just a few years before the outbreak of the Civil War in the famous *Dred Scott v. Sanford* case[2] of 1857. The Supreme Court held that blacks could not become citizens of the United States, nor were they entitled to the rights and privileges of citizenship. The Court also ruled that the Missouri Compromise, which banned slavery in the territories, was unconstitutional. The *Dred Scott* decision had grave consequences. Most observers contend that the ruling contributed to making the Civil War inevitable. (In all fairness, it should be noted that the decision was not unanimous—the Court was divided 6 to 3 over the issue.)

With the emancipation of the slaves in 1863 and the passage of the Thirteenth, Fourteenth, and Fifteenth Amendments following the Civil War, constitutional in-

[1] It may seem ironic that the median wage of blacks today is approximately three-fifths that of whites.
[2] 19 Howard 393 (1857).

equality was ended. The Thirteenth Amendment (1865) states that neither slavery nor involuntary servitude shall exist within the United States. The Fourteenth Amendment (ratified on July 9, 1868) tells us that *all* persons born or naturalized in the United States are citizens of the United States. Furthermore, "No State shall make or enforce any law which shall abridge the privileges or immunities of the citizens of the United States; nor shall any State deprive any person of life, liberty or property without due process of law; nor deny to any person within its jurisdiction the equal protection of the laws." The Fifteenth Amendment seems equally impressive: "The right of citizens of the United States to vote shall not be denied or abridged by the United States or by any State on account of race, color, or previous condition of servitude." As we shall see, though, those words had little immediate effect. Although slavery was legally and constitutionally ended, politically and socially the idea of black inferiority has continued to the present time. In the following sections, we discuss several landmarks in the struggle of black people to overcome this inequality.

The Civil Rights Acts of 1865–1877

At the end of the Civil War, President Lincoln's Republican party controlled the national government and indeed most state governments, and the so-called Radical Republicans with their strong antislavery stance controlled the party. The Radical Republicans pushed through the Thirteenth, Fourteenth, and Fifteenth Amendments to the Constitution (the "Civil War amendments") and, from 1865 to 1877, succeeded in getting Congress to pass a series of civil rights acts that were aimed at enforcing these amendments. Even Republicans who were not necessarily sympathetic to a strong antislavery position wanted to undercut Democratic domination of the South. What better way to do so than to guarantee black suffrage? The civil rights acts that were passed from 1865 to 1877 were also supported by pro-industry legislators who believed that agrarian southern Democrats would impede industrialization.

The first Civil Rights Act under Reconstruction was passed in 1866 over the veto of President Andrew Johnson. That act extended citizenship to anyone born in the United States and gave American Negroes full equality before the law. The act further authorized the president to enforce the law with national armed forces. Many considered the law to be unconstitutional, but such problems disappeared in 1868 with the adoption of the Fourteenth Amendment.

Among the six other civil rights acts in the nineteenth century, one of the more important ones was the Enforcement Act of May 31, 1870, which set out specific

Table 5–2

▽

Median Incomes and Education of Whites, Blacks, and Latinos, 1985

	Median Family Income (in current dollars)	Percentage of Adults Completing 4 Years of High School
White	24,356	39.1
Black	13,875	34.3
Spanish-origin	17,502	27.3

SOURCE: *Statistical Abstract of the United States, 1986*, p. 446.

Dred Scott

Table 5–3

▽

Median Family Income of Whites, Blacks, and Spanish-Origin Americans for 1972, 1976, 1981, and 1985 (in current dollars)

	1972	1976	1981	1985
White	11,549	15,537	23,517	24,356
Black	6,864	9,242	13,266	13,875
Spanish-origin	8,183	10,259	16,401	17,502

SOURCE: *Statistical Abstract of the United States, 1986*, p. 446.

Did You Know?
▽

That the original Constitution failed to describe the status of a citizen or to describe how this status could be acquired?

criminal sanctions for interfering with the right to vote as protected by the Fifteenth Amendment, or by the Civil Rights Act of 1866. Equally important was the Civil Rights Act of April 20, 1872, known as the Anti-Ku Klux Klan Act. This act made it a federal crime for anyone to use law or custom to deprive an individual of his or her rights, privileges, and immunities secured by the Constitution or by any federal law. Section 2 of that act imposed detailed penalties or damages for violation of the act.

The last of these early civil rights acts, known as the Second Civil Rights Act, was passed on March 1, 1875. It declared that everyone is entitled to full and equal enjoyment of public accommodations, theaters, and other places of public amusement, and imposed penalties for violators. Unfortunately, the act was virtually nullified by the *Civil Rights Cases* of 1883 discussed below.

The civil rights acts of the 1870s are of special interest because they were an indication that congressional power or authority applied to official, or government, action and to private action. The theory behind the acts was that if a state government failed to act, Congress could act in its absence. Thus Congress could directly legislate against private individuals who were violating constitutional rights of other individuals when state officials failed to protect those rights. At the time this was a novel theory and not truly accepted until the 1960s.

The Nullification of the Civil Rights Acts

The Civil Rights Cases

The Reconstruction statutes, or civil rights acts, ultimately did little to secure equality for blacks in their civil rights. The Supreme Court invalidated the 1875 Civil Rights Act when it held in the *Civil Rights Cases*[3] of 1883 that the enforcement

[3]109 U.S. 3 (1883).

First reading of the Emancipation Proclamation.

Over 50 percent of black infants are born to unwed black mothers, compared with 12.8 percent of whites.

Over half of black families with children are headed by females with no husband or father present, compared with 15 percent of white female-headed families.

Black teenage unemployment is over 40 percent, compared with 15 percent for white teenagers.

Only 41 percent of black children under 18 live with two parents, compared with 80 percent of white children.

Almost 50 percent of all persons sent to jail are black, yet blacks make up 12 percent of the total U.S. population.

Thirty-four percent of all murder victims in the United States are black males, even though they represent only 5.6 percent of the population.

In 1986, almost 95 percent of black males murdered between the ages of 15 and 35 were killed by another young black male; murder appears to be the leading cause of death among young blacks.

SOURCE: *Statistical Abstracts*, 1985, and *Washington Post*, National Weekly Edition, February 3, 1986, pp. 10–11, and March 17, 1986, p. 7.

clause of the Fourteenth Amendment was limited to correcting actions by states in their official acts; thus the discriminatory acts of private citizens were not illegal ("Individual invasion of individual rights is not the subject matter of the Amendment"). The 1883 Supreme Court decision met with widespread approval throughout most of the United States. Twenty years after the Civil War, the nation was all too willing to forget about the condition of blacks in the prewar South. The other civil rights laws that the Court specifically did not invalidate became dead letters in the statute books, although they were never repealed by Congress.

Plessy v. Ferguson: Separate but Equal

A key decision during this period involved Homer Plessy, a Louisiana resident who was one-eighth black. In 1892, he was riding in a train from New Orleans when the conductor made him leave the car, which was restricted to whites, and directed him to a car for nonwhites. At that time, Louisiana had a statute providing for separate railway cars for whites and blacks.

Plessy went to court, claiming that such a statute was contrary to the Fourteenth Amendment's equal protection of the laws clause. In 1896, the U.S. Supreme Court rejected Plessy's contention, indicating that segregation alone did not violate the Constitution: "Laws permitting, and even requiring their separation in places where they are liable to be brought into contact do not necessarily imply the inferiority of either race to the other."[4] So was born the **separate but equal doctrine.**

For more than half a century, the separate but equal doctrine was accepted as consistent with the equal protection of the laws clause in the Fourteenth Amendment. In practical terms, the separate but equal doctrine effectively nullified this clause. *Plessy v. Ferguson* became the constitutional cornerstone of racial discrimination throughout the United States. Even though *Plessy* upheld segregated facilities in railway cars only, it was assumed that the Supreme Court was upholding segregation everywhere as long as the separate facilities were equal. The result was

Separate but Equal Doctrine
The doctrine holding that segregation in schools and public accommodations does not imply the superiority of one race over another; rather, it implies that each race is entitled to separate but equal facilities.

[4]*Plessy v. Ferguson*, 163 U.S. 537 (1896).

a system of racial segregation, particularly in the South, which required separate drinking fountains, separate seats in theaters, restaurants, and hotels, separate public toilets, and separate waiting rooms for the two races—collectively known as Jim Crow laws.

The End of the Separate but Equal Doctrine

The *Plessy* decision withstood attack by the National Association for the Advancement of Colored People (NAACP), formed in 1909, for nearly half a century. Then, in 1951, Oliver Brown decided that his eight-year-old daughter, Linda Carol, should not have to go to an all-black elementary school, twenty-one blocks from her home when there was a white school only seven blocks away. The NAACP decided to help Oliver Brown, and the results were monumental in their impact on American society. Actually, there was a series of cases, first argued in 1952, contesting state laws permitting or requiring the establishment of separate school facilities based on race. Following the death of Chief Justice Frederick M. Vinson and his replacement by Earl Warren, the Court asked for rearguments.

Brown v. Board of Education

The 1954 unanimous decision in *Brown v. Board of Education of Topeka*[5] established that public school segregation of races violates the equal protection clause of the Fourteenth Amendment. Chief Justice Warren stated that "to separate [blacks] from others of similar age and qualifications solely because of their race generates a feeling of inferiority as to their status in the community that may affect their hearts and minds in a way unlikely ever to be undone." In other words, Warren said that separation implied inferiority, whereas the majority opinion in *Plessy v. Ferguson* had said the opposite. Legal purists still argue with the sociological rather than strictly legal criteria of the *Brown* decision.

Jim Crow laws resulted in the segregation of public facilities, such as this theater.

"With All Deliberate Speed"

The following year, in *Brown v. Board of Education*[6] (sometimes called the second *Brown* decision), the Court asked for rearguments concerning the way in which compliance with the 1954 decision should be undertaken. The Supreme Court declared that the lower courts must ensure that blacks would be admitted to schools on a nondiscriminatory basis "with all deliberate speed." In other words, the high court told lower federal courts that they had to take an activist role in society. The district courts were to consider devices in their desegregation orders that might include "the school transportation system, personnel, [and] revision of school districts and attendance areas into compact units to achieve a system of determining admission to the public schools on a nonracial basis."

Reactions to School Integration

One unlooked-for effect of the "all deliberate speed" decision was that the term *deliberate* was used as a loophole by some jurists who were able to delay deseg-

[5]347 U.S. 483 (1954).
[6]349 U.S. 294 (1955).

regation by showing that they were indeed acting with all deliberate speed but still were unable to desegregate. Another reaction to court-ordered desegregation was "white flight." In some school districts the public school population became 100 percent black when white parents sent their children to newly established private schools, sometimes known as "segregation academies."

The South was not about to let the Supreme Court ruling go unchallenged. Arkansas's Governor Orval Faubus used the state's National Guard to block the integration of Central High School in Little Rock, Arkansas, in September 1957. The federal court demanded that the troops be withdrawn. Finally, President Eisenhower had to nationalize the Arkansas National Guard to quell the violence. Central High became integrated.

The universities in the South, however, remained segregated. When James Meredith, a black student, attempted to enroll at the University of Mississippi in Oxford in 1962, violence flared there as it had in Little Rock. Two men were killed and a number injured in campus rioting. President John Kennedy sent federal marshals and ordered federal troops to maintain peace and protect Meredith. One year later, George Wallace, governor of Alabama, promised "to stand in the school-house door" to prevent two black students from enrolling at the University of Alabama in Tuscaloosa. Wallace was forced to back down when Kennedy federalized the Alabama National Guard.

James Meredith

The Controversy Continues: Busing

In most parts of the United States, school integration is made difficult by housing segregation. Although it is true that a number of school boards in northern districts created segregated schools by the arbitrary drawing of school district lines, the concentration of blacks and other minorities in well-defined geographical locations was the reason for the **de facto segregation** of northern public schools. Whether segregation was de facto or **de jure segregation,** the obvious solution seemed to be

De Facto Segregation

Racial segregation that occurs not as a result of deliberate intentions but because of past social and economic conditions and residential patterns.

De Jure Segregation

Racial segregation that occurs because of laws or administrative decisions by public agencies.

Little Rock Central High School.

Busing

The transportation of public school students from areas where they live to schools in other areas to eliminate school segregation based on residential patterns.

the transporting of some black schoolchildren to white schools and some white schoolchildren to black schools. Increasingly, the courts ordered school districts to engage in such **busing** across neighborhoods. Busing led to violence in some northern cities, as in south Boston where black students were bused into blue-collar Irish Catholic neighborhoods.

Busing is unpopular with all groups. In the mid-1970s, almost 50 percent of the blacks interviewed were opposed to busing and approximately three-fourths of the whites interviewed held the same opinion.[7] Nonetheless, the Supreme Court has upheld a number of busing plans. In 1971, the Court upheld the right of judges to order school busing in the case of *Swann v. Charlotte–Mecklenburg Board of Education*.[8] Two years later in *Keyes v. School District No. 1*,[9] the Court ruled that the Denver school board had intentionally segregated a significant number of students. The Court determined that the Denver school had to completely desegregate the school system. The Keyes decision was reaffirmed in 1979 when the Court upheld crosstown busing plans in Dayton and Columbus, Ohio.[10]

In an apparent reversal of previous decisions, the Supreme Court in June 1986 allowed the Norfolk, Virginia, public school system to end fifteen years of court-

[7]Diane Ravitch, "Busing: The Solution That Has Failed to Solve," *New York Times*, December 21, 1975, Section 4, p. 3.

[8]402 U.S. 1 (1971).

[9]413 U.S. 189 (1973).

[10]*Dayton Board of Education v. Brinkman*, 443 U.S. 526 (1979), and *Columbus Board of Education v. Penick*, 443 U.S. 449 (1979).

Busing in Boston.

ordered busing of elementary schoolchildren.[11] Starting in the fall of 1986, the Norfolk schools were allowed to assign children to schools in their neighborhoods, even though ten of the city's thirty-five elementary schools would become 97 to 100 percent black. The Norfolk school board supported the decision. Its support was prompted by a drop from 32,500 whites attending public schools in 1970 when busing was ordered to less than 14,000 in 1985.

The Civil Rights Movement

▽

The *Brown* decision applied only to public schools. Not much else of the structure of existing segregation was affected. In December 1955, a forty-three-year-old black woman, Rosa Parks, boarded a public bus in Montgomery, Alabama. When it became crowded and several white people stepped aboard, she was asked to move to the rear of the bus. She refused, was arrested, and was fined $10; but that was not the end of the matter. For an entire year blacks boycotted the Montgomery bus line. The protest was headed by a twenty-seven-year-old Baptist minister, Dr. Martin Luther King, Jr. During the protest period, he went to jail;[12] his house was bombed. But in the face of overwhelming odds, King won. In 1956, the district federal court issued an injunction prohibiting the segregation of buses in Montgomery. The era of civil rights protests had begun.

The following year, Martin Luther King formed the Southern Christian Leadership Conference (SCLC). King's philosophy of nonviolent civil disobedience was influenced greatly by Mahatma Gandhi's life and teachings. For the next decade, blacks and sympathetic whites engaged in sit-ins, freedom rides, and freedom marches. In the beginning such demonstrations were often met with violence. When blacks in Greensboro, North Carolina, were refused service at a Woolworth's lunch counter, they organized a sit-in that was aided day after day by sympathetic whites and blacks. Enraged customers threw ketchup on the protestors. Some spat in their faces. But the sit-in movement continued to grow. Within six months of the first sit-in at the Greensboro Woolworth's, hundreds of lunch counters throughout the South were serving blacks.

The sit-in technique was also successfully used to integrate interstate buses and their terminals, as well as railroads engaged in interstate transportation. Although buses and railroads that were engaged in interstate transportation were prohibited from segregating blacks from whites,[13] they only stopped doing so after the sit-in protests.

The civil rights movement, with King at its head, gathered momentum in the 1960s. One of the most famous of the violence-plagued protests occurred in Birmingham, Alabama, in the spring of 1963, when Police Commissioner Eugene "Bull" Connor unleashed police dogs and used electric cattle prods against the protestors. People throughout the country viewed the event on national TV with indignation and horror, and such media coverage played a key role in the process of ending Jim Crow conditions in the United States. The ultimate result was the most important civil rights act in the nation's history, passed in 1964.

In August 1963, Dr. Martin Luther King, Jr., organized a massive March on

[11]Riddick v. School Board of City of Norfolk, 627 F.Supp. 814, injunction denied 106 S.Ct. (1986).

[12]Read his "Letter from the Birmingham Jail" for a better understanding of this period.

[13]See *Morgan v. Commonwealth of Virginia*, 328 U.S. 373 (1946); and *Henderson v. United States*, 339 U.S. 819 (1950).

Highlight

△

"I Have a Dream"

On August 28, 1963, in the centennial year of the Emancipation Proclamation, a long-planned mass mobilization of civil rights supporters took place in the March on Washington for Jobs and Freedom. The march, attended by perhaps 250,000 black and white men and women, was a major event in the civil rights movement and in the leadership of Martin Luther King, Jr., head of the Southern Christian Leadership Conference. The March on Washington helped to generate a political momentum that resulted in the landmark civil rights legislation of 1964 and 1968, and it also propelled Atlanta Baptist minister King to the forefront of the civil rights movement.

Local school bands provided early entertainment for the crowd gathered at the Washington monument marshaling grounds. Joan Baez sang the anthem of the civil rights movement, "We Shall Overcome," and the mood was further enhanced by the songs of Peter, Paul, and Mary and the resounding voice of Odetta. Several minutes before the scheduled 11:30 A.M. starting time for the march to the Lincoln Memorial, the marchers set out behind the Kenilworth Knights, a local drum and bugle corps. The crowd moved too quickly for its leaders, who rushed to keep up with the marchers while marshals and news reporters tried to slow the human flow along Constitution and Independence Avenues.

At the Lincoln Memorial, more entertainers performed for the crowd massed around the reflecting pool and near the memorial steps. Performances of Bobby Darin, Josh White, Bob Dylan, Marian Anderson, Lena Horne, Mahalia Jackson, and others were interspersed with speeches by author James Baldwin, actors Paul Newman, Charlton Heston, Burt Lancaster, Sidney Poitier, Marlon Brando, Sammy Davis, Jr., and Harry Belafonte, Nobel Prize-winner Dr. Ralph Bunche, and sports greats Jackie Robinson and Wilt Chamberlain.

The day's program included speeches by civil rights leaders John Lewis, Roy Wilkins, A. Philip Randolph, and Martin Luther King, Jr. The jobs, education, and antidiscrimination programs called for by earlier speakers were summarized in Dr. King's words:

There will be neither rest nor tranquility in America until the Negro is granted his citizenship rights. The whirlwinds of revolt will continue to shake the foundations of our nation until the bright day of justice emerges. . . . I have a dream that my four little children will one day live in a nation where they will not be judged by the color of their skin but by the content of their character. . . . When we let freedom ring, when we let it ring from every village and every hamlet, from every state and every city, we will be able to speed up that day when all God's children, black men and white men, Jews and Gentiles, Protestants and Catholics, will be able to join hands and sing in the words of that old Negro spiritual, "Free at last! Free at last! Thank God almighty, we are free at last!"

The contribution of Martin Luther King, Jr. to minority rights was officially recognized on October 20, 1983, when President Reagan signed into law an act establishing January 15, Martin Luther King, Jr.'s birthday, as a national holiday beginning in 1986, after originally opposing the legislation.

SOURCES: David L. Lewis, *King: A Critical Biography* (New York: Praeger, 1970), pp. 210–232. Lenwood G. Davis, *I Have a Dream . . . : The Life and Times of Martin Luther King, Jr.* (Westport, Conn.: Negro Universities Press, 1969), pp. 132–140.

Washington for Jobs and Freedom. Before a quarter-million white and black Americans and millions watching on TV, Dr. King gave the world his dream (see Highlight). King's dream was not to be realized immediately. Eighteen days after his famous speech, four black girls attending Bible class in the basement room of the Sixteenth Street Baptist Church in Birmingham, Alabama, were killed by a bomb explosion.

Police dog attacks, cattle prods, high-pressure water hoses, beatings, bombings, and the March on Washington—all of these events led to an environment in which Congress had to act on behalf of blacks in America. So came the second era of civil rights acts, the so-called Second Reconstruction period.

1960s Civil Rights Legislation and Its Implementation

▽

In the wake of the Montgomery bus boycott, public sentiment for stronger civil rights legislation put pressure on Congress and President Dwight David Eisenhower to act. The action taken was relatively symbolic. The Civil Rights Act of 1957 established a Civil Rights Commission and a new Civil Rights Division within the Justice Department. (President Reagan tried to abolish the Commission in 1983; Congress extended its life for another twenty years, after working out a compromise by which the president and congressional leaders would select its members.)

The growing number of demonstrations and sit-ins successfully created further pressure for more legislation through the classic democratic politics of mobilization of public opinion, coordinated with lobbying of political leaders. The Civil Rights

> ## Did You Know?
> ▽
> That during the 1964 Mississippi Summer Project, organized by students to register black voters, there were 1,000 arrests, 35 shooting incidents, 30 buildings bombed, 25 churches burned, 80 people beaten, and at least 6 murders?

The march to Montgomery.

Act of 1960 was passed to protect voting rights. Whenever a pattern or practice of discrimination was documented, the Justice Department, on behalf of the voter, could bring suit even against a state. The act also set penalties for obstructing a federal court order by threat of force and for illegally using and transporting explosives. But the 1960 Civil Rights Act, as well as that of 1957, had little substantive impact.

The same cannot be said about the Civil Rights Acts of 1964 and 1968 and the Voting Rights Act of 1965. Those acts marked the reassumption by Congress of a leading role in the enforcement of the constitutional notion of equality, for *all* Americans, as provided by the Fourteenth and Fifteenth Amendments.

The Civil Rights Act of 1964

As the civil rights movement mounted in intensity, equality before the law came to be "an idea whose time has come," in the words of conservative Senate Minority Leader Everett Dirksen. The 1964 legislation, the most far-reaching bill on civil rights in modern times, forbade discrimination on the basis of race, color, religion, and national origin and barred discrimination in employment on the basis of sex.

The major provisions of the act are as follows:

1. It outlawed arbitrary discrimination in voter registration.
2. It barred discrimination in public accommodations, like hotels and restaurants, whose operations affect interstate commerce.
3. It authorized the federal government to sue to desegregate public schools and facilities.
4. It expanded the power of the Civil Rights Commission while extending its life.
5. It provided for the withholding of federal funds from programs administered in a discriminatory manner.
6. It established the right to equality of opportunity in employment.

Discrimination in housing was not covered by the 1964 act.

Several factors led to the passage of the 1964 act. As we noted, there had been a dramatic change in the climate of public opinion owing to violence perpetrated against protesting blacks and whites in the South. Second, the assassination of President John F. Kennedy in 1963 had, according to some, a significant effect on the national conscience. Many believed the civil rights program to be the legislative tribute that Congress paid to the martyred Kennedy. Finally, the 1964 act could be seen partly as the result of President Lyndon B. Johnson's vigorous espousal of the legislation after his gradual conversion to the civil rights cause.

The act was passed in Congress only after the longest filibuster in the history of the Senate (eighty-three days) and only after cloture was imposed for the first time to cut off a civil rights filibuster.

The Civil Rights Act of 1968

Martin Luther King, Jr. was assassinated on April 4, 1968. Nine days after King's death, President Johnson signed the Civil Rights Act of 1968, which forbade discrimination in most housing and provided penalties for those attempting to interfere with individual civil rights, giving protection to civil rights workers, among others. Although the open-housing provision seemed important at the time, it was made obsolete by that summer when the Supreme Court prohibited discrimination in the sale and rental of all housing, using as a precedent the Civil Rights Act of April 9, 1866.[14] The Court held that Section 1 of the earlier act contains a broad prohibition against any racial discrimination in the sale or rental of property. It therefore forbids private development companies from refusing to rent to an individual simply because she or he is black. The Court noted that racial discrimination "herds men into ghettos and makes their ability to buy property turn on the color of their skin."

Employment and Affirmative Action

Title VII of the Civil Rights Act of 1964 is the cornerstone of employment discrimination law, prohibiting discrimination in employment based on race, color, religion, sex, or national origin. Under Title VII, executive orders were issued that banned employment discrimination by firms that received any federal funding. The 1964 Civil Rights Act created a five-member commission, the **Equal Employment Opportunity Commission (EEOC)**, to administer Title VII.

The EEOC can issue interpretive guidelines and regulations, but these do not have the force of law. Rather, they give notice of the commission's enforcement policy. The EEOC also has investigatory powers: It has broad authority to require the production of documentary evidence, to hold hearings, and to **subpoena** and examine witnesses under oath.

To put teeth in the 1964 law, President Johnson applied the concept of **affirmative action** in 1965. Affirmative action can be defined as remedial steps taken to improve work opportunities for women, racial and ethnic minorities, and other persons considered to have been deprived of job opportunities in the past on the basis of other than work-related criteria.

Affirmative action has come to be embodied in a set of programs, some required by court action, some by national and state legislation, and some by administrative regulation. When a court finds specific discrimination by a particular employer or benefit giver, the offender is ordered to stop the discriminatory policy and take actions that set right previous wrongs.

Reverse Discrimination: Backlash

By the early 1970s, Labor Department regulations imposing numerical employment goals and timetables had been applied to every company that did more than $10,000 worth of business of any sort with the national government. Affirmative action plans were also required whenever an employer had been ordered to develop such a plan by a court or by the EEOC because of past discrimination. Finally, labor unions that had been found to discriminate against women or minorities were required to follow affirmative action plans.

Affirmative action plans were seen to have a negative impact on whites, especially white males, and began to be challenged in the courts. In *McDonald v. Santa Fe Trail Transportation Company*,[15] in 1976, the Supreme Court stated that "Title VII [of the 1964 Civil Rights Act] prohibits racial discrimination against the white petitioners upon the standards as would be applicable were they Negroes." Several

Equal Employment Opportunity Commission (EEOC)

A commission established by the 1964 Civil Rights Act to (1) end discrimination based on race, color, religion, sex, or national origin in conditions of employment and (2) promote voluntary action programs by employers, unions, and community organizations to foster equal job opportunities.

Subpoena

A legal writ requiring a person's appearance in court to give testimony.

Affirmative Action

Policies issued in job hiring that give special consideration or compensatory treatment to traditionally disadvantaged groups in an effort to overcome present effects of past discrimination.

[14]*Jones v. Mayer*, 329 U.S. 409 (1968).
[15]427 U.S. 273 (1976).

Even though the federal government has pursued a policy of affirmative action, the general public has consistently opposed such plans. Here we show the results of a Gallup Poll survey in 1984. These results differ very little from similar surveys done in 1980 and 1977. Nationally, only 10 percent of those interviewed favored preferential treatment of women and minorities over ability as a criterion for employment and college admission. Remarkably, even among women, 84 percent chose ability. Even more surprisingly, minority persons for whom the affirmative action policy was clearly designed supported ability over preferential treatment, although by a smaller margin than among women.

QUESTION: "Some people say that to make up for past discrimination, women and members of minority groups should be given preferential treatment in getting jobs and places in colleges. Others say that ability, as determined by test scores, should be the main consideration. Which point of view comes closer to how you feel on this subject?"

	Preferential Treatment	Ability	No Opinion
National	10%	84%	6%
Sex			
Men	9	85	6
Women	11	84	5
Race			
Whites	8	87	5
Nonwhites	27	64	9
Blacks	28	63	9
Hispanics	17	75	8
Education			
College graduates	11	86	3
College incomplete	9	87	4
H.S. graduates	7	89	4
Less than H.S. graduates	14	75	11

employees had misappropriated the property of the Santa Fe Trail Transportation Company. Although the white employees were discharged, the black employees were reinstated. The issue of voluntary affirmative action programs was not, however, addressed in the *Santa Fe* case.

The Bakke Case

Alan Bakke, a Vietnam veteran and engineer who had been turned down for medical school at the Davis campus of the University of California, discovered that his academic record was better than some of the minority applicants who had been admitted to the program. He sued the University of California regents, alleging **reverse discrimination**. The Davis medical school had held sixteen places out of one hundred for educationally "disadvantaged students" each year, and the administrators at that campus admitted to using race as a criterion for admission for these particular minority slots. At trial in 1974, Bakke said that his exclusion from medical school violated his rights under the Fourteenth Amendment's provision for equal protection of the laws. The trial court agreed. On appeal, the California supreme court agreed also. Finally, the regents of the university appealed to the U.S. Supreme Court.

Reverse Discrimination

The charge that affirmative action programs requiring preferential treatment or quotas discriminate against those who have no minority status.

On June 28, 1978, the Supreme Court handed down its decision in *Regents of the University of California v. Bakke.*[16] The Court did not actually rule against affirmative action programs but did hold that Bakke must be admitted to the UC Davis Medical School because its admission policy had used race as the *sole* criterion for the sixteen "minority" positions. But Justice Lewis Powell, speaking for the Court, indicated that race can be considered "as a factor" among others in admissions (and presumably hiring) decisions. In other words, it is legal to give special consideration to "afflicted minority groups" in an effort to remedy past discrimination. Race can be one of many criteria for admission, but not the only one. So affirmative action programs were upheld as constitutional, but not if they were carried out as they had been at the UC-Davis Medical School.

The Weber Case

In 1979, the issue of reverse discrimination in employment was addressed in *United Steelworkers of America, AFL-CIO-CLC v. Weber.*[17] The lower courts in that case had relied on the *Santa Fe* decision mentioned earlier and on Section 703(j) of the Civil Rights Act of 1964.

Using the language of *Santa Fe* and Section 703(j) as a basis for their decisions, the district court and the court of appeals held that the use of a racial quota to staff an apprenticeship program violated Title VII. What was at issue was Brian F. Weber's complaint that as a white employee in Kaiser Aluminum and Chemical Corporation's plant in Gramercy, Louisiana, he was denied his rightful place in a training program that would have raised his salary had he successfully completed it. Because of the affirmative action program in his union, he was passed over in favor of blacks with less seniority.

Even though the lower courts held in his favor, in 1979 the Supreme Court reversed their decisions. The Court stated that the prohibition against racial discrimination in Title VII must be read against the background of the legislative history of Title VII calling for voluntary or local resolution of the discrimination problems and against the historical context from which the 1964 Civil Rights Act arose.

In other words, the union apprenticeship program at Kaiser Aluminum violated the words of the Civil Rights Act of 1964, but not the spirit. Essentially, any form of reverse discrimination—even explicit quotas—is permissible provided that it is the result of a legislative, executive, or judicial finding of past discrimination.

Brian F. Weber

The Court's Most Recent Record on Reverse Bias

In 1984, in *Firefighters Local v. Stotts,*[18] the Supreme Court said that the layoffs of Memphis firefighters had to go by seniority unless there were black employees who could prove they were victims of racial bias. But in 1986, in *Wygant v. Jackson Board of Education,*[19] the highest court sent the signal that affirmative action could apply to hiring, but not to layoffs. This mixed message involved a case brought by a group of white teachers in Jackson, Michigan, challenging a labor contract that

[16]438 U.S. 265 (1978).
[17]443 U.S. 1963 (1979).
[18]467 U.S. 561 (1984).
[19]106 S.Ct. 1842 (1986).

Integrated firefighting unit in Atlanta.

called for laying off three white teachers for every faculty member belonging to a minority group in order to preserve the school system's racial and ethnic ratios. In a 5–4 vote, the Court's majority said that the Jackson plan violated the Fourteenth Amendment's guarantee of equal protection of the laws. This is the first time that the Reconstruction-era provision had been extended to white plaintiffs. This ruling has the effect of forcing state and local governments to reexamine whether their affirmative action plans for both hiring as well as layoffs are drafted carefully enough to justify preferential treatment for minorities.

In spite of the apparent weakening of affirmative action plans, the Court's actual written decision seemed to repudiate the Reagan administration's attempts to curb the use of numerical goals or quotas. Even though private employees were not affected by the *Wygant* decision (the Fourteenth Amendment applies to actions of state and local governments), the Court's view of the constitutionality of affirmative action in the public sector has in the past shaped its decisions for the private sector.

The Voting Rights Act of 1965

▽

The Fourteenth Amendment provided for equal protection of the laws. The Fifteenth Amendment, ratified on February 3, 1870, stated that "the right of citizens in the United States to vote shall not be denied or abridged by the United States or by any state on account of race, color, or previous condition of servitude." Immediately after the adoption of those amendments, blacks in the South began to participate in political life—but only because of the presence of federal government troops and northern Radical Republicans who controlled the state legislatures.

Historical Barriers to Black Political Participation

But this brief enfranchisement ended after 1877 when southern Democrats regained control of state governments. Social pressure, threats of violence, and the terrorist

TO MONTGOMERY FOR FREEDOM

▽

148

tactics of the Ku Klux Klan combined to dissuade blacks from voting. Southern politicians, using everything except race as a formal criterion, passed laws that effectively deprived blacks of the right to vote.

This was the era of the **white primary** and the "**grandfather clause.**" By using the ruse that political party primaries were private, southern whites were allowed to exclude blacks. The Supreme Court in *Grovey v. Townsend*[20] upheld such exclusion. Indeed, it was not until 1944 in *Smith v. Allwright*[21] that the highest court finally found the white primary to be a violation of the Fifteenth Amendment. The Court reasoned that the political party was actually performing a state function in holding a primary election, not acting as a private group. By being denied a vote in the primary, blacks had been prevented from participating in the selection of public officials from the end of Reconstruction until World War II. The grandfather clause allowed the voting franchise only to those who could prove that their grandfather had voted before 1867. Most blacks were automatically disenfranchised by this provision.

Another device to prevent blacks from voting was the **poll tax,** requiring the payment of a fee to vote. This practice assured the exclusion of poor blacks from the political process. It wasn't until the passage of the Twenty-fourth Amendment, ratified in 1964, that the poll tax as a precondition to voting was eliminated. That amendment, however, applied only to federal elections. In *Harper v. Virginia State Board of Elections,*[22] the Supreme Court declared that the payment of any poll tax as a condition for voting in any election is unconstitutional.

Actually, the poll tax had reduced the voting participation of both whites and blacks in five southern states, but it worked a greater hardship on blacks because there were more poor blacks than whites. Also, the poll tax was unequally enforced among whites and blacks. The result was that poll tax states had turnouts in national elections equal to about 50 percent of those in states not having poll taxes.

One of the more subtle devices used in the South to prevent blacks from voting was the literacy test. Literacy tests, introduced during the second half of the nineteenth century, asked potential voters to interpret (not just read) complicated texts, such as sections of the state constitution, to the satisfaction of local registrars. Voters were sometimes asked to recite from memory parts of the Constitution. At times, prospective voters even had to pass "good character" tests! It is not surprising that even as late as 1960, only 29.1 percent of blacks of voting age were registered in the southern states, in stark contrast to 61.1 percent of whites.

In 1965, Martin Luther King, Jr. took action to change all that. Selma, the county seat of Dallas County, Alabama, was chosen as the site to dramatize the voting rights problem. In Dallas County, only 2 percent of eligible blacks had registered to vote by the beginning of 1965. King organized a fifty-mile march from Selma to the state capital in Montgomery. He didn't get very far. Acting on orders of Governor George Wallace to disband the marchers, state troopers did so with a vengeance—with tear gas, night sticks, and whips.

Once again the national government was required to intervene to force compliance with the law. President Johnson federalized the National Guard and the march continued. During the march, the president went on television to address a special joint session of Congress urging passage of new legislation to assure blacks the right to vote. The events during the Selma march and Johnson's dramatic

Ku Klux Klan cross burning.

White Primary

State primary elections that restrict voting only to whites; outlawed by the Supreme Court in 1944.

Grandfather Clause

A device used by southern states to exempt whites from state taxes and literacy laws originally intended to disenfranchise black voters. It allowed the voting franchise to anyone who could prove that his grandfather had voted before 1867.

Poll Tax

A special tax that must be paid as a qualification for voting. The Twenty-fourth Amendment to the Constitution outlawed the poll tax in national elections, and in 1966 the Supreme Court declared it unconstitutional in all elections.

[20]295 U.S. 45 (1935).
[21]321 U.S. 649 (1944).
[22]383 U.S. 663 (1966).

Richard Hatcher, mayor of Gary, Indiana.

Black voter registration.

speech, wherein he invoked the slogan of the civil rights movement ("We shall overcome"), were credited for the swift passage of the Voting Rights Act of 1965.

Provisions of the Act

The act had two major provisions. The first one outlawed discriminatory voter registration tests like the frequently used literacy test. The second major section authorized federal registration of persons and federally administered voting procedures in any political subdivision or state that discriminated electorally against a particular group.[23] Within one week after the act was passed, forty-five federal examiners were sent to the South. A massive voter registration drive covered the country.

The Voting Rights Act of 1965 was extended to August 1975 in 1970. In 1975, Congress extended the act to August 1982 and it was again extended in 1983. Both in 1970 and in 1975, the law was extended to other states and to other groups, including Spanish-speaking Americans, Asians, and Native Americans, including Alaskan natives. As a result of this act and its extensions and of the large-scale voter registration drives in the South, the number of blacks registered to vote climbed dramatically, until by 1980 55.8 percent of blacks of voting age in the South were registered.

By 1986 the number of registered black voters was more than 11 million. In that same year, there was a total of more than 5,000 black elected officials, including 18 at the national level, 336 at the state level, 2,977 at the local level, 563 in the judiciary, and 1,266 in various local school districts. Many of the largest cities in the United States have black mayors: Chicago, Los Angeles, Philadelphia, and Detroit. In 1984, the Reverend Jesse Jackson became the first black candidate to compete seriously for the Democratic presidential nomination. A renewed effort to register thousands more black and other minority voters helped Jackson achieve an impressive 12 percent of the total primary vote.

[23]In addition, the act indicated that in Congress's opinion the state poll tax was unconstitutional.

Best known as the wife of slain civil rights leader Martin Luther King, Jr., Coretta Scott King was originally interested in a musical career. She studied voice with Metropolitan Opera star Marie Sundelius after receiving her Bachelor of Music degree from the New England Conservatory of Music in 1954.

Coretta Scott King had become an activist in the equal rights movement even before her husband's death. Indeed, she has more than forty years' experience in numerous organizations working for peace and equality. She has amassed an outstanding number of awards in the last twenty-five years, including honorary degrees from a dozen universities, the 1968 Wateler Peace Prize, the 1969 Dag Hammarskjold Award, and the 1971 Leadership for Freedom Award from Roosevelt University.

"Let us continue to dream big dreams and go out and work to fulfill them."

Much of Mrs. King's life was lived under threat of physical harm. During the Montgomery bus boycott of 1956,

she and her husband received constant obscene phone calls and threatening notes. When Mrs. King and her daughter were inside their house, a bomb was thrown onto their front porch, destroying part of the building.

At the August 29, 1983, twentieth anniversary celebration of Martin Luther King's famous "I have a dream" speech, Mrs. King told the crowd, "We still have a dream. We are all here to reaffirm our commitment to peace, justice, brotherhood, and equality. We gather today in nonviolent solidarity."

Hispanics in American Society
▽

The second largest minority group in America can be classified loosely as Hispanics—or individuals of Spanish-speaking background. Even though this minority group represents about 6.5 percent of the American population, its diversity and geographical dispersion have hindered its ability to achieve political power, particularly at the national level. Table 5–4 shows the size of the Hispanic population in the United States and its geographic distribution throughout the country. Clearly, Mexican Americans constitute the majority of the Hispanic population. Of the nearly fifteen million Hispanics in the United States, Mexican Americans number about nine million. The next largest group is the Puerto Ricans, then the Cubans, and finally Hispanics from Central and South America.

Mexican Americans

Mexicans were not brought to the colonies by force. Some of them were even in the southwestern territory of what eventually became the United States before the settlement of the eastern shores by the early English colonists. Indeed, Mexico

Table 5–4

▽

The Hispanic Population by State (1980)

The last national census in 1980 provides the state-by-state distribution of the Hispanic population. California leads the nation with 4.5 million Hispanics, followed by Texas with 3 million and New York with 1.6 million. Florida and Illinois are the two other states with significant Hispanic populations.

Alabama	33,000	Montana	10,000
Alaska	10,000	Nebraska	28,000
Arizona	441,000	Nevada	54,000
Arkansas	18,000	New Hampshire	6,000
California	4,544,000	New Jersey	492,000
Colorado	340,000	New Mexico	477,000
Connecticut	124,000	New York	1,659,000
Delaware	10,000	North Carolina	57,000
Florida	858,000	North Dakota	4,000
Georgia	61,000	Ohio	120,000
Hawaii	71,000	Oklahoma	57,000
Idaho	37,000	Oregon	66,000
Illinois	636,000	Pennsylvania	154,000
Indiana	87,000	Rhode Island	20,000
Iowa	26,000	South Carolina	33,000
Kansas	63,000	South Dakota	4,000
Kentucky	27,000	Tennessee	34,000
Louisiana	99,000	Texas	2,986,000
Maine	5,000	Utah	60,000
Maryland	65,000	Vermont	3,000
Massachusetts	141,000	Virginia	80,000
Michigan	162,000	Washington	120,000
Minnesota	32,000	West Virginia	13,000
Mississippi	25,000	Wisconsin	63,000
Missouri	52,000	Wyoming	24,000

formerly owned California as well as Arizona, New Mexico, Texas, Utah, and most of Colorado during the early 1800s. By 1853, these territories had all been acquired by the United States (by purchase or by war) and were settled mainly by Anglos. (It is interesting to note that the treaty ending the Mexican War in 1845 explicitly guaranteed all former citizens of Mexico then living in United States territory the same liberties, protections, and rights as any other American citizens.)

Mexicans, though, have continued to settle in the United States, immigrating to this country primarily for economic reasons. Even today, in spite of Mexico's spurt of economic growth, per capita income there was only $2,130 in 1980 compared with $9,511 in the United States. Most Mexican Americans still live in the southwestern United States, but many have moved to Indiana, Illinois, Pennsylvania, and Ohio.

Political Participation

Mexican Americans have a very low level of political participation in national elections. In 1983, only 58 percent of Mexican Americans were registered to vote compared with 74 percent of Anglos. Mexican Americans have faced numerous barriers to voting, as have blacks, not the least of which is the language barrier for those unable to read English. The Voting Rights Act extension of 1970 alleviated this problem somewhat by requiring ballots to be printed in both English and Spanish in districts where at least 5 percent of the registered voters are Spanish speaking. In 1984, the Southwest Voter Registration Project tried to mobilize Hispanics as a group by registering them to vote. It had only modest success.

Mexican Americans have also had little success in sending their own representatives to Congress. In 1976, the Hispanic caucus in the House of Representatives consisted of five people—a California Mexican American, two Texan Mexican Americans, the resident commissioner from Puerto Rico, and a Puerto Rican from New York City. In the Hundredth Congress in 1987, the number of Hispanics had risen to fourteen.

Political Organizations

Mexican Americans have not, however, let the American political process pass them by. As far back as 1921, the Orden Hijos de America (Sons of America) was

Did You Know?
▽

That in 1963 there were more than ten thousand demonstrations for racial equality?

formed in San Antonio, Texas. Eight years later, in Corpus Christi, the League of United Latin American Citizens (LULAC) was established. Its goal, then and now, is to facilitate Hispanics integration into American culture using English as the primary language tool. Through numerous court battles LULAC succeeded in removing discriminatory barriers in public facilities, education, and employment in the Southwest for Hispanics.

In the 1960s, the Political Association of Spanish Speaking Organizations (PASO) in Texas, the Mexican American Political Association (MAPA) in California, and the American Coordinating Council on Political Education (ACCPE) entered numerous local political contests to elect Mexican Americans. They did not engage in economic or social struggles, however, viewing such struggles as nonpolitical.

Mexican Americans have not been uniformly in favor of downplaying social and economic inequalities. One of those with different views is Cesar Chavez.

In 1962, in California, Chavez began organizing farm workers into the United Farm Workers and started a five-year strike against Central California grape growers to force them to recognize the union. The UFW organized a nationwide boycott of table grapes. Many responded out of sympathy with the strikers, who called their movement "La Causa." By 1975, Chavez and the UFW had convinced the California legislature to pass a bill that gave farm workers the same rights held by union members elsewhere.

Among the more controversial and well-publicized developments within the Mexican American, or Chicano, movement was the La Raza Unida Party (LRUP). La Raza Unida grew out of the first Chicano National Youth Movement meeting in Colorado in 1968. Chicanos, in forming La Raza Unida, hoped to show Anglo politicians that they were no longer dependent on them. They also desired to make the Chicano community aware of the possibilities of making change. The uniqueness of La Raza Unida lay in its being more than a political party. It was designed as "an ethnic institution that will break the cycle of Chicano repression by a variety of organizational efforts. La Raza Unida is not a vehicle for entering the mainstream of United States society, but is a safeguard for the Mexican American bilingual/bicultural uniqueness."[24] LRUP had some success in Colorado, Arizona, California, and New Mexico, as well as in Texas. Today it is not as active as it was in the 1970s.

Puerto Ricans

Because Puerto Rico is a U.S. Commonwealth, its inhabitants are American citizens. As such, they may freely move between Puerto Rico and the United States. Most of them who come to the continental United States reside in the New York-New Jersey area.

In Puerto Rico, Puerto Ricans use U.S. currency, U.S. mails, and U.S. courts. In Puerto Rico, they are also eligible for U.S. welfare benefits and food stamps, but they pay no federal taxes unless they move to the continental United States. By the late 1970s, almost three-fourths of Puerto Ricans living in Puerto Rico were eligible for food stamps. Those who come to the mainland do not fare much better, because they face economic and language barriers and racial discrimination.

Puerto Ricans have had few political successes on the mainland. There are more than a million Puerto Ricans living in New York City, constituting at least 10

[24]Matt S. Meyer and Feliciano Rivera, *The Chicanos* (New York: Hill and Wang, 1972), p. 277.

percent of the city's population. But only about 30 percent are registered to vote. Other dispiriting statistics show that there are currently only a few Puerto Rican city council members and only one Puerto Rican member of Congress. In New York City's massive bureaucracy, only a small percentage of the administrators are Puerto Rican.

Cuban Americans

Unlike their Hispanic brothers and sisters from Mexico and Puerto Rico, Cuban Americans chose to come to the United States for political, as well as economic, reasons. Many of the emigrés came from the educated middle class, and although they had to leave most of their financial assets behind, their education and training helped them to establish themselves economically with relative ease. In Miami, for example, there are numerous examples of former Cuban professionals who started out as taxi drivers and today own banks, retail stores, and law practices.

In 1980, President Carter allowed more than 150,000 Cubans to enter Florida through the so-called Mariel boatlift. This latest wave of Cuban immigrants were mostly lower class and unskilled. A thousand of them had been released from Cuban prisons and mental institutions. Their ability to be assimilated into even the heavily Latin-accented culture of Miami was noticeably less than that of their earlier compatriots.

A majority of Cuban Americans reside in southern Florida, although some live in New York City and elsewhere. Economically, they constitute a major force in the southern Florida region. Politically, they have been very successful in gaining power within city and county governments, and their political influence will certainly rise as their percentage of the population increases. In particular, in Dade County, it is estimated that (in the not-too-distant future) Hispanics, particularly Cubans, will constitute the majority of the county's population.

Bilingual Education

All Hispanic groups are concerned about the preservation of their language and heritage. Bilingual education programs are supported by many Hispanic groups as a civil right. This claim was established by the Supreme Court in 1974 when it required a school district in California to provide special programs for Chinese students with language difficulties if there were a substantial number of these children.[25]

Native Americans: An American Tragedy

▽

When America was discovered, there were about ten million Native Americans, or "Indians," living in The New World. It is estimated that they inhabited areas from the north slope of Alaska to the southern tip of South America for at least thirty thousand years before Europeans arrived. By 1900, the number of Native Americans in the continental United States had declined to less than half a million owing to the effects of diseases brought to the continent by European immigrants.

[25]*Lau v. Nichols*, 414 U.S. 563 (1974).

Figure 5–2
▽

**Native American and White Family
Earnings Compared**

Percentage of Native American
and white families that earn --

Less than $5,000

16.0
5.6

$5,000-9,999

20.4
11.9

$10,000-19,999

32.0
29.6

$20,000-34,999

23.9
35.1

$35,000 or more

7.9
17.6

☐ = Native American families
☐ = White families

In the latest census, about 1.4 million individuals identified themselves as Indians. The five states with the largest Indian populations are Oklahoma, Arizona, California, New Mexico, and Alaska.

Economic and Social Status

Native Americans have not fared well economically, as is evident in Figure 5–2. From the point of view of health, Indians are even worse off than their economic status shows. Table 5–5 shows that the age-adjusted death rates per 100,000 of the population are two and sometimes three or more times the national average.

The Appropriation of Indian Lands

When the Continental Congress passed the Northwest Ordinance, it stated that "the utmost good faith shall always be observed towards the Indians; their lands and property shall never be taken from them without their consent; and their property rights, and liberty, they shall never be invaded or disturbed, unless in just and lawful wars authorized by Congress." In 1787, Congress designated the Indian tribes as foreign nations to enable the government to sign treaties with them about land and boundaries.

During the next hundred years, many agreements were made with the Indian tribes; however, many were broken by Congress, as well as by individuals who wanted Indian lands for settlement or exploration. In 1830, Congress instructed the Bureau of Indian Affairs to remove all Indian tribes to lands west of the Mississippi River to free the land east of the Mississippi for white settlement. From that time on, Indians who refused to be "removed" to whatever lands were designated for them were forcibly moved. With the passage of the Dawes Act (General Allotment Act) of 1887, the goal of Congress became the "assimilation" of Indians into American society. Each family was allotted acreage within the reservation to

A *Navajo reservation.*

farm, and the rest was sold to whites. The number of acres in reservation status was reduced from 140 million acres to about 47 million acres. Tribes that refused to cooperate with this plan lost their reservations altogether.

The U.S. Senate Subcommittee on Indian Education during the 1969 Congress issued its analysis of what had happened. The report declares:

> A careful review of the historical literature reveals that the dominant policy of the Federal Government toward the American Indian has been one of forced assimilation which has vacillated between the two extremes of coercion and persuasion. At the root of the assimilation policy has been a desire to divest the Indian of his land and resources.[26]

Native American Political Response

Native Americans have been relatively unsuccessful in garnering political power. In the 1960s, the National Indian Youth Council (NIYC) was the first group to become identified with Indian militancy. At the end of the 1960s, a small group of persons identifying themselves as Indians occupied Alcatraz Island, claiming that the island was part of their ancestral lands. In 1972, several hundred Indians marched to Washington and occupied the Bureau of Indian Affairs (BIA). They arrived in a caravan labeled "The Trail of Broken Treaties." In 1973, supporters of the American Indian Movement (AIM) took over Wounded Knee, South Dakota, which had been the site of the massacre of at least 150 Sioux Indians by the U.S. Army in 1890.[27] The goal of these demonstrations was to protest federal policy toward Native Americans.

The seige at Wounded Knee focused the anger of Native Americans on the BIA and the way their affairs were being administered by the agency. The American

[26]U.S. Senate, Subcommittee on Indian Education, *Indian Education: A National Tragedy—A National Challenge*, 91st Cong., 1st Sess. (1969), p. 9.

[27]This famous incident was the subject of Dee Brown's best-selling book, *Bury My Heart at Wounded Knee* (New York: Holt, Rinehart, and Winston), published two years earlier.

Table 5–5

▽

Native Americans: Age-Adjusted Death Rates per 100,000 Population, 1983

	Native Americans (including Alaskans)	All Races
Motor-vehicle accidents	44.6	18.5
All other accidents	38.3	16.8
Alcoholism	28.9	6.1
Homicide	16.4	8.6
Pneumonia, influenza	16.4	11.8
Diabetes	20.5	9.9
Suicide	14.7	11.4
Tuberculosis	3.3	0.5

SOURCE: Indian Health Service, Center for Disease Control, 1986.

▽

157

Highlight

▽
Skeletons in the Smithsonian's Closet

The Smithsonian Museum of Natural History in our nation's capital has large collections of just about everything relating to America's past. Among its collection are fourteen thousand American Indian skeletons. In 1986, an Indian rights organization called the American Indians against Desecration (AIAD) argued that the skeletons are the sacred remains of Indians' ancestors. After all, most of the five hundred or more recognized American Indian tribes believe that the burial place of deceased Indians is indeed a sacred site. The removal, display, and even study of Indian remains, they maintained, violates their religious beliefs and traditions—their civil liberties. AIAD and other groups have asked the Smithsonian to return the skeletons for proper burial. "They do not do this with any other race of people but the red man," said AIAD head Jan Hammill. "Can you imagine if they had dug up white Americans—Catholics, Jews, Protestants—and put them on display in the name of science? It would not be tolerated."*

The issue of Indian skeletons and Indian rights reflects the delicate balance among conflicting interests, beliefs, and rights. Responding to the demands and desires of American Indians, the Oklahoma State Museum recently returned all thirty-six Indian remains in its collections. These were buried at the famous Wounded Knee Cemetery in South Dakota. Other museums are considering similar actions.

*"The Skeletons in the Smithsonian's Closet," *The Washington Post*, National Weekly Edition, March 17, 1986, p. 33.

Indian Policy Review Commission, established by Congress, agreed in its 1977 report that the BIA mishandled Indian money, did not protect Indian property rights, and neglected Indian safety. The Commission recommended that the BIA be replaced by a separate Department of Indian Affairs that would be divorced from the Department of the Interior. The Commission's recommendation was not implemented.

Native Americans today face the continuing problem of dealing with a divided BIA. Some BIA bureaucrats want to maintain the dependency of the Native Americans on the reservation system run by the agency. Recently, however, the BIA has let more and more tribes control the police, job training, educational, and social programs that the BIA used to manage. Nonetheless, there are still numerous conflicts between Indian tribes and the BIA, as well as between them and state governments.

Asian Americans

Because Asian Americans have a relatively high median income, they are typically not thought of as being discriminated against. This certainly was not always the case. The Japanese Exclusion Act of 1882 prevented the Japanese from coming to the United States to prospect for gold or to work on the railroads or in factories in the West. Japanese American students were segregated into special schools after the San Francisco 1906 earthquake so that white children could use their buildings. The 1941 Japanese bombing of Pearl Harbor intensified fear and hatred of the Japanese. Executive Order 9066, signed by President Franklin D. Roosevelt on February 19, 1942, set up "relocation" camps for virtually every Japanese-American living in the United States. The Japanese were required to dispose of their property, usually at below-market prices. It wasn't until 1944 and 1945 that the relocation camps were closed and the prisoners freed after a December 18, 1944, Supreme Court ruling deemed such activity illegal.[28]

Both the Japanese and the Chinese have overcome initial prejudice to lead America's ethnic groups in median income and median education. Recently, however, a new group of Asians have had to fight discrimination—those from Southeast Asia. Almost three-quarters of a million Indo-Chinese war refugees have come into the United States in the last ten years. Like their predecessors, the newer immigrants have quickly increased their median income; only about one-third of all such households receive welfare of any sort. But as with the Chinese and the Japanese, once they become established, they are seen as economic threats.

Melting Pot or Ethnic Stew?

▽

No one really knows when the term *melting pot* was first applied to American society, although the phrase is derived from a play of that name by Israel Zangwill.

[28]See Dylan S. Meyer, *Uprooted American: The Japanese-American and the War Relocation Authority During World War II* (Tucson: University of Arizona Press, 1971).

That American Indians were made American citizens by an act of Congress on June 15, 1924?

Perhaps the last lines of Emma Lazarus' sonnet, "The New Colossus," engraved on a tablet inside the base of the Statute of Liberty, best synthesize the melting-pot idea.

> Give me your tired, your poor,
> Your huddled masses yearning to breathe free,
> The wretched refuse of your teeming shore.
> Send these, the homeless, tempest-tossed to me,
> I lift my lamp beside the golden door!

The earlier ethnic groups that came to the United States in the great waves of immigration that began after the Civil War were first northern Europeans and later eastern and southern Europeans. Then, as now, they were lured by the American Dream—the promise of economic security and freedom. Assimilation was the way by which the American Dream could be achieved.

Today the melting-pot idea is being revised. A new emphasis on ethnic and racial pride has come to the fore with increased Asian and Hispanic immigration and black self-consciousness. Since 1977, four out of five immigrants have come from Latin America or Asia. If current rates continue, Hispanics will overtake blacks as the nation's largest minority by the year 2020. By the year 2030, blacks and Hispanics will comprise 30 percent of the population.

Ben Wattenberg of the American Enterprise Institute in Washington, D.C., says the United States is becoming the world's first "universal nation." We have always claimed to be one, but this really was not true until relatively recently. The "old guard" Anglo-Saxon Protestants will no longer dominate American political life. We may even see intense periods of conflict among blacks and newly arrived Hispanics and Asians as they vie for jobs and political influence. On the other hand, if Hispanics and blacks can form coalitions, perhaps with Asians, their political strength can be increased dramatically, for they will have the numerical strength to make significant changes.

America has been challenged and changed—and culturally enriched—time and again by immigrant peoples speaking other languages and observing different customs. The minority groups discussed here will eventually come to participate fully in the American system, and someday "traditional Americans" may be of Spanish or Asian origin, as well as Anglo-Saxon.

Citizenship and Immigration Rights

A great debate has taken place in recent years over the issue of immigration rights. The questions have included whether illegal immigrants can become citizens, whether employers are liable for hiring illegals, and whether the economy can absorb so many new workers. Legislation passed in 1986 created a new process by which illegal aliens who have resided in the United States since 1982 can apply to become legal residents, and after five more years, citizens. Employers will be required to certify the legal status of alien workers, or face fines. Although the law forbids discrimination against anyone on the basis of national origin, the new rules may, in fact, reinforce prejudices against minorities. Many organizations will be concerned with the way the illegal immigrants are treated by federal and state police and immigration officials. Such groups want to maintain the nation's commitment to relatively free entry to people of all racial, ethnic, religious, political, and income backgrounds. Their goals are fair immigration rules, greater protection for resident illegal aliens, and a more pluralistic and tolerant culture.

You can become involved in this national controversy over immigration and citizenship policy in a number of ways. You can pay attention to the often contradictory policies that are proposed in Congress to deal with the problem. If you feel deeply enough about this issue, you might wish to join action organizations that lobby through influencing public opinion or by exerting direct pressure on Congress and the executive branch. Some of you may wish to help a sanctuary group that provides aid to illegal aliens. (Be aware, however, that such activity may be illegal and could lead to your being prosecuted by the government.) A safer means of taking similar action would be to lobby your local government to enact laws allowing aliens fleeing persecution to live in your community. The following organizations have been involved in the controversy over immigration and citizenship policies. Some groups are generally in favor of the right to immigrate:

Center for Immigrants' Rights
48 St. Marks Place
New York, NY 10003
(212) 505-6890

Citizens Committee for Immigration Reform
1120 Belleview
McLean, VA 22102
(703) 759-3326

National Center for Immigrants' Rights
1636 West Eighth St., Suite 215
Los Angeles, CA 90017
(213) 487-2531

National Immigration Project of the National Lawyers Guild
14 Beacon St., Suite 407
Boston, MA 02108

Other groups that usually support stricter enforcement of existing immigration laws or a more homogenous culture include:

Federation for American Immigration Reform
1424 16th St., N.W., Room 701
Washington, D.C. 20036
(202) 328-7004

U.S. English
1424 16th St., N.W., Suite 714
Washington, D.C. 20036
(202) 232-5200

Chapter Summary

▽

1. Minority rights have often been called civil rights, and the quest for the expansion of minority rights has been called the civil rights movement. It has taken this nation two hundred years to reach a semblance of equality among its citizens, and the effort to expand constitutional guarantees to all individuals continues.

2. Before the Civil War, the Constitution protected slavery. It was confirmed in the *Dred Scott v. Sanford* case in 1857, which held that blacks could not become U.S. citizens, nor were they entitled to the rights and privileges of citizenship. With the emancipation of the slaves in 1861 and the passage of the Thirteenth, Fourteenth, and Fifteenth Amendments to the Constitution, this inequality was legally and constitutionally ended. Politically and socially, however, the badge of inferiority continued.

3. The first civil rights acts, passed from 1865 to 1877, were designed to enforce the civil rights amendments nationally. They ultimately did little to secure equality for blacks.

4. In *Plessy v. Ferguson* (1896), the Supreme Court upheld a "separate but equal" doctrine, which became the constitutional cornerstone of racial discrimination throughout the United States.

5. In *Brown v. Board of Education* (1954), the Supreme Court finally reversed the 1896 decision and declared that enforced racial segregation in public schools was unconstitutional. Southern states continued to resist integration, and segregation continued on a de facto basis. Courts increasingly ordered busing to achieve integration, which has created a major controversy. The controversy continues as the Supreme Court in June 1986 allowed the Norfolk, Virginia, public school system to end fifteen years of court-ordered busing of elementary schoolchildren.

6. By the 1960s, the quest for civil rights had led to a mass political movement with Martin Luther King, Jr. at its head.

7. Congress passed the Civil Rights Act of 1964, which banned discrimination against minorities in public accommodations and employment. The Civil Rights Act of 1968 forbade discrimination in housing.

8. The Equal Employment Opportunity Commission was created by the 1964 act to administer a program of affirmative action designed to increase the hiring of minority workers. Affirmative action was eventually seen to have a negative impact on whites, especially white males. This question of reverse discrimination reached the Supreme Court in the *Bakke* and *Weber* cases.

9. Historically, blacks were effectively excluded from the election process through such methods as the poll tax, the grandfather clause, and literacy tests. The Voting Rights Act of 1965 outlawed discriminatory voter registration tests and authorized federal registration and federally administered voting procedures in any state or political subdivision evidencing electoral discrimination or unduly low registration rates.

10. The second largest minority group in America, Hispanics, or Spanish-speaking individuals, constitutes about 6.5 percent of the American population. Their diversity and geographical dispersion have hindered their ability to achieve political power, particularly at the national level, although a number of Hispanic groups have succeeded in removing some discriminatory barriers.

11. Of the nearly fifteen million Hispanics in the United States, Mexican Americans number about nine million. The next largest group is the Puerto Ricans, followed by the Cubans, then those from Central and South America.

12. Before the arrival of Europeans in America, Native Americans numbered about ten million. War and disease drastically reduced their numbers, and today there are approximately 1.4 million Native Americans. Statistically, they remain the least educated, most economically disadvantaged, and unhealthiest group in America. They have been relatively unsuccessful in garnering political power and face the continuing problem of dealing with a divided Bureau of Indian Affairs.

13. Among Asian Americans, Japanese and Chinese have overcome prejudice to lead America's ethnic groups in median income and median education. Southeast Asian immigrants—three-quarters of a million in the last ten years—have quickly increased their median income; only about one-third of all such households receive welfare of any sort.

14. Since 1977, four out of five immigrants have come from Latin America or Asia. As the ethnic and racial makeup of this country changes, the "old guard" Anglo-Saxon Protestants will no longer dominate American political life. Minority groups will come to participate more fully in the American political system.

Questions for Review and Discussion

▽

1. According to the Supreme Court in *Brown v. Board of Education*, "separate but equal" is "inherently unequal." Why did the Court reject the idea of separate but equal in 1954? Why didn't segregation really provide equal opportunities for blacks in the United States?

2. Even though the North fought the Civil War in part to liberate the slaves, the southern states were able to reestablish white domination within a generation after the war. Why did the North allow the disenfranchisement of the blacks in the South, even though it violated the Constitution? How did the Supreme Court's views of the proper powers of gov-

ernment work to support segregation in the South and industrialization in the North?

3. To what extent can the "American" culture absorb other, non-Anglo-Saxon cultures such as those of the American Indian, the Hispanics, or the Asians? How would "American culture" be changed if we came to have a multilingual, multiethnic society?

4. What is the purpose of affirmative action programs? Is it possible to institute such programs without practicing reverse discrimination?

Selected References
▽

Dee Brown, *Bury My Heart at Wounded Knee* (New York: Holt, Rinehart & Winston, 1971). An important examination of the treatment of Native Americans as the frontier pushed westward.

Stokely Carmichael and Charles V. Hamilton, *Black Power: The Politics of Liberation in America* (New York: Vintage Books, 1967). Classic expression of the politics of racism in the United States and of the struggle to overcome white domination.

Norman Dorsen, *Discrimination and Civil Rights* (Boston: Little, Brown, 1969). This is a classic book of constitutional cases in civil rights and is regularly updated.

Leslie Dunbar, ed., *Minority Report* (New York: Random House, 1984). An interesting book that discusses the impact of government policies on the rights of minorities in the 1980s.

Richard Kluger, *Simple Justice* (New York: Alfred A. Knopf, 1975). The history of the 1954 Supreme Court ruling on Brown v. Board of Education and black Americans' struggle for equality.

Aldon D. Morris, *The Origins of the Civil Rights Movement* (New York: The Free Press, 1985). This interesting book traces the alliances between black groups and the tactics they used in accelerating the civil rights movement in the United States.

Sidney Verba and Gary R. Orren, *Equality in America: The View from the Top* (Cambridge, Mass.: Harvard University Press, 1985). This fascinating book used an elite survey of 2,762 American leaders from a wide range of groups (business, labor, feminists, and so on) to determine the meanings and implications of equality and attitudes about equality in America.

C. Vann Woodward, *The Strange Career of Jim Crow* (New York: Oxford University Press, 1957). The classic study of segregation in the southern United States.

Chapter 6

▽

New Groups, New Demands

Contents

▽

Women's Position in Society: Historical Background
The Continued Struggle for Equal Status
Federal Responses to Sex Discrimination in Jobs
The Status of the Elderly
The Rights of the Handicapped
The Rights and Status of Juveniles
The Rights and Status of Gays

What If . . .
▽
Women's Suffrage
Had Failed

If women had never been granted the right to vote in national elections, there certainly would have been no need to put Rep. Geraldine Ferraro on the Democratic ticket as vice presidential candidate in 1984, partly to appeal to "the women's vote" and to exploit "the gender gap." Neither would members of Congress have seen much reason to add sex discrimination provisions to legislation regulating employment, health benefits, or pension plans. As long as women were not part of legislators' voting constituencies, there would be little need to consider their interests.

It is not possible to know exactly how women's rights would have developed if the suffrage movement had failed. Probably the rights of women would be different in each state. States that have more conservative political traditions might have viewed the role of women in the common-law tradition, in which women were considered to become *femme coverte*, or civilly dead, when they married. This means that all business must be transacted by the husband, women have few property or contractual rights of their own, and husband and wife are considered to be one le-

gal and political unit. In nineteenth-century America, many women and men believed that women should restrict themselves to the domestic sphere, leaving all dealings with the outside world—including political decisions—to their fathers or husbands. The only political role accorded to women was that of instilling patriotic ideals in their children and guiding their family's moral development. Husbands and sons would vote for the women's interest.

In other states, women would probably have the vote for some elections, such as school boards, perhaps property taxes, or city councils. But they still would be "second-class citizens," restricted in political participation to local elections only.

The status of a woman would change if her husband moved from one state to another, depending on the political rights granted by each state. A woman's control over property or rights to the guardianship of children in one state might not be upheld in another. The status of unmarried women would be most problematic.

In general, if women had not achieved the right to vote, their political status would be more similar to that of children than to that of any other group in our society.

▽

In the last several decades, there have been great changes in the status of women and other groups—old and young people, gay men and women—in society and in their respective political rights. These changes reflect both legal reforms and revised social attitudes.

The paramount destiny and mission of women are to fulfill the noble and benign offices of wife and mother. This is the law of the Creator.

Words of centuries ago? Not quite. These words were part of a Supreme Court opinion rendered in the first case tried under the Fourteenth Amendment in 1873. The Court at that time upheld the denial of the right of women to practice law.[1] Although written more than a hundred years ago, the sentiment that it is somehow more "natural" for women (than for men) to tend the household and the children is still very much alive. Old ways of thinking die hard, and those who favor complete equality among men and women—socially, politically, and economically—must still struggle with this age-old cultural tradition regarding the proper status of women in society.

Women's Position in Society: Historical Background
▽

In some ancient civilizations, women were granted a number of rights and privileges. If we look at the Code of Hammurabi, which dates back to the eighteenth century B.C., we see that married women were granted a great deal of personal and financial freedom. Women could get a divorce on the grounds of adultery or cruelty (although a husband could divorce his wife at will), and women were allowed to trade on their own account. Many women were apparently judges, scribes, and elders. In ancient Egypt, the status of women was still higher. There they owned property and mixed freely with men.

In those cultures that formed the basis of Western civilization, however, this was not the case. In the Hebraic culture of the Middle East—which became a part of the Christian heritage in the West—women were regarded as little more than vehicles for the pleasure and/or paternal ambitions of men. They were an order apart from male society and had virtually no political or economic rights. In biblical days, for example, if a woman became widowed, she was left to find her way back to her father's house or to beg for a living—or, in some cases, to starve. In the

[1]*Bradwell v. Illinois*, 16 Wall. 130 (1873).

cultural traditions of Greece and Rome, the situation was not much different. The Greeks and Romans likewise regarded women as social ornaments and childbearing slaves—and occasionally, in Roman times, as "imbeciles."

In the Christian world of the late Middle Ages, women were usually excluded from all public affairs as well as from religious affairs. The church acted on St. Paul's injunction:

The women should keep silence in the Churches. For they are not permitted to speak. [2]

With the growth of towns, however, at least middle-class women improved their social and economic status. They were increasingly allowed to take part in trade and to become members of the medieval craft guilds. At the time of the American Revolution, some women practiced trades, but most accepted their roles as wives or mothers.

The Early Feminist Movement in the United States

Women were considered citizens in the early years of the nation, but they had no political rights. The first political cause in which women became actively engaged was the slavery abolition movement—although male abolitionists felt that women should not take an active role or speak on the subject in public. Separate female and male antislavery societies were founded in many states. When the World Antislavery Convention was held in London in 1840, women delegates were barred from active participation. Responding partly to this rebuff, two American delegates, Lucretia Mott and Elizabeth Cady Stanton, returned from that meeting with plans to work for women's rights in the United States.

In 1848, Mott and Stanton organized the first women's rights convention in Seneca Falls, New York. The three hundred persons who attended approved a declaration of sentiments: "We hold these truths to be self-evident: that all men *and women* are created equal. . . ." In the following twelve years, groups of feminists held seven conventions in different cities in the Midwest and in the East. With the outbreak of the Civil War, however, advocates of women's rights were urged to put their support behind the war effort. Most agreed, and consequently the women's rights movement was held in abeyance for the duration.

Suffrage
Right to vote; franchise.

Elizabeth Cady Stanton.

The Suffrage Issue and the Fifteenth Amendment

"The right of citizens of the United States to vote shall not be denied or abridged by the United States or by any State on account of race, color, or previous condition of servitude." So reads Section 1 of Amendment XV to the Constitution, ratified on March 30, 1870. The campaign for the passage of this amendment split the women's **suffrage** movement. Militant feminists wanted to add sex to "race, color, or previous condition of servitude." Other feminists, along with many men, opposed this view; they wanted to separate black suffrage and women's suffrage to ensure the passage of the amendment. So the women's rights movement became separate from the racial equality movement.

Susan B. Anthony and Elizabeth Cady Stanton formed the National Suffrage Association in 1869. According to their view, women's suffrage was a means to

[2] *I Cor.* 14:34.

achieve major improvements in the economic and social situation of women in the United States. In other words, the vote was to be used to obtain a larger end. Lucy Stone, however, felt that the vote was the only major issue. Members of the American Women's Suffrage Association, founded by Stone and others, traveled to each state, addressed state legislatures, wrote, published and argued their convictions. They achieved only limited success. In 1890, the two organizations quit battling and joined forces. The National American Women's Suffrage Association had only one goal—the enfranchisement of women—but it made little progress.

By the early 1900s, small radical splinter groups were formed, such as the Congressional Union headed by Alice Paul. This organization worked solely for the passage of an amendment to the national Constitution. Willing to use "unorthodox" means to achieve its goal, this group and others took to the streets. There were parades, hunger strikes, arrests, and jailings. Finally, in 1920, seventy-two years after the Seneca Falls convention, the Nineteenth Amendment was passed: "The right of citizens of the United States to vote shall not be denied or abridged by the United States or by any state on account of sex." Women were thus enfranchised.

Although today it may seem that the United States was slow to give women the vote, it was really not too far behind the rest of the world. The first countries to grant women electoral equality with men were New Zealand in 1893, Finland in 1906, Norway in 1913, and Denmark and Iceland in 1915. Toward the end of World War I, or soon after, most of the Western nations—including the United States—granted women the right to vote.

The Continued Struggle for Equal Status
▽

Obviously, the right to vote does not guarantee political power. It has been more than half a century since women obtained the right to vote in most countries of the Western world, yet the number of women who have held high political positions can be counted on one's fingers. Women have become elected heads of state in India, Ceylon, Israel, Bolivia, Argentina, Barbados, and England. There have been a few women ministers in a number of countries, but normally these ministries are concerned primarily with so-called "women's interests," such as family affairs or social welfare. In the United States, we have not yet nominated a woman for president—although the predictions are that we will see one elected in the next half-century. In Congress, the men's club atmosphere prevails. A few women senators have been elected. As of 1987, there were 23 women members of the House of Representatives—only 5 percent of the total. Of the more than 10,000 members of the House of Representatives who have served, only 1 percent have been women. No woman has yet held one of the major leadership positions in the House or in the Senate.

Women have also been meagerly represented in federal political appointments, although this situation is changing. In 1969, President Nixon declared that "a woman can and should be able to do any political job that a man can do." But by the time of his resignation in 1974, he had not appointed a woman to either the cabinet or the Supreme Court. His successor, Gerald Ford, appointed a woman as secretary of housing and urban development. President Carter had three women in his cabinet. Ronald Reagan appointed women to two major cabinet posts and to head the U.S. delegation to the United Nations. He can also be credited with

Susan B. Anthony.

an historic first in his appointment of Sandra Day O'Connor to the Supreme Court in 1981.

Until recently, women have had difficulty getting elected to state offices as well. But this picture too is changing. Several women have been elected to governorships, and many women are running for—and being elected to—positions such as mayor, county commissioner, school board member, and state legislator.

The representation of women in political office does not reflect in their participation as voters. As Table 6–1 indicates, the overall turnout of women voters nationally is about equal to that of male voters.

The National Organization for Women (NOW)

Betty Friedan.

There was a hiatus between the nineteenth-century women's movement in the United States and the current feminist movement that began in the late 1950s. The women's movement of today is referred to by its members as the "second wave." Pioneering this second wave was Betty Friedan, whose book *The Feminine Mystique* detailed "sexism," or "the disease which has no name" in the suburbia of the 1950s.[3]

Although often identified as middle-class, the modern women's movement seeks to define sexism and to eradicate it from all spheres of life for all women. Perhaps the most prominent of the organizations associated with the women's movement is the National Organization for Women (NOW). NOW was formed by Friedan and others who were dissatisfied with the lack of antisex-discrimination activity by the then largest women's organizations—the National Federation of Business and Professional Women's Clubs and the League of Women Voters. The specific issue around which NOW coalesced was the failure of the Equal Employment Opportunity Commission (EEOC) to enjoin newspapers from running separate want ads for men and women. In June 1966, at the third annual Conference of State Commissions on the Status of Women, the attendees demanded a resolution condemning such sex discrimination in employment. They were told that the conference "was not allowed to pass such a resolution" or take any action for that matter. NOW was formed and immediately sent telegrams to the EEOC. After a series of tough battles in 1968, NOW won its war against sex-segregated want ads.

NOW elected Betty Friedan as its first president and adopted a blanket resolution

[3]Betty Friedan, *The Feminine Mystique* (New York: W. W. Norton, 1963).

Table 6–1
▽
Voting and Registration: 1984

Voting participation by females has recently been equal or greater to voting participation by males. Here we can see that in both absolute and percentage terms, females voted and registered more than males in 1984.

	Persons of Voting Age (millions)	Persons Reporting They Registered (millions)	Persons Reporting They Voted (millions)	Persons Registered (percent)
Male	80.3	54.0	47.4	67.3
Female	89.6	62.1	54.5	69.3

SOURCE: *Statistical Abstract of the United States*, 1986, p. 256.

Profile
▽
Eleanor Smeal

Like the president of the United States, the president of the National Organization for Women (NOW) cannot run for a consecutive third term. That rule ended Eleanor Cutri Smeal's reign as head of the most powerful women's rights organization in this country in 1982; however, she was reelected for another term as NOW President in 1985. Smeal continues to be heavily involved in the women's movement. Her career as a feminist leader spans almost two decades.

The daughter of Italian immigrants, Smeal grew up in a family of Democrats. She attended public schools, going on to pursue graduate work in political science and public administration. While recuperating from a back injury for about a year, she read much on the women's movement. Her husband—who had assumed the housekeeping and child-care responsibilities during that time—also became a believer in feminism. They both joined NOW in 1970. From 1971 to 1973, Smeal was president of the NOW chapter in a Pittsburgh suburb. She also helped found the National Women's Political Caucus and became president of the statewide Pennsylvania

"We are a political power, and the message is, we are going to make this nation safe for equality."

chapter of NOW, serving in that capacity until 1975. On April 23, 1977, she was elected president of the national NOW. Ratification of the national Equal Rights Amendment was the top priority of her administration.

Perhaps the most memorable day for Smeal was July 9, 1978, when she led 100,000 people in a march on Washington, D.C., pushing for ERA ratification. She succeeded in getting the ratification deadline extended. The following year, *World Almanac* picked her as one of the twenty-five most influential women in the United States, and in 1980 *Time* magazine included her among the "Fifty Faces of America's Future." That same year she was reelected as president of NOW. In 1982, she stepped down at the end of her second term. Smeal was reelected for an historic third term in 1985 when she won on a platform of continued support for ratification of ERA and the use of large-scale mass actions to revitalize NOW, which had lost more than 100,000 members since she left office in 1982.

Eleanor Smeal's commitment to the struggle for equality is perhaps best summarized by her statement quoted in the *Christian Science Monitor* on September 4, 1979: "I made up my mind that the fight for the equality of women was the most important historical thing I could participate in and would always be important to me."

designed "to bring women into full participation in the mainstream of American society *now*, exercising all the privileges and responsibilities thereof in truly equal partnership with men." NOW grew from its original 300 members to approximately 130,000 members in 1982. It has continued to be one of the leading pressure groups in the struggle for women's rights.

NOW and the Equal Rights Amendment

Perhaps more than any other women's group, NOW has championed the passage of the Equal Rights Amendment (ERA)—the proposed Twenty-seventh Amendment to the U.S. Constitution—which states:

Equality of rights under the law shall not be denied or abridged by the United States or by any state on account of sex.

ERA was first introduced in Congress in 1923 by leaders of the National Women's Party who felt that getting the vote would not be enough to change women's status. After years during which the amendment was not even given a hearing in Congress, it was finally approved by both chambers in 1972.

As we noted in Chapter 2, any constitutional amendment must be ratified by the legislatures (or conventions) in three-fourths of the states before it can become law. Since the early 1900s, most proposed amendments have required that ratification occur within seven years of passage of the amendment by Congress. Supporters of ERA initially had until March 22, 1979, to obtain ratification by thirty-eight states.

ERA had tremendous popular support, not least among those who saw it as a way to invalidate numerous existing state laws that continue to maintain the inferior status of women by discriminating against them in property and contractual rights. By March 22, 1973, ERA had been ratified by thirty states—eight less than were needed. At the same time opposing forces were becoming organized and militant.

Opposition to ERA: The Conservative Reaction

Much of the responsibility for the defeat of ERA rests with the efforts of Phyllis Schlafly. Emphasizing the positive and unique qualities of the traditional role of women in society, Schlafly mobilized the sentiments of many women and men against ERA through the Stop-ERA and the Eagle Forum organizations. Schlafly claimed that pro-ERA groups were hostile to all the values women had traditionally held and to the general welfare of women. During the course of the anti-ERA campaign, Schlafly emphasized the issues of abortion on demand and homosexuality—linking ERA more firmly with a broader range of controversial social issues. She felt the most "cruel and damaging sexual harassment taking place today" was not that which men inflicted on women but rather that which was directed "by feminists and their federal government allies against the role of motherhood and the role of the dependent wife."[4]

The conservative opposition was effective. The necessary thirty-eight states failed to ratify the amendment within the seven-year period, in spite of the support given to ERA in numerous national party platforms and by six presidents and both houses of Congress. NOW boycotted nonratifying states. A number of associations refused to hold their conventions in Las Vegas, Miami Beach, Atlanta, Chicago, Kansas City, and New Orleans because the respective states refused to ratify. Nonetheless, the anti-ERA campaign was successful: As the deadline neared, five approvals were still lacking. Three states rescinded their ratification.[5] Congress decided to extend the deadline to June 30, 1982, but ERA again failed to receive the required number of ratifications.

Schlafly greeted the defeat of ERA with the statement that the bill's failure to pass was "the greatest victory for women's rights since the women's suffrage amendment of 1920."[6] The National Organization for Women and related groups, how-

Phyllis Schlafly.

[4]Phyllis Schlafly's statement before a Senate labor subcommittee in 1981, quoted in the *Los Angeles Herald Examiner*, April 22, 1981, p. 2.

[5]But such rescinding (or taking back one's vote) may not be constitutional. Samuel S. Friedman argued this point in *ERA: May a State Change Its Vote?* (Detroit: Wayne State University Press, 1979).

[6]Majorie P. K. Weiser and Jean S. Arbeiter, *Womanlist* (New York: Atheneum, 1981); and Carol Felsenthal, "Phyllis Schlafly: The Sweetheart of the Silent Majority," in Peter Woll, ed., *Behind the Scenes in American Government* (Boston: Little, Brown, 1983), pp. 85–96.

The May, 1986 primaries in Nebraska resulted in victory for two women candidates for the governorship of that state. Republican Kay Orr received 39% of the vote in a seven-person race and received a congratulatory telephone call from President Reagan after her victory, while Democrat Helen Boosalis obtained 44% against six contenders.

Mrs. Orr, the 47-year-old Republican State Treasurer said, after the primary: "This is an opportunity to tell that what we have in Nebraska are open-minded people." Mrs. Orr was born in Burlington, Iowa and attended the University of Iowa. The daughter of a Swedish farm implement dealer, she remembers that politics was a frequent topic of conversation in her home. She is a Republican activist who cut her political teeth in the 1964 Presidential campaign of Senator Barry

Goldwater. A conservative, she has attended three Republican Party National Conventions as a Reagan delegate, served as co-chair in 1984 on the party platform committee and helped write its anti-abortion plank. She is also opposed to the Equal Rights Amendment because she feels its objectives (women's equality), with which she agrees, could better be achieved through legislation and other means.

Mrs. Boosalis, 66 years old, was born in Minneapolis of Greek immigrants. She studied at the University of Minnesota. After moving to Lincoln, Nebraska where her husband, a plant pathologist, went to work for the University of Nebraska, she became interested in politics through the League of Women Voters and served as president of the local chapter. She ran and served as a member of the Lincoln City Council for 16 years, then ran for

and became mayor of Lincoln—the first woman mayor of a city over 100,000 with a strong mayor form of government. She also became the first woman president of the United States Conference of Mayors. She has also been director of Nebraska's department of aging.

Their primary victories marked the first all-woman gubernatorial race in U.S. history. In the November election, Orr won. In addition to the Orr-Boosalis race there were at least seven women running for Lieutenant Governor, and seventeen women running for the governorship in several states, among them Oregon and Arizona. There were also roughly 50 women running for Congress in 1986.

SOURCE: *New York Times*, May 15, 1986, p. 11; *Time*, May 26, 1986, p. 29; *New Directions for Women*, May/June, 1986, p. 2.

ever, have renewed the struggle. The Equal Rights Amendment has been reintroduced in Congress, and many years of renewed conflict over this issue can be expected. A Gallup poll taken in 1982 (see Table 6–2) showed that the prospects for ERA's future success are bright: 56 percent of Americans who have heard about ERA favored the amendment. Members of Congress may have to respond to this public opinion.

Federal Responses to Sex Discrimination in Jobs
▽

Although ERA did not pass, several efforts have been made by the federal government to eliminate sex discrimination in the labor market both before and after the introduction of the amendment.

Sex Discrimination and Title VII

Sex was included as a prohibited basis for discrimination in the job market under Title VII of the Civil Rights Act of 1964, although Title VII does not cover

Sex Discrimination

Overt behavior in which people are given differential or unfavorable treatment on the basis of sex. Any practice, policy, or procedure that denies equality of treatment to an individual or to a group.

Sex-Plus Discrimination

Harassment on the basis of sex, in violation of Title VII. This includes unwanted physical or verbal conduct or abuse of a sexual nature that interferes with a recipient's job performance or carries with it an implicit or explicit threat of adverse employment consequences.

discrimination based on sexual preferences. Since its enactment, Title VII has been used to strike down so-called protective legislation, which prevents women from undertaking jobs deemed "too dangerous or strenuous by the state." In practice, such protective legislation often "protected" women from higher-paying jobs. Under the Equal Employment Opportunity Commission guidelines, such state statutes may not be used as a defense to a charge of illegal **sex discrimination.**

So-called **sex-plus discrimination** has also been outlawed by Title VII. In April 1980, the EEOC issued its first guidelines on the subject. Under the guidelines, all unwelcome sexual advances, requests, or other physical or verbal conduct of a sexual nature are illegal sexual harassment if submission is a condition of employment or a basis of pay, of promotion, or of other employment decisions. Also, if such unwanted conduct interferes with an employee's job performance or creates an intimidating, hostile, or offensive environment, it is illegal. The courts have gone so far as to hold the employer liable for illegal sexual harassment by supervisors, and EEOC guidelines go one step further—they hold an employer liable for a supervisor's conduct regardless of the employer's knowledge of such conduct or even when the employer has a policy forbidding such conduct.

The right of women to be free from sexual harassment on the job has been increasingly upheld by the Supreme Court in the last few years. In 1986, the Court indicated that creating a hostile environment by sexual harassment, even if job status is not affected violates Title VII.[7] According to Emily Spitzer, an attorney

[7]*Meritor Savings Bank, FSB v. Vinson*, 106 S.Ct. 2399 (1986).

Table 6–2
▽

Results of a Gallup Poll of Opinions on the Equal Rights Amendment, 1982
(in percent)

This opinion poll shows that overall females favored the ERA only by 2 percentage points more than the sample of males polled. Nonwhites, however, favored the ERA greatly relative to whites (77 percent versus 54 percent). Also, Democrats favored the ERA much more than Republicans (64 percent versus 44 percent).

Question: "Do you favor or oppose this amendment [ERA]?"	Favor	Oppose	No Opinion
Gender			
Male	55	36	9
Female	57	33	10
Race			
White	54	36	10
Non-white	77	16	7
Age			
18–24 years	66	27	7
25–29 years	66	23	11
30–49 years	56	35	9
50–64 years	51	39	10
65 and over	45	41	14
Politics			
Republicans	44	46	10
Democrats	64	27	9
Independents	56	33	11

SOURCE: *The Gallup Poll*, 1982.

with the NOW Legal Defense and Education Fund, the 1986 Supreme Court decision "alerts employers and workers that treating women in a sexually harassing manner in the workplace isn't going to be condoned."[8]

Even a required uniform can become the cause for a complaint of sexual abuse. In the case of Judith Marentette, a cocktail waitress in a lounge in Detroit's Metropolitan Airport, the uniform she was required to wear caused her psychological discomfort and led to unpleasant incidents with her customers. Tired of her predicament, Marentette got in touch with the Detroit Women's Justice Center. The center filed an administrative complaint with EEOC, and a class-action suit on behalf of her and thirty-one other airport waitresses was filed against their employer, Michigan Hosts, Inc., under Title VII of the 1964 Civil Rights Act. Although Marentette continued her lawsuit, the immediate result was that the company changed the uniforms to ones that were comfortable and more modest.[9]

In 1978, in a Title VII-based decision, the Supreme Court ruled that an employer (the City of Los Angeles) could not require female employees to make higher pension-fund contributions than male employees earning the same salary.[10] This and similar cases involving differential life insurance premiums for males and females (prohibited by a 1983 ruling) represent another set of issues on which Americans have been slowly redefining gender-based discrimination.[11]

The 1978 Pregnancy Discrimination Act amended Title VII to include job-related discrimination based on pregnancy, childbirth, or related medical conditions. Pursuant to this amendment, health and disability insurance plans must cover pregnancy, childbirth, or related medical conditions in the same way as any other temporary disability. An employer must provide leaves of absence for pregnant women on the same terms and conditions as those given to any other worker for any other temporary disability. Also, simply because a woman is pregnant does not mean that she can be forced to take a maternity leave for any *specified* period of time. As long as she is capable of performing her duties, she must be allowed to work. The 1978 act applies both to married and unmarried women and to any aspect of employment.

For a comparison, note that in Sweden the law provides maternity leave for women workers. Also, in the case of married couples working, either the wife or the husband may stay home to care for the infant for a specified period after the birth. The loss of pay is reimbursed by the health insurance system. Maternal or paternal leaves are also available up to eighteen days when children are sick.[12]

The Equal Pay Act of 1963

The Equal Pay Act was enacted as an amendment to the Fair Labor Standards Act of 1938 and since 1979 has been administered by the Equal Employment Opportunity Commission. Basically, the act prohibits sex-based discrimination in the wages paid for equal work on jobs when their performance requires equal skills, effort, and responsibility under similar conditions. It is job content rather than job

[8]*Wall Street Journal*, June 20, 1986, p. 2.

[9]"Viewpoint," *Glamour*, October 1980, p. 256.

[10]*Los Angeles v. Manhart*, 435 U.S. 702 at 710 (1978).

[11]Congressional Quarterly, *Guide to the U.S. Supreme Court* (Washington, D.C., 1979).

[12]Siv Gustafsson, IV, "Working Life," *In Sweden*, no. 15 (December 17, 1979), published by the Swedish Information Service.

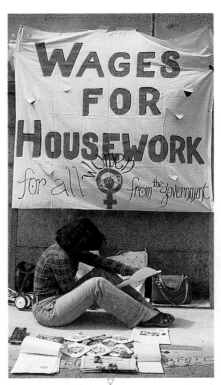

description that controls in all cases. For the equal pay requirements to apply, the act requires that male and female employees must work at the same establishment.

With equal-pay questions, the issue focuses more on the jobs performed by two employees and whether they are substantially equal than on the equivalence of employees' skills and training. But small differences in job content do not justify higher pay for one sex. The courts look to the primary duties of the two jobs. The jobs of a barber and a beautician are considered essentially "equal." So, too, are those of a tailor and a seamstress.

A typical example of sex discrimination in the workplace involved the Minnesota Mining and Manufacturing Company (3M). In August 1982, 3M decided to settle a number of sex-bias suits charging that 3M had discriminated against women in job assignments, wages, promotions, transfers, and other job-related areas. In this case, one thousand women had been forced to take maternity leaves four months before their scheduled delivery dates.[13] The company agreed to pay $2.3 million to some 2,350 women. In addition to the settlement, the company also agreed to help the women gain access to better-paying jobs by providing job counseling, public posting of job openings, and payment for job-related classes.

Comparable Worth

The comparable worth idea is that compensation should be based on the worth of the job to an employer and that factors unrelated to the worth of a job, such as the sex of the employee, should not affect compensation; generally used in the argument that women are entitled to comparable wages for doing work that is different from, but of comparable worth and value to, work done by higher-paid men.

The "Willmar 8," women bank employees picketing for equal pay.

Comparable Worth, or Pay Equity

The concept of **comparable worth,** or pay equity, is that women should receive equal pay, not just for equal (that is, the same) work, but also for work of comparable skill, effort, and responsibility. This is an effort to redress the effects of traditional "women's work" being undervalued and underpaid. Indeed, four out of five women hold jobs that have largely become women's work—for example, secretary (95 percent female), telephone operator (94 percent female), and nurse (96 percent female).

The issue of equal pay for comparable work obtained national attention when municipal workers in San Jose, California, successfully struck in 1981. At that time, a study comparing the skill, effort, and responsibility of all city jobs showed that jobs traditionally held by women had pay rates less than those of comparable jobs held by men. The mayor's secretary, for example, was paid $18,000 for work found to be qualitatively equivalent to that of a senior air-conditioning mechanic earning $31,000. The strike was ended by an agreement to raise the women's pay to the same level of male workers doing comparable work.[14]

In 1981, the Supreme Court ruled that female workers could sue under Title VII even if they were not performing the same jobs as men. In this case, a group of jail matrons in the State of Washington claimed that they did not receive the same salaries as male prison guards; their jobs differed from the men's in that they had fewer prisoners to guard and they also performed clerical tasks. The Court ruled that they could sue on the basis of sex discrimination.[15]

In 1983, the American Federation of State, County, and Municipal Employees filed a lawsuit against the State of Washington, charging that state employees in job categories dominated by women were paid less, on average, than workers in other categories requiring comparable skills and background. According to the

[13]*Monthly Labor Review,* August 1982, p. 58.

[14]*Facts on File, 1981,* July 13, 1981, p. 535.

[15]Barbara Deckard Sinclair, *The Women's Movement,* 3rd ed. (New York: Harper and Row, 1983), p. 12.

Washington State Supreme Court, the "evidence is overwhelming that there has been past historical discrimination against women in employment in the state of Washington and that discrimination has been manifested, according to the evidence, by direct, overt, and institutionalized discrimination."[16] The court ruled that the state would have to make amends. Union officials estimated that the state's liability in this case may reach $500 million.

A public opinion poll taken in 1986 indicated that Americans are divided over the idea of comparable worth. Forty percent of the respondents favored some type of system using comparable worth, but 38 percent said that wages should be established strictly by supply and demand. Women were in favor of a comparable worth system over a supply and demand system by 42 percent to 31 percent. Men opposed it by 46 percent to 38 percent. On the other hand, the same poll showed that almost 90 percent of the people polled supported the idea of equal pay for equal work—regardless of sex, race, age, or other factors, persons doing the same job should receive the same pay.[17]

The question of equal pay for comparable worth is clearly a critical one for employment discrimination cases in the 1980s and 1990s. We are certain to see many groups continuing to press this important concept in the courts.

The Status of the Elderly
▽

A major change in our society is the growing number of people age sixty-five or over, due to our approaching **zero population growth.** Within a few decades, we will no longer be a nation of young people, with its focus on youth culture. The trend to younger and younger presidents of major corporations, universities, and foundations will gradually be reversed. Demographically, we will resemble countries like France, where the unknowing American immediately remarks on how many "old" people there are.

Today, the median age of the population of the United States is twenty-nine and 11.5 percent of the population (28 million) is sixty-five or over. As can be seen in Figure 6–1, it is estimated that by the year 2000 this figure will have reached thirty-three million. Thus the problems of aging and retirement are going to become increasingly important national issues.

Poverty, at least on the surface, appears to be a major problem facing older people in America. Fully 15 percent of people sixty-five and older are earning less than the poverty level. There are a number of explanations for this phenomenon, which we consider in the following pages.

The Burden of Medical Costs

Many older individuals find themselves unable to make ends meet because they suffer from chronic illnesses that require constant attention. Medical expenses associated with such illnesses may be a steady drain on already meager resources. However, since the introduction of Medicare and Medicaid, this problem has been ameliorated to some extent for a large number of senior citizens. Others are able

[16]*American Federation of State, County and Municipal Employees v. State of Washington*, Civil Action No. C82-465T (W. D. Wash., 1983), p. 4.

[17]*Washington Post*, Weekly Edition, March 17, 1986, p. 38.

> ### Did You Know?
> ▽
> That health care for the elderly costs four times what it does for other Americans?

Zero Population Growth

A stable rate of growth in population, where the birth rate equals but does not exceed the mortality rate.

Figure 6–1
▽

Population Projections: Persons Age 65 and Older (in thousands)

SOURCE: *Statistical Abstract of the United States, 1984*, p. 32.

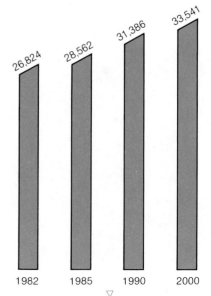

▽
177

Mandatory Retirement
Forced retirement when a person reaches
a certain age.

to take advantage of extensive private medical insurance to avoid being saddled
with extraordinary expenses in cases of catastrophic medical problems.

The Inability to Find Work

Pressure not to hire older people in many companies and other workplaces makes
it extremely difficult for senior citizens to work even when they want to. Also,
union restrictions and minimum wage laws make it difficult, if not impossible, for
senior citizens to find full- or part-time work in lower-paying jobs that they might
be willing to accept if it weren't for the restrictions. Further, the Social Security
program discourages retired people from making extra income. As of 1980, for
every $2 that a Social Security recipient earns up to $6,000 he or she loses $1 of
Social Security benefits. That is an effective tax rate of 50 percent, in addition to
taxes like the federal income tax, Social Security contributions, and state income
taxes. Recipients aged seventy or over can earn any amount and still receive full
benefits.

Age Discrimination in Employment

In spite of their proven productivity, the elderly have suffered from discrimination
in employment for many years. One of their major problems has been **mandatory
retirement.**

Elderly citizens eating at a senior center.

In an interview in *Publishers Weekly*, author and playwright Garson Kanin reflected on the forced retirement of news commentator Eric Sevareid at age sixty-five by CBS:

> I don't think its right for *anyone* to be forced out just because he's committed a birthday. The United States of America watched CBS news for years, watched Eric. No longer. CBS didn't tell us he lost his marbles or got drunk or came in late every night. No; they're saying he got to be 65 and so he had to get out. This visible act conveys to all of us that at 65 a man is no longer useful. A disgraceful myth. I think it *takes* someone of 65—or 70 or 75—to do Eric's job.[18]

Court Actions

In 1976, the Supreme Court, in *Massachusetts Board of Retirement v. Murgia*,[19] upheld a Massachusetts law requiring state troopers to retire at age fifty, reversing a lower court decision that held such a law in violation of the equal protection amendment to the Constitution. Although in this particular case, age was identifiable and discrimination against the elderly was widespread, the Court nonetheless said that in this case age classification could not be considered "suspect." The mandatory retirement rule was valid because it met the rational-basis standard.

Mandatory retirement was also the key issue in *United Air Lines v. McMann* (1977).[20] Harris McMann, a sixty-year-old United Airlines employee, was forced to retire because of a provision in the airline's pension plan. McMann objected to the action, arguing that it violated the 1967 Age Discrimination in Employment Act, which placed mandatory retirement at age sixty-five. A federal appeals court found in his favor. On December 12, 1977, however, the Supreme Court overturned the decision. The Court argued that the pension plan, set up in 1941, was not "a subterfuge to evade the 1976 act since the plan preceded the act by twenty-six years." It therefore did not find the decision unconstitutional.

Congressional Actions

As age was not included within the protections of the 1964 Civil Rights Act, Congress directed the secretary of labor to prepare a report on the problem of age discrimination. In 1965, that report, *The Older American Workers—Age Discrimination in Employment*, documented widespread discrimination. The report served as the impetus for passage of the Age Discrimination in Employment Act of 1967. The act, which applies to employers, employment agencies, and labor organizations and covers individuals between the ages of forty and seventy, prohibits discrimination against individuals on the basis of age unless there is a bona fide occupational qualification reasonably necessary to the normal operation of the particular business.

Specifically, it is against the law to discriminate by age in wages, benefits, hours worked, or availability of overtime. Employers and unions may not discriminate against those between the ages of forty and seventy in providing fringe benefits, such as education or training programs, career development, sick leave, and vacations. It is a violation of the act to publish notices or advertisements indicating a preference limitation or discrimination based on age. Even advertisements that imply a preference for youthful workers over older workers are in violation of the

[18]*Publishers Weekly* Jan. 23, 1978, p. 276.

[19]427 U.S. 307 (1976).

[20]U.S. Va, 98 S.Ct. 444.

Profile
▽
Claude Pepper

Born in Chambers County, Alabama, in 1900, Claude Pepper studied at the University of Alabama and received his law degree from Harvard University in 1924. His political career began with a seat in the Florida house, which he held from 1929 to 1931. In 1936, he gained a seat in the U.S. Senate and served uninterruptedly through 1950 when he was defeated in a primary campaign. In 1962, Pepper was elected to the House of Representatives and has served continuously since that time.

A "crusading liberal" sympathetic with FDR's New Deal, Pepper has always been identified with liberal politics. In his more recent career as representative of Florida's Fourteenth Congressional District, which includes most of Miami and Miami Beach, he has become the leading advocate of the rights of older Americans. As chairman of the Select Committee on Aging, he

"To waste the talents of the older worker is as shameful as it is to waste natural resources."

has worked for a strong and viable Social Security system and was instrumental in pushing through legislation in 1978 that changed the mandatory

retirement age from sixty-five to seventy years of age and banned mandatory retirement for most federal employees. In 1981 Pepper made the following remarks about Social Security before the House of Representatives:

There are many voices sounding the call of retreat. . . . Social Security, they say . . . must be slashed . . . in order to make it possible to cut the taxes of many . . . who hardly need tax reduction as much as the elderly need the benefits they are receiving.*

Pepper relinquished his chairmanship of the Committee on Aging in 1983 to become chairman of the House Rules Committee. From this powerful leadership position, he was able to serve as a strong supporter of the Speaker and to work for the passage of liberal legislation.

*The New York Times Magazine Nov. 29, 1981, p. 126

law. Requesting age on an application is not illegal, but may be closely scrutinized in light of the employer's hiring practices.

The Age Discrimination in Employment Act of 1967 was amended in 1974 to include state and local governments and to furnish protection to most federal employees. More importantly, in 1978, Congress made extensive amendments to the 1967 act, prohibiting mandatory retirement of most employees under age seventy. Many states had already passed similar statutes. In 1986, mandatory retirement rules were finally outlawed, except for a few selected occupations.

The Elderly and Politics

The Elderly as Voters

If we use voter participation as a measure of political involvement, it is clear that the elderly are very active. Table 6–3 shows that of the six age categories listed, the over-sixty-five age group ranks second in voter registration and in actual turnout on election day. Whereas approximately 59 percent of all persons of voting age claim to have voted, in the over-sixty-five category the voting rate is 68 percent.

Table 6-3

Voter Participation by Age Groups, 1984

Voter participation seems to be positively correlated with age, as we can see in this table. The lowest participation is by 18–20 year olds and the highest is by 45–64 year olds.

Age Group	Persons of Voting Age (millions)	Percent Reporting They Registered	Percent Reporting They Voted
18–20	11.2	47.0%	36.7%
21–24	16.7	54.3%	43.5%
25–34	40.3	63.3%	54.5%
35–44	30.7	70.9%	63.5%
45–64	44.3	76.6%	69.8%
65 and over	26.7	76.9%	67.7%

SOURCE: *Statistical Abstract of the United States, 1986,* p. 256.

The Elderly as Legislators

Whereas all other minority groups are very poorly represented in the Senate and in the House, such is not the case for the elderly. In 1985, for example, the Senate had twenty-one members over the age of sixty and the House had seventy-seven. Table 6–4 shows the age categories of members of Congress for selected years.

Table 6–4

Ages of Members of Congress for Selected Years

Congressional Chamber and Year	Under 40	40–49	50–59	60–69	70–79	80 and Over
Representatives						
1971	40	133	152	86	19	3
1973	45	132	154	80	20	2
1975	69	138	137	75	14	2
1977	81	121	147	71	15	—
1979	86	125	145	63	14	—
1981	94	142	132	54	12	1
1983	96	142	131	53	12	1
1985	71	154	131	59	17	1
Senators						
1971	4	24	32	23	16	1
1973	3	25	37	23	11	1
1975	5	21	35	24	15	—
1977	6	26	35	21	10	2
1979	10	31	33	17	8	1
1981	9	35	36	14	6	—
1983	9	35	36	14	6	—
1985	4	27	38	25	4	2

SOURCE: *Statistical Abstract of the United States, 1986,* p. 249.

Maggie Kuhn, the leader of the Gray Panthers.

The Elderly as Activists

Today the elderly work for their interests through a number of active, large, and effective political associations. The National Association of Retired Federal Employees, formed in 1921, currently has 450,000 members. In 1947, the National Retired Teachers' Association was established, and today it has more than half a million members. The largest of these groups is the American Association of Retired Persons, for those aged fifty-five and older, founded in 1958, with a current membership of more than twelve million. The latter two groups have united in a powerful joint effort to ensure beneficial treatment for the elderly by lobbying for legislation at the federal and state levels. They use the same staff in Washington and provide almost the same services to their members, including low-priced group insurance and travel programs.

In 1971, the Gray Panthers was formed to fight ageism, taking as its motto "Age and Youth in Action." It has about a hundred local groups in a number of cities and a staff of six at its Philadelphia headquarters.

The National Council of Senior Citizens, established in 1960, is a politically-oriented group of 3,300 local clubs. It keeps a close watch on congressional legislation affecting the elderly, informs members about important pending votes, and instructs them on how to lobby effectively for or against particular pieces of legislation.

Some of these organizations are more exotic. Flying Senior Citizens of the U.S.A., for example, is a Buffalo (New York)-based group of about 1,500 persons. Its main goal is to petition domestic airlines to allow senior citizens to travel for half fare Monday through Thursday, the off-peak days of the week. They argue that older persons should have this opportunity, as teenagers do, through standby rates.

The National Alliance of Senior Citizens, in contrast to the Flying Senior Citizens, has 450,000 members and addresses thirty different issue areas—from adult education to volunteerism—through its specialized advisory council.

Demonstration by the Gray Panthers.

The Rights of the Handicapped

$\triangledown$

By the 1970s, the handicapped were becoming a political force. In particular, they wanted the right to physical access in order to be able to compete more effectively in the marketplace. This meant modifying physical structures so they could avoid the curbs, stairways, and counters that make mobility difficult for them. A 1978 amendment to the Rehabilitation Act of 1973 established the Architectural and Transportation Barriers Compliance Board. Regulations for ramps, elevators, and the like in all federal buildings were quickly implemented. Cost, however, created somewhat of a backlash. Estimates from as low as $4 billion to more than $7 billion were given as the cost of compliance over the next several decades. Faced with such estimates, the Reagan administration took some steps to rescind previous advances in this area.

Congress passed Public Law 94-142 in 1975. Its official name is the Education for All Handicapped Children Act, but unofficially, it has been referred to as the Bill of Rights for the handicapped. This act guarantees that all handicapped children will receive an "appropriate" education.

What we will continue to observe in the future are the economic trade-offs that have to be made when resources are allocated to benefit specially selected groups in society. It is not enough to state simply that the handicapped (or the elderly or any other disadvantaged group) should be given better treatment in America. How much better the treatment will be is both an economic and then a political question.

The Rights and Status of Juveniles

$\triangledown$

There are sixty-three million children who are American citizens. The definition of *children* ranges from under age sixteen to twenty-one, but however defined, children form a large group of individuals in the United States and have the least amount of rights and protections. The reason for this lack is the common presumption of society and its lawmakers that children are basically protected by their parents. This is not to say that children are the exclusive property of the parents, but rather that an overwhelming case in favor of not allowing parents to control the actions of their children must be presented before the state will intervene.

Voting, Marriage, and the Young

The Twenty-sixth Amendment to the Constitution, ratified on July 1, 1971, reads as follows:

> The right of citizens of the United States, who are eighteen years of age or older, to vote shall not be denied or abridged by the United States or by any State on account of age.

Why age eighteen? Why not seventeen or sixteen? Why did it take until 1971 to allow those between the ages of eighteen and twenty-one to vote?

There are no easy answers to such questions. One cannot argue simply that those under twenty-one, or those under eighteen, are "incompetent." Incompetent at what? Certainly, one could find a significant number of seventeen-year-olds who can understand the political issues presented to them as well as many eligible adults. One of the arguments used for granting suffrage to eighteen-year-olds was

Juvenile being arrested.

Civil Law

The law regulating conduct between private persons over noncriminal matters. Under civil law, the government provides the forum for the settlement of disputes between private parties in such matters as contracts, domestic relations, and business relations.

Criminal Law

The law that defines crimes and provides punishment for violations. In criminal cases, the government is the prosecutor since crimes are against the public order.

Majority

Full age; the age at which a person is entitled by law to the management of his or her own affairs and to the enjoyment of civil rights.

Necessaries

In contracts, necessaries include whatever is reasonably necessary for suitable subsistence as measured by age, state, condition in life, and so on.

▽

that because they could be drafted to fight in the country's wars, they had a stake in public policy. At the time, the example of Vietnam was paramount.

Have eighteen- to twenty-one-year-olds used their right to vote? Yes and no. Immediately after the passage of the Twenty-sixth Amendment, the percentage of eighteen- to twenty-year-olds registering to vote was 58 percent (in 1972), and 48.3 percent reported that they had voted. By the 1980 election, however, only 44.7 percent of this age group had registered and only 35.7 percent had voted.

In the area of marriage, young people in the United States are also selected for age-related regulation: The law determines the minimum age for marriage. Table 6–5 suggests that both gender and age are considered to be important factors in making judgments about when people are considered adults for purposes of marriage. A fourteen-year-old boy or girl may marry with parental consent in Alabama. If the same persons were living in Delaware, however, the girl would have to wait two years and the boy four years longer before having the right to marry.

The Rights of Children in Civil and Criminal Proceedings

Children today have limited rights in civil and criminal proceedings in our judicial system. Different procedural rules and judicial safeguards apply in civil and criminal laws. **Civil law** relates in part to contracts among private individuals or companies. **Criminal law** relates to crimes against society that are defined by society acting through its state legislatures.

Private Contract Rights

Children are defined exclusively by state law with respect to private contract negotiations, rights, and remedies. The legal definition of **majority** varies from eighteen to twenty-one years of age, depending on the state. If an individual is legally a minor, she or he usually cannot be held responsible for contracts entered into. In most states, only contracts entered into for so-called **necessaries** (things necessary

Table 6–5

Minimum Age for Marriage in Selected States (1982)

State	With Parents' Consent		Without Parents' Consent	
	Male	Female	Male	Female
Alabama	14	14	18	18
Delaware	18	16	18	18
Puerto Rico	18	16	21	21
Wyoming	16	16	19	19

for subsistence, as determined by the courts) can be enforced against minors. Also, when minors engage in negligent behavior, typically their parents are liable. If, for example, a minor destroys a neighbor's fence, the neighbors may bring suit against the child's parents, but not against the child.

Criminal Rights

One of the main requirements for an act to be criminal is intent. The law has given children certain defenses against criminal prosecution because of their presumed inability to have criminal intent.

Under **common law** children up to seven years of age were considered incapable of committing a crime because they did not have the moral sense to understand that they were doing wrong. Children between the ages of seven and fourteen were also presumed to be incapable of committing a crime, but this presumption could be rebutted by showing that the child understood the wrongful nature of the act. Today, states vary in their approaches, but all retain this concept. Most states retain the common-law approach, although age limits vary from state to state. Other states have rejected the rebuttable presumption and simply set a minimum age for criminal responsibility.

All states have juvenile court systems that handle children below the age of criminal responsibility who commit delinquent acts. Their aim is allegedly to reform rather than to punish. In states that retain the rebuttable presumption approach, children who are beyond the minimum age but are still juveniles can be turned over to the criminal courts if the juvenile court determines that they should be treated as adults.

Procedural Rights in Criminal Trials

In 1965, if a child were picked up for illegal activities, that child could have been sentenced in juvenile court without a lawyer, without the child's parents being allowed to see the complaint against him or her, and without having counsel being able to cross-examine whoever made the complaint. In addition, in most states the child would have been unable to appeal his or her punishment to a higher court. Basically, the Bill of Rights did not apply to the young.

In 1967, all that changed. In a watershed case, the father of a child who had been sentenced in juvenile court to six years in an industrial school for one obscene phone call took his case all the way to the Supreme Court. The father argued that the Bill of Rights protects children, and noted that his child didn't have a lawyer,

Common Law

Judge-made law that originated in England from decisions shaped according to prevailing customs. Decisions were applied to similar situations and thus gradually became common to the nation. Common law forms the basis of legal procedures in the United States.

Ronald Zamora, age 15, being tried for murder.

the parents couldn't see the complaint against the child, and no one could cross-examine the person who complained that the child had made the obscene phone call. Amazingly, if the child had been an adult (over eighteen), the maximum sentence in the state in which the presumed phone call was made would have been three months in jail or a fine of from $5 to $50.

The Supreme Court, in *In re Gault*, held that

> The Due Process Clause of the Fourteenth Amendment requires that in respect to proceedings to determine [juvenile] delinquency which may result in commitment to an institution in which the juvenile's freedom is curtailed, the child and his parent must be notified of the child's right to be represented by counsel retained by them, or if they are unable to afford counsel, that counsel will be appointed to represent the child.[21]

In its majority opinion the Court, after reviewing reports on juvenile court proceedings, concluded that "juvenile court history has again demonstrated that unbridled discretion, however benevolently motivated, is frequently a poor substitute for principle and procedure." Finally, the Court stated that "under our Constitution, the conditions of being a boy does not justify a **kangaroo court.**"

In spite of *In re Gault*, children still do not have the right to trial by jury or to bail. Also, parents can still commit their minor children to state mental institutions without granting the child a hearing.

The Other Side of the Coin

Although it may be true that minors still do not normally have the full rights of adults in criminal proceedings, they have certain advantages. In felony, manslaughter, murder, armed robbery, and assault cases, juveniles are usually not tried as adults. They may be sentenced to probation or "reform" school for a relatively few years regardless of the seriousness of their crimes. However, most states allow juveniles to be tried as adults (often at the discretion of the judge) for certain crimes such as murder. When they are tried as adults, they are treated to due process of law and tried for the crime, rather than being given the paternalistic treatment reserved for the juvenile delinquent.

The Rights and Status of Gays

▽

Studies by Kinsey and his associates in the late 1940s, and early 1950s, coupled with more recent research, indicate there are perhaps twenty-five million Americans with varying degrees of homosexual orientation.[22] **Gays,** as they are most commonly called, therefore represent one of the most important minorities in the United States. Nonetheless, the rights of gays have only recently surfaced as a major issue on the American political and legal scene.

The Law and Public Attitudes

The status of gays came to national attention in 1977 when Anita Bryant, of Florida orange juice and television commercial fame, organized a "Save Our Children" campaign, whose purpose was to rescind the law protecting gays' legal rights in

Kangaroo Court
A mock hearing in which norms of justice and judicial procedure are ignored.

Gays
A term used to denote homosexuals. (The term *lesbians* denotes homosexual women only.)

[21]*In re Gault*, 387 U.S. 1 (1967).

[22]Rhonda Rivera, "Homosexuality and the Law," in William Paul, James D. Weinrich, John C. Gonsirock, and Mary E. Hoxtedt, eds., *Homosexuality: Social, Psychological, and Biological Issues* (Beverly Hills, Sage, 1982), pp. 25–26.

One of the most adverse developments for the U.S. gay community has been the increasing problem of AIDS, or acquired immune deficiency syndrome. It is virtually always fatal and until recently has affected and been spread primarily by homosexual males and by intravenous drug users or recipients of blood transfusions. When the potential impact of AIDS beyond the gay community became clearer, the politics of AIDS expanded. Children with AIDS were banned from schools by parent groups fearing transmission to their own children. Gays began to experience more job discrimination. Persons who tested positively for the virus were fired from their jobs.

Rumors spread that AIDS could be contracted through touch and by saliva. In at least one case, a man was charged with attempted murder when he told police officers that he had AIDS and then spit at them. Laws mandating the strict quarantine of persons with AIDS were passed in some

states. Anti-AIDS groups, especially religious conservatives, commented that AIDS was God's punishment for homosexuals.

The rights of AIDS victims have be-

come a concern. Gay groups have protested the lack of government effort to help find the cause and a cure. Public opinion on the whole has become more hostile to gay life-styles. The biggest reversal for gays came when the Office of Legal Counsel of the U.S. Department of Justice issued an opinion in June 1986 that said employers could dismiss gays who are determined to be carriers of the virus, when such firing can be justified as a prudent action to protect other employees. These and other developments have blunted the political clout of the sizable gay community. It seems doubtful, for example, that Democratic party candidates in the foreseeable future will seek gay support as openly as did Walter Mondale in his 1984 quest for the presidency. On the other hand, as AIDS affects a larger spectrum of the population, it is probable that public opinion will shift more toward finding a solution rather than assigning blame to gays.

Dade County, Florida. The Dade County law protected homosexuals from discrimination in public accommodations, housing, and employment. Bryant's campaign against the gay community's effort to keep the law on the books was successful. In June 1977, Miami citizens voted 2 to 1 to repeal the law protecting gays. Similar laws were repealed in Eugene, Oregon; Wichita, Kansas; and St. Paul, Minnesota.

Until recently, homosexuality was illegal in virtually every state in the Union. Today only twenty-nine states still have antihomosexual laws on the books. Recent Gallup polls show that 44 percent of Americans believe that private homosexual relations between consenting adults should not be considered illegal. In July 1985, 71 percent felt homosexuals should have equal rights in terms of job opportunities, and 33 percent felt homosexuality should be considered an acceptable alternative life-style. Yet in the summer of 1986, the Supreme Court upheld an antigay law in the state of Georgia that made homosexual conduct between two adults a crime. Justice Byron White, in a written opinion, said that "we are quite unwilling" to "announce . . . a fundamental right to engage in homosexual sodomy."[23]

[23]*Bowers v. Hardwick*, 106 S.Ct. 2841 (1986).

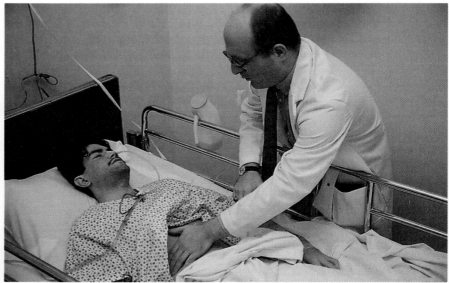

Gays and Politics

The number of gay organizations grew from fifty in 1969 to more than a thousand by the end of the 1970s. These groups have been active in exerting pressure on legislatures, the media, schools, and churches. In 1973, gay organizations succeeded in having the American Psychiatric Association remove homosexuality from its list of disorders. During the 1970s, more than half the states repealed sodomy laws. The Civil Service Commission eliminated its ban on the employment of gays. In 1980, the Democratic party platform included a gay rights plank.[24]

Politicians have not overlooked the potential significance of homosexual issues in American politics. Conservative politicians have been generally critical of gays. Liberals, however, have by and large begun to speak out for gay rights. Walter Mondale, former vice president of the United States and the winning contender for the Democratic party nomination for president in 1984, addressed a gay convention and openly bid for their political support.

In cities such as San Francisco, which is considered to be the gay capital of the United States, and Washington, D.C., the homosexual vote is considered to be a critical factor in politics. In 1979, gay political activist David Scott forced San Francisco Mayor Dianne Feinstein into a runoff primary election. In that same year, active gay voters in Washington, D.C., helped to elect Mayor Marion Barry. In other cities such as Miami, Florida, in 1977 and smaller communities such as Ames, Iowa, in the summer of 1983, ordinances specifically addressing gay rights have been defeated or repealed. Gay bars, apartment houses, public bathhouses, saunas, and other establishments catering to gays have proliferated across the country. Gays have been elected to public office and gays in increasing numbers and from all walks of life declare themselves publicly. Americans clearly appear, though, not to have fully accepted homosexuality as a normal and legitimate way of life. The controversy over the role of gays in American society will continue to occupy a great deal of public debate.

[24]John D'Emilio, *Sexual Politics, Sexual Communities* (Chicago: University of Chicago Press, 1983), pp. 1,238.

When you apply for a job, you may be subjected to a variety of possibly discriminatory practices—based on your race, gender, religion, and the like. You may also be subjected to a battery of tests, some of which you may feel are discriminatory. At both state and federal levels, the government has continued to examine the fairness and validity of criteria used in job applicant screening. If you believe that you have been discriminated against by a potential employer, you may wish to consider the following steps:

1. Evaluate your own capabilities and determine if you are truly qualified for the position.
2. Analyze the reasons that you were turned down (or dismissed); do you feel that others would agree with you, or would they uphold your employer's claims?
3. If you still believe that you have been unfairly treated, you have recourse to several agencies and services.

You should first speak to the personnel director of the company and politely explain that you feel you have not been adequately evaluated. If asked, give the specifics of your concerns. If necessary, go into explicit detail and indicate that you feel that you may have been discriminated against. If a second evaluation is not forthcoming, contact the local branch of your state employment agency. If you still do not obtain adequate help, contact one or more of the following agencies, usually found by looking in your telephone directory under "state government" listings:

1. If a government entity is involved, a state ombudsman or citizen aide who will mediate may be available.
2. You may wish to contact the State Civil Rights Commission, which will at least give you advice if it does not wish to take up your case.
3. The state attorney general's office will normally have a division dealing with discrimination and civil rights.
4. There may be a special commission or department specifically set up to help you, such as a women's status commission or a commission on Hispanic or Asian Americans. If you are a member of such a minority or a woman, contact the staff people of these commissions.
5. Finally, at the national level, you can contact the American Civil Liberties Union and you can also contact the most appropriate federal agency: Equal Employment Opportunity Commission, 2401 E St., NW, Washington, D.C. 20506

Chapter Summary

▽

1. The earliest feminist movement in the United States was entwined with the struggle to abolish slavery. Later, the women's rights movement separated itself from the racial equality movement.

2. About 1870, women's organizations formed with the aim of achieving suffrage for women. In 1920, the Nineteenth Amendment was passed, granting women the right to vote.

3. The current feminist movement began in the late 1950s. The movement seeks to define sexism and to eradicate it from all spheres of life for all women. One of the leading pressure groups for women's rights today is the National Organization for Women (NOW).

4. The proposed Twenty-seventh Amendment to the Constitution (the Equal Rights Amendment, or ERA) states, "Equality of rights under the law shall not be denied or abridged by the United States or by any state on account of sex." Anti-ERA groups, headed by Phyllis Schlafly, were successful in preventing ratification by the necessary number of states.

5. Under Title VII of the Civil Rights Act of 1964, sex discrimination in employment is prohibited. The Supreme Court has indicated in a recent case that creating a hostile environment for sexual harassment even if job status isn't affected also violates Title VII. As amended in 1978 by the Pregnancy Discrimination Act, sex discrimination based on pregnancy, childbirth, or related medical conditions is also prohibited.

6. The Equal Pay Act of 1963 prohibits discrimination in the wages paid for equal work when its performance requires equal skills, effort, and responsibility under similar condi-

▽

tions. The issue of comparable worth is that women should receive equal pay, not just for equal work, but also for work of comparable skill, effort, and responsibility.

7. Of the American population 11.5 percent are sixty-five or older. Many are poor, burdened by medical costs, and unable to find work because of age discrimination in employment. The problems of aging and retirement will become increasingly important as the population continues to age.

8. The Age Discrimination in Employment Act of 1967 prohibits discrimination against individuals on the basis of age unless there is a bona fide occupational qualification reasonably necessary to the normal operation of a particular business. It has been amended to cover state and local governments and to prohibit mandatory retirement of most employees under the age of seventy.

9. The elderly are involved politically through high voter turnout, representation in Congress, and very active political associations.

10. The rights of the handicapped became a political and economic issue in the 1970s and continues to be a controversial issue today.

11. Children form a large group of individuals in the United States but have the least amount of rights and privileges.

12. The Twenty-sixth amendment extended the right to vote in national elections to all persons age eighteen and over.

13. Children have limited rights in civil and criminal proceedings in our judicial system. They are defined exclusively by state law with respect to private contract negotiations, rights, and remedies. States set minimum age requirements for criminal responsibility. The 1967 *In re Gault* decision extended the due process clause to juveniles.

14. The rights of gays, who comprise an estimated 10 percent of the U.S. population, has recently surfaced as a major issue on the American political and legal scene. In certain cities, gays have become politically active, and the homosexual vote is considered a critical factor in politics. Gay political organizations have considerable power. However, Americans have not yet fully accepted homosexuality as a legitimate way of life.

Questions for Review and Discussion
▽

1. What beliefs about the nature of women made granting them the right to vote so difficult? To what extent do some of the same attitudes exist today?

2. Think about the concept of equal pay for comparable work. What kinds of jobs traditionally performed by men would be comparable in effort, skill, and worth, say, to an executive secretary or switchboard operator? How would the economy be affected if the wages for many "women's jobs" were greatly increased?

3. What changes in our patterns of family life and in societal values have led to the political activism of senior citizens? How has the establishment of the Social Security program changed our views of the relationship between government and the elderly?

Selected References
▽

Robert H. Binstock and Ethel Shanas, eds., *Handbook of Aging and the Social Sciences* (New York: Van Norstrand Reinhold, 1976). A comprehensive treatment of specialized topics concerning the elderly in American society.

Sylvia Ann Hewlett, *A Lesser Life: The Myth of Women's Liberation in America* (New York: Morrow, 1986). One of the most controversial books on the women's struggle, it unfavorably compares the record of the United States with other countries, especially in Europe, in the area of women's social support and social legislation (maternity leave and day care, for example).

William W. Lammers, *Public Policy and the Aging* (Washington, D.C.: Congressional Quarterly Press, 1983). The author describes how the rapidly growing older population will affect the development of programs for the elderly. Specific public policies are explored in detail.

Gilbert Y. Steiner, *The Children's Cause* (Washington, D.C.: Brookings Institution, 1976). An analysis of the organizations that lobby for children's rights and programs.

Gilbert Y. Steiner, *Constitutional Inequality: The Political Fortunes of the Equal Rights Amendment* (Washington, D.C.: Brookings Institution, 1985). A case study of the Equal Rights Amendment, this study dissects the difficulties in accomplishing fundamental policy changes through constitutional amendments.

Patricia A. Vardin and Ilene N. Brody, eds., *Children's Rights: Contemporary Perspectives* (New York: Teachers College Press, 1979). A valuable collection of essays on the rights of children in American politics.

3
PEOPLE AND POLITICS

Chapter 7

▽

Public Opinion

Contents

▽

Defining and Measuring Public Opinion

The Qualities of Public Opinion

Measuring Public Opinion: Polling Techniques

How Public Opinion Is Formed

The Political Culture of Americans

Public Opinion about Government

Political Ideology

Public Opinion and the Political Process

What If . . .
▽
Public Opinion Polls Made Law?

In Chapter 1 we noted that in a direct democracy the citizens would make the laws themselves, rather than through elected representatives who do not always see eye-to-eye with public opinion. What if the United States were a direct democracy? What legal and institutional arrangements would remain the same in our society and what might be changed if the outcome of public opinion polls decided basic issues? Judging from some recent Gallup poll results, here are some things that a *majority* of Americans would enact into law:

—Limits on the sale of handguns
—Development of the "star wars" strategic defense initiative program
—Withholding of tax refunds from those who default on federally guaranteed student loans
—A line item veto for the president to veto some items without vetoing an entire bill

—Enactment of "right to die" legislation
—Possession of small amounts of marijuana should be a criminal offense
—Limits on marriage between blacks and whites

—Prohibition of tandem truck rigs on noninterstate roads
—An immediate, verifiable freeze on nuclear weapons
—No additional military aid to El Salvador
—A national presidential primary

—The limiting of house members to twelve years in office
—Adoption of the Equal Rights Amendment
—A ban on school busing
—More financial responsibility for social programs given to state governments
—Consistent imposition of the death penalty for murder
—Prohibition on the hiring of illegal immigrants
—A constitutional amendment to permit prayer in public schools

▽

Clearly, if public opinion were the sole determinant of public policy, there would be some important changes in our laws. In our representative system of government, however, public opinion acts indirectly to determine public policy. It is important to examine how public opinion is measured and the forces that influence the opinions people hold.

I believe that we must always be mindful of this one thing—whatever the trials and the tests ahead, the ultimate strength of our country and our cause will lie, not in powerful weapons or infinite resources of boundless wealth, but will lie in the unity of our people. . . .

What we won when all of our people united must not now be lost in suspicion and distrust and selfishness and politics among any of our people. And believing this as I do I have concluded that I should not permit the Presidency to become involved in the partisan divisions that are developing in this political year. . . .

Accordingly, I shall not seek, and I will not accept, the nomination of my party for another term as your President.[1]

President Johnson shocked the nation with this statement. His decision not to run again in 1968 was—most political scientists agree—the direct result of massive public resistance to a very unpopular war. Consider some of the events that had occurred before Johnson's speech:

— *In 1965*: Demonstrations were held throughout the country against the Vietnam war and President Johnson's policy in Southeast Asia. On October 15th and 16th, protesters demonstrated in forty cities in the United States. In New York City alone, 10,000 to 14,000 people marched down Fifth Avenue chanting slogans like "Hey, hey, LBJ, how many kids did you kill today?" In November, two American pacifists burned themselves to death in an extreme moral gesture against the U.S. role in Vietnam. Arrests of demonstrators were becoming frequent.

— *In 1966*: Demonstrations continued throughout the country. In New York, on March 25, 20,000 to 25,000 protestors held a rally and parade. A day later in San Francisco, about 3,500 demonstrators marched, wearing black armbands and carrying cardboard coffins. The first high school student protest against the war was conducted on April 9 on the Columbia University campus in New York. On June 4, a three-page advertisement in the *New York Times*, costing $20,880 and bearing more than 6,400 signatures, urged the administration to cease all bombing and to terminate the U.S. military presence in Vietnam.

— *In 1967*: Washington was put under increasing pressure to end the war. Large-scale demonstrations multiplied, often focusing on draft offices, on job recruiters on campus for chemical firms producing napalm, or on army and navy recruiters. The largest antiwar demonstration during 1967—and the most violent—was the Lincoln Memorial rally held on October 21–22. It was estimated that 150,000 persons participated, 57 of whom were injured. The Pentagon steps were said to be spattered with the blood of the protestors. Massive demonstrations were also held abroad—in London, Paris, Stockholm, Berlin, Tokyo, Belgrade, Rome, and elsewhere.

— *In 1968*: Demonstrations continued—against the war and against the draft. Some 5,000 women, led by ex-Representative Jeannette Rankin, age eighty-seven, demonstrated at the foot of Capitol Hill and presented the House speaker with a petition to withdraw troops from Vietnam. On March 2, the Justice Department reported 1,424 cases of draft violation in the preceding year. On the day of Johnson's speech declaring he would not seek reelection to the presidency (March 31, 1968), the *New York Times* reported a Gallup poll showing that only 29 percent of Americans approved of Johnson's handling of the war (63 percent disapproved).

These were only a few of the expressions of public disfavor concerning President Johnson's policy in Vietnam. His speech was in part an acknowledgment of the

---

[1]*Public Papers of the President of the United States: Lyndon B. Johnson, 1968–69*, vol. 1 (Washington, D.C.: Government Printing Office, 1970), pp. 475, 476.

power of public opinion in the United States. Public opinion in a democracy (and even in a dictatorship) must be heeded by politicians and government officials alike; for when it is not, politicians may find themselves out of office and governments may topple.

This was effectively what happened to Richard Nixon in August 1974. After the exposure of the Watergate cover-up, coupled with Nixon's firing of Special Prosecutor Archibald Cox and the resignation of Attorney General John Mitchell, the president's approval ratings slipped badly. Just before his resignation, less than one in four adults had a favorable opinion of Nixon's performance in office, and many wanted him to be impeached and tried for criminal conduct.

Defining and Measuring Public Opinion

▽

There is no one public opinion because there are many different "publics." In a nation of more than 230 million people, there may be innumerable gradations of opinion on an issue. What we do is describe the distribution of opinions among the public about a particular question. Thus we define **public opinion** as follows:

Public Opinion

The aggregate of individual attitudes or beliefs shared by some portion of adults. There is no one public opinion because there are many different "publics."

> Public opinion is the aggregate of individual attitudes or beliefs shared by some portion of adults.

Although it might be said, for example, that public opinion favors the passage of the Equal Rights Amendment (ERA), a more accurate description of public opinion on this issue would be that 60 percent of the public supports the amendment, whereas 40 percent opposes it or has no opinion.

How is public opinion known in a democracy? In the case of the Vietnam war, it was made known by numerous antiwar protests, countless articles in magazines and newspapers, and a continuing electronic media coverage of antiwar demonstrations. Normally, however, public opinion becomes known in a democracy through elections and, in some states, initiatives or referenda (see Chapter 19).

New England town meeting.

Other ways are through lobbying and interest group activities, which are also used to influence public opinion.

Public opinion can be defined most clearly by its effect. As political scientist V. O. Key, Jr. said, public opinion is what governments "find it prudent to heed."[2] This means that for public opinion to be effective, enough people have to hold a particular view with such strong conviction that a government feels its actions should be influenced by it.

An interesting question arises as to when *private* opinion becomes *public* opinion. Everyone probably has a private opinion about the competence of the president, as well as private opinions about more personal concerns, such as the state of a neighbor's lawn. We say that private opinion becomes public opinion when the opinion is publicly expressed and if the opinion concerns public issues. When someone's private opinion becomes so strong that the individual is willing to go to the polls to vote for or against a candidate or an issue—or to participate in a demonstration, to discuss the issue at work, to be willing to speak out on local television, or to participate in the political process in any one of a dozen other ways—then that opinion becomes public opinion.

The Qualities of Public Opinion
▽

At the beginning of the Vietnam war, public opinion about its conduct was not very clear, like a camera that is not focused. As the war progressed and U.S. involvement deepened and there was still no successful outcome and no end in sight, public opinion became increasingly clarified. Public opinion has identifiable qualities that change over time. Political scientists have identified at least five specific qualities relating to public opinion: (1) intensity, (2) fluidity, (3) stability, (4) quiescence, and (5) relevance. In addition, political knowledge affects opinion, and the distribution of opinion on an issue indicates the possibilities for conflict or compromise.

Intensity

How strongly people are willing to express their private opinions determines the **intensity** of public opinion. Consider an example that seems to be continually in the news—gun control. Most Americans who have opinions about gun control do not have very strong opinions. A small percentage have extremely intense convictions pro or con. But the average intensity is still quite mild. However, public opinion about the Iranian hostages in 1979 and 1980 was quite intense, on average. Most Americans were in favor of taking drastic measures to free the hostages. Of those who did have an opinion, only a few were just mildly interested in saving the hostages.

Intensity of public opinion is often critical in generating public *action*. Intense minorities can win on an issue of public policy over less intense majorities. There is often a relationship between intensity of opinion and its perceived relevance on the part of public policy makers.

Intensity
The strengths of a pro or con position concerning a public policy or issue. Intensity is often critical in generating public action; an intense minority can often win on an issue of public policy over a less intense majority.

[2]*Public Opinion and American Democracy* (New York: Alfred A. Knopf, 1961), p. 10.

Fluidity

Public opinion can change drastically in a very short period of time. When this occurs, we say that public opinion is fluid.

Before 1976, most Americans felt that defense spending was too high compared with spending for other government programs. By 1978, public opinion began to shift toward spending more on national security. By the 1980 election, when Ronald Reagan accused Jimmy Carter of not being tough enough with the Russians, a large majority of the public felt that defense spending should be increased. After Congress approved Reagan's budget requests for these increases, public support for defense spending began to decline once more. Such **fluidity** in public opinion reflects public awareness of government policy and in turn influences government decision making.

Stability

Many individual opinions remain constant over a lifetime. Taken together, individual opinions that represent a public opinion may also be extremely stable, persisting for many years. Consider the effect of the Civil War on political attitudes in the South. It was the Republicans under Abraham Lincoln who, in the eyes of southerners, were responsible for the Civil War and the ensuing humiliations experienced by a defeated South. Consequently, the South became strongly Democratic. Until recently, it was called the **Solid South** because Democratic candidates always won. We can say that public-opinion in the South in favor of Democrats and against Republicans had great **stability.**

Quiescence

Not all political opinions are expressed by the holders of opinions. There may be potential political opinions—those not yet realized. Political scientists call these **latent,** or quiescent, **public opinions.** Some say, for example, that Hitler exploited the latent public opinion of post-World War I Germany by forming the National Socialist party. The public was ripe for a leader who would militarize Germany and enforce discipline to put Germany back on its feet. Latent public opinion offers golden opportunities for political leaders astute enough to perceive and act politically on it.

When average citizens are asked to respond to highly complex issues about which they have imperfect knowledge, their opinions may remain latent. This was true, for example, of the antiballistic missile (ABM) program debated by the Senate in 1969. A Gallup poll in July of that year indicated that 59 percent of Americans were undecided about the value of the ABM program even though they knew about it. What the views of those citizens would have been if they had been better informed is unknown. Abstract poll questions dealing with a respondent's ideology also produce high proportions of responses indicating that the question deals with something that many people rarely think about.

Relevance

Relevant public opinion for most people is simply public opinion that deals with issues concerning them. If a person has a sick parent who is having trouble meeting

Fluidity

The extent to which public opinion changes over time.

Solid South

A term describing the disposition of the post-Civil War southern states to vote for the Democratic party. (Voting patterns in the South have now begun to change.)

Stability

The extent to which public opinion remains constant over a period of time.

Latent Public Opinion

Unexpressed political opinions that have the potential to become manifest attitudes or beliefs.

medical bills, then the relevant public opinion for that person will be an opinion that is focused on the issues of Medicare and Medicaid. If another person likes to go hunting with his or her children, gun control becomes a relevant political issue. Of course, **relevance** changes according to events. Public concern about inflation, for example, was at an all-time low during the 1950s and early 1960s. Why? because the United States had little if any inflation during that period. Public opinion about the issue of unemployment was certainly relevant during the Great Depression, but not during the 1960s when the nation experienced 102 months of almost uninterrupted economic growth from 1961 to 1969.

Certain popular books can make a particular issue relevant. The publication of *The Population Bomb*[3] by Paul Ehrlich in 1968 heralded nationwide concern with uncontrolled population growth. The population issue, although still far from resolved, is less in the public mind today. Indeed, public opinion polls rarely sample attitudes about it.

Relevance
The extent to which an issue is of concern at a particular time. Issues become relevant when the public views them as pressing or of direct concern to them.

Political Knowledge

People are more likely to base their opinions on knowledge about an issue if they have strong feelings about the topic. Just as relevance and intensity are closely related to having an opinion, individuals who are strongly interested in a question will probably take the time to read about it.

Looking at the population as a whole, the level of political information is quite low. Survey research tells us that slightly less than 46 percent of adult Americans can give the name of their congressperson, whereas 39 percent can name both U.S. senators from their state. Only 30 percent know that the term of their congressional representative is two years, although almost 70 percent know the majority party in Congress. What these data tell us is that Americans do not expend much effort remembering political facts that may not be important to their daily lives.

Americans are also likely to forget political information quite quickly. Facts that were of vital interest to citizens at one point in time lose their meaning after the crisis has passed. In the 1985 *New York Times*/CBS News Survey on Vietnam, marking the tenth anniversary of the end of that conflict, 63 percent of those questioned knew that the United States sided with the South Vietnamese in that conflict. Only 27 percent remembered, however, which side in that conflict launched the Tet offensive, which was a major political defeat for American and South Vietnamese forces.[4]

If political information is perceived to be of no use for an individual or is painful to recall, it is not surprising that facts are forgotten. What is more disturbing is the inability of many citizens to give basic information about current issues. Members of Congress, who represent their constituents on complex and controversial issues, hope their constituents have informed opinions. In a recent poll of U.S. opinion on giving military assistance to the *contra* forces fighting in Nicaragua, only 38 percent of the respondents knew that the United States was supporting the *contras* against the government. Almost half of those surveyed did not know what kind of government controlled Nicaragua, 20 percent correctly identifying it as communist but 19 percent as a right-wing dictatorship.[5] Such a lack of information about an

"Are you uninformed or apathetic?"
"I don't know and I don't care."

"Why Are Your Papers in Order?"
© 1984 by Peter C. Vey.

[3]New York: Ballantine Books, 1968.
[4]*New York Times* Survey, February 23–27, 1985.
[5]*New York Times*, April 15, 1986, p. 4.

issue currently before Congress indicates that many people have not yet been motivated to learn much about important events in Central America.

Consensus and Division

There are very few issues on which most Americans agree. The more normal situation is for opinion to be distributed among several different positions. Looking at the distribution of opinion can tell us how divided the public is on a question and give us some indication of whether compromise is possible. The distribution of opinion can also tell us how many individuals have not thought about an issue enough to hold an opinion.

When a large proportion of the American public appears to express the same view on an issue, we say that a **consensus** exists, at least at the moment the poll was taken. Figure 7–1 shows the pattern of opinion that might be called consensual. Issues on which the public is divided into widely differing attitudes are clearly **divisive** (Figure 7–2). If there is no possible middle position on such issues, we expect that the division will continue to generate political conflict.

Figure 7–3 shows a distribution of opinion that indicates that most Americans either have no information about the issue or are not interested enough to formulate a position. This figure illustrates latent, or quiescent, opinion. Politicians may feel that the lack of knowledge gives them more room to manuever or they may be wary of taking any action for fear that the opinion will crystallize after a crisis. It is possible that this pattern would be the most likely to occur if survey respondents were totally honest. Research has shown that some individuals will express nonexistent opinions to an interviewer on certain topics rather than admit their ignorance.

Figure 7–1

▽

Consensus Opinion: The Space Shuttle

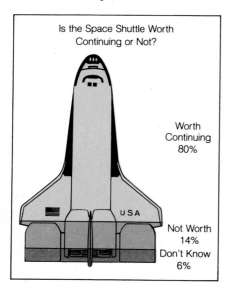

Is the Space Shuttle Worth Continuing or Not?

Worth Continuing 80%

Not Worth 14%
Don't Know 6%

USA

Measuring Public Opinion: Polling Techniques

▽

The History of Opinion Polls

Although some idea of public opinion can be discovered by asking persons we know for their opinions or by reading the "Letters to the Editor" sections in newspapers, most descriptions of the distribution of opinions are based on **opinion polls**. During the 1800s, certain American newspapers and magazines spiced up their political coverage by doing face-to-face straw polls or mail surveys of their readers' opinions. In this century, the magazine *Literary Digest* further developed the technique of opinion polls by mailing large numbers of questionnaires to individuals, many of whom were its own subscribers. From 1916 to 1936, more than 70 percent of the magazine's election predictions were accurate.

Literary Digest, however, suffered a major setback in its polling activities when it predicted that Alfred Landon would win over Franklin Delano Roosevelt in 1936, based on more than two million returned questionnaires. Landon won in only two states. A major problem with the *Digest's* polling technique was its continuing use of nonrepresentative individuals. In 1936, during the Great Depression, those people who were the magazine's subscribers were certainly not representative of the average American.

Several newcomers to the public opinion poll industry accurately predicted Roosevelt's landslide victory. The organizations of these newcomers are still active in the poll-taking industry today: the Gallup poll of George Gallup and Roper and Associates founded by Elmo Roper. Gallup and Roper, along with Archibald Crossley, developed the modern polling techniques of market research. Using personal interviews with small samples of selected voters (a few thousand) they showed they could predict with fair accuracy the behavior of the total voting population. We shall see how this is possible.

Government officials during World War II were keenly interested in public opinion about the war effort and about the increasing number of restrictions put on civilian activities. Improved methods of sampling were used, and by the 1950s a whole new science of survey research developed and spread to Western Europe, Israel, and other countries. Survey research centers sprang up throughout the United States, particularly at universities. Some of these survey groups are the American Institute of Public Opinion at Princeton, New Jersey, the National Opinion Research Center at the University of Chicago, and the Survey Research Center at the University of Michigan.

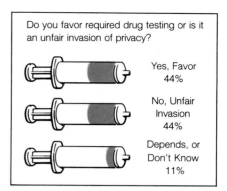

Figure 7–2
▽
Divisive Opinion:
Required Drug Testing

Sampling Techniques

How can interviewing several thousand voters tell us what tens of millions voters will do? Clearly, it is necessary that the sample of several thousand individuals be representative of all voters in the population. Consider an analogy. Let us say we have a large jar containing pennies of various dates and we want to know how many pennies were minted within certain decades—1940–1950, 1950–1960, and so on. There are 10,000 pennies in the jar. One way to estimate the distribution of the dates on the pennies—without examining all 10,000—is to take a representative sample. This sample would be obtained by mixing the pennies up well

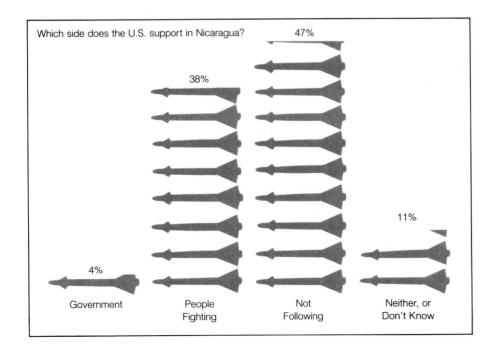

Figure 7–3
▽
Latent Opinion:
Nicaragua

On Saturday evening, October 8, 1983, the annual Iowa Democratic party's Jefferson-Jackson Day dinner at Veterans Memorial Auditorium in Des Moines became the focus of national attention. The important event was a **straw poll** of support for the seven announced Democratic candidates* for the presidency among the six thousand people who had bought tickets to the event.

Each candidate spoke before the audience of party activists. Walter Mondale attacked the record of his leading contender, John Glenn, and emphasized his experience as vice president and member of Congress. Glenn argued for a more centrist party stand on foreign policy and criticized Mondale's reliance on interest group support. Alan Cranston spoke of his support for a mutual and verifiable nuclear freeze.

*Jesse Jackson had not announced his candidacy at that time.

George McGovern promised to end American military actions in Central America and Lebanon and supported a large-scale public works program. Gary Hart derided the straw poll and called for dedication to innovative and creative party policies. Reubin Askew warned not to adopt platforms favoring abortion and opposing right-to-work laws. Ernest Hollings echoed Askew's statements, which were not very well received.

Before the three hours of oratory by these speakers and others, the diners had already voted. The results of the straw poll conducted by the Associated Press were as follows:

Mondale	1,945	48.8%
Cranston	1,534	38.4
Glenn	243	6.1
Hart	146	3.7
McGovern	74	1.9
Askew	35	0.9
Hollings	14	0.4

Are straw polls a useful measure of a candidate's strength among the voters? Probably not. The straw polls in Iowa, Maine, Wisconsin, Massachusetts, and other states early in the Democratic primary campaign were flawed by mass purchases of tickets by campaign coordinators, by the fact that people from other states voted in the polls, and by the respondents being party loyalists rather than average voters. In fact, a scientific public opinion poll at that time showed that rank-and-file Democrats in Iowa gave 46 percent of their votes to Mondale, 27 percent to Glenn, 8 percent to McGovern, 4 percent to Hart, 2 percent each to Cranston and unannounced candidate Jesse Jackson, 1 percent to Askew, and less than 1 percent to Hollings.

Straw Poll

An informal survey of a small group to determine opinion.

and them removing a handful of them—perhaps 100 pennies. The distribution of dates might be as follows:

— 1940–1950:   10 percent
— 1950–1960:   30 percent
— 1960–1970:   60 percent

If the pennies are very well mixed within the jar and if you take a larger sample, the resulting distribution would probably approach the actual distribution of the dates of all 10,000 coins.

The most important principle in sampling, or poll taking, is randomness. Every penny or every person should have an *equal chance* of being sampled. If this happens, then a small sample should be representative of the whole group both in demographic characteristics (age, religion, race, living area, and the like) and in opinions. The most ideal way to sample the voting population of the United States would be to put all voter names into a jar—or a computer—and randomly sample, say, 2,000 of them. However, since this is too costly and inefficient, pollsters have developed other ways to obtain good samples. One of the most interesting techniques is simply to choose a random selection of telephone numbers and interview the respective households. This technique produces an accurate sample at an inexpensive price.

To ensure that the random samples include all living areas—rural, urban, Northeast, South, and so on—most survey organizations randomly choose, say, urban areas that they will consider as representative of all urban areas. Then they randomly select their respondents within that area. A less accurate technique is known as quota sampling. For this type of poll, survey researchers decide how many persons of certain types they need in the survey—such as minorities, women, or farmers—and then send out interviewers to find the necessary number of these types. This method is not only less accurate but it also may be biased if, say, the interviewer refuses to go into certain neighborhoods or will not interview after dark. Generally, the national survey organizations take great care to select their samples randomly because their reputations rest on the accuracy of their results. Usually, the Gallup or Roper polls interview about 1,500 individuals, and their results have a very high probability of being correct—within a margin of 3 percent. The accuracy with which the Gallup poll has predicted political election results is reflected in Table 7–1.

Similar sampling techniques are used in many other, nonpolitical situations. For the Nielsen ratings of TV programs, for example, representative households are selected by the A. C. Nielsen Company and a machine is attached to each household's TV set. The machine monitors viewing choices twenty-four hours a day and transmits this information to the company's central offices. A one-point drop in a Nielsen rating can mean a loss of revenue of millions of dollars to a TV network because a one-point drop indicates about 800,000 fewer viewers are watching a particular show. This means advertisers are unwilling to pay as much for viewing time. Indeed, advertising rates are based in many cases solely on Nielsen ratings. When you consider that only about 3,000 families have that little machine attached to their TV sets, it is apparent that the science of selecting representative samples has come a long way—at least far enough to convince major advertisers to accept advertising fees based on the results of those samples.

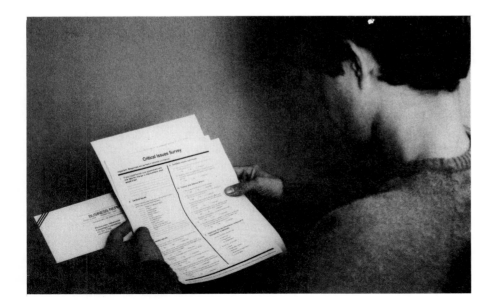

The Polls and the 1984 Election

Public opinion polls that seek to identify the voters' preferences in the presidential election begin long before the primary elections. Usually, polls begin matching potential candidates against each other in the fall of the year before the presidential

Table 7–1
▽
Record of Gallup Poll Accuracy

Year	Gallup Final Survey*		Election Result*		Deviation¹
1984	59.0%	Reagan	59.2%	Reagan	−0.2
1982	55.0	Democratic	56.1	Democratic	−1.1
1980	47.0	Reagan	50.8	Reagan	−3.8
1978	55.0	Democratic	54.6	Democratic	+0.4
1976	48.0	Carter	50.0	Carter	−2.0
1974	60.0	Democratic	58.9	Democratic	+1.1
1972	62.0	Nixon	61.8	Nixon	+0.2
1970	53.0	Democratic	54.3	Democratic	−1.3
1968	43.0	Nixon	43.5	Nixon	−0.5
1966	52.5	Democratic	51.9	Democratic	+0.6
1964	64.0	Johnson	61.3	Johnson	+2.7
1962	55.5	Democratic	52.7	Democratic	+2.8
1960	51.0	Kennedy	50.1	Kennedy	+0.9
1958	57.0	Democratic	56.5	Democratic	+0.5
1956	59.5	Eisenhower	57.8	Eisenhower	+1.7
1954	51.5	Democratic	52.7	Democratic	−1.2
1952	51.0	Eisenhower	55.4	Eisenhower	−4.4
1950	51.0	Democratic	50.3	Democratic	+0.7
1948	44.5	Truman	49.9	Truman	−5.4
1946	58.0	Republican	54.3	Republican	+3.7
1944	51.5	Roosevelt	53.3²	Roosevelt	−1.8
1942	52.0	Democratic	48.0¹	Democratic	+4.0
1940	52.0	Roosevelt	55.0	Roosevelt	−3.0
1938	54.0	Democratic	50.8	Democratic	+3.2
1936	55.7	Roosevelt	62.5	Roosevelt	−6.8

*The figure shown is the winner's percentage of the Democratic–Republican vote except in the elections of 1948, 1968, 1976, and 1980. Because the Thurmond and Henry Wallace voters in 1948 were largely split-offs from the normally Democratic vote, final preelection estimates of the division of the vote were made for the four candidates Truman, Dewey, Wallace, and Thurmond. Therefore, the percentages for Truman shown for 1948 are based on the total vote for the four candidates. In 1968 George Wallace's candidacy was supported by such a large minority that he was clearly a major candidate, and the 1968 percentages are based on the total Nixon–Humphrey–Wallace vote. In 1976, because of interest in McCarthy's candidacy and its potential effect on the Carter vote, the final Gallup poll report included estimates of the share of the vote for Carter, Ford, and McCarthy, as well as an estimate for all other candidates combined. Therefore, the percentages for Carter shown for 1976 are based on the total vote for all candidates. The same is true of 1980 when Anderson's candidacy drew a sizable minority vote.
¹Average deviation for 25 national elections: 2.1 percentage points.
Average deviation for 18 national elections since 1950 inclusive: 1.4 percentage points.
Trend in deviation:

Elections	Average Error
1936–1950	3.6
1952–1960	1.7
1962–1970	1.6
1972–1984	1.2

¹Final report said Democrats would win control of the House, which they did even though the Republicans won a majority of the popular vote.
²Civilian vote 53.3, Roosevelt soldier vote 0.5 = 53.8 Roosevelt. Gallup final survey based on civilian vote.
SOURCE: *The Gallup Report*, August/September 1984, p. 61; *The Gallup Report*, September 1985, p. 33.

contest. In 1983, "test matches" of various candidates against Ronald Reagan showed that several Democrats had a chance to defeat the president, although he was very popular personally. During the primary elections, polls are commissioned every week by the media and by the candidates to find out how each prospective nominee is doing nationally and in the states where primaries are being held. Other polls are taken by researchers at universities like the University of Chicago and the University of Michigan to provide information on people's attitudes for future investigation by political scientists and sociologists. In 1984, some polls suggested that Gary Hart would provide more competition for Mr. Reagan than would Walter Mondale, but it is never possible to foresee the effects of the fall campaign.

From the data given in Figure 7–4, it is easy to see that events can have an impact on public attitudes as measured by the polls. The Gallup data show that Mr. Mondale was almost even with Mr. Reagan immediately after the enthusiastic Democratic convention and that he gained little in the voters' favor after the first presidential debate. On the whole, the poll did accurately measure Mr. Reagan's strong support, and the last poll in the figure closely predicted the final choice of the voters. By the end of 1984, the predictions of the various commercial pollsters became a news story in their own right. By election day, the Harris poll predicted an eleven-point margin between the candidates while USA Today polls showed a 25 percent spread. Almost all of the other polls, however, were accurate within 4 percent of the final vote totals.

Figure 7–4
▽

Tracking the 1984 Election: Gallup Poll Results

SOURCE: Gallup Poll, *Minneapolis Star and Tribune*, Oct. 31, 1984, p. 13A.

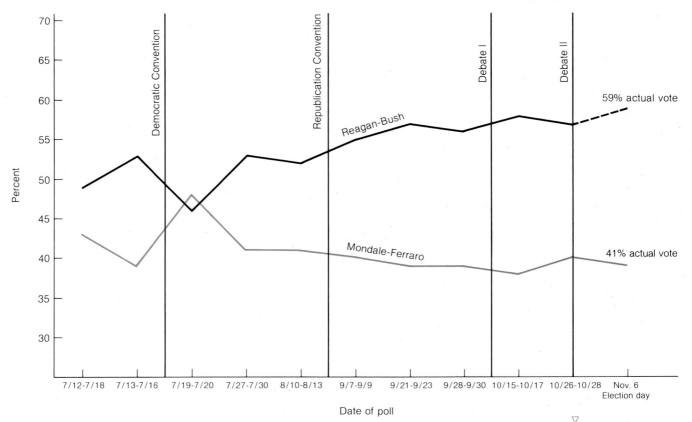

Problems with Opinion Polls

One of the major problems with opinion polls of voter preferences is that they cannot be responsive to rapid shifts in public opinion, unless the polls are taken frequently and up until the last minute. A classic example of opinion polls falling short occurred during the 1980 presidential election when Ronald Reagan overtook President Carter at the last moment.

In addition, because opinion polls can be biased, they must always be interpreted with care. Only when the questions are phrased in a manner that precludes inadvertent bias can we have much faith in the results. Also, when we can see that polls taken at different time periods show a trend, we can increase our faith in them.

Any opinion poll contains sampling error, which is simply the difference between what the sample results show and what the true result would be if everybody had been interviewed. Basically, the greater the number of people who are interviewed and the closer the entire adult population is to being unanimous in their opinion, the smaller the sampling error becomes.

How Public Opinion Is Formed
▽

Most Americans are willing to express opinions on political issues when asked. How do individuals acquire these opinions and attitudes? Most views that are expressed as political opinions are acquired through a process known as **political socialization.** By this we mean that individuals acquire their political attitudes, often including their party identification, through their relationships with their families, friends, and co-workers. The most important influences in that process

Political Socialization
The process by which individuals acquire political beliefs and attitudes.

"Glad you brought that up, Jim. The latest research on polls has turned up some interesting variables. It turns out, for example, that people will tell you any old thing that pops into their heads."

Drawing by Saxon; © 1984 The New Yorker Magazine, Inc.

Highlight

When Polls Are Wrong

Between 1920 and 1932, the *Literary Digest* accurately projected the winners of each presidential election. The poll consisted of approximately ten million voters who received a mailing and returned their responses on presidential preference. In 1936, the results were tallied and reported on October 31: for Landon 57 percent, with 1,293,699 votes; for Franklin D. Roosevelt 43 percent and 972,897 ballots. When American voters actually went to their polling places in November, the results were quite different: Roosevelt got 62.5 percent of the vote and carried every state except Maine and Vermont.

What went wrong? First, the sample was selected from telephone directories and lists of automobile owners, creating a biased sample. Second, of the ten million questionnaires mailed, only about 20 percent responded; thus there was a strong self-selection among those who chose to answer. Third, the time lag between the early September mailing of the questionnaire could not anticipate any changes in voter perception, campaign events, or even world

or national events which by November would cause a shift in voter preferences. Finally, the poll neglected to take into account the fact that in 1936 the United States was still in the throes of a major national crisis. People were shifting allegiances. The New Deal coalition that Roosevelt was constructing recombined different and new groups of people; the working class and the less affluent were rallying behind FDR. The poll underrepresented this constituency and therefore had a disproportionate number of persons who would vote for Landon.

Polling techniques greatly improved in subsequent years. George Gallup, Jr.'s quota sampling technique used census data to identify the necessary percentages of relevant groups in the population (by religion, gender, race, and so on) to make a poll more accurate. Nonetheless, a second and perhaps the most famous erroneous poll occurred in 1948 when Gallup projected that Thomas Dewey would defeat Harry Truman: The poll indicated that Truman would get 44.5 percent of

the vote; he obtained 49.5 percent and won. Another publication, the *Chicago Daily Tribune*, predicted the winner the night before the election with a banner headline that read "DEWEY DEFEATS TRUMAN."

Studies have demonstrated that quota sampling tends to underrepresent certain groups, in particular the poor, minorities, and the less educated, because in filling the assigned quotas, pollsters tend to avoid dangerous neighborhoods and other difficult polling obstacles. An entire quota may be filled from a single, relatively easy location (such as a "nice" apartment building where all of, say, the black quota can be completed). Moreover, in 1948, Gallup did his last poll two weeks before the election, thereby missing a last-minute shift toward Truman. Subsequent polls have tried to correct these flaws by polling up to election day and providing more accurate samples of the electorate.

In spite of great refinements, a third major national polling failure occurred in 1980. Most polls showed the race between Reagan and Carter to be "too close to call." When Reagan beat Carter 51 percent to 41 percent, pollsters and the public were amazed at the magnitude of Reagan's victory. What went wrong? In essence, it was the major enemy of pollsters, last-minute surges. Almost up to election day, relatively large numbers of voters were undecided (some polls showed as many as 13 percent). In hindsight, it appears that almost all of the "undecided" went to Reagan. Polls done closest to election day revealed this trend. In fact, Carter's pollster, Patrick Caddell, looked at his figures the day before the election and told Carter aboard Air Force One that he would not win the election.

Political socialization begins in childhood.

are the following: (1) the family, (2) the educational environment and achievement of the individual, (3) the influence of peers, (4) the influence of religion, (5) economic status, (6) political events, (7) opinion leaders, (8) the media, and (9) race and other demographic traits. In addition to these influences, we also discuss the fairly recent phenomenon of the gender gap in this section.

The Importance of the Family

The family is the most important force in political socialization. Not only do our parents' political attitudes and actions affect our adult opinions but the family links us to other socialization forces. We receive our ethnic identity, our notion of social class, our educational opportunities, and our early religious beliefs in the family. Each of these factors can also influence our political attitudes.

The clearest legacy of the family is partisan identification. If both parents identify with one party, there is a strong likelihood that the children will begin political life with the same party preference. Children do not "learn" such attitudes in the same way as they learn how to ride a bike. Rather, they learn by absorbing their parents' casual comments about political parties, their actions and conversation during election campaigns, and other intended clues.

In their study of political attitudes among adolescents, M. Kent Jennings and Richard G. Niemi[6] probed the partisan attachments of high school seniors and their parents during the mid-1960s. That parents successfully transmit their party identification to their children is evident from Table 7–2. Democratic parents tend to produce Democratic children about two-thirds of the time, and Independent and Republican parents both transmit their beliefs about parties only slightly less well. However, there is still a sizable amount of cross-generational slippage here. In all, Jennings and Niemi found that 59 percent of the children agreed with their parents' party ties.

In a 1973 reinterview of the same children and their parents,[7] Jennings and Niemi found that the younger people had become notably more independent of partisan ties, whereas their parents went through very little change. By 1973 a majority of the children deviated from their parents' partisanship.

[6]*The Political Character of Adolescence: The Influence of Families and Schools* (Princeton, N.J.: Princeton University Press, 1974).

[7]*Generations and Politics* (Princeton, N.J.: Princeton University Press, 1981).

Table 7–2
▽
Student Party Identification by Parent Party Identification (in percent)

High School Students	Parents		
	Democratic	Independent	Republican
Democratic	66	29	13
Independent	27	55	36
Republican	7	17	51

SOURCE: Jennings and Niemi, p. 41.

These researchers also noted wide variance between the attitudes of the parents and children about specific political issues. They investigated parent-student attitudes on four issues: school integration, school prayers, allowing communists to hold elective office, and allowing speeches against churches and religion. There was only a moderate relationship between the two generations' views on the first two issues and virtually no relationship at all on the last two issues.

Educational Influence on Political Opinion

Education is a powerful influence on an individual's political attitudes and on political behavior. Generally, the more education a person receives, the more liberal his or her opinions become. Students who go on to graduate training continue to become more liberal in their opinions. By *liberal*, we mean that the student is more likely to be tolerant of social change, to support social welfare programs, and to think that the United States should be active in international affairs. Individuals who have limited educational backgrounds are more likely to be isolationist in their foreign policy positions, more conservative in their social opinions, and less likely to support civil rights and civil liberties.

Peers and Peer Group Influence

Once a child enters school, the child's friends become an important influence on behavior and attitudes. As young children, and later as adults, friendships and associations in **peer groups** are influential on political attitudes. However, we must separate the effects of peer group pressure on opinions and attitudes in general from peer group pressure on political opinions. For the most part, associations among peers are nonpolitical. It may be overgeneralizing to say that political attitudes are shaped by peer groups. This is more likely to occur when the peer group is actively involved in political activities.

Individuals who join interest groups based on ethnic identity may find, for example, a common political bond through working for the group's civil liberties and rights. Members of a labor union may feel strong political pressure to support certain pro-labor candidates. Black activist groups may consist of individuals who will exert mutual pressure to support government programs that will aid the black population.

Peer Groups

Groups consisting of members sharing common relevant social characteristics. They play an important part in the socialization process, helping to shape attitudes and beliefs.

Religious Influence

Religious associations tend to create definite political attitudes, although why this occurs is not clearly understood. Roman Catholic families tend to be more liberal on economic issues than Protestant families. Apparently, Jewish families are more liberal on all fronts than either Catholics or Protestants.[8] In terms of voting behavior, it has been observed that northern white Protestants mostly vote Republican, whereas northern white Roman Catholics mostly vote Democratic; and everywhere in the United States, Jews mostly vote Democratic. These associations between religious

[8]See Robert S. Erikson, Norman R. Luttbeg, and Kent L. Tedin, *American Public Opinion: Its Origins, Content, and Impact,* 2nd ed. (New York: John Wiley, 1980).

A pervasive influence on public opinion during the 1980 election was exercised by the **Moral Majority.** The president of this strongly conservative Christian political group is the Reverend Jerry Falwell, a Baptist minister. In combination with other major conservative pressure groups, the Moral Majority claimed to have registered three million voters and to have determined the outcomes of many congressional elections, as well as having contributed to Ronald Reagan's victory. Their main effect was in lobbying members of Congress with threats of electoral opposition. This tactic was especially blatant on the issue of school prayer but it was also used to muster opposition to abortion, the Equal Rights Amendment, national health insurance, drugs, and pornography.

On August 21 and 22, 1980, the Moral Majority and its fellow evangelical conservative organizations met in Dallas to drum up national support for its electoral program. They were appealing to the roughly thirty million American voters who believed in a literal interpretation of the Bible and another twenty million "born again" Christians. The Moral Majority was financially well endowed for the elec-

tions. Falwell's *Old Time Gospel Hour,* broadcast from Lynchburg, Virginia, earned about $70 million in 1980, and a sizable amount was spent on lobbying, education, and campaign efforts.

Jimmy Carter sought the help of other evangelical leaders to counter the Moral Majority's influence. Ronald Reagan actively solicited support from Falwell and other conservative religious

leaders. As a tax-exempt organization, the Moral Majority could not directly endorse candidates, although its leaders and its subordinate groups could and did make endorsements. The evangelical leaders generally supported Reagan and targeted liberal and moderate members of Congress for defeat. It was the consensus of many political observers that the Moral Majority and related groups were important factors, at least in certain constituencies, in electing Ronald Reagan to the presidency, contributing to a Republican Senate majority, and defeating House Democrats. Of six liberal Democratic senators specifically targeted by Falwell for defeat, only one (Alan Cranston of California) survived.

On January 3, 1986, Falwell announced the formation of the Liberty Foundation. The Moral Majority became a subsidiary of the new organization. This was done in large part because of increasingly negative public reactions to the image of the Moral Majority and to its political role. A new lobbying group, the Liberty Alliance, was also set up under the Liberty Federation to support conservative views on a wide spectrum of domestic and foreign issues.

Moral Majority

A strongly conservative Christian political group.

background and political attitudes are partly derived from the ethnic background of certain religious groups and the conditions at the time their forebears immigrated to the United States. Germans who immigrated before the Civil War tend to be Republican regardless of their religious background, whereas Eastern European Catholics, who arrived in the late-nineteenth century, adopted the Democratic identity of the cities where they made their homes. The relationship between religion and party affiliation is shown in Table 7–3.

Sometimes a candidate's religion does enter the political picture, as it did in the 1960 presidential election contest between Democrat John Kennedy and Republican Richard Nixon. The fact that Kennedy was a Catholic—the second nominated

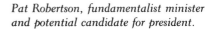
Pat Robertson, fundamentalist minister and potential candidate for president.

by a major party—polarized many voters. Among northern whites, Kennedy was supported by 83 percent of voting Catholics and by 93 percent of Jewish voters but by only 28 percent of the Protestants who voted.

The Influence of Economic Status and Occupation

How wealthy you are and the kind of job you hold are also associated with your political views. Social class differences emerge on a wide range of issues. Poorer people are more inclined to favor government social welfare programs but are likely to be conservative on social issues such as abortion. The upper middle class is more likely to hold conservative economic views although tolerant of social change. People in lower economic strata also tend to be more isolationist on foreign policy issues and are more likely to identify with, and vote for, the Democratic party. Support for civil liberties and tolerance of different points of view tend to be highest among those with higher social status and lowest among those with lower status. Probably, it is educational differences more than the pattern of life at home or work that account for this.

Table 7–3
▽
Religion and Party Affiliation (in percent)

Religion	Republican	Democrat	Independent
Protestant	32	37	29
Catholic	25	41	30
Jewish	14	55	29
Other	23	34	34
None	19	34	39

SOURCE: *The Gallup Report*, May 1985, p. 34.

Generational Effects

Events of a particular time period have a long-lasting effect on the political opinions or preferences of those individuals who came of political age at that time.

Opinion Leaders

Individuals able to influence the opinions of others because of position, expertise, or personality. Such leaders help to shape public opinion either formally or informally.

Media

The technical means of communication with mass audiences. The media have become extremely important in American political life as a means of informing and influencing millions of citizens.

People's political attitudes may be shaped by political events and the nation's reactions to them. In the 1960s and 1970s, the war in Vietnam—including revelations about the secret bombing in Cambodia—and the Watergate break-in and subsequent cover-up fostered widespread cynicism toward government. In one study of the impact of Watergate, Christopher Arterton[9] found that school children changed their image of the president from a "benevolent" to a "malevolent" leader as the scandal unfolded. Negative views also increased about other aspects of politics and politicians.

When the events of an era produce a long-lasting political impact, **generational effects** result. The Vietnam generation, or those voters who came of political age during that conflict, continues to express less patriotic views than those who are older or younger than their group. There is strong evidence that the college-age youth of the 1980s are becoming more attached to the Republican party because of the attractiveness of Ronald Reagan and the improved economic outlook, which they perceive will benefit them.

Opinion Leaders' Influence

We are all influenced by those with whom we are closely associated or whom we hold in great respect—friends at school, family members and other relatives, teachers, and so on. In a sense, these people are **opinion leaders,** but on an informal level; that is, their influence over us is not necessarily intentional or deliberate. Formal opinion leaders, such as a president, a lobbyist, a congressperson, or a news commentator, have it as part of their job to sway people's views. Their interest lies in defining the political agenda in such a way that discussions about policy options will take place on their terms.

Media Influence

Newspapers, television, and other **media** act as sources of information, commentary, and images. Newspapers and news magazines (like *Time* or *Newsweek*) are especially rich sources of knowledge about political issues. Some argue that newspaper editorials normally have a heavily pro-Republican and conservative slant, especially for presidential endorsements, and columnists are often selected to reflect such biases. Journalists are perceived as having a counteracting Democratic and liberal bias. Television, the media source relied on by most Americans, conveys only limited political information about issues or candidates' qualifications. There seems to be no strong partisan or ideological bias in television coverage, although the visual and mental images conveyed by TV clearly have a powerful impact.

The Influence of Demographic Traits

Black Americans show a much stronger commitment than whites to steady or more rapid racial desegregation. Blacks also tend to be more liberal than whites on social

[9]"The Impact of Watergate on Children's Attitudes toward Authority," *Political Science Quarterly*, vol. 89 (June 1974), pp. 269–288.

Profile

▽

Patrick Caddell

Patrick H. Caddell had already worked in five presidential campaigns by the time he reached age thirty-four. One observer has said of him, "Only FDR [four-term president Franklin D. Roosevelt] had more experience campaigning for president." Born in 1950, Caddell lived in the South, mostly Florida and South Carolina. In 1972, Gary Hart, Senator George McGovern's campaign manager, asked "Pat," then a senior in government at Harvard University, to join McGovern's presidential campaign as a pollster. At age twenty-six, he worked on Jimmy Carter's presidential campaign and later became a Carter White House insider, speechwriter, and adviser.

Caddell is part of a new wave of political activists and technicians in the growing ranks of political professionals. Although his political campaigns have centered on Democrats Caddell is a media person, not a party loyalist. His approach is to identify and analyze the political market and then devise a strategy to sell a candidate to the voters.

He has said, "What we've done with polling . . . is that we've provided candidates who have the resources . . . the ability to reach the voters and have a direct contact with the electorate without regard to party or party organization."

Considered strong willed and often abrasive, Caddell has had successes but also more than his share of failures. In 1979, he advised President Carter to give a speech in which the president suggested that the United States was in a period of self-doubt and despair, which Carter, following Caddell's suggestion, called "malaise." The speech,

"I always sense the attitude among policymakers, politicians, and the press that polls that agree with what they want are very good and polls that disagree are very bad."

opposed by Vice President Walter Mondale, was very unpopular. Later, during the 1980 campaign, Caddell urged President Carter to rely on negative campaign themes, focusing on Ronald Reagan's alleged racism and warmongering.

In January 1984, Caddell joined the primary campaign of his former employer, Colorado Senator Gary Hart, as an informal adviser. He proceeded to handle polling for the campaign, but soon began also to structure other aspects of Hart's bid for the Democratic nomination. In particular, Caddell

concluded that Hart was too issue-oriented and "boring." He advised Hart to develop a sharper image, distinguishing himself from Walter Mondale. This led to the development of Hart's "New Ideas" theme. Hart said of Caddell in 1984, "He is a friend and adviser, a very talented man, very intelligent, very creative, possibly a genius."

After Reagan's landslide reelection in 1984, Caddell shifted gears. From his consulting firm, Cambridge Survey Research, he began to diversify his work, adding corporate clients to his list of customers and expanding from polling to the full range of what is called "media work." His clients have included Apple Computer and Coca-Cola, which hired him to help sell their "New" Coke. He advised them to stress a theme similar to the "New Ideas" he had recommended to Hart. Coca-Cola President Brian Dyson, in his speech announcing the new product, talked about reaching out, seeking the promise of the future, and said "The time is right because the mood of America favors change . . ." New Coke was a flop and Coca-Cola found itself instead awash in a wave of tradition, nostalgia, and loyalty for the original Coke (now Coca-Cola Classic). Caddell's analysis that American consumers no longer have product loyalty (much as he argues that voters no longer have party loyalty) proved to be dead wrong in the case of Coca-Cola.

Caddell's distinctive dark beard with a white streak on the right side has become a familiar sight to television viewers. During election years, he is sought out for commentary by the media almost as much as his clients.

Blacks are more likely to support social welfare spending than are whites.

welfare issues, civil liberties, and even foreign policy. Party preferences and voting among blacks since the 1930s have very heavily supported the Democrats.

It is somewhat surprising that a person's chronological age has comparatively little impact on political preferences. Still, young adults are somewhat more liberal than older people on most issues and are considerably more progressive on such issues as marijuana legalization, pornography, civil disobedience, and racial and sexual equality. However, most public opinion polls on the Vietnam war actually found dovish sentiment against the war to be stronger among adults fifty years of age and over than among the youngest adults.

The generally greater conservatism of older Americans may be explained in one or more ways: (1) Simply becoming older makes people more conservative. (2) People carry with them the values they learned when they first became politically aware, which are now considered relatively conservative. (3) People's attitudes are shaped by the events that unfold as they grow up. The most important of these explanations seems to be the third; that is, a person's views are mainly determined by when he or she happened to be born. If an individual grew up in an era of Democratic party dominance, then that person will be more likely to remain a Democrat throughout his or her life.[10]

Finally, attitudes vary from region to region, although such patterns probably are accounted for mostly by social class and other differences. Regional differences are relatively unimportant today. There is still a tendency for the East and West to be more liberal than most of the Midwest and the South and for the South and East to be more Democratic than the West and the Midwest. More important than region is a person's residence—urban, suburban, or rural. Big cities tend to be more liberal and Democratic because of their greater concentration of minorities and newer ethnic groups, and smaller communities are more conservative and, outside the South, more Republican.

The Gender Gap

Until the 1980s, there was little evidence that men's and women's political attitudes were very different. The election of Ronald Reagan, however, soon came to be associated with a **gender gap.** In a May 1983 Gallup poll, 43 percent of the women polled approved of Reagan's performance in office and 44 percent disapproved, versus 49 percent of men who approved and 41 percent who disapproved.[11]

In the 1984 election, the gender gap reappeared but in a modified form. Although the Democrats hoped that women's votes would add significantly to Mondale's totals, a deep split between men and women did not occur. The final polls showed that men voted 61 percent for Reagan and that 57 percent of the women voted for the president. There is some evidence that women's votes did make a difference in other races.

Women also appear to hold different attitudes from their male counterparts on a range of issues other than presidential preferences. They are much more likely to oppose the use of force on domestic issues, such as capital punishment, and on foreign policy issues. A 1982 poll sponsored by the Chicago Council on Foreign Relations showed that only 34 percent of American women favored our government selling military equipment to other nations, whereas 50 percent of men supported this strategy. Other studies have shown that women are more concerned about risks to the environment, particularly from nuclear power, and more supportive of social welfare than are men.[12] These differences of opinion appear to be growing and may become an important factor in future elections at national and local levels.

The Political Culture of Americans

▽

Americans are divided into a multitude of ethnic, religious, regional, and political subgroups. In many cases, members of these groups hold a particular set of opinions about government policies, about the goals of the society, and about the rights of their group and the rights of others. Given the diversity of American society and the wide range of opinions contained within it, how is it that the political process continues to function without being stalemated by conflict and dissension?

[10]Robert Erikson, Norman Luttbeg, and Kent Tedin, *Public Opinion*, 2nd ed., pp. 170–175.

[11]*The Gallup Report*, May, 1983.

[12]Katherine Frankovic, "Sex and Politics—New Alignments, Old Issues," *PS*, 1982, pp. 439–448.

Did You Know?

▽

That public opinion pollsters typically measure national sentiment among the more than 160 million adult Americans by interviewing only about 1,500 people?

Gender Gap

Most widely used to describe the difference between the percentage of votes a candidate receives from women voters and the percentage the candidate received from men. The term was widely used after the 1980 presidential election.

Rock star Bruce Springsteen as an American cultural idol.

On Political Thinking

Political scientists face a difficult puzzle: How can they find out why individuals hold specific political opinions? For example, in 1986, American naval forces in the Mediterranean were ordered to proceed with their manuevers, even though this would mean that American ships and planes would cross the "Line of Death" established by the Libyan leader, Muammar Khaddafi, into the Gulf of Sidra. Public opinion polls showed that not all Americans were sure this was the correct strategy. After the air strike on Libyan posts, Americans were divided about whether this action would slow down or accelerate terrorist activities sponsored by radical Muslim groups. Most Americans had no idea where Libya was located before these incidents, and little information about Libyan-sponsored terrorism. Yet, within a few hours, most Americans had formulated an opinion about what the United States should do. Where do such opinions come from? What factors lead individuals to make a militaristic or a more accommodationist response to the pollster's questions?

The most recent theories about how people form political opinions draws on the work of cognitive psychology. A number of political scientists have suggested that we begin looking at how people think politically in terms of **schema,** which are internal structures that guide and organize the processing of information. Throughout their lifetime, individuals build these schema in their brains on the basis of experience and their environment. Each schema may be thought of as a kind of file drawer of stored information, emotional attachments, and memories of previous interactions with the political system.

These internal structures seem to perform several functions for individuals to help them cope with the political world. They are useful as a way to catalog and store information and enable individuals to retrieve information quickly when needed. For example, when faced with a news report about U.S. congresspersons traveling to Hanoi, most will quickly call forth memories of the Vietnam war.

Since the schema also include emotional reactions to the issue or general topic, the schema shapes future expectations about interactions. Memories and information about a past conservative governor, for example, would create expectations about the behavior of future conservatives in that office.

Perhaps most importantly, schema are very useful to people in processing information received every day. During a presidential election campaign, many schema may come into use for an individual voter. When considering the candidates' political platforms or discussions of issues, the schema on, for example, national security or social welfare programs will be useful in evaluating the candidates' views. The schema directs what kind of new information is to be stored, decides whether the original structure should be altered because of new information, and evaluates the candidate in light of his or her position. Schema may include the person's prior judgement on an issue. In this case, if the voter already thinks that a strong military is a high priority for the nation, the schema helps him or her evaluate what candidates say and probably allows the individual to keep little new information on the subject that does not confirm the already established schema.

Schema theory differs from previous approaches to political thinking in that it does not start with a well-defined ideological spectrum, such as the liberal-conservative continuum, and then seek to find out what proportion of the general public makes political decisions based on its ideological position. Instead, it seeks to understand the possibly wide array of schema that individuals may have and then looks at the linkages among these internal structures. For some individuals, the schema may link to each other to form a pattern close to that of the classic liberal or conservative. For others, the schema may just as well be close to liberal positions on some issues and much closer to conservative positions on others. The approach emphasizes that schema are tools of the mind, not philosophical principles, and that they will change as the individual is exposed to new political situations.

For discussions of this approach, see Pamela Johnston Conover and Stanley Feldman, "Belief System Organization in the American Electorate: An Alternate Approach," in John Pierce and John Sullivan, eds., *The Electorate Reconsidered* (Beverly Hills, Calif.: Sage Publications, 1980).

One explanation is rooted in the concept of the **political culture,** which can be described as a set of attitudes and ideas about the nation and the government. Our political culture is widely shared by Americans of many different backgrounds. To some extent, it consists of symbols, such as the American flag, the Liberty Bell, and the Statue of Liberty. One of the reasons that the renovation of the Statue so strongly engaged the imagination of the citizens is because it symbolizes two major aspects of American political culture: the pursuit of liberty and the fact that most Americans are descended from immigrants who sought liberty and equality.

The elements of our political culture also include certain shared beliefs about the most important values in the American political system. Research by Donald Devine[13] suggests that there is a set of key values that are central to the political culture. Among the most important are three of the values from the revolutionary period: (1) liberty, equality, and property, (2) support for religion, and (3) a high value on community service and personal achievement. The structure of the government, particularly federalism, the political parties, the strength of Congress, and popular rule, were also found to be important values.

The political culture provides a general environment of support for the political system. If the people share certain beliefs about the system and a reservoir of good feeling exists toward the institutions of government, the nation will be better able to weather periods of crisis such as Watergate. This foundation of good will may combat cynicism and increase the level of participation in elections as well. During the 1960s and 1970s, survey research showed that the overall level of **political trust** declined steeply. A considerable proportion of Americans seemed to feel that they could not trust government officials and that they could not count on officials to care about the ordinary person. This index of political trust reached an all-time low in 1980, but since that year has begun to rebound (Table 7–4).

One way to test whether Americans really believe in the values that are central to the political culture is to examine the degree of **political tolerance** they are willing to show toward those who hold quite eccentric views. Researchers asked Americans if they would be willing to permit demonstrations by a number of groups who espouse particular opinions.[14] More than 80 percent of those asked were willing

Schema

In internal cognitive structures, based on experience, which organize and guide the process of information.

Political Culture

That set of beliefs and values regarding the political system which are widely shared by citizens of a nation.

Political Trust

The degree to which individuals express trust in the government and political institutions. This concept is usually measured through a specific series of survey questions.

Political Tolerance

Whether individuals are able to grant civil liberties to groups that have opinions differing strongly from their own.

[13]Donald Devine, *Political Culture of the United States* (Boston, Little, Brown, 1972).

[14]David G. Lawrence, "Procedural Norms and Tolerance: A Reassessment," *American Political Science Review,* 70: 88 (1976).

Table 7–4

▽

Trends in Political Trust

How much of the time do you think you can trust the government in Washington to do what is right—just about always, most of the time, or only some of the time?

	1964	1968	1972	1974	1976	1978	1980	1982	1984*	1986*
Percent saying:										
Always/Most of the time	76	61	53	36	33	29	25	32	46	42
Some of the time/Never	22	36	45	61	63	67	73	64	51	55

*The New York Times/CBS News surveys

SOURCE: The University of Michigan Survey Research Center, National Election Studies

to permit demonstrations opposing crime in the community and pollution. About 60 percent felt that it would be acceptable to permit black militants or radical students to demonstrate, whereas only 40 percent would support efforts to march for the legalization of marijuana. Although we do not find that all Americans are willing to extend political tolerance to groups indiscriminately, it appears that the political culture is strong enough to provide freedom for most points of view.

Public Opinion about Government

A vital component of public opinion in the United States, as it reflects the nation's political culture and the patterns of political socialization in the country, is the considerable ambivalence with which the public regards many major national institutions. Table 7–5 shows trends from 1973 to 1985 in Gallup public opinion polls asking respondents to tell at regularly spaced intervals "how much confidence you, yourself, have" in the institutions listed. Clearly, religious institutions rank high, as does the military. The U.S. Supreme Court, which many people do not see as a particularly political institution although it is clearly involved in decisions with vitally important consequences for the nation, also scores well, as do banks and banking and the public schools. Congress, however, ranks considerably below these other, more highly regarded institutions. Even less confidence is expressed in newspapers, big business, television, and organized labor, all of which are certainly involved directly or indirectly in the political process.

Although people may not have much confidence in government institutions, they nonetheless turn to government to solve what they perceive to be the major

Table 7–5

Confidence in Institutions Trend
(Percentage saying "great deal" or "quite a lot")

QUESTION: I am going to read a list of institutions in American society. Would you please tell me how much confidence you, yourself, have in each one—a great deal, quite a lot, some, or very little?								
	Percent saying "Great Deal" or "Quite a Lot"							
	1985	1984*	1983	1981	1979	1977	1975	1973
Church or organized religion	66%	64%	62%	64%	65%	64%	68%	66%
Military	61	58	53	50	54	57	58	NA
U.S. Supreme Court	56	51	42	46	45	46	49	44
Banks & banking	51	51	51	46	60	NA	NA	NA
Public schools	48	47	39	42	53	54	NA	58
Congress	39	29	28	29	34	40	40	42
Newspapers	35	34	38	35	51	NA	NA	39
Big business	31	29	28	20	32	33	34	26
Television	29	25	25	25	38	NA	NA	37
Organized labor	28	30	26	28	36	39	38	30

*The *Newsweek* Poll, conducted by The Gallup Organization, Inc.
NA = Not asked.

SOURCE: *The Gallup Report*, July 1985.

problems facing the country. Table 7–6 which is based on Gallup polls conducted over the years 1970 to 1985, shows that the leading problems have clearly changed over time. The public tends to emphasize problems that are real, timely, and important. It is not at all unusual to see fairly sudden and even apparently contradictory shifts in public perceptions of what government should do. Note the years 1975–1977 and 1980–1983, when both "high cost of living" and "unemployment" were at the top of the public's action agenda. These two problems are quite possibly contradictory; that is, reducing unemployment, everything else constant, is likely to produce inflationary pressures, and attempts to reduce inflation may have to be accompanied by more people unemployed so as to reduce inflationary pressures arising from demands for higher wages at a time when labor is relatively scarce. In some instances, government cannot respond well to these contradictory demands from the public. Jimmy Carter, for example, was largely unable to resolve this dilemma. On the other hand, Ronald Reagan was much more successful in confronting much the same set of demands from public opinion, although Reagan benefited from very fortunate declines in energy prices and a climate of opinion that would tolerate very high rates of unemployment.

This gives rise to a critically important question: Is government really responsive to public opinion? One study by political scientists Benjamin I. Page and Robert Y. Shapiro[15] suggests that in fact the national government is very responsive to the public's demands for action. In looking at changes in public opinion poll results over time, Page and Shapiro show that when there is a noticeable change in what the public wants to see government do, government policy changes 43 percent of the time in a direction congruent with the change in public opinion, changes in the direction opposite to the change in opinion 22 percent of the time, and 33 percent of the time does not change even when public opinion demands that a change be made. So, overall, the national government could be said to respond to changes in public opinion about two-thirds of the time, and when government policy does change, it is usually (about two-thirds of the time) consistent with the change in public opinion. Page and Shapiro also show, as should be no surprise, that when public opinion changes more dramatically, say by 20 percentage points rather than by just 6 or 7 percentage points, government policy is much more likely to be consistent with the changing public attitudes.

Table 7–6

Most Important Problem Trend 1970–1985

Year	Problem
1985	Fear of war, unemployment
1984	Unemployment, fear of war
1983	Unemployment, high cost of living
1982	Unemployment, high cost of living
1981	High cost of living, unemployment
1980	High cost of living, unemployment
1979	High cost of living, energy problems
1978	High cost of living, energy problems
1977	High cost of living, unemployment
1976	High cost of living, unemployment
1975	High cost of living, unemployment
1974	High cost of living, Watergate, energy crisis
1973	High cost of living, Watergate
1972	Vietnam
1971	Vietnam, high cost of living
1970	Vietnam

SOURCE: *The Gallup Report*, December 1985, p. 14.

Political Ideology

Political candidates and officeholders in the United States are frequently identified as liberals or conservatives. In recent years, variations on these labels include post–Cold War liberals and neoconservatives. These terms refer loosely to a spectrum of political beliefs that are commonly arrayed on a single dimension from left to right. Each of the terms has changed its meaning from its origins and continues to change as the issues of political debate change. In the United States, however, the terms most frequently refer to sets of political positions that date from the Great Depression.

Liberals are most commonly understood to embrace national government solutions to public problems, to believe that the national government should intervene in the economy to ensure its health, to support social welfare programs to assist the disadvantaged, and to be tolerant of social change. Today, liberals are often

[15]"Effects of Public Opinion on Policy," *American Political Science Review*, 77:175–190 (1985).

New York Governor Mario Cuomo, leading Democratic liberal (left); former Senator Barry Goldwater, Republican conservative (right).

identified with pro-women's rights positions, pro-civil rights policies, and opposition to increased defense spending. New York Governor Mario Cuomo and Massachusetts Senator Edward Kennedy are usually tagged as liberals.

In contrast, conservatives usually feel that the national government has grown too large, that the private sector needs less interference from the government, that social welfare programs should be limited, that state and local governments should be able to make their own decisions, and that the nation's defense should be strengthened. Some conservatives express grave concerns about the decline of family life and traditional values in this country; they would not be tolerant of gay rights laws, for example. Arizona Senator Barry Goldwater represented conservatism in the 1960s, whereas Senators Jesse Helms and Strom Thurmond are examples of today's variety.

When asked, Americans are usually willing to identify themselves on the liberal-conservative spectrum. More individuals are likely to consider themselves moderates than either liberal or conservative. As Figure 7–5 shows, the number of conservatives has increased in recent years and the number of liberals has declined.

Most Americans, however, do not fit into the categories as nicely as Edward Kennedy or Strom Thurmond. Such political leaders, who are quite conscious of their philosophical views and who hold a carefully thought out and consistent set of political beliefs can be described as **ideologues.** Partly because most citizens are not highly interested in all political issues and partly because Americans have different stakes in politics, most people have mixed sets of opinions that do not fit into one ideological framework. Election research in the 1950s suggested that only a small percentage of all Americans, perhaps less than 10 percent, could be identified as ideologues. The rest of the public conceived of politics more in terms of the parties or of economic well-being.

Some critics of the American political system have felt that elections would be more meaningful and that the nation could face important policy problems more effectively if Americans were more ideological in their thinking. Public opinion research suggests that for most Americans, political issues are not as important as their daily lives most of the time. There is no evidence to suggest that forces are in place to turn Americans into highly motivated ideological voters.

Ideologue

A term applied to an individual whose political opinions are tightly constrained, that is, who has opinions that are consistent with one another. Ideologues are often described as having a comprehensive world view.

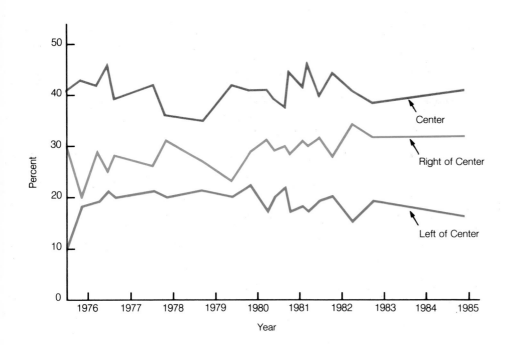

Figure 7–5
▽
**Ideological Self-Identification,
1975–1984**

Public Opinion and the Political Process
▽

Surveys of public opinion, no matter what fascinating questions they ask or how quickly they get the answers, are not equivalent to elections in the United States. Because not all Americans are equally interested in politics or equally informed, public opinion polls can only suggest the general distribution of opinion on issues. Many times, only a few citizens have formulated a preference, and these preferences will be changed by events.

Politicians, whether in office or in the midst of a campaign, see public opinion as important to their careers. The president, as well as governors, mayors, and other elected officials, realize that strong support by the public as expressed in polls is a source of power in dealing with other politicians. It is far more difficult for a senator to say no to the president if he is immensely popular and if polls show approval of his policies. Public opinion also helps political candidates identify the most important concerns among the public and may help them shape their campaigns successfully.

Public opinion is sometimes perceived as acting as a boundary mechanism for public officials. Although it cannot give exact guidance on what the government should do in a specific instance, the opinions measured in polls do set an informal limit on government action. Look at the highly controversial matter of abortion. Most Americans are moderates on this issue; they do not approve of abortions as a means of birth control but they do feel that it should be available under certain circumstances. But sizable groups of individuals express very intense feelings both pro- and anti-abortion. Given this distribution of opinion, most elected officials would rather not try to change policy to favor either of the extreme positions. To do so would clearly violate the opinion of the majority of Americans. In this case, like many others, public opinion does not make public policy; rather, it restrains officials from taking truly unpopular actions. If officials do act in the face of public opposition, the consequences of such actions will be determined at the ballot box.

Getting Involved

▽

How to Read a Public Opinion Poll

We are inundated virtually every day with information from public opinion polls. The polls, often reported to us through television news, the newspaper, *Time* or *Newsweek* magazines, or radio, purport to tell us a variety of things: whether the president's popularity is up or down, whether the public is more willing than before to trust the Russians on arms control agreements, whether gun control is more popular now than previously, or who is leading the pack for the next presidential nomination.

What must be kept in mind during this blizzard of information is that not all the poll results are equally good or equally believable. As a citizen, you need to be aware of what makes one set of public opinion poll results valid and other results useless or even dangerously misleading. You should be able to evaluate the results that are being forced on you by the media or by political groups or candidates.

The first question has to do with how the sample of people who were interviewed were selected. Pay attention only to opinion polls that are based on scientific, or random, samples, in which a known probability was used to select every person who was interviewed. These probability samples, as they are also called, can take a number of different forms. The simplest to understand is known as a simple random sample, in which everybody had an equal chance of being chosen to be interviewed. Other satisfactory ways of selecting samples are systematic samples, in which every tenth person, for example, might be selected from an alphabetized list of names; stratified sampling, in which the pollster has purposely selected a particular proportion or number of poll respondents who are, say, black, Jewish, or farmers and who otherwise might not get sufficient representation in the sample; or cluster sampling, in which people have been interviewed in randomly chosen geographical areas. As a rule, do not give credence to the results of opinion polls like the person-in-the-shopping-mall interviews on local television news segments. The problems with this kind of opinion taking, which is a special version of a so-called accidental sample, are that not everyone had a known or equal chance of being in the mall when the interview took place, and that it is almost certain that the people in the

mall are not a reasonable cross section of a community's entire population (shopping malls would tend to attract people who are disproportionately younger, female, mobile, and middle class). In general, if a pollster can't be specific about the odds of the results of the poll being correct, it means that some nonrandom, or nonprobability sample has been taken and that the results are probably not very useful.

The reason why probability samples are useful whereas nonprobability samples are not is that when you know the odds that the particular sample would have been chosen randomly from a larger population, you can calculate the "sampling error," or the range within which the real results for the whole population would fall if everybody had been interviewed. Well-designed probability samples will allow the pollster to say, for example, that he or she is 95 percent sure that 61 percent of the public, plus or minus 4 percentage points, supports the development of the "Star Wars" Strategic Defense Initiative. The range around the sample result becomes smaller, meaning that the guess about the actual proportion of Star Wars supporters is more precise, as the size of the sample gets bigger. It turns out that if you want to become twice as precise about a poll result, you would need to collect a sample four times as large. This tends to make accurate polls quite expensive and difficult to collect. Typically, national public opinion polls by, for example, the Gallup organization seldom interview more than about 1,500 respondents. With that size sample, Gallup is able to be correct to within about 3 percentage points of the probably true figures.

There are other important points to keep in mind when you are confronted with opinion poll results. How were people contacted for the poll—by mail, by telephone, in person in their homes, or in some other way? By and large, because of its lower cost compared with interviewing people in person, polling firms have recently turned more and more to telephone interviewing. This method can usually produce highly accurate results, but telephone interviews typically need to be short and deal with questions that are fairly easy to answer. Interviews in person are better for getting useful information about why a particular response was given to a question, but they take much longer to complete and are not as useful if results must be generated quickly. Results from mail questionnaires should be taken with a grain of salt, because usually only a small percentage of people complete them and send them back, and the kinds of people who fill them out are typically better educated, with higher incomes and more prestigious jobs, and are therefore not representative of the general population or its likely attitudes.

When you see the results from public opinion polls in this book, they are usually from probability samples, with the results having been gathered in personal interviews or over the telephone. The next time you see an opinion poll anywhere else, ask yourself how the results were collected and whether you want to believe what the poll seems to lead you to conclude.

Chapter Summary

1. Public opinion is the aggregate of individual attitudes or beliefs shared by some portion of adults. It becomes known in a democracy through elections, initiatives, referenda, lobbying, and interest group activities.

2. Public opinion has at least five special qualities: (a) intensity—the strength of an opinion; (b) fluidity—the extent to which an opinion changes; (c) stability—the extent to which an opinion remains constant; (d) quiescence—latent opinions; and (e) relevance—the extent to which an issue is of concern at a particular time.

3. Most individuals remember relatively few political facts. They are most likely to remember political information about issues which are of great interest to them.

4. Consensus issues are those on which there is nearly total agreement within the public. Divisive issues are those on which large segments of the public hold fundamentally opposing views.

5. Most descriptions of the distribution of opinions are based on opinion polls. George Gallup, Elmo Roper, and Archibald Crossley developed modern polling techniques by using personal interviews with careful samples.

6. The most important principle in sampling techniques, or poll taking, is randomness. This ensures that the sample is representative of the whole population.

7. One problem with opinion polls is that they cannot be responsive to rapid changes in public opinion. They may also be biased, and therefore should be interpreted with care.

8. Most people identify with their parents' political parties. An increasing number of young people have entered the electorate as independents, however.

9. The more education a person has, the more liberal and tolerant she or he is likely to be on most social issues, but not on economic issues.

10. Associations in peer groups, particularly when the peer group is politically active, help to determine political attitudes.

11. Other important determinants of political attitudes are religious affiliation, economic status, political events and the nation's reactions to them, opinion leaders, and the media.

12. In general, political attitudes vary with race, age, sex, and region.

13. Although Americans may be divided on specific issues or candidates, most subscribe to a similar set of beliefs about the nation and the government. This set of shared attitudes and values is called the political culture.

14. Most Americans are willing to identify themselves as liberals, moderates, or conservatives, although few individuals really hold the kind of organized beliefs about politics and government that can be called an ideology.

15. Public opinion can play an important part in the political process in election campaigns, in providing support for the President or others, or in limiting the acceptable actions of government officials.

Questions for Review and Discussion

1. How does public opinion influence the formation of national policies? In what ways can public opinion influence the actions of Congress, of the president, and of the Supreme Court? Is public opinion more powerful as a positive force for change or as a negative force opposing change?

2. Think about a current political problem—for example, U.S. policy in Central America. What sources of information do you rely on to form an opinion about this problem? How have the opinions of your parents, your friends, or your teachers affected your own attitudes? To what extent are your views colored by your own political party identification?

3. Do you consider yourself to be a liberal, a conservative, or a moderate on political issues? Try to list all of the beliefs that you hold which create such an identity. To what extent do you feel close to politicians or elected officials who identify themselves in the same way? What evidence could you present that the nation is becoming more conservative or more liberal?

Selected References
▽

George C. Edwards III, *The Public Presidency: The Pursuit of Popular Support* (New York: St. Martin's Press, 1983). A detailed examination of how presidents mold and depend on public opinion.

Charles D. Elder and Roger W. Cobb, *The Political Uses of Symbols* (New York: Longman, 1983). How we react to political symbols with our emotions and intellect and how these symbols structure our political opinions.

Harry Holloway and John George, *Public Opinion: Coalitions, Elites, and Masses*, 2d ed. (New York: St. Martin's, 1986). Public opinion and the 1984 election, shifting forms of conservatism and liberalism, attitudes of elites and the masses, and political socialization as the origin of opinions. Includes discussions of parties, interest groups, and the media, as well as ethnic groups and social class.

Dan D. Nimmo and Charles M. Bonjean, eds., *Political Attitudes and Public Opinion* (New York: David McKay, 1972). A highly useful collection of articles on basic concepts and methods in public opinion, political socialization, consistency of attitudes, the political consequences of public opinion distribution, and attitudes of groups such as blacks, the poor, the unskilled, and students.

Keith T. Poole and L. Harmon Zeigler, *Women, Public Opinion, and Politics: The Changing Political Attitudes of American Women* (New York: Longman, 1985). Focuses on the relationship between attitudes for equality for women and attitudes about other issues, such as regulating the environment or defense spending. Women's political participation, ideological constraint on issues, and candidate preferences are addressed.

Michael Wheeler, *Lies, Damn Lies, and Statistics: The Manipulation of Public Opinion in America* (New York: Dell, 1976). How public opinion polls are used and abused. Attempts to demystify the polling process by demonstrating in nontechnical terms what polls can and cannot do.

Jerry L. Yeric and John R. Todd, *Public Opinion: The Visible Politics* (Itasca, Ill.: F. E. Peacock, 1983). The relationship of public opinion to polling, public policy, and demographic factors.

Chapter 8
▽
Political Parties

Contents
▽
What Is a Political Party?
Why Do People Join Political Parties?
Political Parties in Other Countries
Functions of Political Parties in the United States
A Short History of Political Parties in the United States
The Structure of Political Parties
The Two-Party System in American Politics
The Role of Minor Parties in U.S. Political History
Is the Party Over?

What If . . .

▽

We Had a Multiparty Political System in the United States?

The two-party system is an enduring feature of American government. In most elections, the contest is between two candidates, one from each of the major parties. In modern times, most members of Congress, state legislatures, and every president have been either Democrats or Republicans. Minor third parties have entered the arena, but historically it has been mostly a two-party affair. With few exceptions, the two major parties have accounted for about 90 percent of the total popular vote since the 1800s.

What if we had a multiparty system instead? Actually, such a system is much more common in Western democracies with competing political parties than the two-party system. As a modern, complex society with a wide variety of interests and opinions, it would seem the United States might be a likely candidate for a multiparty system.

Along with such a system, we would probably have proportional representation. Legislative seats would be allocated to parties in proportion to the percentage of votes they won in the nation or a region. If a party or its candidates received 20 percent of the total vote, the party would have 20 percent of the seats in the legislature. It would be unlikely for one party to have exclusive governmental control.

Each party would be like a large interest group. Although still acting like a party, it would perform functions that in a two-party system only an interest group can perform. Parties representing interests would bargain with each other instead of interest groups bargaining with each other within a party. Each party would not have to win support from the large and het-

erogeneous groups they now need, but would achieve success by appealing to special groups.

It is difficult to say how many parties the United States would need to represent the diversity of American society. Would we need five or five hundred? We would likely have parties representing many different groups: a farmer's party, an Hispanic party, a western party, a labor party, and so on. The various groups now working together in coalition within the Democratic and Republican parties might have less reason to seek consensus on issues of public policy. Would a multiparty system achieve truer representation or would it lead to divisiveness?

▽

Thinking about a multiparty system raises a number of questions about the existing American system. Why do we have only two parties and how have they survived for more than one hundred years? Why do American parties take such moderate positions and how do they keep their electoral coalitions united?

What Is a Political Party?

▽

What are you? If that question were asked during a presidential election campaign, the answer would probably be "I'm a Republican" or "I'm a Democrat" or "I'm an Independent."[1] The answer would refer to a person's actual or perceived affiliation with a particular political party. In the United States, being a member of a political party does not require paying dues, passing an examination, or swearing an oath of allegiance. Well, if nothing is really required to be a member of a political party, what then is a **political party?**

A formal definition might be as follows:

> A political party is a group of individuals who organize to win elections, to operate the government, and to determine public policy.

With this definition, we can see the difference between an interest group and a political party. Interest groups do not want to operate government and they do not put forth political candidates—even though they support candidates who will promote their interests if elected or reelected. Another important distinction is that, whereas interest groups tend to sharpen issues, American political parties tend to blur their issue positions in order to attract voters.

A political party is not a **faction** (see Chapter 2). Factions, which historically preceded political parties, were simply groups of individuals who joined together to win a benefit for themselves, like the interest groups of today. They were limited to the period in our political history when there were relatively few elective offices and only a small percentage of the population could meet the requirements for voting. Today, we still use the term *faction*, but only for a particular group within either a political party or some type of organization; for example, we speak of the conservative factions within the Republican and Democratic parties. A faction is founded on a particular philosophy, personality, or even geographical region. Sometimes a faction can be based on a political issue. The main feature differentiating a faction from a political party is that the faction generally does not have a permanently organized structure.

Why Do People Join Political Parties?

▽

People join political parties for different reasons, according to political scientist James Q. Wilson.[2] These include solidary, material, and purposive (or ideological) incentives. Solidary incentives include enjoying the excitement of politics and using politics as a social outlet. Material incentives, such as those that maintained support for big-city political machines, are operative when politics is seen as a means to employment or personal advancement. The jobs often provided an important means of social mobility for aspirants to middle-class life. Finally, ideologically motivated people enter party activities to work for a clear-cut set of issue positions. Principle is more important than winning to those whose incentives are primarily ideological.

Modern political parties are a mixture of these tendencies. In general, "professional" party members, especially candidates for elective office, have different goals than those motivating "amateurs," who are active in party politics only from time to time.

[1]In rare instances the answer might be "I'm a Libertarian" or "I'm a Socialist" or some other less common political group.
[2]*Political Organizations* (New York: Basic Books, 1973).

Political Party

A group of individuals who organize to win elections, to operate the government, and to determine public policy.

Faction

A group or bloc in a legislature or political party acting together in pursuit of some special interest or position.

Democratic convention delegate.

Political Parties in Other Countries

▽

Although the individuals who claim to belong to the major American parties profess a similar political ideology, this is not a requirement for participation. Contrast this situation with membership in political parties in other countries. Members of the Communist party in the Soviet Union, in the People's Republic of China, in Albania, and elsewhere must adhere to rigidly enforced (but often tactically shifting) party lines.

Countries vary widely in their number of political parties and in the way political power is apportioned. Mexico has one dominant political party, but within it are relatively conservative and relatively liberal factions. This party is known as the *Partido Revolucionario Institucional* (Institutional Revolutionary Party), and its somewhat contradictory name conveys the nature of Mexican politics. The party grew out of popular revolutionary struggles in the late nineteenth and early twentieth centuries; today, however, it must address the desires of modern Mexicans for stability.

In Italy, on the other hand, a variety of political parties vie for control and influence. Voters are splintered among the Christian Democrats, the Communists, the Socialists, and a large number of minor parties, including the Social Movement party, the Social Democrats, the Radicals, the Republicans, the Liberals, and the

Proletarian Unity party. Governments normally are formed by coalitions of the Christian Democrats and the Socialists with some of the minor parties.

These different party structures grew out of historical events unique to each nation, as well as electoral laws that may favor either small parties (as in Italy) or only the biggest parties (as in the United States). What we are used to—that is, two relatively moderate political parties alternating in power peacefully—is not likely to exist in countries that have evolved differently from the United States.

Functions of Political Parties in the United States

▽

Political parties in the United States engage in a wide variety of activities. Many of those activities are discussed throughout this chapter. Political parties are expected to do the following, although no single party—state, local, or national—probably does them all.

1. Identify and publicize issues of a political and social nature.
2. Stimulate the public's interest in the political process.
3. Recruit party candidates and enter them in national, state, and local electoral campaigns.
4. Finance political party activity.
5. Accept responsibility for operating government while in power.
6. Provide an organized opposition to the political party operating the government.
7. Attempt to create a consensus that cuts across sectional or social class differences.
8. Provide an avenue for public service careers.

Students of political parties like Leon D. Epstein[3] point out that the major functions of American political parties are carried out by a small, relatively loose-knit **cadre**, or nucleus, of party activists. This is quite a different arrangement from the more highly structured, mass-membership party organization typical of European working-class parties. American parties concentrate on winning elections rather than signing up large numbers of deeply committed, dues-paying members who believe passionately in the party's program.

Cadre
The nucleus of political party activists carrying out the major functions of American political parties.

A Short History of Political Parties in the United States

▽

Political parties in the United States have a long tradition, dating back to the earliest years of this nation's history. The function and character of these political parties, as well as the emergence of the two-party system itself, have much to do with the unique historical forces operating from this country's beginning as an independent nation. It wasn't until the 1790s that political parties emerged in the United States (Figure 8–1). Generally, we can divide the evolution of our nation's political parties into six periods:

1. The creation of parties in the 1790s.
2. The era of one-party rule, or personal politics, in the 1820s.
3. The period from Andrew Jackson's presidency to the Civil War, during which the Democrats and the Whigs were solidly established national parties.

[3]*Political Parties in Western Democracies* (New Brunswick, N.J.: Transaction, 1980).

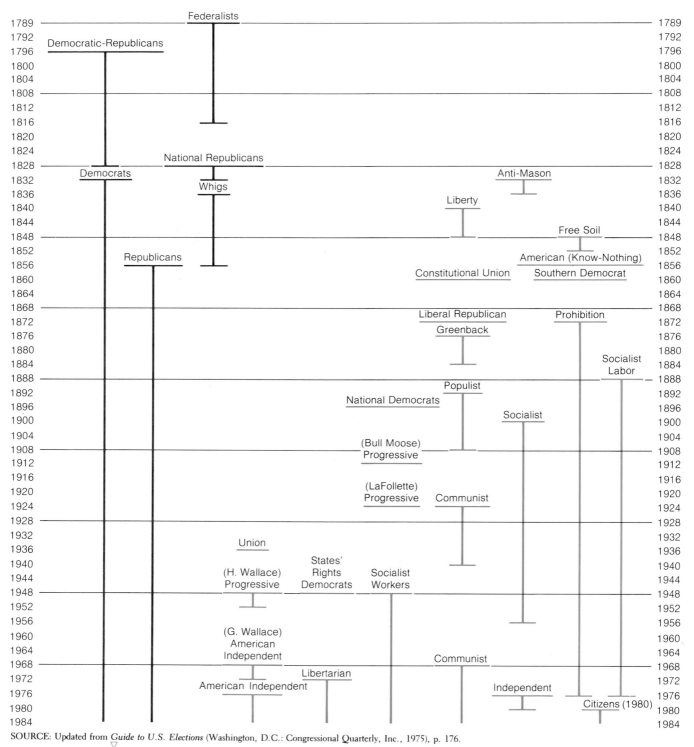

Figure 8–1

American Political Parties Since 1789

MAJOR PARTIES THIRD PARTIES

Federalists

Democratic-Republicans

National Republicans

Democrats

Anti-Mason

Whigs

Liberty

Free Soil

Republicans

American (Know-Nothing)

Constitutional Union   Southern Democrat

Liberal Republican   Prohibition

Greenback

Socialist Labor

Populist

National Democrats

Socialist

(Bull Moose) Progressive

(LaFollette) Progressive   Communist

Union

(H. Wallace) Progressive   States' Rights Democrats   Socialist Workers

(G. Wallace) American Independent

Communist

American Independent   Libertarian

Independent

Citizens (1980)

SOURCE: Updated from *Guide to U.S. Elections* (Washington, D.C.: Congressional Quarterly, Inc., 1975), p. 176.

4. The post-Civil War period, ending in 1896.
5. The progressive period, from 1896 to 1921.
6. The modern period, from Franklin Roosevelt's New Deal until today.

The Formative Years: Federalists and Anti-Federalists

The first partisan political division in the United States occurred after the Constitutional Convention. The **Federalists** proposed adoption of the Constitution, while the **anti-Federalists** were against ratification.

In September 1796, George Washington, who had served as president for almost two full terms, decided not to run again. In his farewell address, he made a somber assessment of the nation's future. Washington felt that the country might be destroyed by the "baneful effects of the spirit of party." He viewed parties as a threat to both national unity and the concept of popular government. Early in his career, Jefferson did not like political parties either. In 1789, he stated, "If I could not go to heaven but with a party, I would not go there at all."[4]

What Americans found out during the first decade or so after ratification of the Constitution was that even a patriot-king (as Washington has been called) could not keep everyone happy. There is no such thing as a neutral political figure who is so fair-minded that everyone agrees with him or her. During this period, it became obvious to many that something more permanent than a faction would be necessary to identify candidates for the growing number of individuals who would be participating in elections. Thus, according to many historians, the world's first democratic political parties were established in this country. Also, in 1800 when the Federalists lost the presidential election to the Democratic Republicans (also known as Jeffersonian), one of the first peaceful transfers of power from one party to another was achieved.

The Era of Personal Politics

From 1816 to 1828, a majority of voters regularly elected Democratic Republicans to the presidency and to Congress. **Two-party competition** did not really exist. This was the so-called **era of personal politics,** when attention centered on the character of individual candidates rather than on party identification. Although opposing the Federalist belief in a stronger, more active central government during elections, the Jeffersonians acquired the Louisiana Territory and Florida, established a national bank, enforced a higher tariff, and resisted European intrusion in the Western Hemisphere. Domestic tranquility was sufficiently in evidence that the administration of James Monroe came to be known as the **era of good feeling.**

National Two-Party Rule: Democrats and Whigs

During the era of personal politics, one-party rule did not prevent Democratic Republican factions from competing against each other. Indeed, there was quite a bit of intraparty rivalry. Finally, in 1824 and 1828, Jeffersonian Republicans who

[4]Letter to Francis Hopkinson written from Paris while he was minister to France. In John P. Foley, ed., *The Jeffersonian Cyclopedia* (New York: Russell & Russell, 1967), p. 677.

Thomas Jefferson

Federalists

The first American political party, led by Alexander Hamilton and John Adams. Many of its members had strongly supported the adoption of the new Constitution and the creation of the federal union.

Anti-Federalists

The anti-Federalists opposed the adoption of the Constitution because of its centralist tendencies and attacked the failure of the Constitution's framers to include a bill of rights.

Two-Party Competition

Two strong and solidly established political parties in competition for political control; both parties have a strong chance of winning an election.

Era of Personal Politics

An era when attention centers on the character of individual candidates rather than on party identification.

Era of Good Feeling

The years from 1817 to 1825 when James Monroe was president and there was, in effect, no political opposition. The term has been continually revived.

Andrew Jackson, founder of the modern Democratic Party.

Democrats

One of the two major American political parties evolving out of the Democratic Republican group supporting Thomas Jefferson.

Whigs

One of the foremost political organizations in the United States during the first half of the nineteenth century, formally established in 1836. The Whig party was dominated by the same anti-Jackson elements that organized the National Republican faction within the Jeffersonian Republicans and represented a variety of regional interests. It fell apart as a national party in the early 1850s.

Republican Party

One of the two major American political parties, which emerged in the 1850s as an antislavery party. It was created to fill the vacuum created by the disintegration of the Whig party. The Republican party traces its name—but not its ideology—to Jefferson's Democratic Republican party.

belonged to the factions of Henry Clay and John Quincy Adams split with Andrew Jackson in those elections. Jackson's supporters and the Clay-Adams bloc formed separate parties as **Democrats** and **Whigs,** respectively. It was under Jackson's leadership that the Jeffersonians changed the name to the Democratic party. That same Democratic party is now the oldest continuing political party in the Western world.

The Whigs were those Jeffersonian Republicans who were often called the "National Republicans." At the national level, the Whigs were able to elect two presidents—William Henry Harrison in 1840 and Zachary Taylor in 1848. However, the Whigs were unable to maintain a common ideological base when the issue of slavery arose in the late 1840s, and the party became increasingly divided. During the 1850s the Whigs fell apart as a national party.

The Post-Civil War Period

The existing two-party system was disrupted by the election of 1860, in which there were four major candidates. Abraham Lincoln, the candidate of the newly formed **Republican party,** was the victor with a majority of the electoral vote, although only 39.9 percent of the popular vote. This newly formed Republican party—not to be confused with the Jeffersonian Republicans—was created in the mid-1850s from the various groups that sought to fill the vacuum left by the disintegration of the Whigs. It took the label of Grand Old Party, or GOP. Its first national convention was held in 1856, but its presidential candidate, John C. Fremont, lost.

After the end of the Civil War, the South became heavily Democratic (the Solid South), and the North became heavily Republican. This era of Republican dominance was highlighted by the election of 1896 when the Republicans, emphasizing economic development and modernization under William McKinley, resoundingly defeated the Democratic and Populist candidate, William Jennings Bryan. The Republicans' control was solidified by winning over the urban working-class vote in northern cities. From the election of Abraham Lincoln until the election of Roosevelt in 1932, the Republicans won all but four presidential elections.

The Progressive Movement

In 1912, a major schism occurred in the Republican party when former Republican President Theodore Roosevelt ran for the presidency as a Progressive. Consequently, there was a significant three-way presidential contest. Woodrow Wilson was the Democratic candidate, William Howard Taft the regular Republican candidate, and Roosevelt the Progressive candidate. The Republican split allowed Wilson to be elected. The Wilson administration, although Democratic, ended up enacting much of the Progressive party's platform. Without any reason to be an opposition party, the Progressive party collapsed in 1921.

Republican Warren Harding's victory in 1920 reimposed Republican domination of national politics until the Republicans' defeat by Franklin Roosevelt in 1932 in the depths of the Great Depression.

The Modern Era: From the New Deal to the Present

Franklin Delano Roosevelt was elected in 1932, reelected in 1936 and 1940 and again in 1944. The impact of his successive Democratic administrations and the New Deal that he crafted is still with us today. Roosevelt used his enormous personal appeal to unify Democrats under his leadership and established direct communication between the president and the public through his radio "fireside chats." It wasn't until 1940 that the Republicans made even a small dent in the Democratic hegemony when Wendell Wilkie reduced Roosevelt's popular vote to 54.8 percent from the 60.5 percent and the 57.4 percent of the two previous elections.

In April 1945, Roosevelt died; Vice President Harry Truman became president through succession, and in 1948 through election. The New Deal coalition, renamed the Fair Deal, continued. It wasn't until Republican Dwight Eisenhower won the 1952 election that the Democrats lost their control of the presidency. The Republicans won again in 1956.

From 1960 through 1968, the Democrats, headed by Kennedy and Johnson, held national power. Republicans again came to power with Nixon's victory in 1968 but lost prestige after the Watergate scandal forced his resignation on August 8, 1974. Although Republican Vice President Ford (the first person ever *appointed* to the vice presidency to become president) took over for the remainder of Nixon's second term, the Republicans were severely damaged by Nixon's resignation. For this and other reasons, the Democrats were back in power in 1976. But Democratic President Jimmy Carter was unable to win reelection against Ronald Reagan in 1980. The Republicans also gained control of the Senate in 1980 and retained it in the elections of 1982 and 1984. In the next presidential election, Ronald Reagan

Handbill for 1860 election.

McKinley campaigning, 1896.

Copyright King Features Syndicate, Inc.

became the oldest man to be elected to the presidency when he garnered a 59 percent majority of the popular vote. He defeated the Democratic ticket of Walter Mondale and Geraldine Ferraro, although his popularity did not give the Republicans much assistance in other elections. The Republicans lost two seats in the Senate and failed to gain enough seats in the House to ensure control. The 1984 reelection of Ronald Reagan appeared to some pollsters to signal the resurgence of the Republican party as a competitive force in American politics as more people declared themselves to be Republicans than in the last several decades.

The Structure of Political Parties

▽

There are two ways to describe the Democratic and Republican parties: in theory and in reality. In theory, each of the American political parties has a standard, pyramid-shaped organization (Figure 8–2). However, the politicians operating within this structure do not find it so simple. The pyramid does not accurately reflect the relative power and strengths of the individual parts of the party organization. If it did, the national chairperson of the Democratic or Republican party, along with the national committee, could simply dictate how the organization was to be run, just as if it were Exxon or Ford Motor Company.

In reality, the formal structure of political parties resembles a layer cake with autonomous strata more than it does a pyramid. Malcolm E. Jewell and David M. Olson point out that

> there is no command structure within political parties. Rather, each geographic unit of the party tends to be autonomous from the other units at its same geographic level.[5]

[5]*American State Political Parties and Elections*, rev. ed. (Homewood, Ill.: Dorsey Press, 1982), p. 73.

National
Convention
(including a
national chairperson
and a national
committee)

National
Party
Organization

State conventions
and committees

State
Party
Organization

County committees

Precinct and ward organizations
(including active, paid and unpaid workers)

Local
Party
Organizations

Party members (those who vote the party ticket)

Figure 8–2

▽

**A Theoretical Structure of the American
Political Party**

The National Party Organization

Each party has a national organization whose clearly institutional part is the **national
convention,** held every four years. The convention is used to nominate the presidential and vice presidential candidates. In addition, the **party platform** is written,
ratified, and revised at the national convention. The platform sets forth the party's
position on the issues and makes promises to initiate certain policies if the party
wins the presidency. Often, platforms represent compromises among the various
factions of a party, in an attempt to make peace before the campaign begins.

After the convention, the platform is frequently neglected or ignored by party
candidates who disagree with it. Since candidates are trying to win votes from a
wide spectrum of voters, it is counterproductive to emphasize the fairly narrow and
sometimes controversial goals set forth in the platform. The work of Gerald Pomper[6]
has shown, however, that once elected, the parties have tried to carry out platform
promises and that roughly three-fourths of the promises eventually become law.
Of course, some general goals, such as economic prosperity, are included in both
parties' platforms.

From 1974 to 1982, a Democratic **miniconvention** was held during nonpresidential election years, but the Republicans did not follow suit. The purpose of
these midterm conferences was to provide a forum for discussing party rules, de-
bating policies and issues, and preparing for the next presidential campaign. In
contrast to the presidential nominating convention, the focus of the miniconvention
was on party business rather than personalities.

Choosing the National Committee

At the national convention, each of the parties formally chooses a national standing
committee, elected by the individual state parties. This **national committee** is

[6]Gerald M. Pomper with Susan S. Lederman, *Elections in America: Control and Influence in Democratic
Politics,* 2d ed. (New York: Longman, 1980).

National Convention

The meeting held every four years by
each major party to select presidential
and vice presidential candidates, to write
a platform, to choose a national committee, and to conduct party business. In
theory, the national convention is at the
top of a hierarchy of party conventions
(the local and state conventions are below it) that considers candidates and issues.

Party Platform

A document drawn up by the platform
committee at each national convention,
outlining the policies, positions, and
principles of the party; it is then submitted to the entire convention for approval.

Miniconvention

A meeting held by the Democratic party
during nonpresidential election years
from 1974 to 1982.

National Committee

A standing committee of a national political party established to direct and coordinate party activities during the four-
year period between national party conventions.

▽

235

The Rise and Fall of the Major Party

No one political party has dominated the American scene since the origin of the republic. Rather, the two most important parties have alternated in being the majority and minority party. Majority status means not only controlling the Congress and winning the presidency a great proportion of the time but also having the largest number of party members at the grass-roots level. Since 1932 and the election of Franklin Roosevelt, the Democratic party has clearly been the dominant party in the American two-party system.

At several distinct moments in history, the dominant party has been overthrown, or replaced by the minority party, and the new majority party has remained in power for more than a generation. Such upheavals, which take place at presidential elections, are usually called "realignments" of the party system. The term *critical realignment* refers to a change in party power that is sudden, accompanied by a particularly intense political campaign, and that sees a number of social groups switch their allegiance from one party to the other permanently. The election of Franklin D. Roosevelt in 1932 is the classic example of such a critical realignment. The dominance of the Republican party since the Civil War was broken, the country was in an economic crisis, and the groups that switched to the Democratic party—blacks, blue-collar workers, Jewish voters—stayed in it for the next forty years.

The question that has intrigued political scientists for the last decade is, "When will the next realignment take place?" In the past, such changes in party balance occurred about every thirty to forty years: 1828, 1860, 1896, and 1932. The Democratic party seemed to be weakening as some traditionally Democratic groups such as white southerners and some ethnics appeared to be tempted by Republican politics, and Republicans took the presidency in 1952, 1956, 1968, 1972, and the first two elections of the 1980s.

The 1980 and 1984 election victories of Ronald Reagan presented a puzzle to political scientists. No large social groups changed their political identity. Polling data showed that large proportions of blacks, union members, Jews, and Catholics continued to vote for the Democratic candidate. Overall figures for party identification, however, showed continual increases for Republicans until, by 1986, the two parties were almost even in their proportions of the electorate. Did the parties realign in the 1980s or did they not?

Work by Helmut Norpoth suggests strongly that a partisan realignment is under way and that it will be long lasting. Realignment, according to Norpoth, is primarily due to the political choices of the youngest generation of voters.[*] Looking at the political identification of voters by the generation in which they were born, he finds increasing Republicanism among voters under thirty years of age, and the younger they are, the more Republican they tend to be. As these new, young Republicans grow older, they become a larger proportion of the electorate, and so the number of Republicans grows.

Given what we know about family influence on party identification, how could Republican children come from the predominantly Democratic families of the 1940s and 1950s? Norpoth believes that although the families declared themselves Democratic, they probably voted for Eisenhower or Nixon during the childhood of these new Republicans. The children learned which party their parents actually voted for, rather than how they identified themselves. When they reached political adulthood, during the zenith of the Reagan years, it was easy for them to adopt a Republican label. Once adopted, it is unlikely that they will change to a Democratic one unless the nation undergoes a political or economic crisis. Thus Norpoth sees a Republican realignment under way, although a gradual one.

[*]Helmut Norpoth, "Party Realignment in the American Electorate: Overdue and Underway?" Paper presented at the Annual Meeting of the American Association for Public Opinion Research, May 1986. For further reading about party realignment, see Walter Dean Burnham, *Critical Elections and the Mainsprings of American Politics* (New York: W. W. Norton, 1970); Angus Campbell et. al., *Elections and the Political Order* (New York: Wiley, 1966); and Everett Ladd and Charles Hadley, *Transformations of the American Party Systems,* 2d ed. (New York: Norton, 1978).

established to direct and coordinate party activities during the following four years. The Democrats include at least two members, a man and a woman, from each state, from the District of Columbia, and from the several territories. Governors, members of Congress, mayors, and other officials may be included as at-large members of the national committee. The Republicans, in addition, add state chairpersons from every state carried by the Republican party in the preceding presidential, gubernatorial, or congressional elections. The national committee members are ratified by the delegations to the national convention.

One of the jobs of the national committee is to ratify the presidential nominee's choice of a national chairperson, who in principle acts as the spokesperson for the party. Even though we have placed the national committee at the top of the hierarchy of party organization (see Figure 8–2), it has very little direct influence. Basically, the national chairperson and the national committee simply plan the next campaign and the next convention, obtain financial contributions, and publicize the national party.

Picking a National Chairperson

In general, the party's presidential candidate chooses the national chairperson.[7] The major responsibility of that person is the management of the national election campaign. In some cases, a strong national chairperson has considerable power over state and local party organizations. There is no formal mechanism with which to exercise direct control over subnational party structures, however. The national chairperson does such jobs as establish a national party headquarters, raise and distribute campaign funds, and appear in the media as a party spokesperson.

The national chairperson, along with the national committee, attempts basically to maintain some sort of liaison among the different levels of the party organization. The fact is that the real strength and power of a national party is at the state level.

The State Organization

There are fifty states in the Union, plus the territories and the District of Columbia, and an equal number of party organizations for each major party. Therefore, there are more than a hundred state parties (and even more if we include local parties and minor parties). Since every state party is unique, it is impossible to describe what an "average" state political party is like. Nonetheless, state parties have several organizational features in common.

This commonality can be described in one sentence: Each state party has a chairperson, a committee, and a number of local organizations. In principle, the **state central committees**—the principal organized structure of each political party within each state—have similar roles in the various states. The committee, usually composed of those members who represent congressional districts, state legislative districts, or counties, has responsibility for carrying out the policy decisions of the party's state convention, and in some states the state central committee will direct the state chairperson with respect to policy making.

Also, like the national committee, the state central committee has control over the use of party campaign funds during political campaigns. Usually, the state central committee has little if any effect on party candidates who are elected. In fact, state parties are fundamentally loose alliances of local interests and coalitions of often bitterly opposed factions.

Although state parties have different power structures, they all provide career opportunities for individuals who want to become national leaders. This was especially apparent in the 1976 and 1980 elections (and administrations) of Jimmy

Frank Fahrenkopf, Republican National Committee Chairman.

State Central Committee

The principal organized structure of each political party within each state. Responsible for carrying out policy decisions of the party's state convention.

---

[7]If that candidate loses, however, the chairperson is often changed.

Unit Rule

All of a state's electoral votes are cast for the presidential candidate receiving a plurality of the popular vote.

Patronage

The practice of exchanging public jobs for political support.

Mayor Richard J. Daley

▽

238

Carter and Ronald Reagan, both of whom had previously been state governors—of Georgia and California, respectively.

State parties also loom importantly in national politics because of the **unit rule,** which awards electoral votes in presidential elections as an indivisible bloc. Presidential candidates concentrate their efforts in states in which voter preferences seem to be evenly divided or in which large numbers of electoral votes are at stake.

In recent years, the Democratic party has dominated state houses across the country. Thirteen governorships were at stake in the 1984 national elections. Eight of these elections were won by Republican candidates. The net effect, however, was an increase of only one governor for the Republicans, to sixteen out of the fifty states. The Republican party made further gains in the statehouse competition in the 1986 elections even though the Democrats took control of the Senate that year. After the votes were counted, the Democrats held the edge in governorships, 26 to 24, their smallest advantage since 1970. Republicans were particularly heartened by their wins in Texas, Alabama, Arizona, and Florida. Three of those four states were traditionally in the Democratic column.

Local Party Machinery: The Grass Roots

The lowest layer of party machinery is the local organization, supported by district leaders, precinct or ward captains, and party workers. Much of the work is coordinated by county committees and their chairpersons. A local party organization is depicted in Figure 8–3. In the past, the institution of **patronage**—rewarding the party faithful with government jobs or contracts—held the local organization together. For immigrants and the poor, the political machine often furnished important services and protections. The big-city party machine was the archetypical example, and Tammany Hall, or the Tammany Society, was perhaps the highest refinement of this political form.

The last big-city local political machine to exercise a great deal of power was run by Chicago's Mayor Richard J. Daley, who was also an important figure in national Democratic politics. Daley, as mayor, ran the Chicago Democratic machine from 1955 until his death on December 20, 1976. Although the machine began to run down in the 1970s as its operators found it increasingly difficult to deliver the vote, a Daley faction prevailed with the election of his successors—Michael Bilandic (1977–79) and Jane Byrne (1979–83). The Daley faction, largely Irish in candidate origin and voter support, was split by the successful candidacy of black Democrat Harold Washington in the racially divisive April 1983 mayoral election. Washington defeated Byrne and Daley's son in the Democratic primary and withstood the defection of many local machine supporters to his Republican opponent, Bernard Epton.

City machines are now dead, mostly because their function of providing social services (and reaping the reward of votes) has been taken over by state and national agencies. This trend began in the 1930s when the social legislation of the New Deal established Social Security and unemployment insurance. The local party machine has little if anything to do with deciding who is eligible to receive these benefits.

Local political organizations, whether located in cities, townships, or at the county level, still can contribute a great deal to local election campaigns. These organizations are able to provide the foot soldiers of politics, individuals who pass out literature and get out the vote on election day, which can be crucial in local elections. In many regions, local Democratic and Republican organizations still control some patronage, such as courthouse jobs, contracts for street repair, and other lucrative construction contracts. Local party organizations are also the most important vehicle for recruiting young adults into political work, since politics at the local level has many opportunities for activists to gain experience.

The Two-Party System in American Politics
▽

It would be difficult to imagine a political system in the United States in which there were four, five, six, or seven major political parties. Of course, the United States has a two-party system, and that system has been around from about 1800 to the present. But considering the range of political ideology among voters and the variety of local and state party machines, the fact that we still have just two major political parties is somewhat unusual.

Strong competition between the parties at the national level has in general not filtered down to the state level. From 1900 to 1980, the Republicans won eleven

Figure 8–3
▽
The Structure of a Typical Local
Party Organization

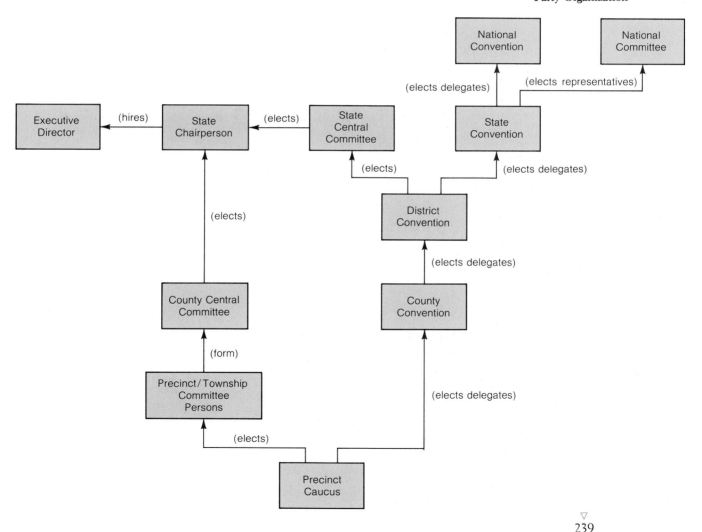

239

Tammany Hall: The Quintessential Local Political Machine

The Tammany Society dominated New York City politics for more than a century. Founded in 1786 with the express purpose of engaging in cultural, social, and patriotic activities, the society evolved into a major political force and became known as Tammany Hall. In the beginning, it organized and provided social services for the largely foreign born who made up the bulk of the Democratic party in New York City. One of its more notorious leaders was William Tweed, head of the so-called Tweed ring whose scandals were unearthed by the *New York Times* in 1871. Readers were entertained and horrified by stories of millions of dollars in kickbacks through the letting of government contracts and the overlooking of civil and criminal violations, as well as phony leases and padded bills that were paid to members of the Tweed ring. As a result of the exposé, Tweed was imprisoned; but the other members of the ring managed to flee the country (as very wealthy men and women). Richard Crocker took over the leadership of Tammany Hall in 1886 and kept it until 1901.

Tammany Hall's influence declined when its slate of candidates was defeated in a reform movement in 1901. It wasn't until Franklin Roosevelt's victory in 1932 that Tammany lost its political clout almost completely—but

TWEEDLEDEE AND SWEEDLEDUM.
(*A New Christmas Pantomime at the Tammany Hall.*)
Clown (to Pantaloon). "Let's Blind them with *this*, and then take *some more.*"
TWEED'S GIFT OF FIFTY THOUSAND DOLLARS TO THE POOR OF HIS NATIVE WARD.—"HARPER'S WEEKLY," JANUARY 14, 1871.

only for a couple of decades. In the 1950s there was a short lived resurgence in the influence of the Tammany Society. It has enjoyed no political influence in New York City politics since then.

presidential elections and the Democrats ten. In state and local elections, however, one-party dominance is the rule in many regions of the United States. The Solid South was almost totally Democratic at all levels of government from 1880 to 1944. The northeastern states and much of the Midwest were solidly Republican from approximately 1860 to 1930. As can be seen in Table 8–1, about 50 percent of the states show one-party dominance even today. In any event, we are still talking about either Democratic or Republican dominance—just two major parties.

Table 8–1
▽

Measure of Party Competition for States, 1961–82

State	Governorship		Senate			House		
	D	R	D	R	Tie	D	R	Tie
Democratic dominant:								
Ala.	22	0	22	0	—	22	0	—
Miss.	22	0	22	0	—	22	0	—
La.	20	2	22	0	—	22	0	—
Ga.	22	0	22	0	—	22	0	—
S.C.	18	4	22	0	—	22	0	—
Ark.	16	6	22	0	—	22	0	—
Tex.	18	4	22	0	—	22	0	—
Democratic majority:								
Md.	20	2	22	0	—	22	0	—
Hawaii	20	2	20	2	—	20	2	—
N.C.	18	4	22	0	—	22	0	—
Fla.	18	4	22	0	—	22	0	—
Ky.	18	4	22	0	—	22	0	—
N.Mex.	16	6	22	0	—	22	0	—
Mo.	16	6	22	0	—	22	0	—
R.I.	16	6	22	0	—	22	0	—
Okla.	14	8	22	0	—	22	0	—
Tenn.	14	8	22	0	—	20	0	2
W.Va.	14	8	22	0	—	22	0	—
Competitive two-party:								
Calif.	14	8	20	0	2	20	2	—
Va.	10	12	22	0	—	22	0	—
Mass.	10	12	22	0	—	22	0	—
Conn.	18	4	20	2	—	14	8	—
Nev.	14	8	16	4	2	18	4	—
Alaska	10	12	14	6	2	18	2	2
Wash.	8	14	22	0	—	12	8	2
N.J.	18	4	10	12	—	16	6	—
Mont.	14	8	16	4	2	10	12	—
Oreg.	4	18	22	0	—	14	8	—
Del.	12	10	14	6	2	12	10	—
Pa.	10	12	10	10	2	12	10	—
Utah	18	4	8	14	—	8	14	—
Wis.	12	10	8	14	—	8	14	—
Mich.	2	20	10	8	4	16	4	2
Nebr.*	14	8	—	—	—	—	—	—
Minn.†	12	10	—	—	—	—	—	—
Ill.	12	10	8	12	2	8	14	—
Ariz.	10	12	10	12	—	8	14	—
Maine	12	6	2	20	—	10	12	—
N.Dak.	20	2	0	22	—	4	18	—
Ohio	6	16	6	14	2	10	12	—
N.Y.	8	14	2	20	—	12	10	—
Iowa	6	16	8	14	—	6	16	—
Ind.	8	14	8	14	—	4	18	—
Kans.	12	10	0	22	—	2	20	—
Idaho	12	10	0	22	—	0	22	—
Republican majority:								
Colo.	10	12	2	20	—	6	16	—
Vt.	10	12	0	22	—	2	20	—
Wyo.	10	12	0	20	2	2	20	—
S.Dak.	8	14	4	18	—	0	20	2
N.H.	10	12	0	16	6	0	22	—

*Nebraska's senate and house have been nonpartisan.
†Minnesota's senate and house have been mostly nonpartisan.

SOURCE: Malcolm E. Jewell and David M. Olson, *American State Political Parties and Elections*, rev. ed. (Homewood, Ill.: Dorsey Press, 1982), p. 27.

Sectional Politics

The pursuit of interests that are of special concern to a region or section of the country.

National Politics

The pursuit of interests that are of concern to the nation as a whole.

Class Politics

Political preferences based on income level and/or social status.

There are several reasons why two major parties have dominated the political landscape in the United States for almost two centuries. These have to do with (1) the historical foundations of the system, (2) the self-perpetuation of the parties, (3) the commonality of views among Americans, (4) the winner-take-all electoral system, and (5) state and federal laws favoring the two-party system.

The Historical Foundation of the Two-Party System

As we have seen, the first two opposing groups in United States politics were the Federalists and the anti-Federalists. The Federalists, who remained in power and solidified their identity as a political party, represented commercial interests—merchants, shipowners, and manufacturers. The anti-Federalists, who gradually became known as the Democratic Republicans, represented artisans and farmers. These interests were also fairly well split along geographic lines, with the Federalists dominant in the North and the Democratic Republicans dominant in the South.

Two relatively distinct sets of interests continued to characterize the two different parties. During Andrew Jackson's time in power, eastern commercial interests were pitted against western and southern agricultural and frontier interests. Before the Civil War, the major split again became North versus South. The split was ideological—over the issue of slavery—as well as economic—the Northeast's industrial interests versus the agricultural interests of the South. After the Civil War and until the 1920s, the Republicans found most of their strength in the Northeast, the Democrats in the Solid South. The West and the Midwest held the balance of power at that time. This period until the 1920s has been called one of **sectional politics.**

Sectional politics gave way to **national politics** as the cities became more dominant and as industry flowed to the South and to the West. Some political scientists classify the period from 1920 to today as one of **class politics,** the Republicans generally finding support among groups of higher economic status and the Democrats appealing more to working-class constituencies.

Self-Perpetuation of the Two-Party System

As we saw in Chapter 7, most children identify with the political party of their parents. Children learn at quite a young age to think of themselves as either Democrats or Republicans. Relatively few are taught to think of themselves as Libertarians or Socialists or even independents. This generates a built-in mechanism to perpetuate a two-party system. According to most studies of the process of political socialization, psychological attachment to party identity intensifies during adulthood.[8]

Also, many politically oriented people who aspire to work for social change consider that the only realistic way to capture political power in this country is to be either a Republican or a Democrat. Of course, the same argument holds for those who involve themselves in politics largely for personal gain. Thus, political parties provide avenues for the expression of the personal ambitions of politicians

[8]See, for example, Lester W. Milbrath, *Political Participation: How and Why Do People Get Involved in Politics?* (Chicago, Ill.: Rand McNally, 1965), pp. 134–135.

and supply government with men and women anxious to serve the public by satisfying their own goals.[9]

The Political Culture of the United States

Another determining factor in the perpetuation of our two-party system is the commonality of goals among Americans. Most Americans want continuing material prosperity. They also believe this goal should be achieved through individual rather than collective initiative. There has never been much support for establishing the government as the owner of the major means of production. Left-wing political movements wish to limit the ownership of private property. Americans take a dim view of such an attitude—private property is considered a basic American institution and the ability to acquire and use it the way one wishes is commonly regarded as a basic American right.

There has never really been a successful movement to change the economic system of **capitalism** in the United States.[10] There has also never been any significant movement to change the country's basic political system. When is the last time you heard somebody seriously suggesting that we have a monarchy? or a dictatorship? or a socialist/communist system? or a feudal system? The fact is that few Americans even deem such a subject worth considering. They are quite content with a republican form of government while occasionally grumbling about the imperfections of its representative democracy.

Another reason we have had a basic consensus about our political system and the two major parties is that we have largely managed to separate religion from politics. Religion was an issue in 1928 when Governor Alfred Smith of New York became the first Roman Catholic to be nominated for the presidency (he was defeated by Republican Herbert Hoover) and again in 1960 when John F. Kennedy was running for president. But religion has never been a dividing force triggering splinter parties. There has never been a major Catholic party or a Protestant party or a Jewish party or a Moslem party.

The major division in American politics has been economic. As we mentioned earlier, the Democrats have been known—at least since the 1930s—as the party of the working class, in favor of government intervention in the economy and more government redistribution of income. The Republican party has been known in modern times as the party of the middle and upper classes and commercial interests, in favor of a more uninhibited workings of the market system and less redistribution of income.

Not only does the political culture support the two-party system but the parties themselves are adept at making the necessary shifts in their platforms or electoral appeal to gain new members. Because the general ideological structure of the parties is so broad, it has been relatively easy for them to change their respective platforms or to borrow popular policies from minor parties to attract voting support. Both parties perceive themselves as broad enough to accommodate every group in society; the Republicans try to woo support from the black community, whereas the Democrats strive to make inroads in professional and business groups.

Did You Know?
▽
That the presidential primary election was originated by the state of Florida in 1904?

Capitalism
An economic and political system based on private ownership of the means of production and a market economy based on supply and demand.

Electoral College
A group of persons called electors who are selected by the voters in each state; this group officially elects the president and the vice president of the United States. The number of electors in each state is equal to the number of each state's representatives in both houses of Congress.

The Winner-Take-All Electoral System

At virtually every level of government in the United States, the outcome of elections is based on the plurality, winner-take-all principle. A plurality system is one in which the winner is the person who obtains the most votes, even if a majority is not obtained. Whoever gets the most votes gets everything. Since most legislative seats in the United States are elected from single-member districts in which only one person represents the constituency, the candidate who finishes second in such an election receives nothing for the effort.

The winner-take-all system also operates in the **electoral college** (see Chapter 10). Each state's electors are pledged to candidates chosen by their respective national party conventions. During the popular vote in November, in each of the fifty states and in the District of Columbia, the voters choose one slate of electors from those on the state ballot. If the slate of electors wins a plurality in a state, *all* the electors so chosen—except in Maine, where electoral votes are apportioned among its U.S. Senate and House seats—then cast their ballots for the presidential and vice presidential candidates of the winning party. That means that if a particular candidate's slate of electors receives a plurality of 40 percent of the votes in a state, that candidate will receive all the state's electoral votes. Minor parties have a difficult time competing under such a system, even though they may influence the final outcome of the election. Because voters know that minor parties can't succeed, they often will not vote for minor party candidates, even if they are ideologically in tune with them.

Not all countries, or all states in the United States, use the plurality, winner-take-all electoral system. Some hold run-off elections until a candidate obtains at least one vote over 50 percent of the votes. Such a system is compatible with multiple parties outside of the United States. Small parties hope to be able to obtain a sufficient number of votes to at least get into a run-off election. Then the small-party candidate can form an alliance with one or more of those parties that did not make the run-off. Such alliances also occur in the United States, but with the plurality system these coalitions must normally be made before the first election since there is no run-off.

Now consider another alternative political system in which there is proportional representation with multimember districts. In West Germany, each party submits its preferred list of candidates in order of preference. If, during the national election, party X obtains 12 percent of the vote, party Y 43 percent of the vote, and party Z the remaining 45 percent of the vote, then in parliament party X gets 12 percent of the seats, party Y gets 43 percent of the seats, and party Z gets 45 percent of the seats. Because even a minor party may still obtain at least a few seats in parliament, the smaller parties have a greater incentive to organize under such electoral systems than they do in the United States.

State and Federal Laws Favoring the Two Parties

Many state and federal election laws offer a clear advantage to the two major parties. In some states, the established major parties need gather only a few signatures to place their candidates on the ballot, whereas a minor party or an independent candidate must get many more signatures. The criterion for making such a distinction is often based on the total party vote in the last general election, penalizing the new political party that did not compete in the election.

Highlight

▽

The Rise of Republicanism in the 1980s

In the aftermath of the Democratic Carter administration, the Republican party found new strength among Americans, particularly among younger, first-time participants in the political process. Ronald Reagan, a telegenic master of public relations, and the leadership of the Republican party undertook a strong, calculated effort to attract new support to their party by an upbeat, positive emphasis on America's strengths and virtues. An improving economy late in Reagan's first term and considerable good luck and success in foreign affairs added to the aura of the Republican party. Public opinion polls showed that Americans believed the Republican party was more likely to keep the nation prosperous and at peace and was at least as able to handle the nation's problems as were the Democrats.

The surge in support for the agenda of the Republican party, or for the nation in general and Ronald Reagan as its leader, was especially apparent among younger adults. Some polls showed that a plurality of first-time voters adopted the Republican label. Even among black voters, where support for the Republican party has been practically nonexistent for decades, 13 percent of those under twenty-five, in a recent *Washington Post*/ABC News Poll, said they are Republicans. College students, who had supported liberal and Democratic causes since the 1960s, voted 60 percent for Reagan in 1984.

The loss of Democratic support and the corresponding increase in Republican strength is also related to changing partisan patterns among white males, particularly those in the South and those who hold conservative, born-again Christian beliefs. In the 1984 election, southern white males voted for Reagan by a 3-to-1 margin and born-again Christians voted for him by a 4-to-1 margin over Mondale. Some Democratic officeholders have been successful in retaining support among these important segments of the Democratic electorate. Among them are former governors Bruce Babbitt of Arizona and Charles Robb of Virginia, and Representative Richard Gephardt of Missouri. The party, however, is internally divided over whether it should change its platform to accommodate more conservative ideas or to continue in its more liberal stance.

Will the Republican party become the dominant, major party in the future? That is, of course, a difficult question to answer. After the individuals who call themselves independents are sorted into party categories depending on which way they lean, the two parties have about equal support, at least within sampling error. One such poll, conducted by the *Washington Post* and ABC News in May 1986, showed that Democrats are by and large less happy with their party. The Republican party scored higher than the Democratic party for its ability to bring about the kind of change the country needs, contributing good ideas for the economy, and engaging in less internal bickering. On all three measures, the Democrats' performance was worse than in a 1984 poll. These doubts about the capacity of the Democratic party to deal with the nation's problems combined with the popularity of Ronald Reagan may lead to more victories for the Republican party in the future, although it will be a number of years before the full effect of the Reagan years is known. The effects of the Iran-*contra* arms scandal may slow or reveerse this process.

SOURCE: *Washington Post*, Weekly Edition, June 16, 1986, p. 37.

At the national level, minor parties face different obstacles. All of the rules and procedures of both houses of Congress divide committee seats, staff members, and other privileges on the basis of party membership. A legislator who is elected on a minor party ticket such as the Liberal party of New York must choose to be counted with one of the major parties to get a committee assignment. The Federal Election Commission (FEC) rules for campaign financing also place restrictions on minor party candidates. Such candidates are not eligible for federal matching funds in either the primary or general election. In the 1980 election John Anderson, running as an independent, sued the FEC for campaign funds, and the Commission finally agreed to repay part of his campaign costs after the election in proportion to the votes he received.

How Do the Democratic and Republican Parties Differ?

The two major American political parties are often characterized as being too much like Tweedledee and Tweedledum, in Lewis Carroll's *Through the Looking Glass*. When both parties nominate moderates for the presidency, the similarities between the parties seem to outweigh their differences. Yet the political parties do generate strong conflict for political offices throughout the United States, and there are significant differences between the parties, both in the characteristics of their members and in their platforms.

"Very Republican. I love it."

Drawing by B. Tobey © 1986 The New Yorker Magazine, Inc.

Although Democrats and Republicans are not divided along religious or class lines to the extent of some European parties, certain social groups are more likely to identify with each. Since the New Deal of Franklin Roosevelt, the Democratic party has appealed to the more disadvantaged groups in society. Black voters are far more likely to identify with the Democrats, as are members of union households, Jewish voters, and individuals who have less than a high school education. Republicans draw more of their support from college graduates, upper-income families, and professionals or businesspersons. In recent years, women have tended to identify themselves as Democrats more than as Republicans.

The coalition of minorities, the working class, and various ethnic groups have been the core of Democratic party support since the presidency of Franklin Roosevelt. The social programs and increased government intervention in the economy that were the heart of Roosevelt's New Deal were intended to ease the strain of economic hard times on these groups. This goal remains important for many Democrats today. In general, Democratic identifiers are more likely to approve of social welfare spending, to support government regulation of business, to approve of measures to improve the situation of minorities, and to assist the elderly with their medical expenses. Republicans are more supportive of the private marketplace, and many feel that the Federal government should be involved in fewer social programs. Table 8–2 shows that the general public shares this view of which groups are served by each party. Identifiers with the Republican party are more conservative in their views on social issues; religion is a major factor in these beliefs.

These differences separating party identifiers are greatly magnified among the leadership of the Democrats and Republicans. Generally, a much greater percentage of Democratic leaders consider themselves to be liberals than their followers, and Republican elites are far more likely to identify their philosophy as conservative than are their followers. Such differences are reflected in the party platforms that are adopted at each party's convention. Democratic platforms recently have stressed equality of opportunity, the government's responsibility to help citizens, and ending

Did You Know?
▽

That in the history of this nation, parties identified as "conservative" and those identified as "liberal" have shared the presidency almost equally?

Table 8–2
▽

Which Party Is Better?

In the view of the public, which party serves the interests of groups in society better?

	Republican	Democrat	Same/ Don't Know
Better for business and professional people	69%	16%	15%
White collar workers	59	23	18
Skilled workers	41	39	20
Small business people	35	45	20
Farmers	31	45	24
Retired people	28	48	24
Unemployed people	26	52	22
Women	25	48	27
Labor union members	24	58	18
Blacks	19	60	21

SOURCE: The Gallup Report, January/February 1985.

Third Party

A political party other than the two major political parties (Republican and Democratic). Usually, third parties are composed of dissatisfied groups that have split from the major parties. They act as indicators of political trends and as safety valves for dissident groups.

Eugene V. Debs, founder of the Socialist party.

tax loopholes for business. Recent Republican platforms seek to ban abortions, oppose quotas to remedy discrimination, and increase defense spending. It is worth noting, however, that the strong differences between the attitudes of party elites and platforms tend to disappear during the election campaign as candidates try to win votes from party members of all ideological persuasions and from independent voters as well.

The Role of Minor Parties in U.S. Political History

▽

Minor parties have a difficult if not impossible time competing within the two-party-dominated American system. Nonetheless, minor parties have had an important place in our political life. Frequently, dissatisfied groups have split from major parties and formed so-called **third parties,**[11] which have acted as barometers of changes in political mood. Such barometric indicators have forced the major parties to recognize new issues or trends in the thinking of Americans. Political scientists also believe that third parties have acted as a safety valve for dissonant political groups, perhaps preventing major confrontations and political unrest.

Historically Important Minor Parties

Most minor parties that have endured have had a strong ideological foundation that is typically at odds with the majority mind-set. Ideology has at least two functions. First, the members of the minor party regard themselves as outsiders and look to one another for support; ideology provides tremendous psychological cohesiveness. Second, because the rewards of ideological commitment are partly psychological, these minor parties do not think in terms of immediate electoral success, and a poor showing at the polls does not dissuade either the leadership or the grass-roots participants from continuing their quest for change in American society. Some of the notable doctrinal third parties that are still active include the following:

1. The Socialist Labor party, started in 1877
2. The Socialist party, founded in 1901
3. The Communist party, started in 1919 as the radical left wing that split from the Socialist party
4. The Socialist Workers' party, a Trotskyite group, started in 1938
5. The Libertarian party, formed in 1972 and still an important minor party

As we can see from their labels, several of these minor parties have been Marxist oriented. The most successful was Eugene Debs's Socialist party, which captured 6 percent of the popular vote for president in 1912 and elected more than a thousand candidates at the local level. About eighty mayors were affiliated with the Socialist party at one time or another. It owed much of its success to the corruption of big-city machines and to antiwar sentiment. Debs's Socialist party was vociferously opposed to American entry into World War I, an opposition shared by many Americans. The other more militant parties of the left (the Socialist Labor, Socialist Workers', and Communist parties) have never enjoyed wide electoral success.

[11]This term is quite erroneous because sometimes there have been third, fourth, fifth, and even sixth parties, but it has endured and we will use it here.

Profile
△
Lyndon H. LaRouche, Jr.

Founder of the National Caucus of Labor Committees, Lyndon H. LaRouche, Jr. leads an organization that placed as many as one thousand members on primary ballots in 1986. LaRouche and his followers are now considered to be an ultrarightist group, although at an earlier period in his life LaRouche held quite different opinions.

Born in 1922 in New Hampshire, Lyndon LaRouche grew up in the family of a shoe-industry executive. He had few friends and immersed himself in philosophy. During the Second World War, LaRouche declared himself a conscientious objector and served in Burma in a noncombatant capacity. Old associates say that he was influenced by Indian socialism during his time in Asia.

Returning to the United States, LaRouche joined the Socialist Labor party and wrote articles on Marxist philosophy. By the late 1960s, he was well known for his lectures in Greenwich Village on Marxist theory. His group of followers were more interested in abstract ideas than in the activities of more militant groups. At one point, some of his followers held leadership positions in the student strike at Columbia University in 1968, although they quarreled with other striking groups.

In the 1970s, LaRouche began to display the suspicion—some would say paranoia—that frequently characterizes strongly ideological groups. This suspicion was directed particularly toward journalists who investigated him and

"The United States of 1776 is not yet fully awakened, but forces within our government and among our citizens are sitting up and rubbing their eyes."

toward his political opponents. He began to set up security forces for his own protection, including the founding of a "counterterrorism" school in Georgia. By the mid-1970s, the La-Rouche position could be better described as right wing than as leftist. LaRouche began to accuse the CIA, the Rockefeller family, and others of plotting against him and his followers. Other LaRouche elements attacked the

Queen of England as sponsoring traffic in drugs.

Since the election of Ronald Reagan in 1980, LaRouche and his followers have attempted to open contacts with the conservatives who serve the president in the National Security Council and other posts. The LaRouche organization maintains its own worldwide intelligence network and has demonstrated the high quality of some of its intelligence reports, although others, such as those accusing British royalty of drug dealing and Walter Mondale of being a Soviet spy, seem to be less trustworthy. Journalists have found that a number of administration officials have met with LaRouche or his representatives to gain access to his intelligence sources. The LaRouche group also maintains contact with a number of Soviet officials and invites them to their seminars. Some critics have suggested that LaRouche's personal conversion from a Marxist position to the far right may not have been genuine.

The most recent strategy of the La-Rouche organization has been to place candidates on the Democratic primary ballot in many states without disclosing their true loyalty. Depending on the relatively low level of information possessed by most voters, especially in primary elections, the LaRouche candidates expect by this means to win several positions on the general election ballot. One major platform position emphasized by these candidates is to play up the threat of AIDS and to identify potential ways to find and quarantine AIDS victims.

At the other end of the ideological spectrum, the Libertarian party supports a laissez-faire capitalist economic program combined with a hands-off policy on regulating matters of moral conduct. Its 1980 presidential nominee, Ed Clark, received more than 900,000 popular votes.

In 1986, another minor party created a sensation by capturing the Democratic nominations for lieutenant governor and secretary of state in Illinois. Supporters of Lyndon LaRouche, an ultraconservative, self-sponsored candidate for president, had submitted petitions for the offices as Democrats and were elected over the candidates of the regular Democratic party in the primary. The LaRouche candidates had spent only a few hundred dollars on their campaigns, running on the platform that AIDS victims should be quarantined and drug dealers subjected to capital punishment. With almost no publicity and unidentified by the news media or the Democratic party, the LaRouche candidates capitalized on their ballot positions and the lack of voter information. Other LaRouche followers have undertaken a similar strategy, several filing as Democratic congressional candidates in California.

Spin-off Minor Parties

Spin-Off Party

A new party formed by a dissident faction within a major political party. Usually, spin-off parties have emerged when a particular personality was at odds with the major party.

The most successful minor parties have been spun off from major parties. The impetus for these **spin-off parties,** or factions, has usually been a situation where a particular personality was at odds with the major party. The most famous spin-off was the Bull Moose Progressive party, which split from the Republican party in 1912 over the candidate chosen to run for president. Theodore Roosevelt rallied his forces and announced the formation of the Progressive party, leaving the regular

Teddy Roosevelt, founder of the Bull Moose Party.

Republicans to support William Howard Taft. Although the party was not successful in winning the election for Roosevelt, it did succeed in splitting the Republican vote so that Democrat Woodrow Wilson won.

Another split in the Republican party occurred in the 1924 election. Robert La Follette was the candidate for a new Progressive party; he was also endorsed by the Socialists, who did not run a candidate of their own that year, and was supported by a number of Democrats. Despite receiving 4.8 million popular votes (16.6 percent), he gained only 13 electoral votes (2.4 percent) and Republican candidate Coolidge was elected.

Among the Democrats in recent years, there have been three splinter third parties: (1) the Dixiecrat (States Rights) party of 1948, (2) Henry Wallace's Progressive party of 1948, and (3) the American Independent party supporting George Wallace in 1968.

The strategy employed by Wallace in the 1968 election was to deny Nixon or Humphrey the necessary majority in the electoral college. Many political scientists (but not all) believe that Humphrey still would have lost to Nixon in 1968, even if Wallace hadn't run, since most Wallace voters would probably have given their votes to Nixon. The American Independent party mostly emphasized racial issues and to a lesser extent foreign policy. Wallace received 9.9 million popular votes and 46 electoral votes.

Governor George Wallace who ran for President on the American Independent party ticket in 1968 and 1972.

Other Minor Parties

There have been numerous minor parties that have coalesced around specific issues or aims. The goal of the Prohibition party, started in 1869, was to ban the sale of liquor. The Free Soil party, in evidence from 1848 to 1852, was dedicated to preventing the spread of slavery.

Some minor parties have had specific economic interests as their reason for being. When those interests are either met or made irrelevant by changing economic conditions, these minor parties disappear. Such was the case with the Greenback party, which lasted from 1876 to 1884. It was one of the most prominent farmer-labor parties that favored government intervention in the economy, specifically the printing of more money to inflate the economy. Similar to the Greenbacks but with broader support was the Populist party, which lasted from about 1892 to 1908. Farmers were the backbone of this party, and agrarian reform was its goal. In 1892, it ran a presidential candidate, James Weaver, who received one million popular votes and 22 electoral votes. The Populists for the most part joined with the Democrats in 1896 when both parties endorsed the Democratic presidential candidate, William Jennings Bryan.

The Impact of Minor Parties

Minor parties clearly have had an impact on American politics. What is more difficult to ascertain is how great that impact has been. Simply by showing that third-party issues were taken over some years later by a major party really doesn't prove that the third party instigated the major party's change. The case for the importance of minor parties may be strongest for the splinter parties. Splinter parties do indeed force a major party to reassess its ideology and organization. There is general agreement that Teddy Roosevelt's Progressive party and La Follette's Progressive party caused the major parties to take up business regulation as one of their major issues.

Calling the United States a two-party system is an oversimplification. The nature and names of the major parties have changed over time, and smaller parties have almost always enjoyed a moderate degree of success. Whether they are splinters from the major parties or expressions of social and economic issues not addressed adequately by factions within the major parties, the minor parties attest to the vitality and fluid nature of American politics.

Is the Party Over?

▽

Figure 8–4 shows **party identification** as measured by standard polling techniques from 1937 to 1985. What is quite evident is the rise of the independent voter combined with a more recent surge of support for the Republican party so that the traditional Democratic advantage in party identification is relatively minor today.

In the 1940s, only about 20 percent of voters classified themselves as independents. By 1975, this number had increased to a third, and more recent polls show it holding steady at about that level. The Democrats have at times captured the loyalty of about half the electorate, and the Republicans until 1960 had more than 30 percent support. By the early 1980s, the Democrats could count on barely 40 percent and the Republicans only a quarter of the electorate. In fact, from 1972 until 1984 Independents constituted the second-largest bloc, the Republicans becoming almost a third party in terms of public support. In reality, recent political history shows an increase in **ticket splitting,** where the independent voter and even large numbers of nominal party backers vote for some Republicans and some Democrats (and for some candidates who run as independents), rather than voting

Party Identification

Linking oneself to a particular political party.

Ticket Splitting

Voting for candidates of two or more parties for different offices. For example, a voter splits her ticket if she votes for a Republican presidential candidate and for a Democratic senatorial candidate.

Figure 8–4

▽

Political Party Identification from 1937 to 1985 (in percent)

SOURCES: *The Gallup Report,* January–February, 1986; *The Gallup Poll: Public Opinion,* 1985, 1984, 1983; *The Gallup Report,* December 1981; *The Gallup Report,* December 1985.

for a party slate. Almost 70 percent of all voters in the presidential election year of 1960 were straight party-ticket voters. According to some researchers, by the 1972 election less than one-third were straight party-ticket voters.[12]

The reasons for the upsurge in independent voters and reduction in party loyalty are less well known, but we can see in Figure 8–5 that the most dramatic increase has come from the ranks of new voters—the young and the previously **disenfranchised.**

The 1984 election saw a continuation of the trend toward ticket splitting and the weakening of party influence on the voters. However, many pollsters saw evidence in the polls that many people were becoming more attached to the Republican party. Until several more elections pass by, it is impossible to know whether the overwhelming popularity of Mr. Reagan will actually translate into more victories nationally for the Republican party. In 1984, though, certain patterns in the preferences of the voters showed signs of change. Among voters under the age of thirty, the number who declared themselves Republicans increased 15 percent since 1976; in the age group thirty to forty-nine, the increase was 11 percent; and among those over fifty, the increase was only 7 percent. If young voters become attached to the Republican party in their first few national elections, their loyalty may lead to a stronger Republican party and, possibly, a more competitive two-party system. It is also possible that Mr. Reagan may yet face the kinds of crises that will cost him political support with these "new Republicans," who may drift back to being independents or Democrats.

[12]See Nie, *The Changing American Voter*, p. 53.

Disenfranchised
The condition of a person when his or her right to vote has been removed. Persons may be disenfranchised if they lose their citizenship, if they fail to register when required, or if they are convicted of certain crimes. Used also to mean those who have never had the right to vote.

Figure 8–5
▽

Distribution of Independents According to Age Cohorts in 1952, 1974, and 1980

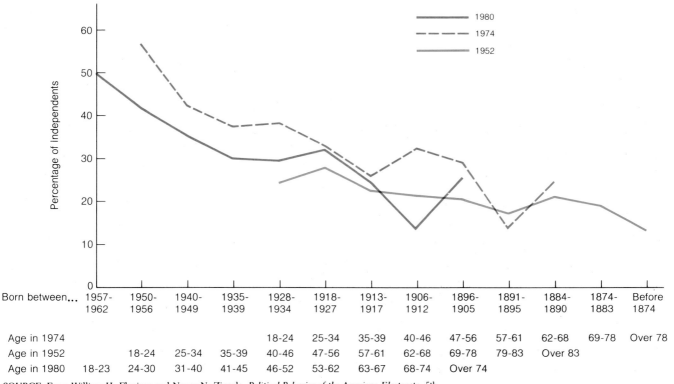

SOURCE: From William H. Flanigan and Nancy N. Zingale, *Political Behavior of the American Electorate*, 5th ed. (Boston: Allyn and Bacon, 1983), p. 62.

▽
253

Electing Convention Delegates

The most exciting political party event, staged every four years, is the national convention. Surprising as it might seem, there are opportunities for the individual voter to become involved in nominating the delegates to the national convention or in becoming such a delegate. For both the Republican and Democratic parties, most delegates must be elected at the local level—either the congressional district or the state legislative district. These elections take place at the party primary election or at a neighborhood or precinct caucus. If the delegates are elected at the primary election, persons who want to run for these positions must file petitions with the board of elections in advance of the election. If you are interested in committing yourself to a particular presidential candidate and running for the delegate position, check with the local county committee or with the party's national committee about the rules you must follow.

It is even easier to get involved in the grass-roots politics of presidential caucuses. In some states, Iowa being the earliest and most famous one, delegates are first nominated at the local precinct caucus. According to the rules announced for the Iowa caucuses in 1984, anyone can participate in the caucus if he or she is eighteen years old, a resident of the precinct, and registered as a party member. These caucuses, as well as being the focus of national media attention in February, select delegates to the county convention who are pledged to specific presidential candidates. This is the first step toward going to the national convention.

At both the county caucus and convention level, both parties try to find younger members to fill some of the seats. Get in contact with the state or county political party to find out when the caucuses or primaries will be held. Then gather local supporters and friends and prepare to join in an occasion where political persuasion and debate are practiced at their best.

For further information about these opportunities (some states have caucuses and state conventions in every election year), contact the state party office or your local state legislator for specific dates and regulations or write to the national committees for their informational brochures on how to become a delegate.

Republican National Committee
Republican National Headquarters
310 1st Street, SE
Washington, D.C. 20003
202-484-6500

Democratic National Committee
Democratic National Headquarters
1625 Massachusetts Avenue, NW
Washington, D.C. 20036
202-797-5900

Chapter Summary

1. A political party is a group of individuals who organize to win elections, to operate the government, and to determine public policy.

2. People join political parties for solidary, material, and purposive (or ideological) reasons.

3. Various party structures throughout the world grew out of historical events unique to each nation. Structures range from one major political party, as in Mexico, to a variety of political parties vying for control, as in Italy.

4. The evolution of our nation's political parties can be divided into six periods: (1) the creation and formation of political parties beginning in the 1790s; (2) the era of one-party rule, or personal politics, in the 1820s; (3) the period from Andrew Jackson's presidency to the Civil War, during which the Democrats and Whigs were the two solidly established national parties; (4) the post-Civil War period, ending in 1896 with solid control by the modern Republican party; (5) the progressive period, from 1896 to 1921; and (6) the modern period, from Franklin Roosevelt's New Deal until today.

5. In theory, each of the American political parties has a standard, pyramid-shaped organization with a hierarchical command structure. In reality, the formal structure resembles a layer cake with autonomous strata more than it does a pyramid.

6. The national party organization holds a national convention every four years to select presidential and vice presidential candidates, to write a party platform, to choose a national committee, and to conduct party business.

7. Each party chooses a national standing committee, elected by the individual state parties, to direct and coordinate party activities during the following four years. A national chairperson is chosen to manage the national election campaign.

8. Each state has a unique party organization, but each has a chairperson, a committee, and a number of local organizations.

9. The local party machinery is made up of district leaders, precinct or ward captains, and party workers. In the past, the local organization was held together by the institution of patronage—rewarding the party faithful with government jobs or contracts and immigrants and the poor with important social services.

10. Two major parties have dominated the political landscape in the United States for almost two centuries. The reasons for this include (a) the historical foundations of the system, (b) the self-perpetuation of the parties, (c) the commonality of views among Americans, (d) the winner-take-all electoral system, and (e) state and federal laws favoring the two-party system.

11. Minor parties have emerged from time to time, often as dissatisfied splinter groups from within major parties that acted as barometers of changes in political moods.

12. Various enduring minor parties arose during this century with strong ideological foundations from both ends of the ideological spectrum.

13. Spin-off parties, or factions, usually have occurred when a particular personality was at odds with the major party, like the Bull Moose Progressives. Numerous other minor parties have formed around single issues, such as the Prohibition party.

14. Minor parties have an impact on American politics by forcing major parties to reassess their ideologies and organizations or to take up particular issues.

15. From 1937 until recently, independent voters have formed an increasing proportion of the electorate, with a consequent decline of strongly Democratic or strongly Republican voters. The upsurge in independent voters has been seen most dramatically among new voters—the young and previously disenfranchised. In the 1980s, support has increased for the Republican party.

Questions for Review and Discussion

1. Some commentators have suggested that political parties are becoming obsolete in the United States. What functions of the parties are now being performed by the media? By the individual candidate or campaign organization? By the national government?

2. Although the political parties seem to have a formal organization and structure, the national offices are usually considered to be unimportant. Why is the power in American parties at the county and state level? Why can't the national party control local parties?

3. What are the major differences on issues and in membership between the Democratic and Republican parties? What elements in the American political system tend to make them both move toward the political center?

Selected References

Alan R. Gitelson, M. Margaret Conway, and Frank B. Feigert, *American Political Parties: Stability and Change* (Boston: Houghton Mifflin, 1984). An up-to-date text giving a good overview of the American party system.

Seymour Martin Lipset, ed., *Party Coalitions in the 1980s* (San Francisco: Institute for Contemporary Studies, 1981). Describes parties as coalitions of voters and interests throughout American history. Special emphasis is placed on the 1980 election and the possible realignment of the electorate.

David R. Mayhew, *Placing Parties in American Politics* (Princeton, N.J.: Princeton University Press, 1986). Using sketches of each of the fifty states, this fascinating book analyzes the form, distribution, and effect of local political parties in the United States.

Steven J. Rosenstone, Roy L. Behr, and Edward H. Lazarus, *Third Parties in America: Citizen Response to Major Party Failure* (Princeton, N.J.: Princeton University Press, 1984). The authors' general theory of third-party voting is based on the factors of major party decline, attractive third-party candidates, and new voters with no loyalty to the two major parties.

James L. Sundquist, *Dynamics of the Party System: Alignment and Realignment of Political Parties in the United States* (Washington, D.C.: Brookings Institution, 1973). An analysis of three major realignments in party strength, why they happened, and what they meant.

Chapter 9

▽

The Media

Contents

▽

The Media's Functions
History of the Media in the United States
The Primacy of Television
The Political Power of the Media
Setting the Public Agenda
Government Regulation of the Media
The Public's Right to Media Access
Bias in the Media

What If . . .

▽

There Were Only One National Network?

"And now, for today's programming on Network One, the U.S. Broadcasting Company. We will feature the president's news conference, the morning session of the U.S. Senate, the environmental show, 'Nature U.S.A.,' the New York City Opera, and the evening news from the White House."

If the United States had only one, government-owned network, such programming might be typical of a day on television. Many other nations, including most of those in Western Europe and the Soviet bloc nations, have government-owned broadcasting systems. In the Soviet Union and other socialist nations, all broadcasting and news is controlled by the state, which means that only news and entertainment programming approved by the state and its carefully chosen editors is accessible to most of the public. Although the United States attempts to provide alternate sources of news to these nations through Radio Free Europe and the Voice of America, few Soviet citizens can receive these broadcasts. As the Chernobyl nuclear reactor explosion demonstrated,

Soviet citizens are often uninformed about serious crises even within their own nation. In that instance, many found out about the disaster from the BBC (the British Broadcasting Corporation), and a few even called London from Moscow with further questions.

If we had government-controlled broadcasting, most likely we would follow the Western European model. No commercials would interrupt programming, but we would also have far fewer programs aimed at pure entertainment, such as game shows, soap operas, sports, or prime-time series like "Dynasty." Generally, government programming tends to be more heavily tilted toward news, reporting of government activities, and programming that "educates" the public. The U.S. Network could be developed

from the existing Public Broadcasting System, with at least one channel emphasizing cultural and educational programs. One channel could be devoted to broadcasting the House of Representatives, the Senate, and other government bodies. It

is doubtful whether any commercial sports such as professional baseball or football would be broadcast, since the goal of these teams is to make money for their owners.

Creation of a single source of news in the United States suggests, of course, the heavy hand of censorship. Such a public network might refrain from any criticism of the administration and probably would do little investigative reporting. Opposing views could be censored or kept from air time altogether. But the European situation suggests a way to counter such suppression of the news. Britons, for example, can hear alternative radio programming, although most of it is rock and roll music, by tuning in to stations on ships located just offshore in the Atlantic. Imagine the possibilities for stations on the Atlantic and Pacific coasts of the United States.

▽

Given our tradition of freedom of the press and freedom of speech, it is unlikely that such a government-controlled network could ever be developed in the United States. Furthermore, the media here have a long tradition of private-sector sponsorship and protection of their right to criticize the government.

Historian Daniel J. Boorstin said, "Nothing is 'really' real unless it happens on television."[1] It is not surprising that in a recent Roper poll, when asked which news source they thought was most credible, most Americans chose the national TV news commentators.[2]

A Gallup poll asked the following question: "How would you rate the honesty and ethical standards of people in these different fields—very high, high, average, low, or very low?" TV reporters and commentators were rated well above journalists, newspaper reporters, business executives, senators, congressmen, and labor union leaders.[3]

Any study of people and politics, including public opinion, political parties, campaigns, elections, and voter behavior, must take as a given the enormous importance that the media have in American politics today. Not only are the newscasters and their programs the most trusted information sources in our society but the media also depend on the political system for much of the news they report.

[1] *The Quotable Quotations Book*, ed. Alec Lewis (New York: Cornerstone Library, 1981), p. 283.
[2] *U.S. News & World Report*, February 21, 1983, p. 49.
[3] *The Gallup Poll*, 1985, pp. 191–193.

T.V. coverage of the 1984 Republican convention.

The relationship between the media and politics can best be described as reciprocal; the media need politics and politicians to report on, and political leaders need the media to campaign, to persuade, and to influence. This mutual dependence has sometimes led each party to feel mistreated. Republican leaders frequently complain that the press is too liberal (that is, too critical of Republicans), whereas Democrats argue that the media are controlled by big business (read "Republicans").

The Media's Functions
▽

The mass media perform a number of different functions in any country. In the United States we can list at least six. Almost all of them can have political implications, and some are essential to the democratic process. These functions are as follows: (1) entertainment, (2) reporting the news, (3) identifying public problems, (4) socializing new generations, (5) providing a political forum, and (6) making profits.

Entertainment

By far the greatest number of radio and television hours are dedicated to entertaining the public. The battle for prime-time ratings indicates how important successful entertainment is to the survival of networks and individual stations. There is no direct linkage between entertainment and politics; however, network dramas often introduce material that may be politically controversial and that may stimulate

Native Americans protest lack of newspaper coverage in San Francisco.

public discussion. One controversial segment of "Cagney and Lacey," a show about two policewomen, treated the topic of abortion; another police show, "Hill Street Blues," portrayed a candidate for mayor who moved into a public housing project and almost lost his life due to violence in the project.

Reporting the News

The mass media in all its forms—newspapers, radio, television, cable, magazines—have as their primary goal the reporting of news. The media convey words and pictures about events, facts, personalities, and ideas. The protections of the First Amendment are intended to keep the flow of news as free as possible because it is an essential part of the democratic process. If citizens cannot get unbiased information about the state of their community and their leaders' actions, how can they make voting decisions? Perhaps the most incisive comment about the importance of the media was that made by James Madison, who said:

A people who mean to be their own governors must arm themselves with the power knowledge gives. A popular government without popular information or the means of acquiring it, is but a prologue to a farce or a tragedy or perhaps both.[4]

Identifying Public Problems

The power of information is important, not only in revealing what the government is doing or is doing wrong, but also in determining what the government ought to do—in other words, in setting the public agenda. The mass media identify public problems, such as the scandal of "missing children," and sometimes help to set up mechanisms to deal with them (in this example, the Missing Children Hotline, "Childfind"). American journalists also work in a long tradition of uncovering public wrongdoing, corruption, and bribery and of bringing such wrongdoing to the public's attention. Closely related to this investigative function is that of pre-

[4]Quoted in "Castro vs. (Some) Censorship," editorial in the *New York Times*, November 22, 1983, p. 24.

'WE HEAR YOUR SON MAY BE A CASUALTY IN THE BEIRUT BOMBING. GIVE US SOME COLOR ON THAT— LIKE ANGUISH, GRIEF, HOW YOU FEEL ABOUT IT...'

Copyright, 1983, Oliphant. Reprinted by permission of Universal Press Syndicate.

Highlight
▽
The Bill Cosby Phenomenon

Bill Cosby and "The Cosby Show" represent a real breakthrough in American television for black performers, as well as a huge success in the TV series genre. In 1986, the show was first in the Nielsen ratings and won an Emmy Award for best comedy and a Peoples Choice Award.

Born in a Philadelphia housing project on July 12, 1937, Cosby dropped out of school in the tenth grade to join the navy. He completed high school through a correspondence course and attended Temple University on a football scholarship. Although he did some stand-up comedy during his teens, it was his costarring role with Robert Culp in the comedy-adventure series "I Spy" that brought him stardom. In the new "Cosby Show," he plays Dr. Cliff Huxtable, whose relationships with his wife, an attorney, and their children, form the story line for the series.

Critics have tried to identify the reasons for the show's great success. Of course, the talents and humor of Cosby

himself are very important ingredients. But beyond this, the immense popularity of the show is based on its representation of traditional, middle-class, American family values. The show

treats "universal" themes of family relations. Avoiding what might be called "black issues," it reaches an enormous audience that empathizes with the situations. (This avoidance of racial problems has drawn criticism from some black leaders.) Also, the show is upbeat. The problems between parents and children are always resolved fairly and sensitively, although the parents keep their authority.

Cosby and his lawyer/wife on the show play roles that clearly depart from the stereotyped portrayals of blacks. Moreover, the family is complete, with both parents living at home and with grandparents on both sides, a stark contrast to the fragmented lives of many American black families.

It is interesting to note that many of the themes of the show—family, parental authority, middle-classness, success, and prosperity—all run parallel to the major themes of recent political campaigns and the presidency of Ronald Reagan.

---

senting policy alternatives. Because public policy is often very complex and difficult to make entertaining, programs devoted to public policy are not often scheduled for prime-time television. Several networks, however, have produced "white papers" on foreign policy and on other issues.

Socializing New Generations

The media are a major influence on the ideas and beliefs of all adults, but particularly the younger generation and recent immigrants. Through the transmission of historical information (sometimes fictionalized), the presentation of American culture, and the portrayal of all the diverse regions and groups in the United States, the media teach young people and immigrants about what it is to be an American. The extensive coverage of elections is a socializing process for these groups.

Providing a Political Forum

As part of their news function, the media also provide a political forum for leaders and the public. Candidates for office use news reporting to sustain interest in their campaigns, whereas officeholders use the media to gain support for their policies or to present an image of leadership. Presidential trips abroad are an outstanding way for the chief executive to get colorful, positive, and exciting news coverage that makes him look "presidential." The media also offer a way for the citizen to participate in public debate, either through letters to the editor or televised editorials. The question of whether more public access should be provided is discussed later in the chapter.

Making Profits

Most of the news media in the United States are private, for-profit corporate enterprises. One of their goals is to make money—for employee salaries, for expansion, and for dividends to the stockholders who own the company. Money is made, in general, by charging for advertising. Advertising revenues are usually directly related to circulation or listener/viewer ratings.

Several well-known outlets are publicly owned—public television stations in many communities and National Public Radio. These operate without commercials and are locally supported and often subsidized by the government and corporations.

Added up, these factors form the basis for a complex relationship among the media, the government, and the public. Throughout the rest of this chapter, we examine some of the many facets of this relationship. Our purpose is to set a foundation for understanding the role of the media in forming public opinion, in organizing political parties, in campaigning, and in voting behavior.

History of the Media in the United States
▽

Many years ago Thomas Jefferson wrote:

> Were it left to me to decide whether we should have a government without newspapers, or newspapers without a government, I should not hesitate a moment to prefer the latter.[5]

Although the media have played a significant role in politics since the founding of this nation, they were not as overwhelmingly important then as they are today. For one thing, politics was controlled by a small elite who communicated personally. For another, during the early 1800s news traveled slowly. If an important political event occurred in New York, it wasn't known until five days later in Philadelphia; ten days later in Hartford, Connecticut; Baltimore, Maryland; and Richmond, Virginia; and fifteen days later in Boston, Massachusetts. Of course, there were one or more newspapers in each major city and they served some of the functions that newspapers do today. Most of these early newspapers were weeklies, but a few daily publications existed also.

Roughly 3,000 newspapers were being published by 1860. Some of these, such as the *New York Tribune*, were mainly sensation-mongers, concentrating on crimes,

[5]Quoted by Richard M. Clurman in "The Media Learn a Lesson," *New York Times*, December 2, 1983, p. 2–A.

scandals, and the like. The *Herald* specialized in self-improvement and what today would be called practical news. Although sensational and biased reporting often created political divisiveness (this was particularly true during the Civil War), many historians believe the growth of the printed media played an important role in unifying the country.[6] A few printed publications stand out as being instrumental in changing the fate of the nation. As we pointed out in Chapter 2, Thomas Paine's *Common Sense* was not only a best-seller (half a million copies) but also a catalyst for the revolt against the mother country. Later *The Federalist Papers* were instrumental in creating the atmosphere necessary for the ratification of the Constitution.

The Rise of the Political Press

Americans may cherish the idea of a nonpartisan press, but in the early years of the nation's history the number of politically sponsored newspapers was significant. The sole reason for the existence of such periodicals was to further the interests of the politicians who paid for their publication. Printing newspapers was relatively expensive in the 1700s and 1800s, and poor transportation meant they could not be widely distributed. As a consequence, political newspapers had a small clientele who paid a relatively high subscription price.

As chief executive during this period, George Washington has been called a "firm believer" in **managed news.** Although acknowledging that the public had a right to be informed, he felt there were some matters that should be kept secret and that news that might damage the image of the United States should not be published. Washington, however, made no attempt to control the press.

Several political periodicals were partially subsidized by the government. No one seemed to think it was improper for government-paid employees to work on partisan newspapers. Indeed, the change to objectivity on the part of the press that we value so much was not due to any increase in idealism; rather, it was the result of a reduction in the cost of printing newspapers and the consequent rise of the self-supported mass-readership daily.

Managed News

Information generated and distributed by the government in such a way as to give government interests priority over candor.

The Development of Mass-Readership Newspapers

Two inventions led to the development of mass-readership newspapers. The first was the high-speed rotary press; the second was the telegraph. Faster presses meant lower per-unit costs and lower subscription prices. The telegraph meant instant access to news between major cities at a low cost. By 1848, the Associated Press had developed the telegraph into a nationwide apparatus for the dissemination of all types of information on a systematic basis.

Along with these technological changes were a growing population and increasing urbanization. Daily newspapers could be supported by a larger, more urbanized populace, even if their price were only a penny. Finally, the burgeoning, diversified economy encouraged the growth of advertising, which meant that newspapers could obtain additional revenues from merchants who seized on the opportunity to promote their wares to a larger public. The days of dependence upon political interests for newspapers were coming to an end.

[6]Richard N. Current, T. Harry Williams, and Frank Freidel, *American History: A Survey* (New York: Alfred A. Knopf, 1979), pp. 299–301.

The Popular Press and Yellow Journalism

Students of the history of journalism have noted a change in the last half of the 1800s, not in the level of biased news reporting, but in its origin. Whereas earlier politically sponsored newspapers expounded a particular party's point of view, most mass-based newspapers expounded whatever political philosophy the owner of the newspaper happened to have. William Randolph Hearst thought the United States should go to war against Spain. He was also interested in selling newspapers. Tensions between the United States and Spain grew over a bloody colonial war the Spanish were fighting in Cuba, and Hearst used this episode to launch his anti-Spanish campaign with screaming headlines. When the U.S. battleship *Maine* exploded in Havana harbor at 9:40 P.M. on February 15, 1898, killing 260 officers and soldiers, Hearst and others wrote such inflammatory articles that President

A cartoon attacking "yellow journalism." William Randolph Hearst (left) and Joseph Pulitzer are lampooned.

Yellow Journalism

A derogatory term for sensationalistic, irresponsible journalism. Reputedly, the term is short for "Yellow Kid Journalism," an allusion to the cartoon "The Yellow Kid" in the old *New York World*, a paper especially noted for its sensationalism.

William McKinley had little choice but to go to war. Spain was blamed for the explosion, even though later investigations could not fix responsibility on anyone.[7]

Even if newspaper heads did not have a particular political axe to grind, they often allowed their editors to engage in sensationalism and **yellow journalism.** Exposing the questionable or simply personal activities of a prominent businessperson, politician, or socialite was front-page material. Newspapers then as today made their economic way by maximizing readership, and as the *National Inquirer* shows today with its more than five million circulation, sensationalism is rewarded by high levels of readership.

The Age of the Electromagnetic Signal

The first scheduled radio program in the United States featured politicians. On the night of November 2, 1920, KDKA-Pittsburgh transmitted the returns of the presidential election race between Harding and Coolidge. The listeners were a few thousand people tuning in on very primitive, homemade sets.

By 1924, there were nearly 1,400 radio stations. But it wasn't until 8:00 P.M. on November 15, 1926, that the electronic media came into its own in the United States. On that night, the National Broadcasting Company (NBC) debuted with a four-hour program broadcast by twenty-five stations in twenty-one cities. The gala evening included one thousand guests, five orchestras, a brass band, nationally known entertainer Will Rogers, and other attractions. Network broadcasting had become a reality.

Even with the advent of national radio in the 1920s and television in the late 1940s, many politicians were slow to understand the significance of the electronic media. The 1952 presidential campaign involved a real role for TV, however, although a relatively minor one. Even though Eisenhower had problems reading a teleprompter that didn't work, his vice presidential running mate put the TV time to good use. Accused of hiding a secret slush fund, Nixon replied to his critics

[7]John Tebbel, *The Media in America* (New York: Thomas Y. Crowell, 1974), pp. 269–272.

Will Rogers, comedian and radio star.

KDKA Radio in Pittsburgh, broadcasting the 1920 presidential election returns.

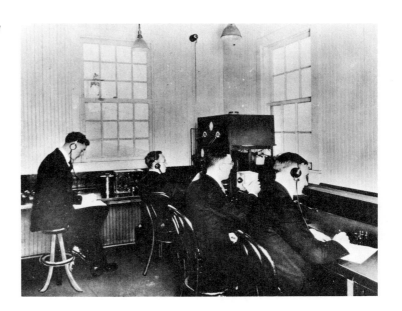

with his famous "Checkers" speech. He denied the attacks, cried real tears, and said the only thing he ever received from a contributor for his personal use was his dog, Checkers. It was a highly effective performance.

Today, television dominates the campaign strategy of every would-be national politician, as well as that of every elected official. Smart politicians figure out ways to continue to be newsworthy, thereby gaining access to the electronic media. Attacking the president's programs is one way; others include holding highly visible hearings on controversial subjects, going on "fact-finding" trips (such as to the island of Grenada after the U.S. invasion in 1983), and gimmicks like Iowa senatorial candidate "Dick" Clark's walking tour of the state of Iowa.

The Revolution in Electronic Media

Just as technological change was responsible for the end of politically sponsored periodicals, technology is increasing the number of alternative news sources today.

The advent of pay TV, cable TV, subscription TV, satellite TV, and the like have completely changed the **electronic media** landscape. When there were basically only three television networks, it was indeed a "wasteland," as federal communications commissioner Newton Minnow once claimed. But now, with dozens of potential outlets for specialized programs, the electronic media are becoming more and more like the printed media catering to specialized tastes. This is sometimes referred to as **narrow casting.** If, for example, you wish to appeal only to health-conscious individuals and there are a sufficient number of them with cable-ready TV, you might be able to have a cable-TV station offering in-depth programs on nutrition, diet, exercise, sports, and the like. You wouldn't have to appeal to the general advertiser; rather, you could find advertising dollars from vitamin manufacturers, health food product manufacturers, and gymnasium equipment manufacturers. Many of these sponsors would never be able to pay the very high prices for thirty seconds on a network TV station (and wouldn't want to because such a small percentage of the total market would be interested in their products), but they could pay the lower-dollar figure for your shows and make a profit in so doing. Why? Because the audience would be specialized—it would consist mainly of those individuals who are good potential purchasers of the sponsor's products.

We can predict that as the cost of entry into the electronic media falls because of, for example, direct satellite transmissions, the diversity of TV shows available for viewers will increase. Part of that diversity will consist of more in-depth news analysis of political happenings.

Electronic Media
Broadcasting media (radio and television). The term derives from their method of transmission, in contrast to printed media.

Narrow Casting
Broadcasting that is targeted to one small sector of the population.

The Primacy of Television

▽

Television is perhaps the most influential of the media. It also is big business. National news TV personalities, such as Dan Rather and Tom Brokaw, earn in excess of $1.5 million per year from their TV news-reporting contracts alone. They are paid so much because they command large audiences, and large audiences command high prices for advertising on national news shows. Indeed, news per se has become a major factor in the profitability of TV stations. In 1963, the major networks—ABC, CBS, and NBC—devoted only eleven minutes daily to national news. By 1986, the amount of time on the networks devoted to news-type programming had increased to three hours. In addition, a twenty-four-hour-a-day news

Veteran anchorman Dan Rather.

cable channel—CNN—started operating in 1980. News is obviously good business.

Television's influence on the political process today is recognized by all who engage in it. Its special characteristics are worthy of attention. Television news is often criticized for being superficial, particularly as compared with the detailed coverage available in the *New York Times,* for example. In fact, television news is constrained by its peculiar technical characteristics, the most important being the limitations of time; stories must be reported in only a few minutes. The most interesting aspect of television is, of course, the fact that it relies on pictures rather than words. Therefore, the videotapes or slides that are chosen for a particular political story have exaggerated importance. The viewer does not know what other photos may have been taken or events recorded except those appearing on his or her screen. Television news can also be exploited for its drama by well-constructed stories. Some critics suggest there is pressure to produce television news that has a "story line," like a novel or movie: The story should be short, have exciting pictures, and have a clear plot.

As you are aware, real life is usually not dramatic, nor do all events have a neat or an easily understood plot. Political campaigns are continuing events, lasting perhaps two years or more. The significance of their daily turns and twists are only apparent later. The "drama" of Congress with its 535 players and dozens of important committees and meetings is also difficult for the media to present. But TV needs dozens of daily three-minute stories. It has been suggested that these formatting characteristics—necessities—of TV increase its influence on political events. For example, news coverage of a single event like the results of the Iowa caucuses or the New Hampshire primary may be the most important factor in which candidate is seen as the "front-runner" in presidential campaigns. To a somewhat lesser extent, newspapers and news magazines are also limited by their formats.

The Political Power of the Media

▽

All forms of the media—television, newspapers, radio, and magazines—have enormous political impact on American society. If they didn't, politicians would not spend so much time and effort trying to get before the cameras or microphones

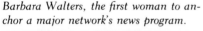

Barbara Walters, the first woman to anchor a major network's news program.

▽

Profile
▽
Ted Koppel

During the Iranian hostage crisis in 1980, ABC instituted a special late evening news show to keep Americans up-to-date on the latest news about the situation. This news show not only attracted a steady viewing audience of about five million Americans but catapulted Ted Koppel to the top ranks of news broadcasters. Although it seemed as if he were a "new face" on TV, Koppel had already built a career in television journalism.

Koppel was born in Britain to a German Jewish family who had escaped from Hitler's Germany. He moved to the United States when he was thirteen and attended school at Syracuse University and Stanford, majoring in journalism. He began his career as a radio journalist and went to work for ABC in 1965. He was a reporter in Vietnam and spent a number of years as a diplomatic correspondent.

In 1976, Koppel took a year off from his career in national television to be

"It's very difficult to overpower an interrupting voice when it shows up inside your head."

the family housekeeper while his wife began law school. Then he worked part-time at ABC until fired from his

job by the new president of the network, Roone Arledge. One night, he substituted for Frank Reynolds on a special broadcast and the network became aware of his ability to interview people.

Koppel is known as a "buttoned down" interviewer, always staying calm and cool while interviewing guests. His show, *Nightline*, consists of interviews with five or six guests with whom he converses, even though they may be located at different points on the globe. He is known to be very intelligent, to do his homework well, and to have a dry wit. When opening the presidential debate in New Hampshire with the eight Democratic candidates in 1984, Koppel began by saying, "The moderator will *try* to have complete control."*

Time January 30, 1984, p. 70.

---

nor spend millions of dollars on paid political announcements. Media influence is most obvious during political campaigns. Because television is the primary news source for the majority of Americans, candidates and their consultants spend much of their time devising strategies to use television to their benefit. Three types of TV coverage are generally used in campaigns for the presidency and other offices: paid-for political announcements, management of news coverage, and campaign debates.

Paid-for Political Announcements

Perhaps one of the most effective **paid-for political announcements** of all time was a short, thirty-second spot created by President Lyndon Johnson's media adviser. In this ad, a little girl stood in a field of daisies. As she held a daisy she pulled the petals off and quietly counted to herself. Suddenly, when she reached number ten a deep bass voice cut in and began a countdown: 10, 9, 8, 7, 6. . . . When the voice intoned "zero" the unmistakable mushroom cloud of an atom bomb began to fill the screen. Then President Johnson's voice was heard: "These are the stakes.

Paid-for Political Announcement
A message about a political candidate conveyed through the media, designed to elicit positive public opinion.

▽
269

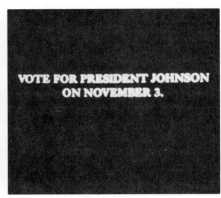

VOTE FOR PRESIDENT JOHNSON ON NOVEMBER 3.

President Johnson's "Daisy Ad."

To make a world in which all of God's children can live, or to go into the dark. We must either love each other or we must die." At the end of the commercial, the message read, "Vote for President Johnson on November 3."

To understand how effective this daisy-girl commercial was, you must remember that Johnson's opponent was Barry Goldwater, a presumably far-right-wing Republican conservative candidate. The implication was that Goldwater would lead the United States into nuclear war. Our involvement in Vietnam was still small. Goldwater, according to his Democratic critics, would surely escalate the war and also create a setting for nuclear confrontation with the Russians. Although the ad was withdrawn within a few days, it has a place in political campaign history as the classic negative campaign announcement.

Management of News Coverage

Using paid-for political announcements to get a message across to the public is a very expensive tactic. Coverage by the news media is, however, free; it simply demands that the campaign assure that coverage takes place. In recent years, campaigns have shown increasing sophistication in providing news for journalists to cover. They are aware that, as Christopher Arterton points out,

> The media and campaigns need each other: journalists define presidential politics as an important story to be reported fully; campaigners want to reach voters through the news reporting process.[8]

[8]"The Media Politics of Presidential Campaigns," in James David Barber, ed., *Race for the Presidency* (Englewood Cliffs, N.J.: Prentice-Hall, 1978), p. 51.

The technique used to establish a successful, paid-for political announcement, a TV ad campaign is really no different from the techniques used to introduce to the public a new detergent or a new car. Making successful TV ads follows a well-known format. The ad maker either has thirty or sixty seconds. In that short amount of time, a message must be communicated in such a way that it is retained. To ensure that the message is retained, it must be repeated a number of times so that the same people see it more than once. Madison Avenue hasn't had to develop any new techniques to sell candidates to voters. A good media adviser will pick up on the most positive personality traits of a candidate and center a TV ad campaign around those traits.

As with any other product being advertised to TV viewers, the placement of political ads is strategically determined by the media consultants. One media expert referred to the advantage of the "intrusion" effect:

My job is to articulate in 30 seconds what the candidate is trying to say in his total campaign, and this is intruded in the middle of a regular television program. The only people who will watch 30 minutes of Jimmy Carter are already for him or dead set against him. They'll watch *Happy Days* instead, so that's where I put my 30 seconds—in the middle of *Happy Days*.*

*James Callaway, president of Holland & Callaway Advertising, Inc., New York, as quoted in *The Nation's Business*, February 1980, p. 33.

To take advantage of the media's interest in campaign politics, whether at the presidential level or perhaps in a Senate race, the campaign staff tries to influence the quantity and type of coverage the campaign receives. First, it is important for the campaign staff to understand the technical aspects of media coverage—camera angles, necessary equipment, timing, and deadlines—and to plan their political events to accommodate the press. Second, the campaign organization learns that political reporters and their sponsors—networks or newspapers—are in competition for the best stories and can be manipulated through granting favors such as a personal interview with the candidate. Third, an important task for the scheduler in the campaign is the planning of events that will be photogenic and interesting enough for the evening news. A related goal, although one that is more difficult to attain, is to convince reporters that a particular interpretation of an event is correct. For example, after **Super Tuesday** on March 20, 1984, *Time* described the result as "not a draw but a split decision. Hart won seven states, Mondale six, 'uncommitted' swept Hawaii, South Carolina and three Kentucky counties that caucused in advance of the rest of the state."[9] Throughout the primary season, candidates tried to get the edge on the media by giving their interpretation of primaries before they occurred, and, in a new twist, newscasters discussed the efforts by the campaigns to persuade the journalists.

Super Tuesday
A football metaphor referring to the date on which a large number of presidential primaries are held throughout the country. In 1984, Super Tuesday was March 20.

The Campaign Technique of Presidential Debates

Perhaps of equal importance to paid-for political announcements on TV is how presidential candidates appear in presidential debates. The first such debate occurred in 1960 between Kennedy and Nixon; the next was in 1976 between Carter and

⁹*Time* March 26, 1984, p. 12.

Ford; then in 1980 Reagan, Carter, and Anderson had a debate, as did vice presidential candidates Bush and Mondale. In 1984, Reagan and Mondale debated twice, and the vice presidential candidates, Ferraro and Bush, debated once.

The 1960 Debates

In 1960, Congress suspended the equal time provision of the Federal Communications Act to allow a series of debates between Vice President Richard Nixon (Republican) and Senator John F. Kennedy (Democrat). There was little question that the relatively unknown Kennedy was the more impressive candidate in these debates. For the first debate, Nixon looked haggard and drawn. Nixon's physical appearance worked against him. He apparently didn't take it seriously enough to make sure that he shaved ahead of time. Substituting "Lazy Shave" powder for a real shave, Nixon went before the camera with a five o'clock shadow. Kennedy's campaign advisers knew the value of a healthy, tanned, well-barbered appearance, and that is what he presented. Nixon also tended to slouch; he looked strained.

Polls taken by Gallup indicated that 43 percent of the respondents felt that Kennedy was the leader in the race after the first debate. By the end of the third debate, Nixon, who held a slight lead over Kennedy in September, was 3 percentage points behind.[10]

The 1976 Debates

It was sixteen years before American TV viewers again had a chance to witness the presidential candidates debate. This time the debate featured a relatively unknown

[10]Theodore H. White, *The Making of the President 1960* (New York: Atheneum Publishers, 1961), pp. 294–295.

A family watching the Kennedy and Nixon debates on T.V., 1960.

Gerald Ford and Jimmy Carter debate in 1976.

former Georgia governor and the then-current president of the United States. We might wonder why any incumbent would agree to such a debate. After all, the incumbent has the upper hand by virtue of being better known, as well as having access to all the publicity outlets that the office of the president allows. Gerald Ford's problem as the Republican incumbent was that the polls already showed him losing at the beginning of the campaign. Ford challenged Democratic candidate Carter to the debate. Carter's advisers quickly urged him to accept.

Of the three debates, a Gallup poll showed that Ford won the first one, Carter won the second, and Carter won the third. There is little doubt in most analysts' minds that the 1976 debates helped Carter win the election by a narrow margin. Ford made some startling verbal errors during the debates, the most flagrant being his statement that the Soviet Union did not dominate Poland.

The 1980 Debates

Since there was a major third-party candidate—John Anderson—in 1980, there were two sets of debates sponsored by the League of Women Voters. Reagan debated John Anderson, a Republican turned independent. Carter refused to debate with what he called two Republicans at once. Then Reagan debated with Carter.

The Reagan-Anderson debate certainly did little to benefit Reagan. But it elevated the status of Anderson as an independent candidate to a level he could not have otherwise obtained. Fully 36 percent of the voters watching thought that Anderson had won the debate; only 30 percent thought Reagan had won it.

The main event, however, was between Reagan and Carter. Both hopefuls were skilled debaters. Reagan, of course, had thirty years of experience as an actor behind him. His ability to appear relaxed seemed at odds with Carter's denunciation of Reagan as a military hawk. How could a hawk be so genial? Reagan also was able to zero in on the Democratic incumbent's main weakness—the state of the economy. According to *Newsweek*, the debate was won by Reagan.[11]

[11]*Newsweek*, November 10, 1980, p. 37.

The Carter-Reagan debate, 1980.

The 1984 Debates

Negotiations for the 1984 debates began after the Democratic and Republican conventions. The incumbent is generally considered to be at a disadvantage in these debates because it places him on an equal footing with the challenger and makes the latter look "presidential." Knowing this, Mondale pushed for many debates (six or seven) while Reagan wanted as few as practical. The two sides finally settled on two presidential debates and one vice presidential debate.

The first debate, on domestic policy, was held in Louisville, Kentucky, on October 7. The result was a victory for Mondale insofar as the polls and com-

Mondale's and Reagan's first debate, 1984.

What's in the News?

Both politicians and the general citizenry are subject to what seems to be endless coverage of election campaigns. No sooner is the president inaugurated than the networks begin speculating on the potential candidates for the next presidential election, four years away. During the election year itself, coverage of candidates, delegate counts, the convention struggles, and even coverage of the media efforts to report on the campaign dominates the news. The question that researchers have tried to answer is to what degree such extensive coverage influences election results. In investigating this question, many researchers have looked carefully at the kind of news actually reported during election campaigns.

Candidates and critics of the media alike charge that the media, particularly television, tend to avoid reporting on the issues of the campaign. If the voters cannot find out what the issue differences are between candidates, how can they make judgments about which candidate would best represent their interests? Research suggests that the criticism is true. Particularly during the primary campaigns, stories about who is winning, or the "horse race," clearly dominate those concerned with issues. Even later in the campaign, when the media carry more stories oriented toward issues, the focus is often on candidate differences on simple, clear-cut issues such as abortion or Social Security payments rather than on large, more complex questions like our overall foreign policy stance. The electronic media admit this but say that such reporting is easier.

"Horse race" journalism changes the kind of stories that become news. Because they are looking for excitement and conflict to report to their readers and viewers, reporters and news producers tend to focus on which candidate seems to be ahead and what the daily strategic decisions of each campaign are rather than what the candidates are saying. The language used in such stories is drawn from sports: "the game plan," "clash," "attack," "offense and defense." Reporting on the campaign becomes very similar in style to reporting on the "Road to the Super Bowl." The polling efforts of the candidates and the media themselves add to this emphasis on "who's ahead." By constantly polling the public on the campaign, the networks and major newspapers are creating news about who is currently winning. In the 1976 election, Thomas Patterson divided all of the media stories about the campaign into substance stories and "game" stories. He found that 50 to 60 percent of all of the stories concerned the game, whereas only 30 to 35 percent focused on issues, policies, and candidate traits.* In 1980, another study showed that 67 percent of the stories on CBS news, during the primaries, were "horse race" stories.

This emphasis on who's winning can be explained by the "melodramatic imperative" of the media. Paul Weaver suggests that news stories about the campaign must be affected by the media's need to entertain their audience. The demand for melodrama emphasizes the unusual story, the exciting development, the unfolding of the plot. As Weaver puts it, the story opens "in the snows of New Hampshire; the plot develops, election by election, until it reaches its *denouement* before the national conventions, not as people who are running for elective office, but as figures deeply and totally embroiled in an all-out struggle."**

Accenting the competition between the candidates tends to cast everything they do and say as part of the struggle. Their issue positions, choices of running mates, decisions to campaign on the road or "to stay in the Rose Garden," and relationships with interest groups are all interpreted as decisions with a strategic purpose: to increase the chances of winning. As one of Carter's campaign aides said, "Reporters are . . . telling Americans no candidate takes any position except to enhance his election prospects. It's automatically assumed that nobody can do anything because he believes it."*** Politicians complain that it becomes impossible to get the media to report their policy initiatives; what gets reported are their blunders on the campaign trail. Yet politicians are not blameless here. All too often, their managers plan campaign events with an eye toward getting the best pictures for the evening news. The question that remains is how this emphasis on the strategy of campaigns influences the minds of the voters.

*Thomas E. Patterson, *The Mass Media Election* (New York: Praeger, 1980).
**Paul Weaver, "Captives of Melodrama," *New York Times Magazine*, August 29, 1976, p. 6.
***Quoted in David L. Swanson, "And That's the Way It Was? Television Covers the 1976 Presidential Campaign," *Quarterly Journal of Speech* (October 1977), p. 246.

mentators agreed that he had carried the day. In the debate, Mondale seemed more at ease, was humorous, had a less "whiny" voice, treated Reagan kindly (at one point saying "I like President Reagan"), and was upbeat, overcoming the idea that he conveyed gloom. Reagan, on the other hand, seemed ill at ease, lost his train of thought, and several times floundered in a maze of facts with which he had been drilled (according to his campaign) in preparation for the debate. This prompted the media, especially the *Wall Street Journal*, to ask if Reagan was affected by his age and thus too old to be reelected.

The second debate, between Vice President Bush and Democratic candidate Geraldine Ferraro, took place in Philadelphia on October 11. The results of this debate were not clear cut. The polls showed that a majority of viewers felt Bush had won, especially in the second half which covered foreign policy (the first half was on domestic issues). Ferraro had apparently toned down her aggressive, "street-wise" style and slowed down her almost slurred, fast-paced speech pattern. Some commentators considered this a mistake because she seemed to be holding back.

In the wake of the first two debates, the polls showed only a slight immediate increase in the approval rating for the Democratic ticket. However, it appeared to inject new life into the Mondale-Ferraro campaign as the size and enthusiasm of crowds at campaign rallies intensified. Moreover, it was said that campaign workers felt encouraged and redoubled their efforts. Campaign contributions began to flow more abundantly into the Democratic coffers.

The third debate took place on October 22 in Kansas City. As expected, Reagan was less intent on facts and figures and stayed closer to broad themes. Several commentators observed that his style was more "vintage Reagan." On the other hand, Mondale was not as relaxed and humorous as he had been in the first encounter. Thus the third debate was deemed to be a draw. Reagan scored high in humor when he answered a question about his age, strength, and stamina by saying, "I will not make age an issue. I will not exploit my opponent's youth and inexperience," which yielded abundant laughter.

How much difference the debates made in the final outcome of the 1984 election is difficult to say because there were no dramatic results from the debates and the wide gap between the Democratic and Republican tickets made the small shifts in voter preference less significant than they would have been in a close race.

A newspaper reporter types up his story on the Mondale campaign.

Investigating the Government

The mass media not only wield considerable power when it comes to political campaigns but they also can, in one way or another, wield power over the affairs of government and over government officials. Perhaps the most notable example in recent times concerns the activities of *Washington Post* reporters Robert Woodward and Carl Bernstein. Assigned to cover the **Watergate break-in,** these two reporters undertook an investigation that eventually led to the impeachment proceedings against President Nixon and later to a best-selling book and a film (*All the President's Men*). Investigative reporting—with its antecedents in the muckraking journalism of the first decades of this century—became increasingly popular and journalism as a career attracted a new crop of inquisitive, probing reporters intent on going beyond the news by digging for hidden facts.

The Media and Public Attitudes

The question of how much influence the media have on public opinion is difficult to answer. Although one of the media's greatest powers is the ability to shape the public agenda by focusing attention on public problems and on particular political leaders, studies have shown that the media may not have as much power to change the minds of the people as has been thought. Generally, individuals watch television or read newspapers with certain preconceived ideas about political issues and candidates. These attitudes and opinions act as a kind of perceptual screen that blocks out information people find uncomfortable or that does not fit with their own ideas.

Voters watch campaign commercials and news about political campaigns with "selective attentiveness"; that is, they only watch those commercials that support the candidate they favor and only pay attention to news stories about their own candidates. This process of selectivity also affects perceptions of the content of the news story or commercial and whether it is remembered. Apparently, the media are most influential with those persons who have not formed an opinion about political candidates or issues. Studies have shown that the flurry of television commercials and debates immediately before election day has the most impact on those voters who are truly undecided. Few voters change their minds under the influence of the media.

The Media and the Presidency

A love-hate relationship clearly exists between the president and the media. During the administration of John F. Kennedy, the president was seen in numerous photos scanning the *New York Times* and the *Washington Post,* as well as other newspapers, each morning to see how the press tallied his successes and failures. This led to frequent jocular comments about his speed-reading ability.

In the United States the prominence of the president is cultivated by a **White House press corps** that is assigned full time to cover the presidency. These reporters even have a lounge in the White House where they spend their days, waiting for a story to break. Most of the time they simply wait for the daily or twice-daily briefing by the president's **press secretary.** Because of the press corps's physical proximity to the president, the chief executive cannot even take a brief stroll around

Did You Know?
▽

That, in 1984, a thirty-second political commercial on ABC's "Monday Night Football" cost $125,000?

Watergate Break-in
The 1972 illegal entry into the Democratic campaign offices engineered by the Nixon reelection campaign.

White House Press Corps
A group of reporters assigned full time to cover the presidency.

Press Secretary
The individual responsible for representing the White House before the media. The press secretary writes news releases, provides background information, sets up press conferences, and so on.

President Franklin D. Roosevelt.

the presidential swimming pool without it becoming news. Perhaps no other nation allows the press such access to its highest government official. Consequently, no other nation has its airwaves and print media so filled with absolute trivia regarding the personal life of the chief executive and his family.

President Franklin D. Roosevelt brought new spirit to a demoralized country and led it through the Great Depression. His radio **"fireside chats"** brought hope to millions. Roosevelt's speeches were masterly in their ability to forge a common emotional bond among his listeners. His decisive announcement in 1933 on the reorganization of the banks calmed a jittery nation and prevented the collapse of the banking industry, that was threatened by a run on banks in which nervous depositors were withdrawing all their assets. His famous Pearl Harbor speech, following the Japanese attack on the U.S. Pacific fleet on December 7, 1941 ("a day that will live in infamy"), mobilized the nation for the sacrifices and effort necessary to win World War II.

Perhaps no president has exploited the electronic media more effectively than has Ronald Reagan. The "great communicator," as he has been called, was never more dramatic than in his speech to the nation following the October 1983 invasion of Grenada. In this address, the president, in an almost flawless performance, appeared to many to have decisively laid to rest the uncertainty and confusion surrounding the event.

The relationship between the media and the president has thus been reciprocal; both institutions have used each other, sometimes positively, sometimes negatively. The presidency and the news media are, however, deeply dependent on each other.

Fireside Chats

Warm, informal talks by Franklin D. Roosevelt to a few million of his intimate friends—via the radio. Roosevelt's fireside chats were so effective that succeeding presidents have been urged by their advisers to emulate him by giving more radio and television reports to the nation.

Public Agenda

Issues that are commonly perceived by members of the political community as meriting public attention and governmental action. The media play an important role in setting the public agenda by focusing attention on certain topics.

Setting the Public Agenda
▽

Given that government officials have in front of them an array of problems with which they must deal, the process of setting the **public agenda** is constant. To be sure, what goes on the public agenda for discussion, debate, and ultimately policy

A Reagan press conference.

action depends on many factors—not the least being each official's personal philosophy.

According to a number of studies, the media play an important part in setting the agenda, as well as in helping government officials to better understand society's needs and desires. W. P. Davison went so far as to claim that diplomats obtain the bulk of their information about what is happening in the world not from other diplomats but from the press.[12]

One of the most dramatic examples of the impact of the media on agenda setting was the ABC made-for-television movie "The Day After," which depicted the effects of nuclear war on Kansas City and the nearby community of Lawrence, Kansas. More than one-hundred million people watched the film on Sunday, November 20, 1983.

The movie was hailed by groups favoring disarmament and by the nuclear freeze movement as a clear message that nuclear war is an unacceptable choice and that nuclear disarmament is essential for the survival of humanity.

Conservative groups, however, claimed that the program played into the hands of the Russians and could weaken U.S. resolve in the face of Soviet military

[12]W. P. Davison, "News and Media and International Negotiation," *Public Opinion Quarterly*, No. 38 (Summer 1974), pp. 174–191.

Filming "The Day After."

expansion. President Reagan said the film underscored the need for a strong nuclear deterrence to prevent the possibility of war.

The world press also reacted, praising the film as an important step in influencing public opinion against the impending deployment of new U.S. Pershing and cruise missiles in Europe.

Activists on all sides mobilized activities around "The Day After." Antinuclear groups purchased air time to promote their efforts. Actor Paul Newman, featured in a spot for the Center for Defense Information, a nuclear-freeze group, invited viewers to write or call in for a "nuclear war prevention kit." The 800-NUCLEAR project raised $200,000 for advertisements featuring U.S. and Soviet generals inflating a balloon, which exploded into a mushroom cloud. A superimposed toll-free number promised information about how to become active in the nuclear freeze movement.

Conservative activist Phyllis Schlafly called the movie a "two-hour political editorial" and asked ABC affiliates for air time for opposing views. The Reverend Jerry Falwell, leader of the Moral Majority, said the program was a "preemptive strike" in the debate over nuclear arms.[13]

"The Day After" seemed to have had less effect on U.S. public opinion than was anticipated, according to the results of the *Washington Post*'s polls taken three weeks before the showing of the film and on the night immediately following the showing. There was only a slight increase in the percentage of those polled who thought President Reagan's plans to build more nuclear weapons had gone too far. Surprisingly, at least to some, there was a decrease (from 57 to 43 percent) in those

[13]*New York Times*, November 17, 1983, p. 8; November 22, 1983, p. 11.

who believed Reagan's handling of foreign affairs was increasing the chances for war. Also somewhat surprisingly, there was only a slight increase in those who approved a freeze on nuclear weapons by both the United States and the Soviet Union (83 to 85 percent).[14]

Government Regulation of the Media
▽

The United States has perhaps the freest press in the world. Nonetheless, regulation of the media does exist, particularly the electronic media. Many aspects of this regulation were discussed in Chapter 4, when we examined First Amendment rights and the press.

The First Amendment and the Press: A Review

The First Amendment simply states that Congress shall make no law abridging the freedom of speech or of the press. Those are powerful and, at first view, all-encompassing strictures on the role of government in relation to the media. Indeed, the First Amendment has restricted the government from censoring news, engaging in prior restraint (preventing the publication of news), and preventing the press from criticizing government officials and government actions in general.

Serious constitutional issues regarding the press have arisen nonetheless. The confidentiality of reporters' sources has been an issue on numerous occasions. Does the government, when it believes that a reporter has information that will help resolve a criminal case, have the right to force the reporter to give up that information? In at least one Supreme Court case, the answer was yes. The reporter could not withhold evidence because the accused person's right to a fair trial required that all evidence be presented.[15]

The Electronic Media and Government Control

The First Amendment does not mention the electronic media—it didn't exist at that time. For many reasons, the government has much greater control over the electronic media than it does over printed media. Through the Federal Communications Commission (FCC), the number of radio stations has been controlled for many years, in spite of the fact of that technologically we could have many more radio stations than now exist. Also, the FCC has created a situation where the three major TV networks have dominated the airwaves. Only recently did the FCC bow to public and political pressure to open up the TV airwaves to all the new technological devices now available. Most FCC rules have dealt with ownership of news media, such as how many stations a network can own.

In general, the broadcasting industry has successfully avoided government regulation of content by establishing its own code. This code consists of a set of rules determined by the National Association of Broadcasters, the lobby for the TV and radio industry, regulating the amount of sex, violence, nudity, profanity, and so forth allowed on the air. It should be noted that abiding by the code is voluntary on the part of networks and stations.

[14]*Washington Post*, December 5, 1983, p. 12.

[15]*Farber and the New York Times v. U.S.*, 84 F(2d) 999 (1978).

Highlight
▽
Satellite Freedom

Since the late 1970s, as many as 2 million households have bought backyard satellite dishes. This equipment enables them to receive satellite-transmitted signals from entertainment channels, corporate conferences, network programs without commercials, and foreign television signals without paying for more than the original equipment.

On January 14, 1986, the Federal Communications Commission ruled that local governments could not pass zoning ordinances to limit use of dishes unless there were "reasonably and clearly defined" health, safety, or aesthetic goals. This ruling was opposed by a number of interest groups that had worked against the unregulated use of dishes. The cable industry, for example, estimated that it lost between $500 million and $700 million annually because dish owners did not have to pay cable fees.

On the next day, January 15, 1986, Home Box Office (HBO) and Cinemax, two of the movie channels, started to scramble their signals to force dish owners to pay subscription fees or buy unscrambling equipment. More than a dozen other cable channels followed. Unscrambling devices, costing about $400, were offered to satellite

dish owners, whereas various bills were introduced into Congress to support free use of the equipment.

At least one enterprising critic of the cable industry took matters into his own hands. An April 27, 1986, the HBO presentation of its feature movie was interrupted by the following message that was displayed on the screens of unsuspecting viewers: GOOD EVENING HBO FROM CAPTAIN MIDNIGHT. $12.95 MONTH? NO WAY! (SHOWTIME/THE MOVIE CHANNEL BEWARE.)

"Captain Midnight" had been able to override the HBO satellite signal going to half a million viewers. Of course, what was demonstrated by this action, apart from a new form of protest, was that orbiting communications satellites, including both civilian and military communications, could be very vulnerable to the high-tech intrusions of resourceful "hackers." The penalty for what Captain Midnight did, under federal criminal law, is a minimum fine of $10,000 and up to a year in jail.

Since 1980, there has been continued public debate over whether the government should attempt to control polling and the "early calling" of presidential elections. On election night in 1980, the networks predicted that Ronald Reagan had been elected before numerous states had closed their polls. In 1984, this controversy over network predictions based on exit polls surfaced again. The concern expressed by many was that voters on their way to vote might not bother since the victor had already been declared. It was feared that the drop in turnout due to these voters would affect state and local races and, because some types of voters such as factory workers are more likely to vote late in the day, the outcomes of elections and referenda might be seriously affected.

In 1984, the networks were careful to say that they would not project winners in any state until the polling places *in that state* were closed. However, with the different time zones and with a concentration of population (and electoral college votes) in the Northeast and Midwest, the networks were able to project a winner by 8:00 P.M., Eastern time, which was 5:00 P.M. on the West Coast. In spite of the fact that anchorpersons were careful to encourage voters to go to the polls and vote on "the many important state and local issues, the outcome of which depend on your vote," there was a great deal of adverse reaction to the practice of "early calling" of the election.

Some legislators and citizens have called for a ban on exit polls or on releasing them before *all* polling places in the continental United States were closed. Others called for a federal law establishing a uniform closing time for voting so that voting would end at the same time all over the country and thus exit polls could not be a factor. Still others suggested self-censorship by the networks or the National Broadcasters Association. The evidence on whether such predictions really affect turnout is mixed. While turnout has been lower than expected in many western states, studies suggest that the early announcement of election results based on exit polls has little effect on election outcomes.

The FCC's Fairness Doctrine

Perhaps the most controversial of all of the rules promulgated by the FCC is its **fairness doctrine.** Under the so-called fairness doctrine, TV and radio broadcasters must present contrasting views on controversial public issues. This means that if you attack John Doe publicly on radio and TV for an action he presumably did that you think has harmed the national interest, John Doe can demand free equal time to reply. Newscasts are exempt from this requirement, however.

Numerous problems exist with the fairness doctrine. One is that there are not only two sides to every story; there may be three, four, or more sides. In other words, not every controversial issue is black or white—there are often many shades

Fairness Doctrine
An FCC regulation requiring that equal broadcast time be made available to legitimate opposing political groups, interests, or individuals.

The Parents Musical Resource Center tries to influence rock music lyrics.

of gray. Also, TV and radio station owners will often avoid controversial issues and statements simply to avoid the obligation to give free time for contrasting views. Of course, the fairness doctrine does not apply to everybody and to every issue. Communists and their viewpoints, for example, are not considered to be under the purview of the fairness doctrine.

At issue is whether the FCC has the right to impose the fairness doctrine on the electronic media while completely ignoring the printed media. There are virtually no restrictions on who may start a newspaper or a magazine and what its content may be. There is no restriction on how much or how little advertising it may carry. There is no restriction on the amount of violence (or sex, in most cases) the publication may contain. About 70 million newspapers are sold every day. Certainly, the influence of newspapers on people's attitudes and behavior is widespread.

Does National Security Justify Suppression of the News?

On October 25, 1983, the United States, supported by the island nations of Antigua, Barbados, Dominica, Jamaica, St. Lucia, and St. Vincent, invaded the island of Grenada. The purpose of the invasion, as stated by the president, was to rescue Americans on the island following a violent coup d'etat and to replace a hard-line Marxist government. No advance notice was given to the media on the planned

Marines invade Grenada, 1983.

operation. Once the assault on Grenada began, no American reporters were allowed on the island for several days. Reporters who tried to get there on a chartered boat were ordered away by the U.S. forces. During the first days of the action, the only source of news was the American military, which provided still photos, film footage, and news bulletins.

The U.S. government claimed that this news blackout was necessary to ensure a surprise attack. The Reagan administration also claimed that newspersons were kept out to guarantee their own safety.

The reaction of the American news media was strong and swift. By denying independent access, the government threatened American freedom and the role that the media play in keeping Americans informed. The media and other observers saw the blackout as censorship, and some denounced the military's control of information about the invasion as a blatant propaganda effort. The Senate voted 53 to 18 to end the restrictions on the media. The American Society of Newspaper Editors declared that "the Defense Department has let down the American people."

The Grenada news blackout raised once again the question of how the public's "right to know" should be balanced against the government's responsibilities to protect the national interest successfully.

An interesting comment on the Grenada press crisis was sounded by Cuban leader Fidel Castro in a Havana speech. Castro mentioned the absence of the U.S. media in the first days of the action and intimated that U.S. public support for the invasion was largely due to this manipulation of the news.[16]

The Public's Right to Media Access
▽

Does the public have a right to **media access?** Both the FCC and the courts have gradually taken the stance that citizens have a right of access to the media, particularly the electronic media. The argument is that the airwaves are public, but because they are used for private profit, the government has the right to dictate how they are used. It does so in many ways. In addition to the fairness doctrine and the equal time rule for candidates, the FCC has also promulgated the **personal attack rule.** This rule allows individuals (or groups) air time to reply to attacks that have previously been aired. Another rule governing access to the airwaves involves the right of candidates opposed by a station to have time to reply to the station's statements about them.

Technology is giving more citizens access to the electronic media, in particular television. As more and more cable operators have more and more time to sell, some of that time will remain unused and will be available for public access. At the same time such developments as citizens' band radio, the video magazine for the millions of videocassette-recorder owners, and other technological changes are making the issue of media access by the public less important. The public increasingly has relatively cheap access to the electronic media, although not in the traditional forms.

Equal Access Law
A law embodied in the Federal Communications Act of 1934 stating that stations selling or giving time to one candidate for public office are required to sell or to give equal time to all legally qualified candidates for the same office. News programs are excluded from this provision.

Media Access
The public's right of access to the media. The FCC and the courts have gradually taken the stance that citizens do have an access right to the media.

Personal Attack Rule
The rule promulgated by the FCC that allows individuals or groups air time to reply to attacks that have previously been aired.

Bias in the Media
▽

Spiro T. Agnew, who resigned the vice presidency during the Nixon administration after having been implicated in a major kickback scheme while governor of Maryland, called the media "nattering nabobs of negativism." Agnew's criticism of the

[16]*New York Times*, November 22, 1983, p. 24.

press was very accurate if you talk to conservatives; not so accurate if you talk to liberals. Relatively few objective studies of media bias have been undertaken to allow us to answer the charges. But Richard Hofstadter, in his extensive study of the 1972 presidential campaign,[17] found that the Democratic candidate, George McGovern, received a few percentage points more coverage than did Nixon. However, according to Hofstadter, Nixon received more favorable stories than McGovern. He concluded that there was no general bias in the media presentation of the 1972 presidential campaign.

Some critics of the electronic media continue to point out their perception of the electronic media's alleged anti-business and pro-government intervention bias. The power of the media and its impact on American society is clearly a controversial and important subject. To what extent the mass media help to clarify issues and to contribute to a more enlightened public, as opposed to distorting and oversimplifying reality, is a topic hotly debated in the United States.

Jonathan Power has said that "the front page is a paper's most precious commodity. It helps set the nation's agenda."[18] If that is the case, then the media have indeed become a force in American politics equal to that of the traditional three branches of government.

[17]Richard Hofstadter, *Bias in the News* (Columbus: Ohio State University Press, 1976).
[18]*The Quotable Quotations Book*, ed. Alec Lewis (New York: Cornerstone Library, 1981), p. 181.

Television and newspapers provide an enormous range of choice for Americans who want to keep informed. Still, critics of the media argue that a substantial amount of programming and print is colored either by the subjectivity of editors and producers or by the demands of profit-making. Few Americans take the time to become critical consumers of the news, either in print or on the TV screen.

To become a critical news consumer, you must practice reading a newspaper with a critical eye toward editorial decisions. For example, what stories are given prominence on the front page of the paper and which ones merit a photograph? What is the editorial stance of the newspaper? Most American papers tend to have moderate to conservative editorial pages. Who are the columnists given space on the "op-ed" page, the page opposite the paper's own editorial page? For a contrast to most daily papers, occasionally pick up an outright political publication such as the *National Review* or *New Republic* and take note of their editorial positions.

Watching the evening news can be far more rewarding if you look at how much the news depends on "video" effects. You will note that stories on the evening news tend to be no more than three minutes long, that stories have excellent videotape will get more attention, and that considerable time is taken up with "happy talk" or human interest stories that tap the emotions of the audience.

Another interesting study you might make is to compare the evening news with the daily paper on a given date. You will see that the paper is perhaps half a day behind the news but that the print story contains far more information. Headlines must take the place of videotape in grabbing your attention. Often stories that appear on the local television news, such as murders and accidents, do not merit space in the paper, probably because they are not unusual occurrences in most larger cities and because the newspaper cannot use pictures of the victims or their relatives.

You can also be a more active consumer by voicing your views and suggestions to the producers of television news or to the editors of newspapers and magazines. These persons are often responsive to criticism and open to constructive suggestions; you might be surprised to find them so accessible.

If you wish to obtain more information on the media and increase your active role as a consumer of the news, you can contact one of the following organizations:

National Association of Broadcasters
1771 N St., N.W.
Washington, D.C. 20036
(202) 293-3500

National Newspaper Publishers Association
970 National Press Bldg.
Washington, D.C. 20045
(202) 662-7324

Accuracy in Media (a conservative group)
1275 K St., N.W., Suite 1150
Washington, D.C. 20005
(202) 371-6710

People for the American Way (a liberal group)
1424 16th St., N.W., Suite 601
Washington, D.C. 20036
(202) 462-4777

Chapter Summary

▽

1. The media are enormously important in American politics today. There is a complex and reciprocal relationship among the media, the government, and the public.

2. The media perform a number of functions, including (a) entertainment, (b) news reporting, (c) identifying public problems, (d) socializing new generations, (e) providing a political forum, and (f) making profits.

3. The media have always played a significant role in American politics. However, in the 1800s news traveled slowly and politics was controlled by a small group who communicated personally. The high-speed rotary press and the telegraph led to self-supported newspapers and mass readership.

4. In contrast to today's ideal of objective news coverage, in the early years of this nation many publications were politically sponsored and contained partisan views.

5. The electronic media (television and radio) are growing

▽

in significance in the area of communications; new technologies, such as cable TV, are giving broadcasters the opportunity to air more specialized programs.

6. The media wield enormous political power during political campaigns and over the affairs of government and government officials by focusing attention on their actions.

7. Mastering the media is critical in today's political campaigns. This is done through paid-for political announcements and expert management of news coverage.

8. Of equal importance for presidential candidates is how they appear in presidential debates.

9. The media play an important role in setting the public agenda and in getting government officials to better understand the needs and desires of American society.

10. The relationship between the media and the president is close; both have used each other—sometimes positively, sometimes negatively.

11. The media in the United States, particularly the electronic media, are subject to government regulation, although the United States has possibly the freest press in the world. Most FCC rules have dealt with ownership of T.V. and radio stations.

12. Perhaps the most questioned rule of the FCC is its fairness doctrine, which requires the broadcast media to give equal time to opposing views on controversial public issues.

13. When the United States invaded the island of Grenada on October 25, 1983, the media were not allowed on the island for national security reasons. This blackout raised the question of how the public's "right to know" should be balanced against the need to protect the national interests.

14. Whether the media clarify and enlighten issues or distort them through biased reporting is a hotly debated topic in the United States. Relatively few objective studies have been undertaken, and answers often depend on personal views or ideological orientations.

Questions for Review and Discussion

1. Explain why the media and political candidates are dependent on each other. Why does this relationship sometimes become antagonistic, especially between the press and the president?

2. Suppose that you are the campaign manager for a U.S. Senate candidate in your state. What kinds of "media events" would you try to set up so that your candidate would get coverage? What meetings, parades, celebrations, and rallies would you have your candidate attend to provide good pictures for TV news? What kinds of assistance could you give to the newspeople to make them generally favorable to your campaign?

3. Compare the coverage of a political event, such as an election, or a speech, such as the State of the Union message, by the newspapers, the news magazines, television, and radio. How are pictures used to convey the story as compared with words? How does "editing" change the content and the effect of such a story?

4. How could the media become more responsive to their readers and viewers? Should there be more opportunities for individual citizens and groups to convey their messages through the media? If there were more opportunities for public access to television, for example, what groups would be most likely to take advantage of them?

5. Should the media be required to provide equal coverage to all of the candidates for an office and for all political parties? Is it fair for the two major political parties to be able to buy or otherwise obtain more coverage in every news medium?

Selected References

David L. Altheide, *Media Power* (Beverly Hills, Calif.: Sage Publications, 1985). Explores how the mass media, especially television, structures our perceptions, expectations, and actions.

Ronald Berkman and Laura W. Kitch, *Politics in the Media Age* (New York: McGraw-Hill, 1986). Investigates the place of the mass media in the new American political landscape. Examines how the media cover the political world, how the political world uses the media, and effects of the media on political behavior.

Edward Epstein, *News from Nowhere* (New York: Random House, 1973). A critical examination of how television news is produced.

Doris A. Graber, *Media Power in Politics* (Washington, D.C.: Congressional Quarterly Press, 1984). This book explores the profound impact of the mass media on the political system. It has both an historical and a topical focus.

Michael Parenti, *Inventing Reality: The Politics of the Mass Media* (New York: St. Martin's Press, 1986). How and why the print and television news media distort important aspects of social and political life. Emphasis is placed on suppression of news, underlying ideological values, mechanisms of information control, media ownership, and the role of newspeople, publishers, advertisers, and the government.

William W. Van Alstyne, *Interpretations of the First Amendment* (Durham, N.C.: Duke University Press, 1984). All about the First Amendment and its relationship to the electronic media.

Chapter 10

▽

Campaigns, Candidates, and Elections

Contents

▽

The People Who Run for Political Office

The Modern Campaign Machine

Campaign Strategy

Campaign Financing and Reform

The Primaries and the Presidential Election

The Electoral College

Voting in National, State, and Local Elections

Legal Restrictions on Voting

Determinants of Voter Choice

Elections and Campaigns: A State of Constant Change

What If . . .

$\triangledown$

Voting Were Compulsory?

Casting a ballot is often seen as the prime symbol of a democracy. It is the way we choose our leaders, a source of legitimacy for our government, and a means by which citizens can influence public policy. For most Americans, voting is the only form of political participation they experience. Yet a large number of Americans do not vote. In 1986, only about one-third of those old enough to vote actually showed up at the polls to select their representatives and senators. In the 1984 presidential election, barely more than half of those eligible actually voted. Voter participation in the United States appears to be much lower than in other democracies, where 80 to 90 percent of the population go to the polls on voting day.

In the United States, our laws give Americans the right to vote, but they do not require us to vote. In some countries, voting is compulsory. What if we had such a law making it compulsory for all eligible citizens to vote, perhaps by levying a fine on those who did not? What would the outcome be if *all* eligible U.S. citizens *had* to vote?

The immediate effects might not be that significant. Studies indicate that nonvoters' attitudes are similar to those of voters, so the results of elections would likely be very much the same. There would be about the same proportion of Democrats, about 4 percent fewer Republicans, and a similar proportion of independent voters.* Since nonvoters are usually less interested in politics and lack firm positions on issues, the new voters would probably not change issue preferences in the electorate. Nonvoters are usually not distinctly liberal or conservative.

The longer-term consequences are harder to calculate, but they may be more significant. Those who stay away from the polls tend to be the least educated, the poor, the young, the elderly, minorities, southerners, and the unemployed. Parties and

*Raymond Wolfinger and Steven Rosenstone, *Who Votes?* (New Haven, Conn.: Yale University Press, 1980), ch. 6.

candidates do not have to make specific appeals to these groups because of their low voter turnout. But if these groups forming distinct constituencies were compelled by law to vote, their interests might be given more attention. Perhaps the population would be on the whole better represented.

Some argue that the country would be worse off if its least-interested and least-informed citizens voted—that people who

consider voting more trouble than it is worth are likely to make poor choices. Further, it would be unhealthy for a democracy to compel people to vote.

Others say that voting is not only a right but an obligation in a country that claims to have a representative government. Through elections, the people express approval or disapproval of the government's actions, and there would be a stronger sense of the government's legitimacy and of the worthiness of its elected officials if everyone voted. They would argue that where almost half the population avoids the polls, democracy functions badly.

$\triangledown$

Who decides to cast a ballot and how a choice of whom to vote for are two essential questions in democratic politics. These questions are influenced by the mechanics of elections, by social and economic factors, and by the flow of political campaigns.

The People Who Run for Political Office

▽

During the spring of 1984, *Time* magazine reported that "the standard campaign day just before any primary includes a couple of events in each of five cities. Mondale may hold one season record: The day before Super Tuesday, he hit eight southern cities in eighteen hours. . . . Hart's Monday, meanwhile, publicly began at the Philadelphia docks for a 7:30 A.M. mingle with longshoremen. At Pittsburgh's airport (four hours after Mondale had touched down there), he met with a group of old people bused out for the occasion, then submitted to three separate TV interviews and a twenty-minute radio call-in show. . . . Indeed, the intensity of this year's primary rigors, physical and emotional, may be unprecedented."[1]

This vignette of the 1984 Democratic primary campaign raises two important questions: Why would anyone want to undergo such an experience, and why does the American political system require such an endurance test? The answer to the first question lies in the forces that motivate individuals to run for office at all levels of government, and the answer to the second lies in the changing nature of the party system. There is no doubt that the prizes of the presidency—power, status, a place in history—make it the most sought-after office in the land. Furthermore, there is an excitement that seems to be intoxicating to the candidate and to the staff in the presidential race. Edmund Muskie described this feeling to journalist Elizabeth Drew:

> It's a very heady business, really, to suddenly find yourself near the top, and to breathe constantly the atmosphere of those who simply take it for granted that you're going to be the next President of the United States.[2]

[1]"Facing the Fatigue Factor," *Time*, April 23, 1984, p. 37.
[2]"Running," *The New Yorker*, December 1, 1975, p. 61.

Gary Hart working the crowd during his 1984 campaign.

Why They Run

People who choose to run for office can be divided into two groups—those who are "self-starters" and those who are recruited, or externally instigated. The volunteers, or self-starters, get involved in political activities to further their careers, to carry out specific political programs, or in response to certain issues or events. The campaign of Senator Eugene McCarthy in 1968 to deny Lyndon Johnson's renomination was rooted in McCarthy's opposition to the Vietnam war. His campaign became the model for many other peace activists in the years that followed.

Issues are important, but self-interest and personal goals—status, career objectives, prestige, and income—are central in motivating some candidates to enter political life. Political scientist Joseph Schlesinger suggests that personal ambition is a major force in politics, as political office is often seen as the stepping stone to achieving certain career goals. A lawyer or an insurance agent may run for office only once or twice and then return to private life with enhanced status. Other politicians may aspire to long-term political office—for example, county offices like commissioner or sheriff that sometimes offer attractive opportunities for power, status, and income and that are in themselves career goals. Finally, we think of ambition as the desire for ever more important offices and higher status. Politicians who run for lower office and then set their sights on Congress or the governorship may be said to have "progressive" ambitions.[3]

Although we tend to pay far more attention to the flamboyant politician or to the personal characteristics of those with presidential ambitions than to their lesser colleagues, it is important to note that there are far more opportunities to run for office than there are citizens eager to take advantage of them. To fill the slate of candidates for election to such jobs as mosquito-abatement district commissioner, the political party must recruit individuals to run. The problem of finding candidates is compounded in states or cities where the majority party is so dominant that the minority candidates have virtually no chance of winning. In these situations, candidates are recruited by party leaders on the basis of loyalty to the organization and civic duty.

Recruited, or externally instigated, politicians often see their entry into politics as a sacrifice of personal interests rather than as a step toward higher office. One of the most famous examples of this recruitment process is the entry of General Dwight D. Eisenhower into the presidential contest in 1952. Both the Democratic and the Republican parties approached "Ike" to become their presidential candidate at a time when the general was looking forward to retirement to his farm in Gettysburg, Pennsylvania. Although Eisenhower eventually chose to run on the Republican ticket, he had no history of political activism and no previous relationship with either party.

Another explanation for the motivation of political candidates is psychological. Harold Lasswell, in a famous study of personality and politics,[4] argues that people may become involved in politics to compensate for personal feelings of inadequacy, which they attempt to alleviate by a career in public life. This conclusion is contradicted by Paul Sniderman, whose study[5] shows that, on the contrary, persons

[3]Joseph Schlesinger, *Ambition in Politics: Political Careers in the United States* (Chicago: Rand-McNally, 1966), p. 6.

[4]Harold D. Lasswell, *Power and Personality* (New York: Viking Press, 1962).

[5]Paul M. Sniderman, *Personality and Democratic Politics* (Berkeley: University of California Press, 1975).

Dwight D. Eisenhower campaigning for president in 1952.

who are active in politics may be better adjusted and more self-confident on the whole than most other Americans.

Who Runs?

There are few constitutional restrictions on who can become a candidate in the United States. As detailed in the Constitution, the requirements for a national office are as follows:

1. President: Must be a natural-born citizen and have attained the age of thirty-five years and be a resident of the country for fourteen years by the time of inauguration.

2. Vice president: Must be a natural-born citizen, have attained the age of thirty-five years, and not be a resident of the same state as the candidate for president.

3. Senator: Must be a citizen for at least nine years, have attained the age of thirty by the time he or she takes office, and be a resident of the state from which elected.

4. Representative: Must be a citizen for at least seven years, have attained the age of twenty-five by the time of taking office, and be a resident of the state from which elected.

The qualifications for state legislators are set by the state constitutions and likewise relate to age, place of residence, and citizenship. (Usually, the requirements for the upper house are somewhat higher than for the lower house.) The legal qualifications for running for governor or other state office are similar.

In spite of these minimal legal qualifications for office at both the national and state levels, a quick look at the slate of candidates in any election—or at the U.S.

House of Representatives—will reveal that not all segments of the population take advantage of these opportunities. Holders of political office in the United States are overwhelmingly white and male. Until this century, politicians were also of northern European origin and predominantly Protestant. Laws enforcing segregation in the South and many border states, as well as laws that denied voting rights to black Americans, made it impossible to elect black public officials in many areas where blacks constituted a significant portion of the population. Since the passage of major civil rights legislation in 1964 and later, the number of black public officials has increased throughout the United States.

Until recently, women were generally considered to be suited only for lower-level offices, such as state legislator and school boards. The last ten years have seen a tremendous increase in the number of women who run for office, not only at the state level, but for the U.S. Congress as well. In 1986, sixty-four women ran for Congress and twenty-three were elected. Whereas blacks were restricted from running for office by both law and custom, women were generally excluded by the agencies of recruitment—parties and interest groups—because they were thought to have no chance of winning or because they had not worked their way up through the party organization. They also had a more difficult time raising campaign funds. Today, it is clear that women are just as likely as men to participate in most political activities, and a majority of Americans say they would vote for a qualified woman or for a black person for president of the United States. The changing attitudes of voters toward women and blacks holding high political office is illustrated in Figure 10–1.

Not only are candidates for office more likely to be male and white than female or black, but they are also likely to be professionals, particularly lawyers, businesspeople, and teachers. Political campaigning and officeholding are simply easier for some occupational and economic groups than for others and they can make a valuable contribution to certain careers. Lawyers, for example, have more flexible schedules than other professionals, can take time off for campaigning, and can leave their jobs to hold public office full time. Furthermore, holding political office

Geraldine Ferraro, the first woman to be nominated for vice president by a major party.

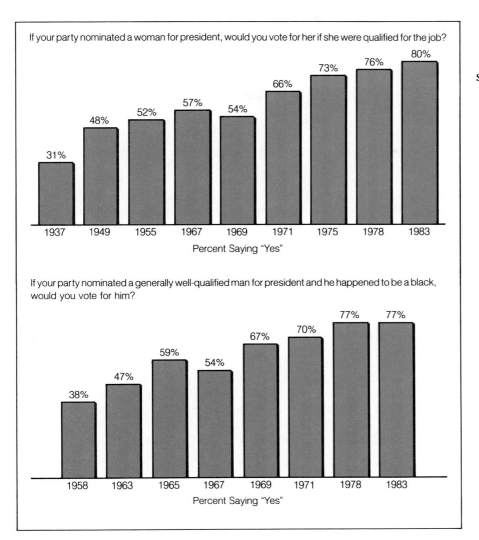

Figure 10–1
▽

Changing Attitudes Toward a Black or Female Presidential Candidate
SOURCE: *The Gallup Poll* 1983, p. 114.

is good publicity for their professional practice, and they usually have partners or associates to keep the firm going while they are in office. Perhaps most importantly, many jobs that lawyers aspire to—federal or state judgeships, state's attorney offices, or work in a federal agency—can be attained by political appointment. Such appointments most likely come to loyal partisans who have served their party by running for and holding office. Personal ambitions, then, are well served for certain groups by entering the political arena, whereas it could be a sacrifice for others whose careers demand full-time attention for many years.

The Modern Campaign Machine
▽

American political campaigns are extravagant, year-long events which produce campaign buttons and posters for collectors, hours of film and sound to be relayed by the media, and eventually winning candidates who become the public officials of the nation. Campaigns are also enormously expensive; the total expenditures for 1986 were estimated at $1 billion for all congressional and local races in that year. Political campaigns exhaust candidates, their staff members, and the journalists covering the campaign—to say nothing of the public's patience.

The Changing Campaign

Campaigns seem to be getting longer and more excessive each year. The costs for candidates, primarily for media coverage, are rising; the candidates announce earlier; and the number of primaries, caucuses, and "beauty contests" increases with each presidential election. The goal of all this frantic activity is the same for all campaigns—to convince voters to choose a candidate or a slate of candidates for office. Part of the reason for the increased intensity of campaigns in the last decade is that they have changed from being party-centered to being candidate-centered in response to changes in the electoral system and to technological innovations.

To run a successful and persuasive campaign, the candidate's organization must be able to raise funds for the effort, to get coverage from the media, to produce and use paid political commercials and advertising, to schedule the candidate's time effectively with constituent groups and prospective supporters, to convey the candidate's position on the issues, to research the opposing candidate, and to get the voters to go to the polls. When party identification was stronger among voters and before the advent of television campaigning, a strong party organization on the local, state, or national level could furnish most of the services and expertise that the candidate needed. Political parties provided the funds for campaigning until the 1970s; parties used their precinct organizations to distribute literature, to register voters, and to get out the vote on election day. Less effort was spent on advertising for a single candidate's positions and character because the party label communicated that information to many of the voters.

One of the most important reasons that campaigns no longer depend on parties is that fewer people identify with them (see Chapter 8). Whereas in 1952, for example, about 47 percent of the voters declared themselves Democrats and 27 percent said they were Republicans, in 1986 only 39 percent claimed to be Democrats while 28 percent were Republicans. In 1952, only 22 percent of the voters were **independent voters;** in 1986 almost 33 percent classified themselves this way. Independent voters include not only those voters who are well educated and issue oriented but also many voters who are not very interested in politics or well informed about candidates or issues. It is during the campaign that such voters can obtain the most information about the political stance of each candidate. James Callaway, media expert and campaign consultant, referred to this marginal group of voters in 1980 when he said:

> I'm convinced that 45 percent of the people will vote one way and 45 percent the other way . . . so that leaves 10 percent who can be reached by television.[6]

There are two other important reasons for the relative weakness of political parties in campaigning. First is the inability of local and state parties to support campaigns financially owing to legal limits placed on campaign contributions and the related public financing of presidential campaigns. Second is the overwhelming importance of the media in campaigns—both for news coverage and for commercials. Media

Independent Voters
Voters who disavow any party affiliation and cast their ballots based on their views of who is the best candidate.

[6]*Nation's Business*, February 1980, p. 33.

Vice President George Bush campaigning with Governor Sununu in New Hampshire.

techniques are much more easily applied to individual candidates than to political parties, although the Republicans—in the first major advertising effort ever conducted by a political party—launched a series of theme commercials in 1980, urging viewers to "Vote Republican for a Change."

The Professional Campaign

Whether the candidate is running for state legislator, for governor, for the U.S. Congress, or for the presidency, every campaign has some fundamental tasks to accomplish. What is most striking about today's campaigns is that many of these tasks are now put into the hands of paid professionals rather than volunteers or amateur politicians.

One of the most important of these professionals is the campaign director or manager who will decide how to organize the effort to accomplish the several tasks of financing the campaign, gaining maximum media coverage, scheduling the campaign events, recruiting assistants for the necessary fieldwork, and conducting research. These are discussed in the following paragraphs.

Financing the Campaign

How will the campaign be paid for? If you are running for president, your eligibility for matching federal funds depends first on your ability to raise private donations. If you must depend totally on contributions, who will plan the coffees, the $100-a-plate dinners, and the solicitation of PAC contributions? You will probably need both a finance director to supervise the entire effort and a skilled accountant to

Highlight

▽

Some Big Spenders in the History of Campaign Spending

Back in 1896 Boies Penrose spent more than half a million dollars (over $8.5 million in today's currency) to win a Senate seat from Pennsylvania. Most of that money went into bribes, because senators were not popularly elected but chosen by the state legislatures.

In 1980 Governor Jay Rockefeller of West Virginia spent more than $12 million on his reelection campaign. His opponent, governor Arch Moore, used this fact to advantage in his slogan, "Make him spend it all, Arch."

In that same year Robert Dornan spent $1.9 million for a third term as Republican congressman from Los Angeles's oceanfront suburbs (he lost), and House majority leader Jim Wright spent $1.2 million to return to Congress (he won). The rest of the top ten campaign spenders in 1980 were as follows:

▽ James Corman, Dem.-California: $905,000 (he lost)
▽ Jack Fields, Rep.-Texas: $800,000 (he won)
▽ John Brademas, Dem.-Indiana: $744,000 (he lost)
▽ Richard Huff, Rep.-Arizona: $700,000 (he lost)
▽ Morris Udall, Dem.-Arizona: $688,000 (he won)
▽ David Robinson, Dem.-Illinois: $675,000 (he lost)
▽ Al Ullman, Dem.-Oregon: $670,000 (he lost)
▽ William Patman, Dem.-Texas: $666,000 (he won)*

*Norman J. Ornstein, Thomas E. Mann, Michael J. Malbin, and John F. Bibby, *Vital Statistics on Congress, 1982* (Washington, D.C.: American Enterprise Institute, 1983).

MAMIE
START PACKING
the
KENNEDYS
are
COMING

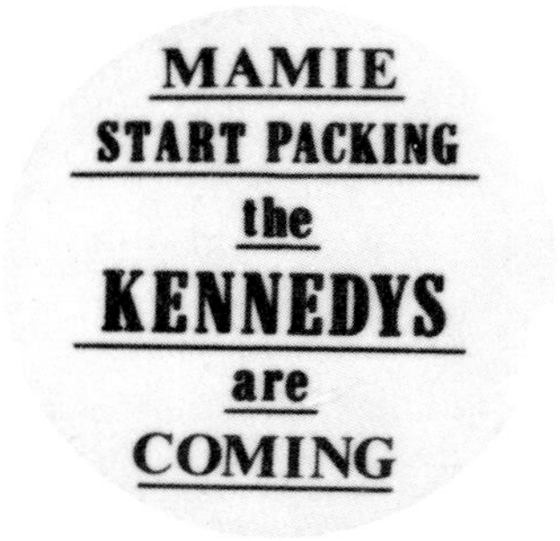

make sure that all campaign finance laws are satisfied. In addition, it would help to have several wealthy friends who will volunteer to solicit contributions from their acquaintances.

Media Coverage

How will you make your issue positions and your qualifications for office known to the voters? The media director must supervise both the design and preparation of commercials for radio, TV, and newspapers, as well as make sure that each of your public appearances is covered on the news. The person who is responsible for news coverage needs to have experience in setting up interesting "photo opportunities" and a good sense of timing: All good news events must happen before 2:30 P.M. so they can make the evening television news.

Scheduling Campaign Events

One of the most vital jobs in a campaign is the proper scheduling of the candidate's appearances. The candidate must meet with all important constituent groups and influential individuals and must be ready to present his or her views at conventions, say, of teachers or businesswomen or even at a high school commencement where there are many parents to listen. The campaign scheduler needs to have the tact to say no to those dates that are of lesser importance and the discretion to know which political invitations must be accepted.

Recruiting Assistants for Fieldwork

In earlier times candidates at every level depended on the party faithful to deliver their literature, to persuade voters, to register voters, and to make sure that likely

*"The question is: Which of his irritating mannerisms can
be used to political advantage?"*

supporters reached the polls. In many parts of the nation, political parties are not strong enough to provide a corps of ready volunteers, nor do many candidates want to be in debt to the local political party. Candidates therefore want to find individuals who will set up local offices, recruit volunteers to go door to door in local areas, and set up phone banks for calling. These efforts may be organized in cooperation with local party officials or in defiance of the local organization.

Conducting Research

Finally, the candidate must consider the issues, the need for research on the opposition (How did she or he vote on specific bills? Who is paying for the opposition's campaign?), and prepare for press conferences and debates. The research director should organize information systems so that speeches can be written stating the candidate's views, voting records are obtainable, and themes for debates are clear.

Campaign Workers

All of these areas of campaign organization can be, and in the past have been, staffed by volunteers or local political activists—or by the candidate's family. However, most contemporary campaigns for higher-level offices (statewide office or the U.S. Congress) hire some outside help to carry out these tasks. Such outside help can be quite expensive. Table 10–1 is a hypothetical listing of campaign personnel and their respective annualized salaries for a typical Republican candidate for the House of Representatives.

Table 10–1

▽

A Hypothetical Republican House Candidate's Professional Campaign Organization

Title	Annualized Salary*
Campaign Manager	$45,000
Finance Chairman	40,000
Press Secretary	30,000
Political Organization Director	30,000
Scheduler	30,000
Volunteer Coordinator	25,000
Office Secretary	20,000
Aide/Companion	20,000
General Consultant	50,000
Media Consultant	50,000
Direct Mail Specialist	30,000
Pollster	30,000

*Estimated by the authors.

▽

Political Consultant

A paid professional hired to devise a campaign strategy and manage a campaign. Image building is the crucial task of the political consultant.

The most sought-after and possibly the most criticized expert is the **political consultant** who for a large fee devises a campaign strategy, thinks up a campaign theme, and possibly chooses the campaign colors and candidate's portrait for all literature to be distributed. It is the paid consultant who suggests new campaign ideas to the candidate day by day and who decides what new advertising spots are needed. The consultants and the firms they represent are not politically neutral; most will work only for candidates from one party or only for candidates of a particular ideological persuasion. There are a couple of so-called "superfirms" that have reached the pinnacle of campaign management. These firms are so effective that they do not go to candidates; rather, the candidates must come to them. Two California firms, Spencer-Roberts and Whitaker and Baker, handle Republican candidates only. It was one of them, Spencer-Roberts, to whom Ronald Reagan went in 1965 when he was thinking about running for governor in California. Reagan chose well. Spencer-Roberts helped him defeat Governor Edmund Brown. For the Democrats, nationally known consultants include Joseph Napolitan Associates, Peter Hart, and Patrick Caddell.

As more and more political campaigns are run exclusively by professional campaign managers, critics of the campaign system are becoming increasingly vociferous. Their worry is this: Professional campaign managers are concerned almost solely with personalities rather than with philosophies and issues. A professional campaign manager is a public relations person. He or she looks at an upcoming election as a contest of personalities rather than as a contest between two opposing parties or opposing principles. According to critics, professional campaign managers are willing to do anything to get their candidate to win, even if this means reshaping the public image of the candidate so that it bears little relation to reality.

Image building is seen to be the crucial task of campaign consultants, and is increasingly necessary to a successful campaign. Using public and private opinion polls as guidelines, consultants mold the candidate's image to meet the campaign's special needs.

Gary Hart's ads created an informal image of the candidate; he was shown wearing cowboy boots, riding horses, and looking windblown—emphasizing his "differentness" from the old-style candidate, Mondale. This type of image construction is a far cry from the "ear to the ground" technique used by party leaders in the past to select candidates and platforms. Yet the alternative to such image building is almost certain failure—regardless of the candidate's stand on significant issues. As Patrick Caddell, Jimmy Carter's pollster and consultant, once lamented; "Too many good people have been defeated because they tried to substitute substance for style."[7]

Image Building

Using public and private opinion polls, the candidate's image is molded to meet the particular needs of the campaign. Image building is done primarily through the media.

Campaign Strategy
▽

The goal of every political campaign is the same: to win the election. In the United States, unlike some European countries, there are no rewards for a candidate who comes in second; the winner takes all. The campaign organization must plan a strategy to maximize the candidate's chances of winning. In making these strategic choices, a number of factors should be considered. One of the most important concerns is how well known the candidate is. If he or she is a highly visible

[7]Quoted in Peter Woll, *Behind the Scenes in American Government: Personalities and Politics* (Boston: Little, Brown, 1983), p. 128.

Profile

▽

Jesse Jackson

Jesse Jackson, born on October 8, 1941, in Greenville, North Carolina, was raised amid deep poverty. He secured his first job at age six delivering stove wood, and at age eleven he was a manager in charge of the wood yard's finances, hiring, and firing. Jackson attended Greenville's public schools and proved to be an outstanding athlete. In 1959, he entered the University of Illinois on a football scholarship but left after one year. He returned to his home state and attended the Agricultural and Technological College of Greensboro. In 1965, he moved to Chicago to enroll in a theological seminary and was ordained a Baptist minister in 1968. He married and now has five children.

Jackson played an important role in the civil rights struggles of the 1960s, leading marches, picketers, and sit-ins. He joined Martin Luther King, Jr. in the Southern Christian Leadership Conference and became a close adviser and field organizer. In 1966, as head of the SCLC's Operation Breadbasket, the conference began a systematic boycott of businesses that it believed exploited blacks.

Soon after King's assassination, which Jackson had witnessed, Jackson petitioned for an appointment to a higher post in the SCLC, but was turned down. After a series of clashes with the SCLC leadership, Jackson, with his characteristic defiance, resigned. Within a few months he announced the formation of Operation PUSH (People United to Save Humanity), a Chicago-based civil rights and economic development organization. He also organized an innovative educational program to increase learning

"Racism, not communism, is the number one threat to our national security."

skills among minority students.

In 1983, Jackson made a series of public appearances throughout the country in voter registration drives, church rallies, and campaign appearances for local candidates. On November 3, 1983, he formally announced his candidacy for the Democratic presidential nomination, proclaiming the need for social justice and economic betterment for the poor and for minorities. Although Jackson was given little chance to win the nomination, he carried his campaign to the national convention. Jackson won two primary elections outright and garnered more than 10 percent of the vote in a number of others.

To consolidate his political position, Jackson began in 1985 and 1986 to expand his political base and visibility.

His political organization, Rainbow Coalition Inc. held a convention in Washington, D.C. in April 1986. One of the surprises of this meeting, attended by more than one thousand people from forty states, was the presence of some labor leaders and white farmers facing foreclosure. Jackson had spoken out about the farm crisis and labor rights, traveling through the Midwest where he met with farmers and showed up at a bitter labor dispute in Austin, Minnesota.

Other activities that kept him in the news included his appearance at the Reagan-Gorbachev summit meeting in Geneva, where he headed a private peace delegation that met for one hour with the Soviet leader, and participation at international meetings against apartheid in South Africa. He also began a campaign to get more blacks into the mass media.

Jackson will likely have an important impact on the March 1988 "southern primary" if he is a candidate for president. Although southern Democrats hope that holding thirteen southern primaries on one day will favor a moderate candidate, Jackson did receive 18 percent of the vote in that region in 1984. Whether or not that success is repeated, Jackson is expected to be a very important factor in the 1988 Democratic party presidential contest.

*Time May 7, 1984, pp. 30–41.

incumbent in the office, there may be little need for campaigning except to remind the voters of the officeholder's good deeds. If, however, the candidate is an unknown challenger or, as in the case of Gary Hart, a largely unfamiliar character attacking a well-known public figure, the campaign must devise a strategy to get the candidate before the public.

In the case of the **independent candidate** or the candidate representing a minor party, the problem of name recognition is serious. There are usually a number of **third-party candidates** in each presidential election (see Table 10–2 for a list of those campaigning in the 1984 presidential race), and such candidates must present an overwhelming case for the voter to reject the major party candidate. Both the Democratic and the Republican candidates use the strategic ploy of labeling third-party candidates as "not serious" and therefore not worth the voter's time.

Independent Candidate

A political candidate who is not affiliated with a political party.

Third-Party Candidate

A political candidate running under the banner of a party other than the two major political parties.

Table 10–2
▽
Third-Party Candidates in the 1984 Presidential Election Campaign

Candidate	Age	Occupation
American		
Delmar Dennis (Tenn.)	44	Book publisher
Traves Brownlee (Del.)	39	Head of Americans for Constitutional Taxation
Citizens		
Sonia Johnson (Va.)	48	Women's rights activist
Richard Walton (R.I.)	56	Free-lance writer
Communist		
Gus Hall (N.Y.)	74	Party general secretary
Angela Davis (Calif.)	40	Political science teacher, author
Independent		
Lyndon H. LaRouche (Va.)	62	Self-described economist
Billy Davis (Miss.)	46	Lawyer and farmer
Independent Alliance		
Dennis L. Serrette (N.J.)	44	Phone technician, union organizer
Nancy Ross (N.Y.)	41	Former school teacher
Libertarian		
David Bergland (Calif.)	49	Lawyer
Jim Lewis (Conn.)	51	Bookbinding sales representative
Populist		
Bob Richards (Texas)	58	Lecturer and real estate developer
Maureen Kennedy Salaman (Calif.)	47	President of the National Health Federation
Prohibition		
Earl F. Dodge (Colo.)	51	National party chairman
Warren C. Martin (Kan.)	75	Farmer and businessman
Socialist Workers		
Mel Mason (Calif.)	41	Ex-Seaside, Calif., city councilor
Andrea Gonzalez (N.Y.)	33	Young Socialist Alliance chairperson
Workers World		
Larry Holmes (N.Y.)	32	Black activist
Gloria La Riva (Calif.)	30	Political activist

SOURCE: Congressional Quarterly, *Weekly Report*, November 3, 1984, p. 2851.

Because neither of the major parties can claim a majority of voters in its camp, the task that faces them is threefold. Each party and its presidential candidate must reinforce the party loyalty of its followers, motivate the undecideds or independents to vote for their candidate, and—the most difficult task—try to convince some followers of the other major party to cross party lines. The Republicans, having the fewer adherents, spend more time and money trying to attract independents and Democrats, whereas the Democrats know they can win if they can secure all of the votes of their party plus a goodly share of the independents. To accomplish these tasks, the campaign organization, whether at the presidential level or otherwise, plans a mix of strategies using the media through campaign appearances, debates, and position papers to sway the voters. One of the first decisions that the candidate and his or her staff must make is whether to emphasize "style" or "substance." A style candidacy focuses on the candidate's personal characteristics or style of action: Characterizing Gary Hart, for example, as the man of new ideas was a bid to convince voters that he was the man for the future. Substance campaigns stress issues and policy positions. Walter Mondale's close ties to labor unions suggested that he supported policies that favor labor.

The Value of Campaign Polls

Since the decision-making power for presidential nominations has shifted from the elites to the masses, one of the major sources of information for both the media and the candidates is polls. Poll taking is widespread during the primaries. Often presidential hopefuls will have private polls taken to make sure there is at least some chance they could be nominated, and if nominated, elected. Also, since the party nominees depend on polls to fine-tune their campaigns, during the presidential campaign itself continual polls are taken, not only by the regular pollsters—Roper, Harris, Gallup, and others—but also privately by each candidate's campaign organization.

Gary Hart left the Senate in 1986 to begin his campaign for the 1988 Democratic presidential nomination.

Jack Kemp, Representative from New York, talking to political supporters.

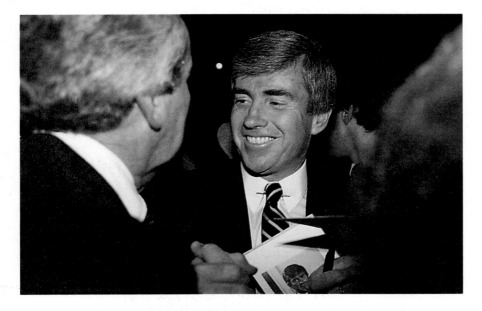

In the 1980 presidential campaign, Jimmy Carter relied on constant rounds of polling conducted by his personal pollster, Patrick Caddell. Candidate Ronald Reagan used the skills of Richard Wirthlin and his staff to measure the pulse of the voters. These private polls, as opposed to the independent public polls conducted by Gallup and others, are for the exclusive and secret use of the candidate and his or her campaign organization. Such polls can tell each candidate what the distribution of public sentiment is on specific issues. A candidate may make a particularly important campaign speech in a major city and immediately afterward have a private poll taken of voters in that city to gauge how that candidate appealed to the voters. As the polls reflect voters' acceptance or nonacceptance of a candidate's personality and/or stand on an issue, that candidate can attempt to change his or her image in a way that appeals to more voters. Polls are already under way to determine people's reactions to potential presidential candidates for 1988 (Table 10–3).

Campaign Financing and Reform
▽

In a book published in 1932 entitled *Money in Elections*, Louise Overacker had the following to say about campaign financing:

> The financing of elections in a democracy is a problem which is arousing increasing concern. Many are beginning to wonder if present-day methods of raising and spending campaign funds do not clog the wheels of our elaborately constructed mechanism of popular control, and if democracies do not inevitably become plutocracies.[8]

Although writing more than fifty years ago, Overacker touched upon a sensitive issue in American political campaigns: the connection between money and elections. It is estimated that $2 billion was spent at all levels of campaigning in 1984.

[8]New York: Macmillan, 1932, p. vii.

Table 10–3
▽
Potential Democratic and Republican Nominees for President
Early returns for 1988, based on an exit poll taken on election day, November 4, 1986.

Whom do you want your party to nominate for president in 1988?			
Republicans		**Democrats**	
George Bush	34%	Gary Hart	26%
Bob Dole	14%	Mario Cuomo	20%
Howard Baker	9%	Jesse Jackson	7%
Jack Kemp	9%	Joseph Biden	2%
Pat Robertson	6%	Bruce Babbitt	1%
Paul Laxalt	2%	Richard Gephardt	1%
Pete du Pont	1%	Sam Nunn	1%
Someone else	15%	Someone else	33%
No answer	11%	No answer	10%

Based on 8,997 voters interviewed at 188 randomly selected polling places throughout the country.

SOURCE: *New York Times*, November 6, 1986, p. 19.

A total of more than $160 million is estimated to have been spent in races for the House of Representatives, $125 million in senatorial races, and $200 million in the presidential campaign. Except for the presidential campaign in the general election, all of the other money had to be provided by the candidates and their families, borrowed, or raised by other means. For the general presidential campaign, most of the money comes from the federal government.

The road to election is long and takes, among other things, a lot of money. That money, as we have seen, is used for TV commercials, media consultants, campaign managers, and a host of other professional services. According to Mat Reese, president of Mat Reese and Associates, a campaign management firm, the single most important barrier in running for the House (and presumably the Senate also) is the ability to pay for a modern campaign. Reese says he spends a lot of his time telling potential candidates that they can't afford to run:

> I've seen a lot of people with $50,000 in cash who can't raise another $250,000. I get almost rich men in here all the time, who say they've got $50,000 or $75,000 of their own money to run for Congress. And I have to be the one to tell them that that isn't enough.[9]

Although the total number of dollars being spent on financing campaigns is certainly not decreasing, the way in which campaigns are financed has changed rather dramatically in the last few years. In the wake of the scandals uncovered after the 1972 Watergate break-in, Congress and the Supreme Court reshaped the nature of political spending. It was discovered during the Watergate investigations that large amounts of money had been illegally funneled to Nixon's Campaign to Reelect the President (CREEP). Congress acted quickly to prevent such a situation occurring again. After all, those who make large campaign contributions presumably require something in return.[10]

[9]Quoted in Walter Shapiro, "A House Full of Millionaires," *Harpers,* no. 265 (July 1982), p. 50.

[10]See Chapter 11 for a discussion of the effective use of campaign contributions from the dairy lobby in obtaining a multimillion-dollar increase in federal dairy support prices.

Corrupt Practices Acts
A series of acts passed by Congress in an attempt to limit and regulate the size and sources of contributions and expenditures in political campaigns.

Hatch Act
Passed in 1939, this act forbids a political committee to spend more than $3 million in any campaign and limits individual contributions to a committee to $5,000. The act was designed to control political influence buying.

Federal Election Campaign Act of 1972
An act to control the raising and spending of funds for political campaigns.

Federal Election Commission
Created by the 1972 Federal Election Campaign Act to enforce compliance with the requirements of the act; the commission consists of six nonpartisan administrators.

There have been a variety of federal **Corrupt Practices Acts** designed to regulate campaign financing. The first, passed in 1925, limited primary and general election expenses for congressional candidates. In addition, it required disclosure of election expenses and in principle put controls on contributions by corporations. However, numerous loopholes were found in the restrictions on contributions and they proved to be ineffective.

In 1939, the **Hatch Act** (Political Activities Act of 1939) was passed in another attempt to control political influence buying. That act forbade a political committee to spend more than $3 million in any campaign and limited individual contributions to a committee to $5,000. Of course, such restrictions were easily circumvented by creating additional committees.

The Federal Election Campaign Acts of 1972 and 1974

It wasn't until the 1970s that more effective regulation of campaign financing was undertaken. The **Federal Election Campaign Act of 1972** essentially eliminated all past laws and instituted a major reform. The act placed no limit on overall spending, but restricted the amount that could be spent on mass media advertising, including television. It limited the amount that candidates and their families could contribute to their own campaigns, and required disclosure of all contributions and expenditures in excess of $100. In principle, the 1972 act limited the role of labor unions and corporations in political campaigns. It also provided for a voluntary $1 check-off on federal income tax returns for general campaign funds to be used by major party candidates (first applied in the 1976 campaign).

But the act still did not go far enough. In 1974, Congress passed another Federal Election Campaign Act. It did the following:

1. Created the **Federal Election Commission,** consisting of six nonpartisan administrators whose duties are to enforce compliance with the requirements of the act.
2. Provided public financing for presidential primaries and general elections. Any candidate running for president who is able to obtain sufficient contributions in at least twenty states can obtain a subsidy from the U.S. Treasury to help pay for primary campaigns. Each major party is given $2 million for the national conventions. The major party candidates have federal support for almost all of their expenses, provided they are willing to accept campaign-spending limits.
3. Limited presidential campaign spending. Any candidate accepting federal support has to agree to limit campaign expenditures to the amount prescribed by federal law.
4. Limited contributions. Citizens can contribute up to $1,000 to each candidate in each federal election or primary; the total limit of all contributions from an individual is $25,000 per year. Groups can contribute up to a maximum of $5,000 to a candidate in any election.
5. Required disclosure. Periodic reports must be filed by each candidate with the Federal Election Commission, listing who contributed, how much was spent, and what the money was spent for.

The 1972 act limited the amount that each individual could spend on his or her own behalf. Senator Jim Buckley of New York challenged that aspect of the law and the Supreme Court declared the provision unconstitutional in 1976.[11]

[11]*Buckley v. Valeo,* 424 U.S. 1 (1976).

The Impact of the 1974 Act

Who would benefit by severe limitations on the amount an individual could spend on her or his own campaign and the total amount that could be spent on a campaign altogether? Obviously, incumbents would benefit by such restrictions. Unfortunately for incumbents, the 1976 Supreme Court decision eliminated restrictions on campaign spending for congressional seats. The Court ruled that the overall campaign-spending ceilings infringed the First Amendment, and in a second opinion it held that it was unconstitutional to restrict in any way the amount congressional candidates or their immediate families could spend on their own behalf: "The candidate, no less than any other person, has a First Amendment right to engage in the discussion of public issues and vigorously and tirelessly to advocate his own election." The Court let stand the 1974 limits on individual contributions and on contributions by groups such as political action committees (PACs). Candidates who do not want to have to depend on the kindness of strangers can simply write checks out for any amount they wish. They can do something else—take out loans.

The Loan Strategy

Let us say you are running for office and are short of funds. You are unable to get funds quickly from your would-be constituents, so you decide to loan your campaign the money. According to William Sweeney, former deputy chairman of the Democratic National Committee, the fastest-growing source of campaign funds is the personal indebtedness of the candidates. The Federal Election Commission doesn't even compile statistics on such matters. Take, for example, Texas Democrat William Patman. In 1980, he loaned his campaign $495,593.15. Cooper Evans, an Iowa Republican, loaned his campaign $440,000. The beauty of loaning money to your own campaign is that after you are elected, you can take ex post facto contributions to pay off the campaign debt to yourself.

The Growth in Political Action Committees (PACs)

The 1974 act, as modified by certain amendments in 1976, allows corporations, labor unions, and special interest groups to set up **political action committees (PACs)** to raise money for candidates. For a PAC to be legitimate, the money must be raised from at least fifty volunteer donors and must be given to at least five candidates in the federal election. PACs can contribute up to $5,000 to each candidate in each election. Each corporation or each union is limited to one PAC. As you might imagine, corporate PACs obtain funds from executives, employees, and stockholders in their firms and unions obtain PAC funds from their members. The relationship between interest groups and PACs is discussed further in Chapter 11.

Political Action Committees (PACs)
Committees set up by and representing corporations, labor unions, or special interest groups; PACs raise and give campaign donations on behalf of the organizations or groups they represent.

The Primaries and the Presidential Election
▽

The American presidential election is the culmination of two different campaigns linked by the parties' national conventions. The **presidential primary** campaign lasts officially from January until June of the election year and the final presidential campaign begins around Labor Day.

Presidential Primary
A statewide primary election of delegates to a political party's national convention to help a political party determine its presidential nominee. Such delegates are either pledged to a particular candidate or unpledged.
▽

Primary elections were first mandated in 1903 in Wisconsin. The purpose of the primary was to open the nomination process to ordinary party members and to weaken the influence of party bosses in the nomination process. However, until 1968, there were fewer than twenty primary elections for the presidency. They were generally **"beauty contests"** in which the contending candidates for the nomination competed for popular votes, but the results had little or no impact on the selection of delegates to the national convention. National conventions were meetings of the party elite—legislators, mayors, county chairpersons, and loyal party workers— who were mostly appointed to their delegations. These party faithful frequently voted as a bloc under the direction of their leaders. Chicago's Mayor Richard Daley was famous for the control he exercised over the Illinois delegation to the Democratic convention. National conventions saw numerous trades and bargains between competing candidates and the leaders of large blocs of delegate votes.

Primary Reform

In recent years, the character of the primary process and the makeup of the national convention have changed dramatically. The mass public, rather than party elites, now controls the nomination process owing to extraordinary changes in the party rules. After the massive riots outside the doors of the 1968 Democratic convention in Chicago, many party leaders pushed for serious reforms of the convention process. They saw the general dissatisfaction with the convention and the riots in particular as stemming from the inability of the average party member to influence the nomination system.

The Democratic National Committee appointed a special commission to study the problems of the primary system. Known as the McGovern-Fraser Commission, the group over the next several years formulated new rules for delegate selection that had to be followed by state Democratic parties. Although some of the state parties did not agree with the rules, the commission held the ultimate threat: If a

Beauty Contest
A term used to describe a form of presidential primary where delegates are selected by the party organization and are not allocated according to popular votes.

Riots outside the 1968 Democratic convention in Chicago.

state did not comply with the rules, its delegation would not be seated at the national convention. This penalty was carried out against Mayor Daley of Chicago in 1972.

The reforms instituted by the Democratic party, and imitated in most states by the Republicans, revolutionized the nomination process for the presidency. The most important changes require that convention delegates cannot be nominated by the elites in either party; they must be elected by the voters in primary elections, in caucuses held by local parties, or at state conventions. Delegates are mostly pledged to a particular candidate, although the pledge is not formally binding at the convention. The delegation from each state must also include a proportion of women, younger party members, and representatives of the minority groups within the party. Finally, there were virtually no special privileges given to elected party officials such as senators or governors; only a handful could attend the convention. In 1984, many of these officials returned to the Democratic convention as super-delegates. These changes in the Democratic rules are detailed in Table 10–4.

Some political scientists believe these presidential primaries perform several useful functions. First, it is through primaries that a relatively unknown candidate,

Table 10–4
▽
Changes in Democratic Convention Rules

The checkmarks indicate that the rules were in force for that year.

	1972	1976	1980	1984
Timing: Restrict delegate selection events to a 3-month period (the "window").			✔	✔
Conditions of Participation: Restrict participation in delegate selection events to Democrats.		✔	✔	✔
Proportional Representation: Ban all types of winner-take-all contests.			✔	
Delegate Loyalty: Give candidates the right to approve delegates identifying with their candidacy.		✔	✔	✔
Bind delegates to vote for their original presidential preference at convention on first ballot.			✔	
Party and Elected Officials: Expand each delegation by 10 percent to include pledged party and elected officials.			✔	✔
Further expand each delegation to include uncommitted party and elected officials ("superdelegates").				✔
Demographic Representation: Encourage participation and representation of minorities and traditionally under-represented groups (affirmative action).	✔	✔	✔	✔
Require delegations to be equally divided between men and women.			✔	✔

SOURCE: *Elections: '84*, Washington, D.C.: Congressional Quarterly Press, 1984, p. 36.

Delegates supporting Jesse Jackson at the 1984 Democratic national convention.

Caucus

A closed meeting of party leaders to select party candidates or to decide on policy. Also, a meeting of party members designed to select candidates and propose policies.

Party members caucus in the firehouse to choose delegates.

such as Gary Hart, can get his or her "bandwagon" going. Primaries also provide an opportunity for candidates to organize their campaigns and to try out different issue positions before the public. The long primary season stretching from February until mid-June can even be regarded as an endurance test, in which the voters can see how candidates stand up under stress. Finally, the primaries may put pressure on an incumbent to change his or her policy. Lyndon B. Johnson decided not to run for the presidency again after the 1968 New Hampshire primary showed he was losing party support.

Critics of the system argue that the primaries drag out the presidential election to such a length that by the time they are over, the public is tired of the whole business. The result is that people may take less interest in the general election.

The states that do not have presidential primaries use the **caucus** to choose convention delegates. The original definition of a caucus is a secret meeting of party leaders for the purpose of nominating the party's candidates. In the early years of this century, the caucus was frequently referred to as "the smoke-filled room." Caucuses are still in use by local parties in many states and counties to determine which candidates will be endorsed by the party in primary elections. For the presidential nominating process, caucuses can be used to nominate the delegates to the national convention or to county and state conventions where the official delegates will be chosen. In the latter case, the caucus must be open to all members of the political party who live within the specified geographic area—precinct, legislative district, or county. These neighbors gather, discuss presidential candidates, decide who the delegates will be, and determine whether the delegates will be pledged to one or more presidential candidates. Some critics of the primary system feel that the caucus is a better way of finding out how loyal party workers feel about the candidates and that its more widespread use would lead to stronger political parties.

Types of Primaries

The two most common types of primaries are the closed primary and the open primary. In addition, there are the blanket primary and the run-off primary.

Closed Primary

In a **closed primary,** the selection of a party's candidates in an election is limited to avowed or declared party members. In other words, voters must declare their party affiliation, either when they register or at the primary election. A closed-primary system makes sure that registered voters cannot cross over into the other party's primary. Why would they want to do so? To nominate the weakest candidate of the opposing party or to affect the ideological direction of that party. Regular party workers favor a closed primary because it promotes party loyalty and responsibility. Independent voters do not like closed primaries because they exclude such voters from participating in the nominating process.

Open Primary

An **open primary** is a direct primary in which voters can vote in either party primary without disclosing their party affiliation. Basically, the voter makes the choice in the privacy of the voting booth. The voter must, however, choose one party's list from which to select candidates. Open primaries place no restrictions on independent voters. Few states use such a system.

Blanket Primary

A **blanket primary** is one in which the voter may vote for candidates of more than one party. Alaska, Louisiana, and Washington all have blanket primaries.

Run-Off Primary

Some states have a two-primary system. If no candidate receives a majority of the votes in the first primary, the top two candidates must compete in another primary, called a **run-off primary.**

A National Presidential Primary?

There have been waves of popular demand for a single, nationwide presidential primary election. Its main advantage is that it would be more efficient than the existing expensive, long-drawn-out, state-by-state system of selecting candidates.

Arguments against a national presidential primary emphasize several factors. First, it might be very difficult for minor candidates to achieve any success when they have to compete everywhere at once with their limited resources. Second, since candidates would not be eliminated from the competition during the primary process, as at present, there would probably be a fragmented national delegate split, which might lead to convention outcomes being decided by the party leaders. (But some feel that party leaders are well-qualified to judge the competing candidates, particularly as to their electability. Throwing the nomination into the convention might increase the influence of parties in the elections overall.) Third, an advantage of the current process is that details of the candidates' views or personality are revealed by having to be on display constantly and under widely varying conditions from state to state. Finally, party organizations might be further weakened by even greater emphasis on candidates in the national media.[12]

[12]These and other arguments are presented in Nelson W. Polsby and Aaron Wildavsky, *Presidential Elections,* 6th ed. (New York: Charles Scribner's, 1984), pp. 223–230.

Closed Primary

The most widely used primary, in which voters may participate only in the primary of the party with which they are registered.

Open Primary

A direct primary where voters may cast ballots in the primary of either party without having to declare their party registration. Once voters choose which party primary they will vote in, they must select among only the candidates of that party.

Blanket Primary

A primary in which all candidates' names are printed on the same ballot, regardless of party affiliation. The voter may vote for candidates of more than one party.

Run-Off Primary

An election that is held to nominate candidates within the party if no candidate receives a majority of the votes in the first primary election.

On to the National Convention

Presidential candidates have been nominated by the convention method in every election since 1832. The delegates are sent from each state and are apportioned on the basis of state representation. There are delegate bonuses for states that had voting majorities for the party in the preceding elections. Parties also accredit delegates from the District of Columbia, Puerto Rico, and the Virgin Islands.

Credentials Committee

A committee used by political parties at their national conventions to determine which delegates may participate. The committee inspects the claim of each prospective delegate to be seated as a legitimate representative of his or her state.

At the convention, each political party uses a **credentials committee** to determine which delegates may participate. The credentials committee usually prepares a roll of all delegates entitled to be seated. Controversy arises when rival groups claim to be the official party organization for a county, district, or state. At that point, the credentials committee will make a recommendation, which is usually approved by the convention without debate or even a roll call. On occasion, conventions have rejected recommendations of the credentials committee, and in some cases the decision has been a decisive factor in the selection of the presidential nominee. At the Republican convention in 1952, two competing delegations supporting Eisenhower and Robert Taft arrived from five different southern states. It was because Eisenhower supporters succeeded in getting the credentials committee to approve their delegates that Eisenhower was nominated.

The Mississippi Democratic party split along racial lines in 1964 at the height of the civil rights movement in the Deep South. Separate all-white and mixed white and black sets of delegates were selected, and both factions showed up at the national convention. After much debate on party rules, the committee decided to seat the pro-civil rights forces and exclude those who opposed racial equality.

Illinois delegation on the convention floor.

The goal of any presidential hopeful at the national convention is to obtain a majority of votes on the earliest ballot. Given that delegates generally arrive at the convention in various states of commitment to presidential candidates, a certain amount of politicking, logrolling, and promising must take place in order to get delegate pledges. Much of this activity has been eliminated by convention reforms in both major parties that typically have required delegates to pledge themselves to a presidential candidate. Consequently, no convention since 1952 has required more than one ballot to choose a nominee. However, much of this is accomplished by a long-drawn-out single ballot during which delegations shift and realign so that the appearance, if not the actuality, of unity may be conveyed to the TV audience.

It is interesting to note that there is no federal regulation of conventions. Each party makes its own rules and polices itself as it sees fit. The typical convention lasts only a few days. The first day consists of speech making, usually against the opposing party. During the second day, there are committee reports, and during the third day, there is presidential balloting. On the fourth day, a vice presidential candidate is usually nominated and the presidential nominee gives the acceptance speech.

The Mechanics of Elections

Australian Ballot

A secret ballot prepared, distributed, and tabulated by government officials at public expense. Since 1888, all states have used the secret Australian ballot rather than an open, public ballot.

The United States uses the **Australian ballot**—a secret ballot that is prepared, distributed, and counted by government officials at the public expense. Since 1888, all states have used the Australian ballot, but before that many states used the alternatives of oral voting and differently colored ballots prepared by the parties. Obviously, knowing which way a person was voting made it easy to apply pressure to change his or her vote, and vote buying was common.

Office-Block and Party-Column Ballots

There are two types of ballots in use in the United States in general elections. The first, called an **office-block ballot** or sometimes a **Massachusetts ballot,** groups all the candidates for each elective office under the title of each office. Politicians dislike the office-block ballot because it places more emphasis on the office than on the party; it discourages straight-ticket voting and encourages split-ticket voting.

A **party-column ballot** is a form of general election ballot in which the candidates are arranged in one column under their respective party labels and symbols. It is also called the **Indiana ballot.** In some states, it allows voting for all of a party's candidates for local, state, and national offices by simply marking a single "X" or by pulling a single lever. Most states use this type of ballot. As it encourages straight-ticket voting, majority parties favor this form. When a party has an exceptionally strong presidential or gubernatorial candidate to head the ticket, the **coattail effect** is increased by the party-column ballot.

Long Versus Short Ballots

During the Jacksonian era, the number of elective offices to be filled increased dramatically on the theory that this was a way to expand democracy. Today, the typical state and local ballot is a **long ballot.** Sometimes it is called a bedsheet ballot or a jungle ballot because of the extremely large number of offices to be

Massachusetts ballot.

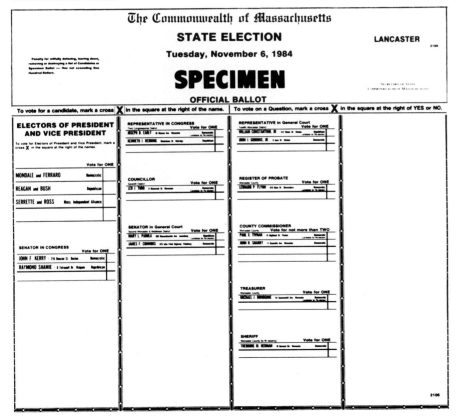

Office-Block Ballot or **Massachusetts Ballot**

A form of general election ballot in which candidates for elective office are grouped together under the title of each office. It emphasizes voting for the office and the individual rather than for the party.

Party-Column Ballot or **Indiana Ballot**

A form of general election ballot in which candidates for elective office are arranged in one column under their respective party labels and symbols. It emphasizes voting for the party rather than for the office or individual.

Coattail Effect

The influence of a popular or unpopular candidate on the electoral success or failure of other candidates on the same party ticket. The effect is increased by the party-column ballot, which encourages straight-ticket voting.

Long Ballot

Sometimes called the "bedsheet ballot" or "jungle ballot," the long ballot is a lengthy list of candidates and is typical in states and localities that have many offices to be filled.

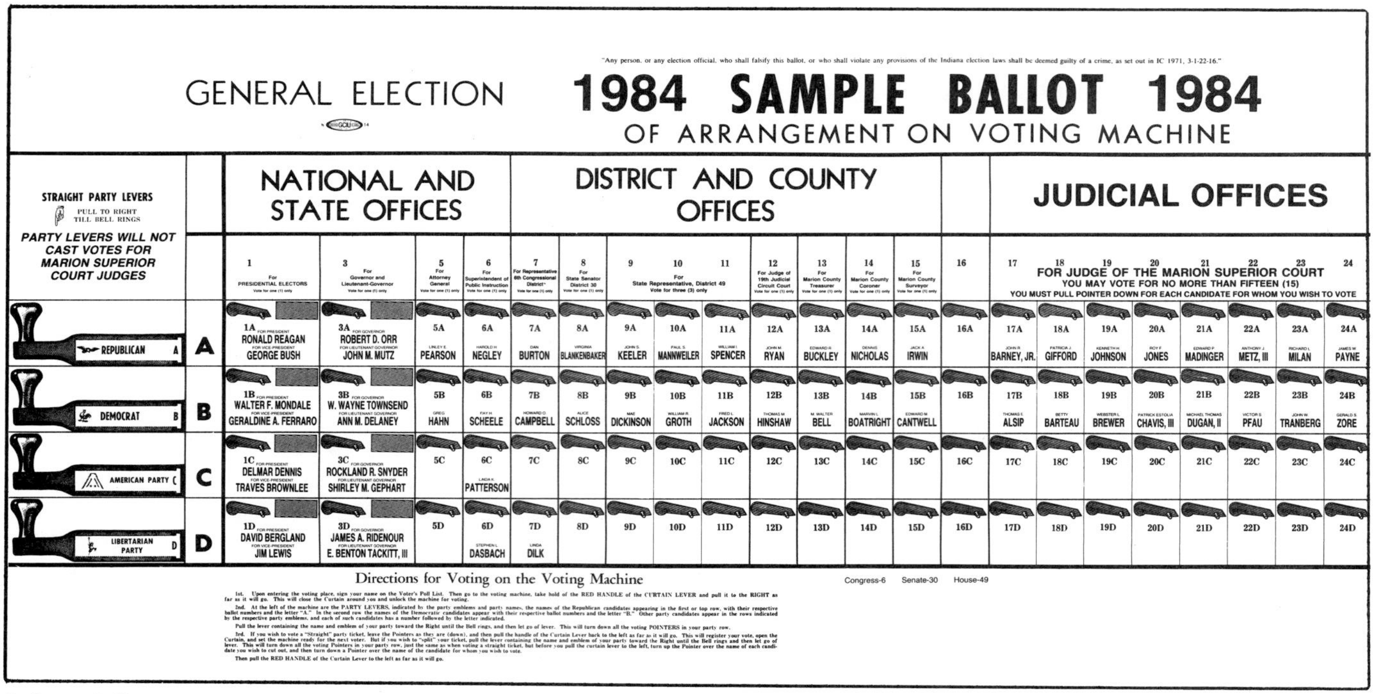

1984 SAMPLE BALLOT 1984
OF ARRANGEMENT ON VOTING MACHINE

"Any person, or any election official, who shall falsify this ballot, or who shall violate any provisions of the Indiana election laws shall be deemed guilty of a crime, as set out in IC 1971, 3-1-22-16."

STRAIGHT PARTY LEVERS	NATIONAL AND STATE OFFICES											DISTRICT AND COUNTY OFFICES							JUDICIAL OFFICES								

STRAIGHT PARTY LEVERS
PULL TO RIGHT TILL BELL RINGS

PARTY LEVERS WILL NOT CAST VOTES FOR MARION SUPERIOR COURT JUDGES

NATIONAL AND STATE OFFICES
DISTRICT AND COUNTY OFFICES
JUDICIAL OFFICES

FOR JUDGE OF THE MARION SUPERIOR COURT
YOU MAY VOTE FOR NO MORE THAN FIFTEEN (15)
YOU MUST PULL POINTER DOWN FOR EACH CANDIDATE FOR WHOM YOU WISH TO VOTE

Column headers:
1 For Presidential Electors — Vote for one (1) only
3 For Governor and Lieutenant-Governor — Vote for one (1) only
5 For Attorney General — Vote for one (1) only
6 For Superintendent of Public Instruction — Vote for one (1) only
7 For Representative 6th Congressional District — Vote for one (1) only
8 For State Senator District 30 — Vote for one (1) only
9 10 11 For State Representative, District 49 — Vote for three (3) only
12 For Judge of 19th Judicial Circuit Court — Vote for one (1) only
13 For Marion County Treasurer — Vote for one (1) only
14 For Marion County Coroner — Vote for one (1) only
15 For Marion County Surveyor — Vote for one (1) only
16
17–24 For Judge of the Marion Superior Court

Row A — REPUBLICAN
1A FOR PRESIDENT RONALD REAGAN / FOR VICE PRESIDENT GEORGE BUSH
3A FOR GOVERNOR ROBERT D. ORR / FOR LIEUTENANT GOVERNOR JOHN M. MUTZ
5A LINLEY E. PEARSON
6A HAROLD H. NEGLEY
7A DAN BURTON
8A VIRGINIA BLANKENBAKER
9A PAUL S. KEELER
10A ROY T. MANNWEILER
11A SPENCER
12A JOHN W. RYAN
13A EDWARD H. BUCKLEY
14A DENNIS NICHOLAS
15A JACK A. IRWIN
16A
17A JOHN R. BARNEY, JR.
18A GIFFORD
19A JOHNSON
20A ROY F. JONES
21A EDWARD F. MADINGER
22A ANTHONY J. METZ, III
23A RICHARD L. MILAN
24A JAMES W. PAYNE

Row B — DEMOCRAT
1B FOR PRESIDENT WALTER F. MONDALE / FOR VICE PRESIDENT GERALDINE A. FERRARO
3B FOR GOVERNOR W. WAYNE TOWNSEND / FOR LIEUTENANT GOVERNOR ANN M. DELANEY
5B GREG HAHN
6B TOM H. SCHEELE
7B HOWARD O. CAMPBELL
8B ALICE SCHLOSS
9B MAX DICKINSON
10B WILLIAM F. GROTH
11B FRED J. JACKSON
12B THOMAS M. HINSHAW
13B M. WALTER BELL
14B MARION I. BOATRIGHT
15B EDWARD W. CANTWELL
16B
17B THOMAS J. ALSIP
18B BETTY BARTEAU
19B WEBSTER L. BREWER
20B PATRICK ESTOLIA CHAVIS, III
21B MICHAEL THOMAS DUGAN, II
22B VICTOR S. PFAU
23B JOHN W. TRANBERG
24B GERALD S. ZORE

Row C — AMERICAN PARTY
1C FOR PRESIDENT DELMAR DENNIS / FOR VICE PRESIDENT TRAVES BROWNLEE
3C FOR GOVERNOR ROCKLAND R. SNYDER / FOR LIEUTENANT GOVERNOR SHIRLEY M. GEPHART
5C
6C PATTERSON
7C 8C 9C 10C 11C 12C 13C 14C 15C 16C 17C 18C 19C 20C 21C 22C 23C 24C

Row D — LIBERTARIAN PARTY
1D FOR PRESIDENT DAVID BERGLAND / FOR VICE PRESIDENT JIM LEWIS
3D FOR GOVERNOR JAMES A. RIDENOUR / FOR LIEUTENANT GOVERNOR E. BENTON TACKITT, III
5D
6D DASBACH
7D LINDA A. DILK
8D 9D 10D 11D 12D 13D 14D 15D 16D 17D 18D 19D 20D 21D 22D 23D 24D

Directions for Voting on the Voting Machine

1st. Upon entering the voting place, sign your name on the Voter's Poll List. Then go to the voting machine, take hold of the RED HANDLE of the CURTAIN LEVER and pull it to the RIGHT as far as it will go. This will close the Curtain around you and unlock the machine for voting.

2nd. At the left of the machine are the PARTY LEVERS, indicated by the party emblems and party names; the name of the Republican candidate appearing in the first or top row, with their respective ballot numbers and the letter "A." In the second row the names of the Democratic candidates appear with their respective ballot numbers and the letter "B." Other party candidates appear in the rows indicated by the respective party emblems, and each of such candidates has a number followed by the letter indicated.

Pull the lever containing the name and emblem of your party toward the Right until the Bell rings, and then let go of lever. This will turn down all the voting POINTERS in your party row.

3rd. If you wish to vote a "Straight" party ticket, leave the Pointers as they are (down), and then pull the handle of the Curtain Lever back to the left as far as it will go. This will register your vote, open the Curtain, and set the machine ready for the next voter. But if you wish to "split" your ticket, pull the lever containing the name and emblem of your party toward the Right until the Bell rings and then let go of lever. This will turn down all the voting Pointers in your party row, just the same as when voting a straight ticket, but before you pull the curtain lever to the left, turn up the Pointer over the name of each candidate you wish to cut out, and then turn down a Pointer over the name of the candidate for whom you wish to vote.

Then pull the RED HANDLE of the Curtain Lever to the left as far as it will go.

Congress-6   Senate-30   House-49

Indiana ballot.

"Punch Card" voting—another form of an Indiana ballot.

filled, candidates to be selected, and issues to decide. Political scientists today are not certain that a long ballot enhances the democratic process. They argue that a long ballot enables political machines to retain power, since voters tend to become apathetic or confused by the ballot and may simply vote a straight ticket as a result.

A **short ballot,** in contrast, contains relatively few offices to be filled by election. New Jersey and Alaska have a short ballot; others are considering it. For national elections, all ballots are short. A person votes for president and vice president, a single representative, and, in one out of three elections, a senator. Advocates of the short ballot argue that municipal, county, and state ballots should be similar to national ballots; a reduction in the number of choices presumably will increase voter participation.

Counting the Votes and Avoiding Fraud

State and local election officials tabulate the results of each election after the polls are closed. Although most votes are tallied electronically, there is still the possibility of voting fraud. To minimize this possibility, the use of canvassing boards is common. A **canvassing board** is an official body that is typically bipartisan. The canvassing boards tabulate and consolidate the returns and forward them to the state canvassing authority, which will usually certify the election of the winners within a few days. A state canvassing board often consists of ex officio members of

Short Ballot

A ballot containing relatively few offices to be filled by election. In national elections, the short ballot is used to vote for, at a maximum, four officials—the president, the vice president, a senator, and a representative. It is also used in some state elections.

Canvassing Board

An official and normally bipartisan group on a county, city, or state level that receives vote counts from every precinct in the area. The state canvassing board obtains the voting results from all local boards, tabulates the figures, and certifies the winners.

Counting the vote by hand.

Poll Watcher

An individual appointed by a political party to scrutinize the voting process on election day. Usually, there are two poll watchers at every voting place, representing the Democratic and the Republican parties, both attempting to ensure the honesty of the election.

Challenge

An allegation by a poll watcher that a potential voter is unqualified to vote or that a vote is invalid; designed to prevent fraud in elections.

Elector

The partisan slate of electors is selected early in the presidential election year by state laws and applicable political party apparatus, and the electors cast ballots for president and vice president. The number of electors in each state is equal to that state's number of representatives in both houses of Congress.

Electoral College

The constitutionally required method for the selection of the president and the vice president. To be elected president or vice president, the candidate must have a majority of the electoral votes (currently, 270 out of 538).

the state government and is usually headed by the secretary of state. Typically, the extensive coverage of election returns by the mass media makes the results known to the public before certification by canvassing boards. It is only in very close elections that the final outcome turns on the official tabulation and certification.

To avoid fraud at the polling places themselves, each party may appoint **poll watchers** to monitor elections. In virtually all polling places throughout the country during partisan elections, major parties have their own poll watchers. Poll watching is particularly important when there is a challenge to an entrenched, local political machine. At any time, a poll watcher may make a **challenge,** which is an allegation that a potential voter is either unqualified or that his or her vote is invalid. Once a challenge is made, a bipartisan group of election judges in each precinct will decide on the merits of the challenge.

Vote fraud is something regularly suspected but seldom proved. Voting in the nineteenth century, when secret ballots were rare and people had a cavalier attitude toward the open buying of votes, was probably much more conducive to fraud than modern elections are. However, stories persist in places like Cook County, Illinois, about dead people miraculously voting, people voting more than once, or opponents' votes sinking into the Chicago River. Such allegations formed part of a continuing debate over the 1960 presidential election, when John Kennedy officially defeated Richard Nixon by only 112,803 popular votes and by 303 to 219 electoral votes. Eleven states were decided by a margin of less than two percentage points. Allegations of fraud, paying off voters, and tampering with vote totals were rampant in Texas, Illinois, and New Jersey—states that were all carried narrowly by Kennedy. Most of the time for most elections, fraud is entirely absent.

The Electoral College

▽

Most voters who vote for the president and vice president think they are voting directly for a candidate. In actuality, they are voting for a slate of **electors** who will cast their ballots in the **electoral college.** Article II, Section 1, of the Constitution outlines in detail the number and choice of electors for president and vice president. The Founding Fathers wanted to avoid the selection of president and vice president by the excitable masses. Rather, they wished the choice to be made by a few supposedly dispassionate, reasonable men (but not women).

The Choice of Electors

Each state's electors are selected during each presidential election year. The selection is governed by state laws and by the applicable party apparatus (Table 10–5). After the national party convention, the electors are pledged to the candidates chosen. The total number of electors today is 538, equal to 100 senators, 435 members of the House, plus 3 electors for the District of Columbia, subsequent to the Twenty-third Amendment, ratified in 1961. Each state's number of electors equals that state's number of senators (two) plus its number of representatives (from one for Alaska, Delaware, North Dakota, South Dakota, Vermont, and Wyoming to forty-five for California.)

Table 10-5

Elector Selection Methods and Ballot Listing

State	Party Convention	Party Committee	Party Primary	Other	Electors' Names Not on Ballot	Electors' Names Appear on Ballot
Ala.	X²				X	
Alaska						X
Ariz.	X		X			X
Ark.	X				X	
Calif.				X³	X	
Colo.				X⁴	X	
Conn.	X²				X	
Del.	X²				X	
Dist. of Col.		X			X	
Fla.				X⁵	X	
Ga.	X⁶	X⁶			X	
Hawaii	X				X	
Idaho	X					X
Ill.	X				X	
Ind.	X				X	
Iowa	X				X	
Kan.	X²					X
Ky.		X¹			X	
La.		X¹				X
Maine	X				X	
Md.	X⁶	X⁶			X	
Mass.		X			X	
Mich.	X				X	
Minn.	X				X	
Miss.			X			X
Mo.	X⁶	X⁶				X
Mont.	X²				X	
Neb.	X				X	
Nev.	X				X	
N.H.	X⁷				X	
N.J.		X			X	
N.M.		X			X	
N.Y.	X²				X	
N.C.	X²				X	
N.D.	X					X
Ohio	X				X	
Okla.	X⁶				X	
Ore.	X⁶	X⁶			X	
Pa.				X⁸	X	
R.I.	X⁷					X
S.C.		X				X
S.D.	X					X
Tenn.		X¹			X	
Texas	X				X	
Utah	X⁷				X	
Vt.	X				X	
Va.	X²					X
Wash.	X⁷				X	
W.Va.	X				X	
Wis.	X				X	
Wyo.	X				X	

SOURCES: *Nomination and Election of the President and Vice President of the United States*, by Thomas M. Durbin and Michael V. Seitzinger (Washington, D.C.: U.S. Government Printing Office, 1980) and from secretaries of state. *Congressional Quarterly Weekly Report*, October 25, 1980, p. 3184.

1. State law allows parties to choose means of selecting electors. Both parties chose to use party committees.

2. State law allows parties to choose means of selecting electors. Both parties chose to use party conventions.

3. California law contains separate provisions for the methods to be used by the Democratic and Republican parties in selecting electors. Each Democratic nominee for U.S. representative and the last two Democratic nominees for U.S. senator designate an elector. Certain Republican officials are designated as electors, and the Republican State Central Committee appoints the remaining electors.

4. State law allows parties to choose means of selecting electors. The state Democratic Party chose to use the party convention method. The state Republican Party chose to have the party chairman select the electors based on recommendations of party officials.

5. In Florida, the governor officially chooses the electors. However, he must choose only those electors selected by the parties' state executive committees.

6. State law allows the parties to choose the method of selecting electors. The state Republican Party chose to use the party convention method, and the state Democratic Party chose to use the party committee method.

7. Although termed a "convention," state law designates the party officials who meet to select electors.

8. Pennsylvania law provides that the national Democratic and Republican parties' presidential nominees name their electors for Pennsylvania.

The Electors' Commitment

If a plurality of voters in a state chooses one slate of electors, then those electors are pledged to cast their ballots later in December at the state capital for the presidential and vice presidential candidates for the winning party.[13] The Constitution does not, however, require the electors to cast their ballots for the candidate of their party.

The ballots are counted and certified before a joint session of Congress early in January. The candidates who receive a majority of the electoral votes (270) are certified as president-elect and vice president-elect. According to the Constitution, in cases where no candidate receives a majority of the electoral vote, the election of the president is decided in the House from among the three highest candidates (decided by a plurality of each state delegation), each state having one vote. The selection of the vice president is determined by the Senate in a choice between the two highest candidates, each senator having one vote. Congress was required to choose the president and vice president in 1801 (Jefferson and Burr), and the House chose the president in 1825 (John Quincy Adams).

It is possible for a candidate to become president without obtaining a majority of the popular vote. There have been numerous minority presidents in our history, including Abraham Lincoln, Woodrow Wilson, Harry S. Truman, John F. Kennedy, and Richard Nixon (in 1968). Such an event can always occur when there are third-party candidates.

Perhaps more distressing is the possibility of a candidate being elected when the candidate's major opposition receives a larger popular vote. This occurred on three occasions—in the elections of John Quincy Adams in 1824, Rutherford B. Hayes in 1876, and Benjamin Harrison in 1888, all of whom won elections without obtaining a **plurality** of the vote.

Criticisms of the Electoral College

Besides the possibility of a candidate becoming president even though his or her major opponent obtains more popular votes, there are other complaints about the electoral college. The Founding Fathers' idea was to have electors use their own discretion to decide who would make the best president. But electors no longer perform the selecting function envisioned by the Founding Fathers, as they are committed to the candidate who has a plurality of votes in the general election.[14]

One can also argue that the current system, which gives all of the electoral votes to whoever has a statewide plurality, is unfair to other candidates and their supporters. The unit system of voting also means that presidential campaigning will be concentrated in those states that have the largest number of electoral votes and in those states where the outcome is likely to be close. All of the other states presumably get second-class treatment during the presidential campaign.

It can also be argued that there is something of a small-state bias in the electoral college, because including Senate seats in the electoral vote total partly offsets the big states' edge in the House. A state such as Alaska (with two senators and one

Plurality

The winning of an election by a candidate who receives more votes than any other candidate but not necessarily a majority. Most national, state, and local electoral laws provide for winning elections by a plurality vote.

"Faithless" Electors

Electors voting for candidates other than those within their parties. They are pledged, but not required by law, to vote for the candidate who has a plurality in the state.

---

[13]An exception to this winner-take-all rule is Maine, where since 1969 two electors are chosen on the basis of the statewide vote and the other two according to which party carries each congressional district.

[14]However, there have been revolts by **"faithless"** electors—in 1796, 1820, 1948, 1956, 1960, 1968, 1972, and 1976.

representative) gets an electoral vote for roughly each 71,000 people, whereas Iowa gets one vote for each 365,000 people and New York has a vote for every half-million inhabitants.

Proposed Reforms

Many proposals for reform of the electoral college system have been advanced. The most obvious is to get rid of it completely and simply to have candidates elected on a popular-vote basis; in other words, a direct election, by the people, for president and vice president. This was proposed as a constitutional amendment by President Carter in 1977, but it failed to achieve the required two-thirds majority in the Senate in a 1979 vote. An earlier effort in 1969 passed the House, but a Senate vote was blocked by senators from small states and the South.

A less radical reform is a federal law that would require each elector to vote for the candidate who has a plurality in the state. Another system would eliminate the electors but retain the electoral vote, which would be given on a proportional basis rather than on a unit basis (winner take all). This method was endorsed by President Nixon in 1969.

The major parties are not in favor of eliminating the electoral college, fearing that it would give minor parties a more influential role. Also, small states are not in favor of direct election of the president because they feel they would be over-whelmed by the large urban vote.

Near crises in the electoral vote method, such as happened with the strong third-party Wallace movement in 1968 or with the close presidential votes of 1960 and 1976, always generate support for major changes. However, such efforts at change have been made in Congress numerous times since 1797, and only the Twelfth Amendment, ratified in 1804, has succeeded.

Voting in National, State, and Local Elections
▽

In 1984, there were 174 million eligible voters. Of that number, 128 million, or 74 percent, actually registered to vote in the general presidential elections. Of those who registered, 92.6 million actually went to the polls. The participation rate during the 1984 presidential election was only 72.4 percent of registered voters and 53.2 percent of eligible voters.

Figure 10–2 shows that the **voter turnout** in the United States compared with that of other countries places Americans in the bottom 20 percent. Figure 10–3 shows voter turnout for presidential and congressional elections from 1868 to 1986. The last "good" year of turnout for the presidential elections was 1960, when almost 65 percent of the eligible voters actually voted. We can also see that voting for U.S. representatives is greatly influenced by whether there is a presidential election in the same year.

The same is true at the state level. When there is a race for governor, more participation occurs both in the general election for governor and in the election for state representatives. Voter participation rates in gubernatorial elections are also greater in presidential election years than when there is no president to choose. Table 10–6 indicates that average turnout is about 14 percentage points higher when a presidential election is held. The figures for Arkansas, New Hampshire,

Voter Turnout

The percentage of citizens taking part in the election process; the number of eligible voters that actually "turn out" on election day to cast their ballot.

Figure 10–2

Voter Turnout in the United States Compared with Other Countries

SOURCE: David Glass, Peverill Squire, and Raymond Wolfinger, "Voter Turnout: An International Comparison," *Public Opinion*, December/January 1984, p. 50.

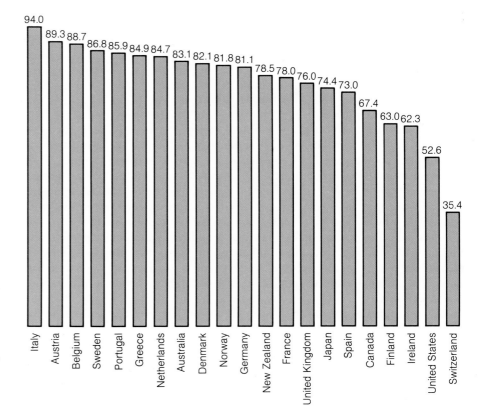

Data as of 1981

Figure 10–3

Voter Turnout for Presidential and Congressional Elections, 1868–1986

SOURCES: Historical Data Archive, Inter-university Consortium for Political and Social Research; U.S. Bureau of the Census, *Statistical Abstract of the United States: 1980*, 101st ed. (Washington, D.C.: U.S. Government Printing Office, 1980), p. 515; William H. Flanigan and Nancy H. Zingale, *Political Behavior of the American Electorate*, 5th ed. (Boston: Allyn and Bacon, 1983), p. 20.

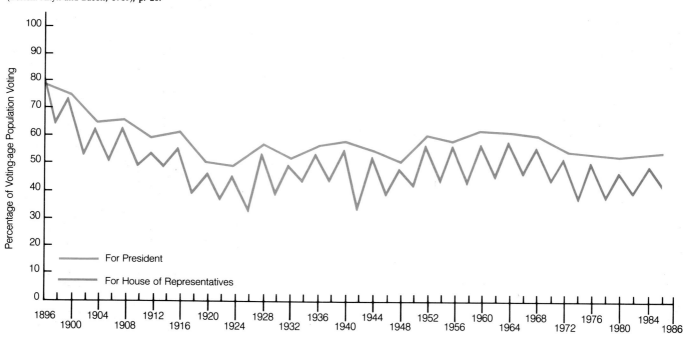

Table 10–6

▽

Voter Participation Rates in Gubernatorial Elections

State	Percentage of Eligible Voting Population Who Actually Voted		State	Percentage of Eligible Voting Population Who Actually Voted	
	Presidential Year (1980)	Nonpresidential Year (1982, unless specified)		Presidential Year (1980)	Nonpresidential Year (1982, unless specified)
Alabama		38.2	Montana	64.5	
Alaska		58.9	Nebraska		47.4
Arizona		35.4	Nevada		35.6
Arkansas	51.5	48.1	New Hampshire	57.2	40.6
California		42.1	New Jersey		42.8**
Colorado		41.7	New Mexico		43.4
Connecticut		44.9	New York		39.0
Delaware	52.1		North Carolina	43.3	
Florida		32.4	North Dakota	64.6	
Georgia		38.9	Ohio		42.6
Hawaii		43.6	Oklahoma		38.1
Idaho		49.3	Oregon		50.4
Illinois		41.6	Pennsylvania		40.8
Indiana	56.1		Rhode Island	57.2	43.3
Iowa		49.1	South Carolina		29.1
Kansas		42.8	South Dakota		57.5
Kentucky		36.9*	Tennessee		36.6
Louisiana		49.7*	Texas		28.7
Maine		54.5	Utah	64.1	
Maryland		35.0	Vermont	56.9	44.1
Massachusetts		46.3	Virginia		36.2**
Michigan		45.7	Washington	57.1	
Minnesota		56.5	West Virginia	53.2	
Mississippi		37.7*	Wisconsin		45.2
Missouri	58.4		Wyoming		47.5
			Average Turnout	56.6	42.6

*1979 election; turnout based on 1978 electorate.
**1981 election; turnout based on 1980 electorate.

Rhode Island, and Vermont—all of which had gubernatorial elections both in 1980 and 1982—clearly show the presidential election impact on the gubernatorial election in the same state.

Now consider local elections. In races for mayor, city council, county auditor, and the like, it is fairly common for only 25 percent or less of the electorate to vote. Is something amiss here? It seems obvious that people would be more likely to vote in elections that directly affect them. At the local level, each person's vote counts more (because there are fewer voters) and the issues—crime control, school bonds, sewer bonds, and so on—touch the immediate interests of the voters. The facts, however, do not fit the theory. Potential voters are most interested in national elections when a presidential choice is involved. Otherwise, voter participation in our representative government is very, very low (and as we have seen, it is not overwhelmingly great even at the presidential level).

The top twenty-five metropolitan areas in the United States today account for more than one-third of all the ballots cast in presidential elections. In most past elections, the Democratic presidential candidates drew large percentages of this urban vote. But between 1976 and 1984, this vote shifted away from the Democratic candidates. In 1976, Democrat Jimmy Carter got more than half of the vote in seventeen of the twenty-five biggest metropolitan areas. In 1984, Republican Ronald Reagan got more than 50 percent of the vote in twenty of the twenty-five. In the 1984 election, votes cast in seventeen of these areas contributed half

or more of the total votes cast in fourteen states plus the District of Columbia. Those fourteen states plus Washington, D.C., contain 243 electoral college votes, only 27 votes less than the 270 necessary to win a presidential election.

These figures mean that the vote in the twenty-five largest metropolitan areas of the U.S. is crucial to winning the plurality of electors in states with the electoral college votes needed to win the presidency. As we noted, the urban-metropolitan vote has been crucial for Democratic party presidential victories. John F. Kennedy in 1960 carried Illinois by only 8,858 votes,

giving him that state's electoral college votes for his presidential victory. Kennedy's almost 200,000 vote edge in Chicago was decisive here. Although the shift away from Democratic candidates has favored Republican presidential aspirants, the same has not been true for other offices: These metro areas have sent twice as many Democrats as Republicans to the U.S. House of Representatives and have elected five times as many Democratic mayors. The urban vote in the 1988 presidential election may tell us whether the shift toward the Republicans is permanent or simply a part of the Reagan phenomenon.

The Effect of Low Voter Turnout

Representative Democratic Government
A democracy in which representatives are empowered by the people to act on behalf of those represented.

There are two schools of thought concerning low voter turnout. Some view the decline in voter participation as a clear threat to our **representative democratic government**. Fewer and fewer individuals are actually deciding who wields political power in our society. Also, low voter participation presumably signals apathy about our political system in general. It also may signal that potential voters simply do not want to take the time to learn about the issues involved. When only a handful of people do take the time, it will be easier, say the alarmists, for an authoritarian figure to take over our government.

Others are less concerned about low voter participation. They believe that a decline in voter participation simply indicates there is more satisfaction with the status quo. Also, they believe that representative democracy is a reality even if a very small percentage of eligible voters vote. If everyone who does not vote believes the outcome of the election will accord with his or her own desires, then representative democracy is working. The nonvoters are obtaining the type of government—with the type of people running it—that they want to have anyway. It has further been suggested that declining voter participation, rather than spelling alarm for the future of American democracy, may really reflect a better-informed voting public. According to political scientists William H. Flanigan and Nancy H. Zingale,

> The high rate of turnout in the nineteenth century may not have resulted from political involvement by an interested, well-informed electorate, but on the contrary it may have

been possible at all only because of low levels of information and interest. During the last half of the nineteenth century, a largely uninformed electorate was aroused to vote by means of extreme and emotional political appeals. . . . [B]y and large, the parties manipulated the electorate—a manipulation possible because the electorate was not well informed.[15]

Factors Influencing Who Votes

A clear association exists between voting and the following characteristics: age, educational attainment, minority status, income level, and the existence of two-party competition.

1. *Age.* Look at Table 10–7 where we show the breakdown of voter participation by age group for the 1984 presidential election. It would appear from these figures that age is a strong factor in determining voter turnout on election day. The reported turnout increases as the age groups become older until the sixty-five-and-over category, where there is a very slight decline. Greater participation with age is very likely due to the fact that older voters are more settled in their lives, are already registered, and have had more time to experience voting as an expected activity.

2. *Educational attainment.* Education also influences voter turnout. In general, the more education you have, the more likely you are to vote. This pattern is clearly evident in the 1984 election results, as we can see in Table 10–8. Reported turnout is 30 percentage points higher for those who have a college education than it is for people who have never been to high school.

3. *Minority status and income level.* Race is important, too, in determining the level of voter turnout. Whites in 1984 voted at a 61 percent rate, whereas the black turnout rate was 56 percent. Differences in income can also lead to differences in voter turnout. Wealthier people tend to be overrepresented in the electorate. In 1984, turnout among whites varied from less than 40 percent of those with annual

[15]*Political Behavior of the American Electorate*, 5th ed. (Boston: Allyn and Bacon, 1983), p. 9.

Table 10–7

▽

Voting in the 1984 Presidential Election by Age Group (in percent)

Age	Reported Turnout
18–24	41
25–44	58
45–64	70
65 and over	68

SOURCE: Bureau of the Census, reported in *National Journal*, Feb. 2, 1985.

Table 10–8

▽

Voting in the 1984 Presidential Election by Education Level (in percent)

Years of School Completed	Reported Turnout
8 years or less	42.9
9–11 years	44.4
12 years	58.7
More than 12 years	71.5

SOURCE: Polsby and Wildavsky, *Presidential Elections* (New York: Charles Scribners' Sons, 1984), p. 29.

Young voters learning to use the voting machine.

Table 10–9

▽

1982 Voting Turnout and State Party
Competition (in percent)

	Average Turnout
Democratic dominant	42.3
Democratic majority	47.5
Competitive two-party	54.1
Republican majority	55.0

SOURCE: *Congressional Quarterly Weekly Report*
41, no. 35 (September 3, 1983), pp. 1771–1871.
Data calculated by U.S. Census Bureau.

Rational Ignorance Effect

When people purposefully and rationally
decide not to become informed on an issue because they realize that their vote
on the issue is not likely to be the deciding one; a lack of incentive to seek the
necessary information to cast an intelligent vote.

family incomes under $5,000 to about 70 percent for people whose annual family incomes were $50,000 and over.

4. Two-party competition. Another factor in voter turnout is the extent to which elections are competitive within a state. Table 10–9 shows the percentage of the electorate voting in 1982—when local rather than national presidential issues tended to predominate—according to the degree of competition in state elections. More competitive states generally have higher turnout rates, although the highest average percentage turnout is for the states that for the past two decades were the most Republican in state elections.

The foregoing statistics reinforce one another. For example, rich, white, educated, more elderly Minnesotans vote more often than poor, nonwhite, uneducated, young people in Texas.

Why Citizens Do Not Vote: The Rational Ignorance Effect

Less than 50 percent of the American electorate can correctly identify the names of their members of Congress. Even fewer are able to name their state representatives, and still fewer can tell where their representatives—either state or national—stand on various issues. It should not be surprising then that the number of nonvoters in our society is so great. To understand why, we must understand the incentives confronting the potential voter. If citizens act as if they believe their vote will not affect the outcome of an election, then they have little incentive to seek the information they need to cast an intelligent vote. The lack of incentive to obtain costly information (in terms of time, attention, and so on) about politicians and political issues has been called the **rational ignorance effect.** That term may seem internally contradictory, but it is not. Rational ignorance involves purposefully and rationally deciding *not* to obtain information—to remain ignorant.

Consider an example of the rationally ignorant farmer. One of the most important factors determining farming profitability is the weather. Does that mean each farmer should become a meteorologist to understand the weather? No. Even if the farmer understands weather, he or she cannot easily avoid its adverse effects. So the farmer might choose to be rationally ignorant about what determines the weather. So too the average voter may decide to remain rationally ignorant about political issues, which she or he feels cannot be affected by knowledge anyway.

If average voters choose to remain rationally ignorant, what determines how they vote when they do vote? According to the rational ignorance theory, voters will simply rely on information that is supplied by candidates and by the mass media. Bits of information picked up from TV news and political advertising, as well as information gleaned from casual conversations with coworkers and friends, will be used as a basis for making a choice among candidates. Few voters will take the time to examine the issues and assess a candidate's likely handling of them. In any event, even those who attempt to find out about issues will have a difficult time.

Since there is such a low probability that an individual's vote will make a difference, it is understandable why voter turnout is so low. The personal payoffs are low. After all, the probability that a single vote will be decisive is almost zero. Why then do even one-third to one-half of U.S. citizens bother to show up at the polls? One explanation is that most citizens receive personal satisfaction from the act of voting. It makes them feel that they are good citizens and that they are doing something patriotic. But that feeling is not overriding. Even among voters who are

On Voting Choices

For the most part, political party identification is the strongest influence on how people vote. Particularly in state and local elections, when voters may have little information about the candidates for some lower offices, party is the cue that the voter seeks. In national elections for president and for congressional seats, the evidence suggests that party is important, but that other sorts of judgments also come into play. After all, since World War II, Republicans have won the White House in six out of ten elections even though they were the minority party. The question that intrigues political scientists is: What factors convince a large proportion of independents and some Democrats to vote for Republican candidates?

If we look at elections over time, one trend becomes evident. The state of the economy influences the outcome of national elections. When the economy is strong, inflation under moderate control, and employment on the upswing, the incumbent president and his party are likely to do well. If the economy is faltering, it is likely that voters will replace the incumbent. President Carter suffered this fate in 1980, whereas President Reagan rode to victory in 1984 on economic good times.

The most straightforward explanation of this phenomenon is called "pocketbook voting," where voters rely on their personal economic experiences as a guide to voting. If no economic crises have struck the family, if jobs are secure, if the economic prospects for the household look good, then voters have no need of much political information to make their voting decisions. The homemaker learns about the record of the incumbent at the grocery store; the wage earner sees it in his or her paycheck. When personal economic fortunes change for the worse—unemployment, high inflation, housing shortages—citizens can easily decide to vote against the party in power. This explanation fits well with our knowledge of most people's relative disinterest in politics.

An alternative explanation has been offered by several political scientists, most notably Donald Kinder and D. Roderick Kiewiet. They looked at the evidence of pocketbook voting using data from polls and concluded that the situation is more complicated than simply personal economic well-being determining voter decisions. They found that even among individuals who said their economic future was not hopeful or who had suffered some reverses, there was no evidence of voting the incumbent out if the *overall* economy was good. Only if a member of the household had lost a job did pocketbook voting occur.

Kinder and Kiewiet claim that most citizens vote according to "sociotropic politics." By this they mean that people make a judgment about the nation's overall economic well-being, rather than their own personal fortunes, and vote for the good of the nation. They may be acting out of largely altruistic motives or they may be projecting their own futures. If the nation does well, eventually they or their children will benefit. Most people do not assign credit or blame for their own personal situation to the incumbent. They see, for example, that factory closings in their town may be the responsibility of management or due to other conditions. Voters make their decisions in national elections based on the larger picture of the nation's health, a picture that the media have a major role in interpreting.

SOURCES: Donald R. Kinder and D. Roderick Kiewiet, "Sociotropic Politics: The American Case," in Richard G. Niemi and Herbert F. Weisberg, eds., *Controversies in Voting Behavior*, 2d ed. (Washington, D.C.: Congressional Quarterly Press, 1984).

registered and who plan to vote, if the cost of voting goes up (in time and convenience), the number of eligible voters will fall. In particular, bad weather on election day means on average a smaller percentage of eligible voters at the polls.

Legal Restrictions on Voting
▽

Legal restrictions on voter registration have existed since the founding of the nation. Most groups in the United States have been involved in the suffrage issue at one time or another.

Franchise

The legal right to vote, extended to blacks by the Fifteenth Amendment, to women by the Nineteenth Amendment, and to people age eighteen and over by the Twenty-sixth Amendment.

Historical Restrictions

In colonial times, only white males with a certain minimum value of property were eligible to vote, leaving the far greater number of Americans ineligible to take part in the democratic process. Since many of government's functions are in the economic sphere and concern property rights and the distribution of income and wealth, the Founding Fathers felt it was appropriate that only people who had an interest in property should vote on these issues. The idea of extending the vote to all citizens was, according to South Carolina delegate Charles Pinckney, merely "theoretical nonsense." Of paramount concern to the backers of the Constitution was that the government should be as insulated as possible from the shifting electoral will of the population. A restricted vote meant a more stable government. An unrestricted vote would result, as Elbridge Gerry of Massachusetts declared at the Constitutional Convention, in "the evils . . . [which] flow from the excess of democracy."

The logic behind this restriction of the **franchise** to property owners was seriously questioned by Thomas Paine in his pamphlet *Common Sense*:

> Here is a man who today owns a jackass, and the jackass is worth $60. Today the man is a voter and goes to the polls and deposits his vote. Tomorrow the jackass dies. The next day the man comes to vote without his jackass and cannot vote at all. Now tell me, which was the voter, the man or the jackass?[16]

It wasn't until the Jacksonian era of the 1830s that the common man (but not woman) began to be heralded as the backbone of democracy. Men without property

[16]Thomas Paine, *Common Sense* (London: H. D. Symonds, 1792), p. 28.

A black citizen registers to vote.

were first given the right to vote in the western states, but by about 1850, most adult males in virtually all the states could vote without any property qualification. North Carolina was the last state to eliminate its property test for voting—in 1856.

Extension of the franchise to black males occurred with the passage of the Fifteenth Amendment in 1870. This enfranchisement was short-lived, however, as the "redemption" of the South by white racists rolled back these gains by the end of the century. As discussed in Chapter 5, only in the 1960s were blacks, both male and female, able to participate in large numbers in the electoral process. Women received full national voting rights with the Nineteenth Amendment in 1920. The most recent extension of the franchise occurred when the voting age was reduced to eighteen by the Twenty-sixth Amendment in 1971.

Current Eligibility and Registration Requirements

Voting requires **registration,** and registration requires satisfying voter qualifications, or legal requirements. These requirements are the following: (1) citizenship, (2) age (eighteen or older), and (3) residence—the duration varying widely from state to state and with types of elections. In addition, most states disqualify mental incompetents, prison inmates, convicted felons, and election law violators.

Each state has different qualifications for voting and registration. In every state except North Dakota, registration must take place before voting. Also, many states still require a personal appearance at an official building during normal working hours to register.[17] In general, a person must register well in advance of an election, although voters in Maine, Minnesota, Oregon, and Wisconsin are allowed to register up to and on election day.

Some argue that these registration requirements are responsible for much of the nonparticipation in our political process. One study[18] showed that they reduce

Registration
The entry of a person's name onto the list of eligible voters for elections. Registration requires meeting certain legal requirements such as age, citizenship, and residency.

[17]Twenty states now allow registration by postcard, however.

[18]Raymond E. Wolfinger and Steven J. Rosenstone, "The Effect of Registration Laws on Voter Turnout," *American Political Science Review*, 72 (March 1978), pp. 22–48.

Registering 18-year-old voters.

national voter turnout by about 9 percent. Certainly, since their introduction in the late nineteenth century, registration laws have had the effect of reducing the voting participation of blacks and immigrants.

The question arises as to whether registration is really necessary. If it decreases participation in the political process, perhaps it should be dropped altogether. Still, as those in favor of registration requirements argue, such requirements may prevent fraudulent voting practices, such as multiple voting or voting by noncitizens.

Determinants of Voter Choice

▽

Political scientists and survey researchers have collected much information about voting behavior. This information sheds some light on which people vote and why people decide to vote for particular candidates. We have already discussed factors influencing voter turnout. Generally, the factors that influence voting decisions can be divided into two groups: socioeconomic and demographic factors, and psychological factors.

Socioeconomic and Demographic Factors

Socioeconomic Status

A category of people within a society who have similar levels of income and similar types of occupations.

The socioeconomic and demographic factors include, but are not limited to, the following: (1) education, (2) income and **socioeconomic status,** (3) religion, (4) ethnic background, (5) sex, (6) age, and (7) geographic region. These influences all reflect the voter's personal background and place in society. Some have to do with the family into which a person is born: race, religion (for most people), and ethnic background. Others may be the result of choices made throughout an individual's life: place of residence, educational achievement, or profession. It is also clear that many of these factors are related. People who have more education are likely to have higher incomes and to hold professional jobs. Similarly, children born into wealthier families are far more likely to have completed college than children from poorer families. Furthermore, some of these demographic factors relate to the psychological factors—as we shall see.

Education

More education seems to be highly correlated with voting Republican. Those who leave school earlier rather than later tend to vote Democratic. As can be seen in Table 10–10, 53 percent of college graduates voted for Reagan in the 1980 election and only 35 percent voted for Carter. About the same percentages characterized the 1968 election between Humphrey and Nixon. The relationship is not invariable, however. In 1964, college graduates voted 52 percent for Democrat Johnson and 48 percent for Republican Goldwater. Typically, those with less education are more inclined to vote for the Democratic nominee. In 1984, Mondale received 43 percent and Reagan 57 percent of the vote from high school graduates, whereas those with only a grade-school education voted 51 percent for Mondale and 49 percent for Reagan.

Income and Socioeconomic Class

If we measure socioeconomic class by profession, then professionals and business-persons, as well as white-collar workers, tend to vote Republican. Manual laborers, factory workers, and especially union members are more likely to vote Democratic. The effects of income are much the same: The higher the income, the more likely it is that a person will vote Republican. Conversely, a much larger percentage of low-income individuals vote Democratic. But there are no hard and fast rules. There are some very poor individuals who are devoted Republicans just as there are some extremely wealthy supporters of the Democratic party. In some recent elections, the traditional pattern did not hold. In 1980, for example, many blue-collar Democrats voted for Ronald Reagan.

Religion

In the United States, Protestants have traditionally voted Republican and Catholics and Jews have voted Democratic. Like the other patterns discussed, however, these too are somewhat fluid. Nixon obtained 52 percent of the Catholic vote in 1972, and Johnson won 55 percent of the Protestant vote in 1964. The Catholic vote was evenly split between Carter and Reagan in 1980, but went heavily for Reagan in 1984. As had been the pattern in the past, Republican candidate Reagan obtained more votes from Protestants than did the Democratic candidates Carter and Mondale.

Ethnic Background

Traditionally, the Irish have voted for Democrats. So too have Slavs, Poles, and Italians. However, Anglo-Saxon and northern European ethnic groups have voted for Republican presidential candidates. These patterns were disrupted in 1980 when Reagan obtained much of his support from several of the traditionally Democratic ethnic groups, with the help of fundamentalist religious groups.

Blacks voted principally Republican until Roosevelt's New Deal. Since then they have largely identified with the Democratic party. Indeed, the Democratic presidential candidates have received, on average, more than 80 percent of the black vote since 1956.

Sex

Until recently, there seemed to have been no fixed pattern of voter preference by sex in presidential elections. One year more women than men would vote for the Democratic candidate; another year more men than women would do so. Some political analysts believe that a "gender gap" became a major determinant of voter decision making in the 1980 presidential election. Ronald Reagan obtained 15 percentage points more than Carter among male voters, whereas women gave about an equal number of votes to each candidate. Polls continued to show greater approval ratings of Reagan among men than women. Several reasons have been advanced for this gender gap, including Reagan's refusal to endorse the Equal Rights Amendment, his aggressive promilitary stance (one study indicates that women are less likely than men to favor military action[19]), the "feminization" of families living in poverty, and the increasing number of women in the work force. In 1984, the gender gap amounted to 9 percent nationally with 64 percent of male voters casting their ballots for Ronald Reagan and 55 percent of the female voters doing the same. The gender gap appeared most strongly in the East, where the difference in support for Mr. Reagan was 10 percent.

[19]Sandra Baxter and Marjorie Lansing, *Women in Politics: The Invisible Majority* (Ann Arbor: University of Michigan Press, 1980), p. 57.

Table 10–10
▽

Vote by Groups in Presidential Elections Since 1956 (in percent)

	1956		1960		1964		1968			1972	
	Stevenson	Ike	JFK	Nixon	LBJ	Goldwater	Humphrey	Nixon	Wallace	McGovern	Nixon
NATIONAL	42.2	57.8	50.1	49.9	61.3	38.7	43.0	43.4	13.6	38	62
SEX											
Male	45	55	52	48	60	40	41	43	16	37	63
Female	39	61	49	51	62	38	45	43	12	38	62
RACE											
White	41	59	49	51	59	41	38	47	15	32	68
Nonwhite	61	39	68	32	94	6	85	12	3	87	13
EDUCATION											
College	31	69	39	61	52	48	37	54	9	37	63
High school	42	58	52	48	62	38	42	43	15	34	66
Grade school	50	50	55	45	66	34	52	33	15	49	51
OCCUPATION											
Professional and business	32	68	42	58	54	46	34	56	10	31	69
White collar	37	63	48	52	57	43	41	47	12	36	64
Manual	50	50	60	40	71	29	50	35	15	43	57
AGE											
Under 30 years	43	57	54	46	64	36	47	38	15	48	52
30–49 years	45	55	54	46	63	37	44	41	15	33	67
50 years and older	39	61	46	54	59	41	41	47	12	36	64
RELIGION											
Protestants	37	63	38	62	55	45	35	49	16	30	70
Catholics	51	49	78	22	76	24	59	33	8	48	52
POLITICS											
Republicans	4	96	5	95	20	80	9	86	5	5	95
Democrats	85	15	84	16	87	13	74	12	14	67	33
Independents	30	70	43	57	56	44	31	44	25	31	69
REGION											
East	40	60	53	47	68	32	50	43	7	42	58
Midwest	41	59	48	52	61	39	44	47	9	40	60
South	49	51	51	49	52	48	31	36	33	29	71
West	43	57	49	51	60	40	44	49	7	41	59
MEMBERS OF LABOR UNION FAMILIES	57	43	65	35	73	27	56	29	15	46	54

Age

Age clearly seems to relate to an individual's voting behavior. Younger voters tend to vote Democratic; older voters tend to vote Republican. It was only the voters under thirty who clearly favored Carter during the Carter-Reagan election in 1980. This trend was reversed in 1984 when voters under thirty voted heavily for Ronald Reagan.

Geographic Region

As we noted earlier, the formerly Solid (Democratic) South has crumbled. In 1972, Republican Nixon obtained 71 percent of the southern vote, whereas McGovern only obtained 29 percent. Reagan drew 52 percent of the southern vote in 1980 and 58 in 1984.

Democrats still draw much of their strength from large northern and eastern cities. Rural areas tend to be Republican (and conservative) throughout the country

Table 10–10

▽

Continued

	1976			1980			1984	
	Carter	Ford	McCarthy	Carter	Reagan	Anderson	Mondale	Reagan
NATIONAL	50	48	1	41	51	7	41	59
SEX								
Male	53	45	1	38	53	7	36	64
Female	48	51	*	44	49	6	45	55
RACE								
White	46	52	1	36	56	7	34	66
Nonwhite	85	15	*	86	10	2	87	13
EDUCATION								
College	42	55	2	35	53	10	39	61
High school	54	46	*	43	51	5	43	57
Grade school	58	41	1	54	42	3	51	49
OCCUPATION								
Professional and	42	56	1	33	55	10	34	66
business	50	48	2	40	51	9	47	53
White collar	58	41	1	48	46	5	46	54
Manual								
AGE								
Under 30 years	53	45	1	47	41	11	40	60
30–49 years	48	49	2	38	52	8	40	60
50 years and older	52	48	*	41	54	4	41	59
RELIGION								
Protestants	46	53	*	39	54	6	39	61
Catholics	57	42	1	46	47	6	39	61
POLITICS								
Republicans	9	91	*	8	86	5	4	96
Democrats	82	18	*	69	26	4	79	21
Independents	38	57	4	29	55	14	33	67
REGION								
East	51	47	1	43	47	9	46	54
Midwest	48	50	1	41	51	7	42	58
South	54	45	*	44	52	3	37	63
West	46	51	1	35	54	9	40	60
MEMBERS OF LABOR UNION FAMILIES	63	36	1	50	43	5	52	48

*Less than 1 percent.

Note: 1976 and 1980 results do not include vote for minor party candidates.

SOURCE: *The Gallup Report*, November 1984, p. 32.

except in the South, where the vote still tends to be heavily Democratic. On average, the West has voted Republican in presidential elections. Except for the 1964 election between Goldwater and Johnson, the Republicans have held the edge in western states in every presidential election since 1956.

Psychological Factors

In addition to socioeconomic and demographic explanations for the way people vote, there are at least three important psychological factors, which are rooted in attitudes and beliefs held by voters. These are (1) party identification, (2) perception of the candidates, and (3) issue preferences.

"Good God! He's giving the white-collar voters' speech to the blue collars."

Drawing by Joseph Farris; © 1984 The New Yorker Magazine, Inc.

Party Identification

With the possible exception of race, party identification has been the most important determinant of voting behavior in national elections. As we pointed out in Chapter 7, party affiliation is influenced by family and peer groups, by age, and by psychological attachment. During the 1950s, independent voters were a little more than 20 percent of the eligible electorate. In the middle to late 1960s, however, party identification began to weaken, and by the 1970s independent voters had become roughly 30 percent of all voters. In 1984, the estimated proportion of independent voters was 32 percent. Independent voting seems to be most concentrated among new voters, particularly among new young voters. Thus we can still say that party identification for established voters is a major determinant in voter choice.

Perception of the Candidates

Another psychological factor, candidate image, seems to be important in a voter's choice for president. We do not know as much about the effect of candidate image as we do about party identification, however, because it is difficult to make systematic comparisons of candidate appeal over time. The evidence is mixed. Data compiled by Warren Miller and others[20] show some important differences in the strength of this factor on voter choice from one election to the next. These researchers found that perceptions of *both* candidates were positive in 1952, 1960, and 1976, whereas in 1956 Eisenhower's image was highly favorable and Stevenson's was neutral. In 1964, very positive ratings for Johnson contrasted with very negative perceptions of Goldwater. Nixon's positive 1968 and 1972 ratings allowed him to defeat his negatively evaluated opponents. In 1980, both Reagan and Carter had negative images. The researchers also determined that, except in 1964 and 1976, Republican candidates were evaluated more favorably by the voters than were the Democratic candidates. To some extent, voter attitudes toward candidates are based on emotions (such as trust) rather than on any judgment about experience or policy.

Issue Preferences

Issues make a difference in presidential and congressional elections. Although personality or image factors may be very persuasive, most voters have some notion of how the candidates differ on basic issues or at least know that they want a change in the direction of government policy. In recent elections, the most important issue areas have been foreign policy, economic policy, and social or life-style issues. Other types of issues that may become extremely important include corruption—personal or governmental—the size of government, civil rights, and social welfare issues.

FOREIGN POLICY ISSUES.   Foreign policy issues have been at the forefront of presidential (and to a lesser extent congressional) campaigns for most of our history.

Both the Republicans and the Democrats have attempted to label each other as the party of war (although the Democrats have had the misfortune of being in office more often when the United States has gone to war). Johnson's use of the

[20]Warren E. Miller, Arthur H. Miller, and Edward J. Schneider, *American National Election Studies Data Sourcebook* (Cambridge, Mass.: Harvard University Press, 1980), pp. 127, 129; Center for Political Studies 1980 National Election Study.

Did You Know?
▽
That, in 1962, Representative Clem Miller, a California Democrat, successfully defended his congressional seat against challenger Don Clausen despite the fact that Miller had died more than a month earlier in a plane crash?

U.S. policy toward terrorism becomes an election issue.

Scenes such as this one of the Iranian hostages were broadcast almost nightly on T.V. and had a disastrous affect on President Carter's reelection campaign in 1980.

Medicare

A health insurance program enacted in 1965 as an amendment to the Social Security Act to provide medical care for the elderly.

daisy commercial is an example of this kind of labeling. In the 1980 election, Carter used ads that described himself as the "peacemaker" and that were illustrated by scenes from the Egyptian-Israeli peace meetings at Camp David.

In the 1984 general election campaign, Mr. Mondale tried to focus attention on Mr. Reagan's "failures" in foreign policy, charging that the Reagan administration was the only one in recent decades that had made no progress toward arms negotiations. The Mondale campaign also used ads to attack the "Star Wars" weapon system proposed by Reagan. However, the majority of voters seemed to feel that the president was more likely to keep the United States out of war.

ECONOMIC ISSUES.   When push comes to shove, bread-and-butter issues seem to determine most voters' preferences. When the economy is doing well, it is much more difficult for a challenger to win over an incumbent. Conversely, when unemployment and/or inflation is high, the contender has a major set of bread-and-butter issues that he or she can use effectively when campaigning.

Democratic campaigns tend to emphasize the social benefits that Democratic administrations have brought to the American people. After all, was it not under Franklin Roosevelt (a Democrat) that we obtained Social Security and unemployment insurance? Was it not under President Lyndon Johnson (another Democrat) that we obtained **Medicare?** The facts speak for themselves: The Democrats have been the party of social reform and social legislation. To the extent that there is less unemployment and less inflation, the issues of income security matter less to most voters. Therefore, the Republicans will usually fare better during an election year if the economy is doing well when they are in power.

SOCIAL ISSUES.   In the last decade, a number of issues have come to be labeled social or life-style issues. As the United States has changed from a traditional family society to one of single parent households, easy divorces, and new living arrangements, a number of groups have been formed to reverse these trends. The Moral Majority was the most vocal of the conservative politico-religious interest groups that support traditional cultural values—the family, the role of women as homemakers, antihomosexuality, antiabortion, and prayer in the public schools. For most political candidates, these issues are difficult to deal with because they regard them as matters of individual conscience, not public policy. No matter what stand a candidate takes, she or he is likely to offend some voter, and since these are moral issues or questions of faith, it is not possible to suggest a compromise. Fundamentalist political groups like the Moral Majority and the National Conservative Political Action Committee (NCPAC) worked to defeat certain liberal senators and representatives by backing candidates who campaigned primarily on social issues rather than on economic or foreign policy questions.

CORRUPTION, WASTE, AND BIG GOVERNMENT.   All candidates seem equal in their ability to find scandal in the background of their opponents. One of the greatest scandals of American presidential campaigning, the Watergate affair, had no effect on the 1972 campaign when it occurred, although it cost Richard Nixon the presidency two years later and led to the defeat of many Republican members of Congress in the 1974 midterm elections.

Government waste has been a campaign issue off and on, although not a major one. On occasion, the party in power will be accused of promoting waste and inefficiency or a government agency may be attacked for procurement decisions. In an interesting political tactic, Senator William Roth of Delaware held a press conference in December 1983 to display his office Christmas tree. It was decorated with parts and small tools purchased by the Defense Department at horrendous cost. Roth claimed that some tools that cost less than $1 in the local hardware store were ordered regularly by the Defense Department at hundreds of dollars each.[21]

In the last several presidential elections, the issue of big government has been highly visible. Reagan especially argued in favor of making the federal government smaller by returning to the states some of the powers that had been acquired by the federal government and by reducing the amount of federal regulation of the business sector. There is no doubt that government has grown enormously since World War II. Since 1978, more than one-third of the **gross national product (GNP)** goes to federal, state and local governments—although much of that is returned to individuals in the form of **transfer payments** (Social Security, unemployment insurance, and welfare). What is interesting, of course, is that what may be a campaign issue may not square with reality after election. In Reagan's case, his anti-big government views were not translated into effective action once in office. In 1980, the federal government's share of GNP was 22.4 percent. By 1984, it was more than 25 percent.

All candidates try to set themselves apart from their opposition on the crucial issues for that election. What is more difficult to ascertain is the relative importance of issues in determining how voters choose one candidate over another. In other words, how much **issue voting** actually occurs? Political scientists do not entirely agree on the answer. Some research has shown that issue voting was important in 1964, 1968, and 1972, and again became moderately important in 1980.

Gross National Product (GNP)
The total market value of all final goods and services produced by the entire economy in a one-year period.

Transfer Payments
Money payments that are made by governments to individuals for which no services or goods are concurrently rendered. Examples are Social Security, unemployment insurance, and welfare payments.

Issue Voting
Voting for a candidate based on how he or she stands on a particular issue.

Elections and Campaigns: A State of Constant Change
▽

Like the field of microcomputers, the field of campaigns and elections is constantly changing and developing. The reforms in the primary and convention systems placed more power in the hands of the ordinary citizen, although the result—the extended primary and caucus system—may be too long, give too much power to the media, and not produce better candidates after all. The news media and advertising are forces that exert great influence on political campaigns. As new techniques to persuade people to buy soap are invented, they surely will be applied to political candidates. As the competition between the networks and cable TV continues to build, the political campaigns will become more like sporting events whose coverage places a premium on sensation and climax. As advertising rates, commercial production, and polling become more expensive, the need for campaign funds will grow. These trends suggest that political campaigning will become more lavish and exhausting than ever before.

On the plus side, if more people become interested in politics and motivated to turn out on election day partly because of media influence, democracy in the United States will be enhanced. There is, however, evidence in Jesse Jackson's presidential campaign that the ideas and symbols of politics are more important than the extravagances. Black turnout in the 1984 primaries set records throughout the nation, and the Reverend Jackson campaigned without television advertising and on a lower campaign budget than anyone had considered possible. Black voters were motivated by the possibility of a black presidential nominee and by the way in which Jackson spoke to their interests. Such a campaign suggests that high technology and high finance are not always essential to the democratic process.

[21]*New York Times*, December 20, 1983, B, p. 8.

In nearly every state, before you are allowed to cast a vote in an election, you must first register. Specific registration laws vary considerably from state to state, and, depending on how difficult state laws make it to register, some states have much higher rates of registration and voting participation than do others.

What do you have to do to register and cast a vote? Most states require that you meet minimum residence requirements. In other words, you must have lived in the state in which you plan to be registered for a specified period of time. You may retain your previous registration, if any, in another state and you can cast an absentee vote if your previous state permits that. The minimum residency requirement is very short in some states, such as one day in Alabama or ten days in New Hampshire and Wisconsin, but in other states, as much as fifty days (in Arizona or Tennessee) must elapse before you can vote. Other states with voter residency requirements have minimum-day requirements in between these extremes. Twenty states do not have any minimum residency requirement at all.

Nearly every state also specifies a closing date by which you must be registered before an election. In other words, even if you have met a residency requirement, you still may not be able to vote if you register too close to the day of the election. The closing date deadline is different in certain states (Connecticut, Delaware, and Louisiana) for primary elections than for other elections. The closing date for registration varies from election day itself (Maine, Minnesota, Oregon, and Wisconsin) up to fifty days (Arizona). Delaware specifies the third Saturday in October as the closing date.

Keep in mind too that in most states your registration can be revoked if you do not vote within a certain number of years. This process of automatically "purging" the voter registration lists of nonactive voters happens every two years in about a dozen states, every three years in Georgia, every four years in more than twenty other states, every five years in Maryland and Rhode Island, every eight years in North Carolina, and every ten years in Michigan. Ten states do not require this purging at all.

What you must do to register and remain registered to vote varies from state to state and even from county to county within a state. In general, you must be a citizen of the United States, at least eighteen years old on or before election day, and a resident of the state in which you intend to register. Using Iowa as an example, you would normally register through the local county auditor. If you move to a new address within the state, you must also change your registration to vote by contacting the auditor. Postcard registrations must be postmarked or delivered to the county auditor no later than the twenty-fifth day before an election. Party affiliation may be changed or declared when you register or reregister, or you may change or declare a party at the polls on election day. Postcard registration forms in Iowa are available at many public buildings, from labor unions, at political party headquarters, at the county auditor's office, or from campus groups. Mobile registrars may be made available by calling your party headquarters or your county auditor.

For more information on voting registration, you should contact your county or state officials, party headquarters, labor union, or your local chapter of the League of Women Voters.

Chapter Summary

1. People may choose to run for political office to further their careers, to carry out specific political programs, or in response to certain issues or events. Others are recruited by political parties, interest groups, close friends, or family.

2. The legal qualifications for holding political office are minimal at both the state and local levels, but most segments of the population do not run for office. Holders of political office are predominantly white and male and are likely to be from the professional class.

3. American political campaigns are lengthy and extremely expensive. In the last decade, they have changed from being party-centered to being candidate-centered in response to technological innovations and decreasing party identification.

4. Candidates have begun to rely less on the party and more on paid professional consultants to perform the various tasks necessary to wage a political campaign. The first person hired is a campaign director who then decides how to accomplish the tasks of financing the campaign, gaining maximum media coverage, scheduling campaign events, recruiting assistants for fieldwork, and conducting research.

5. The crucial task of professional political consultants is image building.

6. The campaign organization devises a campaign strategy to maximize the candidate's chances of winning. Whether to emphasize style or substance is a strategic issue.

7. Candidates use public opinion polls to gauge their popularity and to test the mood of the country.

8. The amount of money spent in financing campaigns is steadily increasing. There have been a variety of Corrupt Practices Acts designed to regulate campaign finance. The Federal Election Campaign Acts of 1972 and 1974 instituted major reforms by limiting spending and contributions. Incumbents have benefited from this legislation.

9. The 1974 act, as amended in 1976, allows corporations, labor unions, and interest groups to set up political action committees (PACs) to raise money for candidates.

10. After the 1968 Democratic convention, the McGovern-Fraser Commission was appointed to study the problems of the primary system. They formulated new rules, which were also adopted by Republicans in many states. These reforms opened up the nomination process for the presidency to all voters.

11. The primary campaign must follow two strategies. First, primaries must be won state by state within the party. Second, after the national convention and the nomination of one person to carry the party standard, candidates must appeal not only to the party faithful but also to independent voters and to those from the opposing party.

12. A presidential primary is a statewide election to help a political party determine its presidential nominee at the national convention. Almost two-thirds of the states and the District of Columbia have some form of primary. Other states use the caucus method of choosing convention delegates.

13. Different types of presidential primaries include the closed primary, the open primary, the blanket primary, and the run-off primary. Some argue for a single, nationwide presidential primary election to replace the state-by-state system.

14. Delegates from each state, apportioned on the basis of state representation, are sent to the national convention. A credentials committee determines which delegates may participate.

15. The United States uses the Australian ballot, a secret ballot that is prepared, distributed, and counted by government officials.

16. The office-block ballot groups candidates according to office. The party-column ballot groups candidates according to party labels and symbols. The typical state and local ballot is a long ballot, which contains a large number of elective offices to be filled. The short ballot, in contrast, contains relatively few offices.

17. To minimize the possibility of voting fraud, the use of a canvassing board to tabulate and certify election returns is common. Each party often appoints poll watchers who may make a challenge if a voter is unqualified or if his or her vote appears invalid.

18. In making a presidential choice on election day, the voter technically does not vote directly for a candidate but chooses between slates of presidential electors. The slate that wins the most popular votes throughout the state gets to cast all the electoral votes for the state. The candidate receiving the majority of the electoral votes (270) wins.

19. It is possible for a candidate to become president without obtaining a majority of the popular vote.

20. Both the mechanics and the politics of the electoral college have been sharply criticized. There are many proposed reforms, including a direct election where candidates are elected on a popular-vote basis.

21. Voter participation in the United States is low (and declining) compared with that of other countries. Some view the decline in voter turnout as a threat to representative democracy, whereas others believe it simply indicates greater satisfaction with the status quo.

22. There is an association between nonvoting and a person's age, education, minority status, and income level. Another factor is the extent to which elections are competitive within a state.

23. Citizens may purposefully and rationally decide not to seek the necessary information they need to cast an intelligent vote because the information is too costly to obtain (in terms

of time, attention, and so on); they may rely instead on information supplied by candidates and through the mass media. Citizens may decide not to vote because they realize that any one person's vote will not make a difference.

24. In colonial times, only white males with a certain minimum amount of property were eligible to vote. The suffrage issue has involved, at one time or another, most groups in the United States.

25. Current voter eligibility requires registration, citizenship, and specified age and residence requirements. Each state has different qualifications. It is argued that these requirements are responsible for much of the nonparticipation in the political process in the United States.

26. Socioeconomic or demographic factors that influence voting decisions include (a) education, (b) income and socioeconomic class, (c) religion, (d) ethnic background, (e) sex, (f) age, and (g) geographic region.

27. Psychological factors that influence voting decisions include (a) party identification, (b) perception of candidates, and (c) issue preferences.

Questions for Review and Discussion
▽

1. Think about the U.S. senators from your own state. How did each begin in politics? To what extent are they "self-starters?" Did either of your senators hold political office before running for the national legislature? What are the major sources of support and campaign funding for each of the senators?

2. What factors have led to the replacement of the old-time politician or political boss by the modern political consultant? Why do such consultants only work for candidates with similar political philosophies as their own? How might this sharing of viewpoints weaken a campaign plan?

3. Suppose you were going to run for election on the Democratic ticket in your community. What demographic groups in the population would you try to recruit as supporters and voters?

4. What is the relationship between the primary elections in the states and the national convention of the political party? Who are the delegates to the national convention and whom do they represent?

5. How would our elections change if we abolished the electoral college and the electoral vote, and held a national popular election for president instead?

Selected References
▽

Paul R. Abramson, John H. Aldrich, and David W. Rohde, *Change and Continuity in the 1984 Elections* (Washington, D.C.: Congressional Quarterly Press, 1986). Past election results and public opinion surveys over the last four decades are used to put the putative realignment of 1984 in perspective. A detailed, timely investigation of what happened in 1984 and what it may mean for the future.

M. Margaret Conway, *Political Participation in the United States* (Washington, D.C.: Congressional Quarterly Press, 1985). The nature and extent of participation in American politics. Factors examined include citizens' life experiences, their psychological orientations to politics, the political environment, the legal context in which participation occurs, and the decision process by which citizens evaluate the costs and benefits of participation.

Everett Carll Ladd, *Where Have All the Voters Gone: The Fracturing of America's Political Parties*, 2d ed. (New York: W. W. Norton, 1982). The "unmaking" of the Republican party, the divisions within the Democratic party, the perils of party reform, Reagan's "brittle mandate," and the prospects for a Republican revival in the 1980s.

Gerald Pomper, with colleagues, *The Election of 1984: Reports and Interpretations* (Chatham, N.J.: Chatham House, 1985). An examination of the 1984 elections from several perspectives—the nomination struggle, issues in the campaign, the presidential election, public opinion, the congressional elections, what Reagan's second term may produce, and the meaning of the election.

Stephen A. Salmore and Barbara G. Salmore, *Candidates, Parties, and Campaigns: Electoral Politics in America* (Washington, D.C.: Congressional Quarterly Press, 1985). Identifies the central characteristics of successful and unsuccessful campaigns and discusses the challenges to the role of the political parties and how the parties have responded.

Chapter 11
▽
Interest Groups

Contents
▽
The Role of Interest Groups
Major Interest Groups
Interest Group Strategies
Regulating Lobbyists
Why Interest Groups Have So Much Power

What If . . .

Interest Groups' Campaign Spending Were Limited to $1.00 Per Member?

This appears to be a period of American political history when money is truly the mother's milk of politics. The 1980 congressional and presidential campaigns cost more than half a billion dollars. The rise of Political Action Committees (PACs) has opened the floodgates for money flowing into campaigns. By 1984, on the average, 30 percent of a Senate candidate's expenses came from PACs. Concern over the impact of money on politics, especially the argument that those politicians receiving the money return the favor, has led to a search for solutions.

What if groups were limited to spending only $1 for each member of the organization on political campaign contributions? Would the role of money in American politics change in dramatic ways? What would be some of the consequences of such a policy?

To begin with, lobby groups would probably begin an aggressive campaign to increase their membership. They would hire even more specialists in membership and fund raising. Today, even though Americans readily join organizations, it is safe to say that most of us simply rely on groups to which we do not belong but with whose objectives we agree to represent us. We may send a few dollars when

asked, but we do not necessarily join formally.

Second, as a result of formal membership in special interest organizations, we would be bombarded with newsletters, telephone polls, and invitations to rallies and demonstrations. Thus Americans would likely be encouraged to become more militant and active in single-issue groups.

Third, the strengths of interest groups traditionally are evaluated by the nature of the group. Mass membership groups have their large numbers as a resource. They can write millions of letters, threaten to vote for the opposition candidate, march in protest, and in other ways make themselves felt in numbers. Other groups that do not have large numbers can use superior organization and money to press for their interests. A strict $1 per member limit on contributions to political campaigns would obviously shift the balance in favor of those organizations with mass memberships.

In 1987, here are some of the immediate consequences of such a campaign contribution provision.

In the area of economic affairs, the AFL-CIO would be permitted to spend $13 million on politics, but the National Association of Manufacturers would be limited to $14,000.

On the very politicized issue of right to life versus freedom of choice, the National Right to Life organization could spend $12 million, while the National Abortion Rights Action League would be confined to $115,000.

In the area of gun control, the National Rifle Association would spend roughly $3 million, whereas the combined gun control lobby groups, National Coalition to Ban Handguns and Handgun Control, Inc., could only spend $300,000.

We can imagine that some groups and individuals would be tempted to inflate the numbers in their ranks. If the history of voting fraud and the growth of PACs are any lesson, monitoring, compliance, and enforcement of the dollar rule would quickly become a nightmare. The Federal Election Commission

(FEC), charged with monitoring election finances, would not only have to check campaign contributions of interest groups against their stated membership numbers but would also have to spot check membership rosters to verify the existence of persons claimed on the lists.

It is quite likely that numerous scandals would erupt as groups were found to have listed names from the telephone directory or a local graveyard on their official membership lists and then spent a dollar on campaigns for each. We would also expect a massive proliferation of new interest groups, some legitimate, but many of them simply cloned from existing organizations and consisting of almost the identical members.

Thus the $1 a member campaign finance reform effort would, in all probability, not significantly reduce the role of money in American politics.

▽

Interest groups are a long-established phenomenon in American politics, operating at the national, state, and local level. What this example illustrates is the way in which such groups might adapt in response to regulations and restrictions. Given the structure of American government, it is inevitable that interests will find a way to be represented.

The Role of Interest Groups

▽

Contrary to the expectations of most political analysts, Congress passed a massive tax reform bill in 1986, an election year. Like other tax bills which have gone before, this piece of legislation was a major source of concern for interest groups representing many sectors of American life. Lobbyists and staff members for interest groups spent long hours waiting outside the committee rooms for a chance to talk to the legislators as they left the meetings. Among the groups which were vitally interested in the legislation were the bankers, stock-brokers, oil and timber interests, professionals, farmers, real estate investors, and state and local governments.

By early summer, it was clear that the bill would emerge from committee with strong bipartisan support. There had been few opportunities for interest groups to influence committee decisions. The groups would have to decide a strategy for lobbying on the floor of Congress. Observers who watch such activities said that the size and complexity of the proposed reforms made the usual coalitions among interest groups hard to form. Some groups, like the American Bankers Association, decided to support the Senate bill unchanged, rather than joining mutual funds groups in opposing changes in Individual Retirement Account (IRA) provisions.

About 150 other groups formed an alliance, calling its organization the 15/27/33 Coalition. This acronym stood for the proposed new tax rate structure. This huge alliance included such diverse groups as Aetna Life insurance, small businesses, and numerous women's groups. All agreed that the proposed measure was a "fair" bill and that the balance of tax rates should not be altered.

Among the groups which lobbied intensively for changes in the bill were representatives of the securities industry, the real estate industry, and elected officials of states and cities. The most successful lobbying group during the summer of 1986 had to be the state and local government officials. The original bill proposed that the deduction of state and local property and sales taxes be abolished. State officials protested strongly that this would be an unfair burden on taxpayers whose states had high property or sales taxes. The final bill kept the deduction for property taxes but eliminated it for sales taxes.

Although the tax reform bill escaped without major changes to benefit special interests, many industries or corporations were aided by the "transition" rules. These 682 rules, which were written into the law to ease the transition from the old law to the new, were buried in the bill. Among the 47 corporations which received rules with a net value of $20 million or more were United Telecom of Kansas City ($234 million savings in taxes), John Deere ($212 million), and Chrysler Corporation ($78 million). These rules, however, provide one-time benefits for specific corporations, not permanent loopholes for entire groups.[1]

What Is an Interest Group?

We have already used the term **interest group,** also called pressure group and sometimes lobby, but have not yet explicitly defined it. We may define this kind of group as follows:

> An interest group is any organized group whose members share common objectives. An interest group actively attempts to influence government policy makers through direct and indirect methods, including the marshaling of public opinion, lobbying members of Congress, and electioneering. Interest groups work to persuade decision makers in all three branches of government.

[1]*Congressional Quarterly Weekly Report*, September 27, 1986, p. 2256.

Interest Group
An organized group of individuals sharing common objectives who actively attempt to influence government policy makers through direct and indirect methods, including the marshaling of public opinion, lobbying, and electioneering.

▽

How Widespread Are Interest Groups?

Alexis de Tocqueville observed in 1834 that "in no country of the world has the principle of association been more successfully used or applied to a greater multitude of objectives than in America."[2] But de Tocqueville could probably not have conceived of the more than 100,000 associations currently existing in the United States in the 1980s. It is estimated that about two-thirds of the U.S. population is formally associated with some type of group. Of course, the majority of these 100,000 groups do not strictly fit our definition of an interest group because they are not actively seeking to change or influence government policy. But we can be sure that the purpose of the roughly 1,200 organizations whose names begin with the word *National* listed in the Washington, D.C., telephone directory is to do just this. To this list, we can add many of the 600 organizations listed in the D.C. telephone directory whose first word is *American* or *Americans*. According to Norman J. Ornstein and Shirley Elder,[3] well over 10,000 separate groups exist for the purpose of influencing government policies.

Alexis de Tocqueville

Major Interest Groups
▽

Three of the most influential types of interest groups in the United States are business, agriculture, and labor. In terms of the amount of campaign funds provided by interest groups, we must add another category—the professional group, particularly the American Medical Association. Also to this list we must add public interest groups and public employee groups. There are also ethnic groups, conservation groups, and organizations to support almost any other cause, as Table 11–1 indicates.

Business Interest Groups

There are thousands of trade organizations, but most of them are quite ineffective in influencing legislation and administrative regulations. Big business pressure groups that are consistently effective number only three: (1) the National Association of Manufacturers, (2) the United States Chamber of Commerce, and (3) the Business Roundtable.

The National Association of Manufacturers (NAM)

The annual budget of the NAM is more than $8 million, which it collects in dues from about 14,000 relatively large corporations. Organized in Cincinnati in 1895 as a predominantly small business association, the NAM became during the Depression of the 1930s primarily a proponent of the interests of large corporations. Of particular interest to the NAM is legislation that affects labor laws, minimum wage rates, corporate taxes, and trade regulations. The NAM's Washington national headquarters staff numbers about one hundred, of whom a dozen are full-time lobbyists.

[2]*Democracy in America*, vol 1, ed. Phillips Bradley (New York: Alfred A. Knopf, 1980), p. 191.

[3]*Interest Groups, Lobbying and Policymaking* (Washington, D.C.: Congressional Quarterly Press, 1978), p. 23.

Table 11–1

▽

Selected Interest Groups Registered as Lobbyists

Bankamerica Corp., BankAmerica Center, San Francisco, Calif. Filed for self 11/28/83. Legislative interest—Not specified. Lobbyist—Nancy Camm, 1800 K St. NW, Washington, D.C. 20006.

Continental Airlines, Houston, Texas. Lobbyist—Akin, Gump, Strauss, Hauer & Feld, 1333 New Hampshire Ave. NW, Washington, D.C. 20036. Filed 11/1/83. Legislative interest—Not specified.

Muckleshoot Indian Tribe, Washington, D.C. Lobbyist—SENSE Inc., 1010 Vermont Ave. NW, Washington, D.C. 20005. Filed 11/28/83. Legislative interest—". . . HR 336. . . ."

Hughes Helicopters Inc., Culver City, Calif. Lobbyist—Andrews & Kurth, 1747 Pennsylvania Ave. NW, Washington, D.C. 20006. Filed 11/18/83. Legislative interest—"Tax legislation."

International Association of Psycho-social Rehabilitation Services, McLean, Va. Lobbyist—Washington Alternatives Inc., 1702 Woodman Drive, McLean, Va. 22101. Filed 12/5/83. Legislative interest—"Mental health legislation impacting on chronically mentally ill adults. Disability legislation, HR 4170/S 467. Appropriations for National Institute of Mental Health. Fair Housing Act."

National Association of Black Owned Broadcasters, Washington, D.C. Lobbyist—James L. Winston, 1730 M St. NW, Washington, D.C. 20036. Filed 12/1/83. Legislative interest—"Amendments to the Communications Act and related legislation."

Distilled Spirits Council of the U.S. Inc., Washington, D.C. Lobbyist—Palumbo & Cerrell Inc., 11 Dupont Circle NW, Washington, D.C. 20036. Filed 11/21/83. Legislative interest— "HR 3870."

Morality in Media Inc., 475 Riverside Drive, New York, N.Y. 10115. Filed for self 11/28/83. Legislative interest—"Effective and constitutional Federal Obscenity legislation . . . S 2136; S 2172 . . . S 2572 . . . S 66 . . . S 57 . . . HR 2106 . . . S 1469 . . . HR 3635. . . ." Lobbyists—Morton A. Hill, Paul J. McGeade, Evelyn Dukovic, Christopher M. Beermann.

U.S. Tobacco Co., 100 W. Putnam Ave., Greenwich, Conn. 06830. Filed for self 11/23/83. Legislative interest—"All legislation that could affect our industry; HR 4114 and S 2162, Employees Stock Ownership Assistance Acts." Lobbyist—Keith Rogers.

American Chamber of Commerce in Germany, Frankfurt, Federal Republic of Germany. Lobbyist—Squire, Sanders & Dempsey, 1201 Pennsylvania Ave. NW, Washington, D.C. 20004. Filed 11/16/83. Legislative interest—". . . HR 1234, S 144, S 414. . . ."

American College of Neuropsycho-Pharmacology, Nashville, Tenn. Lobbyist—Perito, Duerk, Carlson & Pinco, 1140 Connecticut Ave. NW, Washington, D.C. 20036. Filed 11/7/83. Legislative interest—"Legislation supporting biomedical research."

Carolinas Cotton-Growers Association, Raleigh, N.C. Lobbyist— Neal A. Jackson, 1156 15th St. NW, Washington, D.C. 20005. Filed 11/18/83. Legislative interest—"Supporting legislation to permit employer to file judicial claim against USDA for cotton misgrading (S 2067)."

Lockheed Air Terminals Inc., Burbank, Calif. Lobbyist—Morrison & Foerster, 1920 N St. NW, Washington, D.C. 20036. Filed 11/10/83. Legislative interest—". . . Tax Reform Act of 1983 and related tax legislation."

Texas Instruments Inc., 13500 North Central Expressway, Dallas, Texas 75243. Filed for self 11/29/83. Legislative interest—"Matters affecting conduct of business, including but not limited to: Taxation, telecommunications, Defense, Trade, energy, and government relations." Lobbyist—Gary Howell, 1745 Jefferson Davis Highway, Arlington, Va. 22202.

Mitchell Energy & Development Corp., Washington, D.C., and Woodlands, Texas. Lobbyist—Foreman & Dyess, 1920 N St. NW, Washington, D.C. 20036. Filed 11/17/83. Legislative interest— "Natural gas including S 1715 and HR 4722." Lobbyist—Daniel A. Dutko, 412 First St. SE, Washington, D.C. 20003. Filed 11/21/83. Legislative interest—". . . oil and gas matters."

Montana Power Co., Butte, Mont. Lobbyist—James A. Rock, 1730 M St. NW, Washington, D.C. 20036. Filed 11/11/83. Legislative interest—". . . includes but is not limited to . . . Internal Revenue Code, Atomic Energy Act, Federal Power Act, Rural Electrification Act, Reclamation Acts, Flood Control Act, Appropriations Acts, Rivers and Harbors and Flood Control Authorization Acts, Federal Water Pollution Control Act, Clean Air Act, Occupational Health and Safety, Equal Employment Opportunity Act, Employee Retirement Income Security Act, Wild and Scenic Rivers Act, National Energy Act."

Rollins Environmental Services, Wilmington, Del. Lobbyist— O'Connor & Hannan, 1919 Pennsylvania Ave. NW, Washington, D.C. 20006. Filed 11/14/83. Legislative interest—Not specified.

National Association of Personnel Consultants, Alexandria, Va. Lobbyist—Luman & Schoor, 1050 17th St. NW, Washington, D.C. 20036. Filed 11/23/83. Legislative interest—". . . General interest in all matters affecting national employment laws and their impact on the personnel consulting industry. . . . Specific interest in the immigration reform legislation (HR 1510 and S 529)— Support."

The National Organization for Women, Washington, D.C. Lobbyist—Eleanor Smeal and Associates, 2600 Virginia Ave. NW, Washington, D.C. 20037. Filed 11/10/83. Legislative interest— "For the Equal Rights Amendment, H J Res."

Committee for Private Education, Washington, D.C. Lobbyist— Shaw, Pittman, Potts & Trowbridge, 1800 M St. NW, Washington, D.C. 20036. Filed 11/9/83. Legislative interest— "Support tuition tax credit legislation including S 528."

Shipbuilders Council of America, 1110 Vermont Ave. NW, Washington, D.C. 20005. Filed for self 11/11/83. Legislative interest—"Maritime legislation, tax law related thereto, naval shipbuilding, government procurement regulations, maritime related labor, health and environmental." Lobbyist—W. Patrick Morris.

United Federation of Police, Hawthorne, N.Y. Lobbyist—Robert D. Gordon, 117 C St. SE, Washington, D.C. 20003. Filed 12/5/83. Legislative interest—". . . affecting law enforcement."

SOURCE: *Congressional Quarterly Weekly Report*, February 18, 1984, pp. 328–334; March 24, 1984, pp. 678–680.

The U.S. Chamber of Commerce

Sometimes called the National Chamber, this special interest organization represents more than 100,000 businesses. Dues from its members, which include upward of 3,500 local chambers of commerce, approach $30 million a year. In 1977, the National Chamber started the National Chamber Litigation Center—a public interest law firm, having the express purpose of countering what they regarded as antibusiness public interest law firms, one of which was started by Ralph Nader, champion of consumer interests. The National Chamber also organized Citizens' Choice in 1976. The latter is a pressure group specifically designed to influence public opinion against high taxes and "increasing government interference" with individual lives. Citizens' Choice also lobbies in the halls of Congress.

Business Roundtable

Two hundred of the largest corporations in the United States send their chief executive officers to the Business Roundtable. This organization is based in New York, but it does its lobbying in Washington, D.C. Established in 1972, the Roundtable was designed to provide a more aggressive view of business interests in general, cutting across specific industries. Dues paid by the member corporations are determined by the companies' wealth. Roundtable members include American Telephone and Telegraph, General Motors, USX Corporation, and International Business Machines. The Roundtable was instrumental in opposing common-site picketing legislation, the proposed Consumer Protection Agency, automobile emissions standards, and industrial pollution control.

Lobbyists at a reception in Washington.

The Roundtable is considered to be a particularly effective organization because of the high status of its members—the chief executives and presidents of giant corporations. Their strategy is to visit or call legislators in person rather than sending lesser-known lobbyists. Legislators, like most ordinary citizens, tend to be impressed by a personal call from the president of Xerox Corporation, for example.

Other Business-Oriented Pressure Groups

The National Federation of Independent Business represents close to three-quarters of a million small business owners. By taking regular polls of its members, it is able to report their opinion to members of Congress. Also active in lobbying for policy changes that will benefit small business is the National Small Business Association, representing about 45,000 members.

Agricultural Pressure Groups

American farmers and their workers represent only about 3 percent of the United States population. In spite of this, farmers' influence on legislation beneficial to their interests has been enormous. In 1986, American farmers received more than $35 billion in direct and indirect subsidies from the federal government. Farm programs designed to keep farm incomes high involve price supports, target prices, soil conservation, and myriad other policies. Farmers have succeeded in their aims through very strong interest groups. The American Farm Bureau Federation, established in 1919, has three million members. It was instrumental in getting government guarantees of "fair" prices during the Depression in the 1930s.[4] In principle, the Federation, controlled by wealthier farmers, is no longer in favor of government price supports. These farmers, who are engaged in large-scale farming, do not need government price supports to compete effectively.

[4]The Agricultural Adjustment Act of 1933 (declared unconstitutional) was replaced by the 1937 Agricultural Adjustment Act and later changed and amended several times.

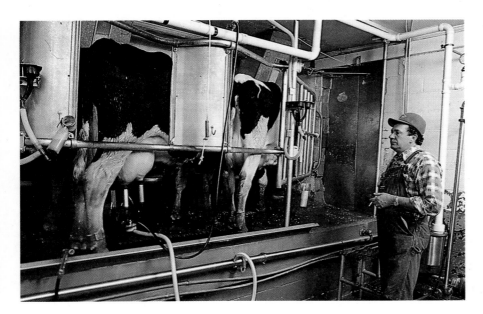

Dairy farmers are one of the best organized agricultural groups.

Highlight
▽
Honey and Money

Between 1982 and 1984, the U.S. Department of Agriculture bought more than 215 million pounds of honey. In 1984 alone, it donated 7 million pounds each month to schools and food programs for low-income families. This program cost $60 million in 1983 and roughly $75 million in 1984. If continued, the program will cost $160 million between 1986 and 1989.

Honey is only one of many agricultural commodities that are supported by federal programs to producers. For nearly forty years (since the 1949 farm bill), the U.S. government has offered price supports to encourage beekeepers to produce honey. In a nutshell, the program consists of loans from the federal government to farmers. When the market price of honey is attractive, farmers sell and repay the loans. Beginning in 1981, however, world honey prices were below the federally guaranteed price, and honey producers began to settle their loans by letting their product go to the government.

In addition to ensuring an abundant supply of honey, the federal program also helps keep up the bee population in the United States, which is ex-

tremely important in assuring the proper pollination of more than one hundred agricultural crops such as apples and oranges. More recently, the distribution of surplus honey has also contributed to the nutrition of low-income people receiving periodic allotments.

On the negative side, the program is costly. Moreover, high domestic support prices and a strong dollar have made U.S. honey far more expensive than imported honey, creating a trade disadvantage and in the long run possibly driving most American beekeepers out of business. Much of the honey now consumed in the United States is imported from China, Mexico, Canada, and Argentina.

On the other hand, it has been estimated that an end to the honey program itself would drive half of the 1,700 commercial beekeepers (there are, all told, 211,700 beekeepers but most do it as a hobby) out of business. At the same time, honey prices would come down by as much as 25 percent.

When the honey subsidy program finally comes to an end, it will affect mostly large producers. For example, a General Accounting Office study in 1985 titled "Federal Price Support for Honey Should Be Phased Out" indicates that one honey producer in North Dakota produced 2.5 million pounds in 1982 and received roughly $1.5 million from the federal government for his product.

Another important agricultural special interest organization is the National Farmers' Union. The NFU was founded in 1902 and claims a membership of more than a quarter of a million today. The oldest farm lobby organization is the National Grange, founded in 1867. With a membership of more than half a million, it finds it support among New England, Middle Atlantic, and, to a lesser extent, Pacific dairy farmers. It champions basically the same causes as the National Farmers' Union, such as higher agricultural support prices.

Labor Interest Groups

Pressure groups representing the **labor movement** date back to at least 1886 with the formation of the American Federation of Labor (AFL). In 1955, the AFL joined

Labor Movement
In general, the term refers to the full range of economic and political expression of working-class interests; politically, it describes the organization of working-class interests.

▽

Strikers outside the Hormel plant in Austin, Minnesota.

forces with the Congress of Industrial Organizations (CIO), and today the combined AFL-CIO is an enormous union with a membership exceeding 15 million workers. In a sense the AFL-CIO is a union of unions. Its political arm is the Committee on Political Education (COPE), which cooperates with the CIO **Political Action Committee (PAC)** and the AFL League for Political Education. COPE's activities are funded by voluntary contributions from trade union members.

COPE has been active in state and national campaigns since 1956. In principle, it is used to educate workers and the general public on issues and candidates of interest to labor. Some critics of COPE allege that trade union members are pressured into making contributions to the organization. Other critics claim that its "education" is simply partisan political propaganda favorable to the Democratic party. The AFL-CIO through COPE has established policies on issues such as Social Security, housing, and health insurance.

Other unions are also active politically. One of the most widely known of these is the International Brotherhood of Teamsters, which was led by Jimmy Hoffa until his expulsion in 1967 because of alleged ties with organized crime. The Teamsters Union was initially established in 1903 and today has a membership of three million and an annual budget of $73 million.

Another independent union is the United Auto Workers, founded in 1935. It now has a membership of 1.5 million with an annual budget of $217 million. Also very active in labor lobbying is the United Mine Workers (UMW) union, representing about 200,000 members.

Political Action Committees (PACs)

Committees set up by and representing corporations, labor unions, or special interest groups; PACs raise and give campaign donations on behalf of the organizations or groups they represent.

Profile

▽

Lane Kirkland

In January 1985, Lane Kirkland stated in a message to American teachers and students,

> What we would most like in Mr. Reagan's second term is an effort to breathe life into the Pledge of Allegiance to the Flag so that this country shall become, in truth, "one nation . . . with liberty and justice for all"—including working people, the young, the old, the sick, and the disadvantaged, and not exclusively those who hold the greatest economic and political power.

With these comments, the president of the AFL-CIO, the largest labor confederation in the country, reasserted the traditional liberal and labor position on justice and economic opportunity.

Kirkland was born in Camden, South Carolina. His father was a cotton buyer and his great-great-grandfather (Thomas Jefferson Withers) was a southern leader in the secession and represented South Carolina in the Confederate Senate. Lane joined the merchant marine in 1940, and after a year entered and later graduated from the Merchant Marine Academy. He joined the AFL-CIO as a researcher in 1948, and gradually worked his way up to executive assistant to union president

"I'm not interested in a candidate who's charming and appealing but is empty of principles or of positions that, in our view, reflect the hopes and aspirations of working people."

George Meany. He was Meany's handpicked successor and was elected president in 1979.

Kirkland differs from the typical image of a hard-talking, blunt, working-class leader such as his predecessor George Meany. He has been called "a southern aristocrat," a leader who uses his inside connections and close friendship with business leaders as a tool for representing unions rather than the

confrontational style more commonly associated with labor unions. He collects Egyptian artifacts and modern art, and likes jazz, gardening, and archeology.

Although he is a Democrat and a liberal on economic matters and civil rights, Kirkland is a strong anticommunist and has been a supporter of increased defense spending. He is a cofounder (1976) of the Committee on the Present Danger, which has advocated increased defense spending. He has also supported legislation to reduce low-priced, foreign imports and thus to protect domestic jobs. This activism on international matters (he has recently been deeply involved in opposing the Reagan policy in Central America) is a reflection of his belief that international affairs should not be left to "a tight incestuous breed of economists and diplomats."

Clearly, however, Kirkland's most pressing challenge is to revive the U.S. labor movement. This is a period when U.S. business must contend with much lower labor costs of overseas competitors. So-called "union bashing," wage and benefit concessions, and a decline in blue-collar jobs have all combined to test the leadership and creativity of labor leaders such as Kirkland.

Labor group pressure on Congress has been only partly successful. Although unions successfully allied themselves with civil rights groups in the 1960s, they lost on such issues as the Taft-Hartley Act of 1948, which put some limits on the right to strike and the right to organize workers. They were also frustrated in their efforts in 1975 and in 1977 to enact a bill designed to facilitate the picketing of construction sites.

The role of unions in American society has declined in recent years, witnessed by a decline in union membership from 1945 to the present (Figure 11–1). The strength of union membership traditionally lay with blue-collar workers. But in the age of automation and with the rise of the **service sector**, blue-collar workers in basic industries (autos, steel, and the like) represent a smaller and smaller

Service Sector

That sector of the economy that provides services—such as food services, insurance, and education—in contrast to that sector of the economy that produces goods.

▽

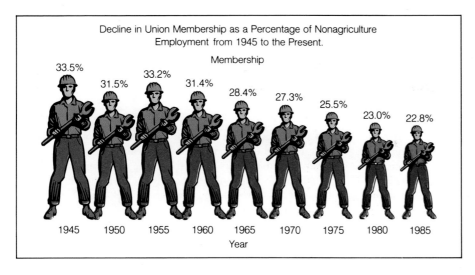

Decline in Union Membership as a Percentage of Nonagriculture Employment from 1945 to the Present.

percentage of the total working population. Because of this decline in the industrial sector of the economy, national unions are looking to nontraditional areas for their membership, including migrant farm workers, service workers, and most recently public employees—such as police and fire-fighting personnel and teachers, including college professors.

Public Employee Pressure Groups

The degree of unionization in the private sector has declined slightly since 1965, but there has been spectacular growth in the unionization of public employees. Membership in the three largest unions of government employees rose almost 40 percent from 1960 to 1984. Table 11–2 shows the number of members in the three largest public employee unions, which grew more than 600 percent from 1960 to 1984.

Both the American Federation of State, County, and Municipal Employees and the American Federation of Teachers are members of the AFL-CIO's Public Employee Department. Originally, the public employee unions started out as social and professional organizations. Today, they have become quite militant and are

Table 11–2
▽
The Growth in Public Employee Unionism

Union Name	1960	1980	1984
American Federation of State, County, and Municipal Employees	185,000	1,098,000	1,200,000
American Federation of Government Employees	70,000	255,000	300,000
American Federation of Teachers	56,000	551,000	580,000
Total	311,000	1,904,000	2,080,000

SOURCE: *Statistical Abstract of the United States, 1984*, p. 400.

The Logic of Collective Action

One puzzle that has fascinated political scientists is the question of why some individuals join interest groups, whereas a great many more Americans do not. Everyone has some interest that could benefit from government action. For many groups, however, those remain unorganized, or **latent interests.** Consider the women's movement. Until the 1960s, the interests of women in equal employment or equal educational opportunities had no representation. Even today, the membership of women's groups such as NOW or Women Employed is but a fraction of the women who share their goals.

It may be, according to the theory of Mancur Olson, that it is simply not rational for individuals to join most groups. His theory of collective action, first published in 1965, is controversial, but it offers an intriguing explanation for interest group membership and strength.

Olson introduces the idea of the "collective good." This concept refers to any public benefit that, if available to any member of the community, cannot be denied to any other member, whether or not he or she participated in the effort to gain the good. For example, women who regard themselves as antifeminists, or at least who would never join such an organization as NOW, still may avail themselves of equal employment opportunities although they never participated in the effort to change the laws. So equal employment is seen as a collective good.

Although collective benefits are usually thought of as coming from such public goods as clean air or the national defense, benefits are also bestowed by the government on subsets of the public. The price subsidies to dairy farmers or loans to college students are examples. Olson uses economic theory to propose that it is not rational for interested individuals to join groups that work for group benefits. In fact, it is often more rational for the individual to wait for others to procure the benefits and then share them.

Using agriculture as an example, Olson suggests that the solution to overproduction is for all farmers to cut production. The rational farmer, however, seeing that his small cutback will not really change the overall output, would be smarter to grow as much as possible so that if others cut production, prices would rise and he would profit from their actions. In the same fashion, individuals who would like government benefits will probably find it more rational to let others invest in the political effort from which they will similarly profit.

If so little incentive exists for individuals to join together, why are there thousands of interest groups lobbying in Washington? Olson's theory holds that if the contribution of an individual *will* make a difference to the effort, then it is worth it to join. Thus smaller groups, which seek benefits only for a small proportion of the population, are more likely to enroll members who will give time and money to the cause. Larger groups, which represent general public interests, like the women's movement or Common Cause, will have a difficult time getting individuals to join.

Olson's theory seems to have considerable validity. Certainly, the smaller, more cohesive groups have a larger presence in Washington than their size would warrant. Furthermore, these groups seem to have highly motivated members who will pressure their representatives to achieve their goals. If this aspect of Olson's theory is true, then smaller interests will always be overrepresented compared with the public interest.

Some larger interest groups, however, are also successful, such as the National Education Association or the AFL-CIO. Olson says that groups can increase their members by offering incentives to them. The NEA, for example, provides information, publications, insurance plans, and educational assistance to teachers. Furthermore, many organizations offer such benefits as free travel services (AAA), free admissions (to zoos, by the Audubon Society), or conventions (the American Legion). It is also true that if the cost of membership is low and the group provides other benefits, such as social opportunities, individuals may join, regardless of rational calculations. For the poorer members of the community, however, any cost of group membership is probably too high. Thus groups tend to be middle- and upper-class organizations.

Olson's theory presents complications for a democratic society. If groups that are smallest are likely to be most cohesive and determined to get benefits, the public interest may be injured. Similarly, if individuals who need the most assistance from the government—the least advantaged—are least likely to organize, policies that extend benefits to them are less likely to be promoted. For further reading on this complex and interesting theory, see Mancur Olson, *The Logic of Collective Action* (Cambridge, Mass.: Harvard University Press, 1965).

often involved in strikes. Many of these strikes are illegal because certain public employees do not have the right to strike and essentially sign a contract so stating. In August 1981, the Professional Air Traffic Controllers Organization (PATCO), in defiance of a court order, went on strike. The issues included wage levels, long hours, excess stress, insensitive Federal Aviation Administration (FAA) management, and other problems. President Reagan, convinced that public opinion was on his side, fired the strikers. Supervisors, nonstrikers, military personnel, and new trainees were rounded up to handle the jobs vacated by the terminated 16,000 air traffic controllers. On July 27, 1982, the union folded as a trustee padlocked the PATCO headquarters office. (A major irony is that PATCO was one of only a few unions to endorse Ronald Reagan's candidacy in 1980.)

Perhaps the most powerful of the pressure groups lobbying on behalf of public employees is the National Education Association, a nationwide organization of about 1.8 million administrators, teachers, and others connected with education. In principle, the aim of the NEA is to maintain and elevate the standards of the teaching profession. The association, however, is intensively involved in lobbying for increased public funding of education. The NEA sponsors regional and national conventions each year and has an extensive program of electronic media broadcasts, surveys, and the like. It is a pressure group, formed and maintained for the benefit of teachers.

Professional Pressure Groups

Numerous professional organizations exist, including the American Bar Association, the Association of General Contractors of America, the Institute of Electrical and Electronic Engineers, the Screen Actors Guild, and others. In terms of money spent on lobbying, however, one professional organization stands out head and shoulders above the rest—the American Medical Association. Founded in 1947, it is now affiliated with more than 2,000 local and state medical societies and has a total membership of 237,000 and an administrative staff of 1,000. Together with the American Dental Association, the AMA spent $3.3 million in 1982 congressional campaign contributions in its efforts to influence legislation.

The AMA's most notable, but largely unsuccessful, lobbying effort was against the enactment of Medicare, which provides health insurance coverage for the elderly. In the early 1960s, the AMA launched a national advertising campaign to convince the public that Medicare was tantamount to "socialized medicine" and that private plans would offer better protection. This indirect lobbying, combined with direct pressure on members of Congress, delayed passage of the legislation until 1965 and ensured that the bill's language would protect and enhance doctors' incomes. More recently, the AMA has lobbied against broader national health insurance coverage and stringent medical cost containment.

Public Interest Pressure Groups

Public interest is a difficult term to define because, as we noted earlier, there are many publics in our nation of more than 230 million. It is nearly impossible for one particular public policy to benefit everybody, which makes it practically impossible to define the public interest. Nonetheless, over the past few decades, a variety of legal and lobbying organizations have been formed "in the public interest."

Latent Interests
Interests that are dormant or unexpressed. The group that holds these interests has never organized nor articulated them.

Public Interest
The best interests of the collective, overall community; the national good, rather than the narrow interests of a self-serving group.

Chapter 11
Interest Groups
▽
351

Ralph Nader

The most well known and perhaps the most effective are those public interest groups organized under the leadership of consumer activist Ralph Nader.

The story of Ralph Nader's rise to the top began in the mid-1960s after the publication of his book *Unsafe at Any Speed*, a lambasting critique of General Motors' purported attempt to keep from the public detrimental information about GM's rear-engine Corvair. Partly as a result of Nader's book, Congress began to consider testimony in favor of an automobile safety bill. GM made a clumsy attempt to discredit Nader's background. Nader sued, the media exploited the story, and when GM settled out of court for several hundred thousand dollars, Nader became the recognized champion of consumer interests. Since then, Nader has turned over much of his income to the various public interest groups he has formed or sponsored. In all, there are more than fifteen national "Naderite" organizations promoting consumer interests.

Partly in response to the Nader organizations, numerous conservative public interest law firms have sprung up that are often pitted against the consumer groups in court. Some of these are the Mountain States Legal Defense Foundation, the Pacific Legal Foundation, the National Right-to-Work Legal Defense Foundation, the Washington Legal Foundation, and the Mid-Atlantic Legal Foundation.

One of the largest public interest pressure groups is Common Cause, founded in 1968, whose goal is to reorder national priorities toward "the public" and to make governmental institutions more responsive to the needs of the public. Anyone willing to pay dues of $15 a year can become a member. Members are polled regularly to obtain information about local and national issues requiring reassessment. Some of the activities of Common Cause have been: (1) helping to assure passage of the Twenty-sixth Amendment (giving eighteen-year-olds the right to vote), (2) achieving greater voter registration in all states, (3) supporting the complete withdrawal of all U.S. forces from South Vietnam, and (4) prompting legislation that would limit campaign spending.

Other public interest pressure groups are active on a wide range of issues. The goal of the League of Women Voters, founded in 1920, is to educate the public on political matters; although generally nonpartisan, it has lobbied for the Equal Rights Amendment and for government reform. The Consumer Federation of America is an alliance of about two hundred local and national organizations interested in consumer protection. The American Civil Liberties Union dates back to World War I when, under a different name, it defended draft resisters. It generally enters into legal disputes related to Bill of Rights issues.

Single-Interest Groups

In recent years, a number of interest groups have formed that are focused on one issue. Among these are the various antiabortion groups like Right To Life and the National Abortion Rights Action League. Narrowly focused groups such as these may be able to call more attention to their respective causes because they have simple and straightforward goals and because their members tend to care intensely about the issue. Thus they can easily motivate their members to contact legislators or to organize demonstrations in support of their policy goals.

Foreign Governments

Home-grown interests are not the only players in the game. Washington, D.C., is also the center for lobbying by foreign governments as well as private foreign interests. Large research and lobbying staffs are maintained by governments of the largest U.S. trading partners, such as Japan, Korea, the Philippines, and the Common Market countries. Even smaller nations such as those in the Caribbean engage lobbyists when vital legislation affecting their trade interests is considered. Frequently, these foreign interests hire ex-representatives or ex-senators to promote their positions on Capitol Hill. Figure 11–2 shows foreign lobby expenditures for selected countries in 1984.

Interest Group Strategies
▽

Interest groups employ a wide range of techniques and strategies to promote their policy goals. Although few groups are successful at persuading the Congress and the president to endorse their programs completely, many are able to prevent legislation injurious to their members from being considered or to weaken such legislation. The key to success for interest groups is the ability to have access to governmental officials. To achieve this, interest groups and their representatives try to cultivate long-term relationships with legislators and government officials. The best of such relationships are based on mutual respect and cooperation. The interest group provides the official with excellent sources of information and assistance, and the official in turn gives the group opportunities to express its views.

The techniques used by interest groups may be divided into those that are direct and indirect. **Direct techniques** include all those ways in which the interest group and its lobbyists approach the officials personally to press their case. **Indirect techniques,** on the other hand, include strategies that use the general public or individuals to influence the government for the interest group.

Direct Techniques

Interest group activities that involve interaction with government officials to further the group's goals.

Indirect Techniques

Strategies employed by interest groups that use a third party, the general public, or other individuals to influence government officials.

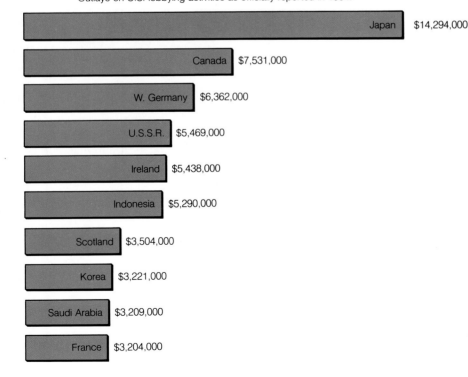

Outlays on U.S. lobbying activities as officially reported in 1984.

Japan $14,294,000
Canada $7,531,000
W. Germany $6,362,000
U.S.S.R. $5,469,000
Ireland $5,438,000
Indonesia $5,290,000
Scotland $3,504,000
Korea $3,221,000
Saudi Arabia $3,209,000
France $3,204,000

Figure 11–2
▽

Foreign Lobby Expenditures
SOURCE: U.S. Department of Justice.

Lobbying

The attempt by organizations or by individuals to influence the passage, defeat, or contents of legislation and of the administrative decisions of government. The derivation of the term may be traced back over a century ago to the habit of certain private citizens who regularly congregated in the lobby outside the legislative chambers before a session to petition legislators.

Lobbyists wait outside a committee room to talk to Congresspersons about the details of the bill.

▽

354

Direct Techniques

Lobbying, publicizing ratings of legislative behavior, and providing campaign assistance, especially through political action committees, are the three main direct techniques used by interest groups.

Lobbying Techniques

As might be guessed, the term **lobbying** comes from the original habit of private citizens regularly congregating in the lobbies of legislative chambers before a session. In the latter part of the nineteenth century, railroad and industrial interests openly bribed state legislators to pass legislation beneficial to their interests, giving lobbying a well-deserved bad name. Today, standard lobbying techniques still involve buttonholing senators and representatives in state capitols and in Washington, D.C., while they are moving from their offices to the voting chambers. Lobbyists, however, do more than that.

Lobbyists engage in an array of activities to influence legislation. These are, at a minimum, the following:

1. Engaging in private meetings with public officials to make known the lobbyist's clients' interests. Although acting on behalf of a client, often lobbyists provide needed information to senators and representatives (and government agency appointees) that they could not hope to obtain on their own. It is to the lobbyist's advantage to provide accurate information so that the policy maker will rely on this source in the future.

2. Testifying before congressional committees for or against proposed legislation.

3. Testifying before executive rule-making agencies, such as the Federal Trade Commission or the Consumer Product Safety Commission, for or against proposed rules.

4. Assisting the legislators or bureaucrats in drafting legislation or prospective regulations. Often, lobbyists can furnish legal advice on the specific details of legislation.

5. Inviting legislators to social occasions such as cocktail parties, boating expeditions, and other events. Most lobbyists feel that contacting legislators in a more relaxed social setting is effective. The extent to which legislators feel obligated to lobbyists for entertaining them is hard to gauge.

6. Providing political information to legislators and other government officials. Often the lobbyists will have better information than the party leadership about how other legislators are going to vote. In this case, the political information they provide may be a key to legislative success.

The Ratings Game

Many interest groups attempt to influence the overall behavior of legislators through their rating systems. Each year, the interest group selects those votes on legislation that it feels are most important to the organization's goals. Legislators are given a score based on the percentage of times that he or she voted with the interest group. The usual scheme ranges from 0 to 100 percent. If a legislator has a score of, for example, 90 percent on the Americans for Democratic Action rating, it means that he supported their positions to a high degree (Table 11–3). Such a high ADA score is usually interpreted as very liberal. The groups that use rating systems range from

Highlight
▽
High-Tech Lobbying

Interest group activity has exploded in recent years. One particularly important aspect of lobbying in this new era is the use of modern technology to enhance the role of pressure groups. Such use is particularly striking in the case of the burgeoning New Right groups on the conservative side of the political spectrum.

Lobbying organizations have for many years employed "grass-roots" tactics for influencing the outcomes of government decisions. These tactics have included soliciting citizens to send letters to members of Congress, mobilizing protest movements, and endorsing or attacking candidates during election campaigns. What is new, exciting, and potentially crucial in the struggle over who will have access to the levers of power in government is the availability of computer-based technology and expanded telecommunications facilities for communicating more effectively and more quickly to targeted segments of the population. Elected representatives may in fact not know which interest group was involved in the "write-your-congressperson" campaign and may even be unaware that any group was behind sophisticated letter-writing efforts in which every letter reads slightly differently and at least appears to have come from a different person with an equally intense interest in the issue at hand. Groups also generate massive telephone call-in efforts with instructions to each caller to indicate a slightly different aspect of an issue that most concerns them. The goal of such campaigns, made possible by computer-controlled mass mailings to targeted citizens, is to produce at least the appearance that the interest group has a massive, unified, intense, and growing block of supporters.

The use of direct-mail methods to solicit small monetary contributions is among the most important reasons for the growth of conservative pressure groups in recent years. This has not only produced a considerable amount of money with which to finance conservative PACs but has also produced very large lists of contributors and activists for future mobilization and has allowed the New Right to bombard average Americans with their views. These lists are readily tapped by the organizers of right-wing groups to generate pressure on Washington officials or on state and local political leaders. The critical thing to understand about the mailing lists, which are maintained by Richard Viguerie in Falls Church, Virginia, is that they allow the pressure groups to bypass the traditional media sources for communicating their views to the general public. As a consequence, individuals who are not in the network of these special interest groups may be caught unawares by major efforts by such groups to push for their views on major issues such as abortion, defense spending, or equal rights.

Not only computers but also advanced television technology has allowed New Right pressure groups to increase their role in American politics. The Rev. Jerry Falwell, leader of the Moral Majority, uses more than six hundred television and radio stations to carry his political messages during his weekly broadcasts of the "Old Time Gospel Hour." Other members of the "electronic church," such as Pat Robertson, have entered directly into electoral politics. Robertson declared that he was a Republican candidate for president in 1988. Fundamentalist electronic ministers also rely on the use of direct-mail techniques. Such ef-

forts resulted, for example, in a million letters and postcards sent to President Reagan supporting a constitutional amendment to allow prayer in public schools.

Business pressure groups have adopted the tactics that have been so successful for the New Right. Apart from the more traditional efforts of soliciting letters, telegrams, and phone calls to elected officials, the Chamber of Commerce has the computer capabilities to send targeted "action calls" in the form of bulletins distributed within particular congressional districts. The chamber has a major high-technology communications system available to send its interpretations of pending legislation and other matters to members; a monthly magazine (*Nation's Business*) with a circulation of 1.25 million; a weekly newsletter, *Washington Report*, sent to nearly a million members and nonmembers of the chamber; a weekly televised syndicated program, "It's Your Business," carried on more than one hundred stations; a radio show, "What's the Issue?" discussing major national topics on more than four hundred stations; and Biznet, a highly ambitious closed-circuit tax-exempt television network, which in theory would allow the chamber to mobilize its members and supporters in only a matter of hours. Satellite television transmission by the U.S. Chamber of Commerce and computer real-time access are also planned. Future developments in high-tech lobbying will be limited only by the speed with which new technological innovations can be put in place.

SOURCE: Allan J. Cigler and Burdett A. Loomis, eds., *Interest Group Policies* (Washington, D.C.: Congressional Quarterly Press, 1983).

Table 11-3

ADA Ratings for 1984

Senator	Highest
Dodd, D., Conn.	100%
Sarbanes, D., Md.	100
Levin, D., Mich.	100
Riegle, D., Mich.	100
Lautenberg, D., N.J.	100
Bingaman, D., N.M.	100
Burdick, D., N.D.	100
Metzenbaum, D., Ohio	100
Pell, D., R.I.	100
Sasser, D., Tenn.	90
	Lowest
Denton, R., Ark.	0
McClure, R., Idaho	0
Symms, R., Idaho	0
Hecht, R., Nev.	0
East, R., N.C.	0
Helms, R., N.C.	0
Nickles, R., Okla.	0
Thurmond, R., S.C.	0
Garn, R., Utah	0
Zorinsky, D., Neb.	10

SOURCE: *Congressional Quarterly Weekly Report*, April 20, 1985, p. 743.

the Americans for Constitutional Action (considered to be conservative) to the League of Conservation Voters (environmental). One group, Environmental Action, identified the twelve legislators having what they saw as the worst records on environmental issues and advertised that list as the "Dirty Dozen."[5] Needless to say, a senator or representative would not want to earn membership on this list.

Campaign Assistance

Interest groups have additional strategies to use in their attempts to influence government policies. Groups recognize that the greatest concern of legislators is to be reelected, so they focus on their campaign needs. Associations with large memberships such as labor unions or the National Education Association are able to provide "manpower" for political campaigns, including precinct workers to get out the vote, volunteers to put up posters and pass out literature, and people to staff telephone banks for campaign headquarters.

In many states, where membership in certain interest groups is large, candidates vie for the group's endorsement in the campaign. Gaining that endorsement may be automatic or it may require that the candidate participate in a debate or interview with the interest group. Endorsements are important because the group usually publicizes its choices in its membership publication and because the candidate can use the endorsement in his or her campaign literature. Traditionally, labor unions such as the AFL-CIO and the UAW have endorsed Democratic party candidates. However, Republican candidates often try to persuade union locals to, at the minimum, refrain from any endorsement. Making no endorsement can then be perceived as disapproval of the Democratic party candidate.

PACs and Political Campaigns

Within the last ten years, the most important form of campaign help from interest groups has become the political contribution from a group's political action committee. The 1974 Federal Election Campaign Act and its 1976 amendments allow corporations, labor unions, and special interest groups to set up PACs to raise money for candidates. For a PAC to be legitimate, the money must be raised from at least fifty volunteer donors and must be given to at least five candidates in the federal election. PACs can contribute up to $5,000 to each candidate in each election. Each corporation or each union is limited to one PAC. As you might imagine, corporate PACs obtain funds from executives in their firms and unions obtain PAC funds from their members.

The number of PACs has grown astronomically, as has the amount they spend on elections. There were about 600 political action committees in 1976; by 1984, there were more than 3,500. Corporate PACs are increasing at a rate greater than other varieties. The total amount of spending by PACs grew from $19 million in 1973 to $265 million in 1983–1984. Of all of the campaign money spent by congressional candidates in 1984, about 35 percent came from PACs.[6] (Table 11–4 lists the PACs that spent the most in congressional races in 1980–1984.)

Interest groups funnel PAC money to candidates who they think can do the most

[5]Bill Keller, "The Trail of the Dirty Dozen," *Congressional Quarterly Weekly Report*, March 21, 1981, p. 510.

[6]Federal Election Commission Press Release, May 19, 1985, "Pacs Support of Incumbents Increases in 1984 Elections," Washington, D.C.

Table 11–4

▽

Top PACs' Spending in Congressional Races 1980–1984

Direct contributions to candidates.

Political Action Committee	1984	1982	1980
1. Realtors Political Action Committee (National Association of Realtors)	$2,429,552	$2,115,135	$1,536,573
2. American Medical Association Political Action Committee	1,839,464	1,737,090	1,348,985
3. BUILD-PAC (National Association of Home Builders)	1,625,539	1,006,628	379,391
4. National Education Association Political Action Committee	1,574,003	1,183,215	283,585
5. UAW V-CAP (United Auto Workers Volunteer Community Action Program)	1,405,107	1,628,347	1,422,731
6. Seafarers Political Activity Donation (Seafarers International Union)	1,322,410	850,514	685,248
7. Machinists Non-Partisan Political League (International Association of Machinists and Aerospace Workers)	1,306,497	1,445,459	847,708
8. Active Ballot Club (United Food and Commercial Workers International Union)	1,271,974	729,213	569,775
9. Committee on Letter Carriers Political Education (National Association of Letter Carriers)	1,234,603	387,915	44,715
10. National Association of Retired Federal Employees Political Action Committee	1,099,243	564,225	8,200
11. Committee for Thorough Agricultural Political Education of Associated Milk Producers Inc.	1,087,658	962,450	738,289
12. Automobile and Truck Dealers Election Action Committee (National Automobile Dealers Association)	1,057,165	917,295	1,035,276
13. Public Employees Organized to Promote Legislative Equality (American Federation of State, County and Municipal Employees)	905,806	496,400	338,035
14. National Association of Life Underwriters Political Action Committee	900,200	563,573	652,112
15. BANKPAC (American Bankers Association)	882,850	947,460	592,960

NOTE: The data are based on a two-year election cycle, and only include direct contributions to candidates for the House and Senate.

SOURCE: *Congressional Quarterly Weekly Report*, June 8, 1985, p. 1117.

good for them. Frequently, they make the maximum contribution of $5,000 per election to candidates who face little or no opposition. The summary of PAC contributions given in Figure 11–3 shows that the great bulk of campaign contributions goes to incumbent candidates rather than to challengers. Corporations are particularly likely to give money to Democrats in Congress as well as to Republicans, because many Democratic incumbents chair important committees or subcommittees. In the Senate, the Republicans held committee chairs until 1986, so they reaped corresponding benefits in PAC money. Why, might you ask, would corporations give to Democrats who may be more liberal than most businesses? Interest groups see PAC contributions as a way to ensure access to powerful legislators, even if they may disagree with them some of the time. PAC contributions are, in a way, an investment in a relationship.

The campaign finance regulations clearly limit the amount that a PAC can give to any one candidate, but there is no limit on the amount that a PAC can spend on an independent campaign, either on behalf of a candidate or party or in opposition to one. One of the most prominent PAC in the United States is the National Conservative Political Action Committee, or NCPAC. This interest group espouses a conservative philosophy, opposing abortion, supporting prayer in school, and supporting a strong defense. In recent elections, NCPAC has targeted specific senators and representatives for defeat, spending large sums of money against them in primary and general elections. In general, NCPAC has not been successful in these efforts since 1980.

Indirect Techniques

By working through third parties, either constituents, the general public, or other groups, interest groups can try to influence government policy. Indirect techniques mask the interest group's own activities and make the effort appear to be sponta-

Figure 11–3

▽

PAC Contributions to Congressional Candidates, 1972–1984

SOURCE: *Congressional Quarterly Weekly Report*, March 22, 1986, p. 657.

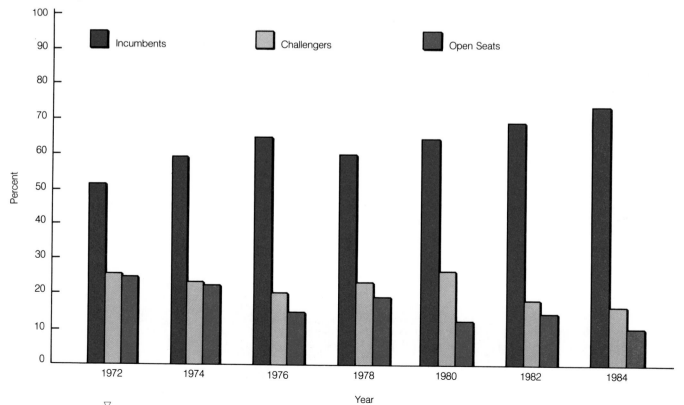

neous. Furthermore, legislators and government officials are often more impressed by contacts from constituents than from the interest group's lobbyist.

Generating Public Pressure

In some instances, interest groups try to produce a "groundswell" of public pressure to influence the government. Such efforts may include advertisements in national magazines and newspapers, mass mailings, television publicity, and demonstrations. Interest groups may commission polls to find out what the public sentiments are and then publicize the results. The intent of this activity is to convince policy makers that public opinion overwhelmingly supports the group's position.

Some corporations and interest groups also engage in a practice that might be called **climate control.** This strategy calls for public relations efforts, often not directly related to a specific political issue or legislation, aimed at improving the public image of the industry or group. Contributions by corporations and groups in support of public television programs, sponsorship of such events as Hands Across America, and commercials extolling the virtues of corporate research are examples of climate control. By building a reservoir of favorable public opinion, groups believe it less likely that their legislative goals will be met with opposition by the public.

Using Constituents as Lobbyists

One of the most effective interest group activities is the use of constituents to lobby for the group's goals. In the "shotgun" approach, the interest group tries to mobilize large numbers of constituents to write or phone their legislators or the president.

Climate Control
Techniques to create a favorable public opinion toward an interest group, industry, or corporation.

Lobbyists at the Capitol reporting to their organizations on the day's legislation.

Often, the group provides postcards or form letters for constituents to fill out and mail. These efforts are only effective on Capitol Hill when there are an extraordinary number of responses, since legislators know that the voters did not initiate the communication on their own.

A more influential variation of this technique uses only important constituents. Known as the "rifle" technique, or the "Utah plant manager's theory," the interest group contacts an influential constituent, for example, the manager of a local plant in Utah, to contact the senator from Utah.[7] Because the constituent is seen as responsible for many jobs or other resources, the legislator is more likely to listen carefully to his or her concerns about legislation than to a paid lobbyist.

Building Alliances

Another indirect technique used by interest groups is to join with other groups concerned about the same legislation in an alliance. Often, these groups will set up a paper organization with an innocuous name, such as the Coalition for American Rivers, to represent their joint concerns. In this case, the sponsoring groups, which included railroads, environmentalists, and others, who opposed the construction of the Alton Lock and Dam, contributed money to the "front" alliance, loaned lobbyists to it in Illinois, and paid the rent for its office.[8] The advantage of an alliance is that it looks as if larger public interests are at stake and it hides the specific interests of the individual groups involved. It is also an efficient device for keeping like-minded groups from duplicating one another's lobbying efforts.

Regulating Lobbyists

▽

In principle, lobbyists are regulated. In 1946, Congress made its first attempt to control lobbyists and lobbying activities through Title III of the Legislative Reorganization Act of 1946, otherwise known as the Federal Regulation of Lobbying Act. The act actually provides for publicity more than for regulation. Its specific provisions are as follows:

1. Any person or organization that receives money to be used principally to influence legislation before Congress must register.
2. Any individual lobbyist or a representative of a group who is registering must, under oath, give his or her name, address, place of employment, salary, amount and purpose of expenses, and duration of employment.
3. Every registered lobbyist must give quarterly reports on his or her activities; these reports are published in the *Congressional Record*.
4. Anyone failing to satisfy the specific provisions of the act can be fined up to $10,000 and receive a five-year prison term.

In a famous case relating to the constitutionality of the lobbying act of 1946,[9] the Supreme Court emphasized that the intention of the act was simply to enable Congress to discover "who is being hired, who is putting up the money, and how

---

[7]Kay Lehman Schlozman and John T. Tierney, *Organized Interests and American Democracy* (New York: Harper and Row, 1986), p. 293.

[8]See T. R. Reid, *Congressional Odyssey* (San Francisco: W. H. Freeman, 1980) for the complete account of such lobbying activities.

[9]*United States v. Harriss*, 347 U.S. 612 (1954).

In 1978, Congress passed the Ethics in Government Act as a reaction to the Watergate scandal during the Nixon administration. The main purpose of the act was to provide for independent investigations of present or former high-ranking government officials, unless the charges filed against an official are judged by the attorney general to be without merit. The act forbids former senior government employees to lobby their former agency on any matter for a year after leaving, to lobby any department for two years on an issue in which they had a direct responsibility, or to lobby for the rest of their lives on issues in which they participated "personally and substantially."

On May 29, 1986, Whitney North Seymour was appointed by a three-judge federal court to serve as a special prosecutor to investigate conflict-of-interest charges against former deputy White House Chief of Staff Michael K. Deaver. Deaver left the White House staff in May 1985 to become a highly paid lobbyist for foreign governments and business corporations. Deaver discussed with Robert McFarlane, the president's national security adviser at the time, some objections his client, the Commonwealth of Puerto Rico, had to a proposed revision in tax laws that would eliminate tax advantages for American businesses that invested in Puerto Rico and that could cause perhaps $600 million in economic losses. McFarlane was at the

Michael Deaver, former member of the White House staff.

time directly involved in looking into the possible revocation of this tax break. This occurred about two or three months after Deaver left office, in violation of the one-year prohibition on direct lobbying of his former White House colleagues.

In addition to these incidents, Deaver's work on behalf of the Daewoo Corporation, a large steel company in South Korea, and the U.S. defense contractor Rockwell International Corporation were also examined, following a series of allegations by Democrats on the Senate Judiciary Committee, by the General Accounting Office, and by

the Office of Government Ethics. Finally, Deaver's work for the government of Canada in its dispute with the United States over acid rain also allegedly violated the 1978 law.

For his efforts, Deaver was paid well by his clients: $105,000 by Canada, $250,000 by Rockwell International, $250,000 by Daewoo, and an undisclosed amount by Puerto Rico.

The Deaver episode highlighted a continuing problem for the Reagan administration, whose high- and middle-level officials have frequently been investigated for improper or unethical conduct. Previous special prosecutors had examined charges against Reagan's former secretary of labor, Raymond Donovan, for taking payoffs and has investigated allegations that Edwin Meese, formerly special counsel to Reagan and later attorney general, had committed eleven violations of government ethics. Both Donovan and Meese were cleared of those charges. Two previous investigations of Carter administration officials by special prosecutors also failed to produce convictions.

The reaction to the Deaver affair in Congress led to attempts to strengthen existing ethics legislation and to extend its coverage to members of Congress, who have been exempted from coverage under previous ethics laws. Nearly two hundred former members of Congress live in and around Washington and commonly act as lobbyists.

much." The Court stated that the lobbying law does not violate due process, freedom of speech or press, or freedom of petition. But the Court narrowly construed the application of the act to only those lobbyists who *directly* seek to influence federal legislation. Any lobbyist indirectly seeking to influence legislation simply through public opinion does not fall within the scope of the activities regulated by the act.

Currently, about 6,500 lobbyists are registered under the act. The act has probably

Did You Know?
▽

That special interest groups often concentrate on preventing legislation rather than promoting it?

had no effect on the amount of money spent on lobbying and the types of activities engaged in by lobbyists. No enforcement agency has been created by Congress, and the public is almost totally ignorant of the publicity given in the quarterly reports. The problem facing Congress, of course, is that any stricter regulation of lobbying will run into constitutional problems because of the potential abridgement of First Amendment rights. Also, as long as the Supreme Court does not view indirect lobbying through attempts to change public opinion as falling under the purview of the act, lobbying will be difficult to control.

After the Watergate scandal, Congress attempted to pass a new bill that would make strict registration and reporting provisions a requirement. This 1976 bill, supported by Common Cause, almost passed, but it failed under the combined attack of business, labor, and, interestingly enough, Ralph Nader. Obviously, public interest groups do not always see eye-to-eye. Whereas Common Cause is most concerned about good government—that is, better procedure—the Nader-type groups are more interested in substantive policy changes.

Why Interest Groups Have So Much Power
▽

It has been claimed that we are a nation of special interests. Organized interest groups have obtained special benefits for their members and blocked legislation that seems to be clearly supported by most citizens. The power of interest groups in the American political system probably results from a number of factors, some of which are inherent in the groups themselves and some of which are derived from the structure of our government.

Not all interest groups have an equal influence on government. As already mentioned, there are many different types of interest groups, and each one has a different combination of resources to use in the policy-making process. Some groups are composed of members who have high social status and enormous economic resources, such as the National Association of Manufacturers. Other groups, such as labor unions, derive influence from their large membership. Still other groups, like farmers or environmentalists, have causes that can claim strong public support even from those people who have no direct stake in the issue. Groups like the Moral Majority and the National Rifle Association are well-organized and have highly motivated members. This enables them to channel a stream of mail toward Congress with a few days' effort.

Even the most powerful interest groups do not always succeed in their demands. Whereas the National Chamber of Commerce may be accepted as having a justified interest in the question of business taxes, many legislators might feel that the chamber should not engage in the debate over the size of the deficit. In other words, groups are seen as having a legitimate concern in the issues closest to their interests but not necessarily in broader issues. This may explain why some of the most successful groups are those that focus on very specific issues—tobacco farming, funding of abortions, handgun control—and do not get involved in larger conflicts.

The structure of American government also invites the participation of interest groups. The governmental system has many points of access or places in the decision-making process where interest groups may focus an attack. If a bill opposed by a group passes the Senate, the lobbying efforts shift to the House of Representatives or to the president to seek a veto. If in spite of all efforts the legislation passes, the group may even lobby the executive agency or bureau that is supposed to implement the law and hope to influence the way in which the legislation is applied. The constitutional features of separation of powers and checks and balances encourage interest groups in their efforts.

The point is often made by lobbyists to members of Congress that interest groups are really constituents. The most legitimate claim of any interest group is that it speaks for the demands and desires of the legislator's constituents. If the group's needs are not met, the district may suffer economically and the members of the group may vote against the legislator in the next election. When the argument is made to a member of Congress that voting against a new weapons system will result in the loss of jobs for constituents, the legislator can easily think of these constituents' votes in terms of the good of the district rather than of interest group pressure.

Is the easy availability of handguns a major cause of crime? Do people have a right to firearms to defend home and hearth? These questions are part of a long-term and heated battle between organized profirearm and antifirearm camps. The disagreements run deep and reflect strong sentiments on both sides. The fight is fueled by the one million gun incidents occurring in the United States each year—the murders, suicides, assaults, accidents, robberies, and injuries in which guns are involved. Proponents of gun control seek new restrictions on gun purchases—if not a ban on them entirely—while decreasing existing arsenals of privately owned weapons. Proponents of firearms are fighting back. They claim that firearms are a cherished tradition, a constitutional right, a vital defense need for individuals. They contend that the problem lies not in the sale and ownership of the weapons themselves but in the criminal use of firearms.

Michael Beard, director of the National Coalition to Ban Handguns, favors a total ban because "the only way to prevent the tragic loss of life—the thirty-two thousand lives a year we're losing to handguns—is to say: We no longer need handguns. They serve no valid purpose, except to kill people." Neal Know, director of the Institute for Legislative Action of the National Rifle Association of America, opposes a ban "because, among other reasons, it wouldn't work. It would not reduce the number of crimes committed. Are we going to assume that a person who will violate a law against rape, robbery, or murder will suddenly obey a gun law? I doubt it. There is no city, no state, no nation that has reduced its crime rate by the enactment of a gun law."*

The debate is intense and bitter. Gun control proponents accuse their adversaries of being "frightened little men living in a pseudomacho myth." Gun control opponents brand the other side as "new totalitarians" intent on curbing individual freedom.

The National Rifle Association, founded in 1871, is currently one of the most powerful single-issue groups on the American political scene. With some two million members and an annual budget of $30 million, the NRA is frequently successful in its efforts to block gun control legislation, elect officials sympathetic to its cause, and defeat candidates supportive of gun control. If you agree with the NRA's position and want to get involved in its efforts in opposition to gun control legislation, contact:

The National Rifle Association
1600 Rhode Island Ave., N.W.
Washington, D.C. 20036
202-828-6000

If, however, you are concerned with the increase in gun-related crimes and feel that stricter gun laws are necessary, you can get involved through these organizations:

Committee for the Study of Handgun Misuse
109 N. Dearborn St., Suite 704
Chicago, IL 60602
312-641-5593

The National Coalition to Ban Handguns
100 Maryland Avenue, N.E.
Washington, D.C. 20002
202-544-7190

Handgun Control, Inc.
810 18th St. N.W., Suite 705
Washington, D.C. 20006
202-638-4723

*"Should Handguns Be Outlawed?" *U.S. News & World Report*, December 22, 1980, p. 23.

Chapter Summary

1. An interest group is an organized group of individuals who share common objectives and who actively attempt to influence government policy.

2. Three of the most influential types of interest groups in the United States are business, agriculture, and labor.

3. Although there has been a decline in the percentage of nonagricultural workers who are union members, unions which represent public employees are increasing in strength.

4. Numerous professional organizations lobby to influence legislation; foremost among them in terms of money spent on lobbying is the American Medical Association (AMA).

5. Over the past decade a variety of legal and lobbying organizations have been formed in the "public interest." The best known and perhaps most effective ones started under the leadership of Ralph Nader.

6. Lobbyists utilize a variety of direct techniques to influence legislation. These include testifying before congressional committees and rule-making agencies, providing information to legislators, making campaign contributions, and rating legislators' performance.

7. Most campaign contributions from interest groups are given through their Political Action Committees (PACs). New PACs are organized every year with the corporate sector leading in growth. PACs give more money to incumbent legislators than to challengers.

8. Interest groups can also use indirect techniques to influence policymaking. Among these are campaigns to influence public opinion, campaigns to generate letters from the public, and using constituents to lobby for their cause.

9. The 1946 Legislative Reorganization Act was the first attempt to control lobbyists and lobbying activities through registration requirements. The Supreme Court narrowly construed it as applying only to lobbyists who directly seek to influence federal legislation.

10. The power of interest groups in the American political system derives partly from the structure of the government, which allows many points of access to the decision-making process, and partly from group characteristics, such as economic resources, social status, membership size, worthiness of the cause, and efficient organization.

Questions for Review and Discussion

1. The American political system is sometimes described as one having "multiple cracks," or points of access for interest groups. If Congress is about to pass a law that adversely affects an interest group to which you belong, how can you lobby against it? How would you plan to lobby Congress, the executive branch, and the Supreme Court? How could you influence public opinion to support your point of view?

2. Think about your own interests—ethnic identity, religious affiliation, occupation, union, profession, hobby interests, and so on. How many interest groups might you belong to? Are you formally a member of any of these? If you are not a member, how are your interests represented? Which group represents the interests of the general public, say, for clean air or for lower automobile prices?

3. At the present time, PACs give disproportionate amounts of campaign contributions to incumbent legislators. How would the political process be changed if PACs were required to give equal amounts to challengers and incumbents, or if there were a limit on the percentage of campaign funds which could come from PACs? Where do PACs get their money?

Selected References

David S. Broder, *Changing of the Guard: Power and Leadership in America* (New York: Simon and Schuster, 1980). The new generation of group leaders and its impact on the future of politics in the United States.

Alan J. Cigler and Burdett A. Loomis, eds., *Interest Group Politics* (Washington, D.C.: Congressional Quarterly Press, 1983). An in-depth discussion of what interest groups are, how they emerge and grow, and how they influence the legislative process.

David H. Everson, *Public Opinion and Interest Groups in American Politics* (New York: Franklin Watts, 1982). The swing to the right in American politics, public opinion and democratic theory, the decline of parties, the mass media in American politics, changes in party identification and voting by groups, and the consequences for making policy decisions in government.

Ronald J. Hrebenar and Ruth K. Scott, *Interest Group Politics in America* (Englewood Cliffs, N.J.: Prentice-Hall, 1982). The foundations of group power, the strategies and tactics of lobbying, the interaction of lobbies and governmental institutions, traditional lobbies and public interest groups, and case studies on the SALT II treaty and energy.

Robert C. Liebman and Robert Wuthnow, eds., *The New Christian Right: Mobilization and Legitimation* (New York: Aldine, 1983). An overview of the new Christian Right, its forms of mobilization, the character of its constituency, the major tenets of its ideology, and the cultural environment in which the movement emerged.

4
POLITICAL
INSTITUTIONS

Chapter 12

▽

The Presidency

Contents

▽

Historical Development of the Presidency
Who Can Become President?
The Process of Becoming President
The Many Powers of the President
The President as Party Chief and Super Politician
The Special Uses of Presidential Power
Abuses of Executive Power: Impeachment
The Executive Organization
The Vice Presidency
Is the Power of the Presidency Increasing or Decreasing?

What If . . .

The United States Had a Plural Executive?

At the Constitutional Convention in Philadelphia in 1787, the delegates were deeply divided over whether the new country should have a strong or a weak executive. One key spokesman for those favoring a weak executive was Edmund Randolph of Virginia who advocated a triple presidency, with each of the three chief executives representing a different section of the country. What if the United States had a plural executive?

Instead of being called the presidency, the executive could be known as the National Council of Government. Elected by direct popular vote, the council would consist of, say, nine members. Six of them would be elected from the majority party, that is, the party receiving the largest vote in the national election. The other three would be from the leading minority party. The council would have a six-year term of office with the six members of the majority party rotating each year in the position of chairperson or president of the council. All nine members would have an equal vote, but the three minority party members could not chair the council. Each of the nine council members would head up a major federal agency.

If such a system had been used in the 1984 presidential election, the National Council of Government might have consisted of six Republicans, probably Ronald Reagan, George Bush, Sen. Robert Dole (then Senate Republican leader), Rep. Jack Kemp, Sen. Paul Laxalt, and Rep. Robert Michel (House Republican leader). There would have been three Democrats on the council—Walter Mondale, Geraldine Ferraro, and either Sen. Gary Hart or the Rev. Jesse Jackson.

What would be the consequences of such a system in the United States? First of all, it would drastically change the nature of national campaigns, probably shifting the emphasis away from the so-called horse race aspect of the primaries, which emphasizes what candidate is ahead in each round of primaries, toward each party building a six-person national ticket. Clearly, the national conventions would also change in nature—the national ticket, having campaigned in primaries, would probably simply be endorsed at the convention. The emphasis thus might be more on programs and issues than on the individual personality of candidates. The role of the political parties would grow and the impact of individuals would be diluted.

Such a system would also have a significant impact on the operation of the executive branch. It could help reduce the terrible load on the single person who now has to carry the presidential burden. It would most likely lead to a greater degree of subject specialization, since each person could concentrate on one of the very complex executive agencies for six years and truly come to understand how it works, what it does, and what it is capable of accomplishing. Imagine, though, how difficult it would be for the Council to agree on major policies. For example, with Ferraro, Jackson, and Mondale on the plural executive, what sort of policy would have been developed, say, toward Nicaragua or the Soviet arms talks? Even if the council majority had decided on one approach, those dissenting would surely have campaigned in the media and Congress against any policy with which they disagreed.

In times of prosperity, stability, and normalcy, such a system might work much like a parliamentary system in Europe (the council would be similar to a European cabinet and the annual rotating chair or president of the council would act like a prime minister). In times of crisis, however, the council might very well be unable to make timely and difficult decisions, leaving the country vulnerable and without strong leadership.

▽

In contrast, the Constitution specifies a president and gives virtually no attention to the role of others in the Executive Branch. Even the vice president does not share the power of the chief executive.

It is ironic that the Founding Fathers, rejecting so emphatically the model of a king, created an office presently invested with authority far beyond that of any surviving king and only to be rivaled by the powers of absolute monarchs.[1]

The office of the presidency of the United States of America is unusual, or rather we should say it is unique—at least in the world of today. In almost all of the democratic nations of Europe, as well as in Japan and Israel, there is a prime minister who is part of a **parliamentary system** of government. In parliamentary systems, the prime minister as chief executive is chosen by the legislature. Once the prime minister is chosen, he or she chooses a government—a set of ministers selected directly from the members of parliament.

Historical Development of the Presidency

▽

We can appreciate the uniqueness of the United States presidency even more when we consider that those attending the Philadelphia Constitutional Convention in 1787 had no working model of such a presidency to follow. They had, to be sure, two models of executive offices that they did *not* want to follow—the British monarchy and the legislative committees under the Articles of Confederation. That is not to say that the concept of monarchy was completely discarded. Indeed, John Jay questioned George Washington about the desirability of choosing a king, and Hamilton, royalist that he was, considered the British monarchy to be the best model of government in the world. But the rest of the delegates at the Philadelphia Convention considered their previous experiences under George III and his colonial governors to be so onerous as to eliminate a monarchy completely as a model for the new United States government.

As the Founding Fathers proceeded with their deliberations, two opposing views became apparent. One view favored a weak executive who would be chosen by Congress for a several-year period and who could, at any time during that limited term, be removed by the legislature. The executive could not veto any of the laws passed by Congress; his primary function would be to carry out the will of the legislature. The other view favored a strong, independent executive exercising significant powers within the new government. Advocates of this view had seen how ineffectual a weak executive was under the Articles of Confederation. Although not willing to accept a monarchy, this group wanted a single executive chosen by some means other than legislative appointment. This person would be removed only for good cause (not simply because of political distaste). He would have veto power over legislation, and, if he did have an executive council, it would be advisory only. Many of those in favor of a strong executive branch clearly had George Washington in mind when they argued their case. They assumed, and rightly so, that Washington would be our first president.

So, retaining the title of president as the chief executive officer of Congress under the Articles of Confederation, the Founding Fathers created an executive branch molded by the desires of those in favor of a strong executive. Rather than being chosen by the legislature, the president is chosen by the electoral college. He does not derive his authority from Congress but from the powers granted to him by the Constitution. His powers are broad and undefined. As stated in Article II, Section 1, of the Constitution: "The Executive Power shall be vested in a President of the United States of America."

[1]Page Smith, *The Constitution: A Documentary and Narrative History* (New York: William Morrow, 1978), p. 528.

Parliamentary System

A system of government in which governmental authority is vested in the legislative body (parliament) and in the cabinet headed by a prime minister or premier. The executive and legislative branches are fused.

The first cabinet—from left to right: Henry Knox, Thomas Jefferson, Edmund Randolph, Alexander Hamilton, and President George Washington.

▽

Profile
▽
George Washington

George Washington was born more than two and a half centuries ago. In spite of voluminous research and the millions of words written about him, he still retains his aura of greatness. Not surprisingly, his contemporaries offered him as much respect as school-children do today.

However, if Washington were alive today and scrutinized with the same standards we use with our contemporary presidents, this aura might be diminished. Consider his reading habits. They certainly weren't as sophisticated as those of John Fitzgerald Kennedy, who, when asked what his ten favorite books were, listed works of biography, history, and politics. Washington, a how-to-do-it expert, enjoyed books about manure and animal husbandry.

Washington was not a world traveler. Indeed, he never went to Europe. He spoke no foreign languages—and he was a poor public speaker. The single outstanding characteristic of his military career was perseverance. It was perseverance that won the Battle of Trenton and brought the Revolution back to life, convincing France to commit herself to the American cause. Military analysts of today, however, do not have high praise for the technical

"I do not conceive we can exist long as a nation without having lodged somewhere a power which will pervade the whole union in as energetic a manner as the authority of the state governments extends over the several states."

expertise of Washington's military campaign. Crossing the Delaware River, his troops couldn't fire their guns be-

cause the powder was soaked by freezing rain. His officers wanted to call off the attack, but his men fought with bayonets. The Battle of Trenton was won because Washington was determined, not because he was a military genius.

In his day, Washington was one of the wealthiest individuals in the nation. He was proud and aristocratic in manner and never attempted to give the impression that he was a great democrat. The story goes that Gouveneur Morris, an old friend and supporter, once put his hand on Washington's shoulder to show his close relationship with the chief executive. Washington removed Morris's hand almost immediately.

Contemporaries of the first president and historians of today agree that Washington had the necessary qualities to be the "father of our country"; Washington was a natural leader. As the chief executive, he organized the administration, maintained dignity in office, and kept the early decisions of the nation free from partisanship.

Who Can Become President?
▽

The requirements for becoming president, as outlined in Article II, Section 1, of the Constitution, are not overwhelmingly stringent:

No person except a natural-born Citizen, or a Citizen of the United States, at the time of the Adoption of this Constitution shall be eligible to the Office of President; neither shall any Person be eligible to that Office who shall not have attained to the Age of 35 Years, and been fourteen Years a Resident within the United States.

The only question that arises about these qualifications relates to the term *natural-born citizen*. Does that mean only citizens born in the United States and its territories? What about a child born to a U.S. citizen (or to a couple who are U.S.

John Fitzgerald Kennedy taking the oath of office.

citizens) while visiting or living in another country? Although the question has not been dealt with directly by the Supreme Court, it is reasonable to expect that someone would be eligible if his or her parents were Americans. The first presidents, after all, were not even American citizens at birth, and others were born in areas that did not become part of the United States until later. This issue became important when George Romney,[2] who was born in Chihuahua, Mexico, made a serious bid for the Republican presidential nomination in the 1960s.

The great American dream is symbolized by the statement that "anybody can become president of this country." It is true that in modern times presidents have included a haberdasher (Truman—for a short period of time), a peanut farmer (Carter), and an actor (Reagan). But if you examine Appendix C, you will see that the most common previous occupation of presidents in this country has been the legal profession. Out of forty presidents, twenty-four have been lawyers.

Although the Constitution states that the minimum-age requirement for the presidency is thirty-five years, most presidents have been much older than that when they assumed office. John F. Kennedy, at the age of forty-three, was the youngest elected president, and the oldest has been Ronald Reagan at age sixty-nine. The average age at inauguration has been fifty-four. There has clearly been a demographic bias in the selection of presidents. All have been male, white, and Protestants, except for John F. Kennedy, a Roman Catholic. Presidents have been men of great stature—like Washington—and men in whom leadership qualities were not so pronounced—such as Harding.

The Process of Becoming President

▽

As we learned in earlier chapters, a presidential election takes place every four years. Major and minor political parties nominate candidates for president and vice president at the national conventions. The nation's voters do not directly elect a

[2]Governor of Michigan from 1963 to 1969.

Highlight

▽

Presidential Elections

No president of the United States has ever been elected by a majority of all adults of voting age, even though many presidents have been elected by very large majorities of votes from citizens who actually cast ballots. As you can see from the accompanying table, Martin Van Buren was elected president by a record low of just 11.4 percent of voting-age Americans in 1836. The proportion of voting-age citizens who have elected presidents has generally increased over time. This has happened largely because of several important extensions of voting rights—the Fifteenth Amendment in 1870, which removed race as a barrier to voting for black males; the Nineteenth Amendment in 1920, which enfranchised women; the Twenty-fourth Amendment in 1964, which abolished the poll tax in federal elections; and the Twenty-sixth Amendment in 1971 lowering the minimum voting age to eighteen. Ronald Reagan was reelected in 1984 with the votes of 32.0 percent of Americans of voting age. Lyndon Johnson, in 1964, came the closest of any president in history to being elected by a majority of the voting-age public, and even he gained the votes of less than 40 percent of those who were old enough to cast a ballot.

These results are especially useful to keep in mind whenever a president lays claim to having received a "mandate" from the people to govern the nation. In reality, no president has ever been elected with sufficient popular backing to make this a serious claim.

Year	Winning Candidate	Percentage of Total Vote	Percentage of Voting-Age Population
1828	Andrew Jackson	56.0	12.4
1832	Andrew Jackson	56.5	11.6
1836	Martin Van Buren	50.8	11.4
1840	William Harrison	52.9	16.9
1844	James Polk	49.5	15.1
1848	Zachary Taylor	47.3	13.5
1852	Franklin Pierce	50.6	13.8
1856	James Buchanan	45.3	13.8
1860	Abraham Lincoln	39.8	12.5
1864	Abraham Lincoln	55.0	13.4
1868	Ulysses Grant	52.8	16.7
1872	Ulysses Grant	55.7	17.8
1876	Rutherford Hayes	47.9	17.8
1880	James Garfield	48.3	17.5
1884	Grover Cleveland	48.5	17.3
1888	Benjamin Harrison	47.9	17.4
1892	Grover Cleveland	46.1	16.1
1896	William McKinley	51.1	18.8
1900	William McKinley	51.7	17.6
1904	Theodore Roosevelt	56.4	16.8
1908	William Taft	51.6	15.4
1912	Woodrow Wilson	41.9	11.7
1916	Woodrow Wilson	49.3	15.8
1920	Warren Harding	60.4	25.6
1924	Calvin Coolidge	54.0	23.7
1928	Herbert Hoover	58.1	30.1
1932	Franklin Roosevelt	57.4	30.1
1936	Franklin Roosevelt	60.8	34.6
1940	Franklin Roosevelt	54.7	32.2
1944	Franklin Roosevelt	53.4	29.9
1948	Harry Truman	49.6	25.3
1952	Dwight Eisenhower	55.1	34.0
1956	Dwight Eisenhower	57.4	34.1
1960	John Kennedy	49.7	31.2
1964	Lyndon Johnson	61.1	37.8
1968	Richard Nixon	43.4	26.4
1972	Richard Nixon	60.7	33.7
1976	Jimmy Carter	50.1	27.2
1980	Ronald Reagan	51.0	26.7
1984	Ronald Reagan	58.7	32.0

president and vice president, but rather cast ballots for presidential electors who then vote for president and vice president in the electoral college. The electors are chosen by all the states and the District of Columbia.

Since the election is governed by a majority in the electoral college, it is conceivable that someone could be elected to the office of the presidency without having a majority of the popular vote. Indeed, in three cases, candidates won elections even though their major opponents received more popular votes. This occurred in the elections of John Quincy Adams in 1824, Rutherford B. Hayes in 1876, and Benjamin Harrison in 1888. In cases where there were more than two candidates running for office, many presidential candidates have won the election with less than 50 percent of the total popular votes cast for all candidates—including Abraham Lincoln, Woodrow Wilson, Harry Truman, John F. Kennedy, and Richard Nixon.

On occasion, the electoral college has failed to give any candidate a majority. At this point, the election is thrown into the House of Representatives, where the president is chosen from among the three candidates having the most electoral college votes. Each state's House delegation has one vote. To win the election, a candidate must receive a majority of the votes that are cast in the House of Representatives. By House rule, each state's vote is given to the candidate preferred by a majority of the state's delegation in the House. In the event that there are an even number of delegates from a particular state and the vote is a tie, that state's vote is not counted.

Only two times in our past has the House had to decide on a president. Thomas Jefferson and Aaron Burr tied in the electoral college in 1800. This happened because the Constitution had not been explicit in indicating which of the two electoral votes was for president and which was for vice president. The **Twelfth Amendment,** ratified on July 27, 1804, clarified the matter. In 1824, the House had to make a choice among William H. Crawford, Henry Clay, Andrew Jackson, and John Quincy Adams. It chose Adams, even though Jackson had more electoral and popular votes.

What if the House fails to choose a president? Then the vice president, who has been chosen by the electoral college—or failing that, chosen by the Senate—becomes president. There is no explicit provision in the Twelfth Amendment or elsewhere in the Constitution about what will happen if neither a president nor a vice president can be selected by Congress. Failure to select a vice president, however, is very unlikely because the Senate makes its choice with all members voting for one of two candidates. A Senate deadlock is still possible. Either a new election could be called or the Speaker of the House could succeed to the presidency until the matter could be resolved.

The Many Powers of the President

▽

The Constitution in Article II delineates the explicit powers that are delegated to the president. These powers define the president as (1) **chief of state,** (2) **chief executive,** (3) **commander in chief** of the armed forces, (4) **chief diplomat,** and (5) **chief legislator** of the United States. Here we examine each of these significant presidential functions, or roles. It is worth noting that one person plays all these roles simultaneously and that the needs of these roles may at times be contradictory.

Did You Know?

▽

That Franklin Roosevelt was remotely related to eleven former presidents, five by blood and six by marriage, and that he was a fifth cousin of Theodore Roosevelt?

Twelfth Amendment
An amendment to the Constitution, adopted in 1804, that specifies the separate election of the president and vice president by the electoral college.

Chief of State
The role of the president as ceremonial head of the government.

Chief Executive
The role of the president as head of the executive branch of the government.

Commander in Chief
The role of the president as supreme commander of the military forces of the United States and of the state national guard units when they are called into federal service.

Chief Diplomat
The role of the president in recognizing foreign governments, making treaties, and making executive agreements.

Chief Legislator
The role of the president in influencing the making of laws.

▽
375

Chief of State

Every nation has at least one person who is the ceremonial head of state. As we pointed out at the beginning of this chapter, in most democratic governments the role of chief of state is given to someone other than the chief executive. In Britain, for example, the chief of state is the Queen. In France, where the prime minister is the chief executive, the chief of state is the president. But in the United States the president is both chief executive and chief of state. According to William Howard Taft, as chief of state the president symbolizes the "dignity and majesty" of the American people. In his capacity as chief of state, the president engages in a number of activities that are largely symbolic or ceremonial in nature, such as the following:

▽ Decorating war heroes
▽ Throwing out the first ball to open the baseball season
▽ Dedicating parks and post offices
▽ Launching charity drives
▽ Receiving visiting chiefs of state at the White House
▽ Going on official state visits to other countries
▽ Making personal telephone calls to congratulate the country's heroes and heroines

Many students of the American political system believe that having the president serve as both the chief executive and the head of state drastically limits the time

Participating in this event is part of being Chief of State.

available to do "real" work. Not all presidents have agreed with this conclusion, however—particularly those presidents who have been able to blend skillfully these two roles with their role as politician. Being chief of state gives the president tremendous public exposure, and when that is positive it helps the president deal with Congress over proposed legislation and increases his chances of being re-elected—or getting his party's candidates elected.

One effect of the president's role as chief of state is that his life is put on public display day in and day out. Everything he does, and everything his family does, has become intensely interesting to the American—and indeed to the world—public. One reason why many Americans are so absorbed by the trivia of presidential activities is that the president is also the personal symbol of the nation, in the same way that kings and queens are. This symbolic role leads to an emotional investment by citizens and explains why, even if the president is not liked by many individuals, they still feel great anxiety when his life is threatened. It seems like a threat to the nation, not just to the person in the office.

Chief Executive

According to the Constitution, "The executive power shall be vested in a President of the United States of America. . . . He may require the Opinion, in writing, of the principal Officer in each of the Executive Departments, upon any Subject relating to the Duties of their respective Offices . . . and he shall nominate, and by and with the Advice and Consent of the Senate, shall appoint . . . Officers of the United States. . . . He shall take Care that the Laws be faithfully exe-cuted, ..."

As chief executive the president is constitutionally bound to enforce the acts of Congress, the judgments of federal courts, and treaties to which the United States is a signator. To assist him in his various tasks as chief executive, the president has a federal bureaucracy (see Chapter 14), which currently consists of some three million civilian employees and which spends over a trillion dollars per year.

The Powers of Appointment and Removal

Since the president is head of the largest bureaucracy in the United States, you might think that he wields enormous power. The president, however, only nom-inally runs the executive bureaucracy, for most of its jobs are protected by **civil service.**[3] Therefore, even though the president has **appointment power,** it is not very extensive, being limited to cabinet and subcabinet jobs, federal judgeships, agency heads, and about two thousand lesser jobs. In Table 12–1, we show what percentage of the total employment in each executive department is available for political appointment by the president.

The president's power to remove from office officials who are doing a poor job or who don't agree with the president is not explicitly granted by the Constitution and has been limited. In 1926, however, a Supreme Court decision prevented Congress from interfering with the president's ability to fire those executive-branch officials that the president had appointed with Senate approval.[4]

Civil Service

A collective term for the body of employ-ees working for the government. Gener-ally, civil service is understood to apply to all those who gain government em-ployment through a merit system.

Appointment Power

The authority vested in the president to fill a governmental office or position. Po-sitions filled by presidential appointment include those in the executive branch, the federal judiciary, commissioned offi-cers in the armed forces, and members of the independent regulatory commissions.

---

[3]See pages 467–472 for a discussion of the Civil Service Reform Act.

[4]*Meyers v. United States,* 272 U.S. 52 (1926).

Table 12–1

Total Employment in Cabinet Departments Available for Political Appointment by the President

Executive Department	Total Number of Employees[1]	Political Appointments Available[2]	Percent
Agriculture	114,361	463	0.40
Commerce	34,302	261	0.76
Defense	1,018,098	549	0.05
Education	5,783	159	2.75
Energy	18,641	170	0.91
Health and Human Services	147,830	234	0.16
Housing and Urban Development	14,921	167	1.12
Interior	73,825	140	0.19
Justice	54,722	364	0.67
Labor	18,795	151	0.80
State	23,795	463	1.95
Transportation	60,946	114	0.19
Treasury	126,421	454	0.36
Total	1,712,620	3,689	0.22

[1]1982.

[2]Includes noncareer employees in the Senior Executive Service.

SOURCES: Committee on Post Office and Civil Service, House of Representatives, 96th Congress, 2nd Session, *Policy and Supporting Positions*, November 18, 1980; *Statistical Abstract of the United States, 1982–83*, p. 266.

The eleven agencies whose directors the president can remove at any time are as follows:

1. ACTION (coordinates volunteer programs)
2. Arms Control and Disarmament Agency
3. Commission on Civil Rights
4. Energy Research and Development Agency
5. Environmental Protection Agency (EPA)
6. Federal Mediation and Conciliation Service
7. General Services Administration (GSA)
8. National Aeronautics and Space Administration (NASA)
9. Postal Service
10. Small Business Administration (SBA)
11. Veterans Administration

In addition, the president can remove all heads of cabinet departments and all individuals in the Executive Office of the President.

Truman spoke candidly of the difficulties a president faces in trying to control the executive bureaucracy. Upon leaving office, he referred to the problems that Eisenhower, as a former general of the army, was going to have: "He'll sit here and he'll say do this! do that! and nothing will happen. Poor Ike—it won't be a bit like the Army. He'll find it very frustrating."[5] Truman went on to say that his job consisted of trying to persuade people to do the things they ought to have sense enough to do without his persuading them.

[5]Quoted in Richard E. Neustadt, *Presidential Power* (New York: John Wiley, 1960), p. 9.

Jimmy Carter and his wife, Rosalyn, walk down Pennsylvania Avenue at his inaugural.

The Power to Grant Reprieves and Pardons

Section 2 of Article II of the Constitution gives the president the power to grant **reprieves** and **pardons** for offenses against the United States except in cases of impeachment. All pardons are administered by the Office of the Pardon Attorney in the Department of Justice. In principle, pardons are granted to remedy a mistake made in a conviction. In addition, pardons are given to offenders who presumably have been rehabilitated.

The Supreme Court upheld the president's right to reprieve in a 1925 case concerning the pardon granted by the president to an individual convicted of contempt of court.[6] The judiciary had contended that only judges had the authority to convict individuals for contempt of court when court orders were violated and that the courts should be free from interference by the executive branch. The Supreme Court simply stated that the president could reprieve or pardon all offenses "either before trial, during trial, or after trial, by individuals, or by classes, conditionally or absolutely, and this without modification or regulation by Congress."[7]

Reprieve

The president has the power to grant a reprieve to postpone the execution of a sentence imposed by a court of law; usually done for humanitarian reasons or to await new evidence.

Pardon

The granting of a release from the punishment or legal consequences of a crime; a pardon can be granted by the president before or after a conviction.

Commander in Chief

The president, according to the Constitution, "shall be Commander in Chief of the Army and Navy of the United States, and of the militia of the several States,

[6]*Ex parte Grossman*, 267 U.S. 87 (1925).
[7]Ibid.

Military aide carrying the "football."

War Powers Act

A law passed in 1973 emphasizing the right of Congress to declare war and spelling out the conditions under which the president can commit troops without congressional approval.

Damage in Tripoli after the American attack in 1986.

when called into the actual service of the United States." In other words, the armed forces are under civilian, rather than military, control.

Certainly the Founding Fathers had George Washington in mind when they made the president the commander in chief. President Washington was in physical command of the troops that put down the Whiskey Rebellion in 1794. Although we no longer expect our president to lead the troops to battle, presidents as commanders in chief have certainly wielded dramatic power. Harry Truman made the awesome decision to drop the atomic bomb on Hiroshima and Nagasaki. Lyndon Johnson ordered bombing missions to North Vietnam, and he personally selected the targets. Nixon decided to invade Cambodia in 1970, and Reagan sent troops to Lebanon and Grenada in 1983 and ordered American fighter planes to attack Libya in 1986 in retaliation for terrorist attacks on American citizens.

The president is the ultimate decision maker in military matters. Everywhere he goes, so too goes the "football"—a briefcase filled with all the codes necessary to order a nuclear attack. When Lyndon Baines Johnson boarded Air Force One to take the oath of office following Kennedy's assassination, an aide with the football was nearby. Only the president has the power to order the use of nuclear force.

In his role as commander in chief, the president has probably exercised more authority than in any of his other roles. Constitutionally, Congress has the sole power to declare war, but the president can send the armed forces into a country in situations that are certainly the equivalent of war. When William McKinley ordered troops into Peking to help suppress the Boxer Rebellion in 1900, he was sending them into a combat situation. Harry Truman dispatched troops to Korea as part of a "police action" in 1950. Kennedy, Johnson, and Nixon waged an undeclared war in Vietnam, where 57,000 Americans were killed and 300,000 were wounded. In none of these situations did Congress declare war.

In an attempt to gain more control over such military activities, in 1973 Congress passed a **War Powers Act**—over President Nixon's veto—requiring that the president consult with Congress before sending American forces into action. Once they are sent, the president must report to Congress within forty-eight hours. Unless the Congress has passed a declaration of war within sixty days or has extended the

sixty-day time limit, the forces must be withdrawn. The War Powers Act was tested in the fall of 1983 when Reagan requested that troops be left in Lebanon. The resulting compromise was a congressional resolution allowing troops to remain there for eighteen months. Shortly after the resolution was passed, however, more than 240 sailors and marines were killed in the suicide bombing of a U.S. military housing compound in Beirut. That event provoked a furious congressional debate over the role American troops were playing in the Middle East and all troops were withdrawn shortly after.

In spite of the War Powers Act, the powers of the president as commander in chief are more extensive today than they were in the past. These powers are closely linked to the president's powers as chief diplomat, or chief crafter of foreign policy.

Chief Diplomat

The Constitution gives the president the power to recognize foreign governments, to make nontreaty agreements with other heads of state, and, with the **advice and consent** of the Senate, to make treaties. In addition, he nominates ambassadors. As chief diplomat, the president dominates American foreign policy.

Recognition Power

An important power of the president as chief diplomat is **recognition power,** or the power to recognize—or refuse to recognize—foreign governments. In his role as ceremonial head of state, the president has always received foreign diplomats. In modern times, the simple act of receiving a foreign diplomat has been equivalent to accrediting the diplomat and officially recognizing his or her government. Such recognition of the legitimacy of another country's government is a prerequisite to diplomatic relations or negotiations between that country and the United States.

Deciding when to recognize a foreign power is not always a simple task. The United States, for example, did not recognize the Soviet Union until 1933—sixteen

Did You Know?

▽

That more than $26 million was spent in 1984 to pay living and security expenses for former presidents Nixon, Ford, and Carter?

Advice and Consent

The power vested in the U.S. Senate by the Constitution (Article II, Section 2) to give its advice and consent to the president concerning treaties and presidential appointments.

Recognition Power

The president's power, as chief diplomat, to extend diplomatic recognition to foreign governments.

The President meets Nicholas Daniloff after the journalist was released by the Soviet Union. He had been charged with spying.

years following the Russian Revolution of 1917. It was only after all attempts—including military invasion of Russia as well as diplomatic isolation—to reverse the effects of that revolution had proved futile that Franklin Roosevelt extended recognition to the new government. U.S. presidents faced a similar problem with the Chinese communist revolution and the emergence of a new communist government in mainland China. The former government had fled to the island of Taiwan, establishing its headquarters there, and there were thus two rival governments—both claiming legitimacy. In December 1978, forty years after the communist victory in China, Jimmy Carter granted official recognition to the People's Republic of China and downgraded diplomatic relations with the rival government of the Republic of China in Taiwan. Nixon's earlier "ping-pong diplomacy"[8] and subsequent trip to China did much to prepare the way for diplomatic recognition of that country by the United States, but Carter's policy nonetheless elicited much criticism from anticommunist hardliners. On April 7, 1979, Carter again used his recognition powers as chief diplomat when he broke diplomatic ties with the revolutionary Khomeini government in Iran.

In 1986, the Reagan administration faced a key decision of whether to continue its support for Ferdinand Marcos, president of the Philippines, or to recognize Corazón Aquino's claim to that office. After the presidential elections, charges of corruption and fraud in the vote count led to demands for Marcos to leave office. Both Marcos and Aquino were sworn in as president on February 25 in separate ceremonies. The Reagan administration, recognizing the fraudulent nature of the election and other evidence of corruption in the Marcos regime, called for Marcos to resign and leave the country. As soon as Marcos and his entourage arrived at an American base in Guam, President Reagan officially recognized the Aquino government and sent a special envoy to discuss the ways in which the United States could aid the Philippines. The president's decision to recognize the new regime

[8]The Nixon administration first encouraged new relations with the People's Republic by allowing a cultural exchange of ping-pong teams.

Ferdinand and Imelda Marcos (right) campaigning for his reelection. Corazón Aquino (left) as the newly elected president of the Phillipines.

immediately was interpreted as a statement of support for government reform and for Mrs. Aquino's political party. Failure to extend diplomatic recognition would have cast grave doubt on the ability of the Aquino administration to survive.

Proposal and Ratification of Treaties

The president has the sole power to negotiate treaties with other nations. These treaties must be presented to the Senate, where they may be modified and must be approved by a two-thirds vote. After ratification, the president can approve of the senatorial version of the treaty. Approval poses a problem when the Senate has tacked on substantive amendments or reservations to a treaty, particularly when such changes may require reopening negotiations with the other signatory governments. Sometimes a president may decide to withdraw a treaty if the senatorial changes are too extensive—as Wilson did with the Versailles Treaty in 1919. Wilson felt the senatorial reservations would weaken the treaty so much that it would be ineffective. His refusal to accept the senatorial version of the treaty led to the eventual refusal of the United States to join the League of Nations.

President Carter was more successful in lobbying for the treaties returning the Panama Canal to Panama by the year 2000 and neutralizing the canal. However, he was unsuccessful in his attempts to gain ratification of the Strategic Arms Limitation Talks treaty, known as SALT II. That treaty, which provided for limits on nuclear-armed, long-range bombers and intercontinental ballistic missiles, encountered fierce opposition from Senate conservatives and from the subsequent Reagan administration. The treaty was withdrawn by President Reagan.

Executive Agreements

Presidential power in foreign affairs is greatly enhanced by the use of **executive agreements** made between the president and other heads of state. Such an agreement does not require Senate approval, although the House and Senate may refuse to

Executive Agreements
International agreements made by the president, without senatorial ratification, with heads of foreign states.

Carter, Sadat and Begin signing the Camp David Accords.

appropriate the funds necessary to implement it. Also, executive agreements can be set aside by the legislature. Whereas treaties are binding on all succeeding administrations, executive agreements are not binding without each new president's consent.

Among the advantages of executive agreements are speed and secrecy. The former is essential during a crisis; the latter is important when the administration fears that open senatorial debate may be detrimental to the best interests of the United States or to the interests of the president. There have been far more executive agreements (about 9,000) than treaties (about 1,300). In 1905, Theodore Roosevelt implemented the Dillingham-Sanchez Protocol, which permitted American control of customs houses in Santo Domingo (now the Dominican Republic), as an executive agreement. In 1970, Richard Nixon did the same in concluding an agreement with the government of Spain to operate military bases. Franklin Roosevelt used executive agreements to bypass congressional isolationists in trading American destroyers for British Caribbean naval bases and in arranging diplomatic and military affairs with Canada and Latin American nations. Many executive agreements contain secret provisions calling for American military assistance or other support.

Chief Legislator

Constitutionally, the president must recommend to the Congress legislation that he judges necessary and expedient. Not all presidents have wielded their power as chief legislator in the same manner. President John Tyler was almost completely unsuccessful in getting his legislative programs implemented by Congress. Presidents Theodore Roosevelt, Franklin Roosevelt, and Lyndon B. Johnson, however, saw much of their proposed legislation put into effect.

In modern times, the president has played a dominant role in creating the congressional agenda. In the president's **State of the Union message,** which is required by the Constitution (Article II, Section 3) and given annually, usually in late January shortly after Congress reconvenes, the president as chief legislator

State of the Union Message

An annual message to Congress in which the president proposes his legislative program. The message is not only to Congress but also to the American people and to the world. It offers the opportunity to dramatize policies and objectives and to gain public support.

Reagan signing the 1985 farm legislation.

presents his program. The message gives a broad, comprehensive view of what the president wishes the legislature to accomplish during the session. It is as much a message to the American people and to the world as it is to Congress, and its impact on public opinion can determine the way Congress responds to the president's agenda.

Getting Legislation Passed

The president can propose legislation, but Congress is not required to pass any of his bills. How then does the president get his proposals made into law? One way, of course, is to draft the bills that he wants to see passed. But perhaps equally important is his power of persuasion. The president writes to, telephones, and meets with various congressional leaders. He makes public announcements to force the weight of public opinion onto Congress in favor of his legislative program. Finally, as head of his party he exercises legislative leadership through the congresspersons of his party.

To be sure, presidents whose party represents a majority in both houses of Congress have an easier time getting their legislation passed than do presidents facing hostile Congresses. But one of the ways in which a president who faces a hostile Congress can still wield power is through his ability to veto legislation.

Saying No to Legislation

The president has the power to say no through his use of the veto,[9] by which he returns a bill unsigned to the legislative body with a **veto message** attached. Since the Constitution requires that every bill passed by the House and the Senate must be sent to the president before it becomes law, the president must act on each bill.

1. If he signs the bill, it becomes law.
2. If he doesn't sign the bill and doesn't send it back to Congress after ten congressional working days, it becomes law.

[9]"Veto" in Latin means "I forbid."

Veto Message
The president's formal explanation of his veto when he returns legislation to the Congress.

President Reagan gives the state of the union address.

3. He can "veto" the bill and send it back to Congress with a message setting forth his objections. The Congress then can change the bill, hoping to secure his approval and repass it, or it can simply reject the president's objections by overriding the veto with a two-thirds roll-call vote of the members present in each house.

4. If the president refuses to sign the bill and Congress adjourns within ten working days after the bill has been submitted to the president, the bill is killed permanently for that session of Congress; and if Congress wishes the bill to be reconsidered, it must be reintroduced during the following session. This is called a **pocket veto.**

Pocket Veto

A special veto power exercised by the chief executive after a legislative body has adjourned. Bills not signed by the chief executive die after a specified period of time. If Congress wishes to reconsider such a bill, it must be reintroduced in the following session of Congress.

Presidents employed the veto power infrequently until the administration of Andrew Johnson, but it has been used with increasing vigor since then (Table 12–2). The total number of vetoes from George Washington through Jimmy Carter has been 2,391, with almost 45 percent of those vetoes being exercised by Franklin Roosevelt, Truman, and Eisenhower.

A veto is a clear-cut indication of the president's dissatisfaction with congressional legislation. It is a very effective tool as well, because it denies the legislative power of the Congress. Nonetheless, Congress rarely overrides a regular presidential veto. Consider that two-thirds of the members of each house who are present must vote to override the president's veto in a roll-call vote. This means that if only one-third plus one of the members voting in one of the houses of Congress do not agree to override the veto, the veto holds. Table 12–2 tells us that it wasn't until the administration of John Tyler that Congress overrode a presidential veto. In the first sixty-five years of American federal government history, out of thirty-five regular vetoes, Congress only overrode one, or less than 3 percent. Overall, only about 4 percent of all vetoes have been overridden.

Measuring the Success of a President's Legislative Program

One way of determining a president's strength is to evaluate his success as chief legislator: A strong president is one who has achieved much of his legislative program; a weak president is one who has achieved little. Using these definitions of strong and weak, it is possible to rank presidents according to their legislative success. Researchers do not, however, have a unified view of measuring the success of the president's legislative program. Look at Figure 12–1. Here we show the percentages of presidential victories measured by congressional votes in situations where the president took a clear-cut position. Based on this information, Kennedy appears to have been the most successful president in recent years. Ford was the least successful. The problem with the data is that they do not indicate how much proposed legislation was subsequently not pursued by the president; nor do they indicate how much legislation the president did not support after he knew he could not win on the original form of a bill he had proposed. The data in Figure 12–1 also do not weigh legislative victories and defeats in terms of their importance to the president's overall program.

Other Presidential Powers

Constitutional Powers

The powers vested in the president by Article II of the Constitution.

Statutory Powers

The powers created for the president through laws established by Congress.

The powers of the president just discussed are called **constitutional powers** because their basis lies in the Constitution. In addition, Congress has established by law, or statute, numerous other presidential powers—such as the ability to declare national emergencies. These are called **statutory powers.** Both constitutional and

Table 12–2

The Use of Veto Power by United States Presidents, 1789–1986

President	All Bills Vetoed	Public and Private Bills		
		Regular Vetoes	Pocket Vetoes	Vetoes Overridden
Washington	2	2	0	0
J. Adams	0	0	0	0
Jefferson	0	0	0	0
Madison	7	5	2	0
Monroe	1	1	0	0
J. Q. Adams	0	0	0	0
Jackson	12	5	7	0
Van Buren	1	0	1	0
W. H. Harrison	0	0	0	0
Tyler	10	6	4	1
Polk	3	2	1	0
Taylor	0	0	0	0
Fillmore	0	0	0	0
Pierce	9	9	0	5
Buchanan	7	4	3	0
Lincoln	7	2	5	0
A. Johnson	29	21	8	15
Grant	93[1]	45	48[1]	4
Hayes	13	12	1	1
Garfield	0	0	0	0
Arthur	12	4	8	1
Cleveland (1st term)	414	304	110	2
B. Harrison	44	19	25	1
Cleveland (2nd term)	170	42	128	5
McKinley	42	6	36	0
T. Roosevelt	82	42	40	1
Taft	39	30	9	1
Wilson	44	33	11	6
Harding	6	5	1	0
Coolidge	50	20	30	4
Hoover	37	21	16	3
F. D. Roosevelt	635	372	263	9

President	All Bills Vetoed	Public Bills			
		Total Vetoed	Regular Vetoes	Pocket Vetoes	Vetoes Overridden
Truman	250	83	54	29	11[2]
Eisenhower	181	81	36	45	2
Kennedy	21	9	4	5	0
Johnson	30	13	6	7	0
Nixon	43[3]	40	24	16[3]	5
Ford	66	63	46	17	12
Carter	31	29	13	16	2
Reagan[4]	52	52	31	21	6

[1]Veto total listed for Grant does not include a pocket veto of a bill that apparently never was placed before him for his signature.

[2]Truman also had one private bill overridden, making a total of 12 Truman vetoes overridden.

[3]Includes Nixon pocket veto of a bill during the 1970 congressional Christmas recess which was later ruled invalid by the District Court for the District of Columbia and the U.S. Court of Appeals for the District of Columbia.

[4]Through 1986.

SOURCES: *Presidential Vetoes, 1789–1976*, compiled by the Senate Library under the direction of J. S. Kimmitt, secretary, and Roger K. Haley, librarian (U.S. Government Printing Office, 1978) and the staff of the Senate Library. Congressional Quarterly, *Guide to Congress*, 3rd ed., 1983; *Congressional Quarterly*, 1985.

Express Powers

Constitutional and statutory powers of the president, which are expressly written into the Constitution or into congressional law.

Inherent Powers

Powers of the president derived from the loosely worded statement in the Constitution that "the executive power shall be vested in the president" and that the president should "take care that the laws be faithfully executed"; defined through practice rather than through constitutional or statutory law.

Patronage

The power to make partisan appointments to office or to public jobs.

statutory powers have been labeled the **express powers** of the president because they are expressly written into the Constitution or into congressional law.

Presidents also have what have come to be known as **inherent powers.** These depend on the loosely worded statement in the Constitution that "the executive power shall be vested in a president" and that the president should "take care that the laws be faithfully executed." The most common example of inherent powers are those emergency powers invoked by the president during wartime. Franklin Roosevelt used his inherent powers to relocate the Japanese living in the United States after the bombing of Pearl Harbor.

The President as Party Chief and Super Politician

▽

The president is by no means above political partisanship, and one of his many roles is that of chief of party. Although the Constitution says nothing about the function of the president within a political party (the mere concept of political parties was abhorrent to most of the Founding Fathers), today the president is the actual leader of his party.

As party leader, the president chooses the national committee chairperson and can try to discipline those party members who fail to support his policies. One way of exerting political power within the party is by the use of **patronage**—appointing individuals to government or public jobs. This power was more extensive in the past, before the establishment of the civil service in 1882 (see Chapter 14), but the president still retains impressive patronage power. As we noted earlier, the president can appoint several thousand individuals to jobs in the cabinet, the White House, and the federal regulatory agencies.

The president has a number of other ways of exerting influence as party chief. He may make it known that he will not appoint a particular congressperson's choice for federal judge, unless that member of congress is more supportive of his legislative

Figure 12–1

▽

Presidential Success Based on Congressional Votes 1953–1985

Most presidents have their greatest successes in the first years of their terms in office.

SOURCE: *Congressional Quarterly Weekly Report,* January 11, 1986, p. 68.

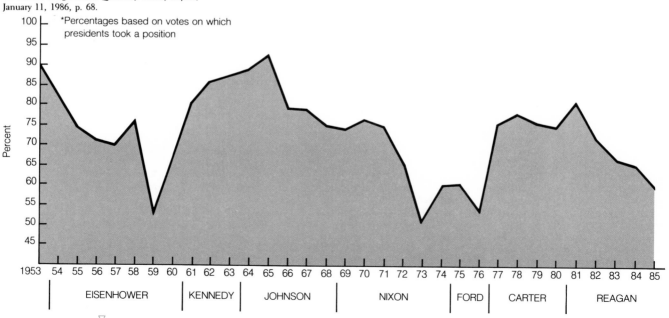

▽

The President's Personality

The legal powers of the presidency, the relationship among the president and Congress, the courts, and the media, and the challenges of history all determine the success and failure of individuals in the White House. Another set of factors influencing the president's achievements is the chief executive's style, personality, and character.

Probably the best-known scheme for analyzing presidential character is that of political scientist James David Barber. Barber suggests we look at two separate dimensions of personality that manifest themselves in the chief executive and that can be traced to early experiences. These two dimensions are (a) the degree of energy and activity a president puts into the job, and (b) whether he likes and enjoys the job. These two characteristics can be further broken down: In work energy, the president can be *active* or *passive*; in attitude toward the job, the president can be *positive* or *negative*.

When these dimensions are laid out as a grid (see the accompanying figure), we discover that Barber's presidential character model offers four different types: Active-Positive, Active-Negative, Passive-Positive, and Passive-Negative.

In Barber's view, the Active-Positives make the best presidents because they have high activity levels and are energetic while at the same time relishing the job. They display a zest for presidential tasks, project high levels of self-esteem, tolerate frustration well, and gain a sense of accomplishment from their work. They are flexible and able to laugh at themselves. Franklin Roosevelt, Harry Truman, John Kennedy, Gerald Ford, and Jimmy Carter were all Active-Positives.

On the other hand, Active-Negatives can be ultimately destructive. Although hardworking and dynamic, they receive little pleasure from politics, see the world as full of enemies, are sensitive to criticism, and are excessively serious, even morose. They may compulsively fix their sights on certain objectives, and in their rigidity ruin themselves or endanger the nation. Among the Active-Negatives were Woodrow Wilson, who could not compromise with the Senate on the League of Nations treaty; Herbert Hoover, who refused to face the economic crisis of the Depression; Lyndon Johnson, who became fixated on the Vietnam war; and Richard Nixon, who was destroyed by Watergate.

Passive-Positives enjoy what they are doing, have an upbeat approach to politics, look for approval from others, but have a laid-back approach to the job. They take regular vacations, work shorter hours, and emphasize sociability. William How-

Presidential Personality

Attitude:
level of enjoyment for the job,
satisfaction, self-esteem, flexibility, humor.

	POSITIVE	NEGATIVE
ACTIVE	**Active-Positive** Flexible, self-confident, enjoys the job, "best" type. Examples: FDR, JFK, Carter	**Active-Negative** Ambitious, driven, high energy but low esteem, feels threatened, "worst" type. Examples: Nixon, LBJ
PASSIVE	**Passive-Positive** Likeable, tolerant, other-directed, little ambition or drive Examples: Taft, Reagan, Harding	**Passive-Negative** Avoids conflict, self-doubting, serves out of duty and responsibility Examples: Eisenhower, Coolidge

Activity Level:
high energy, drive
for accomplishment

Presidential Personality

SOURCE: Adapted from James David Barber, *The Presidential Character*, 3rd ed., Englewood Cliffs, NJ: Prentice Hall, 1985.

ard Taft, Warren G. Harding, and Ronald Reagan fall into this group.

Passive-Negatives consider the presidency to be a duty, focus their efforts on carrying out the law, avoid controversy and conflict, and show little initiative. Recent Passive-Negatives were Calvin Coolidge and Dwight Eisenhower.

Critics of presidential personality studies and Barber's model in particular point out several flaws. First of all, reducing all human behavior to two dimensions is overly simplistic. Such analysis can be criticized as "pop psychology," with little grounding in psychiatry or psychological theory. Second, the possibility exists that presidents may grow and change in office. Finally, even though presidents act as lone individuals, their advisers may well counterbalance their own weaknesses.

Barber's typology does not always seem to match the performance of the presidents he discusses. Kennedy, an Active-Positive, is hard to judge because his death cut short his rec-

ord. Jimmy Carter, also an Active-Positive, is often considered to have been a weak president. Ronald Reagan, although mellow and prone to vacation, is a very active man and has certainly had more significant accomplishments than his Passive-Positive classification would predict. Some critics suggest that Barber selectively chooses evidence on presidential personalities and puts those he likes best in the most favored category. His efforts at analyzing recent presidents may be more subjective than his work with historical figures.

Attempts such as Barber's to identify presidential character, personality, and the role of the individual in the executive office are impressionistic, but they offer useful insights into the actions of past presidents.

SOURCE: James David Barber, *The Presidential Character: Predicting Performance in the White House*, 3d ed. (Englewood Cliffs, N.J.: Prentice-Hall, 1985).

---

program.[10] He may agree to campaign for a particular program or for a particular candidate. The president is often called on to mend party fences—which was the reason for John F. Kennedy's trip to Dallas on November 22, 1963, when he was assassinated.

All politicians worry about their constituencies, and so does the president. The president, however, has numerous constituencies. In principle, he is beholden to the entire electorate—the public of the United States—even to those who did not vote for him. He is certainly beholden to his party constituency because its members put him in office. His constituency also includes members of the opposing party

[10]However, "senatorial courtesy" (see Chapter 13) often puts the judicial appointment in the hands of the Senate.

Reagan campaigning for Kay Orr, Republican candidate for Governor in Nebraska.

whose cooperation he needs. Finally, the president has to take into consideration a constituency that has come to be called the **Washington community**. It is a community that consists of individuals who—whether in or out of political office—are intimately familiar with the workings of government, that thrives on gossip, and that daily measures the political power of the president.[11]

All of these constituencies are impressed by presidents who maintain a high level of public approval, partly because this is very difficult to accomplish. Presidential popularity, as measured by national polls, gives the president an extra political resource to use in persuading legislators or bureaucrats, who realize that in refusing the president, they may be going against public sentiment. President Reagan has shown amazing strength in the public opinion polls for a second-term chief executive. As Figure 12–2 indicates, the president's popularity surpasses even that of Eisenhower, who was genuinely admired by many Americans. A Gallup poll of June 1985 showed that President Reagan was also improving his image in history, with the public ranking him as sixth on the list of the nation's greatest presidents, behind Kennedy, Lincoln, Franklin Roosevelt, Truman, and Washington.[12]

Faced with a crucial election in 1986 which would determine control of the Senate, President Reagan drew on his high standing with the public to campaign for Republican candidates. During the last two weeks of the campaign, the President travelled more than 23,000 miles to urge the voters to "stay the course." He tried to pursuade them to vote for Republican candidates so that his programs would be supported. The voters rejected the President's appeal decisively, defeating seven Republican incumbents, and giving control of the Senate to the Democrats. Like other presidents, Ronald Reagan's popularity was unable to sway votes in an off-year election.

[11]See Richard E. Neustadt, *Presidential Power*, (New York: John Wiley, 1960).
[12]The Gallup Poll, 1985.

Washington Community
Individuals regularly involved with the political circles in Washington, D.C.

Figure 12–2
▽
Reagan and His Predecessors
SOURCE: *Public Opinion*, February/March 1986, pp. 36–39.

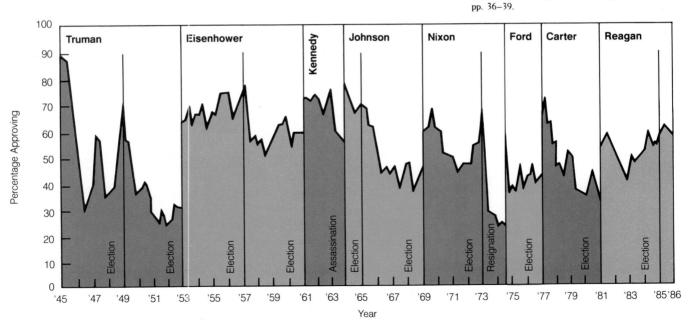

Emergency Powers

Inherent powers exercised by the president during a period of national crisis, particularly in foreign affairs.

Executive Order

A rule or regulation issued by the president that has the effect of law. Executive orders can implement and give administrative effect to provisions in the Constitution, to treaties, and to statutes.

▽

The Special Uses of Presidential Power

▽

The president has at his disposal a variety of special powers and privileges not available to other branches of the U.S. government. These include (1) emergency powers, (2) executive orders, (3) executive immunity, and (4) impoundment of funds.

Emergency Powers

If you were to read the Constitution, you would find no mention of the additional powers that the executive office may exercise during national emergencies. Indeed, the Supreme Court has indicated that an "emergency does not create power."[13] But it is clear that presidents have used their inherent powers during times of emergency, particularly in the realm of foreign affairs. The **emergency powers** of the president were first enunciated in the Supreme Court's decision in *United States v. Curtiss-Wright Export Corporation*.[14] In that case, President Franklin Roosevelt, without authorization by Congress, had ordered an embargo on the shipment of weapons to two warring South American countries. The Court recognized that the president may exercise his inherent powers in foreign affairs and that the national government has primacy in foreign affairs.

Examples of emergency powers are abundant, coinciding with real or contrived crises in domestic and foreign affairs. Abraham Lincoln's suspension of civil liberties at the beginning of the Civil War, his calling of the state militias into national service, and his subsequent governance of conquered areas and even of areas of northern states were justified by claims that such actions were essential to preserve the Union. Franklin Roosevelt declared an "unlimited national emergency" following the fall of France in World War II and mobilized the federal budget and the economy for war preparations.

A more recent example occurred when President Harry S. Truman authorized the federal seizure of steel plants and their operation by the national government in 1952 during the Korean war. Truman claimed he was using his inherent emergency power as chief executive and commander in chief to safeguard the nation's security, as the ongoing steel mill strike threatened the supply of weapons to the armed forces. The Supreme Court did not agree, saying the president had no authority under the Constitution to seize private property or to legislate such action.[15] According to legal scholars, this was the first time a limit was placed on the exercise of the president's emergency powers.

Executive Orders

Congress allows the president (and his administrative agencies) to issue **executive orders** that have the force of law. These executive orders can do the following: (1) give force to legislative statutes, (2) enforce the Constitution or treaties with foreign nations, and (3) establish or modify practices of executive administrative agencies.

[13]*Home Building and Loan Association v. Blaisdell*, 290 U.S. 398 (1934).

[14]229 U.S. 304 (1936).

[15]*Youngstown Sheet and Tube Co. v. Sawyer*, 343 U.S. 579 (1952).

An executive order, then, represents the president's legislative power. The only apparent requirement is that under the Administrative Procedures Act of 1946, all executive orders must be published in the **Federal Register.**

Executive orders have been used to establish some procedures for appointing noncareer administrators, to implement national affirmative action regulations, to restructure the White House bureaucracy, to ration consumer goods and to administer wage and price controls under emergency conditions, to classify government information as secret, and to regulate exports of restricted items. Nearly 13,000 executive orders have been promulgated in a numbered series officially compiled by the State Department, and many more have never been compiled.

Executive Immunity

Another inherent executive power that has been claimed by presidents involves the ability of the president and his executive officials to refuse to appear before, or to withhold information from, Congress or the courts. This is called **executive immunity,** and it relies on the constitutional separation of powers for its basis. Critics of executive immunity believe it can be used to shield from public scrutiny actions of the executive branch that should be open to Congress and to the American public.

Federal Register
A publication of the executive branch which prints executive orders, rules, and regulations.

Executive Immunity
The right of executive officials to refuse to appear before, or to withhold information from, a legislative committee. Executive privilege is enjoyed by the president and by those executive officials accorded that right by the president.

President Richard Nixon.

Limits to executive immunity went untested until the Watergate affair in the early 1970s when the Supreme Court subpoenaed secret tapes containing Richard Nixon's Oval Office conversations during his tenure at the White House. Nixon refused to turn them over, claiming executive immunity. He argued that "no president could function if the private papers of his office, prepared by his personal staff, were open to public scrutiny." In one of the Court's most famous cases, *United States v. Nixon* (1974),[16] the judges unanimously ruled that Nixon had to hand over the tapes to the Court. Executive immunity could not be used to prevent evidence from being heard in criminal proceedings.

Impoundment of Funds

By law, the president proposes a budget and Congress approves it. But there is no clear-cut constitutional indication that the president, as chief executive, is required by law to *spend* all of the funds appropriated by Congress, and many presidents have not done so. In 1803, Thomas Jefferson deferred a $50,000 appropriation for gunboats. Ulysses Grant returned to the Treasury unspent money for public works. In 1932, Herbert Hoover canceled projects funded by Congress. Franklin Roosevelt deferred spending on a number of appropriations to later fiscal years. Truman didn't spend all the money Congress had allocated for the military, nor did Johnson the money allocated for highway construction, nor did Kennedy the money for weapons systems.

The question came to a head during the Nixon administration after a number of confrontations over this issue between the president and an antagonistic, Democratic-controlled Congress. When Nixon vetoed appropriations bills, Congress often overruled his veto. In retaliation, Nixon impounded the appropriated funds and refused to spend them, claiming that he wanted to reduce overall federal spending. As part of its new Budget and Impoundment Control Act of 1974, Congress required that the president spend all appropriated funds, although Congress gave the president some leeway. If the president is not going to spend all appropriated funds, he must tell Congress; and only if Congress agrees within forty-five days can the president withhold spending. If the president simply wishes to delay spending, he must indicate this to Congress. If Congress does not agree, it can pass a resolution requiring immediate spending of the appropriated funds. During the time when Congress was deliberating on the budget bill, cities, states, and certain members of Congress sued President Nixon over the impoundment issue. The Supreme Court in 1975 unanimously ruled that the president had to spend money appropriated by Congress because of his obligation to "take care that the laws be faithfully executed."[17]

Abuses of Executive Power: Impeachment
▽

Impeachment

As authorized by Article I of the Constitution, impeachment is an action by the House of Representatives and the Senate to remove the president, vice president, or civil officers of the United States from office for crimes of "treason, bribery, or other high crimes and misdemeanors."
▽

Presidents normally leave office either because their first term has expired and they did not seek (or win) reelection or because, having served two full terms, they are not allowed to seek reelection (owing to the Twenty-second Amendment, passed in 1951). Eight presidents have left office because of death. But there is still another way for a president to leave office—by **impeachment**. Article I of the Constitution

[16]318 U.S. 683 (1974).

[17]*Train v. City of New York*, 420 U.S. 35 (1975).

394

Highlight

▽

Watergate: A Crime of Power?

On June 17, 1972, at 2:30 A.M., five men were arrested in the headquarters of the Democratic National Committee in the Watergate apartment complex in Washington, D.C. It was obvious from the outset that this was no ordinary burglary. The five men, dressed in business suits and wearing surgical gloves, were also found to have in their possession some extraordinary items: two cameras, forty rolls of film, lock picks, pen-sized tear-gas guns, bugging devices, a walkie-talkie, and nearly $2,300 in cash among them. In the following days and months, as investigations of the Watergate break-in continued, a story was pieced together that shocked the nation.

The five men had been searching for documents that would connect Senator George McGovern, the Democratic nominee for president, with Fidel Castro and thereby discredit McGovern in the eyes of the American public. They were also looking for any information the Democratic National Committee might have stumbled on that could prove embarrassing to the Nixon administration.

Six days after the break-in, President Nixon and his White House chief of staff, H. R. (Bob) Haldeman, formulated a plan by which the Central Intelligence Agency (CIA) would impede the investigation of the affair that was being undertaken by the Federal Bureau of Investigation.

By early 1973, however, a select Senate committee was established, under the chairmanship of Senator Sam Ervin of North Carolina, to investigate the Watergate affair. During the Senate investigation information about the

John Dean testifying at Nixon's impeachment hearing.

White House-sponsored criminal activities and subsequent cover-up began to leak out. John Dean, III, President Nixon's legal counsel, eventually told the committee that the president himself was responsible for the cover-up. The committee also learned that the Oval Office conversations had been tape-recorded.

Archibald Cox, the Watergate special prosecutor in charge of legal investigations into the affair, subpoenaed several of the tapes, an action upheld by the federal district and appeals courts. The "Saturday Night Massacre" ensued, in which Nixon fired Cox, and the attorney general and deputy attorney general were both forced to resign because they refused to obey Nixon's orders to fire Cox. Many of Nixon's closest White House aides were in-

dicted in the scandal, and Nixon himself was named an unindicted coconspirator by the grand jury. A new special prosecutor and Congress subpoenaed a large number of tapes, which the president refused to make available—except in edited form—to Congress. On July 24, 1974, the U.S. Supreme Court ruled that Nixon had to give up the information requested by the special prosecutor. Three days later, the House Judiciary Committee passed the first of three articles of impeachment against President Nixon. On August 9, Nixon resigned, and his vice president, Gerald Ford (who had in turn replaced the first Nixon vice president, Spiro Agnew—who had resigned because it was revealed he had accepted bribes as governor of Maryland), became president.

Nixon leaving the White House after his resignation.

authorizes the House and Senate to remove the president, the vice president, or civil officers of the United States for crimes of "treason, bribery, or other high crimes and misdemeanors." No one has really defined "high crimes and misdemeanors," but at least twice the Congress and the American public were pretty sure that a president had engaged in them.

The authority to impeach is vested in the House of Representatives, and formal impeachment proceedings are initiated there. The power to try impeachment cases rests with the Senate. In the House, a representative must list the charges against the president, vice president, or other civil officer. The impeachment charges are referred either to the Judiciary Committee or to a special investigating committee. If a majority in the House vote for impeachment, then Articles of Impeachment are drawn up, which set forth the basis for the removal of the executive-branch officer. When the president is on trial, the Chief Justice of the United States presides over the Senate. A two-thirds vote of the senators present is required for conviction. The only punishment that Congress can mete out is removal from office and disqualification from holding any other federal office. However, the convicted official is subject to further punishment according to law.

In the history of the United States, no president has ever been impeached and also convicted. The only president who was actually impeached by the House was Andrew Johnson, but he was acquitted by the Senate by the margin of a single vote in 1868. Some argue that Johnson's impeachment was simply a case of partisan politics. Impeachment attempts were made against Tyler (1847), Hoover (1932 and 1933), and Vice President Schuyler Colfax (1873).

The case of Richard Nixon, however, was more serious and certainly less questionable in terms of its political motivation. In 1974, the House was ready to vote on Nixon's impeachment and to send the Articles of Impeachment to the Senate when Nixon resigned.

The Executive Organization

▽

Gone are the days when presidents answered their own mail, as George Washington did. It wasn't until 1857 that Congress authorized a private secretary for the president to be paid by the federal government. Woodrow Wilson typed most of his correspondence, even though he did have several secretaries. At the beginning of FDR's long tenure at the White House, the entire staff consisted of thirty-seven individuals. It wasn't until the New Deal and World War II that the presidential staff became a sizable organization. Today, the executive organization includes a White House Office staff of about six hundred, including some workers who are part-time and others who are detailed from their departments to the White House. The personal presidential staff have such titles as counselor, chief of staff, press secretary, assistant to the president for national security affairs, assistant to the president for public liaison, assistant to the president for legislative affairs, and many others.

The Cabinet

Cabinet

An advisory group selected by the president to aid him in making decisions. The cabinet presently numbers twelve department secretaries and the attorney general. Depending on the president, the cabinet may be highly influential or relatively insignificant in its advisory role.

Although the Constitution does not include the word *cabinet*, it does state that the president "may require the Opinion, in writing, of the principal Officer in each of the executive Departments." Since our first president there has always been an advisory group, or **cabinet,** to which the president turns for counsel. Originally, the cabinet consisted of only four individuals—the secretaries of state, treasury, and war, and the attorney general. Today the cabinet numbers twelve secretaries and the attorney general. Table 12–3 shows the chronological growth of the president's cabinet.

The cabinet may consist of more than the secretaries of the various departments. The president at his discretion can, for example, ascribe cabinet rank to his National Security Council adviser, to the ambassador to the United Nations, or to others. Since neither the Constitution nor statutory law requires the president to consult with his cabinet, its use is purely at his discretion. Some presidents have relied on

Did You Know?

That our tenth president, John Tyler, had fifteen children?

Table 12–3

Cabinet Departments

Department	Function
State (1789)	Foreign policy making and treaties
Treasury (1789)	The federal government's banker
War (1789)	Administration of the Army only (this department was merged with the Department of the Navy and with the addition of the Air Force was called the National Military Establishment in 1947)
Attorney General (1789)	Government's attorney (became the Justice Department in 1870)
Navy (1798)	Administration of the Navy (became part of the National Military Establishment in 1947)
Interior (1849)	Manager of national natural resources, including public lands
Justice (1870)	Government's attorney with attorney general as head
Post Office (1872)	Operation of the mails (became an independent federal agency in 1970)
Agriculture (1889)	Administration of farm programs and, currently, the food stamp program
Commerce and Labor (1903)	Conducts U.S. census, aids business and labor organizations (split into two separate departments in 1913)
Commerce (1913)	Formerly part of Commerce and Labor
Labor (1913)	Formerly part of Commerce and Labor
Defense (DOD) (1949)	Combined departments of Army and Navy with Air Force added
Health, Education and Welfare (HEW) (1953)	Health and welfare programs, Social Security, and education (split in 1980)
Housing and Urban Development (HUD) (1965)	The nation's public housing programs
Transportation (DOT) (1966)	Federally funded highway programs and mass transportation
Energy (DOE) (1977)	Research, atomic energy, and overall national energy policy
Health and Human Services (HHS) (1980)	From HEW
Education (1980)	From HEW

Kitchen Cabinet
The informal advisers to the president.

the counsel of their cabinets more than others. Eisenhower frequently turned to his cabinet for advice on a wide range of governmental policies—perhaps because he was used to the team approach in solving problems. Other presidents have solicited the opinions of their cabinets and then did what they wanted to do anyway. Lincoln supposedly said—after a cabinet meeting in which a vote was seven nays against his one aye—"Seven nays and one aye, the ayes have it."[18] In general, few presidents have relied heavily on the advice of their cabinet members. Carter thought he could put his cabinet to good use and held regular cabinet meetings for the first two years of his tenure. Then he fired three cabinet members and forced two others to resign while reorganizing his "inner government." He rarely met with the members of his cabinet thereafter. In recent years, the growth of other parts of the executive branch has rendered the cabinet relatively insignificant as an advisory board to the president.

Often a president will use a **kitchen cabinet** to replace the formal cabinet as his major source of advice. The term *kitchen cabinet* originated during the presidency of Andrew Jackson, who relied on the counsel of close friends who often met with him in the kitchen of the White House. A kitchen cabinet is a very informal group of advisers who may or may not be otherwise connected with the government, such as Reagan's trusted California coterie.

It is not surprising that presidents only reluctantly meet with their cabinet heads. Often the departmental heads are more responsive to the wishes of their own staffs or to their own political ambitions than they are to the president. They may be more concerned with obtaining resources for their departments than with helping the president achieve his goals. So there is often a strong conflict of interest between the president and his cabinet members. It is likely that formal cabinet meetings are held more out of respect for the cabinet tradition than for their problem-solving value.

[18]Quoted in Thomas E. Cronin, *The State of the Presidency*, 2nd ed. (Boston: Little, Brown, 1980), p. 11.

A satirical treatment of Andrew Jackson's "kitchen cabinet."

The Executive Office of the President

When President Franklin Roosevelt appointed a special committee on administrative management, he knew it would determine that the president needed help. Indeed, the committee proposed a major reorganization of the executive branch. Congress did not approve the entire reorganization, but it did create the **Executive Office of the President (EOP)** to provide staff assistance for the chief executive and to help him coordinate the executive bureaucracy. Since that time, a number of agencies have been created to supply the president with advice and staff help. These are as follows:

▽ The White House Office (1939)
▽ Council of Economic Advisers (1946)
▽ National Security Council (1947)
▽ Office of the United States Trade Representative (1963)
▽ Council on Environmental Quality (1969)
▽ Office of Management and Budget (1970)
▽ Office of Science and Technology Policy (1976)
▽ Office of Administration (1977)
▽ Office of Policy Development (1977)

One of the most important of the agencies within the EOP is the **White House Office,** which includes most of the key personal and political advisers to the president. Among the jobs held by these aides are legal counsel to the president, secretary, press secretary, and appointments secretary. Often the individuals who hold these positions are recruited from the president's campaign staff, and their duties, mainly protecting the president's political interests, are similar to campaign functions.

Several other of the nine offices within the EOP are especially important.

Council of Economic Advisers (CEA)

The Employment Act of 1946 created a three-member **Council of Economic Advisers** to advise the president on economic matters. Their advice serves as the basis for the president's annual economic report to Congress. Each of the three members is appointed by the president and can be removed at will. In principle the CEA was also created to advise the president on economic policy, but for the most part CEAs have functioned to prepare the annual report. Many economists have refused the job, indicating that they do not want to become "part of the team"—unable to express ideas on, say, inflation, unemployment, and interest rates that may be at odds with administration policy. Members of the council are often at odds with members of the president's cabinet. In 1983, the public dispute between CEA Chairman Martin Feldstein and Secretary of the Treasury Donald Regan over the importance of the nearly $200-billion federal budget deficit projected for 1984 resulted in White House displeasure with Feldstein's statements and, in 1984, his resignation.

Office of Management and Budget (OMB)

The **Office of Management and Budget** was originally the Bureau of the Budget, created in 1921 in the Department of the Treasury. Recognizing the importance of this agency, President Franklin Roosevelt moved it into the White House office

---

Executive Office of the President (EOP)
Established by President Franklin D. Roosevelt by executive order under the Reorganization Act of 1939. It currently consists of nine staff agencies that assist the president in carrying out his major duties.

White House Office
The staff agency under the EOP which includes most of the key personal and political advisers of the president. The office facilitates relations with Congress, executive agencies, the media, and the public.

Council of Economic Advisers (CEO)
A staff agency in the Executive Office that advises the president on measures to maintain stability in the nation's economy. Established in 1946, the council develops economic plans and budget recommendations for maintaining the nation's "employment, production, and purchasing power" and helps the president prepare an annual economic report to Congress.

Office of Management and Budget (OMB)
A division of the Executive Office created by executive order in 1970 to replace the Bureau of the Budget. OMB's main functions are to assist the president in preparing the annual budget, to clear and coordinate all departmental or agency budgets, to help set fiscal policy, and to supervise the administration of the federal budget.

in 1939. Nixon reorganized the Bureau of the Budget in 1970 and changed its name to reflect its new managerial function. It is headed by a director who must make up the annual federal budget that the president presents to Congress each January for approval (which is rarely forthcoming without months of haggling over changes). In principle, the director of the OMB has broad fiscal powers in planning and estimating various parts of the federal budget, as all agencies must submit their proposed budget to OMB for approval. In reality, it is not so clear that the OMB can truly affect the greater scope of the federal budget. Although David Stockman, President Reagan's aggressive OMB director, constantly fought against misman-agement and inefficient use of government funds, the overall effect on the total size of the federal budget was not significant. The director's job may be more important as a clearinghouse for legislative proposals initiated in the executive agencies.

National Security Council (NSC)

National Security Council (NSC)
A staff agency in the Executive Office established by the National Security Act of 1947. The NSC advises the president on domestic and foreign matters involving national security.

The **National Security Council** is a link between the president's key foreign and military advisers and the president. Its members consist of the president, the vice president, the secretaries of state and defense, plus other informal members. The NSC has the resources of the National Security Agency (NSA) at its disposal in giving counsel to the president. Included in the NSC is the president's special assistant for national security affairs. Nixon had Henry Kissinger in this post; Carter had the equally visible Zbigniew Brzezinski.

The Vice Presidency
▽

Vice presidents usually have not been overly ecstatic about their position. FDR's vice president for his first two terms, John Nance Garner, said that "the vice presidency isn't worth a pitcher of warm spit." Harry Truman, himself FDR's last vice president, was even more forthright: "[Vice presidents] were about as useful as a cow's fifth tit." Walter Mondale, Carter's hard-working vice president and one of the few who truly took an active role in the executive branch, said, "They know who Amy is, but they don't know me." He was referring to Carter's grammar school-aged daughter.

The Vice President's Job

The Constitution doesn't give much power to the vice president. His only formal duty is to preside over the Senate—which is rarely necessary. He fulfills this obligation when the Senate organizes and adopts its rules and when he is needed to decide a tie vote. In all other cases the president pro tempore manages parliamentary procedure in the Senate. The vice president is expected only to participate informally in senatorial deliberations, if at all.

Traditionally, vice presidents have been chosen by presidential nominees to balance the ticket or to reward or appease party factions. If a presidential nominee is from the North, it is not a bad idea to have a vice presidential nominee from the South or the West. If the presidential nominee is from a rural state, perhaps someone with an urban background would be most suitable as a running mate. If the presidential nominee is strongly conservative or strongly liberal in many of his views, he would do well to have a vice presidential nominee who is more in the middle of the political road.

Vice presidents have infrequently become elected presidents in their own right. John Adams and Thomas Jefferson were the first to do so. Then Martin Van Buren was elected president in 1836 after he had served as Jackson's vice president. Nixon became president in 1968, having been Eisenhower's vice president eight years earlier.

The job of the vice president is certainly not time consuming, even when the president gives some specific task to the vice president. Typically, he spends his time supporting the president's activities. All of this changes, of course, if the president becomes disabled or dies in office.

Presidential Succession

Eight vice presidents have become president because of the death of the president. John Tyler, the first, took over William Henry Harrison's position after only one month. No one knew whether Tyler should simply be a caretaker until a new president could be elected three and a half years later or whether he should actually be president. Tyler assumed that he was supposed to be the chief executive and he acted as such—although he was commonly referred to as "His Accidency." On all occasions since then, vice presidents taking over the position of the presidency because of the incumbent's death have assumed all the presidential powers.

> ### Did You Know?
> ▽
>
> That every president from William Henry Harrison to John Kennedy who was elected on the first year of a new decade died in office (Harrison in 1840, Lincoln in 1860, Garfield in 1880, McKinley in 1900, Harding in 1920, Roosevelt in 1940, and Kennedy in 1960)?

The Reagan assassination attempt of March 31, 1981.

Twenty-fifth Amendment
An amendment to the Constitution adopted in 1967 that establishes procedures for filling vacancies in the two top executive offices and that makes provisions for situations involving presidential disability.

Spiro Agnew, Vice President 1969–1973.

But what should a vice president do if a president becomes incapable of carrying out his duties while in office? When Garfield was shot in 1888, he stayed alive for two and a half months. What was Vice President Chester Arthur's role?

This question was not addressed in the original Constitution. Article II, Section 1, says only that "in case of the removal of the president from office, or of his death, resignation, or inability to discharge the powers and duties of the said office, the same shall devolve on the vice president."

Congress has made numerous attempts to deal with the thorny problem of presidential inability. When Eisenhower became ill a second time in 1958, he entered into a pact with Nixon providing that the vice president could determine whether the president was incapable of carrying out his duties if the president could not communicate. Kennedy and Johnson entered into similar agreements with their vice presidents. Finally, the **Twenty-fifth Amendment** was passed in 1967, establishing procedures in case of presidential incapacity.

The Twenty-fifth Amendment

According to the Twenty-fifth Amendment, when the president believes he is incapable of performing the duties of office, he must inform the Congress in writing. Then the vice president serves as acting president until the president can resume his normal duties. In cases where the president is unable to communicate, a majority of the cabinet, including the vice president, can declare that fact to Congress. Then the vice president serves as acting president until the president resumes his normal duties.

If a dispute arises over the president's ability to discharge his normal functions, a two-thirds vote of Congress is required to install the vice president as acting president; a two-thirds vote is also required to reinstall the president and allow him to resume his duties.

Although President Reagan did not formally invoke the Twenty-fifth Amendment during his surgery for the removal of a cancerous growth in his colon on July 13, 1985, he followed its provisions in temporarily transferring power to the vice president, George Bush. At 10:32 A.M., before the operation began, Reagan signed letters to the speaker of the House and the president pro tem of the Senate directing that the vice president "shall discharge those powers and duties in my stead commencing with the administration of anesthesia to me . . . ." In early evening of that same day, Reagan transmitted another letter to both officials announcing that he was again in charge. During this period, Vice President Bush signed no bills and took no actions as acting president. Although the Reagan administration claimed that the president's action set no precedents, most legal experts saw his acts as the first official use of the Twenty-fifth Amendment.

When the Vice Presidency Becomes Vacant

The Twenty-fifth Amendment also addresses the issue of how the president should fill a vacant vice presidency. Section 2 of the amendment simply states, "Whenever there is a vacancy in the office of the vice president, the president shall nominate a vice president who shall take office upon confirmation by a majority vote of both houses in Congress." This is exactly what occurred when Nixon's vice president, Spiro Agnew, resigned in 1973 because of his alleged receipt of construction contract

On Saturday, July 13, 1985, President Ronald Reagan was operated on at Bethesda Naval Hospital for colon cancer. A two-foot section of Reagan's large intestine was removed. From midmorning until early evening, George Bush was the nation's first "acting president," a status created by the Twenty-fifth Amendment to the Constitution. Before the ratification of that amendment, previous presidents had worked out informal arrangements to delegate authority to their vice presidents in case they were not able to function in office.

This will not be the last case of a serious presidential illness or incapacity, and it certainly was not the first. George Washington was a hypochondriac, suffered from tuberculosis, pneumonia, rheumatism, and had a deformed jaw caused by rotting teeth, which were replaced with wooden dentures. He was disabled for 109 days of his tenure, during which time he could not conduct much official business. Thomas Jefferson suffered from severe

depression and migraine headaches. James Madison was an epileptic.

Several presidents were incapacitated by illness, and their medical problems were kept secret from the public. In July 1893, Grover Cleveland underwent two secret operations for jaw cancer; the public was told only that he had a problem with abscessed teeth.

Woodrow Wilson was debilitated by a stroke in October 1919, but his wife and doctor concealed this fact from the nation. During the seventeen months he was ill, his wife, Edith Wilson, read his documents and decided whom he would see. Congress in the meantime refused to ratify the League of Nations Treaty and passed twenty-eight bills that Wilson never signed.

In the years before the passage of the Twenty-fifth Amendment, the threat of presidential incapacity seemed even greater. Dwight Eisenhower suffered a serious heart attack in 1955, an ileitis operation in 1956, and a stroke in 1957. John Kennedy had serious back problems and suffered from Addison's disease, a form of tuberculosis. Lyndon Johnson underwent a gallbladder operation in October 1965, and Richard Nixon contracted viral pneumonia in July 1973, which kept him hospitalized for eight days.

Clearly, presidential sickness and an emergency succession are real probabilities in American political life.

kickbacks during his tenure as governor of Maryland. Nixon turned to Gerald R. Ford as his choice for vice president. After extensive hearings, both houses confirmed the appointment. Then when Nixon resigned on August 9, 1974, Ford automatically became president and nominated as his vice president Nelson Rockefeller. Congress confirmed Ford's choice. For the first time in the history of the country, both the president and the vice president were individuals who had not been elected to their positions.

Is the Power of the Presidency Increasing or Decreasing?

▽

After the Watergate scandal in 1972 and immediately following the ending of the Vietnam war, many people feared that the American presidency had become far too powerful. As commander in chief, the president could engage U.S. military forces anywhere in the world; his control over the budget process gave him authority over Congress and the executive agencies; and the constant expansion of the Executive Office of the President provided him with better information and assistance than that available to the other branches of government.

Congressional response to this augmented presidential power was quite striking. Among the techniques forged by Congress to maintain a balance of power with the president were the War Powers Act of 1973, which required the president to consult with Congress before committing American troops; the Budget and Impoundment Control Act of 1974, which restrained the president's power to impound funds; and the Case Amendment of 1972, which limited the use of secret executive agreements. Congress also resorted more frequently to the legislative veto to control presidential policy making.

The ability of President Reagan to get his first tax plan and budget passed in 1981 by a Democratic House suggests that the balance of power has not swung too heavily to Congress. In the first six years of his presidency, Reagan reaffirmed the power of the president as commander in chief with his use of military forces in Lebanon and Central America and against Libya. He convinced the Congress to support aid for the *contras* in Nicaragua and to work for and complete serious tax reform. One of the reasons for Mr. Reagan's general success has been his ability to persuade individual legislators. Even more important was his continued strong standing in the polls. As long as any president has support from the public and is able to survive media criticism, he has great latitude of action. If the president's actions are unpopular and his political power weakens, it is likely that his power on Capitol Hill and elsewhere will be more limited. By early 1987 with his performance appraisal slipping badly owing to the Iran arms deal and *contra* supply scandal, Reagan confronted a generally hostile Congress and an increasingly probing media with a considerably weaker power base.

In March 1981, the Reagan administration encountered its first notable public opinion backlash. The issue was U.S. presence in El Salvador. While the White House was emphasizing the overwhelming support for the president's economic recovery program, as evidenced by incoming mail, it was underplaying the mail response to the administration's El Salvador policy. Letters to the White House ran ten to one against sending military aid and advisers to the impoverished, strife-ridden Central American country. The signal to the president was clear: The public was not enthusiastic about the possibilities of U.S. involvement in a foreign war.

Such expressions of public support or opposition are important either to legitimize the administration's actions or to voice disapproval. Although you will probably not have the opportunity to express your personal opinions directly to the president, your views and those of others who think the same way can be brought to his attention. If you strongly agree with, or oppose, certain actions taken by the president, you can contact the White House, addressing your letter as follows:

The President of the United States
The White House
1600 Pennsylvania Ave., N.W.
Washington, D.C. 20500

You could also send a telegram to that address or telephone the White House directly at 202-456-1414.

Another way to communicate your views to the executive branch is to write a letter to the editor of a major newspaper. The White House clips letters from newspapers across the country to provide a digest of public opinion for the president and his staff.

Chapter Summary

▽

1. The office of the presidency of the United States, combining the functions of chief of state and chief executive, is unique. Most democratic nations of Europe have a parliamentary system of government in which the chief executive is chosen by the legislature.

2. Of the two opposing views at the Constitutional Convention, one favored a weak executive who would carry out the will of the legislature and the other favored a strong, independent executive. The office of the presidency was molded by the desires of the latter.

3. Requirements for becoming president, outlined in Article II, Section 1, of the Constitution, concern age, citizenship, and residence.

4. U.S. voters select a president and vice president by casting ballots for presidential electors who in turn cast their ballots in the electoral college.

5. Constitutional powers of the president are set forth in Article II of the Constitution. These include the roles of chief of state, chief executive, commander in chief, chief diplomat, and chief legislator.

6. As chief of state, the president is the ceremonial head of the government of the United States.

7. As chief executive, the president is constitutionally bound to enforce the acts of Congress, the judgments of federal courts, and treaties to which the United States is a signatory. He has the power of appointment and the power to grant reprieves and pardons.

8. As commander in chief of the armed forces, the president exercises a vast array of war powers and is the ultimate decision maker in military matters.

9. As chief diplomat, the president, with the advice and consent of the Senate, makes treaties, recognizes foreign governments, and nominates and receives ambassadors. The president can make executive agreements with other heads of state without senatorial approval.

10. The role of the president as chief legislator includes recommending legislation to Congress, exercising veto power, and informally influencing Congress to pass presidentially sponsored legislation. The evaluation of a president's success is based to a large extent on his success or failure as chief legislator.

11. The Constitution provides that every bill passed by the

House and Senate must be sent to the president before it becomes law. The president has the option to veto the bill and send it back to Congress with a message setting forth his objections. Congress can change the bill and repass it or override the veto with a two-thirds roll-call vote.

12. The president has statutory powers, or those written into law by Congress, and inherent powers, which are defined by practice.

13. Although not set forth in the Constitution, the president is the leader of his political party as well as a politician serving numerous constituencies.

14. The special powers of the president include emergency powers, executive orders, executive immunity, and impoundment of funds.

15. Abuses of executive power are dealt with by Article I of the Constitution, which authorizes the House and Senate to remove the president, the vice president, or civil officers of the United States for crimes of "treason, bribery, or other high crimes and misdemeanors."

16. The executive organization of today includes a White House Office staff of about six hundred.

17. The cabinet, an advisory group selected by the president to aid him in making decisions, today includes twelve department secretaries and the attorney general. Its use and membership is determined by tradition and is at the discretion of the president.

18. The Executive Office of the President was established by Franklin D. Roosevelt by executive order in 1939. The components have changed over the years; today the major staff agencies include the Office of Management and Budget, the White House Office, the Council of Economic Advisers, the National Security Council, the Office of Policy Development, the Office of the United States Trade Representative, the Council on Environmental Quality, the Office of Science and Technology Policy, and the Office of Administration.

19. The vice president is the constitutional officer assigned to preside over the Senate and to assume the presidency in case of the death, resignation, removal, or disability of the president. The vice president participates informally in the Senate, voting only when a tie occurs. Vice presidents have traditionally been chosen to balance the party ticket or to reward or appease party factions.

20. The Twenty-fifth Amendment, passed in 1967, established procedures to be followed in case of presidential incapacity and when filling a vacant vice presidency.

Questions for Review and Discussion

▽

1. The roles of the president often require difficult decisions. What should the president do when Congress sends him a law which violates his own party platform? Think of other situations when the political needs of the president may not be consistent with national needs.

2. The president is frequently seen as the chief legislator of the nation. How much power does he have to get laws passed? What restraints does the Congress have on this role?

3. What is the process for impeaching the president? Can a president be impeached for political reasons—that is, by offending enough members of Congress?

4. Why has the Executive Office of the President grown so dramatically in the last quarter century? Does this existence of so many advisory and staff offices really assist the president in his job?

Selected References

▽

James D. Barber, *The Presidential Character: Predicting Performance in the White House*, 2d ed. (Englewood Cliffs, N.J.: Prentice-Hall, 1977). A masterful typology of the personal traits of presidents and the consequences for how we are governed.

John Hart, *The Presidential Branch* (Elmsford, N.Y.: Pergamon Press, 1987). This book traces the history of the Executive Office from 1857 to the present, analyzing the role of staff power, accountability, and the importance of the Executive Office in the post-Watergate period.

Samuel Kernell, *Going Public: New Strategies of Presidential Leadership* (Washington, D.C.: Congressional Quarterly Press, 1986). This fascinating book explores and describes how presidents have increasingly bypassed the traditional process of bargaining with Congress and have "gone public" with presidential priorities in an effort to bring direct public pressure on Congress.

Raymond Tatalovich and Byron Daynes, *Presidential Power in the United States* (Monterey, Calif.: Brooks/Cole, 1983). An authoritative book summarizing the research on presidential power and action.

John Tebbel and Sara Miles Watts, *The Press and the Presidency* (New York; Oxford University Press, 1985). From Washington to Reagan, this book explores the delicate relationship between the White House and the media, with special emphasis on presidential manipulation of the mass media and implications for the First Amendment.

Chapter 13
▽
The Congress

Contents
Why Was Congress Created?
The Powers of Congress
The Functions of Congress
House-Senate Differences
Congresspersons and the Citizenry: A Comparison
Congressional Elections
Congressional Reapportionment
Pay, Perks, and Privileges
The Committee Structure
The Formal Leadership
How Members of Congress Decide
How a Bill Becomes Law
The Question of Congressional Ethics
New Directions From Old

What If . . .
▽
Bills Could Not Be Amended?

As legislation passes through the labyrinth of the congressional decision-making process, if it survives to emerge as a law, it is almost never unchanged by the committee that considered it or by the two full chambers of Congress, which can each amend it on the floor. Both committee amendments and floor amendments can burden the original bill with Christmas tree-like "ornaments" of some group's or an individual legislator's pet idea or project. The result may be an improvement on the originally proposed legislation, or the net effect may be to gut the bill's provisions or make it the vehicle for an action that it simply was not intended to produce. What would happen, though, if either an amendment to the Constitution or a simple change of the rules of the House and Senate made it impossible for bills to be amended?

The most likely thing that would happen to the decision-making process in Congress is that it would probably become much less collegial. One of the purposes served by the possibility of amending legislation is that more support can be gathered for a legislative proposal if additional members can "sign on" by agreeing to amendments that modify the original terms of the bill to

make it more attractive. The members who introduce bills that could not be amended would have to find other ways of generating support for their legislative initiatives. One way would be to promise in advance to support someone else's legislation in return for support now on their bill. This process, known as logrolling, would probably become more important. However, if logrolling is pursued to this extreme, it might produce a Congress in which everyone is tightly locked in to support or oppose each piece of legislation and in which the members would be unable to reach compromises on legislation unless they worked out very careful negotiations well before the bill was introduced.

Another possible consequence of nonamendable legislation might be the further weakening of party leadership and the heightening of the power held by committee chairs and of personal leadership by strong-willed and respected individual leaders of factions or blocs within Congress. Party leaders as brokers could not negotiate to amend bills. Influential factional leaders would, however, be in a

stronger position because they could bargain with the supporters of a bill for their bloc's vote in return for future return favors.

Control over agenda setting would become all-important, as the president, the chairs of committees, and interest groups would have to struggle to regulate the flow of legislation and would vie with one another for the right to introduce legislation in their preferred version. This "sink or swim" approach to lawmaking introduces the possibility that the political parties may have to take a clear stand on the issues.

Of course, if bills could not be amended, some features of the current congressional decision-making process would almost certainly be simplified. For one thing, less time would probably be taken up in debate on the floor as there would not be any amendments to

debate and to use as attempts to delay the outcome of the final vote. Other stalling tactics may be invented, or members may fall back on tried-and-true methods of holding up passage of legislation they don't like. Another likely simplification would be the elimination of conference committees, as there would be no possibility of different amendments being adopted in the House and the Senate that would have to be compromised. It is reasonable to assume that Congress could thereby operate more quickly and more decisively, although the quality of the decisions made may not be any higher. One intriguing possibility is that with the absence of any possibility for changes in legislation coming out of either chamber, a movement might arise to establish a unicameral legislature or at least a legislature in which one chamber is clearly supreme and the other has only limited ability to influence legislation.

▽

Throughout its history, Congress has been a pre-eminently political body where the arts of bargaining and compromise are practiced daily. Both the House and the Senate tend to prize conflict resolution over speed and efficiency in the legislative process.

Do Americans have much confidence in Congress? According to most polls, there has been some improvement in the reputation of the legislative branch, but it still is less respected than many other institutions of American life. The results of one 1985 poll showed that only 39 percent of the American public expressed either "a great deal" or "quite a lot" of confidence in Congress. Americans showed more confidence in organized religion (66 percent), the military (61 percent), the Supreme Court (56 percent), banks and banking (51 percent), and the public schools (48 percent). People expressed less confidence in newspapers (35 percent), business (31 percent), television (29 percent), and organized labor (28 percent).[1]

Similarly low levels of public approval of Congress's performance have been recorded over an extended period of time. Figure 13–1 illustrates results of Gallup public opinion surveys over a recent eight-year period in response to the question: "Do you approve or disapprove of the way Congress is doing its job?" Although specific events, like the televised Watergate hearings, can produce a temporary upsurge in approval of congressional activity (or inactivity), the dominant pattern is one of chronically low citizen evaluations of the job Congress is doing.

This low level of confidence that Americans have in Congress may or may not be justified. Is it fair to expect Congress to solve all the problems confronting the country today? How could the House and the Senate be made to operate more effectively? Before these and other questions can be answered, we need to understand why this institution was created in the first place and why it has taken on the form that we see today.

Why Was Congress Created?
▽

The founders of the American republic believed that the bulk of the power that would be exercised by a national government should be in the hands of the leg-

[1]The Gallup Poll, 1985, reported in *National Journal*, August 10, 1985, p. 1861.

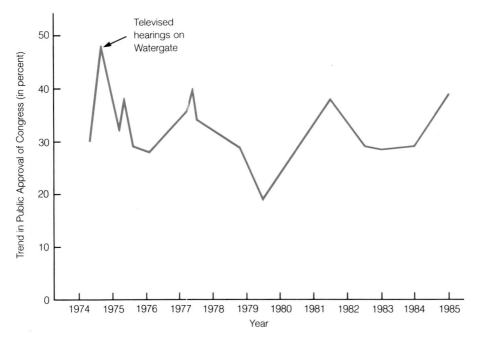

Figure 13–1
▽

**Trend in Public Approval of Congress
(in percent)**

SOURCES: *The Gallup Opinion Index*, 1982; *The Gallup Poll*, 1985.

John Lewis, former civil rights worker, was elected to Congress in 1986.

islature. As you will recall from Chapter 2, the authors of the Constitution were strongly influenced by their fear of tyrannous kings and powerful, unchecked rulers. They were also aware of how ineffective the confederal congress had been during its brief existence under the Articles of Confederation.

The leading role envisioned for Congress in the new government is apparent from its primacy in the Constitution. Article I deals with the structure, the powers, and the operation of Congress, beginning in Section I with an application of the basic principle of separation of powers: "All legislative Powers herein granted shall be vested in a Congress of the United States, which shall consist of a Senate and House of Representatives." These legislative powers are spelled out in detail in Article I and elsewhere.

The **bicameralism** of Congress—its division into two legislative houses—was in part an outgrowth of the Connecticut Compromise, which tried to balance the big-state population advantage, reflected in the House, and the small-state demand for equality, which was satisfied in the Senate. Beyond that, the two chambers of Congress also reflected the social class biases of the founders. They wished to balance the interests and the numerical superiority of the common citizen with the property interests of the less numerous businesspeople, landowners, bankers, and merchants. This goal was achieved by providing in Sections 2 and 3 of Article I that the House of Representatives should be elected directly by "the people," whereas the Senate was to be chosen by the elected representatives sitting in state legislatures.

The elected House, then, was to be the common man's chamber, and the nonelected Senate was to be the chamber of the wealthy, similar to the division between the House of Commons and the House of Lords in England. Also, the House was meant to represent the people, whereas the Senate was meant to represent the states, in accordance with the intent of the Connecticut Compromise. The issue of who counted as part of "the people" for electing members of the House was left up to the states. As a practical matter, the electorate as defined in state laws originally included only property-owning adult white males. Women, blacks, the impoverished, many common workers, and Indians could not vote for congres-

Bicameralism

The division of a legislature into two separate assemblies.

sional representatives. The logic of separate constituencies and separate interests underlying the bicameral Congress was reinforced by differences in length of tenure. Members of the House were required to face the electorate every two years, whereas senators could serve for a much more secure term of six years—even longer than the four-year term provided for the president.

The Powers of Congress

▽

The Constitution is both highly specific and extremely vague about the powers that Congress may exercise. The first seventeen clauses of Article I, Section 8, specify most of the **enumerated powers** of Congress—that is, powers expressly given to that body.

Enumerated Powers

The enumerated powers of Congress include the right to impose taxes and import tariffs, borrow money, regulate interstate commerce and international trade, establish procedures for naturalizing citizens, make laws regulating bankruptcies, coin (and print) money and regulate its value, establish standards of weights and

Enumerated Powers
The powers specifically granted to the national government by the Constitution. The first seventeen clauses of Article I, Section 8, specify most of the enumerated powers of Congress.

measures, punish counterfeiting, establish post offices and postal roads, regulate copyrights and patents, establish lower federal courts, punish piracy and other illegal acts committed on the high seas, declare war, raise and regulate an army and navy, call up and regulate the state militias to enforce laws, to suppress insurrections, and to repel invasions, and govern the District of Columbia.

The most important of the domestic powers of Congress, enumerated in Article I, Section 8, are the rights to collect taxes, to spend money, and to regulate commerce, whereas the most important foreign policy power is the power to declare war. Other sections of the Constitution give Congress a wide range of further powers. Generally, Congress is able to establish rules for its own members, to regulate the electoral college, and to override a presidential veto.

Some functions are restricted to only one house. Under Article II, Section 2, the Senate must advise on and consent to the ratification of treaties, and must accept or reject presidential nominations of ambassadors, Supreme Court justices, and "all other officers of the United States," but may delegate to the president, the courts, or department heads the power to make lesser appointments. Congress may regulate the appellate jurisdiction of the Supreme Court, regulate relations between states, and propose amendments to the Constitution.

The amendments to the Constitution provide yet another source of congressional power. Congress must certify the election of a president and a vice president or itself choose these officers if no candidate has a majority of the electoral vote (Twelfth Amendment), may levy an income tax (Sixteenth Amendment), and determines who will be acting president in case of death or incapacity of the president or vice president (Twentieth Amendment, Sections 3 and 4, and Twenty-fifth Amendment, Sections 2, 3, and 4). In addition, Congress is explicitly given the power to enforce, by appropriate legislation, the provisions of several of the amendments.

The Necessary and Proper Clause

Beyond these numerous specific powers, Congress enjoys the right under Article I, Section 8 (the "elastic" or "necessary and proper" clause), "to make all Laws which shall be necessary and proper for carrying into Execution the foregoing Powers [of Article I], and all other Powers vested by this Constitution in the Government of the United States, or in any Department or Officer thereof." This vague statement of congressional responsibilities has set the stage for a greatly expanded role for the federal government relative to the states and has also constituted, at least in theory, a check on the expansion of presidential powers. By continuing to delegate powers to the executive branch, however, Congress has over time reduced the role it might otherwise play in national and international affairs.

The Constitution provides the foundation of congressional powers. Yet a complete understanding of the role that Congress plays requires a broader study of the functions that the national legislature performs for the American political system.

The Functions of Congress

▽

Congress as an institution of government is expected by its members, by the public, and by other centers of political power to perform a number of functions. Our perceptions of how good a job Congress is doing overall are tied closely to evaluations of whether and how it fulfills certain specific tasks. These tasks include the following:

1. Lawmaking activities
2. Service to constituents
3. Representation of diverse interests
4. Oversight of the manner in which laws are implemented
5. Educating the public about national issues and setting the terms for national debate
6. Resolving conflicts in American society

The Lawmaking Function

The principal and most obvious function of any legislature is **lawmaking**. Congress is the highest elected body in the country charged with making binding rules for all Americans. Lawmaking requires decisions about the size of the federal budget, about issues such as abortion or school busing, and about the long-term prospects for war or peace. This does not mean, however, that Congress initiates most of the ideas for legislation that it eventually considers; the bulk of the bills that Congress acts on originates in the executive branch, and many other bills are traceable to interest groups and party organizations. Through processes of compromise and **logrolling** (offering to support a fellow member's bill in exchange for their promise to support your bill in the future), backers of legislation attempt to fashion a winning majority coalition by making legislative ideas as attractive as possible.

Lawmaking

The process of deciding the legal rules that govern our society. Such laws may regulate minor affairs or establish broad national policies.

Logrolling

An arrangement by which two or more members of Congress agree in advance to support each other's bills.

Senator Jesse Helms, N.C., and Rep. Kika de la Garza, Texas, confer on agricultural legislation.

Service to Constituents

Casework

Personal work for constituents by members of Congress.

Ombudsman

An individual in the role of hearing and investigating complaints by private individuals against public officials or agencies.

Individual members of Congress are expected by their constituents to act as brokers between private citizens and the imposing, often faceless, federal government. **Casework** is the usual form taken by this function of providing service to constituents. The legislator and his or her staff spend a considerable portion of time on casework activity, such as tracking down a missing Social Security paycheck, explaining the meaning of particular bills to people who may be affected by them, promoting a local business interest, or interceding with a regulatory agency on behalf of constituents who disagree with proposed bureaucratic rules and regulations. Legislators and analysts of congressional behavior regard this **ombudsman** role as an activity that strongly benefits the members of Congress. A government characterized by a large, confusing bureaucracy and complex public programs offers innumerable opportunities for legislators to come to the assistance of (usually) grateful constituents. Morris Fiorina suggests somewhat mischievously that senators and representatives prefer to maintain bureaucratic confusion in order to maximize their opportunities for performing good deeds on behalf of their constituents:

> Some poor, aggrieved constituent becomes enmeshed in the tentacles of an evil bureaucracy and calls upon Congressman St. George to do battle with the dragon . . . . In dealing with the bureaucracy, the congressman is not merely one vote of 435. Rather, he is a nonpartisan power, someone whose phone call snaps an office to attention. He is not kept on hold. The constituent who receives aid believes that his congressman and his congressman alone got results.[2]

[2]*Congress: Keystone of the Washington Establishment* (New Haven: Yale University Press, 1977), pp. 44–47.

Senator Dan Quale of Indiana speaks with a group of young constituents.

414

The Representation Function

If constituency service carries with it nothing but benefits for most members of Congress, the function of **representation** is less certain and even carries with it some danger that the legislator will lose his or her bid for reelection. Generally, representation means that the many competing interests in society should be represented in Congress. It follows that Congress should be a body acting slowly and deliberately, whose foremost concern is to maintain a carefully crafted balance of power among competing interests.

The Trustee View of Representation

How is representation to be achieved? There are basically two points of view on this issue. The first approach is that legislators should act as **trustees** of the broad interests of the entire society and that they should vote against the narrow interests of their constituents as their conscience and their perception of national needs dictate. This view is often associated with the eighteenth-century British political philosopher and member of Parliament, Edmund Burke. Perhaps it will come as no great surprise that Burke faced considerable opposition to this view from his constituents in Bristol and subsequently was forced to step down as a legislator.

The Instructed-Delegate View of Representation

A view directly opposite to the Burkean notion of the legislator as trustee is that the members of Congress should behave as **instructed delegates;** that is, they should mirror the views of the majority of the constituents who elected them to power in the first place. On the surface, this approach is plausible and rewarding. For it to work, however, we must assume that constituents actually have well-formed views on the issues that are decided in Congress and, further, that they have clear-cut preferences about these issues. Neither condition is likely to be satisfied often. Most people generally do not have well-articulated views on major issues, and, among those who do, there frequently is no clear majority position but rather a range of often conflicting minority perspectives. In a major study of the attitudes held by members of Congress about their proper role as representatives, Roger Davidson found that neither a pure trustee nor a pure instructed-delegate view was held by most legislators. Davidson's sampling of members of Congress showed that about the same proportion endorsed the trustee (28 percent) and delegate (23 percent) approaches to representation, but the clear preference was for the **politico** position—which combines the perspectives of both the trustee and the delegate in a pragmatic mix.[3]

The Oversight Function

Oversight of the bureaucracy is essential if the decisions made by Congress are to have any force. **Oversight** is the process by which Congress follows up on the laws it has enacted to ensure that they are being enforced and administered in the way Congress intended. This is done by holding committee hearings and investigations, changing the size of an agency's budget, and cross-examining high-level presidential nominees to head major agencies. Also, Congress can refuse to accede to proposed

[3]*The Role of the Congressman* (New York: Pegasus, 1969), p. 117.

Representation
The function of Congress as elected officials to represent the views of their constituents.

Trustees
The idea that a legislator should act according to his or her conscience and the broad interests of the entire society, often associated with the British statesman Edmund Burke.

Instructed Delegates
The concept that legislators are agents of the voters who elected them and that they should vote according to the views of their constituents regardless of their own personal assessments.

Politico
The legislative role that combines the delegate and trustee concepts. The legislator varies the role according to the issue under consideration.

Oversight
The responsibility Congress has for following up on laws it has enacted to ensure that they are being enforced and administered in the way in which they were intended.

Legislative Veto

Provision in a bill reserving to Congress or to a congressional committee the power to reject an act or regulation of a national agency by majority vote; declared unconstitutional by the Supreme Court in 1983.

Agenda Setting

The power to determine which public policy questions will be debated or considered by Congress.

rules and regulations by resorting to the **legislative veto.** Increasingly popular in Congress in recent years—until it was declared unconstitutional by the Supreme Court in 1983—the legislative veto provided that one or sometimes both chambers of Congress could disapprove of an agency rule within a specified period of time by a simple majority vote and thereby prevent its enforcement.

Senators and representatives increasingly see their oversight function as a critically important part of their legislative activities. In part, oversight is related to the concept of constituency service, particularly when Congress investigates alleged arbitrariness or wrongdoing by bureaucratic agencies. Beyond service to constituents, however, oversight is seen by many legislators, and by political scientists like Morris Ogul,[4] as a crucial tool for preserving the balance of power between Congress and the executive branch.

The Public Education Function

Educating the public is a function that is exercised every time Congress holds public hearings, exercises oversight over the bureaucracy, or engages in committee and floor debate on major issues and such topics as political assassinations, aging, drugs, or the concerns of small businesses. In so doing, Congress presents a range of viewpoints on pressing national questions. Congress also decides what issues will come up for discussion and decision; **agenda setting** is a major facet of its public education function.

The Conflict Resolution Function

Congress is commonly seen as an institution for resolving conflicts within American society. Organized interest groups and representatives of different racial, religious, economic, and ideological interests look on Congress as an access point for airing their grievances and possibly for stimulating government action on their behalf. A logical extension of the representation function, this focus on conflict resolution puts Congress in the role of trying to resolve the differences among competing points of view by passing laws to accommodate as many interested parties as possible. Clearly, this is not always achieved. Every legislative decision results in some winners and some losers. However, Congress is commonly regarded as the place to go in Washington to get a friendly hearing or a desired policy result. To the extent that Congress does accommodate competing interests, it tends to legitimize the entire political process by all branches of government.

House-Senate Differences

▽

The preceding functions of Congress describe how that body is expected to perform and what it does as a whole. To understand better what goes on in the national legislature, however, we need to examine the effects of bicameralism, for Congress is composed of two markedly different—although co-equal—chambers. Although the Senate and the House of Representatives exist within the same legislative

[4]Morris S. Ogul, *Congress Oversees the Bureaucracy* (Pittsburgh: University of Pittsburgh Press, 1976), pp. 21–22.

House chamber.

institution, each has developed certain distinctive features that clearly distinguish life on one end of Capitol Hill from conditions on the other (the Senate wing is on the north side of the Capitol building and the House wing is on the south side). A summary of these differences is given in Table 13–1.

Size and Rules

The central difference is simply that the House is much larger than the Senate. There are 435 representatives, plus nonvoting delegates from the District of Columbia, Puerto Rico, Guam, and the Virgin Islands, in the House compared with

Table 13–1
▽
Differences Between the House and the Senate

Some of these differences, such as the term of office, are provided for in the Constitution while others, such as debate rules, developed informally.

House	Senate
Members chosen from local districts	Members chosen from an entire state
Two-year term	Six-year term
Originally elected by voters	Originally (until 1913) elected by state legislatures
May impeach (indict) federal officials	May convict officials of impeachable offenses
Larger (435 voting members)	Smaller (100 members)
More formal rules	Fewer rules and restrictions
Debate limited	Debate extended
Floor action controlled	Unanimous consent rules
Less prestige and less individual notice	More prestige and media attention
Originates bills for raising revenues	Power to "advise and consent" on presidential appointments and treaties
Local or narrow leadership	National leadership

Rules Committee

A standing committee of the House of Representatives that provides special rules under which specific bills can be debated, amended, and considered by the House.

Filibustering

In the Senate, unlimited debate to halt action on a particular bill.

Cloture

A method invoked to close off debate and to bring the matter under consideration to a vote in the Senate.

just 100 senators. This size difference means that a greater number of formal rules are needed to govern activity in the House, whereas correspondingly looser procedures can be followed in the less crowded Senate. This difference is most obvious in the rules governing debate on the floors of the two chambers.

The Senate normally permits extended debate on all issues that arise before it, whereas the House operates with an elaborate system in which its **Rules Committee** normally proposes time limitations on debate for any bill and then a majority of the entire body accepts or modifies those suggested time limits. As a consequence of its stricter debate time limits, and in spite of its greater size, the House is often able to act more quickly on legislation than the Senate.

Debate and Filibustering

According to historians, the Senate tradition of unlimited debate, or **filibustering,** dates back to 1790, when a proposal to move the United States capital from New York to Philadelphia was stalled by such time-wasting tactics. This unlimited debate tradition—which also existed in the House until 1811[5]—is not absolute, however.

Under Senate Rule 22, debate may be ended by invoking **cloture,** or shutting off discussion on a bill. Recently amended in 1975 and 1979, Rule 22 states that debate may be closed off on a bill if sixteen senators sign a petition requesting it and if, after two days have elapsed, three-fifths of the entire membership (sixty votes, assuming no vacancies) vote for cloture. After cloture is invoked, each senator may speak for a maximum of one hour on a bill before a vote is taken.

The Senate made further changes in its filibuster rule in 1979. It extended Rule 22 to provide that a final vote must take place within one hundred hours of debate after cloture has been imposed, and it further limited the use of multiple amendments to stall postcloture final action on a bill.

Prestige

As a consequence of the greater size of the House, representatives generally cannot achieve as much individual recognition and public prestige as can members of the Senate. Senators, especially those who openly express presidential ambitions, are better able to gain media exposure and to establish careers as spokespersons for large national constituencies. To obtain recognition for his or her activities, a member of the House must either survive in office long enough to join the ranks of the leadership on committees or within the party or become an expert on some specialized aspect of legislative policy—such as tax laws, the environment, or education.

Other Differences

Other major differences between the House and the Senate are unrelated to the size of each chamber. The Constitution in Article I provides that members of the House serve shorter terms (two years) than senators (six years). All 435 voting

[5]William J. Keefe and Morris S. Ogul, *The American Legislative Process,* 5th Ed. (Englewood Cliffs, N.J.: Prentice-Hall, 1982).

members of the House must run for reelection in November of even-numbered years, but only about one-third of the Senate seats are contested in the same biennial election. Before passage of the Seventeenth Amendment in 1913, all senators were not even elected by direct popular vote; some were instead appointed by state legislatures. The longer term in office generally gives senators more time to act as national leaders before facing the electorate again.

Government institutions are given life by the people who work in them and shape them as political structures. Who then are the members of Congress and how are they elected?

Congresspersons and the Citizenry—A Comparison

Members of the United States Senate and the United States House of Representatives are not typical American citizens (Table 13–2). Members of Congress are, of course, older than most Americans, partly because of constitutional age requirements and partly because a good deal of political experience is normally an advantage in running for national office. Members of Congress are also disproportionately white, male, Protestant, and trained in higher-status occupations.

Some recent trends in the social characteristics of Congress should be noted, however. The average age of members of the Hundredth Congress is 52.5 years— a slight decline from an average age of 53 three decades ago. More than half the representatives had four or fewer years of congressional experience, and more than half the senators had been in office six years or less. Early retirement of larger numbers of legislators, coupled with the declining average age (until recently) among incoming members, have created this trend.

Table 13–2

Characteristics of the 100th Congress (1987–1989)

	U.S. Population	House	Senate
Average Age	30.6 (median)	50.7	54.4
Percent Non-white	14.4	8.5	0
Religion			
Percent church members	60	98.8	100
Percent Catholic	36.9	28.2	19
Percent Protestant	55.1	58.6	68
Percent Jewish	4.3	6.6	8
Percent Female	51.4	5.2	2
Percent College Educated	17.7	93	100
Occupation			
Percent lawyers and judges	.6	42.3	62
Percent blue collar workers	29.7	0	0
Family Income			
Percent of families earning over $50,000 annually	4.4	100	100
Personal wealth			
Percent of population with assets over $1 million	.7	16	33

Profile

▽

Edward Moore Kennedy

"For all those whose cares have been our concern, the work goes on, the cause endures, the hope still lives, and the dream shall never die."

A member of one of America's most prominent political families, "Ted" Kennedy has long been an important figure in the Senate and among Democratic liberals, as well as the survivor of a tragic family history. Two of his brothers were the victims of assassins: President John F. Kennedy in 1963 and presidential candidate Robert Kennedy in 1968.

Ted Kennedy was born in Boston, Massachusetts, on February 22, 1932, the son of Joseph P. and Rose Kennedy. His multimillionaire father became the ambassador to Great Britain and was active in state and national Democratic politics. After graduating from Milton Academy in 1950, Kennedy received his A.B. degree from Harvard College in 1956. He earned a law degree from the University of Virginia in 1959, following a year's study in the Hague, Holland, at the International Law School. Kennedy enlisted in the U.S. Army as a private and served in France and Germany from June 1951 to March 1953. He was elected to the U.S. Senate on November 6, 1962, to fill the unexpired term of his brother, John. Subsequent reelections to the Senate followed in 1964, 1970, 1976, and 1982.

In the Senate, Ted Kennedy served as assistant majority leader from 1968 to 1971 and was the first chair of the Congressional Technology Assessment Board in 1973 and 1974. Now a senior leader among Senate Democrats, he has been a perennial candidate—potential or active—for the Democratic presidential nomination. In 1983, he decided against entering the presidential race to devote more time to Senate work and to deal with family problems, including his divorce from his wife, Joan. A hard-working and respected senator, Kennedy has successfully sponsored bills on immigration reform, airline deregulation, and reform of the criminal code. In 1979, he succeeded James Eastland of Mississippi as chairman of the Judiciary Committee. With the Republican party gaining control of the Senate in 1980, he lost this position and opted for the ranking minority position on the Labor and Human Resources Committee. After the Democrats regained control of the Senate in 1986, he assumed the chairmanship of that committee.

Kennedy's presidential ambitions and his status within the Senate have been overshadowed by the fatal accident in 1969 involving Mary Jo Kopechne, a young campaign worker, who was killed when a car the senator was driving veered off a bridge at Chappaquiddick Island, Massachusetts. Kennedy's opponents in both parties have long used the incident, and his plea of guilty to leaving the scene of the accident, to blunt efforts to put Kennedy in the White House or in stronger positions of leadership within Congress and the national Democratic party. He remains, nonetheless, a vital force in the politics of the 1980s.

The Protestant domination of Congress has been loosened, with substantial increases being made in the representation of Jews and Roman Catholics. "Higher status" Protestant denominations, notably Episcopalians and Presbyterians, are overrepresented in Congress, whereas Baptists and Lutherans are underrepresented relative to their numbers among American Protestants.

Lawyers are by far the largest occupational group among congresspersons. Sixty-two senators and 184 representatives in the Hundredth Congress reported that they were trained in the legal profession. However, the proportion of lawyers in the House is lower now than at nearly any time in the last thirty years. Members of this Congress reported other previous occupations as follows: 25 in agriculture, 170 businesspersons or bankers, 50 educators, 5 engineers, 28 journalists, 2 labor lead-

ers, 7 law enforcement officers, 4 medical doctors, 114 in politics and public service, 3 clergymen, 5 in aeronautics, 1 in the military, 6 in professional sports, and one actor (Fred Grandy, R. Iowa, who starred in the series *Love Boat*).

Congressional Elections

▽

The process of electing members of Congress is decentralized. Congressional elections are operated by the individual state governments, which must conform to the rules established by the Constitution and by national statutes. The Constitution states that representatives are to be elected every second year by popular ballot, and the number of seats awarded to each state is to be determined by the results of the decennial census. Each state has at least one representative, with most Congressional districts having about a half million residents. Senators are elected by popular vote (since the passage of the Seventeenth Amendment) every six years; approximately one-third of the seats are chosen every two years. Each state has two senators. Under Article I of the Constitution, state legislatures are given control over "the times, places, and manner of holding elections for Senators and Representatives"; however, "the Congress may at any time by law make or alter such regulations. . . ."

Candidates for Congressional Elections

Candidates for seats in Congress are generally recruited by local political party activists. Potential candidates who are selected or self-selected usually have many of the social characteristics shared by their prospective constituents. Religion, race, and ethnic background are especially important considerations here. Prior political experience may be an important asset, especially in states with strong political parties or restrictive nominating systems.

Reasons for Making the Race

At least three major factors are important in determining who will run for congressional office and whether party leaders are willing to recruit someone for the race. As discussed by James David Barber,[6] these are *motivation, resources,* and *opportunity.* Motivation means that a candidate must be able to achieve a sense of self-satisfaction from participating in the contest. It also implies that a candidate must project a positive attitude toward electoral politics. Important resources for the campaign include money, the political skills of the candidate and of his or her supporters, the ability of the candidate and staff to take time off from their jobs and other commitments, and the candidate's access to the mass media. Opportunity relates to such questions as whether an incumbent is running for office, whether many candidates are contending for the same nomination, how strong the opposition party may be in November, and whether the local party activists form a positive image of the candidate.

The Nomination Process

Since the early part of the century, control over the process of nominating congressional candidates has been shifting from party conventions—which reformers charged

Kathleen Kennedy Townsend campaigning for Congress in 1986. She was unable to defeat the incumbent, Marjorie Holt.

[6]*The Lawmakers: Recruitment and Adaptation to Legislative Life* (New Haven: Yale University Press, 1965), pp. 10–15.

"Please, Hobart, would you kindly confine your speeches about the damned deficit to the floor of the Senate? You've already got my vote."

Drawing by Stan Hunt; © 1984 The New Yorker Magazine, Inc.

Highlight

▽

Congress on the Air

After several years of consideration, the House of Representatives voted to begin live television coverage of its proceedings in 1979. Since then, floor debates, committee hearings, and news conferences have been available on many cable systems over the C-SPAN network. At the time, many legislators, including then Speaker of the House, Tip O'Neill, worried about possible adverse effects on the quality and quantity of debate. By 1982, O'Neill reversed his position, stating that the only significant effect on his colleagues was that they showed up with "blue shirts, red ties and 'stickem' on their hair."

Although Howard Baker, the majority leader from 1981 until 1985, strongly urged the Senate to allow television coverage, the upper house did not accept the idea until 1986 when a two-month trial was begun on June 6. Many senators were concerned about possible negative effects of TV coverage. Senator Long of Louisiana, strongly opposed to such coverage, said, "It's very important that we preserve the potential of the Senate . . . to say the unpopular things. Some of those things you can't do before television." Senator Dole, the Republican majority leader, warned on June 2 that "if members play to the camera with gimmicks, filibusters and endless speeches, we have failed the test." Most commentators noted that the only

Opening coverage of the Senate on C-SPAN.

change they saw in the Senate on the first day was some powder applied to bald heads to reduce the shine in the television lights.

The fears of the legislators were probably unfounded. A study of the House on television by Timothy E. Cook found that the more image-conscious legislators, sometimes called the "show horses" of Congress, did not get more television time. Rather, the representatives who appeared more often on television were those who held

leadership positions or more seniority. Television coverage actually allows the party leaders more opportunity to state their case rather than giving more time to those legislators seeking individual exposure.

SOURCE: *Congressional Quarterly Almanac, 1985*, Washington, D.C., 1986; *Congressional Quarterly Weekly Report*, June 7, 1986, p. 1274; and Timothy E. Cook, "House Members as Newsmakers: The Effects of Televising Congress," *Legislative Studies Quarterly*, May 1986, pp. 203–226.

Direct Primaries

An intraparty election in which the voters select the candidates who will run on a party's ticket in the subsequent general election.

Party Identifiers

Those who identify themselves with a political party.

with being corrupt and boss-controlled—to **direct primaries** in which **party identifiers** in the electorate select the candidate who will carry that party's endorsement into the actual election. All fifty states currently use the direct primary to select party nominees for senator or representative. In general, there are more candidates running and the competition is more intense when a party is strong and a November victory is likely.

Who Wins, and Why?

Most candidates win through the effectiveness of their personal organizations, although sometimes with assistance from the state party organization. It is important to realize that congressional candidates have only a loose affiliation to the party at the national and state level. Even the effects of presidential "coattails," in which a victorious president helps bring into office legislators who would not have won otherwise, are minimal. For example, Richard Nixon's smashing victory over George McGovern in 1972, with 61 percent of the popular vote and 520 out of 538 electoral votes, resulted in a gain of only twelve Republican seats in the House.

In midterm congressional elections—those held between presidential contests—voter turnout falls sharply. In these elections party affiliation of the voters who turn out is a stronger force in deciding election outcomes, and the party controlling the White House normally loses seats in Congress. Table 13–3 shows the pattern for midterm elections since 1942. The result is a fragmentation of party authority and a loosening of ties between Congress and the president.

The Power of Incumbency

The power of incumbency in the outcome of congressional elections cannot be overemphasized. Table 13–4 shows that the overwhelming majority of representatives and a smaller proportion of senators who decide to run for reelection are successful. This conclusion holds for both presidential election and midterm election years.

David R. Mayhew[7] argues that the pursuit of reelection is the strongest motivation behind the activities of members of Congress. The reelection goal is pursued in three major ways: by *advertising*, by *credit claiming*, and by *position taking*. Advertising involves using the mass media, making personal appearances with constituents, sending newsletters—all to produce a favorable image and to make the incumbent's name a household word. Members of Congress try to present themselves as informed, experienced, and responsive to people's needs. Credit claiming focuses on the things a legislator claims to have done to benefit his or her constituents—by fulfilling the congressional casework function or by supplying material goods in the form of, say, a new post office or a construction project like a dam or a highway. Position taking refers to explaining why a member of Congress voted the way he or she did, and to making public statements of general support for presidential decisions or specific support for positions on key issues such as gun control or antiinflation policies. Position taking carries with it certain risks, as the incumbent may lose support by disagreeing with the attitudes of large numbers of constituents.

[7]*Congress: The Electoral Connection* (New Haven: Yale University Press, 1974).

Table 13–3

▽

Midterm Losses to the Party of the President: 1942–1986

Seats Lost to the Party of the President in the House of Representatives	
1942	−45 (D)
1946	−55 (D)
1950	−29 (D)
1954	−18 (R)
1958	−47 (R)
1962	− 4 (D)
1966	−47 (D)
1970	−12 (R)
1974	−43 (R)
1978	−11 (D)
1982	−26 (R)
1986	− 5 (R)

▽

Table 13–4
▽

The Power of Incumbency

	Presidential-Year Elections							Midterm Elections						
	1960	1964	1968	1972	1976	1980	1984	1962	1966	1970	1974	1978	1982	1986
House														
Number of incumbent candidates	405	397	409	390	384	398	408	402	411	401	391	382	381	391
Reelected	375	344	396	365	368	361	392	368	362	379	343	358	352	385
Percentage of total	92.6	86.6	96.8	93.6	95.8	90.7	96	91.5	88.1	94.5	87.7	93.7	92.4	98.5
Defeated	30	53	13	25	16	37	16	34	49	22	48	24	39	6
In primary	5	8	4	12	3	6	4	12	8	10	8	5	10	3
In general election	25	45	9	13	13	31	12	22	41	12	40	19	29	3
Senate														
Number of incumbent candidates	29	33	28	27	25	29	29	35	32	31	27	25	30	28
Reelected	28	28	20	20	16	16	26	29	28	24	23	15	28	21
Percentage of total	96.6	84.8	71.4	74.1	64.0	55.2	89	82.9	87.5	77.4	85.2	60.0	93.3	75
Defeated	1	5	8	7	9	13	3	6	4	7	4	10	2	7
In primary	0	1	4	2	0	4	0	1	3	1	2	3	0	0
In general election	1	4	4	5	9	9	3	5	1	6	2	7	2	7

SOURCE: *Statistical Abstract of the United States, 1982–83*, p. 485; *Congressional Quarterly Weekly Report*, 40, no. 45 (November 6, 1982) and 40, no. 44 (October 30, 1982), and 44, no. 45 (November 8, 1986).

The 1986 Congressional Elections

The outcome of the 1986 congressional elections insured much greater difficulty for President Reagan's legislative proposals. The Democrats regained majority control of the Senate by picking up a net of eight seats. Republicans lost the Senatorial seats they had held in Florida, Georgia, Alabama, North Carolina, Maryland, North Dakota, South Dakota, Nevada, and Washington. In contrast, the Democrats lost only one seat in Missouri.

Although pollsters were unable to call this reversal before the election, the results were not too surprising. The Republicans had to defend 22 of their seats while the Democrats had only 12 seats at stake in 1986. A number of the Republican incumbents were first elected in the Reagan landslide in 1980 and were not considered to be very strong candidates on their own. Similarly, some of the Democratic victories in 1986 were very close, suggesting possible trouble for their new class in the 1992 contests.

Exit polls suggested that low turnout among younger voters and independents helped defeat the Republicans. In the South, where Democrats returned to dominance, black voters provided the margin of victory for the new Democratic senators. In many states, the condition of the rural economy also helped the Democrats to victory.

In contrast to the Senate, the House of Representatives was virtually unchanged after the election. Past presidents have suffered, on average, losses of more than 40 seats in their sixth year election. With only losing 5 seats in 1986, Republicans claimed that the voters really were supporting their party.

At Home with House Members

Although opinion polls have shown for at least a decade that the public does not have great confidence in the Congress, such mistrust does not seem to affect congressional elections. More than 90 percent of members of the House who seek re-election are victorious every two years. This puzzle, that we cheerfully reelect our congresspersons although we don't think much of the institution, has intrigued political scientists for some time.

One explanation of the phenomenon is that many congressional districts have been drawn to be safe for one party. This does not, however, account for the ability of the incumbent to fend off primary challenges from within his or her own party. Similarly, the fact that incumbents gain an advantage at the polls through voter recall of their names does not completely explain incumbent staying power, particularly in an age where challengers can make extensive use of the media to become well known.

Another view of why incumbents do so well with their voters is put forth by Richard Fenno in his book, *Homestyle: House Members in Their Districts*. Fenno believes that political scientists usually focus on what legislators do in Washington, D.C., to the exclusion of what they do back in their districts. To investigate the members at home, he spent more than seven years accompanying congresspersons in their home-district travels. His research suggests that an important key to understanding why incumbents are so successful lies in the development of their respective "homestyles."

By interviewing legislators, their aides, and their constituents, Fenno found that each legislator develops a unique style of dealing with the voters in his or her district. It is rooted first in the legislator's perception of the district: Is it a homogenous district or is it quite heterogeneous in class, race, and economic factors? The legislator then thinks about how he or she "fits" that district. Some representatives are so similar to most of the constituents, having been born and bred in the

district, that they feel they understand their constituents' needs intuitively. Others, who do not have a "close fit" to their districts or who have very heterogeneous districts, must develop different homestyles.

According to Fenno, each House member develops a "presentational style" for home use that fits his or her personality and the type of district. Some representatives use a person-to-person style that emphasizes personal contact and informality. As one representative put it, "No one will vote against you if you are on a first-name basis." Other representatives choose to emphasize issues or their own personal views, which may mark them as, say, a maverick or a staunch liberal.

The representative must also decide to whom he or she will make this self-presentation. Fenno suggests that each member sees the constituency as a set of concentric rings, with the closest friends and political advisers at the center, then the strongest supporters within the electorate, the reelection constituency, and finally the entire geographical district. The representative has to decide which of the groups needs to be visited or given extra attention. At some time, the representative must make an appeal to each of them to be reelected.

At the heart of the representative's homestyle is the relationship with constituents. Fenno sees the activities at home as building a certain trust between the legislator and the constituents. Since voters must send off the congressperson to vote on issues with which the public is unfamiliar and since voters really do not expect or desire to keep close watch on the legislator, this relationship rests to some extent on the trust built up by House members in their visits home. This trust is a vital ingredient in the ability of incumbents to be reelected time after time.

SOURCE: Richard F. Fenno, Jr., *Homestyle: House Members in Their Districts* (Boston: Little, Brown, 1978).

Black candidates won a record 23 House seats, all within the Democratic party. Mike Espy, a lawyer, became the first black Representative from Mississippi since the Reconstruction era. Barbara Mikulski, a five-term congresswoman, became the first female Democrat to be elected to the Senate without first succeeding her husband.

The shift in party control of the Senate from Republican to Democratic, combined with continued Democratic dominance in the House, suggested that the president would have a much more difficult time controlling the legislative agenda. The Democratic leadership of the Senate would be able to set their own priorities in legislation. It seems likely that President Reagan will have much more trouble gaining approval for aid to the *contras* in Nicaragua, for funding for the Strategic Defense Initiative (the "Star Wars" system), and for his judicial appointees.

Congressional Reapportionment

▽

By far the most complicated aspect of the mechanics of congressional elections is the issue of **reapportionment,** or the allocation of seats in the House to each state after each census, and **redistricting,** the redrawing of the boundaries of the districts within each state.[8]

In a landmark 6-to-2 vote in 1962, the Supreme Court made reapportionment a **justifiable** (that is, a reviewable) **question** in the Tennessee case of *Baker v. Carr*[9] by invoking the Fourteenth Amendment principle that no state can deny to any person "the equal protection of the laws." This principle was applied directly in the 1964 ruling, *Reynolds v. Sims,*[10] when the Court held that *both* chambers of a state legislature must be apportioned with equal populations in each district. This "one man, one vote" principle was applied to congressional districts in the 1964 case of *Wesberry v. Sanders,*[11] based on Article I, Section 2 of the Constitution.

Severe malapportionment of congressional districts prior to *Wesberry* had resulted in some districts containing two or three times the populations of other districts in the same state, thereby diluting the effect of a vote cast in the larger districts. This system had generally benefited the conservative populations of rural areas and small towns and harmed the interests of the more heavily populated and liberal urban areas. In fact, suburban areas have benefited the most from the *Wesberry* ruling, as suburbs account for an increasingly larger proportion of the nation's population and cities include a correspondingly smaller segment of the population.

Although the general issue of reapportionment has been dealt with fairly successfully by the one man, one vote principle, the specific case of **gerrymandering** has not yet been resolved. This term refers to the legislative boundary-drawing tactics used by Elbridge Gerry, the governor of Massachusetts, in the 1812 elections (Figure 13–2). A district is said to have been gerrymandered when its shape is substantially altered by the dominant party in a state legislature to maximize its electoral strength at the expense of the minority party. This can be achieved by either concentrating the opposition's voter support in as few districts as possible or diffusing the minority party's strength by spreading it thinly across a large number of districts.

In 1986, the Supreme Court heard a case that challenged gerrymandered congressional districts in Indiana. The Court ruled for the first time that redistricting for the political benefit of one group could be challenged on constitutional grounds. In this specific case, *Davis v. Bandemer,* the Court did not, however, agree that the districts were unfairly drawn, since it could not be proven that a group of voters

Redistricting
Redrawing district lines within the states.

Reapportionment
The redrawing of legislative district lines to accord with the existing population distribution.

Justifiable Question
A question that may be raised and reviewed in court.

Gerrymandering
The drawing of legislative district boundary lines for the purpose of obtaining partisan or factional advantage. A district is said to be gerrymandered when its shape is manipulated by the dominant party in the state legislature to maximize electoral strength at the expense of the minority party.

[8]For an excellent discussion of reapportionment, see Keefe and Ogul, *The American Legislative Process,* pp. 68–85.

[9]369 U.S. 186 (1962).

[10]377 U.S. 533 (1964).

[11]376 U.S. 1 (1964).

Figure 13–2

▽

The Original Gerrymander

The practice of "gerrymandering"—the excessive manipulation of the shape of a legislative district to benefit a certain incumbent or party—is probably as old as the republic, but the name originated in 1812.

In that year the Massachusetts legislature carved out of Essex County a district that historian John Fiske said had a "dragonlike contour." When the painter Gilbert Stuart saw the misshapen district, he penciled in a head, wings, and claws and exclaimed: "That will do for a salamander!"—to which editor Benjamin Russell replied: "Better say a Gerrymander"—after Elbridge Gerry, then governor of Massachusetts.

SOURCE: *Congressional Quarterly's Guide to Congress*, 3rd ed. (Washington, D.C.: Congressional Quarterly, 1982), p. 695.

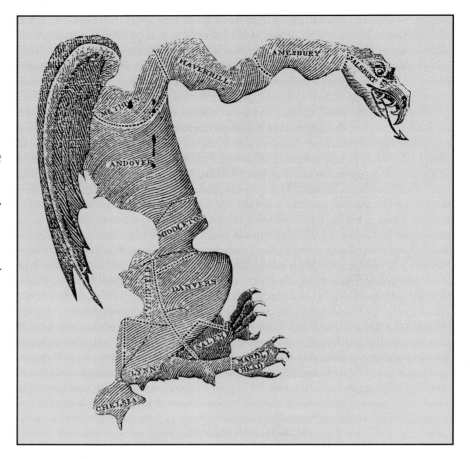

would be consistently deprived of their influence at the polls because of the new districts.[12] Figure 13–3 shows a recent gerrymander.

Pay, Perks, and Privileges
▽

Compared with the average American citizen, members of Congress are well paid. As of 1987, congressional salaries amounted to $77,400 a year. Senators are permitted to earn up to 40 percent of their salaries annually in outside income (representatives are permitted 30 percent)—largely in the form of honoraria for speeches, articles, and public appearances. They also earn income from their accumulated personal assets and may conduct business and legal operations on the side within these limits.

Members of Congress also benefit in other ways from belonging to a select group. They have access to private Capitol Hill gymnasium facilities, get low-cost haircuts, receive free, close-in parking at National and Dulles airports near Washington, and get six free parking spaces in Capitol Hill garages—plus one free outdoor Capitol parking slot. They also avoid parking tickets because of their congressional license plates. Members of Congress are not required to comply with labor laws in dealing with their staffs, eat in a subsidized dining room, and take advantage

[12]*Congressional Quarterly Weekly Report*, July 5, 1986, p. 1523.

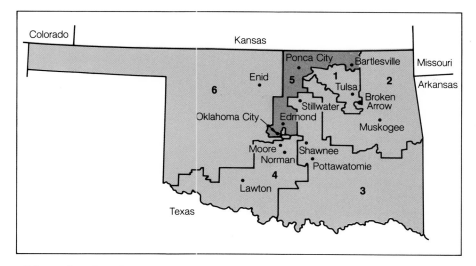

Figure 13–3

▽

A Modern Gerrymander

*After the 1980 census, Oklahoma legisla-
tors redrew their congressional districts in
such a way as to concentrate a large
number of Republicans in the strangely
shaped Fifth District. By lumping the
wealthier suburbs of Oklahoma City with
Bartlesville four counties away, they were
able to create one Republican district
while safeguarding the Democratic majorities in the five other districts.*

SOURCE: Michael Barone and Grant Ujifusa, *Almanac of American Politics 1986*, (Washington,
D.C.: National Journal, 1985).

of free gift and package wrapping, free plants from the Botanical Gardens for their
offices, free medical care, an inexpensive but generous pension plan, liberal travel
allowances, and special tax considerations.

Members of Congress are also granted generous **franking** privileges that permit
them to mail newsletters, surveys, and other letters to their constituents. As Table
13–5 indicates, the costs of congressional mail have risen more than tenfold from
1971 to 1984. Typically, the costs for these mailings rise enormously during election

Franking

A policy that enables members of Congress to send material through the mail
by substituting their facsimile signature
(frank) for postage.

Table 13–5

▽

Costs of Official Mail, 1971–1984

Year	Appropriations (dollars)	Average Unit Cost of Franked Mail (cents)
1971	11,244,000	8
1972	14,594,000	8
1972 supplement	18,400,000	
1973	21,226,480	8.79
1974	30,500,000	9.9
1975	38,756,015	11.4
1976	46,101,000	13.2
Transition period[a]	11,525,000	
1976 supplement	16,080,000	
1977	46,904,000	13.4
1978	48,926,000	12.7
1979	64,944,000	13.98
1980[b]	50,707,000	13.39
1981	52,033,000	
1982	75,095,000	13.94[c]
1983	93,161,000	12.3[c]
1984	107,077,000	12.3[c]

NOTE: 1984 figure does not include supplementals.

a. Reflects change in the fiscal year from July 1 to October 1.

b. Lower figure reflects decrease in bulk mail rates.

c. Estimate.

SOURCE: Norman Ornstein, Thomas E. Mann, Michael J. Malbin, Allen Schick, and John F. Bibby, eds.,
Vital Statistics on Congress 1984–85 (Washington, D.C.: American Enterprise Institute, 1984), p. 131.

Congress has a heavy burden to bear. It is expected to monitor and make intelligent decisions on a wide range of problems both domestic and foreign. Official fact-finding trips overseas by members of Congress are intended to help legislators make wise decisions.

In 1986, the U.S. Congress spent $4.76 million in foreign travel. This doesn't include most of the transportation costs, since transport is most frequently provided by Defense Department aircraft (at costs that are substantially higher than commercial airline rates!). Members of Congress made 426 trips, 347 of them by 262 members of the House and 76 trips by 43 senators. House member trips accounted for the lion's share—more than $4.08 million—of the congressional total.

The favorite place for congresspersons and their staffs to travel to was West Germany, which had 74 visits. In descending order, here were the top ten: Switzerland (67); Italy (62); France (61); the Soviet Union (51); Ireland (37); Israel (30); Spain (28); China (27); England (25); and Brazil (24). Third-world countries were not of great interest to congresspersons, although Barbados, a tranquil island and popular tourist spot in the Atlantic, was visited officially by 11 House members.

Senator Ted Stevens (Rep.-Alaska) was the most assiduous traveler. He went on seven trips and spent $681,232 (again, not including transportation).

One of the most interesting trips, or "junkets," as these foreign excursions are known, was led by House Speaker Thomas "Tip" O'Neill from March 13 to March 18 to Ireland. The press noted that most of the travelers had Irish names, were personal friends of O'Neill's, and, curiously, the dates of the trip allowed the delegation to spend St. Patrick's Day, the most celebrated Irish holiday, in Ireland. The trip cost more than $225,000 dollars, including transportation.

Although some trips seem to have mostly political and entertainment value, others have brought important insights to Congress. In 1985, the observations of legislators who went to the Philippines for the Marcos-Aquino election were crucial in building congressional support for Mrs. Aquino.

years. In May 1986, the Senate passed a resolution that would give each member a fixed mailing allowance for the rest of the year, but there was little expectation that the House, with all of its members up for reelection, would agree.

In recent years, increasingly generous staff support and office costs have also been provided. Each member is assigned office space in one of the three Senate office buildings named after former senators Richard B. Russell (Dem.-Georgia), Everett M. Dirksen (Rep.-Illinois), and Philip A. Hart (Dem.-Michigan) or in one of the three House office buildings named for former Speakers of the House Samuel Rayburn (Dem.-Texas), Joseph Cannon (Rep.-Illinois), and Nicholas Longworth (Rep.-Ohio). Senators are allocated physical office space based on the populations of their states.

Permanent Professional Staffs

Over forty thousand people are employed in the Capitol Hill bureaucracy.[13] About half of this total consists of personal and committee staff members. The personal staff includes office clerks and secretaries; professionals who deal with media relations, draft legislation, and satisfy constituency requests for service; and staffers

[13]Harrison W. Fox, Jr., and Susan Webb Hammond, *Congressional Staffs: The Invisible Force in American Lawmaking* (New York: Free Press, 1977).

who maintain local offices in the member's home district or state. The average Senate office on Capitol Hill employs about thirty staff members, and twice that number work on the personal staff of senators from the most populous states. House office staffs are typically about half as large as those of the Senate.

Congress also benefits from the expertise of the professional staff who work in agencies that were created to produce information for members of the House and Senate—resources comparable to those available to the president and the rest of the executive branch. The Congressional Research Service (CRS), a section of the Library of Congress, is an information and fact-finding center for legislators and their assistants. It furnishes a computer-based record of the contents and current legislative status of major bills that are under consideration. This record can be reviewed by staff members using computer terminals available in most offices. The General Accounting Office (GAO) audits the spending of money by federal agencies, investigates agency practices, and makes policy recommendations to Congress, especially concerning financial activities of the government. The Office of Technology Assessment (OTA), as yet little used, is designed to evaluate national technology policy in such areas as energy and the environment. The Congressional Budget Office (CBO) advises Congress on the anticipated effect on the economy of government expenditures and estimates the cost of proposed policies.

Privileges and Immunities Under the Law

Members of Congress also benefit from a number of legal privileges and immunities. Under Article I, Section 6, of the Constitution, they "shall in all Cases, except Treason, Felony, and Breach of the Peace, be privileged from Arrest during their Attendance at the Session of their respective Houses, and in going to and returning from the same; and for any Speech or Debate in either House, they shall not be questioned in any other Place." While the arrest immunity clause is not really an important provision today, the "speech or debate" clause means that a member may make any allegations or other statements he or she wishes in connection with official duties and not normally be sued for libel or slander or be otherwise subject to legal action.

The Committee Structure

▽

Most of the actual work of legislating is performed by the committees and subcommittees within Congress. With the thousands of bills that are introduced in every session of Congress, no single member can possibly be adequately informed on all the issues that arise. The committee system is a way to provide for specialization, or division of the legislative labor. Members of a committee can concentrate on just one area or topic—such as taxation or energy—and develop sufficient expertise to draft appropriate legislation when called for. The flow of legislation through both the House and the Senate is largely determined by the speed with which the members of these committees act on bills and resolutions.

Commonly known as "little legislatures,"[14] committees usually have the final say on pieces of legislation. Committee actions may be overturned on the floor by the full House or Senate, but this is rarely accomplished. Legislators normally defer

[14]This term is from Woodrow Wilson, *Congressional Government* (New York: Meridian Books, 1956 [first published in 1885]).

Staff member sorts the constituent mail.

Discharge Petition

A procedure by which a bill in the House of Representatives may be forced out of a committee (discharged) that has refused to report it out for consideration by the House. The discharge motion must be signed by an absolute majority (218) of representatives and is used only on rare occasions.

Standing Committee

A permanent committee within the House or Senate that considers bills within a subject area.

Budget committee meeting.

to the expertise of the chairperson and other members of the committee who speak on the floor in defense of a committee decision. Chairpersons of full committees exercise control over the scheduling of both hearings and formal action on a bill and decide which subcommittee will act on legislation falling within their committee's jurisdiction. Committees are very rarely deprived of control over a bill—although this kind of action is provided for in the rules of each chamber. In the House if a bill has been considered by a standing committee for thirty days, the signatures of a majority (218) of the House membership on a **discharge petition** can pry a bill out of an uncooperative committee's hands. From 1909 to 1982, however, although 909 such petitions have been made, only 26 resulted in successful discharge efforts, and of those, 20 passed the House.[15]

Types of Congressional Committees

Over the past two centuries, Congress has created several different types of committees, each of which serves particular needs of the institution.

Standing Committees

By far the most important committees are the **standing committees**—permanent bodies established by the rules of each chamber of Congress that continue from session to session. A list of the standing committees of the One Hundredth Congress is presented in Table 13–6. In addition, most of the standing committees have

[15]*Congressional Quarterly's Guide to Congress,* 3rd ed., p. 426.

Table 13–6

Standing Committees of the One Hundredth Congress

House Committees	Chair	Senate Committees	Chair
Agriculture	Kika de la Garza, D., Tex.	Agriculture, Nutrition, and Forestry	Patrick Leahy, D., Vermont
Appropriations	Jamie Whitten, D., Miss.	Appropriations	John Stennis, D., Miss.
Armed Services	Les Aspin, D., Wis.	Armed Services	Sam Nunn, D., Georgia
Banking, Finance, and Urban Affairs	F. J. St. Germain, D., R.I.	Banking, Housing, and Urban Affairs	William Proxmire, D., Wis.
Budget	William Gray, D., Pa.	Budget	Lawton Chiles, D., Fla.
District of Columbia	Ronald Dellums, D., Ca.	Commerce, Science, and Transportation	Ernest Hollings, D., S.C.
Education and Labor	Augustus Hawkins, D., Ca.		
Energy and Commerce	John Dingell, D., Mich.	Energy and Natural Resources	J. Bennett Johnston, D., La.
Foreign Affairs	Dante Fascell, D., Fla.	Environment and Public Works	Quentin Burdick, D., N.D.
Government Operations	Jack Brooks, D., Texas		
House Administration	Frank Annunzio, D., Ill.	Finance	Lloyd Bentsen, D., Texas
Interior and Insular Affairs	Morris Udall, D., Ariz.	Foreign Relations	Claiborne Pell, D., R.I.
Judiciary	Peter Rodino, Jr., D., N.J.	Governmental Affairs	John Glenn, D., Ohio
Merchant Marine and Fisheries	Walter Jones, D., N.C.	Judiciary	Joseph Biden, Jr., D., Del.
		Labor and Human Resources	Edward Kennedy, D., Mass.
Post Office and Civil Service	William Ford, D., Mich.	Rules and Administration	Wendell Ford, D., Kentucky
		Small Business	Dale Bumpers, D., Ark.
Public Works and Transportation	James Howard, D., N.C.	Veterans Affairs	Alan Cranston, D., Cal.
Rules	Claude Pepper, D., Fla.		
Science and Technology	Robert A. Roe, D., N.J.		
Small Business	John J. LaFalce, D., N.Y.		
Standards of Official Conduct	Julian Dixon, D., Cal.		
Veterans' Affairs	G. V. "Sonny" Montgomery, D., Miss.		
Ways and Means	Dan Rostenkowski, D., Ill.		

created several subcommittees to carry out their work. In the Ninety-ninth Congress, there were 103 subcommittees in the Senate and 139 in the House.[16]

Each standing committee is given a specific area of legislative policy jurisdiction, and almost all legislative measures are considered by the appropriate standing committees. Because of the importance of their work and the traditional influence of their members in Congress, certain committees are considered to be more prestigious than others. If a congressperson seeks to be influential, he or she will usually aspire to a seat on the Appropriations Committee in either chamber or on the Ways and Means Committee in the House. Significant public policy committees are the House Education and Labor Committee and the Senate Foreign Relations Committee.

Each member of the House serves generally on two standing committees, except when that member sits on the Appropriations, Rules, or Ways and Means Committee—in which case he or she serves on only that one standing committee. Each senator may serve on two major committees and one minor committee (only the Rules and Administration Committee and the Veterans Affairs Committee are considered minor).

[16]*Congressional Directory* (Washington, D.C.: Government Printing Office, 1985–86).

Select Committees

Select Committee
A temporary legislative committee established for a limited time period for a special purpose.

A **select committee** is normally created for a limited period of time and for a specific legislative purpose, such as conducting an investigation or study of a public problem like nutrition or aging. Select committees are disbanded when they have reported to the chamber that created them. They rarely create original legislation.

Joint Committees

Joint Committee
A legislative committee composed of members from both houses of Congress.

A **joint committee** is formed by the concurrent action of both chambers of Congress and consists of members from each chamber. Joint committees, which may be permanent or temporary, recently have dealt with the economy, taxation, the Library of Congress, and congressional printing operations. In the past, joint committees have been set up to examine congressional operations, atomic energy, and defense production.

Conference Committees

Conference Committees
Special joint committees appointed to reconcile differences when bills pass the two houses of Congress in different forms.

Conference committees are special cases of joint committees that are formed for the purpose of achieving agreement between the House and the Senate on the exact wording of legislative acts when the two chambers pass legislative proposals in different forms. No bill can be sent to the White House to be signed into law unless it first passes both chambers in identical form. Sometimes called the "third house" of Congress, conference committees are in a position to make significant alterations in legislation and frequently become the focal point of policy debates. This was the case, for example, with the passage of the National Energy Act of 1978, or the tax reform legislation of 1986, both of which required long and difficult negotiations in the House-Senate conference committee to reconcile conflicting versions.

The House Rules Committee

Because of its special "gatekeeping" power over the terms on which legislation will reach the floor of the House of Representatives, the House Rules Committee holds a uniquely powerful position. A special committee rule sets the time limit on debate and determines whether and how the bill may be amended. This practice dates back to 1883. The members of the Rules Committee have the unusual powers to meet while the House is in session, to have its resolutions considered immediately on the floor, and to initiate legislation on its own.

Before 1910, the committee cooperated closely with the House leadership in allowing favored legislation onto the floor. Following a revolt against centralized control over House affairs, the Rules Committee became independent of the leadership, and alternative routes to the floor were found by sponsors of legislation. In the late 1930s, the committee became controlled by a loose but effective combination of conservative Democrats and Republicans who regularly thwarted liberal proposals. An enlargement of the committee in 1961 and repeated efforts by the president and liberal members to make its members less obstructionist has paid off for House liberals and the Democratic leadership.

Since the 1960s, the Rules Committee has been much more accommodating to the wishes of the House's members. No longer is the committee chaired by members such as Howard W. Smith (chairperson of the Rules Committee from 1955 to 1966) who regularly disappeared to his Virginia farm to avoid discussing any legislation he opposed. The chair's power was reduced by the committee after Smith's departure, and subsequent committee heads have seen their independent power slip further.

The Selection of Committee Members

In the House, representatives are appointed to standing committees by the Steering and Policy Committee (for Democrats) and by the Committee on Committees (for Republicans). Committee chairpersons are normally appointed according to the principle of seniority.

The rule of seniority specifies that members with longer terms of continuous service on the committee will be given preference when committee chairpersons—as well as holders of other significant posts in Congress—are selected. The principle of seniority is not a law but an informal, and traditional, process. The **seniority system,** although deliberately unequal, provides a predictable means of assigning positions of power within Congress.

The general pattern until the 1970s was that members of the House or Senate who represented **safe seats** would be continually reelected and would eventually accumulate enough years of continuous committee service to enable them to become the chairpersons of their committees—if their party gained control of the appropriate chamber of Congress. Traditionally, this avenue of access to power benefited southern Democrats and midwesterners within the Republican party, who seldom faced serious, organized opposition either in their own party's primaries or during the general election. This resulted in a predominance of committee chairpersons from the more conservative ranks of both political parties.

In the 1970s, a number of reforms in the chairperson selection process somewhat modified the seniority principle and introduced the use of a secret ballot in electing House committee chairpersons, as well as a greater dispersal of authority within the committees themselves, by establishing rules for the selection of subcommittee chairpersons.

Seniority System
A custom followed in both houses of Congress specifying that members with longer terms of continuous service will be given preference when committee chairpersons and holders of other significant posts are selected.

Safe Seat
A district that returns the legislator with 55 percent of the vote or more.

The Formal Leadership
▽

The limited amount of centralized power that exists in Congress is exercised through party-based mechanisms. Congress is organized by party. When the Democratic party, for example, wins a majority of seats in either the House or the Senate, Democrats control the official positions of power in that chamber, and every committee has a Democratic chairperson and a majority of Democratic members. The same process holds when Republicans are in the majority. Every member of Congress, except for occasionally successful independent candidates, was elected through a partisan electoral process. Senators and representatives therefore usually have some sense of loyalty to their party in Congress.

We consider the formal leadership positions in the House and in the Senate separately, but some broad similarities are apparent in the way that leaders are selected and in the ways they exercise power in the two chambers.

Speaker of the House

The presiding officer in the House of Representatives. The speaker is always a member of the majority party and is the most powerful and influential member of the House.

James C. Wright, speaker of the House.

Majority Leader of the House

A legislative position held by an important party member in the House of Representatives. The majority leader is selected by the majority party in caucus or conference to foster cohesion among party members and to act as spokesperson for the majority party in the House.

Leadership in the House

The Speaker

The foremost power holder in the House of Representatives is the **speaker of the House.** The speaker's position is technically a nonpartisan one, but in fact, for the better part of two centuries, the speaker has been the official leader of the majority party in the House. When a new Congress convenes in January of odd-numbered years, each party nominates a candidate for speaker. In one of the very rare instances of perfect party cohesion, all Democratic members of the House ordinarily vote for their party's nominee, and all Republicans support their alternative candidate.

House leadership is exercised primarily by the speaker, the majority leader, the minority leader, and the majority and minority whips. The election of the speaker thus automatically puts the majority party in control of the powers that are available to that office.

The extent of the speaker's power has varied markedly over time. Throughout most of the nineteenth century, speakers had to share power with groups of powerful members or with key committee chairpersons. Beginning about 1890 and continuing through 1910, speakers gradually consolidated their power and exercised such dictatorial powers as controlling all committee appointments and the agenda. In the aftermath of a revolt in 1910 and 1911, however, these extensive powers of the speaker were substantially reduced.

The influence of modern-day speakers is primarily based on their personal prestige, persuasive ability, and knowledge of the legislative process—plus the acquiescence or active support of other representatives. The major formal powers of the speaker include the following:

1. Presiding over meetings of the House
2. Appointing members of joint committees and conference committees
3. Scheduling legislation for floor action
4. Deciding points of order and interpreting the rules with the advice of the House parliamentarian
5. Referring bills and resolutions to the appropriate standing committees of the House

A speaker may take part in floor debate and vote, as can any other member of Congress, but recent speakers usually have voted only to break a tie.

In general, the powers of the speaker are related to his or her control over information and communications channels in the House. This is a significant power in a large, decentralized institution where information is a very important resource. With this control over communications, the speaker attempts to ensure the smooth operation of the chamber and to integrate presidential and congressional policies.

In 1975, the powers of the speaker were expanded when the House Democratic caucus gave its party's speaker the power to appoint the Democratic Steering Committee, which determines new committee assignments for House party members.

The Majority Leader

The **majority leader of the House** has been a separate position since 1899, transferring to a new office a power that had usually been exercised by the chairperson of the Ways and Means Committee. The majority leader is elected by the caucus of party members to foster cohesion among party members and to act as a spokesperson for the party. The majority leader influences the scheduling of debate and generally acts as chief supporter of the speaker. Majority leaders conduct most procedural debate and also much of the substantive debate on the House floor. They are most deeply involved in debates on the important partisan issues that separate Democrats from Republicans. The majority leader cooperates with the speaker and other party leaders, both inside and outside Congress, to formulate the party's legislative program and to guide that program through the legislative process in the House. The majority leader's post is a very prestigious one because of the power and responsibility inherent in the office and also because, at least among Democrats, future speakers are recruited from that position.

The Minority Leader

The **house minority leader** is the losing candidate nominated for speaker by the caucus of the minority party. Like the majority leader, the leader of the minority party has as his or her primary responsibility maintaining cohesion within the party's ranks. As the official spokesperson for the minority party, he or she consults with the ranking minority members of the House committees and encourages them to adhere to the party platform. The minority leader also acts as a morale booster for the generally less well-informed and usually less successful minority and speaks on behalf of the president if the minority party controls the White House. In relations with the majority party, the minority leader consults with both the speaker and the majority leader on recognizing members who wish to speak on the floor, on House rules and procedures, and on the scheduling of legislation. Minority leaders have no actual power in these areas, however.

Whips

The formal leadership of each party includes assistants to the majority and minority leaders known as **whips**. These positions have existed throughout this century, and over the past fifty years they have developed into a complex network of deputy and regional whips supervised by the chief party whip. The whips assist the party leader by passing information down from the leadership to party members and by ensuring that members show up for floor debate and recorded votes on important issues. Whips conduct polls among party members about their views on major pieces of legislation, inform the leaders about who is a doubtful and who is a certain vote, and may exert pressure on members to support the leader's position. The Democratic whip was historically appointed by the party leader in consultation with a Democratic speaker, whereas the Republican chief whip has been elected by the party caucus since 1965. Beginning with the One Hundredth Congress, though, the position of House Democratic whip will be filled by a vote of the Democratic caucus. In all, several dozen members take part in this formal effort to maintain party discipline.

What Determines the House Leadership's Success

The success of the formal leadership in the House, particularly that of the majority party, depends on several factors. House speakers and leaders must obtain cooperation from the frequently more influential chairpersons of standing committees and avoid obstruction by the Rules Committee in getting bills to the floor. Their ability to function effectively is related to the size and cohesiveness of their legislative party, the extent to which members of the House feel secure enough in office to

House Minority Leader
The party leader elected by the minority party in the House.

Robert H. Michel, House minority leader.

Whips
Assistant floor leaders who aid the majority and minority floor leaders.

Robert Byrd, Majority floor leader.

President Pro Tempore
The temporary presiding officer of the Senate in the absence of the vice president.

Majority Floor Leader
The chief spokesperson of the major party in the Senate who directs the legislative program and party strategy.

Minority Floor Leader
The party officer in the Senate who commands the minority party's opposition to the policies of the majority party and directs the legislative program and strategy of his or her party.

Robert Dole, Minority floor leader.

ignore the leadership's pressure, and the degree of support that the leaders are provided in their party caucus.

Leadership in the Senate

The Senate is less than one-fourth the size of the House. This fact alone probably explains why a formal, complex, and centralized leadership structure is less necessary in the Senate than in the House.

The two highest-ranking formal leadership positions in the Senate are essentially ceremonial in nature. Under the Constitution, the vice president of the United States is the president (that is, the presiding officer) of the Senate and may vote to break a tie. However, the vice president only rarely is present for a meeting of the Senate. In his absence the Senate elects instead a **president pro tempore.** Ordinarily the member of the majority party with the longest continuous term of service in the Senate, the president pro tem does not have powers analogous to those of the speaker of the House, although he or she does appoint, jointly with the speaker, the director of the Congressional Budget Office. The most junior senators are usually chosen by the president pro tem and the majority leader to chair portions of each day's session.

The real leadership power in the Senate rests in the hands of the **majority floor leader,** the **minority floor leader,** and their respective whips. The majority and minority Senate leaders have the right to be recognized first in debate on the floor and generally exercise the same powers available to the House majority and minority leaders. They control the scheduling of debate on the floor in conjunction with the majority party's Policy Committee, influence the allocation of committee assignments for new members or for senators attempting to transfer to a new committee, influence the selection of other party officials, and participate in selecting members of conference committees. The leaders are expected to mobilize support for partisan legislative initiatives or for the proposals of a president who belongs to the same party. They act as a liaison with the White House when the president is of their party, try to get the cooperation of committee chairpersons, and seek to

facilitate the smooth functioning of the Senate through the principle of unanimous consent. Floor leaders are elected by their respective party caucuses.

Leaders of the Senate Democrats potentially have more power than Republican leaders. The Democratic floor leader is simultaneously chairperson of the Conference (caucus) of the Steering Committee, which makes committee assignments, and of the Policy Committee, which schedules legislation for floor action. In contrast, four different Republican senators hold these comparable positions, in a much more decentralized pattern of leadership.

Senate party whips, like their House counterparts, maintain communication within the party on platform positions and try to assure that party colleagues are present for floor debate and important votes. The Senate whip system is far less elaborate than its counterpart in the House, simply because there are fewer members to keep track of.

A list of the formal party leaders of the One Hundredth Congress is presented in Table 13–7.

Did You Know?
▽

That the Constitution does not require that the speaker of the House of Representatives must be an elected member of the House?

Table 13–7
▽
Party Leaders in the One Hundredth Congress

Position	Incumbent	Party/State	Leader Since
HOUSE			
Speaker	Jim Wright	D.-Texas	Jan., 1987
Majority leader	Tom Foley	D.-Wash.	Jan., 1987
Majority whip	Tony Coelho	D.-Cal.	Jan., 1987
Chairperson of the Democratic Caucus	Richard Gephardt	D.-Mo.	Dec., 1985
Minority leader	Robert Michel	R.-Ill.	Dec., 1980
Minority whip	Trent Lott	R.-Miss.	Jan., 1981
Chairperson of the Republican Conference	Jack Kemp	R.-N.Y.	Jan., 1981
SENATE			
President pro tempore	John Stennis	D.-Miss.	Jan., 1987
Majority floor leader	Robert Byrd	D.-W.Va.	Jan., 1987
Assistant majority leader	Alan Cranston	D.-Cal.	Jan., 1987
Secretary of the Democratic Conference	Daniel Inouye	D.-Hawaii	Jan., 1987
Minority floor leader	Robert Dole	R.-Kan.	Jan., 1987
Assistant minority leader	Alan K. Simpson	R.-Wyo.	Jan., 1987
Chairperson of the Republican Conference	John H. Chafee	R.-R.I.	Dec., 1985

Party leaders are a major source of influence over the decisions about public issues that senators and representatives must make every day. We consider the nature of partisan and other pressures on congressional decision making in the next section.

How Members of Congress Decide

▽

Why congresspersons vote as they do is uncertain and controversial. One popular perception of the legislative decision-making process is that legislators take cues from other trusted or more senior colleagues.[17] This model holds that since most members of Congress have neither the time nor the incentive to study the details of most pieces of legislation, they frequently arrive on the floor with no clear idea about what they are voting on or how they should vote. Their decision is simplified, according to the cue-taking model, by quickly checking how key colleagues have voted or intend to vote. More broadly, verbal and nonverbal cues can be taken from fellow committee members and chairpersons, party leaders, state delegation members, or the president.

A different theory of congressional decision making places the emphasis on the policy content of the issues being decided and on the desires of a congressperson's constituents and the pressures brought to bear by his or her supporters.[18] The degree of constituency influence on congressional voting patterns depends on the extent to which a state or district is urbanized, the region and state that a member represents, and the blue-collar proportion of the labor force.

Most people who study the decision-making process in Congress agree that the single best predictor for how a member will vote is his or her party membership.[19] Republicans tend to vote similarly on issues, as do Democrats. Of course, even though liberals predominate among the Democrats in Congress and conservatives among the Republicans, the parties still may have internal disagreements about the proper direction that national policy should take. This was generally true for the civil rights legislation of the 1950s and 1960s, for example, where the greatest disagreement was within the Democratic party between its conservative southern members and its liberal northern wing.

One way to measure the degree of party unity in Congress is to look at how often a majority of one party votes against the majority of members from the other party. Table 13–8 displays the percentage of all roll-call votes in the House and the Senate when this type of party voting has occurred. Note that party voting occurs at a much higher rate in the House in the odd-numbered years, which happen to be the years when congressional elections are not held.

Regional differences, especially between northern and southern Democrats, may overlap and reinforce basic ideological differences among members of the same party. One consequence of the North-South split among Democrats has been the **conservative coalition** policy alliance between southern Democrats and Republicans. This conservative, cross-party grouping can now be counted on to form regularly on votes on controversial issues in Congress. It is usually highly successful.

Table 13–8

▽

Party Voting in Congress

Percentage of all roll calls when a majority of Democratic legislators voted against a majority of Republican legislators.

	House	Senate
1986	57.0	52.0
1985	61.0	50.0
1984	47.1	40.0
1983	55.6	43.6
1982	36.4	43.4
1981	37.4	47.8
1980	37.6	45.8
1979	47.3	46.7
1978	33.2	45.2
1977	42.2	42.4
1976	35.9	37.2
1975	48.4	47.8
1974	29.4	44.3
1973	41.8	39.9

SOURCE: *Congressional Quarterly Weekly Report,* Nov. 15, 1986, p. 2902.

Conservative Coalition

An alliance of Republicans and southern Democrats that can form in the House or the Senate to oppose certain types of legislation.

[17]Donald Matthews and James Stimson, *Yeas and Nays: Normal Decision Making in the U.S. House of Representatives* (New York: John Wiley, 1975).

[18]Aage R. Clausen, *How Congressmen Decide* (New York: St. Martin's Press, 1973).

[19]David Mayhew, *Party Loyalty Among Congressmen* (Cambridge: Harvard University Press, 1966).

How a Bill Becomes Law

▽

Perhaps the best way to understand how a bill becomes a law is to follow a hypothetical law through the process. Consider the fate of a bill to regulate the oil industry. Where did the original idea come from? Undoubtedly, it would originate in the minds of lobbyists and other representatives and rank-and-file members of public interest organizations. Business, labor, farm, and civil rights interest groups are a source of many legislative ideas. Quite possibly, pressure group representatives would convince the right people in the executive branch to endorse the idea. The bulk of legislation considered by Congress originates in the White House or is passed up through the bureaucracy until it gets the president's attention.

Before being placed on the calendar and from there into the hands of the Rules Committee, the bill must be passed by a vote of the Interstate and Foreign Commerce Committee, which is the standing committee with jurisdiction in this case. The bill is referred to that committee on action of the House parliamentarian on the speaker's order. First, a subcommittee appointed by the full committee investigates the bill by holding open hearings and taking testimony from interested public and private officials. The subcommittee then "marks up" the bill—or determines the appropriate language to recommend for the bill. After receiving the subcommittee's report, the standing committee holds further hearings, adopts some amendments to the original wording, and submits both a majority report and a minority report on its actions to the full House.

A similar procedure takes place in the Senate, with some exceptions. There the bill is brought up under the Calendar of Business, which is the official schedule for all legislation of the Senate. The only other Senate calendar, the Executive Calendar, is reserved for treaties and presidential nominations. The bill is placed on the Senate floor, an action scheduled by the majority leader, the majority Policy Committee, and the minority leader. An attempted filibuster may be avoided by some quick behind-the-scenes compromises.

Before reaching the House floor, the bill passes through the Rules Committee. If the chairperson of the Rules Committee and the party leadership supports the

Roll call votes posted in the House.

Figure 13–4

△

How a Bill Becomes Law

This illustration shows the most typical way in which proposed legislation is enacted into law. There are more complicated, as well as simpler, routes, and most bills never become law. The process is illustrated with two hypothetical bills, House bill No. 1 (HR 1) and Senate bill No. 2 (S 2). Bills must be passed by both houses in identical form before they can be sent to the president. The path of HR 1 is traced by a solid line, that of S 2 by a broken line. In practice most bills begin as similar proposals in both houses.

SOURCE: Congressional Quarterly, Inc.

bill, it is reported out with only limited amendments. This major hurdle passed, the bill avoids the graveyard of proposed legislation that the Rules Committee has often been in the past.

Before the House votes on the original language in the bill, it first has to act on a number of amendments proposed as additions or changes. Also, before this first House vote occurs, it is scheduled for floor action under the Union Calendar, the calendar (agenda) that deals with legislation generally related to government finances and the economy. Different types of calendars are used in the House: the House Calendar (for nonfinancial and noneconomic issues), the Consent Calendar (for noncontroversial issues), the Private Calendar (for claims against the United States or private immigration bills), and the Discharge Calendar (for motions to discharge a committee from consideration of a bill).

After floor debate, the House votes to accept its own version of the bill. In this case, the vote has been an electronically recorded roll call. Of course, other methods of voting could have been used, such as voice votes in which members answer in chorus either "aye" or "no" and the chair decides the result. Other methods are division, or standing, votes—in which first the members in favor stand up and are counted by the presiding officer and then those opposed do the same—and teller votes—where members file past tellers selected by the chair who collect from them red ("no") or green ("yes") cards bearing the members' signatures.

In the next stage a conference committee, composed of members of both the Senate and the House, will spend long hours hammering out a language for the bill that will be acceptable to both the senators and representatives sitting on the committee. Much discussion and compromise has been necessary, but agreement is finally reached and the bill passes on to the Senate for its decision. The Senate passes the bill. If a majority in the House has also passed it on this latest vote, the bill will go on to the president for his decision. The president has to decide whether to veto the bill or sign it into law. If he waits ten days, not including Sundays, then the bill will automatically become law even without his signature—as long as Congress is still in session. If Congress ends its session and the president hasn't signed the bill within the ten-day period, then the bill will die from a so-called pocket veto.

Thus the progress of a bill through the halls of Congress. Figure 13–4 traces this route from the clerk through the parliamentarian and speaker to the appropriate standing committee, and so on up to the president (if the bill is passed by both chambers of Congress) for approval. Every stage of the process is characterized by debate and compromise among the members of Congress—within committees and subcommittees, on the floors of both chambers, and in private discussions held among the members.

The Question of Congressional Ethics

△

Ethics is the most serious public relations problem confronting Congress. Perhaps nothing has so tarnished the public's perception of Congress as the revelations concerning the abuse of staff members, the misuse of public funds, and the personal indiscretions of several members of that institution.

Congress's response to revelations of member misconduct has been mixed. The House Democratic caucus in June 1980 voted 160 to 0 to require that chairpersons of committees or subcommittees be automatically stripped of their posts if they

How a Bill Becomes Law

This illustration shows the most typical way in which proposed legislation is enacted into law. The process is illustrated with two hypothetical bills, House bill No. 100 (HR 100) and Senate bill No. 200 (S 200). Bills must be passed by both houses in identical form before they can be sent to the president. The path of HR 100 is traced by a solid line, that of S 200 by a broken line. In practice most bills begin as similar proposals in both houses.

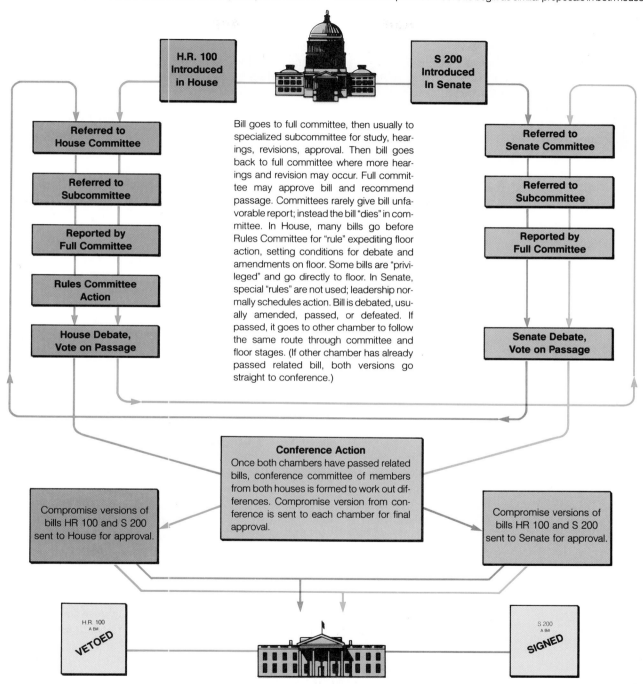

H.R. 100 Introduced in House

S 200 Introduced in Senate

Referred to House Committee

Referred to Subcommittee

Reported by Full Committee

Rules Committee Action

House Debate, Vote on Passage

Bill goes to full committee, then usually to specialized subcommittee for study, hearings, revisions, approval. Then bill goes back to full committee where more hearings and revision may occur. Full committee may approve bill and recommend passage. Committees rarely give bill unfavorable report; instead the bill "dies" in committee. In House, many bills go before Rules Committee for "rule" expediting floor action, setting conditions for debate and amendments on floor. Some bills are "privileged" and go directly to floor. In Senate, special "rules" are not used; leadership normally schedules action. Bill is debated, usually amended, passed, or defeated. If passed, it goes to other chamber to follow the same route through committee and floor stages. (If other chamber has already passed related bill, both versions go straight to conference.)

Referred to Senate Committee

Referred to Subcommittee

Reported by Full Committee

Senate Debate, Vote on Passage

Conference Action
Once both chambers have passed related bills, conference committee of members from both houses is formed to work out differences. Compromise version from conference is sent to each chamber for final approval.

Compromise versions of bills HR 100 and S 200 sent to House for approval.

Compromise versions of bills HR 100 and S 200 sent to Senate for approval.

H.R. 100
A Bill
VETOED

S 200
A Bill
SIGNED

Compromise bill approved by both houses is sent to the president, who can sign it into law or veto it and return it to Congress. Congress may override veto by a two-thirds majority vote in both houses; bill then becomes law without president's signature.

have been censured or indicted on a felony charge carrying a prison sentence of at least two years. This rule can be waived, however, by the same caucus. The House adopted a rule in 1977 (effective in 1979) to limit outside earned income to an amount equal to 30 percent of a member's salary. The same limit had been scheduled to go into effect in the Senate in 1979, but it was delayed until 1983 by a vote conducted quickly at the beginning of the Ninety-eighth Congress. In 1979, both chambers loosened the strict requirements on disclosure of their members' personal income and assets that they had earlier imposed on themselves. The new action replaced stricter disclosure provisions with the more lenient standards of the 1978 Ethics in Government Act. In 1983, another set of rules permitted members to earn tens of thousands of dollars in outside income.

Public financing of congressional campaigns may offer a partial solution to the problems of financial misconduct. Nonetheless, Congress has refused to use tax money or to impose spending limits on its members' campaigns, even though it adopted such provisions for presidential campaigns in 1974. Part of the campaign-funding problem is illustrated by the former congressman who used leftover campaign funds to make a down payment on a fifty-five-foot houseboat in Florida and to finance a limousine carrying the congressional seal. The practice of diverting unused campaign funds to personal use was outlawed in January 1980, but current members of Congress were exempted from coverage by the law.[20]

The extent of public disenchantment with the state of congressional ethics is suggested by a Gallup poll conducted in early 1980.[21] Seventy-eight percent of a national sample answered yes when asked if they believed "there are senators and representatives now serving in Congress who won election by using unethical and illegal methods in their campaigns." Forty percent of the same sample felt that one-fifth or more of the present members of Congress "got there by using unethical or illegal campaign methods." Another Gallup poll taken in May of 1983 showed that the honesty and ethical standards of senators were rated "high" or "very high" by only 16 percent of a national sample of adults. Only 14 percent gave a similar rating to members of the House.[22]

New Directions from Old
▽

Winds of an uncertain change have blown through Congress in the last few years. The old seniority system, once a virtually certain path to power through the committee structure, has been eroded. Power has been decentralized and diffused in many respects, most importantly by the growth of subcommittees. The greater number and increased importance of subcommittees has reduced control over information and material resources formerly in the hands of full committee chairpersons and party leaders.

A response to this fragmentation of power in Congress has been the increased importance of the party caucuses, especially on the Democratic side, though this too has meant that party and committee leaders are more answerable to the will of each party member. Numerous minicaucuses have formed around the specific

[20]*U.S. News and World Report*, March 17, 1980, pp. 61–62.
[21]*The Gallup Poll 1980* (Wilmington, Del.: Scholarly Resources, 1981), p. 65.
[22]*The Gallup Poll 1983* (Wilmington, Del.: Scholarly Resources, 1984), p. 144.

personal or constituency interests of different members of Congress. These sources of inside lobbying include such groups as the Congressional Black Caucus, the New England Congressional Caucus, the Northeast-Midwest Economic Advancement Coalition, the Congresswomen's Caucus, and the Textile Caucus. These groups have appeared in the House but not yet in the Senate.

Many of the recent changes in Congress resulted from reforms that were intended to "liberalize" the legislative body. However, the decentralization of power and increasing importance of individual members has tended to make compromise more difficult and to slow down the legislative process. The function of lawmaking is sometimes sacrificed to the representation of constituency interests as a consequence of making the Congress more democratic.

Congress, especially the House of Representatives, was intended to be the branch of the people. Since it is not possible for each one of us to represent ourself in governmental decision making, we choose representatives to make decisions on our behalf. The concept of representation is basic to any democratic political system.

As a citizen and voting constituent, you are entitled to assistance from your congressperson. If you have problems or questions concerning service from the federal government, he or she may be able to help you. You might, for example, want to contact your senator or representative concerning a Social Security check, a student loan, or veteran's benefits. A very large part of the work of senators and representatives is devoted to personalized work for constituents, or casework. You can locate your representatives' addresses in the *Congressional Directory*, available in most libraries; or, alternatively, you can write to them, addressing your letter as follows:

The Honorable _____
United States House of Representatives
Washington, D.C. 20515

The Honorable _____
United States Senate
Washington, D.C. 20510

But getting involved means more than this. It means more than being a passive recipient of your representative's actions. What Congress does is not determined by Congress alone. Individuals and groups on the outside affect the pace, the choices, and the policies adopted within the halls of Congress. Generally, members of Congress guide themselves by the opinions of the outspoken and organized members of their constituency. So if you want congressional response, be organized and articulate—let your views be known.

If you wish to telephone a member of Congress, call the Capitol Switchboard at (202) 224-3121 and ask to be connected to your congressperson's offices or to the office of a committee or subcommittee of Congress.

Chapter Summary

▽

1. The Founding Fathers, believing the bulk of national power should be in the legislature, set forth the structure, power, and operations of Congress in Article I of the Constitution.

2. Article I, Section 2, of the Constitution says that Congress will consist of two chambers. Partly an outgrowth of the Connecticut Compromise, this bicameral structure established a balanced legislature with the membership in the House of Representatives based on population and the membership in the Senate based on the equality of states.

3. The first seventeen clauses of Article I, Section 8, of the Constitution specify most of the enumerated, or expressed, powers of Congress, including the right to collect taxes, to

spend money, to regulate commerce, and to declare war. Other sections cover a wide range of further powers.

4. Besides its enumerated powers, Congress enjoys the right to "make all Laws which shall be necessary and proper for carrying into Execution the foregoing Powers, and all other powers vested by this Constitution in the Government of the United States, or in any Department or Officer thereof." This is called the necessary and proper clause.

5. Functions of Congress include (a) lawmaking activities, (b) service to constituents, (c) representation of diverse interests, (d) oversight of the manner in which laws are implemented, (e) educating the public about national issues and setting the terms for national debate, and (f) resolving conflicts.

6. There are 435 members in the House of Representatives compared with 100 senators. Owing to its larger size, there are a greater number of formal rules in the House.

7. The Senate tradition of unlimited debate, or filibustering, dates back to 1790 and has been used over the years to frustrate the passage of bills. Under Senate Rule 22, cloture can be used to shut off debate on a bill.

8. Congressional elections are operated by the individual state governments, which must conform to rules established by the Constitution and national statutes.

9. The process of nominating congressional candidates has shifted from party conventions to the direct primaries currently used in all states.

10. Candidates win through the effectiveness of their personal organizations, often with assistance from the state party organization. They have a loose affiliation with the party at the national level. The overwhelming majority of incumbent representatives and a smaller proportion of senators who run for reelection are successful.

11. The most complicated aspect of the mechanics of congressional elections is reapportionment—the allocation of legislative seats to constituencies. The Supreme Court's 1964 one man, one vote rule has been applied to equalize the populations of state legislative and congressional districts.

12. Members of Congress have a personal staff and benefit from the expertise of the professional staff of agencies created to produce information for their use. They enjoy certain legal privileges and immunities.

13. Members of Congress are disproportionately white, male, Protestant, and trained in higher-status occupations, relative to the American population as a whole.

14. Most of the actual work of legislating is performed by committees and subcommittees within Congress. It is the method of dividing legislative, appropriations, and investigatory functions among small, specialized groups.

15. Legislation introduced into the House or Senate is assigned to the appropriate standing committees for review.

16. Select committees are created for a limited period of time for a specific legislative purpose. Joint committees are formed by the concurrent action of both chambers and consist of members from each chamber.

17. Conference committees are special joint committees set up to achieve agreement between the House and the Senate on the exact wording of legislative acts passed by both chambers in different forms.

18. The House Rules Committee sets the rules by which bills may be debated, amended, and considered by the House.

19. The seniority rule specifies that longer-serving members will be given preference when committee chairpersons and holders of other important posts are selected.

20. The foremost power holder in the House of Representatives is the speaker of the House. Other leaders are the House majority leader, the House minority leader, and the majority and minority whips.

21. Formally, the vice president is the presiding officer of the Senate, with the majority party choosing a senior member as the president pro tem to preside when the vice president is absent. Actual leadership in the Senate rests with the majority floor leader, the minority floor leader, and their respective whips.

22. Congresspersons may make decisions by taking cues from trusted party colleagues or by responding to the policy context of issues and the desires of their constituents.

23. A bill becomes law by progressing through both houses of Congress and their appropriate standing and joint committees to the president.

24. Congressional ethics is a problem that Congress has addressed with mixed success.

Questions for Review and Discussion
▽

1. Two of the most important functions of Congress are representation and lawmaking. Think of several instances where these two functions present a conflict for an individual legislator. What should a congressperson do if a vote for a cut in defense spending means reducing jobs in a defense plant in his or her district?

2. Why are so many incumbent congresspersons reelected to office? How do they build so much support in their constituencies? Do voters know enough about congressional activity to make an intelligent choice for their representatives?

3. If legislators in Washington are mostly wealthy, well-educated lawyers, how can they know the needs and desires of their constituents? Would Congress be different if there were more women, minorities, and working-class people elected?

4. What functions does the leadership of the parties perform in Congress? Why is the leadership organization important to individual members?

5. Is the process of lawmaking too complicated? Does it give too many opportunities to minorities to block needed legislation?

Selected References
▽

Michael Barone and Grant Ujifusa, *The Almanac of American Politics* 1986 (Washington, D.C.: National Journal, 1985). A comprehensive summary of current political information on each member of Congress, his or her state or congressional district, recent congressional election results, key votes and ratings of roll call votes by various organizations, and sources of campaign contributions and records of campaign expenditures.

Lawrence C. Dodd and Bruce I. Oppenheimer, *Congress Reconsidered*, 3d ed. (Washington, D.C.: Congressional Quarterly Press, 1985). A collection of up-to-date essays on recent developments in congressional elections, changes in how Congress operates, committee and subcommittee politics, leadership and party politics, effects on public policy, and relationships with the executive branch.

Richard Fenno, Jr., *Home Style: House Members in Their Districts* (Boston: Little, Brown, 1978). A first-hand account of how eighteen members of the House interact with their constituents.

Morris P. Fiorina, *Congress—Keystone of the Washington Establishment* (New Haven: Yale University Press, 1977). An excellent summary of the functions of Congress within the national government.

Louis Fisher, *The Politics of Shared Power: Congress and the Executive* (Washington, D.C.: Congressional Quarterly Press, 1981). Operation of the separation of powers doctrine in practice, emphasizing the president's role as legislator, congressional intervention in administrative matters, and the political and constitutional problems in this sharing of power.

Randall B. Ripley, *Congress: Process and Policy*, 3d ed. (New York: W. W. Norton, 1983). An overview of Congress covering its role in the policy-making environment, historical development, elections, socialization of its members, committees and subcommittees, party leadership, state delegations, ideologically based groups, personal and committee staffs, support agencies, relations with interest groups and constituents, relations with the president and the bureaucracy, access to policy making, and impact on policy.

Chapter 14
▽
The Bureaucracy

Contents
▽

Controlling the Federal Bureaucracy
The Nature of Bureaucracy
The Size of the Bureaucracy
The Organization of the Federal Bureaucracy
Staffing the Bureaucracy
Current Attempts at Bureaucratic Reform
Bureaucrats as Politicians and Policy Makers
The American Bureaucracy

What If . . .
▽
There Were No Civil Service?

Since the civil service began in 1883, many millions of federal employees have been hired by competitive examinations, required to be politically neutral while employed, and enjoyed considerable job security. How would the political system be different if we did away with civil service?

One alternative is to return to the patronage, or "spoils," system of the last century. This would allow presidents to hire and fire public employees at will. An incoming president would direct his staff to find hundreds of thousands of names to replace federal employees.

Generally, presidents would look for three qualifications among these patronage appointees: previous political work for the party and campaign, friendship with the president's political supporters and contributors, and ideological compatibility.

The main advantage of such a system would be that the president could count on these appointees to implement his program. Normal bureaucratic resistance to change would be greatly weakened. Also, the promise of a federal job would be a great incentive for more people to become

active in politics. It would be possible to reward more individuals from disadvantaged backgrounds who cannot pass the current tests. Finally, under a patronage system, the president could greatly increase the number of women and minorities in public service "with a stroke of the pen."

On the other hand, such a spoils system would be the ideal target for corruption and scandal. Bureaucrats would get their jobs because of *whom* they knew, not *what* they could do, which would encourage the hiring of incompetents. Individuals might receive paychecks but never show up for work. Government contracts might be given to political supporters of the president or to other officials rather than to the most competent or lowest bidder. During political campaigns, the resources of the federal government—mailing, funds, contracts, and jobs—could be used to sway voters. In short, the system would be highly politicized and anyone who objected could be summarily fired.

A patronage system would also wreak havoc on long-term projects of federal agencies. Imagine replacing the senior investigators of AIDS at the National Center for Disease Control every four years. How could the FBI continue investigating organized crime if new agents were substituted with every change of administration? In such agencies as the Treasury and the State Department, a high degree of technical knowledge is necessary to perform certain jobs. Patronage appointees would never have the time to acquire such expertise before they were ousted for a new lot of appointees.

▽

The objectives of the civil service have been two: to take politics out of federal government employment and to provide an environment in which professionals, who gain their positions on merit, can carry out the functions of the federal government. Although a patronage system might be more responsive to the political winds, it would be ill-suited to the technical and sophisticated personnel demands of the modern federal bureaucracy.

One day a president of the United States smelled a rat. Actually, he thought he smelled a dead mouse that had died behind a wall near the Oval office. Since the president was expecting some important visitors, he demanded that the mouse be removed. His staffers called the General Services Administration (GSA), the independent agency that is responsible for the maintenance of the White House. The bureaucrats at the GSA claimed that the dead mouse in the White House was not their problem; after all, they had just fumigated for mice. They reasoned that the mouse must have come in from the outside and therefore was under the jurisdiction of the Department of the Interior. But when the bureaucrats at Interior were contacted, they refused to respond, claiming that their jurisdiction ended where the White House walls began.

The irate president demanded to see the responsible individuals from both agencies. He wanted action—and eventually he got it. A special interagency task force was formed to remove the dead mouse from the White House.

A tale of fiction? Unfortunately not. The president in question was James Earl Carter, and the irony was that Carter had campaigned only months earlier on a platform promising to streamline the federal bureaucracy.[1] Carter had not been alone. In the last twenty or thirty years almost every presidential candidate has at one time or another maintained that he would do something about the bureaucracy.

Controlling the Federal Bureaucracy
▽

How successful have all these presidential candidates been at controlling, containing, or altering the federal bureaucracy once they have taken office? The answer is easy—not very successful at all. Reagan claimed he was going to eliminate both the Department of Education and the Department of Energy. He did neither. Carter also claimed he was going to reduce the number of cabinet departments.

[1]*The New York Times*, November 11, 1981, p. 1.

The computer tape library for the Department of Health and Human Services.

Instead, two new ones—the Department of Energy and the Department of Education—were added during his administration.

Presidents have been virtually powerless to affect significantly the structure and operation of the federal bureaucracy. It has been called the "fourth branch of government," even though you will find no reference to the bureaucracy in the original Constitution or in the twenty-six amendments that have been passed since 1787. But Article II, Section 2, of the Constitution gives the president the power to appoint "all other officers of the United States, whose appointments are not herein otherwise provided for," and Article II, Section 3, states that the president "shall take care that the laws be faithfully executed, and shall commission all the officers of the United States." Constitutional scholars believe that the bureaucracy rests on these two sections in Article II.

Presidents have not only found it almost impossible to change the bureaucracy but, more seriously, they have also found that departments and agencies are often able to obstruct the president's own goals. Franklin Roosevelt complained of ideological and personal department opposition during his tenure:

> The Treasury is so large and far-flung and ingrained in its practices that I find it is almost impossible to get the action and results that I want. . . . But the Treasury is not to be compared with the State Department. You should go through the experience of trying to get any changes in the thinking, policy and action of the career diplomats and then you'd know what a real problem was. But the Treasury and the State Department put together are nothing compared with the Na-a-vy.[2]

It soon becomes clear to new administrations that real power in the executive branch lies at least as much with bureaucrats and cabinet officers as it does with the White House. Resistance to John Kennedy's New Frontier was led by "the feudal barons of the permanent government, entrenched in their domains and fortified by their sense of proprietorship."[3] The Nixon administration encountered social service interests within the government "dominated by administrators ideologically hostile to many of the directions of the Nixon administration in the realm of social policy."[4]

Two questions raised by such comments are: what is a bureaucracy, and how does it become so powerful?

The Nature of Bureaucracy

▽

Bureaucracy

A large organization that is structured hierarchically to carry out specific functions.

A **bureaucracy** is the name given to a large organization that is structured hierarchically to carry out specific functions. Generally, most bureaucracies are characterized first and foremost by an organization chart. According to the German sociologist Max Weber, bureaucracies share certain qualities. Every person who works in the organization has a superior to whom he or she reports. The units of the organization are divided according to specialization and the expertise of the employees. There are elaborate rules that everyone in the organization is expected to accept and follow. Finally, tasks are supposed to be done in a neutral manner, that is, for the sake of the organization rather than for personal gain.[5]

[2]Quoted in Marriner Eccles, *Beckoning Frontiers* (New York: Alfred A. Knopf, 1951), p. 336.

[3]Arthur Schlesinger, Jr., *A Thousand Days* (Boston: Houghton Mifflin, 1965), p. 981.

[4]Joel Aberbach and Bert Rockman, "Clashing Beliefs Within the Executive Branch," *American Political Science Review*, 70, no. 2 (June 1976), pp. 456–468.

[5]Max Weber, *Theory of Social and Economic Organization*, ed. Talcott Parsons (New York: Oxford University Press, 1974).

We should not think of bureaucracy as unique to government. Any large corporation or university can be considered a bureaucratic organization. The fact is that the handling of complex problems requires a division of labor. Individuals must concentrate their skills on specific, well-defined aspects of a problem and depend on others to solve the rest of it.

But public or government bureaucracies differ from private organizations in some important ways. Unlike a private corporation like General Motors, public bureaucracies do not have a single set of leaders such as GM's board of directors. Although the president is the chief administrator of the federal system, all bureaucratic agencies are subject to the desires of Congress for their funding, staffing, and, indeed, for their continued existence. Furthermore, public bureaucracies supposedly serve the citizen rather than the stockholder. In a sense each American has a right to feel that he or she should control the bureaucracy. Perhaps it is this aspect of government organization that makes citizens hostile toward government employees when they experience inefficiency and red tape. One other important difference is that government bureaucracies are not organized to make a profit.

Internal Revenue Service employees sorting returns.

Rather they are supposed to perform their functions as efficiently as possible to conserve the taxpayers' dollars. These characteristics, together with the prevalence and size of the government bureaucracies, make them an important factor in American life.

The Size of the Bureaucracy

▽

In 1787, the new government's bureaucracy was miniscule. There were three departments—State (with nine employees), War (with two employees), and Treasury (with thirty-nine employees). This bureaucracy was still small in 1798 when the secretary of state had seven clerks and spent a total of $500 (about $4,500 in 1986 dollars) on stationery and printing. In that year the Appropriations Act allocated $1.4 million to the War Department (or $12.3 million in 1986 dollars).[6]

Times have changed, as we can see in Figure 14–1, which lists the various federal agencies and the number of employees in each. Excluding the military, 2.8 million government employees constitute the federal bureaucracy. That number

[6]Leonard D. White, *The Federalists: A Study in Administrative History 1789–1801* (New York: The Free Press, 1948).

Figure 14–1

▽

Federal Agencies and Their Respective Number of Employees

SOURCE: *Statistical Abstract of the United States, 1986.*

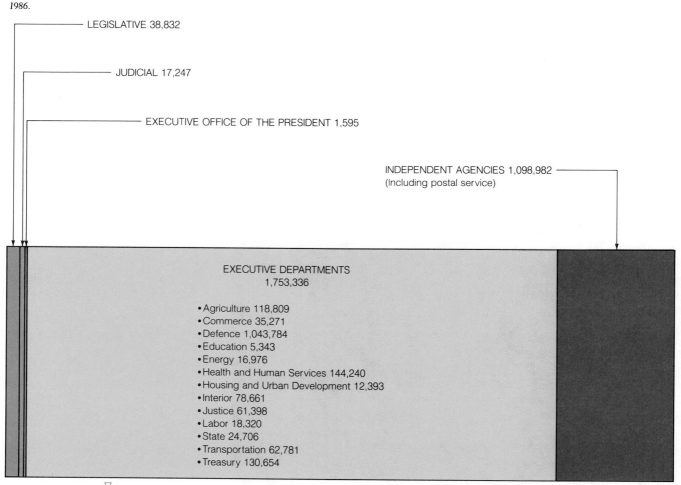

LEGISLATIVE 38,832

JUDICIAL 17,247

EXECUTIVE OFFICE OF THE PRESIDENT 1,595

INDEPENDENT AGENCIES 1,098,982
(Including postal service)

EXECUTIVE DEPARTMENTS
1,753,336

• Agriculture 118,809
• Commerce 35,271
• Defence 1,043,784
• Education 5,343
• Energy 16,976
• Health and Human Services 144,240
• Housing and Urban Development 12,393
• Interior 78,661
• Justice 61,398
• Labor 18,320
• State 24,706
• Transportation 62,781
• Treasury 130,654

Profile
▽
Elizabeth Hanford Dole

"We will continue to pursue the process of deregulation whenever it serves the best interest of the public, but we will remain sensitive to the temporary dislocations that changes in regulatory policy can cause."

When Elizabeth Hanford Dole was named by President Reagan to replace Drew Lewis as the Secretary of Transportation in 1983, she already had held numerous governmental posts. Dole's experience in government started soon after she completed her law degree at Harvard. She began her Washington career as an assistant to Lyndon Johnson's consumer adviser, Betty Furness. In the Nixon administration, she served on the President's Committee on Consumer Interests from 1969 to 1971 and then, in 1973, became the second woman ever named to the Federal Trade Commission. When Ronald Reagan was elected, Dole was called to serve again on the White House staff, this time as a special assistant to the president, whose duties included meeting with special interest groups and building coalitions for administration proposals. Lobbyists who dealt with Mrs. Dole described her as "extremely capable, hard-working, charming, and a good politician."

Elizabeth Hanford Dole was born in North Carolina in 1937. She attended Duke University before going on to law school. Her career in Washington took her from White House jobs to cabinet agencies and then to the Federal Trade Commission, giving her experience in a wide variety of bureaucratic organizations. She brought this experience to the Department of Transportation where she is responsible for dealing with such issues as the sale of Conrail to a private corporation, the deregulation of the airlines, and the improvement of automotive safety. In 1986, the "Dole light," or high brake light, became mandatory in all new cars sold in the United States.

In 1975, as an established Washington lawyer, she married Robert Dole, the Republican senator from Kansas. When Mr. Dole was nominated for vice president on the Ford ticket in 1976, Mrs. Dole campaigned vigorously for him. They became well known as a couple, with her southern charm balancing his sharp wit. At the 1984 Republican convention, Mrs. Dole gave one of the major speeches as the Republicans tried to showcase their female officeholders. Commentators often interviewed the married couple and asked which one would be the candidate for president in 1988 or whether both might run, making it a Dole-Dole ticket. When Mrs. Dole accepted the cabinet position, she was asked whether there would be any conflict of interests in dealing with the chairman of the Finance Committee in the Senate, Mr. Dole. She responded, "There's a lot of interest, but no conflict."

Source for quotes: *Congressional Quarterly Weekly Report*, January 8, 1983, p. 13.

has remained relatively stable for the last several decades. It is somewhat deceiving, however, because there are many others working directly or indirectly for the federal government as subcontractors, consultants, and in other capacities.

But the figures for federal government employment are only part of the story. Figure 14–2 shows the growth in government employment on federal, state, and local levels. Since 1950, this growth has been mainly at the state and local levels, so that if all government employees are counted, a bit under 10 percent of the entire civilian population over age 16 works directly for the government. If we include the military, then 15 percent of the entire labor force is employed directly by government.

The costs of the bureaucracy are commensurately high and growing. The share of the gross national product taken up by government spending was only 8.5 percent in 1929, but today it exceeds 25 percent.

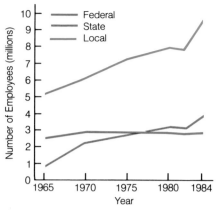

Figure 14–2

▽

Growth in Government Employment on Federal, State, and Local Levels

By the 1980s, there were more local government employees than federal employees, and three times as many state employees.

SOURCE: *Statistical Abstract of the United States, 1986.*

Cabinet Departments

The thirteen departments of the executive branch (State, Treasury, Defense, Justice, Interior, Agriculture, Commerce, Labor, Health and Human Services, Housing and Urban Development, Education, Energy, and Transportation).

Line Organization

Government or corporate units that provide direct services or products for the public.

The Organization of the Federal Bureaucracy
▽

Within the federal bureaucracy are a number of different types of government agencies and organizations. Figure 14–3 outlines the several bureaucracies within the executive branch as well as the separate organizations that provide services to the Congress, to the courts, and to the president directly. In Chapter 12, we discussed those agencies that are considered to be part of the Executive Office of the President.

The executive branch, which employs most of the bureaucrats, has four major types of bureaucratic structures. They are (1) cabinet departments, (2) independent executive agencies, (3) independent regulatory agencies, and (4) government corporations. Each has a distinctive relationship to the president, and some have unusual internal structures, overall goals, and grants of power.

Cabinet Departments

The thirteen **cabinet departments** are the major service organizations of the federal government. They can also be described in management terms as **line organizations.** This means they are directly accountable to the president and are responsible for performing functions of government such as printing money or training troops. These departments were created by Congress when the need for each arose. The first department to be created was State and the most recent one was Education, established in 1979. Although the president might ask that a new department be created or an old one abolished, he has no power to do so without legislative approval from Congress.

Each department is headed by a secretary and several levels of undersecretaries, assistant secretaries, and so on. Figure 14–4 is the organization chart of the Department of Transportation. The president theoretically has considerable control over the cabinet departments since he is able to appoint or fire all of the top officials. However, as Franklin Roosevelt suggested, even cabinet departments do not always respond to the president's wishes. One reason for the frequent unhappiness of presidents with their departments is that the entire bureaucratic structure below the top political levels is staffed by permanent employees, many of whom are committed to established programs or procedures and who resist change. As we can see from Table 14–1, each cabinet department employs thousands of individuals, only a handful of whom are under the control of the president.

Some observers have grouped the cabinet departments according to their closeness to the chief executive. Several of the departments—State, Defense, Justice, and Treasury—are known as the "inner" departments, since they primarily serve the president and their secretaries are often those who are closest politically and personally to the Oval Office. The other departments are sometimes classified as "outer" because their functions deal more with domestic constituency groups and thus their goals may differ from those of the president. Very large and complex departments like Defense, Health and Human Services, and Housing and Urban Development have been called "holding companies" because of the multitude of agencies and interests that are combined within one organization. Such complex departments tend to suffer from internal conflicts as one bureau tries to expand its functions or budget at the expense of another.

The cabinet departments are by far the most important sectors within the federal bureaucracy. The thirteen cabinet departments combined account for 1.6 million

THE GOVERNMENT OF THE UNITED STATES

THE CONSTITUTION

This chart seeks to show only the more important agencies of the government. See text for other agencies.

LEGISLATIVE BRANCH

THE CONGRESS

SENATE   HOUSE

Architect of the Capitol
United States Botanic Garden
General Accounting Office
Government Printing Office
Library of Congress
Office of Technology Assessment
Congressional Budget Office
Copyright Royalty Tribunal

EXECUTIVE BRANCH

THE PRESIDENT

Executive Office of the President

White House Office
Office of Management and Budget
Council of Economic Advisers
National Security Council
Office of Policy Development
Office of the United States
  Trade Representative

Council on Environmental Quality
Office of Science and Technology
  Policy
Office of Administrator

THE VICE PRESIDENT

JUDICIAL BRANCH

The Supreme Court of the
United States

United States Courts of Appeals
United States District Courts
United States Claims Court
United States Court of Appeals for
  the Federal Circuit
United States Courts of International
  Trade
Territorial Courts
United States Court of Military
  Appeals
United States Tax Court
Administrative Office of the
  United States Courts
Federal Judicial Center

DEPARTMENT OF AGRICULTURE

DEPARTMENT OF COMMERCE

DEPARTMENT OF DEFENSE

DEPARTMENT OF EDUCATION

DEPARTMENT OF ENERGY

DEPARTMENT OF HEALTH AND HUMAN SERVICES

DEPARTMENT OF HOUSING AND URBAN DEVELOPMENT

DEPARTMENT OF THE INTERIOR

DEPARTMENT OF JUSTICE

DEPARTMENT OF LABOR

DEPARTMENT OF STATE

DEPARTMENT OF TRANSPORTATION

DEPARTMENT OF THE TREASURY

INDEPENDENT ESTABLISHMENTS AND GOVERNMENT CORPORATIONS

ACTION
Administrative Conference of the U.S.
American Battle Monument Commission
Appalachian Regional Commission
Board for International Broadcasting
Central Intelligence Agency
Civil Aeronautics Board
Commission on Civil Rights
Commission of Fine Arts
Commodity Futures Trading Commission
Consumer Products Safety Commission
Environmental Protection Agency
Equal Employment Opportunity
  Commission
Export Import Bank of the U.S.
Farm Credit Administration
Federal Communications Commission

Federal Deposit Insurance Corporation
Federal Election Commission
Federal Emergency Management
  Agency
Federal Home Loan Bank Board
Federal Labor Relations Authority
Federal Maritime Commission
Federal Mediation and Conciliation
  Service
Federal Reserve System, Board of
  Governors of the
Federal Trade Commission
General Services Administration
Inter American Foundation
Interstate Commerce Commission
Merit Systems Protection Board

National Aeronautics and Space
  Administration
National Capital Planning
  Commission
National Credit Union Administration
National Foundation on the Arts and
  the Humanities
National Labor Relations Board
National Mediation Board
National Science Foundation
National Transportation Safety Board
Nuclear Regulatory Commission
Occupational Safety and Health Review
  Commission
Office of Personnel Management
Panama Canal Commission
Peace Corps

Pennsylvania Avenue Development
  Corporation
Pension Benefit Guaranty Corporation
Postal Rate Commission
Railroad Retirement Board
Securities and Exchange Commission
Selective Service System
Small Business Administration
U.S. Arms Control and Disarmament
  Agency
U.S. Information Agency
U.S. International Development
  Cooperation Agency
U.S. International Trade Commission
Veterans Administration

Figure 14–3
▽
**Organization Chart
of the Federal Government**

SOURCE: *U.S. Government Manual, 1983–84.*

employees, or fully 57 percent of the civilian federal bureaucracy. In terms of spending, the Department of Defense and the Department of Health and Human Services together account for 60 percent of all federal outlays.

Independent Executive Agencies

Independent executive agencies are bureaucratic organizations that have a single function. They are not located within a department and report directly to the president who appoints their chief officials. When a new federal agency is created—the Environmental Protection Agency, for example—a decision is made by the president and Congress about where it will be located in the bureaucracy. In this century, presidents have often asked that a new organization be kept separate or independent rather than added onto an existing department. This is a political decision, which may focus public attention on the new agency by putting it closer to the White House or keep the new group out of a department that may in fact be hostile to its creation. Among the major independent agencies are the following:

Independent Executive Agency
A federal agency having a single function that is not a part of a cabinet department but reports directly to the president.

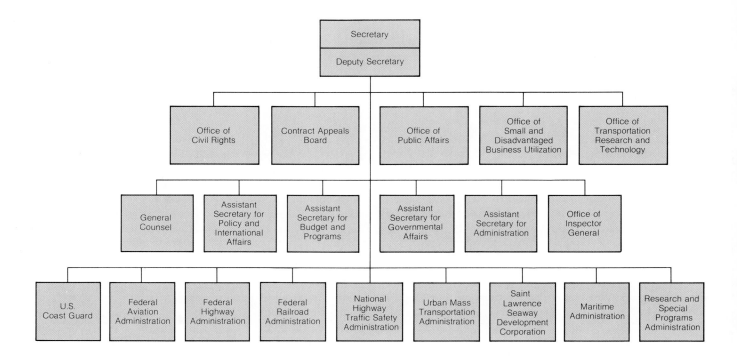

```
┌─────────────────┐
│    Secretary    │
├─────────────────┤
│ Deputy Secretary│
└─────────────────┘
```

| Office of Civil Rights | Contract Appeals Board | Office of Public Affairs | Office of Small and Disadvantaged Business Utilization | Office of Transportation Research and Technology |

| General Counsel | Assistant Secretary for Policy and International Affairs | Assistant Secretary for Budget and Programs | Assistant Secretary for Governmental Affairs | Assistant Secretary for Administration | Office of Inspector General |

| U.S. Coast Guard | Federal Aviation Administration | Federal Highway Administration | Federal Railroad Administration | National Highway Traffic Safety Administration | Urban Mass Transportation Administration | Saint Lawrence Seaway Development Corporation | Maritime Administration | Research and Special Programs Administration |

General Services Administration (GSA)

This independent agency was established in 1949 to centralize purchasing for the federal government and the management of its property and records. The GSA is headed by an administrator, appointed by the president with Senate approval, who has the responsibility for procuring, supplying, and transporting the property and services of all the executive agencies. The administrator of the GSA also is in charge of the acquisition and management of federally owned or leased property, the disposal of service property, and the management of all records. The GSA has more than thirty thousand employees.

Since the GSA is the business arm of the federal government, it has implied powers of oversight. For example, as the major government contractor in the construction industry and elsewhere, it implements national policy by requiring contractors to prove they are complying with Equal Employment Opportunity legislation. It also oversees spending. The GSA has uncovered a number of overcharges and other procurement irregularities in government each year. In 1981, an alleged $1.8 million or 10 percent overcharge was discovered in an $18 million National Aeronautics and Space Administration contract. In another case, a single Defense Department employee was discovered to have falsified more than 3,300 forms and embezzled some $1.8 million in medical funds.

Although the GSA has uncovered a number of abuses in government operations, it has also suffered from internal corruption and malpractice. In 1976, for example, a GSA employee pleaded guilty to defrauding the agency of $300,000 by submitting false bills payable to phony post office addresses. In 1978, it was alleged that the GSA was giving kickbacks to a firm supplying office furniture to the agency and allowing fraudulent contract-bidding practices by that office supply firm. Jay Solomon, head of the GSA, told a Senate subcommittee in 1978 that "the fraud, the thievery . . . and downright abuse of the public trust that have been exposed to this date [at the GSA] are only the beginning."[7]

National Aeronautics and Space Administration (NASA)

This independent government agency was established in 1958 by the National Aeronautics and Space Act. Its primary purpose is to explore the peaceful use of space, and as such it is responsible for building, testing, and operating space vehicles. NASA has four divisions: (1) the Office of Manned Space Flights, (2) the Office of Space Science and Applications, (3) the Office of Advanced Research and Technology, and (4) the Office of Tracking and Data Acquisition. In its early years, NASA at times had extremely large budgets, particularly during its efforts to put a person on the moon. In the last few years, its budget has averaged about $5.7 billion annually.

Veterans Administration (VA)

In 1930, the VA was formed by combining various federal agencies that handled benefits for veterans. Since today there are 28.5 million veterans, including 5.5 million Vietnam-era veterans, the responsibilities of the VA are immense. Indeed, when we add the dependents and survivors of veterans, they make up almost one-half the population. The annual budget for the VA is around $24 billion, $7.6 billion being paid as compensation to disabled veterans. The VA maintains 165 hospitals and 200 outpatient clinics, rehabilitation centers, and nursing homes. The VA hospitals employ about 3 percent of all doctors in the United States and train about 25 percent of the new doctors annually.

Altogether, there are fifty-seven independent executive agencies. Other well-known ones include the Environmental Protection Agency (EPA), the Central Intelligence Agency (CIA), and the Peace Corps.

Table 14–1

▽

Employment in the Executive Branch

Agriculture............	118,809
Commerce	35,271
Defense	1,043,284
Health and Human Services	144,240
Housing and Urban Development	12,393
Interior	78,661
Justice	61,398
Labor	18,320
State	24,706
Transportation	67,781
Treasury	130,654
Environmental Protection Agency ...	13,048
National Aeronautics and Space Administration	22,085
Veterans Administration	239,923

SOURCE: *Statistical Abstract of the United States, 1985–1986*, p. 325.

Independent Regulatory Agencies

The **independent regulatory agencies** are typically responsible for a specific type of public policy. Their function is to make and implement rules and regulations in a particular sector of the economy to protect the public interest. The earliest such agency was the Interstate Commerce Commission (ICC), which was established in 1887 when Americans began to seek some form of government control over the rapidly growing business and industrial sector. This new form of organization, the independent regulatory commission, was supposed to make technical, nonpolitical decisions about rates, profits, and rules that would be for the benefit of all and that did not require congressional legislation. In the years that followed the creation of the ICC, other agencies were created to regulate aviation (the Civil Aeronautics Board, CAB), communication (the Federal Communications Commission, FCC), the stock market (the Securities and Exchange Commission, SEC), nuclear power (the Nuclear Regulatory Commission, NRC), and so on.

The regulatory commissions are administered independently of all three branches of government. Since they were set up because Congress felt it was unable to handle

Independent Regulatory Agency
An agency outside the major executive departments charged with making and implementing rules and regulations to protect the public interest.

[7]Testimony before the Subcommittee on Federal Spending Practices and Open Government (of the Senate), September 19, 1978.

Highlight

▽

NASA and the Space Shuttle Disaster

On Tuesday, January 28, 1986, at 11:38 A.M., the space shuttle *Challenger* lifted off from its launch pad at Cape Canaveral, Florida. Seventy-three seconds later, the shuttle exploded, owing to faulty design of its booster rockets, and the entire crew of seven were killed in full view of the audience and launch personnel on the ground and viewers on television. The explosion was replayed many times over on subsequent news coverage of the disaster.

The National Aeronautics and Space Administration (NASA) had supported and funded the shuttle program ever since President Nixon committed the nation to launching a fleet of shuttles in the early 1970s. After many success-ful flights, NASA had become confident that the shuttle was capable of fulfilling its missions of launching satellites, providing for scientific studies, and developing advanced technology for both civilian and military applications. In the aftermath of the shuttle disaster, however, doubts arose within government and among the public about how NASA ran the shuttle program and how the agency operated internally.

The first evidence of trouble within and for NASA came in the investigation of the shuttle tragedy that was undertaken by a federal commission headed by William P. Rogers, former Secretary of State under President Nixon. The commission uncovered the fact that NASA launch officials had pressured the engineers at the corporation that designed the boosters—Morton Thiokol, in Brigham City, Utah—to give written approval for lift-off despite the engineers' strenuous objections that temperatures at the launch site were too low for the boosters' seals to work properly. The commission later discovered that officials at the Marshall Space Flight Center in Huntsville, Alabama, which is run by NASA, had destroyed records of weekly engineering reports detailing problems with the shuttle's suspect booster rockets after the probe of the accident began. It was clear from the commission's investigation that NASA had glossed over a history of serious safety problems with the seals in the rocket joints dating back to 1977. Waste and inefficiency within the agency went virtually unnoticed by Congress, which was as caught up as the general public in adulation of the NASA programs that had put humans in orbit and on the moon.

Among the problems with NASA's organization specified by the Rogers Commission was the agency's loose managerial structure in which individual flight centers were given too much power to make decisions and to cover up reports of negative developments. The commission recommended that quality control efforts be enhanced through stricter reviews of the critical items on the shuttle, that NASA managers change the system of signing waivers clearing the shuttle for flight when there are documented problems with flight safety, and that a larger role in launch decisions should be given to astronauts, engineers, and flight contractors.

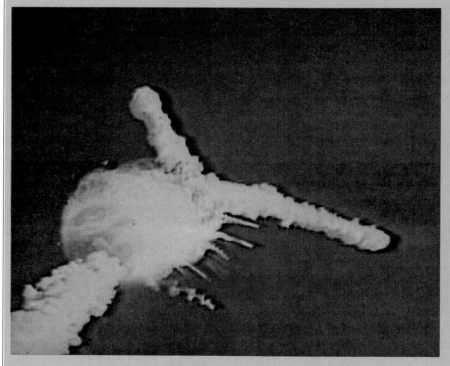

Many of the officials most closely linked to the shuttle's boosters were reassigned or retired, and NASA was given a new administrator, James Fletcher, who had headed the agency previously. On June 13, 1986, President Reagan ordered NASA to implement the Rogers Commission's recommendations as soon as possible. One of the first steps taken by NASA was the creation of an Office of Safety, Reliability, and Quality Assurance that would have authority throughout the agency and that would report directly to the agency's administrator. New directors of the shuttle program and of the Johnson Space Flight Center in Houston were named.

Through all the turmoil, public opinion remained supportive of manned space missions. A Gallup poll taken immediately after the shuttle exploded revealed that 80 percent of a national sample of adults believed that the United States should continue the manned shuttle program, and 69 percent felt that civilian astronauts such as journalists, politicians, and school-teachers should participate in future space shuttle flights. In addition, 79 percent expressed a great deal of confidence or a fair amount of confidence that NASA will be able to prevent similar accidents from happening in the future. Another Gallup poll revealed that 50 percent of the adult public wants spending on the U.S. space program either to remain the same or be increased, whereas only 14 percent favor decreased spending and 5 percent want expenditures on the space program to be ended altogether.

SOURCES: The *Gallup Report*, March, 1986, pp. 10–14; *The Washington Post*, May 26, 1986.

the complexities and technicalities required to carry out specific laws in the public interest, the regulatory commissions in fact combined some functions of all three branches of government—executive, legislative, and judicial. They are legislative in that they make rules that have the force of law. They are executive in that they provide for the enforcement of those rules. They are judicial in that they decide disputes involving the rules they have made (primarily through administrative law judges, discussed in more detail in Chapter 15).

Regulatory commission members are appointed by the president with the consent of the Senate, although they do not report to the president. By law, the members of regulatory commissions cannot all be from the same political party. The president can influence regulatory agency behavior by appointing people of his party or those who share his philosophy when vacancies occur, in particular when the chairpersonship is vacant.

The most important independent regulatory agencies, in order of their creation, are as follows:

1. Interstate Commerce Commission (1887)
2. Federal Reserve System (1913)
3. Federal Trade Commission (1914)
4. Federal Deposit Insurance Corporation (1916)
5. Farm Credit Administration (1933)
6. Federal Communications Commission (1934)
7. Securities and Exchange Commission (1934)
8. National Labor Relations Board (1935)
9. Civil Aeronautics Board (1940, terminated January 1, 1985)
10. Equal Employment Opportunity Commission (1964)
11. Environmental Protection Agency (1970)
12. Consumer Product Safety Commission (1972)

All told, the independent regulatory agencies employ roughly eighty thousand civilians. A number of bureaus and sections within cabinet departments also function as regulatory agencies, such as the Occupational Safety and Health Admin-

Truckers protesting Interstate Commerce Commission regulations.

istration that is part of the Labor Department and the Food and Drug Administration that is part of the Department of Health and Human Services.

Over the last several decades, some observers have concluded that these agencies, although nominally independent of the three branches of the federal government, may in fact not always be so. They contend that many independent regulatory commissions have been "captured" by the very industries and firms that they were supposed to regulate. The results have been less competition rather than more, higher prices rather than lower ones, and less choice rather than more choice for consumers. For example, in 1976, it was estimated that the Interstate Commerce Commission kept freight rates about 40 percent higher than they would have been otherwise by restricting competition within the common carrier trucking industry.[8]

Not surprisingly, the 1980s have been called the era of deregulation. An important part of Reagan's 1980 campaign was his promise to reduce the regulation of American business. But deregulation had already started before Reagan was elected. President Carter pushed for and obtained the Motor Carrier Deregulation

[8]Roger LeRoy Miller and James S. Mofsky, *Legal and Economic Evaluation of Impact Statement Requirements for Regulatory Agencies* (Coral Gables, Fla.: University of Miami, Law and Economics Center, 1976).

Act of 1978. He also appointed a chairperson of the Civil Aeronautics Board who waged a war against the regulation of airline tariffs and routes. The result has been the almost complete deregulation of the airline industry. The CAB ceased to exist on January 1, 1985.

Since the late 1970s, there has been relatively little additional congressionally mandated deregulation—except perhaps in the banking industry, pursuant to the Depository Institutions Deregulation and Monetary Control Act of 1980. Again, this deregulation was initiated before Reagan's election in 1980. Table 14–2 shows the decline in regulatory agency growth from 1970 to the present. Between 1970 and 1980, expenditures by regulatory agencies grew from $1.6 billion to a high of $6.8 billion, but since then such expenditures have grown much more slowly. Moreover, the number of regulatory personnel has declined from 131,500 in 1980 to an estimated 112,300 in 1986.

Did You Know?

That almost 100 million individual income tax returns were filed in 1986?

Government Corporations

The newest form of bureaucratic organization to be adopted in the United States is the government corporation. Although the concept is borrowed from the world of business, distinct differences exist between the public and private types.

A private corporation has shareholders who elect a board of directors, who in turn choose the corporate officers, such as president and vice president. When a

Table 14–2

Regulatory Agency Growth

The following chart shows the changes in expenditures and permanent, full-time personnel for 54 federal regulatory agencies for selected fiscal years. (Figures do not add due to rounding.)

	1970	1980	1984	1985 (est.)	1986 (est.)
Expenditures (in billions)					
Social Regulation					
Consumer health and safety	$ 0.9	$ 2.8	$ 3.1	$ 3.3	$ 3.1
Job safety, other working conditions	0.1	0.8	0.8	0.9	0.8
Energy, environment	0.3	2.2	2.7	3.1	3.2
Subtotal	1.3	5.7	6.6	7.2	7.2
Economic Regulation					
Finance, banking	$ 0.1	$ 0.4	$ 0.8	$ 0.9	$ 0.8
Other industry-specific	0.1	0.3	0.3	0.3	0.3
General business	0.1	0.4	0.5	0.5	0.5
Subtotal	0.3	1.1	1.5	1.7	1.7
Total	$ 1.6	$ 6.8	$ 8.1	$ 8.9	$ 8.9
Personnel (in thousands)					
Social regulation	$65.5	$103.6	$ 87.8	$ 88.4	$ 86.8
Economic regulation	19.9	27.8	25.6	25.3	25.5
Total	$85.4	$131.5	$113.3	$113.7	$112.3

SOURCE: Center for the Study of American Business, Washington University.

Government Corporation

An agency of government that administers a quasibusiness enterprise. Used when an activity is primarily commercial, produces revenue for its continued existence, and requires greater flexibility than permitted for departments.

private corporation makes a profit, it must pay taxes (unless it avoids them through various legal loopholes), and it either distributes part or all of the after-tax profits to shareholders as dividends or plows them back into the corporation to make new investments.

A **government corporation** has a board of directors and managers, but it doesn't have any stockholders. We cannot buy shares of stock in a government corporation. If the government corporation makes a profit, it does not distribute the profit as dividends. Also, if it makes a profit, it does not have to pay taxes; the profits remain in the corporation.

Three of the major federal government corporations are as follows:

Tennessee Valley Authority (TVA)

Created in 1933, TVA is run by a three-person board that is appointed by, and is directly responsible to, the president. The general manager of TVA reports to that board. TVA operates a Tennessee River control system and also generates power for a seven-state region and for the U.S. atomic and space programs. TVA has sold electricity at relatively low rates compared with rates charged by privately owned electric utilities. As such, its rates have been deemed the yardstick by which the fairness of other electricity rates are measured. Critics of TVA claim, however, that the yardstick concept is misguided since TVA does not have to pay federal or state taxes. TVA has about forty-five thousand employees.

U.S. Postal Service

The history of the mail service in the United States dates back to the colonial era when King William of England granted Thomas Neale a patent to set up and maintain a postal system. When Neale died in 1707, the British government took control of the postal service. In 1753, Benjamin Franklin and William Hunter were appointed by the British government as joint postmasters general in the col-

Mail carrier.

onies. The Articles of Confederation gave Congress the exclusive control over the mails.

The Constitution, in Article I, Section 8, expressly gives Congress the power to establish post offices. In 1789, Congress exercised this power and created the Office of Postmaster General within the Treasury Department. Then, in 1792, a Post Office Department was created. In 1829, the postmaster general under President Jackson sat as a member of the cabinet, although it wasn't until 1872 that the Post Office Department officially became part of the executive branch. The post office remained as part of the cabinet until 1970, when President Nixon signed the Postal Reorganization Act. Currently, the U.S. Postal Service is managed by a presidentially appointed, bipartisan board of governors and by a postmaster general and deputy postmaster general selected by the board.

The U.S. Postal Service is by far the largest of the government corporations, employing about 660,000 workers. The reorganization of the post office into the U.S. Postal Service did not change its unprofitable status. From 1971 through 1983, it lost a total of $3 billion. In 1986, despite opposition from the Reagan administration, Congress approved legislation that included almost $1 billion in subsidies for postage rates for nonprofit organizations, newspapers, and other special categories of mail. Subsidizing these rates has always been popular with Congress, although it undercuts the goal of self-sufficiency.

AMTRAK

This railway service, administered by the National Railroad Passenger Corporation, was created in 1970 to help provide an integrated, balanced national and intercity rail passenger service network. It currently controls about twenty-three thousand miles of track, serves 505 stations, employs 18,500 persons, and in 1986 carried more than twenty million people.

AMTRAK was created in response to a declining number of U.S. rail passengers and deteriorating quality of railroad service. Its main objectives have been to renovate track, replace outdated equipment, streamline and reduce revenue-losing routes, and in general elevate U.S. passenger rail service to a position similar to that existing in Europe. Although it is far from reaching that goal, the overall performance is impressive. In 1982, AMTRAK maintained on-time performance 80 percent of the time—better than many other types of public transportation.

AMTRAK, however, has never been able to generate enough revenue to pay for the improvements. Subsidies for the service were set at $616 million in 1986, about the same level as in 1985. President Reagan had proposed eliminating all federal aid to AMTRAK, saying that "the United States government had no business running a railroad—and running it, by the way, hundreds of millions of dollars in the red."[9]

Some of the other government corporations include the Federal Deposit Insurance Corporation, which insures bank deposits; CONRAIL, which is a freight rail service; and the Export-Import Bank, which loans money for foreign trade.

Staffing the Bureaucracy

▽

There are two groups of people whom we may call bureaucrats: political appointees and civil servants. As noted earlier, the president is able to make political appoint-

[9]Speech of December 18, 1985, quoted in *Congressional Quarterly Almanac,* 1985, p. 41–D.

AMTRAK *service.*

Natural Aristocracy

A small ruling clique of the state's "best" citizens, whose membership is based on birth, wealth, and ability. The Jeffersonian era emphasized rule by such a group.

Spoils System

The awarding of government jobs to political supporters and friends; generally associated with President Andrew Jackson.

Merit System

The selection, retention, and promotion of government employees on the basis of competitive examinations.

Cartoon satire on the spoils system.

ments to most of the top jobs in the federal bureaucracy as well as to appoint ambassadors to the most important foreign posts. All of the jobs that are considered "political plums" and that usually go to the politically well connected are listed in *Policy and Supporting Positions*, published by the Government Printing Office after each presidential election. This has been informally (and correctly) called "The Plum Book." The rest of the individuals who work for the national government belong to the civil service and got their jobs through a much more formal process.

A Short History of the Federal Civil Service

When the federal government was formed in 1789, it had no career public servants, but rather consisted of amateurs who were almost all Federalists. When Jefferson took over as president, he found that few in his party were holding federal administrative jobs, so he fired more than one hundred officials, replacing them with members of the so-called **natural aristocracy**—that is, with his own Jeffersonian Republicans. For the next twenty-five years, a growing body of federal administrators gained experience and expertise, becoming in the process professional public servants. These administrators stayed in office regardless of who was elected president. The bureaucracy had become a self-maintaining, long-lived element within government.

To The Victor Belongs the Spoils

When Jackson took over the White House in 1828, he could not believe how many appointed officials (appointed before him, that is) were overtly hostile toward him and his Democratic party. The bureaucracy—indeed an aristocracy—considered itself the only group fit to rule. But Jackson was a man of the people, and his policies were populist in nature. As the bureaucracy was reluctant to carry out his programs, Jackson did the obvious: He fired federal officials—more than had all his predecessors combined. The **spoils system**—an application of the principle that to the victor belongs the spoils—reigned. The northeastern aristocrats were out and the common folk were in. The spoils system was not, of course, a Jacksonian invention. Thomas Jefferson too had used this system of patronage in which the boss, or patron, rewards his workers for the job they did in getting him elected.

In addition to putting his own people on the federal payroll, Jackson decided to reorganize the bureaucracy in order to ensure that his policies were carried out. During his eight years in office, almost every department and bureau was restructured.[10]

The Civil Service Reform Act of 1883

Jackson's spoils system survived for a number of years, but it became increasingly corrupt. Also, the size of the bureaucracy increased by 300 percent between 1851 and 1881. Reformers began to examine the professional civil service that was established in several European countries, which operated under a **merit system**—in which job appointments were based on competitive examinations. The cry for civil service reform began to be heard more loudly.

[10]Matthew A. Crenson, *The Federal Machine: Beginnings of a Bureaucracy in Jacksonian America* (Baltimore, Md.: Johns Hopkins University Press, 1975).

The ruling Republican party was divided in its attitude toward reform, the "stalwart" faction opposing reform of any sort. When President James A. Garfield, a moderate reformer, was assassinated in 1881 by a disappointed office seeker, Charles J. Guiteau, the latter was heard to shout "I am a stalwart, and Arthur is president now!" He was correct: Chester A. Arthur, a stalwart vice president, became president. Ironically, it was under the stalwart Arthur that civil service reform actually occurred—partly as a result of public outrage over Garfield's assassination. The movement to replace the spoils system with a permanent career civil service had the cause that would carry it to victory.

Finally, in 1883, the **Pendleton Act**—the **Civil Service Reform Act**—was passed, bringing to a close the period of Jacksonian spoils. The act established the principle of employment on the basis of open competitive examinations and created the **Civil Service Commission** to administer the personnel service. However, only 10 percent of federal employees were covered by the merit system. Later laws, amendments, and executive orders increased the coverage to more than 90 percent of the federal civil service.

The Hatch Act of 1939

The growing size of the federal bureaucracy created the potential for political manipulation. In principle, a civil servant is politically neutral. But civil servants certainly know that it is politicians who pay the bills through their appropriations and that it is politicians who decide about the growth of agencies. In 1933, when Roosevelt set up his New Deal, a virtual army of civil servants was put on board to staff the numerous new agencies that were created to cope with the problems of the Great Depression. As the individuals who worked in these agencies owed their jobs to the Democratic party, it seemed natural for them to campaign for Democratic party candidates. The Democrats controlling Congress in the mid-1930s did not object. But in 1938, a coalition of conservative Democrats and Republicans took control of the Congress and forced through the **Hatch Act**—the **Political Activities Act**—of 1939.

Pendleton Act (Civil Service Reform Act of 1883)
This law, as amended over the years, remains the basic statute regulating federal employment personnel policies. It established the principle of employment on the basis of merit and created the Civil Service Commission to administer the personnel service.

Civil Service Commission
The central personnel agency of the national government created in 1883.

Hatch Act (Political Activities Act)
This 1939 act prohibits the use of federal authority to influence nominations and elections or the use of rank to pressure federal employees to make political contributions. It also prohibits civil service employees from active involvement in political campaigns.

The assassination of President Garfield by a disappointed office-seeker.

The main provision of this act is that civil service employees cannot take an active part in the political management of campaigns. It also prohibits the use of federal authority to influence nominations and elections and outlaws the use of bureaucratic rank to pressure federal employees to make political contributions.

In 1972 a federal district court declared the Hatch Act prohibition against political activity to be unconstitutional. However, the U.S. Supreme Court reaffirmed the challenged portion of the act in 1973, stating that the government's interest in preserving a nonpartisan civil service was so great that the prohibitions should remain.[11]

The Carter Reforms

The Civil Service Commission has worked well, according to many students of the bureaucracy. But a persistent group of reformers felt it had taken on too many tasks. President Carter, a particularly concerned critic, worked out a reform package with his head of the Civil Service Commission, political scientist Allen K. Campbell. Among the reforms they proposed and that were finally adopted by Congress in its reform bill passed on October 13, 1978, was one splitting the Civil Service Commission into the Office of Personnel Management (OPM) and the Merit Systems Protection Board (MSPB).

The Office of Personnel Management

In charge of hiring for most of the federal agencies, the members of OPM are appointed by the president and confirmed by the Senate. Among the elaborate rules that OPM has established for hiring, promotion, and firing is one requiring competitive examinations for most civil service jobs. Assuming an applicant passes that examination, she or he is then sent to an agency that requires a job with skills that fit the applicant's own. For each federal agency job that is open, the OPM uses the "rule of three," sending three names to the agency for consideration. In general, the agency has to hire someone on this list.

Within the civil service, each individual hired is assigned a general schedule, or GS, rating (Table 14–3). In 1987 the salary range extended from $9619 to $70,800.

The Merit Systems Protection Board

The Merit Systems Protection Board was created as an independent agency with an independent staff, whose goal is to protect the integrity of the federal merit system. The MSPB undertakes studies of the merit system. It hears charges of wrongdoing and appeals of adverse agency actions against civil servants. It can order corrective and disciplinary action against executive agencies (or employees—but that is rare). The MSPB also has an independent legal staff, which investigates prohibited personnel practices and can prosecute officials who violate civil service rules and regulations.

Table 14–3

▽

GS Ratings and Their Respective Minimum Salaries, 1987

Rating	1987 Salary
GS–1	$ 9,619
GS–2	10,816
GS–3	11,802
GS–4	13,248
GS–5	14,822
GS–6	16,521
GS–7	18,358
GS–8	20,333
GS–9	22,458
GS–10	24,732
GS–11	27,172
GS–12	32,567
GS–13	38,727
GS–14	45,763
GS–15	53,830
GS–16	63,135
GS–17	73,958*
GS–18	86,682*

*These rates are applicable to the "super grade" officers but have been limited by Congress to $70,800.

SOURCE: *Current Salary Schedules of Federal Officers and Employees* (Washington, D.C., U.S. Government Printing Office, 1985).

[11]*United States Civil Service Commission v. National Association of Letter Carriers*, 413 U.S. 548 (1973).

The Senior Executive Service

Another major reform of the civil service that President Carter obtained in the 1978 Civil Service Reform Act was the creation of a **Senior Executive Service** (SES), a corps of about 8,500 high-level administrators and managers. The purpose of establishing the SES was to reward top-ranking civil servants for superior performance by making those who choose to join eligible for substantial cash bonuses.

Risk and reward go hand in hand, however, so that anybody who joins the SES has less job tenure and can be transferred more easily within an agency or to another agency. But the lure of cash bonuses for merit has apparently been sufficient to outweigh the decreased job security. Of those eligible to join the SES (approximately seven thousand), 98.5 percent did join—a far greater number than had been anticipated.[12]

Senior Executive Service
A corps of about 8,500 high-level government administrators created in 1978 to provide rewards and incentives for top-ranking civil servants.

The Reagan Reforms

To reduce the size and expense of the federal bureaucracy, President Reagan's fiscal 1983 budget proposed cutting 150,000 workers from nondefense-related agencies

[12]*Civil Service Reform: A Report on the First Year*, Office of Personnel Management (Washington, D.C.: GPO, January 1980), p. 5.

This chart depicts all of the steps necessary to fire a federal Civil Service worker.

by fiscal year 1987 and reducing cost-of-living raises for retired federal employees. These cuts would have reduced the size of the federal budget by nearly $6 billion in 1987 and continued the trend toward declining federal employment. From 1968 to 1983, civilian employment in the executive branch as a percentage of the total civilian work force has fallen from 3.8 to 2.7 percent. According to one congressperson, the budget "is the same old thing"—that is, "hatchet, cut, chop."[13] The easiest way to cut the budget is to simply eliminate government jobs, although the programs they administer may be unchanged. This strategy is politically popular because there is a widespread belief that there are too many bureaucrats.

Current Attempts at Bureaucratic Reform

▽

As long as federal bureaucracy exists, there will continue to be attempts to make it more open, efficient, and responsive to the needs of the American citizen. The most important actual and proposed reforms in the last few years include grade banding, sunshine and sunset laws, and giving more protection to so-called whistleblowers.

Grade Banding

The 1978 Civil Service Reform Act encouraged, among other things, merit pay experiments in the federal government. The China Lake Naval Weapons Center and the Navy Ocean Systems Center, both in California, began an experiment in merit pay in 1980. The practice, called "grade banding," consists of grouping similar occupations together and combining from two to four GS pay levels into broader

[13]Patricia Schroeder (Dem.-Colorado), Chairperson of the House Post Office Civil Service Subcommittee, as quoted in *Congressional Quarterly Weekly Report*, February 13, 1982, p. 257.

"pay bands" or "grade bands." This allows supervisors to have more flexibility in offering starting salaries, rewarding persons for excellence with incentive raises, and penalizing poor performers with low or no pay raises. This can all be done without reclassifying positions into higher GS levels, a process that is cumbersome and that cannot be used to reward individual cases. In a recent poll of the five thousand employees at China Lake, 83 percent said they preferred the new experimental system to the old GS classification.

In May 1986, the Reagan administration proposed to Congress to authorize expanding the China Lake program to other agencies in the hope of moving toward a more flexible system. Opponents of the system include the American Federation of Government Employees and other public unions, which have expressed skepticism about the system, saying that it could be used to reward upper management at the expense of lower-level, generally unionized employees. Congress too has been cautious about the proposal. The Office of Management and Budget has also expressed concern that grade banding will cost more in salaries. Proponents claim, however, that the increased performance, morale, and efficiency resulting from the changes will make up for any increased costs.

Sunshine Laws

In 1976, Congress enacted a significant bill (PL 94-409). This legislation, referred to as the **Government in the Sunshine Act,** required for the first time that all multiheaded federal agencies—about fifty of them—conduct their business, that is, hold their meetings, regularly in public session. The bill defined *meetings* as almost any gathering, formal and informal, of agency members—including conference telephone calls. The only exceptions to this rule of openness are discussions of matters like court proceedings or personnel problems, and these exceptions are specifically listed in the bill.

Government in the Sunshine Act
Requires that all multiheaded federal agencies conduct their business regularly in public session.

Sunset Laws

A potential type of control on the size and scope of the federal bureaucracy is **sunset legislation,** which would place government programs on a definite schedule of congressional consideration. Unless Congress specifically reauthorized a particular federally operated program at the end of a designated period, it would automatically be terminated; that is, its sun would set.

The idea of sunset legislation was first suggested by Franklin D. Roosevelt when he created the plethora of New Deal agencies. His assistant, William O. Douglas, recommended that each agency's charter should include a provision allowing for its termination in ten years. Only an act of Congress could revitalize it. Obviously, FDR's and Douglas's proposal was never adopted. It wasn't until 1976 when a state legislature—Colorado's—adopted sunset legislation for state regulatory commissions, giving them a life of six years before their sun set. Today thirty-five states have some type of sunset law.

In 1978, the Senate passed legislation that would require review of most federal programs every ten years, but since then the House has not passed its own version of the Senate bill.

Sunset Legislation
A law requiring that an existing program be regularly reviewed for its effectiveness and terminated unless specifically extended as a result of this review.

Helping Out the Whistle-Blowers

Whistle-Blower

Someone who brings to public attention gross governmental inefficiency or an illegal action.

George Spanton.

The term **whistle-blower** as applied to the federal bureaucracy has a special meaning; It is someone who blows the whistle on a gross governmental inefficiency or illegal action. One of the most famous whistle-blowers is A. Earnest Fitzgerald, who worked for the Defense Department as a cost analyst. In 1968, Fitzgerald went before a congressional committee claiming that the Lockheed C-5A transport plane had cost more than Congress had appropriated for it. He also pointed out that the plane was not worth the money. Upon close scrutiny, his accusations proved to be accurate, but Mr. Fitzgerald was fired. A court ordered the Defense Department to give him back his job, and a later decision awarded him $350,000 in back pay and damages.[14]

In 1982, another whistle-blower, George Spanton, working as a $50,000-a-year Pentagon auditor, accused Pratt-Whitney Aircraft of overcharging the federal government $150 million. His reward for whistle-blowing was a bitter struggle with his own superiors at the Pentagon's Defense Contract Audit Agency. Spanton's boss tried to get him transferred to another job within the agency, but Spanton filed an appeal with the Merit Systems Protection Board charging that the transfer was in retaliation for his "candid audits." The special counsel to the board supported Spanton and even filed disciplinary charges against Spanton's superiors.

Congress included some protection for whistle-blowers in the 1978 Civil Service Reform Act. Specifically, that act prohibits reprisals against whistle-blowers by their superiors, and it set up the Merit Systems Protection Board as part of this protection. There is little evidence, however, that potential whistle-blowers have truly received much improved protection.

Many federal agencies also have toll-free hot lines that employees can use to report, anonymously, bureaucratic waste and inappropriate behavior. About 35 percent of all calls are followed up. Some result in dramatic savings for the government. The General Accounting Office hot line alone was reported to have generated $9.4 million in savings between January 1979 and September 1980. Further, excluding crank calls, the hot line received more than nine thousand calls during that period, which resulted in three hundred cases of conviction or reprimand.[15]

Bureaucrats as Politicians and Policy Makers

▽

The bureaucracy and its individual employees are supposed to be nonpolitical, but we have seen that political activity is natural within the bureaucratic setting. Although the majority of persons working for an organization are not likely to be politically active, we cannot say that their agencies and departments are politically neutral. The civil service as a whole is interested in survival and expansion because that is how its members stay employed. Each agency and department is also interested in survival and expansion, which means they are constantly, if quietly, battling each other for a share of the budget and to retain or expand their functions and staff. Every agency attempts to gain the good will of the White House and of the Congress for these ends.

[14]Kenneth Bredemeier, "Tapes Show Nixon Role in Firing of Earnest Fitzgerald," *Washington Post,* March 7, 1979.

[15]*Congressional Quarterly Weekly Report,* February 21, 1981, p. 344.

In February 1982, President Reagan named Peter Grace, a successful businessman, to head a study commission that would investigate mismanagement, waste, and inefficiency in the federal government. The commission, which consisted of about 160 top business executives, was supported by volunteer contributions. Two years later, the Grace Commission presented the president with forty reports, totaling twenty-three thousand pages, suggesting changes in government practices that could save the federal government as much as $454 billion.

Among the findings of the Grace Commission were the following:

▽ Although the federal government has a daily cash flow of $6.8 billion, it has no financial assets system to make that money work. This failure to manage the daily money flow costs the government $79 billion. For example, in 1982, the Justice Department seized nearly $317 million in cash and property (boats, homes, and so on), most of this from drug-smuggling activities. The cash (almost $80 million) was not held in interest-bearing accounts, and most of the worth of the property was depreciated before it was finally sold at auction.

▽ The federal government has more than seventeen thousand computers, most of which are obsolete. There is no centralized agency for computer purchases, servicing, and replacement, so each agency has a different computer system. Nearly $20 billion could be saved if a computer management office were in place. For example, the Urban Mass Transportation Administration spent $10 million on a computer to manage the $25 billion it disperses in grants. The commission found that the agency had not kept up its account books, had no central record of who received the grants or for what, and in spite of acquiring the computer system, still kept the financial records by hand.

▽ Other examples of inefficiency cited in the report were the following: (1) The navy purchased 60¢ light bulbs for $511 apiece. (2) The Veterans Administration hospital construction staff consisted of eight hundred people, whereas a comparable private firm employed fifty persons. (3) More than $30 million in Medicare checks were paid out to deceased persons.

In spite of these and many other suggestions and examples, reforms have been very slow in coming. The Grace Commission report has been criticized as being too simplistic and applying private industry cost-benefit practices that are inappropriate for government. Of course, most government agencies have vigorously resisted changes in their practices as well.

SOURCES: *The Grace Commission Report*, 1984; *The Washington Post*, January, 1984; Edward Meadows, "Peter Grace Knows 2,478 Ways to Cut the Deficit," *National Review*, March 9, 1984.

The various bureaucratic agencies of the federal government are specifically prohibited from lobbying Congress directly. However, bureaus and agencies have developed a number of techniques to help them gain political support. Each organization generally maintains a congressional information office, which specializes in helping members of Congress by supplying requested information or solving casework problems. The Defense Department has earned a reputation for being able to create good publicity for itself and thus support on Capitol Hill. When President Reagan asked Congress to approve the sale of AWACS planes to Saudi Arabia, the Pentagon arranged for a plane to be stationed near Washington and invited members of Congress as well as staff members on guided tours to explain its complicated technology. Even the secretaries of the departments are expected to lobby the president for support of their budget and programs. This kind of politicking from people whom the president appointed to support his own objectives can lead to considerable tension between the White House and the departments.

Theories of **public administration** once assumed that bureaucracies do not make policy but only implement the laws and policies promulgated by the president and legislative bodies. A more realistic view of the role of the bureaucracy in policy

Public Administration

The science of managing public organizations.

▽
473

AWACS planes.

making, which is now held by most bureaucrats and elected officials, is that the agencies and departments of government play important roles in policy making. Many government rules, regulations, and programs are in fact initiated by the bureaucracy, based on its expertise and scientific studies. How a law passed by Congress is eventually translated into concrete action—from the forms to be filled out to decisions about who gets the benefits—is usually determined within the department. Even the evaluation of whether a policy achieved its purpose is usually based on studies that are commissioned and interpreted by the agency administering the program.[16]

We can try to understand the bureaucracy's policy making role by examining what has been called the "**iron triangle.**"

Iron Triangle
The three-way alliance among legislators, bureaucrats, and interest groups to make or preserve policies that benefit their interests.

The Iron Triangle

Consider the bureaucracy within the Department of Agriculture. It consists of 114,361 individuals working directly for the federal government and thousands of other individuals who, directly or indirectly, work as contractors, subcontractors, or consultants to the department. Now consider that there are various interest, or client, groups that are concerned with what the federal government does for farmers. Some of these are the American Farm Bureau Federation, the National Cattleman's Association, the National Milk Producers Association, the Corn Growers Association, and the Citrus Growers Association. Finally, go directly to Congress and you will see that there are two major committees concerned with agriculture in the House and in the Senate: the House Committee on Agriculture and the Senate Committee on Agriculture, Nutrition, and Forestry, each of which has seven subcommittees.

Figure 14–5 is a schematic view of the iron triangle of the Department of Agriculture. This triangle, or subgovernment, is an alliance of mutual benefit

[16]See, for example, Francis E. Rourke, ed., *Bureaucratic Power in National Politics* (Boston: Little, Brown, 1965).

among some unit within the bureaucracy, its interest or client group, and committees or subcommittees of Congress and their staff members. The workings of the iron triangle are complicated but well established in almost every subgovernment.

The secretary of agriculture is nominated by the president (and confirmed by the Senate) and is nominally the boss of the Department of Agriculture. But that secretary cannot even buy a desk lamp if Congress does not approve the appropriations for Agriculture's budget. Within Congress, the responsibility for considering the Department of Agriculture's request for funding belongs first to the House and Senate Appropriations committees and to the Agriculture subcommittees under them. The members of those committees, most of whom represent agricultural states, have been around a long time. They have their own ideas about what is appropriate for the Agriculture Department's spending. They have their own program concepts. They carefully scrutinize the ideas of the president and the secretary of agriculture.

Finally, the various interest groups—including producers of farm chemicals and farm machinery, consumer groups, agricultural cooperatives, grain dealers, and exporters—have vested interests in whatever the Department of Agriculture does and in whatever Congress lets the Department of Agriculture do. Those interests are well represented by the lobbyists who crowd the halls of Congress. Many lobbyists have been working for agricultural pressure groups for decades. They know the congressional committee members and Agriculture Department staff extremely well and routinely meet with them. When the president or others propose policies that benefit or harm the natural interests or constituents of groups of the triangle, they present a united front either to pass or to oppose such legislation. Such iron triangles—of which there are many, not only on Capitol Hill, but also in state capitols—at times have completely thwarted efforts by the president to get his programs enacted.

Congressional Control of the Bureaucracy

Is the bureaucracy so strong that Congress cannot control it? Some cynics say yes. But others point out that Congress has a variety of controls over the federal bureaucracy, including the ultimate control—the purse, or the appropriations check. One could reasonably argue that the power of the purse has not been used very often. After all, the size of the federal bureaucratic budget has increased manyfold since, say, World War II. In some instances, Congress may control the bureaucracy by cutting off its funds, but in general it does not. Since bureaucrats know their continued funding is a function of previous funding, they make every effort to assure that previous funding is well spent. Actually, they make sure that any fiscal year's funding is completely spent down to the last penny. If it were not spent, Congress might not provide at least the same amount of funding for the following fiscal year.

Some argue that Congress has encouraged bureaucratic growth by formulating laws that are vague—but vague for a reason. One observer claims that Congress ultimately creates credit for itself by creating an ever-larger bureaucracy with increasingly ill-defined goals:

> Legislation is drafted in very general terms, so some agency, existing or newly established, must translate a vague policy mandate into a functioning program, a process that necessitates the promulgation of numerous rules and regulations and, incidentally, the

Figure 14–5
▽
The Iron Triangle of the Department of Agriculture

Bureaucracy

Interest Groups, Professional Staff, and Lobbyists

Congressional Committees and Staff

trampling of numerous toes. At the next stage, aggrieved and/or hopeful constituents petition their Congressman to intervene in the complex . . . decision processes of the bureaucracy. The cycle closes when the Congressman lends a sympathetic ear, piously denounces the evils of bureaucracy, intervenes in the latter's decisions, and rides a grateful electorate to even more impressive electoral showings. Congressmen take credit coming and going.[17]

If there is any truth to this statement, the probability of our seeing a reduction in the bureaucracy in our lifetimes is quite small.

The American Bureaucracy

▽

Today, the government of the United States is expected to furnish hundreds of services to citizens, to provide an effective national defense, and to carry out national programs ranging from feeding the hungry to regulating the money supply. The only way to accomplish all these tasks is to establish and maintain a large formal organization, namely, a bureaucracy. We have pointed out some of the difficulties this situation creates. Bureaucracies become protective of their own mission and therefore resist change; public bureaucracies receive mixed direction from their two bosses—Congress and the president; the bureaucracy's goals of service and equity may reduce efficiency; and neither of these two branches of government is exempt from trying to use the bureaucracy for its own political purposes. Still, Congress benefits from the bureaucracy's serving it with information and casework, and a president such as Mr. Reagan can depend on the Department of Defense to make an excellent case for its own increases in funding. Furthermore, private corporations and groups that benefit from contracts or services support the bureaucratic organization. With the prospect that bureaucracies in the United States, whether federal, state, or local, will not get smaller in the future, the bureaucracy's task is to create new ways to attract highly qualified people to the civil service and to adopt the most effective and up-to-date management tools that are consistent with public goals.

[17]Morris P. Fiorina, *Congress: Keystone of the Washington Establishment* (New Haven, Conn.: Yale University Press, 1977), p. 49.

The federal government collects billions of pieces of information on tens of millions of Americans each year. These are stored in files and gigantic computers and often exchanged between agencies. You probably have at least several federal records (for example, those in the Social Security Administration, the Internal Revenue Service, and, if you are male, the Selective Service).

The 1966 Freedom of Information Act requires that the federal government release, on your request, any identifiable information it has in the administrative agencies of the executive branch. This information can be about you or about any other subject; however, ten categories of material are exempted (classified material, confidential material dealing with trade secrets, internal personnel rules, personal medical files, and the like). To request material, you must write the Freedom of Information Act officer directly at the agency in question (let's say the Department of Education). You must also have a relatively specific idea about the document or information you wish to obtain.

A second law—the Privacy Act of 1974—gives you access specifically to information the government may have collected about you. This is a very important law because it allows you to review your records on file with federal agencies (for example, with the Federal Bureau of Investigation) and to check those records for possible inaccuracies. Cases do exist in which two people with similar or the same names have had their records confused. In some cases, innocent persons have had crime records from someone else erroneously inserted in their files.

If you wish to look at any records or find out if an agency has a record on you, write to the Agency Head or Privacy Act Officer, address it to the specific agency, state that "under the provisions of the Privacy Act of 1974, 5 U.S.C. 522a, I hereby request a copy of (or access to) . . . ," and then describe the record you wish to investigate.

If you have trouble finding out about your records or wish to locate an attorney in Washington, DC, to help you with this matter, you can contact:

Lawyer Referral Service
Washington Bar Association
1819 H St., N.W., Suite 300
Washington, D.C. 20036
202-223-1484

Chapter Summary

1. Presidents have little power to affect significantly the structure and operation of the federal bureaucracy.

2. Although not directly referred to in the Constitution, the functions of the "fourth branch" of government are implied in Article II, Sections 2 and 3.

3. In theory, bureaucracies are defined by hierarchical organizational charts with clear lines of authority and division of labor.

4. Although government employment at the federal level has remained relatively stable in the past several decades, it has increased at the state and local levels. A large percentage of the labor force is employed directly or indirectly by the government.

5. There are four major types of government organizations where federal bureaucrats are employed: (1) cabinet depart-

ments, (2) independent executive agencies, (3) independent regulatory agencies, and (4) government corporations.

6. The thirteen cabinet departments are the major service organizations of the federal government. They are directly accountable to the president and are responsible for performing broad governmental functions.

7. There are numerous independent agencies, which report directly to the president and have a single function. One example is the General Services Administration, established in 1949 to centralize the purchasing and management of property.

8. Regulatory agencies, also independent of the cabinet departments, are charged with making and implementing rules and regulations designed to protect the public interest. Their functions combine executive, legislative, and judicial powers.

9. Major government corporations include the Tennessee Valley Authority, the United States Postal Service, and AM-TRAK.

10. The federal bureaucracy has a long history, originating with the Jefferson administration's first permanent government organization.

11. In 1828, President Andrew Jackson instituted the spoils system and replaced the bureaucrats with his own political allies.

12. In 1883, Congress passed the Civil Service Reform Act, which was intended to make ability rather than personal or party loyalty the criterion for choosing federal workers. It established the merit system and created the Civil Service Commission to administer personnel services.

13. The Hatch Act of 1939 prohibits civil service employees from taking an active part in political campaigns and prohibits the use of federal authority to influence nominations and elections.

14. President Carter's reform package split the Civil Service Commission into the Office of Personnel Management and the Merit Systems Protection Board. The OMP is the hiring agency, and the MSPB investigates personnel practices.

15. President Carter's 1978 Civil Service Reform Act created the Senior Executive Service to provide rewards and incentives to top-ranking civil servants for superior performance.

16. President Reagan's fiscal 1983 budget proposed cutting 150,000 federal workers by 1987 and reducing cost-of-living raises for retired federal employees to cut the federal deficit.

17. Current attempts at bureaucratic reform include grade banding, grouping similar occupations and combining GS pay levels to allow supervisors more flexibility in personnel dealings; sunshine laws, establishing "openness" in government operations; sunset laws, placing government programs on a definite schedule of congressional consideration; and encouraging individual reporting of bureaucratic wrongdoing and waste.

18. The alliance of congressional committees, bureaucratic agencies, and interest groups that influences policy making has been called "the iron triangle."

19. The ultimate control that Congress has over bureaucracy is the appropriations process.

Questions for Review and Discussion
▽

1. Why did the federal bureaucracy grow so tremendously in the twentieth century? Why has it recently declined while the state and local bureaucracies are continuing to grow?

2. Although Congress often attacks the bureaucracy as overgrown and inefficient, it has done little to reform it. Why is Congress unlikely to make major reforms in the bureaucracy?

3. Tales of $5000 screwdrivers being purchased by the army abound. Who is responsible for such inefficiencies? What role do private interests play in making the government inefficient?

4. If you were on a government commission to streamline the federal bureaucracy, how would you reorganize the departments, independent agencies, and regulatory commissions? Could some of these organizations be combined so that the president would have more direct control over them? Or would you grant them more independence from the president's authority?

Selected References
▽

R. Douglas Arnold, *Congress and the Bureaucracy: A Theory of Influence* (New Haven: Yale University Press, 1979). Presents and tests a theory of how congresspersons influence bureaucrats' decisions about spending money to benefit different constituencies.

A. Lee Fritschler, *Smoking and Politics: Policymaking and the Federal Bureaucracy*, 3d ed. (Englewood Cliffs, N.J.: Prentice-Hall, 1983). Fascinating case study of bureaucrats as the makers of public policy and how they interact with Congress and interest groups.

Cole Blease Graham, Jr. and Steven W. Hays, *Managing the Public Organization* (Washington, D.C.: Congressional Quarterly Press, 1986). This book sharply distinguishes between private and public sector management and thoroughly explores such practical topics as planning, organization, staffing, coordination, reporting, budgeting, and evaluation.

David Lowery and William D. Berry, *Government Growth in the United States* (New York: Praeger, 1986). An excellent effort to review past explanations of government growth and then test empirically the reasons for growth of government in the United States in the post-World War II era.

Kenneth J. Meyer, *Politics and the Bureaucracy: Policymaking in the Fourth Branch of Government* (Monterey, Calif.: Brooks/Cole, 1986). The impact of bureaucracy on policy making (as opposed to simple policy implementation) is explored in this book. Includes suggestions on how to channel, structure, and control bureaucratic policy making.

Bernard Rosen, *Holding Government Bureaucracies Accountable* (New York: Praeger, 1984). The principal focus of this book is the question of accountability of the bureaucracy to the executive, legislative, and judicial branches of government and to interest groups and citizens, with suggestions on how such accountability can be strengthened.

Chapter 15

▽

The Judiciary

Contents

▽

What Is the Law?

The Foundation of American Law: The Courts and *Stare Decisis*

More Recent Sources of Law

Court Jurisdiction

How the Supreme Court Functions

How Federal Judges Are Selected

Who Are the Federal Judges?

Judicial Activism and Judicial Restraint

A Contrast in Courts: The Warren Court and the Burger Court

What Checks Our Courts?

The Proper Role of the Supreme Court

What If . . .

▽

The United States Had a Napoleonic Law Code?

My glory is not to have won forty battles; for Waterloo's defeat will destroy the memory of as many victories. But what nothing will destroy, what will live eternally, is my Civil Code.
—*Napoleon at St. Helena*

In the United States we have fifty-two separate legal systems; those of the fifty states and the District of Columbia and that of the federal court system. There are ninety-five federal district courts, twelve circuit courts of appeal, and the Supreme Court. Our system as a

whole is based on the English system and upon common law. The exception is Louisiana, originally settled by French colonists. Its system is the only sizable enclave of European law in the United States and includes large parts of the Napoleonic Code. Each state judiciary has its own set of legal traditions, principles, and procedures.

The French system is quite different. France is composed of ninety-five metropolitan departments, all subject to a uniform judicial code. The French system, far more than the Anglo-American, became the model for continental Europe. It is based on Roman law and the civil, criminal, penal, commercial, and procedural codes drafted under the direction of Napoleon Bonaparte. This work culminated in the Code Napoleon, still the basis of French law. In fact, for some 150 years there were no major changes in the code—the first significant al-

teration occurred with the Gaullist reforms of 1959 that gave French married women increased property rights.

What if early American lawmakers had decided to fashion the American system after the Napoleonic Code rather than common law? For one thing, our lawyers and judges wouldn't need so many tens of thousands of books. The judge would be bound by the specific provisions of a code and not by previous judicial interpretations and precedents which have built up over the centuries and fill the volumes lining the law libraries.

The system would have the advantage of precision, simplicity, and clear-cut applicability, but would still be subject to interpretations of administrators and judges. Some would argue that this type of codified system would cease to grow and to adapt to changing times and ideas. Justice Holmes maintained:

The provisions of the Constitution are not mathematical formulas having essence in their form; they are organic living institutions transplanted from English soil. Their significance is vital, not formal. It is to be gathered not simply by taking the words and a dictionary, but by considering their origin and the line of their growth. *

▽

As the discussion of the civil code suggests, one of the continuing questions that is faced by the judiciary is exactly what is the law of the land? The answer to that question is influenced by judicial philosophy, by the structure of the courts, and by national politics.

*Gompers v. United States, 233 U.S. 604 (1914), at 610.

What Is the Law?

▽

Supreme Court Justice Oliver Wendell Holmes contended that law was a set of rules that allowed one to predict how a court would resolve a particular dispute— "the prophecies of what the courts will do in fact, and nothing more pretentious, are what I mean by the law." The Greek philosopher Aristotle saw law as a rule of conduct, whereas Plato believed law was a form of social control. British jurist Sir William Blackstone described law as "a rule of civil conduct prescribed by the supreme power in a state, commanding what is right, and prohibiting what is wrong." Although having different emphases, these definitions are not mutually exclusive.

Two major types of law are civil law and criminal law. **Civil law** spells out the rights and duties that exist between persons or between citizens and their governments. When one person infringes on the legally recognized rights of another, civil law is involved. For example, if you walk into your local supermarket and slip on an oily patch that one of the employees forgot to clean up, you can sue for damages if you are hurt (either physically or mentally). You would bring a civil action in a court. You would be the plaintiff and the owner of the supermarket, and/or others, would be the defendant. (Such a case might be called *Jones v. Kareless Supermarket*.)

Criminal law is concerned with a wrong committed against the public as a whole. Criminal acts are prescribed by local, state, or federal government by statute or ordinance—laws that were passed by some legislative body. In a case of criminal law the government seeks to impose a penalty upon an allegedly guilty person, whereas in a civil case one party tries to make the other party comply with a duty or pay for the damages caused by the failure to comply. In criminal cases, crimes are prosecuted by a public official, not by the victims of crime. The plaintiff in a criminal case is not an individual, but rather society as a whole. (A criminal case, for example, might be called *The People of the City of Denver v. Jones*.) Criminal law is directly concerned with punishing the wrongdoer. Crimes are classified as felonies or misdemeanors, according to their seriousness. Felonies are more serious than misdemeanors and are punishable usually by death or by imprisonment in a federal or state penitentiary for more than a year. Misdemeanors are crimes punishable by a fine or by confinement, in most cases for up to a year.

Civil Law

Law that applies to the rights and duties that exist between private persons or between citizens and their governments.

Criminal Law

Law concerned with a wrong committed against the public order and enforced by the government.

Sir William Blackstone (left) and Oliver Wendell Holmes (right).

The Foundation of American Law: The Courts and *Stare Decisis*

Common Law

Judge-made law that originated in England from decisions shaped according to prevailing custom. Decisions were reapplied to similar situations and gradually became common to the nation. Common law forms the basis of legal procedures in the American states.

Precedent

A court rule bearing on subsequent legal decisions in similar cases. Judges rely on precedents in deciding cases.

Stare Decisis

"To stand on decided cases." The policy of courts to follow precedents established by the decisions of the past.

Because of our colonial heritage, most of American law is based on the English legal system. In 1066, the Normans conquered England, and William the Conqueror and his successors began the process of unifying the country under their rule. One of the ways they did this was to establish the King's Court, or Curia Regis. Before the conquest, disputes had been settled according to local custom. The King's Court sought to establish a common or uniform set of rules for the whole country. As the number of courts and cases increased, the more important decisions of each year were gathered together and recorded in yearbooks. Judges settling disputes similar to ones that had been decided before used the yearbooks as the basis for their decisions. If a case was unique, judges had to create new laws, but they based their decisions on the general principles suggested by earlier cases. The body of judge-made law that developed under this system is still used today and is known as the **common law.**

The practice of deciding new cases with reference to former decisions, that is, according to **precedent,** became a cornerstone of the English and American judicial systems and is embodied in the doctrine of *stare decisis* ("to stand on decided cases").

The rule of *stare decisis* performs many useful functions. First, it helps the courts to be more efficient. It would be very time consuming if each judge had to establish reasons for deciding what the law should be for each case brought before the court. If other courts have confronted the same issue and reasoned through the case carefully, their opinions can serve as guides.

Second, *stare decisis* makes for a more uniform system. All courts try to follow precedent, and thus different courts will often use the same rule of law. (However, some variations occur because different states and regions follow different precedents.) Also, the rule of precedent tends to neutralize the personal prejudices of individual judges to the degree that they feel obliged to use precedent as the basis for their decision.

Finally, the rule makes the law more stable and predictable than it would otherwise be. If the law on that subject is well settled, someone bringing a case to court can usually rely on the court to make a decision based on what the law has been.

Sometimes a court will depart from the rule of precedent because it has decided that the precedent is incorrect—for example, that changes in technology, business practice, or society's attitudes require a change in the law. But judges are reluctant to overthrow precedent, and whether they do will depend on the case, the number and prestige of prior decisions, the degree of social change that has occurred, and the identity of the deciding court. (The Supreme Court of the United States, when deciding a constitutional question, is the highest authority in the land and is therefore freer to reverse the direction of the law than a lower court.)

Sometimes there is no acceptable precedent on which to base a decision, or there are conflicting precedents. In these situations, a court will (1) refer to past decisions that may be similar to the current case and decide the case by reasoning through analogy; (2) look at social factors—changes in the status of women, for example—that might influence the issues involved; and (3) consider what the fairest result would be.

Cases that overturn precedent often receive a lot of publicity, and it might seem that they are fairly common. In reality, the majority of cases are decided according to the rule of *stare decisis*.

More Recent Sources of Law

Today, courts have sources other than precedent to consider when making their decisions. These sources are described in the following pages.

Constitutions

The constitutions of the federal government and the states set forth the general organization, powers, and limits of government. The U.S. Constitution is the supreme law of the land. A law in violation of the Constitution, no matter what its source, may be declared unconstitutional and thereafter cannot be enforced. Similarly, the state constitutions are supreme within their respective borders (unless they conflict with the U.S. Constitution or laws and treaties made in accordance with it).

Judicial Review

The process for deciding whether a law is contrary to the mandates of the Constitution is known as **judicial review.** The power of judicial review is not constitutionally mandated. Rather, this judicial power was first established in the famous case of *Marbury v. Madison* (see Highlight, page 484), which determined that the Supreme Court had the power to decide that a law passed by Congress violated the Constitution:

> It is emphatically the province and duty of the Judicial Department to say what the law is. Those who apply the rule to a particular case, must of necessity expound and interpret that rule. If two laws conflict with each other, the courts must decide on the operation of each.
>
> So if the law be in opposition to the Constitution, if both the law and the Constitution apply to a particular case, so that the court must either decide that case conformably to the law, disregarding the Constitution; or conformably to the Constitution, disregarding the law; the court must determine which of these conflicting rules govern the case. This is of the very essence of judicial duty.
>
> If, then, the courts were to regard the Constitution and the Constitution is superior to any ordinary Act of the Legislature, the Constitution, and not such ordinary Act, must govern the case to which they both apply.[1]

The Supreme Court ruled parts or all of acts of Congress to be unconstitutional only 113 times in its history through 1980. State laws, however, have been declared unconstitutional by the Court much more often—about 1,000 times (see Table 15–1). Most of these rulings date from the period after the Civil War, before which time only two acts of Congress were declared unconstitutional. There have been two periods of relatively extensive use of the process of judicial negation—from 1921 to 1940, when a conservative Court upheld private interests over public statutes, and in the 1960s and 1970s, when more liberal justices upheld individual and group rights to racial and political equality.

A recent significant case of judicial review was the ruling by the Supreme Court in 1983 that outlawed the practice of the legislative veto by which one or both chambers of Congress could overturn decisions made by the president or by executive agencies.[2] This single declaration of unconstitutionality affected several

[1]5 U.S. (1 Cranch) 137 (1803).

[2]*Immigration and Naturalization Service v. Chadha*, 77 L.Ed.2nd 317 (1983).

Judicial Review
The power of the courts to declare acts of the executive, legislative, and judicial branches unconstitutional. First established in *Marbury v. Madison.*

Table 15–1

Number of Supreme Court
Rulings on Unconstitutionality

Decade	Congress	State Legislatures
1789–1800	0	0
1801–1810	1	2
1811–1820	0	6
1821–1830	0	8
1831–1840	0	2
1841–1850	0	9
1851–1860	1	8
1861–1870	7	22
1871–1880	4	39
1881–1890	4	43
1891–1900	5	28
1901–1910	9	36
1911–1920	8	102
1921–1930	15	131
1931–1940	14	76
1941–1950	2	50
1951–1960	7	48
1961–1970	20	145
1971–1980	16	181
TOTAL	113	936

SOURCES: For Congressional data: Congressional Quarterly, *The Supreme Court and Its Work* (Washington, D.C.: Congressional Quarterly, 1981), pp. 237–242; for state legislative data complete to July 2, 1980: Library of Congress, *The Constitution of the United States of America: Analysis and Interpretation* (Washington, D.C.: GPO, 1973), pp. 1623–1768, and *1980 Supplement*, pp. S309–S329.

Highlight

▽

Judicial Review—*Marbury v. Madison* (1803)

In the edifice of American public law, the *Marbury v. Madison* decision in 1803 can be viewed as the keystone of the constitutional arch. The story is often told, and for a reason—it shows how seemingly insignificant cases can have important and enduring results.

Consider the facts behind *Marbury v. Madison*. John Adams had lost his bid for reelection to Thomas Jefferson in 1800. Adams, a Federalist, thought the Jeffersonian Republicans would weaken the power of the national government by asserting states' rights. He also feared the anti-Federalists' antipathy toward business. During the final hours of Adams's presidency, he worked feverishly to "pack" the judiciary with loyal Federalists by giving what came to be called "midnight appointments," just before Jefferson took office.

All of the judicial commissions had to be certified and delivered. The task

John Marshall.

of delivery fell on Adams's secretary of state, John Marshall. Out of the fifty-nine midnight appointments, Marshall delivered only forty-two. He assumed that the remaining seventeen would be sent out by Jefferson's new secretary of state, James Madison. Of course, the new administration refused to cooperate in packing the judiciary: Jefferson refused to deliver the remaining commissions. William Marbury, along with three other Federalists to whom the commissions had not been delivered, decided to sue. The suit was brought directly to the Supreme Court seeking a **writ of mandamus,** authorized by the Judiciary Act of 1789.

As fate would have it, the man responsible for the lawsuit, John Marshall, had stepped down as Adams's secretary of state only to become chief justice. He was now in a position to decide the case for which he was responsible.* Marshall was faced with a dilemma: If he ordered the commissions delivered, the new secretary of state could simply refuse. The Court had no way to compel action because it has no police force. Also, Congress was controlled by the Jeffersonian Republicans. It might impeach Marshall for such an action.** But if Marshall simply allowed Secretary of State Madison to do as he wished, the Court's power would be severely eroded.

Marshall stated for the unanimous Court that Jefferson and Madison had acted incorrectly in refusing to deliver Marbury's commission. However, Mar-

*Today any justice who has been involved in the issue before the Court would probably disqualify himself or herself because of a conflict of interest.

**In fact, Congress later did impeach Supreme Court Justice Samuel Chase, although he was not convicted. The charge was abusive behavior under the Sedition Act.

shall also stated that the highest court did not have the power to act as a court of **original jurisdiction** in this particular case, because the section of the law that gave it original jurisdiction was unconstitutional. The Judiciary Act of 1789 specified that the Supreme Court could issue writs of mandamus as part of its original jurisdiction, but Marshall pointed out that Article III of the Constitution, which spelled out the Supreme Court's original jurisdiction, did not mention *writs of mandamus*. In other words, Congress did not have the right to expand the Court's jurisdiction, so this section of the Judiciary Act of 1789 was unconstitutional and hence null and void.

The decision avoided a showdown between the Federalists and the Jeffersonian Republicans. The power of the Supreme Court was enlarged: "A law repugnant to the Constitution is void."

Was the Marshall Court's assump-

James Madison.

tion of judicial review power justified by the Constitution? Whether or not it was, *Marbury v. Madison* confirmed a doctrine that was part of the legal tradition of the time. Indeed, judicial review was a major premise (although not articulated) on which the movement to draft constitutions and bills of rights was ultimately based, as well as being part of the legal theory underlying the Revolution of 1776. During the decade before the adoption of the federal constitution, cases in at least eight states involved the power of judicial review. Also, the Supreme Court had considered the constitutionality of an act of Congress in *Hylton v. U.S.*,*** in which Congress's power to levy certain taxes was challenged. But since that particular act was ruled constitu-

***3 Dallas 171 (1796).

tional, rather than unconstitutional, this first federal exercise of true judicial review was not clearly recognized as such.

In any event, since Marshall masterfully fashioned a decision that did not require anyone to do anything, there was no practical legal point to challenge. It still stands today as a judicial and political masterpiece.

---

dozen separate statutes and reinforced the Court's position as an enforcer of the separation of powers principle.

Even though the Constitution was silent about the question of judicial review, there is no doubt that such a mechanism was and continues to be needed in our federal system. The conflicts and struggles between the national and state governments, and between the branches of government among the various states, must be resolved. When does a particular law overreach the limitations imposed on government by the Constitution? Only a federal judiciary is able to answer such a question, presumably for the good of the nation as a whole rather than for the good of any one particular state.

Writ of Mandamus
An order issued by a court to compel performance of an act.

Original Jurisdiction
The authority of a court to hear a case in the first instance.

Court Jurisdiction
▽

Juris means "law"; *diction* means "to speak." Thus **jurisdiction** is the power to speak the law. Before any court can hear a case, it must have jurisdiction—the

Jurisdiction
Authority vested in the court to hear and to decide a case.

The jury box in a courtroom.

Did You Know?

▽

That only three American presidents, William Henry Harrison, Andrew Johnson, and Jimmy Carter, appointed no Supreme Court justices?

General Jurisdiction
Extends to all types of cases that may be brought before a court within legal bounds.

Special, or Limited, Jurisdiction
Extends to a particular class of cases, such as cases where the amount of money in controversy is below a prescribed sum or cases that are subject to specific exceptions.

During his days as a circuit-riding judge, Chief Justice John Marshall, left, stops at a tavern to talk with local leaders.

power to decide that case—over the person who brings the case or against whom the suit is brought or over the subject matter of the case. Otherwise, it cannot exercise any authority in the case. Jurisdiction is granted in constitutions or by statute.

General Jurisdiction and Special, or Limited, Jurisdiction

The distinction between courts of **general jurisdiction** and courts of **special, or limited, jurisdiction** lies in the subject matter of cases heard. A court of general jurisdiction can decide virtually any type of case. However, a state court cannot decide a federal question, and federal courts normally limit themselves to matters of federal law. Every state has one level of courts of general jurisdiction, which may be called county courts, circuit courts, district courts, or some other name. At both federal and state levels are courts that hear only cases of specialized, or limited, subject matter. One court may handle only cases dealing with divorce or child custody. Another may handle disputes over relatively small amounts of money (a small claims court). Courts of general jurisdiction will not handle cases that are appropriate for these courts of special, or limited, jurisdiction.

Original and Appellate Jurisdiction

The distinction between courts of original jurisdiction and courts of appellate jurisdiction normally lies in whether the case is being heard for the first time. Courts having original jurisdiction are those of the first instance; they are courts

Library of Congress

where the trial of a case begins. In contrast, courts having **appellate jurisdiction** act as **reviewing courts.** In general, cases can be brought to these courts only on appeal from an order or a judgment of a lower court.

The Court Systems in the United States

Today, in the United States, there are fifty-two separate court systems. Each of the fifty states and the District of Columbia has its own fully developed, independent system of courts. In addition, there is a separate federal court system. The federal courts taken as a whole are not superior to the state courts. They are simply an independent and parallel system authorized by Article III, Section 2, of the Constitution to handle matters of particular federal interest. As we shall see, the United States Supreme Court is the final arbiter of all fifty-two systems, at least when questions of U.S. constitutional law are involved. A typical state court system is shown in Figure 15–1.

The Federal Court System

The federal court system is a three-tiered model consisting of (1) trial courts, (2) intermediate courts of appeals, and (3) the Supreme Court. Figure 15–2 shows the organization of the federal court system.

District Courts

Each state has at least one federal **district court.** Congress has divided the country and territories into ninety-five federal judicial districts. (This number will be reduced to ninety-four as the District Court in the Panama Canal Zone is being phased out.) The number of judicial districts can vary over time primarily owing

Appellate Jurisdiction
The authority of a court to review decisions of an inferior court.

Reviewing Courts
Courts of appellate jurisdiction with authority to review decisions of lower courts.

District Courts
The federal court of original jurisdiction where most federal cases begin.

Figure 15–1
▽
The State Judiciary
The arrows indicate normal avenues of appeal.

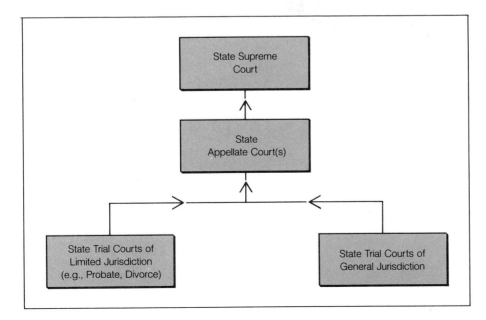

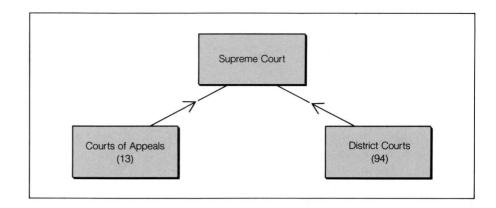

to population changes and corresponding caseloads. Large states like California have more than one. Thus an entire state can comprise a single district, or a state can be divided into several districts. With one exception (the District of Wyoming—which includes sections of Yellowstone National Park located in Montana and Idaho), the districts do not cross state lines. United States district courts are often called federal trial courts. Most federal cases originate in these courts.

U.S. district courts have original jurisdiction in federal matters. There are other trial courts with original, although special (or limited) jurisdiction, such as the U.S. Tax Court, the U.S. Bankruptcy Court, and the U.S. Claims Court. Certain administrative agencies and departments having quasijudicial power also have original jurisdiction; the decisions of these courts can be reviewed by the federal district courts.

U.S. Courts of Appeals

Congress has established eleven judicial circuits (plus the District of Columbia Circuit and the Federal Circuit) that hear appeals from the district (and territorial) courts located within their respective circuits. Figure 15–3 shows the geographical boundaries of these judicial circuits. The decisions of the courts of appeals are final in most cases, but appeal to the Supreme Court is possible. Appeals from some federal administrative agencies, such as the Federal Trade Commission, are also made to the U.S. circuit courts of appeals.

The Supreme Court of the United States

The highest level of the three-tiered model of the federal court system is the Supreme Court of the United States. According to the language of Article III of the U.S. Constitution, there is only one supreme court. All other courts in the federal system are considered "inferior." Congress is empowered to create such other inferior courts as it deems necessary. According to this language, the inferior courts that Congress has created include the U.S. courts of appeal, the district courts, and any other courts of limited, or specialized, jurisdiction.

The Supreme Court of the United States consists of nine justices appointed by the president of the United States and confirmed by the Senate. They receive lifetime appointments (under Article II, they "hold their offices during Good Behavior"). Although the Supreme Court has original, or trial, jurisdiction in rare instances, as set forth in Article III, Section 2, of the Constitution, it functions mostly as an appeals court.

Jurisdiction of Federal Courts

Since the federal government is a government of limited powers, the jurisdiction of the federal courts is limited. Article III of the Constitution established the boundaries of federal judicial power:

Section 2. The judicial power shall extend to all Cases, in Law and Equity, arising under this Constitution, the Laws of the United States, and Treaties made, or which shall be made, under this Authority:—to all Cases affecting Ambassadors, other public Ministers and Consuls;—to all Cases of admiralty and maritime Jurisdiction;—to Controversies to which the United States shall be a Party;—to Controversies between two or more States;— between a State and Citizens of another State;[3]—between Citizens of different States;— between Citizens of the same State claiming Lands under the Grants of different States, and between a State, or the Citizens thereof, and foreign States, Citizens or Subjects.

In all Cases affecting Ambassadors, other public Ministers and Consuls, and those in which a State shall be a Party, the Supreme Court shall have original Jurisdiction. In all the other Cases before mentioned, the Supreme Court shall have appellate Jurisdiction, both as to Law and Fact, with such Exceptions, and under such Regulations as the Congress shall make.

[3]Amendment XI, passed in 1798, prohibits any exercise of federal judicial power in cases brought against a state by citizens of another state and so on.

Figure 15–3
▽

Geographical Boundaries of Judicial Circuit Courts

ADMINISTRATIVE OFFICE OF THE UNITED STATES COURTS
January 1983

Circuit boundaries
State boundaries
District boundaries

The Solicitor General and two assistants enter the Supreme Court building.

In line with the checks-and-balances system of the federal government, Congress has the power to control the number and kind of inferior courts in the federal system. Normally, except in those cases where the Constitution gives the Supreme Court original jurisdiction, Congress can also regulate the jurisdiction of the Supreme Court. Therefore, although the Constitution sets the outer limits of federal judicial power, Congress can set other limits on federal jurisdiction. Furthermore, the courts themselves can promulgate rules that limit the types of cases they will hear.

How the Supreme Court Functions

Which Cases Reach the Supreme Court?

Many people are surprised to learn that in a typical case there is no absolute right of appeal to the United States Supreme Court. The Supreme Court is given original, or trial court, jurisdiction in a small number of situations. Under Article III, Section 2(2), the Supreme Court has original jurisdiction in all cases affecting foreign diplomats and in all cases in which a state was a party. The Eleventh Amendment, passed in 1798, removed from the judicial power of the United States suits commenced by, or prosecuted against, citizens of another state or by citizens or subjects of any foreign state. Therefore, the Supreme Court today rarely acts as a court of original jurisdiction. In all other cases, its jurisdiction is appellate "with such Exceptions, and under such Regulations as the Congress shall make." Although more than 4,500 cases are filed with the Supreme Court each year, the court only hears an average of 300.[4]

There are basically two procedures for bringing a case before the Supreme Court: by *appeal* or by *writ of certiorari*.

Appeal

Under rules set out by Congress, the Supreme Court must review a decision (that is, an individual has an absolute right to appeal) in the following situations:

1. When a federal court of appeals holds a state statute to be invalid because it violates federal law.
2. When the highest state court holds a federal law invalid or upholds a state law that has been challenged as violating a federal law.
3. When a federal court holds an act of Congress unconstitutional and the federal government or one of its employees is a party.
4. When the hearing under appeal is for an **injunction** in a civil (as opposed to criminal) action that Congress requires a district court of three judges to determine.

Theoretically, the Supreme Court is required to hear any appeal that falls within one of these four categories, but it has complete discretion to decide which of these cases require full consideration, including briefs on the merits of the cases and oral arguments before the Court. The Court normally will give full consideration only if four of the nine justices vote to do so.[5] Unless there is sufficient interest in the

Injunction

An order issued by a court in an equity proceeding to compel or restrain the performance of an act by a private individual or government official.

---

[4]There has been some discussion about establishing a new national appellate court to relieve the Supreme Court's workload by taking cases of lesser importance so that the Supreme Court could take on more cases that had important public implications. See Commission on Revision of the Federal Court Appellate System, *Structure and Internal Procedures: Recommendations for Change* (1975).

[5]The "rule of four" is modified when seven or fewer justices participate, which occurs from time to time. When that happens, as few as three justices can grant certiorari or go to a full-scale appeal.

case on the part of the justices, the case will be dismissed. A case can be dismissed because the Court agrees with the lower court's decision, because the federal question presented is not a substantial one, or on some other procedural ground. When a case is dismissed because the higher court agrees with the lower court or because a substantial federal question is lacking, the Court's decision to dismiss has a value as a precedent, and the dismissal can be cited in later cases.[6]

Writ of Certiorari

With a **writ of certiorari,** the Supreme Court orders a lower court to send it the record of a case for review. Often, a party whose case does not fall into one of the four appeal categories just listed will petition the Supreme Court to issue a writ of certiorari. However, even in cases that satisfy one of the four appeal categories, the petitioner may choose for tactical purposes to use the writ of certiorari route to the Supreme Court. Typically, only the petitions that raise the possibility of important constitutional questions or problems of statutory interpretation are granted writs of certiorari. Within these limits, the granting of certiorari is done entirely at the discretion of the Court and seems to depend on factors such as who the petitioners are, the kinds of issues, and the ideologies of the individual justices.

The following situations indicate when the Court will issue a writ, although they are not a limit on the Court's discretion:

1. When a state court has decided a substantial federal question that has not been determined by the Supreme Court before or the state court has decided it in a way that is probably in disagreement with the trend of the Supreme Court's decisions.
2. When two federal courts of appeals are in disagreement with each other.
3. When a federal court of appeals has decided an important state question in conflict with state law, has decided an important federal question not yet addressed by the Court but which should be decided by the Court, has decided a federal question in conflict with applicable decisions of the Court, or has departed from the accepted and usual course of judicial proceedings.

Most petitions for writs of certiorari are denied. A denial is not a decision on the merits of a case, nor does it indicate agreement with the lower court's opinion. (The judgment of the lower court remains, however.) Therefore, denial of the writ has no value as precedent.[7] The Court will not issue a writ unless at least four justices approve of it.

Decisions and Opinions

The United States Supreme Court does not hear any evidence, as is true with all appeals courts. The Court's decision in a case is based upon the abstracts, the record, and the briefs. The attorneys can present oral arguments, after which the case is taken under advisement. When the court has reached a decision, the decision is written. It contains the **opinion** (the court's reasons for its decision), the rules of law that apply, and the judgment. In general, the Court will not **reverse** findings of fact unless the findings are unsupported or contradicted by the evidence. Rather, it will review the record for errors of law. If the Supreme Court feels that a reversible error was committed during the trial or that the jury was improperly instructed,

[6]*Hicks v. Miranda*, 422 U.S. 332, 95 S.Ct. 2281 (1975).
[7]*Singleton v. Commissioner of Internal Revenue*, 439 U.S. 940, 99 S.Ct. 335 (1978).

Writ of Certiorari
An order issued by a higher court to a lower court to send up the record of a case for review. It is the principal vehicle for U.S. Supreme Court review.

Opinion
The statement by a judge or a court of the decision reached in a case tried or argued before them. It expounds the law as applied to the case and details the reasons upon which the judgment was based.

Reverse
To annul or make void a judgment on account of some error or irregularity.
▽

"The Supreme Court says we can tape this if we want."

Remand

To send a case back to the court that originally heard it.

Affirm

To declare that a judgment is valid and right and must stand.

Unanimous Opinion

Agreement of all judges on the same opinion or determination.

Majority Opinion

The views of the majority of the judges.

Concurring Opinion

An opinion, which supports the decision of the majority of the court, prepared by a judge who agrees in general but wants to make or clarify a particular point or to voice disapproval of the grounds on which the decision was made.

Dissenting Opinion

A separate opinion in which a judge dissents from the conclusion reached by the majority of the court and expounds his or her own views about the case.

the judgment will be reversed. Sometimes the case will be **remanded** (sent back to the court that originally heard the case) for a new trial or other proceeding. In many cases, the decision of the lower court is **affirmed,** resulting in enforcement of that court's judgment or decree.

There are four types of written opinions for any particular case decided by the Supreme Court. When all justices unanimously agree on an opinion, the opinion is written for the entire Court (all the justices) and can be deemed a **unanimous opinion.** When there is not a unanimous opinion, a **majority opinion** is written, outlining the views of the majority of the justices involved in the particular case. Often one or more justices who feel strongly about making or emphasizing a particular point that was not made or emphasized in the unanimous or majority written opinion will write a **concurring opinion.** That means the justice writing the concurring opinion agrees with the conclusion given in the unanimous or majority written opinion (concurs) but for different reasons. Finally, in other than unanimous opinions, one or more dissenting opinions are usually written by those justices who did not agree with the majority. The **dissenting opinion** is important because it often forms the basis of the arguments used years later in reversing the majority opinion in a similar case.

The Supreme Court at Work

The Supreme Court, by law, begins its regular annual term on the first Monday in October and usually adjourns in late June or early July of the next year. Special sessions may be held after the regular term is over, but only a few cases are decided in this way. More commonly, cases are carried over until the next regular session.

The Court hears oral arguments on Monday, Tuesday, Wednesday, and sometimes Thursday usually for seven two-week sessions scattered from the first week

Justice Thurgood Marshall with his law clerks.

in October to the end of April or the first week in May. Recesses are held between periods of oral argument to allow the justices to consider the cases and handle other Court business. Oral arguments run from 10 A.M. to noon and again from 1 to 3 P.M., with thirty minutes for each side unless special exception is granted. All statements and the justices' questions are tape recorded during these sessions. Unlike most courts, lawyers addressing the Supreme Court can be questioned by the justices at any time during oral argument.

Deciding a Case: Private Research

All of the crucial work on accepted cases is done through private research and reflection. Each justice is entitled to four law clerks, recent graduates of law schools, who undertake much of the research and preliminary drafting necessary for the justice to form an opinion. It is sometimes suspected that because of their extensive assistance, the law clerks form a kind of junior court in themselves, deciding the fate of appeals and petitions to the Court. Some disgruntled lawyers have even suggested that the Senate no longer confirm the appointment of justices but rather the appointment of law clerks. Such criticism is probably too harsh. Clerks do help in screening the large volume of petitions and in the preliminary research work for cases under review, but the justices make the decisions.

Deciding a Case: The Friday Conference

Each Friday during the annual court term, the justices meet in conference to discuss cases then under consideration and to decide which new appeals and petitions the Court will accept. These conferences take place in the oak-paneled chamber and are strictly private—no stenographers, tape recorders, or video cameras

The Judicial Conference, shown here in the east conference room of the Supreme Court building, oversees the administration of the U.S. courts and recommends changes in rules and policies.

are allowed. There used to be two pages in attendance who waited on the justices while they were in conference, but fear of information leaks caused the Court to stop this practice.[8]

In the justices' conference, certain procedures are traditionally observed. Upon entering the room, each justice shakes hands with all present. The justices then sit by order of seniority around a large, rectangular table. Each case is discussed by each justice in that order, with the chief justice starting the discussion. The chief justice determines the order in which the cases are called, guides the discussion generally, and in most cases sets the tone for a case.

Starting with the Court of John Marshall, after each discussion a vote was taken in reverse order of seniority. Today, the justices seldom vote formally. Rather, the chief justice gets a sense of what the majority wants by listening to the justices' individual arguments. When each conference is over, the chief justice, if he is in the majority, will assign the writing of opinions. When the chief justice is not in the majority, the most senior justice in the majority assigns the writing. Since 1965, decisions have been announced on any day that they are ready to be released. They are usually presented orally, in summary form, in open session by the author of the decision. Other views may be stated by members who have written concurring or dissenting opinions. Cases that are brought on petition or appeal to the Court are scheduled for an oral argument or denied a hearing in a written "orders list" released on Mondays. After the necessary editing and the publication of preliminary prints, the official Court decision is placed in the *United States Reports*, a record of the Court's decisions, which is available in most college libraries.

[8]Even though it turned out that one supposed information leak came from lawyers making educated guesses.

How Federal Judges Are Selected

▽

Federal judges are all appointed. Specifically, Article II, Section 2, of the U.S. Constitution states that the president "shall nominate, and by and with the advice and consent of the Senate, shall appoint . . . judges of the Supreme Court." Congress has provided for the same procedure for staffing other federal courts. In other words, the Senate and the president jointly decide who shall be a federal judge, no matter what the level. That decision, of course, has led to a significant amount of politicking in the selection process.

Nominating Judicial Candidates

Judicial candidates for federal judgeships are usually suggested by the attorney general's office to the president. The Judiciary Committee of the Senate considers the nominees. Of course, the advice of the attorney general's office may be rejected outright by both the president and the entire Senate, as may be the advice of the Senate Judiciary Committee.

Since the Truman administration, the American Bar Association, through its Committee on the Federal Judiciary, furnishes the president with evaluations of those individuals being considered. No president is required to refer any nominees to the committee, but most presidents have done so.

The nomination process—no matter how the nominees are obtained—always works the same way: The president does the actual nomination, transmitting the name to the Senate. The Senate then either confirms or rejects. To reach a conclusion, the Senate Judiciary Committee (operating through subcommittees) invites testimony, both written and oral, at its various hearings. The Judiciary committee of the Senate typically sends a blue slip of paper to each of the two senators in the state where the judgeship is vacant. The blue slip is the means for exercising **senatorial courtesy,** as the senators are given a chance to indicate disapproval (but without actually voicing it) by not returning the blue slip.

District Court Judgeship Nominations

Although the president nominates federal judges, the nomination of district court judges typically originates with a senator or senators of the president's party from the state in which there is a vacancy. If the Committee on the Federal Judiciary of the American Bar Association deems the nominee unqualified, as a matter of senatorial courtesy the president will discuss whether the nomination should be withdrawn with the senator or senators who originated the nomination. Also, when a nomination is politically unacceptable to the president, he will consult with the appropriate senator or senators to indicate his displeasure and to seek an alternative candidate.

Courts of Appeals Appointments

There are fewer courts of appeals than district courts, but courts of appeals handle more important matters—at least from the point of view of the president. Consequently, presidents usually take a keener interest in the nomination process for

Senatorial Courtesy
A Senate tradition allowing a senator (or senators) of the president's party to veto a federal judicial appointment in his (or their) state simply by indicating that the appointment is "personably obnoxious." At that point, the Senate may reject the nomination.

such judgeships. The president culls the Circuit Judge Nominating Commission's list of nominees for potential candidates and also may use this list to oppose senators' recommendations that may be politically unacceptable to him.

The President and Supreme Court Appointments

The nomination of Supreme Court justices belongs solely to the president. That is not to say the president's nominations are always confirmed, however. In fact, almost 20 percent of presidential nominations for the Supreme Court have been either rejected or not acted upon by the Senate. Numerous acrimonious battles over Supreme Court appointments have ensued when the Senate and the president have not seen eye to eye about political matters. The U.S. Senate had a long record of refusing to confirm the president's judicial nominations from the beginning of Jackson's presidency in 1829 to the end of Grant's presidency in 1877. During a fairly long period of relative acquiescence on the part of the Senate to presidential nominations, from 1893 until 1968, only three nominees were not confirmed. From 1968 through 1983, however, there were two rejections of presidential nominees to the highest court. In addition, one of Lyndon Johnson's nominations was not acted on, and his choice for chief justice in 1968—Abe Fortas, a member of the Court—was withdrawn after a question arose during confirmation hearings involving Fortas's association with an industrialist convicted of securities irregularities. That problem resulted in Fortas's eventual resignation from the Court.

The Constitution does not establish any qualifications for members of the Supreme Court, and Congress has not legislated any official requirements for confirmation. Informally, however, there are pressures to select justices who have had legal training, who have had some experience in public service, and who are of good moral character. Two Supreme Court nominees—George H. Williams in 1873 and G. Harold Carswell in 1970—were denied confirmation on the grounds that they were professionally unqualified. In 1969, Clement F. Haynsworth, Jr. was rejected partly because of alleged ethical and financial improprieties. Partisan considerations have been the primary factor, though, in most Senate rejections of presidential nominees, especially when a nominee was proposed by a "lame duck" president who would not serve an additional term. Disagreement on important policy issues has also been a major consideration in Senate rejections.

Abe Fortas.

Who Are the Federal Judges?

▽

The Background of Supreme Court Justices

The make-up of the federal judiciary is far from typical of the American public. Table 15–2 summarizes background information on all of the 103 Supreme Court justices to 1986. In general, the justices' partisan attachments have been mostly the same as those of the president who appointed them. However, there have been some exceptions. Nine nominal Democrats have been appointed by Republican presidents, three Republicans by Democratic presidents, and one Democrat by Whig President John Tyler.[9]

[9]Actually, Tyler was a member of the Democratic party who ran with Harrison on the Whig ticket. When Harrison died, much to the surprise of all the Whigs, Tyler—a Democrat—became president, although they tried to call him "acting president." Thus there are historians who quibble over the statement that Tyler was a Whig.

Table 15–2
▽
Background of Supreme Court Justices

	Number of Justices (103 = Total)
Occupational Position before Appointment	
Private legal practice	25
State judgeship	21
Federal judgeship	22
U.S. Attorney General	7
Deputy or Assistant U.S. Attorney General	2
U.S. Solicitor General	2
U.S. Senator	6
U.S. Representative	2
State governor	3
Federal executive posts	10
Other	3
Religious Background	
Protestant	82
Roman Catholic	8
Jewish	5
Unitarian	7
No religious affiliation	1
Age on Appointment	
Under 40	4
41–50	29
51–60	56
61–70	14
Political Party Affiliation	
Federalist (to 1835)	13
Democrat-Republican (to 1828)	7
Whig (to 1861)	2
Democrat	42
Republican	39
Educational Background	
College graduate	87
Not a college graduate	16
Sex	
Male	102
Female	1
Race	
Caucasian	102
Other	1

SOURCES: Congressional Quarterly, *Congressional Quarterly's Guide to the U.S. Supreme Court* (Washington, D.C.: Congressional Quarterly, 1979); *Congressional Quarterly's Guide to Government, Spring 1983* (Washington, D.C., 1982), pp. 108–109; Leon Friedman and Fred L. Israel, eds., *The Justices of the United States Supreme Court, 1789–1969: Their Lives and Major Opinions*, 4 vols. (New York: Chelsea House, 1969); *Information Please Almanac*, 1983, pp. 633–635.

As you will note, the most common occupational background of the justices has been private legal practice or state or federal judgeships at the time of their appointment. Those ten justices who were in federal executive posts at the time of their appointment held the high offices of secretary of foreign affairs, secretary of state, comptroller of the treasury, secretary of the navy, postmaster general, secretary of the interior, chairman of the Securities and Exchange Commission, and secretary

Profile
▽
Sandra Day O'Connor

On September 21, 1981, history was made when the Senate unanimously confirmed the nomination of Sandra Day O'Connor as the first woman justice of the Supreme Court. Born in El Paso, Texas, she was raised on her grandfather's 162,000-acre Lazy B Ranch near Duncan, Arizona. O'Connor graduated *magna cum laude* from Stanford University with a B.A. degree in economics in 1950. Two years later, she earned her LL.B. law degree from Stanford University Law School where she was an editor of the *Stanford Law Review* and a member of the Order of the Coif, an honorary society. In law school, she was a classmate of one of her future colleagues on the Supreme Court, William H. Rehnquist.

As was common for women professionals in the early 1950s, O'Connor had some difficulty in finding employment where she could use her legal training. After serving briefly as deputy county attorney for San Mateo County California, from 1952 to 1953, she ac-

"A majority of litigants who come before us are people who are essentially unknown, not only to us but even within their own community. We resolve their problems and, in the process, resolve the problems of thousands or millions similarly situated."

companied her husband to Germany during his military service and worked as a civilian attorney for the army. Fol-

lowing a several-year interruption in her career to raise three sons—during which she worked part-time in the law—she became an assistant attorney general for the state of Arizona in 1965.

In 1969, she was appointed to fill a vacancy in the Arizona Senate and retained the seat in the next year's election. She was chosen Senate majority leader as a Republican in 1972—the first woman majority leader in history. Active in Republican politics, O'Connor also cochaired the Arizona committee to Re-Elect the President (Nixon) in 1972. In 1974, she was elected to the Superior Court for Maricopa County, and five years later she was appointed to the Arizona Court of Appeals. On August 19, 1981, President Reagan nominated her as an associate justice to replace Potter Stewart, who had retired. Her first years on the Court have marked her as a conservative justice who believes in a relatively limited role for the Court in making national policy.

of labor. In the "other" category in the table are two justices who were professors of law (including Taft, a former president), and one justice who was a North Carolina state employee with responsibility for organizing and revising the state's statutes.

Most justices were in their fifties when they assumed office, although two were as young as thirty-two and one as old as sixty-six. The average age of newly sworn justices is about fifty-three.

Note also that the great majority of justices have had a college education. By and large, those who didn't attend college or receive a degree lived in the late eighteenth and early nineteenth centuries when a college education was much less common than it is today. In recent years, degrees from such schools as Yale, Harvard, Columbia, and other prestigious institutions have been typical. It is interesting that many of the earlier college-educated justices did not hold their degrees in law. In fact, it was not until 1957 that all the then-current members of the Court were graduates of law schools.

The religious background of Supreme Court justices is strikingly untypical of that of the American population as a whole, even making allowances for changes over time in the religious composition of the nation. Catholics (and certain Protestant denominations, notably Baptists and Lutherans) have been underrepresented, whereas Protestants in general (Episcopalians, Presbyterians, Methodists, and others), as well as Unitarians, have been overrepresented among the justices. Typically, there has been a "Catholic seat" on the Court, with interruptions, and a "Jewish seat" existed without a break from 1916 until 1969, when Fortas resigned.

The Background of Lower Court Judges

Federal district judges and circuit court judges also have distinctive backgrounds. Most are lawyers in private practice or state judges. Many circuit judges were previously district court judges. They tend to be college educated and to have extensive legal education. District court judges are generally appointed in their forties, whereas circuit judges are a few years older, on average.

One study[10] has shown that federal court appointees under Democratic presidents tend to go more to Catholics, Jews, lower-status Protestants, blacks, and women than is the case under Republican administrations. Republicans are more likely than Democrats to appoint white, male, middle- or upper-class, high-status Protestants to the federal bench. Under both Democratic and Republican administrations, federal judicial appointees have had a history of partisan affiliation and possibly activism with the president's party or they have had an established legal record that accords with the president's personal philosophy.

A comparison of the last few presidential administrations is especially revealing in respect to the proportion of women, blacks, and Hispanics named to the federal courts. Table 15–3 shows judicial appointments made to the U.S. district courts during the Johnson, Nixon, Ford, Carter, and Reagan administrations. In his first four years in office, President Reagan appointed 130 district court jurists. Twelve were women, seven were Hispanics—three appointed to the traditionally Hispanic seats in Puerto Rico—and one was black. Jimmy Carter, aided by the 1978 Omnibus Judgeship Act that created 152 new federal judgeships, appointed a total of 14 women, 14 blacks, and 7 Hispanics to district court positions. Including appeals court appointees, these figures rise to 40, 38, and 16, respectively.

[10]Sheldon Goldman and Thomas P. Jahnige, *The Federal Courts As a Political System*, 2nd Ed. (New York: Harper and Row, 1976).

Thurgood Marshall, the first black to serve on the Supreme Court.

Table 15–3
▽
Judicial Appointments to U.S. District Courts (in percentages)

	Women	Blacks	Hispanics
Johnson	1.6	3.3	2.5
Nixon	0.6	2.8	1.1
Ford	1.9	5.8	1.9
Carter	14.1	14.1	6.8
Reagan (1981–84)	9.2	0.8	5.4

SOURCE: Congressional Quarterly *Almanac 1984*, p. 244.

Democrat Harry E. Claiborne was appointed federal district judge from Las Vegas, Nevada, by President Jimmy Carter in 1978. Claiborne was convicted of tax evasion in 1984 for failing to report more than $100,000 in income in both 1979 and 1980. He was given a two-year prison sentence, which he began to serve at the federal detention center in Montgomery, Alabama, in May 1986.

Congress, outraged that the judge refused to resign his lifetime appointment and continued to draw his paycheck of $6,558 a month, began impeachment proceedings. (Impeachment is the first step in the removal of a federal official. The second step is the actual trial to determine the guilt or innocence of the accused and is handled by the Senate.)

On July 22, 1986, the House of Representatives voted unanimously to impeach Judge Claiborne on four charges. Claiborne was accused by the House impeachment in three counts that were based on his felony conviction for tax evasion of "misbehavior" and "high crimes and misde-

Judge Harry Claiborne.

meanors." The fourth count accused the judge of bringing "disrepute on the federal courts and the administration of justice." If the Senate were to find him guilty of any one of the four, he would be forcibly removed from his judgeship and the Senate could bar him from holding future office.

This marked only the fourteenth impeachment vote in the history of the House of Representatives and the first unanimous vote. It was also the first time a federal judge serving time for a felony has faced impeachment (in the past, impeachment has been avoided by resignation). The last impeachment of a federal judge took place in 1936 when Halsted Ritter, U.S. district judge in Florida, was removed from office after the Senate found him guilty of corruption and tax evasion. In 1974, the House Judiciary Committee voted three articles of impeachment against President Richard Nixon; however, Nixon resigned from the presidency before the House of Representatives had a chance to vote on the articles of impeachment.

A special Senate committee heard seven days of testimony and presented its evidence to the Senate in October, 1986. On October 8th, the Senate voted to accept the committee report in lieu of a full trial. The next day Judge Claiborne was found guilty on three of the four counts and was removed from office.

Qualifications of Federal Judges

Most people would probably hope that members of the judiciary were not "common folk." As technical legal matters must be decided all the time, it is reasonable that a qualification for the federal judiciary be membership in the legal profession (even though this is not a legal requirement). Most federal judges have had public experience at some level of government. At a minimum, they have participated in political activities. This is particularly true for members of the Supreme Court. What is less true is judicial experience prior to accepting a federal judgeship. Only about 35 percent of federal district judges have been state judges, and only about 40 percent of federal judges sitting on circuit courts of appeals have had previous judicial experience. Although we might think that the Supreme Court would draw its judges from the pool of the judicially experienced, such is not necessarily the case. A little less than 43 percent of the justices have come from lower federal or state courts. Indeed, numerous chief justices held no prior judicial office, including John Marshall and Earl Warren, although Earl Warren had been attorney general (and governor) of California.

The Effect of Party Affiliation

The only characteristic of Supreme Court appointments that is relatively predictable is that they will be from the same political party as the president who appoints them. The same is generally true for inferior federal courts. Table 15–4 shows the partisan distribution of appointments for five presidents. About 86 percent of Carter's appointments were Democrats, whereas Reagan picked nearly all Republicans and only a handful of Democrats to sit on the federal bench. In the nearly two hundred years of Supreme Court history, fewer than 14 percent of the justices nominated by a president have been from an opposing political party.

Even though presidents attempt to choose nominees for the Supreme Court who share their general political views, they may be fooled. Consider a few examples. Teddy Roosevelt, an opponent of big business, appointed Oliver Wendell Holmes, Jr., who Roosevelt thought had similar views, to the Court. One of Holmes's first votes was against the administration and for business interests.[11] An even more striking example was President Eisenhower's nomination of Earl Warren as chief justice. Eisenhower thought he was nominating a fellow conservative. Warren, however, turned out be one of the most liberal justices in the history of the Supreme Court. When Eisenhower was later asked if he had made any mistakes as president, he reportedly responded: "Yes, two, and they [Warren and Associate Justice William J. Brennen, Jr.] are both sitting on the Supreme Court."

Presidents are stuck with Supreme Court appointees. For all intents and purposes, a Supreme Court justice is there for life or until he or she retires. Supreme Court justices can be impeached, just as presidents can, but this has happened only once, in the case of Samuel Chase. Chase, indicted by Jefferson's Republicans in the House in 1804 for allegedly politicizing the federal bench, was acquitted by the Senate on each of eight counts the following year. Only five lower federal court judges have been removed by impeachment proceedings.

[11]In *Northern Securities Company v. United States*, 193 U.S. 197 (1904).

Samuel Chase.

Table 15–4
▽
Presidential Appointments to Federal Courts by Party

President	Democratic Appointees	Republican Appointees
Franklin Roosevelt	188	6
Dwight Eisenhower	9	165
Lyndon Johnson	159	9
Richard Nixon	15	198
Gerald Ford	12	52
Jimmy Carter	33	14
Ronald Reagan*	157	4

*First term

Judicial Activism and Judicial Restraint

▽

Judicial Activism

A doctrine advocating an active role for the Supreme Court in enforcing the Constitution and in using judicial review. An activist Court takes a broad view of the Constitution and involves itself in legislative and executive matters by altering the direction of activities of Congress, state legislatures, and administrative agencies.

Judicial Restraint

A doctrine holding that the Court should rarely use its power of judicial review or otherwise intervene in the political process.

Judicial scholars like to characterize different Supreme Courts and different Supreme Court justices as being either activist or restraintist. Those advocating the doctrine of **judicial activism** believe the Court should use its power to alter the direction of the activities of Congress, state legislatures, and administrative agencies. Those advocating the doctrine of **judicial restraint** believe the Court should use its powers of judicial review only rarely. In other words, whatever popularly elected legislatures decide should not be thwarted by the Supreme Court so long as such decisions are not unconstitutional.

During the early years of the nation, the Supreme Court certainly was in no position to exercise judicial activism. Indeed, in *The Federalist Papers*, Alexander Hamilton stated that "the judiciary is beyond comparison the weakest of the three departments of power." The Supreme Court during its first decade justified that remark, as it handled few matters and decided only one important case. The weakness of the Court was emphasized by the plans for the new Capitol. No chamber was provided for the Court. When the seat of government was moved to Washington, D.C., the Supreme Court met in a room in the basement beneath the Senate chamber.

Alexis de Tocqueville, an astute French observer of American institutions in the early nineteenth century, appreciated the position of the Court in the American constitutional system, however. He stated that "the supreme court is placed higher than any known tribunal. . . . The peace, the prosperity, and the very existence of the Union are vested in the hands of the seven Federal judges."

Today, many of the Supreme Court's critics believe it should exercise more restraint. They criticize the first *Brown* decision in 1954 (see Chapter 5) on the grounds that the highest court settled a problem that should have been resolved by Congress. Critics of the current courts call them "minilegislatures." They point out, for example, that in *Baker v. Carr*[12] the federal courts wrongly exercised

[12]369 U.S. 69 (1962).

Although Supreme Court justices share a belief in judicial review, some have been more willing to use it than others. Justice Felix Frankfurter (left), for example, emphasized judicial restraint, whereas Chief Justice Warren (right), believed in judicial activism.

jurisdiction over the issue of state legislative districting plans and that the U.S. Supreme Court had no right to intervene in such a state matter. Another activist decision was *Roe v. Wade*,[13] in which the U.S. Supreme Court gave women the right to an abortion during the first trimester of pregnancy, thereby striking down state statutes permitting abortions only in special cases.

A Contrast in Courts:
The Warren Court and the Burger Court
▽

Chief Justices Earl Warren and Warren Burger both set the tone and direction of the Supreme Court's decisions, just as their predecessors had. Although the chief justice is not legally superior to his colleagues except in title and in his slightly higher income, some observers note his capacity to influence the other members of the Court. He directs the Court's business. He directs the work of deciding cases in the conference chamber, where he can call and discuss the individual cases before any of the other justices have a chance to speak. He will, and often does, control the deliberations on each case. The differences between the Warren Court and the Burger Court are in part a product of the views and attitudes of their respective chief justices.

The Warren Court

Earl Warren of California presided over the Supreme Court from 1953 to 1969. The Court he came to was one in which the justices were at odds with one another. Under the previous two chief justices, Harlan F. Stone and Fred M. Vinson, relatively little authority had been exercised by the chief justice. Warren brought to the Court a measure of authority and once again emphasized intellectual rather than personal issues in cases brought before it.

Protecting Personal Rights

If one thing characterized the Warren Court, it was its emphasis on personal rights. Warren stated in 1955 that "when the generation of 1980 receives from us the Bill of Rights, the document will not have exactly the same meaning it had when we received it from our fathers."[14] During his tenure as chief justice, Warren expanded the meaning of personal rights and liberties in cases concerning the freedoms of speech, press, and religion, and the rights of minorities and those accused of crimes.

Scholars view the Warren Court's protection of personal rights as emphasizing (1) human rights over property rights and (2) national standards over state standards in Bill of Rights' matters.

Concerning human and property rights, Warren asserted that individuality had been dwarfed by concentrations of economic power. He sought to strengthen the rights of individuals even if they contradicted community values.

As to the supremacy of national standards, we must remember that as early as 1833 the Supreme Court had ruled that the Bill of Rights was not binding on the states.[15] The process of incorporation of the national Bill of Rights had been gradual

[13]410 U.S. 113 (1973).

[14]"The Law and the Future," *Fortune* Magazine, November 1955; reprinted in *The Public Papers of Chief Justice Earl Warren*, ed. by Henry M. Christman (New York: Capricorn Books, 1966), p. 120.

[15]*Barron v. Baltimore*, 7 Peters 243 (1833).

The Warren Court, 1962.

These citizens display their petition over 1,500 feet long to impeach Earl Warren, 1959.

since 1925 and Warren sought to speed up that process. In *Gideon v. Wainwright*,[16] the Warren Court dealt with the problem of an indigent defendant's constitutional right to have an attorney present in a state court criminal proceeding. Before *Gideon* the Supreme Court had made a distinction between federal proceedings, in which indigents were entitled to have a lawyer, and state proceedings in noncapital cases, where the right was more limited. In *Gideon*, the Warren Court held that the right to counsel was fundamental to a fair trial even at the state level.

In case after case, the Warren Court proceeded to affirm the guarantees in the Bill of Rights as binding on all of the states. Today, almost all of the rights safeguarded by the Bill of Rights are imposed on the states by the due process clause of the Fourteenth Amendment.

Widening The Meaning of Personal Rights

The Warren Court also gave a new meaning to personal rights, particularly in the areas of criminal justice and freedom of expression.

With respect to the rights of criminal defendants, numerous restrictions were imposed on police interrogation. In *Miranda v. Arizona*,[17] the majority of the Warren Court declared that henceforth suspects had to be immediately informed of their right to a court-appointed lawyer, their right to remain silent, and the fact that anything they said could be held against them.

The First Amendment freedom of expression was extended under the Warren Court. The right to use the streets and other public places for public speech was

[16]372 U.S. 335 (1963).
[17]384 U.S. 436 (1966).

applied to using such places for demonstrations and civil rights protests. Many censorship laws were struck down. The publication of so-called obscene materials was given increased protection.

Extending the Civil Rights of Minorities

Another broad area of change under the Warren Court was in the area of minority civil rights. As we noted in Chapter 5, the major action here was the case of *Brown v. Board of Education of Topeka, Kansas* (the so-called *Brown I* decision),[18] the first of several cases striking down the separate-but-equal doctrine. Then the Warren Court required that in *Brown v. Board of Education* (the so-called *Brown II* decision),[19] desegregation of schools had to proceed with all deliberate speed. The school segregation cases are perhaps the main monument to Warren's judicial statesmanship. Warren was able to obtain unanimity in the school segregation decision, a monumental accomplishment considering the different views of the other justices and the fact that Warren was then a neophyte chief justice.

When Earl Warren resigned in 1969, some students of the Supreme Court believed that throughout the history of the United States only the Court of John Marshall (1801–1835) had been so influential in reshaping American law and thus American society.

The Burger Court

During Nixon's 1968 presidential campaign, he promised that if elected he would alter the trend of Supreme Court decisions by appointing "strict constructionists" and judicial conservatives. When Chief Justice Warren retired in 1969, Nixon had his chance. His choice was Warren Burger, a reputedly conservative federal appeals court judge. With Burger's appointment, many expected that the liberalism of the

[18]347 U.S. 483 (1954).
[19]349 U.S. 294 (1955).

The Supreme Court's decision in the Brown v. Board of Education of Topeka, Kansas *case ruled that racially segregated schools were unconstitutional. That decision became the basis for the integration of public schools in the United States.*

Warren Court would be followed by a period of reaction. This seemed particularly likely as six more members of the Court took their leave and were replaced by nominees of Republican presidents—four by Nixon, one by Ford, and one by Reagan. Court watchers anticipated a sharp departure from the path of the new justices' predecessors.

To a certain degree this happened. For example, in its criminal law rulings the Court allowed police to conduct more extensive searches of suspects arrested for traffic offenses.[20] It ruled that even evidence secured illegally by police can be used in grand jury proceedings.[21] It brought to a halt the process of extending to the juvenile court the procedural requirements applicable in other criminal proceedings.[22]

Judicial Activism Continued

Notwithstanding these conservative rulings, judicial activism was not reversed by the appointment of Chief Justice Burger. As the Burger Court began taking some bold policy-making steps, some contended that by any measure the Burger Court was an activist one. The anticipated reversals of the Warren Court regarding school desegregation and the rights of criminal suspects under interrogation never materialized. Instead, they have been accepted as premises established by the Constitution. Another measure of activism is the Court's willingness to declare acts of Congress unconstitutional. In the sixteen terms of its existence, the Warren Court invalidated nineteen provisions of federal statutes; in its first thirteen terms the Burger Court struck down twenty-four.

Some of the Court's more controversial decisions clearly illustrate this activism. The Burger Court upheld the right of women to have abortions in the hotly disputed *Roe v. Wade*[23] case. This case clearly limited the power of states. In *United States v. Nixon*,[24] the Court ordered President Nixon to hand over the White House tapes during the Watergate investigation. In the Pentagon Papers case,[25] the Court held that under all but the most extraordinary circumstances, the president does not have the inherent power to enjoin the publication by news organizations of classified information. In *Regents of the University of California v. Bakke*,[26] the Court upheld the right of universities to take "affirmative action" by including race as a criterion for admission. It ruled in 1983 that racially discriminatory schools are ineligible for tax exemptions.

Vincent Blasi, a law professor at Columbia University, saw the Burger Court's activism as very different from that of the Warren Court. He stated that the "rootless activism" of the Burger Court "has been inspired not by a commitment to fundamental constitutional principles or noble political ideals, but rather by the belief that modest injections of logic and compassion by disinterested, sensible judges can serve as a counterforce to some of the excess and irrationalities of contemporary governmental decision-making."[27]

[20]*U.S. v. Robinson*, 414 U.S. 218 (1973).

[21]*U.S. v. Calandra*, 414 U.S. 338 (1974).

[22]*McKeiver v. Pennsylvania*, 403 U.S. 528 (1971).

[23]410 U.S. 113 (1973).

[24]418 U.S. 683 (1974).

[25]*New York Times Co. v. U.S.*, 403 U.S. 713 (1971).

[26]438 U.S. 265 (1978).

[27]Vincent Blasi, ed., *The Burger Court: The Counter Revolution That Wasn't* (New Haven, Conn.: Yale University Press, 1983), p. 200.

In 1974 the Supreme Court ruled that President Nixon was required to hand over the White House tapes to the special prosecutor in the Watergate investigation. Here Nixon is shown during a television broadcast with transcripts of the tapes in the background.

Blasi contended that the Burger Court was moderate, pragmatic, and "centrist"— seeking middle-of-the-road doctrines that offered something to adherents on both sides of a social controversy. This was in contrast to the energetic moral vision that gave impetus to the activism of the Warren Court. Because of the pragmatic attitude of the Burger Court, its decisions did not always fall into neat unambiguous patterns of liberalism or conservatism. For example, when the Burger Court affirmed an order of the Pittsburgh Commission on Human Relations, an order that directed a newspaper to classify its help-wanted ads without regard to sex, was it a liberal triumph promoting sexual equality or a conservative attack on the freedom of the press?[28] In certain areas, the Court has consolidated the landmark advances of the Warren years. In other areas, a mild retrenchment has taken place.[29]

Blasi concluded, "Much of the time the Court seems to be drifting. It adds up to a curious but nonetheless intriguing period in the history of a remarkable institution."[30]

Liberal or Conservative?

The most widely used criteria for judging the ideological tendency of the Supreme Court is its overall direction—liberal or conservative. As we have seen, the predecessor of the Burger Court, the Warren Court, was considered liberal. The Burger Court, on the other hand, can be viewed as being much less consistent in its findings. The general conclusion is that so-called centrist justices held the balance of power and therefore the Court did not move decisively either to the right (conservative) or to the left (liberal). (Figure 15–4 shows how the Burger Court voted on six key issues.) If one can talk of the Burger Court, it will be remembered

[28]See *Pittsburgh Press Co. v. Pittsburgh Comm. on Human Relations*, 413 U.S. 376 (1973).

[29]Blasi, *op. cit.*, p. xiii.

[30]*Ibid.*

Figure 15–4

How the Burger Court
Voted on Six Key Issues

Justice	Marshall	Brennan	Blackman	Stevens	Powell	White	O'Connor	Burger	Rehnquist
Age in 1986	77	80	77	66	78	69	56	78	61
Year Appointed	1967	1956	1970	1975	1972	1962	1981	1969	1972

ABORTION
Roe vs. Wade (1973)
Does a woman have a Constitutional right to choose to have an abortion?

YES	YES	YES	YES	YES	NO	YES	YES	NO
			(William Douglas)			(Potter Stewart)		

PORNOGRAPHY
Miller vs. California (1973)
May a carefully circumscribed criminal statute ban works it defines obscene?

NO	NO	YES	NO	YES	YES	NO	YES	YES
			(William Douglas)			(Potter Stewart)		

DEATH PENALTY
Gregg vs. Georgia (1976)
May the death penalty be imposed constitutionally under certain circumstances?

NO	NO	YES	YES	YES	YES	YES	YES	YES
					(Potter Stewart)			

LIBEL
Herbert vs. Lando (1979)
Does the First Amendment ever prevent a libel plaintiff from obtaining internal communications about the editorial process?

YES	YES	NO	NO	NO	NO		NO	NO

RELIGION
Lynch vs. Donnelly (1984)
Does a publicly funded créche in a Christmas display violate the constituional separation of church and state?

YES	YES	YES	YES	NO	NO	NO	NO	NO

CRIMINAL LAW
U.S. vs. Leon (1984)
Can evidence be used in a criminal trial if it was seized by police in good-faith reliance on an improper warrant?

NO	NO	YES	NO	YES	YES	YES	YES	YES

 = LIBERAL VOTE

= CONSERVATIVE VOTE

as a moderate court—neither retrenching nor avant garde. Its legacy, according to University of Texas Law Professor Scott Powell, is that "It met the hard cases, decided the finer points, and didn't push things along any further."[31]

The Rehnquist/Reagan Court

Ronald Reagan's nomination of William H. Rehnquist in 1986, the strong anchor of the Supreme Court's conservative wing, as the nation's sixteenth chief justice fairly cemented the future conservative leaning of that institution. In addition, Reagan proposed Antonin Scalia, another conservative judge, to the Court. With four sitting justices more than seventy-seven years of age that year and two in failing health, the question remains, how soon will the next change occur? When we consider that Reagan will have appointed about half of the 744 federal judges by the time his term ends, the transformation of the federal judiciary to a more conservative body cannot be questioned. We can expect that some of the conservative trends started under the Burger Court will continue under Rehnquist. The rights of criminals, for example, were trimmed under Burger. With Rehnquist taking the lead, there are probably six votes for further cuts. With respect to abortion, the last ruling leaving it intact was won by a narrow margin of 5 to 4. *Roe v. Wade* has only five defenders left on the Court. One departure and the balance will shift, perhaps inviting new state restrictions on a woman's right to choose an abortion. Affirmative action may be another area of change. The Burger Court voted in favor of some race-conscious remedies. The Rehnquist Court may not. With respect to capital punishment, one barrier recently fell when death penalty foes were allowed to be excluded from juries. Some believe that only a few procedural questions are unresolved and that under the Rehnquist Court the pace of executions will quicken.

A note of caution is in order here. Dwight David Eisenhower chose Earl Warren for his conservative views. But the Warren Court was known as a liberal court. In other words, there is no guarantee that a presidential appointee will reflect the president's views. Moreover, there is no guarantee that Rehnquist and Scalia will

[31]Quoted in *Time*, June 30, 1986, p. 36.

The Rehnquist Court, 1986.

Profile
▽
Chief Justice Rehnquist

On Tuesday, June 17, 1986, Warren Burger, chief justice of the Supreme Court, announced that he would retire after seventeen years of service. President Ronald Reagan named Supreme Court Justice William Rehnquist to replace Burger as chief justice. Rehnquist had been on the Supreme Court since 1971, when he was nominated by Richard Nixon. Since that time, he has been viewed as one of the Court's most conservative members. He faced a hard confirmation fight in the Senate because of his conservative views.

His background includes a B.A. from Stanford University, a Master's degree in political science from Harvard, and a degree from Stanford Law School where he graduated first in his class in 1952. He clerked for Supreme Court Justice Robert Jackson in 1952 and 1953 and then practiced law in Arizona, where in 1964 he worked on conservative Barry Goldwater's presidential campaign. Under the Nixon administration in 1969, he became a

"It is basically unhealthy to have so much authority concentrated in a small group of lawyers who have been appointed to the Supreme Court and enjoy virtual life tenure."

deputy attorney general and later, head of the Department of Justice, Office of Legal Counsel, where he successfully defended the government's program of

secret surveillance of anti-Vietnam war groups in the United States.

On many issues, Rehnquist is an almost doctrinaire conservative. For example, he has been the leader in the Court conservatives' efforts to narrow the interpretation of defendants' rights in criminal cases. In recent decisions, he has dissented forcefully when the court reaffirmed womens' rights to abortion.

Personal acquaintances say that Rehnquist is affable and friendly, with great skills at interpersonal relations. One University of Virginia law professor has indicated that he is one of the brightest justices ever to sit on the bench because he writes with style, force, and assurance, as no one else has in recent times. "It is hard to match his agility in shaping a record and marshalling arguments to reach a conclusion."*

*Quoted in *U.S. News & World Report*, June 30, 1986, p. 18, by Professor of Law A. E. Dick Howard, University of Virginia.

form a lasting alliance, even though they are sometimes referred to as the "dynamic duo." Within any institution made up of people, relationships depend not just on similarity of views but also on personal chemistry. The odds are, though, that we will have a conservative court for a while to come. Shortly after the Rehnquist and Scalia appointments, a leading student of the Supreme Court noted that "if the Republicans hold the White House and the Senate through 1992, we are likely to have five Rehnquists on the Supreme Court—and that would be an extraordinary state of affairs."[32] When the Democrats regained Senate control after the 1986 elections, this possibility became somewhat less likely.

[32]Remarks by Professor Jeffrey Stone of the University of Chicago Law School, reported in *U.S. News & World Report*, June 30, 1986, p. 19.

What Checks Our Courts?

▽

Our judicial system is probably the most independent in the world. But the courts do not have absolute independence, for they are part of the political process. Political checks limit the extent to which courts can exercise judicial review and engage in an activist policy. These checks are exercised by the legislature, the executive, other courts, and the public.

Legislative Checks

Courts may make rulings, but often the legislatures at local, state, and federal levels are required to appropriate funds to carry out the court's rulings. When such funds are not appropriated, the court in effect has been checked. A court, for example, may decide that prison conditions must be improved. But then a legislature has to find the funds to carry out such a ruling.

Courts' rulings can be overturned by constitutional amendments at both the federal and state levels. Many of the amendments to the U.S. Constitution check the state courts' ability to allow discrimination, for example. Recently, though, proposed constitutional amendments created by a desire to reverse courts' decisions on school prayer and abortion have failed.

Finally, legislatures can pass new laws to overturn courts' rulings. This may happen particularly when a court makes a ruling in the absence of a relevant statute. The legislature can then pass a new statute to negate the court's ruling.

Executive Checks

Presidents have the power to change the direction of the Supreme Court and the federal judiciary, for the president can appoint new judges who in principle have philosophies more in line with that of the president. Also, a president, governor, or mayor can refuse to enforce courts' rulings. In a famous statement, President Andrew Jackson, in response to Chief Justice Marshall's ruling that a state could not pass laws governing Indians on their own territory within the state, said, "John Marshall has made his decision. Now let him enforce it."

The Rest of the Judiciary

Higher courts can reverse the decisions of lower courts. Lower courts can put a check on higher courts, too. The Supreme Court of the United States, for example, cannot possibly hear all of the cases that go through the lower courts. Lower courts can and have ignored, directly or subtly, Supreme Court decisions by deciding in the other direction in particular cases. Only if a case goes to the Supreme Court on appeal or certiorari can the Supreme Court correct the situation.

The Public Has a Say

History has shown members of the Supreme Court that if its decisions are noticeably further ahead or at odds with a national consensus, then it will lose its support and some of its power. Perhaps the best example was the Dred Scott decision of 1857 in which the Supreme Court held that blacks could not become citizens of the United States, nor were they entitled to the rights and privileges of citizenship. The Court ruled, in addition, that the Missouri Compromise banning slavery in the territories was unconstitutional. Most observers contend that the Dred Scott ruling contributed to making the Civil War inevitable.

Observers of the court system believe that because of the sense of self-preservation of the judges, they are forced to develop a sense of self-restraint. Some observers even argue that such sense of self-restraint is more important than the other checks just discussed.

Changing the Legal System

Although impressed by the power of judges in American government, Alexis de Tocqueville stated:

> The power is enormous, but it is clothed in the authority of public opinion. They are the all-powerful guardians of a people which respects law; but they would be impotent against public neglect or popular contempt.*

The court system may seem all-powerful and too complex to be influenced by one individual, but its power nonetheless depends on our support. A hostile public has many ways of resisting, modifying, or overturning rulings of the court. Sooner or later a determined majority will prevail. Even a determined minority can make a difference. As Hamilton suggested in *Federalist Paper* no. 1, the people will always hold the scales of justice in their hands, and ultimately all constitutional government depends on their firmness and wisdom.

One example of the kind of pressure that can be exerted on the court system began with a tragedy. On a spring afternoon in 1980, thirteen-year-old Cari Lightner was hit from behind and killed by a drunk driver while walking in a bicycle lane. The driver turned out to be a forty-seven-year-old man with two prior drunk-driving convictions. He was at that time out on bail for a third arrest. Cari's mother, Candy, quit her job as a real estate agent to form MADD (Mothers Against Drunk Driving) and launched a personal campaign to stiffen penalties for drunk-driving convictions.

The organization grew to 20,000 members with 91 regional offices and a staff of 160. Outraged by the estimated 26,000 lives lost every year because of drunk driving, the group not only seeks stiff penalties against drunk

Democracy in America, vol. 1 (New York: Schocken Books, 1961), p. 166.

drivers but also urges police, prosecutors, and judges to crack down on such violators. MADD, by becoming involved, has gotten results. Owing to their efforts and the efforts of other citizen-activist groups, many states have responded with stronger penalties and deterrents. If you feel strongly about this issue and want to get involved, contact the following:

MADD
5330 Primrose, Suite 146
Fair Oaks, CA 95628
916-966-6233

Several other organizations have been formed by people who want to change or influence the judicial system. A few of them are as follows:

Legal Defense Research Institute
733 N. Van Buren
Milwaukee, WI 53202
414-272-5995

HALT—An Organization of Americans for Legal Reform
201 Massachusetts Ave., NE
Suite 319
Washington, D.C. 20002
205-546-4258

National Legal Center for the Public Interest
1101 17th St., NW
Washington, D.C. 20036
202-296-1683

If you want information about the Supreme Court, contact the following by telephone or letter:

Clerk of the Court
The Supreme Court of the United States
1 First St., NE
Washington, D.C.
202-393-1640

Chapter Summary

1. Civil law spells out the rights and duties that exist between persons or between citizens and their government. Criminal law is concerned with wrongs committed against the public as a whole.

2. Because of our colonial heritage, most American law is based on the English legal system.

3. The body of judge-made law based on decisions in earlier cases is known as common law.

4. The doctrine of *stare decisis* means that judges attempt to follow precedents established by decisions of the past. The doctrine helps courts to be more efficient, uniform, and stable.

5. The U.S. Constitution is the supreme law of the land. State constitutions are supreme within their respective borders.

6. The process of deciding whether a law is contrary to the mandates of the Constitution is known as judicial review. This judicial power, first established in *Marbury v. Madison* (1803), is not often exercised.

7. For a court to exercise valid authority, it must have jurisdiction over the person against whom the suit is brought or over the subject matter of the case.

8. Courts of general jurisdiction can decide almost every type of case. At both the federal and state levels, there are courts that handle only cases of specialized, or limited, subject matter.

9. Courts having original jurisdiction are those of the first instance. Those having appellate jurisdiction act as reviewing courts.

10. The federal court system is a three-tiered model consisting of (a) trial courts, (b) intermediate courts of appeals, and (c) the Supreme Court.

11. Article III of the Constitution establishes the boundaries of federal judicial power. Federal courts are normally restricted to so-called federal questions.

12. The Supreme Court rarely acts as a court of original jurisdiction. In all other cases, its jurisdiction is appellate. The two procedures for bringing a case before the Supreme Court are by appeal and by writ of certiorari.

13. The Supreme Court conveys its decisions in written form. The decision contains the opinion (the Court's reason for its decision), the rules of law that apply, and the judgment.

14. The president appoints federal judges with the advice and consent of the Senate. The nomination of district court judges typically originates with a senator or senators of the president's party from the state in which there is a vacancy.

15. Almost 20 percent of presidential nominations for the Supreme Court have been either rejected or not acted on because of partisan considerations, lack of professional qualifications, or disagreement on important policy issues.

16. The makeup of the federal judiciary is far from typical of the American public. Most judges are white, male, Protestant, over age fifty, and college educated.

17. Presidents usually appoint judges from their own political party.

18. Supreme Courts are characterized as either activist or restraintist. Those advocating judicial activism believe the Court should use its power to alter the direction of the activities of Congress, state legislatures, and administrative agencies. Those advocating judicial restraint believe the Court should use its power of judicial review only rarely.

19. The Warren Court, presided over by Chief Justice Earl Warren from 1953 to 1969, emphasized personal rights over property rights and national standards over state standards in Bill of Rights matters. It also extended the civil rights of minorities.

20. Since the 1969 appointment of Chief Justice Burger, the political complexion of the Court has changed, but judicial activism has not been reversed. This activist role raises the important question of the proper role of the Supreme Court in the future.

21. Ronald Reagan appointed William H. Rehnquist as the nation's sixteenth Chief Justice and added another conservative to the Supreme Court, Antonin Scalia. Many of the conservative trends started under the Burger Court will undoubtedly continue under Rehnquist.

22. There are numerous checks on our courts. They include (a) legislative checks, (b) executive checks, (c) checks by the rest of the judiciary, and (d) checks by the public.

Questions for Review and Discussion

1. Define "judicial review." Does the Supreme Court "legislate" using this power? In what areas has the Court made major policy decisions by judicial review?

2. An old political saying declares that "the Supreme Court follows the election returns." What factors in the nomination process, the decision process, and, indeed, the power of the Court itself make this true?

3. What are the benefits of being a member of the federal judiciary? Why is this such a sought-after position? How would you go about planning a career in the judicial branch?

4. Why is it possible for the law to change radically within a few decades? For example, after World War II, the Communist party was illegal, women were barred from many activities in our society, and the races were legally segregated in many parts of the country. All of those conditions are now legally reversed, mostly due to Court decisions. How does the Court shape our ideas of what is right? Or what is fair?

Selected References

Alan Barth, *Prophets with Honor: Great Dissents and Great Dissenters in the Supreme Court* (New York: Alfred A. Knopf, 1974). Six cases in which dissenting justices had their views vindicated years later when the Court reversed itself.

Robert A. Carp and C. K. Rowland, *Policymaking and Politics in the Federal District Courts* (Knoxville: University of Tennessee Press, 1983). The authors argue that the administration of justice in district courts can be significantly affected by the president's appointments.

Sheldon Goldman and Thomas P. Jahnige, *The Federal Courts as a Political System*, 3d ed. (New York: Harper and Row, 1985). Using the systems analysis approach, this book examines inputs, conversions, outputs, feedback, and other processes in a dynamic investigation of the complicated interrelationships of the federal courts' "political system."

Elder Witt, *A Different Justice: Reagan and the Supreme Court* (Washington: Congressional Quarterly Press, 1986). This book describes and analyzes how the Reagan administration has looked at the Supreme Court as an instrument for reshaping the federal government. It also provides excellent profiles on the justices, in particular Sandra Day O'Connor.

Bob Woodward and Scott Armstrong, *The Brethren: Inside the Supreme Court* (New York: Simon and Schuster, 1979). A detailed, behind-the-scenes account of Supreme Court decision making on cases dealing with abortion, busing, the Nixon tapes, and obscenity.

5
PUBLIC POLICY

Chapter 16

▽

Political Economy

Contents

▽

Monetary and Fiscal Policy

The Budget Process

The Federal Tax System

When Spending Exceeds Revenues: The Public Debt

The Long Road to a Balanced Budget: Gramm-Rudman

What If . . .

The Federal Budget Had to Be Balanced?

On December 12, 1985, President Reagan signed a balanced budget act setting targets for budget reductions and revenue monitoring in order to accomplish a balanced budget by 1991. One of the biggest problems with a balanced budget is that a large proportion of federal spending is extremely difficult to cut because it is allocated to fixed items such as interest on the federal public debt and contracts that are outstanding. Other programs are difficult to cut because of ethical or political reasons (for example, Social Security, food stamps, or defense spending). Yet many observers felt that the 1986 federal budget deficit of over $200 billion was burdensome as well as dangerous to the economic well-being of the United States. What are some ways to balance the federal budget?

The first and apparently easiest way to accomplish a balanced budget would be to raise taxes. The income and corporate tax would simply be increased to a rate that would cover expenditures. Tax increases, however, depend on the willingness of politicians to raise taxes and on the willingness of Americans to reelect politicians who favor tax hikes.

A second approach would be to proceed with the normal budgetary process of taking the most conservative estimates on revenues coming in and passing spending bills that match projected federal income.

A third way of balancing the budget would be to set

automatic spending cuts that would accompany revenue shortfalls, without the need for congressional action.

A mandatory balancing of the federal budget by constitutional amendment is another way expenditures and revenues could be brought into line. One of the dangers of this approach, however, is the rigidity it imposes on the federal government. What if a national emergency such as war or a major nuclear disaster were to occur suddenly? How would the government legally be able to secure the necessary resources to deal with such a crisis?

In principle, the federal budget does have to be balanced by the government's fiscal year 1991. The reality, however, is that Congress is finding ways to play with the numbers to show a smaller deficit than actually exists. There are some critics of the American governmental process who contend that no matter what law is passed, we will never see a federal budget that is truly balanced again.

Politics and economics certainly go hand in hand, particularly in a nation in which government—federal, state, and local—controls more than 40 percent of **gross national product (GNP)**. Political economy is the analysis and formulation of public policies that have to do with the economic questions facing our nation, such as how to deal with inflation, unemployment, high interest rates, international trade deficits, and the like—all important issues in American society.

In this chapter, we look at how political economy involves management of the national economy to satisfy the national goals of low inflation, low unemployment, and steady economic growth. We then examine the budget process, which is rapidly becoming the most important policy process in national government. Next, taxation, or how revenue is raised, is analyzed by itself and as a component of fiscal and other social policies. Finally, we examine the struggle with large federal government deficits, an increasing public debt, and the general problem of the shortfall of revenues for the government.

Chapter 16
Political Economy
▽

Gross National Product
The total value of all *final* goods and services produced in this nation during one year.

Monetary and Fiscal Policy
▽

The basic tools that the federal government uses to manage the national economy are monetary policy and fiscal policy. **Monetary policy** includes regulating the amount of money, or cash, in circulation—a responsibility of the Federal Reserve Board. **Fiscal policy,** which is a responsibility of the president and Congress, consists of changing federal government taxes and spending to affect the rate of growth of the total demand for goods and services in the economy.

Monetary Policy

To understand monetary policy, we must look at one of the major economic institutions in this country—the **Federal Reserve System,** also known as the "Fed." The Federal Reserve Act of 1913 created the Federal Reserve System, consisting of twelve district banks, to which commercial banks could belong. The purpose of the system is to regulate the distribution of currency to member banks.

From the point of view of managing the national economy, the Federal Reserve System, particularly its **Federal Open Market Committee (FOMC),** attempts to "ride against the wind." When the economy is overheated and inflation is picking up, the Fed cuts back on the rate of growth of the money supply. This takes dollars out of circulation so that individuals and businesses choose to spend less because interest rates increase and make credit more expensive. Less demand pressure on suppliers of goods and services means that prices won't rise as much. When the economy is in the doldrums—a **recession**—the Fed will "prime the pump" by increasing the rate of growth of money in circulation; this fuels a desire to spend more on goods and services because interest rates fall and consumer and business credit becomes less expensive. Of course, if too much money is put into circulation, then inflationary pressures arise. Presidents often lambast the chairman of the Board of Governors of the Federal Reserve System for keeping too tight a rein on economic growth, but the response is predictable: If too much money is put in circulation, too much inflation will result.

Monetary Policy
Controlling the amount of currency in circulation and the availability of credit.

Fiscal Policy
The use of government spending and taxation policies to influence the level of economic activity, the rate of inflation, and economic growth.

Federal Reserve System
The public banking regulatory system that establishes the banking policies and influences the amount of credit available and currency in circulation. Determines the nation's general monetary and credit policies.

Federal Open Market Committee (FOMC)
A major policy-making unit in the Federal Reserve System that directs so-called open-market operations, where U.S. government bonds are bought and sold in order to carry out monetary policy directives.

Recession
The period during which overall economic activity has slowed down. A time when there is increased unemployment in the economy and increased business bankruptcies.

Paul Volcker, chairman of the Federal Reserve Board.

Incomes Policy

An attempt by government to reduce the rate of increase in prices and wages. Also known as *price controls*, where there is a cap put on the prices of specific goods and services throughout the country.

The Federal Reserve Board.

Full Employment Without Inflation: Incomes Policy

Starting in the 1960s, many government officials and economists believed it was possible to maintain full employment while preventing higher rates of inflation through application of an **incomes policy,** that is, putting a cap on wage and price increases. Incomes policy, or price controls, can be either voluntary or mandatory. During the Kennedy and Johnson administrations, government economic advisers counseled using voluntary wage and price "guideposts" to keep prices from rising.

On August 1, 1971, President Richard Nixon instituted the first mandatory wage and price freeze in American peacetime history. That freeze lasted for ninety days. Then, in varying phases over a several-year period, his administration "decontrolled" prices. For the most part, wage and price controls as an antiinflationary measure have been unpopular, even though at first the majority of businesspeople and economists favored the Nixon controls.

The Politics of Monetary Policy

Although the Federal Reserve Board is, in principle, completely independent of the president and Congress, in the past it has tended to act in a partisan way in dealing with inflation versus unemployment. In general, the boards under Republican administrations have been more concerned about controlling inflation than boards under Democratic administrations and consequently have followed "tighter" monetary policies. Significant exceptions to this generalization have occurred, however, especially with the administrations of Kennedy, Nixon, and Carter.

Fiscal Policy

Monetary policy is largely carried out by an independent Federal Reserve System. Fiscal policy is determined by Congress and the presidency and the interaction of those two institutions. Traditional fiscal policy is to lower taxes during times of

Highlight

▽

The "Misery Index"

Almost everybody is convinced that unemployment and high rates of inflation are social evils. A meaningful measure of economic discomfort might be obtained by combining these two together. The late Arthur Okun of the Brookings Institution and former chairman of the Council of Economic Advisers constructed such a discomfort index for the economy by combining the unemployment rate and the annual rate of change in consumer prices. Until the 1980s, the discomfort index grew dramatically, as can be seen in the data in the accompanying table. In 1965, the discomfort index was only 6.6 percent; the estimate for 1980 was a whopping 19.5 percent! In 1980, presidential candidate Ronald Reagan aptly called this the "misery index." Since 1980, the index has trended downward, mainly because of lower rates of inflation.

Okun's Index

Year	% Rate of Unemployment	Annual % Rate of Inflation	Discomfort Index
1965	4.5	2.1	6.6
1966	3.8	3.2	7.0
1967	3.8	3.3	7.1
1968	3.6	4.8	8.4
1969	3.5	6.1	9.6
1970	4.9	5.5	10.4
1971	5.9	3.4	9.3
1972	5.6	3.4	9.0
1973	4.9	8.8	13.7
1974	5.6	12.2	17.8
1975	8.5	7.0	15.5
1976	7.7	4.8	12.5
1977	7.0	6.8	13.8
1978	6.0	9.0	15.0
1979	5.8	13.3	19.1
1980	7.1	12.4	19.5
1981	7.5	8.9	17.4
1982	9.5	3.9	13.4
1983	9.5	3.8	13.3
1984	8.0	5.2	13.2
1985	7.3	3.9	11.2
1986	7.0	2.9	9.9

recession and to raise them during times of inflation. Alternatively, fiscal policy can include increasing government spending, generally by borrowing to increase total demand in the economy during times of recession and decreasing government spending during times of inflation. But fiscal policy can also include targeting specific industries or groups of individuals. For example, public works programs like the Civilian Conservation Corps (CCC) and the Works Progress Administration (WPA) during the Depression and the Comprehensive Employment and Training Act (CETA) in the 1970s were designed to use federal tax dollars directly to employ unemployed individuals.

The government formally took on the responsibility of reducing unemployment when it passed the Employment Act of 1946, which reads as follows:

> The Congress hereby declares that it is the continuing policy and responsibility of the Federal Government to use all practicable means consistent with its needs and obligations and other essential considerations of national policy, with assistance and cooperation of industry, agriculture, labor and State and local governments to coordinate and utilize all its plans, functions, and resources for the purpose of creating and maintaining, in a manner calculated to foster and promote free competitive enterprise and the general welfare, conditions under which there will be afforded useful employment opportunities, including self-employment, for those able, willing, and seeking to work and to promote maximum employment, production, and purchasing power.

Did You Know?

▽

That the first income tax law was passed in 1862 to support the Civil War but was eliminated in 1872 only to be brought back in 1913 by the Sixteenth Amendment to the Constitution, which made it permanent?

The effect of this legislation was to require the federal government to monitor the unemployment rate and the overall state of the economy.

Not surprisingly, debates over the size of federal government spending often center on the necessity of stimulating the economy during periods of recession.

Current Fiscal Policies

Current fiscal policies have run the range from specific programs designed to reduce unemployment in inner-city ghettos to broad attempts at stimulating the economy. For example, Reagan pushed through a tax rate reduction in 1981 that was designed to increase the incentive for workers to work more and for businesses to invest more. Part of the impetus for the sweeping Tax Reform Act of 1986, in which tax rates were lowered dramatically and many loopholes were eliminated, was to increase the rate of economic growth. This was done by simplifying personal and business life with respect to the tax code and by further increasing incentives for individuals to work harder because they would be able to take more income home by giving less money to the federal government.

Fiscal Policy and the Federal Budgeting Process

The preceding discussion of fiscal policy might give the impression that there is some overall, overriding policy that a single agency puts into effect for the benefit of the nation as a whole. But as we shall see, fiscal policy is multilayered and the federal budget process is complex because no single agency is responsible for such policy. The budget authority is divided between the president and Congress. Budget policy also serves many other goals besides attempting to provide for low inflation, low unemployment, and higher economic growth. Other goals that are faced by budget policy makers are national security and social equity, for example. Another goal is pure political ambition.

Actually, the national goals of full employment, price stability, and economic growth often carry very little weight in the real budgetary process within Congress. Tax and spending decisions are made in dozens of subcommittees dominated by interest groups and client politics—helping the folks back home. One former chairman of the Council of Economic Advisers, Herbert Stein, said, "The basic fact is that we have no long-run budget policy—no policy for the size of deficits and for the rate of growth of the public debt over a period of years."[1]

The Political Business Cycle and Monetary and Fiscal Policy

A number of researchers have noticed a correlation between presidential elections, monetary and fiscal policy, and rates of unemployment and inflation, which they call a political business cycle. The political business cycle also seems to exist in other countries, according to Edward Tufte, a political scientist from Yale University.[2]

[1]Herbert Stein, "After the Ball," *AEI Economist*, December, 1984, p. 2.

[2]See Edward Tufte, *Political Control of the Economy* (Princeton, N.J.: Princeton University Press, 1978).

Highlight

▽

The Great Depression, 1929–1941

On October 24, 1929, commonly called "Black Thursday," the New York Stock Exchange suffered through the first of a series of steep declines that made the nation and much of the world aware that a major economic catastrophe was in progress. From 1929 to 1933, the nation's unemployment rate shot up from 3.2 percent to an astronomical 25.2 percent, and income per person (in then current dollars) fell from $846 to $442. Public and private construction fell by nearly three-fourths, the business failure rate increased by 50 percent, and thousands of banks and hundreds of thousands of business firms closed by the time the Depression hit bottom in 1933.

In this climate of nearly total economic collapse, Republican President Herbert Hoover was voted out of office and replaced by the "New Deal" Democratic administration of Franklin Roosevelt. Roosevelt promised aid to farmers, public development of electric power, a balanced federal budget, and government regulation of private economic power, which many people blamed for causing the Depression. He temporarily closed the nation's banks to thwart depositors' panicky withdrawal of funds and implemented measures to economize on government spending. Under his prodding, Congress enacted a bold series of relief measures.

Congress passed legislation in 1933 to create the Federal Emergency Relief Administration, which gave money to state relief agencies; the Civilian Conservation Corps (CCC), which employed as many as 500,000 young men at a time in flood control and reforestation work; the Agricultural Adjustment Administration (AAA), which aimed to raise farm prices and farmers' incomes

Wall street during the stock market crash.

through farm commodity subsidies; the Public Works Administration (PWA) to encourage building and construction; the National Recovery Administration (NRA) to regulate labor and fair trade practices; the Tennessee Valley Authority (TVA) to provide flood control, energy, and regional planning for a large segment of lower-income Americans living in Appalachia; and the Securities and Exchange Commission (SEC) to regulate stock market practices. Other legislation established maximum hours of work, minimum wages, guarantees of labor-management collective bargaining, and abolition of child labor in interstate commerce.

In 1935, the Social Security Act was passed and the Works Progress Administration (WPA) was created. WPA em-

ployed more than two million workers and added billions of dollars to the economy.

Subsequent opposition from the Supreme Court and from conservative Republicans and many southern Democrats in Congress limited the effectiveness of these and other programs of Roosevelt's New Deal. The Depression and its direct economic and political consequences effectively ended by 1941, as the United States rebuilt its industrial base for a wartime economy. Clearly, however, many of the political and economic institutions of today, as well as the debate over their usefulness, can be traced to these events of the Great Depression and the political responses to that crisis.

The Theory of a Political Business Cycle

A theory of the political business cycle rests on two premises: (1) The electorate dislikes inflation and unemployment. (2) The electorate is myopic (short-sighted). Consequently, if an incumbent president follows the political business cycle, he should pursue restrictive monetary and fiscal policy *early* in his administration. The short-run effect of such restrictive monetary and fiscal policy is to raise the unemployment rate, but it will also help reduce the rate of inflation. About eighteen months before the next presidential election, the president should then switch to expansionary monetary and fiscal policy. On election day, in the best of all possible worlds under this political business cycle theory, the economy will be experiencing a low unemployment rate as a result of the short-run effects of the expansionary monetary and fiscal policies. It will also be experiencing less inflation because the economy will still be in a favorable position brought about by the previous restrictive monetary and fiscal policies. The full inflationary consequences of the expansionary policies which had started eighteen months before the election will not be felt until after the election.

The Evidence

The evidence is somewhat inconclusive about whether the political business cycle strategy is actually followed. Nonetheless, the presidential elections of 1956, 1964, 1972, and 1984 all had the basic pattern of unemployment and inflation predicted by the political business cycle, and the incumbents Eisenhower, Johnson, Nixon, and Reagan won by landslides. The elections of 1960, 1968, 1976, and 1980 did not have the political business cycle pattern and, as predicted, the White House changed hands in 1960 and 1968, and Ford and Carter lost.

The Budget Process

▽

One technical definition of a **budget** is given by Aaron Wildavsky: *the translation of financial resources into human purposes*. Certainly, the budgeting process that the individual family uses has little resemblance to the budget process of the federal government. Budget authority is divided between the president and Congress, and budget policy serves many goals. Let's briefly look at the complicated federal budget process (Figure 16–1).

Presidential Budgeting

Budget

The translation of financial resources into human purposes or, otherwise stated, a policy document that allocates taxes and government expenditures.

Fiscal Year

The twelve-month period that is used for bookkeeping, or accounting, purposes. Usually the fiscal year does not coincide with the calendar year. For example, the federal government's fiscal year runs from October 1st through September 30th.

The federal government operates on a **fiscal year** running from October through September, so that fiscal 1989, or FY89, runs from October 1, 1988, through September 30, 1989.[3] Eighteen months before a fiscal year starts, the executive branch begins preparing the budget. The Office of Management and Budget (OMB) receives advice from the Council of Economic Advisers (CEA) and the Treasury Department. OMB outlines the budget and then sends it to the various departments and agencies. Bargaining follows, in which, to use only two of many examples, the Department of Health and Human Services argues for more welfare spending

[3]Note that state and municipal budgets can have different fiscal years.

and the armed forces argue for more defense spending. The OMB in principle is supposed to be a fiscally conservative force.

OMB's Spring and Fall Preview

Even though OMB has only six hundred employees, it is known as one of the most powerful agencies in Washington. It assembles the budget documents and monitors the agencies throughout each year. Every year, it begins the budget process with a **spring preview,** in which it requires all of the agencies to review their programs, activities, and goals. At the beginning of each summer, the director of OMB sends out a letter instructing agencies to submit their requests for funding for the next fiscal year. By the end of the summer, each agency must submit a formal request to OMB.

In actuality, the "budget season" begins with the **fall review.** At this time, OMB looks at budget requests and in almost all cases routinely cuts them back. Although OMB works within guidelines established by the president, specific decisions are often left to the director and his associates. By the beginning of November, the director's review begins. He meets with cabinet secretaries and budget officers. Time becomes crucial. The budget must be completed by January to go to the printer to be included in the *Economic Report of the President.*

What the President Does

The budget is submitted to the Congress in the president's name. Although presidents are not involved in all of the complexities of the budgeting process, through-

Spring Preview

The beginning phase of the budgeting process for the federal government, occurring in the spring and during which all of the executive agencies are required to review their programs, goals, and activities.

Fall Review

The second phase of the budgeting process, occurring in the fall when the Office of Management and Budget examines each executive agency's budget request that was formulated during the summer.

Figure 16–1
▽
The Budget Cycle

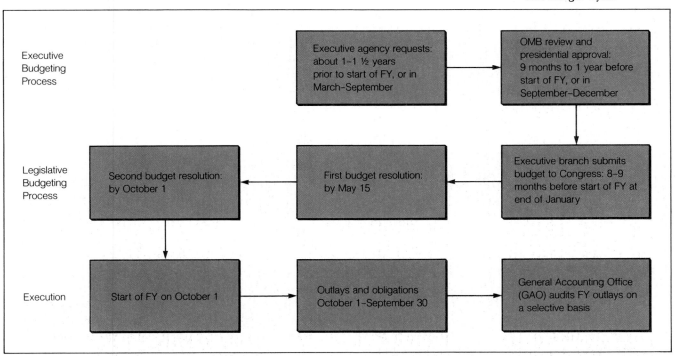

out this budgeting phase, the president is bombarded by requests from various agencies and interest groups, all wishing to increase spending. Every pressure group and every agency starts the budgeting year with high expectations. Simply owing to limited resources, the president has to disappoint many individuals and groups.

If the president has little concern about what is actually happening with the budget, the director of the OMB and his associates, as well as senior White House staff members, typically fill in the power vacuum. Some presidents have taken an active part in reducing government spending by requesting a **deferral,** which is a proposal that funds not be spent that year, or a **rescission,** which is a proposal that funds be given back to the Treasury. Unless Congress passes a motion against, deferrals are automatically accepted. Rescissions, on the other hand, require congressional approval.

One power that the president has is his ability to veto **appropriations bills.** Budget resolutions create spending authority, but only become binding on the congressional committees that create the spending authority through appropriations bills. Such bills can be vetoed by the president.

The press is fond of talking about "the president's budget." The buck, of course, stops at his desk. But all of the agencies and the OMB and the White House staff have an impact on the budget. Another impact comes from so-called uncontrollable expenses, such as mandatory entitlement programs such as Social Security. Finally, the state of the economy may affect the budget in ways that the president and his staff have no way of changing or predicting.

Congressional Budgeting

In January, nine months before the fiscal year starts, the president takes whatever OMB has finally come up with and submits it to Congress. Then the congressional budgeting process takes over. Congressional committees and subcommittees look at the proposals from the executive branch. The Congressional Budget Office (CBO) advises the different committees on economic matters, just as the OMB and the CEA advise the president. The **first budget resolution** by Congress is supposed to be passed in May. It sets overall revenue goals and spending targets and, by definition, the size of the deficit (or surplus, if that were ever to occur again).

During the summer, bargaining among all the parties involved takes place. Spending and tax laws that are drawn up during this period are supposed to be guided by the May congressional budget resolution. By September, Congress is supposed to pass its **second budget resolution,** one that will set "binding" limits on taxes and spending for the fiscal year beginning October 1. Bills passed before that date that do not fit within the limits of the budget resolution are supposed to be changed.

In actuality Congress has not passed a complete budget by October 1 since 1978. Congress does not follow its own rules. Budget resolutions are passed late, and when they are passed they are not treated as binding. Since 1978, each fiscal year has started without a budget. Every agency then operates on the basis of **continuing resolutions,** which enable the agencies to keep on doing whatever they were doing the previous year with the same amount of funding. Even continuing resolutions have not always been passed on time. Federal workers have had to be sent home until money was appropriated to pay them (see Highlight).

Deferral

A request by the president to defer the spending of funds during a specific fiscal year.

Rescission

A proposal by the president that funds be given back to the Treasury.

Appropriations Bills

Bills granting an agency the permission to spend funds that have already been authorized in specific amounts for specific purposes.

First Budget Resolution

A resolution passed by Congress in May setting overall revenue and spending goals and, hence, by definition, the size of the deficit for the following fiscal year.

Second Budget Resolution

A resolution passed by Congress in September which sets "binding" limits on taxes and spending for the next fiscal year beginning October 1st.

Continuing Resolutions

Temporary laws that Congress passes when various appropriations bills have not been decided by the beginning of the new fiscal year on October 1st.

The Five Decision Categories in Congressional Budget Making

We can break down congressional budget making into five decision categories. They are as follows:

1. Total budget: The House and Senate, through their respective budget committees, pass a *concurrent budget resolution*. A concurrent budget resolution does not need the signature of the president. Such a resolution does not create spending authority, however.

2. Authorizations: These are the legislative authority for each program. Authorizations must be passed before money can be appropriated. Authorizing committees in Congress report authorizations.

3. Appropriations: Through appropriations, Congress creates the spending authority allowing the government to operate. The House and Senate Appropriations Committees (and their specialized subcommittees), exercise the "power of the purse." (The congressionally approved budget is actually thirteen separate appropriations bills.)

4. Revenues: The Senate Finance Committee and the House Ways and Means Committee write tax legislation. Tax bills are considered separately from spending legislation.

5. Oversight and review: The General Accounting Office (GAO) and the Congressional Budget Office (CBO), along with the appropriations and authorization committees in Congress, monitor the way money is spent each year.

Supplemental Appropriations

The budget process does not stop simply because the budget has been passed. **Supplemental appropriations** are made for additional programs throughout the year. Sometimes these are programs created in response to new emergencies. Table 16–1 shows a sample of the larger items in the FY86 Supplemental Appropriation bill which added $9.7 billion in new budget authority. The president and Congress end up modifying the budget so much before and during the fiscal year that what actually occurs has little to do with what was proposed.

Supplemental Appropriations
Those appropriations authorized by Congress after the total budget has been passed. They can occur any time throughout the fiscal year.

▽
529

Table 16–1
▽

Highlights of the 1986 Supplemental Appropriations Bill

Commodity Credit Corporation	$5.3 billion
Embassy Security	$702 million
NASA	$531 million
IRS	$340 million
VA compensation & pensions	$272 million
Disaster Relief	$250 million
Forest Firefighting	$165 million
Philippine Aid	$150 million
Student Aid Pell Grants	$146 million

SOURCE: *Congressional Quarterly Weekly Report*, July 5, 1986, p. 1550.

Nonpolitical Budgeting: The Uncontrollables

Uncontrollables

The spending that Congress, in principle, cannot control unless it changes an entire program.

Entitlements

Programs providing benefits to individuals who have an established legal right to them, e.g., Medicare, Medicaid, and Social Security. Entitlements are sometimes classified as synonymous with uncontrollables.

Depending on which estimate you use, at least half, if not more, of the federal budget consists of **uncontrollables,** that is, spending items that Congress cannot control unless it is willing to change entire programs. Uncontrollables are also sometimes called **entitlements**—programs that provide benefits to individuals who have an established legal right to them. They include Medicare, Medicaid, Social Security, government employee and military personnel pensions, veterans' benefits, and interest on the public debt. To a lesser degree, welfare and food stamp programs, as well as unemployment benefits, are considered entitlements. They are uncontrollable to the extent that they depend on external factors, such as the level of economic activity in the nation, which determines the amount of employment and unemployment. Entitlements affect about 30 percent of all Americans—three out of every ten Americans get benefits from the government.[4]

If we add all uncontrollables plus all of defense spending, what is left that is "controllable" is only about 9 percent of the total federal budget. That is really most of the budget that Congress and the president have to work with.

Our Federal Tax System
▽

The budgeting process is complex and goes on all the time. So too is the process by which revenues are raised in order for the federal government to be able to spend as it chooses. Now is a particularly appropriate time to examine the system of taxation at the federal level, since the passage of the Tax Reform Act of 1986 represents the first complete major overhaul of the system since 1954. Let us first take a look at the types of taxes and their importance in our federal tax system.

The Types of Taxes

Off-budget Items

Expenditures undertaken by the federal government that do not directly appear on the federal government's official budget.

Backdoor Funding

The sum total of federal government expenditures undertaken by using contract, loan guarantee, and borrowing authority.

As you can see in Figure 16–2, personal income taxes are the most important category of revenue raisers for the federal government, accounting for 43 percent

[4]See United States Census Bureau, *Survey of Income and Program Participation*, published quarterly.

Congress grants two kinds of spending authority—legislative and budget. The legislative authority that Congress gives an executive agency is permission to go ahead and do something, and it often sets a ceiling on the amount of money that can be spent. Budget authority, on the other hand, authorizes the *actual* money, and it normally requires an appropriation.

There are three other ways for Congress to grant budget authority, as follows:

1. Contract authority. An authorization committee proposes legislation giving an executive agency the authority to contract with private firms or state governments. Once a contract has been made, the Appropriations Committee cannot deny the money needed to pay off the contract.

2. Loan guarantee authority. Such authority has been legislated for student loans, the Chrysler Corporation, the city of New York, and Lockheed Corporation among others. Small Business Administration loans are also included under this authority.

3. Borrowing authority. Federal loans have increased at a dramatic rate since 1970. These are often called **off-budget items,** the largest one being the Federal Financing Bank, which cur-rently has a total of more than $130 billion in loans outstanding. It is the second largest "bank" in the United States, making loans to other government agencies, such as the Rural Telephone Bank and the United States Railway Association.

Contract, loan guarantee, and borrowing authority are known collectively as **backdoor funding.** Loan guarantees to students alone amounted to more than $40 billion in 1986. That's a backdoor that has been open quite frequently.

of all revenues obtained. This was not always the case. For example, in 1927, they accounted for less than 26 percent of all federal revenues.

Second in importance is Social Security, and third is the corporate income tax. Corporations are generally taxed on the difference between their total revenues, or receipts, and their expenses. Other taxes, which today represent less than 8 percent of federal revenues, are state taxes, sale and excise taxes, and taxes on imported goods.

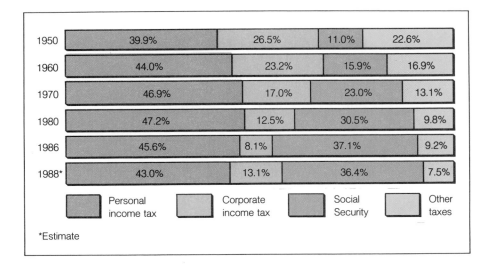

*Estimate

Figure 16-2
▽
Where Uncle Sam Gets His Money
Estimated figures for FY 1988 show that the personal income tax provides more than 43 percent of federal revenues, with Social Security taxes following at 36 percent. The corporate income tax, however, generates only little more than 13 percent of federal revenues.

SOURCE: *Statistical Abstract of the United States, 1986 and authors' estimates.*

Proportional Tax System

A system of taxation in which the same percentage of income is paid by everyone on every dollar that is taxed. Also called a *flat rate* tax system.

Progressive Tax System

A system of taxes in which the higher the income, the larger is the percentage of income paid on taxes.

Tax Bracket

A specified interval of income to which a specific and unique tax rate is applied. In a progressive taxation system, the higher the tax bracket, the greater the tax rate applied to that higher tax bracket.

Regressive Taxation

A system of taxes in which the higher the income, the smaller is the percentage of income paid as taxes.

Horizontal Equity

Equity that exists when those with equal paying abilities pay the same amount of tax regardless of how it was earned or who earned it.

Vertical Equity

Equity that exists when those with a greater ability to pay bear a heavier tax burden than those with a smaller ability to pay; in other words, unequals are treated unequally.

What Is a Fair Type of Tax System?

Philosophers, politicians, economists, political scientists, and concerned laypersons have debated the fairness of different types of tax systems from time immemorial. There is no way to tax that can satisfy everyone. Should the rich be taxed more than the poor? If the answer is yes, should they be taxed more than in proportion to their relative income differences than the poor? Although we cannot answer these questions, we can establish a framework for a discussion of them. First we look at proportional, progressive, and regressive taxation, then examine horizontal versus vertical equity, and finally examine several different principles of imposing a "fair" tax.

Three Types of Taxation

A **proportional tax system** simply means that as an individual's income goes up, so too do his or her taxes in *exactly* the same proportion. If, for example, we have a flat rate tax of 20 percent, then all income, whether it be $100 or $100 million, is taxed at 20 percent.

Under a **progressive taxation system,** as an individual's income increases, the percentage of income paid in taxes increases. For example, the first $100 might be taxed at 10 percent, but the second $100 at 20 percent, and the third $100 at 30 percent. As the individual moves into a higher **tax bracket,** the rate paid on the income earned in that bracket is higher than that paid in the previous bracket.

Regressive taxation is the opposite of progressive taxation. As income increases, a smaller and smaller percentage is taken away in taxes. To use the same example, the first $100 might be taxed at 30 percent, the second at 20 percent, and third at only 10 percent.

In the United States, we currently have a progressive tax system in which, subject to many qualifications, individuals are faced with a tax rate of 15 percent up to a certain income level, which varies depending on marital status, and rises to 28 percent above that.[5]

Horizontal Versus Vertical Equity

Consider a person who works at a regular job 37.5 hours a week and makes an annual salary of $20,000. Consider another person who doesn't work for wages, but rather is a stock market trader who at the end of the year has made trading profits of $20,000. If we impose the rule of **horizontal equity**, the tax law should treat the $20,000 earned by the salaried worker the same way it treats the $20,000 of trading profits earned by the stock trader. In other words, the rule of horizontal equity dictates that equal incomes should be taxed equally.

The concept, or rule, of **vertical equity** deals with unequals. Unequals should be treated unequally, meaning that people who make lots of income should not be taxed in the same manner as those who make very little income. Even if we accept the rule of vertical equity, an operational issue still remains: How should unequals be treated? The two most popular theories consistent with vertical equity are that taxes should be based on each individual's ability to pay and that taxes should be based on each individual's benefits received from government activities.

[5]Actually, there is a third tax rate of 33 percent that applies to those individuals making relatively high incomes. It is disguised in the form of surtaxes and reductions in personal exemptions on which no tax previously was paid.

Ability-to-Pay Principle

The taxing principle that states that individuals should pay taxes according to their ability to pay has been popular for at least several thousand years. This principle of taxation may be simple to state, but it is certainly not easy to put into effect. We all agree that an individual who earns $20,000 per year is better able to pay taxes than an individual who earns only $2,000 per year. A serious question remains: How much greater is the first person's ability to pay than the second person's ability to pay? No one has yet come up with a functionally meaningful way of measuring ability to pay.

Benefits-Received Principle

According to this principle, individuals should be taxed in proportion to the benefits they receive from government services. Those who receive numerous benefits should pay more than those who receive few services. For example, individuals who drive frequently on toll roads are charged according to use. This is a situation in which it is relatively easy to collect money based on benefits received. On the other hand, in many situations it is much cheaper to collect through taxes. For example, the gasoline tax collected by the federal government is based on the benefits-received principle. Those who use roads and highways more presumably purchase more gas. Clearly, this is an imperfect method of applying the benefits-received principle of taxation, but it seems to be preferable to any other.

IRS checks.

Tax Reform

President Reagan came into office with a pledge to pull the country out of its economic doldrums by increasing incentives for individuals to work and to invest. In 1981, Congress approved the president's program for a reduction in tax rates. In 1986, in part as a continuation of Reagan's push for lower tax rates, virtually the entire tax code of the federal government was rewritten. Some of the basic changes were as follows:

1. A simplification of the tax tables for individuals, from one with fourteen separate rates depending on income to one with two rates, as mentioned earlier
2. An increase in the base level of income below which individuals pay no taxes
3. The elimination of many deductions, such as interest paid on consumer loans
4. The elimination of the special lower rate applied to long-term profits (called capital gains) derived from the sale of stocks and bonds and other assets held for more than six months
5. A reduction in the top corporate tax rate from 46 percent to 34 percent
6. The elimination of certain tax benefits that businesses were able to take before, such as the investment tax credit.

Although there is no question that many individuals will benefit from the Tax Reform Act of 1986, tax reform by its very nature helps some people while it hurts others. Indeed, tax reform involves political decisions at all levels.

The Politics of Tax Reform

Tax reform raises basic value questions and centers on the moral issue of fairness. All tax laws, just as any legislation, reflect the values we hold and that as a nation we try to promote. Consider a simple example. Family taxpayers were able to deduct $1,080 for every dependent; the Tax Reform Act of 1986 increased that deduction to $2,000. What is the message of this decision? It is implicitly indicating that children are desirable and that American society should bear part (albeit a small part) of the cost of raising children.

We can similarly examine just about every provision of the tax code. The debate that was carried on before the Tax Reform Act of 1986 was and will continue to be a debate on the relative importance of different values. We pointed out that the new tax code eliminates the lower tax rates applied to long-term capital gains. Policy makers in the past were implicitly indicating that the contribution to society made by investors had a higher value than contributions made by hourly wage earners. The tax code allows state and local income and property taxes to be deducted from income before federal income taxes are assessed. This implicitly favors more government activity at the state and local levels. The elimination of the deduction of interest payments for consumer credit is a statement that we wish to see less of a credit society than we have in the past.

The Players in the Tax Reform Debate

Many players contributed to the latest tax reform debate. They included President Ronald Reagan and a number of legislators. Senator Bill Bradley (D.-New Jersey) initiated the current generation of tax reform legislation and chaired the Senate

President Reagan signing the 1986 Tax Reform Bill.

Democratic Task Force on Tax Reform. Senator Robert Packwood (R.-Oregon), as chairman of the Senate Finance Committee, presided over the creation of the committee's tax reform bill. His counterpart in the House was Representative Daniel Rostenkowski (D.-Illinois), chairman of the House of Representatives Ways and Means Committee, which drafted its version of the tax reform bill. Representative Jack R. Kemp (R.-New York) popularized the idea of cutting taxes to promote greater economic growth.

There were, of course, many other players, including economists, political scientists, legal scholars, and concerned citizens, who voiced their opinions in letters and in debates.

The Basic Question of Fairness

Look at Figure 16–3, which gives the results of a 1985 public opinion poll on how fair taxes have been. Of those queried, 69 percent believed that middle-income families were paying too much in income taxes; 59 percent felt that those who earned all their income from salary or wages were paying too much; and 57 percent felt that lower-income families were paying too much. Quite clearly, Americans on average have not believed that the tax system has been fair. One of the basic noneconomic, nongrowth-oriented results of the Tax Reform Act of 1986 is a fairer tax system. The old tax system allowed some taxpayers to manipulate it and to significantly reduce their income tax. This was especially evident among upper-income taxpayers who had the greatest latitude for such tax planning. For example, Internal Revenue Service statistics for 1982 showed that large numbers of individuals with incomes in excess of $200,000 were paying less than 15 percent of their income in taxes, whereas some individuals making the same amount of money were paying more than twice that amount in income taxes. This would seem to

Figure 16–3

▽

Are Taxes Fair?

SOURCE: Survey by the Roper Organization (Roper Report 85–2), January 5–19, 1985. From *Public Opinion*, February/March 1985, p. 23; reprinted with permission of the American Enterprise Institute.

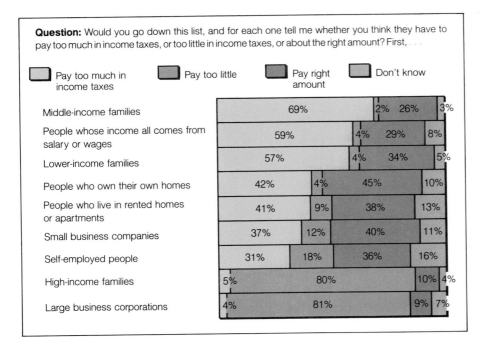

Question: Would you go down this list, and for each one tell me whether you think they have to pay too much in income taxes, or too little in income taxes, or about the right amount? First, . . .

Pay too much in income taxes | Pay too little | Pay right amount | Don't know

	Pay too much	Pay too little	Pay right amount	Don't know
Middle-income families	69%	2%	26%	3%
People whose income all comes from salary or wages	59%	4%	29%	8%
Lower-income families	57%	4%	34%	5%
People who own their own homes	42%	4%	45%	10%
People who live in rented homes or apartments	41%	9%	38%	13%
Small business companies	37%	12%	40%	11%
Self-employed people	31%	18%	36%	16%
High-income families	5%	80%	10%	4%
Large business corporations	4%	81%	9%	7%

be an indication of an unfair system. In fact, the system violated both horizontal equity and vertical equity, because some upper-income persons were paying little or no taxes, whereas lower and middle-income persons were paying a significant share of their incomes in taxes.

Many observers believe that one of the greatest impacts of tax reform is an increased support for the constitutional system in America. Inequality in taxation has promoted the belief that government itself is unfair and less deserving of allegiance. The newest federal tax system provides for both greater horizontal and greater vertical equity. If Congress does not significantly alter the new tax system by continually adding changes that benefit only special interest groups, then perhaps we will see increased support for our government's leaders.

When Spending Exceeds Revenues: The Public Debt
▽

Every time the federal government appropriates and spends more in total in a year than it collects in revenues from taxes and other sources, it runs a **budget deficit.** To pay for the budget deficit, it issues debt instruments in the form of **U.S. Treasury bonds.** The sale of these bonds to private individuals, corporations, pension plans, foreign governments, foreign businesses, and foreign individuals creates additions to the public, or national, debt.

Table 16–2 shows what has happened to the public debt over time. That table, however, is misleading. It does not take two important variables into account: inflation and increases in population. Look at Figure 16–4. Here we show the per capita public debt of the United States corrected for inflation. As you can see, it reached its peak during World War II and fell steadily until the mid-1970s. What has happened since then is, of course, the real issue of concern to politicians and the public alike.

Is the Public Debt a Burden?

We often hear talk about the burden of the public debt. Some argue that the government is eventually going to go bankrupt, but that, of course, cannot be the case. As long as the government has the taxing ability to pay for interest payments on the public debt, it will never go bankrupt. What happens is that when Treasury bonds come due, they are simply "rolled over." That is to say, if a $1 million Treasury bill comes due today, the U.S. Treasury pays it off and reissues another $1 million bond.

What about the interest payments? Interest payments are paid by taxes, so what we are really talking about is taxing some people to pay interest to others who loan money to the government. This cannot really be called a burden to all of society. There is one hitch, however. Not all of our interest payments are paid to Americans. An increasing amount is paid to foreigners, because foreigners own almost 20 percent of the public debt. So it is no longer true that we "owe it all to ourselves."

Consider another factor that is extremely important. Even though we are paying interest payments to ourselves, for the most part, the more that the federal government borrows, the greater the percentage of the federal budget that is committed to interest payments. The ever-increasing portion of the budget committed to interest payments reduces the federal government's ability to purchase public goods in the future, such as more parks. Indeed, if you wish to do a simple projection

Budget Deficit

The difference between what the government collects from taxes and other sources and what the government spends.

U.S. Treasury Bonds

Securities that are evidence of debt that the federal government owes to those who paid for such securities.

Table 16–2
▽
**Gross Public Debt
of the Federal Government**

Year	Total (billions of current dollars)
1935	28.7
1940	43.0
1945	258.7
1950	257.4
1955	274.4
1960	286.3
1965	317.3
1970	370.9
1975	544.1
1976	631.9
1977	709.1
1978	780.4
1979	833.8
1980	914.3
1983	1,382.0
1986	2,011.6

SOURCE: U.S. Office of Management and Budget.

Highlight

▽

Republicans: Fiscal Conservatives?

From 1929 through 1987, the U.S. Government has had only 13 budget surpluses totaling $67.1 billion and thirty-seven deficits totaling $1.567 trillion. An interesting question revolves around whether Democratic or Republican administrations run higher deficits. Typically, Republicans are known as fiscal conservatives. Consequently, we would expect Republican administrations to run fewer and lower federal budget deficits than Democratic administrations. Such is not the case. In terms of surpluses and deficits, the Hoover, Eisenhower, Nixon, Ford, and Reagan administrations (through

FY87) have had four surpluses and twenty-one deficits. Democrats Roosevelt, Truman, Kennedy, Johnson, and Carter produced five surpluses and twenty-seven deficits.

The real test, though, is in the *cumulative* budget deficits over each president's term, expressed as a *proportion* of total output of goods and services. The accompanying table shows that the average cumulative budget deficit as a proportion of total national output of goods and services since Hoover. If we eliminate the World War II years of Roosevelt, who do you call a fiscal conservative?

Cumulative Budget Deficits as a Proportion of Total National Output of Goods and Services

HOOVER (R)	1.7%
ROOSEVELT (D)	14.0
TRUMAN (D)	.2
EISENHOWER (R)	.5
KENNEDY (D)	1.1
JOHNSON (D)	.9
NIXON (R)	1.2
FORD (R)	3.6
CARTER (D)	2.1
REAGAN (R)	4.4
(through FY 1987)	

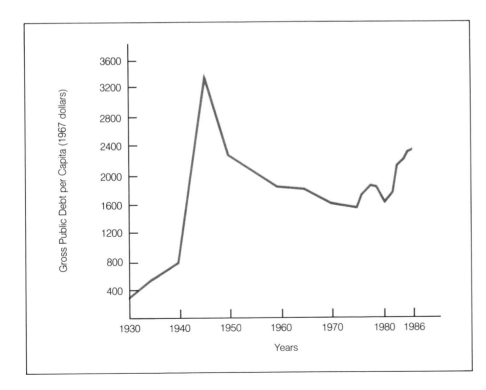

Figure 16–4

▽

Per Capita Public Debt of the United States in Constant 1967 Dollars

The public debt jumped during World War II, has fallen since then by more than one-third, and has recently started to rise.

SOURCE: U.S. Department of the Treasury.

Chapter 16
Political
Economy
▽
537

Is The Budget Deficit a Red Herring?

The federal government has been operating in the red for sixteen years. Federal budget deficits have become a way of life, but recently they have increased at what appears to be an alarming rate. Citizens and politicians alike are concerned. According to some analysts, however, the size of the budget deficit is simply a red herring—it is beside the point. The real point at issue is the size of government, not how it is financed.

How We Finance Government

There are basically three ways to finance government expenditures: (1) taxing, (2) borrowing, and (3) creating money.

1. Taxation is a tried and true method of government finance that few Americans have difficulty understanding. A tax is very clearly a transfer of control over income from the individual to the government. What you pay in taxes, you obviously cannot spend yourself.
2. Borrowing is the second most important method of government finance. The Treasury sells a bond to the public (or to foreigners or their governments). Treasury borrowings occur whenever there are deficits. When an investor decides to purchase one of the newly issued Treasury bonds—decides to loan money to the federal government—that private investor is by necessity *not* loaning money to a private corporation. Consequently, whenever there is a deficit and the federal government borrows money from the private sector, the private sector, in a roundabout way, is giving up resources to the government sector.
3. Sometimes the federal government pays for the goods and services it buys by creating money.* When the government creates money, there are more dollars in circulation chasing a limited supply of goods. The result is inflation (although this is certainly not the only cause of inflation).

*It does so in a rather indirect manner. The Treasury sells government bonds to pay for the deficit, and the Federal Reserve System purchases some of those government bonds in the open market. The Federal Reserve, however, purchases the bonds by creating money, that is, paying for U.S. Treasury bonds that it purchases in the open market by, in essence, writing a check on itself. The proceeds from that check are used in the economy to purchase real goods and services, but the Fed never actually had any funds to cover the check. It has the ability to "write up" reserve accounts. This is the meaning of "money creation" by the Fed. Money creation does not, as is commonly thought, occur when the U.S. Treasury prints more $1 and $5 bills that the public uses as cash.

Ultimately There Is a Trade-off

The end result of all three types of financing is always the same—the government sector controls and uses more resources and the private sector uses fewer resources. Therefore, according to critics of the deficit dilemma, the real issue is not the size of the *deficit*, but rather the size of the *government*. If total government spending is, say, 35 percent of all spending (gross national product, or GNP), then what does it matter how that government spending was financed? After all, does the private sector really care how the government sector took control of resources? Is not the true issue the trade-off between government spending and private spending, the proportion of total spending that is left over for the private sector after the government takes its "fair share"? Conservative political scientists, historians, economists, and government watchers often answer yes to those questions. Conservative economist Milton Friedman, for example, has pointed out in many of his popular writings that the federal government deficit is indeed a red herring. He nonetheless favors a balanced budget amendment to the U.S. Constitution because he believes that forcing the federal government to raise taxes to equal federal government outlays exactly would give better information to the paying public. In other words, if the federal government is going to use a third of GNP, Friedman would like taxpayers to know that fact of life directly. Taxpayers would pay one-third of all of their income in taxes in total rather than having the government fool them by letting them pay several hundred billion dollars less in taxes directly and either taking away from the private sector by crowding out private investment (borrowing) or by increasing the rate of inflation through money creation.

The Long Road to a Balanced Budget: Gramm-Rudman

Balancing the budget has been a priority item in political debate for many years. Although waning in importance now, a movement has been afoot to have a constitutional convention to draft a balanced budget amendment to the U.S. Constitution. Two-thirds of the state legislatures need to petition the Congress for a convention to be called. To date, the required thirty-four legislative petitions have not been filed.

Perhaps as an alternative to a constitutional amendment for balancing the budget, in December, 1985 Congress passed the Gramm-Rudman-Hollings Act, also called the Balanced Budget and Emergency Deficit Control Act of 1985. Its goal was no less than a balanced budget by FY91. Figure 16–5 shows the deficit goals. As can be seen, the impact of Gramm-Rudman, as it is commonly called, is supposed to grow as the decade progresses. In the beginning of 1986, it was estimated that budget cuts of at least $54 billion were needed to meet Gramm-Rudman's mandate that the 1987 def-icit not exceed $144 billion. According to Gramm-Rudman, if Congress doesn't meet the targets, the **sequestration process** must start on August 15 when the Congressional Budget Office and the Office of Management and Budget estimate the amount that must be cut to bring the next fiscal year budget in compliance with the law. By October 15, a final list of automatic cuts is to go out, unless Congress has acted to bring the projected budget deficit within $10 billion of the specified goal.

of current trends into the future, some time in the next century the federal government will be spending almost 100 percent of its budget on interest payments! This, of course, will not occur, but it highlights the problem of running larger and larger deficits and borrowing more and more money to cover them.

The Problem of "Crowding Out"

Although it may be true that we owe the public debt to ourselves (except for what is owed to foreigners), there is another issue involved in having a large public debt that is made up of a series of annual federal government budget deficits. Each time the federal government runs a deficit, we know that it must go into the financial marketplace and borrow the money. This is the process during which the U.S. Treasury sells U.S. Treasury bonds. It is called public debt financing. Public debt financing in effect "crowds out" private borrowing. Consider that to borrow, say, $200 billion, the federal government must bid for lendable funds in the marketplace just like any business does. It bids for these lendable funds by offering to pay higher interest rates. Consequently, interest rates are increased when the federal government runs large deficits and goes out to borrow money to cover them. Higher interest rates can stifle or slow business investment, which reduces the rate of economic growth.

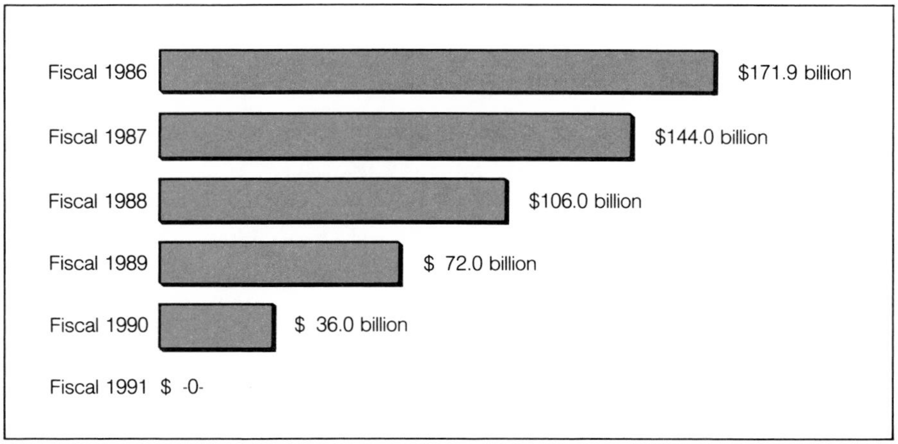

Sequestration Process
The process by which spending cuts are imposed on different aspects of the federal government budget in order to meet specific deficit reduction goals as mandated by the Gramm-Rudman-Hollings Act of 1985.

Figure 16–5
▽
Gramm-Rudman-Hollings Act
Deficit Reduction Requirements

Fiscal 1986	$171.9 billion
Fiscal 1987	$144.0 billion
Fiscal 1988	$106.0 billion
Fiscal 1989	$ 72.0 billion
Fiscal 1990	$ 36.0 billion
Fiscal 1991	$ -0-

Profile
▽
William Philip Gramm

"I get in battles to win because I think the battles are important. The people of Texas . . . elected me to win. And I do that."

Philip Gramm was born on July 8, 1942, at Fort Benning, Georgia, the son of Sergeant and Mrs. Kenneth Gramm. He received a B.A. degree in business administration in 1964 and the Ph.D. degree in economics in 1967 from the University of Georgia. From 1967 to 1978, he taught economics at Texas A&M University. He has written extensively on issues of economics and energy policy.

Gramm unsuccessfully sought the Democratic nomination for U.S. senator from Texas in 1976. Presenting himself as a conservative alternative to Senator Lloyd Bentsen, Gramm failed in his initial bid for national office principally because he was relatively unknown and not very well financed. He was elected as a Democrat to the U.S. House of Representatives in 1978 and was reelected to the House in 1980 and 1982, although he had to survive a strong primary challenge in 1982 from Jack Teague, who charged Gramm with abandoning the Democratic party's commitment to the underprivileged and the middle class.

While a member of the House, Gramm offended his fellow Democrats, not only by his strong support for the Reagan administration's fiscal and social policies, but also by his assertive, self-confident style. He was coauthor, together with Republican Representative Delbert L. Latta of Ohio, of the so-called Gramm-Latta budget resolution, which was adopted by the House on May 7, 1981. In fact, it was Gramm who brought the Reagan budget to the floor of the House in 1981. Later that same year, he and Latta again teamed up on the Gramm-Latta II Omnibus Reconciliation Act, which changed existing law to reduce the level of expenditures for 250 federal government programs, mandated the administration's proposed tax cut, and implemented the administration's economic recovery program. Gramm-Latta II was designed as a nominally bipartisan measure to trump the House Democratic leadership's proposed $37 billion in specific spending cuts worked out through the House Budget Committee.

Gramm resigned from the House early in 1983 after being denied his seat on the House Budget Committee because of his work with the Reagan administration and with conservative Republicans in the House during his previous term. Gramm was reelected in a special election on February 12, 1983, as the first Republican ever elected from the Sixth Congressional District of Texas. In 1984, Gramm handily defeated Democrat Lloyd Doggett to win a U.S. Senate seat. Gramm has been and continues to be a controversial force within the federal government.

Testing the Constitutionality of Gramm-Rudman

Representative Mike Synar (D.-Okla.), a member of the House-Senate Conference Committee on the Gramm-Rudman-Hollings Act, wrote in a provision that allows members of Congress to challenge the act in court. Once the act was passed, he immediately put this provision into use. Synar and eleven other members of Congress joined suit claiming that the law violates the Constitution's principle of separation of powers. The court combined Synar's case with an action brought by the National Treasury Employees Union challenging a provision of the law that suspended a January 1, 1986, cost-of-living payment for retired federal workers. The Synar-NTEU suit challenged the roles assigned to the General Administration Office, the Congressional Budget Office, and the Office of Management and

Budget. Gramm-Rudman instructs the CBO and the OMB jointly to determine whether the deficit in any given year is likely to be higher than permitted. When it is, the comptroller general who directs the GAO, must prepare a list of spending cuts—half from defense and half from nondefense items. These cuts must then be implemented by the president. The comptroller general is a servant of Congress, so the issue is whether an employee of Congress can mandate presidential actions.

A lower federal court agreed that the American system of checks and balances does *not* allow government agencies independent of political accountability. The case was brought to the Supreme Court, which ruled that the key deficit-reduction provision of the Gramm-Rudman law was unconstitutional.[6] The court ruled 7–2 that the law's automatic deficit-reduction mechanism improperly empowered the comptroller-general—an officer of Congress—to make the cuts needed to meet the act's spending limits. The Supreme Court's decision did not, however, invalidate the entire act. Rather, it left it up to Congress itself to make the cuts necessary to meet the Gramm-Rudman provisions. The task could no longer be assigned to a non-elected official.

Congress Reacts

Congress reacted accordingly. On July 17, 1986, it reaffirmed $11.7 billion in spending cuts for the 1986 fiscal year that had been made under the Gramm-Rudman law in March, but had been declared unconstitutional. The vote was considered a first test of congressional resolve to live within the law's deficit-cutting guidelines. The cuts that were approved amounted to 4.9 percent in defense program reductions and 4.3 percent in domestic cuts. A few cost-of-living increases in federal pensions and some other programs were canceled.

We must note, however, that what Congress did in an attempt to get within $10 billion of the required $144 billion Gramm-Rudman-Hollings deficit requirement was mainly window-dressing. It sold some government assets and changed accounting rules to make the final budget look "right." By the middle of October, 1986, it still hadn't passed a final *total* budget, but a $576 billion omnibus spending bill signed by President Reagan had health, science, education, and law-enforcement areas receiving large increases that more than restored the cuts mandated by the Gramm-Rudman deficit reduction law. Prospects at that time were not rosy for the ability of Congress to meet the following fiscal year's Gramm-Rudman deficit reduction cuts. It was estimated that Congress would have to cut spending by more than $50 billion in the following fiscal year to do so. No one at that time had much hope for such a draconian spending reduction.

[6]Bowsher v. Synar, 92 L.Ed.2nd. 583 (1986).

In this chapter, we have talked about the federal budgetary process as a complex system that involves many players. The ultimate test of the effectiveness of the federal budgetary process is how it affects each individual American. One way for you to take stock of how the federal government affects your life is as follows: (1) List what you have as assets. (2) List what you do during the day as activities. Then note the extent to which government is involved in your life—and at what cost. The emphasis should always be on the services that must be paid for, either directly or indirectly.

Consider the following example:

1. Rode bicycle to class—highway usage. How are the highways paid for? Who paid for them?

2. Checked out book from public library—Who paid for that library? Who owns it?
3. Received student loan—a subsidy from the government. Who ultimately paid for it?
4. Went to class—On average, in the United States, taxpayers pay approximately 70 percent of the cost of higher education and students and their families directly pay only 30 percent.
5. Got groceries—How much of the meat was government inspected?

Where else did government intervene?

Chapter Summary

▽

1. Monetary policy includes regulating the amount of money in circulation and is the responsibility of the Federal Reserve Board, whereas fiscal policy, which involves changing federal government taxes and spending, is the responsibility of the president and Congress.

2. Federal Reserve policy is carried out by the Federal Open-Market Committee (FOMC), which determines the rate of growth of the supply of money in circulation.

3. On occasion, in order to stop inflation, price controls (sometimes called incomes policy) have been imposed. In particular, President Richard Nixon imposed them for the first time in peace-time history in 1971.

4. Fiscal policy includes overall changes in tax structure, such as occurred in 1981 and, more importantly, in 1986, as well as specific programs to create increased demand or employment in certain sectors of the economy. The federal budgeting process, however, does not relate specifically to fiscal policy because policy makers also are worried about interest groups and client politics (getting reelected).

5. Some researchers argue that there is a political business cycle in which an administration goes into office using restrictive monetary and fiscal policy for about eighteen months. Then the administration switches to expansionary monetary and fiscal policy, so that on election day the economy will be experiencing a low unemployment rate and will have not yet felt the effects of expansionary policy in the form of more inflation. There is some evidence that the political business cycle theory does predict well.

6. The federal budget process involves presidential budgeting and congressional budgeting.

7. Presidential budgeting starts with the spring preview, during which all executive agencies must review their programs, activities, and goals. By the end of the summer, the fall review, undertaken by the Office of Budget and Management, occurs with OMB looking at budget requests and typically cutting them back.

8. The president is often not directly involved in the budget, but may request deferrals or rescissions.

9. Congressional budgeting starts in January when the president takes his final proposed budget to Congress. Congress comes up with its first budget resolution by May. During the summer, bargaining within Congress results in the second budget resolution which, in principle, sets binding limits on taxes and spending for the fiscal year beginning October 1st. Not since 1978 has the second budget resolution been passed in time for the new fiscal year. Therefore, every year since then, there has been a continuing resolution under which the government has operated for at least a short period.

▽

10. Authorizations are the legislative authority for each program and must be passed before money can be appropriated. Appropriations create the spending authority allowing the executive branch to operate. There are thirteen separate appropriations bills.

11. So-called backdoor funding involves contract, loan guarantee, and borrowing authority.

12. Of the three types of tax systems—proportional, progressive, and regressive—the United States federal personal income tax system is progressive, in which those who make higher incomes, in principle, pay a higher percentage of their incomes in taxes.

13. The Tax Reform Act of 1986 simplified tax tables for individuals by going from fourteen separate rates to two rates. It also increased the base level of income below which individuals pay no taxes and eliminated numerous deductions and special rates applied to long-term profits. The corporate income tax top rate was reduced from 46 percent to 34 percent.

14. All tax reform involves politics and values. Every provision of the Tax Code has involved a debate about the relative importance of different values, such as whether home owning should be encouraged by allowing the interest paid on mortgages to be deducted from income before taxes are paid. There are always numerous players in tax reform debates and the debate that occurred prior to the Tax Reform Act of 1986 was no exception.

15. Whenever the federal government spends more than it receives, it runs a deficit. The deficit is taken care of by U.S. Treasury borrowing. This adds to the public debt of the federal government. Although the public debt has grown dramatically, when corrected for increases in population and inflation, it fell from the end of World War II to the middle of the 1970s. Since then, it has increased and has created concern by both citizens and politicians alike.

16. One problem with annual federal government deficits is that when the Treasury goes out to borrow money to pay for them, it increases interest rates, thereby crowding out private investment because private investors are unwilling to pay the higher cost of borrowing money.

17. In an attempt to force the federal government budget to be balanced, Congress passed the Gramm-Rudman-Hollings Balanced Budget and Emergency Deficit Control Act of 1985. In principle, the budget must be balanced by the federal government's fiscal year 1991. During the first year that Gramm-Rudman was in effect, Congress attempted to meet its requirements by a variety of stop-gap measures, including selling federally-owned assets and changing accounting rules. It is not clear that it will be able to meet the budget deficit reduction requirements in the future, however.

Questions for Review and Discussion
▽

1. Which is more important, monetary or fiscal policy? How much influence does the president or Congress have on monetary policy?

2. It is often argued that we do not have a "fair" federal tax system. Do you agree or disagree? If you disagree, how would you change our system to make it fairer?

3. Does it matter which way the federal government takes spending power from you to finance its activities? That is to say, do you care whether the federal government taxes you for the full amount of federal government expenditures every year, or runs a deficit?

4. How can Congress pass a law to balance the budget with specific budget deficit reductions and not live up to its own legislation?

Selected References
▽

William P. Avery and David P. Rapkin, eds., *Political Economy* (White Plains, N.Y.: Longman, 1982). Excellent articles that cover the major forces at work in the world, concentrating on economywide issues, politics, policy, and ideology.

Dwight R. Lee, ed., *Taxation and the Deficit Economy* (San Francisco: Pacific Institute, 1986). This book forthrightly addresses the issue of taxes and public policy in the United States and includes specific recommendations for ending the federal deficit and reforming domestic economic policies.

Lance T. LeLoup, *Budgetary Policies*, 3d ed. (Brunswick, Ohio: Kings' Court Communications, Inc., 1986). An overview of the federal budget process and the nature of budgetary decisions.

The President's Council of Economic Advisers, *Economic Report of the President* (Washington, D.C.: Government Printing Office, annually). Details current issues of monetary and fiscal policy each year.

Irene S. Rubin, *Shrinking the Federal Government: The Effect of Cutbacks in Five Federal Agencies* (White Plains, N.Y.: Longman, 1985). Analyzes the process and impact of federal cutback policies in the areas of public health, employment training, community planning, urban mass transit, and the Office of Personnel Management.

David A. Stockman, *The Triumph of Politics: Why the Reagan Revolution Failed* (New York: Harper & Row, 1986). President Reagan's former director of the Office of Management and Budget reveals the inner workings, conflicts, personalities, and failures of the Reagan administration in this much-talked-about and controversial book.

▽

Chapter 17
▽
Domestic Policy

Contents
▽
Providing Income Security for Retirement: Social Security

Providing for Medical Care: Medicare and Medicaid

Poverty on the Rise?

Providing Income Security for Farmers

Labor-Management Regulation

Regulating Worker Safety and Health

Energy and the Environment

What If . . .
Nuclear Power Were Banned in the U.S.?

On Monday, April 28, 1986, technicians at a Swedish nuclear power plant detected abnormally high radiation readings on their computer screens. Further checks indicated that workers, as well as the soil and plants outside the plant, gave Geiger counter readings five times the normal levels. At first, the Swedes feared it might be the malfunctioning of one of their own twelve nuclear power plants. After other readings were taken and wind patterns studied, however, it became clear there had been a nuclear accident in the Soviet Union.

The name Chernobyl has by now become synonymous with the dangers of nuclear radiation. The aftermath of this meltdown at a nuclear power plant is raising serious doubts about the future of nuclear energy in the West. What if nuclear power were banned in the United States?

In 1986, the United States had 101 operating commercial nuclear reactors. All but fourteen states had at least one reactor—Illinois had nine, the largest number of any state. These reactors generated 17 percent of the nation's total electricity. But, as Chernobyl demonstrated, the United States did not have a monopoly on nuclear

power. In 1986, 375 commercial nuclear power plants were in operation around the world; another 157 were on order. Many countries have committed themselves to nuclear energy and generate a large proportion of their electricity from this source—France, 65 percent; Belgium, 60 percent; Sweden, 50 percent; Taiwan, 52 percent; and Japan, 26 percent.

The shutdown of nuclear reactors in the United States would obviously necessitate finding alternative electrical energy sources, most likely coal or oil. Although nuclear power poses a potential risk, it has been pointed out that since 1955 only four people in the United States have died from nuclear power-related accidents. On the other hand, during that same period, almost seven thousand people have died in coal-mining accidents (most coal is used to generate electric power). If nuclear reactors were shut down, the danger of nuclear radiation would decrease; however, the fact is that in 1986, fifteen nuclear power plants were operating in Canada alone—with another two each in Mexico and

Cuba. The United States would still be vulnerable to nuclear accidents.

Some additional effects of abandoning nuclear power would be the danger of renewed dependency on oil-producing countries. This could pose a threat to the American economy and might even become a matter of national security. Abandoning nuclear research would impair the develop-

ment of advances in medicine and other applications of nuclear energy, such as irradiating food to kill dangerous parasites and other contaminants and developing ways of extending the shelf life of food.

Antinuclear activists such as the Coalition of Environmental-Safe Energy Organizations insist that any risk of nuclear accident is unacceptable. Nuclear power plants in the vicinity of a city like Chicago, for example, with a population of more than 3 million, pose a nightmarish possibility of disaster. Shutting down these plants would prevent such a risk. Moreover, one of the more complicated effects of generating nuclear power is the problem of what to do with nuclear waste materials. Abandoning nuclear power would eliminate the need to find storage and disposal facilities for this dangerous material

If nuclear power were banned in the United States, the cost of electricity would definitely go up. Less research that might be beneficial in other areas, such as in medicine, would be undertaken. On the other hand, a lot of Americans would definitely sleep more soundly at night.

The title of this chapter, Domestic Policy, is all-encompassing. It includes just about anything the government does to help individuals and groups in our domestic economy. Domestic policy has often been named social welfare policy—defined as direct or indirect government financial subsidies to individuals. But domestic policy means even more—for example, regulating how businesses act, regulating how labor unions act, establishing safety standards for workers and requirements that firms reduce the amount of pollution they put into the environment.

Domestic policy in the United States does not follow some master plan. No overall agenda guides policy makers. The United States does not have a welfare state with a coordinated set of programs to help the poor, for example. There is not a czar of business regulation who dictates consistent policy for all businesses. Consequently, we cannot start with an overall theory of domestic policy and then fill in the examples of how this theory is applied to every area of the economy. Rather, we are forced to look at a sampling of the most important domestic policies that affect Americans today. We have chosen to look at the provision of income security as a major part of our domestic policy and within this category to examine programs to help the poor and the sick and to provide income security for our farmers. With respect to regulation, we have chosen two areas of concern: labor-management regulation and regulations affecting energy and the environment.

Domestic policy is often a response to problems that build up gradually and finally cry out for a solution. It is easy to look backward and ask, Why didn't we do something earlier? But it is not always so easy to see these problems while they are developing.

Providing Income Security for Retirement: Social Security

▽

During the depths of the Great Depression in the 1930s, it became painfully apparent that many people had not been able to provide for themselves in cases of emergency. Nearly a fourth of the work force was unemployed, and a large percentage of the elderly population who could not rely on its children for support

FDR signing the Social Security Act legislation.

became destitute. In an effort to prevent a recurrence of this kind of suffering, Congress passed the Social Security Act, which was signed by President Franklin Roosevelt on August 14, 1935. The act, which included unemployment and old-age insurance plus survivor's benefits, instituted one of the most important social insurance programs in the history of the United States.

How It Works

The Social Security Act levied a payroll tax on wages paid by all employers. This tax was initially 1 percent, but rose to 3 percent after 1937. Although it is not clear how effective the Social Security provisions were during the early years of the program, today we have ample evidence of how Social Security works. All wage earners who are covered start paying Social Security taxes as soon as they become employed. The basic rate in 1987 is 7.15 percent for the first $43,800 of income earned.

Social Security is essentially an income transfer program financed by compulsory payroll taxes levied on employer and employees, whereby those who are employed transfer income to those who are retired. The worker pays for Social Security while working and receives the old-age benefits after retirement. When the insured worker dies, benefits accrue to his or her survivors. Special benefits also provide for disabled workers. In addition, Social Security now includes Medicare, a health insurance program for the elderly, which will be discussed later.

Social Security, which is a form of social insurance, is technically known as Old Age and Survivors Disability Insurance, or OASDI.

The Economic and Political Crisis Facing Social Security

Senior citizen inquiring about social security.

In January 1940, when the first Social Security monthly benefits were distributed, only twenty-two thousand people received payments. Today, well over 90 percent of people aged sixty-five or older are receiving Social Security benefits or could receive them if they were not still working. Today, more than 14 percent of the entire population is receiving all or part of its income from the Social Security Administration. Raising enough revenues to support this system has posed a major challenge to the federal government in recent years. In 1977, the Social Security system was threatened with bankruptcy, so Congress passed a $227 billion Social Security tax increase in hopes of solving the problem. Claude Pepper, Democratic representative from Florida and a major advocate for the elderly, was confident that the tax increase would "strengthen the Social Security system, not just for the immediate future, but far into the next century."[1]

In addition to raising taxes to salvage Social Security, other policies were adopted as part of a larger reform package. Several cuts in benefits were made. The death benefit (to assist with funeral expenses) was eliminated. The college education payment to children aged eighteen to twenty-two of deceased contributors was abolished. The minimum base payment which guaranteed all eligible participants in the system a minimum payment regardless of income or contributions was abolished, limiting Social Security payments to those at the bottom of the income scale. The other policy change was legislation providing more incentives for individuals to contribute to private pension plans. In general, this allowed individuals

[1]Quoted by Douglas Bandow in "The Faulty Foundations of Social Security," *Wall Street Journal*, April 25, 1983, p. 27.

to put $2,000 of income into an Individual Retirement Account (IRA), to be fully deductible before income taxes are paid.

At the same time, the trustees of the Social Security Trust Fund declared the program to be sound until the year 2030. By 1983, however, taxes had to be increased again to provide sufficient funding. Again, almost all members of Congress were confident that after the 1983 increase the system would be sound for seventy-five or more years—although Speaker of the House Tip O'Neill thought only twenty-five or thirty years was a more accurate estimate.

How Did the Short-Term Crisis Occur?

How could the system suddenly run out of reserves as it did in the late 1970s? The answer lies partly with politics and partly with economics. From 1939 to 1976, Congress found it politically attractive to give the beneficiaries of Social Security increased payments without increasing Social Security tax rates enough to compensate. The political argument centered around a shift away from thinking of government old-age benefits as a social insurance program that was to *supplement* other income sources for the elderly, such as private savings or company pension plans. Instead, government officials and citizens have increasingly regarded Social Security as the *primary* source of an adequate retirement income. Thus, what we witnessed was Congress changing the formula virtually every year to raise the benefits. Congress also saw fit to index benefits to changes in the cost of living (rate of inflation). When we had high inflation in the 1970s and early 1980s, Social Security benefits rose accordingly. Then too, both the eligibility and the benefits available have expanded rapidly. Finally, we cannot forget that people are living longer now. It is little wonder that the Social Security Administration looked like it was going to run out of money in the late 1970s.

Now for the Long Run

As we saw, a number of things were done in the early 1980s to fix the short-term problem. But what about the long run? The birthrate is declining, longevity is increasing, and the average retirement age is falling. What all that means is there will be fewer and fewer workers to support a larger number of retirees. Consider Figure 17–1. In 1945, each retiree was supported by forty-two workers; in 1965, each retiree was supported by five workers; in 1987, the number had fallen to 3. By the year 2030, it is estimated that each retiree will be supported by only two members of the labor force! Stated another way, by the year 2030 every working couple will have to support itself, its children, and one retired person. Estimates of the tax this may require vary from two to three times the 7.15 percent paid in today.

There certainly are options available for dealing with this problem even if they are politically unacceptable. One option would be to increase the retirement age at which people become eligible for Social Security. This change would keep people working longer. Another option is to reduce benefits paid to retirees.

Providing for Medical Care: Medicare and Medicaid

In 1963, a popular actor of the time, Ronald Reagan, made a recording to help the American Medical Association (AMA) with its greatest fight—its effort to halt the "socialist threat" of government-supported health insurance. A quarter of a

> ## Did You Know?
> ▽
> That approximately 30 million Americans were living below the poverty line in 1986?

Figure 17–1

▽

Workers Supporting Retirees

*A certain number of retirees receiving So-
cial Security are supported by a certain
number of members of the labor force.
You can see that it has dropped from
forty-two in 1945 to three in 1987.*

SOURCE: Social Security Administration.

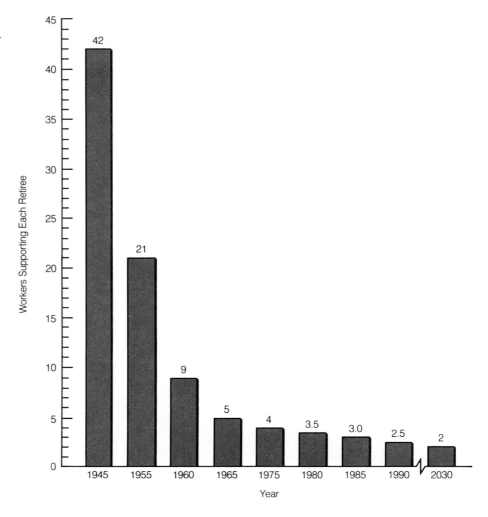

Medicare

A federally funded medical insurance
program that was added to the Social Security Act of 1935 in 1966.

Medicaid

Health care payments for the needy regardless of age. It is state-administered
and the particulars differ from state to
state. Some are generous; others are not.

decade later, such health insurance—**Medicare**—is a reality and President Reagan
was still in the struggle, this time trying to prevent increases in federal government
spending on health programs. However, the AMA was urging Congress *not* to cut
back on Medicare and other federally provided health programs.

Some people believe that the most important social welfare program to emerge
in the 1960s was the Medicare Act of 1965. Britain had already created a national
health insurance service under its Labour government in 1945. Although President
Harry S. Truman had proposed national health care insurance at the same time,
he had little success in convincing Congress. It was not just the AMA that was
worried about "socialized" medicine. When Lyndon Johnson was elected in 1964,
he finally had the majorities in Congress necessary to support such a program.
Medicare was later expanded to include **Medicaid,** which extended medical assistance to the poor as well as the elderly. The Medicare/Medicaid bill passed Congress
by large majorities. Today, more than fifty million people receive benefits under
this law. Medicare benefits extend to about 12 percent of the population, and
Medicaid benefits to almost 8 percent.

▽

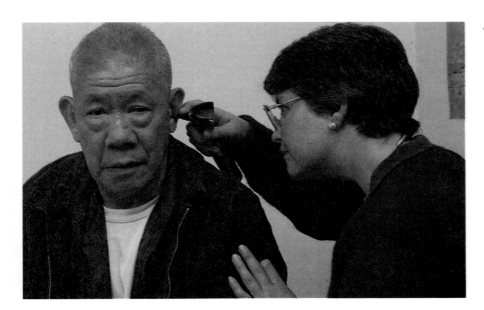

The Medicare program became effective on July 1, 1966, as an addition to the Social Security Act, and it has been amended a number of times. It consists of two parts: Part A is compulsory hospitalization insurance and is financed by contributions from employees and employers, similar to Social Security; Part B is supplemental medical insurance to help pay for the cost of doctors' services, as well as other medical costs, for participants age sixty-five and over. There is a nominal monthly charge for this service. Medicaid is state administered, so Medicaid in some states may seem very generous and in others practically nonexistent.

Basically, the financing of Medicare comes from the same pool of funds that financing for Social Security comes from. That means the same long-run problems exist—benefits will probably not be as generous for future generations relative to contributions paid as they have been for past and are for the current generation. In addition, a problem that will continue to plague Medicare is the inflationary cost associated with new medical technology. Congress has responded to that problem by proposing a "health cost containment" bill, which would basically be medical care price controls. Other observers have recommended a network of federally owned hospitals, similar to the Veterans Administration hospitals, to cut costs of the program.

Social Security, Medicare, and Medicaid deal with the elderly. While roughly 14 percent of the elderly suffer from problems of poverty, they are not the only ones. As we see in the next section, poverty still exists in the United States, it is a problem, and the political system has attempted to deal with it in important, although not always successful, ways.

Poverty on the Rise?

▽

Poverty exists today, as it has always existed in the United States. In the history of governmental concern, it appears as if poverty really wasn't discovered until the 1960s, when during the 1960 presidential campaign, John Kennedy appeared shocked at the real poverty he observed traveling through West Virginia. He pledged, if elected, to do "something." Kennedy's concern and mounting public debate about the issue, especially Michael Harrington's influential book *The Other America*, helped put poverty on the policy agenda. Poverty became tied to the civil rights struggle. Lyndon Johnson declared a "War on Poverty" when he became president, which took shape through several laws, including the Economic Opportunity Act of 1964. This act established new services and agencies to help the poor directly. Additional legislation that was passed during the Johnson period included:

1. Head Start, giving poor preschool children social and educational experiences equivalent to those obtained by more affluent children.
2. Work-study programs, to aid poor college students.
3. The Neighborhood Youth Corps, giving youth on-the-job experience.
4. Literacy programs, to help adults compete in the job market.

In spite of massive funds expended to fight poverty, using the official government definition and estimates of those in poverty, we see in Figure 17–2 that the number of poor have increased since 1978. Today, more than one in every eight American families can be considered poor. To understand how this anomaly could occur in the land of plenty, we have to first start with the official definition of poverty.

Defining Poverty

Being poor means not having enough income, but how much is "enough"? The government states that poverty exists when people have inadequate income to provide the necessities of life—food, clothing, and housing. In 1985, a family of four fell below the poverty level if it had income of less than $10,989. This poverty line changes depending on the size of the family and other special characteristics. It increases to take account of inflation. It also rises over the long run because our concept of poverty changes. Consider that the official definition of poverty in the United States exceeds the average income of a majority of the world. Also consider that $10,989 in 1985 would have been regarded in colonial times as a very nice

Figure 17–2
▽
Poverty on the Rise
SOURCE: U.S. Dept. of Commerce.

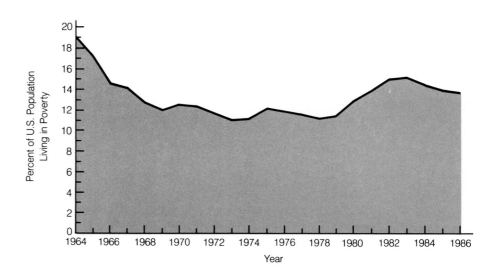

income (even after we correct for inflation). In fact, historically the current poverty level would have been considered an acceptable level of income as late as the 1930s.

Who Are the Poor?

The incidence of poverty is not uniform throughout different socioethnic or geographic groups in the United States. For example, there is a higher incidence of poverty in the South than in the North. There is a higher incidence of poverty among those with less than a grade school education than among those with a high school diploma or better. Figure 17–3 shows the percentage of each group in poverty in 1979 and in 1985. You can see from this graph that blacks have an almost three times greater probability of living in poverty than whites. Those from fatherless families have a higher probability of being poor than those in a household with both parents. Being black and in a single-parent family means that a person has better than a 50 percent chance of being below the poverty line.

Except for the elderly, poverty for each category in Figure 17–3 has increased since 1979. But look at Table 17–1, where we show welfare or public assistance

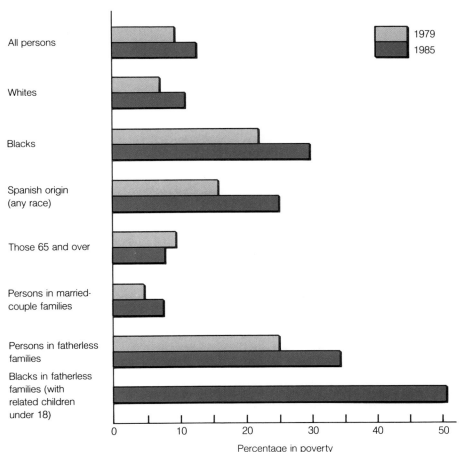

Figure 17–3
▽
Incidence of Poverty, 1979 and 1985
The incidence of poverty increased for almost all groups from 1979 to 1985.

SOURCE: U.S. Department of Commerce, Bureau of the Census, "Estimates of Poverty, Including the Value of Non-Cash Benefits," Technical Paper 51, p. xviii; and Technical Paper 52, pp. xi, xiv, 20.

Table 17–1
▽

Income Transfer Programs

	Public Expenditures (billions of current dollars)			
	1965	**1979**	**1981**	**1986**
Social insurance				
Cash benefits:				
Social security	$16.5	$102.6	$137.0	$188.6
Unemployment insurance	2.5	11.2	18.7	23.7
Workers' compensation	1.8	9.9	14.8	16.1
Veterans' disability compensation	2.2	6.8	7.5	11.4
Railroad retirement	1.1	4.3	5.2	6.1
Black lung	†	0.6	0.9	1.0
In-kind benefits:				
Medicare	†	29.1	38.4	66.8
Welfare (public assistance)				
Cash benefits:				
Aid to families with dependent children (AFDC)	1.7	10.8	12.8	8.3
Supplemental security income (SSI)§	2.7	6.8	8.5	8.6
Veterans' pensions	1.9	3.6	4.1	3.8
General assistance	0.4	1.2	1.5	
In-kind benefits:				
Medicaid	0.5	21.8	27.6	24.1
Food stamps	0.04	6.8	9.7	12.6
Housing assistance	0.3	4.4	6.6	10.7
Total expenditures	31.5	219.9	293.2	381.8
Total expenditures as a percentage of GNP	4.6%	9.1%	10.0%	9.5%

†Nonexistent.

§Prior to 1972, Aid to the Blind, Aid to the Permanently and Totally Disabled, and Old Age Assistance.

SOURCE: Sheldon Danziger, Robert Haveman, and Robert Plotnick, "How Income Transfer Programs Affect Work, Savings and the Income Distribution: A Critical Review," *Journal of Economic Literature*, September 1981, table 1 and *Economic Report of the President*, 1986.

programs available to the nation's lower income groups. These consist of Aid to Families with Dependent Children (AFDC), Supplemental Security Income (SSI), veterans' pensions, and general assistance. That total was $219.9 billion in 1979 and increased to $381.8 billion in 1986. So we are faced with an anomaly—rising public assistance payments and increasing poverty, as defined by the government.

Other Basic Programs for the Poor

In addition to Social Security, Medicare, and Medicaid, a variety of other programs are designed to help America's poor.

Supplemental Security Income (SSI) and Aid to Families with Dependent Children (AFDC)

A large number of poor persons do not qualify for Social Security benefits. They are assisted through other programs. Starting in 1974, a federally financed and

Poverty-Welfare Curve
The curve that shows the trade-off between welfare spending per capita and the percentage of population living in poverty. According to some researchers, the poverty-welfare curve shows a decrease in the percentage of the population living in poverty as welfare spending increases up to a certain point, and then shows an *increase* in the percentage of population living in poverty as welfare spending goes up even more.

Is There a Poverty-Welfare Curve?

Some researchers have examined the economic incentives facing individuals who have the choice between working or not working and receiving different types of welfare payments. Consider the public housing program under which families pay 25 percent of their income in rent. For every dollar more that they earn, they must pay 25 cents more in rent. That means they have a negative incentive to earn more money income because of the "cost" of earning that extra income. As it turns out, welfare families end up losing a significant portion of their benefits as they make higher money income. They are faced with an implicit tax that often exceeds the actual tax that higher-income earners pay. In one study of welfare benefits and implicit taxes in California, an increase in monthly gross wages from $400 to $500 actually *reduced* spendable income by $21. That means an implicit tax rate of 121 percent. Such negative incentives can help explain why individuals in poverty would rationally choose to draw welfare instead of working. (The negative incentive effects mentioned here cannot, however, explain why people are poor in the first place.)

Professors Richard Vedder and Lowell Gallaway of Ohio University have tried to quantify what they call the **poverty-welfare curve.** They looked at the rate of poverty among children and compared high welfare-benefit states with low welfare-benefit states. The result is seen in the accompanying figure. At zero benefits, the percentage of the population living in poverty was somewhere between 15 and 20. As the federal welfare spending per capita rose to $140, the percentage of the population living in poverty reached its low of 13.8. As welfare spending per capita has increased, the percentage of the population living in poverty has also increased.*

*Richard Vedder and Lowell Gallaway, "AFDC and the Laffer Principle," *Wall Street Journal*, Wednesday, March 26, 1986, p. 26.

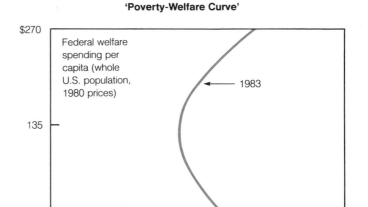

'Poverty-Welfare Curve'

Federal welfare spending per capita (whole U.S. population, 1980 prices)

← 1983

Percent of Population Living in Poverty

They concluded that when federal public assistance to the poor was modest, increases in that assistance were related to more, not less, poverty. The federal government has found itself "paying people to be poor," these researchers claim. From 1972 to 1986, public assistance has added 5.7 million Americans to the poverty role—more of us have voluntarily chosen to be poor, according to Vedder and Gallaway. They estimate that in many states welfare benefits that are obtainable by the poor for having a child exceed the additional cost of rearing the child up to about age twelve. "The numbers indicate that having poor children is a potentially profitable activity."

administered Supplemental Security Income (SSI) program was instituted. The purpose of SSI is to establish a nationwide minimum income for the aged, the blind, and the disabled.

The AFDC is a state-administered program, partially financed by federal grants. This program provides aid to families in which dependent children do not have the financial support of the father because of desertion, disability, or death.

An applicant for food stamps.

Negative Income Tax
A system designed to help the poor in which those below a certain income level receive direct payments from the government in the form of a negative income tax, or cash payment.

Food Stamps

In 1964, at the beginning of the program, about 367,000 Americans were receiving food stamps. By 1986, there were more than 20 million recipients. The annual cost jumped from $860,000 to more than $12 billion. Individuals on strike and also many college students are eligible for the food stamp program.

A congressional committee found that by 1975 one in every fourteen persons was estimated to be using food stamps. The food stamp program has become a major part of the welfare system in the United States. Although it has been and continues to be a method of supporting better nutrition among the poor, in retrospect it seems to have also been used to shore up the nation's agricultural sector by distributing "surplus" food through retail channels.

Additional Programs

A wide range of other programs exist to support the poor. They include rent subsidies, legal aid, family planning, school lunches, and student grants and loans. At any one time, at the federal level, there exist more than 150 separate programs, many of them overlapping. Indeed, so many programs have been started that some critics of our welfare system argue that virtually all programs should be eliminated and replaced with straight cash payments to those below the poverty level. This could be done via a **negative income tax,** which is a system of transferring income to the poor by giving them an income subsidy depending on how far below a "target" income their earned income lies.

Why Are People Poor?

As this chapter's Critical Perspective indicates, some of the decisions that individuals in poverty make not to work depend on the negative incentives imposed on them by the welfare system. But why are individuals poor in the first place? Why has there been a rise in poverty? Some of the factors that need to be considered are the following:

1. Increased unemployment: In 1946, so-called full employment was defined as 3.5 percent unemployment. In 1950, it was 4 percent; in 1960, 5 percent; in 1970, 6 percent. Today, about 6.5 percent unemployment is defined as full employment. Perhaps the economy is simply not generating enough jobs to keep everybody working.
2. Lack of educational training: Those who most need vocational or technical training may have least access to it.
3. Business locations: Businesses have been reluctant to locate in inner cities where there is high unemployment, thus reducing the income-earning possibilities of the poor.
4. "Feminization" of poverty: The lowest-paying "pink collar" jobs (clerks and retail sales) are still slotted for women, many of whom remain part of the poverty syndrome.
5. Ethnic and gender discrimination: The continuing effects of such discrimination are apparent if we look at the Bureau of Labor Statistics data, which show that women and minorities with the same jobs and the same skills are still paid less than white males in the *same* jobs.

Many poor are also homeless.

Poverty has existed in the rural sectors of America for many years. To fight such poverty, the government since the early days of the Depression has enacted income security programs for farmers. We now examine some of those programs.

Providing Income Security for Farmers

▽

It has been said that farmers have the worst of all possible worlds. They sell everything they produce at wholesale and buy everything they need at retail. Farmers as a group have always held a special place in American politics. This should not be surprising, since farmers were the largest single group in the United States during all of this country's formative years. For many years, more than 90 percent of Americans in the work force were engaged in some form of agricultural pursuit. It was not until 1884 that less than 50 percent of American workers were in the agricultural sector. Today, only about 3 percent of American workers are officially considered in agriculture. But that 3 percent, particularly the very wealthy among them, have had a disproportionate influence on federal government legislation during the twentieth century. The variety of programs aimed at providing income security for farmers of all types is impressive.

A Short History of the Farmers' Dilemma

Before World War I, the United States had about twenty years of relatively continuous agricultural prosperity. During the war, increased demand for agricultural products brought the "golden age of American farming" to its peak. Many foreign countries demanded our agricultural products because they were using all their productive facilities to fight the war. The sharp depression in 1920 brought the golden age to an abrupt halt. Even though the economy picked up in 1921 and through the "roaring twenties," agriculture never shared in the remaining years of prosperity. Europeans reduced their demand for U.S. agricultural exports as they increased their own productive capacities in farming. Also, the United States put high tariffs on all imported goods, restricting the flow of imports. Since other countries were not able to export as many goods to us as before, they were in no position to import as much from us as before. Since exports are what any country uses to pay for its imports, the less it is able to export, the less it is able to import.

Then the Great Depression hit, and its effect on American farming was disastrous. Farm prices and farm incomes fell sharply. It was at this time that massive farm programs were put into operation. In 1929, the Federal Farm Board was created and given a budget of $1.5 million ($10.2 million in 1987 dollars) to begin price stabilization operations for poor farmers. The Farm Board was supposed to use the money to support the price of farm products, and thereby farmers' incomes, by buying crops to keep their prices from falling. Then, when the Great Depression got into full swing, the government instituted a system of **price supports.** At one time or another, there has been some form of price supports for wheat, feed grains, honey, cotton, tobacco, rice, peanuts, soybeans, dairy products, and sugar.

Problems with Current Farm Programs

Surprisingly, the area of federal spending that has increased the most over the last five years has not been defense or social programs but agricultural assistance programs. For example, from 1981 to 1985, defense spending increased 55 percent, whereas outlays for agricultural price supports increased by 340 percent. For the fiscal year ending September 30, 1986, farmers received **deficiency payments** of about $26 billion. Deficiency payments are an open-ended entitlement program that is second only in size to Social Security.

Deficiency Payments and Target Prices

The system of deficiency payments works with **target prices.** The target price for corn, for example, in 1986 was $3.03 a bushel. The loan level for corn was $1.86 a bushel. Whenever the market price hits the loan level, the federal treasury pays the corn growers the difference between $3.03 and $1.86, or $1.17 a bushel. In 1986, about 8.4 billion bushels of corn qualified for this deficiency payment.

The Dairy Program

In 1986, the federal government decided that there were too many cows. Its solution was to pay dairy farmers to go out of business for at least five years. About 14,000 farmers responded. The cost to the government was $1.8 billion. But, of course, that meant a lot of cattle had to be slaughtered, putting downward pressure on beef prices, so the government decided it had to buy up 400 million pounds of beef.

The remaining 200,000 surviving dairy farmers are improving their efficiency every day. Feed costs have dropped and milk production, rather than contracting, has expanded. By the summer of 1986, the federal government owned 627 million pounds of surplus cheese, 242 million pounds of butter, and 828 million pounds of dried milk.

Price Supports

Minimum prices set by the government. To be effective, price supports must be coupled with a mechanism to rid the market of "surplus" goods that arise whenever the supported price is greater than the market-clearing price.

Deficiency Payments

The difference between a target price that the government sets for a particular crop and the market price that the crop fetches.

Target Price

A price set by the government that it wishes farmers to receive for particular products. Target prices are typically set above market prices. Any difference is made up by government in direct payments to farmers in the form of deficiency payments, described above.

Price Supports and Surpluses

Any type of price supports that attempt to keep prices above those that would prevail in the absence of government intervention will create surpluses. The preceding examples can be multiplied a hundredfold since price supports have been instituted in the United States. So long as price supports exist, there will always be a "farm program" that includes surpluses.

Who Benefits from Price Supports?

Have the tens of billions of dollars in price supports and other income security programs helped farmers? Of course, many farmers have been helped, but there is a basic economic reality attached to any program that pays farmers in relation to the amount that they produce (or could produce). Low-income farmers are, by definition, those who produce very little. Therefore, they benefit very little from price supports and similar programs. Under current law, no grower is supposed to receive more than $50,000 a year in federal deficiency payments, but the big producers have easily avoided that restriction. Historically, the benefits of agricultural programs have been greatly skewed toward the owners of very large farms. Owners of farms with sales of less than $10,000, for example, received less than 4 percent of the benefits from price supports in 1986. Indeed, to supplement shrinking farm income, small farmers are earning three times more income from off-farm employment. In other words, the poor farmers are really part-time farmers and have not been helped very much (if at all) by farm income security programs.

Surplus corn in Minnesota.

▽

559

Stretched between rising costs and sluggish sale prices, many small American farmers borrowed more and more during the early 1980s. Today, farm debt in the United States totals almost $250 billion. Many fear that the American institution of the family farm will disappear. We have noted that the income security programs for farmers are benefiting large farmers rather than small farmers. In the face of rising debt and increasing competition, small farmers are getting out of business. They are selling their land and putting their money in the bank rather than trying to run an uneconomical unit. The result of the decline of the small family farm is an agricultural sector that is becoming increasingly concentrated in few hands. Today, 1 percent of farms produce 25 percent of the nation's agricultural product. "In the next two decades, the market share of these farms is expected to reach 50 percent of the total."*

Also, much of the farm land small farmers are selling is being turned into airports, shopping centers, housing developments, recreational facilities, and industrial parks. It is estimated that by the year 2000, twenty million acres of

*Anwar S. Kahn and Nozar Hashemzadeh, *The Institute for Socioeconomic Studies*, Fall 1983.

current and potential farm land will be swallowed up by rural and urban development. Is there hope for small farmers? Probably not. They do not have the political base or the economic leverage to influence their futures. This means that the future of farming lies with agribusiness—large corporations running increasingly large farms.

The new agricultural bill passed in the summer of 1986 cut price supports for major crops, but it increased direct federal handouts to farmers who agreed to idle part of their land. Of course, the richer farmers have the most land

to idle. Under the new farm law, only about 17 cents out of every federal dollar being spent goes to full-time farmers in desperate straits. Fifteen percent of all federal handouts will continue to go to farmers with net worth exceeding $1 million. Farmers will continue to add to the already bursting bins of government "surplus" crops. At the beginning of 1987, the United States had enough wheat to make twenty-seven loaves of bread for each of the world's almost five billion inhabitants.

Labor-Management Regulation
▽

The labor union is an accepted American institution, but it was not always so. Indeed, the first permanent federation of labor on a national scale did not appear in this country until 1852 (the National Typographic Union formed in Cincinnati in May of that year). From the Civil War to President Franklin D. Roosevelt's New Deal, labor's struggle for the right to organize unions to engage in **collective**

bargaining was a hard and slow road. In 1869, the Knights of Labor was formed; by 1886 the organization had a membership of about 800,000. Among its demands were an eight-hour workday, equality of pay for men and women, and the replacement of the free enterprise system with a socialist system. The American Federation of Labor (AFL)—a federation of craft unions—was formed in 1886 under the leadership of Samuel Gompers (a cigar maker). By the beginning of World War I, the AFL claimed it was the voice of the majority of organized labor.[2] The business community opposed the union movement, and for much of the period preceding World War I, the government supported business opposition by offering the use of police personnel to break strikes. The courts upheld many of these police actions and even ruled that unions violated antitrust laws by acting in restraint of trade—that is, by acting as monopolies.

Labor's Political Agenda

During its early period from 1886 to 1928, labor's political agenda was primarily focused on winning free universal public education, public school vocational training, minimum wages, unemployment insurance, workers' compensation, the eight-hour day, government old-age pensions, the abolition of child labor, and factory inspection safety laws, at both the state and local level. Labor achieved significant victories during this period in the northern industrial states (Illinois, Massachusetts, Pennsylvania), but many of these victories, such as the minimum wage, were taken away by federal courts and the U.S. Supreme Court. That is one reason why labor shifted its attention from the state and local level to the federal level in the 1930s.

It is worth mentioning that American labor's "political philosophy," from the early AFL period to this day, has differed quite markedly from that of most other labor movements throughout the world. The American labor movement made the conscious decision *not* to form an independent labor or socialist political party but

[2]The Congress of Industrial Organizations (CIO) was founded in 1937–38 as a competing and more militant confederation of industrial unions. It merged with the AFL to form the AFL-CIO in 1955.

Collective Bargaining
Bargaining between management of a company or a group of companies and management of a union or a group of unions for the purpose of setting a mutually agreeable contract on wages, fringe benefits, and working conditions for *all* employees in the union(s). Different from individual bargaining, where each employee strikes a bargain with his or her employer individually.

Samuel Gompers.

Children working in a glass factory in 1908.

rather to use its influence to reward friends and punish enemies of labor on an individual "nonpartisan" basis—a philosophy called "Gomperism," after AFL founder Sam Gompers.

During World I, Wilsonian liberalism set an important precedent within the Democratic party and for the New Deal during the 1930s. Under the necessity of securing labor's cooperation in the war effort, the government not only encouraged union membership but it also forced employers to make concessions during bargaining and it placed labor officials on various planning and policy boards. These gains were lost during the 1920s (a period very similar to the 1980s for labor) when the labor movement went into a steep decline. But the labor movement was to have a resurgence under Roosevelt.

Labor Legislation

By 1920, union membership had increased to more than 500,000. But it was not until the depths of the Great Depression that labor-management relations were institutionalized by a number of important pieces of congressional legislation.

Norris-LaGuardia Act of 1932

Yellow-Dog Contract

An anti-union device fostered by management. In such a contract, workers agree to remain nonunion as a condition of employment. Violation of the yellow-dog contract exposed a worker to a lawsuit by his or her employer, the result of which might be a court-imposed fine or, in some cases, imprisonment.

At the depths of the Great Depression, Congress passed the Norris-LaGuardia Act granting labor the right to organize into unions. Most of the act was declared unconstitutional by the Supreme Court. One of the act's most important provisions was to outlaw the **yellow-dog contract,** which requires individual workers to sign a contract swearing that they are not members of a union and will not join one while employed.

National Labor Relations Act of 1935

The National Labor Relations Act (NLRA), otherwise known as the Wagner Act, is considered the true start of the regulation of labor-management relations in the United States. Indeed, the Wagner Act has been called labor's Magna Carta. It withstood a constitutional test in the Supreme Court in 1937. The NLRA guaranteed workers the right to organize unions or join unions that already existed and outlawed various unfair business practices (for example, interfering in internal union business or not bargaining in good faith). It set up the National Labor Relations Board (NLRB) to hear and adjudicate accusations by labor of unfair business practices. Later, under the Taft-Hartley Act which is discussed later, the board also included unfair labor practices within its purview.

The Forty-Hour Work Week and the Prohibition Against Child Labor

Minimum Wage

An hourly wage rate below which employers cannot pay covered workers. Minimum wages are imposed by federal, state, and local laws.

In 1938, Congress passed the Fair Labor Standards Act. It established a forty-hour work week and required time and a half to be paid for overtime. It also established a **minimum wage** for workers employed by companies engaged in interstate commerce.

Two years later, in 1940, the Federal Labor Standards Act was passed. Among other things, this law prohibited the use of child labor by industry.

Profile

▽

Florence Kelley

Florence Kelley was born into a Scotch-Irish Presbyterian Philadelphia family on September 12, 1859. Her father, William Darrah Kelley, was a judge from 1846 to 1856 on the Court of Common pleas in Philadelphia. From 1860 until his death in 1890, he was a member of the U.S. House of Representatives as a Republican.

Florence attended Cornell University, where she gravitated toward the social sciences, founded the Social Science Club, and earned Phi Beta Kappa graduation honors in 1882. Her senior thesis was on the subject of "Law and the Child." Barred from studying law in the United States because of her sex, she attended the University of Zurich, in Switzerland, where she delved into the writings of Karl Marx and translated Friedrich Engels's epochal work, *Condition of the Working Class in England.*

She joined the famous social reformer Jane Addams in the Hull House settlement work in Chicago in 1891, and was later commissioned by the governor of Illinois, John Peter Altgeld, to prepare a study of the Chicago slums and to report on the use of child labor in sweatshops. A child labor law was enacted through her efforts. The law included a provision for the establishment of a new state department of factory inspection, which Kelley was selected to head. The problems that

"The noblest duty of the republic is that of self-preservation by so cherishing all of its children that they, in turn, may become enlightened, self-governing citizens."

she encountered with the district attorney's office in this official capacity impelled her to earn an LL.B. degree in law at Northwestern University in 1894. Her insistence on publicizing the problems associated with child labor resulted in another law limiting the employment of minors and the enactment of a law providing for the compulsory education of all children, including those at work. She resigned as factory inspector in 1897.

In 1899, Florence Kelley became general secretary in New York of the National Consumers' League, which she had helped to found. The rest of her life was dedicated to the work of the league through editing its publications, helping to organize a large number of local chapters, and speaking before other groups. Kelley continued to seek radical reforms in the employment and education of children, women's working conditions, health standards in factories, workers' living standards, and minimum wages. Her 1905 book, *Some Ethical Gains Through Legislation,* helped lead to the establishment in 1912 of the federal Children's Bureau.

Kelley was a major writer in the field of social reform, contributing reports and articles regularly to journals. In addition to her 1905 book, she wrote *Modern Industry* (1913), edited Edmond Kelly's *Twentieth Century Socialism* (1910), and compiled *The Supreme Court and Minimum Wage Legislation* and *Comment of the Legal Profession on the District of Columbia Minimum Wage Case* (1925).

A true believer in human equality and social justice, Florence Kelley was a socialist and a Quaker. She died in Germantown, Pennsylvania, on February 17, 1932, in the depths of the Great Depression.

The Taft-Hartley Act of 1947

The Taft-Hartley Act, otherwise called the Labor Management Relations Act, has been termed the "slave labor act" by some union people. Among other things, it allows individual states to pass their own **right-to-work laws.** A right-to-work law makes it illegal for union membership to be a requirement for continued employment in any establishment.

Right-to-Work Laws

Laws that make it illegal to require union membership as a condition of continuing employment in a particular firm.

▽

Closed Shop

A business enterprise in which an employee must belong to the union before he or she can be employed and must remain in the union after employment.

Union Shop

A business enterprise that allows non-union members to become employed, conditional on their joining the union by some specified date after employment begins.

Jurisdictional Dispute

A dispute by two or more unions over which should have control of a particular jurisdiction, such as a particular craft or skill or a particular firm or industry.

Sympathy Strike

A strike by a union in response to, or in sympathy with, another union's already existing strike.

Secondary Boycott

A boycott of companies or products sold by companies that are dealing with a company that has already been struck.

More specifically, the act outlaws the **closed shop,** which requires that a worker must join a union before employment can be obtained. A **union shop,** on the other hand, is legal; a union shop does not require membership as a prerequisite for employment, but it can, and usually does, require that workers join the union after a specified amount of time on the job. (Even a union shop is illegal in twenty-one states with right-to-work laws.)

Jurisdictional disputes, sympathy strikes, and secondary boycotts are made illegal by this act as well. A **jurisdictional dispute** involves two or more unions fighting (and striking) over which should have the right to organize in a particular trade, craft, or industry. For example, should a carpenter working for United States Steel be part of the steelworkers' union or the carpenter's union? A **sympathy strike** occurs when one union strikes in sympathy with another union's problems or another union's strike. If the retail clerks' union in an area is striking grocery stores, teamsters may refuse to deliver products to those stores in sympathy with the retail clerks' demands for higher wages or better working conditions. A **secondary boycott** is the boycotting of a company that deals with a struck company. If union workers strike a baking company, then the boycotting of grocery stores that continue to sell that company's products is a secondary boycott. The secondary boycott brings pressure against third parties to force them to stop dealing with an employer who is being struck.

In general, the Taft-Hartley Act outlawed unfair labor practices by unions, such as "make-work" rules and the requirement that unwilling workers join a particular union. Perhaps the most famous aspect of the Taft-Hartley Act is its provision against strikes that are believed to imperil the national safety or health. Presidents have on occasion used this provision, much to the chagrin of the unions involved. President Truman used its provisions for seizing the steel mills in 1948. President Nixon applied the act's eighty-day injunction order to striking longshoremen in 1971. President Eisenhower took the same action against striking steelworkers in 1959; President Carter applied the injunction against striking coal miners in 1978.

The Landrum-Griffin Act of 1959

Internal union business procedures became more strictly regulated with the passage of the Landrum-Griffin Act (officially known as the Labor-Management Reporting

The results of a municipal workers strike in Philadelphia.

and Disclosure Act). The act regulates union elections, requiring regularly scheduled elections of officers and the use of secret ballots. Ex-convicts and communists are prohibited from holding union office. Moreover, union officials are made accountable for union property and funds. Any union officer who embezzles union funds violates a federal law. Finally, the act laid out certain rights of union members—the right to attend and participate in union meetings, to nominate officers, and to vote in most union proceedings.

Regulating Worker Safety and Health
▽
OSHA

In 1970, Congress created the Occupational Safety and Health Administration (OSHA) to regulate hazards in the workplace. In the first four years of operation, OSHA wrote more than four thousand standards, filling a total of eight hundred pages in the Code of Federal Regulations. OSHA has been one of the more severely criticized regulatory agencies, partly because of the too-hasty promulgation of its rules, the overlapping levels of regulation, and the lack of any single overriding criterion for evaluating its rules. When a rule was first drawn up, OSHA often deleted references to circumstances where the standard would be applied. This led to the creation of rules that, although appropriate in limited situations, were applied to all situations. For example, when OSHA rule makers neglected to describe the circumstances surrounding the prohibition of using pond ice in drinks for workers who were cutting ice in ponds, the stated general rule—if enforced—would have prohibited *all* employees from putting ice in drinking water. Thus a reasonable rule that would have reduced the possibility of contaminated pond ice being consumed by ice cutters became an unreasonable rule.

The separate levels of regulation have also contributed to OSHA's difficulties. One level is a general duty clause that requires employers to provide a workplace "free from recognized hazards that are causing or are likely to cause death or serious physical harm" to employees.[3] The next level of regulation is also general but applies to a specific category of situations such as protective shields for machines.[4] The third level is more rigid and mandates particular performance requirements for individual machines or work stations. The fourth and most complex level sets out detailed specifications—for example, the exact distances between moving parts of machines and shields, the number of fasteners, and other technical input.

When these regulations are superimposed, they often create new hazards while eliminating an old one. For example, a work rest intended to help support a tool must be placed one-eighth of an inch from a grinding wheel. When large objects are being ground, however, a work rest that close to the wheel may interfere with proper operation and actually may decrease safety. In such cases, an adjustable work rest would be an improvement, and this one-eighth-of-an-inch OSHA rule results in thousands of violations.

Protection for Workers on the Decline

The Reagan administration has put less emphasis on the federal imposition of worker safety rules than previous administrations. Also, in an attempt to reduce

[3]Public Law 92-573, Section 5.

[4]See, for example, *Code of Federal Regulations*, vol. 29, sec. 1910, 212(a).

large government deficits, the Reagan administration cut back many of its programs, including worker protection.

A report on federal policies affecting American workers submitted to the Joint Economic Committee by Sar Levitan and Isaac Shapiro of the George Washington University Center for Social Policy Studies claimed that federal programs developed over the past fifty years for the protection of American workers had been seriously eroded since President Reagan took office. This report, released at the beginning of the summer of 1986, states that the Reagan administration has "executed a full-scale retreat in virtually every area of government activity affecting the well-being of American workers."[5] OSHA and Bureau of Labor Statistics indicate that work-related accidents have increased over the last six years owing to cuts in inspection and enforcement.

Energy and the Environment
▽

On April 26, 1986, the Chernobyl nuclear power plant in the Soviet Union blew its top, channeling the blast and debris upward into the atmosphere. The accident was apparently caused by human error. In any event, coolant was lost and the reactor critically overheated, causing the ensuing explosion. Estimates of future cancer deaths from the radiation range from 6,500 according to the Soviets, to 24,000 according to the International Atomic Energy Agency, and to 45,000 according to the Natural Resources Defense Council.

A less serious disaster occurred at Three-Mile Island nuclear power plant near Harrisburg, Pennsylvania, on March 28, 1979, when a malfunctioning valve set off an intricate chain of mechanical and human failures. During this time, the core of the nuclear reactor was uncovered, and some melting occurred. The world has thus already faced the possibility of the "China Syndrome" in a nuclear melt-down.

[5]Sar Levitan and Isaac Shapiro, *Protecting American Workers: An Assessment of Government Programs* (Washington, D.C.: Bureau of National Affairs, 1986).

The nuclear plant at Chernobyl.

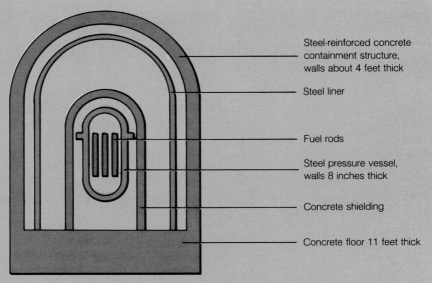
Nuclear Power

At first, nuclear power seemed destined to become a major source of energy in the United States—both cheap and renewable. On December 27, 1966, the *Wall Street Journal* headlined a front-page article, "Shape of the Future: Huge Nuclear Facilities Will Help the U.S. Meet Surging Power Demands," which included the following statements:

Nuclear waste in Washington.

Radioactive Wastes

Material—in gaseous, liquid, or solid form—that is a by-product of all the processes in the nuclear fuel cycle. It emits ionizing radiation and is damaging to all living organisms. Radioactive waste is classified as low-level, intermediate-level, and high-level waste.

Victims of the disaster at Chernobyl.

Researchers say the earth still holds enough of the fossil fuels—coal, oil, and gas—to keep homes and factories humming for centuries . . . and ultimately there will be almost limitless supplies of power from nuclear plants, expected eventually to be the cheapest source of energy almost everywhere on the globe . . . By 1980, according to Atomic Energy Commission Chairman Glenn Seaborg, atomic capacity may reach as much as 110 million kilowatts, a fifth of the total electric capacity the U.S. is expected to have then. By 2000, Mr. Seaborg continues, nuclear reactors will account for half the nation's electric capacity.

Nuclear power no longer seems to be the desirable energy source it once was thought to be. First, nuclear power plants have quadrupled, and sometimes sextupled, in cost compared with ten years ago. New environmental restrictions and additional safety requirements have raised their construction costs enormously, whereas increased concerns over safety, requiring more frequent shutdowns, have seriously reduced the percentage of capacity at which nuclear power plants have been able to operate. Today, many experts believe that the cost per kilowatt hour for nuclear power plants is higher than the cost per kilowatt hour for coal-fired electricity plants. Even if the cost were less than for coal-fired plants, it would not be sufficiently less to justify constructing a nuclear power plant.

Secondly, there is the great unsolved problem of how to dispose of radioactive wastes. **Radioactive wastes** are highly toxic. They must be kept isolated for literally thousands of years. No one knows today how the job can best be done, and even if we did, we do not know what the long-run costs would be. There is also the related problem of dismantling nuclear reactors when their useful life ends—every forty years or so. The questions are the same as for waste disposal.

Finally, the great debate over the safety of nuclear power has continued since the Three Mile Island episode in 1979 and the Chernobyl episode in 1986. A major related issue is the liability for nuclear accidents. Who should pay, and how much should they pay, if and when a nuclear accident occurs? Early in the era of nuclear power, Congress passed the Price-Anderson Act setting a $560 million limit on electric utilities' insurance liability in the case of any nuclear accident. No such cap on accidents involving competing energy sources exists.

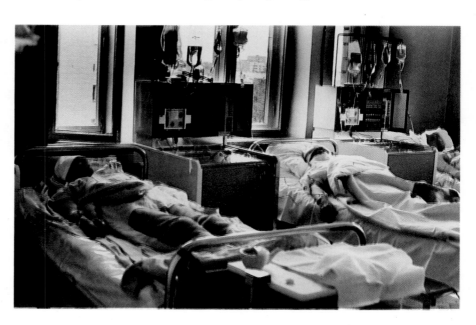

For years, vintners have used yeast to make wine and farmers have selectively bred livestock. Today, you can take living organisms, put them in the production process, isolate certain microbes or splice genes, and *voilà*, you've created a new kind of organism for a specific purpose. That is biotechnology. The effects of today's biotechnology on the environment, the economy, and public health are starting to worry people, though, and a new political debate has begun.

A live, genetically altered virus has been injected without government authorization into pigs in Illinois, and field tests are scheduled for pesticides developed through the use of recombinant DNA. By 1988, farmers should be able to buy a bovine growth hormone that may increase milk production in cows by up to 40 percent, causing a reduction in milk prices and affecting the number of dairy farmers who can stay in business. Proponents of such actions see dramatic benefits, including higher crop yields and healthier, more marketable livestock. They even see a cleaner environment through elimination of pesticides. But critics of the technology are everywhere. They include Washington activist Jeremy Rifkin, the Humane Society, and even the Reverend Jerry Falwell's Moral Majority. Critics fear this biotechnology could produce disastrous ecological problems.

In partial answer to the critics, the White House Domestic Council approved and sent to President Reagan on May 20, 1986, a new set of rules for regulating the biotechnology industry. The policy holds that each biotechnology product should be considered separately, with some exempted from regulation altogether and others assigned for regulation by specific agencies. The White House Biological Science Coordinating Committee (BSCC) is designated under the new regulatory provisions as the permanent coordinator of federal biotechnology policy. Detailed implementation will be left to the EPA, the Department of Agriculture, and the FDA. Further political actions, highlighted by strong lobbying both for and against widespread application of biotechnology, are certain to follow.

Critics of the nuclear power industry point out that such a liability limitation has encouraged the building of more nuclear power plants than would otherwise have been done. The Price-Anderson Act actually constitutes a hidden subsidy of nuclear power by the U.S. government. The critics want electric utilities to bear full responsibility for any nuclear accident, no matter how great. (Actually, many of the critics want *no* nuclear power because of safety problems.) The issue of full liability for nuclear accidents will continue to be raised.

The Environment

We face crucial trade-offs with respect to energy. Everyone realizes that energy is scarce and that many of our nonrenewable resources are jeopardized by excessive consumption. Therefore, alternative, often cheaper, sources of energy are sought for heating, for example. Energy efficiency can be improved if we are willing to relax pollution standards for factories and automobiles. But what is the appropriate **trade-off**? As a nation, must we worry more about conserving energy and less about a clean environment? Or should we worry more about a clean environment and less about energy?

The energy-environment trade-off is a constant issue because virtually all future energy development will entail an environmental hazard. If we use too much of our nonrenewable resources, then we will face worldwide resource exhaustion. If we use coal, we will pollute the air and harm the environment. If we use nuclear

Trade-Off
What has to be given up in order to get something else.

power, we are faced with problems of operational safety and nuclear waste disposal. This energy-ecology trade-off is relatively new to the American political and economic scene.

In American government, the energy-ecology balance had been a nonissue until recently. The nod had always been given to energy development with little thought to environmental concerns. The national government (as well as state governments) promoted automobile use without regard for long-term air quality. The nationally subsidized interstate highway system gave us almost fifty thousand miles of highway at a cost of at least $70 billion. The issue of public safety and nuclear power was largely ignored by the Atomic Energy Commission in the 1950s and only became a serious issue in the last ten to fifteen years.

The energy-ecology balance, however, is shifting. Fewer Americans are concerned about "running out of gas" and more of them are concerned about cleaner air and water.

The Government's Response to Pollution Problems

Government has been responding to pollution problems since before the American Revolution, when the Massachusetts Bay Colony issued regulations to try to stop the pollution of Boston Harbor. In the nineteenth century, states passed laws controlling water pollution after scientists and medical researchers convinced most policy makers that dumping sewage into drinking and bathing water caused disease. At the national level, the Water Pollution Control Act of 1948 provided that research and assistance be given to the states, but little was done. In 1952, the first state air-pollution law was passed in Oregon. Again at the national level, the Air Pollution Control Act of 1955 gave some assistance to states and cities. Table 17–2 describes the major environmental legislation in the United States.

Air pollution over the Capitol building in Washington, D.C.

Table 17–2
▽

Major Federal Environmental Legislation

1899 Refuse Act
Made it unlawful to dump refuse into navigable waters without a permit. A 1966 court decision made all industrial wastes subject to this act.

1947 Federal Insecticide, Fungicide and Rodenticide Act
Enacted to protect farmers from fraudulent claims of salespersons. Required registration of poisons.

1955 Federal Water Pollution Control Act
Set standards for treatment of municipal water waste before discharge. Revisions to this act were passed in 1965 and 1967.

1963 Clean Air Act
Assisted local and state governments in establishing control programs and coordinated research.

1965 Clean Air Act Amendments
Authorized establishment of federal standards for automobile exhaust emissions, beginning with 1968 models.

1965 Solid Waste Disposal Act
Provided assistance to local and state governments for control programs and authorized research in this area.

1965 Water Quality Act
Authorized the setting of standards for discharges into waters.

1967 Air Quality Act
Established air quality regions, with acceptable regional pollution levels. Required local and state governments to implement approved control programs or be subject to federal controls.

1967 Federal Insecticide, Fungicide and Rodenticide Amendments
Provided for licensing of pesticide users. (Further authority granted through 1972 revision.)

1970 National Environmental Quality Act
Established Council for Environmental Quality for the purpose of coordinating all federal pollution control programs. Authorized the establishment of the Environmental Protection Agency to implement CEQ policies on a case-by-case basis.

1970 Clean Air Act Amendments
Authorized the Environmental Protection Agency to set national air pollution standards. Restricted the discharge of six major pollutants into the lower atmosphere. Automobile manufacturers were required to reduce nitrogen oxide, hydrocarbon, and carbon monoxide emissions by 90 percent (in addition to the 1965 requirements) during the 1970s. Set aircraft emission standards. Required states to meet deadline for complying with EPA standards. Authorized legal action by private citizens to require EPA to carry out approved standards against undiscovered offenders.

1970 Resource Recovery Act
Authorized government assistance for the construction of pilot recycling plants. Authorized the development of control programs on national level.

1970 Water Quality and Improvement Act
Required local and state governments to carry out standards under compliance deadlines.

1972 Federal Water Pollution Control Act Amendments
Set national water quality goal of restoring polluted water to swimmable, fishable waters by 1983.

1972 Noise Control Act
Required EPA to establish noise standards for products determined to be major sources of noise. Required EPA to advise the Federal Aviation Administration on acceptable standards for aircraft noise.

1972 Pesticide Control Act
Required that all pesticides used in interstate commerce be approved and certified as effective for their stated purposes. Required certification that they were harmless to humans, animal life, animal feed, and crops.

1974 Clean Water Act
Originally called the Safe Water Drinking Act, this law set (for the first time) federal standards for water suppliers serving more than twenty-five people, having more than fifteen service connections, or operating more than sixty days a year.

1975 Federal Environmental Pesticide Control Act Amendments
Established 1977 as the deadline for registration, classification, and licensing of approximately 50,000 pesticides. This deadline was not met.

1976 Resource Conservation and Recovery Act
Encouraged conservation and the recovery of resources. Put hazardous waste under government control. Disallowed the opening of new dumping sites. Required that all existing open dumps be closed or upgraded to sanitary landfills by 1983. Set standards for providing technical, financial, and marketing assistance to encourage solid waste management.

1977 Clean Air Act Amendments
Changed deadline for automobile emission requirements from 1975 to 1978 to 1980–1981.

1977 Amendments to Clean Water Act
Revised list of toxic pollutants and set new policies for review. Required that pollutants be monitored "by best available technology" that is economically feasible.

1977 Federal Water Pollution Control Act Amendments
Authorized extension of the 1972 regulations.

1980 Toxic Waste Superfund Act
Established a fund to clean up toxic waste dumps.

An oil spill in the Gulf of Mexico.

The National Environmental Policy Act

The year 1969 marks perhaps the true start of national government involvement in pollution problems. In that year, the conflict between oil exploration interests and environmental interests literally erupted when a Union Oil Company's oil well six miles off the coast of Santa Barbara, California, exploded, releasing 235,000 gallons of crude oil. The result was an oil slick, covering an area of eight hundred square miles, that washed up on the city's beaches and killed plant life, birds, and numerous fish. Hearings in Congress revealed that the Interior Department did not know which way to go in the energy-environmental trade-off. Congress did know, however, and passed the National Environmental Policy Act in 1969. This landmark legislation established, among other things, the **Council for Environmental Quality (CEQ)**. Also, it mandated that an **environmental impact statement (EIS)** be prepared for every recommendation or report on legislation or major federal action that significantly affected the quality of the environment. The act therefore gave citizens and public interest groups concerned with the environment a weapon against unnecessary and inappropriate use of our resources by government.

Acid Rain: A Current Environmental Policy Question

At the beginning of 1984, five states and three national environmental groups said they planned to sue the Environmental Protection Agency, hoping to force action on the problem of **acid rain.** The Clean Air Act amendments, they contended, require that the EPA reduce pollution from coal-burning, electricity-generating plants. They maintained that the EPA and factories in the Midwest had been lax in applying the necessary pollution-abatement standards. According to these groups, the result has been acid rain—rain that has a high sulfur content, such as in Wheeling, West Virginia, where it is about on a par with the acid content of stomach acid, or in Jockeybush Lake in the Adirondacks, where it is not much less acidic than vinegar. In parts of Canada and the Northeast particularly, acid rain is thought to be responsible for killing fish and blighting forests.

Council for Environmental Quality

An organization that recommends to the president policies that might improve the environment. It was created in 1969 by the National Environmental Policy Act.

Environmental Impact Statement (EIS)

A statement first required by the 1969 National Environmental Policy Act. That act directed federal agencies to consider the impact on the environment of all major activities and to include in every recommendation a written analysis of that effect as well as alternatives to the proposal.

Acid Rain

Rain containing a high sulfur content.

Congress has not wanted to act according to the experts, primarily because of the regionally devisive nature of the problem. Most scientists believe that acid rain is caused when sulfur and other pollutants, primarily from coal-fired electric power plants, factories, and cars, are carried a long distance in the atmosphere. If indeed it is the coal-fired electric utility plants in the Midwest that are causing the problem in the Northeast, then the customers of the midwestern utilities are going to have to foot the bill. But, of course, they do not want to do so, and the midwestern utilities do not want to assume the costs of cleaning up the sulfur emissions from electric power generation. A lot of money is involved. Cost estimates for the major bills circulating in Congress range between $3 and $8 billion annually.[6]

Even within the Reagan administration, there was no unanimity about how to solve the problem. In 1984, Office of Management and Budget Director David Stockman argued that the proposed acid rain control programs would cost thousands of dollars per pound of fish saved, whereas Environmental Protection Agency Administrator William Ruckelshaus wanted some kind of program to placate environmentalists. National environmental policy is a function of scientific fact, interest group pressure, and politics at the highest level.

[6]Andy Pasztor, "Congress Seen Unlikely to Act on Acid Rain," *The Wall Street Journal*, January 12, 1984, sect. 2, p. 1.

Energy will undoubtedly be among the more important domestic issues in the coming decades. Ultimately, every energy policy involves environmental questions. Not only is this issue central to our everyday lives, but also, it is argued, the fate of the planet may hang in the balance of decisions made about energy production and environmental protection. To make things more complicated, these parallel struggles of coping with energy problems and preserving our environment tend to work at cross-purposes. In pursuit of secure and abundant energy, clean air, water, and land—as well as people—are sometimes sacrificed.

Over all decisions about nuclear energy hang memories of Three Mile Island, Chernobyl, continuous low-level radiation, the hazards of radioactive waste, and the threat of worldwide proliferation of nuclear weapons. Reliance upon oil raises the problem of continuing pollution and of committing the economic well-being of our nation to the decisions of other nations. Increasing reliance on coal means encouraging an industry that is hazardous to its workers, as well as increasing the possibility of severe environmental damage through deglaciation and acid rain.

When objectives clash, difficult political trade-offs must be made. To a large group of environmentalists in this country, the choice is clear. Through citizen action groups, environmentalists have challenged the government on these and other issues. They argue that if we want to improve or even preserve our quality of life, we must stop environmental degradation.

New fears that Reagan administration policies would threaten a decade of progress in curbing pollution added thousands of members to the ranks of environmental organizations. Many felt that the administration was giving industry dangerous leeway to get around environmental regulations. Some were concerned with expanding nuclear energy plants without a concurrent plan to dispose of nuclear wastes. Some were critical of the Environmental Protection Agency's revisions in assessing the dangers of new pesticides. Others were angered with the drive to open up more of the nation's natural resources to commercial development and mineral exploration.

Although these diverse groups work on a host of issues from solar power to mass transit and from wildlife preservation to population control, they are bound by certain commonly held beliefs. Brock Evans describes the traditional goals of the environmental movement:

> We have always sought the highest quality management of public lands for the full spectrum of multiple uses, so that the lands will not be abused but will be passed on to the future intact and not ravaged by short-term exploitation.
>
> We have always sought special reservations of our finest scenic vistas, our superlative natural and historic wonders, the remnants of once-vast wilderness . . . because they are part of our culture, history, and traditions too.
>
> We have always sought the highest degree of protection for our native wildlife in parks, refuges, and wilderness areas, and through high-quality management . . . so that future generations as well as our own can enjoy this abundance.*

If you feel strongly about these issues and want to get involved, contact the following groups:

Sierra Club
530 Bush St.
San Francisco, CA 94108

National Audubon Society
1130 5th Ave.
New York, NY 10038

National Parks Conservation
  Association
1701 18th St., NW
Washington, D.C. 20009

Wilderness Society
1901 Pennsylvania Ave., NW
Washington, D.C. 20006

National Wildlife Federation
1412 16th St., NW
Washington, D.C. 20006

Environmental Defense Fund
1525 18th St., NW
Washington, D.C. 20036

Natural Resources Defense
  Council
917 15th St., NW
Washington, D.C. 20005

Friends of the Earth
620 C St., SE
Washington, D.C. 20003

*Brock Evans, "The Environmental Community: Response to the Reagan Administration Program," delivered to the National Symposium on Public Lands and the Reagan Administration, Denver, Colorado, November 19, 1981, and published in *Vital Speeches*, February 1, 1982, p. 231.

Chapter Summary

1. The Social Security Act was passed in 1935 and now covers almost all Americans with some sort of social insurance for retirement and for medical payments after retirement.

2. The Social Security Administration has faced numerous financial crises as benefits have increased faster than the taxes levied. In the future, there may be additional Social Security crises as the percentage of the population eligible for Social Security rises and the percentage of the population working and paying into Social Security falls.

3. Medicare, part of the Social Security program, became effective on July 1, 1966 and provides for hospitalization insurance financed by contributions from employers and employees similar to Social Security contributions. The states operate Medicaid, which is a health insurance program for the poor regardless of age.

4. In spite of rising expenditures on poverty elimination, the percentage of persons officially classified as poor has risen in the United States since 1978. Currently more than one in eight Americans is classified as poor.

5. Other basic programs for helping the poor include Supplemental Security Income (SSI) and Aid to Families with Dependent Children (AFDC), as well as food stamps and housing subsidies. There are over 150 separate programs, many of them overlapping.

6. The reason we may have observed more individuals entering the ranks of the poor is because of (a) increased unemployment, (b) lack of educational training, (c) the feminization of poverty, and (d) ethnic and gender discrimination.

7. Income security for farmers is created through a variety of programs designed to support the price of agricultural crops or pay farmers subsidies in the form of deficiency payments for crops that they sell below government-specified target prices. Price supports will always create surpluses with which the government must contend.

8. Since price support programs and deficiency payments for farmers relate to potential total farm output, large farms benefit the most. The truly needy farmers obtain a very small percent of all farming sector government benefits.

9. Labor-management relations are governed by a variety of federal legislation, including the Norris-LaGuardia Act of 1932, the National Labor Relations Act of 1935 (the Wagner Act), the Fair Labor Standards Act of 1938, the Federal Labor Standards Act of 1940, the Taft-Hartley Act (Labor-Management Relations Act) of 1947, and the Landrum-Griffin Act of 1959.

10. Some states have right-to-work laws which make it illegal for union membership to be a requirement for continued employment. Most states allow a union shop to be legal because membership is not a prerequisite for employment.

11. Worker safety and health is regulated by the Occupational Safety and Health Administration (OSHA), which was created in 1970. OSHA creates rules and regulations that employers must follow and enforces them by sending out observers to find violations. It then fines offenders.

12. Concern about energy and the environment increased in 1986 because of a large nuclear power plant accident at Chernobyl in the Soviet Union. Nuclear power was seen as a major future source of energy in the United States, but because of accidents and increased requirements for safety devices, the cost of nuclear power no longer makes it the most viable long-run choice for energy production. There is also grave concern about radioactive waste and what must be done with it.

13. All improvement in our environment involves a trade-off. That is to say, a cleaner environment usually means less of other things because it requires resources to make our environment cleaner.

Questions for Review and Discussion

1. If you are planning for your retirement some forty years from now, do you think it is wise to consider other sources of income besides Social Security?

2. How can it be possible to spend more to alleviate poverty while at the same time have the percentage of the population defined as poor going up?

3. It has been said that current government programs to help the farmer only benefit rich farmers because these programs are based on total amount of potential output. Can you think of an alternative way to help poor farmers besides those described in the text?

4. Anti-union critics claim that unions are simply another form of monopoly and should be outlawed. Do you agree or disagree?

5. Why is it said that it is impossible to have a cleaner environment without incurring a trade-off?

Selected References

Energy and Environment, The Unfinished Business. (Washington, D.C.: Congressional Quarterly Press, 1985). This compendium discusses the debate between the Reagan administration and Congress over energy policy, in particular, conservation versus regulation with a focus on how regional issues and interests impact on those issues.

Eli Ginsberg, ed., *U.S. Health Care System: A Look to the 1990s* (Totowa, N.J.: Roman and Littlefield, 1985). An excellent review of the major areas of American health care, such as public attitudes, care provider issues, advanced medical technology, and cost-benefit analysis.

Michael Harrington, *The New American Poverty* (New York: Penguin Books, 1985). A powerful and controversial examination of the nature of poverty in the United States, this book reveals new characteristics of the nation's poor in blue-collar communities, among illegal immigrants, and single mothers.

James P. Lester and Ann O'M. Bowman, eds., *The Politics of Hazardous Waste Management* (Durham, N.C.: Duke University Press, 1983). A massive anthology of original research on a serious and controversial subject.

R. Shep Melnick, *Regulation and the Courts* (Washington, D.C.: Brookings Institution, 1984). This book analyzes the effects that court decisions have had on federal air pollution policy.

Morgan O. Reynolds, *Power and Privilege: Labor Unions in America* (New York: Universe Books, 1974). A critique of the role of labor unions and their functions.

James Ridgeway, *The Politics of Ecology* (New York: E. P. Dutton, 1970). Proposes changes in corporate power to alleviate the problem of pollution, with a focus on political sources of support for those who damage the environment.

Chapter 18
▽
Foreign and Defense Policy

Contents
▽
The United States Is Just a Part of the World

What Is Foreign Policy?

A Short History of U.S. Foreign Policy

Who Makes Foreign Policy?

The Military-Industrial Complex

Limiting the President's Power

Foreign Economic Policy

Multinational Corporations: A New Force in Foreign Policy

The Nuclear Freeze Movement

What If . . .

▽

The United States Withdrew from the United Nations?

As one of the charter members of the United Nations, with the power to veto decisions of the Security Council, the United States has had a longstanding interest in the operation of the U.N. The financial obligation of this membership is considerable—about $336 million in 1984. Apart from general U.N. activities, the money helps to sustain the Food and Agricultural Organization, the International Atomic Energy Agency, the International Civil Aviation Organization, the International Telecommunications Union, the United Nations Educational, Scientific, and Cultural Organization (from which the United States withdrew early in 1985), the World Health Organization, the World Meteorological Organization, and other agencies. Nearly $70 million more was given in 1982 for U.N. military peacekeeping forces.

If the United States were to pull out of the U.N., much or all of these expenditures would be saved. New

York City would be spared the trouble of providing police protection and other services for the eighteen-acre headquarters site in Manhattan along the East River. Possible espionage and other diplomatic incidents involving U.N. personnel would also be avoided.

There would also be major drawbacks to an American withdrawal. The United States would lose a propaganda forum for promoting its actions and attacking the policies of its opponents. An important avenue for resolving conflicts peacefully would virtually cease to exist, and key U.N. agencies that assist in world health, agriculture, international finance, education, and other areas might well collapse. The United States would be perceived by allies and enemies alike as resigning its world leadership role. Whether the interests of the rest of the world or even the national interest of the United States would be served by a U.S. withdrawal from the U.N. is doubtful.

▽

Once considered an isolationist nation, the United States now plays a role as a world leader. Our foreign and defense policy must take into account our national goals, our economic needs, and our view of both friends and enemies abroad.

For a period of six weeks in the spring of 1986, the foreign policy decisions of the United States in a number of areas, and specifically the actions of Ronald Reagan, held center stage. Late in February, the Philippines saw *both* Ferdinand Marcos and Corazon Aquino sworn in as president following an election marked by fraud and intimidation. The Reagan administration, after years of American support for Marcos, urged the former ally to resign, and offered him safety in the United States. The recognition of the Aquino government by the United States was a major victory for her political movement.

Even as the Marcos entourage settled into quarters in Hawaii, the spotlight turned to Central America. President Reagan had requested $70 million in military aid and $30 million in humanitarian aid for the *contras* fighting against the Sandinista government of Nicaragua. On March 20, the House of Representatives rejected his request. The president lobbied hard for this measure in between official meetings with Brian Mulroney, the prime minister of Canada, who was in Washington for a two-day summit meeting. The primary focus of the Reagan-Mulroney talks was the problem of acid rain.

Three days after the House vote, attention shifted to the Middle East where the U.S. Sixth Fleet was conducting exercises in the Mediterranean. The fleet purposely crossed into the Gulf of Sidra, a body of water that Libya had claimed as its own. After Libyan forces fired missiles at American warplanes, the United States responded by attacking Libyan ships and missile positions. The United States had previously ordered Americans to leave Libya after the terrorist attacks on the Rome and Vienna airports. On March 27, the Senate approved the president's request for aid to Nicaragua, sending the bill back to the House. The Senate action followed rumors that Nicaraguan troops had entered Honduras to attack the contra forces. Nicaragua denied the charge.

Yet another terrorist attack took place on April 2, when a bomb exploded on a TWA jet flying from Rome to Athens, killing four passengers, all Americans. On April 5, a bomb destroyed a West Berlin nightclub frequented by U.S. service personnel, killing two individuals. This terrorist act precipitated the president's

The Berlin night club destroyed by terrorist bombing on April 5, 1986.

Damage caused by the American attack on Libya.

decision to send American warplanes to attack Tripoli, the Libyan capital, on April 14. Except for the British, who allowed U.S. planes to use bases in England to stage the attack, all of its European allies criticized the American action. Later, however, most of the European nations tightened up their own security arrangements and began intense efforts to locate terrorists within Europe.

This brief chronology only hints at our nation's global involvement. Whether the issue is protecting Americans abroad, countering unfriendly governments in Central America, or improving the chances of democracy in Asia, United States interests are affected and United States foreign policy must be shaped accordingly. The place of the president as a premier foreign policy maker is clear. Using his powers as chief diplomat, Ronald Reagan gave support to Aquino; as chief legislator, he lobbied Congress for the *contra* cause; and, as commander in chief, the president ordered military forces to attack Libya.

The United States Is Just a Part of the World

▽

Although the events that occurred in the spring of 1986 may seem atypical, the president of the United States, as well as Congress—and occasionally the federal judiciary—is constantly faced with making decisions affecting the rest of the world.

The United States is part of the world, and as such is dependent on what the rest of the world does. It is equally true that the rest of the world depends on the United States. We are indeed interdependent—all 5 billion of us who people the 58.5 million square miles of land on the globe.

Economic Interdependence

Table 18–1 shows world trade in different countries as a percentage of gross national product. Some countries, such as the Netherlands, derive a large percentage of their GNP from world trade. The United States has a relatively small percentage of its GNP accounted for by world trade. But still, consider what would happen if we were no longer allowed to import goods from other countries: Tea and coffee drinkers would have to switch to postum. Chocolate would be out of the question; carob would have to do. We would have no pepper and no Scotch whiskey. When the supply of some goods that we import is cut off—as happened with OPEC's 1973 oil embargo—the results can be almost devastating.

What about exports? If we weren't able to export to other countries, the following would happen:

1. The economy would lose about $30 billion in foreign sales for food and live animals, most of that for grains.
2. The coal, petroleum, and other mineral fuels industries would lose more than $8 billion in sales.
3. More than $20 billion in chemicals would go unsold.
4. Nearly $85 billion would be lost to manufacturers of machinery and transport equipment such as cars or airplanes.
5. Textile industry sales would decrease by about $3.5 billion.

Military Interdependence

The United States is militarily interdependent with many other nations. As a leader in the Western alliance system, the U.S. is party to at least five major collective mutual defense assistance treaties, such as the North Atlantic Treaty Organization (NATO). To preserve peace, or at least a setting for negotiations, U.S. marines were sent into Lebanon in 1983. The United States sells about $16 billion worth of arms each year to foreign governments and gives more than that away.

In view of the fact that this country spends 30 percent of its federal budget on defense and maintains half a million troops overseas, it is clear that the U.S. is intimately and inexorably involved in what happens in the rest of the world.

Cultural Interdependence

As we pointed out in Chapter 5, the United States does not consist of white, Anglo-Saxon Protestants only. There are in fact dozens of ethnic groups within our borders that have to some extent maintained cultural ties with their country of origin. Also, every year about half a million immigrants obtain permanent residence in the United States. Occasionally, entire ethnic communities are formed within a short period of time. This happened when Haitians left their country in great numbers

Did You Know?
▽
That in 1985, the Soviet Union and Warsaw Pact nations had an estimated 43,000 tanks and more than 4 million military personnel as compared with the 13,000 tanks and 2.6 million military personnel of the United States and NATO forces in Europe?

Table 18–1
▽
World Trade in Various Countries as a Percentage of Gross National Product

Country	Exports as a % of GNP
Argentina	8.6%
Australia	13.8
Brazil	6.8
Canada	24.6
Czechoslovakia	11.0
Egypt	9.5
France	18.0
East Germany	12.6
West Germany	26.9
India (1981)	4.5
Japan	13.2
Netherlands	48.0
Nigeria	28.5
USSR	5.1
United Kingdom	20.7
United States	9.1

SOURCE: *Handbook of Economic Statistics, 1986,* Central Intelligence Agency, Directorate of Intelligence.

Foreign Policy

A nation's external goals and the techniques and strategies used to achieve them.

Diplomacy

The total process by means of which states carry on political relations with each other; settling conflicts among nations by peaceful means.

Economic Aid

Assistance to other nations in the form of grants, loans, or credits to buy American products.

Technical Assistance

Sending experts with technical skills in agriculture, engineering, or business to aid other nations.

Foreign Policy Process

The steps by which external goals are decided and acted on.

National Security Policy

Foreign and domestic policy designed to protect the independence and political and economic integrity of the United States; policy that is concerned with the safety and defense of the nation.

National Security Council (NSC)

A board created by the 1947 National Security Act to advise the president on matters of national security.

from 1980 to 1982 and came to Florida and when communities of Vietnamese sprang up almost overnight on the West Coast after the United States, for humanitarian and political reasons, agreed to accept about 200,000 refugees.

In short, the United States is a tremendous importer of foreign culture. But the United States also exports American culture—especially pop culture. American popular music has had a tremendous influence, not only in Britain, but also in almost every country of the world. British rock stars, such as the Rolling Stones and the Beatles, have paid tribute to their American progenitors—Chuck Berry and Buddy Holly, for example. American clothing fads quickly travel to western Europe and beyond. The sports-look mania of tennis shoes, jogging shoes and jogging clothes, not to mention the ubiquitous blue jeans, are America's contribution to international culture. For better or worse, the American love for fast food eventually caught on in Western Europe; today even the once-conservative Japanese eat at McDonald's in Tokyo.

What Is Foreign Policy?

▽

As our cultural, military, and economic interdependence with the other nations of the world has increased, it has become even more important for the United States to establish and carry out foreign policies to deal with external situations and to carry out our own national goals. By **foreign policy,** we mean both the goals we want to achieve in the world and the techniques and strategies to achieve them. For example, if one national goal is to achieve stability in the Caribbean basin and to encourage the formation of democratic governments there, U.S. foreign policy in that area may be carried out with the techniques of **diplomacy, economic aid, technical assistance,** or military intervention. Sometimes foreign policies are restricted to statements of goals or ideals, such as helping to end world poverty, whereas at other times foreign policies are comprehensive efforts to achieve particular objectives.

United States foreign policy is established through the **foreign policy process,** which usually originates with the president and those agencies that advise him on foreign policy matters. Foreign policy formulation is often affected by congressional action and national public debate.

National Security Policy

We should not confuse foreign policy with national security policy, which is one aspect of the former. A more specialized concept, **national security policy** is designed primarily to protect the independence and the political integrity of the United States. It concerns itself with the defense of the United States against actual or potential (real or imagined) enemies, domestic or foreign.

U.S. national security policy is based on determinations made by the Department of Defense, the Department of State, and a growing number of other federal agencies, including the **National Security Council (NSC).** The NSC acts as an advisory body to the president, but it has increasingly become a rival to the State Department in influencing the foreign policy process. This was particularly evident when it was revealed, in November 1986, that the Reagan administration had largely by-passed the Department of State (and Congress) in using the NSC to direct sales of U.S. military equipment to Iran.

Diplomacy

Diplomacy is another aspect of foreign policy, but is not coterminous with it. Diplomacy involves all of a nation's external relationships, from routine diplomatic communications to summit meetings among heads of state. More specifically, diplomacy refers to the settling of disputes and conflicts among nations by peaceful methods. Diplomacy is the set of negotiating techniques by which a nation attempts to carry out its foreign policy.

The United States historically has not been seen as good at diplomacy. Indeed, many American lawmakers justified an isolationist approach to foreign affairs in the past because the United States presumably lacked the diplomatic ability to negotiate successfully with experienced "Old World" diplomats. The results of several diplomatic conferences during World War II with the Soviet Union further strengthened the notion that Americans were not diplomatically adept.[1]

We can understand the foreign and defense policies of today more easily if we look briefly at the history of the United States in world affairs.

George Shultz, Secretary of State.

A Short History of U.S. Foreign Policy

▽

American foreign policy falls into a number of distinct periods throughout the nation's relatively short history. They are as follows: (1) the formative years, (2) nineteenth-century isolationism, (3) World War I, (4) post-World War I isolationism, (5) World War II, (6) the cold war, (7) détente, and (8) post-détente.

The Formative Years

United States foreign policy dates back to the colonial uprising against the British Crown. The Declaration of Independence formalized the colonists' desired break from Britain. Then on September 3, 1783, the signing of the Treaty of Paris not only ended the eight-year War of Independence but also accorded to the United States recognition as an independent nation by the rest of the world. In addition, the Treaty of Paris probably helped to reshape the world, for the American colonies were the first to secure independence against a "superpower."

Foreign policy was largely negative during the formative years. Remember that the new nation was operating under the Articles of Confederation. The national government had no right to levy and collect taxes, no control over commerce, no right to make commercial treaties, and no power to raise an army (the army was dismantled in 1783). Our lack of international power was clearly evident when the U.S. was unable to obtain American hostages that had been seized in the Mediterranean by Barbary pirates, but ignominiously had to purchase the hostages in a treaty made with Morocco.

The Founding Fathers had a basic mistrust of corrupt European governments. George Washington said it was the United States's policy "to steer clear of permanent alliances," and Thomas Jefferson echoed this sentiment when he said America wanted peace with all nations but "entangling alliances with none." This was also a logical position at a time when the United States was so weak militarily that it

---

[1]Roosevelt's meetings with Stalin at Yalta and Potsdam in 1945 have been routinely interpreted, especially by conservatives, as diplomatic victories for the U.S.S.R.

could not directly influence European development. It chose instead to believe that the United States would set a moral standard that Europe could follow. Moreover, being protected by oceans that took weeks to traverse certainly allowed the nation to avoid entangling alliances. During the 1700s and 1800s, the United States generally stayed out of European conflicts and politics.

Nineteenth-Century Isolationism

The United States's role as a world power began in the early 1800s, nonetheless. President James Monroe, in his message to Congress on December 2, 1823, stated that this country would not accept foreign intervention in the Western Hemisphere. In return, the United States would not meddle in European internal affairs. The **Monroe Doctrine** was the underpinning of the United States's isolationist foreign policy throughout the nineteenth century—the **period of isolationism.** More recently, however, the Monroe Doctrine, among other things, was used to justify the invasion of Grenada in the Caribbean in October, 1983.

The Beginning of Interventionism and World War I

Although the nineteenth century was not completely devoid of American **interventionism** in the rest of the world, it was a relatively quiet period in terms of foreign involvement. In 1812, the United States went to war with Great Britain over the ostensible issue of the British navy preying on American commerce. In 1846, President James K. Polk provoked Mexico into war with the United States when he ordered the army to occupy disputed territory along the Rio Grande River.

Monroe Doctrine

The policy statement included in President Monroe's 1823 annual message to Congress, which included three principles: (1) European nations should not establish new colonies in the Western Hemisphere, (2) European nations should not intervene in the affairs of independent nations of the Western Hemisphere, and (3) the United States would not interfere in the affairs of European nations.

Period of Isolationism

A period of abstaining from an active role in international affairs or alliances, which characterized most of the nineteenth century.

Interventionism

Involvement in foreign affairs; actions directed at changing or preserving the internal political arrangements of other nations.

A 1912 painting shows President James Monroe explaining the Monroe Doctrine to a group of government officials.

As a result of the Mexican War, the United States acquired New Mexico, Arizona, California, and other western lands.

But the real end of isolationism started with the Spanish-American War in 1898. Winning that war gave the United States possession of Guam, Puerto Rico, and the Philippines (which gained independence in 1946). Although the United States returned to a policy of isolationism following the Spanish-American War, it lasted only for a brief time—until World War I (1914–18). Still, reluctant to entangle this country with European internal politics, the United States didn't enter the war until late. In his reelection campaign of 1916, President Woodrow Wilson ran on the slogan, "He kept us out of war." But not for long. On April 6, 1917, the United States declared war on Germany because it was evident to Wilson that, without help, the Allies would be defeated and that American property and lives would be attacked by German submarines. Wilson also sought to promote American democratic ideals in Europe and to end international aggression through the United States's entry into the war.

Post-World War I Isolationism

President Wilson was determined that World War I would be the "war to end war." Before the war ended Wilson proposed to secure a just and lasting peace through promulgation of his **Fourteen Points.** They included **open diplomacy,** freedom of the seas, removal of economic barriers, international supervision of colonies, and the creation of a League of Nations. Although ultimately a failure, the Fourteen Points were a useful propaganda instrument during the last phase of World War I, helping to prop up sagging Allied morale.

The signing of the Treaty of Versailles in 1919 formally ended the war, providing among other things for the League of Nations. Wilson went on a cross-country tour to stimulate support for U.S. participation in the league, but was unsuccessful. The Senate refused to ratify it and the United States did not join the league.

In the 1920s, the U.S. did indeed go "back to normalcy," as President Warren G. Harding urged it to do. U.S. military forces were largely disbanded, defense spending dropped to about 1 percent of GNP, and the nation once more retreated into isolationism. International power politics ceased to be an issue in U.S. foreign policy—if in fact the country can be said to have had a foreign policy.

World War II—The Era of Internationalism

Isolationism was permanently shattered and relegated to its place in history by the bombing of the U.S. naval base at Pearl Harbor, Hawaii, on December 7, 1941. The surprise attack by the Japanese resulted in the deaths of 2,403 American servicemen and the wounding of 1,143 others. Eighteen warships were sunk or seriously damaged, and 188 planes were destroyed at the airfields. Tales of the horrors experienced by the wounded survivors quickly reached American shores. The American public was outraged. President Roosevelt immediately declared war on Japan, and the United States entered World War II.

This unequivocal response was certainly due to the nature of the provocation. American soil had not been attacked by a foreign power since the burning of Washington, D.C., by the British in 1814. World War II marked a permanent change in American foreign policy. It also produced a permanent change in the

Fourteen Points

The summarization of Woodrow Wilson's aims and hopes for postwar peace, calling for open diplomacy, freedom of the seas, removal of economic barriers, international supervision of colonies, and the creation of a League of Nations.

Open Diplomacy

The substance of point one of Woodrow Wilson's Fourteen Points—open treaties openly arrived at.

The atomic bomb explodes over Nagasaki on August 9, 1945.

size of the American government. Except for brief periods during the Civil War and World War I, defense spending had been a fairly trivial part of the gross national product. By the end of World War II in 1945, defense spending had increased to almost 40 percent of GNP. The number of United States overseas military bases increased from three at the beginning of 1940 to almost 450 by the end of World War II. National security had become a priority item on the federal government's agenda.

The United States was the only country to emerge from World War II with its economy intact, and even strengthened. The Soviet Union, Japan, Italy, France, Germany, Britain, and a number of minor participants in the war were all economically devastated. The United States was also the only country to have control over operating nuclear weapons. President Harry S. Truman had personally made the decision to use two atomic bombs to end the war with Japan on August 6 and August 9, 1945. (Historians still dispute the necessity of this action, which ultimately killed more than 100,000 Japanese civilians and left an equal number permanently injured.) The United States had truly become the world's superpower.

The End of World War II and the Beginning of the Cold War

On June 26, 1945, in San Francisco, a multilateral treaty, serving as the charter for the United Nations Organization, was signed. Ultimately, it was ratified by fifty-one nations, mainly those united against Germany and Japan, and was put into effect on October 24, 1945. This time the United States could not ignore the need for international cooperation to handle security threats to itself and the rest

The United Nations General Assembly hall.

of the world. The majority of Americans were in favor of joining the United Nations. But the seeds of suspicion and mistrust between the two most powerful nations—the United States and Russia—had already been sown. The Marshall Plan was partly a response to a perceived communist threat. Other responses followed.

The Marshall Plan

After World War II, American financial assistance to other countries was generously extended. The United States financed approximately three-quarters of the United Nations Relief and Rehabilitation Program, which gave $4 billion worth of food, clothing, and medical services to war-ravaged Europe. In the three years following the end of the war, the United States provided about $17 billion in aid to Europe, or about $50 billion in today's dollars.

By 1948, it became clear to Secretary of State George Marshall that more was needed to stimulate the European economies. In a famous address at Harvard University, in June, 1948, Marshall outlined a plan to speed up Europe's recovery—and so was born the **Marshall Plan.** The plan established the European Recovery Program, which granted more than $13 billion in foreign aid over four years, mostly in the form of equipment and supplies produced in the United States. Many observers contend that the Marshall Plan was instrumental in the dramatic growth of Europe's productive capacity during the late 1940s and early 1950s. The massive influx of economic assistance also reduced Soviet influence in Western Europe.

Marshall Plan

A proposal made by Secretary of State George C. Marshall in 1948 for a vast program of American economic aid to reconstruct the war-devastated economies of Western Europe. It was accepted by Congress, and sixteen nations in Western Europe received significant economic aid in the form of grants, loans, and supplies from 1948 to 1952.

▽

587

Security Pacts

Mutual military assistance agreements.

Soviet Bloc

The Eastern European countries with communist regimes.

Cold War

The ideological, political, and economic impasse that existed between the United States and the Soviet Union following World War II.

Iron Curtain

The term used to describe the division of Europe between the Soviet Union and the West. Popularized by Winston Churchill in a speech portraying Europe as being divided by an iron curtain, with the nations of Eastern Europe behind the curtain and increasingly under Soviet control.

Mutual Security Pacts

During the first few years after the close of World War II, the United States entered into mutual military assistance agreements, or **security pacts,** with a number of nations throughout the world (Figure 18–1). The most famous of these is the North Atlantic Treaty Organization (NATO), formed in 1949, which pledges its fourteen European signatories and the United States to mutual military defense against Russia. In all, the United States currently has mutual military assistance agreements involving more than fifty nations.

Confrontation with the Soviet Union

The United States had become an uncomfortable ally of the Soviet Union after the latter had been invaded by Hitler. Soon after the war ended, relations between the Soviets and the West deteriorated. The Soviets wanted a weakened Germany, and to achieve this they insisted that the country be divided in two, with East Germany becoming a buffer for Russia. Little by little, the Soviets supported friendly governments in Eastern European countries, which collectively have become known as the **Soviet bloc.** In response, the United States encouraged the rearming of Western Europe. The "**cold war**" had begun.[2]

In Fulton, Missouri, on March 5, 1946, Winston Churchill, in a striking metaphor, declared that from the Baltic to the Adriatic Seas "an iron curtain has descended across the [European] continent." The term **iron curtain** became even more appropriate when the Soviets built a wall separating East Berlin from West Berlin on August 17–18, 1961.

[2]See John Lewis Gaddis, *The United Nations and the Origins of the Cold War* (New York: Columbia University Press, 1972).

The Berlin Wall.

Figure 18–1

▽

U.S. Security Pacts

Nations with which the United States has signed mutual defense pacts.

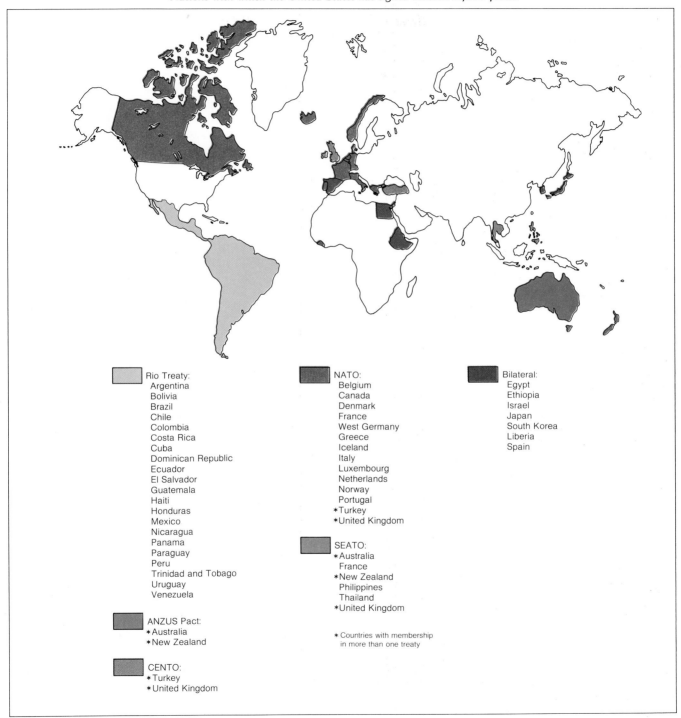

Rio Treaty:
Argentina
Bolivia
Brazil
Chile
Colombia
Costa Rica
Cuba
Dominican Republic
Ecuador
El Salvador
Guatemala
Haiti
Honduras
Mexico
Nicaragua
Panama
Paraguay
Peru
Trinidad and Tobago
Uruguay
Venezuela

ANZUS Pact:
*Australia
*New Zealand

CENTO:
*Turkey
*United Kingdom

NATO:
Belgium
Canada
Denmark
France
West Germany
Greece
Iceland
Italy
Luxembourg
Netherlands
Norway
Portugal
*Turkey
*United Kingdom

SEATO:
*Australia
France
*New Zealand
Philippines
Thailand
*United Kingdom

* Countries with membership
  in more than one treaty

Bilateral:
Egypt
Ethiopia
Israel
Japan
South Korea
Liberia
Spain

SOURCE: U.S. Department of State, *Treaties in Force* (Washington, D.C.: GPO, 1982).

▽

589

Who Started the Cold War?

There are the good guys and the bad guys. Our nation spends money for national defense, whereas their nation spends money for aggression and domination. At least, this is the orthodox view of the United States and the Soviet Union since the beginning of the cold war.

According to orthodox interpretations of history, the Soviet Union has had world domination as its central policy goal since the Russian Revolution. Although the U.S. was allied with the Soviet Union during World War II, that relationship was undercut by Soviet activities at the end of the war. Their refusal to allow elections in the European countries that they liberated from the Nazis, their military occupation of some of those nations, and their anti-American propaganda all served notice of their true intentions. Since the postwar period, many Soviet actions have reaffirmed this view: the crushing of the Hungarian revolt in 1956 and of opposition in Poland in 1956 and 1981, the invasion of Czechoslovakia in 1968, and the invasion of Afghanistan in 1979.

The United States, in this scenario, is the leader of the free world and defender of democratic government and economic freedom. To meet the Soviet threat, the United States must present a strong military presence, secure international respect, and work to limit Soviet expansion. This is the "containment" theory. Its objective is to balance Soviet power.

But not everyone subscribes to the good-guy/bad-guy version of the cold war. Revisionist historians and political scientists point out that the West can be seen as responsible for the hostility between the two camps. Many actions taken by the United States since the Russian Revolution have increased the suspicion of the Russians and added to their own insecurity. This view sees the Russians as responding to an external threat. The West—the United States and NATO—has ringed Soviet borders with armies, rockets, and weapons, and the Soviets have responded by building a buffer zone in the Eastern bloc nations.

Some scholars attribute the cold war to misperceptions held by the superpowers. Starting out as suspicious allies, each expected that the other had evil intentions and, as events unfolded, their worst suspicions were confirmed. The Soviets saw the Marshall Plan as a way to deprive them of their share of the victory over Germany. They resented the close cooperation between the British and the Americans and the fact that the United States did not keep them informed about the development of the atomic bomb. The organization of NATO threatened the Soviets militarily.

Each side continues to regard the other as aggressive, motivated by an all-consuming ideology, and their own efforts as purely defensive. Such differences in perceptions make attempts to reach agreement on such complex issues as arms control even more difficult.

Containment: A New Foreign Policy

In 1947, a remarkable article was published in *Foreign Affairs*. The article was signed by "X." The actual author was George F. Kennan, chief of the policy-planning staff for the Department of State. The doctrine of **containment** set forth in the article became—according to many—the Bible of Western foreign policy. "X" argued that whenever and wherever the Soviets could successfully challenge Western institutions, they would do so. He recommended that our policy toward the Soviets be "firm and vigilant containment of Russian expansive tendencies."[3]

The containment theory was enunciated quite clearly in the **Truman Doctrine,** which was part of President Harry S. Truman's historic address to Congress on March 12, 1947. In that address, he announced that the United States must help countries where a communist takeover seemed likely, and he proposed the Greek-Turkish aid program specifically to counter Soviet influence in the eastern Mediterranean. He put the choice squarely before Congress—it either supported those

Containment

U.S. diplomatic policy adopted by the Truman administration to "build situations of strength" around the globe to contain communist power within its existing boundaries.

Truman Doctrine

The policy adopted by President Harry Truman in 1947 to halt communist expansion in southeastern Europe.

[3]Mr. X., "The Sources of Soviet Conduct," *Foreign Affairs*, July 1947, p. 575.

measures required to preserve peace and security abroad or it would risk widespread global instability and perhaps World War III.[4]

During the cold war, there had never been any direct military confrontation between the United States and the Soviet Union. Rather, confrontations among "client" nations were used to carry out the policies of the superpowers. Only on occasion has the United States directly entered into a conflict in a significant way. Two such occasions were in Korea and Vietnam.

In 1950, North Korean troops were embroiled in a war with South Korea. President Truman asked for and received a Security Council order from the United Nations for the North Koreans to withdraw. The Soviet Union was absent from the council on that day and did not participate in the discussion. Truman then authorized the use of American forces in support of the South Koreans. For the next three years, American troops were engaged in a land war in Asia—nominally a United Nations effort in which the Americans were the principal combatants. When General MacArthur, commander of the UN forces, attacked North Korea, the People's Republic of China responded with a massive influx of troops. The war became a stalemate and a political liability to President Truman. One of Dwight Eisenhower's major 1952 campaign promises was to end the Korean war—which he did. An armistice was signed on July 27, 1953. However, American troops have been stationed in South Korea ever since.

U.S. involvement in Vietnam began shortly after the end of the Korean conflict. When the French army in Indochina was defeated by the communist forces of Ho Chi Minh and the two Vietnams were created in 1954, the Americans assumed the role of supporting the South Vietnamese government against the communist North. John Kennedy sent 16,000 "advisers" to help South Vietnam, and after Kennedy's death, Lyndon Johnson greatly increased the scope of that support. American forces in Vietnam at the height of U.S. involvement totaled more than 500,000 troops. Over 56,000 Americans were killed and more than 300,000 were wounded in the conflict. The debate over the United States's presence in Vietnam

[4]*Public Papers of the Presidents of the United States: Harry S. Truman, 1947* (Washington, D.C.: GPO, 1963), pp. 176–180.

American soldiers in Korea.

Profile
▽
George F. Kennan

Although he was a career diplomat and intellectual rather than a political leader, George Frost Kennan probably has had more influence on the shape of American foreign policy since World War II than any other American. Kennan, born in 1904 in Milwaukee, Wisconsin, received his college education at Princeton University. After graduating, he entered the foreign service and spent the next twenty years as a career foreign service officer, holding assorted posts in Eastern Europe. When the United States first extended diplomatic recognition to the Soviet Union in 1933, Kennan went to Moscow with the new ambassador as a consular officer. Thus began Kennan's lifelong involvement in U.S.–U.S.S.R. relations.

At the outbreak of the Second World War, Kennan was serving in the U.S. embassy in Berlin. He was interned by the Nazi government for a year and then released. In 1944, he returned to Moscow as the minister-counselor of the embassy. As part of his duties in Moscow, he sent a cablegram to the State Department in 1946 outlining his recommendations for U.S. policy toward the Soviets after the war. This cablegram led to his assuming the post of director of policy planning for the State Department and the publication of his ideas in an article in the prestigious periodical *Foreign Affairs.*

The article in *Foreign Affairs,* which was signed by "X," recommended that the United States must act to "contain' Soviet expansion whenever and wherever it occurred. Published at precisely the moment when the Soviet Union

"Every government is in some respects a problem for every other government, and it will always be this way so long as the sovereign state, with its supremely self-centered rationale, remains the basis of international life."

George F. Kennan

was attempting to consolidate its control over the Eastern European nations and to weaken pro-American elements in Greece and Italy, the containment policy suggested in the article became the cornerstone of American policy toward Russia. Throughout the decade of the 1950s, American policy was based

on signing treaties and constructing alliances to "contain" the Soviet Union. The creation of NATO and the stationing of American troops in Europe was also based on this strategy.

George Kennan, however, has criticized the way in which containment has been understood by government officials. In his view, the article was not meant to create an official policy stance toward the Soviets but to suggest tactics for dealing with their specific actions. He has steadfastly argued that American policy makers are too concerned with idealistic goals in foreign policy and with originating moralistic policies. In his view, the most important part of foreign policy is the application of diplomatic techniques and the choice of specific policies to achieve one's goals.

Besides his contributions to the foreign policy of the United States, Kennan has had a long and distinguished career as an author and historian. He is the only American to be both a foreign service officer and a member of the American Academy of Arts and Letters. Winner of numerous prizes for his books, Kennan continues past the age of eighty to publish his views on how the United States should deal with the Soviet Union in the nuclear age. In a recent work, he declared that "there is no issue at stake in our political relations with the Soviet Union . . . which would conceivably be worth a nuclear war."*

*Stanley Hoffman, "Kennan's Passionate Realism," *Atlantic,* December 1982, p. 96.

Helicopters in Vietnam.

divided the American electorate and spurred congressional efforts to limit the ability of the president to commit forces to armed combat. After a peace treaty was signed in 1973 and the prisoners of war were returned, the United States seemed unclear about its national security goals and its commitment to the old containment view of dealing with communism.

Confrontation in a Nuclear World

Nuclear power has spread throughout the world. The United States, the Soviet Union, India, China, Britain, France, and several other countries all have the capability of detonating nuclear bombs. It is estimated that the two superpowers have enough nuclear bombs to destroy everyone at least twice and maybe three times. Obviously, confrontation between the United States and Russia could take on world-destroying proportions. Perhaps the closest we came to such a confrontation was the Cuban missile crisis in 1962. For thirteen days, the United States and Russia were close to nuclear war. The Soviets had decided to place offensive missiles ninety miles off the American coast in Cuba. On October 14, 1962, an American U-2 spy plane photographed the missile site being built. Immediately, the executive committee of the National Security Council met to discuss ways to get the missiles out of Cuba before they became operational. President Kennedy and his advisers rejected the possibility of armed intervention, setting up a naval blockade around the island instead. When Soviet vessels, apparently carrying nuclear warheads, appeared near Cuban waters, the confrontation reached its height. After intense negotiations between Washington and Moscow, the Soviet ships turned around on October 25, and on October 28 the Soviet Union announced the withdrawal of its missile operations from Cuba. In exchange, the United States agreed not to invade Cuba.

Most other confrontations between the superpowers, as well as those among the lesser powers, have not come anywhere near to threatening a devastating nuclear war. The conflicts in Vietnam and Korea were both limited wars involving major powers but without the use of nuclear weapons. Even more likely are conflicts between smaller nations or civil insurrections such as that which is taking place in El Salvador, where combatants are supported and given supplies by the U.S., the Soviet Union, or Cuba although their troops are not directly involved.

A Period of Détente

The French word **détente** means a relaxation of tensions between nations. By the end of the 1960s, it was clear that some efforts had to be made to reduce the threat of nuclear war between the United States and the Soviet Union. The Soviet Union had gradually begun to catch up in the building of strategic nuclear delivery vehicles in the form of bombers and missiles, thus balancing the nuclear scales. In the parlance of nuclear strategy, both nations had acquired **mutual assured-destruction (MAD)** capabilities. Theoretically, this meant that if the forces of both nations were approximately equal, neither would chance a war with each other.

The development of **antiballistic missiles (ABMs)** made the balance unstable. With ABMs, each side could shoot down the other's intercontinental nuclear warhead missiles. The United States also began to put **multiple, independently targetable warheads (MIRVs)** on a single missile, making it impossible for any ABM defensive system to eliminate completely the possibility of nuclear attack. This policy expanded our nuclear **first-strike capabilities** without requiring the production of new missiles. These developments in weapons technology made arms control negotiations to reduce the possibility of war imperative.

As the result of protracted negotiations, in May 1972, the United States and the Soviet Union signed the **Strategic Arms Limitation Treaty (SALT I)**. That treaty "permanently" limited the development and deployment of the ABM, and it limited for five years the number of offensive missiles each country could deploy. The treaty negotiations were only one part of the détente policy developed by Secretary of State Henry Kissinger and President Nixon. Kissinger felt that with the two superpowers becoming equal in weaponry, the best hope for avoiding war was to increase contacts between the new nations, thus creating economic, social, and scientific relationships that would reduce tensions. Under the Kissinger-Nixon policy, new scientific and cultural exchanges were arranged with the Soviets, and new opportunities for Jewish emigration out of the Soviet Union were arranged.

The policy of détente was not limited to relationships with the Soviet Union. Seeing an opportunity to capitalize on the increasing tensions between the Soviet Union and the People's Republic of China, Kissinger secretly began negotiations to establish a new relationship with that nation. After some minor cultural and sports exchanges, President Nixon eventually visited the People's Republic and set the stage for the formal diplomatic recognition of that country during the Carter administration. Again, the new relationship was intended to increase cultural, economic, and scientific exchanges with the Chinese, reducing international tensions with that superpower.

A Change in Direction?

Historians will certainly mark the late 1970s as the end of détente. Communist military activities increased. The Soviets intervened in Afghanistan on December 27, 1979. The Carter administration, unilaterally and without consulting Congress, retaliated by restricting grain sales to the Soviet Union and by prohibiting Americans

Détente

A French word meaning relaxation of tension. Characterizes U.S. Soviet policy as it developed under President Nixon and Henry Kissinger. Stresses direct cooperative dealings with cold war rivals but avoids ideological accommodation.

Mutual Assured Destruction (MAD)

A theory that if the United States and the Soviet Union had extremely large and invulnerable nuclear forces that were somewhat equal, then neither would chance a war with the other.

Antiballistic Missiles (ABMs)

A defense system designed to protect targets by destroying the attacking airplanes or missiles before they reach their destination.

Multiple, Independently Targetable Warheads (MIRVs)

Multiple warheads carried by a single missile but directed to different targets.

First-Strike Capabilities

The launching of an initial strategic nuclear attack before the opponent has used any strategic weapons.

Strategic Arms Limitation Treaty (SALT I)

A treaty between the United States and the Soviet Union to stabilize the nuclear arms competition between the two countries. SALT I talks began in 1969 and agreements were signed on May 26, 1972.

President Nixon signs the SALT I Treaty.

from participating in the Olympic Games that were to be held in Moscow in 1980. Beginning in December 1981, the Polish communist regime, backed by the Soviets, crushed the growing Solidarity labor union movement—which had demanded extensive economic, social, and political freedoms—and established martial law.

Many people saw evidence of United States ineffectiveness when the country allowed fifty-two Americans to be kept hostage by Iran for 444 days—a period of time that finally ended on President Ronald Reagan's inauguration day, Tuesday, January 20, 1981. Before this date we had suffered even more frustration when, on October 24, 1980, a military mission failed in its goal of rescuing the hostages. Instead, eight American crewmen were killed in a collision between a helicopter and a transport plane.

By the time President Reagan began to formulate his foreign policy, it was quite obvious that the American public was ready to sanction a stronger military stance if it could be convinced that U.S. interests were directly involved. The president sent the Marines into Lebanon in 1983—and even after over 240 of them were killed in a particularly gruesome suicide bombing of the marine compound in Beirut, the American public was slow to demand that the nation limit its involvement in the Middle East. Indeed, when he sent thousands of Marines and paratroopers to invade the tiny Caribbean island of Grenada on October 24, 1983, the American public and Congress approved the president's action. Few American lives were lost and the mission was described by the media as a success. In 1985, the president again demonstrated his willingness to use force. American jet fighters successfully forced the Egyptian plane carrying the terrorists who had hijacked an American ship and killed one American passenger to land in Sicily, where the terrorists were arrested.

MX Missiles.

After the bombing of the Marine head-quarters in Beirut.

Terrorism

The hijacking of TWA flight 847 on June 21, 1985, illustrated both the complexities of foreign policy and the frustration that terrorism causes for officials and the general public. An American plane bearing mostly American passengers returning from vacations abroad was selected by terrorists to be held hostage for the return of more than seven hundred Moslem prisoners held by the Israelis. The terrorists chose an American target deliberately, knowing that the United States had influence over the Israeli government but would be reluctant to exercise it, thus embarrassing both the United States and Israel. The situation was made even more difficult by the delicacy of the diplomatic and military conditions in Beirut, where the plane and thirty-nine of its hostages spent two weeks. As the capital of Lebanon, where no political faction has complete political control, the situation was beyond the reach of the United States diplomatically. It appeared impossible to rescue the hostages regardless of the size and capability of the U.S. defense establishment because the hostages were scattered throughout civilian homes in the city. Any military action would surely kill innocent Lebanese and endanger the Americans. The hostages were placed under the protection of the Amal militia and their leader, Nabih Berri, who receives his political support from President Assad of Syria. Negotiations among all parties finally freed the hostages seventeen days after the hijacking. In a strange turn of international affairs, the United States gave its thanks to the Syrians, who are allied with the Soviet Union, for getting the hostages out of Beirut. The Israelis freed the prisoners in the weeks that followed, insisting they

Rapid Deployment Force
Military unit trained for quick action and kept in a state of readiness.

▽

Highlight

▽

Are United States Defenses Spread Too Thin?

The accompanying map details the deployment of American forces at the end of October 1983. Some students of national security have begun to ask whether America isn't spreading itself too thin. The United States is obligated by treaty to defend Japan, South Korea, Central and Southeast Asia, Latin America, and Western Europe—including Greece and Turkey—a total of about fifty nations. The United States has pledged to use its military might to keep oil from the Middle East flowing to the "free" world. What if a military response became necessary? Could the United States carry out significant military actions with its army, navy, air force, and marines spread throughout the world?

In principle, the United States' **rapid deployment force**, could, for example, counteract a Soviet invasion of Iran by sending in 55,000 military personnel (three and one-third army divisions)—who would have tanks, armored personnel carriers, mortars, machine guns, and antipersonnel weapons—plus one and one-half marine amphibious units and seven air force fighter wings with about 500 planes. The *rapid* in *rapid deployment force* means that this could be done over a period of weeks.

Unfortunately, after getting into Iran it would be difficult to sustain these forces during any protracted campaign, because of the difficulty of supplying them with food, fuel, and ammunition.

Should the United States try to lighten its military load? Or should it simply expand its military might with more personnel and machines? This is an important issue in the continuing debate over national security, a debate that is carried out in Congress as well as in the executive branch of government.

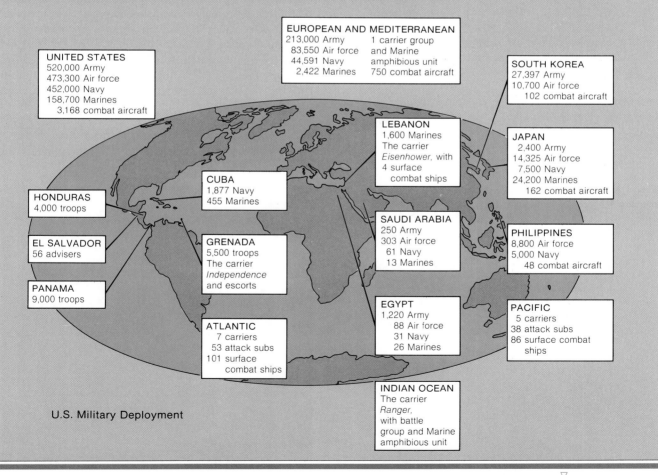

EUROPEAN AND MEDITERRANEAN
213,000 Army
83,550 Air force
44,591 Navy
2,422 Marines
1 carrier group and Marine amphibious unit
750 combat aircraft

UNITED STATES
520,000 Army
473,300 Air force
452,000 Navy
158,700 Marines
3,168 combat aircraft

SOUTH KOREA
27,397 Army
10,700 Air force
102 combat aircraft

LEBANON
1,600 Marines
The carrier *Eisenhower*, with 4 surface combat ships

JAPAN
2,400 Army
14,325 Air force
7,500 Navy
24,200 Marines
162 combat aircraft

HONDURAS
4,000 troops

CUBA
1,877 Navy
455 Marines

EL SALVADOR
56 advisers

GRENADA
5,500 troops
The carrier *Independence* and escorts

SAUDI ARABIA
250 Army
303 Air force
61 Navy
13 Marines

PHILIPPINES
8,800 Air force
5,000 Navy
48 combat aircraft

PANAMA
9,000 troops

ATLANTIC
7 carriers
53 attack subs
101 surface combat ships

EGYPT
1,220 Army
88 Air force
31 Navy
26 Marines

PACIFIC
5 carriers
38 attack subs
86 surface combat ships

INDIAN OCEAN
The carrier *Ranger*, with battle group and Marine amphibious unit

U.S. Military Deployment

Did You Know?

▽

That the CIA is estimated to employ more than sixteen thousand individuals, with about five thousand in the clandestine services?

were under no pressure from the Americans to do so, and the political situation in Beirut showed no change.

After the seizure of the *Achille Lauro*, an Italian cruise ship, and the attack on the Rome airport, the United States acted forcefully against terrorists. On April 14, 1986, at 12:13 P.M., fifty-seven U.S. aircraft including refueling tankers and F-111 bombers left England on a southwest course that took them along the coast of France, Portugal, and Spain, through the Straits of Gibraltar, and into the Mediterranean Sea. This trip of 2,800 miles was necessary because France had refused to allow the U.S. aircraft to fly the direct route over French territory.

Once in the Mediterranean, they were joined by fourteen aircraft launched from the U.S. aircraft carriers *Coral Sea* and *America*, which had been positioned off the coast of Libya. This combined air strike force then quickly made its way to land, guided by the most sophisticated radar and communications systems in the U.S. arsenal. At 7:00 P.M., they struck at numerous targets in and around the Libyan capital of Tripoli and the city of Benghazi. The raid lasted eleven minutes and thirty seconds, after which the aircraft returned, respectively, to England and their carriers. One U.S. aircraft and its two crew members were lost in the mission and roughly thirty-seven Libyans died and many more were injured in the attack.

The Reagan administration chose to launch this armed strike against Libya because its leader, Colonel Gadaffi, had become the most visible and vocal supporter of terrorist activity against the United States. He acknowledged supporting terrorist training camps, harboring terrorist leaders in his country, and supplying funds for their actions. The United States hoped this strike would accomplish several goals. It would send a message to the world that the United States would not allow attacks on its citizens to go unpunished. Also, the attack might destabilize Gadaffi's regime in Libya, if he were not killed during the raid. With the European nations refusing to assist the United States in this attack, the Reagan administration wanted to set an example for them and pressure them to increase their own efforts against terrorism.

After the raid, the United States was widely criticized in the European press, the media pointing out that Syria was as heavily implicated in recent terrorist

Marilyn Klinghoffer, wife of the murdered American hostage, leaving the Achille Lauro.

activity as was Libya. Europeans also feared the United States would force Gadaffi to retaliate, probably within Europe. The British public generally disapproved the decision by Margaret Thatcher to allow the American planes to take off from British bases. Although critical, many European nations tightened their own security efforts and deported many Libyan and other Middle Eastern citizens who may have been connected to terrorist activity. Americans canceled their European travel plans by the thousands while such nations as Italy and West Germany tried to convince American tourists that their nations were safe. For the short run, terrorist activities declined and Col. Gadaffi remained subdued.

The Iranian Connection

Beginning in 1984, terrorist groups operating in Beirut, Lebanon, began kidnapping American and European citizens and holding them hostage. The groups responsible for these kidnappings often tried to negotiate for the release of fellow terrorists held in prison by other nations. The official United States policy was the same as that of other nations: no negotiations should be held because it would encourage further terrorist activities. Numerous religious and other world leaders tried to persuade the terrorist groups to release their captives. One of the most prominent among these was Terry Waite, an emissary of the Archbishop of Canterbury.

Col. Gadaffi of Libya.

Mr. Waite's efforts appeared to be instrumental in the release of Rev. Benjamin Weir, in September, 1985. Nine months later, a Catholic priest, Father Martin Jenco, was released and returned to the United States. The third hostage to be released was David Jacobson, an official of the American University in Beirut, who was freed on November 2, 1986, just prior to the American elections. Terrorists claimed to have killed a fourth hostage, William Buckley, who was said to be the CIA chief in Beirut. Two other Americans remained captives: Terry Anderson, an American correspondent, and Thomas Sutherland, the Dean of Agriculture at American University of Beirut.

Two days after the 1986 election, news stories suggested that the United States had sent a private envoy Robert McFarlane, who had previously served as national security adviser to Mr. Reagan, on secret missions to Iran to negotiate a deal for the hostages. Within a few days, it becomes known that the United States had been involved in arms shipments to Iran in return for improved relations with that nation and help in freeing the hostages. Mr. Reagan, in a televised address, acknowledged the strategy, saying that he had authorized the transfer of small shipments of arms to Teheran, even though the United States had imposed a ban on any arms shipments to that nation since 1980.

As the story unfolded, it became more complex and more politically damaging to the Reagan presidency. The money for the arms shipments was, evidently, deposited in Swiss bank accounts which were controlled by a member of the National Security Council staff, Col. Oliver North, and by a retired general, Major General Richard Secord. The profit from the arms sales was to be used for aiding the contra forces in Nicaragua. These funds were possibly used to buy armaments for that rebel force during the months when the Congress had forbidden any military assistance to the *contras*. The President quickly dismissed Oliver North from his staff as well as National Security Adviser, John M. Poindexter, who had known about the contra funds. Both men sought protection under the Fifth Amendment in their first appearances at congressional committees.

Col. Oliver North (left) and John M. Poindexter (right).

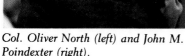

President Franklin D. Roosevelt signs the declaration of war against Japan on December 8, 1941.

Congressional hearings showed that the plan to aid the *contras* was kept from the Secretary of State and from the Secretary of Defense, although the role of the CIA was not as certain. The immediate political reaction to the disclosure of the scheme was an enormous 21 percent drop in the president's public approval rating. Both houses of Congress as well as the FBI launched investigations into the transactions and the President asked for the appointment of a special prosecutor to look into any wrong-doing. The possibility that the Iranian-contra connection would fatally damage Ronald Reagan's last two years in office was obvious to both Democrats and Republicans on Capitol Hill.

Who Makes Foreign Policy?

▽

Is foreign policy made by the president, by the Congress, by joint executive and congressional action? There is no easy answer to this question because, as constitutional authority Edwin S. Corwin once observed, the Constitution created an "invitation to struggle" between the president and Congress for control over the foreign policy process. Let us look first at powers given to the president by the Constitution.

Constitutional Powers of the President

The Constitution confers on the president broad powers that are either explicit or implied in key constitutional provisions. Article II vests the executive power of the government in the president. The presidential oath of office given in Article II, Section 1, requires that the president must "solemnly swear" to "preserve, protect and defend the Constitution of the United States."

In addition, and perhaps more importantly, Article II, Section 2, designates the president as "Commander in Chief of the Army and Navy of the United States." Starting with Abraham Lincoln all presidents have interpreted this authority dynamically and broadly. Indeed, since the Washington administration, the United States has been involved in at least 125 undeclared wars that were conducted under presidential authority. In 1846, President Polk provoked Mexico into a war. Teddy

President Reagan meeting with President Aquino.

Roosevelt sent the navy on a cruise around the world (presumably to impress Japan with the nation's naval power). Before entering World War II, FDR ordered the navy to "shoot on sight" German submarines that appeared in our Western Hemisphere security zone. Truman personally made the decision to drop atomic bombs on Japan. It was also Truman who ordered American armed forces in the Pacific to enter into North Korea's conflict with South Korea. Eisenhower threatened China and North Korea with nuclear weapons if the Korean peace talks were not successfully concluded. From Eisenhower through Nixon, chief executives increasingly embroiled the United States in a war in Vietnam.

Article II, Section 2, of the Constitution also gives the president the power to make treaties, provided that two-thirds of the senators present concur. Presidents have mostly been successful in getting treaties through the Senate. In addition to his formal treaty-making powers, the president makes use of **executive agreements.** Since the Second World War, executive agreements have accounted for almost 95 percent of the understandings reached between the United States and other nations.

Executive agreements have a long and significant history. Franklin Roosevelt made his destroyer base deal with Great Britain in 1940 by executive agreement. More significant in their long-term effects were the several agreements he reached with the U.S.S.R. and other countries, especially at Yalta and Potsdam, during the Second World War. The government of South Vietnam and the government of the United States, particularly under Eisenhower, Kennedy, and Johnson, made a series of executive agreements in which the United States promised to support the former. All in all, between 1946 and 1985 about eight thousand executive agreements with foreign countries were made. There is no way to get an accurate count because perhaps several hundred of these agreements have been secret.

An additional power conferred on the president in Article II, Section 2, is the right to appoint ambassadors, other public ministers, and consuls. In Section 3 of that article, the president is given the power to recognize foreign governments through receiving their ambassadors.

Executive Agreement

A binding international obligation made between chiefs of state without legislative sanction.

Informal Techniques of Presidential Leadership

Other broad sources of presidential power in the American foreign policy process are tradition, precedent, and the president's personality. The president has a host of informal techniques that give him overwhelming superiority within the government in foreign policy leadership.

First, he has access to information. More information is available to the president from the CIA, the State Department, and the Defense Department than to any other governmental authority. This gives him the ability to make quick decisions—and he often uses it.

Second, the president is a legislative leader. As a legislative leader he can influence the amount of funds that are allocated for different programs. For example, he can try as both Reagan and Carter did to increase defense spending and decrease nondefense spending.

Third, the president can influence public opinion. President Theodore Roosevelt once said:

> People used to say to me that I was an astonishingly good politician and divined what the people are going to think. . . . I did not "divine" how the people were going to think; I simply made up my mind what they ought to think and then did my best to get them to think it.[5]

The president is without equal in this regard, partly because of his ability to command the media. Depending on his skill in appealing to patriotic sentiment (and sometimes fear), he can make people think that his course in foreign affairs is right and necessary. Public opinion seems to be impressed often by the president's decision to make a United States commitment abroad. Presidents normally, although certainly not always, receive the immediate support of the American people when reacting to (or creating) a foreign policy crisis.

Ronald Reagan succeeded, where his predecessors had often failed, in building up and maintaining a very high level of public support for his performance in office. On foreign policy matters, however, Reagan's policies evoked a wide range of both favorable and unfavorable reactions from the American public. Among Reagan's more popular actions was the air raid on Libya on April 14, 1986. Seventy-one percent of the respondents in a Gallup survey taken within a few days after the bombing approved of the action, 68 percent supported the raids even if it turned out that the action would not reduce future acts of terrorism, 52 percent favored either future bombings of Libyan oil fields or instigating a military coup against Libyan leader Muammar Gadaffi, and 62 percent believed that President Reagan made wise use of military forces generally to solve foreign policy problems.

Finally, the president can morally commit the nation to a course of action in foreign affairs. As the head of state and the leader of one of the most powerful nations on earth, once he has made a commitment for the United States, it is difficult for Congress or anyone else to back down on that commitment.

Sources of Foreign Policy Making Within the Executive Branch

There are at least four sources of power in foreign policy making within the executive branch, in addition to the president. These are (1) the Department of State, (2) the

[5]Sidney Warren, *The President as World Leader* (New York: McGraw-Hill, 1964), p. 23.

Secretary of State Shultz meets with his Russian counterpart, Eduard Shevarnadze.

National Security Council, (3) the intelligence community and informational programs, and (4) the Department of Defense.

The Department of State

In principle, the State Department is the executive agency that is most directly concerned with foreign affairs. It supervises U.S. relations with the nearly two hundred independent nations around the world and with the United Nations and other multinational groups, such as the Organization of American States (OAS). It staffs embassies and consulates throughout the world. Figure 18–2 is an organization chart of the Department of State. It has about 24,000 employees. This may sound impressive, but it is small compared with, say, the Department of Health and Human Services with its 140,000 employees. Also, the State Department had an annual operating budget of only $2.6 billion in fiscal year 1984— the smallest budget of all thirteen executive agencies.

When a new president is elected, he usually tells the American public that he regards his new secretary of state as the nation's chief foreign policy adviser. Nonetheless, the State Department's preeminence in foreign policy has declined rather dramatically since World War II. The State Department's image within the White House Executive Office and Congress (and even other governments) is quite poor— a slow, plodding, bureaucratic maze of inefficient, indecisive individuals. There is even a story about how Soviet Premier Nikita Khruschev urged Kennedy to

Figure 18–2
▽
Organization Chart of the U.S. Department of State

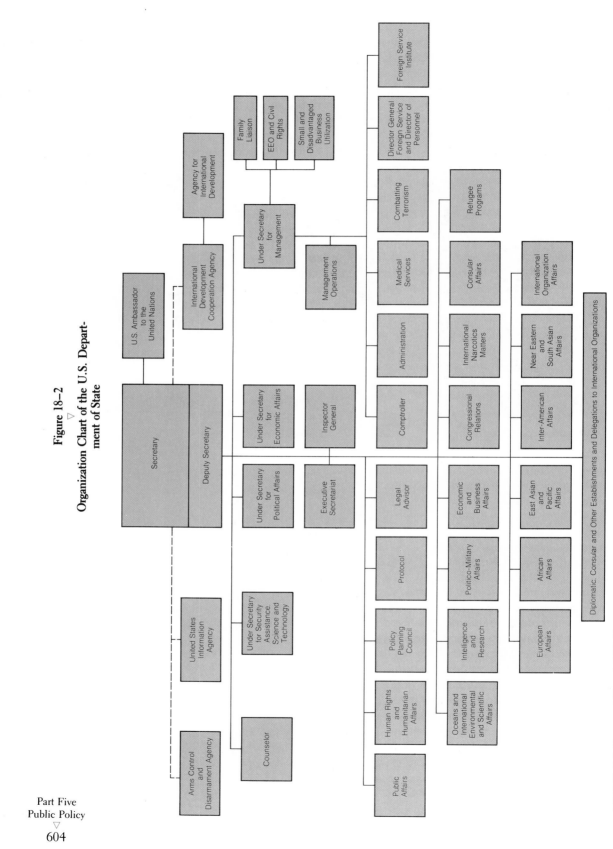

SOURCE: *U.S. Government Manual*, 1983–84.

formulate his own views rather than to rely on State Department officials who, according to Khruschev, "specialized in why something had not worked forty years ago."[6] In any event, since the days of Franklin Roosevelt, the State Department has been bypassed and often ignored when crucial decisions are made.

It is not surprising that the State Department has been overshadowed in foreign policy. It has no natural domestic constituency like, for example, the Department of Defense, which can call on defense contractors for support. Instead, the State Department has what might be called **negative constituents**—U.S. citizens who openly oppose American foreign policy. Also, within Congress, the State Department is often looked upon as an advocate of unpopular, costly foreign involvement. It is often called "the Department of Bad News."

The National Security Council

The job of the National Security Council (NSC), created by the National Security Act of 1947, is to advise the president on the integration of "domestic, foreign, and military policies relating to the national security." Its larger purpose is to provide policy continuity from one administration to the next. As it has turned out, the NSC—consisting of the president, the vice president, the secretaries of state and defense, the director of emergency planning, and often the chairman of the joint chiefs of staff and the director of the CIA—is used in just about any way the president wants to use it. Eisenhower made frequent use of the NSC. Kennedy convened it infrequently and on an informal basis. When Nixon was elected, he decided to reestablish the NSC as the principal forum for presidential examination of foreign policy issues. During the Reagan administration, the NSC played a central role in funneling private aid to the *contra* forces in Central America and in arranging the arms deal with Iran.

The role of national security adviser to the president seems to fit the wearer. Recent role players have come into conflict with heads of the State Department. Henry A. Kissinger, Nixon's flamboyant and aggressive national security adviser, rapidly gained ascendancy over William Rogers, the secretary of state, in foreign policy. Finally, to settle the conflict, Nixon made Kissinger secretary of state during his second term as well as national security adviser. When Carter became president, he appointed Zbigniew Brzezinski as national security adviser, who openly competed with Secretary of State Cyrus Vance (who apparently had little power). Reagan has also had difficulty with the tension between these two positions; his first choice as secretary of state, General Alexander Haig, resigned after a number of disputes with White House staff; and his national security adviser, Richard Allen, left office after questions were raised about his relationship with some Japanese business interests.

The Intelligence Community

No discussion of foreign policy would be complete without some mention of what is generally known as the **intelligence community**. This consists of the forty or more government agencies or bureaus that are involved in intelligence activities— informational and otherwise. On January 24, 1978, President Carter issued Ex-

[6]Theodore C. Sorensen, *Kennedy* (New York: Harper and Row, 1965), pp. 554–555.

Negative Constituents

U.S. citizens who openly oppose government policies.

Intelligence Community

The government agencies involved in gathering information about the capabilities and intentions of foreign governments and engaging in covert activities to further American foreign policy aims.

▽

ecutive Order 12036 in which he formally defined the official major members of the intelligence community. They are as follows:

1. Central Intelligence Agency (CIA)
2. National Security Agency (NSA)
3. Defense Intelligence Agency (DIA)
4. Offices within the Department of Defense
5. Bureau of Intelligence and Research in the Department of State
6. Federal Bureau of Investigation (FBI)
7. Army intelligence
8. Air Force intelligence
9. Department of the Treasury
10. Drug Enforcement Administration (DEA)
11. Department of Energy

The CIA was created as part of the National Security Act of 1947. The National Security Agency and the Defense Intelligence Agency were created by executive order. Until recently, Congress voted billions of dollars for intelligence activities with little knowledge of how the funds were being used. Only twice did the intelligence activities of the agency attract public attention. In 1960, an American U-2 spy plane was shot down over the Soviet Union and its pilot, Gary Powers, captured. Eisenhower at first denied that the U-2 was a spy plane but later admitted that the United States was indeed taking aerial reconnaissance photos of the U.S.S.R. Again, in 1961, when the Bay of Pigs invasion of Cuba failed, even though Kennedy took the blame it was clear that he had been misled by the CIA.

Intelligence activities consist mostly of overt information gathering as well as covert actions. Covert actions, as the name implies, are done secretly and rarely does the American public find out about them. In the late 1940s and early 1950s, the CIA covertly subsidized anticommunist labor unions in Western Europe. The CIA covertly aided in the overthrow of the Mossadegh regime in Iran, which allowed the restoration of the Shah in 1953. The CIA helped to overthrow the Arbenz government of Guatemala in 1954 and apparently was instrumental in destabilizing the Allende government in Chile from 1970 to 1973.

During the mid-1970s, the "dark side" of the CIA was at least partly uncovered when the Senate, under Senator Frank Church (Dem.-Idaho), undertook an investigation of its activities. One of the major findings of the Senate Select Committee on Intelligence was that the CIA had routinely spied on American citizens domestically—a strictly prohibited activity. Consequently, the CIA came under the scrutiny of six, and later eight, oversight committees within Congress, which restricted the scope of its activity. However, by 1980, the CIA regained much of its lost power to engage in covert activities. The legislation requiring the agency to report covert operations to eight congressional committees was repealed. A new law permitted the chief executive to decide whether congressional committees would receive prior notification of covert activities. In general, the CIA's relationship to Congress reverted to that of the 1960s.

In addition to intelligence activities, U.S. foreign policy also makes use of propaganda and information programs. The United States Information Agency (which for a while was called the United States International Communication Agency) is part of an attempt to spread information and propaganda throughout the world on behalf of the American government. One of its major efforts is the Voice of America, a worldwide radio network that broadcasts news and information from an American point of view. Under the Reagan administration, this activity was expanded. In 1983, Congress passed a bill authorizing Radio Marti to transmit specifically to Cuba.

The Department of Defense

The Department of Defense (DOD) was created in 1947 to bring all of the various activities of the American military establishment under the jurisdiction of a single department headed by a civilian secretary of defense. At the same time, the joint chiefs of staffs, consisting of the commanders of each of the military branches and a chairman, was created to formulate a unified military strategy. The organization of the DOD is given in Figure 18–3. The DOD is huge. It has more than one million civilian employees and more than two million military personnel. It has an annual budget that in fiscal year 1987 was over $300 billion. Since much of this budget is spent on contracts with civilian firms, it is not surprising that a somewhat symbiotic relationship has developed between civilian defense contractors and the DOD.

The Military-Industrial Complex

▽

Civilian fear of "the generals" and the relationship between the defense establishment and arms manufacturers dates back many years. In the 1930s, Franklin Roosevelt raised the specter of mammoth improper military influence in the domestic economy. On the eve of a Senate investigation of the munitions industry,

Military Industrial Complex
The mutually beneficial relationship between the armed forces and defense contractors.

The Pentagon.

Figure 18–3
▽
Organization of the U.S. Department of Defense

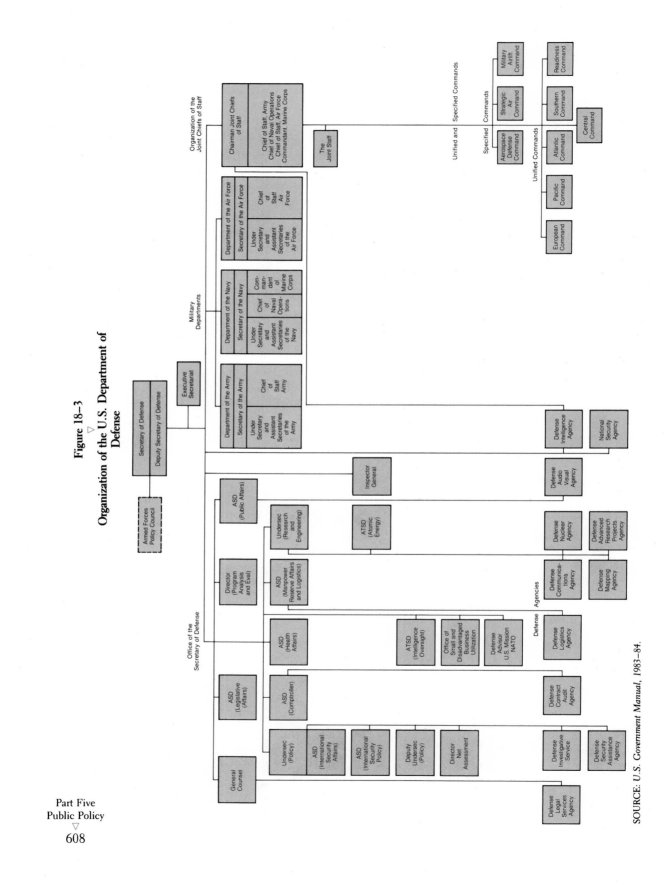

SOURCE: *U.S. Government Manual, 1983–84.*

he said that the arms race was a "grave menace . . . due in no small measure to the uncontrolled activities of the manufacturers and the merchants of the engines of destruction and it must be met by the concerted actions of the people of all nations."

Eisenhower's Farewell to the Nation

During his eight years in office, the former five-star general of the army experienced firsthand the kind of pressure that could be brought against him and other policy makers by arms manufacturers. (Ike's secretary of defense had said, "What's good for General Motors is good for the country.") Eisenhower determined to give the country a solemn and, as he saw it, necessary warning of the consequences of this influence. On January 17, 1961, in his last official speech, he said:

> This conjunction of an immense military establishment and a large arms industry is new in the American experience. The total influence—economic, political, even spiritual— is felt in every city, every State house, every office of the Federal government. We recognize the imperative need for this development. Yet we must not fail to comprehend its grave implications. Our toil, resources, and livelihood are all involved; so is the very structure of our society.
>
> In the councils of government, we must guard against the acquisition of unwarranted influence, whether sought or unsought, by the military-industrial complex. The potential for the disastrous rise of misplaced power exists and will persist. . . . Only an alert and knowledgeable citizenry can compel the proper meshing of the huge industrial and military machinery of defense with our peaceful methods and goals, so that security and liberty may prosper together.[7]

A Symbiotic Relationship

The relationship between prime defense contractors and the Pentagon is close and seems to be getting closer all the time. Not only does the Pentagon support a large sector of our economy through defense contracts but it also supplies a large number

[7]Congressional Quarterly, *Almanac* (Washington, D.C.: Congressional Quarterly, 1961), pp. 938–939.

of key executives to large defense-contracting firms. Senator William Proxmire has criticized the "incestuous hiring" that industry engages in among retired army officers and high Pentagon officials. A 1969 survey showed that Lockheed Aircraft had 210 former DOD employees; the Boeing Company, 169; McDonnell Douglas Corporation, 141; General Dynamics Corporation, 113; and North American Rockwell Corporation, 104.

The military establishment also has a powerful political arm. The Department of Defense employs almost 350 lobbyists on Capitol Hill; it maintains some 2,850 public relations representatives in the United States and in foreign countries.

The close relationship between the Pentagon and defense contractors has led one staunch critic, economist John Kenneth Galbraith, to hypothesize the following:

> Where a corporation does all or nearly all of its business with the Department of Defense; uses much plant owned by the government; gets it working capital in the form of progress payments from the government; does not need to worry about competitors for it is the sole source of supply; accepts extensive guidance from the Pentagon on its management; is subject to detailed rules as to its accounting; and is extensively staffed by former service personnel, only the remarkable flexibility of the English language allows us to call it private enterprise. Yet this is not an exceptional case, but a common one. We have an amiable arrangement by which the defense firms, part of the public bureaucracy, are largely exempt from its political and other constraints. [8]

Limiting the President's Power

▽

One of the major outcomes of the Vietnam war was a new interest in the balance of power between Congress and the president on foreign policy questions. Sensitive to public frustration over the long and costly war and angry at Richard Nixon for some of his other actions as president, Congress attempted to establish some limits on the power of the president in setting foreign and defense policy. In 1973, Congress passed the War Powers Act over President Nixon's veto, limiting the president's use of troops in military action without congressional approval (see Chapter 12). Most presidents, however, have not interpreted the "consultation" provisions of the act as meaning that Congress should be consulted before military action is taken. Instead, Ford, Carter, and Reagan have ordered troop movements and then informed congressional leaders. Critics note that it is quite possible for a president to commit troops to a situation from which the nation could not withdraw without incurring heavy political losses, whether or not Congress is consulted.

In recent years, Congress has also exerted its authority to limit or deny the president's requests for military assistance to Angolan rebels and to the government of El Salvador, for new weapons like the B-1 bomber, and for weapons sales through a legislative veto over sales greater than $50 million (although recent court decisions have left the veto technique in doubt). In general, Congress has been far more cautious in supporting the president where military involvement of American troops is possible, although it has largely supported the Reagan administration's requests for defense budget increases.

At times the Congress can take the initiative in foreign policy. In 1986, the Congress initiated and passed a bill instituting economic sanctions against South

U.S. advisers in El Salvador.

▽

[8]John Kenneth Galbraith, *The Military Budget and National Economic Priorities*, Pt. 1 (Washington, D.C.: GPO, 1969), pp. 5–6.

Africa to pressure that nation into ending apartheid. President Reagan vetoed the bill but the veto was overridden by large majorities in both the House and the Senate.

Foreign Economic Policy

▽

As we noted, the United States is increasingly dependent on other nations in trade and other economic affairs. One task of American foreign policy is to protect American economic interests and to find new markets for American products overseas. As part of our national security policy, the government must also regulate the flow of goods and technology to nations that might use these products for military purposes.

One of the techniques of foreign economic policy is **export control**. Certain items, for example, are not permitted to be sold or shipped to the Soviet Union. Recently, the government announced that some of the simpler personal computers could be exported to communist countries although more sophisticated computer systems cannot. Of course, export controls can also be used as a direct diplomatic response. After the invasion of Afghanistan by the Soviet Union, President Jimmy Carter placed an embargo on shipments of American wheat to Russia. However, many experts express doubts about the long-range effectiveness of any type of export controls.

In recent years, many American industries have suffered declines in sales and worker layoffs because their products have not been able to meet foreign competition. American steel has been largely replaced by cheaper Japanese steel; electronic goods also come mostly from Japan, shoes from Taiwan and Brazil, cloth from the Far East, and so on. When a domestic industry is severely injured by foreign competition, interests representing both management and labor often seek relief from Congress and the president. One technique is to place a high duty on imported goods, raising their price; another is to provide retraining for workers in affected industries. The enormous success of Japanese automobiles in the U.S. market and the consequent decline of American car sales led to an agreement between the United States and Japan to limit the import of cars through a quota system. One result of this agreement was to increase the price of the limited supply of Japanese cars and to permit Detroit-based manufacturers to raise the prices of American cars as well. In the future, such agreements may be made within a single corporation if Japanese and American manufacturers are joined in a multinational enterprise.

Multinational Corporations: A New Force in Foreign Policy

▽

The emergence of **multinational corporations (MNCs)** in the 1960s has had a strong impact on foreign policy, simply because the MNCs are often more powerful economically than the countries in which they reside—as may be seen in Table 18–2. The network of MNCs is worldwide, and over three-fourths of them are affiliates of corporations based in the United States, the United Kingdom, France, and the Federal Republic of Germany. Eight of the ten largest of the multinational corporations are based in the United States.

Although the bulk of MNC activities is located in developed market economies, about one-third of the total stock of foreign direct investment is received by the

---

Did You Know?

▽

That the largest trading partner of the United States is Canada?

Export Control

Restricting exports to another nation for security or other reasons.

Multinational Corporations (MNCs)

Corporations with a number of foreign subsidiaries operating in various countries.

Table 18–2

▽

A Comparison of U.S. Corporate Assets and Other Countries' GNPs (1982) (in billions of dollars)

India	161.6
American Telephone & Telegraph	148.2
Netherlands	138.1
BankAmerica Corporation	122.2
Citicorp	114.9
Argentina	100.6
Belgium	83.0
Chase Manhattan Corporation	80.9
Federal National Mortgage Association	73.5
South Korea	71.0
Prudential	66.7
Exxon	62.3
Taiwan	48.9
Algeria	42.5
General Motors	41.4
American Express	28.3
Iraq	27.1
Chile	25.6
Bangladesh	14.1
Zimbabwe	5.4

SOURCE: GNPs are from *Handbook of Economic Statistics, 1983,* Central Intelligence Agency, Directorate of Intelligence, September 1983. Corporate assets are from *Fortune 500, 1983,* Time Inc.

▽

Highlight
▽
The Roller-Coaster Dollar

For tourists traveling to Europe, the best news is a strong dollar. When the United States dollar is strong against European currencies, the tourist can expect to get real bargains in shopping and accommodations. In contrast, to some American businesses and most farmers, a strong dollar is bad news. If the dollar is strong, then it costs more for other nations to buy our manufactured goods and our surplus farm products, so exports fall. But the American consumer usually gets more bargains, especially in the electronic goods purchased from Asia and in clothing. Congress has reacted to the plight of business by considering protectionist legislation that would keep some foreign goods out of the market or force up their prices. The administration has felt that protectionist legislation simply triggers retaliation from other nations.

Beginning in September 1985, the Reagan administration began to work on lowering the value of the dollar. At a meeting with the Group of Five (the G-5), Treasury Secretary Baker convinced Britain, France, Japan, and West Germany to take steps to lower the dollar's value. As the accompanying table indicates, those steps have had some effect, although the U.S. trade representative, Clayton Yeutter,

The Cost of Foreign Money

Following is a comparison of the dollar's strength against the currencies of the other nations in the so-called Group of Five. The chart shows how many yen, marks, and francs could be bought for a U.S. dollar, and how many dollars it took to buy a British pound.

	Japanese Yen	German Mark	French Franc	British Pound
1971	347.9	3.5	5.5	2.43
1973	271.7	2.7	4.5	2.45
1975	296.8	2.5	4.3	2.22
1977	268.5	2.3	4.9	1.75
1979	219.1	1.8	4.3	2.12
1981	220.5	2.3	5.4	2.02
1983	237.5	2.6	7.6	1.51
1985	238.5	2.9	9.0	1.34
12/15/86	162.7	2.0	6.6	1.43

SOURCE: International Monetary Fund

felt the dollar would have to fall further to improve exports.

International monetary matters are never simple. Although American businesses, particularly the automotive industry, are pleased with the fall of the dollar, the Japanese are extremely concerned. As the table indicates, the dollar has weakened against the yen for a number of years. As a result, the price of video recorders has increased 10 percent in the United States since the G-5 meeting, the prices of Japanese cars are climbing, and a number of

Japanese manufacturers are in serious financial trouble and are pressuring their government for relief.

There is little agreement on the solution for these currency imbalances. Although some critics of the present system want to return to fixed currency rates, most simply want to limit the wilder swings in the world monetary system.

SOURCE: *Congressional Quarterly Weekly Report*, February 22, 1986, pp. 460–464.

developing countries in Africa, Asia, the Middle East, and Central and South America. United States MNC affiliates and investments have been concentrated primarily in Central and South American countries.

Some scholars have estimated that by the end of the twentieth century, international trade will be dominated by three hundred large corporations, the great majority of which will be American owned. The question arises as to whether these large corporations can wield sufficient political power to alter the course of international economics and even international politics. The problem for the United

States government is how to influence these giants when their activities affect or conflict with U.S. foreign or domestic policy goals.

Economists disagree about the extent to which multinationals benefit or harm the economies and political systems of the countries where they operate. They can be credited with speeding up economic development in the host country. They employ local workers, often giving better benefits, wages, and training than are given those who work for local firms. They probably upgrade the standard of living for some citizens of the nation and change the technical level of expertise overall.

However, multinational corporations have been accused of taking all of their profits out of less-developed nations and investing them back home, of earning exorbitant profits, and of using the cheaper labor of these nations to offset high labor costs in Europe or the United States. This, of course, becomes a domestic political problem, and there have been periodic demands by affected segments of the work force for Congress to regulate such activity. Finally, multinationals have occasionally attempted to influence the political system of the nations where they are established. In 1986, a number of American MNCs severed their connections with South African subsidiaries in protest against that nation's apartheid policies. Such political pressures by private corporations can either work in support of U.S. policy or against it.

Japanese cars being unloaded for sale in the United States.

Students and faculty protest school closings in South Africa.

The Nuclear Freeze Movement

Former Secretary of Defense Robert S. McNamara wrote in the fall of 1983 in *Foreign Affairs* that the United States and NATO should renounce their current reliance on the threat to use nuclear weapons because they are "totally useless and serve no military purpose." He reiterated the feeling of many students of national security that the strategic use of nuclear weapons against the Soviet Union would be an act of suicide. McNamara's article couldn't have come at a worse time for the Reagan administration because it was just on the verge of deploying the controversial Pershing II and cruise missiles in Western Europe. Figure 18–4 pictures the nuclear landscape at the beginning of 1984.

Figure 18–4

▽

**The Nuclear Landscape
at the Beginning of 1984**

SOURCE: *Newsweek*, October 24, 1983, p. 38.

NATO's new deployment will respond to the Soviet buildup of SS-20 missiles and to the preponderance of Soviet warheads aimed not at the United States but at Western Europe.

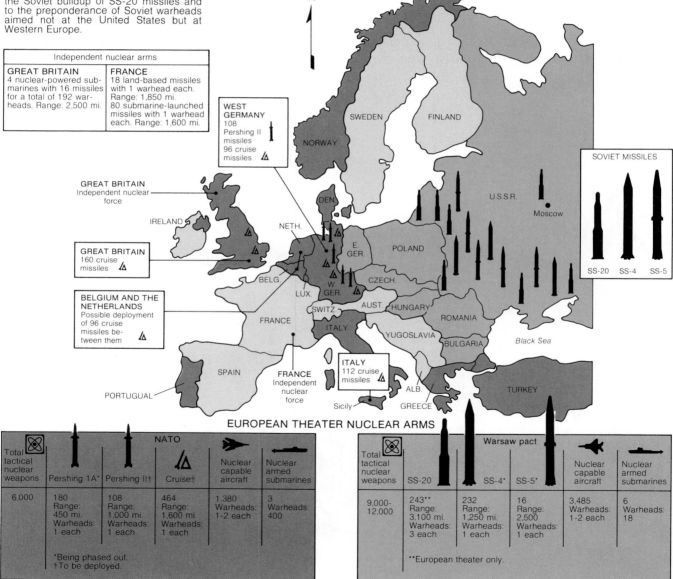

EUROPEAN THEATER NUCLEAR ARMS

Would Nuclear War Be World Suicide?

When nuclear weapons first became an issue, a number of scientists claimed that the world could survive nuclear war. At a conference entitled "The World After Nuclear War" held in Washington, D.C., during the week of November 7, 1983, just the opposite conclusion was given in a report representing two years of work by one hundred physicists, biologists, and atmospheric scientists from around the world. Using computer-modeled nuclear exchanges ranging from 100 megatons (250 Pershing missiles) to 500 megatons (less than half the world's nuclear arsenal), the scientists claimed that in the 500-megaton scenario, the intense heat from the blast would set off firestorms that would ignite everything flammable throughout the entire world. The air would be filled with poisonous fumes of carbon monoxide, dioxins, and cyanides. The nuclear fireball when it reached the stratosphere would destroy 50 percent of the ozone layer. After about a week, darkness would descend as 200 million tons of smoky debris created a "blacktop highway three miles up." Only about 5 percent of the normal sunlight would reach the earth. No region of the planet would be spared—not even the Southern Hemisphere. The conclusion was that nuclear exchange is futile. A nuclear war, according to these scientists, would be the last war.

Anti-nuclear weapons demonstration.

Impetus for a Nuclear Freeze

In 1983, a Louis Harris & Associates public opinion poll was taken to find out whether the public wanted the United States to negotiate a **nuclear freeze** with the Soviet Union and to ban the future production, storage, and use of nuclear weapons. The results showed overwhelming support for such a freeze (Table 18–3). By 1984, more than two hundred cities had passed resolutions against the use of nuclear weapons. Numerous demonstrations were held against the deployment of Pershing missiles in Western Europe. Concurrently, the Reagan administration had practically brought arms control discussions with the Soviet Union to a standstill. The Soviets' destruction of a Korean airliner, killing all 269 aboard, on September 1, 1983, was used to justify the new tough stance. Reagan pledged that "if the Soviets sit down at the bargaining table seeking genuine arms reduction, there will be arms reduction. . . . [But] the governments of the West and their people will not be diverted by misinformation and threats. The time has come for the Soviet Union to show proof that it wants arms control in reality, not just in rhetoric."

What Reagan was referring to was the inability to agree on monitoring such agreements. Reagan had a whole list of Soviet breaches of previous arms control

Nuclear Freeze

A halt in the development, production, and deployment of nuclear weapons.

Table 18–3
▽
Support for a Nuclear Freeze

Q. Would you oppose a congressional resolution that would call on the U.S. to negotiate a nuclear freeze with the Soviet Union under which both sides would ban the future production, storage, and use of nuclear weapons?						
		Consider self			Voted for	
A.	TOTAL	REPUBLICAN	DEMOCRAT	INDEPENDENT	REAGAN	CARTER	OTHER
FAVOR	81%	77%	83%	83%	79%	87%	83%
OPPOSE	15	20	13	14	17	9	15
NOT SURE	4	3	4	3	4	4	2

SOURCE: Louis Harris & Associates, Inc., for *Business Week*, May 16, 1983, p. 14.

Star Wars weaponry.

agreements, such as the United States's discovery that the U.S.S.R. had constructed a new battle management radar facility, purportedly in violation of the Antiballistic Missile Treaty, and the sighting of a new ICBM not permitted under SALT I.

In 1983, President Reagan publicly announced his strategic defense initiative (SDI), popularly known as "Star Wars," a defense against nuclear missiles that is based in outer space. Reagan and others in his administration argued that the program would deter nuclear war by shifting the emphasis of defense strategy from offensive to defensive weapons systems. Critics of the program, however, believed it would simply make the arms race more intense, be very expensive, and probably would not be technically feasible. Early public opinion polls on the issue suggested that the public was closely divided on the merits of the Star Wars proposal.

In November 1985, President Reagan and Mikhail Gorbachev, the Soviet leader, held summit talks in Geneva. The two men agreed to reestablish cultural and scientific exchanges and to continue the arms control negotiations. Progress towards an agreement has been slow. Although the United States, the other NATO nations and the Soviet Union agreed to new measures to reduce the possibility of accidental hostilities in 1986, no new nuclear arms treaty has been signed. A second Gorbachev-Reagan meeting in Reykjavik, Iceland in October, 1986 came close to achieving an agreement on massive reductions in, and possibly the elimination of, strategic nuclear weapons. A confused post-summit climate, however, left both sides irritated and charging that the other nation's policymakers were not negotiating in good faith.

President Reagan and Mr. Gorbachev in Iceland.

There are some 50,000 nuclear warheads in the world. They are a pit into which the whole world can fall—a nemesis of all human intentions, actions, and hopes. We must bend our efforts toward ridding the world of them. The alternative is to risk surrendering ourselves to absolute and eternal darkness: a darkness in which no nation, no society, no ideology, no civilization will remain, in which never again will a child be born; in which never again will human beings appear on the earth, and there will be no one to remember that they ever did.*

The early 1980s saw the nation's attention turn to nuclear war. Millions of Americans responded to appeals from doctors, lawyers, nurses, scientists, teachers, and priests who called for a nuclear freeze—a halt to the testing, production, and further deployment of nuclear warheads, missiles, and other delivery systems. People demanded a greater voice in the formulation of nuclear weapons policy. The nationwide grass-roots movement to stop the nuclear arms race was endorsed by hundreds of town meetings, dozens of city councils, and nine state legislatures. Today, there is organized nuclear-freeze activity in almost every state. The movement's scope was dramatically illustrated in the June 1982 disarmament rally in New York City, which drew an estimated 700,000 people, making it the largest political demonstration in U.S. history. As one observer noted, the movement demonstrates "that the creaky machinery of democracy can be made to work if the people demand it, and if they think the stakes are high enough."**

The campaign's biggest victories have been on a local level, and its most valuable asset has been citizen action. It is estimated that there are more than one thousand antinuclear groups in the country. If you feel strongly about

this issue and want to get involved, you can contact one of the following:

Nuclear Weapons Freeze Campaign
National Clearinghouse
4144 Lindell Blvd., Suite 404
St. Louis, MO 63108
314-533-1169

Nuclear Information and Resource Center
1536 16th St., N.W.
Washington, D.C. 20036
202-483-0045

Clergy and Laity Concerned
198 Broadway, Room 302
New York, NY 10038
212-964-6730

But despite the rapid spread of the antinuclear movement, no consensus exists about how to proceed and indeed whether a freeze proposal is a good plan at all. Some argue that the freeze is simplistic and impractical, that a freeze would lock the United States into a position of permanent strategic inferiority and vulnerability vis-a-vis the Soviet Union, and that it could also weaken U.S. bargaining leverage that the planned deployment of new weapons would provide. The freeze, it is argued, would freeze solutions, not problems, because the arms race reflects rather than causes political instabilities. If you support this position or want more information, you can contact one of the following organizations:

American Security Council (ASC)
Washington Communications Center
Boston, VA 22713
703-825-8336

Coalition for Peace Through Strength
Boston, VA 22713
703-825-1776

American Conservative Union (ACU)
38 Ivy St., S.E.
Washington, D.C. 20003
202-546-6555

---

*From one of three *New Yorker* articles by Jonathan Schell, excerpted and introduced into the *Congressional Record* by Senator Alan Cranston, *Proceedings and Debates of the 97th Cong., 2nd Sess., Senate Congressional Record*, 128:34, Tues., March 30, 1982, Washington, D.C.

**Edward F. Feighan, "The Freeze in Congress," in *The Nuclear Freeze Debate*, Paul M. Lok and William J. Taylor, Jr. eds. (Boulder, Colo.: Westview Press, 1983), p. 30.

Chapter Summary

▽

1. The United States is economically, militarily, and culturally interdependent with the rest of the world.

2. Foreign policy includes our national goals and the techniques used to achieve them. National security policy, which is one aspect of foreign policy, is designed to protect the independence and the political and economic integrity of the United States. Diplomacy involves the nation's external relationships and is an attempt to resolve conflict without resort to arms.

3. During the 1700s and 1800s, the United States had little international power and generally stayed out of European conflict and politics.

4. The nineteenth century has been called the period of isolationism. The Monroe Doctrine of 1823 stated that the United States would not accept foreign intervention in the Western Hemisphere and would not meddle in European affairs.

5. The end of the period of isolationism started with the Spanish-American War of 1898. The first major entanglement in European politics began when the U.S. entered World War I on April 6, 1917.

6. Following the signing of the Treaty of Versailles in 1919, the United States once more retreated into isolationism, rejecting membership in the League of Nations and largely disbanding its military forces.

7. Isolationism was permanently shattered with the Japanese attack on the U.S. naval base at Pearl Harbor, Hawaii, on December 7, 1941. President Roosevelt immediately declared war on Japan, involving the United States directly in World War II.

8. World War II marked a permanent change in American foreign policy. The United States was the only country to emerge from the war with its economy intact and the only country with operating nuclear weapons.

9. In 1945, the United Nations was formed. In 1948, the Marshall Plan was established to stimulate the European economies and thereby contain the spread of communism. The United States also entered into numerous mutual security pacts.

10. Soon after the war ended, the cold war with the Soviet Union began. A policy of containment, which assumed an expansive Soviet Union, was enunciated in the Truman Doctrine.

11. Since the spread of nuclear weapons throughout the world, we have entered an era of limited wars. The closest the U.S. has come to a nuclear confrontation was during the Cuban missile crisis in 1962.

12. Following the frustrations of the Vietnam war and the apparent arms equality of the United States and Russia, the United States was ready for détente. As the arms race escalated, arms control became a major foreign policy issue.

13. The latter 1970s marked the end of the period of détente. As Reagan began formulating his foreign policy, it was evident that the American public was ready to sanction a stronger military stance if it could be convinced that national interests were directly involved.

14. The formal power of the president to make foreign policy derives from the Constitution, which makes the president responsible for the preservation of national security and designates him as commander in chief of the army and navy. Presidents have interpreted this authority broadly. They also have the power to make treaties and executive agreements.

15. The president also has a host of informal techniques that give him overwhelming superiority in foreign policy leadership.

16. In principle, the State Department is the executive agency most directly involved with foreign affairs. In the last several administrations, it has often been bypassed, however.

17. The National Security Council advises the president on the integration of "domestic, foreign, and military policies relating to national security." Presidents' use of the NSC has varied.

18. The intelligence community consists of forty or more government agencies engaged in intelligence activities varying from information gathering to covert actions.

19. The Department of Defense was created in 1947 to bring under the jurisdiction of a single department headed by a civilian secretary of defense all of the various activities of the American military establishment.

20. Civilian concern about the relationship between the defense establishment and arms manufacturers dates back to the 1930s. In 1961, President Eisenhower cautioned the nation to beware of the military-industrial complex in his famous farewell address to the nation.

21. The DOD has been criticized for too close a relationship with prime defense contractors.

22. One task of American foreign policy is to protect American economic interests. Export controls and import quotas are techniques that have been used with varying degrees of success.

23. The emergence of multinational corporations has had a strong impact on foreign policy because they are often more powerful economically than the countries in which they reside. MNCs are seen by some as beneficial for host countries, but criticized by others for exploiting the host countries.

24. Many scientists have concluded that the world could not survive a nuclear war. Public support of a nuclear freeze with the Soviet Union is quite strong.

Questions for Review and Discussion

▽

1. Some critics have argued that the United States alternates between internationalism and isolationism, never quite able to decide whether to take a leadership role. What historical experiences might account for this indecisiveness? What would be the consequences for American citizens and for the world community if the United States did withdraw from world affairs?

2. Which branches and agencies of the national government are influential in making foreign policy? Think of at least one issue or foreign policy question on which the Departments of State and Defense would be likely to hold different views. What are the sources of power in foreign policy decision making that would determine which department might be more influential?

3. Foreign economic policy is increasingly important, not only for the United States, but also for its allies and for the less-developed nations. Should economic policy be used as a tool to serve other foreign policy goals, as in the grain embargo, or should economic policy only serve the cause of American prosperity?

4. The vast majority of Americans favor negotiations for a nuclear freeze. Why is it so difficult for the two superpowers to begin these negotiations? To what extent do domestic political concerns within each nation affect these negotiations?

Selected References

▽

Richard J. Barnet and Ronald E. Müller, *Global Reach: The Power of the Multinational Corporations* (New York: Simon and Schuster, 1975). An interesting account of the power and role of these economic giants in world affairs.

Cecil V. Crabb, Jr., and Pat M. Holt, *Invitation to Struggle: Congress, the President and Foreign Policy* (Washington, D.C.: Congressional Quarterly, 1980). A well-presented analysis of the conflict between Congress and the president in the foreign policy arena.

Richard E. Feinberg. *The Intemperate Zone: The Third World Challenge to U.S. Foreign Policy* (New York: W. W. Norton, 1983). This excellent study analyzes the implications of a more assertive and active third world.

Raymond L. Garthoff, *Détente and Confrontation: American-Soviet Relations from Nixon to Reagan* (Washington, D.C.: Brookings Institution, 1985). Both Soviet and U.S. foreign policy perspectives are examined from 1969 to 1984 to help readers understand the development of the most powerful factor in U.S. foreign policy and draw conclusions about the future of U.S.-Soviet relations.

James M. McCormick, *American Foreign Policy and American Values* (Itasca, Ill.: F. E. Peacock, 1985). An up-to-date, comprehensive discussion of the foundations and principles of U.S. foreign policy.

U.S. Foreign Policy: The Reagan Imprint (Washington, D.C.: Congressional Quarterly Press, 1986). This is a very compact and fact-filled compendium of current American foreign policy with special focus on regional issues, arms control, international trade, and economics.

6
STATE AND LOCAL POLITICS

Chapter 19
▽
State and Local Government

Contents
▽

State and Local Government Spending
Paying for State and Local Government
The U.S. Constitution and the States
State Constitutions
The State Executive Branch
The State Legislature
The State Judiciary
How Local Government Operates

What If . . .

Every State Had the Same Constitution?

Each state has at least a slightly different set of constitutional provisions that determine how its government operates and how its citizens are treated. What might happen if each state had exactly the same constitution? One possible set of implications can be found in the Model State Constitution, drafted by the National Municipal League.

One characteristic of the mythical uniform constitution would be brevity. The model is less than ten thousand words in length, and that figure includes optional language covering alternative government structures. It begins with a brief preamble, affirming support for the U.S. Constitution and pledging that state power will be used for the public benefit. A bill of rights closely follows the federal standard. Enumerated state powers and functions are neither a grant to, nor a limitation on, the states; state governments have all powers not denied them either by the model constitution or by the national Constitution. Anyone can vote or run for office who is of sufficient age and a resident of the state for three months, who is literate in an acceptable language, and who is not barred for reasons of mental incompetency or a felony conviction. Elections would be in odd-numbered years.

The state legislature would have one chamber (with a bicameral alternative), with one member per district. Terms of office would be the same as for Congress: two years for the lower house (assembly) and six years for the upper body (senate). Redistricting would be done every ten years by the governor, subject to review by the state supreme court. Special or local legislation would be severely limited, and bills appropriating funds could not have unrelated amendments attached to them. Postaudits of state spending would be controlled by the legislature.

The governor would have fifteen days to decide whether to veto a bill, and his or her veto could be overridden by a two-thirds legislative vote. Governors also would be able to line veto appropriations bills, that is, veto specific items. There would be no restrictions on the number of four-year terms he or she could serve. The governor would appoint and remove the heads of all administrative departments.

The state courts would have a unified organization based on the federal model. Judges would be appointed by the governor, with the advice and consent of the legislature, or, alternatively, they would be chosen by the governor from a list compiled by a nominating commission.

Local governments would be given broad grants of authority, including home rule. Public education would specifically be a function of local government. A merit system would be used for government appointments and promotions. Amendments could be proposed easily, by initiative or by the legislature, and ratified in statewide elections.

Some states already incorporate many of these suggestions in their constitutions, but there are still important differences among states on exactly how to structure and operate their governments.

▽

Because we have a federal system, state and local governments can take a wide variety of forms. In this chapter, we examine some of the differences in government structure and politics that reflect local traditions and demands.

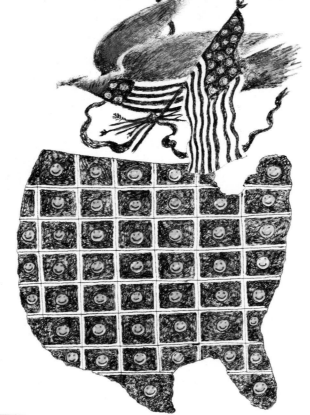

The national government was created by design, and thirteen states had of necessity to be included in the system, as did the relatively large number of local units of government in 1787. But the rest of the units—other states, cities, townships, special districts—were all created later, willy-nilly, in response to irresistible political and economic demands in Congress and in the state legislatures . . . there was no stopping their creation. And the process, below the state level at least, has not yet come to a halt. The same pressures that have always been present are still at work to bring new local units of government into existence.

With no foreordained plan from which to build, and no clear guidelines to help the old and the new units adjust to one another (how would such a plan and such guidelines have been drawn up?), so many contenders for power produce a great deal of overlapping, duplication, and conflict, as well as waste of effort and resources.[1]

The United States has more separate governmental units than most other countries in the world. When political scientists use the term *hyperpluralism*, they often point to the existence of the nearly eighty thousand separate governmental units in the United States to demonstrate the concept. **Hyperpluralism** is an exaggerated form of **pluralism** in which government is so decentralized and authority so fragmented that it doesn't get anything done. It may seem that way, particularly at the local level, but actually the almost eighty thousand governments in the United States, minus the federal government and the fifty state governments, do most of what people think government does—provide education, police protection, public health facilities, and the like. Indeed, most individuals come into contact with government workers only at the state and local levels. Although government employment at the federal level has been declining in recent years, at the state and local level the number of civilian employees in government has been increasing—from 9.9 percent of the entire civilian work force in 1963 to 12.8 percent in 1986. In 1986, over thirteen million American civilians worked directly for state and local governmental units, and millions of others worked indirectly for—or were contractors and consultants to—state and local governments. Just from a practical

[1]Richard H. Leach, *American Federalism* (New York: W. W. Norton, 1970), pp. 47–48.

Hyperpluralism

An exaggerated form of pluralism in which government is so decentralized and authority so fragmented that it doesn't get anything done.

Pluralism

A political doctrine in which autonomous groups in society actively compete in the decision-making process for resources and services.

Emergencies such as this California flood are state responsibilities.

Table 19–1

▽

State Expenditures (in percentages)

Education is the largest category of state spending and local spending.

Education	26.66
Public welfare	21.04
Highways	15.51
Health and hospitals	10.28
Interest on general debt	4.32
Natural resources	3.80
Corrections	2.46
Financial administration	2.03
General control	1.67
Social insurance administration	1.63
Police	1.48
General public building	.59
Air transportation	.30
Housing and urban renewal	.28
Water transport and terminals	.24
Libraries	.10
Other	7.61

SOURCE: Tax Foundation: *Facts and Figures on Government Finance, 1986.*

point of view, a knowledge of how these governments operate is relevant for every citizen, for they are the governments that every citizen must deal with almost on a daily basis.

State and Local Government Spending

▽

Examining the spending habits of a household often gives relevant information about the personalities and priorities of the household members. Examination of the expenditure patterns of state and local governments can likewise be illuminating. In Table 19–1, we show state expenditures for the latest fiscal year for which data are available. In Table 19–2, we show the same data for municipalities. There is a clear-cut pattern. State and city expenditures are concentrated in the areas of education, public welfare, highways, health, and police protection. Education is the biggest category of expenditure, particularly at the local level. Contrast this expenditure pattern with the federal government, which allocates only about 4 percent of its budget to education.

Paying for State and Local Government

▽

In 1986, state and local expenditures totaled $575 billion. These expenditures had to be paid for somehow. Until the twentieth century, almost all state and local expenditures were paid for by state and local revenues raised within state borders. Starting in the twentieth century, however, federal grants to state and local governmental units began to pay some of these costs. In the year 1902, federal grants to state and local governments accounted for 0.7 percent of state and local revenues. By 1970, they accounted for 18 percent. As we pointed out in Chapter 3, this shift has come about because of increased federal grants-in-aid and general revenue sharing. By 1986, these two forms of federal aid accounted for almost 22 percent of state and local revenues.

State and local governments in general are very willing to accept federal money. Indeed, they have entire staffs who devote all of their time to obtaining grants. For obvious reasons politicians usually prefer to obtain money through federal, rather than direct state or local, taxation.

Raising Revenue

Figure 19–1 (a) shows the percentages of taxes in various categories raised by state governments and (b) gives the same information for local governments. By far the most important tax at the state level is the **general sales tax,** and at the local level, the **property tax.** Whereas the federal government obtains more than 43 percent of its total revenues from the personal income tax, states only obtain about 13 percent this way. In 1986, there were still eight states that did not have a personal income tax. Other taxes assessed by states include corporate income taxes, at the state level, and fees, permits, and licenses at both the state and local government level, as well as death and gift taxes at the state level.

A tremendous amount of variation exists in state and local taxes collected. Look at the average taxes collected per person for all the states in Table 19–3. This table shows us that among the states levying the highest taxes are Alaska, Massachusetts, New York, and California. Those levying the lowest taxes are Tennessee, Arkansas, and Mississippi.

Table 19–2

▽

Local Expenditures (in percentages)

Education	44.88
Public welfare	7.06
Health and hospitals	6.78
Highways	5.66
Police	5.08
Interest on general debt	3.84
Sewerage	3.72
General control	2.58
Fire protection	2.44
Parks and recreation	2.42
Housing and urban renewal	1.80
Sanitation (other than sewerage)	1.44
Financial administration	1.26
General public building	1.25
Correction	.89
Air transportation	.76
Libraries	.72
Natural resources	.64
Water transport and terminals	.30
Parking facilities	.21
Other	6.27

SOURCE: Tax Foundation: *Facts and Figures on Government Finance, 1986.*

General Sales Tax

A tax levied as a proportion of the retail price of a commodity at the point of sale.

Property Tax

A tax on the value of real estate; limited to state and local governments and a particularly important source of revenue for local governments.

Figure 19–1

▽

Taxes Raised by State and Local Governments

States are generally dependent on sales taxes while towns and cities depend on property taxes.

SOURCE: *Book of the States, 1984–1985,* p. 344.

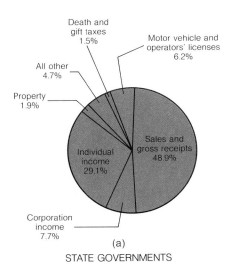

(a)
STATE GOVERNMENTS

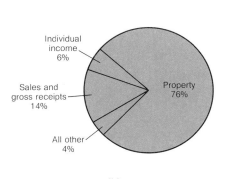

(b)
LOCAL GOVERNMENTS

Table 19–3

Average Taxes Paid Per Capita for All States and the District of Columbia

Alaska	4,908	Oklahoma	1,123
Wyoming	2,443	North Dakota	1,100
District of Columbia	2,132	Ohio	1,100
New York	1,189	Virginia	1,094
Minnesota	1,473	Maine	1,082
Hawaii	1,457	Arizona	1,064
New Jersey	1,457	Louisiana	1,051
Connecticut	1,434	New Mexico	1,041
Massachusetts	1,425	Texas	1,033
Wisconsin	1,393	Georgia	973
Michigan	1,370	West Virginia	972
Maryland	1,350	Florida	968
California	1,337	Utah	963
Washington State	1,306	New Hampshire	951
Rhode Island	1,295	Missouri	931
Delaware	1,273	South Dakota	914
Illinois	1,255	North Carolina	911
Oregon	1,229	Indiana	905
Nevada	1,214	Kentucky	888
Montana	1,179	South Carolina	878
Iowa	1,171	Idaho	875
Pennsylvania	1,169	Alabama	806
Colorado	1,166	Tennessee	803
Nebraska	1,146	Arkansas	771
Vermont	1,138	Mississippi	769
Kansas	1,129		

SOURCE: *Statistical Abstract of the United States*, 1986, p. 272.

The Era of Tax Revolt

In the last two decades where the taxes have grown rapidly, citizens have made relatively successful attempts at limiting levels of state taxation and state expenditures. In 1976, Michigan voters were offered Proposal C, which set a limit of 8.3 percent of the total personal income of Michigan citizens as the size of the state government revenues. Tennessee in 1978 approved a tax limitation by a better than 64 percent margin. This set tax revenues at the same percentage of total state personal income that existed in 1977.

Enter Proposition 13

Perhaps the most famous tax limitation or reduction measure was California's Proposition 13, which was passed by 65 percent of the voters in 1978. That proposition placed a ceiling on property taxes at 1 percent of market value as of March 1, 1975. Further, it limited increases in assessed valuation to 2 percent per year, unless two-thirds of the voters subsequently decided otherwise. Finally, it prohibited full reassessment of the property's value except when the property was sold.

The immediate impact of Proposition 13 was a decrease in property taxes, although two-thirds of the tax reductions went to commercial interests, not to residential taxpayers. The cuts in government spending did not become noticeable until 1980 when the state of California had exhausted its surplus funds. Across-

Proposition 13 supporter.

Profile

▽

Tom Bradley

Tom Bradley became the first black American to become mayor of a predominantly white city when he was elected mayor of Los Angeles in 1973. During the 1984 primary campaign, Bradley was one of the candidates considered by Walter Mondale for a vice presidential running mate. Bradley's rise to political prominence is, in many ways, a classic American success story.

Born in 1917 on a cotton plantation in East Texas, Bradley was one of seven children. At the age of seven, he moved to Los Angeles with his family. His mother took work as a domestic, while his father worked at a variety of unskilled jobs. Young Tom had his own newspaper route at the age of nine and was an all-city athlete in high school. Although discouraged from attending college by his advisers, he earned an athletic scholarship to UCLA.

In 1940, Bradley dropped out of college to get a job with the Los Angeles Police Department. During his twenty-one year career with the department, he held a number of posts and completed a law degree at night school. He retired from the force in 1961 to prac-

"I prefer to work quietly behind the scenes rather than get into a big public debate that accomplishes nothing . . . [I am] fiscally conservative and liberal on other issues. You cannot pin me down."

Tom Bradley

tice law. Two years later, he became the first black member of the Los Angeles City Council by being elected from a racially integrated district.

In 1969, Bradley had firsthand experience with the disadvantages of a "runoff" primary system. With thirteen candidates running in the Democratic primary against the incumbent mayor, Sam Yorty, Bradley took the plurality of the vote, 42 percent to Yorty's 26 percent. Since no one had received a majority of the vote, a runoff primary was held. Charging Bradley with being a black radical and recalling images of the Watts riots, Yorty defeated Bradley in the election, 53 percent to 47 percent.

Bradley was determined to succeed in his drive for the office. Four years later, after spending a great deal of time becoming known to the voters and hiring David Garth as his media expert, Bradley defeated Yorty to become mayor. He has been reelected three times since that time. His term as mayor has emphasized programs to improve mass transit in Los Angeles, efforts to ensure racial peace, increasing federal grants to the city, and balancing the municipal budget. He has twice run unsuccessfully as the Democratic nominee for governor of California.

---

the-board cuts were made in all departments except prisons, hospitals, and veterans' homes. County government and schools, receiving less state aid, cut expenditures by 10 percent. The tax revolt in California was only one of many. In the twenty-one states that allow voter initiatives, fifteen voted on tax limitation proposals. Of these, eleven passed. States that do not have initiatives are much less likely to enact similar legislation.

Effects of Tax Limitation Measures

Critics of limiting state taxes and spending point out that such restrictions might undermine essential programs like police protection and schools. Critics also point out that putting a percentage limitation in the state constitution will eventually turn out to be as troublesome as it has been in other cases where specific figures have been embedded in ordinances, building codes, and other legislation.

That the first black mayors of big cities were Richard G. Hatcher of Gary, Indiana, and Carl B. Stokes of Cleveland, both elected in 1967?

By 1986, the enthusiasm for tax rollback had diminished. Voters in several states defeated proposals to limit taxes and public services. In general, 1986 saw more voter approvals of bond issues than in recent years, particularly those which were earmarked for environmental purposes.

The U.S. Constitution and the States
▽

We live in a federal system in which there are fifty separate state governments and one national government. The U.S. Constitution gives a broad range of powers to state governments. It also prohibits state governments from engaging in certain activities. The U.S. Constitution never explicitly stated what the states may actually do. Rather, state powers were simply reserved, or residual—states may do anything they are not prohibited from doing by the Constitution or anything that is not expressly in the realm of the national government.

The major reserved powers of the states are the powers to tax, spend, and regulate intrastate commerce, or commerce within a given state. The states also have general **police power,** meaning they can impose their will on their citizens in the areas of safety (through, say, traffic laws), health (immunizations), welfare (child-abuse laws), and morals (censorship of pornographic materials).

Police Power

Authority to promote and safeguard the health, morals, safety, and welfare of the people.

The Massachusetts gun law is an example of police power.

Restrictions on state and local governmental activity are implied by the Constitution in Article VI, paragraph two:

> This Constitution, and the Laws of the United States, which shall be made in Pursuance thereof; and all Treaties made, or which shall be made, under the Authority of the United States, shall be the Supreme Law of the Land; and the Judges in every State shall be bound thereby, any Thing in the Constitution or Laws of any State to the Contrary notwithstanding.

In other words, it is the Constitution that is the supreme law of the land, and no state or local law can be in conflict with the Constitution or with laws made by the national Congress or by treaties entered into by the national government. Judicially, the U.S. Supreme Court has been the final arbiter of those conflicts arising between the national government and state governments.

State Constitutions
▽

The U.S. Constitution is a model of brevity, although at the cost of specificity. State constitutions, however, are typically models of excessive length and detail. The U.S. Constitution has endured for two hundred years and has been amended only twenty-six times. State constitutions are another matter. Louisiana has had eleven constitutions; Georgia, nine; South Carolina, seven; and the states of Alabama, Florida, and Virginia, six. The number of amendments that have been submitted to voters borders on the absurd. For example, by 1985, the citizens of Alabama had been asked to approve 656 amendments—of which they adopted 452. Table 19–4 offers comparative information on state constitutions.

Why Are State Constitutions So Long?

According to historians, the length and mass of detail of many state constitutions reflects the loss of popular confidence in state legislatures between the end of the Civil War and the early 1900s. During that period, forty-two states adopted or revised their constitutions. Those constitutions that were adopted before or after are shorter and contain fewer restrictions on the powers of state legislatures. Another, equally important reason for the length and detail of state constitutions is that the constitution makers apparently have had a difficult time distinguishing between constitutional and statutory law. Does the Louisiana state constitution need an amendment to declare Huey Long's birthday a legal holiday? Is it necessary for the state constitution of South Dakota to authorize a cordage and twine plant at the state penitentiary? Does the Alabama constitution have to include a thirteen-and-a-half-page amendment establishing the "Alabama Heritage Trust Fund"? Does Article XX of the California constitution need to discuss the tax-exempt status of the Huntington Library and Art Gallery? The U.S. Constitution contains no such details. It leaves to the legislature the nuts-and-bolts activity of making specific statutory laws.

There is another reason for the lengthiness of state constitutions. They are basically political documents that attempt to reflect the desires and needs of various groups within a state.

Table 19–4

General Information on State Constitutions

State or Other Jurisdiction	Number of Consti- tutions*	Dates of Adoption	Effective Date of Present Constitution	Estimated Length (number of words)	Number of Amendments Submitted to Voters	Adopted
Alabama	6	1819, 1861, 1865, 1868, 1875, 1901	Nov. 28, 1901	1742,000	656	452
Alaska	1	1956	Jan. 3, 1959	13,000	28	20
Arizona	1	1911	Feb. 14, 1912	28,876(a)	187	104
Arkansas	5	1836, 1861, 1864, 1868, 1874	Oct. 30, 1874	40,720(a)	156	71(b)
California	2	1849, 1879	July 4, 1879	33,350	756	449
Colorado	1	1876	Aug. 1, 1876	45,679	227	108
Connecticut	4	1818(c), 1965	Dec. 30, 1965	9,564	24	23
Delaware	4	1776, 1792, 1831, 1897	June 10, 1897	19,000	(d)	115
Florida	6	1839, 1861, 1865, 1868, 1886, 1968	Jan. 7, 1969	25,100	63	41
Georgia	10	1777, 1789, 1798, 1861, 1865, 1868, 1877, 1945, 1976, 1982	July 1, 1983	25,000(a)	11 (e)	10
Hawaii	1(f)	1950	Aug. 21, 1959	17,453(a)	85	77
Idaho	1	1889	July 3, 1890	21,500	183	103
Illinois	4	1818, 1848, 1870, 1970	July 1, 1971	13,200	7	3
Indiana	2	1816, 1851	Nov. 1, 1851	9,377(a)	65	36
Iowa	2	1846, 1857	Sept. 3, 1857	12,500	48	45(g)
Kansas	1	1859	Jan. 29, 1861	11,865	107	80(g)
Kentucky	4	1792, 1799, 1850, 1891	Sept. 28, 1891	23,500	54	26
Louisiana	11	1812, 1845, 1852, 1861, 1864, 1868, 1879, 1898, 1913, 1921, 1974	Jan. 1, 1975	36,146(a)	24	15
Maine	1	1819	March 15, 1820	13,500	181	153(h)
Maryland	4	1776, 1851, 1864, 1867	Oct. 5, 1867	41,134	227	195
Massachusetts	1	1780	Oct. 25, 1780	36,690(a,i)	141	116
Michigan	4	1835, 1850, 1908, 1963	Jan. 1, 1964	20,000	41	15
Minnesota	1	1857	May 11, 1858	9,500	203	109
Mississippi	4	1817, 1832, 1869, 1890	Nov. 1, 1890	23,500	124	54
Missouri	4	1820, 1865, 1875, 1945	March 30, 1945	42,000	100	62
Montana	2	1889, 1972	July 1, 1973	11,866(a)	17	10

*The constitutions referred to in this table include those Civil War documents customarily listed by the individual states.

(a) Actual word count.

(b) Eight of the approved amendments have been superseded and are not printed in the current edition of the constitution. The total adopted does not include five amendments that were invalidated.

(c) Colonial charters with some alterations served as the first constitutions in Connecticut (1638, 1662) and in Rhode Island (1663).

(d) Proposed amendments are not submitted to the voters in Delaware.

(e) Estimated length of the printed constitution, which includes only provisions of statewide applicability. Local amendments comprise most of the total constitution.

(f) As a kingdom and a republic, Hawaii had five constitutions.

(g) The figure given includes amendments approved by the voters and later nullified by the state supreme court in Iowa (three), Kansas (one), Nevada (six) and Wisconsin (two).

(h) The figure does not include one amendment approved by the voters in 1967 that is inoperative until implemented by legislation.

(i) The printed constitution includes many provisions that have been annulled. The length of effective provisions is an estimated 24,122 words (12,490 annulled) in Massachusetts and 11,399 words (7,627 annulled) in Rhode Island.

(j) The constitution of 1784 was extensively revised in 1792. Figures show proposals and adoptions since 1793, when the revised constitution became effective.

(k) The figures do not include submission and approval of the constitution of 1889 itself and of Article XX; these are constitutional questions included in some counts of constitutional amendments and would add two to the figure in each column.

(l) The figures include one amendment submitted to and approved by the voters and subsequently ruled by the supreme court to have been illegally submitted.

(m) Certain sections of the constitution were revised by the limited constitutional convention of 1967–68. Amendments proposed and adopted are since 1968.

(n) Of the estimated length, approximately two-thirds is of general statewide effect; the remainder is local amendments.

(o) Of the 628 proposed amendments submitted to the voters, 130 were of general statewide effect and 496 were local; the voters rejected 83 (12 statewide, 71 local). Of the remaining 543, the General Assembly refused to approve 100 (22 statewide, 78 local), and 443 (96 statewide, 347 local) were finally added to the constitution.

SOURCE: *Book of the States*, 1986–87, p. 14–15.

Table 19–4

▽

General Information on State Constitutions *(Continued)*

State or Other Jurisdiction	Number of Constitutions*	Dates of Adoption	Effective Date of Present Constitution	Estimated Length (number of words)	Number of Amendments Submitted to Voters	Adopted
Nebraska	2	1866, 1875	Oct. 12, 1875	20,048(a)	276	183
Nevada	1	1864	Oct. 31, 1864	20,770	165	100(g)
New Hampshire	2	1776, 1784	June 2, 1784	9,200	271j)	141(j)
New Jersey	3	1776, 1844, 1947	Jan. 1, 1948	17,086	48	36
New Mexico	1	1911	Jan. 6, 1912	27,200	213	104
New York	4	1777, 1822, 1846, 1894	Jan. 1, 1895	80,000	270	203
North Carolina	3	1776, 1868, 1970	July 1, 1971	11,000	30	24
North Dakota	1	1889	Nov. 2, 1889	31,000	208(k)	119(k)
Ohio	2	1802, 1851	Sept. 1, 1851	36,900	241	142
Oklahoma	1	1907	Nov. 16, 1907	68,800	254(l)	114(l)
Oregon	1	1857	Feb. 14, 1859	25,965	347	174
Pennsylvania	5	1776, 1790, 1838, 1873, 1968(m)	1968(m)	21,675	24(m)	19(m)
Rhode Island	2	1842(c)	May 2, 1843	19,026(a,i)	84	44
South Carolina	7	1776, 1778, 1790, 1861, 1865, 1868, 1895	Jan. 1, 1896	22,500(n)	638(o)	454(o)
South Dakota	1	1889	Nov. 2, 1889	23,300	178	92
Tennessee	3	1796, 1835, 1870	Feb. 23, 1870	15,300	55	32
Texas	5	1845, 1861, 1866, 1869, 1876	Feb. 15, 1876	62,000	430	283
Utah	1	1895	Jan. 4, 1896	17,500	121	73
Vermont	3	1777, 1786, 1793	July 9, 1793	6,600	206	49
Virginia	6	1776, 1830, 1851, 1869, 1902, 1970	July 1, 1971	18,500	19	16
Washington	1	1889	Nov. 11, 1889	29,400	139	76
West Virginia	2	1863, 1872	April 9, 1872	25,600	96	59
Wisconsin	1	1848	May 29, 1848	13,500	161	118(g)
Wyoming	1	1889	July 10, 1890	31,800	90	51
American Samoa	2	1960, 1967	July 1, 1967	6,000	13	7
No. Mariana Islands	1	1977	Oct. 24, 1977	—	—	—
Puerto Rico	1	1952	July 25, 1952	9,281(a)	6	6

*The constitutions referred to in this table include those Civil War documents customarily listed by the individual states.

(a) Actual word count.

(b) Eight of the approved amendments have been superseded and are not printed in the current edition of the constitution. The total adopted does not include five amendments that were invalidated.

(c) Colonial charters with some alterations served as the first constitutions in Connecticut (1638, 1662) and in Rhode Island (1663).

(d) Proposed amendments are not submitted to the voters in Delaware.

(e) Estimated length of the printed constitution, which includes only provisions of statewide applicability. Local amendments comprise most of the total constitution.

(f) As a kingdom and a republic, Hawaii had five constitutions.

(g) The figure given includes amendments approved by the voters and later nullified by the state supreme court in Iowa (three), Kansas (one), Nevada (six) and Wisconsin (two).

(h) The figure does not include one amendment approved by the voters in 1967 that is inoperative until implemented by legislation.

(i) The printed constitution includes many provisions that have been annulled. The length of effective provisions is an estimated 24,122 words (12,490 annulled) in Massachusetts and 11,399 words (7,627 annulled) in Rhode Island.

(j) The constitution of 1784 was extensively revised in 1792. Figures show proposals and adoptions since 1793, when the revised constitution became effective.

(k) The figures do not include submission and approval of the constitution of 1889 itself and of Article XX; these are constitutional questions included in some counts of constitutional amendments and would add two to the figure in each column.

(l) The figures include one amendment submitted to and approved by the voters and subsequently ruled by the supreme court to have been illegally submitted.

(m) Certain sections of the constitution were revised by the limited constitutional convention of 1967–68. Amendments proposed and adopted are since 1968.

(n) Of the estimated length, approximately two-thirds is of general statewide effect; the remainder is local amendments.

(o) Of the 628 proposed amendments submitted to the voters, 130 were of general statewide effect and 496 were local; the voters rejected 83 (12 statewide, 71 local). Of the remaining 543, the General Assembly refused to approve 100 (22 statewide, 78 local), and 443 (96 statewide, 347 local) were finally added to the constitution.

SOURCE: *Book of the States,* 1986–87, p. 14–15.

The Constitutional Convention and the Constitutional Initiative

Constitutional Initiative
An electoral device whereby citizens can propose a constitutional amendment through initiatory petitions signed by the required number of registered voters.

Two ways to effect constitutional changes are the state constitutional convention and the constitutional initiative. As of 1981, at least 230 state constitutional conventions had been used to write an entirely new constitution or to attempt to amend an existing one. A unique feature of the constitutions of seventeen states is the **constitutional initiative.**[2] An initiative allows citizens to place a proposed amendment on the ballot without calling a constitutional convention. The number of signatures required to get a constitutional initiative on the ballot varies from state to state; it is usually between 5 to 10 percent of the total number of votes cast for governor in the last election. The states where the initiative process has been used most frequently are California and Oregon. Relatively few initiative amendments are successfully approved by the electorate. California's Proposition 13, already discussed, was a very successful exception.

The State Executive Branch

▽

All state governments in the United States have executive, legislative, and judicial branches. Here the similarity ends. State governments do not always have strong executive branches. Also, as we have noted, in some states citizens can initiate legislation.

A Weak Executive

During the colonial period, governors were appointed by the Crown and had the power to call the colonial assembly into session, recommend legislation, exercise veto power, and dissolve the assembly. The colonial governor acted as commander in chief of each colony's military forces, and the governor was head of the judiciary.

Not surprisingly, when the colonies revolted against English rule, that revolt centered on the all-powerful colonial governors. When the first states were formed after the Declaration of Independence, hostility toward the governor's office assured a weak executive branch and an extremely strong legislative branch. By the 1830s, the state executive office had become more important. Since Jackson's presidency, all governors (except in South Carolina) have been directly elected by the people. Simultaneously, there was an effort to democratize state government by popularly electing other state government officials as well.

Under the tenets of Jacksonian democracy, the more public officials who are elected (and not appointed), the more democratic (and better) the system. The adoption of the long ballot (see Chapter 10) was the result. Even today, some states have numerous state offices with independently elected officials. Michigan, for example, has thirty-six. The problem with the long ballot is that the direct election of so many executive officials means it is likely that no one will have much power because each official is working to secure his or her own political support. Only if the elected officials happen to be able to work together cohesively can they get much done.

[2]These states are as follows: Arizona, Arkansas, California, Colorado, Florida, Illinois, Massachusetts, Michigan, Missouri, Montana, Nebraska, Nevada, North Dakota, Ohio, Oklahoma, Oregon, and South Dakota.

In some states, the voters have at times chosen a governor from one political party and a lieutenant governor from another. This happened in California in 1978, in Missouri in 1980, and in Iowa in 1982 and 1986. These situations can result in making the governor unwilling to leave the state to keep the lieutenant governor from exerting power during his or her travels.

Reforming the System

Most states follow the practice of electing numerous executive officials. Nonetheless, the authority of the office of the governor has been exercised with increasing frequency in recent years. Governors have become a significant force in legislative policy making. The governor, in theory, enjoys the same advantage that the president has over Congress in his or her ability to make policy decisions and to embody these in a program for the state legislative body to act on. How the governor exercises this ability often depends on his or her powers of charm and persuasion. A strong personality can make for a strong executive office.

Reorganization of the state executive branch to achieve greater efficiency has been attempted at numerous times and in many states. In the 1950s, thirty-five states created their own reorganization commissions, patterned after the national commission on organization of the executive branch of the national government that was chaired by former President Hoover. Their administrative reforms typically involved compressing numerous, fragmented governmental agencies into more hierarchical and streamlined systems to increase efficiency or to end obsolete agencies.

There are many obstacles to reorganizing state executive branches. Voters do not want to lose their ability to influence politics directly. Both the voters and the legislators are fearful that reorganization will concentrate too much authority in the hands of the governor. Finally, many believe that numerous governmental functions, such as control of the highway program, should remain administrative rather than political.

Massachusetts governor Michael Dukakis.

Item Veto
The power exercised by the governors of most states to veto particular sections or items of an appropriations bill, while signing the remainder of the bill into law.

The Governor's Veto Power

The veto power of the president of the United States gives him immense leverage. Simply the threat of a presidential veto often means that legislation will not be passed by Congress. In some states, governors have stronger veto power than in others, and in some states, governors have no veto power at all. Some states give the governor veto power but give him or her only five days in which to exercise it. About twenty states give the governor a pocket veto power (see Chapter 12).

In forty-three states, the governor has some form of **item veto** power on appropriations. If the governor in such a state does not particularly like one item, or line, in an appropriations bill, he or she can veto that item. In twelve states, the governor can reduce the amount of the appropriation, but not completely. Nineteen states give governors the ability to use the item veto on more than just appropriations. Contrast this power with that of the president, who must veto the entire piece of legislation or leave it intact.

Off-Year Election of Governors

Increasingly, state elected officials, including the governor, are isolating themselves from national politics. They have been able to do this because of the tendency of states to elect their governors and other executive officials in off-presidential election years. For example, in 1984, fully thirty-seven states did not have gubernatorial elections. In 1920, only twelve states did not have gubernatorial elections in presidential election years.

The purpose behind this shift has been to weaken the influence of national politics over state politics. For example, if a Democratic candidate for governor is running during a presidential election year when the Democratic candidate for president is obviously going to achieve a landslide victory, the Democratic gubernatorial candidate has a much better chance of winning also.

Although this argument certainly has validity, there is a cost to such isolation from presidential politics. The cost is less voter participation in statewide elections. On average, only 75 percent of the voters who vote during the presidential election years vote during off-presidential election years.

The State Legislature
▽

Although there has been a move in recent years to increase the power of governors, state legislatures are still an important force in state politics and state governmental decision making. The task of these assemblies is to legislate on such matters as taxes and the regulation of business and commerce, school systems and the funding of education, and welfare payments. Allocation of funds and program priorities are vital issues to local residents and communities, and conflicts between regions within the state or between the cities and the rural areas are common.

State legislatures have been criticized for being less professional and less effective than the U.S. Congress. It is true that state legislatures sometimes spend their time considering trivial legislation (such as joggers' headphones in Iowa in 1983), and lobbyists often have too much influence in state capitals. At the same time, state legislators are often given few resources to work with. In many states, legislatures are limited to meeting only part of the year, and in some the pay is a disincentive to real service. In at least eight states, state legislators are paid under $10,000 per year. A complete list of state legislators' salaries is given in Table 19–5.

Table 19–5

Characteristics of State Legislatures

	Seats in Senate	Length of Term	Seats in House	Length of Term	Years Sessions Are Held	Salary*
Alabama	35	4	105	4	annual	$ 10 (d)
Alaska	20	4	40	2	annual	46,800
Arizona	30	2	60	2	annual	15,000
Arkansas	35	4	100	2	odd	7,500**
California	40	4	80	2	even	33,732
Colorado	35	4	65	2	annual	17,500
Connecticut	36	2	151	2	annual	13,000
Delaware	21	4	41	2	annual	20,000
Florida	40	4	120	2	annual	18,000
Georgia	56	2	180	2	annual	10,000
Hawaii	25	4	51	2	annual	15,600
Idaho	42	2	84	2	annual	30 (d)
Illinois	59	—‡	118	2	annual	32,500
Indiana	50	4	100	2	annual	11,600
Iowa	50	4	100	2	annual	14,600
Kansas	40	4	125	2	annual	52 (d)
Kentucky	38	4	100	2	even	100 (d)
Louisiana	39	4	105	4	annual	16,800**
Maine	35	2	151	2	even	7,500***
Maryland	47	4	141	4	annual	21,000
Massachusetts	40	2	160	2	annual	30,000
Michigan	38	4	110	2	annual	36,520
Minnesota	67	4	134	2	odd	22,350
Mississippi	52	4	122	4	annual	10,000
Missouri	34	4	163	2	annual	19,524
Montana	50	—‡	100	2	odd	52.13 (d)
Nebraska†	49	4	—	—	annual	4,800
Nevada	21	4	42	2	odd	104 (d)
New Hampshire	24	2	400	2	annual	200 (b)
New Jersey	40	—‡	80	2	annual	25,000
New Mexico	42	4	70	2	annual	75 (d)
New York	61	2	150	2	annual	43,000
North Carolina	50	2	120	2	odd	8,400
North Dakota	53	4	100	2	odd	90 (d)
Ohio	33	4	99	2	annual	31,659
Oklahoma	48	4	101	2	annual	20,000
Oregon	30	4	60	2	odd	9,300
Pennsylvania	50	4	203	2	annual	35,000
Rhode Island	50	2	100	2	annual	5 (d)
South Carolina	46	4	124	2	annual	10,000
South Dakota	35	2	70	2	annual	3,200****
Tennessee	33	4	99	2	odd	12,500
Texas	31	4	150	2	odd	7,200**
Utah	29	4	75	2	annual	65 (d)
Vermont	30	2	150	2	odd	300§
Virginia	40	4	100	2	annual	11,000
Washington	49	4	98	2	annual	13,700
West Virginia	34	4	100	2	annual	6,500
Wisconsin	33	4	99	2	annual	27,202
Wyoming	30	4	64	2	annual	75 (d)

*Salaries annual unless otherwise noted as (d), per day or (b), biennium.
**Plus per diem.
****For odd year; $2,800 for even year.
‡Terms vary from two to four years.
***For odd year; $4,000 for even year.
†Unicameral legislature.
§Per week.

SOURCE: Adapted from *Book of the States*, 1986–87 (Lexington, Ky.: Council of State Governments, 1986).

> **Did You Know?**
>
> That nine states have no minimum age and fourteen states have no U.S. citizenship requirements for a person to run for governor?

We have seen earlier how a bill becomes law in the U.S. Congress. A similar process occurs at the state level. Figure 19–2 traces "how an idea becomes a law" the Florida legislature. Similar steps are followed in other states (note that Nebraska has a unicameral legislature, so there is no second chamber process).

Legislative Apportionment

Drawing up legislative districts—state as well as federal—has long been subject to gerrymandering—creative cartography designed to guarantee that one political party maintains control of a particular voting district (see Chapter 13). In Figure 19–3 we see a particularly bizarre example—the proposed sixty-ninth Assembly District for the State of California, drawn up by the California legislature to create a Democratic district in Orange and Los Angeles counties.

The Supreme Court indicated in 1982 that malapportioned state legislatures violate the equal protection clause of the Fourteenth Amendment.[3] In a series of Supreme Court cases that followed, the grossest examples of state legislative malapportionment were eliminated. The Burger Court, however, allowed "benevolent, bipartisan gerrymandering" in certain states. Indeed, in 1977, the Supreme Court held that the state had an obligation imposed under the 1965 Voting Rights Act to draw district boundaries to maximize minority legislative representation.[4]

Does the issue of malapportionment matter? Some researchers believe it does. One study concluded that "reapportionment is making differences in state spending

[3]In *Baker v. Carr* (1962).

[4]*United Jewish Organizations of Williamsburg v. Cary*, 430 U.S. 144 (1977).

Figure 19–2

How an Idea Becomes a Law

SOURCE: Allen Morris, *The Florida Handbook 1983–1984*. 19th ed. (Tallahassee, Fl.: Peninsular Publishing Co., 1983), pp. 84–85.

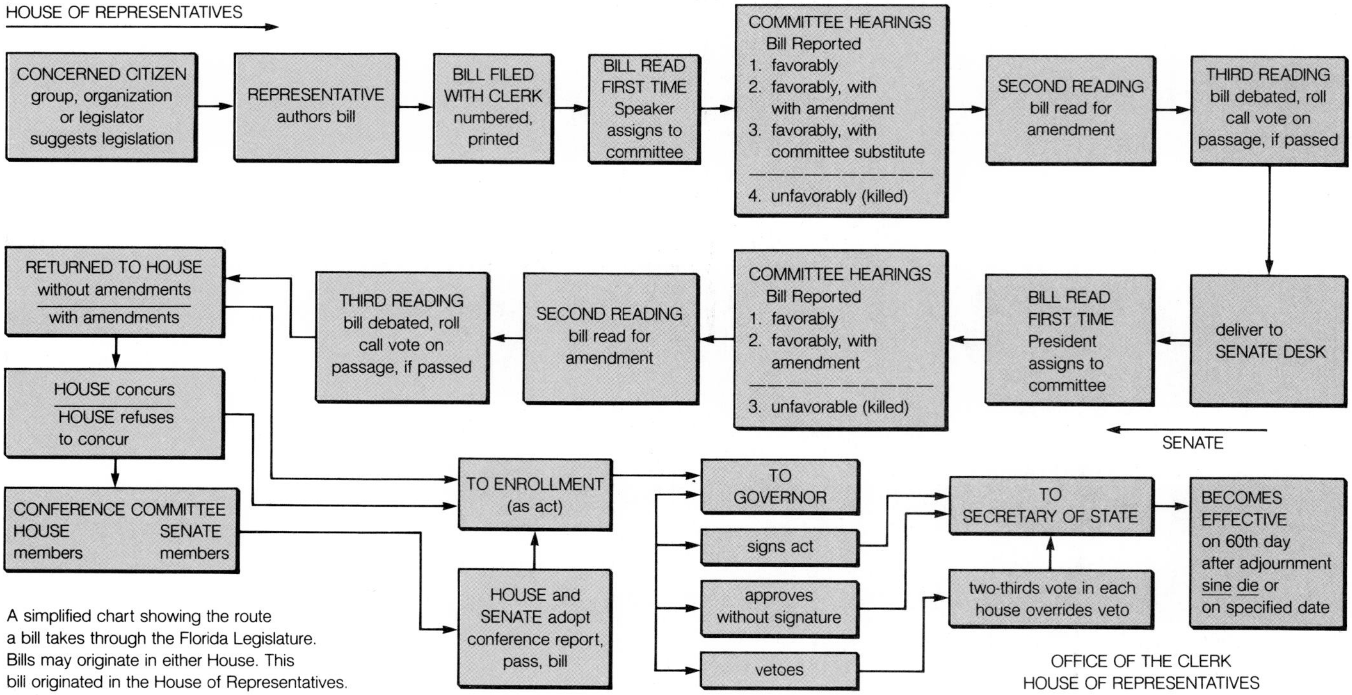

A simplified chart showing the route a bill takes through the Florida Legislature. Bills may originate in either House. This bill originated in the House of Representatives.

in the direction of less discrimination against metropolitan areas."[5] But others, including political scientist Thomas Dye, have concluded that "on the whole, the policy choices of malapportioned legislatures are not noticeably different from the policy choices of well-apportioned legislatures."[6] Dye was particularly referring to state public policies on health, education, highways, welfare, and taxation.

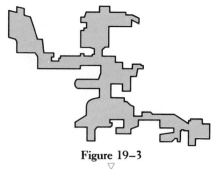

Direct Democracy: The Initiative, Referendum, and Recall

There is a major difference between the legislative process as outlined in the U.S. Constitution and the legislative process as outlined in the various state constitutions. Many states exercise a type of direct democracy through the initiative, the referendum, and the recall—procedures that allow voters to directly control the government.

Figure 19–3
▽
Proposed Sixty-ninth Assembly District in California

SOURCE: Gordon E. Baker, "Redistricting in the Seventies: The Political Thicket Deepens," *National Civic Review* (June 1972), p. 281.

The Initiative

This technique lets citizens bypass legislatures by proposing new statutes or changes in government for citizen approval. Most states that have citizen legislative initiative require that the initiative backers circulate a petition to place the issue on the ballot and that, say, 7 percent of the registered voters in the last gubernatorial election sign the petition. If enough signatures are obtained, then the issue is put on the ballot. Twenty-one states use the legislative initiative, typically those states where political parties are relatively weak and where nonpartisan groups are strong. Some major initiatives that have been passed include a 1980 Washington state ban on out-of-state nuclear waste, a 1982 Massachusetts requirement that voters approve any future nuclear plant construction, and the adoption of laws requiring refunds on beverage cans and bottles in Maine and Michigan in 1976.

The Referendum

The **referendum** is similar to the initiative, except that the issue (or constitutional change) is initially proposed by the legislature and then directed to the voters for their approval. The referendum is most often used for approval of local school bond issues and for amendments to state constitutions. In a number of states that provide for the referendum, a bill passed by the legislature may be suspended by obtaining the required number of voters' signatures on petitions. A statewide referendum election is then held, and if the majority of the voters disapprove of the bill, it is no longer valid.

The referendum was not initially intended for regular use, and indeed it has been used infrequently in the past. Its opponents argue that it is an unnecessary check on representative government and that it weakens legislative responsibility. In recent years, the referendum has become increasingly popular as citizens have attempted to control their state and local governments. Interest groups have been active in sponsoring the petition drives necessary to force a referendum. Thirty-seven states provided for the referendum as of 1982.

Referendum

An electoral device whereby legislative or constitutional measures are referred to the voters for approval or disapproval.

[5]H. George Fredrickson and Yong Hyo Cho, " 'Sixties' Reapportionment: Is It Victory or Delusion?" *National Civic Review* (February 1971), p. 78.

[6]Thomas R. Dye, "Malapportionment and Public Policy in the States," *Journal of Politics* 27 (August 1965), p. 599.

Recall

A procedure enabling voters to remove an elected official from office before his or her term has expired.

A fairly regular focus of state referenda has been various versions of an equal rights amendment. Referendum elections were held in Florida and Nevada in 1978, in Iowa in 1980, and in Vermont in 1986 on proposals for a state equal rights amendment. In each state, the proposal was rejected by the voters. Another example of the referendum was the decision by Alaskan voters in 1976 to move the state capital from Juneau to the little town of Willow. Funding for the move, however, was defeated in a 1982 referendum. The 1986 elections saw decisions on referenda on a wide variety of issues in the states. The voters in five states approved lotteries, the voters in Kansas approved parimutuel betting on horse and dog races, and California voters passed a measure making English the official state language.

The Recall

The **recall** is directed at public officials who are deemed incompetent or grossly unethical in their conduct. Voters may circulate a petition calling for the removal of such an official, and if a petition obtains a sufficient number of signatures (usually that number is quite high—say, 25 percent of the votes cast in the last gubernatorial election), then a recall election is held. The recall is authorized mainly in western states. So far only one governor has been recalled from office— Lynn Frazier of North Dakota in 1922. (Later, he was elected to the U.S. Senate in that same state.)

The recall is mainly used as a threat. Proponents of the recall in the fourteen states in which it exists argue that the possibility of recall prevents outrageously inappropriate official behavior. Its opponents argue that it makes officeholders a prey of well-financed special interest groups. In 1984, antitax groups in Michigan succeeded in recalling two Democratic members of the state legislature and were successful in replacing them with newly elected Republicans. Those changes shifted the balance of party control in one house of the legislature (the Senate).

The State Judiciary

▽

Each of the fifty states, as well as the District of Columbia, has its own separate court system (which is in addition to the federal courts—see Chapter 15). Figure 19–4 shows a hypothetical model of the state court system. It appears quite similar to the model of the federal court system, with its three levels of courts—trial courts, intermediate courts of appeal, and a supreme court. Again, the trial courts are of two types: those having limited jurisdiction and those having general jurisdiction.[7] Cases heard before these courts can be appealed to the state appellate court and ultimately to the state supreme court.

State courts confront severe problems of underfunding and overwork. Lack of funds—due to an increased case load, inflation, and fiscal conservatism in state governments—has slowed down and occasionally even threatened to shut down operations. State courts annually process about 100 million cases, three-quarters of which involve traffic offenses and about 10 percent of which involve alleged criminal activity. Short on judicial personnel and delayed by often complex cases with lengthy appeals, the state courts are often unable to function efficiently or

[7]See Chapter 15 for a definition of these terms.

fairly. The consequence is all too often a resort to plea-bargained convictions or a denial of justice to plaintiffs in civil and criminal cases.

The state courts of last resort are usually called simply supreme courts, although they are also labeled the supreme judicial court (Maine and Massachusetts), the court of appeals (Maryland and New York), the court of criminal appeals (Oklahoma and Texas, which also have separate supreme courts), or the supreme court of appeals (West Virginia). Judges for these highest courts may be chosen either at large from the state as a whole or by judicial district. Chief justices may be chosen by the public in an election, by fellow justices, by gubernatorial appointment with or without legislative approval, by a judicial nominating commission, by seniority, by rotation, or by the legislature. Terms of the chief justice and associate justices range from six years to life, though typically a limit of a certain number of years is set.

All states have major trial courts, commonly called circuit courts, district courts, or superior courts. The number of judges and their terms in office vary widely. Many, though not all, states have intermediate appellate courts between the trial courts of original jurisdiction and the court of last resort. These are usually called the courts of appeal. Salaries of state judges also vary widely, but higher pay is given to appellate and supreme court members.

State judges may be removed by a variety of means, including judicial inquiry commissions, action by fellow judges, impeachment by the legislature or through a concurrent resolution, recall by the electorate, or action by the governor on request of the legislature. In 1986 the chief justice of the State Supreme Court, Rose Bird, was removed from office by the voters. She had firmly opposed the imposition of the death penalty. Not all states establish qualifications for state judges, though nearly all require U.S. citizenship and legal training, and many require a minimum residency period in the state, a minimum age (as low as eighteen in Wisconsin), years of legal experience, being a qualified voter, and personal traits such as good character.

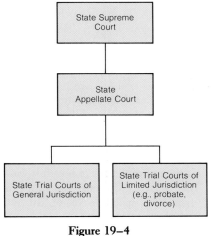

Figure 19–4
▽
The State Court System

California Supreme Court Chief Justice Rose Bird was not recertified by the voters in 1986.

How Local Government Operates
▽

Local governments are difficult to describe because of their great dissimilarities and because, if we include municipalities, counties, towns, townships, and special districts, there are so many of them. We limit the discussion here to the most important types and features of local governments.

The Legal Existence of Local Government

The U.S. Constitution makes no mention of local governments. Article IV, Section 4, states that "the United States shall guarantee to every State in this Union a Republican Form of Government. . . ." Actually, then, the states do not even have to have local governments. Consequently, every local government is a creature of the state. The state can create a local government and the state can terminate the right of a local government to exist. Indeed, states have often abolished entire counties, school districts, cities, and special districts. Since World War II, almost twenty thousand school districts have gone out of existence as they were consolidated with other school districts.

Profile
▽
Henry Cisneros

After Walter Mondale's nomination at the Democratic convention seemed assured in 1984, Mondale began the search for a vice presidential candidate. One of the names which quickly rose to the top of the list of hopefuls was that of Henry Cisneros, the young and dynamic Hispanic mayor of San Antonio, the ninth largest city in the United States.

The success of Cisneros and the current economic prosperity of his city are both recent phenomena. Up until recent years, the Hispanic population of San Antonio, a city which was founded in 1718, had been excluded from political power. The town itself was economically stagnant with many poverty-stricken neighborhoods. In 1974, Hispanic leaders formed an activist community organization to force the city government to improve the poor neighborhoods. At about the same time, a business group formed an organization to promote the rapid development of San Antonio. The two groups ousted the old city leadership and began a bitter struggle within the city council over the distribution of services. Cisneros,

"There isn't an alternative to trickle-down economics. If the city works, the people work."

elected as a councilman in 1975, worked to bring peace to the warring factions.

A native of San Antonio, Cisneros grew up in the *barrio*, the son of a retired federal employee. After graduating from Texas A&M University, he

earned a Master's degree from Harvard and a Ph.D. in public administration from George Washington University. During the Nixon administration, he spent a year as a White House Fellow in a program which recognizes extraordinary young Americans. In 1974, he returned to his native city with his family to begin a political career.

To become mayor, Cisneros had to defeat a wealthy insurance agent. The campaign styles of the two candidates provided quite a contrast; Cisneros drove himself around the neighborhoods in a 1972 Volkswagen Beetle and preached economic development, while his opponent, arriving in a new Lincoln, talked about cautious growth. Cisneros's approach not only attracted the Hispanic community but also many of the Anglo businesspersons who wanted rapid expansion. In April 1981, Dr. Cisneros was swept into office with 62 percent of the vote. As one observer of the young campaigner put it, "Henry is the guy who can heal the wounds. He's acceptable to people on both sides of the tracks."*

*Time, April 13, 1981, p. 59.

Dillon's Rule

The narrowest possible interpretation of the legal status of local governments, outlined by Judge John F. Dillon who in 1911 stated that a municipal corporation can exercise only those powers expressly granted by state law.

Since the local government is the legal creature of the state, does that mean the state can dictate everything the local government does? For many years that seemed to be the case. The narrowest possible view of the legal status of local governments follows **Dillon's rule,** outlined by John F. Dillon in his *Commentaries on the Law of Municipal Corporations.* He stated that municipal corporations may possess only powers "granted in express words . . . [that are] necessarily or fairly implied in or incident to the powers expressly granted."[8] Cities governed under Dillon's rule have been dominated by the state legislature. Those communities wishing to obtain the status of a municipal corporation have simply petitioned the state legislature for a charter. The charter has typically been extremely narrow.

[8]John F. Dillon, *Commentaries on the Law of Municipal Corporations,* 5th ed. (Boston: Little, Brown, 1911), I, Sec. 237.

Snow removal in New York city.

In a revolt against state legislative power over municipalities, the home rule movement began. It was based on **Cooley's rule**, derived from an 1871 decision by Michigan Judge Thomas Cooley,[9] and stating that cities should be able to govern themselves. Since 1900, about four-fifths of the states have allowed **municipal home rule**, but only with respect to local concerns—where no statewide interests are involved. A municipality must choose to become a **home rule city**; otherwise, it operates as a **general law city**. In the latter case, the state makes certain general laws relating to cities of different sizes, which are designated as first class cities, second class cities, or towns. Once a city by virtue of its population receives such a ranking, it follows the general law put down by the state. Only if it chooses to be a home rule city can it avoid such state government restrictions. In most states only cities with populations of 2,500 or more can choose home rule.

Local Governmental Units

There are four major types of local governmental units: municipalities, counties, towns and townships, and special districts.

Municipalities

As of 1986, there were about nineteen thousand municipalities within the fifty states. Almost all municipalities are fairly small cities. Only about five hundred

[9]*People v. Hurlbut*, 24 Mich. 44 (1871).

Cooley's Rule

The view that cities should be able to govern themselves, presented in an 1871 decision by Michigan Judge Thomas Cooley.

Municipal Home Rule

The power vested in a local unit of government to draft or change its own charter and to manage its own affairs.

Home Rule City

A city with a charter allowing local voters to frame, adopt, and amend their own charter.

General Law City

A city operating under general state laws that apply to all local government units of a similar type.

County

The chief government set up by the state to administer state law and business at the local level. Counties are drawn up by area, rather than by rural or urban criteria.

New England Town

Combines the roles of city and county into one governmental unit in the New England states.

Town Meeting

The governing authority of a town. Qualified voters may participate in the election of officers and in the passage of legislation.

cities have populations over fifty thousand, and only six municipalities (Chicago, Detroit, Houston, Los Angeles, New York, and Philadelphia) have populations over a million. In 1986 all the municipalities combined spent about $100 billion—primarily for water supply and other utilities, police and fire protection, and education. More than half of municipal tax revenues come from property taxes. Municipalities rely very heavily on financial assistance from both the federal and state governments.

Counties

The difference between a **county** and a municipality is that a county may not be created at the behest of its inhabitants. The state sets up counties on its own initiative to serve as a political extension of the state government. Counties apply state law and administer state business at the local level. Counties are not municipal corporations, even though in some states the law treats counties as involuntary, quasi-municipal corporations.

County governments, of which there are almost three thousand within the United States, vary from Los Angeles County, California, with eight million people, to Loving County, Texas, with less than one hundred people. San Bernardino County, California, has more than twenty thousand square miles—half the size of Pennsylvania—but Bristol County, Rhode Island, comprises only twenty-five square miles.

County governments' responsibilities include zoning, building regulations, health, hospitals, parks, recreation, highways, public safety, justice, and record keeping. Typically, when a municipality is established within a county, the county withdraws most of its services from that municipality; for example, the municipal police force takes over from the county police force. County governments are extremely complex entities, a product of the era of Jacksonian democracy and its effort to bring government closer to the people. There is no easy way to describe their operation in summary form. Indeed, the county has been called by one scholar "the dark continent of American politics."[10]

Towns and Townships

A unique governmental creation is the **New England town**—not to be confused with the word *town* used as just another name for a city. In Maine, Massachusetts, New Hampshire, Vermont, and Connecticut, the unit called the town combines the roles of city and county into one governing unit. A New England town typically consists of one or more urban settlements and the surrounding rural areas. Consequently, counties have little importance in New England. In Connecticut, for example, they are simply geographic units.

From the New England town comes the tradition of the annual **town meeting**, where direct democracy was—and continues to be—practiced. Each resident of a town is summoned to the annual meeting at the town hall. Those who attend levy taxes, pass laws, elect town officers, and appropriate money for different activities.

Normally, few residents show up for town meetings today unless a high-interest item is on the agenda or unless their family members want to be elected to office. The town meeting takes a day or more, and few citizens are able to set aside such a large amount of time. Because of the declining interest in town meetings, many

[10]Henry S. Gilbertson, *The County, the "Dark Continent of American Politics"* (New York: National Short Ballot Association, 1917).

New England towns have adopted a **town manager system,** in which the voters simply elect three **selectmen** to represent the citizens who then appoint a professional town manager. The town manager in turn appoints other officials.

   Townships operate somewhat like counties. Where they exist there may be several dozen within a county, and they perform the same functions that the county would do otherwise. Indiana, Iowa, Kansas, Michigan, Minnesota, New Jersey, New York, Ohio, Pennsylvania, and Wisconsin all have numerous townships. A township is not the same thing as a New England town because it is meant to be a rural government rather than a city government. Moreover, it is never the principal unit of local government—as are New England towns. The boundaries of most townships are based on federal land surveys of the 1780s, which mapped the land into six-mile squares called townships. They were then subdivided into thirty-six blocks of one square mile each called sections. Along the boundaries of each section a road was built.

   Although townships have few functions left to perform in many parts of the nation, they are still politically important in others. In some metropolitan areas, townships are the political unit that provides most public services to residents who live in suburban but unincorporated areas.

Special Districts

The most numerous form of local government is the special district, which includes school districts. In 1986, there were about 43,500 special districts, of which slightly less than 15,000 were school districts. Special districts are one-function governments (Figure 19–5). After school districts, districts for fire protection are the most numerous. There are also districts for mosquito control, cemeteries, and numerous other concerns. Special districts may be called authorities, boards, corporations—and even districts.

   One important feature of special districts is that they cut across geographical and governmental boundaries. Sometimes special districts cut across state lines, as does,

Town-Manager System
Form of city government in which voters elect three selectmen who then appoint a professional town manager who in turn appoints other officials.

Selectmen
The governing group of a town.

Township
Rural units of government based on federal land surveys of the American frontier in the 1780s. They have significantly declined in importance.

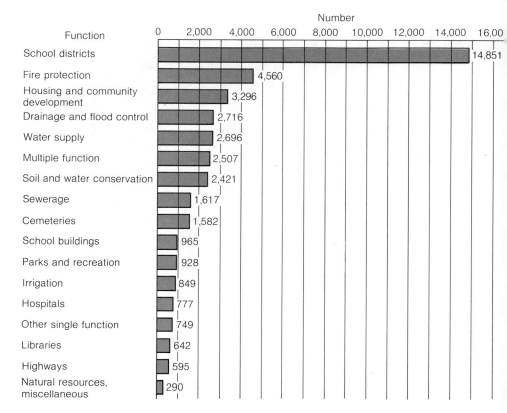

Number

Function	Number
School districts	14,851
Fire protection	4,560
Housing and community development	3,296
Drainage and flood control	2,716
Water supply	2,696
Multiple function	2,507
Soil and water conservation	2,421
Sewerage	1,617
Cemeteries	1,582
School buildings	965
Parks and recreation	928
Irrigation	849
Hospitals	777
Other single function	749
Libraries	642
Highways	595
Natural resources, miscellaneous	290

Interstate Compact

An agreement between two or more
states to cooperate on a policy or problem such as sharing water resources must
first be approved by Congress.

for example, the Port of New York Authority, which was established by an **interstate
compact** between New Jersey and New York. A mosquito control district may cut
across both municipal lines and county lines. A metropolitan transit district may
provide bus service to dozens of municipalities and to several counties.

Except for school districts, the typical citizen is not very aware of most special
districts. Indeed, most citizens don't know who furnishes their weed control, mosquito control, water, or sewage control. Part of the reason for the low profile of
special districts is that special district administrators are appointed, not elected, and
therefore receive little public attention.

Consolidation of Governments

With approximately eighty thousand separate and often overlapping governmental
units within the United States, the trend in recent years toward consolidation is
understandable. **Consolidation** is defined as the union of two or more governmental
units to form a single unit. Typically, a state constitution or a state statute will
designate consolidation procedures.

Consolidation

The union of two or more governmental
units to form a single unit.

Functional Consolidation

The cooperation of two or more units of
local government in providing services to
their inhabitants.

Consolidation is often recommended for metropolitan-area problems, but to
date there have been few consolidations within metropolitan areas. The most
successful consolidations have been **functional consolidations**—particularly of city
and county police, health, and welfare departments. In some cases, functional
consolidation is a satisfactory alternative to the complete consolidation of governmental units. The most successful form of functional consolidation was started in

▽
646

1957 in Dade County, Florida. The county, now called Metro, is a union of twenty-six municipalities. Each municipality has its own governmental entity, but the county government operates under a home rule charter. The county, or Metro, has authority to furnish water, planning, mass transit, and police services and to set minimum standards of performance. The governing body of Metro is an elected thirteen-member board of county commissioners, which appoints a county manager and an attorney.

A special type of consolidation is **councils of government (COGs)**, voluntary organizations of counties and municipalities that attempt to tackle areawide problems. More than two hundred COGs have been established, mainly since 1966. The impetus for their establishment was and continues to be federal government grants. COGs are an alternative means of treating major regional problems that various communities are unwilling to tackle on a consolidated basis either by true consolidation of governmental units or by functional consolidation.

The power of COGs is advisory only. Each member unit simply selects its council representatives who report back to the unit after COG meetings. Nonetheless, today there are several COGs that have begun to have considerable influence on regional policy. These include the Metropolitan Washington Council of Governments, the Supervisors' Inter-County Commission in Detroit, and the Association of Bay Area Governments in San Francisco.

Councils of Governments (COGs)
Voluntary organizations of counties and municipalities concerned with areawide problems.

How Municipalities Are Governed

We can divide municipal representative governments into four types: (1) the commission plan, (2) the council-manager plan, (3) the mayor-administrator plan, and (4) the mayor-council plan.

The Commission Plan

This form of municipal government consists of a commission of three to nine members who have both legislative and executive powers. The salient aspects of the commission plan are as follows:

1. Executive and legislative powers are concentrated in a small group of individuals, who are elected at large on a (normally) nonpartisan ballot.
2. Each commissioner is individually responsible for heading a particular municipal department, such as the department of public safety.
3. The commission is collectively responsible for passing ordinances and controlling spending.
4. The mayor is selected from the members of the commission (an office that is only ceremonial).

The commission plan, originating in Galveston, Texas, in 1901, had its greatest popularity during the first twenty years of this century. It appealed to municipal government reformers, who looked upon it as a type of business organization that would eliminate the problems that they believed to be inherent in the long ballot and in partisan municipal politics. Unfortunately, vesting both legislative and executive power in the hands of a small group of individuals means that there are no checks and balances on administration and spending. Also, since the mayoral office is ceremonial, there is no provision for strong leadership. Not surprisingly, only about one hundred cities today use the commission plan—Tulsa, Salt Lake City, Mobile, Topeka, and Atlantic City are a few of them.

Mayor of Carmel, California, Clint Eastwood.

▽
647

Did You Know?

▽

That, in 1979, a liberal group of Texas state senators called "the Killer Bees" hid from the leadership and the Texas Rangers for five days to thwart a quorum needed to pass a bill they opposed? (The bill died.)

The Council-Manager Plan

In this form of municipal government, a city council appoints a professional manager who acts as the chief executive. He or she is typically called the city manager. In principle, the manager is simply there to see that the general directions of the city council are carried out. The important features of the council-manager plan are as follows:

1. A professionally trained manager can hire and fire subordinates and is responsible to the council.
2. The council or commission consists of five to seven members, elected at large on a nonpartisan ballot.
3. The mayor may be chosen from within the council or from outside, but he or she has no executive function. As with the commission plan, the mayor's job is largely ceremonial. The city manager works for the council and not the mayor (unless, of course, the mayor is part of the council).

Today about two thousand cities use the council-manager plan. About one-third of the cities with populations above 5,000 and about one-half of the cities with populations above 25,000 operate with this type of plan. Only four large cities of more than 500,000 people—Cincinnati, Dallas, San Antonio, and San Diego—have adopted the plan.

The major defect of the council-manager scheme, as with the commission plan, is that there is no single, strong political executive leader. It is therefore not surprising that large cities rarely use such a plan.

The Mayor-Administrator Plan

In this municipal government plan, the mayor is an elected chief executive. He or she has an appointed administrative officer whose function is to free the mayor from routine administrative tasks, such as personnel direction and budget supervision. In some cities, the mayor may appoint the chief administrative officer without city council approval.

The mayor-administrator plan is often used in large cities where there is a strong mayor. It has some features of the council-manager plan but vests political leadership in the mayor.

Mayor-Council Plan

This plan completely separates executive and legislative functions. The mayor is elected as chief executive officer; the council is elected as the legislative body. This traditional separation of powers allows for checks and balances on spending and administration.

About 50 percent of American cities use some form of the mayor-council plan. There are strong-mayor plans and weak-mayor plans, depending on the charters or laws and the tradition in a particular city. Most recently, the mayor-council plan has lost ground to the council-manager plan in small and middle-sized cities.

Machine Versus Reform in City Politics

For much of the later nineteenth and early twentieth centuries, many major cities were run by "the machine." The machine was an integrated political organization

Highlight

▽

Three Tables and Some Chairs—$180,000

In the latter part of the nineteenth century, a powerful urban political machine emerged in New York City under the leadership of William Marcy ("Boss") Tweed. The Tweed Ring, as it was called, worked through Tammany Hall, the Democratic party headquarters in New York, and extended its influence like an octopus into city government, the state legislature, the governor's office, the courts, the police, and even the crime underworld. The greatest resource of this formidable political machine was patronage—the granting of jobs and contracts. Drawing on a vast pool of the poor and recent immigrants, buying votes and controlling the ballot boxes, Tammany Hall continued to flourish until the press and its political opponents began to expose its abuse of power and a reform movement (relying in part on the passage of civil service reform laws that undermined its patronage base) eroded its power base at the turn of the century.

Today's news stories about unwarranted costs for military hardware and overpriced toilet seats, coffee makers, hammers, and so forth have their parallel in the Tweed Ring's procurement practices more than a century ago, as the following passage relates:

One of the Ring's greatest "accomplishments" was the "construction" of the County Courthouse in downtown Manhattan. (You will understand shortly why accomplishments and construction are in quotation marks.) The small 3-story building cost more than four times as much as the British Houses of Parliament and nearly twice as much as the whole of Alaska. In the 13 years between 1858 and 1871 more than $13 million was spent on the (then still unfinished) building. The contracts let on the building were padded beyond belief. For example, the city paid $179,729.60 for only 3 tables and 40 chairs. The James Ingersoll Company, a favorite of the Ring, was paid $5,691,144.26 for furniture, carpets, and shades for the building. John Keyser, the

plumber, received nearly $1.5 million for plumbing and gaslight fixtures. "Lucky" George Miller, Tweed's carpenter, received $460,000 for lumber worth only $48,000. J. McBride Davidson charged over $500,000 for safes (door locks cost $2,676.75). One Republican reformer complained that more money was spent on these furnishings than it cost to run the entire U.S. mail service and almost three times as much as the expenses necessary to maintain the entire diplomatic corps for two years.

In spite of a cost of over $13 million and 13 years of construction, by 1871 . . . the building was still unfinished. The office of the Bureau of Arrears of Taxes, one of the largest rooms, had no roof. Other offices were uncarpeted. The walls were filthy and the plaster peeling. The whole atmosphere of the building was one of corruption.*

*Source: Richard D. Bingham, *State and Local Government in an Urban Society* (New York: Random House, 1986), p. 323.

---

in which each city block within the municipality had an organizer, each neighborhood had a political club, each district had a leader, and all of these parts of the machine had a boss—such as Richard Daley in Chicago, Edward Crump in Memphis, or Tom Pendergast in Kansas City. The machine became a popular form of city political organization in the 1840s, when the first waves of European immigrants came to the United States to work in urban factories. Those individuals, often lacking the ability to communicate in English, needed help; and the machine was created to help them.[11] The urban machine drew on the support of the dominant ethnic groups to forge a strong political institution that was able to keep the boss (the mayor) in office year after year.

The machine was oiled by **patronage**—rewarding faithful party workers and followers with government employment and contracts. The party in power was often referred to as the patronage party.[12] Loyal voters were rewarded with deliveries

Patronage

Rewarding faithful party workers and followers with government employment and contracts.

[11]See Harvey W. Zorbaugh, *The Gold Coast and the Slum: A Sociological Study of Chicago's Near North Side* (Chicago: University of Chicago Press, 1929).

[12]See, for example, Harold F. Gosnell, *Machine Politics: Chicago Model* (Chicago: University of Chicago Press, 1937).

Harold Washington, a "reform" mayor.

of Thanksgiving turkeys or coal at Christmas in return for their continued support for machine candidates. The power of the machine lay in its ability to control votes, and the votes of new immigrants from Europe or from rural America were especially crucial.

According to sociologist Robert Merton,[13] the machine offered personalized assistance to the needy, helped to establish local businesses, opened avenues of upward social mobility for the underprivileged, and afforded a locus of strong political authority and responsibility. More critical of the political machine are Edward Banfield and James Wilson, who argue that

> machine government is, essentially, a system of organized bribery. The destruction of machines . . . permit[s] government on the basis of appropriate motives, that is, public-regarding ones. In fact it has other highly desirable consequences—especially greater honesty, impartiality, and (in routine matters) efficiency.[14]

When the last of the big city bosses, Mayor Richard Daley of Chicago, died in December 1976, with him died an era that had lasted well over one hundred years. The big city machine began to be in serious trouble in the 1960s, when community activists organized to work for municipal government. Soon a government of administrators rather than politicians began to appear. Fewer offices were elective; more were appointive—presumably filled by technicians who had no political axes to grind, payoffs to make, or patrons to please.

Switching from a political to an administrative form of urban government was a way to break up the centralized urban political machine. In some cities, the results have been beneficial to most citizens. In others, decentralization has gone so far that there is no strong leader who can pull together discordant factions to create and follow a coherent policy. Consequently, in cities with a greatly decentralized government typified by numerous independent commissions and boards, a lot that should be done doesn't get done, particularly when an areawide problem is involved. This is an especially severe problem for less economically privileged people, who used to be able to rely on machine-sponsored activities and on the machine's political clout to help them compete against more well-to-do citizens for a share of the city's services. Reform is in some ways a middle-class preoccupation, whereas the less advantaged may find themselves better served by machine politics.

[13]*Social Theory and Social Structure* (Glencoe, Ill.: Free Press, 1957), pp. 71–81.
[14]Edward C. Banfield and James Q. Wilson, *City Politics* (New York: Vintage Books, 1963), p. 125.

Organizing in Your Community

The political arena is filled with issues that concern you. What government does or fails to do in the areas of education, health, employment, crime, and inflation all affect you, your family, and your friends. Your sense of adventure, concern, curiosity, or injustice may urge you to take an active part in the government of a society with which you might not be particularly content. Yet getting involved on the national level may seem complicated, and national issues may not be of immediate concern. You may not even know exactly where you stand on many of those issues.

However, every week decisions are being made in your community that directly affect your local environment, transportation, education, health, employment, rents, schools, utility rates, freedom from crime, and quality of life. The local level is a good place to begin discovering who you are politically.

Many possibilities are open to creative and concerned citizen activists on the local level. Citizen groups are burgeoning throughout the country. Groups of neighbors have demonstrated repeatedly how much they can accomplish, whether it is restoring a rundown neighborhood, protecting their homes, or fighting crime. These citizens may at first feel helpless or unqualified, but as they accomplish their aims, they begin to know the exhilaration that comes from gaining more control over the conditions that affect their lives rather than feeling helpless under the pressure of inexorable forces.

One way of organizing on the local level has been through "self-help" efforts like neighborhood crime watches. Alarmed and frightened by surges in lawlessness and shrinking police budgets, citizens have begun joining forces to rid their communities of crime. In cooperation with local law enforcement officials, they encourage participation in community crime prevention, which may involve a few people observing street activities or may feature highly organized citizen patrols. If you want information on crime-watch programs in your area, contact:

National Association of Town Watch
P.O. Box 769
Havertown, PA 19083
215-649-6662

Another example is the vocal neighborhood organization known as ACORN, the Association of Community Organizations for Reform Now. With chapters in twenty-six states, ACORN has built a broad constituency around issues common to many neighborhoods—housing shortages, high utility rates, hazardous, abandoned buildings, crime, and job opportunities. They advocate a stronger local neighborhood voice for low- and moderate-income families and more power over economic, political, and social institutions in their communities. They have proved to be a thorn in the side of several state and local legislatures. If you are concerned with such issues and want to find out more about this type of community involvement, contact:

ACORN
628 Baronne Street
New Orleans, LA 70113
504-523-1691

Finally, check in your own community for citizen action groups.

Chapter Summary

1. The United States has more separate governmental units than most other countries in the world.

2. State and local expenditures are concentrated in the areas of education, public welfare, highways, health, and police matters.

3. Starting in the twentieth century, federal grants began to pay for part of the cost of state and local governmental units.

4. The most important tax at the state level is the general sales tax and at the local level the property tax. There is tremendous variation in the rate of state and local taxation.

5. The 1970s and 1980s saw numerous tax revolts, one of the most famous of which was California's Proposition 13. Critics of limiting state taxes point out that such restrictions may undermine essential programs, such as police protection and schools.

6. The Constitution does not explicitly indicate what the states may do, but does say that no state or local law can be in conflict with the Constitution or with national laws. The major reserved powers of the states are to tax, spend, regulate interstate commerce, and exercise police power.

7. State constitutions are generally lengthy and frequently amended. Seventeen states permit constitutional initiatives allowing citizens to place a proposed amendment on the ballot.

8. All state governments have executive, legislative, and judicial branches, but differ from national government in many important ways.

9. Most states follow the practice of electing numerous executive officials, but governors have become a significant force in legislative policy making in recent years. Reorganization of the executive branch for greater efficiency has been attempted in numerous states.

10. Because most states elect governors in off-presidential election years, state officials are more able to isolate themselves from national politics. This practice has also meant less voter participation in these years.

11. Most state governors have some form of veto power, especially of specific items in an appropriations bill.

12. Legislatures usually hold the bulk of state governmental power. Their main task is to legislate on such matters as taxes, education, welfare, and regulation of business and commerce.

13. Malapportionment was the rule rather than the exception within the states until 1962, when the Supreme Court ruled that malapportioned state legislatures violated the equal protection clause of the Fourteenth Amendment. The Burger Court has allowed "benevolent, bipartisan gerrymandering" in certain states.

14. Many states exercise a type of direct democracy through the initiative, the referendum, and the recall.

15. Each state has a separate court system, which is similar to the model of the federal court system with its three levels of courts—trial courts, intermediate courts of appeal, and a supreme court.

16. There is no mention of local governments in the U.S. Constitution. Thus each local government is a creature of the state.

17. For many years, the legal status of local governments was based on Dillon's rule that municipal corporations may possess only powers expressly granted by state law.

18. The view that cities should be able to govern themselves was presented in an 1871 decision by Michigan Judge Thomas Cooley. Since 1900, about four-fifths of the states have allowed municipal home rule, but only with respect to local concerns.

19. The four major types of local governmental units are municipalities, counties, towns and townships, and special districts.

20. Recent years have seen a trend toward consolidation of governments—the union of two or more governmental units to form a single unit—to cope with metropolitan-area problems.

21. Municipal representative governments are of four types: the commission plan, the council-manager plan, the mayor-administrator plan, and the mayor-council plan. About 50 percent of American cities use some form of mayor-council plan. Most recently, the mayor-council plan has lost ground to the council-manager plan in small and middle-sized cities.

22. The urban machine derived its power from immigrant groups to whom it gave jobs and services. The machines began in the 1840s and endured until the 1970s. Cities then began switching from a political to an administrative form of government as a way to break up the centralized urban political machine.

Questions for Review and Discussion

1. One of the main thrusts of the Reagan administration has been to cut back federal spending on social programs. The philosophy underlying this effort is that the people and the states can decide for themselves whether they want these programs to continue. Which federal social programs do you think the states are most likely to fund at the old levels, and which might be cut?

2. What are some of the features of state governments that give greater control to the voters? To what extent do these features limit the flexibility and effectiveness of state government?

3. The structures and practices of state governments vary widely, revealing many adaptations of the national institutions. What reasons can you give for the unique features of state governments?

4. Some people suggest that the reason we have more than eighty thousand local governmental units is that Americans fear placing too much power in any centralized structure. What are some of the advantages and disadvantages of having multiple governments, particularly within one urban area? What functions of government would be easiest to consolidate? Which functions do you think the voters are least likely to grant to any form of metro government or centralized authority?

Selected References

Edward C. Banfield and James Q. Wilson, *City Politics* (New York: Vintage books, 1963). A classic on competing interests and ideas in city life.

Thad L. Beyle and Lynn Muchmore, eds., *Being Governor: The View from the Office* (Durham, N.C.: Duke University, 1983). Original insights into how governors perform their job.

Richard D. Bingham, *State and Local Government in an Urban Society* (New York: Random House, 1986). An excellent and detailed discussion of the institutions, processes, and policy issues of state and local government, including valuable and interesting short case studies.

Mike Royko, *Boss: Richard J. Daley of Chicago* (New York: Signet Books, 1971). The personal and social forces of the Chicago Democratic party machine and the leadership of its famous mayor.

Jack Treadway, *Public Policymaking in the American States* (New York: Praeger, 1985). This book is an extensive literature review of more than 120 studies and provides the reader with an excellent overview of the mix of government, politics, and the socioeconomic environment and its implications for state policy making.

Appendix A

▽

The Declaration of Independence

In Congress, July 4, 1776.

A Declaration by the Representatives of the United States of America, in General Congress assembled. When in the Course of human Events, it becomes necessary for one People to dissolve the Political Bands which have connected them with another, and to assume among the Powers of the Earth, the separate and equal Station to which the Laws of Nature and of Nature's God entitle them, a decent Respect to the Opinions of Mankind requires that they should declare the causes which impel them to the Separation.

We hold these Truths to be self-evident, that all Men are created equal, that they are endowed by their Creator with certain unalienable Rights, that among these are Life, Liberty, and the Pursuit of Happiness—That to secure these Rights, Governments are instituted among Men, deriving their just Powers from the Consent of the Governed, that whenever any Form of Government becomes destructive of these Ends, it is the Right of the People to alter or to abolish it, and to institute new Government, laying its Foundation on such Principles, and organizing its Powers in such Forms, as to them shall seem most likely to effect their Safety and Happiness. Prudence, indeed, will dictate that Governments long established should not be changed for light and transient Causes; and accordingly all Experience hath shewn, that Mankind are more disposed to suffer, while Evils are sufferable, than to right themselves by abolishing the Forms to which they are accustomed. But when a long Train of Abuses and Usurpations, pursuing invariably the same Object, evinces a Design to reduce them under absolute Despotism, it is their Right, it is their Duty, to throw off such Government, and to provide new Guards for their future Security. Such has been the patient Sufferance of these Colonies; and such is now the Necessity which constrains them to alter their former Systems of Government. The History of the present King of Great-Britain is a History of repeated Injuries and Usurpations, all having in direct Object the Establishment of an absolute Tyranny over these States. To prove this, let Facts be submitted to a candid World.

He has refused his Assent to Laws, the most wholesome and necessary for the public Good.

He has forbidden his Governors to pass Laws of immediate and pressing Importance, unless suspended in their Operation till his Assent should be obtained; and when so suspended, he has utterly neglected to attend to them.

He has refused to pass other Laws for the Accommodation of large Districts of People, unless those People would relinquish the Right of Representation in the Legislature, a Right inestimable to them, and formidable to Tyrants only.

He has called together Legislative Bodies at Places unusual, uncomfortable, and distant from the Depository of their Public Records, for the sole Purpose of fatiguing them into Compliance with his Measures.

He has dissolved Representative Houses repeatedly, for opposing with manly Firmness his Invasions on the Rights of the People.

He has refused for a long Time, after such Dissolutions, to cause others to be elected; whereby the Legislative Powers, incapable of Annihilation, have returned to the People at large for their exercise; the State remaining in the mean time exposed to all the Dangers of Invasion from without, and Convulsions within.

He has endeavoured to prevent the Population of these States; for that Purpose obstructing the Laws for Naturalization of Foreigners; refusing to pass others to encourage their Migrations hither, and raising the Conditions of new Appropriations of Lands.

He has obstructed the Administration of Justice, by refusing his Assent to Laws for establishing Judiciary Powers.

He has made Judges dependent on his Will alone, for the Tenure of their offices, and the Amount and payment of their Salaries.

He has erected a Multitude of new Offices, and sent hither Swarms of Officers to harrass our People, and eat out their Substance.

He has kept among us, in Times of Peace, Standing Armies, without the consent of our Legislatures.

He has affected to render the Military independent of, and superior to the Civil Power.

He has combined with others to subject us to a Jurisdiction foreign to our Constitution, and unacknowledged by our Laws; giving his Assent to their Acts of pretended Legislation:

For quartering large Bodies of Armed Troops among us:

For protecting them, by a mock Trial, from Punishment for any Murders which they should commit on the Inhabitants of these States:

For cutting off our Trade with all Parts of the World:

For imposing Taxes on us without our Consent:

For depriving us, in many cases, of the Benefits of Trial by Jury:

For transporting us beyond Seas to be tried for pretended Offences:

For abolishing the free System of English Laws in a neighbouring Province, establishing therein an arbitrary Government, and enlarging its Boundaries, so as to render it at once an Example and fit Instrument for introducing the same absolute Rule into these Colonies:

For taking away our Charters, abolishing our most valuable Laws, and altering fundamentally the Forms of our Governments:

For suspending our own Legislatures, and declaring themselves invested with Power to legislate for us in all Cases whatsoever.

He has abdicated Government here, by declaring us out of his Protection and waging War against us.

He has plundered our Seas, ravaged our Coasts, burnt our towns, and destroyed the Lives of our People.

He is, at this Time, transporting large Armies of foreign Mercenaries to compleat the works of Death, Desolation, and Tyranny, already begun with circumstances of Cruelty and Perfidy, scarcely paralleled in the most barbarous Ages, and totally unworthy the Head of a civilized Nation.

He has constrained our fellow Citizens taken Captive on the high Seas to bear Arms against their Country, to become the Executioners of their Friends and Brethren, or to fall themselves by their Hands.

He has excited domestic Insurrections amongst us, and has endeavoured to bring on the Inhabitants of our Frontiers, the merciless Indian Savages, whose known Rule of Warfare, is an undistinguished Destruction, of all Ages, Sexes and Conditions.

In every state of these Oppressions we have Petitioned for Redress in the most humble Terms: Our repeated Petitions have been answered only by repeated Injury. A Prince, whose Character is thus marked by every act which may define a Tyrant, is unfit to be the Ruler of a free People.

Nor have we been wanting in Attentions to our British Brethren. We have warned them from Time to Time of Attempts by their Legislature to extend an unwarrantable Jurisdiction over us. We have reminded them of the Circumstances of our Emigration and Settlement here. We have appealed to their native Justice and Magnanimity, and we have conjured them by the Ties of our common Kindred to disavow these Usurpations, which, would inevitably interrupt our Connections and Correspondence. They too have been deaf to the Voice of Justice and of Consanguinity. We must, therefore, acquiesce in the Necessity, which denounces our Separation, and hold them, as we hold the rest of Mankind, Enemies in War, in Peace, Friends.

We, therefore, the Representatives of the UNITED STATES OF AMERICA, in General Congress Assembled, appealing to the Supreme Judge of the World for the Rectitude of our Intentions, do, in the Name, and by the Authority of the good People of these Colonies, solemnly Publish and Declare, That these United Colonies are, and of Right ought to be, Free and Independent States; that they are absolved from all Allegiance to the British Crown, and that all political Connection between them and the State of Great-Britain, is and ought to be totally dissolved; and that as Free and Independent States, they have full Power to levy War, conclude Peace, contract Alliances, establish Commerce, and to do all other Acts and Things which Independent States may of right do. And for the support of this declaration, with a firm Reliance on the Protection of divine Providence, we mutually pledge to each other our lives, our Fortunes, and our sacred Honor.

Appendix B

▽

Constitution of the United States of America*

We the People of the United States, in Order to form a more perfect Union, establish Justice, insure domestic Tranquility, provide for the common defence, promote the general Welfare, and secure the Blessings of Liberty to ourselves and our Posterity, do ordain and establish this Constitution for the United States of America.

Article I.

SECTION 1.   All legislative Powers herein granted shall be vested in a Congress of the United States, which shall consist of a Senate and House of Representatives.

SECTION 2.   The House of Representatives shall be composed of Members chosen every second Year by the People of the several States, and the Electors in each State shall have the Qualifications requisite for Electors of the most numerous Branch of the State Legislature.

No Person shall be a Representative who shall not have attained to the Age of twenty five Years, and been seven Years a Citizen of the United States, and who shall not, when elected, be an Inhabitant of that State in which he shall be chosen.

Representatives and direct [Taxes][1] shall be apportioned among the several States which may be included within this Union, according to their respective Numbers [which shall be determined by adding to the whole Number of free Persons, including those bound to Service for a Term of Years, and excluding Indians not taxed, three fifths of all other Persons].[2] The actual Enumeration shall be made within three Years after the first Meeting of the Congress of the United States, and within every subsequent Term of ten Years, in such Manner as they shall by Law direct. The Number of Representatives shall not exceed one for every thirty Thousand, but each State shall have at Least one Representative; and until such enumeration shall be made, the State of New Hampshire shall be entitled to chuse three, Massachusetts eight, Rhode Island and Providence Plantations one, Connecticut five, New York six, New Jersey four, Pennsylvania eight, Delaware one,

---

*The spelling, capitalization, and punctuation of the original have been retained here. Brackets indicate passages that have been altered by amendments to the Constitution.

[1]Modified by the Sixteenth Amendment.

[2]Modified by the Fourteenth Amendment.

Maryland six, Virginia ten, North Carolina five, South Carolina five, and Georgia three.

When vacancies happen in the Representation from any State, the Executive Authority thereof shall issue Writs of Election to fill such Vacancies.

The House of Representatives shall chuse their Speaker and other Officers; and shall have the sole Power of Impeachment.

SECTION 3.   The Senate of the United States shall be composed of two Senators from each State [chosen by the Legislature thereof],[3] for six Years; and each Senator shall have one Vote.

Immediately after they shall be assembled in Consequence of the first Election, they shall be divided as equally as may be into three Classes. The Seats of the Senators of the first Class shall be vacated at the Expiration of the second Year, of the second Class at the Expiration of the fourth Year, and of the third Class at the Expiration of the sixth Year, so that one third may be chosen every second Year [and if Vacancies happen by Resignation, or otherwise, during the Recess of the Legislature of any State, the Executive thereof may make temporary Appointments until the next Meeting of the Legislature, which shall then fill such Vacancies].[4]

No Person shall be a Senator who shall not have attained to the Age of thirty Years, and been nine Years a Citizen of the United States, and who shall not, when elected, be an Inhabitant of that State for which he shall be chosen.

The Vice President of the United States shall be President of the Senate, but shall have no Vote, unless they be equally divided.

The Senate shall chuse their other Officers, and also a President pro tempore, in the Absence of the Vice President, or when he shall exercise the Office of President of the United States.

The Senate shall have the sole Power to try all Impeachments. When sitting for that Purpose, they shall be on Oath or Affirmation. When the President of the United States is tried, the Chief Justice shall preside: And no Person shall be convicted without the Concurrence of two thirds of the Members present.

Judgment in Cases of Impeachment shall not extend further than to removal from Office, and disqualification to hold and enjoy any Office of honor, Trust, or Profit under the United States: but the Party convicted shall nevertheless be liable and subject to Indictment, Trial, Judgment, and Punishment, according to Law.

SECTION 4.   The Times, Places and Manner of holding Elections for Senators and Representatives, shall be prescribed in each State by the Legislature thereof; but the Congress may at any time by Law make or alter such Regulations, except as to the Places of chusing Senators.

[The Congress shall assemble at least once in every Year, and such Meeting shall be on the first Monday in December, unless they shall by Law appoint a different Day.][5]

SECTION 5.   Each House shall be the Judge of the Elections, Returns, and Qualifications of its own Members, and a Majority of each shall constitute a Quorum to do Business; but a smaller Number may adjourn from day to day, and may be authorized to compel the Attendance of absent Members, in such Manner, and under such Penalties as each House may provide.

[3]Repealed by the Seventeenth Amendment.

[4]Modified by the Seventeenth Amendment.

[5]Changed by the Twentieth Amendment.

Each House may determine the Rules of its Proceedings, punish its Members for disorderly Behaviour, and, with the Concurrence of two thirds, expel a Member.

Each House shall keep a Journal of its Proceedings, and from time to time publish the same, excepting such Parts as may in their Judgment require Secrecy; and the Yeas and Nays of the Members of either House on any question shall, at the Desire of one fifth of those Present, be entered on the Journal.

Neither House, during the Session of Congress, shall, without the Consent of the other, adjourn for more than three days, nor to any other Place than that in which the two Houses shall be sitting.

SECTION 6.   The Senators and Representatives shall receive a Compensation for their Services, to be ascertained by Law, and paid out of the Treasury of the United States. They shall in all Cases, except Treason, Felony and Breach of the Peace, be privileged from Arrest during their Attendance at the Session of their respective Houses, and in going to and returning from the same; and for any Speech or Debate in either House, they shall not be questioned in any other Place.

No Senator or Representative shall, during the Time for which he was elected, be appointed to any civil Office under the Authority of the United States, which shall have been created, or the Emoluments whereof shall have been encreased during such time; and no Person holding any Office under the United States, shall be a Member of either House during his Continuance in Office.

SECTION 7.   All Bills for raising Revenue shall originate in the House of Representatives; but the Senate may propose or concur with Amendments as on other Bills.

Every Bill which shall have passed the House of Representatives and the Senate, shall, before it become a Law, be presented to the President of the United States; If he approve he shall sign it, but if not he shall return it, with his Objections to the House in which it shall have originated, who shall enter the Objections at large on their Journal, and proceed to reconsider it. If after such Reconsideration two thirds of that House shall agree to pass the Bill, it shall be sent together with the Objections, to the other House, by which it shall likewise be reconsidered, and if approved by two thirds of that House, it shall become a Law. But in all such Cases the Votes of both Houses shall be determined by Yeas and Nays, and the Names of the Persons voting for and against the Bill shall be entered on the Journal of each House respectively. If any Bill shall not be returned by the President within ten Days (Sundays excepted) after it shall have been presented to him, the Same shall be a Law, in like Manner as if he had signed it, unless the Congress by their Adjournment prevent its Return in which Case it shall not be a Law.

Every Order, Resolution, or Vote to which the Concurrence of the Senate and House of Representatives may be necessary (except on a question of Adjournment) shall be presented to the President of the United States; and before the Same shall take Effect, shall be approved by him, or being disapproved by him, shall be repassed by two thirds of the Senate and House of Representatives, according to the Rules and Limitations prescribed in the Case of a Bill.

SECTION 8.   The Congress shall have Power To lay and collect Taxes, Duties, Imposts and Excises, to pay the Debts and provide for the common Defence and general Welfare of the United States; but all Duties, Imposts and Excises shall be uniform throughout the United States;

To borrow Money on the credit of the United States;

To regulate Commerce with foreign Nations, and among the several States, and with the Indian Tribes;

To establish a uniform Rule of Naturalization, and uniform Laws on the subject of Bankruptcies throughout the United States;

To coin Money, regulate the Value thereof, and of foreign Coin, and fix the Standard of Weights and Measures;

To provide for the Punishment of counterfeiting the Securities and current Coin of the United States;

To establish Post Offices and post Roads;

To promote the Progress of Science and useful Arts, by securing for limited Times to Authors and Inventors the exclusive Right to their respective Writings and Discoveries;

To constitute Tribunals inferior to the supreme Court;

To define and punish Piracies and Felonies committed on the high Seas, and Offences against the Law of Nations;

To declare War, grant Letters of Marque and Reprisal, and make Rules concerning Captures on Land and Water;

To raise and support Armies, but no Appropriation of Money to that Use shall be for a longer Term than two Years;

To provide and maintain a Navy;

To make Rules for the Government and Regulation of the land and naval Forces;

To provide for calling forth the Militia to execute the Laws of the Union, suppress Insurrections and repel Invasions;

To provide for organizing, arming, and disciplining the Militia, and for governing such Part of them as may be employed in the Service of the United States, reserving to the States respectively, the Appointment of the Officers, and the Authority of training the Militia according to the discipline prescribed by Congress;

To exercise exclusive Legislation in all Cases whatsoever, over such District (not exceeding ten Miles square) as may, by Cession of particular States, and the Acceptance of Congress, become the Seat of the Government of the United States, and to exercise like Authority over all Places purchased by the Consent of the Legislature of the State in which the Same shall be, for the Erection of Forts, Magazines, Arsenals, dock-Yards, and other needful Buildings;—And

To make all Laws which shall be necessary and proper for carrying into Execution the foregoing Powers, and all other Powers vested by this Constitution in the Government of the United States, or in any Department or Officer thereof.

SECTION 9.   The Migration or Importation of such Persons as any of the States now existing shall think proper to admit, shall not be prohibited by the Congress prior to the Year one thousand eight hundred and eight, but a Tax or duty may be imposed on such Importation, not exceeding ten dollars for each Person.

The privilege of the Writ of Habeas Corpus shall not be suspended, unless when in Cases of Rebellion or Invasion the public Safety may require it.

No Bill of Attainder or ex post facto Law shall be passed.

[No Capitation, or other direct, Tax shall be laid, unless in Proportion to the Census or Enumeration herein before directed to be taken.][6]

No Tax or Duty shall be laid on Articles exported from any State.

No Preference shall be given by any Regulation of Commerce or Revenue to the Ports of one State over those of another: nor shall Vessels bound to, or from, one State, be obliged to enter, clear, or pay Duties in another.

[6]Modified by the Sixteenth Amendment.

No Money shall be drawn from the Treasury, but in Consequence of Appropriations made by Law; and a regular Statement and Account of the Receipts and Expenditures of all public Money shall be published from time to time.

No Title of Nobility shall be granted by the United States: And no Person holding any Office of Profit or Trust under them, shall, without the Consent of the Congress, accept of any present, Emolument, Office, or Title, of any kind whatever, from any King, Prince, or foreign State.

SECTION 10.   No State shall enter into any Treaty, Alliance, or Confederation; grant Letters of Marque and Reprisal; coin Money; emit Bills of Credit; make any Thing but gold and silver Coin a Tender in Payment of Debts; pass any Bill of Attainder, ex post facto Law, or Law impairing the Obligation of Contracts, or grant any Title of Nobility.

No State shall, without the Consent of the Congress, lay any Imposts or Duties on Imports or Exports, except what may be absolutely necessary for executing its inspection Laws; and the net Produce of all Duties and Imposts, laid by any State on Imports or Exports, shall be for the Use of the Treasury of the United States; and all such Laws shall be subject to the Revision and Controul of the Congress.

No State shall, without the Consent of Congress, lay any Duty of Tonnage, keep Troops, or Ships of War in time of Peace, enter into any Agreement or Compact with another State, or with a foreign Power or engage in War, unless actually invaded, or in such imminent Danger as will not admit of delay.

Article II.

SECTION 1.   The executive Power shall be vested in a President of the United States of America. He shall hold his Office during the Term of four Years, and, together with the Vice President, chosen for the same Term, be elected, as follows.

Each State shall appoint, in such Manner as the Legislature thereof may direct, a Number of Electors, equal to the whole Number of Senators and Representatives to which the State may be entitled in the Congress; but no Senator or Representative, or Person holding an Office of Trust or Profit under the United States, shall be appointed an Elector.

[The Electors shall meet in their respective States, and vote by Ballot for two Persons, of whom one at least shall not be an Inhabitant of the same State with themselves. And they shall make a List of all the Persons voted for, and of the Number of Votes for each; which List they shall sign and certify, and transmit sealed to the Seat of the Government of the United States, directed to the President of the Senate. The President of the Senate shall, in the Presence of the Senate and House of Representatives, open all the Certificates, and the Votes shall then be counted. The Person having the greatest Number of Votes shall be the President, if such Number be a Majority of the whole Number of Electors appointed; and if there be more than one who have such Majority, and have an equal Number of Votes, then the House of Representatives shall immediately chuse by Ballot one of them for President; and if no Person have a Majority, then from the five highest on the List the said House shall in like Manner chuse the President. But in chusing the President, the Votes shall be taken by States, the Representation from each State having one Vote; A quorum for this Purpose shall consist of a Member or Members from two thirds of the States, and a Majority of all the States shall be necessary to a Choice. In every Case, after the Choice of the President, the Person having the greater Number of Votes of the Electors shall be the Vice President.

But if there should remain two or more who have equal Votes, the Senate shall chuse from them by Ballot the Vice President.][7]

The Congress may determine the Time of chusing the Electors, and the Day on which they shall give their Votes; which Day shall be the same throughout the United States.

No person except a natural born Citizen, or a Citizen of the United States, at the time of the Adoption of this Constitution, shall be eligible to the Office of President; neither shall any Person be eligible to that Office who shall not have attained to the Age of thirty five Years, and been fourteen Years a Resident within the United States.

[In Case of the Removal of the President from Office, or of his Death, Resignation or Inability to discharge the Powers and Duties of the said Office, the same shall devolve on the Vice President, and the Congress may by Law provide for the Case of Removal, Death, Resignation or Inability, both of the President and Vice President, declaring what Officer shall then act as President, and such Officer shall act accordingly, until the Disability be removed, or a President shall be elected.][8]

The President shall, at stated Times, receive for his Services, a Compensation, which shall neither be encreased nor diminished during the Period for which he shall have been elected, and he shall not receive within that Period any other Emolument from the United States, or any of them.

Before he enter on the Execution of his Office, he shall take the following Oath or Affirmation: "I do solemnly swear (or affirm) that I will faithfully execute the Office of President of the United States, and will to the best of my Ability, preserve, protect and defend the Constitution of the United States."

SECTION 2.   The President shall be Commander in Chief of the Army and Navy of the United States, and of the Militia of the several States, when called into the actual Service of the United States; he may require the Opinion, in writing, of the principal Officer in each of the executive Departments, upon any Subject relating to the Duties of their respective Offices, and he shall have Power to grant Reprieves and Pardons for Offences against the United States, except in Cases of Impeachment.

He shall have Power, by and with the Advice and Consent of the Senate, to make Treaties, provided two thirds of the Senators present concur; and he shall nominate, and by and with the Advice and Consent of the Senate, shall appoint Ambassadors, other public Ministers and Consuls, Judges of the supreme Court, and all other Officers of the United States, whose Appointments are not herein otherwise provided for, and which shall be established by Law; but the Congress may by Law vest the Appointment of such inferior Officers, as they think proper, in the President alone, in the Courts of Law, or in the Heads of Departments.

The President shall have Power to fill up all Vacancies that may happen during the Recess of the Senate, by granting Commissions which shall expire at the end of their next Session.

SECTION 3.   He shall from time to time give to the Congress Information of the State of the Union, and recommend to their Consideration such Measures as he shall judge necessary and expedient; he may, on extraordinary Occasions, convene both Houses, or either of them, and in Case of Disagreement between them, with Respect to the Time of Adjournment, he may adjourn them to such Time as he shall think proper; he shall receive Ambassadors and other public Ministers; he

[7]Changed by the Twelfth Amendment.

[8]Modified by the Twenty-fifth Amendment.

shall take Care that the Laws be faithfully executed, and shall Commission all the Officers of the United States.

SECTION 4.   The President, Vice President and all civil Officers of the United States, shall be removed from Office on Impeachment for, and Conviction of, Treason, Bribery, or other high Crimes and Misdemeanors.

Article III.

SECTION 1.   The judicial Power of the United States, shall be vested in one supreme Court, and in such inferior Courts as the Congress may from time to time ordain and establish. The Judges, both of the supreme and inferior Courts, shall hold their Offices during good Behaviour, and shall, at stated Times, receive for their Services a Compensation, which shall not be diminished during their Continuance in Office.

SECTION 2.   The judicial Power shall extend to all Cases, in Law and Equity, arising under this Constitution, the Laws of the United States, and Treaties made, or which shall be made, under their Authority;—to all Cases affecting Ambassadors, other public Ministers and Consuls;—to all Cases of admiralty and maritime Jurisdiction;—to Controversies to which the United States shall be a Party;—to Controversies between two or more States;[—between a State and Citizens of another State;—][9] between Citizens of different States;—between Citizens of the same State claiming Lands under Grants of different States, [and between a State, or the Citizens thereof, and foreign States, Citizens or Subjects.][10]

In all Cases affecting Ambassadors, other public Ministers and Consuls, and those in which a State shall be a Party, the supreme Court shall have original Jurisdiction. In all the other Cases before mentioned, the supreme Court shall have appellate Jurisdiction, both as to Law and Fact, with such Exceptions, and under such Regulations as the Congress shall make.

The Trial of all Crimes, except in Cases of Impeachment, shall be by Jury; and such Trial shall be held in the State where the said Crimes shall have been committed; but when not committed within any State, the Trial shall be at such Place or Places as the Congress may by Law have directed.

SECTION 3.   Treason against the United States, shall consist only in levying War against them, or, in adhering to their Enemies, giving them Aid and Comfort. No Person shall be convicted of Treason unless on the Testimony of two Witnesses to the same overt Act, or on Confession in open Court.

The Congress shall have Power to declare the Punishment of Treason, but no Attainder of Treason shall work Corruption of Blood, or Forfeiture except during the Life of the Person attainted.

Article IV.

SECTION 1.   Full Faith and Credit shall be given in each State to the public Acts, Records, and judicial Proceedings of every other State. And the Congress may by general Laws prescribe the Manner in which such Acts, Records and Proceedings shall be proved, and the Effect thereof.

[9]Modified by the Eleventh Amendment.
[10]Modified by the Eleventh Amendment.

SECTION 2. The Citizens of each State shall be entitled to all Privileges and Immunities of Citizens in the several States.

A Person charged in any State with Treason, Felony, or other Crime, who shall flee from Justice, and be found in another State, shall on Demand of the executive Authority of the State from which he fled, be delivered up, to be removed to the State having Jurisdiction of the Crime.

[No Person held to Service or Labour in one State, under the Laws thereof, escaping into another, shall, in Consequence of any Law or Regulation therein, be discharged from such Service or Labour, but shall be delivered up on Claim of the Party to whom such Service or Labour may be due.][11]

SECTION 3. New States may be admitted by the Congress into this Union; but no new State shall be formed or erected within the Jurisdiction of any other State; nor any State be formed by the Junction of two or more States, or Parts of States, without the Consent of the Legislatures of the States concerned as well as of the Congress.

The Congress shall have Power to dispose of and make all needful Rules and Regulations respecting the Territory or other Property belonging to the United States; and nothing in this Constitution shall be so construed as to Prejudice any Claims of the United States, or of any particular State.

SECTION 4. The United States shall guarantee to every State in this Union a Republican Form of Government, and shall protect each of them against Invasion; and on Application of the Legislature, or of the Executive (when the Legislature cannot be convened) against domestic Violence.

Article V.

The Congress, whenever two thirds of both Houses shall deem it necessary, shall propose Amendments to this Constitution, or on the Application of the Legislatures of two thirds of the several States, shall call a Convention for proposing Amendments, which, in either Case, shall be valid to all Intents and Purposes, as part of this Constitution, when ratified by the Legislatures of three fourths of the several States, or by Conventions in three fourths thereof, as the one or the other Mode of Ratification may be proposed by the Congress; Provided that no Amendment which may be made prior to the Year One thousand eight hundred and eight shall in any Manner affect the first and fourth Clauses in the Ninth Section of the first Article; and that no State, without its Consent, shall be deprived of its equal Suffrage in the Senate.

Article VI.

All Debts contracted and Engagements entered into, before the Adoption of this Constitution shall be as valid against the United States under this Constitution, as under the Confederation.

This Constitution, and the Laws of the United States which shall be made in Pursuance thereof; and all Treaties made, or which shall be made, under the

[11]Repealed by the Thirteenth Amendment.

Authority of the United States, shall be the supreme Law of the Land; and the Judges in every State shall be bound thereby, any Thing in the Constitution or Laws of any State to the Contrary notwithstanding.

The Senators and Representatives before mentioned, and the Members of the several State Legislatures, and all executive and judicial Officers, both of the United States and of the several States, shall be bound by Oath or Affirmation, to support this Constitution; but no religious Test shall ever be required as a Qualification to any Office or public Trust under the United States.

Article VII.

The Ratification of the Conventions of nine States shall, be sufficient for the Establishment of this Constitution between the States so ratifying the Same.

Done in Convention by the Unanimous Consent of the States present the Seventeenth Day of September in the Year of our Lord one thousand seven hundred and Eighty seven and of the Independence of the United States of America the Twelfth. IN WITNESS whereof we have hereunto subscribed our Names,

Go. WASHINGTON
Presid't. and deputy from Virginia

Attest
WILLIAM JACKSON
Secretary

DELAWARE
Geo. Read
Gunning Bedfordjun
John Dickinson
Richard Basset
Jaco. Broom

MASSACHUSETTS
Nathaniel Gorham
Rufus King

CONNECTICUT
Wm. Saml. Johnson
Roger Sherman

NEW YORK
Alexander Hamilton

NEW JERSEY
Wh. Livingston
David Brearley.
Wm. Paterson.
Jona. Dayton

PENNSYLVANIA
B. Franklin
Thomas Mifflin
Robt. Morris
Geo. Clymer
Thos. FitzSimons
Jared Ingersoll
James Wilson.
Gouv. Morris

NEW HAMPSHIRE
John Langdon
Nicholas Gilman

MARYLAND
James McHenry
Dan of St. Thos. Jenifer
Danl. Carroll.

VIRGINIA
John Blair
James Madison Jr.

NORTH CAROLINA
Wm. Blount
Richd. Dobbs Spaight.
Hu. Williamson

SOUTH CAROLINA
J. Rutledge
Charles Cotesworth
  Pinckney
Charles Pinckney
Pierce Butler.

GEORGIA
William Few
Abr. Baldwin

Articles in addition to, and amendment of the Constitution of the United States of America, proposed by Congress and ratified by the Legislatures of the several states, pursuant to the Fifth Article of the original Constitution.

Amendment I [12]

Congress shall make no law respecting an establishment of religion, or prohibiting the free exercise thereof; or abridging the freedom of speech, or of the press; or the right of the people peaceably to assembly, and to petition the Government for a redress of grievances.

Amendment II

A well regulated militia, being necessary to the security of a free State, the right of the people to keep and bear arms, shall not be infringed.

Amendment III

No Soldier shall, in time of peace be quartered in any house, without the consent of the owner, nor in time of war, but in a manner to be prescribed by law.

Amendment IV

The right of the people to be secure in their persons, houses, papers, and effects, against unreasonable searches and seizures, shall not be violated, and no warrants shall issue, but upon probable cause, supported by oath or affirmation, and particularly describing the place to be searched, and the persons or things to be seized.

Amendment V

No person shall be held to answer for a capital, or otherwise infamous crime, unless on a presentment or indictment of a Grand Jury, except in cases arising in the land or naval forces, or in the militia, when in actual service in time of war or public danger; nor shall any person be subject for the same offence to be twice put in jeopardy of life or limb; nor shall be compelled in any criminal case to be a witness against himself, nor be deprived of life, liberty, or property, without due process of law; nor shall private property be taken for public use, without just compensation.

Amendment VI

In all criminal prosecutions, the accused shall enjoy the right to a speedy and public trial, by an impartial jury of the State and district wherein the crime shall have been committed, which district shall have been previously ascertained by law, and to be informed of the nature and cause of the accusation; to be confronted with the witnesses against him; to have compulsory process for obtaining witnesses in his favor, and to have the assistance of counsel for his defence.

Amendment VII

In Suits at common law, where the value in controversy shall exceed twenty dollars, the right of trial by jury shall be preserved, and no fact tried by jury, shall be otherwise re-examined in any Court of the United States, than according to the rules of the common law.

[12]The first ten amendments were passed by Congress on September 25, 1789, and were ratified on December 15, 1791.

Amendment VIII

Excessive bail shall not be required, nor excessive fines imposed, nor cruel and unusual punishments inflicted.

Amendment IX

The enumeration in the Constitution, of certain rights, shall not be construed to deny or disparage others retained by the people.

Amendment X

The powers not delegated to the United States by the Constitution, nor prohibited by it to the States, are reserved to the States respectively, or to the people.

Amendment XI—(Ratified February 7, 1795)

The Judicial power of the United States shall not be construed to extend to any suit in law or equity, commenced or prosecuted against one of the United States by Citizens of another State, or by Citizens or Subjects of any Foreign State.

Amendment XII—(Ratified June 15, 1804)

The Electors shall meet in their respective states, and vote by ballot for President and Vice-President, one of whom, at least, shall not be an inhabitant of the same state with themselves; they shall name in their ballots the person voted for as President, and in distinct ballots the person voted for as Vice-President, and they shall make distinct lists of all persons voted for as President, and of all persons voted for as Vice-President, and of the number of votes for each, which lists they shall sign and certify, and transmit sealed to the seat of the government of the United States, directed to the President of the Senate;—The President of the Senate shall, in the presence of the Senate and House of Representatives, open all the certificates and the votes shall then be counted;—The person having the greatest number of votes for President, shall be the President, if such number be a majority of the whole number of Electors appointed; and if no person have such majority, then from the persons having the highest numbers not exceeding three on the list of those voted for as President, the House of Representatives shall choose immediately, by ballot, the President. But in choosing the President, the votes shall be taken by states, the representation from each state having one vote; a quorum for this purpose shall consist of a member or members from two-thirds of the states, and a majority of all states shall be necessary to a choice. [And if the House of Representatives shall not choose a President whenever the right of choice shall devolve upon them, before the fourth day of March next following, then the Vice-President shall act as President, as in the case of the death or other constitutional disability of the President.][13]—The person having the greatest number of votes as Vice-President, shall be the Vice-President, if such number be a majority of the whole number of Electors appointed, and if no person have a majority, then from the two highest numbers on the list, the Senate shall choose the Vice-President; a quorum for the purpose shall consist of two-thirds of the whole number of Senators, and a majority of the whole number shall be necessary to a choice. But no person

[13]Changed by the Twentieth Amendment.

constitutionally ineligible to the office of President shall be eligible to that of Vice-President of the United States.

Amendment XIII—(Ratified on December 6, 1865)

SECTION 1.   Neither slavery nor involuntary servitude, except as a punishment for crime whereof the party shall have been duly convicted, shall exist within the United States, or any place subject to their jurisdiction.

SECTION 2.   Congress shall have power to enforce this article by appropriate legislation.

Amendment XIV—(Ratified on July 9, 1868)

SECTION 1.   All persons born or naturalized in the United States, and subject to the jurisdiction thereof, are citizens of the United States and of the State wherein they reside. No State shall make or enforce any law which shall abridge the privileges or immunities of citizens of the United States; nor shall any State deprive any person of life, liberty, or property, without due process of law; nor deny to any person within its jurisdiction the equal protection of the laws.

SECTION 2.   Representatives shall be apportioned among the several States according to their respective numbers, counting the whole number of persons in each State, excluding Indians not taxed. But when the right to vote at any election for the choice of electors for President and Vice President of the United States, Representatives in Congress, the Executive and Judicial officers of a State, or the members of the Legislature thereof, is denied to any of the male inhabitants of such State, being [twenty-one][14] years of age, and citizens of the United States, or in any way abridged, except for participation in rebellion, or other crime, the basis of representation therein shall be reduced in the proportion which the number of such male citizens shall bear to the whole number of male citizens twenty-one years of age in such State.

SECTION 3.   No person shall be a Senator or Representative in Congress, or elector of President and Vice President, or hold any office, civil or military, under the United States, or under any State, who having previously taken an oath, as a member of Congress, or as an officer of the United States, or as a member of any State legislature, or as an executive or judicial officer of any State, to support the Constitution of the United States, shall have engaged in insurrection or rebellion against the same, or given aid or comfort to the enemies thereof. But Congress may by a vote of two-thirds of each House, remove such disability.

SECTION 4.   The validity of the public debt of the United States, authorized by law, including debts incurred for payment of pensions and bounties for services in suppressing insurrection or rebellion, shall not be questioned. But neither the United States nor any State shall assume or pay any debt or obligation incurred in aid of insurrection or rebellion against the United States, or any claim for the loss or emancipation of any slave, but all such debts, obligations and claims shall be held illegal and void.

[14]Changed by the Twenty-sixth Amendment.

SECTION 5. The Congress shall have power to enforce, by appropriate legislation, the provisions of this article.

Amendment XV—(Ratified on February 3, 1870)

SECTION 1. The right of citizens of the United States to vote shall not be denied or abridged by the United States or by any State on account of race, color, or previous condition of servitude.

SECTION 2. The Congress shall have power to enforce this article by appropriate legislation.

Amendment XVI—(Ratified on February 3, 1913)

The Congress shall have power to lay and collect taxes on incomes, from whatever source derived, without apportionment among the several States, and without regard to any census or enumeration.

Amendment XVII—(Ratified on April 8, 1913)

The Senate of the United States shall be composed of two Senators from each State, elected by the people thereof, for six years; and each Senator shall have one vote. The electors in each State shall have the qualifications requisite for electors of the most numerous branch of the State legislatures.

When vacancies happen in the representation of any State in the Senate, the executive authority of such State shall issue writs of election to fill such vacancies: *Provided*, That the legislature of any State may empower the executive thereof to make temporary appointments until the people fill the vacancies by election as the legislature may direct.

This amendment shall not be so construed as to affect the election or term of any Senator chosen before it becomes valid as part of the Constitution.

Amendment XVIII—(Ratified on January 16, 1919)

SECTION 1. After one year from the ratification of this article the manufacture, sale, or transportation of intoxicating liquors within, the importation thereof into, or the exportation thereof from the United States and all territory subject to the jurisdiction thereof for beverage purposes is hereby prohibited.

SECTION 2. The Congress and the several States shall have concurrent power to enforce this article by appropriate legislation.

SECTION 3. This article shall be inoperative unless it shall have been ratified as an amendment to the Constitution by the legislatures of the several States, as provided in the Constitution, within seven years from the date of the submission hereof to the States by the Congress.[15]

Amendment XIX—(Ratified on August 18, 1920)

The right of citizens of the United States to vote shall not be denied or abridged

---

[15]The Eighteenth Amendment was repealed by the Twenty-first Amendment.

by the United States or by any State on account of sex.

Congress shall have power to enforce this article by appropriate legislation.

Amendment XX—(Ratified on January 23, 1933)

SECTION 1.   The terms of the President and Vice President shall end at noon on the 20th day of January, and the terms of Senators and Representatives at noon on the 3d day of January, of the years in which such terms would have ended if this article had not been ratified; and the terms of their successors shall then begin.

SECTION 2.   The Congress shall assemble at least once in every year, and such meeting shall begin at noon on the 3d day of January, unless they shall by law appoint a different day.

SECTION 3.   If, at the time fixed for the beginning of the term of the President, the President elect shall have died, the Vice President elect shall become President. If a President shall not have been chosen before the time fixed for the beginning of his term, or if the President elect shall have failed to qualify, then the Vice President elect shall act as President until a President shall have qualified; and the Congress may by law provide for the case wherein neither a President elect nor a Vice President elect shall have qualified, declaring who shall then act as President, or the manner in which one who is to act shall be selected, and such person shall act accordingly until a President or Vice President shall have qualified.

SECTION 4.   The Congress may by law provide for the case of the death of any of the persons from whom the House of Representatives may choose a President whenever the rights of choice shall have devolved upon them, and for the case of the death of any of the persons from whom the Senate may choose a Vice President whenever the right of choice shall have devolved upon them.

SECTION 5.   Sections 1 and 2 shall take effect on the 15th day of October following the ratification of this article.

SECTION 6.   This article shall be inoperative unless it shall have been ratified as an amendment to the Constitution by the legislatures of three-fourths of the several States within seven years from the date of its submission.

Amendment XXI—(Ratified on December 5, 1933)

SECTION 1.   The eighteenth article of amendment to the Constitution of the United States is hereby repealed.

SECTION 2.   The transportation or importation into any State, Territory, or possession of the United States for delivery or use therein of intoxicating liquors, in violation of the laws thereof, is hereby prohibited.

SECTION 3.   This article shall be inoperative unless it shall have been ratified as an amendment to the Constitution by conventions in the several States, as provided in the Constitution, within seven years from the date of the submission hereof to the States by the Congress.

Amendment XXII—(Ratified on February 27, 1951)

No person shall be elected to the office of the President more than twice, and no person who has held the office of President, or acted as President, for more than two years of a term to which some other person was elected President shall be elected to the office of President more than once. But this Article shall not apply to any person holding the office of President when this Article was proposed by the Congress, and shall not prevent any person who may be holding the office of President, or acting as President, during the term within which this Article becomes operative from holding the office of President or acting as President during the remainder of such term.

Amendment XXIII—(Ratified on March 29, 1961)

SECTION 1.   The District constituting the seat of Government of the United States shall appoint in such manner as the Congress may direct:

A number of electors of President and Vice President equal to the whole number of Senators and Representatives in Congress to which the District would be entitled if it were a State, but in no event more than the least populous State; they shall be in addition to those appointed by the States, but they shall be considered, for the purposes of the election of President and Vice President, to be electors appointed by a State; and they shall meet in the District and perform such duties as provided by the twelfth article of amendment.

SECTION 2.   The Congress shall have power to enforce this article by appropriate legislation.

Amendment XXIV—(Ratified on January 23, 1964)

SECTION 1.   The right of citizens of the United States to vote in any primary or other election for President or Vice President, for electors for President or Vice President, or for Senator or Representative in Congress, shall not be denied or abridged by the United States, or any State by reason of failure to pay any poll tax or other tax.

SECTION 2.   The Congress shall have power to enforce this article by appropriate legislation.

Amendment XXV—(Ratified on February 10, 1967)

SECTION 1.   In case of the removal of the President from office or of his death or resignation, the Vice President shall become President.

SECTION 2.   Whenever there is a vacancy in the office of the Vice President, the President shall nominate a Vice President who shall take office upon confirmation by a majority vote of both Houses of Congress.

Section 3.

Whenever the President transmits to the President pro tempore of the Senate and the Speaker of the House of Representatives his written declaration that he is unable to discharge the powers and duties of his office, and until he transmits to them a written declaration to the contrary, such powers and duties shall be discharged by the Vice President as Acting President.

SECTION 4.   Whenever the Vice President and a majority of either the principal officers of the executive departments or of such other body as Congress may by law provide, transmit to the President pro tempore of the Senate and the Speaker of the House of Representatives their written declaration that the President is unable to discharge the powers and duties of his office, the Vice President shall immediately assume the powers and duties of the office as Acting President.

Thereafter, when the President transmits to the President pro tempore of the Senate and the Speaker of the House of Representatives his written declaration that no inability exists, he shall resume the powers and duties of his office unless the Vice President and a majority of either the principal officers of the executive department or of such other body as Congress may by law provide, transmit within four days to the President pro tempore of the Senate and the Speaker of the House of Representatives their written declaration and the President is unable to discharge the powers and duties of his office. Thereupon Congress shall decide the issue, assembling within forty-eight hours for that purpose if not in session. If the Congress, within twenty-one days after receipt of the latter written declaration, or, if Congress is not in session, within twenty-one days after Congress is required to assemble, determines by two-thirds vote of both Houses that the President is unable to discharge the powers and duties of his office, the Vice President shall continue to discharge the same as Acting President; otherwise, the President shall resume the powers and duties of his office.

Amendment XXVI [1971]

SECTION 1.   The right of citizens of the United States, who are eighteen years of age or older, to vote shall not be denied or abridged by the United States or by any State on account of age.

SECTION 2.   The Congress shall have power to enforce this article by appropriate legislation.

Appendix C

▽

The Presidents of the United States

	Term of Service	Age at Inauguration	Political Party	College or University	Occupation or Profession
1. George Washington	1789–1797	57	None		Planter
2. John Adams	1797–1801	61	Federalist	Harvard	Lawyer
3. Thomas Jefferson	1801–1809	57	Democratic-Republican	William and Mary	Planter, lawyer
4. James Madison	1809–1817	57	Democratic-Republican	Princeton	Lawyer
5. James Monroe	1817–1825	58	Democratic-Republican	William and Mary	Lawyer
6. John Quincy Adams	1825–1829	57	Democratic-Republican	Harvard	Lawyer
7. Andrew Jackson	1829–1837	61	Democrat		Lawyer
8. Martin Van Buren	1837–1841	54	Democrat		Lawyer
9. William H. Harrison	1841	68	Whig	Hampden-Sydney	Soldier
10. John Tyler	1841–1845	51	Whig	William and Mary	Lawyer
11. James K. Polk	1845–1849	49	Democrat	U. of N. Carolina	Lawyer
12. Zachary Taylor	1849–1850	64	Whig		Soldier
13. Millard Fillmore	1850–1853	50	Whig		Lawyer
14. Franklin Pierce	1853–1857	48	Democrat	Bowdoin	Lawyer
15. James Buchanan	1857–1861	65	Democrat	Dickinson	Lawyer
16. Abraham Lincoln	1861–1865	52	Republican		Lawyer
17. Andrew Johnson	1865–1869	56	Nat'l. Union†		Tailor
18. Ulysses S. Grant	1869–1877	46	Republican	U.S. Mil. Academy	Soldier
19. Rutherford B. Hayes	1877–1881	54	Republican	Kenyon	Lawyer
20. James A. Garfield	1881	49	Republican	Williams	Lawyer
21. Chester A. Arthur	1881–1885	51	Republican	Union	Lawyer
22. Grover Cleveland	1885–1889	47	Democrat		Lawyer
23. Benjamin Harrison	1889–1893	55	Republican	Miami	Lawyer
24. Grover Cleveland	1893–1897	55	Democrat		Lawyer
25. William McKinley	1897–1901	54	Republican	Allegheny College	Lawyer
26. Theodore Roosevelt	1901–1909	42	Republican	Harvard	Author
27. William H. Taft	1909–1913	51	Republican	Yale	Lawyer
28. Woodrow Wilson	1913–1921	56	Democrat	Princeton	Educator
29. Warren G. Harding	1921–1923	55	Republican		Editor
30. Calvin Coolidge	1923–1929	51	Republican	Amherst	Lawyer
31. Herbert C. Hoover	1929–1933	54	Republican	Stanford	Engineer
32. Franklin D. Roosevelt	1933–1945	51	Democrat	Harvard	Lawyer
33. Harry S. Truman	1945–1953	60	Democrat		Businessman
34. Dwight D. Eisenhower	1953–1961	62	Republican	U.S. Mil. Academy	Soldier
35. John F. Kennedy	1961–1963	43	Democrat	Harvard	Author
36. Lyndon B. Johnson	1963–1969	55	Democrat	Southwest Texas State	Teacher
37. Richard M. Nixon	1969–1974	56	Republican	Whittier	Lawyer
38. Gerald R. Ford‡	1974–1977	61	Republican	Michigan	Lawyer
39. James E. Carter, Jr.	1977–1981	52	Democrat	U.S. Naval Academy	Businessman
40. Ronald W. Reagan	1981–	69	Republican	Eureka College	Actor

*Church preference; never joined any church.

†The National Union Party consisted of Republicans and War Democrats. Johnson was a Democrat.

**Inaugurated Dec. 6, 1973, to replace Agnew, who resigned Oct. 10, 1973.

‡Inaugurated Aug. 9, 1974, to replace Nixon, who resigned that same day.

§Inaugurated Dec. 19, 1974, to replace Ford, who became President Aug. 9, 1974.

Religion	Born	Died	Age at Death	Vice-President	
1. Episcopalian	Feb. 22, 1732	Dec. 14, 1799	67	John Adams	(1789–1797)
2. Unitarian	Oct. 30, 1735	July 4, 1826	90	Thomas Jefferson	(1797–1801)
3. Unitarian*	Apr. 13, 1743	July 4, 1826	83	Aaron Burr	(1801–1805)
				George Clinton	(1805–1809)
4. Episcopalian	Mar. 16, 1751	June 28, 1836	85	George Clinton	(1809–1812)
				Elbridge Gerry	(1813–1814)
5. Episcopalian	Apr. 28, 1758	July 4, 1831	73	Daniel D. Tompkins	(1817–1825)
6. Unitarian	July 11, 1767	Feb. 23, 1848	80	John C. Calhoun	(1825–1829)
7. Presbyterian	Mar. 15, 1767	June 8, 1845	78	John C. Calhoun	(1829–1832)
				Martin Van Buren	(1833–1837)
8. Dutch Reformed	Dec. 5, 1782	July 24, 1862	79	Richard M. Johnson	(1837–1841)
9. Episcopalian	Feb. 9, 1773	Apr. 4, 1841	68	John Tyler	(1841)
10. Episcopalian	Mar. 29, 1790	Jan. 18, 1862	71		
11. Methodist	Nov. 2, 1795	June 15, 1849	53	George M. Dallas	(1845–1849)
12. Episcopalian	Nov. 24, 1784	July 9, 1850	65	Millard Fillmore	(1849–1850)
13. Unitarian	Jan. 7, 1800	Mar. 8, 1874	74		
14. Episcopalian	Nov. 23, 1804	Oct. 8, 1869	64	William R. King	(1853)
15. Presbyterian	Apr. 23, 1791	June 1, 1868	77	John C. Breckinridge	(1857–1861)
16. Presbyterian*	Feb. 12, 1809	Apr. 15, 1865	56	Hannibal Hamlin	(1861–1865)
				Andrew Johnson	(1865)
17. Methodist*	Dec. 29, 1808	July 31, 1875	66		
18. Methodist	Apr. 27, 1822	July 23, 1885	63	Schuyler Colfax	(1869–1873)
				Henry Wilson	(1873–1875)
19. Methodist*	Oct. 4, 1822	Jan. 17, 1893	70	William A. Wheeler	(1877–1881)
20. Disciples of Christ	Nov. 19, 1831	Sept. 19, 1881	49	Chester A. Arthur	(1881)
21. Episcopalian	Oct. 5, 1829	Nov. 18, 1886	57		
22. Presbyterian	Mar. 18, 1837	June 24, 1908	71	Thomas A. Hendricks	(1885)
23. Presbyterian	Aug. 20, 1833	Mar. 13, 1901	67	Levi P. Morton	(1889–1893)
24. Presbyterian	Mar. 18, 1837	June 24, 1908	71	Adlai E. Stevenson	(1893–1897)
25. Methodist	Jan. 29, 1843	Sept. 14, 1901	58	Garret A. Hobart	(1897–1899)
				Theodore Roosevelt	(1901)
26. Dutch Reformed	Oct. 27, 1858	Jan. 6, 1919	60	Charles W. Fairbanks	(1905–1909)
27. Unitarian	Sept. 15, 1857	Mar. 8, 1930	72	James S. Sherman	(1909–1912)
28. Presbyterian	Dec. 29, 1856	Feb. 3, 1924	67	Thomas R. Marshall	(1913–1921)
29. Baptist	Nov. 2, 1865	Aug. 2, 1923	57	Calvin Coolidge	(1921–1923)
30. Congregationalist	July 4, 1872	Jan. 5, 1933	60	Charles G. Dawes	(1925–1929)
31. Friend (Quaker)	Aug. 10, 1874	Oct. 20, 1964	90	Charles Curtis	(1929–1933)
32. Episcopalian	Jan. 30, 1882	Apr. 12, 1945	63	John N. Garner	(1933–1941)
				Henry A. Wallace	(1941–1945)
				Harry S. Truman	(1945)
33. Baptist	May 8, 1884	Dec. 26, 1972	88	Alben W. Barkley	(1949–1953)
34. Presbyterian	Oct. 14, 1890	Mar. 28, 1969	78	Richard M. Nixon	(1953–1961)
35. Roman Catholic	May 29, 1917	Nov. 22, 1963	46	Lyndon B. Johnson	(1961–1963)
36. Disciples of Christ	Aug. 27, 1908	Jan. 22, 1973	64	Hubert H. Humphrey	(1965–1969)
37. Friend (Quaker)	Jan. 9, 1913			Spiro T. Agnew	(1969–1973)
				Gerald R. Ford**	(1973–1974)
38. Episcopalian	July 14, 1913			Nelson A. Rockefeller§	(1974–1977)
39. Baptist	Oct. 1, 1924			Walter F. Mondale	(1977–1981)
40. Disciples of Christ	Feb. 6, 1911			George Bush	(1981–)

Appendix D

▽

Federalist Papers #10 and #51

#10

▽

Among the numerous advantages promised by a well-constructed Union, none deserves to be more accurately developed than its tendency to break and control the violence of faction. The friend of popular governments never finds himself so much alarmed for their character and fate as when he contemplates their propensity to this dangerous vice. He will not fail, therefore, to set a due value on any plan which, without violating the principles to which he is attached, provides a proper cure for it. The instability, injustice, and confusion introduced into the public councils have, in truth, been the mortal diseases under which popular governments have everywhere perished, as they continue to be the favorite and fruitful topics from which the adversaries to liberty derive their most specious declamations. The valuable improvements made by the American constitutions on the popular models, both ancient and modern, cannot certainly be too much admired; but it would be an unwarrantable partiality to contend that they have as effectually obviated the danger on this side, as was wished and expected. Complaints are everywhere heard from our most considerate and virtuous citizens, equally the friends of public and private faith and of public and personal liberty, that our governments are too unstable, that the public good is disregarded in the conflicts of rival parties, and that measures are too often decided, not according to the rules of justice and the rights of the minor party, but by the superior force of an interested and overbearing majority. However anxiously we may wish that these complaints had no foundation, the evidence of known facts will not permit us to deny that they are in some degree true. It will be found, indeed, on a candid review of our situation, that some of the distresses under which we labor have been erroneously charged on the operation of our governments; but it will be found, at the same time, that other causes will not alone account for many of our heaviest misfortunes; and, particularly, for that prevailing and increasing distrust of public engagements and alarm for private rights which are echoed from one end of the continent to the other. These must be chiefly, if not wholly, effects of the unsteadiness and injustice with which a factious spirit has tainted our public administration.

By a faction I understand a number of citizens, whether amounting to a majority or minority of the whole, who are united and actuated by some common impulse of passion, or of interest, adverse to the rights of other citizens, or the permanent and aggregate interests of the community.

There are two methods of curing the mischiefs of faction: the one, by removing its causes; the other, by controlling its effects.

There are again two methods of removing the causes of faction: the one, by destroying the liberty which is essential to its existence; the other, by giving to every citizen the same opinions, the same passions, and the same interests.

It could never be more truly said than of the first remedy that it was worse than the disease. Liberty is to faction what air is to fire, an aliment without which it instantly expires. But it could not be a less folly to abolish liberty, which is essential to political life, because it nourishes faction than it would be to wish the annihilation of air, which is essential to animal life, because it imparts to fire its destructive agency.

The second expedient is as impracticable as the first would be unwise. As long as the reason of man continues fallible, and his is at liberty to exercise it, different opinions will be formed. As long as the connection subsists between his reason and his self-love, his opinions and his passions will have a reciprocal influence on each other; and the former will be objects to which the latter will attach themselves. The diversity in the faculties of men, from which the rights of property originate, is not less an insuperable obstacle to a uniformity of interests. The protection of these faculties is the first object of government. From the protection of different and unequal faculties of acquiring property, the possession of different degrees and kinds of property immediately results; and from the influence of these on the sentiments and views of the respective proprietors ensues a division of the society into different interests and parties.

The latent causes of faction are thus sown in the nature of man; and we see them everywhere brought into different degrees of activity, according to the different circumstances of civil society. A zeal for different opinions concerning religion, concerning government, and many other points, as well of speculation as of practice; an attachment to different leaders ambitiously contending for preeminence and power; or to persons of other descriptions whose fortunes have been interesting to the human passions, have, in turn, divided mankind into parties, inflamed them with mutual animosity, and rendered them much more disposed to vex and oppress each other than to co-operate for their common good. So strong is this propensity of mankind to fall into mutual animosities that where no substantial occasion presents itself the most frivolous and fanciful distinctions have been sufficient to kindle their unfriendly passions and excite their most violent conflicts. But the most common and durable source of factions has been the various and unequal distribution of property. Those who hold and those who are without property have ever formed distinct interests in society. Those who are creditors, and those who are debtors, fall under a like discrimination. A landed interest, a manufacturing interest, a mercantile interest, a moneyed interest, with many lesser interests, grow up of necessity in civilized nations, and divide them into different classes, actuated by different sentiments and views. The regulation of these various and interfering interests forms the principal task of modern legislation and involves the spirit of party and faction in the necessary and ordinary operations of government.

No man is allowed to be a judge in his own cause, because his interest would certainly bias his judgment, and, not improbably, corrupt his integrity. With equal, nay with greater reason, a body of men are unfit to be both judges and parties at the same time; yet what are many of the most important acts of legislation but so many judicial determinations, not indeed concerning the rights of single persons, but concerning the rights of large bodies of citizens? And what are the different classes of legislators but advocates and parties to the causes which they determine? Is a law proposed concerning private debts? It is a question to which the creditors are parties on one side and the debtors on the other. Justice ought to hold the balance between them. Yet the parties are, and must be, themselves the judges; and the most numerous party, or in other words, the most powerful faction must be expected to prevail. Shall domestic manufacturers be encouraged, and in what degree, by restrictions on foreign manufacturers? are questions which would be differently decided by the landed and the manufacturing classes, and probably by neither with a sole regard to justice and the public good. The apportionment of taxes on the various descriptions of property is an act which seems to require the most exact impartiality; yet there is, perhaps, no legislative act in which greater opportunity and temptation are given to a predominant party to trample on the rules of justice. Every shilling with which they overburden the inferior number is a shilling saved to their own pockets.

It is in vain to say that enlightened statesmen will be able to adjust these clashing interests and render them all subservient to the public good. Enlightened statesmen will not always be at the helm. Nor, in many cases, can such an adjustment be made at all without taking into view indirect and remote considerations, which will rarely prevail over the immediate interest which one party may find in disregarding the rights of another or the good of the whole.

The inference to which we are brought is that the *causes* of faction cannot be removed and that relief is only to be sought in the means of controlling its *effects*.

If a faction consists of less than a majority, relief is supplied by the republican principle, which enables the majority to defeat its sinister views by regular vote. It may clog the administration, it may convulse the society; but it will be unable to execute and mask its violence under the forms of the Constitution. When a majority is included in a faction, the form of popular government, on the other hand, enables it to sacrifice to its ruling passion or interest both the public good and the rights of other citizens. To secure the public good and private rights against the danger of such a faction, and at the same time to preserve the spirit and the form of popular government, is then the great object to which our inquiries are directed. Let me add that it is the great desideratum by which alone this form of government can be rescued from the opprobrium under which it has so long labored and be recommended to the esteem and adoption of mankind.

By what means is this object attainable? Evidently by one of two only. Either the existence of the same passion or interest in a majority at the same time must be prevented, or the majority, having such coexistent passion or interest, must be rendered, by their number and local situation, unable to concert and carry into effect schemes of oppression. If the impulse and the opportunity be suffered to coincide, we well know that neither moral nor religious motives can be relied on as an adequate control. They are not found to be such on the injustice and violence of individuals, and lose their efficacy in proportion to the number combined together, that is, in proportion as their efficacy becomes needful.

From this view of the subject it may be concluded that a pure democracy, by which I mean a society consisting of a small number of citizens, who assemble and administer the government in person, can admit of no cure for the mischiefs of faction. A common passion or interest will, in almost every case, be felt by a majority of the whole; a communication and concert results from the form of government itself; and there is nothing to check the inducements to sacrifice the weaker party or an obnoxious individual. Hence it is that such democracies have ever been spectacles of turbulence and contention; have ever been found incompatible with personal security or the rights of property; and have in general been as short in their lives as they have been violent in their deaths. Theoretic politicians, who have patronized this species of government, have erroneously supposed that by reducing mankind to a perfect equality in their political rights, they would at the same time be perfectly equalized and assimilated in their possessions, their opinions, and their passions.

A republic, by which I mean a government in which the scheme of representation takes place, opens a different prospect and promises the cure for which we are seeking. Let us examine the points in which it varies from pure democracy, and we shall comprehend both the nature of the cure and the efficacy which it must derive from the Union.

The two great points of difference between a democracy and a republic are: first, the delegation of the government, in the latter, to a small number of citizens elected by the rest; secondly, the greater number of citizens and greater sphere of country over which the latter may be extended.

The effect of the first difference is, on the one hand, to refine and enlarge the public views by passing them through the medium of a chosen body of citizens, whose wisdom may best discern the true interest of their country and whose patriotism and love of justice will be least likely to sacrifice it to temporary or partial considerations. Under such a regulation it may well happen that the public voice, pronounced by the representatives of the people, will be more consonant to the public good than if pronounced by the people themselves, convened for the purpose. On the other hand, the effect may be inverted. Men of factious tempers, of local prejudices, or of sinister designs, may, by intrigue, by corruption, or by other means, first obtain the suffrages, and then betray the interests of the people. The question resulting is, whether small or extensive republics are most favorable to the election of proper guardians of the public weal; and it is clearly decided in favor of the latter by two obvious considerations.

In the first place it is to be remarked that however small the republic may be the representatives must be raised to a certain number in order to guard against the cabals of a few; and that however large it may be they must be limited to a certain number in order to guard against the confusion of a multitude. Hence, the number of representatives in the two cases not being in proportion to that of the constituents, and being proportionally greatest in the small republic, it follows that if the proportion of fit characters be not less in the large than in the small republic, the former will present a greater option, and consequently a greater probability of a fit choice.

In the next place, as each representative will be chosen by a greater number of citizens in the large than in the small republic, it will be more difficult for unworthy candidates to practise with success the vicious arts by which elections are too often carried; and the suffrages of the people being more free, will be more likely to center on men who possess the most attractive merit and the most diffusive and established characters.

It must be confessed that in this, as in most other cases, there is a mean, on both sides of which inconveniencies will be found to lie. By enlarging too much the number of electors, you render the representative too little acquainted with all their local circumstances and lesser interests; as by reducing it too much, you render him unduly attached to these, and too little fit to comprehend and pursue great and national objects. The federal Constitution forms a happy combination in this respect; the great and aggregate interests being referred to the national, the local and particular to the State legislatures.

The other point of difference is the greater number of citizens and extent of territory which may be brought within the compass of republican than of democratic government; and it is this circumstance principally which renders factious combinations less to be dreaded in the former than in the latter. The smaller the society, the fewer probably will be the distinct parties and interests composing it; the fewer the distinct parties and interests, the more frequently will a majority be found of the same party; and the smaller the number of individuals composing a majority, and the smaller the compass within which they are placed, the more easily will they concert and execute their plans of oppression. Extend the sphere and you take in a greater variety of parties and interests; you make it less probable that a majority of the whole will have a common motive to invade the rights of other citizens; or if such a common motive exists, it will be more difficult for all who feel it to discover their own strength and to act in unison with each other. Besides other impediments, it may be remarked that, where there is a con-

sciousness of unjust or dishonorable purposes, communication is always checked by distrust in proportion to the number whose concurrence is necessary.

Hence, it clearly appears that the same advantage which a republic has over a democracy in controlling the effects of faction is enjoyed by a large over a small republic—is enjoyed by the Union over the States composing it. Does this advantage consist in the substitution of representatives whose enlightened views and virtuous sentiments render them superior to local prejudices and to schemes of injustice? It will not be denied that the representation of the Union will be most likely to possess these requisite endowments. Does it consist in the greater security afforded by a greater variety of parties, against the event of any one party being able to outnumber and oppress the rest? In an equal degree does the increased variety of parties comprised within the Union increase this security. Does it, in fine, consist in the greater obstacles opposed to the concert and accomplishment of the secret wishes of an unjust and interested majority? Here again the extent of the Union gives it the most palpable advantage.

The influence of factious leaders may kindle a flame within their particular States but will be unable to spread a general conflagration through the other States. A religious sect may degenerate into a political faction in a part of the Confederacy; but the variety of sects dispersed over the entire face of it must secure the national councils against any danger from that source. A rage for paper money, for an abolition of debts, for an equal division of property, or for any other improper or wicked project, will be less apt to pervade the whole body of the Union than a particular member of it, in the same proportion as such a malady is more likely to taint a particular county or district than an entire State.

In the extent and proper structure of the Union, therefore, we behold a republican remedy for the diseases most incident to republican government. And according to the degree of pleasure and pride we feel in being republicans ought to be our zeal in cherishing the spirit and supporting the character of federalists.

#51

▽

To what expedient, then, shall we finally resort, for maintaining in practice the necessary partition of power among the several departments as laid down in the Constitution? The only answer that can be given is that as all these exterior provisions are found to be inadequate the defect must be supplied, by so contriving the interior structure of the government as that its several constituent parts may, by their mutual relations, be the means of keeping each other in their proper places. Without presuming to undertake a full development of this important idea I will hazard a few general observations which may perhaps place it in a clearer light, and enable us to form a more correct judgment of the principles and structure of the government planned by the convention.

In order to lay a due foundation for that separate and distinct exercise of the different powers of government, which to a certain extent is admitted on all hands to be essential to the preservation of liberty, it is evident that each department should have a will of its own; and consequently should be so constituted that the members of each should have as little agency as possible in the appointment of the members of the others. Were this principle rigorously adhered to, it would require that all the appointments for the supreme executive, legislative, and judiciary magistracies should be drawn from the same fountain of authority, the people, through channels having no communication whatever with one another. Perhaps such a plan of constructing the several departments would be less difficult in practice than it may in contemplation appear. Some difficulties, however, and some additional expense would attend the execution of it. Some deviations, therefore, from the principle must be admitted. In the constitution of the judiciary department in particular, it might be inexpedient to insist rigorously on the principle: first, because peculiar qualifications being essential in the members, the primary consideration ought to be to select that mode of choice which best secures these qualifications; second, because the permanent tenure by which the appointments are held in that department must soon destroy all sense of dependence on the authority conferring them.

It is equally evident that the members of each department should be as little dependent as possible on those of the others for the emoluments annexed to their offices. Were the executive magistrate, or the judges, not independent of the legislature in this particular, their independence in every other would be merely nominal.

But the great security against a gradual concentration of the several powers in the same department consists in giving to those who administer each department the necessary constitutional means and personal motives to resist encroachments of the others. The provision for defense must in this, as in all other cases, be made commensurate to the danger of attack. Ambition must be made to counteract ambition. The interest of the man must be connected with the constitutional rights of the place. It may be a reflection on human nature that such devices should be necessary to control the abuses of government. But what is government itself but the greatest of all reflections on human nature? If men were angels, no government would be necessary. If angels were to govern men, neither external nor internal controls on government would be necessary. In framing a government which is to be administered by men over men, the great difficulty lies in this: you must first enable the government to control the governed; and in the next place oblige it to control itself. A dependence on the people is, no doubt, the primary control on the government; but experience has taught mankind the necessity of auxiliary precautions.

This policy of supplying, by opposite and rival interests, the defect of better motives, might be traced through the whole system of human affairs, private as well as public. We see it particularly displayed in all the subordinate distributions of power, where the constant aim is to divide and arrange the several offices in such a manner as that each may be a check on the other—that the private interest of every individual may be a sentinel over the public rights. These inventions of prudence cannot be less requisite in the distribution of the supreme powers of the State.

But it is not possible to give to each department an equal power of self-defense. In republican government, the legislative authority necessarily predominates. The remedy for this inconveniency is to divide the legislature into different branches; and to render them,

by different modes of election and different principles of action, as little connected with each other as the nature of their common functions and their common dependence on the society will admit. It may even be necessary to guard against dangerous encroachments by still further precautions. As the weight of the legislative authority requires that it should be thus divided, the weakness of the executive may require, on the other hand, that it should be fortified. An absolute negative on the legislature appears, at first view, to be the natural defense with which the executive magistrate should be armed. But perhaps it would be neither altogether safe nor alone sufficient. On ordinary occasions it might not be exerted with the requisite firmness, and on extraordinary occasions it might be perfidiously abused. May not this defect of an absolute negative be supplied by some qualified connection between this weaker department and the weaker branch of the stronger department, by which the latter may be led to support the constitutional rights of the former, without being too much detached from the rights of its own department?

If the principles on which these observations are founded be just, as I persuade myself they are, and they be applied as a criterion to the several State constitutions, and to the federal Constitution, it will be found that if the latter does not perfectly correspond with them, the former are infinitely less able to bear such a test.

There are, moreover, two considerations particularly applicable to the federal system of America, which place that system in a very interesting point of view.

First. In a single republic, all the power surrendered by the people is submitted to the administration of a single government; and the usurpations are guarded against by a division of the government into distinct and separate departments. In the compound republic of America, the power surrendered by the people is first divided between two distinct governments, and then the portion allotted to each subdivided among distinct and separate departments. Hence a double security arises to the rights of the people. The different governments will control each other, at the same time that each will be controlled by itself.

Second. It is of great importance in a republic not only to guard the society against the oppression of its rulers, but to guard one part of the society against the injustice of the other part. Different interests necessarily exist in different classes of citizens. If a majority be united by a common interest, the rights of the minority will be insecure. There are but two methods of providing against this evil: the one by creating a will in the community independent of the majority—that is, of the society itself; the other, by comprehending in the society so many separate descriptions of citizens as will render an unjust combination of a majority of the whole very improbable, if not impracticable. The first method prevails in all governments possessing an hereditary or self-appointed authority. This, at best, is but a precarious security; because a power independent of the society may as well espouse the unjust views of the major as the rightful interests of the minor party, and may possibly be turned against both parties. The second method will be exemplified in the federal republic of the United States. Whilst all authority in it will be derived from and dependent on the society, the society itself will be broken into so many parts, interests and classes of citizens, that the rights of individuals, or of the minority, will be in little danger from interested combinations of the majority. In a free government the security for civil rights must be the same as that for religious ·rights. It consists in the one case in the multiplicity of interests, and in the other in the multiplicity of sects. The degree of security in both cases will depend on the number of interests and sects; and this may be presumed to depend on the extent of country and number of people comprehended under the same government. This view of the subject must particularly recommend a proper federal system to all the sincere and considerate friends of republican government, since it shows that in exact proportion as the territory of the Union may be formed into more circumscribed Confederacies, or States, oppressive combinations of a majority will be facilitated; the best security, under the republican forms, for the rights of every class of citizen, will be diminished; and consequently the stability and independence of some member of the government, the only other security, must be proportionally increased. Justice is the end of government. It is the end of civil society. It ever has been and ever will be pursued until it be obtained, or until liberty be lost in the pursuit. In a society under the forms of which the stronger faction can readily unite and oppress the weaker, anarchy may as truly be said to reign as in a state of nature, where the weaker individual is not secured against the violence of the stronger; and as, in the latter state, even the stronger individuals are prompted, by the uncertainty of their condition, to submit to a government which may protect the weak as well as themselves; so, in the former state, will the more powerful factions or parties be gradually in-duced, by a like motive, to wish for a government which will protect all parties, the weaker as well as the more powerful. It can be little doubted that if the State of Rhode Island was separated from the Confederacy and left to itself, the insecurity of rights under the popular form of government within such narrow limits would be displayed by such reiterated oppressions of factious majorities that some power altogether independent of the people would soon be called for by the voice of the very factions whose misrule had proved the necessity of it. In the extended republic of the United States, and among the great variety of interests, parties, and sects which it embraces, a coalition of a majority of the whole society could seldom take place on any other principles than those of justice and the general good; whilst there being thus less danger to a minor from the will of a major party, there must be less pretext, also, to provide for the security of the former, by introducing into the government a will not dependent on the latter, or, in other words, a will independent of the society itself. It is no less certain than it is important, notwithstanding the contrary opinions which have been entertained, that the larger the society, provided it lie within a practicable sphere, the more duly capable it will be of self-government. And happily for the *republican cause*, the practicable sphere may be carried to a very great extent by a judicious modification and mixture of the *federal principle*.

Publius
(James Madison)

Glossary

A

ABSCAM SCANDALS In 1979 the Federal Bureau of Investigation ran an operation called **ABSCAM** (an acronym for "Arab scam") in which agents videotaped members of Congress accepting bribes from a man posing as an Arab business executive. Seven members of the House of Representatives and one senator were indicted and convicted.

ABSOLUTISTS Those who interpret the First Amendment freedom of speech clause literally.

ACID RAIN Rain containing a high sulfur content.

ACTIONABLE Furnishing grounds for a lawsuit.

ACTUAL MALICE Knowing intent to commit harm to others.

ADMINISTRATIVE AGENCIES The primary interpreters and enforcers of many legislative statutes that focus on business regulation. These agencies may be a part of the traditional administrative branch of the government or established independently of the executive branch.

ADMINISTRATIVE LAW The branch of law that governs the activities of administrative agencies, establishes their methods of procedure, and determines the scope of judicial review of agency practices and actions.

ADVICE AND CONSENT The power vested in the U.S. Senate by the Constitution (Article II, Section 2) to give its advice and consent to the president concerning treaties and presidential appointments.

AFFIRM To declare that a judgment is valid and right and must stand.

AFFIRMATIVE ACTION Job hiring policies that give special consideration or compensatory treatment to traditionally disadvantaged groups in an effort to overcome present effects of past discrimination.

AGENDA SETTING The power to determine which public policy questions will be debated or considered by Congress.

AID TO FAMILIES WITH DEPENDENT CHILDREN (AFDC) Financial aid provided under the categorical assistance program of the Social Security Act of 1935 for children who lack adequate support but who are living with one parent or relative.

ALIEN AND SEDITION ACTS Four acts passed in 1798 by the Federalist Party designed to curb criticism of the government.

ANTI-FEDERALISTS The anti-Federalists opposed the adoption of the Constitution in 1787 because of its centralist tendencies and attacked the failure of the Constitution's framers to include a bill of rights.

ANTIBALLISTIC MISSILES (ABMs) A defense system designed to protect targets by destroying attacking airplanes or missiles before they reach their destination.

APPELLATE JURISDICTION The authority of a court to review decisions of an inferior court.

APPOINTMENT POWER The authority vested in the president to fill a governmental office or position. Positions filled by presidential appointment include those in the executive branch, the federal judiciary, commissioned officers in the armed forces, and members of the independent regulatory commissions.

APPROPRIATIONS BILLS Bills granting an ageancy the permission to spend funds that have already been authorized in specific amounts for specific purposes.

ARISTOCRATIC CLASS A small, privileged class of people who hold their position by virtue of their religious, political, or economic power.

AUSTRALIAN BALLOT A secret ballot prepared, distributed, and tabulated by government officials at public expense. Since 1888 all states have used the secret Australian ballot rather than an open, public ballot.

AUTHORITY An agency that is generally recognized and accepted as having the deciding voice. For most societies, government is the ultimate authority in the allocation of values.

B

BACKDOOR FUNDING The sum total of federal government expenditures undertaken by using contract, loan guarantee, and borrowing authority.

BAD-TENDENCY RULE Speech or other First Amendment freedoms may permissibly be curtailed if there is a possibility that such expression might lead to some "evil."

BEAUTY CONTEST A term used to describe a form of presidential primary where delegates are selected by the party organization and have to support the candidate who wins the most popular votes.

BICAMERAL LEGISLATURE A legislature made up of two chambers or parts. The United States Congress, composed of the House of Representatives and the Senate, is a bicameral legislature.

BICAMERALISM The division of a legislature into two separate assemblies.

BILL OF RIGHTS The first ten amendments to the United States Constitution. They contain a listing of the rights a person enjoys and which cannot be infringed upon by the government, such as the freedoms of speech, press, and religion.

BLANKET PRIMARY A primary in which all candidates' names are printed on the same ballot, regardless of party affiliation. The voter may vote for candidates of more than one party.

BLOCK GRANTS Federal programs which provide funding to the state and local governments for general functional areas such as criminal justice or mental health programs.

BOARD OF GOVERNORS The operating authority of the Federal Reserve System. Consists of seven members appointed by the president and confirmed by the Senate who determine general monetary and credit policies and oversee the operation of the twelve district Federal Reserve banks and member banks throughout the country.

BUDGET The translation of financial resources into human purposes or, otherwise stated, a policy document that allocates taxes and government expenditures.

BUDGET DEFICIT The difference between what the government collects from taxes and other sources and what the government spends.

BUREAUCRACY A large organization that is structured hierarchically to carry out specific functions.

BUSING The transportation of public school students from areas where they live to schools in other areas to eliminate school segregation based on residential patterns.

C

CABINET An advisory group selected by the president to aid him in making decisions. The cabinet presently numbers twelve department secretaries and the attorney general. Depending on the president, the Cabinet may be highly influential or relatively insignificant in its advisory role.

CABINET DEPARTMENTS The thirteen departments of the executive branch (State, Treasury, Defense, Justice, Interior, Agriculture, Commerce, Labor, Health and Human Services, Housing and Urban Development, Education, Energy, and Transportation).

CADRE The nucleus of political party activists that carries out the major functions of American political parties.

CANVASSING BOARD An official and normally bipartisan group on a county, city, or state level that receives vote counts from every precinct in the area. The state canvassing board obtains the voting results from all local boards, tabulates the figures, and certifies the winners.

CAPITALISM An economic and political system based on private ownership of the means of production and a supply-demand market economy.

CAPITALIST ECONOMICS An economic system in which individuals privately own productive resources.

CAPITALIST NATIONS Those nations whose political philosophies advocate an economic system based on private ownership of the means of production and on a supply-demand market economy. Based on the *laissez-faire* theory, this doctrine emphasizes the absence of government restraints on ownership, production, and trade.

CARTEL An alliance between states or businesses to maintain solidarity on trade or price issues. The bargaining power of the members of the cartel is thus enhanced beyond the sum of their individual strengths.

CASE LAW Comprises the rules of law announced in court decisions; the aggregate of reported cases that forms a body of jurisprudence.

CASEWORK Personal work for constituents by members of Congress.

CATEGORICAL GRANTS Federal grants-in-aid to states or local governments which are for very specific programs or projects.

CAUCUS A closed meeting of party leaders or members to select party candidates or to decide on policy.

CEASE-AND-DESIST ORDER An administrative or judicial order commanding a business firm to cease conducting the activities that the agency or court has deemed to be "unfair deceptive acts or practices."

CHALLENGE An allegation by a poll watcher that a potential voter is unqualified to vote or that a vote is invalid; designed to prevent fraud in elections.

CHECKS AND BALANCES A major principle of the American governmental system whereby each branch of the government exercises a check upon the actions of the others. Various safeguards and devices in the Constitution prevent too great a concentration of power in any one person or group of persons. The most important "check" is the fact that the national government is composed of three separate branches: the executive, the legislative, and the judicial.

CHIEF DIPLOMAT The role of the president in recognizing foreign governments, making treaties, and making executive agreements.

CHIEF EXECUTIVE The role of the president as head of the executive branch of the government.

CHIEF LEGISLATOR The role of the president in influencing the making of laws.

CHIEF OF STATE The role of the president as ceremonial head of the government.

CIVIL LAW The law regulating conduct between private persons over noncriminal matters. Under civil law the government provides the forum for the settlement of disputes between private parties in such matters as contracts, domestic relations, and business relations.

CIVIL SERVICE A collective term for the body of employees working for the government. Generally, civil service is understood to apply to all those who gain government employment through a merit system.

CIVIL SERVICE COMMISSION The central personnel agency of the national government created in 1883.

CLASS POLITICS Political preferences based on income level and/ or social status.

CLEAR AND PRESENT DANGER TEST The test proposed by Justice Holmes for determining when government may restrict free speech. Restrictions are permissible, he argued, only when speech provokes a "clear and present danger" to the public order.

CLIMATE CONTROL Techniques to create a favorable public opinion toward an interest group, industry, or corporation.

CLOSED PRIMARY The most widely used primary election, in which voters may participate only in the primary of the party with which they are registered.

CLOSED SHOP A business enterprise in which an employee must belong to the union before he or she can be employed and must remain in the union after employment.

CLOTURE A method invoked to close off the debate and to bring the matter under consideration to a vote in the Senate.

COATTAIL EFFECT The influence of a popular or unpopular candidate on the electoral success or failure of other candidates on the same party ticket. The effect is increased by the party-column ballot, which encourages straight-ticket voting.

COLD WAR The ideological, political, and economic impasse that existed between the United States and the Soviet Union following World War II.

COLLECTIVE BARGAINING Bargaining between management of a company or a group of companies and management of a union or a group of unions for the purpose of setting a mutually agreeable contract on wages, fringe benefits, and working conditions for *all* employees in the union(s). Different from individual bargaining, where each employee strikes a bargain with his or her employer individually.

COMMANDER IN CHIEF The role of the president as supreme commander of the military forces of the United States and of the state national guard units when they are called into federal service.

COMMERCE CLAUSE The section of the Constitution in which Congress is given the power to regulate trade among the states and with foreign countries.

COMMERCIAL SPEECH Advertising statements which have increasingly been given First Amendment protection.

COMMON LAW Judge-made law that originated in England from decisions shaped according to prevailing customs. Decisions were applied to similar situations and thus gradually became common to the nation. Common law forms the basis of legal procedures in the United States.

COMMON PROPERTY Property and resources that are not privately owned and are available for common use.

COMPARABLE WORTH The comparable worth idea is that compensation should be based on the worth of the job to an employer and that factors unrelated to the worth of a job, such as the sex of the employee, should not affect compensation; generally used in the argument that women are entitled to comparable wages for doing work that is different from, but of comparable worth and value to, work done by higher-paid men.

COMPLIANCE Accepting and carrying out authoritative decisions.

CONCURRENT MAJORITY A principle advanced by John C. Calhoun whereby democratic decisions could be made only with the concurrence of all major segments of society. Without that concurrence, a decision should not be binding on those whose interests it violates.

CONCURRING OPINION An opinion which supports the decision of the majority of the court, prepared by a judge who agrees in general but wants to make or clarify a particular point or to voice disapproval of the grounds on which the decision was made.

CONFEDERAL SYSTEM A league of independent states, each having essentially sovereign powers, wherein the central government created by such a league has only limited powers over the states.

CONFEDERATION A political system in which states or regional governments retain ultimate authority except for those powers they expressly delegate to a central government. A voluntary association of independent states, in which the member states agree to limited restraints on their freedom of action.

CONFERENCE COMMITTEES A special joint committee appointed to reconcile differences when a bill passes the two houses of Congress in different forms.

CONFLICT RESOLUTION Making determinations in cases where the public's attitudes are sharply divided.

CONSENSUS General agreement among the citizenry on an issue; public opinion shows that most people give the same response when there is a consensus.

CONSENT OF THE GOVERNED The government is based on the consent or will of the people and can be abolished by them.

CONSENT OF THE PEOPLE The idea that governments and laws derive their legitimacy from the consent of the people living under them.

CONSERVATIVE COALITION An alliance of Republicans and

southern Democrats that can form in the House or the Senate to oppose certain types of legislation.

CONSOLIDATION The union of two or more governmental units to form a single unit.

CONSTITUTIONAL INITIATIVE An electoral device whereby citizens can propose a constitutional amendment through initiatory petitions signed by the required number of registered voters.

CONSTITUTIONAL POWERS The powers vested in the president by Article II of the Constitution.

CONSUMER PRICE INDEX (CPI) An index showing changes in the average price of a "basket" of goods purchased by consumers. The CPI compares each year's price to a base year to determine the relative increase or decrease in the price level.

CONSUMERISM The consumer movement to assure the safety and reliability of products.

CONTAINMENT U.S. diplomatic policy adopted by the Truman administration to "build situations of strength" around the globe to contain communist power within its existing boundaries.

CONTINUING RESOLUTIONS Temporary laws that Congress passes when various appropriations bills have not been decided by the beginning of the new fiscal year on October 1st.

CONVENTION A national meeting of the political parties held to choose a presidential and vice presidential candidate.

COOLEY'S RULE The view that cities should be able to govern themselves, presented in an 1871 decision by Michigan Judge Thomas Cooley.

COOPERATIVE FEDERALISM The theory that the states and the national government should cooperate in solving problems.

CORRUPT PRACTICES ACTS A series of Acts passed by Congress in an attempt to limit and regulate the size and sources of contributions and expenditures in political campaigns.

COUNCIL FOR ENVIRONMENTAL QUALITY An organization that recommends to the president those policies that might improve the environment. It was created in 1969 by the National Environmental Policy Act.

COUNCIL OF ECONOMIC ADVISORS A staff agency in the Executive Office that advises the president on measures to maintain stability in the nation's economy. Established in 1946, the council develops economic plans and budget recommendations for maintaining the nation's "employment, production, and purchasing power" and helps the president prepare an annual economic report to Congress.

COUNCILS OF GOVERNMENT (COGs) Voluntary organizations of counties and municipalities concerned with areawide problems.

COUNTY The chief government set up by the state to administer state law and business at the local level. Counties are drawn up by area, rather than by rural or urban criteria.

CREDENTIALS COMMITTEE A committee used by political parties at their national conventions to determine which delegates may participate. The committee inspects the claim of each pro-

spective delegate to be seated as a legitimate representative of his or her state.

CRIMINAL LAW The law that defines crimes and provides punishment for violations. In criminal cases the government is the prosecutor, since crimes are against the public order.

CRUDE OIL Oil from an underground petroleum reservoir that has been freed from natural gas but has not yet undergone further processing.

CULTURE Habitual modes of thought and behavior characteristic of a particular society; everything that a people consciously creates.

D

DE FACTO SEGREGATION Racial segregation that occurs not as a result of deliberate intentions but because of past social and economic conditions and residential patterns.

DE JURE SEGREGATION Racial segregation that occurs because of laws or administrative decisions by public agencies.

DEFAMATION OF CHARACTER Wrongfully hurting a person's good reputation. The law has imposed a general duty on all persons to refrain from making false, defamatory statements about others.

DEFERRAL A request by the president to defer the spending of funds during a specific fiscal year.

DEFICIENCY PAYMENTS The difference between a target price that the government sets for a particular crop and the market price that the crop fetches.

DELEGATE SELECTION The process, not primarily through elections, of choosing representatives to party conventions.

DEMOCRACY A system of government in which ultimate political authority is vested in the people. Derived from the Greek words *demos* ("the people") and *kratos* ("authority").

DEMOCRATS One of the two major American political parties that evolved out of the Democratic Republican group supporting Thomas Jefferson.

DÉTENTE A French word meaning relaxation of tension. Characterizes U.S. Soviet policy as it developed under President Nixon and Henry Kissinger. Stresses direct cooperative dealings with cold war rivals but avoids ideological accommodation.

DILLON'S RULE The narrowest possible interpretation of the legal status of local governments, outlined by Judge John F. Dillon who in 1868 stated that a municipal corporation can exercise only those powers expressly granted by state law.

DIPLOMACY The total process by means of which states carry on political relations with each other; settling conflicts among nations by peaceful means.

DIRECT DEMOCRACY A system of government in which political decisions are made by the people directly, rather than by their elected representatives; probably possible only in small political communities.

DIRECT PRIMARIES An intraparty election in which the voters select the candidates who will run on a party's ticket in the subsequent general election.

DIRECT TECHNIQUES Interest group activities that involve interaction with government officials to further the group's goals.

DISCHARGE PETITION A procedure by which a bill in the House of Representatives may be forced out of a committee (discharged) that has refused to report it out for consideration by the House. The discharge motion must be signed by an absolute majority (218) of representatives and is used only on rare occasions.

DISENFRANCHISED The condition of a person when his or her right to vote has been removed. Persons may be disenfranchised if they lose their citizenship, if they fail to register when required, or if they are convicted of certain crimes. Used also to mean those who have never had the right to vote.

DISSENTING OPINION A separate opinion in which a judge dissents from the conclusion reached by the majority of the court and expounds his or her own views about the case.

DISTRICT COURTS The federal court of original jurisdiction where most federal cases begin.

DIVERSITY OF CITIZENSHIP Cases involving lawsuits where (1) citizens are of different states, or (2) the controversy is between a state, or the citizens thereof, and foreign states, citizens, or subjects.

DIVISIVE Public opinion is polarized between two quite different positions.

DUAL CITIZENSHIP The condition of being a citizen of two sovereign political units; being a citizen of both a state and the nation.

DUAL FEDERALISM A system of government in which each of the states and the national government remain supreme within their own spheres. The doctrine looks upon nation and state as coequal sovereign powers and holds that acts of states within their reserved powers could be limitations on the powers of the national government.

E

ECONOMIC AID Assistance to other nations in the form of grants, loans, or credits to buy American products.

ECONOMIC REGULATION The regulation of business practices by government agencies.

EFFICIENCY STANDARD A mandatory standard of efficiency set up for energy conservation.

ELASTIC CLAUSE OR NECESSARY AND PROPER CLAUSE The clause in Article I, Section 8, which grants Congress the power to do whatever is necessary to execute its specific powers.

ELECTOR The partisan slate of electors is selected early in the presidential election year by state laws and applicable political party apparatus, and the electors cast ballots for president and vice president. The number of electors in each state is equal to that state's number of representatives in both houses of Congress.

ELECTORAL COLLEGE A group of persons called electors who are selected by the voters in each state; this group officially elects the president and the vice president of the United States. The number of electors in each state is equal to the number of each state's representatives in both houses of Congress.

ELECTORATE All citizens entitled to vote.

ELECTRONIC MEDIA Broadcasting media (radio and television). The term derives from their method of transmission, in contrast to printed media.

EMBARGO A government restriction on trade. Aside from war, embargos may be used to exert political or economic pressure on another country.

EMERGENCY POWERS Inherent powers exercised by the president during a period of national crisis, particularly in foreign affairs.

ENTITLEMENTS Programs providing benefits to individuals who have an established legal right to them, e.g., Medicare, Medicaid, and Social Security. Entitlements are sometimes classified as synonymous with uncontrollables.

ENUMERATED POWERS The powers specifically granted to the national government by the Constitution. The first seventeen clauses of Article I, Section 8 specify most of the enumerated powers of Congress.

ENVIRONMENTAL IMPACT STATEMENT (EIS) A statement first required by the 1969 National Environmental Policy Act. That act directed federal agencies to consider the impact on the environment of all major activities and to include in every recommendation a written analysis of that effect as well as alternatives to the proposal.

EQUAL ACCESS LAW A law embodied in the Federal Communications Act of 1934 stating that stations selling or giving time to one candidate for public office are required to sell or to give equal time to all legally qualified candidates for the same office. News programs are excluded from this provision.

EQUAL EMPLOYMENT OPPORTUNITY COMMISSION (EEOC) A commission established by the 1964 Civil Rights Act to (1) end discrimination based on race, color, religion, sex, or national origin in conditions of employment and (2) promote voluntary action programs by employers, unions, and community organizations to foster equal job opportunities.

EQUALITY A concept that all people are of equal worth.

EQUALIZATION A method for adjusting the amount of money which a state must put up to receive federal funds which takes into account the wealth of the state or its ability to tax its citizens.

ERA OF GOOD FEELING The years from 1817 to 1825 when James Monroe was president and there was, in effect, no political opposition. The term has been continually revived.

ERA OF PERSONAL POLITICS An era when attention centers on the character of individual candidates rather than on party identification.

ESPIONAGE ACT An act passed in 1917 prohibiting espionage, sabotage, and obstruction of the war effort.

ESTABLISHMENT CLAUSE The part of the First Amendment prohibiting the establishment of a church officially supported by the national government. It is applied to questions of state and local government aid to religious organizations and schools, of the legality of allowing or requiring school prayers, and of the teaching of evolution versus fundamentalist theories of creation.

EXECUTIVE AGREEMENT A binding international obligation made between chiefs of state without legislative sanction.

EXECUTIVE IMMUNITY The right of executive officials to refuse to appear before, or to withhold information from, a legislative committee. Executive privilege is enjoyed by the president and by those executive officials accorded that right by the president.

EXECUTIVE OFFICE OF THE PRESIDENT Established by President Franklin D. Roosevelt by executive order under the Reorganization Act of 1939. It currently consists of nine staff agencies that assist the president in carrying out his major duties.

EXECUTIVE ORDER A rule or regulation issued by the president that has the effect of law. Executive orders can implement and give administrative effect to provisions in the Constitution, to treaties, and to statutes.

EXPORT CONTROL Restricting exports to another nation for security or other reasons.

EXPRESS POWERS Constitutional and statutory powers of the president, which are expressly written into the Constitution or into congressional law.

EXTERNAL GOALS National goals concerning economic, political, military, and other relations outside the United States.

EXTRADITE To surrender an accused criminal to the authorities of the state from which he or she has fled; to return a fugitive criminal to the jurisdiction of the accusing state.

EXTRAORDINARY MAJORITY A majority which is greater than 50% plus one. For example, ratification of amendments requires the approval of two-thirds of the House and the Senate and three-fourths of the states.

F

FACTION A group or bloc in a legislature or political party who act together in pursuit of some special interest or position.

FAIRNESS DOCTRINE An FCC regulation requiring that equal broadcast time be made available to legitimate opposing political groups, interests, or individuals.

"FAITHLESS" ELECTORS Electors voting for candidates other than those within their parties. They are pledged, but not required by law, to vote for the candidate who has a plurality in the state.

FALL REVIEW The second phase of the budgeting process, occurring in the fall when the Office of Management and Budget examines each executive agency's budget request that was formulated during the summer.

FEDERAL ELECTION CAMPAIGN ACT OF 1972 An act to control the raising and spending of funds for political campaigns.

FEDERAL ELECTION COMMISSION Created by the 1972 Federal Election Campaign Act to enforce compliance with the requirements of the act; the Commission consists of six nonpartisan administrators.

FEDERAL OPEN MARKET COMMITTEE (FOMC) Composed of the members of the Federal Reserve Governors and five representatives of the Federal Reserve banks who determine monetary policy actions for the Federal Reserve System.

FEDERAL QUESTIONS The interpretation and application of cases arising under the Constitution, acts of Congress, or treaties. Jurisdiction in cases where a federal question is involved is given to the federal courts.

FEDERAL REGISTER A publication of the executive branch which prints executive orders, rules, and regulations.

FEDERAL RESERVE SYSTEM The private-public banking regulatory system, which establishes the banking policies and influences the amount of credit available and currency in circulation. Determines the nation's general monetary and credit policies.

FEDERAL SYSTEM A system of government in which power is divided by a written constitution between a central government and regional, or subdivisional, governments. Each level must have some domain in which its policies are dominant and some genuine political or constitutional guarantee of its authority.

FEDERALISTS The first American political party, led by Alexander Hamilton and John Adams which evolved in the later phases of George Washington's presidency. Many of its members had strongly supported the adoption of the new Constitution and the creation of the federal union.

FILIBUSTERING In the Senate, unlimited debate to halt action on a particular bill.

FIRESIDE CHATS Warm, informal talks by Franklin D. Roosevelt to a few million of his intimate friends—via the radio. Roosevelt's fireside chats were so effective that succeeding presidents have been urged by their advisers to emulate him by giving more radio and television reports to the nation.

FIRST BUDGET RESOLUTION A resolution passed by Congress in May setting overall revenue and spending goals and, hence, by definition, the size of the deficit for the following fiscal year.

FIRST-STRIKE CAPABILITY The launching of an initial strategic nuclear attack before the opponent has used any strategic weapons.

FISCAL POLICY The use of government spending and taxation policies to influence the level of economic activity, the rate of inflation, and economic growth.

FISCAL YEAR A period of twelve months, which can begin at any time during the calendar year, used by businesses for accounting purposes; the federal government's accounting period, or fiscal year, runs from October 1 to September 30 of the following year.

FLUIDITY The extent to which public opinion changes over time.

FOOD STAMP PROGRAM This operates through in-kind transfer payments to give the poor a means to obtain better nutrition.

FOREIGN POLICY A nation's external goals and the techniques and strategies used to achieve them.

FOREIGN POLICY PROCESS The steps by which external goals are decided and acted upon.

FOSSIL FUELS A collective term for all fuels derived through the fossilization process from past living organisms. Natural gas, coal, and petroleum are examples of fossil fuels.

FOURTEEN POINTS The summarization of Woodrow Wilson's aims and hopes for postwar peace, calling for open diplomacy, freedom of the seas, removal of economic barriers, international supervision of colonies, and the creation of a League of Nations.

FRANCHISE The legal right to vote, extended to blacks by the Fifteenth Amendment, to women by the Nineteenth Amendment, and to people age 18 or older by the Twenty-sixth Amendment.

FRANKING A policy that enables members of Congress to send material through the mail by substituting their facsimile signature (frank) for postage.

FRATERNITY From the Latin *fraternus* ("brother"), the term *fraternity* came to mean, in the political philosophy of the eighteenth century, the condition in which each individual considers the needs of all others; a brotherhood. In the French Revolution of 1789, the popular cry was "liberty, equality, and fraternity."

FREE EXERCISE CLAUSE That part of the First Amendment constraining Congress from prohibiting the free exercise of religion.

FULL FAITH AND CREDIT CLAUSE A section of the Constitution that requires states to recognize one another's laws and court decisions. It ensures that rights established under deeds, wills, contracts, and other civil matters in one state will be honored by other states.

FUNCTIONAL CONSOLIDATION The cooperation of two or more units of local government in providing services to their inhabitants.

FUNGIBLE COMMODITIES Commodities that are available from different producers.

G

"GAG" ORDERS Orders issued by judges restricting publication of news about a trial in progress or a pretrial hearing to protect the accused's right to a fair trial.

GAS-GUZZLER TAX A tax imposed on low-mileage cars.

GAYS A term used to denote homosexuals. (The term *lesbians* denotes homosexual women only.)

GENDER GAP Most widely used to describe the difference between the percentage of votes a candidate receives from women voters and the percentage of the candidate received from men. The term was widely used after the 1980 presidential election.

GENERAL JURISDICTION Extends to all types of cases that may be brought before a court within legal bounds.

GENERAL LAW CITY A city operating under general state laws that apply to all local government units of a similar type.

GENERAL SALES TAX A tax levied as a proportion of the retail price of a commodity at the point of sale.

GENERATIONAL EFFECTS Events of a particular time period have a long-lasting effect on the political opinions or preferences of those individuals who came of political age at that time.

GERRYMANDERING The drawing of legislative district boundary lines for the purpose of obtaining partisan or factional advantage. A district is said to be gerrymandered when its shape is manipulated by the dominant party in the state legislature to maximize electoral strength at the expense of the minority party.

GOVERNMENT Individuals, institutions, and processes that make society's rules about conflict resolution and the allocation of resources and that possess the power to enforce them.

GOVERNMENT CORPORATION An agency of government that administers a quasibusiness enterprise. Used when an activity is primarily commercial, produces revenue for its continued existence, and requires greater flexibility than permitted for departments.

GOVERNMENT IN THE SUNSHINE ACT Requires that all multiheaded federal agencies conduct their business regularly in public session.

GRANDFATHER CLAUSE A device used by southern states to exempt whites from state taxes and literacy laws originally intended to disenfranchise black voters. It allowed the voting franchise to anyone who could prove that his grandfather had voted before 1867.

GREAT COMPROMISE The compromise between the New Jersey and the Virginia Plans which created one chamber of the Congress based on population and one chamber which represented each state equally.

GROSS NATIONAL PRODUCT (GNP) The total market value of all final goods and services produced by the entire economy in a one-year period.

GUARANTEED ANNUAL INCOME A plan to eliminate poverty by giving all families falling below the poverty line a straight cash payment.

H

HABITS OF COMPLIANCE Learned obedience without thinking much about power or legitimacy, although these reinforce such habits.

HATCH ACT (POLITICAL ACTIVITIES ACT) Passed in 1939, this act forbids a political committee to spend more than $3 million in any campaign and limits individual contributions to a committee to $5,000. The act was designed to control political influence buying.

HOME RULE CITY A city with a charter allowing local voters to frame, adopt, and amend their own charter.

HORIZONTAL EQUITY Equity that exists when those with equal paying abilities pay the same amount of tax regardless of how it was earned or who earned it.

HOUSE MINORITY LEADER The party leader elected by the minority party in the House.

HYPERPLURALISM An exaggerated form of pluralism in which government is so decentralized and authority so fragmented that it doesn't get anything done.

I

IDEOLOGUE A term applied to an individual whose political opinions are tightly constrained, that is, who has opinions that are consistent with one another. Ideologues are often described as having a comprehensive world view.

IMAGE BUILDING Using public and private opinion polls, the candidate's image is molded to meet the particular needs of the campaign. Image building is done primarily through the media.

IMPEACHMENT As authorized by Article I of the Constitution, impeachment is an action by the House of Representatives and the Senate to remove the president, vice president, or civil officers of the United States from office for crimes of "treason, bribery, or other high crimes and misdemeanors."

INALIENABLE RIGHTS Rights held to be inherent in natural law and not dependent on government; as asserted in the Declaration of Independence, the rights to "life, liberty, and the pursuit of happiness."

INCOME MAINTENANCE PROGRAMS Government transfer programs designed to provide a uniformly adequate standard of living.

INCOMES POLICY An attempt by government to reduce the rate of increase in prices and wages. Also known as *price controls*, where there is a cap put on the prices of specific goods and services throughout the country.

INCORPORATION THEORY The view that the protections of the Bill of Rights are incorporated into the Fourteenth Amendment's protection against the state government.

INDEPENDENT CANDIDATE A political candidate who is not affiliated with either the Democratic or the Republican parties.

INDEPENDENT EXECUTIVE AGENCY A federal agency having a single function that is not a part of a Cabinet department but reports directly to the president.

INDEPENDENT REGULATORY AGENCY An agency outside the major executive departments charged with making and implementing rules and regulations to protect the public interest.

INDEPENDENT VOTERS Voters who disavow any party affiliation and cast their ballots based on their views of who the best candidate is.

INDIRECT TECHNIQUES Strategies employed by interest groups that use a third party, the general public, or other individuals to influence government officials.

INFLATION A sustained rise in prices.

INHERENT POWERS Powers of the president derived from the loosely worded statement in the Constitution that "the executive power shall be vested in the president" and that the president should "take care that the laws be faithfully executed"; defined through practice rather than through constitutional or statutory law.

INITIATIVE A procedure whereby voters can propose a law or a constitutional amendment.

INJUNCTION An order issued by a court in an equity proceeding to compel or restrain the performance of an act by an individual or government official.

INSTITUTIONS Long-standing, identifiable structures or associations that perform functions for society.

INSTRUCTED DELEGATES The concept that legislators are agents of the voters who elected them and that they should vote according to the views of their constituents regardless of their own personal assessments.

INTELLIGENCE COMMUNITY The government agencies involved in gathering information about the capabilities and intentions of foreign governments and engaging in covert activities to further American foreign policy aims.

INTENSITY The strength or intensity of a pro or con position concerning a public policy or issue. Intensity is often critical in generating public action; an intense minority can often win on an issue of public policy over a less intense majority.

INTEREST GROUP An organized group of individuals sharing common objectives who actively attempt to influence government policy makers through direct and indirect methods, including the marshaling of public opinion, lobbying, and electioneering.

INTERNATIONAL ENERGY AGENCY (IEA) An international agency which is supposed to coordinate energy policy among its member nations. It is an organization of oil-consuming nations.

INTERPOSITION The act in which a state places itself between its citizens and the national government as a protector, shielding its citizens from any national legislation that may be harmful to them. The doctrine of interposition has been rejected by the federal courts as contrary to the national supremacy clause of Article VI in the Constitution.

INTERSTATE COMPACT An agreement between two or more states to cooperate on a policy or problem such as sharing water resources.

INTERVENTIONISM Involvement in foreign affairs; actions directed at changing or preserving the internal political arrangements of other nations.

IRON CURTAIN The term used to describe the division of Europe between the Soviet Union and the West. Popularized by Winston Churchill in a speech portraying Europe as being divided by an iron curtain, with the nations of Eastern Europe behind the curtain and increasingly under Soviet control.

IRON TRIANGLE The three-way alliance among legislators, bureaucrats, and interest groups to make or preserve policies which benefit their interests.

ISSUE VOTING Voting for a candidate based on how he or she stands on a particular issue.

ITEM VETO The power exercised by the governors in all but a few states to veto sections or items of an appropriations bill.

J

JIM CROW LAWS State laws enforcing racial segregation in public accommodations and conveyances.

JOINT COMMITTEE A legislative committee composed of members from both houses of Congress.

JUDICIAL ACTIVISM A doctrine advocating an active role for the Supreme Court in enforcing the Constitution and in using judicial review. An activist Court takes a broad view of the Constitution and involves itself in legislative and executive matters by altering the direction of activities of Congress, state legislatures, and administrative agencies.

JUDICIAL RESTRAINT A doctrine holding that the Court should rarely use its power of judicial review or otherwise intervene in the political process.

JUDICIAL REVIEW The power of the Supreme Court or any court to declare federal or state acts unconstitutional. First established in *Marbury v. Madison.*

JURISDICTION Authority vested in the court to hear and to decide a case.

JURISDICTIONAL DISPUTE A dispute by two or more unions over which should have control of a particular jurisdiction, such as a particular craft or skill or a particular firm or industry.

JUSTIFIABLE QUESTION A question that may be raised and reviewed in court.

K

KANGAROO COURT A mock hearing in which norms of justice and judicial procedure are ignored.

KEYNOTE SPEECH The first major speech at the party convention which sets out the theme of the meeting.

KITCHEN CABINET The informal advisers to the president.

KU KLUX KLAN A white supremacist organization founded in 1865 by a small group of ex-Confederate soldiers to resist Reconstructionist policies and to restore state sovereignty.

L

LABOR MOVEMENT In general, the term refers to the full range of economic and political expression of working-class interests; politically, it describes the organization of working-class interests.

LAISSEZ-FAIRE The economic theory popularized by Adam Smith that calls for a hands-off policy by the government in economic affairs. Rejects state control and regulation and emphasizes economic individualism and a market economy.

LATENT INTERESTS Interests that are dormant or unexpressed. The group that holds these interests has never organized nor articulated them.

LATENT PUBLIC OPINIONS Unexpressed political opinions that have the potential to become manifest attitudes or beliefs.

LAWMAKING The process of deciding the legal rules that govern our society. Such laws may regulate minor affairs or establish broad national policies.

LEGISLATIVE VETO Provision in a bill reserving to Congress or to a congressional committee the power to reject an act or regulation of a national agency by majority vote; declared unconstitutional by the Supreme Court in 1983.

LEGISLATURE A government body primarily responsible for the making of laws.

LEGITIMACY A status conferred by the people upon the government's officials, acts, and institutions through their belief that the government's actions are an appropriate use of power by a legally constituted governmental authority following correct decision-making policies; regarded as rightful and entitled to compliance and obedience on the part of citizens.

LIBEL Defamation of character in writing.

LIBERTY The greatest freedom of individuals that is consistent with the freedom of other individuals in the society.

LIMITED GOVERNMENT A form of government based on the principle that the powers of government should be clearly limited either through a written document or through wide public understanding; characterized by institutional checks to ensure that governments serve the public rather than private interests.

LINE ORGANIZATION Government or corporate units which provide direct services or products for the public.

LOBBYING The attempt by organizations or by individuals to influence the passage, defeat, or contents of legislation and administrative decisions of government. The derivation of the term may be traced back over a century to the habit of certain private citizens who regularly congregated in the lobby outside the legislative chambers before a session to petition legislators.

LOGROLLING An arrangement by which two or more members of Congress agree in advance to support each other's bills.

LONG BALLOT Sometimes called the "bedsheet ballot" or "jungle ballot," the long ballot is a lengthy list of candidates and is typical in states and localities that have many offices to be filled.

M

MAJORITY Full age; the age at which a person is entitled by law to the management of his or her own affairs and to the enjoyment of civil rights.

MAJORITY FLOOR LEADER The chief spokesperson of the major party in the Senate who directs the legislative program and party strategy.

MAJORITY LEADER OF THE HOUSE A legislative position held by an important party member in the House of Representatives. The majority leader is selected by the majority party in caucus or conference to foster cohesion among party members and to act as spokesperson for the House.

MAJORITY OPINION The views of the majority of the judges.

MAJORITY RULE A basic principle of democracy asserting that the greatest number of citizens in any political unit should select officials and determine policies.

MANAGED NEWS Information generated and distributed by the government in such a way as to give government interests priority over candor.

MANDATE A term which means overwhelming public support for an official and his or her policies.

MANDATORY RETIREMENT Forced retirement when a certain age is reached.

MARSHALL PLAN A proposal made by Secretary of State George C. Marshall in 1948 for a vast program of American economic aid to reconstruct the war-devastated economies of Western Europe. It was accepted by Congress, and sixteen nations in Western Europe received massive economic aid in the form of grants, loans, and supplies from 1948–1952.

MATCHING FUNDS For many categorical grant programs, the state must put up or "match" the federal funds. Some programs only required the state to raise 10% of the funds while others approach an even share.

MEDIA The technical means of communication with mass audiences. The media have become extremely important in American political life as a means of informing and influencing millions of citizens.

MEDIA ACCESS The public's access right to the media. The FCC and the courts have gradually taken the stance that citizens do have an access right to the media.

MEDICAID Health care payments for the needy regardless of age. It is state-administered and the particulars differ from state to state. Some are generous; others are not.

MEDICARE A health insurance program enacted in 1965 as an amendment to the Social Security Act to provide medical care for the elderly.

MERIT SYSTEM The selection, retention, and promotion of government employees on the basis of competitive examinations.

MILITARY-INDUSTRIAL COMPLEX The mutually beneficial relationship between the armed forces and defense contractors.

MINICONVENTION A meeting held by the Democratic party during nonpresidential election years since 1974.

MINIMUM WAGE An hourly wage rate below which employers cannot pay covered workers. Minimum wages are imposed by federal, state, and local laws.

MINORITY FLOOR LEADER The party officer in the Senate who commands the minority party's opposition to the policies of the majority party and directs the legislative program and strategy of his or her party.

MONARCHY A form of government in which the supreme power of the state is exercised, or ceremonially held, by one person of a royal family, such as a queen, king, or emperor.

MONETARY POLICY Controlling the amount of currency in circulation and the availability of credit.

MONROE DOCTRINE The policy statement included in President Monroe's 1823 annual message to Congress, which included three principles: (1) European nations should not establish new colonies in the Western Hemisphere, (2) European nations should not intervene in the affairs of independent nations of the Western Hemisphere, and (3) the United States would not interfere in the affairs of European nations.

MORAL MAJORITY A strongly conservative Christian political group.

MULTINATIONAL CORPORATIONS (MNCs) Corporations with a number of foreign subsidiaries operating in various countries.

MULTIPARTY SYSTEM An electoral system, usually based on proportional representation, that requires a coalition of several parties to form a majority to run the government. Numerous parties seriously compete for and actually win seats in the legislature. The multiparty system is typical of continental European democracies.

MULTIPLE, INDEPENDENTLY TARGETABLE REENTRY VEHICLES (MIRVs) Multiple warheads carried by a single missile but directed to different targets.

MUNICIPAL HOME RULE The power vested in a local unit of government to draft or change its own charter and to manage its own affairs.

MUTUAL ASSURED DESTRUCTION (MAD) A theory that if the United States and the Soviet Union had extremely large and invulnerable nuclear forces that were somewhat equal, then neither would chance a war with each other.

N

NARROW-CASTING Broadcasting which is targeted for one small sector of the population.

NATIONAL COMMITTEE A standing committee of a national political party established to direct and coordinate party activities during the four-year period between national party conventions.

NATIONAL CONVENTION The meeting held every four years by each major party to select presidential and vice presidential candidates, to write a platform, to choose a national committee, and to conduct party business. In theory the national convention is at the top of a hierarchy of party conventions (the local and state conventions are below it) which considers candidates and issues.

NATIONAL POLITICS The pursuit of interests that are of concern to the nation as a whole.

NATIONAL SECURITY COUNCIL (NSC) A board created by the 1947 National Security Act to advise the president on matters of national security.

NATIONAL SECURITY POLICY Foreign and domestic policy designed to protect the independence and political and economic integrity of the United States; policy that is concerned with the safety and defense of the nation.

NATURAL ARISTOCRACY A small ruling clique of the state's "best" citizens, whose membership is based on birth, wealth, and ability. The Jeffersonian era emphasized rule by such a group.

NATURAL RIGHTS Rights held to be inherent in natural law, not dependent on governments. John Locke stated that natural law, being superior to human law, specifies certain rights of "life, liberty, and property." These rights, slightly altered to become "life, liberty, and the pursuit of happiness," are asserted in the Declaration of Independence.

NECESSARIES In contracts, necessaries include whatever is reasonably necessary for suitable subsistence as measured by age, state, condition in life, and so on.

NEGATIVE CONSTITUENTS U.S. citizens who openly oppose government policies.

NEGATIVE INCOME TAX A system of transferring income to

the relatively poor by taxing them negatively—that is, by giving them an income subsidy that varies according to how far below a "target" income their earned income is.

NEGATIVE SANCTION Withholding something of value—freedom, cooperation, or recognition—or threatening to do so.

NEW ENGLAND TOWN Combines the roles of city and county into one governmental unit in the New England states.

NEW FEDERALISM A plan to limit the national government's power to regulate and to restore power to state governments. Essentially, the new federalism was designed to give the states an increased ability to decide for themselves how government revenues should be spent.

NONABSOLUTISTS Those who hold that there are exceptions to the First Amendment when restrictions on freedom of speech can be imposed.

NUCLEAR FREEZE A halt on the development, production, and deployment of nuclear weapons.

NULLIFICATION The act of nullifying or rendering void. Basing his argument on the assumption that ultimate sovereign authority rested with the several states, John C. Calhoun asserted that a state had the right to declare a national law to be null and void and therefore not binding on its citizens.

O

OFF-BUDGET ITEMS Expenditures undertaken by the federal government that do not directly appear on the federal government's official budget.

OFFICE-BLOCK BALLOT OR MASSACHUSETTS BALLOT A form of general election ballot in which candidates for elective office are grouped together under the title of each office. It emphasizes voting for the office and the individual rather than for the party.

OFFICE OF MANAGEMENT AND BUDGET (OMB) A division of the Executive Office created by executive order in 1970 to replace the Bureau of the Budget. OMB's main functions are to assist the president in preparing the annual budget, to clear and coordinate all departmental or agency budgets, to help set fiscal policy, and to supervise the administration of the federal budget.

OFFSET POLICY A policy requiring a company that wants to build a plant to work out a corresponding reduction in pollution at some existing plant in the same area.

OMBUDSMAN An individual in the role of hearing and investigating complaints by private individuals against public officials or agencies.

OPEN DIPLOMACY The substance of point one of Woodrow Wilson's Fourteen Points—open treaties of peace openly arrived at.

OPEN PRIMARY A direct primary where voters may cast ballots in the primary of either party without having to declare their party registration. Once voters choose which party primary they will vote in, they must vote for only the candidates of that party.

OPINION The statement by a judge or a court of the decision reached in a case tried or argued before them. It expounds the law

as applied to the case and details the reasons upon which the judgment was based.

OPINION LEADERS Individuals able to influence the opinions of others because of position, expertise, or personality. Such leaders help to shape public opinion formally or informally.

OPINION POLL A method of systematically questioning a small, selected sample of individuals who are deemed representative of the total population. Widely used by government, business, university scholars, political candidates, and voluntary groups to provide reasonably accurate data on public attitudes, beliefs, expectations, and behavior.

ORGANIZATION OF PETROLEUM EXPORTING COUNTRIES (OPEC) An organization founded in 1960 by third-world, oil-rich nations in response to price-cutting policies of multinational oil companies and dissatisfaction with what they considered to be inequitable concession agreements. The collective efforts of this cartel climaxed in 1973–74 when, as a result of the Yom Kippur war and a greater awareness of the industrialized nations' dependence on imported oil, OPEC members implemented an oil embargo which was followed by a massive price increase.

ORIGINAL JURISDICTION The authority of a court to hear a case in the first instance.

OSTRACISM The act of banishing a citizen from his or her society by the common consent of the acting political authority; the most severe penalty awarded in the ancient Greek city-states.

OVERBREADTH When a law is so broad that it prohibits, among other things, protected speech.

OVERSIGHT The responsibility Congress has for following up on laws it has enacted to ensure that they are being enforced and administered in the way in which they were intended.

P

PAID-FOR POLITICAL ANNOUNCEMENT A commercial message about a political candidate conveyed through the media, designed to elicit public opinion.

PARDON The granting of a release from the punishment or legal consequences of a crime; a pardon can be granted by the president before or after a conviction.

PARLIAMENTARY SYSTEM A system of government in which governmental authority is vested in the legislative body (parliament) and in the cabinet headed by a prime minister or premier. The executive and legislative branches are fused.

PARTICULATES Air pollution in the form of particles of solid matter.

PARTY-COLUMN BALLOT or INDIANA BALLOT A form of general election ballot in which candidates for elective office are arranged in one column under their respective party labels and symbols. It emphasizes voting for the party rather than for the office or individual.

PARTY IDENTIFICATION Linking oneself to a particular political party.

PARTY IDENTIFIERS Those who identify themselves as involved with a political party sharing their interests.

PARTY PLATFORM A document drawn up by the platform committee at each national convention, outlining the policies, positions, and principles of the party; it is then submitted to the entire convention for approval.

PATRONAGE Rewarding faithful party workers and followers with government employment and contracts.

PEER GROUPS Groups consisting of members sharing common relevant social characteristics. They play an important part in the socialization process, helping to shape attitudes and beliefs.

PENDLETON ACT (CIVIL SERVICE REFORM ACT OF 1883) This law, as amended over the years, remains the basic statute regulating federal employment personnel policies. It established the principle of employment on the basis of merit and created the Civil Service Commission to administer the personnel service.

PERIOD OF ISOLATIONISM A period of abstaining from an active role in international affairs or alliances, which characterized most of the nineteenth century.

PERMIAN BASIN DECISION A decision of the Federal Power Commission which set prices for natural gas.

PERSONAL-ATTACK RULE The rule promulgated by the FCC that allows individuals or groups air time to reply to attacks that have previously been aired.

PLURALISM A political doctrine in which autonomous groups in society actively compete in the decison-making process for resources and services.

PLURALITY The winning of an election by a candidate who receives more votes than any other candidate but not necessarily a majority. Most national, state, and local electoral laws provide for winning elections by a plurality vote.

POCKET VETO A special veto power exercised by the chief executive after a legislative body has adjourned. Bills not signed by the chief executive die after a specified period of time. If Congress wishes to reconsider such a bill, it must be reintroduced in the following session of Congress.

POLICE POWER The authority to legislate for the protection of the health, morals, safety, and welfare of the people. In the United States police power is a reserved power of the states. The federal government is able to legislate for the welfare of its citizens only through specific congressional powers such as interstate commerce.

POLITICAL ACTION COMMITTEES (PACS) Committees set up by and representing corporations, labor unions, or special interest groups; PACs raise and give campaign donations on behalf of the organizations or groups they represent.

POLITICAL CONSULTANT A paid professional hired to devise a campaign strategy and manage a campaign. Image building is the crucial task of the political consultant.

POLITICAL CULTURE The pattern of political beliefs and values characteristic of a community or population.

POLITICAL PARTY A group of individuals who organize to win elections, to operate the government, and to determine public policy.

POLITICAL SOCIALIZATION The process through which individuals learn a set of political attitudes and form opinions about social issues. The family and the public school system are two of the most important forces in the political socialization process.

POLITICAL SYSTEM A set of institutions, practices, and policies through which political questions are resolved.

POLITICAL TOLERANCE Whether individuals are able to grant civil liberties to groups that have opinions differing strongly from their own.

POLITICAL TRUST The degree to which individuals express trust in the government and political institutions. This concept is usually measured through a specific series of survey questions.

POLITICO The legislative role that combines the delegate and trustee concepts. The legislator varies the role according to the issue under consideration.

POLITICS According to David Easton, the "authoritative allocation of values" for a society; according to Harold Lasswell, "who gets what, when, and how" in a society.

POLL TAX A special tax that must be paid as a qualification for voting. The Twenty-fourth Amendment to the Constitution outlawed the poll tax in national elections, and in 1966 the Supreme Court declared it unconstitutional.

POLL WATCHER An individual appointed by a political party to scrutinize the voting process on election day. Usually, there are two poll watchers at every voting place, representing the Democratic and the Republican parties, both attempting to ensure the honesty of the election.

POPULAR SOVEREIGNTY The natural rights concept that ultimate political authority rests with the people.

PORK-BARREL LEGISLATION Appropriations made by a legislative body providing public money for local projects not critically needed but desired by members of the constituencies of congressional members.

POSITIVE LAW Laws made in and by legislatures to fit a particular circumstance.

POSITIVE SANCTION Giving something of value—status, material goods, or psychological support.

POVERTY-WELFARE CURVE The curve that shows the trade-off between welfare spending per capita and the percentage of population living in poverty. According to some researchers, the poverty-welfare curve shows a decrease in the percentage of the population living in poverty as welfare spending increases up to a certain point, and then shows an *increase* in the percentage of population living in poverty as welfare spending goes up even more.

POWER The ability to cause others to modify their behavior and to conform to what the power holder wants.

PRECEDENT A court rule bearing on subsequent legal decisions in similar cases. Judges rely on precedents in deciding cases.

PREFERRED-POSITION TEST A court test used in determining the limits of free expression guaranteed in the First Amendment in which a more rigorous standard of review is required for First

Amendment cases because of the importance of that amendment.

PRESIDENT PRO TEMPORE The temporary presiding officer of the Senate in the absence of the vice president.

PRESIDENTIAL PRIMARY A statewide primary election of delegates to a political party's national convention to help a political party determine its presidential nominee. Such delegates are either pledged or unpledged to a particular candidate.

PRESS SECRETARY The individual responsible for representing the White House before the media. The press secretary writes news releases, provides background information, sets up conferences, and so on.

PRICE-ANDERSON ACT A 1957 law which provides for government back-up of companies which insure nuclear reactors.

PRICE DISCRIMINATION Selling different units of identical products at different prices.

PRICE SUPPORTS Minimum prices set by the government. To be effective, price supports must be coupled with a mechanism to rid the market of "surplus" goods that arise whenever the supported price is greater than the market-clearing price.

PRIMARY ELECTIONS Elections which are held to choose the nominees for an office.

PRIME MINISTER The head of the cabinet in a parliamentary system of government, selected from the membership of the parliament.

PRIOR RESTRAINT Restraining an action before the activity has actually occurred. It involves censorship as opposed to subsequent punishment.

PRIVILEGES AND IMMUNITIES A section of the Constitution requiring states not to discriminate against each other's citizens. A resident of one state cannot be treated as an alien when in another state; he or she may not be denied such privileges and immunities as legal protection, access to courts, travel rights, or property rights.

PROGRESSIVE INCOME TAX SYSTEM A tax system in which, as a person earns more income, a higher percentage of the additional dollars is taxed. Such a tax system taxes those earning higher incomes more heavily than those in lower-income brackets.

PROJECT GRANT An assistance grant that can be applied for directly by state and local agencies; established under the national program grant. Project grants allow Congress (and the administration) to bypass state governments and thereby to place the money directly where it is supposedly the most needed.

PROJECT INDEPENDENCE President Nixon's 1973 proposal for making the U.S. independent of foreign sources of energy by 1985.

PROPERTY As conceived by the political philosopher John Locke, a natural right superior to human law (laws made by government).

PROPERTY TAX A tax on the value of real estate; limited to state and local governments and a particularly important source of revenue for local governments.

PROPORTIONAL REPRESENTATION An electoral system that allocates seats in the legislative body to representatives of various political parties depending on each party's share of the popular vote. The procedure allows minority parties to obtain some representation and often leads to a multiplicity of parties and groups in the legislature. Proportional representation is used most frequently in European democracies and in a small number of American cities.

PROPORTIONAL TAX SYSTEM A system of taxation in which the same percentage of income is paid by everyone on every dollar that is taxed. Also called a *flat rate* tax system.

PUBLIC ADMINISTRATION The science of managing public organizations.

PUBLIC AGENDA Issues that are commonly perceived by members of the political community as meriting public attention and governmental action. The media play an important role in setting the public agenda by focusing attention on certain topics.

PUBLIC INTEREST The best interests of the collective, overarching community; the national good, rather than the narrow interests of a self-serving group.

PUBLIC OPINION The aggregate of individual attitudes or beliefs shared by some portion of adults. There is no one public opinion because there are many different "publics."

PUBLIC POLICIES Policies reflecting various courses of action chosen by government officials.

PURCHASING POWER The quantity and quality of products or services your dollar can buy; the purchasing power of your dollar may be more today, for example, than it will be tomorrow—given inflation.

R

RADIOACTIVE WASTE Material—in gaseous, liquid, or solid form—which is a by-product of all the processes in the nuclear fuel cycle. It emits ionizing radiation and is damaging to all living organisms. Radioactive waste is classified as low-level, intermediate-level, and high-level waste.

RAPID DEPLOYMENT FORCE Military unit trained for quick action and kept in a state of readiness.

RATE OF UNEMPLOYMENT Rate used to denote the number of involuntarily unemployed.

RATIFICATION Formal approval and consent by an authorized political body.

RATIONAL IGNORANCE EFFECT When people purposefully and rationally decide not to become informed on an issue because they realize that their vote on the issue is not likely to be the deciding one; a lack of incentive to seek the necessary information to cast an intelligent vote.

REAPPORTIONMENT The redrawing of legislative district lines to recognize the existing population distribution.

RECALL A procedure allowing the people to vote to dismiss an elected official from state office before his or her term has expired.

RECESSION A period of time during which the rate of growth in business activity is consistently less than its long-term trend or is negative.

RECOGNITION POWER The president's power, as chief diplomat, to extend diplomatic recognition to foreign governments.

RECONSTRUCTION The period following the Civil War when the Reconstruction Acts were passed to reconstruct the southern government and to grant full citizenship to blacks.

REDISTRIBUTION OF INCOME Policies designed to redistribute income from upper-income to lower-income groups by, for example, taxing some individuals to pay for welfare payments to others.

REDISTRIBUTIVE PROGRAMS Programs which shift funds or benefits from wealthier groups to poorer ones.

REDISTRICTING Redrawing district lines within the states.

REFERENDUM An electoral device whereby legislative or constitutional measures are referred to the voters for approval or disapproval.

REGIME The government of a specific leader or a mode of government; used mainly to refer to foreign governments or eras.

REGISTERED VOTERS Citizens who have met certain legal requirements necessary to registration and who have registered prior to election day.

REGISTRATION The entry of a person's name onto the list of eligible voters for elections. Registration requires meeting certain legal requirements such as age, citizenship, and residency.

REGRESSIVE TAXATION A system of taxes in which the higher the income, the smaller is the percentage of income paid as taxes.

RELEVANCE The extent to which an issue is of concern at a particular time. Issues become relevant when the public views them as pressing or of direct concern to them.

REMAND To send a case back to the court that originally heard it.

REPRESENTATION The function of Congress as elected officials to represent the views of their constituents.

REPRESENTATIVE ASSEMBLY A legislature composed of individuals who represent the population.

REPRESENTATIVE DEMOCRACY A form of government in which representatives elected by the people make laws and policies.

REPRESENTATIVES Those empowered to act on behalf of the people.

REPRIEVE The president has the power to grant a reprieve to postpone the execution of a sentence imposed by a court of law; usually done for humanitarian reasons or to await new evidence.

REPUBLICAN GOVERNMENT A government that operates through elected representatives of the people.

REPUBLICAN PARTY One of the two major American political parties, which emerged in the 1850s as an anti-slavery party. It was created to fill the vacuum created by the disintegration of the Whig party. The Republican party traces its name—but not its ideology—to Jefferson's Democratic Republican party.

RESCISSION A proposal by the president that funds be given back to the Treasury.

RESERVES The material that can actually be extracted or recovered with current technology and cost restraint.

RESOURCE The material that actually exists. Resources are not reserves.

REVENUE-SHARING PROGRAM A program in which the federal government allocates funds to states and cities with virtually no strings attached. Recipient governments can use the funds in any way they see fit.

REVERSE To annul or make void a judgment on account of some error or irregularity.

REVERSE DISCRIMINATION The charge that affirmative action programs requiring preferential treatment or quotas discriminate against those who have no minority status.

REVIEWING COURTS Courts of appellate jurisdiction with authority to review decisions of lower courts.

RIGHT-TO-WORK LAWS Laws that make it illegal to require union membership as a condition of continuing employment in a particular firm.

RULE-MAKING POWERS Powers of administrative agencies to make and enforce business regulations.

RULES COMMITTEE A standing committee of the House of Representatives that provides special rules under which specific bills can be debated, amended, and considered by the House.

RUN-OFF PRIMARY An election that is held to nominate candidates within the party if no candidate receives a majority of the votes in the first primary election.

S

SAFE SEAT A district that returns the legislator with 55 percent of the vote or more.

SCHEMA In internal cognitive structures, based on experience, which organize and guide the process of information.

SECESSION The act of formally withdrawing from membership in an alliance; withdrawal of a state from the federal union.

SECOND BUDGET RESOLUTION A resolution passed by Congress in September which sets "binding" limits on taxes and spending for the next fiscal year beginning October 1st.

SECONDARY BOYCOTT A boycott of companies or products sold by companies that are dealing with a company that has already been struck.

SECTIONAL POLITICS The pursuit of interests that are of special concern to a region or section of the country.

SECURITY PACTS Mutual military assistance agreements.

SELECT COMMITTEE A temporary legislative committee established for a limited time period for a special purpose.

SELECTMEN The governing group of a town.

SENATORIAL COURTESY An informal Senate rule, which requires that the president seek the approval of his nominee for a federal appointment from the senator of the nominee's state.

SENIOR EXECUTIVE SERVICE A corps of about 8,500 high-level government administrators created in 1978 to provide rewards and incentives for top-ranking civil servants.

SENIORITY SYSTEM A custom followed in both houses of Congress that specifies that members with longer terms of continuous service will be given preference when committee chairpersons and holders of other significant posts are selected.

SEPARATE BUT EQUAL DOCTRINE The doctrine holding that segregation in schools and public accommodations does not imply the superiority of one race over another; rather, it implies that each race is entitled to separate but equal facilities.

SEPARATION OF POWERS The principle of dividing governmental powers among the executive, the legislative, and the judicial branches of government.

SERVICE SECTOR That sector of the economy that provides services—such as food services, insurance, and education—in contrast to that sector of the economy that produces goods.

SERVICE TO CONSTITUENTS FUNCTION One function of members of Congress, which consists of doing personal casework for constituents.

SEX DISCRIMINATION Overt behavior in which people are given differential or unfavorable treatment on the basis of sex. Any practice, policy, or procedure that denies equality of treatment to an individual or to a group.

SEX-PLUS DISCRIMINATION Harassment on the basis of sex, in violation of Title VII. This includes unwanted physical or verbal conduct or abuse of a sexual nature that interferes with a recipient's job performance or carries with it an implicit or explicit threat of adverse employment consequences.

SHORT BALLOT A ballot containing relatively few offices to be filled by election. In national elections the short ballot is used to vote for, at a maximum, four officials—the president, the vice president, a senator, and a representative. It is also used in some state elections.

SLANDER The public uttering of a statement that holds a person up for contempt, ridicule, or hatred, where the defamatory statement is made to, or within the hearing of, persons other than the defamed party.

SLIDING-SCALE TEST Used as a criterion in cases where a careful examination of the facts of each individual case must be undertaken.

SOCIAL CONFLICT Disagreements arising in society because of differing beliefs, values, and attitudes; conflicts over society's priorities and competition for scarce resources.

SOCIAL CONTRACT An agreement between individuals to establish a government and to abide by its rules. Early theorists saw the social contract as an agreement between the ruler and the people.

SOCIALIST NATIONS Those nations whose political philosophies advocate economic collectivism through governmental or worker group ownership of the means of production and distribution of goods. Basic aims are to replace competition for profit with cooperation and social responsibility and to secure an equitable distribution of income.

SOCIOECONOMIC CLASS A category of people within a society who have similar levels of income and similar types of occupations.

SOLID SOUTH A term describing the disposition of the post-Civil War southern states to vote for the Democratic party. Voting patterns in the South have begun to change.

SOVIET BLOC The Eastern European countries with communist regimes.

SPEAKER OF THE HOUSE The presiding officer in the House of Representatives. The Speaker is always a member of the majority party and is the most powerful and influential member of the House.

SPECIAL, OR LIMITED, JURISDICTION Extends to a particular class of cases, such as cases where the amounts of money in controversy is below a prescribed sum or cases that are subject to specific exceptions.

SPIN-OFF PARTY A new party formed by a dissident faction within a major political party. Usually, spin-off parties have emerged when a particular personality was at odds with the major party.

SPOILS SYSTEM The awarding of government jobs to political supporters and friends. Generally associated with President Andrew Jackson.

SPRING PREVIEW The beginning phase of the budgeting process for the federal government, occurring in the spring and during which all of the executive agencies are required to review their programs, goals, and activities.

STABILITY The extent to which public opinion remains constant over a period of time.

STAGFLATION A period of simultaneous high unemployment (economic stagnation) and rising prices (inflation).

STANDING COMMITTEE A permanent committee within the House or Senate that considers bills within a subject area.

STARE DECISIS "To stand on decided cases." The policy of courts to follow precedents established by the decisions of the past.

STATE CENTRAL COMMITTEE The principal organized structure of each political party within each state. Responsible for carrying out policy decisions of the party's state convention.

STATE OF THE UNION MESSAGE An annual message to Congress in which the president proposes his legislative program. The message is not only to Congress but also to the American people and to the world. It offers the opportunity to dramatize policies and objectives and to gain support through public opinion.

STATUTORY LAW Those laws that are laid down in statutes—laws enacted by Congress or a state legislature.

STATUTORY POWERS The powers created for the president through laws established by Congress.

STRATEGIC ARMS LIMITATION TREATY (SALT I) A treaty between the United States and the Soviet Union to stabilize the nuclear arms competition between the two countries. SALT I talks began in 1969 and agreements were signed on May 26, 1972.

STRATEGIC PETROLEUM RESERVE Established in 1975, the

▽

695

SPR is an emergency supply of oil maintained by the government.

STRAW POLL An informal survey of a small group to determine opinion.

STRIP-MINING A method of mining—also called open-cast mining—in which material is stripped from the surface without recourse to mine shafts or tunnels. It can have extremely detrimental environmental consequences.

SUBPOENA A legal writ requiring a person's appearance in court to give testimony.

SUBSTANTIVE LEGISLATION Laws that regulate specific issues or set up policies, as compared to procedural laws such as budgets or appropriations.

SUFFRAGE Right to vote; franchise.

SUNSET LEGISLATION A law requiring that an existing program be regularly reviewed for its effectiveness and terminated unless specifically extended as a result of this review.

SUPER TUESDAY A football metaphor referring to the date on which a large number of presidential primaries are held throughout the country. In 1984 Super Tuesday was March 20.

SUPPLEMENTAL APPROPRIATIONS Those appropriations authorized by Congress after the total budget has been passed. They can occur any time throughout the fiscal year.

SUPPLEMENTAL SECURITY INCOME (SSI) A federally financed and administered program established in 1974 to establish a nationwide minimum income for the aged, the blind, and the disabled.

SUPPLY-SIDE ECONOMICS An economic theory holding that reducing taxes and government spending on social welfare and reducing government regulation will stimulate saving and investment and increase the total supply of goods and services.

SUPREMACY CLAUSE The constitutional provision that makes the Constitution and federal laws superior to all state and local legislation.

SUPREMACY DOCTRINE A doctrine that asserts the superiority of national law over state or regional laws. This principle is rooted in Article VI of the Constitution, which provides that the Constitution, the laws passed by the national government under its constitutional powers, and all treaties comprise the supreme law of the land.

SYMBOLIC SPEECH Nonverbal expression of beliefs, which are given substantial protection by our courts.

SYMPATHY STRIKE A strike by a union in response to, or in sympathy with, another union's already existing strike.

SYNFUELS Synthetic fuels. Synthetic crude oil is made from coal by liquefaction. Synthetic natural gas, or substitute natural gas, is made from fossil fuels.

T

TARGET PRICE A price set by the government that it wishes farmers to receive for particular products. Target prices are typically set above market prices. Any difference is made up by government

in direct payments to farmers in the form of deficiency payments, described above.

TAX BRACKET A specified interval of income to which a specific and unique tax rate is applied. In a progressive taxation system, the higher the tax bracket, the greater the tax rate applied to that higher tax bracket.

TECHNICAL ASSISTANCE Sending experts with technical skills in agriculture, engineering, or business to aid other nations.

THIRD PARTY A political party other than the two major political parties (Republican and Democratic). Usually, third parties are composed of dissatisfied groups that have split from the major parties. They act as indicators of political trends and as safety valves for dissident groups.

THIRD-PARTY CANDIDATE A political candidate running under the banner of a party other than the two major political parties.

TICKET-SPLITTING Voting for candidates of two or more parties for different offices. For example, a voter splits her ticket if she votes for a Republican presidential candidate and for a Democratic senatorial candidate.

TOWN-MANAGER SYSTEM Form of city government in which voters normally elect three selectmen who then appoint a professional town manager who in turn appoints other officials.

TOWN MEETING The governing authority of a town. Qualified voters may participate in the election of officers and the passage of legislation.

TOWNSHIP Rural units of government based on federal land surveys of the American frontier in the 1780s. They have significantly declined in importance.

TRADE-OFF A compromise between divergent but mutually necessary elements, such as energy and the environment.

TRAGEDY OF THE COMMONS The overuse and destruction of common property resources.

TRANSFER PAYMENTS Money payments that are made by governments to individuals for which no services or goods are concurrently rendered. Examples are Social Security, unemployment insurance, and welfare payments.

TRANSFER SYSTEMS Government payments in cash or in kind made directly to individuals to increase their income. Examples are Social Security, food stamps, and Medicare.

TRANSFERS IN KIND Transfer payments in the form of goods or services—such as food stamps, low-cost housing, and government-provided education.

TRUMAN DOCTRINE The policy adopted by President Harry Truman in 1947 to halt communist expansion in southeastern Europe.

TRUSTEES The idea that a legislator should act according to his or her conscience and the broad interests of the entire society, often associated with the British statesman, Edmund Burke.

TWELFTH AMENDMENT An amendment to the Constitution, adopted in 1804, that specifies the separate election of the president and vice president by the electors.

TWENTY-FIFTH AMENDMENT An amendment to the Constitution adopted in 1967 that establishes procedures for filling vacancies in the two top executive offices and that makes provisions for situations involving presidential disability.

TWO-PARTY COMPETITION Two strong and solidly established political parties in competition for political control; both parties have a strong chance of winning an election.

TWO-PARTY SYSTEM An electoral system based on the division of voter loyalties between two major political parties; the traditional British system, which has been adopted in many Commonwealth countries and by the United States.

U

UNANIMOUS OPINION Agreement of all judges on the same opinion or determination.

UNICAMERAL LEGISLATURES Legislatures with only one legislative body, as compared to bicameral (two-house) legislatures, such as the United States Congress. Nebraska is the only state in the Union with a unicameral legislature.

UNCONTROLLABLES The spending that Congress, in principle, cannot control unless it changes an entire program.

UNION SHOP A business enterprise that allows non-union members to become employed, conditional on their joining the union by some specified date after employment begins.

UNIT RULE The practice among some state delegations to the national convention of voting in a bloc for a single presidential candidate, regardless of individual preference.

UNITARY SYSTEM A centralized governmental system in which local or subdivisional governments exercise only those powers given to them by the central government.

UNIVERSAL SUFFRAGE The right of all people to vote for their representatives.

U.S. TREASURY BONDS Securities that are evidence of debt that the federal government owes to those who paid for such securities.

V

VERTICAL EQUITY Equity that exists when those with a greater ability to pay bear a heavier tax burden than those with a smaller ability to pay; in other words, unequals are treated unequally.

VETO MESSAGE The president's formal explanation of his veto when he returns legislation to the Congress.

VOTER TURNOUT The percentage of citizens taking part in the election process; the number of eligible voters that actually "turn out" on election day to cast their ballot.

W

WAR POWERS ACT A law passed in 1973 emphasizing the right of Congress to declare war and spelling out the conditions under which the president can commit troops without congressional approval.

WASHINGTON COMMUNITY Individuals regularly involved with the political circles in Washington, D.C.

WATERGATE BREAK-IN The 1972 illegal entry into the Democratic campaign offices engineered by the Nixon re-election campaign.

WHIGS One of the foremost political organizations in the United States during the first half of the nineteenth century, formally established in 1836. The Whig party was dominated by the same anti-Jackson elements that had organized the national Republican party and represented a variety of regional interests. It fell apart as a national party in the early 1850s.

WHIPS Assistant floor leaders who aid the majority and minority floor leaders.

WHISTLE-BLOWER Someone who brings to public attention gross governmental inefficiency or an illegal action.

WHITE HOUSE OFFICE The staff agency under the Executive Office of the President, which includes most of the key personal and political advisers of the president. The office facilitates relations with Congress, executive agencies, the media, and the public.

WHITE HOUSE PRESS CORPS A group of reporters assigned full time to cover the presidency.

WHITE PRIMARY State primary elections that restrict voting only to whites; outlawed by the Supreme Court in 1944.

WINDFALL-PROFITS TAX A tax on the profits of the domestic oil industry. The purpose was to recapture for general use some of the profits the oil companies were expected to receive as a result of price deregulation.

WRIT OF CERTIORARI An order issued by a higher court to a lower court to send up the record of a case for review. It is the principal vehicle for U.S. Supreme Court review.

WRIT OF MANDAMUS An order issued by a court to compel performance of an act.

Y

YELLOW-DOG CONTRACT An anti-union device fostered by management. In such a contract, workers agree to remain nonunion as a condition of employment. Violation of the yellow-dog contract exposed a worker to a lawsuit by his or her employer, the result of which might be a court-imposed fine or, in some cases, imprisonment.

YELLOW JOURNALISM A derogatory term for sensationalistic, irresponsible journalism. Reputedly, the term is short for "Yellow Kid Journalism," an allusion to the cartoon "The Yellow Kid" in the old *New York World*, a paper especially noted for its sensationalism.

Z

ZERO-BASED BUDGETING A technique that requires budget planners to begin each budget with zero dollars and justify each item in the budget.

ZERO POPULATION GROWTH A stable rate of growth in population, where the birth rate equals but does not exceed the mortality rate.

Index

▽

Ability-to-pay principle (of taxation), 533
Abortion rights, 57, 118–119
Abrams v. United States, 107
Achison, David, 402
Acid rain, 572–573
ACORN, 651
Acquired Immune Deficiency Syndrome
    (AIDS), 187, 249, 250
ACTION, 378
Actionable, 113
Actual malice, 113
Adams, Frederick U., 53
Adams, John, 15, 47, 105, 231, 401, 484
Adams, John Quincy, 77, 232, 318, 375
Administrative Procedures Act of 1946, 393
Advice and consent, 381
Accuracy in Media (AIM), 287
Advisory Commission on Intergovernmental
    Relations, 82
AFSCME, 176–177, 471
Affirmative action, 24, 145
AFL-CIO, 340, 347, 348, 349, 356
Age discrimination, 178–80
Age Discrimination in Employment Act of
    1967, 179, 180, 444
Agencies, federal, 454, 457–463
    executive, 378
    regulatory, 459–463
Agenda setting, 416
Agnew, Spiro, 285, 395
Agricultural Adjustment Act (AAA), 525
Agricultural interest groups, 345–346
Agriculture, Department of, 397, 456, 459,
    569
Aid to Families with Dependent Children
    (AFDC), 83, 554–555
AIDS, 187, 249, 250
Air Pollution Control Act of 1955, 570
Air Quality Act of 1967, 571
Alien Act, 105

Alien and Sedition Acts of 1798, 105
Alien Enemies Act, 105
All the President's Men, 277
Altgeld, John P., 563
Amendment process, 51–52, 54, 408
Amendments:
    Eleventh (U.S. court jurisdiction), 490
    Twelfth (election of president), 319, 375,
        412
    Thirteenth (abolition of slavery), 132, 134,
        135
    Fourteenth (equal protection), 79, 100–101,
        114, 123, 132, 134, 135, 137, 138,
        144, 146, 148, 167, 427, 638
    Fifteenth (universal male suffrage), 79, 132,
        134, 135, 136, 148, 149, 168–169,
        374
    Sixteenth (income tax), 412
    Seventeenth (direct election of senators),
        419, 421
    Eighteenth (Prohibition), 51, 52
    Nineteenth (women's right to vote), 327,
        374
    Twenty-First (repeal of Prohibition), 51, 52
    Twenty-Second (limiting presidential term),
        394
    Twenty-Third (number of electors), 316
    Twenty-Fourth (ending poll tax), 149, 374
    Twenty-Fifth (presidential incapacity), 402,
        403, 410
    Twenty-Sixth (voting age of 18), 183, 184,
        327, 352, 374
    Twenty-Seventh (Equal Rights), 52, 54, 57,
        171–172, 196, 329
    Twenty-Eighth (congressional representation
        of District of Columbia), 54
    See also Bill of Rights
American Association of Retired Persons
    (AARP), 182
American Bankers Association, 341

American Bar Association, 351, 495
American Civil Liberties Union (ACLU), 116,
    123, 127, 189, 352
American Conservative Union (ACU), 617
American Coordinating Council on Political
    Education (ACCPE), 154
American Dental Association, 351
American Farm Bureau Federation, 345, 474
American Federation of Labor (AFL), 346,
    561
American Federation of State, County, and
    Municipal Employees (AFSCME), 176–
    177, 471
American Federation of Teachers (AFT), 349
American Indian Movement (AIM), 157
American Indian Policy Review Commission,
    158
American Indians against Desecration (AIAD),
    158
American Institute of Public Opinion (AIPO),
    201
American Life Lobby, 57
American Medical Association (AMA), 342,
    351, 549–550
American Nazi Party, 116
American Psychiatry Association, 188
American Security Council (ASC), 617
Americans for Constitutional Action, 356
Americans for Democratic Action (ADA), 354
American Society of Newspaper Editors, 285
American Women's Suffrage Association, 169
AMTRAK, 465
Anderson, John, 272, 273
Anderson, Terry, 599
Andrews, Charles M., 32
Anthony, Susan B., 168
Antiballistic missiles (ABMs), 594
Antiballistic Missile Treaty, 616
Anti-Federalists, 46, 47, 77, 231, 242, 484
Anti-Ku Klux Klan Act, 136

▽

Appeals, to Supreme Court, 490–491
Appeals courts, 488, 495–496
Appellate jurisdiction, 486–487
Appointment power, 377–378
Apportionment, legislative, 638–639
Appropriations bills, 528
Appropriations Committee, 433, 529, 530
Aquino, Corazón, 382–383, 579, 580
Aristocracy, natural, 466, 430
Aristotle, 24, 481
Arms Control and Disarmament Agency, 378
Arledge, Roone, 269
Armstrong, William, 439
Arterton, Christopher, 212, 270
Arthur, Chester, 402
Articles of Confederation, 30, 37–39, 40, 41, 42, 43, 45, 48, 71, 77, 78, 371, 410, 415, 465, 583
Asian-Americans, 22, 133, 134, 159
Askew, Reubin, 202
Assad, Hafez, 596
Assembly, right of, 115–116
Associated Press, 264
Association of Community Organizations for Reform Now (ACORN), 651
Association of General Contractors, 351
Athenian model of direct democracy, 12–13
Australian ballot, 312
Authority:
  budget, 531
  legislative, 531

Babbitt, Bruce, 245
"Baby Doe" rule, 119–120
Backdoor funding, 531
Bad-tendency rule, 108
Baker, Howard, 423
Baker v. Carr, 502
Bakke, Alan, 146
Balanced Budget and Emergency Deficit Control Act, 539
Ballots, 312–315
  Australian, 312
  Indiana, 313
  long, 313–314
  Massachusetts, 313
  office-block, 313
  party-column, 313
  short, 313, 315
Banfield, Edward, 650
Bankruptcy Court, 488
Banks, Dennis, 73
Barber, James David, 289–290, 422
Barron v. Baltimore, 100
Barry, Marion, 188
Bay of Pigs invasion, 606
Beard, Michael, 364
Beauty contest, 296, 308
Benefits-received principle (of taxation), 533
Bentsen, Lloyd, 540
Bergland, David, 302

Bernard, Alvin, 126
Bernstein, Carl, 277
Berri, Nabih, 596
Betts v. Brady, 123
Bicameralism, 410–411
Bicameral legislature, 42
Bilandic, Michael, 238
Bilingual education, 155
Bill of Rights, 21, 49–50, 99–116, 352, 503–504
  defined, 99
  freedom of expression, 105–112
  freedom of the press, 281
  freedom of religion, 101–104
  incorporation theory and, 100–101
  nationalization of, 99–100
  right to assemble, 115–116
  right to petition the government, 115–116
Biotechnology, 569
Black, Hugo, 113
Black Caucus, 445
Blackmun, Harry A., 110, 119
Blacks, 134–150
  affirmative action and, 145
  civil rights movement and, 141–143
  Declaration of Independence and, 22
  employment of, 145–148
  mean income of, 135
  as percentage of population, 133
  as political candidates, 295
  political opinions of, 212, 214
  political participation of, 148–150, 294
  reverse discrimination and, 145–148
  in schools, 138–141
Blackstone, Sir William, 481
Blanket primary, 311
Blasi, Vincent, 506–507
Block grants, 85–86
Board of Governors of the Federal Reserve, 521, 522
Boorstin, Daniel J., 259
Boycott, secondary, 564
Brademas, John, 298
Bradley, Tom, 629
Bradley, William, 534
Brandeis, Louis, 107, 108, 117
Brennan, William J., Jr., 113, 501
Brokaw, Tom, 267
Brookings Institution, 522
Brown, Edmund G., Jr., 73, 300
Brown, Linda Carol, 138
Brown, Oliver, 138
Brown v. Board of Education of Topeka, 138, 140, 505
Brownlee, Travis, 302
Bryan, Rich, 91
Bryan, William Jennings, 232, 251
Bryant, Anita, 186
Brzezinski, Zbigniew, 605
Buchanan, James, 387
Buckley, Jim, 306
Buckley, William, 599

Budget authority, 531
Budget, federal, 520, 532
  deferral and, 528
  deficit, 536, 538
  defined, 526
  fall review of, 527
  spring preview of, 527
Budget and Impoundment Control Act of 1974, 394, 404
Budget resolutions:
  concurrent, 529
  continuing, 528
  first, 528
  second, 528
Bull Moose Progressive Party, 250
Bureaucracy, 449–478
  congressional control of, 475–476
  control of, 451–452
  defined, 452
  history of, 466–468
  nature of, 452–454
  organization of, 455–465
  reform of, 470–476
  size of, 454–455
  staffing of, 465–470
  whistle-blowers and, 472
Bureau of Indian Affairs (BIA), 157
Burger, Warren, 111, 112, 114, 123, 491, 495
Burger Court, 503, 505–509, 510, 638
Burke, Edmund, 415
Burr, Aaron, 15, 318, 375
Bush, George, 292, 370, 402, 403
Business cycle, political:
  evidence of, 526
  theory of, 526
Business interest groups, 342–345
Business Roundtable, 342, 344–345
Busing, 139–140
Byrd, Robert C., 439
Burne, Jane, 238

Cabinet, 378, 396–398, 456–457
Cabot, John, 32
Caddell, Patrick, 207, 213, 300, 304
Cadre, 229
Calendar of Business, 441
Calhoun, John C., 77, 78
Campaign consultants, 300
Campaigns, 291–307
  changes in, 296–297
  finance reform for, 304–307
  financing of, 297–298, 304–307, 340
  issues in, 333–335
  machinery of, 295–300
  media and, 271–276, 298, 300
  organization of, 299
  polls and, 303–304
  primaries and, 307–316
  professional, 297–299
  strategy for, 300–306
  workers for, 298–299

Campbell, Allen K., 468
Candidates:
    blacks as, 294–295
    image of, 300, 332–333
    independent, 303
    lawyers as, 294–295
    motivation of, 291–293
    qualifications of, 293–295
    selling of, 271
    third-party, 303
    voter perception of, 332–333
    women as, 294–295
Cannon, Joseph G., 430
Canvassing board, 315
Canton, 16
Capitalism, 243
Capital punishment, 124–126
Capitol Switchboard, 446
Carswell, C. Harold, 496
Carter, Jimmy, 19, 66, 155, 169, 198, 206,
    207, 210, 213, 219, 233, 245, 271, 272,
    273, 300, 304, 319, 322, 325, 328, 329,
    330, 333, 334, 373, 382, 383, 386, 387,
    389, 390, 400, 451, 462, 468, 469, 486,
    499, 500, 501, 526, 537, 564, 594, 602,
    605, 610
Case amendment, 404
Casework, 414
Castro, Fidel, 285, 395
Categorical grants, 84–85
Caucus, 310
Center for Defense Information, 280
Center for Immigrants' Rights, 161
Central Intelligence Agency (CIA), 106, 395,
    459, 598, 599, 600, 602, 605, 606
Certiorari, writ of, 491
Chafee, John H., 439
Challenge, 316
Chase, Samuel, 501
Chavez, Cesar, 154
Checks and balances, 44, 45
Cheney, Dick, 439
Chernobyl, 566, 567, 574
Chicano National Youth Movement, 154
Chief diplomat, 375, 381–384
Chief executive, 375–379
Chief legislator, 375, 384–386
Chief of state, 375, 376–377
Children, rights of, 184–186
Children's Bureau, 563
China syndrome, the, 566
Church, Frank, 606
Church, separation from state, 101–105
Churchill, Winston, 588
Church-related schools, 104
Cities, 322, 643–644, 647–650
Citizen's Choice, 344
Citizens Committee for Immigration Reform,
    161
Citizenship:
    dual, 100
    of minorities, 135

requirements for, 23
Citrus Growers Association, 474
Civil Aeronautics Board (CAB), 459, 461,
    463, 525
Civil Conservation Corps (CCC), 523
Civil law, 184, 481
Civil liberties, 97–129
    freedom of expression, 105–112
    freedom of the press, 113–115
    freedom of religion, 101–104
    rights of accused vs. rights of society, 120–
        124
    right to abortion, 119–120
    right to assemble and petition the
        government, 115, 116
    right to privacy, 117–118
Civil Rights Acts, 135–140, 143–145, 147
Civil Rights Cases, 136–137
Civil Rights Commission, 143, 144, 188, 378
Civil rights movement, 113, 141–143
Civil service, 377, 388, 466–468, 450
Civil Service Commission, 467, 468
Civil Service Reform Act of 1883, 467
Civil Service Reform Act of 1978, 469, 470,
    472
Civil War, 50, 73, 77–79, 132, 134, 135,
    137, 168, 198, 210, 229, 232, 242, 392,
    560, 586, 631
Civil War amendments, 135
Claims Court, 188
Clark, "Dick," 267
Clark, Ed, 249
Classified Information Procedures Act, 106
Class politics, 242
Clay, Henry, 232, 375
Clean Air Acts, 571, 572
Clean Water Act, 571
Clear and present danger test, 107
Clergy and Laity Concerned, 617
Cleveland, Grover, 387, 403
Climate control, 359
Closed primary, 311
Closed shop, 564
Cloture, 418
Coalition for American Rivers, 360
Coalition for Environment-Safe Energy
    Organizations, 546
Coalition for Peace through Strength, 617
Coalition of Northeast Governors, 89
Coattail effect, 313
Cochran, Thad, 439
Code of Federal Regulations, 565
Code of Hammurabi, 167
Coercive Acts, 34
Cold War, 219, 386–594
Colfax, Schuyler, 396
Collective bargaining, 561
Colonial America, 31–49
    British rule of, 33–35
    Continental Congresses of, 34–36
    Declaration of Independence, 35–36
    early settlements in, 31–33

Columbus, Christopher, 4
Commander in chief, 375, 379–381
Commerce and Labor Department, 397
Commerce clause, 75
Commerce, Department of, 397, 456, 459
Commercial speech, 110
Commission plan, 647
Committee for the Study of Handgun Misuse,
    364
Committee on Political Education (COPE),
    347
Committee on the Present Danger, 348
Committees, 431–435
    conference, 434
    joint, 434
    select, 434
    selection of members in, 435
    standing, 432–433
    structure of, 431–434
    types of, 432–435
Common Cause, 352, 362
Common law, 185, 482
Common Sense, 34–35, 264, 326
Communist Party, 248
Comparable worth, 176–177
Compliance, 11
    habits of, 11–12
Comprehensive Employment and Training Act
    (CETA), 522
Computers, and lobbying, 355
Concurrent majority, 77, 78
Concurrent powers, 70
Concurring opinion, 492
Confederal system of government, 63–64
Confederation, 31, 37
Conference committee, 434
Conflict:
    political, 23–24
    resolution, 416
    social, 9–11
Congress, 407–448
    bicameralism of, 410–411
    bureaucracy and, 475–476
    creation of, 409–411
    functions of, 412–416
    House-Senate differences, 416–419
    lawmaking by, 413, 441–442
    leadership of, 435–440
    new directions in, 444–445
    powers of, 411–412
    public confidence in, 409
    seniority system in, 435
Congressional Budget Office (CBO), 431, 438,
    528, 529
Congressional committees. See Committees
Congressional Directory, 446
Congressional elections, 421–427
    candidates for, 294, 421–424
    incumbents in, 424
    in 1986, 425–427
Congressional ethics, 442–443
Congressional reapportionment, 427–428

Congressional Record, 360
Congressional Research Service (CRS), 431
Congress of Industrial Organizations (CIO), 347
Congress of the Confederation, 38, 39
Congresspersons:
  characteristics of, 181, 419–421
  contacting, 446
  decision making by, 440
  election of, 421–427
  pay of, 428–430
  perks of, 428–430
  privileges and immunities of, 431
  service to constituents by, 414
  staffs of, 430–431
Congresswomen's Caucus, 445
Connecticut Compromise, 43–44, 410
Connor, Eugene, 141
CONRAIL, 465
Consensus, 200
Consent Calendar, 442
Consent of the governed, 36
Consent of the people, 13, 33
Conservative coalition, 440
Conservatives for a Constitutional Convention, 57
Consolidation, 646–647
Constituents, as lobbyists, 359–360
Constitution, 29–59
  amendment process, 51–52, 54
  as basis for American federalism, 67–70
  changes in, 51–56
  commerce clause of, 75–76
  custom and usage in, 55–56
  drafting of, 39–45
  elastic clause of, 69
  English background of, 4
  establishment clause of, 102
  free exercise clause of, 104
  full faith and credit clause of, 71
  on governmental powers, 16, 68–70
  on government structure, 16
  interpretation of, 55–56
  liberty and, 21
  national convention provision of, 54–55
  necessary and proper clause of, 69, 74, 75
  preamble to, 1
  president's foreign policy making powers and, 600–601
  privileges and immunities under, 71–72
  ratification and, 30, 31, 45–49
  republican form of government in, 13–14
  on state government, 641
  states and, 630–631
  supremacy clause of, 72–73
  See also Amendments; Bill of Rights; State constitutions
Constitutional Congress, 15
Constitutional Convention, 5, 31, 39–45, 64, 65, 67, 371, 634
Constitutional Convention Procedures Act, 55

Constitutional democracy, 16
Constitutional initiative, 634
Constitutional monarchy, 8
Constitutional power, 386–388
Consultants, political, 300
Consumer Federation of America, 352
Consumer Product Safety Commission (CPSC), 354, 461
Containment, 590–593
Continental Congresses, 34–36, 37, 40
Convention delegates, election of, 254
Conventions, political, 51, 235–237, 312
Cook, Timothy E., 423
Cooley, Thomas, 643
Cooley's rule, 643
Coolidge, Calvin, 387, 390
Cooperative federalism, 80–81
Corman, James, 298
Corn Growers Association, 474
Corporations:
  government, 463–465
  multinational, 611–613
Corrupt Practices Acts, 306
Corwin, Edwin S., 600
Council for Environmental Quality, 399, 572
Council-manager plan, 648
Council of Economic Advisors (CEA), 399, 522, 524, 526, 528
Councils of Government (COGs), 647
Counties, 644
Courts, 485–515
  of appeals, 488, 489, 495–496
  district, 487–488, 495, 499, 500
  federal, 487–494
  jurisdiction of, 489–90
  reviewing, 487
  state, 640–41
  See also Law; Supreme Court
Cox, Archibald, 196, 395
Cox v. New Hampshire, 116
Cranston, Allan, 202, 210, 439
Crawford, William H., 375
Credentials Committee, 312
Criminal law, 189, 481
Criminal rights:
  of accused, 120–124
  of juveniles, 184–186
Crocker, Richard, 240
Crossley, Archibald, 201
Crump, Edward, 649
Cuban Americans, 155
Culp, Robert, 262
Culture, 18
  See also Political culture
Cuomo, Mario, 8, 221

Dahl, Robert A., 46
Dairy program, 558
Daley, Richard J., 238, 308, 309, 649, 650
D'Amato, Alfonse M., 8

Davidson, J. McBride, 649
Davidson, Roger, 415
Davis, Angela, 302
Davis, Billy, 302
Davis v. Bandemer, 427
Davison, W. P., 277
Dawes Act, 156
Dayton, Jonathan, 41
Dean, John, III, 118, 395
Death penalty, 124–126
Deaver, Michael K., 361
Debates:
  in Congress, 418
  political, 271–276
Debs, Eugene, 107, 248
Debt, public, 536–541
  burden of, 536–539
  financing, 539
  Gramm-Rudman-Hollings Act, 540–541
  per capita, 537
  See also Political economy
Declaration of Independence, 15, 35–36, 47, 99, 634
Defamation of character, 112
Defense, Department of, 397, 456, 457, 459, 602, 606, 607
Defense Intelligence Agency, 606
Defense policy. *See* Foreign policy
Deferral (and federal budget), 528
Deficiency payments, 558
Delegates, instructed, 415
Democracy:
  constitutional, 16
  defined, 12
  direct, 12–14, 639–640
  ideal vs. real, 16–18
  origins of, 12–13
  pluralism and, 18
  representative, 14, 16
Democratic National Committee, 254, 302, 308, 394
Democratic Republicans, 231, 242
Democratic Task Force on Tax Reform, 535
Democrats, 231–232
  in 1986 elections, 6–9
  political culture and, 243
  See also Political parties
Demographic traits, 212–215
Dennis, Delmar, 302
Depository Institution Deregulation and Monetary Control Act of 1980, 463
Deregulation, 463
Detente, 594
Deukmejian, George, 73
Devine, Donald, 217
Dewey, Thomas E., 207
Dickenson, John, 99
Dillingham-Sanchez Protocol, 384
Dillon, John F., 642
Dillon's rule, 642
Diplomacy, 582, 583

Direct democracy, 639–640
  Athenian model of, 12–13
  defined, 12
  founders' fear of, 13–14
  state and local government and, 639–640
Direct-mail methods, and lobbying, 355
Direct primaries, 424
Dirksen, Everett M., 144, 430
Discharge Calendar, 442
Discharge petition, 432
Discrimination:
  age, 178–180
  reverse, 24
  sex, 173–177
  sex-plus, 174
  what to do with, 189
  See also Minorities; Minority rights
Disenfranchised person, 253
Dissenting opinion, 492
District courts, 487–488, 495, 499, 500
Districts, special, 645–646
Dixiecrat Party, 251
Dodge, Earl F., 302
Doe v. Bolton, 119
Doggett, Lloyd, 540
Dole, Elizabeth Hanford, 455
Dole, Robert, 370, 423, 439, 455
Domestic policy, 545–576
  energy and the environment, 566–574
  farmers, income security protection for, 557–559
  labor-management regulation, 560–565
  medical care, 549–551
  poverty, 551–557
  Social Security, 547–549
  worker health and safety, 565–566
Donovan, Raymond, 361
Dornan, Robert, 298
Douglas, William O., 113, 117, 471
Douglass, Frederick, 134
Dred Scott v. Sanford, 134, 512
Drew, Elizabeth, 291
Dual citizenship, 100
Dual federalism, 80
Dye, Thomas, 639
Dyson, Brian, 213

Eagle Forum, 57, 172
Eastland, James, 420
Easton, David, 9, 10
Economic aid, 582
Economic policy. See Domestic policy;
  Political economy
Economic regulation, 80
Economic Report of the President, 527
Education, Department of, 397, 456
Education and Labor Committee, 433
Ehrlich, Paul, 199
Eisenhower, Dwight D., 139, 143, 233, 236,
  266, 292, 312, 386, 387, 390, 391, 392,

402, 403, 501, 509, 526, 537, 564, 591,
  600, 606, 609
Elastic clause, 69
Elazar, Daniel J., 66
Elderly, 177–182
  political opinions of, 180–182
  rights of, 178–182
Elder, Shirley, 342
Elections, 304–335
  ballots, 312–315
  congressional, 6–9, 320, 421–427
  fraud prevention, 315–316
  mechanics of, 312–315
  national convention, 312
  presidential, 374
  primaries, 307–311
  vote counting, 315–316
  voter turnout for, 319–325
  See also Voters; Voting
Electoral College, 44, 244, 316–319, 375
Electorate, 5
Electors, 316
  commitment of, 318
  "faithless," 318
Electronic media, 267, 285–286
  See also Media; Television
Elites, 17
Elite theory, 17
Elitism, 17
Emergency powers of the president, 392
Energy, Department of, 606
Energy, and the environment, 566–574
  energy-environment tradeoff, 569–570
  nuclear power, 567–569
  pollution, 571
Energy Research and Development Agency,
  378
Enforcement Act of 1870, 135
Engel v. Vitale, 102
Engels, Friedrich, 563
Enlightened despotism, 24
Entitlements, 530
Enumerated powers, 411–412
Environment, 566–574
  energy-environment tradeoff, 569–570
  government regulation and, 570–573
  nuclear power, 567–69
  pollution, 571
  working for a clean, 574
Environmental Defense Fund, 574
Environmental impact statement (EIS), 572
Environmental legislation, 571
Environmental Protection Agency (EPA), 457,
  459, 461, 569, 570, 572, 573, 574
Epperson v. Arkansas, 104
Epstein, Leon D., 229
Epton, Bernard, 238
Equal access law, 285
Equal Employment Opportunity Commission
  (EEOC), 145, 170, 174, 175, 189, 461
Equalization, 85

Equal Pay Act of 1963, 175–176
Equal Rights Amendment (ERA), 52, 54, 57,
  71–72, 196, 210, 329
Equity:
  horizontal, 532
  vertical, 532
Era of good feeling, 231
Era of personal politics, 231
Ervin, Sam, 395
Espionage Act, 106–107
Espy, Mike, 426
Establishment clause, 102
Ethics, congressional, 142–143
Ethics in Government Act of 1978, 361
Ethnic groups, 134
European Recovery Program, 587
Evans, Brock, 574
Evans, Cooper, 307
Exclusionary rule, 122, 124
Executive agencies, independent, 456–459
Executive agreements, 383–384, 600
Executive branch:
  foreign policy making by, 602–607
  state, 634–637
  See also Presidency; Presidential powers
Executive Calendar, 441
Executive immunity, 393–394
Executive Office of the President (EOP), 399–
  400
Executive orders, 392–393, 606
Export control, 611
Express powers, 68, 371, 388
Expression, freedom of, 105–112
Extradition, 72, 73
Extraordinary majorities, 64

Factions, 41–42, 227
Fair Labor Standards Act of 1938, 175, 562
Fairness doctrine, 115, 283–284
"Faithless" electors, 318
Fall review (of federal budget), 527
Falwell, Jerry, 19, 210, 280, 569
Farber, Myron, 114
Farm Credit Administration, 461
Farm programs, 557–559
  history of, 557–558
  problems with, 558–559
  who benefits from, 559
Faubus, Orville, 139
Federal Aviation Administration (FAA), 351
Federal budget, 520, 532
  See also Budget, federal; Political economy
Federal budget process, 526–530
Federal Bureau of Investigation (FBI), 106,
  395, 477, 600, 606
Federal civil service, 466–468
Federal Commission on Pornography, 111
Federal Communications Commission (FCC),
  115, 281, 282, 283–285, 459, 461
Federal courts, 487–494

Federal deficit, 536, 538
Federal Deposit Insurance Corporation
    (FDIC), 461, 465
Federal Election Campaign Acts of 1972 and
    1974, 306–307, 356
Federal Election Commission (FEC), 246,
    306, 307, 340
Federal Emergency Relief Administration, 525
Federal Environmental Pesticide Control Act
    Amendments, 571
Federal government:
    constitutional powers of, 68–70
    state governments vs., 72–81
    supremacy of, 72–73
    See also Bureaucracy; Government
Federal Insecticide, Fungicide, and
    Rodenticide Act of 1947, 570
Federalism, 62–94
    constitutional basis for, 67–70
    contemporary issues concerning, 91–92
    cooperative, 80–81
    defined, 80
    dual, 80
    fiscal side of, 84–88
    historical reasons for, 64
    horizontal, 70–72
    new, 82–84
    regionalism vs., 88–90
    "shifting," 86
Federalist Papers, 13, 46, 67, 264, 502, 513
Federalists, 15, 46, 47, 75, 77, 231, 466, 484
Federal Mediation and Conciliation Service,
    378
Federal Open Market Committee (FOMC),
    521
Federal Register, 393
Federal Regulation of Lobbying Act, 360
Federal Reserve Act of 1913, 521
Federal Reserve Board. See Board of
    Governors of the Federal Reserve
Federal system, 64
Federal Trade Commission (FTC), 354, 455,
    461
Federal Water Pollution Control Act of 1955,
    571
Federation for American Immigration Reform,
    161
Feinstein, Dianne, 188
Feldstein, Martin, 399
Felton, Rebecca Latimer, 169
Feminine Mystique, The, 170
Feminist movement, 169–177
Fenno, Richard, 426
Ferraro, Geraldine, 166, 234, 276, 370
Fields, Jack, 298
"Fighting words," 112
Filibustering, 418
Fillmore, Millard, 387
Finances, public. See Political economy
Fiorina, Morris, 414
Firefighters Local v. Stotts, 147

First National Bank v. Belotti, 110
First-strike capabilities, 594
Fiscal policy, 521, 522–526
Fiscal year, 83
Fitzgerald, A. Earnest, 472
Flanigan, William H., 322
Fletcher, James, 461
Fluidity, of public opinion, 198
Flying Senior Citizens of the U.S.A., 182
Foley, Thomas S., 439
Food and Drug Administration (FDA), 462,
    569
Food stamp program, 556
Force Bill, 78
Ford, Gerald, 272, 273, 386, 387, 389, 395,
    403, 455, 499, 501, 506, 526, 537, 610
Foreign policy, 577–619
    as campaign issue, 333–334
    changing directions of, 594–595
    Cold War and, 586–594
    containment, 590–591
    defined, 582–583
    detente, 594
    diplomacy and, 583
    economic, 611
    executive branch sources of, 602–607
    history of, 583–600
    interdependence of nations and, 581–582
    Iran and, 599–600
    isolationism, 584, 585
    military-industrial complex and, 607–610
    multinational corporations, 611–613
    national security policy, 582
    nuclear freeze movement and, 614–615
    presidential leadership techniques and, 602
    president's power and, 600–601, 610–611
    terrorism, 596
    United Nations and, 578
Foreign policy process, 582
Fortas, Abe, 496
Fourteen Points, 585
Franchise, 326–327
    See also Voting rights
Franking, 429
Franklin, Benjamin, 41, 47, 464
Fraternity, 22
Frazier, Lynn, 640
Freedom of Information Act of 1966, 477
Freedoms. See Civil liberties
Free exercise clause, 104
Free speech, 105–112
Free Soil Party, 251
Fremont, James C., 232
Friedan, Betty, 170
Friedman, Milton, 538
Friends of the Earth, 91, 574
Full faith and credit clause, 71
Fulton, Robert, 75
Functional consolidation, 646
Fundamental Orders of Connecticut, 33
Funds, impoundment of, 394

Furness, Betty, 485

Gag orders, 113–114
Galbraith, John Kenneth, 610
Gallaway, Lowell, 555
Gallup, George, 200, 207
Gallup poll, 19, 26, 173, 187, 194, 198, 201,
    203, 204, 212, 218, 219
Gandhi, Rajiv, 141
Gannett Company, Inc. v. De Pasquale, 114
Garfield, James A., 387, 401, 402, 467
Garner, John Nance, 400
Garreau, Joel, 86
Garth, David, 629
Gay rights, 186–188
Gender gap, 215, 329
General Accounting Office (GAO), 346, 431,
    472, 529
General Allotment Act of 1887, 156
General jurisdiction, 486
General law city, 643
General sales tax, 627
General Services Administration (GSA), 378,
    451, 458–459
Generational effects, 212
Gephardt, Richard, 245, 439
Gerry, Elbridge, 42, 427, 428
Gerrymandering, 427, 428, 429
Gibbons, Thomas, 75–76
Gibbons v. Ogden, 75–76
Gideon, Clarence Earl, 123
Gideon v. Wainwright, 123, 504
Gitlow v. New York, 108
Glaser, Norm, 91
Glenn, John, 202
Goldberg, Arthur J., III, 113
Goldman, Emma, 60
Goldwater, Barry, 220, 270, 328, 331, 333,
    510
Gompers, Samuel, 561, 562
Gorbachev, Michail, 616
Government:
    confederal system of, 63–64
    defined, 11
    direct, 12–44
    employment, 454–456, 468, 469–471
    federal system of, 64 (see also Federalism)
    importance of, 542
    limited, 16
    media and, 277, 284–285
    principles of democratic, 16
    representative democratic, 329–330
    republican, 14, 16
    right to petition the, 115–116
    unitary system of, 63
    See also Federal government; Local
        government; State government
Government corporations, 463–465
Government in the Sunshine Act, 471
Government Printing Office, 466

Governors, 634–636
Grace Commission, 473
Grace, Peter, 473
Grade banding, 470–471
Gramm-Latta budget resolution, 540
Gramm-Rudman-Hollings Act of 1985, 538–
 549, 540–541
Gramm, William P., 540
Grandfather clause, 149
Grant, Ulysses, 132, 394
Grants:
 block, 85–86
 categorical, 84–85
 project, 85
Gray Panthers, 182
Great Compromise, 43
Great Depression, the, 80–82, 200, 219, 232,
 342, 345, 389, 467, 522, 525, 547, 562
Greenback Party, 251
Grenada invasion, 267, 278, 284–285, 595
Griswold v. Connecticut, 117
Gross national product (GNP), 335, 521, 526
Grovey v. Townsend, 149
Guiteau, Charles J., 467
Gun control, 364

Habits of compliance, 11–12
Haig, Alexander, 605
Haldeman, H. R., 395
Hall, Gus, 302
HALT, 513
Hamilton, Alexander, 15, 17, 39, 41, 42, 49,
 50, 75, 231, 502, 512
Hammurabi, Code of, 167
Hancock, John, 36
Handgun ban, 364
Handgun Control, Inc., 340, 364
Handicapped, rights of, 183
"Hands across America" project, 5
Harding, Warren, 107, 232, 307, 387, 390,
 401, 585
Harper v. Virginia State Board of Elections,
 149
Harrington, Michael, 552
Harris, Louis, 205, 614
Harrison, Benjamin, 318, 375
Harrison, William Henry, 387, 401, 486
Harris poll, 205, 303, 614
Hart, Gary, 91, 202, 205, 213, 292, 300,
 302–303, 304, 310, 370
Hart, Peter, 300
Hart, Philip A., 430
Hatch Act of 1939, 306, 467, 468
Hatcher, Richard G., 630
Hayes, Rutherford B., 375, 387
Haynsworth, Clement F., Jr., 496
Head Start, 522
Health and Human Services, Department of,
 397, 456, 457, 459, 526, 603
Health. *See* Worker health and safety

Hearst, William Randolph, 265
"Heckler's" veto, 112
Helms, Jesse, 220
Help Abolish Legal Tyranny (HALT), 513
Hispanics, 23, 499, 642
Hitler, Adolf, 198, 588
Hoffa, Jimmy, 347
Hofstadter, Richard, 286
Hollings, Ernest, 202
Holmes, Larry, 302
Holmes, Oliver Wendell, 106, 108, 480, 481,
 501
Home rule city, 643
Homosexual rights, 186–188
Hoover, Herbert, 243, 387, 389, 394, 396,
 525, 537, 634
Horizontal equity, 532
Horizontal federalism, 70–72
House Calendar, 442
House committees, 433
House of Representatives:
 creation of, 410–411
 debate in, 418
 lawmaking in, 441–442
 leadership of, 436–438
 majority leader of, 436–437
 minority leader of, 437
 prestige of, 418
 rules of, 418
 Senate vs., 416–419
 size of, 417–418
 Speaker of, 436
 whips in, 437
 See also Congress
House Rules Committee, 434–435
Housing and Urban Development,
 Department of, 397, 456
Huff, Richard, 298
Human Life Amendment, 57
Humphrey, Hubert, 251, 328, 387
Hunter, William, 464
Hylton v. United States, 485
Hyperpluralism, 625

Idaho Environment Council, 91
Ideologue, 220
Ideology, political, 219–220
Image building, 300
Immigration and Naturalization Service (INS),
 476
Immigration rights, 161
Impeachment, 394–395, 500
Implied powers, 69
Impoundment of funds, 394
Inalienable rights, 22, 36
Income distribution, 10
Income security, 547–549
Income tax. *See* Taxation, federal; Taxes,
 federal
Income transfer program, 554

Incomes policy, 521
Incorporation theory, 100
Incumbency, 424
Independent candidate, 303
Independent executive agencies, 457–459
Independent regulatory agencies, 459–463
Independent voters, 296, 332
Indiana ballot, 313
Indians. *See* Native Americans
Inherent powers, 68, 388
Initiative, 13, 639
Injunction, 74, 490
In re Gault, 186
Institute of Electrical and Electronic
 Engineers, 351
Institutions, 5
Instructed delegates, 415
Integration, of schools, 138–141
Intelligence community, 605–607
Intensity, of public opinion, 198
Interest groups, 339–365
 agricultural, 345–346
 business, 342–345
 defined, 341
 direct techniques of, 354–358
 foreign governments and, 352–353
 indirect techniques of, 358
 labor, 346–349
 lobbying by, 354, 355
 number of, 342
 power of, 362–363
 professional, 351
 public employee, 349–351
 public interest, 351–352
 role of, 341
 single-interest, 352
 strategies of, 353
Interior, Department of the, 397, 456, 459,
 572
Internal Revenue Service (IRS), 11, 117, 477,
 535
International Atomic Energy Agency, 566
Internationalism, 585–586
Interposition, 77
Interstate Commerce Commission (ICC), 459,
 461, 462
Interstate compacts, 72, 646
Interstate extradition, 72, 73
Interstate Oil and Gas Compact of 1935, 72
Interventionism, 584–585
"Intolerable Acts," 34
Iranian connection (foreign policy), 599–600
Iranian hostage crisis, 269
Iron curtain, 588
Iron triangle, 474–475
Isolationism, 584–585
Issue voting, 333–335

Jackson, Andrew, 77, 229, 242, 375, 387,
 396, 398, 465, 466, 511, 634
▽

Jackson, James, 76
Jackson, Jesse, 19, 150, 301, 335, 370
Jacobson, David, 599
Janklow, William, 73
Jay, John, 48, 67, 371, 501
Jefferson, Thomas, 7, 15, 35, 101, 105, 231, 318, 375, 385, 387, 394, 401, 403, 466, 484, 583
Jeffersonians, 231–232
Jenco, Martin, 599
Jennings, M. Kent, 208–209
Jewell, Malcolm E., 234
Jim Crow laws, 79, 138, 141
Johnson, Andrew, 135, 386, 387, 486
Johnson, Lyndon B., 85, 144, 145, 149, 195, 233, 269, 270, 292, 310, 331, 333, 334, 374, 380, 384, 387, 389, 402, 403, 455, 499, 501, 522, 526, 537, 550, 552, 591, 600
Johnson, Sonia, 302
Joint committee, 434
Joint Economic Committee, 566
Judges, 495–501
    background of, 496–500
    party affiliation of, 501
    qualifications of, 500–501
    selection of, 495
    state, 641
Judicial activism, 502–503, 506–507
Judicial restraint, 502–503
Judicial review, 55, 483–485, 502–503
Judiciary, 479–515
    court jurisdiction, 485–490
    federal courts, 487–494
    federal judges, 495–501
    state, 487, 640–641
    See also Law; Supreme Court
Judiciary Act of 1789, 484
Judiciary Committee, 495
Jurisdiction, 485–490
    appellate, 486–487
    defined, 485–486
    federal, 489–490
    general, 486
    limited, 486
    original, 484, 486–487
    special, 486
Jurisdictional dispute, 564
Justice, Department of, 397, 456, 459, 510
Justiciable question, 427
Juveniles, rights of, 183–186

Kangaroo court, 186
Kanin, Garson, 179
Karst, Kenneth, 100
Kelley, Florence, 563
Kelley, William D., 563
Kelly, Edmond, 563
Kemp, Jack, 370, 439, 535
Kennan, George F., 590, 591

Kennedy, Edward ("Ted"), 220, 420
Kennedy, John F., 139, 144, 210, 233, 243, 271, 277, 318, 319, 322, 372, 373, 375, 380, 386, 387, 389, 390, 391, 392, 401, 402, 403, 420, 452, 501, 522, 537, 551–552, 591, 593, 600, 603, 605, 606
Kennedy, Joseph P., 420
Kennedy, Robert F., 420
Kennedy, Rose, 420
Key, V. O., Jr., 197
Keyes v. School District No. 1, 140
Keyser, John, 649
Khaddafi, Muam, 216, 598, 602
Kiewit, D. Roderick, 325
"Killer Bees," the, 648
Kinder, Donald, 325
King, Coretta Scott, 151
King, Martin Luther, Jr., 19, 141, 142, 143, 149, 157, 300
Kinsey, Alfred, 186
Kirkland, Lane, 348
Kissinger, Henry, 594, 605
Kitchen cabinet, 398
Knights of Labor, 561
Know, Neal, 364
Kopechne, Mary Jo, 420
Koppel, Ted, 269
Korean War, 392, 591
Kuhn, Maggie, 182
Krushchev, Nikita, 603
Ku Klux Klan, 79, 149

Labor, Department of, 397, 456, 459, 556
Labor, 560–565
    interest groups, 346–349
    legislation, 562–565
    movement, 346
    political agenda of, 561–562
Labor-management regulation, 560–561
Labor-Management Reporting and Disclosure Act, 564–565
La Follette, Robert, 251
Land management groups, 91–92
Landon, Alfred, 207
Landrum-Griffin Act of 1959, 564
La Raza Unida Party (LRUP), 149
La Riva, Gloria, 302
La Rouche, Lyndon H., Jr., 249, 250, 302
Lasswell, Harold, 10, 292
Latent interests, 351
Latent public opinion, 198
Latta, Delbert L., 540
Law, 480–485
    civil, 184, 481
    common, 185, 482
    compliance with, 11
    criminal, 184, 481
    Napoleonic Code of, 480
    positive, 100
    precedents in, 482

recent sources of, 483–485
Roman, 4
See also Judiciary; Supreme Court
Lawmaking:
    committees and, 431–435
    as congressional function, 412
    process, 441–442
Lawyer Referral Service, 477
Laxalt, Paul, 370
League of Conservation Voters, 356
League of Nations, 383, 389, 403, 585
League of United Latin American Citizens (LULAC), 154
League of Women Voters, 170, 336, 352
Lee, Richard Henry, 37
Lee, Robert E., 132
Legal Defense Fund, 127
Legal Defense Research Institute, 513
Legislation:
    environmental, 571
    presidency and, 375, 384–386
    sunset, 471
    veto of, 385–387
Legislative apportionment, 638–639
Legislative authority, 531
Legislative Reorganization Act of 1946, 360
Legislative veto, 416
Legislature:
    bicameral, 42
    defined, 12
    state, 636–640
    unicameral, 37
    See also Congress
Legitimacy, 11, 135
Lemon v. Kurtzman, 104
Levitan, Sar, 566
Lewis, Drew, 455
Lewis, Jim, 302
Libel, 113
Liberal, 209
Libertarian Party, 248
Liberty, 15, 21
Liberty Alliance, 210
Liberty Amendment Committee of the U.S.A., 57
Liberty Federation, 210
Liberty Weekend, 1986, 5
Lightner, Candy, 513
Lightner, Cari, 513
Limited government, 16
Limited jurisdiction, 486
Lincoln, Abraham, 77, 134, 198, 232, 318, 375, 387, 391, 352, 398, 401, 600
Line organization, 456
Literacy tests, 149
Literary Digest, 200, 207
Livingston, Robert, 75
Lobbying, 354, 355
    computers and, 355
    ratings game and, 355
Lobbying groups, 445

Lobbyists:
  constituents as, 359–360
  registered, 343
  regulation of, 360–362
Local government, 641–651
  city politics, 647–650
  consolidation of, 646–647
  legal existence of, 641–643
  spending by, 627
  taxation by, 627–630
  units of, 643–646
Locke, John, 22, 99
Logrolling, 413
Long ballot, 313–314
Longworth, Nicholas, 430
Lott, Trent, 439

MacArthur, Douglas, 591
McCarthy, Eugene, 292
McClean v. Arkansas, 104
McCulloch, James William, 74
McCulloch v. Maryland, 69, 73, 74–75, 79
*McDonald v. Santa Fe Trail Transportation
  Company*, 145–146
McFarlane, Robert, 361, 599
McGovern, George, 202, 213, 286, 300, 395
McGovern-Fraser Commission, 308
McKinley, William, 232, 266, 380, 387
McMann, Harris, 179
McNamara, Robert, 614
MADD, 513
Madison, James, 13, 39, 41, 42, 44, 48, 50,
  51, 67, 261, 287, 403, 484
Madisonian model of government, 44
Magazines, 268
  See also Media
Maine, Sir Henry, 51
Majority:
  age of, 184
  concurrent, 77, 78
  extraordinary, 64
Majority floor leader (Senate), 438
Majority leader of the House, 436–437
Majority opinion, 492
Majority rule, 16
Malice, 113
Managed news, 264
Mandamus, writ of, 484–485
Mandatory imperatives, 49
Mandatory retirement, 178–179, 180
Mapp, Dollree, 121
Marbury, William, 484
Marbury v. Madison, 94n., 55, 483, 484–485
Marcos, Ferdinand, 382, 430, 579
Marentette, Judith, 175
Marriage, minimum ages for, 184
Marshall, George, 587
Marshall, John, 49, 74, 75, 76, 79, 100, 484,
  494, 501, 505, 511
Marshall Plan, 581, 590

Martin, Luther, 42
Martin, Warren C., 302
Marx, Karl, 563
Mason, George, 42, 49
Mason, Mell, 302
Massachusetts ballot, 313
Massachusetts Board of Retirement v. Murgia,
  179
Massachusetts Body of Liberties, 33
Matching funds, 85
Mayflower Compact, 33
Mayhew, David R., 424
Mayor-administrator plan, 648
Mayor-council plan, 648
Meany, George, 348
Media, 257–88
  bias in, 285–286
  campaigns and, 271–276, 298
  electronic, 267, 285–286
  freedom of press and, 113–135
  functions of, 260–263
  government and, 277
  government regulation of, 281–285
  history of, 263–267
  magazines, 268
  newspapers, 109, 113–114, 212
  politics and, 271–274
  power of, 267–278
  presidency and, 277
  press, 113–115, 263–266
  public agenda and, 278–281
  public opinion and, 212
  television, 212, 266–286
Media access, 285
Media consultants, 271
Medicaid, 177, 430, 549–551
Medical care, 549–551
Medicare, 177, 334, 530, 548–551
Medicare Act of 1965, 550
Meecham, Ralph, 529
Meese, Edwin, 361
Menendez, Pedro, 35
Mercer, John Francis, 42
Meredith, James, 139
Merit system, 466
Merit Systems Protection Board (MSPB), 468,
  472
Merton, Robert, 650
Mexican American Political Association
  (MAPA), 154
Mexican Americans, 133–134, 151–154
Michel, Robert H., 370, 439
Mikulski, Barbara, 426
Military-industrial complex, 607–610
Miller, George, 649
Miller, Warren, 333
Miller v. California, 111, 112
Miniconvention, 235
Minnow, Newton, 267
Minorities, 131–163
  Asian Americans, 134, 159

  blacks, 134–150
  elderly, 177–182
  ethnic, 134
  gays, 186–188
  Hispanics, 134, 151–155, 642
  juveniles, 183–186
  Native Americans, 155–158
  poverty and, 553–554
  religious, 134
  women, 16, 166–177
Minority floor leader (Senate), 438
Minority leader of the House, 437
Minority rights, 131–163
  affirmative action, 24, 145
  age discrimination, 178–180
  Civil Rights Acts, 135–140, 143–145, 147,
    175, 179, 444
  civil rights movement, 113, 141–143
  criminal rights of juveniles, 183–186
  gay rights, 186–188
  Jim Crow laws, 79, 138
  mandatory retirement, 178–179, 180
  political participation, 145–148
  in schools, 138–141
  separate-but-equal doctrine, 137–138
  sex discrimination, 173–177
  suffrage, 16, 166, 168–169
Miranda, Ernesto, 121–122
Miranda v. Arizona, 121–122, 504
"Misery Index," 522
Missing Children Hotline, 261
Missouri Compromise, 134
Mitchell, John, 109, 196
Model Constitution Act, 624
Molasses Act of 1733, 33
Monarchy, constitutional, 8
Mondale, Walter, 188, 202, 205, 212, 213,
  234, 245, 271, 274–276, 291, 300, 303,
  328, 334, 370, 400
Monetary policy, 521–522
Money in Elections, 304
Monroe, James, 231, 387, 584
Monroe Doctrine, 584
Montesquieu, Charles de, 48
Moore, Arch, 298
Moral Majority, 210, 280, 334, 362, 569
Morison, Samuel Eliot, 33
Morris, Gouverneur, 41, 372
Mothers against Drunk Drivers (MADD), 513
Motion pictures, and free speech, 115
Motor Carrier Deregulation Act of 1978, 462
Mott, Lucretia, 168
Movement for Economic Justice, 57
Mulroney, Brian, 579
Multinational corporations (MNCs), 611–613
Multiparty political system, 226
Multiple independently targetable warheads
  (MIRVs), 594
Municipal home rule, 643
Municipalities, 643–644, 647–650
Muskie, Edmund, 291

Mutual assured destruction (MAD), 594
Mutual security pacts, 588

NAACP v. Alabama, 116
Nader, Ralph, 352, 362
Napoleonic Code, 480
Napolitan, Joseph, Associates, 300
Narrow casting, 267
National Abortion Rights Action League, 57,
    340, 352
National Aeronautics and Space
    Administration (NASA), 378, 459, 460
National American Women's Suffrage
    Association, 169
National Alliance of Senior Citizens, 182
National Association of the Advancement of
    Colored People (NAACP), 116, 134
National Association of Broadcasters, 281,
    283, 287
National Association of Manufacturers (NAM),
    340, 342, 362
National Association of Retired Federal
    Employees, 182
National Association of Town Watch, 651
National Audubon Society, 574
National Cattleman's Association, 92, 474
National Caucus of Labor Committees, 249
National Center for Immigrants' Rights, 161
National chairperson, 237
National Chamber of Commerce, 344, 362
National Coalition to Ban Handguns, 340,
    364
National committees, 235–237
National Conservative Political Action
    Committee (NCPAC), 334, 358
National Consumers League, 563
National convention, 51, 235–237, 312
National Council of Senior Citizens, 182
National Education Association (NEA), 351,
    356
National Environmental Policy Act of 1969,
    572
National Environmental Quality Act of 1970,
    571
National Farmers' Union (NFU), 346
National Federation of Business and
    Professional Women's Clubs, 170
National Federation of Independent Business,
    345
National Grange, 346
National Indian Youth Council (NIYC), 157
National Labor Relations Act of 1935, 562
National Labor Relations Board (NLRB), 461
National Legal Center for the Public Interest,
    513
National Milk Producers Association, 474
National Municipal League, 624
National Newspaper Publishers Association,
    287
National Opinion Research Center, 201

National Organization for Women (NOW),
    170–172
National Parks Conservation Association, 574
National politics, 242
National Public Lands Task Force, 92
National Railroad Passenger Corporation, 465
National Recovery Administration, 525
National Republicans, 232
National Rifle Association (NRA), 16, 340,
    362, 364
National Right to Life, 340
National school system, 62
National Security Act of 1947, 605, 606
National Security Agency, 106, 400, 606
National Security Council (NSC), 400, 582,
    593, 599, 605
National security policy, 582
National Small Business Association, 345
National Wildlife Federation, 574
National Women's Political Caucus, 171
Native Americans, 4, 22, 23, 133, 155–158
NATO, 581, 588, 590, 592, 614
Natural aristocracy, 466
Naturalization Act, 105
Natural Resources Defense Council, 566, 574
Natural rights, 36, 99
Navigation Acts, 33
Navy, Department of, 397
Neale, Thomas, 464
Nebraska Press Association v. Stuart, 114
Necessaries, 185
Necessary and proper clause, 69, 74, 75, 412
Negative constituents, 605
Negative income tax, 556
New Deal, 80–81, 180, 207, 233, 238, 247,
    329, 396, 467, 471, 525, 560, 562
New England Congressional Caucus, 495
New England town, 13, 644
New federalism, 82–84
New Jersey plan, 43
News:
    being a critical consumer of, 287
    managed, 264
    suppression of, 284–285
Newspaper correspondents, 276
Newspapers, 264, 298
    circulation of, 263
    development of, 263–266
    freedom of the press and, 113–115
    political, 264
    public opinion and, 212, 277
    yellow journalism and, 265–266
    See also Media
New York Times Co. v. Sullivan, 113
New York Times Co. v. United States, 109
Nielsen, A. C., Company, 203
Niemi, Richard G., 208–209
Nixon, Richard, 82, 86–87, 117–118, 169,
    196, 210, 233, 236, 251, 266, 271, 277,
    285, 286, 305, 218, 238, 330, 333, 334,
    375, 380, 382, 387, 389, 394, 395, 396,

    400, 402, 403, 424, 452, 455, 460, 465,
    498, 499, 500, 505, 506, 510, 521, 522,
    526, 537, 564, 594, 605, 610, 642
Noise Control Act of 1972, 571
Norpoth, Helmut, 236
Norris-La Guardia Act of 1932, 562
North Atlantic Treaty Organization (NATO),
    581, 588, 590, 592, 614
Northeast-Midwest Economic Advancement
    Coalition, 89, 445
North, Oliver, 599
Northwest Ordinance, 15, 38, 156
Nuclear freeze, 614–616, 617
Nuclear Information and Resource Center,
    617
Nuclear power, 546, 566–570
Nuclear Regulatory Commission (NRC), 459
Nuclear Weapons Freeze Campaign, 617
Nullification, 77

Obscenity, 110–112
Occupational Safety and Health
    Administration (OSHA), 444, 565, 566
O'Connor, Sandra Day, 170, 498
Office-block ballot, 313
Office of Administration, 399
Office of Government Ethics, 361
Office of Management and Budget (OMB),
    399–400, 471, 526, 527, 528, 539, 573
Office of Personnel Management (OPM), 468
Office of Science and Technology, 399
Office of Technology Assessment (OTA), 431
Ogden, Aaron, 75–76
Ogul, Morris, 416
Okun, Arthur, 522
Old Age and Survivors Disability Insurance
    (OASDI), 548–549
Olmstead v. United States, 117
Olson, David M., 234
Ombudsman, 414
Omnibus Crime Control and Safe Streets Act,
    122
Omnibus Reconciliation Act, 540
O'Neill, Thomas P., Jr. ("Tip"), 423, 430,
    439, 549
OPEC, 581
Open diplomacy, 584
Open primary, 311
Opinion, 491
Opinion leaders, 212
Opinion polls, 200–206
    accuracy record of, 207
    defined, 200
    Gallup, 19, 26, 173, 187, 194, 198, 201,
        203, 204, 212, 218, 219, 259, 272,
        303, 304, 391, 409, 461, 602
    Harris, 205, 303, 614
        history of, 200–201
        how to read, 222–223
        in 1984 elections, 204–205

in 1986 elections, 6, 7
presidential campaigns and, 303–304, 332–333
problems with, 206
Roper, 201, 203, 259, 303
sampling techniques of, 202–203
straw, 202
Orden Hijos de America (Sons of America), 153
Organization of American States (OAS), 603
Organization of Petroleum Exporting Countries (OPEC), 581
Original jurisdiction, 484, 486–487
Ornstein, Norman J., 342
Other America, The, 552
Overacker, Louise, 304
Oversight, congressional, 415–416

Packwood, Robert, 535
Page, Benjamin I., 219
Paid-for political announcements, 269–270
Paine, Thomas, 34–35, 264, 326
Parks, Rosa, 141
Parliamentary system, 371
Party-column ballot, 313
Party identification, 208–209, 236, 252, 331–332
Party identifiers, 424
Party platform, 235
Paterson, William, 298, 307
Patman, William, 298, 307
Patronage, 238, 388, 450, 649
Paul, Alice, 169
Pay equity, 176–177
Peace Corps, 459
Peer groups, 204
Pelton, Ronald, 106
Pendergast, Tom, 649
Pendleton Act, 467
Pennsylvania Charter of Privileges, 33
Pennsylvania Frame of Government, 33
Penrose, Boies, 298
Pentagon, 609–610
Pentagon Papers, 109, 506
People for the American Way, 287
Pepper, Claude, 180, 548
Period of isolationism, 584
Personal-attack rule, 285
Pesticide Control Act of 1972, 571
Philadelphia Convention. See Constitutional Convention
Pierce, Franklin, 387
Pilgrims, 32–33
Pinckney, Charles, 15, 326
Plato, 481
Plessy, Homer, 137
Plessy v. Ferguson, 137–138
"Plum Book," the, 466
Plural executive, 370
Pluralism, 18, 625

Plurality, 318
Pocket veto, 386
Poindexter, John M., 599
Police power, 79, 630
Political action committee (PAC), 297, 307, 340, 347, 355, 356–358
Political Activities Act of 1939, 306, 467
Political Association of Spanish Speaking Organizations (PASO), 154
Political business cycle. See Business cycle, political
Political conflict, 23–24
Political consensus, 21–23
Political consultant, 300
Political conventions, 51, 235–237, 312
Political culture:
    American, 18–24, 215–218, 243
    defined, 12
Political economy, 519–543
    budget process, 526–530
    congressional budgeting, 528–529
    federal tax system, 530–536
    fiscal policy, 521, 522–526
    monetary policy, 521–522
    nonpolitical budgeting, 530
    presidential budgeting, 526–528
    public debt, 536–541
    supplemental appropriations, 529
Political ideology, 219–220
Political machines, 238–239, 240
Political parties, 226–256
    anti-Federalists, 46, 47, 77, 231, 242, 484
    appointment of Supreme Court justices and, 501
    budget deficits and surpluses and, 537
    defined, 227
    Federalists, 15, 46, 47, 75, 231, 242, 484
    Free Soil Party, 251
    functions of, 229
    history of, 229–234
    identification with, 6, 208–209, 236, 331–332, 424
    Jeffersonians, 231–232
    local organization of, 235–237
    in other countries, 228–229
    progressives, 232, 250–251
    Prohibition Party, 251
    reasons for joining, 227
    spin-off, 250–251
    state organization of, 237–238
    structure of, 234–239
    third, 248
    two-party system and, 231–232, 239–244
    voting in Congress and, 440
    weakening influence of, 252–253
    Whigs, 231–232
    See also Democrats; Republicans
Political profile, 26
Political socialization, 19, 22–23, 206
Political tolerance, 217
Political trust, 217

Politico, 415
Politics, 9–10
    class, 242
    media and, 271–274, 298
    national, 242
    sectional, 242
Policy and Supporting Positions (The "Plum Book"), 466
Polk, James K., 387, 584
Pollard, Jonathan, 106
Polls. See Opinion polls
Poll tax, 149
Pollution, 571
Poll watchers, 316
Pomper, Gerald M., 235
Popular press, 265–266
Popular sovereignty, 22
Population statistics, 177
Populist Party, 251
Positive law, 100
Postal Reorganization Act, 465
Postal Service, 378, 397, 464, 465
Poverty, 551–557
    AFDC and, 555
    food stamps and, 556
    incidence of, 554–555
    increase in, 551–552
    minorities and, 553–554
    negative income tax and, 556
    reasons for, 556–557
    Social Security and, 554–555
Poverty-welfare curve, 555
Powell, Lewis, 147
Power, Jonathan, 286
Power(s), 12
    appointment, 377–378
    concurrent, 69
    of Congress, 411–412
    constitutional, 386
    enumerated, 411–412
    express, 68, 388
    of federal government, 68–69
    federal vs. state, 72–81
    implied, 69
    inherent, 69, 388
    police, 79
    removal, 377–378
    reserved, 69–70
    separation of, 44
    of state government, 69–70
    statutory, 386–388
    See also Presidential powers
Powers, Gary, 606
Precedent, 482
Preferred-position test, 108
Pregnancy Discrimination Act of 1978, 175
Presidency, 369–405
    attitudes toward black or female candidates for, 295
    executive organization of, 396–400
    historical development of, 371

incapacity, 402
influencing the, 405
media and, 277–278
qualifications for, 298, 372–373
powers of, 375–388
succession, 401–402
Presidential campaigns:
financing of, 297–298, 304–307
issues and, 333–335
machinery of, 295–300
media and, 298
polls and, 303–304, 332–333
primaries and, 307–312
strategy for, 300–304
third-party candidates in, 303
Presidential personality, 389–390
Presidential powers:
abuses of, 394–395
appointment, 377–378
chief diplomat, 375, 381–384
chief executive, 375–379
chief legislator, 375, 384–386
chief of state, 375, 376–377
commander in chief, 375, 379–381
constitutional, 386
emergency, 392
executive, 371
executive agreements, 383–384
executive immunity, 393–394
executive orders, 392–393
express, 388
foreign policy making, 600–601, 610–611
impoundment of funds, 394
inherent, 388
limiting, 610–611
party chief, 388–391
proposal and ratification of treaties, 383
recognition, 381–383
removal, 377–378
reprieves and pardons, 379
uses of, 393–394
veto, 385–387
Presidential primaries, 307–311
Presidential succession, 401–402
President pro tempore, 438
Press:
freedom of, 113–115, 281
political, 263–264
public opinion and, 212
yellow journalism and, 265–266
Press secretary, 277
Pressure groups. See Interest groups
Price-Anderson Act, 569
Price supports, 353, 559
Primaries:
blanket, 311
closed, 311
direct, 424
open, 311
presidential, 307–312
reform and, 308–310

run-off, 311
white, 149
Prior restraint, 108, 109
Privacy, right to, 117–118
Privacy Act, 117, 477
Privacy Protection Study Commission, 117
Private Calendar, 442
Privileges and immunities, 71–72
Proclamation of 1763, 33
Professional Air Traffic Controllers
     Organization (PATCO), 351
Progressive taxation system, 532
Progressives, 232, 250–251
Prohibition Amendment, 51, 52
Prohibition Party, 251
Project grant, 85
Property, 21, 22
Property tax, 627, 628–629
Proposal C (Michigan), 628
Proposition 13 (California), 628–629, 634
Proxmire, William, 610
Public administration, 473
     See also Bureaucracy
Public agenda, 278–279
Public debt. See Debt, public
Public education, 416
Public employee pressure groups, 349–351
Public interest, 351
Public interest pressure groups, 351–352
Public Lands Institute, 92
Public opinion, 193–223
     defined, 196
     fluidity of, 198
     formation of, 206–215
     intensity of, 197
     interest groups and, 339–365
     latent, 198
     measurement of, 200–206
     media and, 212, 277
     qualities of, 197–200
     relevance of, 198–199
     stability of, 198
     See also Opinion polls
Public policies, 24
     See also Domestic policy; Foreign Policy
Public Works Administration (PWA), 525
Puerto Ricans, 154–155

Quiescence, of public opinion, 198

Radical Republicans, 135, 148
Radio, 115, 263, 266–267, 298
Radio Marti, 607
Raleigh, Sir Walter, 31
Randolph, Edmond, 42, 370
Rapid deployment force, 597
Ratification, 5, 45, 46, 48–49
Ratings game, and lobbying, 354–357
Rational ignorance effect, 324

Rayburn, Sam, 430
Reagan, Ronald, 66, 86, 142, 143, 233, 236,
     245, 262, 348, 361, 370, 373, 374, 380,
     381, 387, 398, 402, 403, 455, 465, 501,
     549, 550
budget and, 537, 540
bureaucracy and, 469, 471, 473, 477
campaigns of, 282, 273–286, 300
economy and, 462–526
environment and, 573, 574
foreign policy of, 334, 348, 382–383, 404,
     405, 579, 580, 595, 598, 599, 600,
     602, 605, 606, 610, 611, 612, 614
gender gap and, 215, 329
labor and, 565, 566
media and, 273–286, 278, 280, 300
Moral Majority and, 210
new federalism of, 82–84, 85, 335
PATCO and, 351
political appointments of women, 169–170
public opinion and, 5–6, 198, 205, 207,
     212, 213, 219, 281, 333, 390, 391
on school prayer, 103
tax reform and, 534
Supreme Court and, 498, 499, 501, 506,
     509
in television debates, 273–286
veto power and, 387
voter support of, 253, 322, 325, 328, 329,
     330
Reapportionment, 427–428
Recall, 13, 640
Recession, 521
Recognition power, 381–383
Reconstruction, 79, 149
Redistricting, 427
Reese, Mat, 305
Referendum, 13, 639–640
Refuse Act of 1899, 571
Regan, Donald, 399
Regents of the University of California v.
     Bakke, 147, 506
Regents' Prayer Case. See Engel v. Vitale
Regionalism, vs. federalism, 88–90
Registered voters, 319
Registration for voting, 327–328
Regulatory agencies, 459–463
Rehnquist, William H., 498, 509–510
Rehnquist/Reagan Court, 509–510
Relevance, of public opinion, 199
Religion:
     American political culture and, 19
     politics and, 243
     public opinion and, 209–211
     voting behavior and, 329
Religious freedom, 101–104
Religious minorities, 134
Remand, 492
Representation, 415
Representative assembly, 32
Representative democracy, 14

Representative democratic government, 322
Representative function, of Congress, 415
Reprieve, 379
Republicanism, rise of, 36–377
Republican National Committee, 254
Republicans, 232–234
    anti-Royalists as, 37
    in 1986 elections, 6–9
    Radical, 135, 148
    See also Political parties
Rescission, 528
Reserved powers, 69–70
Resolution of Independence, 35
Resource Conservation and Recovery Act of
    1976, 571
Resource Recovery Act of 1970, 571
Retirement, mandatory, 178–179, 180
Revenue-sharing program, 80, 86, 88
Reverse, 491
Reverse discrimination, 145–148
Reviewing courts, 487
Reynolds v. Sims, 427
Richards, Bob, 302
Richmond Newspapers v. Virginia, 114
Rifkin, Jeremy, 569
Rights:
    inalienable, 15
    minority, 131–163
    natural, 36, 99
    property, 22
    voting, 16
    See also Civil liberties
Right to Life organization, 352
Right-to-work laws, 563
Robb, Charles, 245
Robertson, Pat, 19
Robinson, David, 298
Rockefeller, Jay, 298
Rockefeller, Nelson, 403
Roe v. Wade, 118, 119, 502
Rogers, William, 460, 461, 605
Roman law, 4
Romney, George, 373
Roosevelt, Franklin D., 80–82, 85, 159, 180,
    200, 207, 213, 231, 232, 233, 236, 240,
    247, 249, 281, 278, 329, 334, 375, 382,
    384, 386, 387, 388, 389, 391, 392, 394,
    396, 399, 400, 401, 452, 456, 467, 471,
    501, 525, 548, 560, 562, 600, 602, 605,
    607
Roper and Associates, 201
Roper, Elmo, 201
Roper poll, 201, 203, 259, 303
Ross, Nancy, 302
Ross, Nellie Taylor, 640
Rostenkowski, Daniel, 535
Roth, William, 324, 325
Roth v. United States, 110–111
Ruckelshaus, William, 573
Rule of seniority, 435
Rules Committee, 418, 434–435

Rule 22, 418
Run-off primary, 311
Russell, Richard, 430
Rutledge, John, 41

Sabotage Act, 107
Safe seats (congressional), 425
Safety. *See* Worker health and safety
Sagebrush Rebellion, 91, 92
Salaman, Maureen Kennedy, 302
Sales tax, 627
SALT, 383, 594
Schema, 216, 217
Schlafly, Phyllis, 57, 172, 280
Schlesinger, Joseph, 292
School districts, 645–646
School prayer, 102–104
Schools:
    bilingual education in, 155
    church-related, 104
    integration of, 138–141
Scott, David, 188
Screen Actors Guild, 351
Search and seizure laws, 127
Secession, 77
Secondary boycott, 564
Secord, Richard, 599
Sectionalism, 65–66
Sectional politics, 242
Securities and Exchange Commission (SEC),
    459, 461, 497, 525
Security pacts, 588, 589
Sedition Act, 105, 107
Segregation, 139
    See also Minority rights
Select committee, 434
Select Committee on Aging, 180
Selective Service, 477
Selectmen, 645
Senate:
    creation of, 410–411
    filibustering in, 418
    House vs., 416–419
    lawmaking in, 441–442
    leadership of, 438–440
    majority floor leader of, 438
    minority floor leader of, 438
    president pro tempore of, 438
    prestige of, 418
    rules of, 418
    size of, 417–418
    whips in, 439
    See also Congress
Senate committees, 433
Senate Rule 22, 418
Senatorial courtesy, 459
Senators, qualifications of, 293
    See also Congresspersons
Senior Executive Service (SES), 469
Seniority system, 435

Separate-but-equal doctrine, 137–138
Separation of powers, 44
Sequestration process, 539
Serette, Dennis L., 302
Service sector, 348–349
Service to constituents function of Congress,
    414
Sevareid, Eric, 179
Sex discrimination, 173–177
Sex-plus discrimination, 174
Shapiro, Isaac, 566
Shapiro, Robert, 219
Shays, Daniel, 39
Shays's Rebellion, 39
Sherman, Roger, 43
"Shifting" federalism, 86
Short ballot, 313, 315
Sierra Club, 91, 574
Simants, E. C., 114
Simpson, Allan K., 439
Single-interest groups, 352
Slander, 112
Slaughterhouse Cases, 100
Slavery, 15, 36, 43–44
Sliding-scale test, 108
Small Business Administration, 378
Smeale, Eleanor, 171
Smith, Alfred, 243
Smith, Howard W., 435
Smith v. Allwright, 149
Snowbelt, 88–90
Social conflict, 9–11
Social contract, 33
Socialist Labor Party, 248
Socialist Party, 106, 248
Socialist Workers' Party, 248
Social Security, 170, 180, 238, 334, 335, 529,
    530, 531, 548–549, 551, 554
Social Security Act, 525, 548, 551
Social Security Administration, 117, 477, 549
Solid South, 198
Sons of America, 153
Southern Christian Leadership Conference
    (SCLC), 141
Southern Governors' Association, 90
Southwest Voters Registration Project, 153
Soviet bloc, 588
Soviet Union, confrontation with, 588–589,
    593–594
Spanton, George, 472
Speaker of the House, 436
Special districts, 645–646
Special jurisdiction, 486
Speech, freedom of, 105–112
Spencer-Roberts, 300
Spin-off parties, 250–251
Spitzer, Emily, 174
Spoils System, 466
Spring preview (of federal budget), 527
Stability, of public opinion, 198
Stamp Act, 33, 34

Standing committees, 432–433
Stanton, Elizabeth Cady, 168
Stare Decisis, 482
"Star Wars" Strategic Defense Initiative, 8, 222, 334, 427, 616
State central committees, 237
State constitutions, 624, 631–634
State, Department of, 397, 456, 603–605, 606
State government, 621–641
  constitutional powers of, 68–70
  executive branch of, 634–636
  federal government vs., 72–81
  judiciary, 487, 640–641
  legislature, 636–640
  spending by, 626–630
  taxation by, 627–630
  U.S. Constitution and, 631–632
State of the Union message, 384–385
State legislators, 636–637
State political organizations, 237–238
States:
  extradition between, 73
  party competition for, 241
  privileges and immunities in, 71–72
  settlement of differences between, 72
Statutory powers, 386–388
Stein, Herbert, 524
Stevens, Ted, 430
Stewart, Potter, 498
Stockman, David, 400, 573
Stokes, Carl B., 630
Stone, Harlan F., 503
Stone, Lucy, 169
Strategic Arms Limitation Treaty (SALT), 383, 594
Strategic Defense Initiative ("Star Wars"), 7, 222, 334, 427, 616
Straw poll, 202
Strike, sympathy, 564
Stuart, Gilbert, 428
Suarez, Xavier, 636
Subcultures, 23–24
  See also Minorities
Subpoena, 145
Succession, presidential, 401–402
Suffrage, 16, 168
  universal, 16
  women's, 16, 166, 168–169
Sugar Act of 1764, 33
Sunbelt, 88–90
Sunbelt Council, 89
Sundquist, James, 54
Sunset legislation, 471
Sunshine laws, 471
Superior courts, 641
Super Tuesday, 271, 291
Supplemental Security Income (SSI), 554–555
Supremacy clause, 72–73
Supremacy doctrine, 43
Supreme Court, 488, 490–494, 503–510, 631
  appeals to, 490–491
  Burger Court, 505–509

cases reaching, 490–491
checks on, 511–512
Constitution and, 488
decisions and opinions, 491–492
Friday conference of, 493–494
functions, 490–494
judicial activism of, 502, 506–507
judical review of, 55, 483–485, 502–503
Rehnquist/Reagan Court, 509–510
research of, 493
schedule of, 492–494
Warren Court, 503–505
writ of certiorari and, 491
Supreme Court justices:
  appointment of, 488, 496, 505–506, 509–510
  background of, 496–499
  party affiliation of, 501
  qualifications of, 500–501
Survey Research Center, 201
Sutherland, Thomas, 599
Swann v. Charlotte Mecklenberg Board of Education, 140
Sweeney, William, 307
Symbolic speech, protection of, 108, 110
Sympathy strike, 564

Taft, Robert, 312
Taft, William Howard, 232, 251, 387, 389–390
Taft-Hartley Act of 1948, 348, 563–564
Tammany Hall, 238, 240, 649
Taney, Roger, 79
Target price, 558
Tariff Acts, 77, 78
Tawney, R. H., 47
Taxation:
  ability-to-pay principle of, 533
  benefits-received principle of, 533
  fairness of federal, 535–536
  progressive, 532
  proportional, 532
  regressive, 532
Tax bracket, 532
Tax Court, 488
Taxes:
  federal, 530–536
  income, 463
  limitations on, 628–630
  poll, 149
  property, 627, 628–629
  reform and, 533–535
  sales, 627
  types of, 530–531
Tax Reform Act of 1986, 7, 341, 524, 530, 533–536
Tax returns, 535
Tax revolts, 628–630
Taylor, Zachary, 387, 402
Teague, Jack, 430
Teamsters Union, 347

Technical assistance, 582
Television, 115–116
  campaigns and, 271–276, 298
  congressional coverage by, 423
  debates on, 271–276
  government regulation of, 281–285
  primacy of, 267–268
  public agenda and, 278–281
  revolution in, 267
  See also Media
Tennessee Valley Authority (TVA), 464, 525
Terrorism, 596–599
Textile Caucus, 445
Thatcher, Margaret, 599
Third party, 248
Third-party candidate, 303
Thompson, Charles, 36
Three Mile Island, 566, 567, 574
Thurmond, Strom, 220, 439
Ticket splitting, 252–253
Tilden, Samuel J., 242
Title VII of Civil Rights Act of 1964, 173–175
Tocqueville, Alexis de, 342, 502, 573
Tolerance, political, 217
Town, 644–645
Town manager system, 645
Town meeting, 644
Township, 645
Toxic Waste Superfund Act of 1980, 571
Tradeoff, 569
Trading with the Enemy Act, 107
Transfer payments, 335, 554
Transportation, Department of, 397, 456, 459
Treasury, Department of the, 397, 399, 456, 459, 606
Treaties, 383
Treaty of Paris, 583
Treaty of Versailles, 585
Trial rights, 121, 185
Truman, Harry S., 207, 233, 318, 373, 375, 380, 386, 387, 389, 391, 392, 400, 495, 537, 550, 564, 586, 590, 591, 600
Truman Doctrine, 590
Trustees, 415
Trust, political, 217
Tufte, Edward, 524
Tugwell, Rexford G., 53
Tweed, William, 240
Two-party competition, 231, 324
Two-party political system, 231
Tyler, John, 384, 386, 387, 396, 397, 401, 496

Udall, Morris, 298
Ullman, Al, 298
Unanimous opinion, 492
Unicameral legislatures, 37
Uncontrollables, 530
Union Calendar, 442
Unions, 346–351, 562–566
  See also Labor

Union Shop, 564
Unitary system of government, 63
United Air Lines v. McMann, 179
United Auto Workers (UAW), 347, 356
United Farm Workers of America, 154
United Mine Workers (UMW), 347
United Nations, 578, 586
United States Reports, 494
United States v. Curtis Wright Export Corporation, 69 n.4, 392
United States v. Leon, 124
United States v. Nixon, 394, 506
United States v. The Washington Post, 109
United Steelworkers of America, AFL-CIO-CLC v. Weber, 147
United Telecom, 341
Unit rule, 238
Universal suffrage, 16
Urban Mass Transportation Administration, 473
U. S. Bankruptcy Court, 488
U. S. Chamber of Commerce, 342, 344
U. S. Claims Court, 488
U. S. Committee for Energy Awareness, 567
U. S. Courts of Appeals, 488, 489
U. S. English, 161
U. S. Information Agency (USIA), 606
U. S. Tax Court, 488

Van Buren, Martin, 374, 387, 401
Vance, Cyrus, 605
Vedder, Richard, 555
Vertical equity, 532
Veterans Administration (VA), 378, 459, 473
Veterans Affairs Committee, 433
Veto:
  governor's, 636
  "heckler's," 112
  legislative, 416
  pocket, 386
Veto message, 385
Vice president, 400–403
  job of, 400–401
  presidential succession and, 401–402
  as presiding officer of the Senate, 438
  qualifications for, 293
  selection of, 402–403
Vietnam War, 195, 196, 197, 199, 212, 214, 216, 270, 292, 389, 403, 510, 591–595, 610
Vinson, Frederick M., 138
Virginia Declaration of Rights, 49, 50
Virginia House of Burgesses, 25
Virginia House of Delegates, 15
Virginia Plan, 42–43
Voice of America (VOA), 606
Vote counting, 315–316
Voters:
  age of, 181, 323
  education of, 323, 328
  ethnic background of, 329

income of, 328–329
independent, 296, 332
party competition and, 324
party identification of, 236, 332
race of, 323–324
registered, 319
religion of, 329
sex of, 329
socioeconomic status of, 328
turnout of, 319–325
Voting, 319–335
  choices, 325
  compulsory, 290
  demographic and socioeconomic factors in, 323–324, 328–331
  getting involved in, 336
  in gubernatorial elections, 321
  issue preferences in, 333–335
  legal restrictions on, 325–328
  in 1984 presidential elections, 320, 324
  psychological factors in, 331–334
  rational ignorance and, 324
  registration for, 327–328
  See also Elections; Voters
Voting patterns, 319–324, 328–335
Voting rights, 16
Voting Rights Act of 1965, 144, 148, 150, 153

Waite, Terry, 599
Walker, Arthur J., 106
Walker, John, 106
Walker, Michael, 106
Wallace, George, 139, 149, 251, 319
Wallace, Henry, 251
Walton, Richard, 302
War, Department of, 397
War Powers Act, 380, 381, 404, 610
Warren, Earl, 138, 501, 503–505, 509
Warren Court, 503–505, 509
Washington, George, 34, 39, 41, 67, 231, 264, 371, 372, 380, 386, 387, 391, 402, 503, 583
Washington, Harold, 238
Washington community, 391
Watergate break-in, 196, 212, 217, 233, 277, 305, 324, 362, 389, 395, 403, 506
Water Pollution Control Act of 1948, 570
Water Quality Act of 1965, 571
Water Quality and Improvement Act of 1970, 571
Wattenberg, Ben, 160
Ways and Means Committee, 433, 436, 529–535
Weaver, James, 251
Weber, Brian F., 147
Weber, Max, 452
Webster, Daniel, 76, 78
Webster-Calhoun debate, 78
Weir, Benjamin, 599
Welfare. *See* Domestic policy
Welsh v. United States, 105
Wesberry v. Sanders, 427

Western Coalition for Public Lands Clearinghouse, 92
Whigs, 231–232
Whips, 437, 439
Whistle-blowers, 473
White, Byron, 187
White, John, 31
White House Domestic Council, 569
White House Office, 396, 399, 603
White House press corps, 277
White House staff, 396
White primary, 149
Whitaker and Baker, 300
Wildavsky, Aaron, 526
Wilderness Society, 92, 574
Wilkie, Wendell, 233
Williams, George H., 496
Williamson, Richard S., 85
Wilson, Edith, 403
Wilson, James, 42
Wilson, James Q., 227, 650
Wilson, Woodrow, 232, 251, 272, 318, 375, 383, 387, 389, 396, 403, 585
Wirthlin, Richard, 304
Withers, Thomas Jefferson, 348
Woodhull, Victoria, 53
Women, 167–177
  Declaration of Independence and, 169–177
  feminist movement of, 169–177
  historical position of, 167–169
  political opinions of, 215
  as political candidates, 294–295
  right to vote, 16, 166, 168–169
  sex discrimination in employment, 173–177
  voting patterns of, 170
Woodward, Robert, 277
Worker health and safety, 565–566
  decline in, 565
  OSHA and, 565
Works Progress Administration (WPA), 522, 525
World Antislavery Convention of 1840, 168
World War I, 107, 198, 248, 272, 352, 557, 561–562, 584, 586
World War II, 149, 201, 278, 325, 392, 396, 475, 585–589, 600, 603
Wright, James C., Jr., 298, 439
Writ of certiorari, 491
Writ of mandamus, 484, 485
Wygant v. Jackson Board of Education, 147, 148

Yellow-Dog Contract, 562
Yellow journalism, 265–266
Yeutter, Clayton, 612
Yorty, Sam, 629

Zangwill, Israel, 159
Zero population growth, 177
Zingale, Nancy H., 322
Zurcher v. Stanford Daily, 114

▽

Photo Credits